CASSELL COMPANION TO

Theatre

CASSELL COMPANION TO
Theatre

CASSELL

A CASSELL BOOK

First published as *Brewer's Theatre* in 1994:
this revised and updated edition 1997
by Cassell
Wellington House
125 Strand
London WC2R 0BB

First paperback edition 1999

Distributed in the United States by
Sterling Publishing Co., Inc.
387 Park Avenue South
New York, NY 10016
USA

British Library Cataloguing-in-Publication Data
A catalogue record for this book is available from the British Library

ISBN 0-304-35317-5

Compiled and typeset by Market House Books Limited, Aylesbury
Printed and bound in Great Britain by
Mackays of Chatham plc, Chatham, Kent

Contents

Compiled and typeset by:

Market House Books Ltd

Written and edited by:

Jonathan Law
John Wright
Mark Salad
Alan Isaacs
David Pickering
Rosalind Fergusson
Fran Alexander
Amanda Isaacs
Jenny Roberts
Lynn Thomson
Peter Lewis

Preface

The *Cassell Companion to Theatre* offers lively, illuminating, and up-to-date guidance to the world of the drama, past and present. While providing authoritative coverage of all the essential topics, it also finds room for much fascinating and out-of-the-way information not usually included in conventional reference books. The approach is deliberately eclectic, with an emphasis on the humorous and quirky.

The book aims to cover all aspects of theatrical life, language, and legend. It provides a glossary of words and phrases ranging from technical terms to actors' slang and jargon, while also giving clear explanations of the major schools and genres from *Old Comedy* to *environmental theatre*. Facts, anecdotes, and legends about the great personalities of the theatre from *Aeschylus* to *Ayckbourn* are an important feature of the book, as are plot summaries of and key information about the world's best-known plays. The book also explores the eventful histories of some of the most famous theatre buildings and companies. Finally, there are numerous miscellaneous entries ranging from accounts of *theatre ghosts* to a list of actors' *taboos and superstitions*. We have tried to be as inclusive as possible in our definition of theatre; hence the unusually wide coverage of both popular and folk theatre (from *mummers' play* to *music hall* and *striptease*) and the rich theatrical traditions of non-Western cultures.

The idiosyncratic style and unusually wide range of the book can be explained in part by its origin. The *Cassell Companion* is a revised and updated version of *Brewer's Theatre*, one of several modern reference books that draw their inspiration from Dr Ebenezer Cobham Brewer's famous *Dictionary of Phrase and Fable*, first published by Cassell in 1870. Enormously successful in its own day and kept in print ever since, Brewer's *Dictionary* is a cornucopia of useful and curious information, combining etymology, folklore, and literary allusion with a wealth of anecdotal and historical material. Our aim has been to preserve the essence of Dr Brewer's approach in a companion to world drama that is at once thoroughly contemporary and truly catholic.

To this end we have chosen to follow the original Brewer's system of grouping linguistically related but conceptually unconnected terms under a common headword; the main heading *green*, for instance, is followed by *green carpet*, *green man*, and *green umbrella*, amongst other miscellaneous subheadings. The curious juxtapositions thrown up by this system provide one of the chief pleasures of the original *Dictionary* and, we hope, of this book. Cross-references are indicated by the use of SMALL CAPITALS.

J.L.
1997

The Dictionary

A

Abbey Theatre A theatre founded in Dublin in 1904. The Abbey, which was built at the instigation of W. B. YEATS and Lady GREGORY and financed initially by Annie HORNIMAN, became the home of the Irish National Dramatic Society. It presented the first peformances of works by Yeats, Gregory, SYNGE, George Russell (known as AE), and (later) Sean O'CASEY, amongst others. Audiences tended to be vociferous and easily offended: the first productions of Synge's THE PLAYBOY OF THE WESTERN WORLD (1907) and O'Casey's THE PLOUGH AND THE STARS (1926) were both greeted with riots. In 1924 the Abbey became the first state-subsidized theatre in the English-speaking world. A fire destroyed the original building in 1951 but a new playhouse was subsequently built, opening in 1966.

abbot. Abbot of Unreason *See* LORD OF MISRULE.

Abbot's Bromley Horn or **Antler Dance** One of the rare European animal dances surviving from remote times. Originally danced on Twelfth Day at Abbot's Bromley, Staffordshire, it now takes place on the first Monday after 4 September. The six dancers, all male as in MORRIS DANCES, hold antlers (three of which are painted blue or red and three white) to their heads as they dance. It may originally have been a form of fertility rite since the dancers go the round of neighbouring farms before the dance.

Abbott, George (1887–1995) US playwright and director of musicals. A supreme craftsman, he did most of his best work collaborating on and rewriting plays for Broadway. His biggest hit came in 1938 with the musical *The Boys from Syracuse* (*see under* BOY). Abbott wrote the book and directed; the music was by Richard RODGERS and Lorenz Hart. It was not seen in London until 1963, in a production directed by the 75-year-old Abbott.

His first success was *The Fall Guy* (1925), cowritten with James Gleason. Other hits included *Love 'em and Leave 'em* (1926), *Broadway* (1926; with Phillip Dunning), *Coquette* (1927), starring Helen Hayes, *Three Men on a Horse* (1935; with John Cecil Holm), *Where's Charley?* (1948; with Frank Loesser), *The Pajama Game* (1954; with Richard Bissell and music by Richard Adler and Jerry Ross), *Damn Yankees!* (1955; music by Adler and Ross), and *Giorello* (1959; music by Jerry Bock and Sheldon Harnick). Abbott also directed Rodgers and Hart's *Pal Joey* (1940), which made Gene Kelly a star, and *High Button Shoes* (1947).

In 1966 the Adelphi Theatre on Broadway was renamed the George Abbott Theatre in his honour. He lived to the age of 107.

abele spelen The earliest vernacular plays of the Netherlands, possibly the earliest in Europe. They developed in the 13th century from an amalgamation of mime with the ballads and lays of the minstrels. The subject matter was almost always drawn from chivalric romance. The *abele spelen* were generally followed by bawdy farces, called *sotternmieën* or *kluchten*.

The earlier Dutch LITURGICAL DRAMA has not survived, but three *abele spelen* are extant from the 14th century, including the tragedy *Lanseloet van Denemarken*. The only surviving example from the 15th century is *Spiegel der Minnen* by Colijn van Rijssele.

Abigail A traditional name for a lady's maid. The usage derived from the play *The Scornful Lady* (1616) by Beaumont and Fletcher, in which Abigail is a 'waiting-gentlewoman'. It is thought that in choosing the name the authors had in mind the biblical Abigail, who frequently refers to herself as "thine handmaid" (*I Samuel* xxv, 24–28).

The character was enormously popular and the forerunner of a whole race of superior women servants. Similar characters with the same name appeared in works by Swift, Fielding, Smollett, and many others. The usage was given a new impetus during the reign of Queen Anne, when Mrs Masham (whose real name was Abigail Hill) attracted great notoriety as a favourite of the queen and as an enemy of Sarah Churchill. The tradition had petered out by 1800, although the name remained common among Black slaves in the American South. The equivalent name for a valet or manservant was ANDREW.

above *See* STAGE DIRECTION.

Abram-man or **Abraham cove** In Tudor and early Stuart times, a sham maniac who wandered about begging. To **sham Abraham** meant to feign illness in order to dodge work.

Inmates of Bedlam who were not dangerous were kept in the 'Abraham Ward' and occasionally allowed out in distinctive dress and permitted to beg. This gave an opportunity to many imposters. According to Richard Head's *The Canting Academy* (1674) they used to beg alms but "for all their seeming madness, they had wit enough to steal as they went along."

They feature in *King Lear* and in Fletcher and Massinger's *Beggar's Bush* (*c.* 1622), which features a "ragged regiment" of beggars.

Absolute, Captain. A bold despotic character, determined to have his own way, in Sheridan's THE RIVALS (1775). The name was sometimes used of any such person.

absurd. ***Absurd Person Singular*** A black comedy by Alan AYCKBOURN, often considered his best work. It was first performed in 1972 at the STEPHEN JOSEPH THEATRE IN THE ROUND, Scarborough, where Ayckbourn is artistic director. It transferred the following year to the Criterion Theatre, London, where it became one of five Ayckbourn plays running simultaneously in the West End.

The three acts feature three parties, in three kitchens, on three successive Christmas Eves. In each case the action takes place away from the main group of guests; Ayckbourn called *Absurd Person Singular* his first "offstage action play". In the first act the abrasive Sidney and his wife Jane play host to their neighbours Geoffrey and Eva and Ronald and Marion. The action is pure farce, with flyspray mistakenly used as a room freshener, guests locked outside, and numerous personal misunderstandings. At the second party, given by Geoffrey and Eva, Geoffrey tells his wife that he intends to leave her on Boxing Day. She tries unsuccessfully to commit suicide but none of the guests notices. Geoffrey goes for a doctor as the drunken guests sing 'On the First Day of Christmas'. The last act takes place in Ronald and Marion's kitchen, with Marion drunk and ill in her bedroom. The party ends with frenzied dancing to a Scottish reel.

Absurd, Theatre of the A theatrical genre of the 1950s and 1960s, in which accepted stage conventions were largely abandoned in order to present a view of the world as meaningless and incomprehensible. The phrase was coined by the theatre critic Martin Esslin in 1961, who saw in the plays of BECKETT, IONESCO, and others a reflection of the philosophical concept of the Absurd popularized by existentialist writers such as Albert Camus. Ionesco's one-act play THE BALD PRIMA DONNA (1950) is perhaps the earliest play to be recognizably absurdist in its style and preoccupations, while Beckett's WAITING FOR GODOT (1953) is the quintessential work in the genre. Other playwrights to be associated with the style included the Frenchman Arthur ADAMOV and the American Edward ALBEE. The impression of a coherent movement was largely the result of an accidental similarity of theme and treatment and by the 1960s the leading writers had already begun to take different paths.

> The reason why Absurdist plays take place in No Man's Land with only two characters is primarily financial.
>
> ARTHUR ADAMOV.

Abydos Passion Play *See* TRIUMPH OF HORUS.

Accesi A company of Italian actors founded in about 1590 to perform works of the COMMEDIA DELL'ARTE. By 1600 they had come under the leadership of Pier Maria Cecchini. Leading actors with the company included the renowned Harlequin Tristano Martinelli, Flamineo Scala, and Silvio Fiorillo (who joined in 1621). In 1608 the company gave a series of performances in France, finding much acclaim at the French Court. The Accesi eventually joined forces with Francesco Andreini's family troupe, which also toured France. However, the two companies separated after the wives of Cecchini and Andreini began to quarrel, and Cecchini retained the Accesi name.

Accidental Death of an Anarchist A black comedy by the Italian playwright Dario FO, first performed in 1979 in Varese. The play holds the record as Britain's longest-running alternative theatre presentation; in 1980–81 the Belt and Braces Company gave 622 performances of the play at Wyndham's Theatre, London, seen by more than 400,000 theatregoers.

The play is based on the true case of the anarchist Guiseppe Pinelli, who fell to his death from a window at police headquarters while being interrogated; officials said he jumped. Fo's play makes use of a Fool, who impersonates a Captain of Police, thereby exposing the inconsistencies in the police's version. In one ending, the Fool is himself thrown to his death and resurrected. In another, he escapes by threatening to send a tape of police testimony to the press.

Acharnians, The A comedy by ARISTOPHANES, first performed in 425 BC in Athens. His earliest complete extant drama, it won the first prize at the Lenaean Festival.

The Acharnians is a satire on the Peloponnesian War in which the hero, the old farmer Dicaeopolis, weary of the fighting, makes his own private peace treaty with the Spartans. This arrangement is furiously denounced by the chorus of old charcoal burners of Acharnae, but Dicaeopolis's life begins to improve as he trades with the old enemy. The play mocks Athenian values: one scene shows a wealthy Boeotian asking to buy a typical Athenian souvenir and ending up with an informer; another shows a poor Megarian selling his two daughters (disguised as pigs) to keep them from starving. Aristophanes also included lines alluding to his own impeachment the previous year for attacking the demagogue Cleon and his followers in his play *Babylonians.*

The play also mentions the EKKYKLEMA, an early piece of theatrical machinery consisting of a wheeled platform. When a character knocks on Euripides's door and asks him to come out, the dramatist replies that he is not at leisure. The annoyed visitor replies: "At least be wheeled out."

acoustics The characteristics of a theatre, auditorium, or other room that affect sound transmission and its fidelity. The most important factors are the size of the interior, the shape of the ceiling (which reflects most of the sound), and the sound-absorbing properties of carpets, etc. A theatre's PROSCENIUM ARCH is also a major determinant.

The ancient Greeks and Romans built their outdoor theatres in quiet locations; the Greeks improved the sound reception by seating the audience on steep hillsides, while the Romans used elevated platforms. The Greeks also introduced PERIAKTOI – prisms that could be angled to deflect sound towards the audience.

The Italian opera house introduced excellent acoustics for music by eliminating the domed ceiling, draping boxes to dampen reverberations, and adding baroque ornamentation, which diffused the sound.

The spoken word presented more difficult problems. The Elizabethans placed a small roof over the stage to deflect sound downwards. However, later and larger theatres often allowed architectural flourishes to come before acoustical considerations. When VANBRUGH'S large Queen's Theatre opened in 1705 at the Haymarket, its concave roof meant that only one in 10 words was heard distinctly. Thomas Betterton's company, who had moved there from Lincoln's Inn Fields Theatre, had to return to their old venue until alterations could be made. The late recognition of the value of the convex roof was particularly important when projection acting was replaced by more realistic conversational styles. Convex devices have also been hung from the ceiling, as in London's Royal Albert Hall. Acoustics experts have also found that sound quality is improved by a horseshoe-shaped auditorium. In modern theatres with sound-absorbing ceilings, electrical amplification is needed for proper acoustics.

Acres, Bob A character in Sheridan's THE RIVALS (1775), whose courage always "oozed out at his fingers' ends." A coward is sometimes called 'a regular Bob Acres'.

acrobatics The performance by an entertainer of feats requiring physical agility or coordination. Acrobatics has had an important role in many comic traditions and remains a mainstay of the CIRCUS. It is of ancient origin: acrobats performed leaps, somersaults, and vaults at Egyptian feasts, and Greece had itinerant acrobats in the 7th century BC. *The Tumbler of Our Lady* was a popular 12th-century fabliau about an acrobat. Later the COMMEDIA DELL'ARTE depended upon acrobatic skills, as did the English HARLEQUINADE.

The basic move is the **salto**, or leap. In its advanced forms this can be dangerous. In

1842 an attempt at a triple *salto mortale*, or death-defying leap, ended in a fatality at the Van Amburgh Circus (it was finally mastered in 1860 by the American Billy Dutton). Devices used in leaping have gone from the ancient springboard to the flying trapeze, invented in 1859 by the Frenchman Jules LÉOTARD.

Other moves include the **antipodean**, in which one acrobat lies on his back and juggles with another. A development of this is the so-called **Risley Stunt**, invented by Professor Richard Risley of Carlisle, in which two children somersault from foot to foot of a prone partner. A **perch act** involves one acrobat performing balancing moves on the top of a pole held by a second. Another form of acrobatics is **wire-walking**, which has often been used for spectacular entertainment; in 1859 the Frenchman BLONDIN walked blindfolded on a rope over Niagara Falls.

Acrobatic skills are essential to slapstick comedy. In the late 1880s the young Fred KARNO had a juggling and tumbling act with Monsieur Alvene, a well-known 'gymnast and equilibrist'. However, Karno soon made a discovery:

> It came to me that Alvene and I were breaking our arses doing fancy acrobatics for a bit of polite applause, when what the customers liked best was when we were larking about and falling on our bottoms.

Karno went on to become a famous impresario of slapstick comedy.

Actors of the legitimate theatre also learn some acrobatic moves as part of their training.

act One of the major structural divisions of a play. The end of an act, which can contain several scenes, is often indicated by the lowering of the curtain (in PROSCENIUM ARCH theatres) or by raising the house lights. In ancient Greece tragedies were divided into five acts, a convention that was reinforced by Horace (65–8 BC) in his *Ars Poetica*. Ben Jonson introduced this convention to the English stage, leading later editors to divide Shakespeare's tragedies into five acts. Comedies are usually written in three acts. Modern drama tends to employ a more varied structure: Tom Stoppard's *The Real Inspector Hound* (1967) and Edward Bond's *The Pope's Wedding* (1962) are examples of full-length plays that have no divisions into acts.

ACT American Conservatory Theatre. The largest regional repertory company in America, based at San Francisco's 1456-seat Geary Theatre with performances also at the Marine Memorial Theatre. The 50-member company, which performs both classical and modern works, is committed to an educational and experimental role.

ACT was founded in 1965 at the Pittsburgh Playhouse by the flamboyant actor William Ball (1931–), already acclaimed for staging an OFF-BROADWAY production of Chekhov's *Ivanov* (1958). He created a 'dashing style' for the new company but soon fell out with the Pittsburgh management; ACT toured for a year before settling in San Francisco, where it opened with Molière's *Tartuffe* (1966). In 1970 Allen Fletcher began to direct the company's training programme and in 1978 it began to offer a master's degree in acting.

The company overcame a 1973 deficit of $900,000 by trimming its size and repertoire. Its productions have since ranged from *Hamlet* to Feydeau's *A Flea in Her Ear* and Albee's *A Delicate Balance*.

act-drop *See* CURTAIN.

actor A person who acts in a play, film, etc., especially one who does so professionally. The term used to be reserved for male actors but is now used increasingly of women also.

The first actor known to us by name is THESPIS (6th century BC), who is usually considered the founder of the profession. In ancient Greece acting was considered an honourable occupation. This was less so in ancient Rome, although some performers, most notably the comedian Quintus ROSCIUS Gallus (120–62 BC), are known to have enjoyed a high social position.

This situation changed with the adoption of Christianity as the state religion. Thereafter actors were deprived of their legal rights and forced into virtual slave labour for theatre managers. Professional acting did not revive until the 16th century, with the advent of the COMMEDIA DELL'ARTE companies. The early travelling actors often endured miserable poverty. In 1603 the Spanish writer Augustin de Rojas Villandrando wrote:

> They sleep in their clothes, go barefoot, are always hungry, rid themselves of their fleas amid the grain in summer and do not feel them on account of the cold in winter.

In Elizabethan England the first professional company was organized by James Burbage (*see* BURBAGE FAMILY). Unlicensed performers, however, were still classified as vagabonds and liable to imprisonment. In 1597 the Lord Mayor of London objected to a proposed theatre because it would portray vice, attract depraved spectators, and spread disease. Audiences were often just as hostile, sometimes forcing actors to halt an unpopular performance and start another play. Poor acting resulted in a bombardment with oranges, nuts, tiles, and even benches. In Catholic countries actors were refused the sacraments and denied Christian burial (*see* LECOUVREUR, ADRIENNE).

In the 18th century the status of the acting profession was greatly enhanced by David GARRICK, who, according to Edmund Burke, "raised the character of his profession to the rank of a liberal art". Other great British actors of the 18th and 19th centuries include Sarah SIDDONS, Edmund KEAN, and Henry IRVING. The profession finally achieved full respectability when Irving was knighted in 1895. In 1970 Laurence OLIVIER became the first theatrical knight to be raised to the peerage.

Despite this late-won respectability, actors continue to attract their share of derogatory comment (the following are all from 20th-century sources):

> Acting is therefore the lowest of the arts, if it is an art at all.
>
> GEORGE MOORE: *Mummer-Worship.*

> At one time I thought he wanted to be an actor. He had certain qualifications, including no money and a total lack of responsibility.
>
> HEDDA HOPPER: *From Under My Hat.*

> Scratch an actor and you'll find an actress.
>
> DOROTHY PARKER.

> An actor's a guy who, if you ain't talking about him, ain't listening.
>
> MARLON BRANDO.

> They didn't act like people and they didn't act like actors. It's hard to explain. They acted more like they knew they were celebrities and all.
>
> J. D. SALINGER: *The Catcher in the Rye.*

> A talented actor is as rare as an arsehole in the face.
>
> THOMAS BERNHARD: *The Showman.*

See also ACTRESS.

actor-manager An actor who manages his own company, generally both directing and starring in its productions. This arrangement dominated the 19th-century English stage, with the actor-managers Henry IRVING and Beerbohm TREE achieving particular prominence. Irving managed the Lyceum Theatre with some 600 employees, while Tree managed three theatres, the Comedy, the Haymarket, and Her Majesty's. The authority of actor-managers began to wane at the turn of the century with the rise of independent non-acting directors. Notable 20th-century exceptions to this trend include the appointment in 1944 of OLIVIER and Richardson as co-directors of the Old Vic and Olivier's appointment in 1962 as director of the National Theatre Company. The tradition of the touring actor-manager has more recently been revived by Kenneth BRANAGH, who founded the Renaissance Theatre Company in 1986.

Actor Prepares, An The usual English title of Konstantin STANISLAVSKY's treatise (1926) on the psychology of acting. This title was used for a 1936 abridgement published in America. A more literal translation of the Russian title would have been *An Actor's Work on Himself*. The US edition was used as the basis for training in the METHOD, a psychological system of acting based on Stanislavsky's theories.

Actors' Studio The New York-based workshop for professional actors founded in 1947 by Elia KAZAN, Robert Lewis, and Cheryl Crawford. Under the artistic direction of Lee STRASBERG (from 1948), the Studio became known as the US home of the METHOD school of acting and nurtured many leading theatre and film stars, including Marlon Brando. The Studio is primarily a forum for exploration and experimentation, away from the pressures of commercial production. The costs are met by voluntary subscription, and membership is by invitation following audition.

actress A female who acts in a dramatic performance. Respectable women did not act in the classical drama of Greece and Rome, although prostitutes and slaves sometimes appeared in MIME. On the English stage female parts were always taken by boys until the Restoration. Actresses had been introduced to the French and Italian theatres somewhat earlier. In 1611 the traveller Thomas Coryate noted of his stay in Venice: "When I went to a theatre I observed certain things that I never saw before; for I saw women act". Outstanding early actresses include Italy's Isabella Andreini (Isabella Canali; 1562–1604), who developed the role of the *inamorata* (young girl in love), France's Madeleine Béjart (1618–72), cofounder with Molière of the Illustre-Théâtre, and Germany's Caroline Neuber (1697–1760), or Die Neuberin, who also managed.

England's first professional actress was Margaret Hughes (1643–1719), Prince Rupert's mistress, who made her public debut on 3 December 1660 at the Vere Street theatre in Killigrew's *The Moor of Venice*. The audience gave an enthusiastic ovation when informed by the prologue that a woman would appear. Actresses were officially licensed to appear in English theatres in 1662:

> Whereas, women's parts in plays have hitherto been acted by man in the habits of women...we do permit and give leave for the time to come that all women's parts be acted by women.
> Charles II's licence of 1662.

Other early actresses to take London by storm were Nell GWYNN (1650–87), the mistress of Charles II, and two names extolled in PEPYS's diary, Mrs Knepp (d. 1677) and Mrs Betterton (Mary Saunderson; d. 1712). Edward Kynaston (d. 1706) seems to have been the last actor to take female parts in serious drama.

One of Britain's greatest tragic actresses was Sarah SIDDONS (1755–1831). During her last performance – *Macbeth* in 1812 – the audience were so moved that they stood on benches and demanded (successfully) that the play end with her last scene. America's first native-born actress was Charlotte CUSHMAN. The first legitimate actress to appear totally nude on the British stage was Maggie Wright, when she played Helen of Troy in the Royal Shakespeare Company's 1968 production of *Dr Faustus*.

> For an actress to be a success she must have the face of Venus, the brains of Minerva, the grace of Terpsichore, the memory of Macaulay, the figure of Juno, and the hide of a rhinoceros.
> ETHEL BARRYMORE.

Acts of the Apostles A group of French miracle plays written between 1452 and 1478 by Simon Gréban, probably with his brother Arnoul. The stories of the travels, teachings, and martyrdom of Christ's apostles were collected in a manuscript containing 61,968 lines.

For over 70 years the plays were presented by the CONFRÉRIE DE LA PASSION, an association of amateur actors, at a site just outside the walls of Paris. In 1541, however, the Confrérie was charged with adding apocryphal material along with farces and pantomimes. The Church authorities protested that the performances encouraged "neglect of divine service, indifference in almsgiving and charity, adultery and incessant fornication, scandals, mockery and scorn". Even priests were said to hurry through services in order to see the plays. These attacks had little effect on the plays' popularity; in 1545 the *Acts of the Apostles* was played every Sunday for seven straight months. Three years later, however, when the Confrérie moved to a new permanent home at the HÔTEL DE BOURGOGNE they were prohibited from performing religious works.

act-tune Music played between the acts of a play. Such musical interludes were especially important in the Elizabethan and Restoration theatre. The composer Henry Purcell supplied act-tunes for such plays as *King Arthur* (1691) and *The Fairy Queen* (1692). Introductory music for a play was known as the **curtain-tune**.

Adamov, Arthur (1908–70) Russian-born French playwright, who became one of the leading exponents of the Theatre of the ABSURD in the 1950s. Adamov, who did not begin writing for the theatre until the late 1940s, was heavily influenced by the dramatic works of Strindberg. His first play, *La Parodie*, was written in 1947 but not performed until 1952. The play, which features a large handless clock towering over the set, satirizes man's attempts to find the elusive meaning of existence. In 1950 *The Large and Small Manoeuvre* and *The Invasion* were both staged. Major acclaim only arrived, however, with the 1953 production of the Kafkaesque PROFESSOR TARANNE, which concerns a university professor who can no longer maintain his public character. *Ping Pong* (1955), another well-known work, revolves around a pinball machine and the obsession of the central characters with this futile game of chance. The play marks a move away from Adamov's dream world towards the more overtly political concerns that such later works as the Brechtian *Paolo Paoli* (1957), about the turn-of-the-century trade in ostrich feathers, and SPRING '71 (1961), which provides an account of the Paris Commune of 1871. *Off Limits* (1968), set in America at the time of the Vietnam War, and *If Summer Returned* (1970) were his last plays before his suicide. The private neuroses that informed the nightmarish world of his plays are detailed at length in his autobiographical works *The Confession* (1946) and *Man and Child* (1968).

ADC The Amateur Dramatic Club. A theatre group founded in 1855 by F. C. Burnand (1836–1917), a Cambridge undergraduate, who later became a playwright and editor of *Punch*. It revived acting at the University, where no plays had been performed since the Puritans closed the theatres in 1642 (*see* INTERREGNUM). The ADC, which celebrated its centenary in 1955, continues to develop actors for the professional stage, having already contributed such talent as Michael Redgrave (*see* REDGRAVE FAMILY). George Rylands (1902–), lecturer and fellow of King's College, Cambridge, directed many of its most successful productions.

Adding Machine, The An expressionist play by Elmer RICE, first performed in 1923 in New York. The play is a satire on automation. Rice's anti-hero, Mr Zero, is a bookkeeper who represents the average man's dehumanization by the machine age. He is nagged by his wife, rejected at the office by the pretty Daisy, and after 25 years of faithful service finds himself replaced by an adding machine. Mr Zero murders his employer and is subsequently tried and executed. In heaven, he meets Daisy who has committed suicide and now confesses her love. However, he is informed by heavenly sources that after a "cosmic laundering" he will be sent back to earth as a mindless machine operator.

ad libbing In theatrical and broadcasting parlance, to depart from the script and improvise. It is often resorted to in emergencies, such as the absence of an essential prop or a failure to remember the correct lines. The term derives from the Latin **ad libitum**, literally, at pleasure.

Admirable Crichton, The A comedy by J. M. BARRIE, first performed in 1902 in London. It examines the disparity between natural talent and social status. When an upper-class family and their servants are shipwrecked on an island, Crichton, the butler, emerges as the natural leader of the group. However, when rescuers arrive he resumes his original inferior position.

The name was originally bestowed on James Crichton (1560–85), the Scottish traveller, scholar, and swordsman by Sir Thomas Urquhart (1611–60) in his book *The Exquisite Jewel*. Harrison Ainsworth was much indebted to Urquhart for his novel *The Admirable Crichton* (1837). The name is sometimes used to mean a person of all-round talents.

Admiral's Men An English theatre company formed in 1585 with Admiral Lord Howard as its patron. Their large repertory of plays included several by Marlowe. With Edward ALLEYN as their leading actor, they performed at the THEATRE with Strange's Men in 1590; after an argument with the landlord BURBAGE both companies moved to the ROSE THEATRE.

The Admiral's Men lost several good actors to the CHAMBERLAIN'S MEN when the latter were formed in 1594, but Alleyn continued to lead them as an independent company. He retired in 1597 but returned three years later when the company moved to the Fortune playhouse under their new name of Prince Henry's Men. In 1612 they became the Palsgrave's Men under their new patron the Elector Palatine. The company lost all of its costumes and playbooks when the Fortune burned down in 1621. It disbanded 10 years later, after the plague had greatly reduced theatre-going.

advertisement curtain In the British theatre of the late 19th and early 20th centuries, an inner CURTAIN lowered between acts that carried the advertisements of companies and local shops sponsoring the theatre. This practice mostly occurred in provincial and small London theatres.

advice to actors

> Speak the speech, I pray you, as I pronounced it to you, trippingly on the tongue; but if you mouth it, as many of your players do, I had as lief the town-crier spoke my lines. Nor do not saw the air too much with your hand, thus; but use all gently: for in the very torrent, tempest, and – as I may say – whirlwind of passion, you must acquire and beget a temperance, that may give it smoothness. O! it offends me to the soul to hear a robustious periwig-pated fellow tear a passion to tatters, to very rags, to split the ears of the groundlings, who for the most part are capable of nothing but inexplicable dumb-shows and noise: I would have such a fellow whipped for

o'erdoing Termagant; it out-herods Herod: pray you, avoid it.
WILLIAM SHAKESPEARE: *Hamlet*.

When in doubt, shout – that's the motto.
CEDRIC HARDWICKE, recalling the advice of a 19th-century stage manager.

Just know your lines and don't bump into the furniture.
NOËL COWARD.

AE The pseudonym of the Irish dramatist and writer George William Russell (1867–1935). It was derived as a contraction of 'aeon', a word to which he attributed great mystical significance. Russell's considerable and varied output includes several volumes of poetry and the play *Deirdre* (1902). He also helped to found Dublin's ABBEY THEATRE.

A-effect *See* ALIENATION EFFECT.

Aeschylus (525–456 BC) The father of Greek tragic drama, usually considered the first great writer in the Western theatrical tradition. Only seven plays, of over 70 known titles, are extant. These are THE PERSIANS (472 BC), SEVEN AGAINST THEBES (469 BC), PROMETHEUS BOUND (*c*. 460 BC), THE SUPPLIANT WOMEN (*c*. 460 BC), and the ORESTEIA trilogy (458 BC), comprising *Agamemnon, Choephoroi*, and *Eumenides*. He also wrote numerous SATYR-PLAYS, which have only survived in fragmentary form.

Aeschylus's work is powerful and operatic, using majestic but often innovative language. His attitude to Greek society and religion was generally conservative, although he boldly depicted the sufferings of men and woman when moral systems, and the gods themselves, are in conflict.

Legend says he was killed by a tortoise dropped by an eagle (to break the shell) on his bald head (mistaken for a stone).

Aeschylus of France Prosper Jolyot de Crébillon (1674–1762). The name reflects his high standing in the 18th century, when his tragedies were compared with those of Racine. Today his works are regarded as overly melodramatic and are rarely revived. As court censor (from 1735) he was involved in a protracted feud with VOLTAIRE.

after. afterpiece A brief play, often a farce, offered as comic relief after a full-length tragedy in the 18th-century British theatre. Those who wished to see only the afterpiece were usually charged half-price. It tended to appeal to the less sophisticated part of the audience. One theatre-goer in 1806 was amazed to see a play go "eight and twenty nights without the buttress of an afterpiece".

After the Fall A play about love and responsibility by the US playwright Arthur MILLER. It is often considered his best work. Elia Kazan directed the original production at the Washington Square Theatre, New York, in 1964, when it opened the first season of the Vivian Beaumont Repertory Company (which the following year became the Lincoln Center Repertory Company). It was performed at the Belgrade Theatre, Coventry in 1967.

Most believe, but Miller denies, that the play was based on his failed marriage to the Hollywood sex symbol Marilyn Monroe. The play's main female character, Maggie, is given less love than she needs and commits suicide. Monroe's death, a suspected suicide, had occurred only two years earlier, and some critics suggested that Miller could have waited longer before releasing the work.

The setting is a courtroom where Quentin, a 40-year-old lawyer, addresses the audience directly about the traumas of his life, which are depicted in a series of scenes. These show his indifference to Maggie's tragic pleas for attention and his doomed relationships with other women, including Louise, another ex-wife, and a German girlfriend who harbours guilt about the Holocaust.

Agate, James (1877–1947) British theatre critic, whose reviews appeared in the *Sunday Times* from 1923 until his death. He credited George Bernard SHAW as his inspiration, saying, "The articles signed 'G.B.S.' in *The Sunday Review* made me determine that one day I would be a dramatic critic."

In 1928 Agate used his fortnightly theatre talk on the BBC to promote R. C. Sherriff's JOURNEY'S END, which had just opened. He claimed that he had advised the manager to cancel it because the public was utterly unworthy of such a play. Abusive letters poured in from listeners and people rushed to the box office. He often used the incident as an example of the power of exaggeration.

Agate's one attempt to write a play himself was a disaster. Having collaborated on a comedy, *Blessed Are The Rich*, he persuaded friends to put up several thousand pounds for its production at the Vaudeville Theatre in 1928. When the curtain fell the audience lured Agate onstage with polite applause then roared their disapproval with loud shouts of 'Rubbish!'. The play lasted 13 performances and attracted many actors and playwrights who enjoyed this revenge on their previous tormentor.

He was notoriously difficult to please. Only Henry Irving and Sarah BERNHARDT were accorded the accolade of greatness. His sister May Agate (1892–1960) had studied with Bernhardt and appeared with her in Paris and London. Agate's pen could be florid when he contemplated the French actress:

> You would know a scene of Sarah Bernhardt's if you met it in your dreams. To say of the very greatest actress of this type that she is always herself is obviously to mean that whatever quality she expresses will be expressed in its highest power.

It also could be sharp, as in his review of Charles LAUGHTON's London performance as *Henry VIII* in 1933:

> Mr. Laughton came to Sadler's Wells with all his blushing film vulgarities thick upon him.

agitprop A derogatory term for a type of theatre that uses propaganda and tendentious argument to influence its audience's political attitudes. It is often applied to the activities of left-wing touring companies. A prime example was New York's LIVING THEATRE, which toured Europe in the 1960s with a message of anarchy and revolution. In its own work, *Paradise Now* (1968), the audience was urged to take the struggle onto the streets.

The term *agitprop* derives from the Soviet Union's Department of Agitation and Propaganda, which was set up in 1920 by the Central Committee of the Communist Party. Travelling agitprop abounded in Russia and spread throughout Europe. In 1950–51 and again in the 1960s, the Chinese workers' theatres produced their own version of agitprop.

agon An ancient Greek theatrical term for the central conflict in classical TRAGEDY. The word meant a 'contest' or 'struggle'; originally it had the specific meaning of a contest for a prize at the public games.

Aguecheek, Sir Andrew A straight-haired country squire, stupid even to silliness, self-conceited, living to eat, and wholly unacquainted with the world of fashion. He is the companion of Sir Toby BELCH in Shakespeare's TWELFTH NIGHT.

Ah! Wilderness An uncharacteristic play by Eugene O'NEILL, being a nostalgic comedy about his youth (later depicted so bitterly in *Long Day's Journey into Night*). The plot follows 17-year-old Richard Miller during his two-day passage to manhood in a local bar. The play opened on Broadway in 1933; the star was George M. COHAN, making his comeback at the age of 55. Despite receiving an overwhelming ovation and rave reviews, Cohan scowled and groaned, "Imagine my reciting lines by Eugene O'Neill! Why, he ought to be on the stage reciting lines by me!"

O'Neill's plays were generally thought too long and he fought to keep every minute. When the curtain fell on one early performance of *Ah! Wilderness*, the stage hands demanded overtime. After much persuasion, O'Neill delighted the management by agreeing to trim 10 minutes; however, this turned out to be a 10-minute intermission.

aisle sitters US slang for theatre CRITICS. From the notion that someone sitting in the aisle of a theatre could escape from a boring play before the end or leave to send copy to his newspaper without disturbing other theatregoers.

Aktie Tomaat (Dutch: Action Tomato) A radical movement in Dutch theatre in the late 1960s and early 1970s. It was sparked by an incident in 1969, when students of the Toneelschool (Amsterdam's School of Drama) threw tomatoes at actors performing with the Nederlandse Comedie in Amsterdam's municipal theatre. The action was intended as a protest against the bland socially irrelevant productions offered by the Dutch theatrical establishment. Another source of complaint was the allegedly dictatorial role of the director.

The campaign emphasized the social function of drama. New works were written and produced to appeal to sections of the population that had been neglected by the mainstream theatre. Improvisation was encouraged as a way of developing new themes and the creative role of the actor was stressed. Several new democratically organized theatre companies emerged, including Amsterdam's WERKTEATER, the

Sater educational theatre, and the Toneel environmental theatre. *See also* VORMINGSTONEEL.

Aladdin A tale from the *Arabian Nights*, best known in Britain as a subject for PANTOMIMES. Aladdin obtains a magic lamp; when the lamp is rubbed a genie appears, who will comply with even the most extravagant requests. For Aladdin, the genie has a splendid palace built. As the owner of the palace Aladdin marries the daughter of the sultan of China, who disposes of the lamp, and his palace is transported to Africa. He subsequently recovers the lamp and returns with both wife and palace to China to live happily for many years.

Albee, Edward (Franklin) (1928–) US dramatist. Albee was born in Washington, DC, the adoptive grandson of a vaudeville theatre manager of the same name. He first came to public attention with a run of successful one-act plays, *The Zoo Story* (1959), *The Sandbox* (1960), and THE AMERICAN DREAM (1961), which led to his being classed with the writers of the Theatre of the ABSURD. Albee's reputation was firmly established, however, by the Broadway success of his first full-length play WHO'S AFRAID OF VIRGINIA WOOLF? (1962), a campus play exploring the savage love-hate relationship of a college professor and his wife. In 1966, it was made into a successful film starring Richard Burton and Elizabeth Taylor. A DELICATE BALANCE (1964) won Albee his first Pulitzer Prize, the second being awarded almost a decade later for *Seascape* (1975). His later plays, which tend to be somewhat abstract and experimental, have on the whole been less successful with audiences and critics. An exception was *Three Tall Women*, which won Albee his third Pulitzer Prize in 1994. Albee has adapted several works for the stage, including Nabokov's *Lolita* (1981), as well as directing a number of plays off-Broadway.

Albert the Great A nickname given to Albert CHEVALIER, a great favourite of the Victorian and Edwardian MUSIC HALLS. The nickname probably arose by analogy with *Albert the Good*, a name for Albert, the Prince Consort.

Albery Theatre An Edwardian theatre in St Martin's Lane, London, that was once home to the OLD VIC. It was known as the New Theatre until 1973. Charles Wyndham, manager of the Criterion Theatre for 23 years, owned property between Charing Cross Road and St Martin's Lane. On the Charing Cross Road side he built Wyndham's Theatre and, when he failed to sell the rest of the land, built the New Theatre opposite. It opened in 1903. Seating 876, it was the first theatre in London with 'electrical flying scenery'. The original Louis XVI decor remains, with portrait medallions of French kings and queens in the auditorium and sculptured cupid figures (representing peace and music, and winter and summer) on both sides of the proscenium.

The theatre's first great triumph came in 1924 with Sybil Thorndike's performance in Shaw's *Saint Joan*. In 1935 the theatre saw the longest ever run of *Romeo and Juliet*; the outstanding cast of Olivier, Gielgud, Ashcroft, and Evans gave 186 performances. From 1944 to 1950 it was home to the OLD VIC, whose own theatre had been bombed. Some of Olivier's greatest work was seen here, including his *Richard III* (1944) and *Oedipus* (1945). Richardson found equal glory with his Falstaff in *Henry IV, Parts I* and *II* (1945).

The theatre's longest run, however, was Lionel Bart's musical *Oliver!*, which opened in 1960 for 2618 performances (revived in 1977 for a three-year run). The Andrew Lloyd Webber and Tim Rice musical *Joseph and the Amazing Technicolour Dreamcoat* opened here in 1973. That year the New Theatre changed its name to the Albery to honour Sir Bronson Albery, a former manager, as well as to avoid confusion with the New London Theatre.

Alchemist, The A satirical comedy by Ben JONSON, first performed in 1610 at the Globe Theatre. The plot concerns the attempts of three rogues – the alchemist Subtle, the butler Face, and the whore Dol Common – to fleece gullible people in the house of Face's absent master, Lovewit. They distribute alchemical and astrological advice and even perform magic rituals for their customers (at one point summoning up the 'Queen of the Fairies'). Lovewit returns unexpectedly, however, and the law officers are summoned. The alchemist is found to have fled, while Face remains in his master's good graces by arranging a marriage for him. Jonson's delight in trickery and practical jokes is evident throughout. The play also presents a serious moral about human greed and gullibility.

The Alchemist has attracted some of Britain's best serious actors into comedy. David Garrick played Abel Drugger, one of the duped customers, as did Alec Guinness in 1947 at the Old Vic, when critic Kenneth TYNAN wrote of watching "his wistful, happy eyes moving in dumb wonder..." Ralph Richardson was Face in the same production. In more recent revivals Subtle has been played by Leo McKern (1962) and Ian McKellen (1977).

Aldrich, Louis *See* OHIO ROSCIUS *under* ROSCIUS.

Aldridge, Ira *See* AFRICAN ROSCIUS *under* ROSCIUS.

Aldwych Theatre A theatre in the West End of London known for its productions of both farces and Shakespeare. It was built as one of a pair with the Waldorf Theatre (now the Strand Theatre) when slums were cleared away for two new roads, The Aldwych and Kingsway, in 1905. The 1089-seat theatre opened with the musical *Bluebell in Fairyland*, written by and starring Seymour Hicks, one of the theatre's owners.

In 1911 the Aldwych saw the first English performance of a Chekhov play, *The Cherry Orchard*, while during World War I it was converted into a club for Australian servicemen. The first of Ben TRAVERS's famous **Aldwych farces**, *A Cuckoo in the Nest*, was presented in 1925. The series, which also included *Rookery Nook* (1926) and *Thark* (1927), featured a regular cast headed by Robertson Hare, Mary Brough, Tom Walls, and Ralph Lynn. Other successes included Lillian Hellman's *Watch on the Rhine* (1942) and Tennessee Williams's *A Streetcar Named Desire* (1949), with Vivien Leigh.

As the London home of the ROYAL SHAKESPEARE COMPANY from 1960 to 1982, the Aldwych staged such celebrated productions as Peter Brook's *Marat/Sade* (1964) and *A Midsummer Night's Dream* (1970) as well as the eight-and-a-half-hour *Nicholas Nickleby* (1980). The Aldwych also played host to the annual WORLD THEATRE SEASON from 1964 until 1973. The Aldwych has also seen two particularly disastrous productions. William Douglas Home's *Ambassador Extraordinary* (1948), about a visiting Martian, provoked boos from the gallery. Referring to the play's anti-Cold War message, Home made the startling prediction that "if they don't learn the lesson of compromise taught tonight [in his play], in six month's time that gallery won't be here". The gallery was still there 30 years later when the RSC's production of Steve Gooch's *The Women-Piraces: Ann Bonney and Mary Read* (1978) was loudly booed and garnered such reviews as "Yo-ho-ho and a bottle of twaddle". It closed after 19 performances.

Now under US ownership, the Aldwych has more recently enjoyed success with Tom Stoppard's *Hapgood* (1988) and an acclaimed revival of Albee's *Who's Afraid of Virginia Woolf?* (1996).

Alexandre le Grand A tragedy by Jean RACINE that made his name but led to a breach with his supporter MOLIÈRE. Molière produced the play at the Palais-Royal in 1665, a year after staging Racine's first play, *La Thébaïde ou les frères ennemis*, with moderate success. *Alexandre le Grand* quickly proved popular and seemed destined for a long run. Two weeks after opening, however, Racine secretly took the play to a rival company, the Comédiens du Roy, who performed it at the HÔTEL DE BOURGOGNE with Floridor, the greatest tragic actor of the time, in the lead role. When Molière found out, he severed relations with Racine and never spoke to him again. The Hôtel de Bourgogne became the venue for all Racine's subsequent tragedies.

The plot of *Alexandre le Grand* focuses on the conflict between Alexander the Great, presented as a paragon of magnanimity, and two Indian kings, Porus and Taxile. When Racine published the play in 1666 he dedicated it to Louis XIV, the 'Alexander' of that age.

Alhambra A popular MUSIC HALL in Leicester Square, London, that for 76 years presented most of the great British stars of song and comedy. The venue was opened in 1854 as a 3500-seat exhibition centre named the Royal Panopticon of Science and Art. Four years later it became the Alhambra Palace then, after alterations, the Alhambra Music Hall. The name would later change to the Albambra Palace of Varieties and, finally, the Alhambra Theatre.

In 1861 the Alhambra introduced the spectacular French acrobat Jules LÉOTARD to London audiences. It was also the first British theatre to present the French cancan, an indiscretion that briefly cost the Alhambra its licence. The music hall burned down in 1882 but was quickly rebuilt and reopened a year later, establishing a reputation for lavish revues and ballets. Diaghilev's Ballets Russes performed there in 1911 and on several later occasions. Comedy stars to head the Alhambra bill included George Robey and Violet Loraine, who were seen together in *The Bing Boys Are Here* (1916), and Gracie Fields, who made her name in the revue *Mr. Tower of London* (1923). The building was demolished in 1936. The site, on the east side of the square, is now occupied by the Odeon cinema.

The original Alhambra (Arab. *Kal'-at al hamra*, the red castle) is a citadel and palace built at Granada by the Moorish kings in the 13th century. The Alhambra theatre was famous for its ornate Moorish-style architecture.

Ali Baba The hero of a story in the *Arabian Nights* that has become a favourite subject for PANTOMIME. Ali Baba sees a band of robbers enter a cave by means of the magic password "Open Sesame". When they have gone away he enters the cave, loads his ass with treasure and returns home. The Forty Thieves discover that Ali Baba has learned their secret and resolve to kill him, but they are finally outwitted by the slave-girl Morgiana, who pours boiling oil into the jars in which they are hiding.

alienation effect (Ger. *Verfremdungseffekt*) The term coined by Bertolt BRECHT for his technique of deliberately limiting the degree to which both actors and audience identify with the drama. Brecht's intention was to jolt the sensibilities of all concerned in order to sharpen their objectivity and awareness. He achieved this alienation effect in various ways, including the use of third person or past-tense narrative, spoken stage directions, unusual or subversive stage design, as well as the use of songs, placards, etc. One common device was for an actor to step out of character during a scene to address the audience.

all. ***All for Love; or, the World Well Lost*** A tragedy in blank verse by John DRYDEN, first performed in 1677 in London. The plot is derived from Shakespeare's ANTONY AND CLEOPATRA, but with Dryden expanding the last hours of the doomed lovers into a five-act drama that focuses on the conflict between love and honour. *All for Love* is the most successful example of an English tragedy influenced by classical French drama. The UNITIES of time, place, and action are strictly observed. The result is a taut well-constructed work that lacks the sweep and grandeur of Shakespeare's treatment. The tone is also noticeably bleaker. Nevertheless, it has some excellent poetry and provides rich acting parts. It is the most frequently revived of Dryden's plays.

All God's Chillun Got Wings Eugene O'NEILL's play about the marriage between a Black man and a White woman. It caused outrage when first performed in 1924 at the Provincetown Playhouse, New York, in a production starring Paul ROBESON and Mary Blair. Newspapers carried the headline "White Actress Kisses Negro's Hand" after this occurred on stage. O'Neill, his children, and the cast, all received death threats.

Before the play opened, O'Neill and the Provincetown management decided to revive his earlier play *The Emperor Jones* in "an attempt to focus the attention of the public on an actor instead of a controversy". Robeson won acclaim in the role of the Black emperor, but this did nothing to stem the outrage after the opening of *All God's Chillun Got Wings*. O'Neill countered with a press statement:

> Prejudice born of an entire ignorance of the subject is the last word in injustice and absurdity. The Provincetown Playhouse has ignored all criticism not founded on a knowledge of the play and will continue to ignore it...All we ask is a square deal...We demand this hearing.

New York's district attorney tried to ban the play but had to concede that no law was being violated. Instead, he banned the use of child actors and their lines were read by the stage manager throughout the run.

All My Sons A play by Arthur MILLER that proved his first success, winning the New York Drama Critics' Circle Award for Best Play. First performed in 1947 in New York, *All My Sons* is an Ibsenian drama about war profiteering. Set in the aftermath of World War II, the story centres upon 60-year-old Joe Keller, whose partner Deever is serving a prison sentence for knowingly fitting P40 fighter planes with defective engines, causing the deaths of 21 pilots. Although Keller had instigated the crime, he had been released owing to lack of evidence. Deever's son, George, visits and reveals the truth to Keller's son, Chris. A letter then reveals that

Keller's other son, Larry, whom everyone supposes to have been killed in action, had in fact committed suicide on learning of his father's crime. Faced with this truth, Keller shoots himself in the head and dies.

The play was later made into a Hollywood film starring Edward G. Robinson as the father. In the 1981 London revival Colin Blakely played Joe with Rosemary Harris as his wife.

Despite the seriousness of the theme, the first production of *All My Sons* ended with one of those stage pranks beloved by actors. On its last night, the leading man reached for his packet of cigars to find a packet of cocktail sausages in its place.

All-Russian Theatrical Society (VTO) A Russian actor's union established in 1883 to protect working conditions and pay. Dramatists and composers were protected by a subsidiary organization, the Union of Stage Workers. The actress Alexandra Yablochkina (1868–1964) was president of the All-Russian Theatrical Society from 1916 until her death.

All's Well that Ends Well A comedy by SHAKESPEARE, first performed at an unknown date between 1596 and 1604. Owing to its sombre introspective quality, the play is traditionally classed with Shakespeare's 'dark comedies' or 'problem plays'. It has only 14 speaking parts, making it, with *Twelfth Night*, the least populated play by the Bard.

The plot is based on a tale in Boccaccio's *Decameron*. The King of France is cured of a mystery illness by a physician's daughter, HELENA. As a reward, he offers her any bachelor of the court as her husband. She chooses the arrogant BERTRAM, who, regarding her as beneath him, runs away to the wars. Later he writes tauntingly that he will wed Helena only when she obtains the ring from his finger and has his child. She travels to Florence and asks Diana, whom Bertram has pursued, to pretend to submit to him. In the dark, Helena replaces Diana in bed and successfully entreats Bertram to give her his ring. When Bertram returns to Paris, the king has him arrested, believing that he has killed Helena. In the play's last moments the pregnant Helena arrives wearing Bertram's ring, so all ends well.

Alleyn, Edward (1566–1626) English actor and manager, who began his theatrical career with Worcester's Men in about 1583 before moving to the ADMIRAL'S MEN in about 1587, both companies being managed by the Elizabethan impresario Philip HENSLOWE. Alleyn was especially admired for his portrayals of MARLOWE's Dr Faustus and Tamburlaine.

In 1592 Alleyn married Henslowe's stepdaughter Joan Woodward, being thereafter closely associated with Henslowe's business affairs. He became a part owner in both the Rose and Fortune Theatres, as well as becoming involved in some of Henslowe's other enterprises (which included bull-baiting arenas and brothels).

It appears that Alleyn's fortunes prospered sufficiently for him to be able to retire before the age of 40; thereafter he devoted himself to charitable work, founding (1619) the College of God's Gift at Dulwich, which he later endowed with his personal papers, which give a unique insight into the business side of the Elizabethan theatre. Following the death of Joan in 1623, Alleyn married Constance, the daughter of the Dean of St Paul's, John Donne.

> Alleyn's fortune proceeded no doubt from marrying three wives, each of whom brought a handsome fortune, partly from the success of his theatre, partly from his being keeper of the King's wild beasts, and master of the Royal Bear Garden, and partly from his being a most rigid and penurious economist, which character he so strictly enjoined himself, that he was the first pensioner in his own charity.
>
> CHARLES DIBDIN.

alt. ***Altweibermuehle*** (Ger. Mill for Old Women) A Tirolean FASTNACHTSSPIEL in which a group of old men drag their wives to a miraculous mill that can transform them into young and desirable women. After the treatment, however, the wives refuse to return to their husbands unless they reform their behaviour. The plot dates from the 16th century. It is also found in 18th- and 19th-century Yugoslavian folk-paintings.

Altwiener Volkstheater (Ger. Old Viennese folk theatre) A type of improvised folk comedy popular in the Viennese theatre of the early 18th century. It was popularized mainly by the Austrian actors Joseph Stranitsky (1676–1726) and Gottfried Prehauser (1699–1769). Derived from the HAUPT- UND STAATSAKTIONEN, the *Altwiener Volkstheater* featured the wild antics of the Bavarian peasant clown HANSWURST. The genre fell out of favour in the mid 18th century.

alternative theatre *See* COLLECTIVE CREATION; COMMUNITY THEATRE; FRINGE THEATRE; OFF-BROADWAY; OFF-OFF-BROADWAY.

Alvin Theatre A New York theatre on West 52nd Street that opened in 1927 with Gershwin's musical comedy *Funny Face*. The theatre's name combined the first names of the owners, Alex Aarons and Vinton Freedley. Its seating capacity of 1344 makes it ideal for large musicals. In the 1930s the Alvin staged a string of hit musicals including Gershwin's *Porgy and Bess* (1935), Kaufman and Hart's *I'd Rather Be Right* (1937), and George Abbott's *The Boys from Syracuse* (1938). Fred Astaire, Ginger Rogers, and Ethel Merman all starred at the theatre. Later successes have included *A Funny Thing Happened on the Way to the Forum* (1962), a musical based on the plays of Plautus starring Zero Mostel, Sondheim's *Company* (1970), and *Annie* (1977).

The Alvin has also presented serious drama, such as O'Neill's *Mourning Becomes Electra* (1931), Maxwell Anderson's *Mary of Scotland* (1933), and Robert Sherwood's *There Shall Be No Night* (1940), with the LUNTS.

Amadeus Peter SHAFFER's hit play about the life and death of Wolfgang Amadeus Mozart. It opened in 1979 at the Olivier Theatre in a production directed by Peter Hall, transferring to Her Majesty's Theatre in 1981. The play also took Broadway by storm in 1980. *The Sunday Times*, however, called it "tripe". Simon Callow created the role of Mozart, who is presented as a uniquely gifted buffoon. The intense role of Salieri, his conscientious but mediocre rival, was played by Paul Scofield at the Olivier, Frank Finlay at Her Majesty's, and Ian McKellen in New York. A 1983 film version directed by Miloš Forman won eight Oscars, including Best Picture and Best Actor (Murray Abraham as Salieri).

The work takes its central idea from Pushkin's play *Mozart and Salieri*, which suggested that Mozart was poisoned by his rival. In Shaffer's play Mozart goes into a physical and moral decline as Salieri undermines his position at the Austrian court and becomes senior composer. Salieri also attempts to drive the more gifted composer mad by posing as the ghost of his dead father. Years later Salieri himself goes mad and writes a confession to the murder of Mozart.

amateur theatre Drama in which the performers and stage workers receive no payment other than some expenses. Amateur theatre has contributed greatly to the cultural life of areas that seldom see professional companies and has strong links with the FRINGE THEATRE. It has been an important nursery of talent for the professional theatre in most countries.

The early 20th century saw a growing interest in amateur theatre in Britain and REPERTORY companies soon began to merge elements of the amateur and professional traditions. In 1955, the NATIONAL YOUTH THEATRE was founded by the director Michael Croft to promote amateur productions featuring child actors. Today amateur theatre thrives in university societies, such as the Oxford University Dramatic Society (OUDS), and in local societies, who often perform in their own LITTLE THEATRES.

The British Theatre Association (BTA), founded in 1919 by Geoffrey Whitworth (1883–1951) as the British Drama League, coordinates amateur drama throughout the country. The National Operatic and Dramatic Association (NODA), established in 1899, is another British organization that oversees amateur theatre groups. The International Amateur Theatre Association, based at The Hague, was founded in 1952 under the British actor and director E. Martin Browne (1900–80).

Ambassadors Theatre An intimate London theatre that became home to small-scale revues and Agatha Christie's record-breaking play THE MOUSETRAP. Designed as a pair with the next-door St Martin's Theatre, it opened in 1913. Seating only 460, it is decorated in Louis XVI style; the auditorium is adorned with ambassadorial crests.

The Ambassadors originally specialized in revues. It was the first theatre in England to introduce the 'intimate revue', a form which became hugely popular during World War II. Many of these, such as *Sweet and Low* (1943), starred Hermione Gingold. During the war the theatre also remained open for matinee performances of the Ballet Rambert.

On 25 November 1952 the Ambassadors presented the first performance of *The*

Mousetrap, which ran there for more than 21 years with 8862 performances. It later moved next-door to the St Martin's Theatre, where it still runs. Post-*Mousetrap* productions at the Ambassadors have varied widely, ranging from the RSC's 1987 success with Christopher Hampton's *Les Liaisons dangereuses* to the *From A Jack to A King* (1992) a "rock 'n' roll rave" by Bob Carlton.

Ambigu, Théâtre de l' A theatre in Paris that opened in 1769 on the Boulevard du Temple as a venue for children's plays and puppet shows. From 1797 onwards it became a leading theatre for melodramas by such writers as Pixerecourt and Bouchardy. It burned down in 1827 and was rebuilt in 1828 on the Boulevard Saint-Martin, where more successful melodramas were produced, including works by Hugo and Dumas *père* (*see* DUMAS FAMILY). The second Ambigu was demolished in 1971.

American. American Academy of Dramatic Arts The oldest DRAMA SCHOOL in America and still one of the best training grounds for US actors. It was founded (as the Lyceum Theatre School of Acting) in 1884 in New York by the theatre designer and playwright Steel MacKaye and others. The Academy is today affiliated with the State University of New York and offers junior and senior classes in acting.

American Actors' Equity Association *See* EQUITY.

American Company A US theatre company that played a major part in the development of early American drama and had a virtual monopoly on US stage performances for many years. The company was assembled in 1763–64 in Charleston by David Douglass from former members of the elder Hallam's troupe, including his widow and son (*see* HALLAM FAMILY). It was soon housed in the John Street Theatre, New York, under the joint management of John Henry, Lewis Hallam, and John Hodgkinson. In 1796 William DUNLAP became manager after bringing in the first Joseph Jefferson (*see* JEFFERSON FAMILY) as the leading actor. The company had no serious rival until 1794, when Tomas Wignell, their former leading man, formed his own troupe and opened the Chestnut Street Theatre in Philadelphia.

The American Company was the first to stage a professional production of a play by an American, Thomas Godfrey; his tragedy *The Prince of Parthia* was presented for one night at the Southwark Theatre, Philadelphia, in 1767. The company's repertoire included several by Dunlap, such as *The Father; or, American Shandyism* (1789) and *André* (1798). In 1798 it moved to New York's Park Theatre but was disbanded in 1805 after Dunlap went bankrupt and retired. The theatre was taken over by a member of the company, Thomas Abthorpe Cooper.

American Conservatory Theatre *See* ACT.

American Dream, The A one-act play by Edward ALBEE, first performed in 1961 in New York. It takes a satirical look at the tensions that underlie everyday middle-class family life in America. Set in an average living-room, the plot centres on Mommy, Daddy, and Grandma. The latter fearfully awaits the arrival of the "van man", who will one day come and take her away. A visit by Mrs Barker, chairman of a woman's club, reminds Grandma that 20 years ago this same woman brought Mommy and Daddy a bundle of joy from the Bye Bye Adoption Agency. This child was unloved and soon died. After Mrs Barker leaves, a handsome young man (the American Dream) appears seeking work. He tells Grandma that he is incomplete, having no emotions since being separated at birth from his identical twin brother. When Mrs Barker returns, Grandma tells her to pretend that the American Dream is Mommy and Daddy's adopted child, now grown up. This pleases everyone, but Mommy has a funny feeling that the young man somehow seems familiar.

American Educational Theatre Association *See* ATA.

American Laboratory Theatre An acting school and production group established in 1924 in New York by Richard Boleslavsky (1889–1937), who was soon joined by Maria Ouspenskaya (1876–1949). Both were former pupils of STANISLAVSKY at the MOSCOW ART THEATRE. Boleslavsky had already taught the METHOD acting system for a year at New York's Neighbourhood Playhouse after appearing in the Moscow Art Theatre's first Broadway season.

The Laboratory Theatre, which lasted until 1929, was the primary advocate of Stanislavsky's theories in America. Among its pupils were Lee STRASBERG, who became director of the New York Actors' Studio in 1951 and made it home to the Method, and Harold Clurman (who later complained that the Method produced "a kind of constipation of the soul"). Strasberg and Clurman were among the founders of the GROUP THEATRE in 1931.

American Museum A Broadway theatre opened by P. T. BARNUM as a museum in 1841. It became a theatre in 1849 and, after being enlarged and refurbished, reopened a year later with W. H. Sedley-Smith's moralistic melodrama *The Drunkard*, which had a record run. Cultural events were also staged, such as concerts by the opera singer Jenny Lind. Personal financial problems forced Barnum to sell the theatre in 1855 but he was able to repurchase it six years later. In the 1860s, plays were largely displaced by boxing, oddities, and freak shows, including the midget General Tom Thumb. The building burned down in 1865.

Barnum briefly operated from the Winter Garden before opening his **New American Museum** later that year in the former Chinese Rooms on Broadway. A variety of shows were presented, including Van Amburgh's menagerie in 1867, but plays continued to be performed. This theatre also burned down, during a performance of Harriet Beecher Stowe's *Uncle Tom's Cabin* in 1868. Barnum never rebuilt it.

American National Theatre and Academy *See* ANTA.

American Place Theatre A New York theatre company now based at 111 West 46th Street in the rear of the Stevens Building facing Sixth Avenue. In 1971 this underground complex was presented to the company for an annual lease of $5, because zoning laws allow the builder of a skyscraper to add storeys if a theatre is included.

The company mounted its first productions at St Clement's Church on West 46th Street. Its founders, Wynn Handman, who is still the artistic director, and the Reverend Sidney Lanier, pastor of the church, dedicated the company to the presentation of works by living US playwrights. When the company moved to its present location in 1971, the experimental theatre group, **Sub-Plot** was also formed. In 1978 the Women's Project was created by Julia Miles, who assists Handman.

The company's 10-month season includes both full productions and works-in-progress. Among its acclaimed productions have been *Killer's Head* by Sam Shepherd in 1975.

American Negro Theatre A US theatre group founded in 1940 to promote Black productions and actors under the direction of the playwright Abram Hill. The first production, Theodore Browne's *Natural Man*, was staged at the New York Public Library in 1941. Later offerings included two plays by Hill, *Walk Hard* (1944) and *On Strivers' Row* (1946) and, at the Harlem Children's Center in 1949, Synge's *Riders to the Sea*. The company's greatest success was Philip Yordan's *Anna Lucasta*, starring Frederick O'Neal, which opened on Broadway in 1944 and ran for nearly three years. It opened in London in 1947 with equal success. The American Negro Theatre toured England and Europe in 1953 but was disbanded on its return to America.

American Repertory Theatre The title of two US production companies. The first was founded in 1946 in New York by three actress-directors, Cheryl Crawford (1902–86), Eva Le Gallienne (1899–1991), and Margaret Webster (1905–72) (*see* WEBSTER FAMILY). The company, modelled on Le Gallienne's earlier Civic Repertory Company, was not a financial success and closed after one season of six plays given in an old theatre on Columbus Circle. Webster directed and appeared in the opening production of *Henry VIII*, as well as in Barrie's *What Every Woman Knows*, Shaw's *Androcles and the Lion*, and Ibsen's *John Gabriel Borkman*.

The current American Repertory Theatre (ART) is a professional company established in 1979 at Harvard University by Robert Brustein (1927–), who had earlier founded the Yale Repertory Theatre. It is dedicated to performing new US plays, neglected works, and innovative productions of the classics. ART's directors have included Joanne Akalaitis (1937–) and Robert Wilson (1942–). Their work has often been unconventional. Samuel Beckett threatened legal action in 1984 when Akalaitis set his *Endgame* in an abandoned subway tunnel. In 1986 Wilson combined Euripides's *Alcestis* with a Japanese KYŌGEN play and added laser projections. More conventional productions have included the Tony Award-winning musical *Big River* (1985), which transferred to Broadway.

American Shakespeare Theatre A theatre in Stratford, Connecticut, that is home to a famous annual summer drama festival featuring the works of Shakespeare and other classics. The venue, an octagonal structure with a THRUST STAGE and a 1534-seat auditorium was designed by Edwin Howard to resemble the original GLOBE THEATRE. The organization was founded in 1951 under Lawrence Langner as the American Festival Theatre and opened in 1955 with an eight-week season beginning with *Julius Caesar*. Spring performances for students were first added in 1959.

The current name was adopted in 1972. Five years later the Connecticut Center for the Performing Arts was formed to bring in touring companies and guest artists. The latter have included Christopher Plummer, Jessica Tandy, Katharine Hepburn, James Earl Jones, and Alfred Drake. Plummer and Jones appeared together in 1981, as Iago and Othello, respectively. The following year, however, the American Shakespeare Theatre filed for bankruptcy with debts of nearly $2 million. Various financial solutions were devised to allow its continued existence.

American Theatre Association *See* ATA.

amphitheatre A theatre or concert hall with a central arena surrounded by circular or semicircular seating. Examples include the Royal Albert Hall, London, and Madison Square Garden, New York. Sometimes the term is used for the first tier in the gallery of a theatre. The word is from the Greek meaning 'double theatre'; it arose because the first Greek theatres were semicircular or semioval, rather than having seats all around the acting area. The amphitheatres of the Romans, built in cities throughout the Empire, were often used for dramatic performances as well as for such spectacles as gladiatorial contests. Famous amphitheatres include the Colosseum in Rome, opened in 80 AD, whose four-storey structure could accommodate about 50,000 spectators on its marble seats.

Amphitryon In classical legend, a prince of Thebes whose wife, Alcmena, was seduced by Jupiter. The fruit of their union was Hercules. The story has been adapted for the stage in numerous versions.

Amphitruo, a one-act comedy by PLAUTUS, is the earliest known dramatization of the story. First performed in about 190 BC, it is the only parody of mythological themes to have survived from the Roman theatre. The farcical plot provided the basis for such later versions as Heywood's *The Silver Age* (1613), Molière's *Amphitryon* (1668), Dryden's *Amphitryon* (1690; mostly adapted from Molière), and Giraudoux's *Amphitryon 38* (1929).

In a prologue, Mercury explains that Jupiter is in love with Alcmena. While Amphitryon is waging war, Jupiter assumes his identity and Mercury disguises himself as Sosia, Amphitryon's loyal slave. Jupiter's real identity is made clear to the audience by a gold tassel on his hat, and Mercury's by a helmet plume. The plot involves the unexpected return of Amphitryon and Sosia to Thebes and a riotous confusion of identities all round. When Amphitryon questions his wife's fidelity, Jupiter appears as himself to confess that he has made her pregnant.

Amphitryon 38 Jean GIRAUDOUX's best-known play, first performed in 1929 in Paris. It was adapted for the English stage by S. N. Behrman and produced in 1937 in New York, where the LUNTS played Jupiter and Alcmena; it opened a year later in London. The title arose from Giraudoux's belief that his was the 38th version of the Amphitryon legend.

le véritable Amphitryon A phrase from Molière's *Amphitryon* that has become semi-proverbial in France.

Le véritable Amphitryon
Est l'Amphitryon où l'on dine.

In the play Jupiter, in the likeness of Amphitryon, visits his house and gives a banquet; but Amphitryon comes home and claims the honour of being master of the house. As far as the servants and guests are concerned, however, the person who provides the feast is the real host.

Anatomist, The A play by James BRIDIE that established his reputation as a dramatist when it was produced in 1930, first in Edinburgh and then at the Westminster Theatre, London. Bridie was actually Dr Osborne Henry Mavor, a Scottish physician; his plot involved the true story of the Scottish anatomist, Dr Robert Knox, who conspired with the body snatchers Burke and Hare to obtain cadavers for dissection. In the play, Burke murders a disreputable woman whose corpse is recognized on the dissection table by Knox's assistant. He is disturbed by the anatomist's unconcern about how the bodies are obtained. When Hare turns King's Evidence, Burke is convicted of the murder and hanged. Knox is implicated and flees but is eventually rescued by his students.

Anderson, Maxwell (1888–1959) The prolific US playwright, whose works included historical plays, verse dramas, comedies, and musicals. He worked briefly as a journalist before enjoying his first stage success with *What Price Glory* (1924; with Laurence Stallings), about a World War I soldier. *Night Over Taos* (1932) was the first production by the GROUP THEATRE in New York. In 1933 Anderson scored a double triumph with *Both Your Houses*, a satire on political corruption that won a PULITZER PRIZE, and *Mary of Scotland*, in which Mary was played by Helen Hayes. The latter was the first of his poetic historical dramas, the others being *Elizabeth the Queen* (1930) and *Anne of the Thousand Days* (1948).

Some of Anderson's best plays dealt with contemporary subjects: these included *Winterset* (1935), about the Sacco-Vanzetti murder case of the 1920s, and *High Tor* (1936), a satire on materialism. With the composer Kurt Weill he wrote the musicals *Knickerbocker Holiday* (1938) and *Lost in the Stars* (1949).

In 1946 the then-unknown Marlon Brando appeared in Anderson's *Truckline Café*, about a returning GI who murders his wife. Harold Clurman, the director, was mystified by the actor: "He read poorly, his head sunk low on his chest as if he feared to divulge anything. He mumbled for days." Both Anderson's wife and agent wanted Brando fired, but the playwright told his director to persevere with him. One day, Clurman made him shout his lines in the empty theatre while climbing a rope hanging from a gridiron. Brando became furious during the session but thereafter spoke up.

Andrew A name used in old plays for a valet or man-servant. *Compare* ABIGAIL.

Merry Andrew *See under* MERRY.

Androcles and the Lion A two-act comedy by George Bernard SHAW. It was first produced in 1913 in London, starring Harley Granville-Barker and his wife, Lillah McCarthy. The brief play, which explores religious sentiment, was published with a lengthy preface on Christianity. When first produced it was criticized as being somewhat light and frivolous.

The plot is based on an old tale recorded by Aulus Gellius (*c.* 130–180 BC). Androcles was a runaway Christian slave who took refuge in a cavern. A lion entered and, instead of tearing him to pieces, lifted up his forepaw so that Androcles could remove from it the thorn that was troubling him. The slave, being subsequently captured, was doomed to fight with a lion in the Roman arena. It so happened that the same lion was led out against him, and recognizing his benefactor, showed towards him every demonstration of love and gratitude.

Shaw's play focuses on the different ways in which Androcles and his fellow Christians face death. He depicts Caesar as persecuting Christians merely for short-term political motives.

Andromaque The play by Jean RACINE that established his reputation as a great tragic dramatist. It was first performed in 1667 before the king and queen in the queen's apartments, with Racine's mistress Thérèse Du Parc in the title role. In this play Racine broke decisively from the conventions of baroque theatre with his fast and ingeniously simple plot. The play was produced by Molière, who staged it using elaborate machinery and the new Italian painted scenery.

The plot draws upon Euripides's play of the same name and on an incident in Virgil's *Aeneid*. Having slain Hector in the Trojan War, Pyrrhus has abducted his wife, Andromaque. She agrees to marry Pyrrhus in order to save her son's life. The marriage, however, infuriates Hermione, daughter of Helen of Troy, to whom Pyrrhus was pledged. She has him murdered and then commits suicide over his body.

Contemporary critics argued that Racine had used *Andromaque*, which shows love overwhelming and destroying all, to pander to the audience's taste for pure passion. Particularly poignant are Andromaque's devotion to her dead husband and the fierce reproaches of Hermione to Pyrrhus.

angel A financial backer, especially a major one, of a play or other theatrical entertainment. The term, first heard in America in the 1920s, originally referred to someone who donated money to a politician's campaign; it was soon picked up by theatre people and became so commonplace on Broadway that it lost its political meaning.

The first known financial backers of drama were the *choregoi* (*see* CHOREGUS), or rich patrons, of the ancient Greek theatre, who underwrote the expenses of the drama festivals.

Angry Young Men A term applied by journalists to a number of young British dramatists and novelists in the later 1950s. Although the writers were not part of any organized movement, their work shared a number of characteristics, in particular an aggressive dissatisfaction with the social and moral values of post-war British society. Their concentration on the lives of the middle and working classes was something of a departure from the concerns of the previous generation of writers, who were generally from, and wrote about, the upper strata of English society. Principal figures associated with the term include Arnold WESKER, and especially John OSBORNE, whose play LOOK BACK IN ANGER (1956) is usually seen as the quintessentially 'Angry' work. Stylistically there is an emphasis on naturalism and the language of ordinary people. *See also* KITCHEN SINK.

animal impersonator A performer who adopts the guise of an animal. Animal impersonation formed a part of primitive rituals in many cultures. Early English examples are the HOBBY HORSE in the MUMMERS' PLAY and the ABBOT'S BROMLEY HORN DANCE. In the Greek theatre Aristophanes used animal choruses in several of his works, including THE BIRDS (414 BC) and THE FROGS (405 BC).

PANTOMIME and variety have featured various animal roles from Dick Whittington's cat to Dobbin, the two-man horse; the latter dates back to the COMMEDIA DELL'ARTE of the 16th century. In 1902 Charlie Chaplin and Jack Melville did the Dobbin act in a pantomime presented by Fred KARNO's company at the Hippodrome Theatre in Stockport. In the legitimate theatre, Arthur Lupino (*see* LUPINO FAMILY) was an acclaimed animal impersonator, being chosen by Sir J. M. Barrie to play Nana, the dog, in the original production of PETER PAN (1904).

Animation Culturelles, Centres d' *See* CENTRES DRAMATIQUES.

Ankiya Nat (Hind. act drama) A form of religious theatre found in the Indian state of Assam that honours Vishnu's manifestation as Krishna. The genre was created by Sankaradeva (*c.* 1449–1568), who wrote many such plays and urged all religious leaders to write at least one drama. Performances occur at religious festivals. The amateur companies have about 15 actors, who are often monks. Men play all the roles in monastery performances, while women may participate in community productions. The roles of Krishna and his brother Balarama are played by boys, who are said to be possessed by the gods during their performances.

An *Ankiya Nat* drama lasts from about 9 p.m. until sunrise the next day. It is traditionally held in the *nam-ghar*, or prayer hall, of a monastery. The acting and dancing occurs within a narrow corridor marked off by ropes with the audience on both sides. At one end is the shrine containing the sacred text *Bhagavata Purana* and opposite is the *agni-gad*, or archway of lights, through which the actors enter. Characters wear colourful costumes and crowns to show their station in life. Demons and animals are represented by effigies of bamboo and papier-mâché up to 15 feet tall and manipulated by several actors.

Preliminaries include drumming, dances, and songs praising Krishna. When these are completed, the *sutradhara*, or stage manager, enters to the accompaniment of fireworks and dancing. He sings, dances, and recites from the play. Krishna then makes his entrance and dances towards the shrine. Next comes the play itself, which dramatizes the conflict between good and evil. The stage manager remains to give directions to both the actors and musicians and to interpret the action for the audience. The entertainment is concluded with more songs and dances.

Anna Christie A tragicomedy by Eugene O'NEILL, about a fallen woman redeemed by love. The first performance was given in New York in 1921; later that year it was seen in London with Pauline Lord in the title role. It was later made into a film starring Greta Garbo. In 1979 The Royal Shakespeare Company staged an excellent revival at the Warehouse Theatre with Susan Tracy as Anna.

O'Neill probably derived the story from Theodore Dreiser's novel *Sister Carrie* (1900). The play begins with Anna, a prostitute, searching for her estranged father, a seaman, on the New York docks. She finds him in charge of a coastal barge and accepts his invitation to move in, keeping her past a secret. Later they save the lives of four sailors and Anna falls in love with one, a loud Irishman named Mat Burke. She refuses Mat's proposal of marriage and confesses her past to him and her father. Mat comes to the barge meaning to kill Anna but instead offers to marry her. The happy ending has come in for much criticism.

Annie A musical with book by Thomas Meehan, lyrics by Martin Charnin, and music by Charles Strouse. Based on the popular US comic-strip character Little Orphan Annie, it was first performed in 1977 at the ALVIN THEATRE, New York and won a Tony Award as the best musical. It opened a year later at London's Victoria Palace Theatre.

Annie lives in a dismal orphanage run by the horrid Miss Hannigan. One Christmas the secretary of the millionaire Oliver Warbucks chooses her to be a guest at his mansion. The abrasive Warbucks is so delighted with the girl that he takes her to the White House to meet President Roosevelt, who immediately conceives his New Deal when Annie sings 'Tomorrow'. Warbucks then offers $50,000 if Annie's real parents will come forward. Miss Hannigan's brother Rooster and his girlfriend arrive with forged papers. Their plot is foiled, however, when FDR produces an FBI report proving that Annie's parents are dead. 'Daddy' Warbucks adopts Annie and sees that her orphan friends are liberated. Apart from 'Tomorrow', the songs include 'Something Was Missing', and 'You're Never Fully Dressed Without a Smile'.

Annie Get Your Gun Irving BERLIN's fast-paced musical about the sharpshooter ANNIE OAKLEY. Its New York premiere was in 1946 with the brassy-voiced Ethel MERMAN in the lead. The first British production a year later starred Dolores Gray and gave the London Coliseum its longest ever run (1304 performances). It has been revived numerous times, the last West End production being in 1992 at the Prince of Wales Theatre (with Kim Criswell winning rave reviews as Annie).

The story follows Annie as she joins BUFFALO BILL's Wild West Show and becomes the main attraction, even outshooting the famed marksman Frank Butler. Love ensues but is blocked by pride on both sides. Annie finally loses a big shooting contest to Frank when Chief Sitting Bull bends her rifle sights. Male pride is restored and the love match sealed. (The required male triumph does not go down well with many audience members today.)

Berlin's music includes Sioux Indian dances as well as such hits as 'Anything You Can Do', 'I Got the Sun in the Morning', 'Doing What Comes Naturally', and the show-business anthem 'There's no Business like Show Business'.

Annie Oakley US slang for a complimentary ticket. The term probably arose because a punched ticket was thought to resemble the bullet-riddled playing cards used as targets by the markswoman Annie Oakley (Phoebe Anne Oakley Mozee; 1860–1926). Annie's fame became worldwide when she toured Europe in 1887 with Buffalo Bill's WILD WEST SHOW. She became the eponymous heroine of the stage musical *Annie Get Your Gun* (1946).

Anouilh, Jean (1910–87) French dramatist, whose play ANTIGONE, produced in Paris during the German occupation, brought him international fame at the end of World War II. His works offer a generally gloomy view of humanity, recurring themes being the loss of innocence, the inevitability of compromise, the difficulty of distinguishing between reality and illusion, and the impossibility of real human contact (especially in marriage).

Anouilh entered the theatre in 1931 as secretary to Louis JOUVET, principal director with the Comédie des Champs-Élysées. His own work was much influenced by Molière and Jean Giraudoux. His first play, *The Ermine*, was produced in 1932 by Lugné-Poë, but he attracted little attention until 1937, when TRAVELLER WITHOUT LUGGAGE, a sombre piece about an ex-soldier, was staged in Paris.

Anouilh's output is usually divided into the romantic *pièces roses*, such as THIEVES' CARNIVAL (1938); the tragic *pièces noires*, such as *La Sauvage* (*The Restless Heart*; 1938); the witty *pièces brillantes*, such as *La Répétition, ou l'amour puni* (*The Rehearsal*; 1950), the bitter *pièces grinçantes*, such as THE WALTZ OF THE TOREADORS (1952), and the historical *pièces costumées*, such as *L'Alouette* (THE LARK; 1953), about Joan of Arc, and *Becket, or the Honour of God* (1959).

His later works were more whimsical. Kenneth Tynan noted, "He uses fairy-tale or mythical plots of bald simplicity to make his people disrobe their souls." *La Grotte* (*The Cavern*; 1961), a work showing the influence of Pirandello, was seen at the Strand Theatre, London, in a production starring Alec McCowan, while *Hurluberlu ou le réactionnaire amoureux* (1959) was produced at the 1966 Chichester Festival as *The Fighting Cock*. *Antoine* (1969) was hailed as a late masterpiece. His last play, *The Navel*, was produced in 1981 when he was 71.

ANTA American National Theatre and Academy. The national theatre organization that Congress established under Franklin Roosevelt's administration in 1935 to provide a tax-free "people's project, organized and conducted in their interest, free from commercialism". A self-supporting organization run by its own members, it became the US centre for the INTERNATIONAL THEATRE INSTITUTE in 1948. Two years later it acquired the Guild Theatre in New York, which it renamed the Anta Playhouse. The venue was later leased to provide needed funds, although ANTA maintained offices there. In 1968 the Anta Playhouse was given to the nation (under the National Council on the Arts) as a performing arts centre operated by ANTA for non-profit-making theatre groups.

In 1963 ANTA financed the building of the shed-like Washington Square Theatre as a temporary home for the Lincoln Center repertory company. It opened in 1964 with the premiere of Arthur Miller's AFTER THE FALL. The musical *Man of La Mancha* ran there from 1965 until 1968, when the venue was demolished.

Anthony Street Theatre A theatre that stood on Worth Street, New York famous as the venue for Edmund KEAN's first appearance in that city. Originally a circus, it reopened in 1812 as the Olympic Theatre with a company led by two British-born US actors, Charlotte Melmoth and William Twaits. Circus acts continued to appear there. The first season saw the US premiere of M. G. ('Monk') Lewis's equestrian melodrama *Timour the Tartar*. In 1813 the theatre was redecorated and renamed the Anthony Street Theatre (the following year it changed its name to the Commonwealth Theatre and then to the Pavilion Theatre before reverting to the Anthony Street).

After the PARK THEATRE was destroyed by fire in 1820, its company moved to the Anthony Street, where they brought in the celebrated British actor Edmund Kean. After his appearance in the title role of *Richard III*, the *New York Evening Post* called him "the most complete actor, in our opinion, that ever appeared on our boards". Tickets were in such demand that they were auctioned and the profits given to charity. The company left when the Park reopened in 1821; the Anthony Street Theatre closed and was demolished.

Antigone (1) A one-act tragedy by SOPHOCLES, first performed in 422 BC in Athens. It is set in the aftermath of the Theban civil war. Polyneices, the son of King Oedipus and the rebel leader in the war, was amongst those killed. Creon, Oedipus's brother-in-law, now rules Thebes and refuses to allow Polyneices to be buried. Antigone, Oedipus's daughter, defies the ban but is caught and brought before the king. Although she insists that her obligation to her brother comes before her duty to the state, Creon sentences her to be buried alive. His son Haemon, who loves Antigone, pleads for her pardon and the king finally relents. She has already committed suicide, however, and Creon cannot prevent further suicides by his son and his queen. He is left shattered by sorrow and guilt. With its powerfully presented theme of the conflict between public and private loyalties, the play has proved perennially relevant. It has inspired numerous later versions.

(2) The tragedy by Jean ANOUILH that first established his international reputation. It opened in 1944 in German-occupied Paris, where it enjoyed a great but controversial success. The play was widely interpreted as a parable of wartime France. Some felt that it was anti-Nazi in its emphasis on private conscience and personal loyalty in the conduct of Antigone, while others saw a defence of the Vichy government in the sympathetic portrayal of the authoritarian Creon. Anouilh's Chorus concludes:

> Tragedy is clean, it is restful, it is flawless. In tragedy nothing is in doubt and everyone's destiny is known.

In the 1949 Old Vic production at London's New Theatre, Laurence Olivier played the Chorus and his wife Vivien Leigh played Antigone. The role finally brought her recognition as a fine tragedian.

anti-masque *See* MASQUE.

Antony and Cleopatra SHAKESPEARE's tragedy of doomed love, first performed in 1607. It was replaced for years on the English stage by Dryden's retelling of the story, ALL FOR LOVE (1677); Shakespeare's play was only revived in 1849. Famous duos to have played the parts include Godfrey Tearle and Edith Evans in 1946 at the Piccadilly Theatre, Laurence Olivier and Vivien Leigh in 1951 at the St James's, and Michael Redgrave and Peggy Ashcroft in 1953 at Stratford-upon-Avon. In 1978 at the Old Vic, John Turner and Barbara Jefford became the first couple to appear in both Shakespeare's and Dryden's plays.

The play is set in 37 different locations, the most for any work by Shakespeare. He included some teasing lines for the boy actors who would play Cleopatra, making the queen say at one point:

> I shall see
> Some squeaking Cleopatra boy my greatness
> I' the posture of a whore.

Anything Goes A musical with lyrics and music by Cole PORTER and book by Howard Lindsay, Russel Crouse, P. G. Wodehouse, and Guy Bolton. It opened on Broadway in 1934 at the ALVIN THEATRE and starred Ethel Merman as the nightclub singer Reno Sweeney. The *New York Times* review said "If Ethel Merman did not write 'I Get a Kick Out of You' and also the title song of the show, she has made them hers now by the swinging gusto of her platform style."

The plot involves Reno's friendship with Billy Crocker, who still yearns for his ex-fiancée Hope. Reno sails for England on the same ship as Hope; Billy, following her, stows away with the help of the devious Dr Moon, who is wanted by the FBI as 'Public Enemy Number 13'. When they arrive in London, Billy is horrified to learn that Hope plans to wed Sir Evelyn Oakleigh for his money. A business deal comes through, however, and Billy suddenly has the wealth to keep Hope. In the meantime, Sir Evelyn falls for Reno and the FBI reclassifies Dr Moon as 'harmless', upsetting his pride. Porter's songs include 'Anything Goes', 'You're the Tops', 'I Get a Kick Out of You', and 'All Through the Night'.

APA The Association of Producing Artists. During its ten-year existence (1960–70), this New York repertory company provided the widest cross-section of drama to be seen in America. Its eclectic repertory included works by Shakespeare, Shaw, Chekhov, Pirandello, and Ionesco.

Founded by Ellis Rabb, the APA formed a liaison with the OFF-BROADWAY Phoenix Theatre. The company won high critical praise but was sometimes accused of relying upon proven successes. It failed to receive an adequate subsidy and financial problems eventually forced it to close.

Apollo. Apollo Theatre The third theatre to be built on London's Shaftesbury Avenue. Opened in 1901 by Harry Lowenfeld, the Apollo has maintained its French Renaissance exterior and the ornate auditorium decorated in pink, turquoise, and gold. The theatre's badge, seen in the dress circle, features a group of German gypsies that lived on the Lowenfeld family estate in Poland.

The Apollo concentrated on musicals until 1913 (hence the special orchestra pit design). Cicely Courtneidge made her London debut here in *Tom Jones* (1907) and the Pélissier Follies were based at the theatre from 1908 to 1912. Other notable productions included a series of comedies (1934–37) written by Walter Hackett and George Broadhurst for Hackett's US actress wife Marion Lorne, Robert Sherwood's *Idiot's Delight* (1938), and Rattigan's *Flare Path* (1942). John Dighton's farce *The Happiest Days of Your Life* opened in 1948 and ran for 605 performances; in 1962 Marc Camoletti's air-hostess comedy *Boeing, Boeing* began its run of 2035 performances at the Apollo. John Gielgud appeared in 1968 as the headmaster in Alan Bennett's *Forty Years On*.

More recently the Apollo, now managed by the Stoll Moss Theatres, has presented Peter Shaffer's *Lettice and Lovage* (1987) starring Maggie Smith, Alfred Uhry's *Driving Miss Daisy* (1988), and Keith Waterhouse's *Our Song* with Peter O'Toole.

Apollo Victoria Theatre A theatre in Wilton Road, London. It was built in 1930 as the New Victoria, a 'super cinema' with an 'atmospheric' auditorium in blue and green designed to give the impression of an underwater world. In 1980 the building was converted into a concert hall and the Apollo Victoria Theatre, which opened in 1981. Unusually, its spacious foyer runs right through the building opening on both Wilton Road and Vauxhall Bridge Road; it also features inlaid doors and humorous carved reliefs in nooks and crannies.

The first production was a revival of Rodgers and Hammerstein's *The Sound of Music*. Since 1984 it has been the home of Andrew LLOYD WEBBER's *Starlight Express*, which in 1993 became the second-longest-running musical in British theatre history.

Appius The name given to the critic and playwright John Dennis (1657–1734) in Alexander Pope's *Essay on Criticism* (1711). Dennis was the author of the unsuccessful tragedy *Appius and Virginia* (1709). Although a severe critic himself, he was extremely sensitive to criticism from others, a fact alluded to in Pope's lines:

> But Appius reddens at each word you speak,
> And stares, tremendous! with a threatening eye,
> Like some fierce tyrant in old tapestry.

True to form, Dennis took this censure to heart, replying with a furious attack on Pope that the latter considered "perfectly lunatic". The feud raged for some twenty years. In 1717 Pope again satirized Dennis in the play *Three Hours after Marriage*, in which he appears as the character Sir Tremendous. More than ten years later, Dennis's fury had still not abated. He wrote to the *Daily Journal* (11 June 1728):

> Let us take the intitial and final letters of his Surname, *viz.*, *A. P-E*, and they give you the Idea of an *Ape*.–*Pope* comes from the Latin word *Popa*, which signifies a little Wart; or from *Poppysma*, because he was continually *popping* out squibs of wit, or rather *Po-pys-mata*, or *Po-piams*.

However, when Dennis was dying in poverty Pope wrote a prologue for his BENEFIT performance. Although Dennis's plays are now forgotten he is remembered for his criticism and for his invention of the 'thunder run' (*see* THUNDER).

Apple Cart, The A political comedy by George Bernard SHAW, first performed in 1929 in Warsaw and given its British premiere at that year's MALVERN FESTIVAL. The leading role of King Magnus, which is longer than Hamlet's, was written for Cedric Hardwicke. In 1986 Peter O'Toole played Magnus in a memorable revival.

Set in England in 1962, the play discusses the relationship between the monarchy and elected government and examines the morality of party politics. At the time critics felt that Shaw was sending a message to Ramsay MacDonald's socialist government.

The plot centres upon King Magnus, who is given an ultimatum by prime minister Proteus and his corrupt cabinet: the king must stop public speaking, manipulating the press, and otherwise using his influence, or the government will curtail his remaining powers. Magnus, however, is clever enough to outwit the politicians, threatening to upset the apple cart by renouncing all his titles in order to enter parliament. Proteus and his cabinet, aware of the king's charm and popularity, withdraw the ultimatum.

apron or **forestage** A part of the stage that projects in front of the PROSCENIUM ARCH and curtain. It was a Restoration development from the Elizabethan platform stage (*see* THRUST STAGE). Christopher Wren's new Drury Lane theatre opened in 1674 with a semi-oval stage that projected 10 feet forward, allowing actors to be clearly heard throughout the large auditorium.

Apron stages have been added to the Old Vic Theatre and at Stratford-upon-Avon in order to produce Elizabethan and Restoration plays in a historically accurate fashion. They are also seen in other venues, especially those used by academic and experimental companies.

Aquarium Theatre *See* IMPERIAL THEATRE.

aquatic drama A type of dramatic spectacle, popular in the 18th and 19th centuries, in which the acting area was filled with water and naval battles etc. were staged. The vogue originated in Paris, where it was popularized by circuses and the New Aquatic Theatre. In London aquatic dramas, often featuring historical engagements such as the Battle of Trafalgar, were staged at such major theatres as Drury Lane, Covent Garden, and Sadler's Wells. At Sadler's Wells, which briefly changed its name in the 1830s to the Aquatic Theatre, a large tank was filled from the New River.

More recently, Alan Ayckbourn's black comedy *Way Upstream* (1982) required a riverboat floating on real water.

arc Informal name for a carbon arc spotlight, the earliest form of electric LIGHTING used in theatres. Employing two carbon electrodes, it provided an intense (though flickering) beam. The arc was invented in 1809 by Sir Humphry Davy, who also helped develop the LIMELIGHT. It was used as an experiment in an 1846 production of *Prophète* at the Paris Opera but did not come into general theatrical use until about 1870. By the 1880s the arc had been replaced by Thomas Edison's incandescent lamp.

Arcadia A play by Tom STOPPARD, which opened at the Royal National Theatre in London in 1993. The action, with alternate scenes in the first decade of the 19th century and the last decade of the 20th century, takes place in the same room of an arcadian stately home. The young daughter of the 19th-century family has a bent for mathematics considered prophetic by all but her 20th-century kinsman, a mathematician preoccupied with the study of variations in a population of grouse. In the 19th century, Lord Byron visits from his nearby home, Newstead Abbey; the consequences of his visit are plausibly but chaotically misinterpreted by a visiting history don in the 20th century. Elements of farce and a search for the identity of the hermit (who occupied the hermitage in the park) are interspersed with expositions of the influence of the second law of thermodynamics on Newtonian mechanics and the design and layout of English parklands.

Arch Street Theatre One of America's early theatres, opened in 1828 in Philadelphia by the US actor William B. Wood. It immediately engages in fierce competition with the Walnut Street Theatre and the Chestnut Street Theatre, being a factor in the latter's bankruptcy. Under the forceful management (1860–92) of Mrs John Drew (*see* DREW FAMILY) the Arch Street's stock company presented both classic and contemporary works, becoming a great success both commercially

Arden. John Arden (1930–) British dramatist, noted for his politically challenging and linguistically rich plays in the tradition of Brecht; he has written for radio and television as well as for the stage. Since 1965, he has collaborated on many works with his wife, the Irish playwright Margeretta D'Arcy.

Arden's first professionally produced play was a radio drama, *The Life of Man*, broadcast in 1956. In the late 1950s Arden was associated with the ROYAL COURT THEATRE, where his stark anti-war play SERJEANT MUSGRAVE'S DANCE opened in 1959. The play was something of a commercial failure at the time, but has been frequently revived since. It was during the 1960s that Arden produced most of his major stage works; these include *The Happy Haven* (1960), *The Workhouse Donkey* (1963), which concerns municipal corruption in Arden's native Barnsley, *Armstrong's Last Goodnight* (1964), which drew parallels between contemporary political events in the Congo and machinations in medieval Scotland, and *Left-Handed Liberty* (1965).

In 1972 Arden and D'Arcy had a major argument with the RSC about the staging of their Arthurian play *The Island of the Mighty*. The argument culminated in Arden picketing the theatre and vowing that he would not write for the British stage again. Although he has since written plays for both the radio and the stage, he has not returned to the theatrical mainstream. Many of his plays of the 1970s are didactically Marxist in character. In the 1980s he began a second career as a novelist. *See also* LONGEST PLAYS *under* LONG.

Arden of Faversham A play (printed in 1592) once attributed to Shakespeare and possibly written by Thomas KYD. The earliest English domestic melodrama, it is based on the murder of Thomas Arden, Mayor of Faversham, Kent (1548). The play follows the actual events fairly closely. Arden's wife Alice, in love with a tailor called Thomas Mosby, plotted to murder her husband, with the aid of two ruffians known as Loosebagg (in the play, Shakebag) and Black Will. After several foiled attempts, Arden was killed as he played draughts in his parlour with Mosby. In the play the murderers rush in on the signal "Now I take you", when Mosby takes one of Arden's pieces. Three of the murderers were apprehended: Alice was burnt at Canterbury, Mosby was hanged at Smithfield, and Black Will was burnt at Flushing. Loosebagg escaped.

George Lillo's play of the same name was completed after his death (1739) by Dr John Hoadly and acted in 1759.

The story appeared in Holinshed's *Chronicles* (1577). Arden's half-timbered house in Faversham is still standing.

Forest of Arden A wooded tract of country in north Warwickshire, formerly part of a large forest covering much of the West Midlands (in his topographical poem *Polyolbion* Michael Drayton describes it as stretching from the Severn to the Trent). It is the probable setting of Shakespeare's AS YOU LIKE IT, although some writers have suggested that he meant the Ardennes region of France and Belgium (several of the play's characters have French names). The *Arden Shakespeare* is the standard modern scholarly edition of the plays. Shakespeare's mother was one Mary Arden.

arena An open area for acting or entertainment placed in the centre of an auditorium with seats on all sides; also a theatre, concert hall, etc. designed on this principle (in America this is known as an **arena theatre**). The word, which is Latin for sand, came to mean the central performing area of an ancient Roman AMPHITHEATRE.

Arena Stage An 800-seat theatre in Washington, DC, at 6th Street and Maine Avenue, NW, designed by Harry Weese in 1961 as a THEATRE-IN-THE-ROUND. It was built with grants from several organizations (including the Ford Foundation) and opened that year with a production of Brecht's *The Caucasian Chalk Circle*. The resident Arena Stage Company has earned high praise for its productions of new US and European works, classic revivals, and musicals.

The company was founded in Washington in 1950 by six people from George Washington University, including Professor Edward Mangum and Zelda Fichandler. The first season was presented in-the-round at a cinema. Fichandler soon took over as the company's director and manager, positions she still holds (sharing the latter post with her husband, Thomas, since 1961).

In 1956 the company transferred to an old brewery and remained there until its move to the Arena Stage. In 1970 a modified THRUST STAGE theatre, the **Kreeger Theatre**, was added, and soon afterwards a cabaret, the Old Vat Room. The facilities are also home to the COMMUNITY THEATRE group **Living Stage**.

Ariel An "airy spirit" in Shakespeare's THE TEMPEST. According to the play Ariel was enslaved to the witch Sycorax, who overtasked him, and in punishment for not doing what was beyond his power, shut him up in a pine-rift for twelve years. PROSPERO liberated him and was subsequently served by the spirit in all his plans. At the end of the play he sets Ariel free.

The name comes from a Hebrew word signifying 'lion of God'. In demonology, it has a long history as the name of a spirit. Thus Ariel is one of the seven angelic 'princes' in Heywood's *Hierarchie of the Blessed Angels* (1635) and one of the rebel angels in Milton's *Paradise Lost* (1667). Ariel also features as a sylph, the guardian of Belinda, in Pope's *Rape of the Lock* (1712). In astronomy, Ariel is a satellite of Uranus.

Ariel was also the name of the boat in which Percy Bysshe Shelley drowned in the Bay of Lerici in July 1822. He had chosen the name in allusion to his favourite play. His tombstone carries three lines from one of Ariel's songs in *The Tempest*:

> Nothing of him that doth fade,
> But doth suffer a sea change
> Into something rich and strange.

Aristophanes (*c.* 450–*c.* 385 BC) The great Athenian comic dramatist. His earlier plays are the only examples of the OLD COMEDY to have survived intact. In his last works he developed the more subtle and subdued style known as MIDDLE COMEDY. Aristophanes's plays are colourful, imaginative, and highly irreverent. His humour ranges from razor-sharp political satire and entertaining blasphemy, to the most obvious sexual innuendos and jokes about bodily functions. Although he was enormously popular in his heyday and his work is a perennial favourite amongst classical students, the difficulty of writing really funny translations and his uninhibited coarseness have prevented his work from finding a wider modern audience. Only 11 of his numerous works are extant, the best-known being THE ACHARNIANS, THE CLOUDS, THE FROGS, THE BIRDS, THE KNIGHTS, LYSISTRATA, and THE PEACE.

The English or **modern Aristophanes** A name bestowed on Samuel Foote (1722–77), the author and actor-manager. *See under* ENGLISH.

The French Aristophanes A name sometimes given to MOLIÈRE.

Arlecchino The most famous of the ZANNI characters of the Italian COMMEDIA DELL'ARTE. Wearing a black mask and dressed in a multicoloured patched suit, he was alternately foolish and quick-witted. From this ragged comic servant developed the more elegant English Harlequin. The first Italian Arlecchino was probably Tristano Martinelli (1557–1630); another famous interpreter of the part was Giuseppe Biancolelli (1637–88). The character was known as **Arlequin** in later French comedy and was then transformed in the early 18th century into HARLEQUIN, the magic-making lover of Columbine in the English harlequinade.

Arms and the Man A play by George Bernard SHAW, first performed in 1894 in the Avenue Theatre, London. The financial backing for the production came from Annie HORNIMAN, who founded the ABBEY THEATRE in Dublin. The only hiccup in the first night's performance was the moment when an actor mistakenly referred to the British army instead of the Bulgarian. Despite this, the play was rapturously received. When Shaw took his bow as author, he was greeted with cheers and a solitary boo. Shaw remarked:

> I quite agree with you, my friend, but what can we two do against a whole houseful of the opposite opinion?

Shaw once described the play as "one joke after another, it's a firecracker". The plot makes light of both love and war. It follows a Swiss mercenary soldier, Bluntschli, as he takes refuge in the bedroom of the young Raina Petkoff. She is intrigued by his prosaic view of war (he fills his cartridge case with chocolates) as contrasted with the romantic approach of her fiancé Sergius. Raina helps Bluntschli escape. When he returns with her father's coat, she chooses him over Sergius. The story was later adapted for the musical *The Chocolate Soldier* (by Oscar Straus).

In 1944 Olivier and Richardson opened their first Old Vic season with *Arms and the Man*. Richardson was highly praised as Bluntschli but Olivier got such bad reviews as the conventional Sergius (a part he admitted to hating) that he almost quit acting.

Arne, Susanna Maria *See* CIBBER FAMILY.

Arrabal, Fernando (1932–) Moroccan-born Spanish dramatist, poet, and film-maker, who writes in French and is now resident in Paris. Much of Arrabal's writing is informed by his traumatic childhood experiences during the Spanish Civil War, in which his Catholic mother apparently betrayed his Republican father to the Nationalists. His works deal with themes of violence, exile, and betrayal in a style that is often grotesque and shocking.

Following the publication of his first collection of plays in 1958 Arrabal became associated with the burgeoning Theatre of the ABSURD. Arrabal would later apply the label **Théâtre Panique** to his work – because it was intended to provoke psychological shock amongst the audience. In 1959 he produced his most experimental work, *Theatrical Orchestration*, which contains no dialogue whatsoever. Strong anti-Catholic sentiments are to be found in a number of his plays: *Car Cemetry* (1964), for example, includes a blasphemous parody of the crucifixion. Other plays include *The Architect and the Emperor of Assyria* (1967), *And They Put Handcuffs on the Flowers* (1969), a protest against political oppression written after his own imprisonment by the Franco regime, and *The Ballad of the Ghost Train* (1974). Arrabal has also written a novel, several volumes of poetry, essays, and screenplays, as well as directing a number of films.

arras Tapestry, so called from the French town of Arras, once famous for its manufacture. When rooms were hung with tapestry, this provided an obvious hiding place for anyone wishing to conceal him or herself; this is a frequent device in Elizabethan drama. In Shakespeare, for example, Hubert hides the two villains hired to put out Arthur's eyes behind an arras (*King John*, IV, i); Polonius is slain by Hamlet while concealed behind the arras (*Hamlet*, III, iv); Falstaff hides behind it in Ford's house (*The Merry Wives of Windsor*, III, iii); etc.

Arsenic and Old Lace A chaotic black comedy by Joseph Kesselring, first performed in 1941 in New York, where it ran for 1444 performances. The London production, which opened the following year in the Strand Theatre, ran for 1337 performances with Lilian Braithwaite and Mary Jarrold as the lethal heroines. The play was filmed by Frank Capra in 1942 with Cary Grant as Mortimer.

The story involves two elderly sisters, Abby and Martha Brewster, whose angelic looks hide the fact that they cure the loneliness of gentlemen callers by murdering them with poisoned elderberry wine. Upstairs lives their insane brother Teddy who, believing he is Teddy Roosevelt, is digging the Panama Canal in the basement (where 11 bodies are buried). Their brother Mortimer (a theatre critic) discovers the horrific secret and decides he cannot marry his girlfriend since insanity runs in the family. At the story's end, Teddy and his sisters leave for the lunatic asylum and tell Mortimer that he is not after all related to them, enabling him to marry.

Artaud, Antonin *See* CRUELTY, THEATRE OF.

Artists of Dionysus *See under* DIONYSUS.

arts. **Arts Councils** The four Arts Councils of England, Scotland, Wales, and Northern Ireland; they are the main national funding bodies for the arts in Britain. In the field of drama they have fostered the growth of repertory, encouraged new playwrights, subsidized ticket prices, and assisted commercial theatres with 'partly educational' productions.

The Councils also give grants and awards to hundreds of companies throughout Britain, the chief recipients being the Royal National Theatre and the Royal Shakespeare Theatre. Recent cutbacks in central funding have seen regional arts associations assume more responsibility for supporting community and young people's theatres. Since 1995 the Arts Councils have been responsible for allocating about 20% of those funds from the National Lottery designated for 'good works'.

The Arts Councils evolved from the Council for the Encouragement of Music and the Arts (CEMA), which was set up in 1940 (with grants from the Pilgrim Trust and the Treasury) to bring drama, opera, ballet, concerts, and other entertainment to areas whose populations had increased because of wartime evacuation.

In 1946 CEMA was replaced by the Arts Council of Great Britain, created by Royal Charter to "develop a greater knowledge, understanding, and practice of the Fine Arts" as well as to make them more accessible to the public and to improve artistic standards. The Council was now funded on a permanent basis, mostly by an annual grant-in-aid from the Treasury. The Arts Councils of Scotland and Wales became independent in 1994 (that for Northern Ireland having always been autonomous).

Arts Laboratory An experimental London theatre opened in 1968 in Drury Lane by the American Jim Haynes, who later remarked, "My artistic policy was to try to never say the word no." It was used by such radical fringe theatre companies as the Pip Simmons Theatre Group and the People Show (who as part of their first production there locked the audience in cages). The staging area was a curtained off section of a long room. The building also contained a basement cinema, in which the audience sat or lay on the foam-rubber floor (described as the biggest bed in London). The Laboratory's association with student rebellion and the drug culture led to its being refused Arts Council assistance; it closed the following year.

Arts Theatre A small London theatre in Great Newport Street. It began in 1927 as one of the private theatre clubs formed to exploit a loophole in British censorship. An early success (1928) was John Van Druten's *Young Woodley*, a play banned in public theatres by the Lord Chamberlain. Between 1942 and 1950 manager Alec Clunes developed a "pocket National Theatre", offering such new plays as Christopher Fry's *The Lady's Not for Burning*. In 1955 Peter Hall presented the British premiere of Beckett's *Waiting for Godot*. Other notable premieres included Anouilh's *Waltz of the Toreadors* (1956) and Pinter's *The Caretaker* (1960). The Royal Shakespeare Company presented a six-month experimental season at the Arts Theatre in 1962.

Carl Jenner's Unicorn Theatre for Children took over the venue in 1967. In the 1970s the Unicorn presented new plays for children while leasing the venue to visiting companies for evening performances; this produced such successes as Tom Stoppard's *Dirty Linen* (1976), which ran for 1667 performances, and John Godber's *Teechers* (1988). In 1992 the Reduced Shakespeare Company offered *The Complete Works of William Shakespeare*, with 37 plays abridged into two hours.

Ashcroft, Dame Peggy (Edith Margaret Emily Ashcroft; 1907–91) British actress, once described by J. B. Priestley as "the best all-round actress on the English-speaking stage". With the exception of Lady Macbeth, she played every major Shakespearean heroine, many opposite John Gielgud. After losing her father in World War I she was brought up by her mother, an amateur actress. She attended the Central School of Dramatic Art, making her debut in 1926 in Barrie's *Dear Brutus* at the Birmingham Repertory Theatre.

She was Desdemona to Paul Robeson's Othello in 1930 at the Savoy Theatre. Two years later, her Juliet, given at the Old Vic, was considered one of the great performances of modern times. In 1937 she made her Broadway debut in Maxwell Anderson's *High Tor* then returned to London for Gielgud's 1937–38 season at the Queen's Theatre, in which she played several roles, notably Irina in Chekhov's *Three Sisters*.

Just prior to World War II, Ashcroft played in Gerhart Hauptmann's *Before Sunrise* with the German actor Werner Krauss. When he appeared on stage, the booing forced down the curtain, and a pale Ashcroft then appeared to address the audience: "There are about 30 British actors and actresses in this company, and all of us feel most deeply the honour which has been conferred upon us in acting with the distinguished artist who is a visitor in our midst. I appeal to you to give him and us a fair chance." The play then went on to a great ovation and excellent reviews.

In 1942 she played with Gielgud in Wilde's *The Importance of Being Earnest*; *The Times* wrote of her performance that she was "a jewel changing colour with the light, now innocently olive-green, now an audacious pink". In 1954 Ashcroft won great acclaim in the title role of Ibsen's *Hedda Gabler* at the Westminster Theatre; a year later she acted the part in Oslo, receiving King Haakon's Gold Medal. During the 1950s she also began to take roles in contemporary plays, including Miss Madrigal in Enid Bagnold's *The Chalk Garden* in 1956 (the year she was created DBE).

She was a founding member of the ROYAL SHAKESPEARE COMPANY in 1961, later becoming a director; her roles with the company included Queen Margaret in Peter Hall's WAR OF THE ROSES cycle (1963–64). In 1962 a 700-seat theatre was named after her in Croydon. Her later successes included Samuel BECKETT's *Happy Days* in 1974 and the RSC's *All's Well That Ends Well* at the Barbican in 1982.

Ashcroft's few films include *A Passage to India*, for which she won an Academy Award as Best Supporting Actress in 1984.

aside In a play, a comment addressed to the audience rather than to the other characters, who are supposed not to have heard it. The device is popular in melodramas, comedies, and pantomimes; it is often accompanied by an exaggerated gesture, such as a hand held over the mouth. John Wells's topical comedy *Anyone for Denis?* (1981) contains the following exchange between prime minister Margaret Thatcher and a woman admiral:

> ADMIRAL: Oh, Leader, when all these bungling incompetents let you down, remember there is a shoulder here for you to weep upon. We women must stick together!
>
> MAGGIE: (aside) I'll bet she said the same to Edward Heath.

Asphaleian system In the Victorian theatre, a hydraulic system for raising or lowering the stage floor. Introduced in 1884 in Austria-Hungary, the iron mechanism used hydraulic pistons under the floor, which was divided into large individual platforms. Besides moving up and down, each platform could be tilted.

assistant stage manager (ASM) A member of the production team who assists the STAGE MANAGER in meeting the needs of the director and cast. The duties can be handled by one person, but large productions will have three assistant stage managers. The various jobs include being responsible for prompting and making sure that the actors' moves coincide with the director's decisions, placing props and furniture on stage, calling actors to the stage for cues or entrances, and controlling backstage lights and those on stage during scene changes, etc.

Association of Producing Artists *See* APA.

Astley's Amphitheatre A London theatre famous in the 18th and 19th centuries for its exhibitions of horsemanship and EQUESTRIAN DRAMAS. Philip Astley (1742–1814), a horse trainer and former calvary officer, opened it in 1769, with his charger Gibraltar. Astley also built 19 similar amphitheatres throughout Britain, Ireland, and France, including the Astley Amphitheatre in Paris (1782).

His original wooden building on Westminster Bridge Road had an unroofed stage until 1784. The venue burned down four times in 47 years, first in 1794, after which it reopened as the Royal Grove Amphitheatre, and for a second time in 1803, after which it reopened as the Royal Amphitheatre of Arts.

In 1825 a former equestrian performer, Andrew Ducrow (1793–1842), became joint owner despite being illiterate, and he added melodrama to the bill. Two more destructive fires followed in 1830 and

1841, after which William Batty reopened it as Batty's Amphitheatre. The next manager, William Cookes, turned Shakespeare's *Richard III* into an equestrian drama, even creating a leading role for Richard's horse, White Surrey.

Dion Boucicault took over in 1863 and renamed the venue the Theatre Royal, Westminster, presenting premieres of his own plays and works by Sir Walter Scott with little success. The following year E. T. Smith restored the name of Astley's and the US actress Adah Isaacs MENKEN played there in the highly successful equestrian drama *Mazeppa* (1823), an adaptation of Lord Byron's poem, in which she appeared "in a state of virtual nudity when bound to the back of the wild horse".

In 1871 the circus proprietors John and George Sanger assumed control, enlarged the venue, and renamed it Sanger's Grand National Amphitheatre. By 1893 the building was closed after being declared unsafe; it was demolished two years later.

Astor Place riot A riot that took place at the Astor Place Opera House in New York on 10 May 1849 as a result of the long-standing rivalry between the great British tragedian William MACREADY and his US counterpart Edwin FORREST.

The rivalry began in 1836, when Forrest first appeared on the London stage in parts Macready considered his own. Although Macready never saw Forrest perform, his comment was ominous: "It would be stupid and shallow hypocrisy to say that I was indifferent to the result." For a man with an ungovernable temper, this showed considerable restraint.

In 1843 Macready began his own lengthy tour of America; in an unguarded moment he reacted incautiously to a newspaper article that compared his talent to that of his rival: "Let him be an American actor – and a great American actor – but keep on this side of the Atlantic, and no one will gainsay his comparative excellence." After Forrest heard Macready's remark he took to playing the same roles as Macready, in the same town, on the same nights.

The conflict escalated during Forrest's second tour of Britain, in 1846; as a member of the audience for Macready's *Hamlet*, Forrest began to hiss. Personal pique erupted into international scandal: "I feel I cannot *stomach* the United States as a nation", Macready wrote.

The climax of the affair came with Macready's US tour of 1848–49. On 7 May 1849, at the Astor Place Opera House, Macready, playing Macbeth, was openly jeered; the performance ended with the audience throwing eggs and chairs onto the stage. The New York management, embarrassed by the episode, persuaded Macready to repeat the role three days later. On this occasion, order within the theatre was maintained throughout the performance, but outside an angry mob confronted the assembled riot police. When the police lost control of the mob, 60 mounted militiamen were called to the scene, followed by the infantry, with bayonets fixed. The reading of the Riot Act, twice, failed to calm the incensed rioters; the order to fire was given. As a result 22 rioters died and 36 were wounded. Macready himself slipped out of the theatre and escaped to Boston: he never acted in America again. The theatre itself closed for repairs but, now known as the 'Massacre Opera House', it failed to prosper, finally shutting its doors for ever on 12 June 1850.

As You Like It A comedy by SHAKESPEARE, written *c.* 1599, date of first performance unknown. Tradition says the Bard himself played the role of Adam, the old and faithful retainer. Based on Thomas Lodge's *Rosalynde* (1590), the play is set in the contrasting worlds of Frederick's oppressive court and the Forest of ARDEN. The plot concerns the romantic tribulations of four couples: Orlando and ROSALIND, Oliver and Celia, Touchstone and Audrey, and Silvius and Phebe. The characters represent various attitudes to love. Silvius is all sentiment, while Touchstone parodies sentiment. Although deeply in love herself, Rosalind mocks romantic excess; when Orlando says he will die of love, she has her doubts: "Men have died from time to time, and worms have eaten them, but not for love." Melancholy Jaques derides everything, and his famous speech reduces life to a farce full of stock theatrical characters:

> All the world's a stage,
> And all the men and women merely players:
> They have their exits and their entrances,
> And one man in his time plays many parts,
> His acts being seven ages.

In the 18th century *As You Like It* provided choice roles for such actors as Charles Macklin, Charles Kean, and Mrs Siddons. Modern actors to have excelled in the play include Laurence Olivier, Michael Redgrave, Edith Evans, Vanessa Redgrave, Katherine Hepburn, and George C. Scott. An all-male production at the Old Vic in 1967 featured Ronald Pickup, Charles Kay, Richard Kaye, and Anthony Hopkins as Rosalind, Celia, Phebe, and Audrey respectively. It provoked Olivier to snap at rehearsal, "Shouldn't the women be wearing breasts?"

When Nigel Playfair directed the play in 1919 at the STRATFORD MEMORIAL THEATRE, he courted controversy by substituting authentic Shakespeare for local theatrical tradition: amongst other changes he threw out an ancient stuffed stag always used in the play and restored Shakespearean lines always left out. Play-goers were outraged. One woman approached the designer, Lovat Fraser, in town waving her fist: "Young man, how dare you meddle with our Shakespeare."

ATA American Theatre Association. A US theatre organization, located at 1010 Wisconsin Avenue, NW, in Washington, DC, that supports educational and noncommercial theatre. It was founded in 1936 as the American Educational Theatre Association and reorganized under its present name in 1986.

The ATA founded the annual American College Theatre Festival, a competition granting awards at regional and national festivals. Although it supports the activities of more than 2000 drama departments and schools in US colleges and universities, it is not wholly an educational organization. The seven ATA divisions are: the American Community Theatre Association, the Army Theatre Arts Association, the National Association of Schools of Theatre, the National Children's Theatre Association, the Secondary School Theatre Association, the University and College Theatre Association, and the University Resident Theatre Association.

Atelier, Théâtre de l' A theatre in Paris near the Montmartre district. It opened in 1822 as the Théâtre des Élèves, specializing in melodrama and vaudeville; it was later converted into a cinema. In 1922 the actor, director, and producer Charles Dullin (1885–1949) took it over as a home for the avant-garde company he had formed three years earlier. The theatre's reputation grew as Dullin presented the first French production of a play by Pirandello and works by such dramatists as Marcel Achard and Jean Cocteau, including the latter's *Antigone* in 1922. Dullin also ran a drama school in the theatre that provided one of France's best training grounds for actors.

Louis Jouvet (1887–1951) also directed works at the theatre. André Barsacq (1909–73), who began his career at the Atelier under Dullin, succeeded him as manager after World War II.

atellana A type of partly improvised FARCE popular in the early Roman theatre. It was named after its birthplace, the town of Atella in southern Italy. Its coarse rustic humour derived from its original purpose of amusing local people on market day (early *atellanae* have such titles as *The Farmer* and *The She-Goat*). The five main characters, each of whom wore distinctive masks and costumes, were the fat Bucco, the rural Maccus, the hunchback Dossennus, the ogre Manducus, and old Pappus. Scholars have remarked on the similarities to the early form of the COMMEDIA DELL'ARTE.

When the Atellan farce moved to Rome it gradually lost its impromptu nature. It achieved a more sophisticated literary status in the first century BC, when the dramatists Pomponius and Novius began to write down the plots of the short comedies and to use them as curtain-raisers. Under the dictator Sulla (138–78 BC) the *fabula atellana* was the only indigenous Roman drama. It later evolved into, and was replaced by, MIME.

Athalie Jean RACINE's last play, often considered his finest. It was commissioned after his retirement from the commercial stage by Madame de Maintenon, Louis XIV's morganatic wife, for the girls' school she ran and presented at Versailles in 1691. Despite its beautiful chorus passages, Louis XIV disliked the play because Racine had departed from his usual theme of praising the monarchy, promoting instead the views of the Jansenist cult that had educated him. Louis later dispersed the religious group. The first public performance was not until 1716, the year after Louis's death. The tragedy subsequently became a centrepiece in the repertoire of the Comédie-Française.

The plot concerns Athalie, the first queen of Jerusalem, who worships the pagan god Baal. Having already murdered her own grandchildren, she orders the massacre of those who worship Jehovah. The one grandchild to escape was Joash. When Athalie encounters him, she has one moment of weakness and rejects advice to kill him. This hesitation, a miracle from God, leads to her downfall.

Athénée, Théâtre de l' A theatre in Paris. As the Athénée-Comique it was originally known for melodrama and light entertainment. In 1934 the director Louis JOUVET took over the Athénée and began to produce serious plays by Molière and Jean Giraudoux amongst others. The theatre's leading position declined after Jouvet's death in 1951.

Athenian drama Greek theatre of the 5th and 4th centuries BC. The period saw the evolution of both tragedy and comedy through two great annual competitions held in Athens: the city DIONYSIA for tragedies and the LENAEA for comedies. It also supplied the first major Western dramatist whose work survives in AESCHYLUS, two more great tragic poets in SOPHOCLES and EURIPIDES, and the OLD COMEDY of Aristophanes.

During the period the emphasis on religious themes and abstract issues found in the early plays increasingly gave way to individual character analysis. The chorus's role was reduced and more actors brought upon the stage. Basic props and scenery were also introduced. The first plays were staged in the ORCHESTRA in Athens market but as the popularity of drama grew, performances shifted to the steep Acropolis hill, where wooden, then stone, seats were installed. The development of MIDDLE COMEDY and then NEW COMEDY in the later 4th century BC had an important influence on ROMAN DRAMA. *See also* GREEK DRAMA.

Atkinson, Brooks (1894–1984) The drama critic for the *New York Times* from 1926 until 1960 (except during World War II, when he was a war correspondent in China and Russia). Atkinson was respected for his penetrating reviews and was credited with the ability to make or break shows. He received a Tony Award for distinguished achievement in the theatre and when he retired the Mansfield Theatre on Broadway was renamed the Brooks Atkinson Theatre in his honour (1960).

Atkinson could be effusive in his praise, as when describing Beatrice LILLIE in *Oh, Please* (1926) as "an incomparable comedienne in the highly intelligent vein of Charlie Chaplin", or saying of Ethel MERMAN's performance in *Gypsy*: "her personal magnetism electrifies the whole theatre." At the same time he was no respecter of reputations, noting of Charles LAUGHTON's *Galileo* in 1947: "His pompous acting and his overbearing attitude towards the drama reduced epic theatre to the level of exhibitionism." He also savaged Laurence OLIVIER and Vivien LEIGH's performances in *Romeo and Juliet* in 1940 (which had been highly praised in Chicago): "Much scenery, no play. Although Miss Leigh and Mr Olivier are handsome young people, they hardly act the parts at all, and Mr Olivier in particular keeps throwing his part away." Reviewing a British actress named April who had opened on Broadway he noted sharply: "Oh, to be in England, now that's April's here."

audition A method of casting a play, especially for secondary roles or in amateur productions, in which actors compete for parts. An audition is run by the stage manager; its content may range from an informal chat to set readings from classical and modern pieces or from the play to be cast. Actors are often called to perform before the director and others at 10-minute intervals. The nerve-wracking ritual is known derisively within the profession as the **cattle call**; the fact that many actors are auditioned for each part has produced the cliche 'Don't call us, we'll call you'. The musical *A Chorus Line* (1975) concerns a group of actors auditioning for a Broadway show.

Audley. We will John Audley it A theatrical phrase meaning to abridge, or bring to a conclusion, a play in progress. It is said that an 18th-century travelling showman named Shuter used to lengthen out his performances until sufficient newcomers were waiting for the next house. An assistant would then call out, "Is John Audley here?" and the play was brought to an end as soon as possible.

Augustan drama The NEOCLASSICAL DRAMA of the mid 17th century in France and of a slightly later period in England. In France it is represented by the great works of

Corneille, Racine, and Molière, and in England by the plays of John Dryden, William Congreve, Joseph Addison, and others. The original *Augustan Age* was the Golden Age of Latin literature, so called from the Emperor Augustus, in whose reign (27 BC–14 AD) Horace, Ovid, Virgil, Livy, Propertius, etc., flourished.

aulaeum *See* CURTAIN.

Aunt Edna A fictional theatregoer conceived by Terence RATTIGAN as the epitome of the matinée audience he had to please. She later became a widely recognized embodiment of all the forces that the ANGRY YOUNG MEN of the 1950s sought to displace. Rattigan introduced her in his preface to the second volume of his *Collected Plays* (1953):

> A nice respectable, middle-class, middle-aged maiden lady, with time on her hands and the money to help pass it...Let us call her Aunt Edna...Aunt Edna is universal...She is also immortal.

Aureng-Zebe A tragedy by John DRYDEN, first produced in 1675 in London. It was his last rhymed heroic play, a genre with which he had become disillusioned. In its dedication he wrote "I desire to be no longer the Sisyphus of the Stage; to roll up a stone with endless labour...which is perpetually falling down again."

The plot is loosely based on events in the India of Dryden's own day. Aureng-Zebe seizes the Indian empire from his father and his brothers. The hero maintains exemplary virtue in the midst of a chaotic world in which his stepmother lusts after him and his father seeks the woman he himself loves.

author's night In the 17th- and 18th-century English theatre, a BENEFIT performance whose proceeds went to the playwright. This was usually the third night of a production (if it lasted that long). Samuel Johnson was given the proceeds of the 3rd, 6th, and 9th nights of *Irene* (1749), as was Oliver Goldsmith for *The Good-Natured Man* (1768).

Autolycus A rascally pedlar in Shakespeare's THE WINTER'S TALE. A trickster and petty thief, the character owes much to the rogue literature popular at the time.

The original Autolycus was the son of Mercury and the craftiest of thieves. He stole his neighbours' flocks and altered their marks; but Sisyphus outwitted him by marking his sheep under their feet. Shakespeare's Autolycus remarks:

> My father named me Autolycus; who being, as I am, littered under Mercury, was likewise a snapper-up of unconsidered trifles.
>
> *The Winter's Tale* (IV, ii).

auto sacramental The Spanish equivalent of the English MYSTERY PLAY. This vernacular religious drama dates back to about 1200 and derived from the Latin LITURGICAL DRAMA. The plays were acted on temporary open-air stages or wagons at Church festivals, especially at the feast of Corpus Christi. The event began with a procession of choirs, priests bearing the Host beneath a canopy, royalty and nobles, and finally the actors. Prayers were said at the stage before the performance. The main religious allegory was usually preceded by a prologue and a farce and followed by concluding songs or dances.

About 400 of the 1200 plays written by Lope de VEGA were *autos sacramentales*, but the most celebrated writer in the genre was Pedro CALDERÓN de la Barca. His numerous religious works were staged in Madrid from 1650 onwards; the best known is *El gran teatro del mundo*, which develops the idea that the world is a stage on which each person plays the role written for him or her by God. The *autos sacramentales* continued long after mystery plays had died away in England and France, but they became less and less religious in their content and were finally prohibited by royal command in 1765.

Avignon Festival A major French theatre festival that by 1990 had assumed the status of that nation's "premier cultural event". It was founded in 1947 by Jean VILAR, who that year appeared at Avignon in the first French version of Shakespeare's *Richard II*. The open-air production was staged with special music and lighting but without scenery on a platform stage in the courtyard of the Palace of the Popes. The festival became an annual July event and grew quickly. In 1951 Vilar revived the THÉÂTRE NATIONAL POPULAIRE and subsequently brought the company to the festival each year.

Vilar's festival productions were large-scale but emphasized the individual actor and made use of sparse platform settings. Attention was focused upon the performers through elaborate costumes and special lighting. Early successes included Corneille's *Le Cid* and Heinrich von Kleist's *Prinz Friedrich von Homburg* (both 1951) and Beaumarchais's *The Marriage of Figaro* (1956).

In the 1960s the festival expanded rapidly; in 1968 it had 12 official venues and many 'off-off-Festival' ones and staged about 300 productions. This diversity continued after Vilar's death in 1971, with contributions by the major French companies, fringe theatre groups such as New York's radical LIVING THEATRE, and offerings from French-speaking Third World countries. The 1985 festival saw the premiere of Peter Brook and Jean-Claude Carrière's adaptation of the Sanskrit epic, MAHABHARATA.

Awake and Sing A play by the US dramatist Clifford ODETS. It was first performed in 1935 by the GROUP THEATRE at the Belasco Theatre, New York. Its success led to Odets being acclaimed as the country's most promising playwright. The story concerns a shrewd Jewish mother who rules her working-class family with an iron hand. She breaks up her son's love affair and pushes her daughter towards a loveless marriage. In the end, however, her daughter defies her by eloping with a gangster.

Ayckbourn, Sir Alan (1939–) The most popular British playwright since Noël Coward and one of the most prolific. His comedies have been translated into some 30 languages, and in 1975 he had five plays running simultaneously in London's West End. Since 1970 Ayckbourn has been the artistic director (now unpaid) of the STEPHEN JOSEPH THEATRE IN THE ROUND at Scarborough, where most of his plays have been premiered. He was knighted in 1997.

Ayckbourn's comic dissection of middle-class English mores often reveals the underlying loneliness and despair of his characters. Recent works have become blacker. He noted, "I think inevitably as you write about people, you scrape away the outer layers and you get to darknesses", also commenting "People tend to be a lot warier of me now. They don't invite me for dinner as much." His works are often ingeniously constructed: THE NORMAN CONQUESTS (1974) is a trilogy of comedies using the same set and variations on the same plot, SISTERLY FEELINGS (1980) provides the audience with a choice of four versions, while *Intimate Exchanges* (1984) has more than 30 scenes that can be arranged in 16 possible versions.

Born in London, Ayckbourn joined Donald Wolfit's company as both actor and stage manager at the age of 18. He later worked as an actor and director for Stephen Joseph at his theatre-in-the-round in Scarborough and at the Victoria Theatre, Stoke-on-Trent. Joseph encouraged him to write plays for both theatres; Ayckbourn's first comedy, *Mr Whatnot*, was seen in London in 1964 after opening the previous year at the Victoria. Almost all of his subsequent works have been premiered in Scarborough before transferring to the West End. In 1967 he found acclaim with RELATIVELY SPEAKING, produced at the Duke of York's Theatre, London, after its Scarborough opening. Its suburban setting and acrimonious relationships set the pattern for Ayckbourn's future hits. HOW THE OTHER HALF LOVES (1970) starred Robert Morley at the Lyric Theatre and subsequently toured Canada and Australia. TIME AND TIME AGAIN followed in 1972 at the Comedy Theatre, while the great success ABSURD PERSON SINGULAR (1973) was first produced at the Criterion. In 1974 *The Norman Conquests* opened at the Globe Theatre and *Absent Friends* began its run at the Garrick Theatre.

His later works included the five playlets in *Confusions* (1976), BEDROOM FARCE (1977), JUST BETWEEN OURSELVES (1977), JOKING APART (1979), TEN TIMES TABLE (1978), *Taking Steps* (1980), WAY UPSTREAM (1982), the musical *Making Tracks* (1983; with Paul Todd), and A CHORUS OF DISAPPROVAL (1985). Recent plays have included *The Revenger's Comedies* (1991), *Wildest Dreams* (1993), and *Haunting Julia* (1994).

aye, aye, that's yer lot A catchphrase associated with the comedian and variety artist Jimmy Wheeler, who in the 1940s and 1950s used it to sign off at the end of his routine.

B

Bacchus *See* DIONYSUS.

What has that to do with Bacchus? What has that to do with the matter in hand? When THESPIS founded the Greek drama by introducing recitations into the Bacchic vintage songs, the innovation was allowed to pass, as long as the subject of recitation bore on the exploits of Bacchus; but when, for variety's sake, he wandered to other subjects, the Greeks pulled him up with the exclamation, "What has that to do with Bacchus?"

Bacchae, The EURIPIDES's last play, written in exile in Macedonia and produced posthumously in 405 BC in Athens. This one-act tragedy is Euripides's most frequently revived play, mainly because of the psychological intensity with which it presents the conflict between Dionysus (Bacchus), god of ecstasy, wine, and fertility, and the puritanical King Pentheus.

When Dionysus brings his cult to Thebes, Pentheus (*penthos* in Greek means 'sorrow') spurns the god and imprisons his abandoned female followers, declaring "in all matters, self-control resides in our own natures". The god then appears in human form to lure the king to the rites where, disguised as a woman, Pentheus secretly watches the orgiastic rituals. In a blood frenzy, the Bacchae mistake the King for a lion cub and rip him apart with their hands, led by his own mother who parades her son's head in triumph. This play is often taken as a parable about the dangers of repression.

According to one (dubious) legend, Euripides himself was torn apart by mad dogs shortly after writing the dismemberment scene. The play was never finished.

In 55 BC when the Roman consul Crassus was slain by the Parthians they allegedly staged a special performance of *The Bacchae* using Crassus's severed head as a prop: at the play's climax the frenzied Bacchant women sing:

> We've hunted down a mighty chase
> today,
> And from the mountain bring the noble
> prey....

back. **backcloth** *See* CLOTH.

backing flat *See* FLAT.

backstage In theatres with proscenium stages, the area behind the proscenium arch out of view of the audience. This usually includes the wings, dressing rooms, workshops, and storerooms. The term can also refer to these areas in non-proscenium theatres.

A **backstage musical** or **play** is one that deals with the lives, love affairs, rivalries, etc., of theatrical performers during a show. Typically, the actors find their real-life preoccupations mirrored in their stage roles. Famous examples include Michael Frayn's *Noises Off* (1982) and the Cole Porter musical *Kiss Me Kate* (1948).

Back to Methuselah A long fantasy play by George Bernard SHAW, first performed in 1922 by the Theatre Guild in New York. Edith Evans created the roles of the Serpent and the She-Ancient. Shaw considered it his finest play, but it is seldom seen today, being too monumental for normal commercial handling. The drama, five linked plays, covers human history from the Garden of Eden to the year 31290. Shaw expounds his idea of 'creative evolution' through the Serpent, who tells Eve:

> You imagine what you desire; you will what you imagine; and at last you create what you will...

In the year 2170 "the thing happens" when two characters from the 1920s sequence are found to be still alive: humanity has at last achieved the longevity needed to acquire wisdom.

Back to Methuselah was the source of a phrase used by John F. Kennedy (1917–63) and his brother Robert (1925–68) and often credited to them. When the Serpent tries to seduce Eve, he says:

> You see things; and you say 'Why?' But I dream things that never were; and I say 'Why not?'

Another line from the play became a catchphrase for Malcolm Fraser, the former prime minister of Australia (1975–83): "Life wasn't meant to be easy." In the play Shaw's He-Ancient declares:

> Life is not meant to be easy, my child; but take courage: it can be delightful.

Baconian theory The thesis (first put forward by the Rev. James Wilmot in 1805) that the plays of SHAKESPEARE were in fact written by Sir Francis Bacon. This most persistent of literary red herrings is based on the assumption that Shakespeare could not have possessed the knowledge and culture revealed in his works and thrives upon our ignorance of his life. In 1887 Ignatius Donnelly published *The Great Cryptogram*, which professed to show that cryptograms in the plays revealed Bacon as the undoubted author; the cryptographic method was further advanced by Sir Edwin Durning-Lawrence and others. Some have gone further, arguing that 'Shakespeare' was a wholly fictitious concept improvised to disguise the political thoughts of Bacon, Raleigh, and Sidney; proof, it is said, of this claim will be found in the playwright's grave (as yet unopened). Bacon has also been credited with the *Essays* of Montaigne, Burton's *Anatomy of Melancholy*, and the plays of Christopher Marlowe. However absurd it may seem, the theory has had many distinguished converts over the years, including Henry James and Mark Twain. W. S. Gilbert, who thought little of Sir Herbert Beerbohm Tree's performances of Hamlet, suggested that the issue might be resolved once and for all by having both Bacon's and Shakespeare's coffins dug up; whichever corpse turned first in his grave at hearing Tree's recitation would be the true author.

Several other candidates for the authorship have since been proposed, including Elizabeth I herself. In this century the Baconian theory has been rivalled by the so-called **Oxfordian theory**, according to which the plays were written by a minor poet, Edward De Vere, the 17th earl of Oxford (*see* OXFORD'S MEN). Proposed in the 1920s by the unfortunately named T. J. Looney, the theory has found a recent advocate in Enoch Powell. The most striking recent theory was that proposed in 1989 by Colonel Gaddafi, the Libyan leader. According to him, there existed definite proof that the author was an Arab, called 'Sheikh Speare'.

baiting A form of entertainment in which animals are tormented and killed for the pleasure of the spectators. It has existed in many countries. In ancient Rome gladiators known as *venationes* and *bestiarii* fought herds of exotic animals in the arenas. In the Middle Ages bulls were baited for hygienic reasons before their slaughter. The sports of bear-baiting and bull-baiting, in which these animals were chained to a stake and harassed by dogs, were introduced to England in about the 13th century as an aristocratic pleasure. Henry VIII licensed public animal fights and Elizabeth I was an avid supporter of bear-baiting. Although the Puritans outlawed baiting, three bear-gardens are known to have existed in Restoration London, and it was not until 1835 that Parliament legally abolished the unsavoury practice.

The Elizabethan theatre had close connections with baiting. When playhouses closed on Sundays, the Bear Garden, situated next to Shakespeare's GLOBE THEATRE, provided the only entertainment in town.

In 1583 an overflowing crowd caused the Bear Garden to collapse. It was rebuilt in grand style in 1598 and subsequently managed by Philip HENSLOWE, the owner of the Fortune, Hope, and Rose playhouses. He provided such 'entertainment' as the baiting of bears and bulls by dogs and even the whipping of a blind bear. In 1604 the actor Edward ALLEYN became Royal Keeper of Bulls and Mastiffs.

Scholars have suggested that Shakespeare used bears from the adjacent amphitheatre in *The Winter's Tale*, which includes the famous stage direction "Exit pursued by a bear". The Bard and his fellow actors were also familiar with the names of individual bears: in *The Merry Wives of Windsor*, the character Slender speaks of seeing 'Sanderson' loose 20 times.

Bajazet (1) In Marlowe's TAMBURLAINE THE GREAT an Ottoman sultan who is defeated in battle by Tamburlaine and subsequently carried about in an iron cage by his captor. Bajazet eventually beats out his brains on the bars of his prison. The character is based on the historical Bayezid I (ruled 1389–1403), who was defeated and captured by Timur in 1402. There is, however, no evidence for the story of the cage.

The caged sultan also appears in Nicholas Rowe's anti-Catholic play *Tamerlane* (1701), in which he partly represents Louis

XIV of France and his conqueror William III of England. For over a century the play was performed each 5 November, the anniversary of William's landing in Britain.

(2) A tragedy by RACINE that set a new fashion by using subject matter from recent Turkish history. It was first performed in 1672 in Paris; although Racine was criticized in some quarters for treating an oriental story in classical style, the play was a great success.

Set in 1638 in Constantinople, the plot concerns the sultan's younger brother, Bajazet, who weds the possessive and violent sultana Roxane in order to gain the throne. When Bajazet falls in love with the innocent Atalide, a young Ottoman princess, Roxane has him murdered. The play's atmosphere is one of intrigue and passion.

Roxane provided a famous role for RACHEL, who wore an approximation of Turkish dress as part of her campaign for historical accuracy in costumes.

Baker, Sarah (*c.* 1736–1816) English theatre proprietor, famous for her indomitable energy and enterprise during a career of more than 50 years. Although she could barely read and write, she managed a circuit of 10 theatres in Kent.

Sarah was the daughter of a touring actress and began her career with a puppet show. She married an actor in about 1761 but was widowed eight years later; to support her three children, she managed her mother's company before forming her own. Edmund Kean appeared with her troupe early in his career. She established a touring circuit in Kent and the whole family regularly presented comedies and tragedies. From about 1789 onwards she built her own theatres, eventually owning venues in Canterbury, Rochester, Faversham, Maidstone, Tunbridge Wells, Deal, Folkestone, Sandwich, Sittingbourne, and Lewes.

As well as contributing sound effects, Mrs Baker personally collected admission fees for the pit, boxes, and gallery. She then stuffed the receipts in her large front pocket and carried them to her room to be added to the money kept in large china punch bowls on the top shelf of an old bureau. Mistrusting banks, she carried her savings from town to town, once keeping a £200 note in her pocket for seven years.

Mrs Baker found various ingenious ways of overcoming her literacy problems. The critic Edward Dutton Cook (1829–83) described her method of creating a playbill by cutting out the titles of a play, an interlude, and a farce from old posters and sewing them together "avoiding the use of pen and ink". Other occasions proved more embarrassing, especially when she had to replace the prompter. On one such evening, her leading actor James Gardner was playing the role of Gradus in the farce *Who's the Dupe?* In a scene where Gradus pretends to speak Greek, Gardner's mind went blank. He glanced towards the PROMPT SIDE, but Mrs Baker was mute, puzzling over the playbook. "Give me the word, Madam," he whispered, but she only replied, "It's a hard word, Jim." With desperation, he asked for the next word. "That's harder," she replied. "The next," appealed Gardner. "Harder still!" she snapped, then hurled the book on stage and called, "There, now you have them all. Take your choice."

balcony A US and Canadian term for any CIRCLE or GALLERY in the auditorium of a theatre.

Balcony, The An expressionist play in nine scenes by Jean GENET, first performed in 1957 in London. In the 1960 Paris production, Marie Bell gave a noted performance as the madame, Irma. Set in a brothel, the play compares the sex games of prostitutes and their clients with the shams of conventional society. The clients play out the roles of bishop, general, and judge, while the prostitutes assume the guises of virgin, thief, and queen; meanwhile the madame watches everything on closed-circuit television. When a revolution overthrows the government those inside the brothel are urged to act out their roles to amuse the public. These are played out so realistically, however, that the borderline between illusion and reality becomes impossible to discern.

Bald Prima Donna, The A one-act play by IONESCO, first performed in Paris in 1950, that was subsequently recognized as the first major work in the Theatre of the ABSURD. This debut piece introduced many of the themes that were to characterize both Ionesco's own later works and those of other Absurdist writers. Principal among these was an awareness of the deficiencies of language as a means of communication. This aspect of the play is said to have been inspired by Ionesco's reading of English language phrase books. Audiences were at first bemused by the author's rejection of all theatrical conventions, but in time they responded to the desperate humour of the piece. The play's long residency at the Théâtre de la Huchette in Paris, beginning in the early 1950s, made it one of the world's longest-running plays. In America the piece is known as *The Bald Soprano*.

Bale, John (1495–1563) English dramatist who penned 21 plays in defence of the Reformation, formed his own company of travelling players, and eventually became the Bishop of Ossory in Ireland. His most famous work, *Kynge Johan*, was published in 1536 but revised for Edward VI and again for Queen Elizabeth I. It is usually considered the first English historical play, representing a transition between the medieval MORALITY PLAY and the chronicle plays of the Elizabethans.

The play presents John as a heroic figure who rescues Widow England from the clutches of an oppressive Church, declaring that his duty is to God and not to the foreign Pope. A number of historical characters appear as morality figures; thus the Pope is represented by the character Usurped Power, the Archbishop of Canterbury by Sedition, and Cardinal Pandulphus by Private Wealth. Bale's major source was William Tyndale's *Obedience of a Christian Man* (1528). Bale also used the INTERLUDE for religious and political propaganda. The vehemence of his controversial writings earned him the nickname *Bilious Bale*. His life provided the basis for John ARDEN's historical novel *Book of Bale* (1988).

ballad opera A type of musical drama popular in the 18th century, in which spoken dialogue was interspersed with songs set to well-known tunes. The form began as a parody of Italian opera and remained satirical, often attacking contemporary political figures. Gay's *The Beggar's Opera* (1728; *see under* BEGGAR) remains the most famous example. A year later Charles Coffey produced *The Beggar's Wedding* and the same author's play *The Devil to Pay* (1731) also became a popular ballad opera when cut to one act. When translated into German (as *Der Teufel ist los*; 1743) this inspired the development of the parallel *Singspiele* tradition there.

The ballad opera style was revived by the success of Isaac BICKERSTAFFE's *Love in a Village* in 1762, but this and such later works as Sheridan's THE DUENNA (1775) are not true ballad operas, their music having been specially composed.

Balzac of the Muscovite merchant A nickname given to the Russian dramatist Alexander OSTROVSKY. *See also* BANKRUPT, THE.

banana A slang term for a comedian. The term originated in US BURLESQUE, with the best or senior comedian being the 'top banana' followed by the 'second banana', 'third banana', etc. The term was apparently suggested by the banana-shaped clubs filled with air or water that burlesque comedians used to hit one another over the head. These implements may be related to the phallic symbols used in comedy performances in the ancient Greek and Roman theatres.

Bancrofts, the The English actor-manager Sir Squire Bancroft (1841–1926) and his actress-manager wife, the former Marie Effie Wilton (1839–1921). While managing the Prince of Wales' Theatre and the Haymarket, London, they introduced the dramatists Tom Robertson, A. W. Pinero, and Tom Taylor to play-goers. They initiated the vogue for CUP-AND-SAUCER DRAMA and DRAWING-ROOM DRAMA and promoted realistic scenery and more naturalistic styles of acting. The Bancrofts also raised the financial standing of actors, paying the highest salaries in London and providing their actresses with personal wardrobes.

Marie Wilton came from a family of actors and first appeared on stage at the age of six, playing the Emperor of Lilliput in the pantomime *Gulliver's Travels*. She specialized in male roles in BURLESQUE pieces, notably at the Strand Theatre where Charles Dickens called her "the cleverest girl I have ever seen on the stage in my time". Unable to escape being typecast, she borrowed £100 and persuaded the dramatist Henry J. Byron to join her in leasing the tatty Queen's Theatre (known as the DUST HOLE). She redecorated the venue and renamed it the Prince of Wales' Theatre, opening in 1865.

Squire Bancroft was educated privately until his father's early death forced him to earn a living. He joined the Theatre Royal, Birmingham in 1861 and met his future wife in repertory in Liverpool. He played 346 different parts during his four years with stock companies before joining her company at the Prince of Wales' for the opening.

Squire became joint manager when Byron left and the venue developed into London's leading house for comedy. The Bancrofts, who married in 1867, set a new fashion by presenting only one play in an evening. In 1869, when all seats to a revival of Sheridan's *The School For Scandal* were booked, they presented one of London's first matinees.

When the venue became too small, the Bancrofts moved to the Haymarket in 1880. There was a near riot, however, because they had switched the cheap seats from the pit to the second circle and replaced them with expensive stalls. The howls of protest and cries of 'Where's the pit?' lasted for more than 20 minutes.

The Bancrofts retired in 1885, but Squire returned in 1889 to appear opposite Irving at the Lyceum. In 1893 Marie joined him in *Diplomacy* at the Garrick Theatre, and Queen Victoria commanded them to perform the play at Balmoral that same year. Squire, who received a knighthood in 1897, was later president of the Royal Academy of Dramatic Art (*see* RADA), where he is now honoured by the presentation of the **Bancroft Gold Medal**.

Bandi Nata A form of traditional theatre in India's eastern state of Orissa. It presents legends associated with Bandi, the wife of the god Krishna, especially stories of her self-sacrifice in allowing him to frolic with Radha, her sister-in-law.

The plays, most of which last about three hours, combine drama, humour, dances, and songs, with accompaniment by the *dhol* drum. They are performed by untouchables from the central and western areas of Orissa. The actors mingle with the audience during the performance, joining the action only when they have lines.

Bankhead, Tallulah (1902–68) US actress known for her flamboyant style on and off stage and for her habitual husky-voiced greeting of 'Dahling'. Although superb in *femme fatale* roles, she was frequently accused of being more personality than actress. Tallulah was born in Alabama, the daughter of a US Congressman, and at 15 won a contest in a film magazine that sent her to New York. A year later she made her theatrical debut there in *The Squab Farm*.

It was in London, however, that she found fame, with her performance in *The Dancers* at Wyndham's Theatre in 1923. With her acid wit and outrageous style, she instantly became the toast of the town. Shops promoted Tallulah hats, dresses, and hair styles. Queues formed 48 hours in advance for unreserved seats and police once had to disperse 2000 admirers from the stage door. During her seven years in London she took the lead in some 15 plays, including COWARD's *Fallen Angels* (1925). The Master always thought her charming but embarrassing. During an evening at Chez Paree, Coward recalled: "Tallulah screamed and roared and banged the table, etc., and I wished the floor would open."

After returning to New York in 1933 she enjoyed two of her greatest successes as Regina in Hellman's *The Little Foxes* (1939) and Sabina in Wilder's *The Skin of Our Teeth* (1943). When she played the Queen in *The Eagle Has Two Heads* (1947) she had the then-unknown Marlon Brando dismissed from the cast because she disliked his attitude. He opened that same season in *A Streetcar Named Desire*, the work that made his reputation.

For years Tennessee WILLIAMS begged her to perform in his plays. Tallulah consistently refused because the works shocked her; finally, in 1956, she agreed to play Blanche in *A Streetcar Named Desire*. Eventually her life of three-day parties, smoking, alcohol, and cocaine took its toll. Her last performance was in 1964 as Mrs Goforth in Williams's *The Milk Train Doesn't Stop Here Anymore*; the play ran for five disastrous nights before closing.

Tallulah's performances veered from brilliance to calamity. The notices for her performance of Shakespeare's Cleopatra (1937) were particularly miserable; undaunted, she used to read them gleefully out loud, including John Mason Brown's opinion that "Miss Bankhead barged down the Nile last night as Cleopatra – and sank" and George Jean Nathan's comment "Miss Bankhead played the Queen of the Nil." *See also* CAMPBELL, MRS PATRICK.

> She was always a star, but only intermittently a good actress.
>
> BRENDAN GILL in *The Times*, 4 August 1973.

> A day away from Tallulah Bankhead is like a month in the country.
>
> *Show Business Illustrated*, 17 October 1961.

Bankrupt, The A play by the Russian dramatist Alexander OSTROVSKY that was banned for 13 years because it offended the traders of Moscow. Written when the author was 25 years old, it was first performed in 1849 at the Maly Theatre, Moscow (*see* HOUSE OF OSTROVSKY *under* HOUSE) and caused an immediate outcry with its exposure of bogus bankruptcies among the city's merchants. It was later renamed *It's All in the Family*, sometimes also translated as *It's A Family Affair*, *We'll Settle It Among Ourselves*.

The Bankrupt was among the plays that earned Ostrovsky the nickname of the **Balzac of the Muscovite merchant**. It also resulted in him being dismissed from the civil service and placed under police supervision. Although the play could not be performed, it circulated in manuscript form and became well known.

> All the characters in the play...are first-rate villains. The dialogue is filthy. The entire play is an insult to the Russian merchant class.
>
> Censor's report on Ostrovsky's *The Bankrupt*.

Baptiste Stage name of Jean-Gaspard Deburau (also known as Jan Kašpar Dvořák; 1796–1846), France's most famous PIERROT. Born into a family of Bohemian acrobats, he took over the role of the Pierrot at Paris's tiny Théâtre des Funambules on the Boulevard du Temple in about 1811. Baptiste transformed the character into a melancholy and innocent, almost childlike, figure; as a result of his popularity, Pierrot displaced HARLEQUIN as the main character in pantomime. In the part Baptiste wore a new style of white face, a black skullcap (in place of the traditional large hat), and a costume of loose white trousers and blouse (with large buttons but without the traditional ruffles at the neck). He played the part for 35 years until his death, when his son Charles Deburau (1829–73) inherited the role.

Barber of Seville, The A comedy of intrigue by BEAUMARCHAIS, first produced in Paris in 1775; it had been banned from the stage for several years owing to its criticism of the aristocracy. The play introduced as the barber the famous character of FIGARO, who later appeared in several sequels. An opera by Paisello appeared in 1780 but was eclipsed by Rossini's *Barbiere di Siviglia*, with words by Sterbini. The latter was hissed on its first appearance in 1816 under the title of *Almaviva*.

Barbican, the An entertainment complex in the City of London housing two theatres, a concert hall (the home of the London Symphony Orchestra), two exhibition halls, art galleries, a public library, three cinemas, bars, and restaurants. The Barbican Centre for Arts and Conferences was opened on 3 March 1982 by Queen Elizabeth II, who described it as "one of the wonders of the modern world". The complex was built on a World War II bombsite and named after the former Roman fortifications in the area.

The Barbican has been the London home of the ROYAL SHAKESPEARE COMPANY since 1982, with many productions transferring from the RSC's home base in Stratford. The first of these, given in the Barbican Theatre, was *Henry IV, Part I*, starring Joss Ackland as a brilliant Falstaff. The 1166-seat auditorium has three circles and the stage positioned in front of the Proscenium Arch; as a result the most distant seat is only 65 feet away. Scenery is stored above the stage in a 109-foot fly tower, one of the tallest in the world.

Smaller-scale RSC productions are given in The Pit, a flexible studio theatre that seats around 200 people on three or four sides according to the production, with no set seating plan. Originally intended as a rehearsal room, The Pit receives transfers from the RSC's small Stratford theatre, the Other Place.

The building itself (by Chamberlin, Powell, and Bon) has frequently been reviled, both for its ugliness and its confusing and impractical design:

> Cosy as an international airport, welcoming as a bank vault, the place set new standards in the degree of torture people will endure in pursuit of an evening's entertainment.
>
> IRVING WARDLE: *The Independent on Sunday* 23 Feb. 1992.

Bard or **Bard of Avon, the** William SHAKESPEARE, who was born and buried at Stratford-upon-Avon. It became customary to refer to Shakespeare in this way in the mid-to-late 18th century.

> For the bard of all bards was a Warwickshire Bard.
>
> DAVID GARRICK: 'Song' (1785).

bardolatry Excessive or idolatrous admiration for Shakespeare. The term was popularized by George Bernard SHAW in the early 20th century.

Bardolph One of FALSTAFF's inferior officers. Falstaff calls him "the knight of the burning lamp", because his nose is so red, and his face "so full of meteors". He is a low-bred drunken swaggerer, without principle, and "poor as a church mouse". The character appears in *Henry IV, Parts I* and *II*, *Henry V*, and *The Merry Wives of Windsor*. In *Henry V* he is hanged on the orders of the king (as Prince Hal, his former drinking crony) for robbing a church.

Barefoot in the Park A comedy by Neil SIMON that opened in 1963 in New York and ran for 1530 performances. A 1967 film starred Robert Redford and Jane Fonda. The plot concerns a newlywed couple, Corrie and Paul Bratter, who move into a rented apartment on 48th Street in New York. The five flights of stairs defeat most visitors, including Corrie's mother, but the couple settle in happily with the eccentric residents. Soon, however, the quarrelling begins: Corrie calls her husband a stuffed shirt because he will not walk barefoot in the park in freezing weather. Despite a disastrous evening at an Albanian restaurant with Corrie's mother, the couple draw back together and rekindle their love.

barker A person employed by a troupe of entertainers to address passers-by in a loud voice to attract their custom. This mode of publicity is usually associated with fairground or other open-air performances of an unsophisticated nature. The tradition can, however, be traced back to the theatres of ancient Greece and Rome. The main character in Rodgers and Hammerstein's musical CAROUSEL (1945) is the New England fairground barker, Billy Bigelow.

barn. barndoor or **barndoor shutters** A pair of spotlight shutters used to limit the spill from a light and to adjust the beam's size and shape on the stage.

barnstormer A strolling player, and hence any second-rate actor, especially one with an exaggerated declamatory style. From the itinerant actors who performed in village barns.

In America the term has been extended to someone, such as a politician, carrying out a speaking tour in rural areas, etc.

Barnum, P(hineas) T(aylor) (1810–91) The greatest US showman and publicist of his day. His numerous fraudulent exhibits earned him the nickname the PRINCE OF HUMBUGS. Despite this, Barnum established strict moral codes for his shows, led a respectable family life, and founded a model workers' community in East Bridgeport, Connecticut.

Barnum began his show business career in 1834 in New York. In 1841 he purchased Scudder's AMERICAN MUSEUM in that city and opened it as Barnum's American Museum, a venue for 'moral' plays, dioramas, and such curiosities as the first live hippopotamus seen in New York, a fake mermaid, and the midget General TOM THUMB (Charles Stratton), who toured Europe in 1844. In 1849 the museum became a stock company, and the following year he brought the 'Swedish Nightingale' Jenny Lind over for a US singing tour.

Barnum remained director of the museum until 1865. Six years later, at the age of 60, he set up his great CIRCUS and menagerie, which in 1881 merged with that of his rival James Bailey to become the three-ring Barnum and Bailey's Circus billed as "The Greatest Show on Earth". It was sold to the Ringling Brothers in 1907. The hit musical *Barnum* (1981) was based on his career (*see* PALLADIUM).

Barnwell, George The subject of the 17th-century ballad (collected in Bishop Percy's *Reliques*) that formed the basis of George Lillo's prose tragedy *The London Merchant, or the History of George Barnwell*, produced in 1731. Barnwell was a London apprentice, who fell in with a wanton in Shoreditch, named Sarah Millwood, to whom he gave £200 of his master's money in return for her favours. He next robbed his uncle, a rich grazier in Ludlow, and beat out his brains. Having spent the money, Sarah turned him out; each informed against the other and both were hanged. *See also* BÜRGERLICHES TRAUERSPIEL.

Baron, Michel *See* ROSCIUS OF FRANCE *under* ROSCIUS.

Barrault, Jean-Louis (1910–94) French actor, director, and manager, who studied acting under Charles Dullin (making his debut in Dullin's 1931 production of *Volpone*) and mime under Etienne Decroux. In 1940 Barrault joined the Comédie-

Française, where he met his future wife, the actress Madelaine Renaud, with whom he formed (1946) the Renaud-Barrault Company at the Théâtre Marigny. Barrault and Renaud remained at the Marigny for a decade, during which they established a high reputation with a broad range of productions. In 1956 the company moved to the Théâtre Sarah Bernhardt, before subsequently moving to the Palais-Royal. From 1959 to 1968 Barrault was director of the Théâtre National de l'ODÉON, which was renamed the Théâtre de France during this period. Many of his productions at this time were of plays by such contemporary dramatists as Beckett and Ionesco.

During the student riots of 1968 Barrault allowed protestors to occupy the Théâtre de France, which they used as a headquarters and as a forum for debate. When this led to his dismissal, Barrault returned to the independent theatre, where he staged a production of *Rabelais* (1969), his own adaptation of *Gargantua and Pantagruel*. In 1970 Barrault helped Peter BROOK to establish the INTERNATIONAL CENTRE FOR THEATRE RESEARCH in Paris.

From 1980 onwards Barrault was based at the Théâtre du Rond Point, Paris, where he staged both new productions and revivals of his earlier successes, including a 1985 production of Corneille's *Le Cid*. Barrault has also appeared in numerous films since his screen debut in 1936, most notably Marcel Carne's epic of 19th-century theatrical life *Les Enfants du Paradis* (1944), in which he played the great mime artist DEBURAU.

barrel *See* BATTEN.

barrel system *See* DRUM-AND-SHAFT.

Barretts of Wimpole Street, The A play by Rudolf Besier based on the true love story of the poets Elizabeth Barrett and Robert Browning. It was first performed in 1930 in London with Gwen Ffrangcon-Davies as Elizabeth. The following year it opened on Broadway with a strong performance by Katherine CORNELL who began her management of the Empire Theatre with the production. It ran for a year and then toured 77 US cities, providing Cornell with her most famous role. The critic Brooks Atkinson wrote that Cornell's "wild sensitivity... charges the drama with a meaning beyond the facts it records". The cast also included a dog in the role of Elizabeth Barrett's beloved Flush.

Set in 1845 in the London home of Edward Moulton-Barrett, the tyrannical father of the invalid Elizabeth, the play shows his domination of the large family. When the handsome young poet Robert Browning is attracted to Elizabeth's poetry, visits, and eventually proposes, she is fearful of her father's reaction. When he strikes her sister for asking permission to marry, Elizabeth secretly weds Browning and they prepare to leave. In his fury, Moulton-Barrett orders her dog, Flush, to be destroyed.

In 1964 the musical *Robert and Elizabeth* (book by Fred G. Morrit and Ronald Millar and music by Ron Grainer) was produced in London with June Bronhill and Keith Michell in the lead roles. The songs included 'Moon in My Pocket' and 'In A Simple Way'.

Barrie, Sir J(ames) M(atthew) (1860–1937) Scottish playwright and novelist, whose lasting fame derives from the children's fantasy PETER PAN. Although Barrie's more sentimental offerings led to his being described as "sugar without the diabetes" by the US theatre critic George Jean Nathan, he also wrote a variety of plays ranging from social comedies to a tragedy.

The son of a handloom weaver, Barrie studied at Edinburgh University before becoming a journalist. His first theatrical success came in 1892 with the short farce *Walker, London*. In 1897 he adapted *The Little Minister* from his own book and became close to Sylvia Llewellyn Davies and her five sons, for whom he devised his stories of Peter, the boy who would not grow up. In 1902 Barrie enjoyed success with the costume drama QUALITY STREET and the social comedy THE ADMIRABLE CRICHTON, about a butler who emerges as the natural leader of a group of castaways, which includes his former employers, on a desert island.

Peter Pan was first staged in 1904 at the Duke of York's Theatre, London, with Nina Boucicault as Peter; this established the role as one for actresses. The play was revived in London each Christmas from 1905 to 1940, when the tradition was interrupted by the war. When a dinner partner once suggested "Not all your plays are successes, I suppose, Sir James," the playwright retorted, "No, some Peter out and some Pan out."

In 1908 Barrie wrote another popular social comedy, WHAT EVERY WOMAN KNOWS. *Dear Brutus* (1917), often considered Barrie's finest work, shows nine people being given a second chance at life but bungling it once again. The tragedy *Mary Rose* (1920), about the problems caused by a girl who does not grow up, shows the other side of the *Peter Pan* syndrome.

His last play, the biblical *The Boy David* (1936), was written for the Austrian actress Elisabeth BERGNER, who played David. In Bergner's opinion, the play's failure precipitated Barrie's death the next year. Barrie, however, left £2000 to "my loved Elisabeth Bergner for the best performance ever given in any play of mine".

Barry, Elizabeth (1658–1713) British actress, generally considered the first woman to achieve excellence in her profession. She entered the Restoration theatre as a protégée of the Earl of Rochester (whose child she later bore), making her debut in 1673 in a revival of Lord Orrery's heroic drama *Mustapha*. Mrs Barry excelled in tragedy, having a strong voice and plump figure, and often appeared opposite Thomas BETTERTON. She was known for her hard character, miserly ways, and fiery temper; during a production of Nathaniel Lee's *The Rival Queens* she allegedly stabbed and wounded a rival actress on stage. Her lovers were supposedly legion. "Should you lie with her all night," complained one Tom Brown, "she would not know you next morning unless you had another five pounds at her service."

Mrs Barry created more than 100 roles, including two of Thomas Otway's heroines, Monimia in *The Orphan* (1680) and Belvidera in *Venice Preserv'd* (1682). She was also Zara in Congreve's only tragedy, *The Mourning Bride* (1697). She retired in 1710. Her death three years later was apparently the result of a bite from her favourite lapdog who, unknown to her, had become rabid.

Barrymores, the A distinguished US acting family, consisting of Ethel Barrymore (1879–1959) and her brothers Lionel Barrymore (1878–1954) and John Barrymore (1882–1942). They were the children of the actress Georgiana Drew (*see* DREW FAMILY) and the British actor Maurice Barrymore (1847–1905). The Drew-Barrymore clan inspired the 1927 Broadway comedy *The Royal Family* by George S. Kaufman and Edna Ferber.

Ethel Barrymore began her career as a pianist. She made her theatrical debut in 1894 in the company managed by her grandmother, Mrs John Drew. Three years later she played London with Henry Irving in *The Bells* and in 1901 became a Broadway star in *Captain Jinks of the Horse Marines*. A remarkable beauty, Ethel soon became the darling of the stage, the title **glamour girl** being first coined for her. When Winston CHURCHILL proposed marriage she declined, later explaining "My world was the theatre." She was also noted for her wit. When a critic pointed out that an actress known for her bad language was playing in a theatre with poor acoustics, Ethel commented "Now she can be obscene and not heard."

Ethel was also praised for her performances in Ibsen's *A Doll's House* (1905), Pinero's *Trelawny of the 'Wells'* (1911), and such Shakespearean roles as Ophelia, Portia, and Juliet. In 1928 the Shuberts opened the Ethel Barrymore Theatre with the actress starring in *The Kingdom of God*. In 1940 she crowned her career in Emlyn Williams's *The Corn is Green*, which ran for four years. She subsequently abandoned the theatre for the cinema. Her daughter Ethel Barrymore Colt (1912–77) became an opera singer.

Lionel Barrymore, who called acting "the family curse", reluctantly went on the stage at 15 after tutoring by his grandmother. As he later wrote:

> Neither Jack nor myself...preferred the stage...Yet it seemed that we had to be actors. It was as if our father had been a street cleaner, and had dropped dead near a fire hydrant, and we went out to pick up the shovel and broom and continue his work.

He abandoned the theatre for three years in 1906–09 in order to paint in France, later starring with his brother, John, in *Peter Ibbetson* (1917) and *The Jest* (1919). In 1926 Lionel turned permanently to Hollywood, where he made nearly 200 films. He published an autobiography, *We Barrymores*, in 1951.

His younger brother **John Barrymore** preferred love affairs and drinking to acting. He became noted for his comedy roles before making a stunning transition to tragedy in Galsworthy's *Justice* (1916). One of the first MATINEE IDOLS, he became known as **the Great Profile** on account of his striking good looks. His electrifying *Hamlet* (1922) ran for a record 101 performances; members of the

PLAYERS' CLUB were upset because he had not stopped at 99 in respect for Edwin Booth's record 100 performances. John returned to the role in 1925 at London's Haymarket. One evening, rather the worse for drink, he rushed from the stage to vomit. Later, at the GARRICK CLUB, he was congratulated for having so movingly expressed Hamlet's grief by retiring from the stage.

He had a furious temper. One evening, when coughing interrupted his lines, he returned in the second act and reached inside his coat for a large fish. "Here you damned walruses," he shouted, hurling the fish at the audience, "busy yourselves with this, while we go on with the play." He once wrote:

> My only regret in the theatre is that I could never sit out front and watch me.

John was lazy and, at the peak of his stage career, abandoned it for films. Both his daughter Diana Barrymore (1921–60) and his son John Barrymore Jr (1932–) had bright acting careers ruined by alcohol and drugs. His granddaughter, Drew Barrymore (1975–), suffered a similar fate after becoming well-known at the age of seven for her appearance in the film *E.T.* (1982).

Barrymorishly An adverb coined by *Time* magazine to describe the captivating stage presence of Ethel Barrymore.

Barter Theatre The first state-subsidized theatre and oldest professional repertory venue in America. It is located at Abingdon, Virginia, a town of some 4500 residents; audiences usually contain a large proportion of tourists. Built as a Presbyterian church in 1833, the building is America's second oldest theatrical structure (the oldest is Philadelphia's WALNUT STREET THEATRE). The interior was redecorated in 1951 with fittings from the Empire Theatre in New York, which closed that year. Actors whose early careers were boosted by stints at the Barter include Gregory Peck, Patricia Neal, and Ernest Borgnine.

The Barter Theatre was established during the Depression. It was the inspiration of Robert Porterfield, an unemployed actor from Virginia, who decided that he would not starve if theatre-goers could "trade ham for Hamlet", bartering food for their entertainment. With 22 colleagues and scenery begged from a touring company, Porterfield arrived in Abingdon to open the theatre in 1933. The price of admission was 40 cents or the equivalent in produce. Porterfield told the local population, "With vegetables you cannot sell, you can buy a good laugh." At the end of the first season the company had a profit of $4.35 and two barrels of jelly (and the actors recorded a collective weight gain of over 300 pounds).

The Barter's first production was John Golden's *After Tomorrow* in 1933. Later successes have included Shakespeare's *Twelfth Night* in 1947, *Talley's Folley* in 1981, and *Steel Magnolias* in 1988.

In 1946 the state legislature approved an annual appropriation and the designation of the Barter as 'The State Theatre of Virginia'. Porterfield died in 1971 and was succeeded by the current artistic director, Rex Partington, who began his acting career at the Barter in 1950. Bartering for the price of a ticket, still technically permitted, has passed into history.

Bartholomew. Bartholomew Fair A fair opened annually at Smithfield, London, on St Bartholomew's Day (24 August) from 1133 to 1752; after the reform of the calendar it began on 3 September. It was removed to Islington in 1840 and was last held in 1855. One of the great national fairs dealing in cloth, livestock, etc., accompanied by a variety of amusements and entertainments, it long held its place as a centre of London life. The Puritans failed to suppress it.

Ben JONSON's *Bartholomew Fair* was first acted on St Bartholomew's day 1614. The play gives a vibrant bustling picture of the fair and the wide cross-section of London life that attends; the characters include showmen, rogues, dupes, fashionable gallants, and a gaggle of censorious Puritans. In the play's climactic scene the hypocritical Zeal-of-the-land Busy is worsted in a debate about the morality of the theatre.

> Here's that will challenge all the fairs,
> Come buy my nuts and damsons and
> Burgamy pears!
> Here's the *Woman of Babylon, the Devil and the Pope*.
> And here's the little girl just going on
> the rope!
> Here's *Dives and Lazarus*, and the
> *World's Creation*;
> Here's the Tall Dutchwoman, the like's
> not in the nation.
> Here is the booths where the high Dutch
> maid is,

Here are the bears that dance like any ladies;
Tat, tat, tat, tat, says little penny trumpet;
Here's Jacob Hall, that does so jump it, jump it;
Sound trumpet, sound, for silver spoon and fork.
Come, here's your dainty pig and pork!
Wit and Drollery (1682).

Bartholomew pig A very fat person. At Bartholomew Fair one of the chief attractions used to be a pig, roasted whole and sold piping hot. Doll Tearsheet calls FALSTAFF:

Thou whoreson little tidy Bartholomew boar-pig.
Henry IV, Part II, (II, iv).

Basilisco A braggart. Basilisco was a cowardly bragging knight in the tragedy *Solyman and Perseda* (*c.* 1588), often attributed to Thomas KYD. In Shakespeare's *King John* the bastard Faulconbridge says to his mother, who asks him why he boasted of his ill-birth, "Knight, knight, good mother, Basilisco-like" i.e. my boasting has made me a knight.

bat The lath wand traditionally sported by HARLEQUIN. The word comes from French *batte*, a wooden sword.

batten A length of wood or metal that is used to hang lights or scenery, to stiffen a FLAT or board, or to join flats together. A metal batten is sometimes called a **barrel** or **spot bar** in Britain and a **pipe** or **pipe batten** in America. One common type of light batten comprises a series of floodlights mounted in a row of compartments and connected to three or four different circuits for colour mixing. This is known in Britain as a **compartment batten** or **magazine batten** and in America as a **strip light** or **border light**. The arrangement provides a more even but dimmer light than individual floodlights.

Bayes A character in THE REHEARSAL (1671), by George Villiers, the 2nd Duke of Buckingham, designed to satirize the poet and playwright John DRYDEN. The name alludes to the bay laurel of the laureateship, Dryden having been appointed poet laureate in 1668.

Dead men may rise again, like Bayes's troops, or the savages in the Fantocini In the ludicrous play-within-a-play in *The Rehearsal* a battle is fought between foot-soldiers and great HOBBY HORSES. At last DRAWCANSIR kills all on both sides. When asked how they are to go off, Bayes (the author) replies, "As they come on – upon their legs", upon which they all jump up alive again.

Baynes, Arthur *See* STAINLESS STEPHEN.

Bayreuth A city in Bavaria, Germany, famous for its association with the composer Richard Wagner (1813–83) and as the site of his theatre, Das Festspielhaus. Although Bayreuth already possessed a magnificent opera house when Wagner settled there, he was determined to build a new type of theatre capable of presenting his monumental music dramas, particularly the *Ring* cycle. Its strikingly plain design, the work of the architect Gottfried Semper (1803–79), broke with tradition in several respects. The fan-shaped auditorium had 31 rows of seats on a single slope like a Greek theatre; there were no grand boxes or special seating areas. The stark simplicity proved to be a major influence on later theatre design.

Das Festspielhaus was constructed just outside town and opened in 1876 with the complete *Ring* cycle, presented as part of the first Bayreuth Festival. This proved so costly that the theatre did not present another performance for six years. It closed during World War I, resuming Festival performances in 1924. There was another closure from 1945 until 1951, when the management of the Festival was resumed by Wagner's two grandsons.

Beaton, Sir Cecil (1904–80) British photographer and theatrical designer. Beaton began his photographic career while still a student at Harrow, subsequently specializing in portraits of the rich and famous. He became a close friend of Wallis Simpson, serving as the official photographer at her wedding (1936) to the former Edward VIII. Turning to stage design, he worked on several ballets and revues before providing costumes and scenery for major West End productions. His opulent designs drew on many sources, ranging from the gilded salons of Buckingham Palace to his own grandparents' upholstery.

His first great success was John Gielgud's 1945 production of *Lady Windermere's Fan*, for which he created a yellow silk boudoir and long corridors hung with ancestral portraits. For Pinero's *The Second Mrs Tanqueray* (1950) he recreated the grandeur of stately homes in the 1890s as well as a series of lavish gowns for Eileen Herlie. He worked with Noël Coward on *Quadrille* (1952) before moving to Broadway, where he carried out most of his later work.

Beaton's finest work for the stage was undoubtedly that for the Lerner and Loewe musical MY FAIR LADY (1956); the Ascot scene was considered particularly stunning. His designs were also used in the film version, earning him an Academy Award.

Beaton was also a compulsive diarist who wrote thousands of words a day; his journals contain many sharp comments on his theatrical friends. After seeing Mrs Patrick CAMPBELL in *Tanqueray* at the Pier Theatre in Bournemouth in 1924, he wrote, "Mrs. Pat was incredibly huge and terrible. Repulsive! She was twice as large as any man on the stage. She is most amusing, the old brute, when she takes her call. She waddles to the footlights and leans forward, holding up her skirt with one hand, and bowing with a terrible sneer on her face."

Beaton was knighted in 1972.

Beatrice In Shakespeare's MUCH ADO ABOUT NOTHING the rebellious lover of BENEDICK. Born under a "dancing star", Beatrice is perhaps the gaiest and most capricious of Shakespeare's heroines. Ellen TERRY gave a particularly notable performance in the role at the Lyceum Theatre in 1882.

Beaumarchais, Pierre-Augustin Caron de (Pierre-Augustin Caron; 1732–99) The last brilliant playwright of the French theatre before the Revolution of 1789. He is often credited with hastening that event with his two irreverent plays THE BARBER OF SEVILLE (1775) and THE MARRIAGE OF FIGARO (1784). Both are better known today in their operatic versions, Rossini's *Il Barbiere di Siviglia* (1816) and Mozart's *Le Nozze di Figaro* (1786). Although Beaumarchais's later works were failures, his writing influenced such subsequent playwrights as Eugène Scribe and Georges Feydeau.

An early campaigner for authors' rights, he battled the Comédie-Française to secure ROYALTY payments and regularized the practice through the Société des Auteurs, which he founded in 1777. He also won the right for authors to have a say in casting and was the first dramatist to add detailed stage directions to his scripts.

Beaumarchais was born in Paris, the son of a clockmaker. At the age of 19 he invented the escapement watch mechanism still used today. The Beaumarchais name was taken from the estate of the first of his three wives. He bought a judgeship in 1763 but lost it when his financial dealings led to a court case.

After several theatrical failures, Beaumarchais found success with his first comedy of intrigue, THE BARBER OF SEVILLE. The Comédie-Italienne rejected it because their leading actor was a former barber. The Comédie-Française accepted it in 1772 but the work's criticism of the aristocracy led to a ban on performances. However, Beaumarchais earned permission to stage the provocative play in 1775, having recently undertaken a secret mission to Vienna for Louis XVI, which ended in his imprisonment. In 1775 he was sent to London to recover secret French plans to invade England and during the American War of Independence he was involved in sending volunteers and provisions to the colonists.

Beaumarchais had further trouble producing THE MARRIAGE OF FIGARO, sometimes called the most subversive play ever written. Its attacks on the decadent nobility led to a banning order from the king. Public opinion, however, demanded its performance and it opened in 1784 at the Comédie-Française. Shortly afterwards, the naive Marie Antoinette played Rosina in *The Barber of Seville* in her Court Theatre, inviting Beaumarchais to attend.

Following the Revolution Beaumarchais was imprisoned and narrowly escaped the guillotine. His mistress obtained his release and he escaped to Hamburg. He returned to France in 1796 but died three years later, still writing furiously in an attempt to regain his fortune.

Beaumont, Sir Francis (1584–1616) English playwright, mainly remembered for his successful collaboration with John FLETCHER, their works being more popular than Shakespeare's in their day. The two bachelors lived together on Bankside and "had one wench in the house between them", according to John Aubrey in *Brief Lives*.

Beaumont was the son of Francis Beaumont, a justice of common pleas in Leicestershire. He left Oxford without a degree and studied at the Inner Temple before turning to writing. He enjoyed success with *The Woman Hater* (1606) but made his name the following year with THE KNIGHT OF THE BURNING PESTLE, a parody of chivalrous romances that also made fun of the play-going citizen and his wife.

He began to collaborate with Fletcher in about 1606–08, being always the dominant partner. Their first success came in 1609 with *Philaster; or, Love Lies Bleeding*, followed a year later by *The Maid's Tragedy* and *A King and No King* in 1611. Together they wrote at least six plays; in a further seven or eight cases the attribution is probable but not certain.

After marrying an heiress in 1613, Beaumont retired to live in Kent. He is buried in Westminster Abbey.

Beaux' Stratagem, The A comedy by George FARQUHAR, first performed in 1707 in London. Lacking funds, he sketched out the plot in one evening at the urging of his friend, the actor Robert Wilks. It was on the stage within six weeks, but Farquhar died after its third night.

The plot concerns two young gentlemen, Francis Archer and Thomas Aimwell, who seek their fortunes in the country having spent their inheritances in the city. They arrive at Lichfield and learn from the evil innkeeper Will Boniface of the wealthy widow Lady Bountiful and her lovely daughter Dorinda. In order to infiltrate the household Aimwell passes himself off as his elder brother, Lord Aimwell, and Archer pretends to be his servant. Soon they are adored by Dorinda and her sister-in-law, Mrs Sullen, who is married to a drunk. When a gang led by the innkeeper tries to rob the house, Archer and Aimwell thwart their efforts and are acclaimed as heroes. Aimwell, now engaged to Dorinda, reveals his true identity just as news arrives that his brother has died and the title is genuinely his. Dorinda forgives him and grants a fortune to Archer to marry Mrs Sullen, now that her disreputable husband has agreed to end their marriage.

The Beaux' Stratagem has been regularly revived in the 20th century. When John Clements and his wife Kay Hammond starred in a 1949 production at the Phoenix Theatre it ran for 532 performances, a record for a classic revival.

Beckett, Samuel (1906–89) Irish playwright and novelist who was awarded the Nobel Prize for Literature in 1969. His plays, which often dispense with plot, action, and even character, are the most celebrated works associated with the Theatre of the ABSURD. Their bleak vision of the futility of human existence in an indifferent universe is offset by humour and stoicism.

Born near Dublin, he moved to Paris in 1928, where he began to write poetry, essays, and stories under the influence of his friend James Joyce. After further spells in Dublin and London, he settled permanently in Paris in 1937; most of his best-known works were written initially in French.

Beckett wrote a series of novels in relative obscurity before finding sudden fame when his first play *En attendent Godot* (WAITING FOR GODOT) was produced (by Roger Blin) in Paris in 1953. The work achieved an immediate *succès de scandale*. In 1957 came the one-act *Fin de partie* (ENDGAME), produced a year later in London with the monologue KRAPP'S LAST TAPE.

Oh! les beaux jours (HAPPY DAYS) is a monologue for an actress buried up to her waist – subsequently up to her neck – in sand. It had its debut in 1961 in New York and was seen in London a year later. In 1976 the play opened the National Theatre building on the South Bank of the Thames in a production starring Peggy ASHCROFT. Beckett had sat in on rehearsals when Ashcroft first performed the work in 1974 and showed his characteristic obsession with detail. His minute directions to the extremely experienced and instinctive Ashcroft, on which hand to use to unpack a handbag and what to do with her hat and glasses, nearly ended their collaboration – fortunately she had a month to recover before opening night.

"I was in hospital once," Beckett once told Harold Pinter. "There was a man in another ward, dying of throat cancer. In the silence, I could hear his screams continually. That's the only kind of form my work has."

bedroom farce A type of broad comedy that depends upon chaotic and compromising situations featuring loss of clothing, mistaken identities, and double entendre. The *Whitehall farces*, many of which featured Brian Rix, are amongst the best-known British examples of the genre; some of the *Aldwych farces* of Ben Travers also come into the category.

Bedroom Farce A two-act comedy by Alan AYCKBOURN, first performed in 1977 at the National Theatre. The play concerns three married couples and takes place in their bedrooms, shown simultaneously on stage with the action switching rapidly from one to another.

Beefsteak Club A London club, frequented by wits and theatre people, where refreshment was limited to steaks and beer or wine; it was established in 1709, with a gridiron as its badge. In 1735 the Sublime Society of Steaks was inaugurated when Lord Peterborough dined there with John Rich (*see* RICH FAMILY), manager of the Covent Garden Theatre. Peterborough was so delighted with the steak that he proposed to repeat the entertainment every Saturday. The Sublime Society continued to meet there until the fire of 1808, when it moved to other premises. The 'Steaks' included many famous actors until its members lost interest – it came to an end in 1867. The modern Beefsteak Club was founded in 1876.

Beerbohm, Sir Max (1872–1956) British theatre critic and playwright, the half-brother of the actor-manager Beerbohm TREE. In 1898 he became drama critic of the *Saturday Review*, succeeding George Bernard Shaw. In 1908 he reviewed a London performance by the US actress Florence Kahn (1877–1951); they married later that year. Beerbohm also wrote fiction, including the novel *Zuleika Dobson* (1911), and drew caricatures, including a famous one of Oscar Wilde.

Beerbohm's one-act play *A Social Success* was produced in 1913 with George Alexander in the lead. He also turned one of his own short stories into the one-act CURTAIN RAISER *The Happy Hypocrite*; this achieved great success at the Royalty Theatre in 1900 with Mrs Patrick Campbell. On the opening night (which Beerbohm spent in hiding in the Metropole Hotel, Brighton), he confided to a friend that he did not "give a damn" if the critics liked it or not because "the public, after all, is the final court of appeal".

A three-act version of *The Happy Hypocrite* by Clemence Dane was produced in 1936 at His Majesty's Theatre. This starred Ivor NOVELLO as a fat dissolute man who recovers his self-respect when he falls in love. It proved the handsome star's least successful role and the play closed in three months.

Beerbohm's reviews often showed his Edwardian prejudices; for example, he wrote that Eleanora DUSE had a "great egoistic force. In a man I should admire this tremendous egoism very much indeed. In a woman it only makes me uncomfortable. I dislike it. I resent it. In the name of art, I protest against it." He preferred the gentle Ellen Terry (*see* TERRY FAMILY) who "always reminds me of a Christmas-tree decorated by a Pre-Raphaelite." When Sarah BERNHARDT played the role of Hamlet in 1899 in London, Beerbohm wrote: "The customs-house officials at Charing Cross ought to have confiscated her sable doublet and hose." Writing about the Tivoli, he said "The aim of the music hall is, in fact, to cheer the lower classes up by showing them a life uglier and more sordid than their own."

On one occasion the actor John Drew (*see* DREW FAMILY), who had shaved off his moustache for his current role, met Beerbohm in the lobby of a London theatre but could not recall his name. Beerbohm recognized him at once and commented: "Oh, Mr Drew, I'm afraid you don't know me without your moustache."

After World War I Beerbohm retired to Rapallo, in northern Italy, where he was often to be seen in the gardens of the Villino Chiaro in his white linen suit. His near neighbour was Rex HARRISON, who once asked the critic for a suitable Italian name for his house. On Beerbohm's suggestion he called it 'Villa San Genesio', after the patron saint of the theatre.

Beestons, the The actor-manager Christopher Beeston (1570–1638), a leading figure in the early 17th-century English theatre, and his son William Beeston (1606–82), who also acted and managed.

Christopher Beeston, who sometimes called himself Christopher Hutchinson, made his stage debut with Strange's Men and probably also appeared with the Lord Chamberlain's Men. In 1598 he appeared in Ben Jonson's *Every Man In His Humour* at London's Curtain Theatre along with Shakespeare and Richard Burbage. In 1602 Beeston performed with Worcester's Men and remained with the company when it became QUEEN ANNE'S MEN a year later. He subsequently became their business manager and in 1616 gave up acting to become manager of the COCKPIT THEATRE, which he converted into a covered private theatre. He housed his old company at the venue and allowed others to lease it. Beeston owned two-thirds of the theatre's shares and began the practice according to which the theatre manager also owned the costumes and the playscripts. After it burned down in 1617, Beeston rebuilt the theatre as the Phoenix and brought in Prince Charles's Men.

Beeston was a close friend of Thomas Heywood, also of Queen Anne's Men, and put on several of his plays. After the plague of 1625 had disrupted the profession, Beeston formed QUEEN HENRIETTA'S MEN. He disbanded them when the plague returned in 1636, but the following year obtained a royal warrant to bring together young players as the King's and Queen's Boys, usually known simply as Beeston's Boys (*see* BOY COMPANIES).

William Beeston, who had acted under his father, became master of the King's Company of boy players at Salisbury Court before 1642. Following his father's death, he took over Beeston's Boys and appeared with them at the Cockpit. After the closure of the theatres during the Puritan INTERREGNUM, he re-established the company at Salisbury Court but was forced to close in 1649 when the army wrecked the interior. He was also imprisoned for staging an unlicensed play. However, some suspected him of betraying actors to the authorities (*see* ILL BEEST).

After the Restoration, he reopened Salisbury Court and led a company there until 1664. Beeston was therefore one of the few theatrical figures to bring an essentially Elizabethan training into the Restoration era.

beggar. Beggar's daughter of Bednall Green, Bessee the The subject of a play by Henry Chettle and John Day (1600), another by Sheridan Knowles (1834), and a musical play by Robert Dodsley (1791). All three were based on an old ballad of this name (included in Bishop Percy's *Reliques*). The beautiful Bessee had four suitors – a knight, a gentleman of fortune, a London merchant, and the son of the innkeeper at Romford. She told them that they must obtain the consent of her father, the poor blind beggar of Bethnal Green, whereupon they all slunk off except the knight, who went to ask the beggar's leave to wed the "pretty Bessee". The beggar gave her £3000 for her dower, and £100 to buy her wedding gown. At the wedding feast he explained to the guests that he was Henry, son of Sir Simon dc Montfort.

Beggar's Opera, The A BALLAD OPERA by John Gay that opened at Lincoln's Inn Fields Theatre, London, in 1728. The idea originated with Jonathan Swift, who suggested to Gay that a Newgate prison pastoral "might make an odd pretty sort of thing". Since the play's great success brought its producer John Rich (*see* BEEFSTEAK CLUB) an £800 profit, London wits said *The Beggar's Opera* "made Gay rich and Rich gay". Gay's sequel, *Polly*, was banned until 1777 when it opened at the Haymarket in an expurgated version by the elder George Colman (*see* COLMAN FAMILY).

The Beggar's Opera satirized both the conventions of Italian opera and contemporary politics. Almost all the topical references are missed by modern audiences, but at the time the character of Macheath, the highwayman, was widely understood to represent the prime minister Sir Robert Walpole. This influenced Walpole's decision to introduce the 1737 Licensing Act, placing tighter controls on the stage (*see* GOLDEN RUMP, THE; LICENCE).

The play's English airs, selected and arranged by Pepusch, have always been a major part of its appeal. Frederic Austin rearranged the music for a 1920 production at the Lyric Theatre, Hammersmith, while in 1948 Benjamin Britten adapted it for Sadler's Wells. In 1928 Bertolt Brecht used the story as the basis of his THE THREEPENNY OPERA with music by Kurt Weill (including the famous 'Mack the Knife').

The play is described by the Beggar who presents it as a "fine moral tale". It begins with Peachum, a receiver of stolen goods, expressing horror that his daughter Polly has married the highwayman, Macheath. Peachum deals with the situation by informing against his new son-in-law. Macheath escapes, however, and goes to a brothel where he is betrayed by Jenny Diver, arrested, and sent to Newgate. Lucy Lockit, the jailer's daughter, becomes pregnant by Macheath and helps him escape. Lucy and Polly argue about who is the rightful wife. This hardly disturbs Macheath who muses (in a satire on Walpole, who married his mistress on his wife's death):

> How happy could I be with either,
> Were t'other dear charmer away!

Macheath is again caught. He is about to be hanged when the crowd demands a reprieve. The Beggar tells the audience that the piece must be realistic but then decides that a happy ending will ensure a longer run and a larger profit; consequently a messenger enters with a royal pardon for Macheath, who embraces Polly.

Behan, Brendan (1923–64) Irish playwright, who produced only two complete plays in his short turbulent life. Behan joined the IRA at the age of 14 and spent much of his youth in borstal and prison. His inventive dramas show the influence of Brecht and are notable for their rich use of vernacular. His first play, *The Quare Fellow* (1954), originally performed in a Gaelic version in Dublin, found wide acclaim when produced, by Joan LITTLEWOOD's Theatre Workshop in 1958. It ran for a total of 452 performances at the Theatre Royal, Stratford East, and at Wyndham's Theatre in the West End. It tells the story of a 'quare fellow' awaiting execution in an Irish prison; the title character is only talked about and never appears on stage. The play is thought to have influenced the campaign that led to the abolition of capital punishment in Britain.

Behan's tragicomedy *The Hostage* (1957) was also premiered in Gaelic before being successfully presented by Littlewood's group in 1959. The plot concerns an English soldier held prisoner by terrorists in an Irish brothel and eventually murdered. Audiences were also drawn to the theatre by the wild speeches Behan used to make from the stage. Although Behan was now a celebrity he added little to his achievement, wasting his talents in raconteurship and self-destructive drinking bouts. A third play, *Richard's Cork Leg*, was left unfinished at his death but performed in 1972 at the Abbey Theatre.

Behn, Aphra (1640–89) British playwright and novelist, probably the first Englishwoman to earn her living as a writer. She seems to have spent part of her youth in Guiana, where her father may have been a colonial official. After returning to England she married (1666) a wealthy Dutch merchant, who nevertheless left her in poverty on his death.

To support herself, she worked briefly as a British spy in the Netherlands – a position she acquired through the playwright and impresario Sir Thomas KILLIGREW. Thereafter she turned to writing, producing some 15 plays in the remaining two decades of her life. The first of these was the tragicomedy *The Forced Marriage; or, the Jealous Bridegroom* presented at Lincoln's Inn Fields Theatre in 1670 with Thomas Betterton in the lead role.

She made her name, however, with her comedies of intrigue, the first of these being THE ROVER; *or, the Banished Cavalier* (1677), about exiled English cavaliers rampaging through Europe. The central character was modelled upon the Earl of Rochester. Other successful comedies included *The Roundheads; or, the Good Old Cause* (1681), *The City-Heiress; or, Sir Timothy Treat-All* (1682), and *The Lucky Chance* (1686).

In 1687 Mrs Behn used the characters and conventions of the *commedia dell'arte* as the basis for a farce featuring Anthony Leigh as Scaramouche and Thomas Jevon as Harlequin. It was the first of England's many HARLEQUINADES, the genre that evolved into PANTOMIME.

Mrs Behn also wrote a well-received novel *Oroonoko, or the History of the Royal Slave* based on her early years in the West Indies; it was adapted for the stage (by Thomas Southerne) in 1695. Amongst her other achievements, she introduced milk punch into England.

Belasco, David (David Valasco; 1854–1931) Flamboyant US actor-manager and playwright. Perhaps his greatest contribution to the US theatre was his long successful fight (with Sarah Bernhardt and others) against the monopoly of the THEATRICAL SYNDICATE.

Belasco's career began in San Francisco. In 1882 he moved to New York to become stage manager at the Madison Square Theatre and from 1885 to 1890 held the same position at the Lyceum. His own plays included *The Girl I Left Behind Me* (1893), the Civil War drama *The Heart of Maryland* (1895), *Madame Butterfly* (1900), and *The Girl of the Golden West* (1905); the latter two were turned into operas by Puccini. In 1902 he acquired the Republic Theatre, renaming it the Belasco Theatre, and in 1907 built and opened the Stuyvesant Theatre, which likewise became the Belasco Theatre in 1910.

Belasco's productions blended melodrama with realism. He was the first to conceal footlights in the search for naturalism. For *The Governor's Lady* (1912) he built an exact replica of a restaurant on stage. To recreate a cheap theatrical boarding-house, he went to one in New York and bought the entire interior, even the broken gas fixtures.

He was equally famous for his experimental lighting. In his production of *The Darlings of the Gods* one lighting effect lasted seven minutes. For *The Girl of the Golden West* he experimented for three months to get the exact colours of a California sunset over the Sierra Nevada mountains.

Belasco had many eccentricities and strong opinions. He carried a briefcase inscribed in gold letters: 'The Play I Am Now Writing'. He banned brightly coloured flowers, especially red ones, from his productions because he felt they caused a distraction. During rehearsals, he could be a tyrant. "He tortured his actors," said critic Brooks Atkinson, "He stuck a pin in Frances Starr's beguiling behind to make her scream dramatically." He also kept a cheap watch always on hand to throw to the floor in front of the actors and stamp on when frustrated.

Once a playwright pestered Belasco at length to take his new play, finally begging, "Isn't there some way you can put it on stage?" Belasco impatiently snapped, "Give me the script." He flipped it to an assistant and ordered: "Chop this up and use it as the snowstorm tonight."

Belch, Sir Toby A reckless roistering jolly knight in Shakespeare's TWELFTH NIGHT. Fond of drinking, dancing, and singing, he is an enemy of the censorious MALVOLIO. The name is sometimes used of a happy-go-lucky carouser.

Belgrade Theatre A theatre founded in Coventry in 1958 – the first new British theatre to be opened after World War II. It was named in recognition of a gift of timber from Belgrade, Yugoslavia, that was used in its construction. The Belgrade was the first of Britain's CIVIC THEATRES. Its resident company presents an annual staging of the Coventry Cycle of MYSTERY PLAYS.

bell. ***Bell, Book, and Candle*** A comedy about witchcraft in modern Manhattan by the US playwright John Van Druten (1901–57); it opened in New York in 1950. The plot concerns Tony Henderson, a publisher, who rents an apartment in the house of the alluring Gillian Holroyd and her aunt. Both the women, it turns out, are witches, and Gillian uses her powers to win Tony away from his fiancée (and her enemy). If she falls in love, however, she will blush and cry, losing her magical ability. When she reveals her powers to Tony, he storms out and gets another witch to break the spell. Later when he returns to pay Gillian his back rent, she blushes and starts to cry. He realizes that they are in love.

The first London production was mounted in 1954 at the Phoenix Theatre and starred Rex HARRISON and his then wife, Lilli Palmer. The theatre became a battleground when Palmer found out about her husband's new love (and wife-to-be) Kay Kendall. The two stars had amazing rows backstage followed by periods when they would only communicate through notes passed back and forth by the stage manager. None of this, however, affected their tender love scenes on stage.

It was during *Bell, Book, and Candle* that Harrison received the offer to star in Broadway's *My Fair Lady*. The play's producer, Binkie Beaumont, agreed to release him in return for £25,000, along with 1.5% of the Broadway and touring grosses, and the British and Continental rights for *My Fair Lady*. The deal went through. If it had failed, the part of Henry Higgins may well have gone to Cary Grant.

Bells, The Leopold Lewis's English adaptation of *Le Juif polonais*, a melodrama by Erckmann-Chatrian. It was first performed in 1871 at the Lyceum Theatre, London, when it made Henry IRVING famous overnight. Irving persuaded the theatre's US manager, H. L. Bateman, to stage the piece after the Lyceum's season opened disappointingly. Its success established Irving as the leading tragedian of his time, made him the chief power in Bateman's company, and saved the theatre's fortunes.

The plot involves Matthias, a respectable burgomaster, who is haunted by the undiscovered murder and robbery he has committed on a Polish Jew. Matthias has horrid visions of the Jew and keeps hearing the ringing bells of his sleigh. Irving's insight into this tortured character enabled him to hold his audience spellbound.

However, *The Bells* was also the final straw that broke his marriage to Florence O'Callaghan, who was a month away from giving birth to their child when the play opened. They were returning home in a cab after the opening-night celebrations, when Florence, who hated the theatre, suddenly asked him, "Are you going on making a fool of yourself like this all your life?" Irving stopped the carriage, got out, and never once saw her again.

Irving later toured widely with the play, making his New York debut in the piece in 1883; he even played the strenuous role during his last illness, despite doctors' warnings. After Irving's death, the critic A. B. Walkley paid tribute to the man who "set our ears ringing with the 'chink-chink' of the Polish Jew's sleigh bells...."

Bellower Quin Nickname of the English actor James Quin (1693–1766), referring to his bombastic style. Few could match Quin in loudness of voice or costume. He made his debut in 1712 at the Smock Alley Theatre, Dublin, and two years later became an overnight success at Drury Lane when he stood in for a sick actor in Rowe's *Tamerlane*. He consolidated his reputation in Shakespearean roles, becoming especially renowned for his Falstaff. A product of the heroic school of acting, 'Bellower Quin' came to seem a rather laughable and outdated figure in the more restrained era of David GARRICK. "If the young fellow is right," snorted Quin of Garrick, "I and the rest of the players have been all wrong."

Quin was noted for his stubbornness and short temper, which was often turned on Charles MACKLIN, his fellow actor at Lincoln's Inn Fields. This was somewhat reckless, since Macklin eventually killed an actor for arguing over a wig.

below *See* STAGE DIRECTION.

Benedick A young gentleman of Padua in Shakespeare's MUCH ADO ABOUT NOTHING. Though adopting the pose of a confirmed bachelor with no romantic interest in women ("...would you have me speak after my custom, as being a profess'd tyrant to their sex?"), he is easily manipulated into falling in love with BEATRICE.

benefit A special performance of a play in which the night's receipts go to an actor or theatrical personality (often ill or retiring) or to a charity or other worthy cause. Benefits were first introduced in the 17th century, with the proceeds generally going to an actor, playwright, or member of the staff. The first English recipient was the actress Elizabeth Barry in 1687. David Garrick donated all of the proceeds from his last appearance in 1776 to his fund for destitute actors. Most modern benefits are for registered charities or worldwide relief efforts. In 1991 Covent Garden held a special benefit for the ballet star, Dame Margot Fonteyn, who was destitute and suffering from cancer. *See also* BESPEAK PERFORMANCE.

Bennett, Alan (1934–) British actor and playwright, who first came to prominence as a star of the Cambridge Footlights revue BEYOND THE FRINGE. His reputation was firmly established with the success of his first play *Forty Years On* (1968), in which John Gielgud starred as the retiring headmaster of a minor public school. *Getting On* (1971) investigated the disillusionment of a Labour MP, while *Habeas Corpus* (1973), with Alec Guinness, was a farcical exposure of British sexual inhibitions. *The Old Country* (1977), again with Guinness, portrayed a British spy exiled in the Soviet Union.

Bennett has consolidated his reputation as a keen observer of social mores, especially amongst the respectable working classes in his native north of England, with his writing for television. His greatest resource as a writer is a shrewd ear for the oddities of everyday conversation. *Talking Heads* (1988), a series of monologues for TV, was particularly highly praised. He has continued to write for the stage, often appearing in his own plays. More recent dramas have included the double bill *Single Spies* (1988; *A Question of Attribution, An Englishman Abroad*), in which he played the traitor Anthony Blunt, and *The Madness of George III* (1991, adapted for the cinema in 1995). *Writing Home*, a collection of essays and diaries, became a bestseller in 1994.

Bergner, Elisabeth (1900–86) Austrian actress, who made her name in Berlin in the 1920s before becoming a star in Britain and America. Born in Vienna, she made her stage debut in Zürich and later worked under Max Reinhardt at the Deutsches Theatre before moving into films. In 1933 she married the producer-director Paul Czinner. When Alexander Korda invited the couple to Britain to make *Catherine the Great*, Bergner saw this as an opportunity to avoid Hitler, who had just come to power: "I thought, good, I shall go to England and when we return it will all have blown over." When asked to tour the English provinces she snapped, "What is Birmingham?" Nevertheless, she made her British stage debut at the Opera House, Manchester, in 1933 and later that year appeared in London to great acclaim. When she became ill, the producer

C. B. Cochran closed the theatre for three weeks.

In 1936 she told J. M. BARRIE that her greatest artistic experience had been seeing Rembrandt's painting *David Playing the Harp for Saul.* Barrie was so moved that he wrote *The Boy David* for Bergner, who hoped that playing the title role would change her elfin image (she was then 36). The play, Barrie's last, flopped and Bergner fled to Switzerland, refusing to return for a COMMAND PERFORMANCE.

Bergner spent the war years in Hollywood and on Broadway. When she returned to Britain in 1950 *The Daily Telegraph* noted sourly: "Five years after the last bomb has fallen, she has elected to return." In 1963 she was awarded the Schiller Prize "for outstanding contributions to the cultural life of Germany". Ten years later, at the age of 73, she was triumphant in *Cat's Play* by Istvan Orkeny at the Greenwich Theatre; the critics still referred to her "coy Peter Pan little figure".

Berkoff, Steven (1937–) British playwright, actor, and director, who founded (1968) the London Theatre Group. His early work with the company included several adaptations of Franz Kafka, notably *Metamorphosis* (1969), which Berkoff staged using a striking variety of techniques, including mime and acrobatics. The play was subsequently (1989) taken to Broadway and is regularly revived by Berkoff at the Edinburgh Festival.

Berkoff's first completely original play, *East* (1975), used blank verse and the trappings of high tragedy to depict life in London's East End; it was successfully transferred to the National Theatre. In *Greek* (1979) he gave a feminist twist to the Oedipus myth, while in *West* (1983) he used the Beowulf story to attack the British class system. Subsequent plays have included *Sink the Belgrano!* (1986), which uses Shakespeare's *Henry V* to comment on a controversial incident during the Falklands War, *Kvetch* (1987), a comedy about a neurotic Jewish salesman, and *Acapulco* (1992). With his menacing appearance, Berkoff has also been in demand as a Hollywood villain, notably in the Bond film *Octopussy* (1983).

Berkoff's intensely physical and never knowingly understated form of theatre has found both admirers and detractors. His own contempt for the critics emerges vividly from *Free Association* (1996), a memoir.

Berlin, Irving (Israel Baline; 1888–1989) US composer of songs, film scores, and Broadway musicals. His masterpieces, both of which starred Ethel MERMAN were ANNIE GET YOUR GUN (1946) and CALL ME MADAM (1950).

Berlin was born in the Siberian village of Temun, the son of a rabbi; at the age of four he saw his family home burned down during a pogrom. Within a year the Baline family had arrived at New York's Ellis Island and settled into the city's Lower East Side. Israel began to write songs while working as a newsboy and singing waiter, finding success with 'Alexander's Ragtime Band' in 1911. Later hits included 'White Christmas' and 'God Bless America'.

Berlin's first Broadway hit was *Watch Your Step* (1914), in which he introduced ragtime to the stage. This was followed in 1918 by *Yip, Yip, Yaphank*, which included the popular 'Oh, How I Hate to Get Up in the Morning'. In 1933 he wrote *As Thousands Cheer*, which included 'Easter Parade'.

Berlin's music also featured in revues, including the ZIEGFELD FOLLIES and *The Music Box Revue* staged at his own Music Box Theatre. He lived to be over 100, having composed nearly 1,000 songs. The songwriter Jerome Kern commented, "Irving Berlin has no place in American music...he is American music."

Berliner Ensemble The German theatre company founded by Bertolt BRECHT in East Berlin in 1949. The company, established at the invitation of the East German Government, became the focus for much of the most important work then taking place in European theatre, not least in its productions of its founder's own plays and its assimilation of his theories of EPIC THEATRE. After Brecht's death in 1956 it was taken over by his widow, Helene Weigel, and after her death in 1971 by their daughter, Barbara Brecht-Schall. Subsequently the Ensemble's reputation declined sharply, with the interventionist style of Barbara Brecht-Schall coming in for particular criticism. In 1992 five leading directors from the former West Germany (including Peter Palitzsch and Peter Zadek) were called in to save the company from collapse; the Ensemble, formerly funded by the East German state, became a limited company.

Bernadon A stock character of the 18th-century Viennese theatre. An impetuous youth, Bernadon was developed by the Austrian actor Joseph Kurz (1715–84) from the peasant clown HANSWURST. Kurz's improvised 'Bernadoniades' ran their course within his lifetime.

Bernhardt, Sarah (Henriette Rosine Bernard; 1844–1923) One of the stage's most admired and tempestuous actresses. Born in Paris, the illegitimate daughter of a courtesan, Sarah was a sickly tubercular child, who considered becoming a nun. She changed her mind after being taken to the COMÉDIE-FRANÇAISE to see Racine's *Britannicus* and subsequently spent two years training at the Conservatoire. She made her stage debut in 1862, taking the lead in Racine's *Iphigénie* at the Comédie-Française. Always difficult, she was dismissed for fighting with an actress backstage. Sarah, noted for her romantic looks and melodious voice, began a series of love affairs with famous men, including Prince Henri de Ligne, who gave her a son.

Her first great triumph came in 1868, when she played in Dumas's *Kean* at Paris's Odeon Theatre. Admirers would assemble outside the theatre to unfasten the horses from her carriage and pull her home themselves. She was becoming the most talked-about woman in Paris and her parties drew such guests as the Prince of Wales and Oscar Wilde, who wrote *Salomé* (in French) for her.

This growing renown led to her reinstatement at the Comédie-Française, where in 1874 she gave the most sublime performance of her career as Racine's Phèdre. She was one of the stage's most versatile actresses, even playing Hamlet. Other famous roles included Marguerite Gautier in Dumas's *La Dame aux camélias*.

Sarah gave her first London performance in 1879 at the Gaiety Theatre, where she thrilled the British audience as Cleopatra. This was despite taking opium for a fever one evening and forgetting 200 lines. In 1880 she likewise conquered America, giving 157 performances in 51 cities from Montreal to New Orleans. At the age of 71 she had a diseased leg amputated but continued to act, performing as the 18-year-old Joan of Arc with a wooden leg.

Bertinazzi, Carlo *See* CARLIN.

Bertram, Count of Roussillon The young nobleman beloved by HELENA, the heroine of Shakespeare's ALL'S WELL THAT ENDS WELL. Described by Dr Johnson as "a man noble without generosity, and young without truth," he has always been one of the least popular of Shakespearean heroes.

bespeak performance A special performance of a play chosen by patrons, in which the night's receipts go to someone connected with the theatre or are shared among the cast. Bespeak performances originated as a form of BENEFIT during the 17th century and were especially popular during the Victorian era.

Betterton, Thomas (1635–1710) English actor-manager usually considered the leading figure of the Restoration stage. He adapted several of Shakespeare's works and in his day was unrivalled for his Hamlet, Lear, and Sir Toby Belch. He created about 130 new characters for the stage and was the first actor buried in Westminster Abbey.

The son of Charles I's cook, Betterton became a member of John Rhodes's company, which in 1660 reopened the Cockpit at Drury Lane. The next year he joined DAVENANT's company at Lincoln's Inn Fields to appear in *Love and Honour*; for his performance as Prince Alvaro, Charles II loaned Betterton his coronation suit.

In the same year he first played Hamlet, a role he would return to with acclaim until the age of 74, making him the oldest Hamlet ever. Despite having small eyes, a low voice, and an "ill figure...clumsily made", Betterton was immensely powerful in the role. He was renowned for actually turning white when he met the Ghost in Act I. His fellow actor Barton Booth, playing the Ghost, was so astonished by Betterton's reaction that he was unable to continue for several moments. "Instead of my awing him," Booth later recalled, "he terrified me." Other actors were similarly affected. Robert Wilks, playing in *The Maid's Tragedy* with Betterton, was so struck by his dignity that he could barely say a word.

Davenant died in 1668, and Betterton led the company to the Dorset Garden Theatre; in 1682 it merged with the company at DRURY LANE. In 1695 he successfully reopened the theatre in Lincoln's Inn Fields with the premiere of Congreve's *Love for Love*. In 1705 he moved to the new Queen's Theatre in the Hay, a building designed by John Vanbrugh, whose play *The Confederacy* Betterton produced there.

Betterton was a close friend of Archbishop Tillotson, who once asked him why his own sermons could never move the congregation as much as the actor's words affected the audience. "That I think is easy to be accounted for," said the actor. "'Tis because you are only *telling* them a story, and I am *showing* them facts."

Betty, William Henry *See* ROSCIUS, YOUNG *under* ROSCIUS.

beyond. ***Beyond the Fringe*** A satirical revue by Cambridge undergraduates (*see* FOOTLIGHTS CLUB) that became a legendary hit in Britain and America and launched its four performers as international stars. It was co-written by Jonathan Miller and Alan BENNETT, who were joined on stage by Dudley Moore and Peter Cook. The short memorable sketches, delivered by the four wearing dark suits, satirized everything from church sermons and Shakespearean productions to capital punishment; Cook also performed a gruesome imitation of the then Prime Minister Harold Macmillan. Introduced at the 1959 Edinburgh Fringe (hence the title), the revue moved a year later to Edinburgh's Lyceum Theatre and then in 1961 to London's Fortune Theatre. It subsequently ran for a year at the John Golden Theatre on Broadway, captivating US audiences. "It became a very chic show in New York," noted Cook. "Its very Englishness gave it built-in snob appeal." In London the revue ran for six years with a changing cast.

Beyond the Horizon A naturalistic tragedy by Eugene O'NEILL. It was premiered in 1920 in New York's Morosco Theatre, and established O'Neill's reputation, winning the Pulitzer Prize. Set in rural New England, the story concerns two sons of the farmer James Mayo. Andrew, the older, plans to marry their childhood neighbour, Ruth Atkins, and take over the family farm. Robert, a dreamer, wishes to go to sea but first confesses his love to Ruth, who surprises both families by returning it. The brothers then find their fortunes reversed: Robert wins Ruth and stays on the farm while Andy goes to sea, a departure that kills his father. However, Robert knows nothing of business and the farm goes to ruin along with his marriage. When Andy returns, Ruth plans to reveal her love for him, but before she does so he insensitively tells her that he never really loved her. Andy leaves the couple, who fall into despair as first Robert's mother and then their daughter Mary dies. When Andy next returns, Robert too is dying. Andy is now left with Ruth, but it is too late for happiness.

Bhagavata Mela An Indian form of drama honouring the god Vishnu. It is performed annually in late April or early May in the village of Melattur in the Tamil-speaking region of Tanjore, although a few nearby villages give short versions during festivals. It first appeared in about 1502 in Andhra Pradesh, being derived from the KUCHIPUDI dance drama; subsequently Venkatarama Sastri (1759–1847) wrote about a dozen works in the style in order to spread Hinduism. The *Bhagavata Puranas* are epic stories about the incarnations of Vishnu while a *mela* is a troupe of singers or dancers. The plays combine dialogue, song, and dance.

The performance in Melattur before the Varadraja Perumala Temple honours Vishnu's violent man-lion incarnation. A stage is raised in the street and the temple deity is carried in a grand procession through the village. The performance begins in the morning, with the entrances of the *konangi*, or clown, the musicians, and a boy wearing the mask of Ganapatri, the elephant-headed god of good fortune. The actors, all men, then make elaborate ritual entrances and perform classical dances before the main action begins.

The actor portraying Vishnu as man-lion fasts and prays before donning his magical mask. On stage, he enters into a trance and must be restrained by attendants to protect other actors. After the performance ends in the early hours, another temple is visited, where the actor removes his mask and falls into another trance until revived by water.

Bhamakalapam The name of a play and a theatrical genre found throughout the Indian state of Andhra Pradesh, where it is acted by travelling troupes. *Bhama* is a shortening of Satyabhama, the beautiful but jealous wife of Lord Krishna, and *kalapam* means 'dialogue' or 'argument'. Siddhendra Yogi created it in the 17th century as a devotional form for all-male KUCHIPUDI companies. Although *Bhamakalapam* features the full range of feminine dancing movements, or *lasya*, it retains the tradition of using only male dancers. The form was long patronized by local landowners but is now in danger of disappearing from modern India.

Although some scholars also refer to the genre as *Vithi Natakam* it is distinct from the area's street drama, *Veedhi Natakam*.

Bhand Jashna (Kashmiri. Clown Festival) A form of rural theatre that has existed for centuries in the northern Indian state of Kashmir. Improvised farces and satires are performed in Kashmiri with a leavening of Hindustani, Urdu, Punjabi, and other languages depending on the locality. Although on the surface the plays are semi-historical works about folk heroes, in practice the main purpose is to satirize everyone in the village, from poor peasants to corrupt government officials.

Performances are staged in the open air and commence with a prayer, or *poozapath*, honouring Allah. The clowns, or *maskharas*, then make their entrances through the audience to the accompaniment of music. Their costumes include colourful headdresses.

Bhavai A type of bawdy and satirical rural theatre formerly popular in western India. Its emphasis on humour makes it unique in the traditional Indian theatre. The stories depict the vices and virtues of various types in village society but usually centre on figures from history or Hindu mythology. The genre has been introduced to cities by urban troupes who have successfully adapted its social and political satire, but the rural form now barely survives.

According to legend, *Bhavai* was created by the Brahmin priest Asaita Thakar in the 14th century. He was excommunicated for dining with a young Hindu woman; her Muslim captor, knowing this was forbidden, had agreed to release her only if such a meal took place. Asaita then turned to song and dance, forming the *bhaviyas*, the first strolling players in Gujarat, who still perform the *Bhavai* by hereditary right. *Bhavai* stories, known as *vesa* (costume), were not published until the 19th century. Up to 360 once existed, but few survive today.

The plays are performed at religious festivals, especially Navaratri, the festival of Bahucharaji, the patroness of *Bhavai* actors. Performances are held in a temple courtyard or adjacent street. A torch is lit to symbolize the presence of the goddess and the performance begins at about 10 pm with music featuring (amongst other instruments), *Bhavai's* unique *bhungals*, or copper pipes. In the preliminaries, dances are performed by actors dressed as the elephant-headed god Ganapatri, the goddess Kali, and a grotesque Brahmin priest who speaks obscenities and dances with clumsy movements. The regular drama follows.

Bibiena family An Italian family of theatre architects and scene designers. They were the most influential designers of the 18th century, introducing towering perspective scenery and the baroque style to European opera houses.

The family's association with the stage was begun by **Giovanni Maria Galli** (1625–65), known as Il Vecchio. His eldest son, **Ferdinando** (1657–1743), worked as a young man in the Teatro Farnese in Bologna. There he introduced his angle perspective (**scena per angolo**), which revolutionized staging, replacing one vanishing point with several. In 1708 he was summoned to Barcelona to direct festivities at the wedding of the future Emperor Charles VI, who in 1711 named him as court architect in Vienna. There he also designed scenery for the opera. He returned to Bologna in 1717 and built the royal theatre at Mantua in 1731.

Ferdinando's brother, **Francesco** (1659–1737), worked throughout the Continent before becoming the ducal architect at Mantua. His buildings include the grand theatre in Nancy and the Teatro Filarmonico in Verona (both 1708–09). In 1716 Francesco and Ferdinando together designed settings for an outdoor celebration to mark the birth of a son to Charles VI. The stage was built over a large canal and at one point divided to show gilded naval vessels floating on the water below. "The theatre is so large that it is hard to carry the eye to the end of it" wrote Lady Mary Wortley Montagu to Alexander Pope.

Ferdinando's eldest son, **Alessandro** (1687–1769), became in 1719 an architect and painter at the court of the elector of the Palatinate. Ferdinando's second son, **Giuseppe** (1696–1757) became the family's most respected artist, working with his father on designs for operas, plays, and dances. He seems to have been the first to introduce transparent scenery lit from behind. Ferdinando's third son, **Antonio** (1697–*c.* 1774), designed the Teatro Communale at Bologna in 1755 and the Teatro dei Quattro Cavalieri in Pavia in 1773. He followed his father as the Viennese court architect.

Giuseppe's son, **Carlo** (1728–87), collaborated with his father on the Bayreuth Opera House, and subsequently worked throughout Europe, including London. One of his stage settings can still be seen at the Drottningholm Theatre museum (*see* THEATRE MUSEUM).

Bickerstaffe, Isaac (*c.* 1733–*c.* 1812) Irish dramatist; as a writer of light musical works Bickerstaffe was, in his day, considered to be the equal of John Gay.

In 1760 Bickerstaffe's BALLAD OPERA *Thomas and Sally; or, the Sailor's Return*, with music by Thomas Arne, was staged at Covent Garden. The two men collaborated again on LOVE IN A VILLAGE (1762), which is probably the earliest example of an English comic opera. *The Maid of the Mill* (1765) and *The Royal Garland* (1768), both with music by Samuel Arnold, brought Bickerstaffe further success. He also wrote several works in collaboration with Charles DIBDIN, including *Lionel and Clarissa*.

Bickerstaffe's success was cut short in 1782, however, when he was forced to flee the country owing to allegations of sodomy, which at that time was punishable by hanging. Bickerstaffe fled to France, where it seems he lived in poverty and obscurity for a further 30 years. The 1782 *Biographia Dramatica* stated that Bickerstaffe was "...living at some place abroad, to which a deed without name has banished him..."

Bidesia In India, a form of theatre performed in the villages of the northeastern state of Bihar. Dating from the early 20th century, it was supposedly created by Bhikhari Thakur, a barber, who left his home and his profession to tour Bihar with a company of itinerant actors. A *bidesia* is a person who emigrates from his homeland. The plays deal with the everyday trials and tribulations of villagers, including the constant clash between traditional rural values and the new thinking of the towns.

big. Big bird, to get the *See under* BIRD.

Big Four, the Nickname for two actors and two actresses who dominated the New York stage in the late 19th century. They were John Drew (*see* DREW FAMILY), James Lewis, of whom little is known, Ada Rehan (Ada Crehan; 1860–1916), who changed her name following a printer's error and whose most famous role was Katharina in *The Taming Of The Shrew* (1887), and Mrs G. H. Gilbert (Ann Hartley; 1821–1904), who specialized in playing eccentric spinsters. The four appeared regularly at DALY'S THEATRE.

Bill of Divorcement, A The first and most successful play by Clemence DANE. A sensitive study of a young woman's fear of hereditary madness, it is also an attack on the British divorce laws for not admitting insanity as sufficient grounds for divorce. First performed in 1921 in London, it made a star of Maggie Albanesi in the lead role of Sydney Fairfield; sadly, Albanesi died only two years later. It opened in New York in the same year, providing Katharine Cornell with her Broadway debut. The Hollywood film version starred John Barrymore (*see* BARRYMORES) and introduced Katherine Hepburn.

Billy Liar A comedy by Keith Waterhouse and Willis Hall, based on Waterhouse's earlier novel. It was first performed in 1960 in London, with Albert Finney and Tom Courtenay in the leading roles. The play concerns Billy Fisher, 19, a lower-middle-class lad who has big dreams of fame and fortune but lacks the talent or gumption to realize them. To survive his dull northern-English life, he lies and fantasizes, causing grief to his family, friends, and employer (an undertaker). In his daydreams he supposes himself to be various important or glamorous figures, including a general, a doctor, and a politician. When Billy becomes engaged to two girls at the same time, he loses control. One of them, Barbara, comes to tea with his family to announce their wedding plans, but runs into his other fiancée, Rita, and a row ensues. Billy's mate, Arthur Crabtree, warns him that Rita's brother is on the warpath, so Billy sets off to become a television scriptwriter in London with a third girlfriend, Liz. However, he misses the train.

bio-mechanics A theatrical method developed by the avant-garde Russian director V. E. MEYERHOLD, in which actors were totally controlled by the director's decisions. Meyerhold used no proscenium or curtain for his productions and created a bare forestage on which he manoeuvred the players like puppets. He had been trained in the MOSCOW ART THEATRE but subsequently rebelled against the STANISLAVSKY school of acting by telling his actors to suppress their personal emotions in order to concentrate on gesture and movement. They acted without make-up and all wore blue overalls.

Meyerhold first used bio-mechanics in a production of Ferdinand Crommelynck's *The Magnificent Cuckold* in 1922. In Gogol's *The Government Inspector* (1926) he went so far as to replace his actors with dummies in the last scene. The individualistic Meyerhold eventually fell into disfavour with the Soviet authorities. In 1938 he and his wife were arrested; both subsequently died in circumstances that have never been properly explained.

bird. bird, to get the To be hissed off stage; the expression was originally to **get the big bird**, i.e. goose. It is now used much more generally, to mean to be rejected or dismissed.

Birds, The The buoyant comedy by ARISTOPHANES that is usually considered his masterpiece. It was first performed in 414 BC in Athens, when the war against Sparta was going well. The play's heroes, Peisthetaerus and Euelpides, leave Athens to create a utopia named **Cloud-cuckooland** between heaven and earth with the help of the birds. They have abandoned their beloved city for one reason, as Euelpides says:

> Aye, the cicalas chirp upon the boughs
> One month, or two; but our Athenians chirp
> Over their lawsuits all their whole life long.

The Birds is Aristophanes's most gentle work to survive, never mentioning the war or attacking public policy. Some critics, however, see a cleverly disguised political commentary, in which Peisthetaerus is the archetypal manipulative politician and the birds are the public who are always duped. The play may also criticize the Athenians for believing that they can accomplish anything – with the utopia in the sky representing the defeat of Sparta.

Birnam Wood The wood that moves to Dunsinane Hill in Shakespeare's MACBETH, thus heralding the central character's downfall as prophesied by the three witches.

The prophecy, which is fulfilled when Macduff's men carry branches from the wood to conceal their numbers, has a close historical parallel in the fate of the evil Lord Soulis of Hermitage Castle, Borders. He was warned by a spirit called Redcap Sly to "beware of the coming tree" and, sure enough, was captured by his enemies who had similarly camouflaged themselves with branches. He was subsequently wrapped in a piece of lead and boiled to death. Redcap Sly is said still to haunt the ruins of Hermitage Castle.

Birthday Party, The Harold PINTER's first full-length play; it opened in 1958 at the Arts Theatre, Cambridge, and transferred to the Lyric Theatre, Hammersmith. With its enigmatic dialogue, unrevealed motives, and powerful suggestions of menace, the play is now considered one of Pinter's best and most characteristic works. At the time, however, it was savaged by London critics and earned only £260 from its first week at the Lyric. Pinter thought the production, directed by Peter Wood, was bad.

The story focuses on Stanley Webber (originally played by Richard Pearson) who is the only resident at the boarding house run by Meg and Petey. One day they are visited by two sinister strangers, Nat Goldberg and Seamus McCann, who tell Meg that it is Stanley's birthday. They present him with a toy drum which he beats wildly. Stanley, who fears the two men, tries to convince them that he is someone else. Later that evening, they remove his glasses, harshly question him, and make him participate in a game of blind man's buff. The next morning, the men take a confused Stanley away. Petey watches them go, and later tells Meg what a fantastic birthday party it has been.

Bishop of Broadway Nickname for David BELASCO, the US actor-manager and playwright who directed or produced over 300 Broadway plays.

Bitter Sweet Noël COWARD's most popular musical, an operetta that opened in 1929 at Her Majesty's Theatre and transferred to the Palace Theatre for a total 697 performances. Unlike Coward's nonmusical comedies, however, this sentimental romance has not enjoyed a modern revival.

The action begins in 1929, during a party at the home of Lady Shayne. One of the guests, Dolly Chamberlayne, has fallen for an orchestra leader although she is engaged to a peer of the realm. This distresses Lady Shayne, and the scene shifts to 1875 to reveal that she too loved a musician, the Austrian Carl Linden, and turned her back on her fiancé, a distinguished diplomat. Their simple life in Austria ended when Linden was killed in a duel with a cavalry officer who had tried to seduce her. She subsequently dedicated herself to performing his songs throughout Europe. Lord Shayne became entranced with her, and she married him for companionship. In the last act, set in 1895, Lady Shayne is seen hosting a group, including her former fiancé, at the same house as the 1929 party.

Coward's songs included 'The Call of Life', 'I'll See You Again', 'Zigeuner', 'Ladies of the Town', 'If Love Were All', and 'Tarara Boom-de-ay':

> Tarara boom-de-ay,
> Tarara boom-de-ay,
> We are the most effectual,
> Intellectual
> Movement of the day.

black. ***Black Crook, The*** A work usually considered America's first true musical. The show underwent a strange transformation before opening in 1866 at Niblo's Garden in New York. It was originally meant to be a serious Faustian melodrama but the theatre manager, William Wheatley, changed his mind when the New York Academy of Music burned down just before a French ballet troupe was scheduled to dance there. Wheatley took the scenery and the 100 girls, dressed them in scanty corps de ballet outfits, and brought in Giuseppi Operti to supply tunes; his melodrama became a melodrama-ballet-musical.

Despite lasting more than five hours, this rousing mixture of spectacle, dance, and drama proved a booming success, bringing in $1 million, running for 475 performances, and becoming the most popular US production of the 19th century. It played in New York off and on until 1903. Wheatley's follow-up, *The White Fawn*, was less successful, but he was able to retire comfortably on the fortune earned from *The Black Crook*.

In 1954 the composer Sigmund Romberg retold the story of the staging of *The Black Crook* in his own musical, *The Girl in Pink Tights*.

Black-Ey'd Susan A NAUTICAL DRAMA by Douglas Jerrold (1803–57), subtitled *All in the Downs*. It was first staged in London in 1829 at the Surrey Theatre, running for 400 performances. T. P. Cooke was acclaimed in the leading role of William, a sailor who returns from the sea to find his faithful wife, Susan, pursued by his own captain. William strikes the officer and is sentenced to death, but is saved by a last-minute reprieve.

Black-Ey'd Susan was the first play produced when the Royal Coburg Theatre reopened in 1833 as the Royal Victoria – soon renamed the OLD VIC.

Blackfriars Theatre The name of two private theatres built in the ruins of Blackfriars Priory, near the north bank of the Thames in London. They were amongst the first candle-lit indoor theatres in London, allowing performances in bad weather and during the winter.

The first small theatre was built in 1576 by Richard Farrant, master of the choirboys of Windsor. After his death in 1581 it was used by other BOY COMPANIES until 1584, when the space was leased as lodgings.

In 1596 James Burbage attempted to open a second venue on the site suitable for his company from the THEATRE. His plans were obstructed by officials, and he died before the work was completed in 1600 by his sons Richard and Cuthbert Burbage, who leased the venue for eight years to the Children of the Chapel Royal. Cuthbert eventually became co-owner of the rectangular theatre, which had benches for the audience and made use of special painted scenery. The KING'S MEN became the resident company in 1608 and lured the nobility with plays by Shakespeare, Jonson, Beaumont, and Fletcher. The theatre was closed in 1642 by the Puritans and demolished in 1655.

black-out Originally a theatrical term, dating from the early 1920s, meaning to extinguish the lighting to darken the whole stage. It is now largely associated with its World War II use, when it was obligatory throughout Great Britain to cover all windows, etc., before dark so that no gleam of light could be seen from outside. This essential air raid precaution was called the *Black-out*.

Blacks, The A play by Jean GENET. Described by the author as 'a clown show', it is a leading example of the THEATRE OF CRUELTY. It was first produced in 1959 in Paris, opening two years later in London and New York, where it enjoyed a long run.

Genet uses a violent play-within-a-play to explore the nature of racial intolerance. From an upper level, a group of Whites (Black actors wearing masks) watch a group of Blacks below doing their ritual dances. A Black master of ceremonies,

Archibald Absolom Wellington, introduces a drama in which Blacks rape and ritually murder a White woman. When news arrives that Blacks everywhere are rising up against Whites, the Black players kill and mutilate the White audience on the platform. The dead Whites then get up to join the Blacks, and Archibald preaches on the foolishness of racial hatred. The actors put on white masks and depart for hell.

Blin, Roger (1907–84) French actor and director, who was originally drawn to the theatre because he believed that acting might help him to overcome his stammer. During the 1930s Blin worked with Charles Dullin, Antonin Artaud, and Jean-Louis BARRAULT; after the war he became closely associated with the avant-garde, directing plays by ADAMOV, whom he virtually discovered, GENET, whom he greatly popularized, and BECKETT. The French language premiere of WAITING FOR GODOT (1953), was directed by Blin, who also played the character of Pozzo. Blin was also noted for designing his own sets, a practice he considered integral to the directorial process.

Blithe Spirit Nöel COWARD's comedy about a troublesome ghost. It opened in 1941 at the Piccadilly Theatre and ran for four and a half years before enjoying a lengthy run in New York. The original cast included Margaret Rutherford, Kay Hammond, and Fay Compton. The story focuses on Charles, a cynical writer who accidentally summons the ghost of his first wife, Elvira, at a séance. She tries to kill him but mistakenly kills his new wife, so Charles now has two ghosts to nag him. Some objected to the risque dialogue, including Graham Greene who found the play "a weary exhibition of bad taste".

Coward underwent one of the most frustrating experiences of his career when CBS decided to broadcast a live production of *Blithe Spirit* in 1955. The sponsor, Ford Motors, tried to censor the more risque lyrics and several lines. Neither did Coward like the leading actress, Claudette Colbert, whom he found "bossy" and "*extremely* tiresome". She insisted on keeping one side of her face to the cameras at all times, causing all scene groupings to be rearranged. After one rehearsal, during which she repeatedly fluffed her lines, she assured Coward that she knew them backwards. "And that's exactly the way you are saying them this morning," he fumed. At such moments, Coward thought of his CBS cheque and murmured to himself "Thirty thousand pounds, thirty thousand pounds, thirty thousand pounds!"

blocking A stage in the rehearsal process during which actors are positioned on the set and their movements are plotted, with special attention to SIGHTLINE problems. Each movement is noted in the PROMPT BOOK with a number in the 'move column' and the same number next to the word in the script when the move occurs. During blocking sessions, the floor is marked out to indicate the size of the stage and the position of furniture, doors, windows, etc. Blocking is done with actors reading from the script.

Blondin (Jean François Gravelet; 1824–97) One of the most famous acrobats of all time. His greatest feat was in 1859, when he crossed the Niagara Falls on a tightrope, embellishing the performance by repeating it blindfolded, wheeling a barrow, twirling an umbrella, and carrying a man on his back. He made a fortune by this feat and soon after settled in England, where he gave performances until old age forced him to retire.

blood. Blood and Flea Pit Local nickname for the Lyric Opera House in Hammersmith, London, before Nigel Playfair relaunched it in 1918 as the LYRIC THEATRE.

blood and thunder Melodrama, sensational and blood-curdling stuff. An originally US expression, dating from the mid 19th century.

Blood Brothers A long-running musical by Willy RUSSELL. *Blood Brothers* opened in 1983 at the Liverpool Playhouse and transferred to London, where the *Sunday Express* called it "a milestone in British musicals". It was revived in 1988 and nine years later was still running at the Phoenix Theatre.

Mrs Johnstone, a domestic, is expecting twins after being deserted by her husband. Her employer Mrs Lyons adopts one baby, and they agree to keep the two boys in ignorance since it is said that twins parted at birth will die if they know the truth. In later life Mickey Johnstone and Edward Lyons meet and become 'blood brothers'. They both fall for the same girl, Linda, who marries Mickey. Edward attends college and becomes a councillor, while Mickey loses his job and is jailed after turning to crime.

When released, he becomes addicted to tranquillizers. Edward finds him a job and a house, but Mrs Lyons informs Mickey that his wife is having an affair with Edward. Mickey walks into a meeting his twin is attending and fatally shoots him before he in turn is shot by the police.

Russell's songs include 'Marilyn Monroe', 'Shoes upon the Table', and 'My Child'.

blood tub *See* GAFF.

Blood Wedding A poetic tragedy by Federico GARCÍA LORCA, first performed in 1933 in Madrid. It opened in New York in 1935 as *Bitter Oleander* and in London in 1939 as *The Marriage of Blood*; it was translated as *Blood Wedding* by the poet Roy Campbell for revivals in London in 1947 and New York two years later. The play was the first of Lorca's great trilogy of folk tragedies, being followed in 1934 by *Yerma* and in 1945 by *The House of Bernarda Alba*.

Based on a true news story, the play explores the conflict between love and duty. It opens on the eve of an arranged wedding between Andalusian gypsies, as the bridegroom's mother recalls to her son how her husband and other son were murdered. She is fearful because the bride was once engaged to Leonardo (the only named character), a member of the family who committed the murder. Leonardo still loves the bride although his wife is now pregnant. The next day, the couple are married but the bride then flees with Leonardo; as they declare their doomed love a beggar woman gives them the 'eye of death'. Leonardo and the bridegroom kill each other; the bride then offers herself to the mother to be killed.

blue *See* BORDER.

blue bird of happiness The phrase derives from Maurice MAETERLINCK's symbolist play *L'oiseau bleu* (1909), produced in London in 1910. A dream-like allegory, it tells the story of a boy and girl seeking 'the blue bird', a symbol of happiness.

Blue Blouses Soviet workers' theatre groups of the 1920s that toured with stylized AGIT-PROP plays laden with official propaganda. The name referred to the loose blue smocks worn by factory workers. Boris Yuzhanin founded the first troupe in 1923 at the Moscow Institute for Journalism. The companies presented a type of LIVING NEWSPAPER, using songs and sketches to review current events from a communist perspective.

By the mid 1920s more than 5,000 troupes of professional and amateur Blue Blouses existed with some 100,000 members. Plays were presented in factories, clubs, government halls, and outdoor settings. The well-known playwright and poet Sergei Tretyakov (1892–1939) promoted the groups but spoke out against the heavy didacticism. In 1927 the Soviet authorities merged the Blue Blouses with the more conventional TRAM drama organization.

The Chinese workers' theatres created in 1950 after the Russian example also included groups known as Blue Blouses. Even in America the workers' theatre movement included one company named the Blue Blouses.

boards, the The stage; the acting profession. To *go on the boards* is to become an actor or an actress.

Boar's Head Tavern The haunt of FALSTAFF, Prince Hal, and their low-life companions in Shakespeare's *Henry IV* plays. The tavern used to stand in Eastcheap, London. Destroyed in the Great Fire, it was rebuilt and annual Shakespeare Dinners were held there until 1784. It was demolished in 1831 to make way for one of the approaches to London Bridge. Washington Irving has an essay, 'The Boar's Head Tavern, Eastcheap', in his *Sketch Book*.

boat truck A wheeled platform, also called a **truck** or **wagon**, used to move properties and scenery on and off stage. A **scissor stage** contains two boat trucks that sweep in and out of the acting area, and a **wagon stage** has rails and lifts for boat trucks to move across the stage or back and forth to the cellar.

Bobadil, Captain A military braggart in Ben Jonson's EVERY MAN IN HIS HUMOUR. The name was probably derived from Francisco de Bobadilla, the first governor of Santo Domingo, who in 1500 sent Columbus home in chains. It is sometimes used of any boastful or vainglorious soldier.

Bobèche and Galimafré The stage names of the French comic actors Antoine Mandelot (1791–1840) and Auguste Guérin (1790–1870) respectively. Bobèche wore a red jacket and grey tricorn hat topped by a butterfly antennae. He was joined by Galimafré at a booth at the Boulevard du Temple fairground in Paris, where they revived the

18th-century PARADES; they also played in private homes. However, Napoleon was not amused by Bobèche's topical political jokes, and the actor was forced into exile, returning after the Restoration to a renewed but brief success. He subsequently moved into the provinces as a manager. Galimafré retired from performing in 1814, joining the stage staff at the Théâtre de la Gâité and then the Opéra-Comique in Paris. A play based on their lives was written by the Cogniard brothers and produced in 1837 at the Théâtre du Palais-Royal.

Bobo *See* PASO.

boffo A US slang term from the theatrical world meaning excellent. Apparently derived from BOX OFFICE (i.e. box-office success), it is widely used by journalists.

Bolt, Robert (Oxton) (1924–95) British dramatist and screenwriter, who first achieved success with his play *Flowering Cherry* (1957), starring Ralph Richardson and Celia Johnson, which ran for over 400 performances at the Haymarket. Bolt's reputation was confirmed with the success of A MAN FOR ALL SEASONS (1960), dealing with the life and death of Sir Thomas More. Later works included VIVAT! VIVAT REGINA! (1970), which concerns the relationship between Elizabeth I and Mary Queen of Scots, and *State of Revolution* (1977). Bolt also wrote a number of works for children (including *The Thwarting of Baron Bolligrew*, 1966) and several screenplays for the film director David Lean. In his later years he wrote little, having been severely disabled by a stroke. He was married (twice) to the actress Sarah Miles.

Bommalattam A type of puppet theatre only performed in south India, in Tamil Nadu and in northern Karnataka. Its origin is unknown, but performances are normally held at temple festivals or other religious celebrations. The stories, mainly from the *Puranas*, are told in dialogue, song, and dance, with time kept by a cymbal player and drummer and music from a harmonium player. The *ottu*, a wind instrument, is also used in the Mysore plays.

The puppets (which are sometimes used as magic dolls to ward off evil and bring rain) stand from one- to three-feet tall and resemble the more popular KATHPUTLI dolls of north India. They are manipulated by strings to the head, back, arms, and legs, with rods sometimes used for arms and legs. The manipulators, who wear bells on their ankles, stand behind and above the dolls; the acting area is created by black cloth stretched to form a PROSCENIUM ARCH.

The genre is sometimes known as GOMBEYATTA, which is also the name of the shadow puppet theatre of Karnataka.

Bond, Edward (1935–) British socialist playwright, whose unsparing works have sometimes provoked outrage from audiences, critics, and censors. His first play, *The Pope's Wedding* (1962), was presented at the Royal Court Theatre on a Sunday night without scenery. In 1965 SAVED was refused a licence by the LORD CHAMBERLAIN, primarily for an infanticide scene; the subsequent dispute contributed to the abolition of theatrical censorship in Britain. Bond's *Early Morning* (1968) was the last play to be banned by the Lord Chamberlain. The offending scenes included one portraying a lesbian relationship between Queen Victoria and Florence Nightingale. Threatened with prosecution, the theatre gave only one more performance after opening night – a 'critics' dress rehearsal', with 'guests' admitted free through a side door. Censorship was ended in 1968, and the following year the Royal Court revived both plays as part of an Edward Bond season.

In the 1970s Bond became accepted as an important voice within the British theatre. Particularly well received were *Lear* (1971), a savage reworking of Shakespeare's play, and *Bingo* (1973), in which he attacks Shakespeare for failing to be more politically aware. In 1978 his work *The Woman*, based on a Greek tragedy, became the first new play to be premiered at the National's Olivier Theatre. Subsequent works included the commercially successful *Restoration* (1981; revived 1988). In the later 1980s, however, Bond's rather stern brand of left-wing didacticism seemed increasingly out of key with the times and few of his plays reached the London stage (although he continued to be well respected in Europe). His more recent plays include *September* (1990) and *In the Company of Men* (1996).

book In musicals, the basic script, not including the lyrics of the songs. The term is also applied to the script of any play.

book ceiling A stage ceiling made up of two flats hinged together. This device was formerly used in a BOX SET.

book flat Two FLATs hinged together, known in America as a **two-fold.** This arrangement will stand without additional support. To 'book' a flat means to close a book flat.

book-holder *See* PROMPTER.

booking office Another name for the box office (*see under* BOX). The name arose because in earlier times tickets sold at booking offices were written out and entered up in the books by clerks.

book-keeper In the Elizabethan theatre, a member of the company whose primary purpose was to keep and protect copies of the play from rival companies. In the absence of strong copyright laws, the book-keeper would copy out an actor's part and give him only his own lines and the required cues. After a rehearsal or a performance, the actor returned the text to the book-keeper. This control of valuable original texts by a few individuals may have been the cause of so many Elizabethan plays being lost.

book wing A revolving device of attached wing flats, usually four, upon which different scenes are constructed. These scenes can then be changed by rotating the book wing like the pages of a book.

boom A BATTEN upon which stage lighting is mounted, positioned either vertically in the wings or horizontally over the acting area. The term is also used for the light itself.

booth A portable or temporary theatre, as formerly used by itinerant actors throughout Europe. They first came into common use in the 15th century, when religious dramas were often staged using a row of raised booths in which episodes from the Bible were enacted. With the advent of secular drama, booth theatres began to appear at marketplaces and country fairs, a tradition lasting until the 20th century. The booth was often a large tent with a small raised platform at the entrance, upon which a brief scene or entertainment (such as the French PARADE) was performed to entice audiences into the tent. Miniature booths were also employed as puppet theatres for Punch and Judy shows, etc.

Booth family A distinguished US theatrical family – father, three sons, and a grandson – whose contribution to serious 19th-century drama was overshadowed by John Wilkes Booth's assassination of President Abraham Lincoln.

Junius Brutus Booth (1796–1852) Born in London, the son of a lawyer, he joined a group of strolling players while still in his teens. Despite a poor physical appearance, he began to play Shakespearean roles on the London stage from 1817, becoming a rival of Edmund KEAN, who usually bested him. He led a tempestuous love life, fathering two illegitimate children before he was 17. In 1821 he left his wife and emigrated to America with a flower-seller, by whom he had 10 children. He repeated his London successes with US audiences, becoming especially celebrated for his Richard III and Shylock. He later suffered from bouts of madness and once yelled at a shocked Boston audience, "Take me to a lunatic asylum!" He continued to tour successfully with his sons, however. He died from a virus after drinking water from the Mississippi.

Junius Brutus Booth (1821–82) The namesake of his father, he began acting in his father's productions in 1835 and subsequently joined the Bowery Theatre stock company. After his brother assassinated Lincoln, Junius was arrested as a possible conspirator. He eventually went to California to become a theatrical impresario. His son Sydney Barton Booth (1873–1937) was also an actor and vaudeville star.

Edwin Thomas Booth (1833–93) The most talented son of Junius Brutus Booth senior, Edwin won an international reputation for his performances in Shakespearean tragedy. He first appeared on stage in 1849 at the Boston Museum, playing Tressel to his father's Richard III. In 1851 his father refused to perform one evening and Edwin took his place, playing Richard III at the age of 18. After his father's death, Edwin played many of Booth senior's classic roles before finally coming into his own in Boston and New York. His most acclaimed roles included Hamlet (which he once played for 100 consecutive nights) and Shylock.

Although he had a long-standing drink problem, which sometimes cost him jobs, he became manager of New York's Winter Garden Theatre in 1863 and appeared there with his brothers, Junius and John Wilkes, in *Julius Caesar* (ironically, about the assassination of a national leader). When his brother assassinated Lincoln and was shot in turn, Edwin was devastated and retired for nine months.

Edwin built Booth's Theatre at 23rd Street and Sixth Avenue in New York, opening it in 1869 playing Romeo to the Juliet of his second wife, Mary McVicker. His poor business sense, however, led to bankruptcy in 1873 and the loss of the theatre. He recouped his fortune by touring internationally. In 1882 he and Irving alternated in the parts of Othello and Iago at the Lyceum Theatre, London. Possibly his most successful appearances were made in Germany in 1883. In 1888 he founded the Players' Club in New York and became its first president.

John Wilkes Booth (1838–65) The assassin of President Lincoln was the most handsome and vivacious of the Booth brothers. "I must have fame" he had declared as a youth. He made his debut as Richmond in *Richard III* in 1855 and achieved his first triumph in *The Apostate* (1860), in which his acting was so reminiscent of his father that spiritualists suggested that Junius Booth's spirit had returned. His intense style of acting caused a sensation when he played Richard III in 1882 in New York; he also broke all records at the Boston Museum playing Pescara in *The Apostate*.

He was, however, constantly in trouble for his Southern sympathies during the American Civil War; he was frequently threatened with dismissal and once had to swear allegiance to the Union after cursing the government while playing in St Louis. He assassinated President Lincoln on 14 April 1865, during a production of *Our American Cousin* in FORD'S THEATRE. Twelve days later he was cornered in a burning barn and shot.

Borachio A name used by several Elizabethan dramatists for a drunkard. A *borachio* was a name for a wine bottle made of goat-skin; hence, one who fills himself with wine (Sp. *borracha*; Ital. *borraccia*).

In Shakespeare's MUCH ADO ABOUT NOTHING, Borachio is a villainous follower of Don John. At one point he plays upon his own name:

> I will, like a true drunkard, utter all to thee.

border A narrow curtain, painted cloth, flat, etc. hung across the top of the stage behind the PROSCENIUM ARCH. Borders originated in Italy and by the 17th century were standard stage devices in England and on the Continent.

Originally known as a **top drop**, the overhead border concealed lighting and other equipment from the audience's view. When the bottom edge is cut to shape, it is called a **cloud border**, and if painted like a cloudy sky, it is called a CLOUDING, a **sky border**, or a **blue**. In the early 19th century this was often replaced by such illusionistic devices as the PANORAMA and DIORAMA. Other framing pieces on stage include a **tree border** painted to resemble foliage, and a border **tail** or **leg** which is a cloth or narrow flat hanging down at each end to mask the wing and help form an arch over the scene.

border light *See* BATTEN.

born in a trunk A proud theatrical description of the children of actors, especially those who go into the profession themselves. The image is of a constantly travelling troupe, whose offspring could well be born in a trunk in a hotel room, if not a railway station.

borscht belt or **borscht circuit** A string of hotels in the Catskill Mountains of New York state, which constitute a circuit for summer holiday entertainers. Many of the hotels have a predominantly Jewish clientele, to whom they serve borscht, a Russian soup made from beetroots.

bottling In the Elizabethan theatre, the practice by strolling players of taking a collection in a bottle or other container from the audience rather than charging an admission price. This was the usual practice at performances in London INNS. After James Burbage (*see* BURBAGE FAMILY) built the first permanent playhouse, the THEATRE, and began to pay salaries, most professional companies gave up bottling.

Bottom the Weaver One of the Athenian artisans who rehearse and present the play of *Pyramus and Thisbe* in Shakespeare's A MIDSUMMER NIGHT'S DREAM. Shakespeare has drawn him as profoundly ignorant, brawny, mock heroic, and with an overweening conceit. He offers to play every part in the play: hence a Bottom the Weaver is a man who fancies he can do everything, and do it better than anyone else. When the spirit PUCK places an ass's head on his shoulders TITANIA, queen of the fairies, also under a spell, caresses him as an Adonis.

The name is appropriate to a weaver, as one meaning of *bottom* is a ball of thread.

Boucicault family. **Dion Boucicault** (Dionysius Lardner Boursiquot; 1822–90) Irish playwright, actor, and director. He wrote some 200 plays, becoming one of the great names of the 19th-century theatre on both sides of the Atlantic and a favourite of Queen VICTORIA. She wrote in her diary, "Mr Boucicault, who is very handsome and has a fine voice, acted very impressively. I can never forget his livid face and fixed look." She later commissioned a watercolour of him for Windsor Castle.

Born in Dublin, Boucicault began acting and writing as Lee Morton; his LONDON ASSURANCE, which opened in 1841 at Covent Garden, became one of the century's most popular comedies. He later provided Charles Kean with a great success with his adaptation of THE CORSICAN BROTHERS (1852). Boucicault then eloped to New York with Kean's ward, becoming a US citizen in 1873.

In America he made his name with *The Poor of New York* (retitled wherever it played, so that in e.g. London it became *The Poor of London*). He became the first writer seriously to dramatize the lives of US Blacks with *The Octoroon* (1859). The production included the spectacular burning of a Mississippi riverboat – an example of what Boucicault termed 'sensation drama'. His other works included plays with Irish settings including *The Colleen Bawn* (1860), based on the murder of an Irish girl by a British officer, and *The Shaughraun* (1875), the most popular Irish play of the century.

Boucicault was an innovator who pioneered the matinee performance, the BOX SET, and fireproof scenery. Despite his own plagiarism, he lobbied Congress for new COPYRIGHT protection, which became law in 1856. He was an indefatigable worker who suggested his tombstone should read: "His first holiday".

Boucicault's second wife was the Scottish-born actress **Agnes Kelly Robertson** (1833–1916). After eloping with Boucicault to America, she starred in most of his plays, winning particular acclaim as Jeanie Deans in *The Trial of Effie Deans* (1863), a dramatization of Scott's *The Heart of Midlothian*. In 1888 her husband, whose many affairs she had ignored, claimed they had never been legally wed. He then married Louise Thorndyke, an actress 44 years his junior, in what was probably a bigamous union. Agnes continued to act, making her final appearance in London in 1896 in a revival of Boucicault's *The Colleen Bawn*.

Dot Boucicault (Darley George Boucicault; 1859–1929) The elder son of Dion Boucicault and Agnes Robertson. He acted in his father's company before becoming the actor-manager of the Duke of York's Theatre, London, (1901–15). He was especially acclaimed for his role as Sir William Gower in Pinero's *Trelawney of the 'Wells'*. His wife was the actress Irene Vanbrugh.

Nina Boucicault (1867–1950), the daughter of Dion Boucicault and Agnes Robertson. She too began her career in her father's company, playing Eily O'Connor in *The Colleen Bawn* in 1885. Her second role was as Kitty Verdun in the original production of Brandon Thomas's *Charley's Aunt*. In 1904 she became the first Peter Pan in Barrie's famous play for children.

Boulevard theatres A series of theatres built on the Boulevard du Temple, Paris, from about 1760 onwards. A number of troupes had previously occupied fairground locations there (*see* FAIRGROUND ENTERTAINMENT). By the end of the century, such troupes as Audinot's, Nicolet's, the Théâtre des Associés, and the Variétés-Amusantes had acquired elaborate buildings. The Ambigu-Comique opened in 1769 as a children's and marionette theatre, and the Variétés-Amusantes opened in 1785 as the city's best theatre, eventually becoming the home of the COMÉDIE-FRANÇAISE.

During the 19th century the Boulevard theatres provided mainly popular melodrama; they later became more experimental in their production methods and were active in promoting new playwrights. Later boulevard theatres included the Gaîté (1805), the Porte-Saint-Martin (1810), Gymnase (1820), and Vaudeville (1868).

Famous boulevard actors incuded Mme Dorval (1798–1849) who specialized in melodrama at the Porte-Saint-Martin, Bocage (Pierre-François Tousez; 1797–1863), who played great lovers and eventually managed the Odéon, the pantomimist BAPTISTE, who developed the character of Pierrot at the Théâtre des Funambules, and Frédérick (Antoine-Louis-Prosper Lemaître; 1800–76), who first appeared at the Variétés-Amusantes as a pantomime lion, and later turned the stock villain of the melodrama into a comic caricature at the Odéon and Porte-Saint-Martin.

The Boulevard, with its sideshows, fireworks, and cafés, was sometimes nicknamed the **Boulevard of Crime**, after its portrayal in the melodramas of Guilbert de Pixerecourt (1773–1844), who became director of the Gaîté. Successful authors of Boulevard plays included Georges Feydeau (1862–1921), celebrated for his numerous farces, Eugène Labiche (1815–88), who turned out more than 170 light comedies, and Marcel Achard (Marcel-Auguste Ferréol; 1899–1974) who wrote sentimental love stories.

Although the theatres were demolished during a redevelopment of the Boulevard du Temple in 1862, the terms **Boulevard theatre** and **Boulevard play** continued to be used of popular Parisian drama – especially the farces and domestic dramas of the early 20th century.

Bowdler, Thomas (1754–1825) British physician and editor, who took it upon himself to produce an edition of Shakespeare's plays, expurgated of all words and plots "which cannot with propriety be read aloud in a family". His 10-volume *Family Shakespeare*, in which all profanities and obscenities were omitted, was published in 1818. Bowdler believed that by such editing "the transcendant genius of the poet would undoubtedly shine with more unclouded lustre". Some plays defied all Bowdler's attempts to make them 'decent'; in *Measure for Measure*, for instance, he was obliged to print a warning about the language, whilst *Othello* defeated him entirely, prompting him to admit that it was "unfortunately little suited to family reading" and best transferred "from the parlour to the cabinet". By 1838 the terms **bowdlerize** and **bowdlerization** had become widely used for all similar expurgations. Bowdler's own work was widely appreciated; in 1894 no less a person than Algernon Swinburne said of his efforts: "No man ever did better service to Shakespeare." By 1900 there were nearly 50 'gelded' versions of Shakespeare's plays in circulation, practitioners of bowdlerization by then including such luminaries as Lewis Carroll and Noah Webster. A curious fact about Dr Bowdler's works is that he was not the motivating force behind them: that 'honour' goes to his sister, Henrietta Maria Bowdler. That she preferred the expurgated works to be credited to her brother was typical of her modesty; she was so easily upset that when she visited the opera she kept her eyes averted from the stage to avoid seeing any 'indecorous' dancing.

Bowery Theatre A former New York theatre that made the name of Edwin FORREST and over the years presented such varied fare as classic drama, pantomime, melodrama, burlesque, and German-language works. This was despite the Bowery burning down six times within a century (including three times in the nine years 1836–45).

The theatre opened in 1826 as the New York Theatre, Bowery, managed by the actor George H. Barrett and his partner Gilbert. Lit by gas, it opened with Thomas Holcroft's *The Road to Ruin* before introducing its audiences to Forrest, who made his first appearance as Othello.

In 1828 the Bowery burned down but reopened three months later under Thomas Hamblin, who introduced the first continuous runs of plays and remained there until 1850. The Bowery burned down again in 1836, 1838, and 1845. In 1858 George L. Fox and James W. Lingard began to present their melodramas and pantomimes at the Bowery. During the Civil War, it was occupied by troops and presented circus acts. The venue subsequently turned to BURLESQUE, before closing in 1878; when it reopened a year later it was as the Thalia Theatre, a home to German-language works. Further fires occurred in 1923 and 1929, when the theatre closed permanently.

Another Bowery Theatre, later renamed the Stadt Theatre, opened in 1835 with circus acts and later introduced drama and German operas. In 1859 Fox and Lingard opened the New Bowery Theatre, which enjoyed a notable success with *Uncle Tom's Cabin*. This theatre was also destroyed by fire in 1866.

box *See* AUDITORIUM.

Box and Cox A phrase that can best be explained by the story behind it. Mrs Bouncer, a deceitful lodging-house landlady, let the same room to two men, Box and Cox, who unknown to each other occupied it alternately, one being out at work all day, the other all night. It is from the farce by J. M. Morton (1811–91) called *Box and Cox* (adapted from the French).

box office The office in the foyer of a theatre where tickets are purchased. Also called the **ticket office** or **booking office**, it is generally open from 10 a.m. until the evening performance and is run by the box-office manager and his assistants. The term also refers to the evening's receipts from ticket sales. A consistently successful play or performer may be described as 'good box office' (*see* BOFFO).

The earliest form of box office in Britain was the 'pay box' introduced in the 18th century. Most theatres had three of these small cubicals to collect money from customers in the pit, boxes, and gallery.

box set A naturalistic set of a room comprising three continuous walls with usable doors and windows and possibly a ceiling. It was introduced to the English stage in 1832 by the manager of Covent Garden, Madame VESTRIS, for W. B. Vernard's *The Conquering Game.* Flats replaced the painted backcloth with its wings and sky borders. This innovation inspired T. W. Robertson to pen the first drawing-room dramas, such as *Society* (1865). Box sets continued to be popular in the first half of the 20th century, but their use has since declined with the modern move away from the PROSCENIUM ARCH to a THRUST STAGE.

Cumbersome and elaborate box sets have caused actors much grief. Doors and windows stick; walls collapse. Rex Harrison was nearly knocked into the orchestra pit during the New York run of *My Fair Lady* (1956), when a hoisted set fell and sent blocks of wood tumbling across the stage. Box sets also create additional backstage work. The record for opening and closing a sliding door apparently goes to Julie Rutherford, stage manager of John Wells's *Anyone for Denis* (1981) at London's Whitehall Theatre. She did this 54 times in each performance, eventually logging up 20,592 openings and closings.

boy. Boy Bishop In medieval Europe, a boy chosen to oversee festival merrymaking at schools, colleges, cathedral choirs, etc. In England this usually occurred on St Nicholas's day (December 6) or during the New Year Celebrations (when it was sometimes called the Feast of Boys). In France it usually occurred as part of the FEAST OF FOOLS. The boys selected their Boy Bishop, a *dominus festi*, to lead processions and preside at feasts and burlesque Church services. Latin plays were performed. The boy held office for up to three weeks and other boys served as his prebendaries. If he died in office he was buried *in pontificalibus*. Probably the reference is to the boy Jesus sitting in the temple among the doctors. The custom was abolished by Henry VIII in 1541, revived in 1552, and finally abolished by Elizabeth I. Some scholars link the Feast of Boys to the beginnings of English secular drama.

boy companies In the Elizabethan theatre, companies of choir boys who acted semi-professionally and gained a great popular following. The first such companies came from the Chapels Royal in London and Windsor and from St Paul's Cathedral. They performed masques and disguisings at court until 1576 when Richard Farrant (d. 1580), master of the Windsor choirboys, adapted Blackfriars Theatre for their use. The same venue was used by the Boys of St Paul's, boys from OXFORD'S MEN, and by the Children of the Chapel.

Boy companies soon acquired a quasi-professional status and at the turn of the century their popularity often outstripped that of adult companies. The irritation this caused is evident from Shakespeare giving Hamlet a line denouncing boy actors as "little eyases". The boys gave several first performances of major plays, incuding Ben Jonson's *Cynthia's Revels* (1600) and *The Poetaster* (1601) (both of which starred Nathan Field and William Ostler, who later became leading adult actors) and works by John Lyly, George Chapman, and others.

The public infatuation with child actors had run its course by 1615, although such groups as BEESTON's Boys continued to perform into the Restoration era.

Boyfriend, The A musical by Sandy Wilson (1924–). An affectionate parody of the musicals of the 1920s, it was first performed in 1953 at the Player's Theatre, a London theatre club, before transferring to Wyndham's Theatre for a run of more than five years with 2084 performances. It opened on Broadway in 1954 for another long run. In 1967 it was revived in London with great success. A film version was made by Ken Russell (1971).

The story is set in Mme Dubonnet's finishing school, where every proper young lady requires a boyfriend. None exists for Polly Browne, however, because her wealthy father considers all men fortune-hunters. The Carnival Ball is approaching, and Polly (pretending to be a secretary) invites Tony, a simple messenger-boy, to be her date. He accepts, not revealing that he is actually the Hon. Tony Brockhurst. After various confusions among the debutantes and their beaux at the ball, Polly and Tony have their true identities revealed and are delighted to find that their growing love is socially acceptable. Wilson's songs include 'The Boyfriend', 'Won't You Charleston with Me?', 'I Could Be Happy with You', and 'Sur le Plage'.

Boys from Syracuse, The A musical comedy by George ABBOTT (book), Lorenz Hart (lyrics), and Richard Rodgers (music) based on Shakespeare's THE COMEDY OF ERRORS. It opened in New York in 1938 at the Alvin Theatre. *The Boys from Syracuse* retained only two of the Bard's original lines:

> ...the venom clamours of a jealous woman
> Poisons more deadly than a mad dog's tooth.

The plot, however, stays close to Shakespeare's story of separated twins and multiple mistaken identities. The songs included 'This Can't Be Love', 'Falling in Love with Love', and 'Sing for Your Supper'.

bozze A type of early stage LIGHTING introduced in the 17th century for the Italian theatre. It consisted of a glass globe with handles containing a wick. *Bozzi* were sometimes placed behind bottles or glasses containing coloured liquid so that the light would produce atmospheric colour effects such as a sunset.

brace *See* STAGE BRACE *under* STAGE.

Bracegirdle, Anne (1663–1748) One of Britain's first professional actresses. She was trained for the stage by Thomas BETTERTON. By 1688 she was appearing at Covent Garden, where she began to acquire a reputation for comedy. She was involved in a scandal in 1692 when the actor and playwright William Mountford (1664–92) was murdered on the instructions of a Captain Hill in a dispute for her love.

Mrs Bracegirdle later enjoyed a more secure love life as the mistress of William Congreve. She created Congreve's Angelica opposite Betterton's Valentine in *Love For Love* (1695) as well as Millimant in his *The Way Of The World* (1700). She is thought to have been the first woman to play Portia in *The Merchant of Venice*. She retired in 1707 as a gesture to the rising young actress Anne OLDFIELD, who succeeded her as Millament and in other roles.

Braithwaite, Dame (Florence) Lilian (1873–1948) British actress, noted for her sentimental and light-comedy roles. She made her professional debut in South Africa and subsequently acted in Shakespeare with Frank Benson's company and in lighter works with George Alexander's company at the St James' Theatre. Her most acclaimed roles included the society mother in Noël Coward's *The Vortex* (1924) and one of the murderous old ladies in *Arsenic and Old Lace* (1942). After one wartime performance of the latter play, she had to take refuge during a particularly prolonged air-raid. Asked the next day if she was exhausted, Braithwaite replied, "Certainly not. We were £50 up last night."

She was playing a part based on Mrs Patrick CAMPBELL in Ivor Novello's *Party*, when she ran into Mrs Pat herself, who was leaving on tour. "Oh, Lilian, I hear you are a perfect *tour de force* playing me!" said Mrs Pat, "and here I am forced to tour!" But Braithwaite had as quick a wit as Campbell. A young actress once expressed regret that Braithwaite was in the matinee audience because "I always feel I must save myself for the evening performance." Braithwaite shook her head: "I didn't think you saved anything." Commenting on actress Yvonne Arnaud, who had put on weight, she noted, "It's still the dear little face we all loved so in *By Candle Light*." After a pause, she added, "But there's another face round it."

Branagh, Kenneth (1961–) British actor and director, who at the age of 25 co-founded the Renaissance Theatre Company. He was born in Belfast, where his father was a joiner and his mother a mill worker. In 1970 the family moved to England; during summer holidays the young Branagh hitchhiked with a tent to Stratford-upon-Avon to see the productions. In 1979 he won a scholarship to the Royal Academy of Dramatic Art (*see* RADA).

Branagh acted on television before making his London debut in Julian Mitchell's *Another Country* at the Greenwich Theatre. For this he won two 'most promising newcomer' awards. In 1983 he presented a one-man show, *The Madness*, which flopped disastrously at the Upstream Theatre Club in London. One performance saw only 12 customers in the 150-seat auditorium. "And six of them," Branagh recalled, "were my family."

In 1984 he joined the Royal Shakespeare Company at Stratford, and received rave reviews as the lead in *Henry V* (at 23 the youngest actor the RSC had ever cast in the role). As usual, Branagh took special pains to grasp the part, even arranging a meeting with Prince Charles to understand what it is like to be royal. During one performance when he reached for gloves at his belt and found them missing, he trudged about the stage ad-libbing, "I bethinkst myself that I did have some gloves...but see, alas, they are not here..." Eventually a stagehand produced them.

In 1986 Branagh invested £25,000 to found (with David Parfitt) the **Renaissance Theatre Company**. He called it "a company that would fully exploit the actor's imagination and energy". In 1988 the company presented *Hamlet, Much Ado About Nothing*, and *As You Like It* in the provinces and the West End. It also invited actors to direct, leading to successful productions by Judi Dench, Geraldine McEwan, and Derek Jacobi. That year, the company made its first film, *Henry V*, starring and directed by Branagh. One critic called his performance "comparable in stature to Olivier's". The following year he made a highly publicized marriage to the actress Emma Thompson (1959–) and published his autobiography at the age of 28. His subsequent films as actor-director include *Much Ado About Nothing* (1993), in which he co-starred with Thompson, and a four-hour version of *Hamlet* (1997) that opened to decidedly mixed reviews. He separated from Thompson in 1995.

Brand A poetic tragedy by Henrik IBSEN, published in 1866 and first performed in 1885 in Copenhagen. It was seen in New York in 1910 and in London two years later. Ibsen originally wrote it as a narrative poem but later adapted it for the theatre. The work, a bleak exploration of the Norwegian character, established Ibsen's European reputation and earned him a state author's annuity that gave him financial security.

The play is set in 19th-century Norway. Brand, a fanatical pastor, will sacrifice everything, including his family, for the Church. He urges his mother without success to renounce her wealth, and when his child becomes ill from lack of sunlight, he refuses to move to warmer climes as this would mean leaving his congregation. When the child dies, Brand calls it God's will. His wife Agnes also dies. Brand now plans to build a new church and leads his flock into the mountains, where the harsh weather soon induces despair among the brethren. Members of his congregation reject his leadership and stone him. Brand has a vision of his wife asking him to compromise, but he cannot. He dies in an avalanche caused by a gypsy, who believes that Brand is Christ.

bread and circuses Free food and entertainment. *Panem et circenses* were, according to Juvenal's *Satires*, the two things the Roman populace desired.

Break a leg! Traditional wish of good luck among performers in the theatre, since a wish of 'good luck' is considered a jinx. *See* TABOOS AND SUPERSTITIONS.

Brecht, Bertolt (1898–1956) German playwright, poet, and director; one of the most influential theatrical figures of the 20th century.

Brecht's earliest dramas were written just after the end of World War I while he was a medical student at Augsburg. The first of these to reach the professional stage (though not the first to be written) was *Drums in the Night* (1922). Telling the story of a soldier coming home from the war, the play was a success and subsequently transferred to Berlin. In Berlin, Brecht became (1924), an assistant to Max REINHARDT and collaborated with Erwin PISCATOR at the DEUTSCHES THEATER. Brecht's next plays, *Baal* (1923) and *In the Jungle of the Cities* (1923), show the influence of expressionism. MAN IS MAN (1926), marked the beginning of Brecht's experiments with the innovatory ALIENATION EFFECT and may be seen as the first stage in the development of his theory of EPIC THEATRE.

In the late 1920s Brecht began to collaborate with Kurt Weill, resulting in the classic musicals *The Rise and Fall of the City of Mahagonny* (1927), THE THREEPENNY OPERA (1928), *Happy-End* (1929), and *The Seven Deadly Sins* (1933). His conversion to Marxism during this period added an element of rather bleak didacticism to such plays as *He Who Says Yes* (1929), *He Who Says No* (1930), and *The Measures Taken* (1930).

In 1932 Brecht was placed on the Nazi Party's list of decadent writers; the following year, when Hitler came to power, he and his wife Helene Weigel fled to Denmark. After some wandering they finally (1941) made their way to America. During this unsettled period Brecht wrote most of his finest plays, including GALILEO (1943, written 1938), THE GOOD PERSON OF SETZUAN

(1943, written 1938–40), MOTHER COURAGE AND HER CHILDREN (1941, written 1939), and *The Resistible Rise of Arturo Ui* (1957, written 1941). The principal work of Brecht's American period was THE CAUCASIAN CHALK CIRCLE (1948, written 1944–45).

In 1947 Brecht was summoned before a meeting of the House Un-American Activities Committee and gave a cleverly evasive performance. Brecht and his wife subsequently left America, moving briefly to Zürich before returning to Berlin in 1949. In Berlin, Brecht and Weigel were offered their own theatre as well as a considerable subsidy; this enabled them to form the BERLINER ENSEMBLE, to which Brecht devoted much of his remaining time. Following his death, the Ensemble, which had established a high European reputation, continued to be managed by his widow.

Amongst Brecht's other writings were collections of poetry and essays upon the theatre, including the highly influential treatise *Organon für das Theater* (1949), in which he expounded many of his theories.

breeches part A leading male role that is played by an actress. In Britain, this was particularly common in the romantic comedies of the earlier 18th century. Roles in which female characters temporarily disguise themselves as men (as ROSALIND does in *As You Like It*) are not strictly speaking breeches parts.

Celebrated English examples of actresses playing breeches parts are Peg WOFFINGTON as Sir Harry Wildair in Farquhar's *The Constant Couple* and Mrs Mountfort as Macheath in Gay's *The Beggar's Opera*. In Victorian times, Madame VESTRIS was noted for playing male roles. The tradition survives in the convention that the PRINCIPAL BOY in pantomime is played by a young woman. *See also* FEMALE IMPERSONATOR.

Breezy Bill Nickname for the popular actor William TERRISS.

Brentford. Like the two kings of Brentford smelling at one nosegay Said of people who were once rivals, but have become reconciled. The allusion is to THE REHEARSAL (1672), by George Villiers, Duke of Buckingham. At one point in the absurd play-within-a-play presented by BAYES "the two kings of Brentford enter hand in hand". Moreover, the actors make them enter "smelling at one nosegay".

Brenton, Howard (1942–) British dramatist, noted for his controversial political plays. Brenton's first full-length play to be professionally produced was *Revenge*, staged at the ROYAL COURT THEATRE in 1969. He became resident dramatist at the Royal Court in 1972, following on from David HARE. Brenton and Hare collaborated on the writing of *Brassneck* in 1973. Other significant plays from this period include *The Churchill Play* (1973), a fierce attack on the cult of the wartime leader, and *Epsom Downs* (1977), which uses the occasion of Derby Day to present a critical panorama of British society.

In 1980 Brenton found himself at the centre of a major controversy when his play THE ROMANS IN BRITAIN opened at the National Theatre. The play, in which the British role in Northern Ireland is compared to the Roman occupation of Britain, caused outrage, largely as a result of a scene featuring a male rape. In 1985 Brenton collaborated again with Hare on *Pravda*, a boisterous satire on the tabloid press, which opened at the National Theatre with Anthony HOPKINS in the lead. Brenton has also made several translations for the stage, including Brecht's *Galileo* and Büchner's *Danton's Death*. His more recent works include *Moscow Gold* (1990; with Tariq Ali), *Berlin Bertie* (1992), and *One Once* (1994).

bridge A platform used to work on lighting and scenery. An extension of the FLIES, it can be raised and lowered and in the US is sometimes called an **elevator**. A **catwalk** is a narrow bridge between the 'fly floors' over each set of wings used to adjust scenery.

Bridie, James (Osborne Henry Mavor; 1888–1951) Scottish doctor who became a noted playwright and co-founder in 1943 of the Glasgow Citizens' Theatre. A pioneer of the so-called 'play of ideas', Bridie greatly invigorated the Scottish theatre with his 40-or-so plays and in 1950 founded the College of Drama in the Royal Scottish Academy of Music, Glasgow. His plays tended to suffer from loose construction and weak final acts. He excused himself by stating "Only God can write last acts, and He seldom does."

His first great success, THE ANATOMIST (1930), was followed by *Tobias and the Angel* (1931), *Jonah and the Whale* (1932), and *A Sleeping Clergyman* (1933). His anti-fascist play *King of Nowhere*, presented by the Old

Vic Company at the New Theatre in 1938, starred Olivier as a half-mad actor who escapes from an asylum and becomes the leader of a dangerous new political party.

Many of Bridie's plays dealt with religion and the supernatural and required unusual special effects. In *Jonah and the Whale*, Jonah sat crosslegged in the belly of the whale under a red light while a dozen amplifiers blasted the auditorium. Bridie's stage direction states: "The audience is to be deafened by the bellowing noise and hyptonised by the small, impassive, red-lit figure on the stage."

A late success came in 1949 when Edith Evans played Lady Pitts in his controversial *Daphne Laureola*. Reviewers on both sides of the Atlantic loved her performance and disliked Bridie's play.

For the 1950 Edinburgh Festival Bridie wrote *The Queen's Comedy*, often considered his best work. He continued writing until the year of his death.

Bridie's son, Ronald Mavor, was also a playwright, best remembered for *A Private Matter* (1973) about an author writing a biography against the wishes of his subject's family. The production was one of the first to feature full male nudity.

Brigadoon A musical fantasy by Alan Jay Lerner and Frederick Loewe that opened on Broadway in 1947. The cast, which included Eli Wallach, attended Lee Strasberg's METHOD acting class during its run. The London production opened two years later and a film was made in 1954. *Brigadoon* is the name of a magical Scottish village that appears only once a century. It is stumbled upon by two contemporary Americans, Tommy and Jeff, who are told that the village will disappear forever if a native leaves but that a stranger may stay if he loves a villager. Although Tommy has become infatuated with the beautiful Fiona, both Americans decide to return to New York. Tommy soon discovers that he has made a mistake and leaves his American fiancée to find the village again. His strong love reawakens it long enough for him to enter.

The songs, composed by Loewe with lyrics by Lerner, include 'Almost Like Being in Love', 'The Heather on the Hill', 'Come to Me, Bend to Me', and 'I'll Go Home with Bonnie Jean'.

Brighton Beach Memoirs A comedy by Neil SIMON that was based on his youth in New York. It was first performed on Broadway in 1983 at the Eugene O'Neill Theatre, which Simon owns; the play became one of his most successful transfers to London, being seen at the National Theatre in 1986 and transferring the same year to the Aldwych Theatre.

The story, set in Brooklyn in 1937, concerns a poor but respectable Jewish family. The 14-year-old son, Eugene Jerome, is a budding writer who is discovering sex with advice from his big brother Stanley. Their father, Jack, has to hold down two jobs at once to support both his own family and his widowed sister-in-law Blanche and her daughters Nora and Laurie. He finally has a minor heart attack. Stanley narrowly escapes being fired for his principles and then loses a week's wages in a game of poker. His father forgives him and promises to teach him the game. Nora has been offered a Broadway audition, but when her mother insists that she attend college instead she reluctantly agrees. Next comes good and bad news: the family's Polish cousins have escaped the Nazis, but all seven will be moving into the house in a week's time.

bristle trap *See* STAR TRAP *under* STAR.

British. British Actors' Equity Association *See* EQUITY.

British Theatre Association (BTA) An organization that supports and helps to coordinate amateur drama in Britain. It has more than 5000 members, including professional affiliations. Originally named the **British Drama League** (BDL), it was founded in 1919 by Geoffrey Whitworth (1883–1951), who directed it until 1948.

The BTA organizes an annual Conference on Theatre and an annual Festival of Community Drama. It maintains an extensive reference library and, for members, a lending library. Other services include training for amateur actors and producers, an information and advisory service, a junior league providing lectures and courses for young people, a Theatregoers' Club in London, and the publication of *Drama*, a critical quarterly magazine.

Related organizations in the British Isles include the Scottish Community Drama Association (1926), the Amateur Drama Council in Ireland (1952), and the Amateur

Drama Association in Wales (1965). The International Amateur Theatre Association, based in The Hague, was created in 1952 by the actor and director E. Martin Browne.

Broadway A term for New York's commercial theatre, equivalent to the WEST END when referring to London theatre. The name comes from the street that runs through the heart of Manhattan and has been applied to theatres clustering in side streets from West 44th to 50th streets. All mainstream theatre in New York, however, is described as being 'on Broadway'.

Broadway first became synonymous with theatre in the 1850s. When extravagant lighting was introduced some 40 years later it acquired the nickname the **Great White Way**. The district had around 80 theatres when at the height of its prestige in the 1920s. More recently it has specialized in large musicals or small comedies following the decline of serious drama and the advent of competition from OFF-BROADWAY and OFF-OFF-BROADWAY. In all, New York now has some 400 theatres.

Broken Jug, The A one-act comedy by the eccentric German dramatist Heinrich von KLEIST. He finished the play in 1805, during a sojourn in Switzerland, where he had intended to become a farmer. *The Broken Jug* was a failure when first produced in 1808 by Goethe at the Weimar Court Theatre but is now regarded as one of the greatest comic works in the German language. It has been seen in English in a shortened version and there is also a version in Scots titled *The Chippit Chantie*.

The story centres on Adam, a rogueish village magistrate whose disregard for truth is comparable to Falstaff's. To his great concern, he suddenly finds himself presiding over the trial of an innocent man accused of a crime that he himself committed. In 1958 Sir Donald WOLFIT directed and played the leading role at the Lyceum Theatre, Edinburgh, opposite George Curzon as a visiting councillor. Wolfit was known both for his penny-pinching and his horror of being upstaged. At one point during the run the actress Nan Munro, playing a witness, began to eat an apple during some of Wolfit's best lines. The next day he told his stage manager not to buy any more apples: "Cut them. I'm not paying three and six a week for her to go 'Chwap-Chwap' and kill my laughs!"

Brook, Peter (1925–) British theatre director, noted for his strikingly original productions. The child of Russian emigrés, Brook made his debut at the age of 18 with a production of Marlowe's *Dr Faustus*. In 1945 Brook was invited to direct Paul Scofield in *King John* at the Birmingham Repertory Theatre, following this with a celebrated production of *Love's Labours Lost* (1946) at Stratford-upon-Avon (again with Scofield). Further successes included Anouilh's *Ring Round the Moon* (1950), Otway's *Venice Preserv'd* (1953), *Hamlet* (1955), *The Power and the Glory* (1956), and *The Family Reunion* (1956).

Brook was made a codirector of the newly formed Royal Shakespeare Company in 1962, directing later that year a highly acclaimed production of *King Lear* (with Scofield once again). Other successes with the RSC included Peter Weiss's MARAT/SADE (1964), Seneca's *Oedipus* (1968), and a famous production of *A Midsummer Night's Dream* (1970), featuring an all-white set and the use of circus skills.

In 1970 Brook founded, with Jean-Louis BARRAULT, the INTERNATIONAL CENTRE FOR THEATRE RESEARCH, a company of international performers with whom he has toured extensively. His later productions include a nine-hour adaptation of the Indian epic THE MAHABHARATA (1985), a pared down version of *Carmen* (1989), and *Qui est la?* (1995), a reworking of *Hamlet*.

Brooke, Gustavus Vaughan *See* DUBLIN ROSCIUS *under* ROSCIUS.

Brooks Atkinson Theatre A New York theatre on West 47th Street between Broadway and Eighth Avenue. It opened in 1926 as the Mansfield Theatre, its first major production being Ansky's *The Dybbuk*, presented by the Moscow Habimah Players. In 1930 Marc Connelly's *The Green Pastures* was a great hit; later productions included two London imports, Gordon Sherry's *Black Limelight* (1936) and Robert Ardrey's *Thunder Rock* (1939).

During World War II the theatre was converted into a production centre for radio and television broadcasts. When it reopened in 1960 it was renamed the Brooks Atkinson Theatre to honour the *New York Times* critic, who had just retired (*see* ATKIN-

SON, BROOKS). In 1961 Neil Simon's *Come Blow Your Horn* was a great success. Rolf Hochhuth's controversial play denouncing Pope Pius XII for not helping the Jews during World War II, *The Deputy (Der Stellvertreter*; seen in London the previous year as *The Representative*) was mounted there in 1964. Subsequent productions have included Bernard Slade's *Same Time, Next Year* in 1975 and Lanford Wilson's *Talley's Folly* in 1980.

Brothers Bollox Two characters in *The Sod's Opera*, an anonymous piece of Victorian erotica that has sometimes (most unconvincingly) been attributed to GILBERT AND SULLIVAN. As well as the title characters it features such *dramatis personae* as Scrotum, an aged and wrinkled servant. The work has never been performed in public.

Browning Version, The A one-act play by Terence RATTIGAN, first performed in 1948 at the Phoenix Theatre, London. It was one of two plays presented under the title *Playbill*, the other being the short comedy *Harlequinade* (about actors rehearsing *Romeo and Juliet* for a tour of the provinces). Critics gave mixed reviews to *Harlequinade* but hailed *The Browning Version* as a "70-minute masterpiece".

When Rattigan offered the major role to John GIELGUD during a walk in New York's Central Park, the famous actor replied, "I'll have to be so very careful about what I do now, Terry, my dear. The public have seen me in so much first-class stuff, do you think they would accept me in anything second-rate?" Rattigan was shattered at having his work thus described; in the event the role was triumphantly played by Eric Portman.

The plot concerns Andrew Crocker-Harris, an ill and unsuccessful schoolmaster, who is asked by the headmaster to step down in favour of a younger man. Crocker-Harris is hated by his students who call him 'The Himmler of the Lower Fifth', and by his wife, who is having an affair with a younger master. One student, however, shows respect and sympathy, presenting him with a copy of Robert Browning's translation of the *Agamemnon*. Crocker-Harris comes to terms with his failures, ignores his wife's taunts, and tells the headmaster that he will not yield his position.

Bruno, Giordano (1548–1600) The ill-fated Italian philosopher and scientist who wrote one play, *Il Candelaio* (*The Candlemaker*), which was banned in his own lifetime and not performed for nearly 400 years. The play, a satire attacking corruption, was finally given a professional performance in Italy in 1965 in a shortened modernized version.

Born at Nola near Naples, Bruno travelled throughout Europe, publishing *Il Candelaio* in Paris and visiting London and Oxford where he met the poet Sir Philip Sidney. On his return to Italy, he was arrested and imprisoned for his unorthodox religious ideas, which included a belief in the harmony of the human soul and nature. After seven years in prison he was burned at the stake when the Inquisition in Rome named him a heretic.

Bruno's philosophy is thought to have influenced the writings of Shakespeare and Ben Jonson amongst others. His life was depicted in Morris West's play *The Heretic* (1970).

BTA *See* BRITISH THEATRE ASSOCIATION.

Bucco A stock character of the Roman ATELLANA; he appears to have been a fat rustic clown. Pomponius wrote two plays in which he was the main character.

Büchner, Georg (1813–37) German playwright, who was a major influence on both NATURALISM and EXPRESSIONISM, despite writing only three plays (one unfinished) before his death at the age of 23. Born at Goddelau, the son of an army doctor, Büchner studied medicine at Strasbourg and Giessen. He was a political radical who founded a revolutionary society and had to flee to Strasbourg. In 1836 he began to teach natural science in Zürich but died a year later of typhoid fever.

His plays, which reacted against the romanticism of Schiller and others, are filled with morbid pessimism, violence, and a deep sympathy for the oppressed. His first work, *Dantons Tod* (DANTON'S DEATH), written in 1835 but not staged until 1903 in Berlin, took a sombre look at the French Revolution. In Britain, it enjoyed an impressive revival at the National Theatre in 1971 under the direction of Jonathan Miller. *Leonce und Lena* was another attack on romanticism, written in 1836, published in 1850, but not performed until 1885 in

Munich. The incomplete WOYZECK, written in 1836 and first performed in 1913 in Vienna, has been acclaimed as the forerunner of the social dramas of the last decade of the 19th century. The plot concerns the insanity and eventual suicide of the title character.

Buffalo Bill Nickname of William Frederick Cody (1846–1917), the American showman and frontiersman. He earned his nickname after killing, at his estimate, 4280 buffaloes in 18 months, while supplying food for labourers constructing the Kansas Pacific Railway in 1867–68. Born in Iowa, Cody worked variously as a horse wrangler, pony-express rider, and prospector in the Pikes Peak gold rush. During and after the American Civil War, he served in the US cavalry as a scout in campaigns with General Custer. In 1876 Cody killed the Cheyenne chief, Yellow Hand, in a duel; he later commented "Jerking his war-bonnet off, I scientifically scalped him in about five seconds."

Cody's fame was largely based on *The Buffalo Bill Stories*, five-cent novels that often took his heroic actions into the realm of fantasy. He was a superb showman who capitalized on the publicity in 1883 by organizing a spectacular Wild West Show that travelled throughout the US; the show featured cowboys and Indians, sharpshooters, and rodeo roughriders. Among the troupe's performers was the markswoman Annie Oakley, the eponymous heroine of *Annie Get Your Gun* (*see under* ANNIE).

bufo The Cuban and Caribbean version of the Spanish SAINETE. Bufos blend comedy, music, and satire and deal mainly with the working classes. The *bufos cubanos* were generally political satires, often on the theme of illusion and reality. They enjoyed great popularity at the turn of the century but had disappeared by the 1920s, being replaced by the ZARZUELA. Some 30 years later, the genre was resurrected by Fidel Castro's regime as a propaganda vehicle.

Bugaku A form of Japanese mask play with music and dancing that was imported from China and India in the 7th century. The subject matter is based on religious texts. *Bugaku* had a great influence on the development of the more varied NŌ drama. It is a highly formal theatrical art, the movements of the performers, who wear the costume of the early period, being rigidly prescribed by tradition. Until the post-war era performances were restricted to the royal court and certain religious festivals.

built stuff A theatre term for three-dimensional objects built for a scene, such as a ROSTRUM, a piece of furniture, a mantelpiece, or landscape features such as trees and rocks. The construction is often of chicken wire, canvas, and papier-mâché.

bums on seats Theatre slang for members of the audience, generally used in calculations of its size, as in "Olivier could always put bums on seats".

Bunny Nickname of the British comedy actor J. Robertson Hare (1891–1979), who became a star of the Aldwych Farces of the 1920s and the 1930s.

Bunraku Puppet Theatre An ancient Japanese puppet theatre that is one of the world's most sophisticated and realistic forms of puppetry. The genre began in the 11th century, reached its height of popularity in the 18th century, but is now only performed at one theatre in Osaka.

Named after the puppet-master Vemura Bunrakuken (1737–1810), the theatre uses dolls that are from one-half to two-thirds full size. The stylized three-act dramas deal with historical or domestic themes and are performed on full-size stages complete with scenery. A speaker stands at the right of the stage to recite the *joruri*, or dramatic narrative; this role is considered so exhausting that each act has a different narrator. Located next to the speaker are *samisen* musicians.

Each principal puppet character has three visible manipulators on stage. The chief operator wears a ceremonial samurai kimono and inserts his left hand into the puppet's back, controlling the facial expression by means of a rod attached to the eyes, mouth, and eyebrows. The assistant operators are dressed in black and wear black hoods. A lesser character has only one manipulator.

The manipulators begin their training in childhood, do not participate in plays until in their twenties, and are not given major characters to control until middle-aged. They must memorize numerous conventions: a woman puppet steps forward on her right foot but a man on his left; a puppet steps forward to ask a question, back to refuse a request.

The best-known playwright for the *Bunraku* was Chikamatsu (1653–1724), who wrote plays for both the puppet theatre and for the KABUKI, many being performed by both. One of Chikamatsu's plays, *The Double Suicide* (1703), caused so many double suicides in Japan that the government banned plays on the theme.

Burbage family The English actor-manager James Burbage (*c.* 1530–97) and his two sons, the actor-manager Cuthbert Burbage (*c.* 1566–1636) and England's first great actor Richard Burbage (*c.* 1567–1619).

James Burbage began his career in about 1572 as a joiner and actor with Leicester's Men. In 1576 he leased land in Shoreditch, London, and erected the THEATRE, England's first permanent playhouse. In 1577 he built a second theatre in Shoreditch called the Curtain (because it was constructed on land known as Curten Close or Courtein). The CHAMBERLAIN'S MEN, a cooperative of the Burbage family and the leading actors, appeared there on a regular basis and some scholars believe *Romeo and Juliet* was first performed there in about 1595.

In 1596 Burbage converted part of a former Dominican friary into the indoor BLACKFRIARS THEATRE. The local residents, however, secured an injunction, and Burbage died before it opened. His sons inherited Blackfriars and leased it to a boys' company (*see* BOY COMPANIES).

Cuthbert Burbage began as an actor but became involved in management when he and his brother inherited the theatres. A dispute arose with the landowner when the Theatre's land lease expired in 1597, and Cuthbert led the fight. While the landlord was absent, the brothers dismantled their theatre and used the wood to build the famous GLOBE THEATRE on Bankside, forming a syndicate with Shakespeare and others.

Richard Burbage made his debut at the Theatre with the ADMIRAL'S MEN when aged about 18. Although short and stout, by 1594 he was the leading actor with the Chamberlain's Men. At the Globe, under his brother's management, he created such Shakespearean parts as Hamlet, Lear, Macbeth, and Othello. As Richard III (his first major role) he became particularly celebrated for his death scene. A Bosworth innkeeper supposedly took his guests to Bosworth Field and would point out the spot where Burbage cried: "A horse! A horse! My kingdom for a horse!"

Burbage also appeared in the first productions of works by John Webster, including the role of the evil Ferdinand in *The Duchess of Malfi*, and Ben Jonson, Thomas Kyd, Francis Beaumont, and John Fletcher. His name was synonymous with acting during his lifetime and for long afterwards. A character in Jonson's *Bartholomew Fair* asks, "Which is your Burbage now?...your best actor?" Burbage was also an accomplished painter, and some attribute the Chandos portrait of Shakespeare to him. The Bard left Burbage a small remembrance in his will. When Burbage died, Richard Flecknoe (d. 1678) wrote:

> No more young Hamlet, old Hieronymo;
> King Lear, the grieved
> Moor, and more beside, that lived in
> him, have now for ever died.

Emlyn Williams made Burbage a character in his play *Spring 1600* (1934). *See also* RICHARD III.

Bürgerliches Trauerspiel (Ger. Bourgeois Tragedy) A German theatrical genre of the late 18th century, largely inspired by English domestic tragedies, such as those of George Lillo (1693–1739). Lillo's *The London Merchant; or the History of George Barnwell* (1731; *see* BARNWELL, GEORGE) had a direct influence on the first important *Bürgerliches Trauerspiel*, LESSING's *Miss Sara Sampson* (1755). Lessing later contributed *Emilia Galotti* (1772) to the genre, while Schiller also described his *Love and Intrigue* (1783) as a *Bürgerliches Trauerspiel*.

The genre treated the homes of the German bourgeoisie, then increasing in status and power, as apt settings for heroic conflicts once restricted to aristocratic milieux. The *Bürgerliches Trauerspiel* thus foreshadowed the plays of Henrik Ibsen, Gerhard Hauptmann, and the naturalist playwrights of the latter half of the 19th century.

Burgtheater Austria's national theatre, in Vienna opposite the Rathaus (City Hall). It maintains one of the leading companies in the German-speaking world. In 1776 Emperor Josef II decreed the theatre would become the home of a new Hof-und-Nationaltheater company; this would perform serious drama instead of the popular comedy that had reigned for more than 30 years (*see* ALTWIENER VOLKSTHEATER).

The Burgtheater's first manager was Josef von Sonnenfels (1733–1817), who brought in new Austrian plays modelled on classical French and German works, as well as such renowned actors as Germany's Friedrich SCHRÖDER. Sonnenfels built up an impressive reputation for the theatre during his 38 years as manager, being succeeded in 1814 by Josef Schreyvogel (1768–1832), who furthered his reforms and discovered Austria's greatest Romantic dramatist, Franz GRILLPARZER. In 1849 Heinrich Laube (1806–84) took over. Under his management the theatre pioneered the BOX SET and popularized the French WELL-MADE PLAY.

The company moved to a new building in 1888. Here the poet and playwright Anton Wildgans (1881–1932) presented mainly expressionist works between the wars. The building was severely damaged during World War II but reopened in 1955 under the poet, actor, and director Berthold Viertel (1885–1955). The present company performs chiefly classical works.

burla A slapstick interlude of the COMMEDIA DELL'ARTE that was longer than the LAZZO. It was usually unrelated to the plot and often involved a simple practical joke played on the fool by the clown. The words BURLETTA and BURLESQUE were derived from *burla*.

Burleigh's nod A nod or shake of the head conveying great meaning without words. In Sheridan's THE CRITIC a mock tragedy called *The Spanish Armada* is presented by the author, Mr Puff. Lord Burleigh, a character in the play-within-a-play is supposedly too weighed down with affairs of state to communicate with anything but a portentous nod. Each time he moves his head Puff explains his meaning, for instance: "By that shake of the head he gave you to understand that...if there was not a greater spirit shown...the country would at last fall a sacrifice to the hostile ambition of the Spanish monarchy." The real Lord Burleigh (1520–98) was Elizabeth I's chief minister for many years.

burlesque. English burlesque In the English theatre of the late 17th and 18th century, a burlesque was a comic imitation of a popular play or type of play. The parody was generally fairly crude, often involving a reversal of expected roles, with heroes acting as buffoons, etc.

The first English burlesque was the comedy THE REHEARSAL (1671) by George Villiers, Duke of Buckingham, which mocked Dryden, Otway, and heroic Restoration drama. In the 18th century burlesque works became crueller and more defamatory. Examples include John Gay's THE BEGGAR'S OPERA (1728), which ridiculed the conventions of opera, Henry Fielding's TOM THUMB (1730), Henry Carey's "most tragical tragedy" CHRONONHOTONTHOLOGOS (1734), and Sheridan's THE CRITIC (1779), which satirized both the amateur actor and heroic bombast:

> Go call a coach, and let a coach be called
> And let the man who calls it be the caller
> And in his calling, let him nothing call,
> But coach! coach! coach! Oh! for a
> coach, ye gods!

In the 19th century burlesque became kinder and more frivolous, with works such as H. J. Byron's *The Corsican 'Bothers'; or, the Troublesome Twins* (1869), a gentle satire of Boucicault's *The Corsican Brothers*.

The GAIETY THEATRE long thrived on the talents of its famous burlesque quartet Nellie Farren, Edward Terry, Kate Vaughan, and E. W. Royce, who first appeared together in Byron's *Little Don Caesar de Bazan* (1876). In 1889 another Gaiety foursome – Fred Leslie, C. Danby, Ben Nathan, and Fred Storey – appeared dressed as ballerinas for a *pas de quatre* in *Ruy Blas; or, the Blasé Roué*. Henry Irving protested when he realized that one of the 'girls' was made-up to resemble himself; the make-up was subsequently changed.

Other exponents of Victorian burlesque included James Robinson Planche and W. S. Gilbert, before his partnership with Sullivan helped to replace burlesque with light opera and musical comedy. It was deprived of many of its favourite targets when the new naturalistic style of drama was introduced by the playwright Tom Robertson. However, traces of the genre remain in the short scenes of 20th-century REVUE and to a lesser degree in pantomime.

Closely related to the burlesque was the EXTRAVAGANZA which had no particular target for its satire but made fun of myths and folk tales.

American burlesque US burlesque has no relation to the English variety. The genre originated in 1868, when the English actress Lydia Thompson presented a show featuring a chorus line of 'British Blondes'.

The chorus line was used by Michael Bennett Leavitt (1843–1935) as the basis for burlesque shows that set the pattern for the genre in America.

The shows had a standard three-part format, opening with songs and comic sketches called 'bits', following this with an **oilo** (meaning 'potpourri') segment of variety acts such as acrobats, magicians, ventriloquists, and dog acts, and ending with more music as well as burlesque sketches on politics and current plays (the only similarity with English burlesque). The final number was always entitled the 'Extra Added Attraction'.

Burlesque was the training ground for many later stars, including the singer Al Jolson, the comedian W. C. Fields, and the comedienne Fanny Brice. Burlesque performers appeared in New York 'burleycue' houses and on two national circuits that arose after the turn of the century.

The genre's staple was always beautiful girls, whether as dancers or in comic skits, but with the advent of STRIPTEASE in the 1920s sex gradually took over the programme. It was introduced to lure back audiences captured by the fledgling cinema, and this it initially did with such sophisticated performers as Gypsy Rose LEE. Most stripping, however, was of the sleazy variety, and burlesque's low reputation became even lower, leading to bans in many cities. Prohibition had already severely damaged the genre and it effectively came to an end when New York banned burlesque houses in 1942. Some lingered into the 1960s, however, with anaemic programmes of striptease, second-rate comics, and low-budget films.

burletta A type of comic opera or musical farce that provided a legal loophole for unlicensed theatres in the mid-18th and 19th centuries. Under British law, any three-act play with a minimum of five songs was considered a burletta and could be performed in an unlicensed theatre. Playwrights thus took any drama, including Shakespeare's works, adapted the length and added enough songs and dances to meet the criteria. The burletta disappeared from the playbills when the minor theatres were freed from strict licensing laws by the 1843 Theatres Act.

burrakatha (Hind. *tambura* story) A genre of 20th-century Indian drama, especially popular in the rural areas of Andhra Pradesh, where more than 200 troupes exist. It evolved from the art of roving minstrels, of *jangams*, who sang of the god Shiva and later added secular material. *Burrakatha* stories were originally improvised but are now written down and learnt. In the 1940s the left-wing Indian People's Theatre Association (IPTA) employed *Burrakatha* for political purposes, and today the genre is used by both the government and by opposition parties. Most *Burrakatha* performers will work for any political persuasion as a professional duty.

In the drama, the *kathakudu*, or lead performer, dances and plays a *tambura* stringed instrument while reciting a story about a mythological, historical, or socio-political subject. He also keeps time with two hollow rings filled with metal balls. He is joined by two other performers who play *dakki* earthen drums. The drummer on his right, the *rajkiya*, makes comments on contemporary political and social issues. The one on the left, the *hasyam*, provides comic relief by telling jokes. The performance continues for up to three hours; longer works may take place over several evenings.

Burton, Richard (Richard Walter Jenkins; 1925–84) British actor, who took his stage name from his guardian Philip Burton. Born in Pontrhydyfen, South Wales, the twelfth of 13 children of a miner, he made his stage debut at the Royal Court Theatre, Liverpool, in Emlyn Williams's *The Druid's Rest* (1944). During World War II the RAF sent him on a short course at Oxford University, where he was discovered by the don Nevill Coghill and appeared in an OUDS production of *Measure for Measure*. When asked by the producer Binkie Beaumont if he would return to acting after the war, Burton said, "I might go back to the mines. That's where I really belong."

Instead, he returned to the boards in 1949 to star in THE LADY'S NOT FOR BURNING at the Globe Theatre. He was frequently in trouble with the management for his sexual escapades and practical jokes. The following year, he made his Broadway debut with the play at the Royale Theatre. In 1951 Burton joined the Shakespeare Memorial Theatre company at Stratford to play Prince Hal in *Henry IV*. "Burton is a still brimming pool, running deep", wrote the critic Kenneth Tynan (who was later knocked down by Burton after he criticized an actress).

After making several films in Hollywood, he joined the Old Vic in 1953, giving audiences "a rugger-playing Hamlet" according to critic David Lewin. In 1955 his Henry V won the *Evening Standard* Best Actor Award and in 1960 his Broadway performance as King Arthur in the Lerner and Loewe musical CAMELOT won a Tony Award.

He returned to Broadway in 1964 to star in John Gielgud's production of *Hamlet*, giving a performance of "electrical power and sweeping vitality" according to the *New York Times*. This became the most profitable Shakespearean production in Broadway's history, while Burton broke the record for successive performances of Hamlet with 185.

In 1966 he appeared with his second wife Elizabeth Taylor in an Oxford production of Marlowe's *Dr Faustus* to raise money for OUDS; Burton later gave a further £50,000 to renovate the OXFORD PLAYHOUSE. Burton and Taylor were divorced in 1970 and remarried briefly in 1975. The two appeared together again in a disastrous Broadway revival of *Private Lives*.

Burton was once called "the Frank Sinatra of Shakespeare" because of his celebrity status, but most critics felt he never lived up to his early promise and blamed this on his addiction to alcohol. He often became bored on stage and claimed he only acted in Shakespeare as "a kind of duty". Once during his famous Broadway *Hamlet*, having been told that German adoption officials were in the audience, he began his "To be or not to be" soliloquy in German. During a performance of *Camelot*, seeing audience members leaving early during a heavy snowfall, Burton came to the front of the stage and called, "Hey, book a cab for me too, will you?"

business In theatrical parlance business or **biz** means a piece of incidental action or by-play carried out for a dramatic or comic effect. In practice, it is often used to distract the audience's attention from the actor who is supposed to be the focal point of the scene. Business usually takes the form of fiddling with a prop or part of a costume. It is generally the creation of the actor who plays the part, although certain pieces of business have been handed down by tradition. The term is a shortened form of **stage business**. Comedians often refer to physical falls and feats as business or **knockabout business**.

busk To improvise or ad lib. It is from this word that *busker*, meaning a street singer or performer, is derived.

buskin Tragedy. The Greek tragic actors used to wear a thick-soled boot or *cothurnus* to elevate their stature. Sophocles is said to have introduced the custom to distinguish the principal actors from the chorus, who wore low shoes. The *cothurnus* somewhat resembled the later European buskin, a sandal-like covering for the foot and lower leg. *Compare* SOCK.

> Or what (though rare) of later age
> Enobled hath the buskind stage.
>
> MILTON: *Il Penseroso*.

buttered slide A routine of the English HARLEQUINADE, in which a slippery slide caused shopkeepers to fall headlong when chasing shoplifters (who had previously prepared it). When the harlequinade was reduced to being an AFTERPIECE to the new fairytale PANTOMIME this and similar routines disappeared. *Chambers' Journal* of 1864 complained: "Do you reflect upon the painful fact the English Boys are now growing up wholly ignorant of the nature and efficacy of the Buttered Slide?"

Buttons In the pantomime of CINDERELLA, Buttons, the page, is a stock character. Traditionally he wears a jacket remarkable for a display of small round buttons, as close together as they can be fixed, from chin to waist. In Britain, Buttons is an archaic slang term for any page boy, because of the buttoned jackets they often wore.

> So at last Mrs Casey, her pangs to
> assuage,
> Having snapped off his buttonses,
> curried the page.
>
> WALTER DE LA MARE: *Buttons*.

C

cabaret A form of intimate nightclub or restaurant entertainment, usually accompanying a meal; it was especially popular in Germany in the 1930s and in Britain and America in the 1960s. The word refers both to the venue and to the entertainment or floor show. The performance usually combines music, dancing, comedy skits, and other forms of light entertainment.

The term 'cabaret' originated in 17th-century France, when it meant a drinking house. Modern cabaret developed from MUSIC HALL during the first boom in nightclubs and cabarets just before World War I. A leading London venue was the Hotel Metropole, where in 1922 the 'Midnight Follies' broke all cabaret records. British licensing laws permitted an audience seated at tables to consume food and alcoholic drinks that could not be served in a theatre auditorium. London's HIPPODROME became a cabaret restaurant in 1958, renaming itself the Talk of the Town.

Between the wars, German cabaret drew such leading artistic figures as Bertolt Brecht. The atmosphere of pre-war Berlin cabaret was captured by Christopher Isherwood's book *Goodbye to Berlin* (1929). This was the basis for John van Druten's play *I Am a Camera* (1951) and the Broadway musical *Cabaret*.

Cabaret The musical by Fred Ebb, John Kander, and Joe Masteroff, opened on Broadway in 1966 with Lotte Lenya in the lead; it won the Tony award as Best Musical. Two years later the London production, starring Judi Dench who sang "with a voice like fractured glass", won the *Evening Standard* Award. The 1972 film version earned Oscars for Liza Minnelli and Joel Grey. The songs, with lyrics by Ebb and music by Kander, included 'Cabaret', 'Willkommen', 'Tomorrow Belongs to Me', and 'The Money Song'.

The story concerns Clifford Bradshaw, a young American writer, who arrives in Berlin in 1929 and meets Sally Bowles, an English chanteuse who works in the Kit Kat Klub. Cliff grows fond of her and tries to take her away from the growing Nazi menace, but Sally chooses to remain; he writes down the first of his reminiscences as his train departs.

Caesar and Cleopatra A history play by George Bernard SHAW, first performed in 1906 in Berlin and subsequently in New York. Shaw presents Caesar as a powerful man who succumbs to the cunning wiles of the 16-year-old CLEOPATRA (a part written for Mrs Patrick CAMPBELL, then in her early forties). In the plot, Cleopatra flees to the desert to escape Caesar. When they meet at the Sphinx she at first mistakes him for an ordinary soldier. When the Roman Pothinus tries to warn Caesar that Cleopatra will betray him, she has him murdered. Caesar eventually pacifies her by promising to bring the handsome Mark Antony from Rome.

Shaw, who was in his forties when he wrote the play, later said, "I think I was a trifle too young for the job, but it was not bad for a juvenile effort." He wrote it while recovering from an injured foot and broken arm on the Isle of Wight, often lying on a clifftop with his crutches beside him to do so. The Sphinx scene was suggested by a French picture he had seen 30 years before.

He felt that Cleopatra was an easy part to play but not Caesar. "Whoever can play the fourth act of it can play anything," he noted. "Whoever can't, can play nothing."

café. ***café chantant*** The most popular type of venue for VARIETY entertainment in early 19th-century France. In the 1770s Parisian taverns called *musicos* introduced singers; during the Revolution they were licensed by the National Assembly and multiplied in the districts around the Palais-Royal and the Boulevard du Temple. When the theatres were suppressed during the First Empire, the *musicos* were replaced by *cafés chantants*, open-air summer theatres that became immensely popular; Paris had about 200 by 1850. The performers, however, had the legal status of fairground entertainers and were forbidden to wear stage costumes until 1867. The *cafés chantants* expanded during the Second Empire but began to be replaced in the 1860s by the *cafés concerts* (*see* CAF' CONC').

caf' conc' Shortened form of *café concert*, a type of venue that presented VARIETY entertainment in late 19th-century and early 20th-century Paris. It replaced the CAFÉ CHANTANT in the 1860s, offering romantic ballads and nonsensical choruses known as *scies*. The typical venue was a long room with a high stage. The two most popular, the Eldorado and the Alcazar, presented such stars as Thérésa, Polin, and Mayol. In the mid 1860s some *caf' conc'* houses became *cafés spectacles*, adding farces and operettas to the bill; by the turn of the century the largest had assumed the English designation of 'music halls'. They died out in the 1920s. In 1949 an amateur *caf' conc'* tried to revive the style of entertainment without success.

Calderón (de la Barca), Pedro (1600–81) Spanish playwright, the chief successor to Lope de VEGA. Calderón's nearly 200 works are more cerebral and stylized than Lope's and many turn on the now remote concept of the *pundonor* (point of honour). Nevertheless, he is usually considered the most important Spanish dramatist owing to his skill in constructing plots, his intellectual power, and his ability to create outstanding characters. His output encompassed comedies, tragedies, CLOAK-AND-SWORD PLAYS, histories, romances, philosophical dramas, and religious works. He has had a major influence on European drama: English adaptations include Wycherley's *The Gentleman Dancing-Master* (1672), while Goethe produced translations for the Court Theatre at Weimar.

The son of a government official, Calderón began to write plays at the age of 14. In 1623 he abandoned his religious studies to turn out works for the royal palace. Between 1625 and 1640 he wrote his best comedies of intrigue (*see* COMEDY OF INTRIGUE) and such tragedies as THE SURGEON OF HIS OWN HONOUR; 1635, depicting the grimness of a society ruled by a rigid code of honour, and *The Mayor of Zalamea* (1640), about a father's revenge on the seducer of his daughter.

In 1636 Philip IV made Calderón a Knight of the Military Order of St James. The following years saw the production of some of his finest religious plays, such as *The Wonder-Working Magician* (*El mágico prodigioso*; 1637), inspired by the life of St Cyprian, and the AUTO SACRAMENTAL *The Great Theatre of the World* (1641). Of his secular plays, *Life is a Dream* (1638) is regarded as the best; it depicts the mental state of a prince released from life-long imprisonment.

When Philip IV's newly built palace of Buen Retiro opened in 1640, Calderón began to produce elaborate spectacles using the new Italian lighting and perspective scenery. In 1648 he wrote his first ZARZUELA, the two-act *The Garden of Falerina*, in which spoken and sung dialogue alternate. His first opera, the one-act *The Purple of the Rose*, was produced in 1660.

After being ordained in 1651, Calderón announced that he would write no more plays. The king, however, commanded him to write for the court theatre; as a result he produced *The Daughter of Air* (1653), dealing with the conflict between passion and reason. In 1666 Calderón became the king's chaplain of honour and concentrated on writing *auto sacramentales* (66 have survived).

calf-skin A calf-skin coat, buttoned down the back, as worn by jesters. In Shakespeare's *King John* (III, i) Constance says scathingly to the Archduke of Austria:

> Thou wear a lion's hide! Doff it for shame,
> And hang a calf's skin on those recreant limbs!

Caliban In Shakespeare's THE TEMPEST, the deformed half-human son of the devil Setebos and the witch Sycorax; he becomes a reluctant slave to Prospero. Both repulsive and pathetic, he is given some of the play's most memorable poetry.

The name is sometimes applied to any uncouth or boorish person.

call A backstage term used in three different ways. It usually means the call or warning that tells actors and stage crew how much time is left before the curtain rises. However, it can also mean the work and rehearsal notices on the CALL BOARD; it is sometimes used as a short form of CURTAIN CALL.

call board A backstage notice board, located near the STAGE DOOR, upon which messages are posted for the cast and stage crew. These include schedules for rehearsals and other work sessions, as well as the dreaded 'Notice' announcing the end of the play's run.

call-boy A boy employed in theatres to call actors in time for them to appear on the stage. (The female equivalent is not usually referred to as a call-girl.)

call doors *See* PROSCENIUM DOORS.

Call Me Madam A musical by Irving BERLIN, first performed in 1950 in New York starring Ethel MERMAN. The story, by Howard Lindsay and Russel Crouse, is suspiciously similar to that of Victor Herbert's 1904 musical *It Happened in Nordland*. It involves a Washington hostess, Sally Adams, who is appointed ambassador to the tiny country of Lichtenburg, where she falls in love with the foreign minister, Cosmo Constantine. Sally is recalled because of her outrageous behaviour at court, but Cosmo becomes prime minister and pledges his love to her.

President Harry Truman was a featured character in the musical, and Berlin was prophetic in writing the song 'They Like Ike'; two years later, Dwight Eisenhower campaigned successfully for the US presidency using the slogan 'I Like Ike'. Other songs included 'It's a Lovely Day Today', 'You're Just in Love', and 'The Best Thing for You'.

don't call us, we'll call you A phrase supposedly used by theatre directors to say goodbye to unsuccessful applicants at AUDITIONS. The implication is, of course, that no call will be made. The phrase, which dates from the 1940s, is now often used in a jocular way to get rid of anyone offering to sell something or provide a service. It is often shortened to *don't call us*.

Călus A ritual dance of Romania, in which the all-male dancers fall into trances and supposedly heal people who are possessed by evil spirits. It is performed at Whitsuntide. In a Muntenian version, the dances alternate with brief comic plays whose central character is a clown wearing a phallus. Although he is described as a mute, the clown chatters away about such subjects as sex and money. During the period of performance, the dancers avoid social contact and abstain from sexual intercourse.

Cambridge Theatre A London theatre in the Seven Dials area of the West End. It opened in 1930 and was noted for the modern simplicity of its architecture and decor. *The Stage* commented: "The beautiful, if somewhat peculiar decorative scheme appears to be Teutonic, and is strangely reminiscent of the then strange futuristic sets in German films immediately after the war of 1914–18." The Cambridge, which seats 1273, was refurbished in 1950, leaving a few mementos from the thirties, such as the engraved mirrors in one bar.

The new theatre opened with a performance of *Charlot's Masquerade* starring Beatrice Lillie. It has since presented an unusually varied programme, including drama, revue, musicals, opera, ballet, and even Sunday concerts. It hosted the Comédie-Française in 1934 and the New London Opera Company from 1946 to 1948. The Cambridge has been home to the new D'Oyly Carte Opera Company since 1988.

Successful productions have included William Douglas Home's *The Reluctant Debutante* (1955), which ran for 752 performances, Willis Hall and Keith Waterhouse's *Billy Liar* (1960–62), the Tommy Steele musical *Half A Sixpence* (1963–64), Ingmar Bergman's National Theatre production of Ibsen's *Hedda Gabler* (1970), Jonathan Miller's production of Chekhov's *Three Sisters* (1976), and the musical *Chicago* (1979). More recent productions have included *Return to the Forbidden Planet*, winner of the 1990 Laurence Olivier Award for Best Musical, which ran until January 1993.

Cambyses. King Cambyses' vein A style of grandiloquent bombastic acting. The term is used by FALSTAFF in *Henry IV, Part I* when explaining how he would give a passionate speech. Shakespeare is referring to a tragicomedy of the time, *Cambyses King of Persia* (*c.* 1569) by Thomas Preston (*fl.* 1570), which is written in this manner.

Camelot A musical about King Arthur's Court by Alan Jay Lerner and Frederick Loewe. It was first produced on Broadway in 1960 with Richard BURTON, who won a Tony Award, as King Arthur, and Julie Andrews as Guenevere. It opened in London's Drury Lane Theatre in 1964.

The story begins with the young Arthur tumbling out of a tree onto Guenevere, the girl who has been chosen as his queen. They fall in love. Some years later Arthur dreams up the idea of the Round Table and his motto of 'Might for Right'. All goes well until the self-righteous French knight Lancelot du Lac falls in love with the queen. Arthur is imprisoned for a night by the fairy Morgan le Fey, leaving Guenevere and Lancelot alone. They compromise themselves and Arthur reluctantly sentences Guenevere to be burned at the stake, in accordance with the law. Lancelot rescues her from this grisly fate but slays a number of knights doing so. Nevertheless, when Arthur meets Lancelot on the battlefield, they embrace. Lancelot leaves and Guenevere departs for a nunnery. Arthur then meets a young boy, Tom of Warwick, and urges him to spread the word about the glory that had been Camelot.

The songs (music by Loewe, lyrics by Lerner) include 'In Camelot', 'Where Are the Simple Joys of Maidenhood', 'If Ever I Should Leave You', 'I Loved You Once in Silence', and 'What Do the Simple Folk Do?'.

The name Camelot was applied retrospectively to the administration (1961–63) of US President John F. Kennedy, whose glamorous image and youthful vigour had briefly inspired hopes of a golden age in America's history. At the time of Kennedy's inauguration, the Lerner–Loewe musical had recently opened on Broadway. Shortly after Kennedy's assassination, his widow told an interviewer that the president had particularly liked the title song:

> Once there was a fleeting wisp of glory
> Called Camelot...
> Don't let it be forgot
> That once there was a spot
> For one brief shining moment that was known
> As Camelot.

Campbell, Mrs Patrick (Beatrice Stella Tanner; 1865–1940). British actress, who became famous overnight as Paula in Pinero's THE SECOND MRS TANQUERAY, presented at the St James's Theatre, London, in 1893. She was also the first Agnes Ebbsmith in Pinero's *The Notorious Mrs Ebbsmith* (1895) and the original Eliza in SHAW's PYGMALION (1914), a part she played when she was nearly 50. Although by this time she had lost her looks and become fat and slovenly, Shaw fell deeply in love with her.

At the age of 19 she turned down a music scholarship to marry Patrick Campbell. Her London debut was in 1890 in *A Buried Talent* at the Vaudeville Theatre; in 1900 she took over the management of the Royalty Theatre for two years. Although MRS PAT (as she was always known) won great acclaim in her three famous roles, her performances were notoriously uneven, especially in Shakespeare: when she played Juliet at the Lyceum Theatre in 1895, she cut the difficult speeches.

Her temper was famous, and fellow actors dreaded her tantrums and sharp tongue. She said of Tallulah BANKHEAD's popularity in London: "She's always skating on thin ice, and the British public wants to be there when it breaks." When Alexander WOOLLCOTT introduced Mrs Pat to a rival actress, she held the woman's hand and whispered audibly to Woollcott, "I thought she was dead." In later years, Woollcott called her a "sinking ship firing upon her rescuers". One New York critic was less kind: "What chance does mere skill at trivial comedy stand against the recollection of a once lovely woman become fat and yellow?"

> If only you could write a true book entitled WHY, THOUGH I WAS A WONDERFUL ACTRESS, NO MANAGER OR AUTHOR WOULD EVER ENGAGE ME TWICE IF HE COULD POSSIBLY HELP IT, it would be a best seller. But you couldn't. Besides, you don't know. I do.
>
> GEORGE BERNARD SHAW, letter to Mrs Patrick Campbell, 11 August 1913.

Can-Can A two-act musical by Cole PORTER with book by Abe Burrows. It opened on Broadway in 1953 starring the French actress Lilo and ran for nearly three years; the first London production was also a great success. However, the 1981 Broadway revival closed after only five performances, with a loss of more than $2 million. Superstitious cast members attributed the failure to the GYPSY ROBE, a good-luck charm that had been passed from one Broadway musical to the next for thirty years but disintegrated during *Can-Can*'s brief run.

Set in turn-of-the-century Paris, the story involves the handsome judge Aristide Forestier, who is assigned to investigate the provocative can-can dancing at a nightclub. Predictably, he falls for the owner, La Mome Pistache, and arranges an investigative visit by a panel of judges, with a view to legalizing the dance. Equally predictably, the judges are enchanted by the young *grisettes*. The play ends, with monotonous predictability, with Forestier marrying Pistache. The sub-plot includes a farcical duel fought over the rooftops of Paris.

The songs include 'I Love Paris', 'C'est Magnifique', 'Allez-vous En', and 'It's All Right with Me'.

Candida A comedy by George Bernard SHAW, first performed in 1895 at South Shields and subsequently (1900) at London's Royal Court Theatre with Harley GRANVILLE-BARKER. The female lead was written for Janet Achurch; Shaw reneged on a promise to Ellen Terry (*see* TERRY FAMILY) that she could play the role on alternate nights. Its successful revival at the Royal Court in 1904 began a partnership between Granville-Barker and J. E. Vedrenne that produced a total of 10 Shaw plays there over the next three years.

Shaw said he wrote *Candida* in several small notebooks on the top decks of London buses. Although the play was much influenced by Ibsen, Shaw also took characters and ideas from Charles Reade's curtain-raiser *Nance Oldfield*, about the love between a poetic youth and a mother-figure. Shaw called his work "THE Mother Play" and added: "Candida is a work of genius though the Candidamaniacs have always overpraised it. Every word of Candida is written with my heart's blood."

It has often been revived, since it is the cheapest Shaw play to stage, having only one interior set and a cast of six. It is also probably his best constructed work. A 1937 production at the Globe Theatre ran for three months with Nicholas Hannen and his wife, Athene Seyler, in the lead parts. The 80-year-old Shaw spent hours at rehearsals (though he was not the director) making the actors repeat the lines over and over again until they met with his approval. In 1946 Marlon Brando and Katharine Cornell starred in a Broadway production.

The play explores the conflict between romance and practical sense. Candida is the wife of the Reverend James Morrell, a benevolent but smug Christian Socialist. Her simple and parochial life is complicated when the young poet Eugene Marchbanks falls wildly in love with her. The poet seems easily the more fragile of the two men, but Candida, recognizing the depth of his commitment to poetry, chooses to support the weaker man – her husband.

Candour, Mrs A character in Sheridan's THE SCHOOL FOR SCANDAL (1777). A terrifying female back-biter, she conceals her venom under an affectation of amiable frankness.

Canterbury Music Hall One of the most popular music halls in late 19th-century London. It was built in 1852 in Lambeth by Charles MORTON on the site of a skittle alley belonging to his tavern, the Canterbury Arms. Morton began by presenting classical music and ballad singing, but switched to comedy with such success that he was able to increase the theatre's size to seat 1500 people. He gave up the business in 1867. After reconstruction in 1876 the theatre became known as Canterbury Hall; famous patrons included the Prince of Wales (later Edward VII). Many of the great stars of music hall performed here. However, the Canterbury faded with the genre in the 20th century and was destroyed in 1942 by a wartime bomb.

cap. **cap and bells** The insignia of a professional fool or jester. A person who is the butt of the company, or who makes himself ridiculous, is sometimes said to *wear the cap and bells.*

fool's cap A conical cap with feather and bells, such as licensed fools used to wear.

Čapek, Karel (1890–1938) Czech dramatist, novelist, and essayist. The son of a country doctor, Čapek began writing in his youth and was published by the age of 14. After studying philosophy in Prague, Berlin, and Paris, he settled, in 1917, in Prague, where his first play, *The Brigand*, was performed in 1920. This was followed by the expressionist fantasy RUR (1921), which concerned the dangers of unconsidered technological escalation and introduced the word 'robot' into the English language. THE INSECT PLAY (1922), an allegorical piece written in collaboration with his brother Josef, achieved international success, productions being quickly staged both in Britain and America. A sequel to *RUR*, *Adam the Creator* (1927), also written with Josef, dealt with man's attempts to rebuild the world after its virtual destruction by robots. Two later plays, *The White Scourge* (1937) and *The Mother* (1938), dealt with the subjects of war and dictatorship and expressed Čapek's fears about the rise of fascism in Europe. Čapek did not live to see the fulfilment of his worst fears, dying before the outbreak of World War II and his brother's death in Belsen (1945).

Capitano, Il One of the earliest stock characters of the COMMEDIA DELL'ARTE. Sharing many characteristics of the braggart soldier of Roman comedy, the MILES GLORIOSUS, Il Capitano was probably a caricature of the Spanish and French mercenaries who overran Italy in the 16th century. The character's bombastic claims to military greatness and amatory prowess were often exposed as a sham through asides delivered by his squire. Although actors who played the role would often make slight alterations to the Capitano's name, costume, and personality, the basic character remained the same. *See also* SCARAMUCCIA.

captain. ***Captain Brassbound's Conversion*** A play by George Bernard SHAW, first produced in 1900 by Harley Granville-Barker at the Royal Court Theatre. Shaw wrote the part of Lady Cicely Waynflete for Ellen Terry (*see* TERRY FAMILY), with whom he had corresponded for years but never met. The role was therefore based on Terry's personality as Shaw perceived it from their correspondence. When they finally met at rehearsals, they found they could not converse as easily as they had written.

The disappointment seemed to carry over to opening night. According to the critic Max Beerbohm (who had replaced Shaw at the *Saturday Review*): "Miss Ellen Terry was duly vivacious last Tuesday. But she was, also, very nervous. I should not like those of the rising generation who saw the performance to imagine that Miss Terry was within measurable distance of her best...."

The work was published as one of Shaw's *Three Plays for Puritans*, the others being *The Devil's Disciple* (1897) and *Caesar and Cleopatra* (1906). The plot concerns Lady Cicely Waynflete's visit to Morocco with her brother-in-law, Sir Howard Hallam. They are escorted by his nephew, the young pirate Captain Brassbound. As Hallam has stolen the estate of Brassbound's father and caused his mother's death, the pirate has him kidnapped. When a rescue party arrives to seize Brassbound, Cicely reveals the truth and he is freed. Brassbound decides to return to piracy and, although she has fallen for him, Lady Cicely is greatly relieved to see him go.

Captain Cauf's Tail In Yorkshire, the chief MUMMER who led his following from house to house on PLOUGH MONDAY. He was fantastically dressed, with a cockade and many coloured ribbons; and he always had a genuine calf's (*cauf's*) tail fixed behind.

Caretaker, The The play that established Harold PINTER as a major playwright; it is still his best known work. Having only three parts, it was first performed in 1960 at the Arts Theatre Club, London, with Alan Bates as Mick, Peter Woodthorpe as Aston, and Donald Pleasance as Davies.

The story revolves around the shabby old tramp Davies, who has been given somewhere to stay by Aston. The latter has recently had electroconvulsive therapy in a mental institution. Davies constantly invents new excuses for not leaving and is caught looking through Aston's personal belongings by Mick, Aston's brother. Davies's real relationship with the brothers is mysterious: one minute Mick accuses Davies of being an intruder and the next calls him an old friend. Aston returns to offer the tramp the job of caretaker. Davies tries to play the brothers off against each other. Eventually both reject his ploys and he is evicted.

Carlin Nickname of the Italian actor Carlo Bertinazzi (1713–83), who in 1741 joined the COMÉDIE-ITALIENNE at the HÔTEL DE BOURGOGNE, Paris, succeeding Tommaso Vicentini (1682–1739) in the role of Arlequin. One of the few Italian actors still performing with the company at that time, he has been called the last great Arlequin. His admirers included David Garrick.

Carmen Jones Oscar Hammerstein's 1943 reworking of Bizet's opera for an all-Black cast. The setting is transferred from the cigarette factory in Seville to a parachute factory in the Southern US; the bullfighter Escamillo becomes a boxer named Husky Miller. The faithless Carmen is finally stabbed to death by Joe, her sweetheart, outside the boxing ring. The songs, many of which are based on Bizet's score, include 'Beat Out Dat Rhythm on a Drum', 'Dat's Love', and 'My Joe'.

Carnival The season immediately preceding Lent that ends on Shrove Tuesday; in many Roman Catholic countries it is devoted to amusement. The word is formed from the Latin *caro, carnis*, flesh; *levare*, to remove; signifying the abstinence from meat during Lent. The earlier word *carnilevamen* was altered in Italian to *carnevale*, as though connected with *vale*, farewell – farewell to flesh.

In some cities the celebrations involved theatrical and acrobatic displays and the wearing of elaborate masks and costumes. Byron described the Venetian carnival in *Beppo*:

And there are dresses splendid, but
fantastical,
Masks of all times and nations, Turks
and Jews,
And harlequins and clowns, with feats
gymnastical,
Greeks, Romans, Yankee-doodles, and
Hindoos;
All kinds of dress, except the
ecclesiastical.

carnival play *See* FASTNACHTSSPIEL.

Caroline drama English drama during the reign of Charles I (1625–49). Several of the so-called decadent playwrights of the JACOBEAN DRAMA continued to write into the new reign, notably John Ford, who produced such bloody tragedies as *'Tis Pity She's a Whore* (1627). James SHIRLEY wrote both tragedies and comedies of manners, the latter including *The Lady of Pleasure* (1635), while Richard Brome, another Jacobean, contributed such comedies as *A Jovial Crew* (1641). The veteran dramatist Thomas Heywood had by this time settled down as the writer of pageants for the Lord Mayor's Show.

Caroline drama is particularly noted for its pastorals and elaborate court MASQUES. Charles I and Henrietta Maria sometimes danced and participated in these royal entertainments. *Chloridia*, the last collaboration between Ben Jonson and Inigo JONES was staged in 1631. There was little theatrical activity outside London during Charles's reign, although Milton's masque COMUS was presented at Ludlow Castle in 1634. The theatres were closed by the Puritans in 1642 (*see* INTERREGNUM).

Carousel RODGERS AND HAMMERSTEIN's musical about love and death in a New England fishing town. It opened on Broadway in 1945 as a THEATRE GUILD production. Hammerstein acknowledged it as his favourite and critics generally agree, feeling that the integration of music, dancing, and story is unequalled. The songs include 'Carousel Waltz', 'If I Loved You', 'June Is Bustin' Out All Over', and 'You'll Never Walk Alone'.

The story is an adaptation of Ferenč Molnár's play *Liliom* (1909), about a carnival barker in Budapest. Apart from moving the setting to America, Rodgers and Hammerstein changed little. Billy Bigelow, the fairground barker, marries Julie, sometimes beats her, but becomes reformed when their daughter, Louise, is born. While attempting a robbery to support his family, Billy is killed. In heaven he is given one day on earth to do something good for his daughter. He returns home and gives her a star from heaven.

The last scene was called "an impertinence" by the US critic Eric Bentley, who added: "I refuse to be lectured by a musical comedy scriptwriter on the education of children, the nature of the good life, and the contribution of the American small town to the salvation of souls."

carpenter's scene In the Victorian theatre, a short scene acted in front of a backcloth while the stage crew changed the set behind it. This was felt to be an improvement on the blackout introduced for scenery changes by David Garrick. It was no longer necessary once the practice of lowering the front curtain between scene changes was standardized. Today the carpenter's scene only remains in the Pantomime or spectacular musical, where it is often a short musical number.

carpet cut A narrow slot in the stage floor to secure the edge of a carpet or stage cloth (by hinged flaps) so actors will not trip over it.

carriage-and-frame system A method of changing scenery quickly (also called the **chariot-and-pole system**) first used by Giacomo Torelli (*see* GREAT MAGICIAN) in 17th-century Italy. WINGS or FLATS were suspended just above the stage on a frame that projected below the floor through a long slit. The frame rested on a wheeled platform or carriage on rails. As a piece of scenery was rolled off on the underground rail, a duplicate carriage, connected by ropes moving in opposite directions, brought on the replacement. This was driven by a counterweight system that could be operated by "a single boy of 15 years". An operational carriage-and-frame system still exists at the Drottningholm Theatre and Museum near Stockholm (*see* THEATRE MUSEUM).

Cartel, the The cartel of French directors – Louis Jouvet (1887–1951), Gaston Baty (1885–1952), Charles Dullin (1885–1949), and Georges Pitoëff (1887–1939) – appointed in 1936 by the state to run the

COMÉDIE-FRANÇAISE. All four had been successful in creating new directions for the French theatre in the 1920s and their work at the Comédie-Française had an important influence on later experimental drama.

Caste A play by Tom ROBERTSON, first performed in London in 1867 at the Prince of Wales' Theatre. It is regarded as the best of Robertson's CUP-AND-SAUCER DRAMAS, which introduced a new REALISM in the era of MELODRAMA. *Caste* was one of the short titles Robertson employed as a deliberate contrast to more pretentiously named contemporary works (*see* SHORTEST TITLES).

The play uses the story of Esther Eccles, a ballerina who marries into the aristocratic family of the Hon. George D'Alroy to attack class prejudice. The couple live happily for six months until George is stationed in India and reportedly killed. His mother demands custody of her grandson from the now empoverished Esther who refuses, saying she will return to dancing to support herself and the child. George suddenly reappears, delighted to learn of his child and about Esther's independence. Before the final curtain several characters have denounced the folly of snobbery.

cat. cat-and-mouse dialogue *See* STICHOMYTHIA.

cat-call A kind of whistling noise sometimes used by theatre audiences, etc., to express displeasure or impatience.

> I was very much surprised with the great consort of cat-calls...to see so many persons of quality of both sexes assembled together in a kind of caterwauling.
> JOSEPH ADDISON; *The Spectator*, No. 361.

Cat on A Hot Tin Roof Tennessee WILLIAMS's drama about a troubled Southern family bullied by its terminally ill patriarch. The play opened on Broadway in 1955, winning the Pulitzer Prize. Its London run began in 1957 at the Comedy Theatre. The plot concerns the family of Big Daddy, a rich cotton-plantation owner. His son, Brick, is an alcoholic who has become impotent because his wife, Maggie 'the cat', once seduced his best friend. Maggie desperately wants to produce an heir for Big Daddy's fortune; the play ends with her attempt to arouse Brick's sexual interest.

Cats A musical by Andrew LLOYD WEBBER that sets poems from T. S. Eliot's *Old Possum's Book of Practical Cats* to music and dance. Directed by Trevor Nunn, it was first staged in 1981 at the New London Theatre, winning the *Evening Standard* Award for Best Musical. *Cats* began its 16th year at the theatre in 1996, thereby becoming the world's longest-running musical ever. It is the only work to have been presented at the theatre since it opened (it was formerly a Thames television studio). The musical has been staged with great success worldwide.

catwalk *See* BRIDGE.

catastrophe A Greek word that literally means a turning upside down (from *kata* downwards; *strephein*, to turn). It was originally used of the sudden change that produces the *dénouement* of a drama, which is often a 'turning upside down' of the earlier part of the plot.

> All the actors must enter to complete and make up the catastrophe of this great piece.
> SIR THOMAS BROWNE: *Religio Medici.*

> Pat! he comes like the catastrophe of the old comedy.
> SHAKESPEARE: *King Lear* (I, ii).

catharsis A concept defined by Aristotle in his *Poetics*. Catharsis is the purging of the emotions of an audience through the feelings of pity and terror evoked by witnessing a tragedy.

Aristotle might have felt his theory vindicated by the first performance of Freidrich von Schiller's DIE RÄUBER (1787), at which audience members embraced one another, wept, and fainted.

Cathleen ni Houlihan A one-act play by W. B. YEATS (with some help from Lady GREGORY), first produced in 1902 in Dublin by the Irish National Dramatic Society. Two years later it was one of three plays that opened the ABBEY THEATRE, becoming a staple in its repertory. Based in part on an old Irish ballad, it aroused fervent nationalistic feeling with its story of an old woman (a traditional symbol of Ireland) who urges Michael, a young peasant, to assist her in her struggle to reclaim the "four green fields" that have been stolen from her by a stranger. At the end of the play Michael decides to abandon his fiancée and follow Cathleen to the death. In the play's final lines Michael's father asks another character if he has seen an old woman on the road and receives the reply:

> I did not, but I saw a young girl, and she had the walk of a queen.

Yeats later worried about the inflammatory effect the play may have had. In one of his last poems he asked himself:

Did that play of mine send out
Certain men the English shot?
W. B. YEATS: 'Man and Echo'.

Caucasian Chalk Circle A play by Bertolt BRECHT written between 1943 and 1945, premiered in 1948 in Northfield, Minnesota, and first performed in German by the Berliner Ensemble in 1954. It has enjoyed frequent revivals, including an acclaimed 1962 production by the Royal Shakespeare Company at the Aldwych Theatre in London. In Britain it has proved the most popular of Brecht's works with student and amateur groups.

The play, set in Caucasia in the aftermath of World War II, shows the victory of love and expediency over the law. The plot concerns a group of villagers who decide to take over their valley to grow fruit. To justify this, they enact the ancient story of the maid Grusche, who rescues and raises a child deserted by its aristocratic mother. When the real mother demands it back (for legal purposes), Grusche takes the case before a mysterious judge who applies the 'chalk test'. He decides that the 'true' mother is the one who can pull the child out of the chalk circle, and this turns out to be Grusche. The moral is that just as the child belongs to the woman who will truly cherish it, the valley belongs to the villagers.

Cavalcade A patriotic (but anti-war) play by Noël COWARD, first performed in 1931 at Drury Lane. It presents a panorama of British life from 1899 to 1930 through the history of the upper-class Marryot family. An enormous cast was required for the spectacular production. The songs included 'Lover of My Dreams', 'All the Fun of the Farm', 'Twentieth Century Blues', and 'The Girls of the C.I.V.'.

King George V, who could seldom be coaxed into a theatre, was lured by Queen Mary to see *Cavalcade*; and he reluctantly admitted that he actually enjoyed it.

The 1932 film version won three Academy Awards but was denounced by the US critic Pauline Kael as "an orgy of British self-congratulation."

Cavittu Natakam (Tamil: step play) A form of Christian theatre in the south Indian state of Kerala. It originated in the 16th century and has survived with the support of the Roman Catholic Church. Most plays are in Tamil, although members of the all-male troupes speak Malayalam as their first language. The *Cavittu Natakam* incorporates elements of the martial arts and acrobatics, with the actors stamping their feet in vigorous dancing movements. Costumes are colourful Indian versions of historical Western dress; evil characters often wear sunglasses. Actors playing kings come from selected Christian families and family status also determines other roles. An *asan*, or teacher, trains the actors and manages the productions. *Cavittu Natakam* is seldom seen today, except in central Kerala during the major church festivals from Advent through to Easter.

The subjects are the historical or legendary heroes of Christian tradition, including saints, biblical figures, Charlemagne, and St George. One famous work, *The Play of Charlemagne*, requires 80 characters to perform the story over 15 nights. It was derived from Ariosto's *Orlando Furioso* and includes great battle scenes.

The stage is raised in a village or town near a church. At each end of the acting area are tall platforms reached by ladders, and from these lofty heights the kings hold court. Entrances are made from a door on the right and exits through one on the left. A central opening reveals the chorus and musicians, who perform backstage. The main instruments are drums and large bell-brass cymbals. During the performance the *katiyakkaran*, or clown, amuses the audience and interprets the action in Malayalam. He also makes sarcastic remarks about the teacher, who remains on stage during the performance, setting the tempo with hand cymbals and sometimes giving cues with a whistle.

ceiling cloth *See* CLOTH.

Céleste, Madame The French dancer, pantomimist, and actress Céline Céleste (1814–82), who began as a successful child star in Paris. At the age of 13 she made her stage debut in New York with a troupe of dancers and, although plain in looks, won excellent reviews for her graceful dancing. Three years later she opened in London in dancing and pantomime; she subsequently made the city her home. Her first speaking part on the British stage came in 1838. She often played French characters, such as Madame

Defarge in an adaptation of Dickens's *A Tale of Two Cities* (1860).

She was briefly a manager of London's Adelphi Theatre with the elder Ben Webster (*see* WEBSTER FAMILY). She gave her farewell performance in 1874, returning four years later for one performance at Drury Lane, in which she revived her acclaimed role of Miami in John Buckstone's *The Green Bushes; or a Hundred Years Ago*.

Celestina, La A dialogue novel that is the only known work by Fernando de Rojas (1465–1541); it was first published in about 1499 in 16 acts and expanded to 22 acts in 1502. Subtitled 'the Tragi-Comedy of Calisto and Melibea', it is usually considered the most important example of 15th-century Spanish dramatic writing. *La Celestina* was one of the first works to combine romance with an everyday domestic setting. It has been adapted for the stage in several languages. An English version was produced in about 1530 by John Rastell, whose *An Interlude of Calisto and Melibea* is one of the first English comedies. He gave the story a happy ending. A century later it was translated by James Mabbe (1572–1642) as *The Spanish Bawd* (1631). Modern revivals of de Rojas's work include a 1993 production by the Actors' Touring Company.

The plot tells how Calisto, a wealthy gentleman, falls in love with the modest Melibea. To overcome her shyness, he employs the old procuress Celestina to lure her from her virtuous life. Celestina is later murdered by Calisto's servants, Parmeno and Sempronio, in order to steal her fee. The play ends with an orgy of death; Parmeno and Sempronio are executed for their crime; and Calisto is killed while meeting secretly with Melibea, who thereupon commits suicide.

cellar The space beneath the stage. It is used for storage and to house machinery used to change scenery and create special effects. The area is also employed to elevate and lower an actor through a TRAP. Since Continental theatres often had framed backgrounds that had to be lowered beneath the stage, their cellars were sometimes very deep; by comparison the average British cellar was relatively shallow.

When the Ghost in *Hamlet* cries out from beneath the stage, the Prince jokes nervously about "this fellow in the cellarage" (V, i).

Celle Castle A castle in the town of Celle, between Hannover and Hamburg, that contains the oldest theatre in Germany. The baroque theatre seats 330 and was opened in 1674, mostly as a venue for opera. Plays were presented for the Hannoverian Court each summer until 1705. It was reopened in 1772, drawing such stars as Sophia Schroder (1714–92). The theatre fell into general disuse during the 19th century but in 1935 was restored with an expanded stage and modern scenery; it escaped damage during World War II. In 1950 a permanent repertory company took up residence. *See also* ČESKÝ KRUMLOV.

Cenci, The A tragedy in verse by Percy Bysshe Shelley (1792–1822). Published in 1819, it was banned by the LORD CHAMBERLAIN and first performed in 1886 in Paris. In 1888 it was given a single private performance in London by the Shelley Society, with Alma Murray as Beatrice. Although Shelley provided some of the best dramatic verse since the Elizabethans, the play was never a great success, owing to its lack of dramatic action and a style and construction that provoked unflattering comparisons with Shakespeare (although Shelley said his main influence was CALDERÓN).

Despite this, it has often been revived, notably by Sybil THORNDIKE in 1922 and again in 1926. The former production was the first at the New Theatre under the management of Thorndike and her husband Lewis Casson. It was during one of the matinees that George Bernard Shaw, wanting to write a drama about Joan of Arc, saw Thorndike in the trial scene and told his wife, "I'll write the play now. I've found the woman who can play it." A year later she became famous in the title role of *Saint Joan* (1923). In the Cassons's 1926 production of *The Cenci*, they gave the 18-year-old Laurence OLIVIER the minor role of Orsino's servant (27 words) after Olivier's father asked them to keep an eye on his son.

The plot is based on the true story of Beatrice Cenci's trial and execution in 1599 for the murder of her father, Count Francesco Cenci. Shelley emphasized his wickedness and the sufferings of Beatrice.

censorship For most of its history the theatre has been subjected to state censorship for political, religious, or moral reasons.

In Britain control of both plays and theatres was exerted through licensing (*see*

LICENCE) until the Theatres Act of 1968. This system was controlled from 1494–1737 by the MASTER OF THE REVELS and subsequently by the LORD CHAMBERLAIN. Even in the 20th century, the heavy hand of the censor denied British audiences the chance to see works by Shaw, Ibsen, O'Neill, and Bond.

The lowest point in English theatrical history was the Puritan INTERREGNUM (1642–60), during which all the theatres were closed. After the licence of the Restoration period a new era of timidity was ushered in by Jeremy COLLIER's *A Short View of the Immorality and Prophaneness of the English Stage* (1698).

Although America has never had an office of national censorship or any legislation dealing specifically with drama, the state and local police are empowered to act on complaints about obscenity under laws covering literary works. The tradition of BURLESQUE was eventually killed by repeated police raids after STRIPTEASE began to dominate the fare.

The Russian theatre has a long history of suppression, censorship being particularly heavy during the reigns of Catherine II (1762–96) and Alexander I (1801–25) as well as under the Soviet regime. Leading theatrical figures to perish during the Stalinist terror included V. E. MEYERHOLD.

centre. **Centre 42** A cultural organization intended to make the arts more widely accessible, primarily through trade-union support and involvement. It was founded in 1961 by Arnold WESKER, who was also its artistic director until his decision to dissolve the organization in 1970. Centre 42 staged productions in the Round House, a former railway building in Camden, London, from 1968.

Centres Dramatiques A number of theatre companies set up in the French provinces after 1945 under a government-sponsored scheme known as **Décentralisation Dramatique**. The first centres were opened in 1947 in Strasbourg and St-Étienne. Some of the leading companies have been Jean Dasté's Comédie de St-Étienne, the Comédie de l'Ouest based in Rennes, the Compagnie de Caen, and the Grenier de Toulouse, which celebrated its 20th anniversary in 1969 by moving into a new theatre in the city.

The establishment of regional theatre centres gave a much needed boost to provincial drama in France. The companies are usually based in university towns and draw talent from local amateur groups. They tour the region and perform classic French plays as well as contemporary and foreign works. Although the Centres Dramatiques have made a significant impact on the nation's theatre, modern French dramatists prefer to open in Paris and new plays are seldom performed in the regions.

centrestage The middle area of a stage (usually the middle third from right to left). When an actor faces the audience, 'centrestage right' is to his right and 'centrestage left' is to his left. Figuratively, 'to be centre stage' means to be the centre of attention. *See also* UPSTAGE; DOWNSTAGE.

Cervantes (Saavedra), Miguel de (1547–1616) Spanish novelist and playwright. Although he wrote more than 30 plays, he is best known for his satirical romance *Don Quixote de la Mancha* (1605–15). It has been adapted for the stage on numerous occasions: a 1694 version by Thomas D'Urfey included incidental music by Purcell, an 1895 adaptation by W. G. Wills starred Henry Irving, the 1965 Broadway musical *Man of La Mancha* ran for three years, and in 1969 the National Theatre produced James Saunders's *The Travails of Sancho Panza*.

Cervantes was the fourth of seven children of an apothecary-surgeon. He served in the army and began writing after being wounded in his left hand ("to the greater glory of the right") during the battle of Lepanto (1571). Four years later he was captured by pirates and held as a slave in Algiers for five years.

Cervantes's early plays were too literary to be theatrical. For many years he gave up writing for the stage, but returned to drama late in life. Only 18 of his plays survive, all but two of which were published in a volume of eight comedies and eight comic interludes (*entremeses*) in 1615. The latter were his greatest contribution to Spanish drama. The full-length comedies include *Pedro de Urdemalas*, while the best interludes are *El viejo celoso* and *El retablo de las maravillas*. He also wrote (*c*. 1580–90) the Senecan tragedy *El cerco de Numancia*, a patriotic piece about a Spanish city resisting a siege by the Roman army, and a true account of his experiences with the pirates, *El trato de Argel*. Cervantes said his own favourite work was the CLOAK-AND-SWORD PLAY *La Confusa*.

Cervantes and Shakespeare died on the same day, April 23, 1616.

Český Krumlov A castle in Czechoslovakia that contains one of Europe's oldest theatres. Built in 1766 in the baroque style, the small theatre has a proscenium and four traps in the floor. It has 10 sets, painted by the Viennese artists Jan Wetschela and Leo Markla, that are apparently the oldest surviving scenery in the world. The scenes, which use perspective effects developed by the BIBIENA FAMILY, provide general backgrounds such as a palace, forest, and harbour. Many items of the original stage machinery, such as ropes and winches for quick scenery changes, still survive. Despite its fragile condition, the theatre is occasionally used for productions. *See also* CELLE CASTLE.

chair. chairman In British MUSIC HALL, the master of ceremonies who introduced the acts with a bang of his gavel accompanied by lively patter and witty comments to the audience. The role had mostly disappeared by the end of the 19th century.

Chairs, The A one-act tragic farce by Eugene IONESCO. It was first performed in 1952 in Paris and produced in London in 1957. The play's theme, according to Ionesco, is nothingness. The curtain goes up on two empty chairs in a large empty room; we later learn that this is situated high up in a tower surrounded by water. The only characters to appear are an Old Man, an Old Woman, and a deaf-mute Orator. The elderly married couple talk about their meaningless lives and the people they have known, adding further empty chairs for 'characters' that are never seen or heard. The Old Man chats to his childhood girlfriend, and the Old Woman flirts with an engraver. An invisible Emperor also comes in and finally the visible but mute Orator who, the Old Man informs his unseen guests, will save mankind. The elderly couple then leap off the tower to their deaths. Left alone, the Orator writes nonsense on a blackboard, bows to the audience, and exits, leaving the stage crowded with empty chairs.

Chaita Ghoda Nata In India, a simple improvised drama about mythological figures that is acted by the fishermen of the eastern state of Orissa. The evening entertainment, which includes humorous episodes, takes place in the spring under a full moon. All the roles are performed by three actors; the *rauta* who is the main singer and comments on the stories, the *rautami*, a female impersonator who also sings and dances, and a performer who dances as a horse. They are accompanied by two musicians playing the drums and cymbals.

Chamberlain's Men The Elizabethan theatre company for which SHAKESPEARE acted and wrote most of his plays, eventually becoming a leading shareholder. Ben Jonson also wrote for them. Founded in 1594, the company became the most successful troupe of its day with Richard Burbage (*see* BURBAGE FAMILY) as its leading actor; they were originally based at the THEATRE built by Richard's father, James Burbage. The comedians William Kempe and Robert Armin created most of Shakespeare's clowns and fools.

In 1599 the company moved to the new GLOBE THEATRE. Two years later, they risked serious political consequences by performing Shakespeare's RICHARD II (about the deposition of a king) at the time of the Earl of Essex's unsuccessful rebellion. They escaped with an admonishment and probably toured the provinces for a while. The company quickly returned to favour, playing at the court of Elizabeth I shortly before her death. In 1603 they were renamed the **King's Men** after the accession of James I. They took over the second Blackfriars Theatre in 1608 but continued to play at the Globe until 1613, when it burned down after a performance of Shakespeare's HENRY VIII. It was rebuilt the following year, enabling the company to stage Webster's *The Duchess of Malfi*.

After Shakespeare's death in 1616 and Burbage's in 1619, many of the actors moved to other companies. In 1623 two members, John Heminge and Henry Condell, collected 36 of Shakespeare's plays together and published the famous FIRST FOLIO. The two men also acted as the company's business managers, in which role they were succeeded in about 1630 by Joseph Taylor and John Lowin.

In 1624 the company's production of Middleton's *A Game of Chess* was banned and the players admonished after a complaint by the Spanish ambassador. On the death of James I (1625) the King's Men came under the patronage of his successor, Charles I, who protected them from a Puritan attempt to close Blackfriars Theatre. Queen Henrietta Maria was an especially keen supporter of the company, who made court appearances at the indoor Cockpit-in-Court at Whitehall and elsewhere. Philip Massinger became their main dramatist and was succeeded on his death (1640) by James Shirley. In 1642 the King's Men disbanded when the Puritans closed the theatres (*see* INTERREGNUM).

Chambers of Rhetoric (*Rederijkers Kamers*) Associations of rhetoricians in the Low Countries during the 15th to 17th centuries, who organized festivals and performed in the equivalents of the English MYSTERY PLAY and MORALITY PLAY. The idea for such associations originated in the 12th century in northern France; the Chambers of Rhetoric showed this French influence most clearly in their guild-like organization. During the 15th century the emphasis was on farce; only one play with a romance theme by a *Rederijker* survives, Colijn van Rijssele's *Spiegel der Minnen*.

Local towns commissioned Chambers of Rhetoric to organize religious and secular festivals. They also ran national festivals and drama competitions. A winner in 1470 was Pieter Doorlant's morality play *Elckerlyc*, the basis for the English EVERYMAN (1500). The miracle play *Mariken van Nieumeghen* (1500) is one of the earliest works to feature a play-within-a-play; it deals with a sinful woman who is converted by an outdoor pageant.

Champagne Charlie The nickname of George Leybourne (Joe Saunders; 1842–84), the music-hall performer who popularized a song of the same title. He first sang it in 1867 at the Canterbury Music Hall, London. When J. J. Poole, musical director of the Metropolitan Music Hall, saw his performance there, he dubbed Leybourne "a regular lion of a comic", thereby coining the music-hall term LION COMIQUE.

Although Leybourne himself was a Midlands mechanic who first sang in East End taverns, his stage character was a whiskered man-about-town with monocle and fur collar. His songs praised the delights of drink and he lived the part off-stage, drinking only champagne, dressing extravagantly, and driving a carriage-and-four.

By the 1880s Leybourne's popularity and health were declining. His last years were spent managing and chairing smaller halls; he was sometimes joined on stage by his daughter, Florrie, for a short routine.

The character in the song was suggested by the original Champagne Charlie, the 4th and last Marquess of Hastings. He was the most notorious spendthrift and wastrel of the mid-19th century. One night he lost three games of draughts for £1,000 a game. He then cut a pack of cards for £500 a cut, and lost £5,000 in an hour and a half. He paid both debts before he left the room.

Champmeslé, La Madame Champmeslé (Marie Desmares; 1642–98), one of France's first tragic actresses, famous for creating the traditional 'touching voice' of the Paris stage. She became the mistress of RACINE and, according to contemporary gossip, several of the nobility. She began acting at the Théâtre du Marais in Paris and in 1665 married the actor Charles Chevillet Champmeslé (1642–1701), who had written several light comedies. In 1670 both joined the Théâtre de l'HÔTEL DE BOURGOGNE.

La Champmeslé created many famous roles, including the heroines of Racine's *Bérénice* (1670) and *Phedre* (1677). Although she acted in the older declamatory style, her voice was famous. One contemporary wrote that "She shows so much art in the use of it...her heart really seems to be full of the passion which is only in her mouth." In 1680 the Champmeslés were founding members of the COMÉDIE-FRANÇAISE, where she became the leading lady, playing opposite Michel Baron (1653–1729) until her death.

Changeling, The A tragedy by Thomas MIDDLETON and William Rowley. It was first performed in 1622 in London but not published until 1653. The plot is based on John Reynolds's *God's Revenge against Murther* (1621). The main character is Beatrice, whose father, the governor of Alicant, orders her to marry Alonzo de Piracquo. Before the wedding, however, she falls for a visiting nobleman, Alsemero, and arranges for the ugly servant De Flores to murder Alonzo. When this is accomplished she offers him gold but, to her disgust, De Flores demands her instead: "Can you weep Fate from its determined purpose?" he asks her. "So soon may you weep me." Beatrice submits and subsequently marries Alsemero. To disguise the fact that she is not a virgin, she has her maid take her place on the wedding night. Although De Flores murders the maid to prevent exposure, he and Beatrice are overheard conferring and brought before the governor; De Flores mortally wounds Beatrice before committing suicide.

The play's title comes from the comic subplot (written by Rowley) in which Antonio and Franciscus pretend to be changelings (madmen) in order to make advances to Isabella, wife of the doctor of a lunatic asylum.

Chapman, George (1560–1634) English poet and dramatist, also noted for his translations of the *Iliad* and the *Odyssey* (which inspired Keats's sonnet 'On First Looking into Chapman's Homer'). Chapman, who is thought to have served as a soldier in his youth, began to write plays for the Admiral's Men in the 1590s; his earlier works include the comedy *An Humorous Day's Mirth* (1597), which influenced Ben JONSON's *Every Man in His Humour* (1598). Most of Chapman's surviving plays date from the first decade of the 17th century, the tragedy *Bussy D'Ambois* (1604) and its sequel *The Revenge of Bussy D'Ambois* (1610) being usually considered his best work.

In 1605, in collaboration with Ben Jonson and John Marston, Chapman wrote EASTWARD HO!, a play that King James I found so offensive to his fellow Scots that he had Chapman and Marston imprisoned for their part in it. Chapman was also threatened with imprisonment in 1613 for *Chabot, Admiral of France*, which offended the French Ambassador. *Eastward Ho!* has proved to be Chapman's most frequently revived work, although Jonathan Miller directed a revival of *Bussy D'Ambois* at the Old Vic in 1988.

Although little is known for certain about Chapman's life and character, his somewhat shadowy relationships with other writers of the period have prompted much speculation. In particular, he has often been identified as the 'rival poet' alluded to in Shakespeare's *Sonnets* and as the model for the pedant Holofernes in *Love's Labours Lost* (1594) and the scurrilous Thersites in *Troilus and Cressida* (1601). Chapman has also been associated with the so-called 'School of Night', a supposed coterie of freethinkers and occultists that also included Christopher MARLOWE and Sir Walter Raleigh. Intriguingly, Chapman claimed that his translations of Homer had been inspired and guided by the poet's ghost.

chariot-and-pole system *See* CARRIAGE-AND-FRAME SYSTEM.

charivari In the 18th century, a procession of noisy street dancers, singers, maskers, and drummers. The participants included the wild man Hellequin, whose name evolved into HARLEQUIN, dissolute monks who exposed their behinds, and demons beating on pots and pans (still part of the FASTNACHTSSPIEL performed in Basel, Switzerland).

The charivari began in the 14th century as the 'chalvaricum', a loud disturbance organized to show the community's displeasure at irregular or unconventional marriages (such as those between partners of unequal status). In England, a similar uproar occurred at the weddings of butchers, when it was performed good-naturedly by their co-workers, who created a racket with cleavers and marrow-bones. Soon society weddings were demanding this unique ceremony.

In 1832 Charles Philipon founded a French daily publication *Le Charivari* with the intention of ridiculing the foibles of society. The name was adopted as a subtitle by the former English magazine *Punch* when it began in 1841.

The word itself is French, from a Late Latin word meaning 'headache'.

Charley's Aunt A farce by Brandon Thomas, first performed in London in 1892 at the Royalty Theatre in Soho. It ran for four years and 1466 performances with W. S. Penley as the cross-dressing Lord Fancourt Babberley. Many years later the play provided the first professional role for the 19-year-old Rex HARRISON; in 1927 he earned £8 a week playing the girl-crazy Jack Chesney in a 16-week touring version. Frank Loesser turned *Charley's Aunt* into the successful Broadway musical *Where's Charley?*

The story follows two scheming Oxford undergraduates, Jack Chesney and Charles Wykeham, in their attempts to lure a pair of girls, Kitty Verdun and Amy Spettigue, into their rooms to meet "Charley's aunt" from Brazil "where the nuts come from". The aunt, however, is a male friend, Lord Fancourt-Babberly (played in a 1955 production by Frankie Howerd). 'Babbs' enjoys getting close to the girls but has to dodge the attentions of Amy's uncle Stephen. The action becomes more confused when the real Aunt Donna Lucia suddenly shows up under an assumed name.

In Britain, Charlie's Aunt is a press nickname for Princess Margaret, who is, of course, the aunt of Prince Charles.

still running – like *Charley's Aunt* A phrase applied to any popular and long-running play or film, or anything or anyone else that shows a stubborn longevity. It alludes to the long run and frequent revivals of the farce *Charley's Aunt*. In the 1960s it was to some extent replaced by a phrase alluding to another record-breaking theatrical production, 'still running – like the MOUSETRAP'.

Chauve-Souris A highly successful revue produced by the Russian theatre director Nikita Balieff; it was first performed in 1908 at the Chauve-Souris Club in Paris. The revue was brought to London in 1921 by Charles B. COCHRAN and opened in New York the following year. *Chauve-Souris* consisted of burlesques, songs, and pantomime; many of the sketches were mimes based on popular ballads, prints, and engravings. The production was richly designed and costumed in the style of a Russian ballet. The title (literally 'bald mouse') is a French word for a bat.

Cheeky Chappie The nickname of the music-hall comedian Max Miller (1895–1963). The epithet, which appeared on bills advertising his act from 1924, alluded to the risqué nature of his performance, in particular his use of the *double entendre*. 'Clean' gags were described as coming from his 'white book' and 'dirty' gags as coming from his 'blue book'; according to his biographer, however, the books themselves were only notional.

Chekhov, Anton (1860–1904) Russian dramatist and short-story writer. The grandson of a serf and son of a failed grocer, Chekhov began writing humorous sketches and articles as a medical student at Moscow University. After his graduation in 1884 he began to practise medicine but continued to produce short stories and journalism, acquiring something of a lowbrow following.

Chekhov began to make his name in the theatre with a series of successful one-act farces, including *The Bear* and *Swan Song* (both 1888); he claimed to have written the latter in just over an hour. His earliest full-length plays, the gloomy IVANOV (1887) and *The Wood Demon* (1889), were, however, notably unsuccessful. This failure to become a serious dramatist may have influenced his decision to undertake a 6000-mile journey across Siberia to report on the notorious penal settlement of Sakhalin in 1890.

In about 1892 Chekhov bought an estate at Melikhovo, about 50 miles outside Moscow. During his six years at Melikhovo Chekhov produced many of his finest short stories as well as his first mature dramatic work, THE SEAGULL. When produced in 1896 at the Alexandrinsky Theatre, St Petersburg, *The Seagull* proved a catastrophic failure; Chekhov, distressed by this experience, vowed to stop writing for the stage. The following year he suffered a lung haemorrhage and tuberculosis was diagnosed. In 1898, however, he was persuaded to allow the recently formed MOSCOW ART THEATRE to revive *The Seagull*. The production was as successful as the first had been disastrous. In the remaining five years of Chekhov's life the Moscow Art Theatre also staged UNCLE VANYA (1899), a reworking of *The Wood Demon*, THREE SISTERS (1901), and THE CHERRY ORCHARD (1904), shortly after the production of which Chekhov died. Within ten years of his death Chekhov's plays were being staged to considerable critical interest in both Britain and America, though it was not until the mid 1920s that they became commercially successful. With their depiction of the ennui and inconsequence of much of daily life, their unobtrusive symbolism, and their blend of comedy with an underlying sense of anguish, Chekhov's four late masterpieces have had a profound influence on 20th-century Western drama.

Cherry Orchard, The CHEKHOV's last play, generally regarded as his masterpiece. The tragicomedy was first staged in 1904 at the Moscow Art Theatre under STANISLAVSKY, whose influential production emphasized the vein of melancholy in the play to the detriment of the comedy. The first London production was put on by the Stage Society in 1912.

The story concerns the ineffectual attempts of Madame Lyubov Ranevsky and her family to save their estate, with its glorious cherry orchard, from bankruptcy. They are horrified when Lopakhin, a suitor to her stepdaughter, suggests levelling the orchard to develop a holiday resort. Other plans fail, however, and the estate is auctioned. Surprisingly, Lopakhin is the buyer, and the family prepares to move out. In the final scene workmen begin to chop down the orchard. The play is sometimes seen as a parable about the doom of the Russian landowning class.

One memorable revival was the Old Vic's 1933 production directed by Tyrone Guthrie and starring Charles Laughton, James Mason, Elsa Lanchester, and Flora ROBSON. The production suffered a near disaster when Robson tripped over a rug and fell flat on her face. She quickly got back on her feet but the audience showed no reaction. Later in her dressing room, she asked visiting Hollywood producer James Whale why nobody had laughed. "But why?" he shrugged. "We all thought, 'How very Russian'."

Chestnut Street Theatre One of the earliest US theatres. It was built in Philadelphia by the US actor Thomas Wignell for a company he had brought over from England and opened in 1794. The theatre was a copy of the Theatre Royal at Bath and the first in America to incorporate the English style of proscenium. In 1816 it became one of the first theatres to be lit by gas. The company, which produced a series of successful light comedies, included three members of the JEFFERSON FAMILY.

After Wignell's death, the theatre was managed by William Wood (1779–1861) and the elder William Warren (1767–1832). Fire damage closed it from 1820 to 1822 and six years later, when Wood retired, it went bankrupt. This was mostly due to competition from the WALNUT STREET THEATRE (opened 1811) and Mrs John Drew's Arch Street Theatre (*see* DREW FAMILY). The Chestnut Street Theatre was destroyed by fire in 1855 and rebuilt in 1863: it closed in 1910 and was finally demolished in 1917.

The Chestnut Street was one of the two US theatres known as **Old Drury** (the other being New York's PARK THEATRE).

Chevalier. Albert Chevalier (1861–1912) British music-hall performer, whose popular cockney songs earned him the nickname **coster's laureate**. He began his music-hall career at the London Pavilion in 1891, having previously acted in burlesque and melodrama. His best-known songs included 'Knocked 'Em in the Old Kent Road'. *See also* ALBERT THE GREAT; OLD DUTCH.

Maurice Chevalier (1888–1972) French music-hall artist and actor whose talent, debonair charm, and deliberately exaggerated French accent won him international fame and regular performances in London and New York. He gave his 1949 autobiography the title *The Man in the Straw Hat*, a reference to the tilted boater he frequently sported.

Chevalier was born in the Parisian slum of Ménilmontant, where his mother was a poor Flemish lacemaker. He began singing bawdy songs in disreputable Paris cafes at the age of 13 and then moved into music hall. In 1907 he toured the halls with the writer Colette, who later described him as an isolated person who sacrificed everything for his performance. From 1909 to 1913 he appeared on the stage of the Folies-Bergères with the actress and singer MISTINGUETT who, though 13 years his senior, became his lover. Other famous ladies with whom he is said to have had relationships include Marlene Dietrich.

During World War I Chevalier was wounded, taken prisoner, and awarded the Croix de Guerre. In 1919 he made his London debut in the revue *Hullo, America!*. During the 1920s and 1930s he made frequent trips to Hollywood to make films. After World War II *Life* magazine named Chevalier as a Nazi collaborator, although little evidence was provided. It is true that he had sung on the German-controlled radio in Paris, but he also entertained French prisoners.

Chevalier enjoyed his greatest international success with his role in Lerner and Loewe's film musical *Gigi* (1958), released when he was 70. At 82 he unsuccessfully attempted suicide.

chew up the scenery A phrase meaning to overact. It originally appeared in a 1930 theatre review by Dorothy Parker (1893–1967), the US writer and wit, who described one actor as "more glutton than artist...he commences to chew up the scenery." When the director Harold French saw Rex Harrison in *Heroes Don't Care* (1936), he commented: "I thought he did chew up the scenery a bit that night, probably the overconfidence of an actor knowing the run is nearing its end." The phrase has now entered the general language, meaning to dramatize events or oneself inappropriately.

Chicano theatre Drama by and for US citizens of Mexican origin. Plays may be in Spanish, English, or a mixture of both. The plots focus on the experiences of Mexican-Americans, especially their problems in adjusting to a White English-speaking country. Issues dealt with include racial discrimination, unemployment, drug abuse, education, and housing. The troupes are often made up of students from colleges and universities.

Spanish-language drama in North America can be traced back to the arrival of the conquistadors, who staged religious plays for the natives. Such a performance took place in 1598 in present-day El Paso, Texas, during an expedition led by Juan de Oñate. After the United States was established, the Spanish-language theatre continued in the southwest, with centres in California (Los Angeles and San Francisco) and Texas (San Antonio, El Paso, and Laredo). By World War II it had spread to New York, Chicago, and other major cities, where specialist venues presented Spanish plays and ZARZUELAS.

The current Chicano theatre was a product of the 1960s civil rights movement. The director and playwright **Luis Valdéz** (1940–) is credited with its foundation. A student activist and a member of the San Francisco Mime Troupe, Valdéz joined César Chávez during his nationally publicized migrant farmworkers' strike in the vineyards of Delano, California, in 1965. Valdéz used improvised political theatre to support the cause, presenting a series of one-act revolutionary works called *actos*. He went on to establish the company El Teatro Campesino (Farmworkers' Theatre). In 1978 his *Zoot Suit* was premiered in Los Angeles and became the first Chicano offering to transfer to Broadway.

El Teatro Campesino provided a model for other troupes, such as Adrian Vargas's Teatro de la Gente in San Jose, California (1967), the Teatro de los Barrios in San Antonio, Texas (1969), and Joe Rosenberg's Teatro Bilingue in Kingsville, Texas (1972). In 1971 a national Chicano theatre organization called TENAZ (El Teatro Nacional de Aztlán) was created to sponsor annual festivals for companies from the US and Latin America.

Chicano theatre is a part of the broader category of **Hispanic American theatre**, which has expanded rapidly since the 1960s. A survey in 1985 listed 101 Hispanic companies: 29 Chicano, 28 Puerto Rican, 24 Cuban, and 20 of other ethnic groups. The best known New York companies include the Puerto Rican Traveling Theatre, INTAR, and Repertorio Espagnol.

Chichester Festival An annual summer drama festival in Chichester, Sussex, inspired by the Shakespeare Festival Theatre in Stratford, Ontario. It was organized by Chichester's ex-mayor Leslie Evershed-Martin, an amateur actor. Local citizens had pledged £42,000 by the time Laurence OLIVIER accepted the appointment as the first director. He was offered £5,000 a year but only accepted £3,000.

The theatre, built in 1962, seats 1394 on three sides of a hexagonal auditorium (which Olivier helped to design). It was Britain's first large open-stage theatre. The Festival opened that year with a 10-week season. Olivier starred in the productions and assembled a repertory company that was to provide the nucleus for the NATIONAL THEATRE: Sybil Thorndike, her husband Lewis Casson, Michael Redgrave, Fay Compton, Joan Greenwood, John Neville, Nicholas Hannen, and his wife Athene Seyler.

Despite this array of talent, the Festival began disastrously. The first production, Buckingham's farce *The Chances*, drew poor reviews. Worse notices followed the second offering, *The Broken Heart*, which featured Olivier as a jealous nobleman. Half the seats went unsold and the critic Kenneth Tynan wrote an open letter to Olivier blaming his management and saying, "all is not well with your dashing hexagonal playhouse, something has clearly gone wrong."

The third try, Chekhov's *Uncle Vanya*, began just as badly with missed cues and mismatched sound effects. Joan Greenwood, pregnant under a heavy costume, burst into tears after a hiss from the audience. Sybil Thorndike and Lewis Casson suffered one night from the lack of a curtain. When Thorndike got up to leave the scene with Casson, she noticed him asleep in his chair. "Waffles, Waffles," she called, using his character's name. When he continued to slumber, she yelled, "Lewis! Wake up you silly old fool!". He leaped up fearfully and they exited.

Just as it seemed that the Festival itself was in jeopardy, great reviews appeared and *Uncle Vanya* became the hit of the season. Olivier, however, became drunk at the cast party and railed at Evershed-Martin, calling him a rich "theatrical ignoramus" who had founded Chichester to get a knighthood.

The second season was a thorough success, opening with Shaw's *Saint Joan* and featuring a revival of *Uncle Vanya*. Olivier, who became director of the National Theatre in 1963, was succeeded at Chichester by John Clements, who was followed by Keith Michell in 1974, Peter Dews in 1978, and Patrick Garland in 1980.

Hits transferring from the Festival to the West End have included Peter Shaffer's 1964 epic, *The Royal Hunt of the Sun* and T. S. Eliot's *The Cocktail Party* in the 1968 production with Alec Guinness.

Chicken Soup with Barley The first of Arnold WESKER's trilogy of plays about an East End Jewish family, the Kahns. It was first performed in 1958 at the Belgrade Theatre, Coventry, and subsequently transferred to the Royal Court Theatre in London. The other plays of the trilogy are *Roots* (1959) and *I'm Talking About Jerusalem* (1960).

Chicken Soup with Barley follows the Kahn family from 1936 to 1956. Sarah is energetic and emotional, a passionate socialist, while her friendly husband, Harry, is a tiresome political sloth. Sarah fights a long losing battle as Harry's apathy slides into senility. Her son, Ronnie, follows in his father's footsteps, spurning his mother's pleas that he should become politically active.

children. The Children or **Babes in the Wood** An old story found in a ballad collected in Bishop Percy's *Reliques* and also in a crude melodrama, printed in 1601 and attributed on the title-page to Rob Yarington. The full title of this publication was *Two Lamentable Tragedies; the one of the murder of Maister Beech, a chandler in Thames-streete, etc. The other of a young child murthered in a wood by two ruffians, with the consent of his unkle.* It is uncertain which is earlier, the play or the ballad.

The story is that the master of Wayland Hall, Norfolk, left a little son and daughter in the care of his wife's brother; both were to have money, but if the children died first the uncle was to inherit. After twelve months the uncle hired two ruffians to murder the babes; one of them relented and killed his partner, leaving the children in a wood. They died during the night and robins covered them over with leaves.

All things now went badly for the wicked uncle; his sons died, his barns burned down, his cattle died, and he finally perished in jail. After seven years the ruffian was arrested for highway robbery and confessed the whole affair.

A version of the story in which the birds' ministrations save the children's lives provides the basis of the PANTOMIME *Babes in the Wood*.

Children of the Chapel One of the famous BOY COMPANIES of the Elizabethan theatre. Its young actors, who included Ezekiel Fenn, Nathan Field, and Salathiel Pavy, gave the first performances of major works by Jonson, Middleton, Beaumont, and Marston.

The choirboys of the Chapels Royal of Windsor and London were first organized into an acting company by William Cornish (*fl.* 1509–23) to amuse the young Henry VIII. A later master was the playwright Richard Edwardes (*c.* 1523–66), who wrote the tragicomedy *Damon and Pithias* (1565). In 1576 Richard Farrant, deputy master of the Chapel Children, created an indoor theatre for the company in the ruins of the Blackfriars monastery (*see* BLACKFRIARS THEATRE). Under the dramatist John Lyly, who took over in 1580, the company performed several plays with the rival Boys of St Paul's, including Lyly's own *Campaspe* and *Sapho and Phao*. In 1601 the company was drawn into the so-called 'war of the theatres' on the side of Ben Jonson, when they performed in his play *The Poetaster*, which ridiculed John Marston. The latter responded with satires performed by the Boys of St Paul's.

The company began to fall out of favour with James I in 1605, after performing Jonson, Chapman, and Marston's *Eastward Ho!*, which contained some rude remarks about the Scots. The Children of the Chapel moved to the Whitefriars Theatre in 1609 before disbanding in 1615.

children's companies *See* BOY COMPANIES.

Children's Hour, The The first play by the US dramatist Lillian HELLMAN, dealing with the then controversial subject of lesbianism. It was premiered in 1934 in New York and two years later in London; the film version (1961) starred Shirley MacLaine and Audrey Hepburn.

Set in New England, the story involves Karen and Martha, two friends who run a small boarding school for girls. Their neurotic student Mary Tilford runs home to her grandmother, Amelia Tilford, and justifies this by accusing the two women of being lesbians. Mrs Tilford withdraws Mary and other parents do the same as the rumour spreads. Karen's fiancé, Dr Joseph Cardin, is able to find inconsistencies in Mary's story, but she blackmails a fellow pupil into corroborating her lie. The school goes bankrupt and closes. Dr Cardin proposes to Karen but she now has doubts about her sexual preferences. Martha, suffering from the same doubts, commits suicide. Mrs Tilford finally discovers the lie and offers Karen money, but it is too late.

children's theatre Drama productions staged specifically for young people, a feature of the 20th-century theatre. The British director and theatre manager Caryl Jenner (1917–73) was the first to establish a professional theatre for children in this country. She formed several touring companies under the title of the English Theatre for Children and in 1962 established the Unicorn Theatre for Young People at the ARTS THEATRE CLUB London. Plays presented there included Marged Smith's *The Wappy Water Bus* (1965) and John Arden's *The Royal Pardon, or the Soldier Who Became an Actor* (1967). The Unicorn Theatre has also organized workshops for children in such subjects as clown skills and scenery painting.

Britain's NATIONAL YOUTH THEATRE, founded in 1955, established the Shaw Theatre Company in 1971 to perform plays suitable for young audiences. The YOUNG VIC was opened in 1970 as a theatre specifically for young audiences.

Children's theatre has also flourished in America and Continental Europe. The famous BARTER THEATRE in Abingdon, Virginia has set aside a building for productions for children. In France, Chancerel's short-lived Théâtre de l'Oncle Sebastien (1935–39) had a particularly impressive record. Communist states also used the form to indoctrinate young minds.

Chips with Everything A play about life in the RAF by Arnold WESKER. It was first performed in London in 1962 at the Royal Court Theatre, directed by John Dexter, and opened on Broadway a year later. Wesker uses the division between the officers and the other ranks in the Royal Air Force as a microcosm of the British class system and shows the damage it does to individuals.

Set in an RAF station, the plot focuses on an educated upper-class man who rebels against the system by joining the ranks. Although the officers attempt to humiliate and break him, Pip steadfastly remains with his mates who eat "chips with everything". Pip finally gives in when the officers accuse him of seeking power and status among the lower classes. He rejoins the establishment and successfully averts a rebellion by the airmen against their poor treatment.

The phrase 'chips with everything' is often used to epitomize working-class eating habits. Soggy chips, liberally sprinkled with salt and vinegar, are often seen as the hallmark of British working-class tourists abroad.

Chirgwin, George H. *See* WHITE-EYED KAFFIR *under* WHITE.

Chocolate Coloured Coon Stage nickname for G(eorge) H(enry) Elliott (1884–1962), the music-hall comedian, singer, dancer, and pantomime performer. He was especially known for soft-shoe dancing and for the song 'I Used to Sing for the Silvery Moon'. He spent some time in the US with a MINSTREL SHOW, returning to England in 1902 to make his first London appearance at Sadler's Wells Theatre. He replaced Eugene STRATTON as the leading black-faced singer of 'coon' songs.

choregus The patron of the CHORUS in the ancient Athenian drama. At Oxford University the title was formerly given to the assistant of the Professor of Music. *See also* CORYPHAEUS; LITURGY.

choreography The art of devising and directing dances for the ballet or musical theatre. Choreography developed alongside the art of ballet, one of the best known early exponents being Charles Louis Beauchamp at the court of Louis XIV. One of the most original and controversial choreographers of modern dance was the American Martha Graham, whose work greatly affected the dancing seen in plays and films. The modern energetic style of stage dancing was introduced to the US theatre with Rodgers and Hammerstein's OKLAHOMA!. In 1957 Jerome Robbins combined classical ballet with jazz rhythms in his choreography for *West Side Story*.

chorus A group of actors who support the principal performers and enhance the audience's understanding of the play by explaining the action, expressing opinions, or asking questions.

The ancient Greek drama developed from choral lyrics performed in honour of DIONYSUS. These DITHYRAMBS, performed by a chorus of 50 actors, are first mentioned in the 7th century BC. THESPIS was supposedly the first actor to detach himself from the chorus. In the ATHENIAN DRAMA of the 5th and 4th centuries BC the role of the chorus was gradually reduced and that of the principals enhanced. AESCHYLUS reduced the chorus from 50 to 12, while SOPHOCLES limited its role to commenting on the main action. The chorus contributed bawdy songs and lively dancing to the plays of the OLD COMEDY; for some works, notably ARISTOPHANES's *The Birds* and *The Frogs*, it was elaborately costumed. In later Greek drama the chorus was sometimes replaced by interludes featuring singers and dancers. Roman plays usually had no chorus.

In Greece the expense of training and outfitting the chorus was met by the CHOREGUS, a wealthy Athenian citizen who was elected to this position of honour. Like the principal actors, members of the chorus enjoyed various privileges including exemption from military service.

The chorus survived into the later European theatre in various forms. In Elizabethan drama the role was frequently undertaken by a single actor. Shakespeare used such a chorus to great effect in *Henry V* (*c.* 1599) while in *The Spanish Tragedy* (1592), Thomas Kyd used the characters of Revenge and a Ghost as choruses to comment on the action. In the 20th century, T. S. Eliot revived the Greek chorus for his MURDER IN THE CATHEDRAL (1935), in which the Women of Canterbury comment on the meaning of the action. The Stage Manager in Thornton Wilder's OUR TOWN (1938) is effectively a one-man chorus.

In musical shows the chorus appears in choreographed numbers and crowd scenes. The 'chorus line' of beautiful women dancing in unison was introduced in America in the late 19th century (*see* BURLESQUE). The US MUSICAL COMEDY gave the chorus a major role.

Many non-Western theatrical traditions have made use of choruses. In the Japanese NŌ play the chorus of six to ten persons (who wear traditional *samurai* costume) serve virtually the same function as the Greek chorus.

Chorus Line, A A Broadway musical by Marvin Hamlisch (music) and Edward Kleban (lyrics) that became a great success despite having virtually no plot and only one memorable song. The first production was in 1975 at the New York Public Theatre. This won a Pulitzer Prize and the Tony Award for Best Musical despite one New York critic declaring on opening night, "The paltriness of the music was hideously apparent." The show also triumphed in London's West End, winning the *Evening Standard* Award. Sir Richard Attenborough made a film adaptation of the musical in 1985.

The slim plot involves dancers auditioning for the chorus line of a Broadway show. After reducing the candidates to 17 for eight parts, the director-choreographer Zach asks them to talk about themselves, which they do in energetic song and dance. Among the winners is his ex-girlfriend Cassie, of whom he has been especially critical.

Christie, Dame Agatha (1890–1976) British writer of detective stories, who produced over 20 works for the stage. She has earned a place in theatre history by writing the world's longest continuously running play, THE MOUSETRAP, which opened in 1952 and was still going in 1997.

The first of her works to be staged was *The Murder of Roger Ackroyd* (1926), adapted in 1928 as *Alibi* for the Prince of Wales' Theatre. Her first original play, *Black Coffee*, opened in 1930 at the Embassy Theatre. In 1943 she adapted *Ten Little Niggers* (1939) for the St James's Theatre. She said it "set me on the path of being a playwright as well as a writer of books", although *The Times* claimed, "This is not a play. It is a kind of theatrical game." It ran for 260 performances in London and a former 425 performances on Broadway.

Christie's playwriting career hit a low when her 1946 adaptation of *Death on the Nile* (1937) ran at New York's Plymouth Theatre for only 12 performances (as *Hidden Horizon*). The critic Brooks Atkinson called it 'dull in theme, dull in story, dull in the acting'. This failure was followed by a great hit, the 1949 adaptation of *The Murder at the Vicarage* (by Moie Charles and Barbara Toy) which ran for 1776 performances at the Playhouse, London.

Christie had another hit with her adaptation of the short story *The Hound of Death* (1933), renamed *Witness for the Prosecution*. Critics called it her best piece of stagecraft. "I can safely say that that was the only first night I have enjoyed" she later wrote. Her last work for the stage, produced in 1972 when she was 82, was *Fiddlers Three*, a comedy-thriller that opened in Guildford but never transferred to the West End.

Her private life created its own mystery. In 1914 she married Archibald Christie, whose name she used throughout her writing career, despite the fact that they were divorced in 1928 and she subsequently married the archaeologist Max Mallowan. In 1926 Christie disappeared from view for several weeks, leading to a nationwide police hunt. She was finally found in a health resort, apparently suffering from amnesia. A full explanation of this episode has never been given; some regarded it as a publicity stunt, others as a genuine attack of amnesia, perhaps brought on by her failing marriage.

Christy Minstrels For many years in the mid 19th century theatre-goers in London and New York were entertained by the troupe of black-faced minstrels organized by the US Christy brothers (1815–1862). To an accompaniment of various stage-Negro antics they sang plantation songs while Bones, Sambo, and other stock characters of the MINSTREL SHOW cracked innocuous jokes. Stephen Collins Foster provided their best songs, of which *Beautiful Dreamer* is the most famous. They were succeeded by the Moore and Burgess Minstrels and other troupes of the same genre.

> Q: Why is it almost certain that Shakespeare was a broker?
>
> A: Because he furnished so many stock quotations.

The Merry Book of the Moore and Burgess Minstrels.

Chronomastix A character in Ben JONSON's masque *Time Vindicated to Himself and to his Honours* (1623), intended as a satire upon the poet George Wither. Wither was often in trouble with the government for his verses and his irrepressible self-esteem. Charles Lamb later observed: "Wither seems to have contemplated to a degree of idolatry his own possible virtue", while his outrageous personal motto *Nec habeo, nec careo, nec curo* ("Nor have I, nor want I, nor care I") was the cause of one of his several stays in prison. Although his song 'Shall I, wasting in despair' has been much admired, he was also the author of poems notorious for their insipid awfulness. Memorable stanzas include:

> She would me 'Honey' call,
> She'd – O she'd kiss me too.
> But now alas! She's left me
> Falero, lero, loo.

The Puritan tone of some of his later verse was also controversial and the chief element satirized by Jonson. When the Civil War came, Wither sold his house to pay for a troop of horse, which he led until captured in 1639. His execution seemed inevitable until Sir John Denham, the Royalist poet and playwright (who had himself lost land to Wither's troops) intervened. As Denham explained to the king, it was not fellow-feeling for a writer in distress that had prompted his charity but simply "that so long as Wither lived, Denham would not be accounted the worst poet in England."

Chrononhotonthologos A BURLESQUE by the English dramatist Henry Carey (d. 1743), first produced in 1734. It was subtitled *The Most Tragical Tragedy that ever was Tragediz'd by any Company of Tragedians*. The bombastic title character is the King of Queerummania; the name is sometimes used for any self-important person who delivers an inflated address. Another pompous character is named Aldiborontiphoscophornio.

Chuanju The opera of Sichuan province, China. Its origins can be traced back to the 17th century. The music blends various regional styles while the drama combines elements of KUNQU from the main Chinese theatre with the truly native *dengxi*, a folk drama with mask dances. At the beginning of the 20th century extensive reforms were made by the actor and instructor Kang Zhilin (1870–1931). He managed the Sanqing (Three Celebrations) Company, the most famous Sichuan Opera troupe, formed in 1912. The genre has received support from the communist regime (except during the Cultural Revolution). Since 1983 the Sichuan Province *Chuanju* Research Institute has maintained more than 2000 texts of plays.

Although some Sichuan stage techniques were introduced to the Peking Opera, the *Chuanju* retains a number of unique traditions. One of these is the acrobatic move in which an actor touches his forehead with his foot, leaving a third 'eye' there.

Chu Chin Chow One of London's longest running musical comedies, written by Oscar Asche with music by Frederic Norton. It opened in 1916 at His Majesty's Theatre and ran for 2238 performances over nearly five years. Asche devised the plot, a retelling of *Ali Baba and the Forty Thieves* (*see* ALI BABA), in a Manchester hotel room and completed the play three weeks later. When Beerbohm Tree, manager of His Majesty's, first saw the revealing costumes during a rehearsal, he shook his head and commented, "I see – more navel than military." Asche played Abu Hassan, the robber chief, and made a personal profit of more than £200,000 on a production that cost £5,356.

The story is about the clever robber, Abu Hassan, who disguises himself to gain entry into rich homes. He is welcomed into Kasim Baba's house in the guise of Chu Chin Chow, a rich Chinese merchant. Kasim's brother, Ali Baba, eventually finds Abu Hassan's secret cave of treasures, Sesame, and robs it. Hassan tries to recover his fortune by smuggling his men into Ali Baba's house in jars of oil, but the plot fails.

The songs included 'I Am Chu Chin Chow of China', 'Marjanah's Song', 'Open Sesame!', and 'The Cobbler's Song'.

Churchill, Sir Winston (1874–1965) British statesman and leader of the free world in its opposition to Nazi Germany. Churchill, for most of his life, had other preoccupations than the theatre. However, in the late 1920s, when Churchill was out of office, George Bernard SHAW sent him two tickets for the first night performance in London of his play *Saint Joan*. With the tickets came a note: "I enclose two tickets, one for yourself and one for a friend – if you have one". Churchill sent a note back regretting that he had a previous engagement on that evening. "Would it be possible", he added, "for you to let me have tickets for the second night – if there is one".

Churchill also had a family connection with the theatre. His daughter Sarah was a successful actress, and for a time was married to the entertainer Vic Oliver, of whom Churchill disapproved. It is said that on one occasion Oliver asked Churchill if he admired any of his wartime enemies. "Yes", growled Churchill, "Mussolini – he had the courage to have his son-in-law shot". (Count Ciano, husband of the Duce's daughter, was convicted of treason and executed in 1944.)

Numerous plays have made use of Churchillian images or of extracts from his wartime speeches to establish period. In others, Churchill himself has appeared, notably in the less than successful 1980s musical *Winnie*. Howard BRENTON's *The Churchill Play* (1974) opens with Churchill rising from his coffin at his lying-in-state, while Rolf HOCHHUTH's controversial *Soldiers* (1967) has Churchill conspiring to murder the Polish General Sikorski. Perhaps most outrageous is the role Churchill plays in Joe Orton's WHAT THE BUTLER SAW (1969). Early in the play, a statue of the wartime leader is damaged by an exploding gas main. As the play ends the cast gather reverentially round as the demented psychiatrist Dr Rance opens the cigar box in which the statue's private parts have been preserved:

> How much more inspiring if, in those dark days, we'd seen what we see now.
> Instead we had to be content with a cigar – the symbol falling far short, as we all realize, of the object itself.

See also EMPIRE PROMENADE.

Cibber family The British actor-manager, playwright, and poet laureate Colley Cibber (1671–1757) and his children, the actor Theophilus Cibber (1703–58) and the actress Charlotte Charke (1710–60). Theophilus's second wife Susanna Maria Arne (1714–66) was also an actress.

Colley Cibber was born in London, the son of a Danish sculptor, and in 1690 joined Thomas BETTERTON's company at Drury Lane. In one of his first roles, as a messenger to Betterton, Cibber became so nervous that he spoilt the whole scene. Betterton demanded that Cibber forfeit part of his salary. Told that Cibber was paid nothing, Betterton replied, "Then put him down 10 shillings a week and forfeit him 5 shillings."

Cibber's first great success was in his own play *Love's Last Shift* (1696), usually considered the first sentimental comedy. He also played in Vanbrugh's *The Relapse* (1697), a sequel to this play. His successes as a writer included *The Careless Husband* (1704), in which Anne OLDFIELD made her name. He also produced numerous adaptations, including a version of RICHARD III (1700) that held the stage until Irving restored the original in 1871. Cibber's version contained the infamous line, "Off with his head! So much for Buckingham!" In 1710 he became part of the famous TRIUMVIRATE that managed Drury Lane.

Cibber was generally disliked because of his rudeness. After speaking the line "I was then in Rome" in one performance, he suddenly went blank and waited for the prompter's aid. When none came, he dragged the man by the collar to the footlights growling, "Hang you, you scoundrel, what was I doing in Rome? Why don't you tell me?"

He was appointed (a much ridiculed) poet laureate in 1730 and retired from the stage four years later. His autobiography *Apology for the Life of Mr Colley Cibber, Comedian* (1740) gives a valuable description of theatre life during his time.

Theophilus Cibber began to act at the age of 16 and came to specialize in Irish and eccentric roles. He was notorious for his unreliability and dissolute behaviour. On one occasion he fought a harmless duel with his fellow actor James Quin (*see* BELLOWER QUIN). On another he fled abroad to escape creditors but was bailed out by his long-suffering wife, Susanna Arne. His career later declined and he sank into poverty. In 1758, while sailing to make an appearance at Dublin's Smock Alley Theatre, he was drowned in a shipwreck.

His wife, **Susanna Maria Arne**, was the sister of the composer Thomas Arne. In 1736 her budding career as an actress was almost destroyed by scandal, owing to a bizarre plot by her husband, who deliberately led her into an affair with her friend, William Sloper, and then brought an action against them both. Nevertheless, she went on to become an acclaimed tragic actress and one of Garrick's leading ladies at Drury Lane. She also excelled in comedy, making her final performance as Lady Bute in Vanbrugh's *The Provok'd Wife*.

Charlotte Charke, Colley Cibber's daughter, was a wild and rebellious child. She apparently took to the stage to avoid her cruel husband. Renowned for her eccentricities, she often imitated her father on stage and once rubbed fish over his face during a performance. She preferred male roles, such as Captain Macheath in *The Beggar's Opera*. Once, she disguised herself as a man and robbed her father at gunpoint on the highway. Her autobiography, *A Narrative of the Life of Mrs. Charlotte Charke*, appeared in 1755.

Cid, Le A tragicomedy by CORNEILLE. Its first performance in 1637 in Paris is usually considered the inception of the classical French theatre. The play's success provoked fierce attacks from Corneille's rivals and critics, ostensibly because he took liberties with the UNITIES; the ensuing pamphlet war, which culminated in the play's suppression, came to be known as the *querelle du Cid*. Nevertheless, the play established Corneille as the leading dramatist of the day. In the first production the great actor MONTDORY played the title role (his most acclaimed part) at his Théâtre du Marais.

The play was based on *Las mocedades del Cid*, a chronicle play about the exploits of the Spanish hero by Guillen de Castro y Bellvis. The plot, in which a son avenges an insult to his elderly father by killing his fiancée's father, is typical of the Spanish *pundonor* (point of honour) drama, in which action is emphasized over character and morality is black and white.

The historical El Cid was Roderigo or Ruy Diaz de Bivar (*c.* 1040–99), also called El Campeador, the champion of Christianity against the Moors. His exploits, real and legendary, form the basis of many Spanish romances and chronicles. The title is a corruption of *seyyid*, Arabic for lord.

Cinderella Heroine of a fairy tale of very ancient, probably Eastern, origin, found in German literature in the 16th century and popularized by Perrault's *Contes de ma mère l'oye* (1697). In Britain the story is a favourite subject for PANTOMIME.

Cinderella is drudge of the house, while her elder sisters go to fine balls. At length, a fairy enables her to go to the prince's ball; the prince falls in love with her, and she is found again by means of a glass slipper which she drops, and which will fit no foot but her own.

The glass slipper has been conjectured as a fur or sable slipper, supposedly from *pantoufle de vair*, not *de verre*.

The pantomime version adds such characters as Baron Stonybroke and the page BUTTONS and uses the two Ugly Sisters (played by men) as the main source of comedy.

cine. cinematographic A term used in the early 20th-century British theatre to describe the new fashion for realism on stage. It alludes to the advent of the first motion pictures. Max BEERBOHM, reviewing the first production of John Galsworthy's *Justice* in 1910, wrote in the *Saturday Review*: "'Cinematographic' they call it. So it is, in a sense. We really do, in seeing it, have the sensation of seeing reproduced exactly things that have happened in actual life. In the first act of *Justice* we do not feel that we are seeing an accurate presentment of the humdrum of a lawyer's office: we are *in* a lawyer's office. We are haunted by it all afterwards as by an actual experience..."

cine-variety A mixed bill of variety acts and films offered in the late 1920s in Britain. The short-lived scheme was devised to keep stage comedians in work during the early heyday of talking films.

Cinthio, Il Popular name for the Italian novelist, poet, and playwright Giovanni Battista Giraldi (1504–73), derived from his academic name of Cynthius. His moralistic works supplied plots for at least two of Shakespeare's plays, while his habit of adding happy endings to his tragedies virtually created the genre of TRAGICOMEDY. A native of Ferrara, Giraldi assumed the chair of rhetoric there in 1541, later moving to Turin and Pavia.

Giraldi's first play was the Senecan horror tragedy *Orbecche* (1541), premiered in his own home before the Duke of Ferrara and his court. He later moved towards a more romantic style of tragedy in *Didone* (1542), *L'Altile* (1543), *Cleopatra* (1543), and *Epizia* (1547), the last supplying Shakespeare with the plot for *Measure for Measure*. The Bard also took the story of *Othello* from Giraldi's *Disdemona and the Moor*. Shakespeare's contemporaries Robert Greene and James Shirley similarly borrowed ideas, as did playwrights in France and Spain.

The plots of Giraldi's plays were among the 112 short stories that he collected in his *Hecatommithi* (1565), a work in the tradition of Boccaccio's *Decameron*.

circle In British theatres, a level of seating above the main area of the auditorium but below the GALLERY; it is often subdivided into the DRESS CIRCLE and upper circle.

Circle-in-the-Square A New York THEATRE-IN-THE-ROUND that opened in 1951 at 5 Sheridan Square for productions by Jose Quintero's Loft Players. The opening play was Richardson and Berney's *Dark of the Moon*; subsequent successes included Tennessee Williams's *Summer and Smoke* (1952) and Truman Capote's *The Grass Harp* (1953). The theatre closed in 1954 as a fire hazard but reopened in 1956 with a revival of O'Neill's *The Iceman Cometh*, directed by Quintero. Some critics thought it superior to the original production and the Circle-in-the-Square became a popular OFF-OFF-BROADWAY venue.

The theatre was demolished in 1960, forcing the company to move to a remodelled music hall on Bleecker Street, subsequently renamed the Circle-in-the-Square, Downtown. The opening play was Genet's *The Balcony*. Later productions included Dylan Thomas's *Under Milk Wood* (1961), Thornton Wilder's *Three Plays for Bleecker Street* (1962), and Athol Fugard's *Boesman and Lena* (1970). In 1972 the company moved to the new Joseph E. Levine Theatre, where it now produces four plays each year. Recent successes have included the musical *I'm Getting My Act Together and Taking It on the Road* (1978) and *As Is*, one of the first dramas to deal with AIDS.

Circle, The A "perfectly serious comedy" by W. Somerset MAUGHAM, often considered his best play. First produced in 1921 in London, it has often been revived, notably in John Gielgud's 1944 repertory season at the Haymarket, when it proved the year's most popular play. Yvonne Arnaud played Lady Kitty Champion-Cheney, Cecil Trouncer was her deceived husband, Gielgud her priggish son, and Leslie Banks her ageing lover. Maugham wrote a note from America to the producer, Binky Beaumont, saying he appreciated his 10% royalty but was not interested in seeing the play again.

The action takes place at a party, at which Lord Champion-Cheney meets Kitty, the wife who deserted him 30 years ago and destroyed his political career. She is still accompanied by Lord Portreus, her lover. Although Lord Champion-Cheney has enjoyed his carefree unmarried life, he is worried because his son's wife, Elizabeth, seems ready to repeat history by eloping with a young businessman. With the help of his wife and her lover he convinces Arnold that he should give Elizabeth her freedom, this being the best way to bring her to her senses. Elizabeth and her lover disappear, and the audience are left wondering if Lord Champion-Cheney's cleverness will pay off.

circuit A group of theatres regularly visited in turn by touring companies. Such circuits grew up in the early 18th century when most provincial towns could not support a permanent theatre. Each company developed its own circuit of towns easily reached from their home base. The circuits were known by the names of their counties or major cities, such as Aberdeen, Manchester, Newcastle, and Suffolk.

The circuit system served as a training ground for actors and developed many outstanding provincial managers. Tate Wilkinson (1739–1803) managed a company for 30 years on the York circuit (which included Hull and Leeds); his autobiography was titled *The Wandering Patentee* (1795). The company run by Sarah BAKER virtually made the Kent circuit its own in the late 18th century, to the extent that Baker built a theatre at each of the 10 stops of her troupe.

VAUDEVILLE circuits developed in America in the late 19th century, taking the names of the conglomerates that had theatre monopolies; these included the Orpheum circuit from Chicago to California and the Keith-Albee circuit in the eastern and midwestern states.

circus An entertainment featuring acrobats and other skilled performers, clowns, and animals. In ancient Rome the word *circus* (meaning ring) referred both to the arena and to the athletic contests, chariot races, gladiatorial combats, acrobatics, wrestling, etc., that took place there. Wild animals were first exhibited in 186 BC at the Circus Maximus and were soon employed to fight one another or humans.

When the modern circus developed in Britain in the late 18th century the main emphasis was on equestrian feats. The famous bareback rider Philip Astley found that riding in a circle created a centrifugal force that aided balance. He devised the horse ring and in 1769 opened ASTLEY'S AMPHITHEATRE in London, soon adding clowns and acrobats. The name 'circus' was first used in the modern sense in 1782, when the Royal Circus was established by Charles Hughes, a former rider at Astley's.

John William Ricketts opened America's first circuses in 1793 in Philadelphia and New York. When travelling fairground performers saw the popularity of this new entertainment, the first tented circuses were created. In Europe, where circus managers preferred permanent buildings, close associations with the theatre were retained. In the 18th century AQUATIC DRAMA and DOG DRAMA were developed in Paris while EQUESTRIAN DRAMA was highly popular in Britain.

The horse remained the mainstay of the circus until the mid 19th century, when menageries were added. The flying trapeze, invented in 1859, soon became a regular feature.

The late 19th century saw an increase in spectacular shows. The US showman P. T. BARNUM went into the circus business in 1870; ten years later he combined with James Bailey and in 1881 the two introduced the first three-ringed circus. The Greatest Show on Earth, as it became known, toured Europe between 1899 and 1902 with a 60-coach circus train. Acts included trapeze artists, acrobats, jugglers, wire-walkers, stilt-walkers, clowns, performing horses, elephants, lions and tigers, sea lions, dogs, and other animals. Barnum and Bailey's was bought by their main competitor, the Ringling Brothers Circus, in 1907. In 1956 Ringling's gave up its vast 'Big Top' tent for permanent buildings.

Recent protests about the use of performing animals have led to some circuses using only human acts, such as juggling and acrobatics. The late 1980s and 1990s also saw the advent of 'alternative' circus, as represented by the anarchic French troupe Archaos.

citizen comedy Elizabethan and Jacobean plays that satirized the manners, social customs, and financial dealings of London's new prosperous merchant class. This popular genre attracted such leading playwrights as Thomas Dekker, Philip Massinger, Ben Jonson, Thomas Middleton, Thomas Heywood, Francis Beaumont, and John Fletcher.

The period was one of economic and social upheaval in which a trading class of entrepreneurs developed into an established middle class. Accordingly, citizen comedy is characterized by plots about social-climbing and greed, with characters marrying for money, tricking heirs out of their fortunes, and dreaming up schemes to get rich quickly. There is much good-natured moralizing.

Typical examples of the genre include THE SHOEMAKER'S HOLIDAY (1599) and *Old Fortunatus* (1600) by Dekker, EASTWARD HO! (1605), a collaboration between Marston,

Jonson, and Chapman Beaumont's THE KNIGHT OF THE BURNING PESTLE (1607), and Middleton's *A Chaste Maid in Cheapside* (1611).

The political conflict between Charles I and Parliament led to darker themes in citizen comedy and its decline prior to the Civil War and INTERREGNUM.

City Dionysia *See* DIONYSIA.

civic theatre In Britain, a system (also called **municipal theatre**), by which theatres managed by a trust receive public funds from local government in order to enrich the cultural life of the community.

Britain's first civic theatre, the BELGRADE THEATRE in Coventry, was established in 1958 by the city council and leased to an independent trust mostly made up of city councillors. The Lyceum, Edinburgh, which opened in 1883, became Scotland's first civic theatre in 1965. Most such theatres are given total artistic freedom despite their subsidies. Many are now kept in business by a combination of local government funding, Arts Council grants, and money raised by the theatre; in 1993 the Greenwich Theatre, London, for example, received £140,000 from local authorities, £185,000 from the Arts Council, and raised £700,000 itself.

Other civic theatres include Manchester's Library and Forum Theatres, owned and operated as repertory theatres by the city council, the Alhambra Theatre, Bradford, established as a regional centre for touring companies by the local authority, and The Playhouse, Nottingham, a theatre built with funds loaned by local government.

In America the term usually refers to publicly funded amateur groups, such as the LITTLE THEATRES.

Clairon, Mlle Stage name of Claire-Josèphe-Hippolyte Léris de la Tude (1723–1803), an excellent French actress. She began as a singer and minor performer at the Comédie-Italienne, where she drew praise from David Garrick. In 1743 she made an acclaimed debut with the Comédie-Française in the title-role of Racine's PHÈDRE. Five years later she made a success of the weak tragedy *Denys le Tyran* by Jean-François Marmontel (1723–99), whose mistress she became. She subsequently performed as leading lady to the celebrated actor Henri-Louis Lekain (1729–78) in such plays as VOLTAIRE's *L'Orphelin de la Chine* (1755), in which she wore a simple robe with loose sleeves in an effort to reform stage costumes. In the 1750s Marmontel persuaded Madame Clairon to drop her declamatory style of acting for a more natural delivery, which she accomplished after tutoring from the encyclopedist and critic Denis Diderot (1713–84).

Madame Clairon retired from the stage after refusing to perform in a play with a disgraced actor – a dispute that led to her imprisonment. She survived with help from Voltaire and in 1773 was invited to the court of the Margrave of Anspach where she wrote her *Mémoires et réflexions sur l'art dramatique* (1799). She died in poverty.

Clandestine Marriage, The A comedy by David GARRICK and George Colman the Elder (*see* COLMAN FAMILY), first performed in 1766. A row developed between the two authors when Garrick refused to play the role of Lord Ogleby. The part was created by Tom King (1730–1804) and became a much sought-after role. The 1975 CHICHESTER FESTIVAL saw an acclaimed revival with Alistair Sim in his last role; the production went on to become a big hit in the West End.

The story concerns the secret marriage of Fanny Sterling and her father's clerk, Lovewell. Her wealthy father has arranged a marriage between Fanny's sister and Sir John Melvil, the nephew of Lord Ogleby. Melvil and Ogleby arrive to make arrangements, but Melvil now expresses his love for the more attractive Fanny. Fearing to reveal her marriage, she fends him off and appeals to Ogleby who, mistaking this for an advance, proposes marriage himself. When Lovewell is discovered in Fanny's bedroom, however, Lord Ogleby defends the couple and brings about a happy ending.

claque A body of hired applauders at a theatre, etc. The practice was first systematized by a M. Sauton, who in 1820 established in Paris an office to secure the success of dramatic performances. The manager ordered the required number of *claqueurs*, who were divided into *commissaires*, who committed the piece to memory and noisily pointed out its merits; *rieurs*, who laughed at the puns and jokes; *pleureurs*, chiefly women who held their handkerchiefs to their eyes at the emotional parts; *chatouilleurs*, whose role was to keep the audience in good humour; and *bisseurs*, who were to cry 'bis' or encore.

Claque is also the French for an opera-hat, and the word was sometimes used in this sense by 19th-century English writers.

Cleopatra (69–30 BC) Queen of Egypt, being joint ruler with and wife of her brother Ptolemy Dionysius until his death. In 48 BC she was driven from the throne but was reinstated in 47 by Julius Caesar, by whom she had a son. In 41 Mark Antony fell under her spell and repudiated his wife Octavia. When he was defeated at Actium by Octavius (the future emperor Augustus), he committed suicide. Cleopatra followed suit, supposedly by means of the bite of an asp.

The most famous and fascinating woman of the ancient world, Cleopatra has appeared on the stage in numerous guises. The "infinite variety" of Shakespeare's Cleopatra – a woman of fleeting moods and ambiguous motives who nevertheless achieves tragic grandeur in death – makes this perhaps the most challenging female role in the English theatre (*see* ANTONY AND CLEOPATRA). Cleopatra also appears as a leading character in Samuel Daniel's Senecan tragedy *Cleopatra* (1594), Dryden's ALL FOR LOVE, and Shaw's CAESAR AND CLEOPATRA, in which she is presented as a spoilt teenager.

Clive, Kitty (Catherine Raftor; 1711–85) British actress, who excelled in farce, burlesque, and low comedy. She made her debut as a singer at Drury Lane. Colley Cibber (*see* CIBBER FAMILY) discovered her comic talents in 1729, when she played Phillida in his *Love in a Riddle*.

Kitty became a famous comedian and wrote several short farces herself. Her portrait was painted by such leading artists as Hogarth. She remained at Drury Lane for most of her career, enjoying a sweet-and-sour relationship with David GARRICK. Although they admired each other's acting, he angered Kitty by refusing to let her play high comedy and tragedy. She was once seen standing in the wing cursing Garrick's acting, which had just brought tears to her eyes. Suddenly angry at her emotions, she rushed off thundering, "Damn him, he could act a *gridiron*."

On another occasion she was in a play with the celebrated Ned Shuter, who one evening had to be replaced by Thomas Weston. As the substitute entered, the furious audience began chanting "Shuter! Shuter!". Each time Weston attempted to speak his lines, the cries redoubled: "Shuter! Shuter!". Finally the hapless actor pointed at the patient Kitty, and asked, "Why should I shoot her? She plays the part very well." The house rippled with appreciative laughter and respectfully let him continue.

When Kitty retired in 1769 her admirer Horace Walpole presented her with a small house called 'Clive's Den' at Strawberry Hill near Twickenham. There her charm and wit were relished by such devotees as Dr Johnson.

cloak-and-sword play (*comedia de capa y espada*) A type of 17th-century Spanish play characterized by romantic adventure, intrigue, and duelling. No matter how tragic the main plot, there was always a comic subplot. Spanish dramatists who contributed to the genre included Lope de VEGA and Tirso de Molina.

Originally, the cloak and sword signified no more than the rank of the chief characters. However, the characters often disguised themselves with their cloaks and became involved in intrigues, revenges, and plots that necessitated frequent use of their swords. There was often a final duel. Because of this, in France (and through French influence in England) a cloak-and-sword play came to denote a play of swashbuckling adventure. The plays were also sometimes called **cloak and dagger plays**. By association, the undercover and often melodramatic activities of those involved in espionage, etc., came to be called *cloak and dagger operations*.

close. closure of the theatres *See* INTERREGNUM.

We never closed Slogan associated with the WINDMILL THEATRE, London, which, under its proprietor Vivian Van Damm, was the only London theatre to remain open throughout the whole of the Blitz in 1940. It did in fact close in 1964 for conversion to a cinema and again in 1981 for further refurbishment.

closet drama A play intended for reading rather than performance on stage. SENECA's dramas were probably written to be read aloud and include extravagant scenes that would be very difficult to stage.

During the Romantic and Victorian era many established poets wrote closet dramas (*see* POETIC DRAMA); some have actually been produced, with varying degrees of success. Laurence OLIVIER had a crashing failure in 1928 with Tennyson's verse play *Harold*, published during the poet's lifetime but never before performed. When Olivier, then 20, appeared in the play wearing a long blonde wig he was anxious to make an impression in his first leading London role; however, Tennyson's "tediously undramatic text" doomed his best efforts.

cloth A large section of canvas or similar material that hangs from the flies as painted scenery. It is called a **sky cloth** when coloured blue to represent the sky. A **ceiling cloth** is used to create a ceiling for a BOX SET (in which role it superseded the BOOK CEILING). A **backcloth** is suspended at the rear of a scene while a **frontcloth** usually hangs far downstage, where it is often used to hide a scene change. A cloth was formerly called a **drop** in Britain and sometimes still goes by this name in America.

cloud. Cloud-Cuckoo-Land The *Nephelococcygia* of THE BIRDS, by Aristophanes; an imaginary city built in the air by the birds. Hence any impractical Utopian scheme.

clouding A BORDER painted with a cloudy sky. In England they were frequently used in 17th-century court masques such as Inigo JONES's *Salmacida Spolia* (1640), which employed 'side-clouds' as well. Cloudings continued to be used into the mid-18th century. They could often be moved sideways by hooked poles to reveal a bright sky behind.

Clouds, The A comedy by ARISTOPHANES, first performed in 423 BC in Athens. It is an attack on 'modern' education and the morals taught by the sophists. In the play Socrates and his pupils are ridiculed and their school, the *Phrontisterion* ('Thinking Shop') is eventually burned to the ground. Scholars have often wondered why Aristophanes chose Socrates as an example of a false philosopher; some believe he was selected simply because of his fame.

The chorus's entrance song is considered one of Aristophanes's finest lyrics; in the translation by B. B. Rogers (1916) it runs:

Clouds of all hue,
Rise we aloft with our garments of dew.
Come from old Ocean's unchangeable bed,
Come till the mountain's green summits we tread,
Come to the peaks with their landscapes untold,
Gaze on the Earth with her harvest of gold...

The Clouds also contains a curious example of the *parabasis*, or choral address to the audience. At one point the chorus steps forward to berate the audience for its poor taste in withholding first prize from some of Aristophanes's plays in previous contests.

clown The clown of circus and PANTOMIME, in his baggy costume, whitened face, grotesque red lips, and odd little tuft of black hair, probably derives ultimately from the devil as he appeared in medieval miracle plays. He is also the descendant of many court fools and jesters and of the characters of the COMMEDIA DELL'ARTE. Of all the clowns, Joseph GRIMALDI (1779–1837) and the Swiss GROCK (1880–1959), were outstanding.

In the plays of Shakespeare and the Elizabethans the term 'clown' is usually reserved for a slow-witted buffoon, such as the anonymous clowns in *Othello* and *Antony and Cleopatra* and the gravediggers in *Hamlet*. Purveyors of witty sophisticated humour, such as Feste in *Twelfth Night* and Touchstone in *As You Like It*, are called fools (*see* COURT FOOL).

send in the clowns A phrase said when something goes wrong, meaning 'keep things going' or 'the show must go on'. It comes from the circus where, if there was an accident, backstage drama, or other problem, the clowns were sent into the ring to divert the audience. The expression dates from the 1930s. 'Send in the Clowns' is the title of an evocative song by the US composer Stephen SONDHEIM, first heard in his 1973 musical *A Little Night Music*.

coal. Coal Hole *See* SONG-AND-SUPPER ROOMS.

coaling Theatrical slang for telling phrases and speeches, as, 'My part is full of *coaling lines*.' Possibly from *cole*, an old cant term for money, such a part being profitable.

Cochran, Sir Charles B(lake) (1872–1951). The leading British impresario of his day and the most famous producer of revues between the wars. His shows ranged from boxing to the Diaghilev ballet. He advanced the careers of Noël Coward, Beatrice Lillie, Gertrude Lawrence, and Jack Buchanan, and introduced Londoners to HOUDINI, Elisabeth Bergner, Sarah Bernhardt, and Eleonora Duse, amongst others. He was knighted in 1948.

Cochran, universally known as *Cockie*, enjoyed taking a high profile. His rival impresario, Binkie Beaumont, once said, "I love anonymity. I haven't the temperament to be a Cochran." The 1973 musical comedy *Cockie* by Peter Saunders was based on Cochran's life and opened in London at the Vaudeville Theatre. The impresario was played by Max Wall.

Cochran made his stage debut at the Royal Clarence Music Hall, Dover, at the age of 16; his one song was so bad that the manager refused to pay him. Two years later he went to New York and wore the sole off a boot seeking work. His first US job was playing seven parts in the revue *Round the World in Eighty Days*. In 1897 he produced Ibsen's *John Gabriel Borkman* on Broadway. He returned to London in 1902.

Cochran's first revue was the intimate *Odds and Ends* (1914) at the Ambassadors Theatre. After the war he mounted a series of lavish productions at the London Pavilion with his chorus of 'Young Ladies'; these included *As You Were* (1918) and *London, Paris and New York* (1920). His revues emphasized wit as well as dancing and spectacle; Noël Coward wrote three pieces for him, including *Cochran's 1931 Revue*.

More high-brow productions included London's first Eugene O'NEILL play, *Anna Christie* (1925). This led to his bankruptcy, but Cochran bounced back by producing seven of Coward's most successful plays, including *Private Lives* (1930) and *Cavalcade* (1931). After World War II Cochran had a hit with the musical comedy *Bless the Bride* (1947) but otherwise failed to keep up with changes in public taste. He published several volumes of memoirs including *Cock-a-Doodle-Do* in 1941.

Cochran was generous to his actors. When Elisabeth Bergner became ill during her London debut in 1933, he closed *Escape Me Never* for three weeks and paid the company throughout. When *Private Lives* moved from Edinburgh to its London opening, the trip was "swathed in luxury" by Cochran, with first-class railway carriages and hotels for the company.

Cochran's attitude to young actresses supposedly created the term 'casting-couch'. Young girls who attracted him would be given a 'special audition' in his office where he had installed a large comfortable sofa behind his desk.

> When things were good, he resembled a rooster; when bad, a benign bishop.
>
> VIVIAN ELLIS

Cockaigne An imaginary country of laziness and luxury, also known as **Lubberland**. The concept dates back to the early Middle Ages. In this shirkers' paradise salaries are paid for sleeping, rivers flow with wine, houses are made of cake and sugar, buttered birds fall from the sky, and pigs run around with forks already inserted. Cockaigne has provided themes for European folk dramas and carnivals, and many playwrights have mentioned it. In JONSON's *Bartholomew Fair* (1614), for instance, one character asks another how she expects to find a pig without looking for it: "Will it run off o' the spit into our mouths, think you? As in Lubber-land?"

The derivation of 'Cockaigne' is uncertain, although it might come from the German *kuchen* meaning cake. The name Cockaigne has also been applied humorously to east London as the land of the Cockneys (as in Elgar's *Cockaigne* overture).

Cockpit Theatre A theatre in Drury Lane, London, originally built for cockfighting in 1609. Christopher BEESTON turned it into a private theatre in 1616 by adding a roof and renovating the interior. His company planned to move there in 1617, but the Cockpit was destroyed by fire when apprentices on a riotous Shrove Tuesday spree set it ablaze.

Beeston rebuilt the venue and renamed it the Phoenix, subsequently leasing it to several companies, including in 1635 the strolling players of the French actor Floridor. Beeston's own company of boy actors, Beeston's Boys, moved into the theatre following his death in 1638. During the Puritan INTERREGNUM the theatre staged illegal performances and was raided by soldiers in 1649. William DAVENANT, however, won official approval to stage 'plays with music', such as *The Cruelty of the Spaniards in Peru* (1658) and *Sir Francis Drake* (1659).

On the Restoration the theatre was reopened by John Rhodes, a former prompter at Blackfriars Theatre who had been appointed Keeper of the Cockpit in 1644. His small company included Thomas BETTERTON and other young players who later became famous, but his licence was withdrawn after one year when the PATENT THEATRES came into being. Thereafter the theatre lost audiences to the new Drury Lane. It closed in 1665.

There was also a private **Cockpit-in-Court** theatre in Whitehall, so called because it was converted from a cockpit in about 1604. The KING'S MEN and other companies performed there for the court and later for the public (until 1664).

Cocktail Party, The T. S. ELIOT's verse drama about marital illusions. It was first performed at the 1949 Edinburgh Festival with Alec GUINNESS as the Harley Street psychiatrist Sir Henry Harcourt-Reilly and opened in London the next year with Rex HARRISON. Guinness played the role with austerity and Harrison with warm charm. When Harrison confessed to the director, Martin Browne, that he could not grasp what some of Eliot's lines meant, Browne told him not to worry because the audience would not understand them either. Eliot himself was deeply concerned about the play's symbolism, even asking that Harrison keep his arms down to 45 degrees to "avoid the crucifixion suggestion."

Based in part on the *Alcestis* of EURIPIDES, the play is set at a cocktail party hosted by Edward and Lavinia Chamberlayne, both of whom have lovers. The psychiatrist shows the couple and Edward's lover, Celia, how they have all lived an illusion. Following his advice, the Chamberlaynes are reconciled and Celia seeks salvation as a missionary in the East, where she is crucified on an anthill by tribesmen. The psychiatrist sees the death as a predestined event and does not blame himself at all:

> You will have to live with these
> memories and make them
> Into something new. Only by acceptance
> Of the past will you alter its meaning.

Cocteau, Jean (1889–1963) French writer who won acclaim as a playwright, critic, poet, novelist, film director, and artist. His plays ranged from classical tragedy to romantic melodrama but usually dealt with themes of love and death. Cocteau was the son of two wealthy lawyers. Although medically disqualified for military duty, he fought in World War I under an assumed name. In his early twenties he was challenged by Diaghilev to collaborate on a work for the Ballet Russe in Paris, and helped to create *Parade*, which opened in 1917.

Cocteau found acclaim in 1922 with his adaptation of Sophocles's ANTIGONE, directed by Charles Dullin with a set by Picasso. This was followed by *Orphée* (1924) directed by Georges Pitoëff. The next decade saw his powerful MONODRAMA *La Voix Humaine* (1930), *La Machine Infernale* (1934), based on the story of Oedipus and directed by Louis Jouvet, and *Les Parents Terribles* (1938; seen in London in 1951 as *Intimate Relations*).

Cocteau's greatest international success was the romantic costume drama, *L'Aigle à deux têtes* (1946), which opened in Paris with Edwige Feuillère in the role of the Queen. Later that year it enjoyed a long run at the Lyric Theatre, Hammersmith, where Eileen Herlie made her name in the same part. It was also successful on Broadway.

After World War II, Cocteau concentrated on writing for the cinema. He died of a heart attack after hearing that his friend Edith Piaf had died earlier that day.

Cohan, George M(ichael) (1878–1942) US vaudeville's most famous showman in the first decade of the century, Cohan was the embodiment of American flag-waving brashness. The pint-sized entertainer was an actor, songwriter, dancer, playwright, and manager. In 1940 President Roosevelt presented him with a Congressional Medal, the nation's highest civilian award, for writing the wartime songs 'Over There' and 'It's A Grand Old Flag', and in 1959 New York erected a statue to him at the corner of Broadway and 46th Street.

His other songs included 'I'm A Yankee Doodle Dandy' and 'Give My Regards To Broadway'. He could not write music and had to whistle his tunes to a transcriber. Cohan also needed peace and quiet to compose; after he became famous, he would sometimes hire a carriage on a train to work overnight, not caring what the destination was.

Cohan was born on July 3 but always gave the date as July 4, Independence Day. As a child, he appeared on stage with his parents and sister as 'The Four Cohans' and soon began writing songs and skits. He made his adult debut at the Savoy Theatre in his own play, *The Governor's Son* (1901). Later hits included *Little Johnny Jones* (1904), about an American jockey in England, *George Washington, Jr* (1906), *Over There* (1917), an all-star revue to raise money for the Red Cross, *The Song and Dance*

Man (1923), and *American Born* (1925). He opened his own George M. Cohan theatre in 1911.

Late in his career, he starred as Nat Miller in Eugene O'Neill's AH! WILDERNESS (1933) and upset the playwright by interpolating new lines of his own each night. In 1968 Joel Grey starred in *George M*, a Broadway musical based on Cohan's life, while the 1943 film musical *Yankee Doodle Dandy* starred James Cagney as the entertainer.

Cohan often wondered how he succeeded:

> As a dancer, I could never do over three steps. As a composer I could never find use for over four or five notes in my musical numbers. As a violinist, I could never learn to play above the first position. I'm a one-key piano player, and as a playwright, most of my plays have been presented in two acts for the simple reason that I could seldom think of an idea for a third act.

collective creation A method of creating new plays through the collaboration of actors and other company members with a dramatist. Some collective groups have a director who makes final decisions, but the full company's ideas are considered throughout the play's development and staging. British companies based on collective creation have included the People Show (founded in 1966), Pip Simmons Theatre Group (1968), and Welfare State International (1968).

Collective creation was probably practised to some degree by the 16th-century COMMEDIA DELL'ARTE troupes and Elizabethan companies. The modern movement was pioneered by New York's LIVING THEATRE, formed in 1947 by Julian Beck and Judith Malina. The reaction against commercial and bureaucratic methods of production gathered pace during the 1960s, when small alternative theatre groups proliferated. Improvisation became fashionable and collective creation was an apt way of catering for it.

Experimentation on stage was a strong point with such groups as the Performance Group in New York (1967) and the Mabou Mimes in Nova Scotia, Canada (1970). Other companies had explicit political aims, such as El Teatro Campesino (1965), which supported Chicano migrant farm workers (*see* CHICANO THEATRE), and the Free Southern Theatre (1963) of New Orleans, which advocated Black civil rights. In the 1970s and 1980s collective creation became the norm for Feminist Theatre companies such as At the Foot of the Mountain in Minneapolis and the Women's Experimental Theatre in New York.

Collier, Jeremy (1650–1726) English clergyman, who in 1698 published a bitter and influential condemnation of the Restoration stage. His *Short View of the Immorality and Profaneness of the English Stage* accused such leading playwrights as Dryden, Vanbrugh, and Otway of mocking the Church and using profane language.

The outburst touched a nerve with the public and several of the accused were goaded into publishing defences of their work; the resulting controversy lasted for more than 10 years. Dryden was obliged to print a 'confession' of his faults and d'Urfey and CONGREVE were prosecuted. The actor Thomas Betterton and the actress Mrs Bracegirdle were fined and the protests of all the victims were swept away on a tide of public indignation. Perhaps the chief sufferer was Congreve who, after issuing a reply to Collier's criticisms in which he described playwriting as "a difficult and thankless study", wrote virtually nothing more for the stage. Collier's attack, and the ensuing controversy, helped to bring about the demise of the Restoration tradition and to usher in a new era of timid gentility on the stage. Over a century later Byron was to lament in *Don Juan*:

> The days of Comedy are gone, alas!
> When Congreve's fool could vie with
> Molière's *bête*:
> Society is smooth'd to that excess,
> That manners hardly differ more than
> dress.

Colman family George Colman the elder (1732–94) and his son George Colman the younger (1762–1836), both of whom were playwrights and managed COVENT GARDEN.

The elder Colman was a friend of David GARRICK, whose name appeared on the title page of Colman's first play, the farce *Polly Honeycombe*. It was first performed in 1760 at Garrick's Drury Lane, and Colman admitted writing it the following year, after the success of his play *The Jealous Wife*. His most acclaimed work was the comedy *The Clandestine Marriage* (1766), cowritten with Garrick, who caused a rift with Colman when he refused to act in it.

Colman and three partners bought the patent to Covent Garden in 1767. During his management Oliver Goldsmith's only two plays were premiered: *The Good-Natured Man* was coolly received in 1768, but *She Stoops to Conquer* was a great success in 1773. Three years later Colman took over the HAYMARKET and ran it for 18 years until his death. During that time he produced several plays by his son, including the successful comic opera *Inkle and Yarico* (1787).

The younger Colman became manager of Covent Garden in 1794 and remained there for nine years. His plays included *The Iron Chest* (1796), based on Godwin's gothic novel *Caleb Williams*; Edmund Kean revived it in 1816, finding a great tragic part in the character of Sir Edward Mortimer.

Colman was also a successful writer of comedy, creating such memorable characters as Dr Pangloss in *The Heir-at-Law* (1797), and Dennis Brulgruddery in *John Bull; or, The Englishman's Fireside* (1803). In 1817 he wrote *The Actor of all Work; or, First and Second Floor*, a drama with an innovative set that showed two rooms simultaneously.

Colman was known to be extravagant and unstable both financially and in his personal life, having secretly married Clara Morris, a young actress, in 1784. He was nevertheless appointed Examiner of Plays in 1824 and remained in the post until his death, demonstrating a surprisingly strict sense of propriety in judging new works for the stage.

Colosseum The great Flavian AMPHITHEATRE of ancient Rome, said to be named after the colossal statue of Nero that stood close by in the Via Sacra. It was begun by Vespasian in 72 AD and for 400 years was the scene of gladiatorial contests. The name has since been applied to other amphitheatres and places of amusement, such as the LONDON COLISEUM. *Compare* PALLADIUM.

colour wheel A metal wheel attached to the front of a spotlight and rotated manually or automatically to change circles of coloured gel and project different colours of light onto the stage.

Columbine A stock character in the English HARLEQUINADE (and later the PANTOMIME), deriving ultimately from the COMMEDIA DELL'ARTE, in which she was a comic serving girl. In the Harlequinade she was the daughter of PANTALOON and the sweetheart of HARLEQUIN; like him, she was supposed to be invisible to mortal eyes. In Italian *Columbina*, meaning dove-like, is a pet name for a lady-love.

comedia In the 17th-century Spanish theatre, any full-length play.

comedia a fantasia *See* TORRES NAHARRO.

comedia a noticia *See* TORRES NAHARRO.

comedia de capa y espada *See* CLOAK-AND-SWORD PLAY.

comedian. ***Comedians*** A play by the British dramatist Trevor GRIFFITHS, first performed in 1975 at the Nottingham Playhouse. Griffiths uses a story about aspiring stand-up comedians making their first public appearance at a bingo hall to explore the social function of humour.

The student comedians arrive at their Manchester classroom to receive last words of wisdom from their teacher, Eddie Waters, before moving on to the hall. The group includes an insurance agent, a milkman, an Irish docker, and a Jew. Performing between bingo sessions, the comedians have uneven success with their jokes; some deliberately pander to the racial and sexual prejudices of the audience. By contrast, the radical Gethin Price presents a strange politically aggressive act that involves dummies and blood. When the group returns to class for evaluation, the student Bert Challoner berates Price for his "repulsive" act. After everyone else departs, Price and Waters stay behind to discuss what humour means and how it should be used.

comedian's graveyard Nickname for the Glasgow Empire, a venue that was notoriously tough on English comedians. The joke name became reality in 1918 when Mark Sheridan, a singer of comic songs ('I Do Like to Be Beside the Seaside'), received such a poor reception that he walked to Kelvin Grove Park after the show and shot himself.

The comedian Eric Morecambe said he knew top English performers who would "rather have open-heart surgery than face Glasgow". His partner Ernie Wise recalled:

> I can remember coming off at Glasgow one night to the sound of our own footsteps! And the fireman said: "They're beginning to like you".

Other famous names to have played at the Empire include Charlie Chaplin and W. C. Fields.

comédie. ***comédie-ballet*** A 17th-century French genre in which scenes of dialogue alternated with ballet and music. It became especially popular during the 1660s at the court of Louis XIV, where courtiers participated in the entertainment. An extravagant example was *Pleasures of the Enchanted Island* (1664), for which the palace of the enchantress Alcine was constructed on a stage in the middle of a lake at Versailles and then destroyed by fire as part of the performance.

MOLIÈRE refined the *comédie-ballet* by enlarging the role of the dialogue in such works as *The Bores* (1661) and *The Forced Marriage* (1664). Another leading exponent of the genre was the composer Jean-Baptiste Lully (1632–87), who subsequently founded the French opera. Operetta and opera eventually superseded the *comédie-ballet.*

Comédie-Française The French national theatre. The oldest and most renowned of Europe's state-subsidized theatres, it is also known as the **Théâtre-Français** and **La Maison de Molière**. Louis XIV founded it by decree in 1680, and a company was formed by merging the troupes from the HÔTEL DE BOURGOGNE and the Théâtre du Marais (with which MOLIÈRE's Théâtre de Guénégaud had already merged). The new company converted a tennis court into a theatre and used this for their performances until 1770. They subsequently played at the Salles des Machines in the Tuileries until 1789, when they moved to their new theatre, the Odéon, on the Left Bank.

In the same year, however, the French Revolution split the company in two: the conservatives, under François-René Molé, became the Théâtre de la Nation, while the more revolutionary became the Théâtre de la République under François-Joseph TALMA. The two groups reunited in 1803 at Talma's Théâtre de la Révolution.

Following a decree issued by Napoleon in 1812, the Comédie-Française was reorganized along lines proposed by Molière in 1658. These make it a cooperative in which the actors hold shares. A new member is hired at a fixed salary on probation as a *pensionnaire*; he or she may become a *sociétaire* only when a full member dies or resigns. *Sociétaires* are eligible for a pension upon retirement. The Comédie-Française underwent some reorganization in 1945, with the administrative head now being appointed by the minister of education.

Although the theatre's repertory is based on the French classics, modern plays are also produced. The Comédie-Française is acclaimed for its splendid ensemble performances led by the nation's most famous actors; in the 20th century these have included Sarah BERNHARDT and Jean-Louis BARRAULT. More recently foreign directors have sometimes been invited to give the company a more international outlook, including the Englishman Terry Hands who since 1972 has directed such works as *Richard III, Twelfth Night,* and *Murder in the Cathedral.*

Comédie-Italienne A general name used from about 1680 for companies presenting the Italian COMMEDIA DELL'ARTE in France. Italian troupes had first come to Paris in the 16th century, performing at the Salle du Petit-Bourbon and the Palais-Royal before settling into the HÔTEL DE BOURGOGNE in 1680. Louis XIV subsequently gave permission for the Italian companies to act in French, despite strong opposition from the Comédie-Française. The French playwrights Charles-Rivière Dufresny and Jean-François Regnard wrote a series of comedies (often in collaboration) for the Comédie-Italienne from 1688 onwards.

The Comédie-Italienne companies were banished from France in 1697 for offending Madame de Maintenon, the king's mistress, with their production of *La Fausse Prude.* After Louis's death in 1715, they returned to the Hôtel de Bourgogne under Lélio (Luigi Riccoboni) and created a new style of acting that combined Italian exuberance with French elegance. In particular, the companies excelled in the sophisticated comedies of MARIVAUX. By this time, however, the companies had become Italian in little more than name, the last Italian actor being CARLIN (1713–83).

In the mid 18th century they began to exploit the fashionable new genre of *opera buffa* (comic opera). Carlo GOLDONI, who wrote over 200 plays, settled in Paris to direct the Comédie-Italienne in the 1760s. In 1783 the company moved to a new theatre on the street now known as the Boulevard des Italiens; they merged with the Théâtre Feydeau to form the Opéra-Comique in 1801.

comédie larmoyante (Fr. sentimental comedy) A type of sentimental comedy that became fashionable in the 18th-century French theatre. It was popularized by Pierre Claude Nivelle de La Chausée (1692–1754) in some 40 moralistic dramas that included *La Fausse Antipathie* (1733), *Le Préjugé à mode* (1735), and *Mélanide* (1741). His usual formula was to place ordinary characters in an unhappy situation that nevertheless works out happily.

La Chaussée's plays were translated into German, Italian, Dutch, and English. The influence of *comédie larmoyante* was especially strong in Germany. It Britain it influenced the milder comedy of sentiment that superseded the witty and outrageous COMEDY OF MANNERS of the Restoration era.

comédie rosse A type of bitter comedy staged by André Antoine (1858–1943) at his THÉÂTRE LIBRE, a private theatre club in Paris, in the late 19th century. Many were written by the dramatists Henri Becque (1837–99) and Georges Ancey (Georges Mathevon de Curnieu; 1860–1917). Examples include Becque's *Les Corbeaux* (1882), an exposure of greed, and *La Parisienne* (1885), which focuses on the amorality of the main character. Ancey's contributions included *Les Inséparables* (1889), in which two friends share a mistress and *L'Écoles des veufs* (1889), in which the same mistress is shared by a father and his son. The plays were mainly staged using amateur actors and naturalistic scenery.

The notoriety of the *comédies rosses* gave the Théâtre Libre a bad name and generally helped to discredit the burgeoning naturalist movement with the general public (*see* NATURALISM). Even liberal playgoers were repelled by the tone of some of the works and the way in which vice went unpunished and virtue unrewarded. At the same time they helped to liberalize attitudes concerning what was permissible on the stage. Now considered uninspired, the plays are very rarely revived.

comedy A work characterized by humour and a happy ending. The term (Gr. *komē-ōdē*) originally meant a village song, referring to Greek village merrymakings, in which songs still have a conspicuous place. Greek comedy appears to have originated from such village revels and certain elements of the festivities connected with the worship of DIONYSUS. The use of a CHORUS may have derived from the practice of revellers masquerading as birds, frogs, fishes, etc.

Greek comedy is traditionally subdivided into three periods; the boisterous OLD COMEDY of ARISTOPHANES, the transitional MIDDLE COMEDY, and the NEW COMEDY of MENANDER. The latter was the main influence on the development of the COMEDY OF INTRIGUE during the early Roman era. The tradition of classical comedy disappeared during the medieval period (although many mystery plays contain elements of rough farce) to be revived at the Renaissance in the COMMEDIA DELL'ARTE. In the 16th and 17th centuries writers such as SHAKESPEARE, Lope de VEGA, and MOLIÈRE, raised the genre to the highest level of literary art, blending poetry and wit with a profound moral and psychological insight. *See also* TRAGEDY.

Comedy of Errors, The An early comedy by SHAKESPEARE, possibly his first experiment in the genre. It was first performed in 1594 at Gray's Inn Hall, London, where records refer to "a company of base and common fellows" that probably included the Bard. With 1777 lines, it is his shortest play. Theodore Komisarjevsky directed a modern-dress version at Stratford in 1938, while Peter Hall mounted an acclaimed Royal Shakespeare Company production at The Warehouse in 1976. The play was made into a Broadway musical comedy in 1938 by George Abbott, Lorenz Hart, and Richard Rodgers as *The Boys from Syracuse* (*see under* BOY).

The plot derives from Plautus's *Menaechmi* (*see* MENECHMIANS), which was itself based on an earlier Greek model. The story begins when the elderly Aegeon from Syracuse puts ashore in Ephesus; because there is enmity between the cities, he is sentenced to die unless he finds the money for a ransom by nightfall. Asked why he came to Ephesus, Aegeon explains how he lost his wife and one of their identical twin sons years ago in a storm at sea, together with one of a pair of twin servants. More recently, his remaining son and the remaining servant had set out to find their brothers only to go missing themselves. So Aegeon had followed. Unknown to him, both sons and both servants are now in Ephesus. The existence of two sets of twins with the same names in the same city causes multiple confusions before the entire family is reunited and Aegeon is freed.

comedy of humours A form of comedy based on the 'humours' or fixed personality traits of the characters. The genre became popular in the late 16th century. The best-known English examples are Ben JONSON's *Every Man in his Humour* (1598) and *Every Man out of his Humour* (1599). Other English playwrights to attempt the comedy of humours included Francis Beaumont in such works as *The Woman-Hater* (1606), John Fletcher in *The Scornful Lady* (1613), and Thomas Shadwell in *The Sullen Lovers; or, The Impertinents* (1668).

The term 'humours' refers to the medieval belief that an individual's character was determined by the proportion of four cardinal humours or fluids in his body: blood, phlegm, choler or yellow bile, and melancholy or black bile. Hence the expressions sanguine, phlegmatic, choleric, and melancholic.

comedy of intrigue A form of comedy in which the humour flows from complicated relationships and contrived situations. It originated in the classical Roman theatre, where a typical comedy might involve a noble youth caught up in an impossible love affair with a slave girl, only to find that she was swapped as a child and is actually of his class. The 17th-century Spanish theatre saw numerous plays about the romantic intrigues of young adventurers (*see* CLOAK-AND-SWORD PLAY). The genre was further developed in France by Molière and in England by Shakespeare and the writers of Restoration Comedy. English examples include Aphra Behn's topical comedy *The Feign'd Curtizans; or, A Night's Intrigue* (1678).

comedy of manners A form of sophisticated comedy that satirizes the pretentious trifling of the upper classes. The genre can be traced back to the Greek NEW COMEDY but in its modern form was essentially created by MOLIÈRE in such plays as *Les Précieuses ridicules* (1658) and *Le Médecin malgré lui* (1666).

In England the genre flowered after the Restoration, following the success of George Etherege's *The Comical Revenge; or, Love in a Tub* (1664). English examples include Wycherley's THE GENTLEMAN DANCING MASTER (1671), Vanbrugh's THE PROVOK'D WIFE (1697), Congreve's THE WAY OF THE WORLD (1700), Farquhar's THE BEAUX' STRATAGEM (1707), Goldsmith's SHE STOOPS TO CONQUER (1773), and Sheridan's THE SCHOOL FOR SCANDAL (1777). In the last, Lady Teazle berates her husband for denying her "little elegant expenses":

> LADY TEAZLE For my part, I should think you would like to have your wife thought a woman of taste.
>
> SIR PETER Aye – there again – taste! Zounds! madam, you had no taste when you married me!
>
> LADY TEAZLE That's very true, indeed, Sir Peter; and, after having married you, I am sure I should never pretend to taste again.

The elegant wit of the comedy of manners was revived in the late 19th century by Oscar Wilde in such plays as *Lady Windermere's Fan* (1892) and *The Importance of Being Earnest* (1895). In the 20th century some of the plays of Noël Coward, such as *Private Lives* (1930), belong to this genre.

comedy of morals A form of comedy that highlights and condemns behaviour that is considered socially unacceptable. Moral didacticism was a feature of classical Roman comedy, especially in the *fabula togata* (*see* FABULA). Ben Jonson described comedy as being "a thing throughout pleasant and ridiculous and accommodated to the correction of manners." Molière was of the same opinion; his TARTUFFE (1664), a satirical attack on religious hypocrisy, is perhaps the epitome of the comedy of morals.

Comedy Theatre A small London theatre in Panton Street in the West End. Until its redecoration in 1954, the Comedy boasted London's oldest Victorian auditorium, designed by Thomas Verity in a French Renaissance style with rich moulding finished in white and gold. Today the Comedy seats 780 in a cosy drawing-room atmosphere. It opened in 1881 with Audran's *The Mascotte*.

In 1956 the New Watergate Theatre Club was formed to present unlicensed plays at the theatre; these included Tennessee Williams's *Cat on a Hot Tin Roof* (1957) and Peter Shaffer's *Five Finger Exercise* (1959). Male nudity featured in *Fortune and Men's Eyes* (1968) and female nudity in *Steaming* (1981). In 1969 *There's a Girl in my Soup* continued its record run of 2547 performances at the Comedy, having transferred from the Globe. A successful revival of Pinero's *Trelawny of the 'Wells'* opened in 1992.

command performance A performance of a play, solo act, or other entertainment requested by a monarch or head of government. Although many kings and queens enjoyed theatrical presentations at court, it was Queen VICTORIA who formalized the command performance; in 20 years

(1881–1901) she arranged some 30 private events at Windsor Castle. Today command performances are normally given to raise funds for charities.

Command performances are not restricted to the legitimate theatre. The Royal Command Variety Performance at the PALLADIUM theatre in London has always included popular entertainers. The tradition began in 1912, when the theatre manager Oswald Stoll arranged a variety performance at the LONDON COLISEUM for King George V and Queen Mary. The performers included Harry TATE, 'the one-eyed Kaffir', LITTLE TICH, and Vesta TILLEY. When the latter made a daring appearance in trousers, Queen Mary averted her eyes from the stage.

commedia. commedia dell'arte A comic theatrical genre that evolved in 16th-century Italy and went on to enjoy success throughout Europe. Performances, which consisted of improvisations based around skeletal scenarios, employed stock characters such as PANTALOON, IL CAPITANO, IL DOTTORE, and the ZANNI, all of whom were distinguished by masks and emblematic costumes. Players, who usually specialized in one role, would often make slight alterations to masks and costumes in order to customize the character.

The first troupes emerged around the mid-16th century performing (in contrast to the COMMEDIA ERUDITA) comedy suited to popular taste in the commonly spoken language of the time. The first famous *commedia dell'arte* company was the GELOSI, who began performing in 1568. The next 50 years saw the emergence of other notable troupes, including the DESIOSI, the CONFIDENTI, the ACCESI, and the FEDELI. *Commedia dell'arte* troupes are known to have toured France in the early 1570s, and the Gelosi, who were summoned to play before the Royal Court at Blois in 1577, are known to have played in Paris. The Italian companies proved sufficiently popular in France for a permanent home to be established for them at the HÔTEL DE BOURGOGNE, Paris, in 1680. (*See* COMÉDIE-ITALIENNE). The *commedia dell'arte* also flourished in Spain, Eastern Europe, Germany, and England, and influenced the development of the comic drama in most European countries. In England its influence can be seen in the works of JONSON and SHAKESPEARE, as well as in the development of the PANTOMIME and PUNCH AND JUDY show. By the end of the 18th century the genre had lost much of its vitality, having become somewhat over stylized and divorced from everyday life; consequently it drifted out of fashion. The 20th century, however, has seen a revival of interest in the genre, possibly as a reflection of discontent with naturalistic theatre.

commedia erudita In 16th-century Italy, a more scholarly version of the COMMEDIA DELL 'ARTE. Unlike the latter, it was performed to educated audiences and used written scripts, many derived from the comedies of Plautus and Terence. A representative play is Machiavelli's *La Mandragola* (1520), a satire on Florentine society in which a corrupt priest helps a woman's husband, lover, and mother to betray her.

Other writers in the genre were Bernardo Bibbiena, whose *La Calandria* (1506) was adapted from Plautus's *Menaechmi*, Pietro Aretino, who based his *Il Marescalco* (1533) on Plautus's *Casina*, Giambattista Della Porta, who wrote over 30 plays of this kind, and the poet Lodovico Ariosto.

community theatre A theatrical organization or type of drama designed to cater to audiences alienated by or disenfranchised from the conventional and commercial theatre. Community theatre emerged in the 1960s in an attempt to attract a wider and more disparate audience and to create a forum in which subjects ignored by mainstream drama could be debated. Some organizations, such as the London based Inter-Action, concentrated upon taking the theatre to schools, factories, and remote areas of the country. Other organizations, such as Gay Sweatshop and Black Theatre Co-Operative, concentrated on addressing issues affecting particular groups, such as homosexuals or racial minorities.

In the late 1970s another form of community theatre arose based on the idea of the **community play**. Pioneered in the Dorset area by the dramatist Ann Jellicoe, a founder of the Colway Theatre Trust, the community play involves the creation of a dramatic work based on some aspect of a community's local history. These works are usually produced using local people as performers and technical assistants, though often under the guidance of a professional director and playwright. Notable community plays commissioned by Jellicoe include Howard Barker's *The Poor Man's Friend*

(1981), and David Edgar's *Entertaining Friends* (1985), set in Dorchester.

In America the term community theatre is virtually synonymous with the LITTLE THEATRES.

compartment batten *See* BATTEN.

composite setting *See* MULTIPLE SETTING.

comstockery The vigorous suppression of books, plays, and other literature deemed to be salacious or corrupting, as advocated by the New York Society for the Suppression of Vice, whose moving spirit was Anthony Comstock (1844–1915). The word was coined by George Bernard SHAW. *See also* Thomas BOWDLER.

Comus (Gr. *komos*, carousal) In Milton's MASQUE of this name, the god of sensual pleasure, the son of Bacchus and Circe.

In the masque, the elder brother is meant for Viscount Brackley, the younger brother is Thomas Egerton, and the Lady is Lady Alice Egerton, children of the Earl of Bridgewater, at whose castle in Ludlow it was first presented in 1634. The action concerns Comus's unsuccessful attempt to lure the Lady away from the path of abstinence and virtue.

concert party In the early 20th century, a summer family variety programme in Britain, especially one presented at seaside resorts or in public parks. The show featured popular songs, dances, and comedy sketches. In 1980s business jargon the term came to mean an illegal combination of two or more persons who buy or sell shares in a company to influence its market value.

Conchobar In ancient Irish legend a king of Ulster at the opening of the Christian era. He was uncle and guardian of CUCHULAIN and also responsible for the upbringing of Deirdre; his passion for her eventually led to her flight and death. He is said to have died of anger on hearing of Christ's crucifixion. He appears as a character in several works of the Irish Dramatic Renaissance, including plays by Yeats, Synge, and AE. The authentic pronunciation of the name is disputed (Conohore and Crohore being the most popular suggestions). *See also* DEIRDRE OF THE SORROWS.

Confidenti An Italian COMMEDIA DELL 'ARTE company founded in 1574 that toured Italy, France, and Spain for many years. From about 1580 it was led by Giovanni Pellesini (1526–1612), famous for his role as Pedrolino. In 1604 some members of the GELOSI troupe joined after the death of Isabella Andreini. By 1610 Falmineo Scala, known as Flavio, had led the Confidenti back to Italy under the patronage of Giovanni de Medici. The troupe was disbanded in 1621, whereupon some members returned to Paris to join the FEDELI company. *See* COMÉDIE-ITALIENNE.

Confrérie de la Passion An amateur theatre company founded in Paris in 1402 to perform religious plays. It came to exert a virtual control over Parisian drama for most of the 16th and 17th centuries. The company, who performed works such as the ACTS OF THE APOSTLES in a disused hall outside the walls of Paris, were granted a theatrical monopoly in the city in 1518. This would prove a major obstacle to the expansion of professional theatre in Paris.

By 1748 the company had built a new theatre on the ruins of the palace of the Dukes of Burgundy; this would become the famous Théâtre de l'HÔTEL DE BOURGOGNE. As they were on the point of moving in, however, the Church finally reacted to the company's sometimes irreverent productions and banned it from presenting the religious works that formed its traditional repertory. The Confrérie de la Passion stopped producing its own plays in about 1570 and leased the theatre to other groups, including Valleran-Lecomte's company. It would not allow other companies to settle permanently in Paris, however. The Confrérie lost its monopoly in 1675 and disbanded a year later.

Congreve, William (1670–1729) English playwright, the most sophisticated exponent of the COMEDY OF MANNERS during the Restoration era. Congreve wrote five plays before he was 30. His first, THE OLD BACHELOR, was an enormous success at Drury Lane in 1693, in a production starring Thomas Betterton and Mrs Bracegirdle. According to Congreve he wrote the play to amuse himself during a convalescence.

The Double Dealer (1694) was not so well received but in 1695 he produced another hit, LOVE FOR LOVE (again with Betterton and Mrs Bracegirdle), to open the new LINCOLN'S INN FIELDS THEATRE. Its success secured his reputation and earned him a share in the theatre. His promise to write at least one play a year for the theatre of which he was now a part owner, was unfortunately not fulfilled.

Congreve's only tragedy, *The Mourning Bride* (1697), was his most popular work during his lifetime but is now rarely seen. It starred Mrs Bracegirdle as Almeria, a part that became much coveted by tragic actresses.

In 1700 THE WAY OF THE WORLD, a highly sophisticated and complex work that is now considered his masterpiece, was coolly received. This failure, together with his continued discomfort at having been attacked in Jeremy COLLIER's influential pamphlet *A Short View of the Profaneness and Immorality of the English Stage* (1698), persuaded him to retire. (Congreve had replied to Collier with little effect in *Amendments of Mr Collier's False and Imperfect Citations.*)

Voltaire later visited him and accused him of wasting his genius. Congreve told him he wished to be visited as a gentleman, not as an author. To this Voltaire replied that if Mr Congreve were only a gentleman, he would not have bothered to call upon him.

Congreve was by all accounts a warm man who won the love and respect of his many friends. John Dryden called him the equal of Shakespeare, Alexander Pope dedicated his translation of the *Iliad* to him in 1715, and John Gay called him an "unreproachful man." When he died he left nearly all of his £10,000 estate to his mistress, Henrietta, the second Duchess of Marlborough, who arranged for his burial in Westminster Abbey. Congreve was said to be the father of her second daughter.

> The charms of his conversation must have been very powerful, since nothing could console Henrietta Dutchess of Marlborough, for the loss of his company, so much as an automaton, or small statue of ivory, made exactly to resemble him, which every day was brought to table. A glass was put in the hand of the statue, which was supposed to bow to her grace and to nod in approbation of what she spoke to it.
>
> THOMAS DAVIES: *Dramatic Miscellanies* (1784).

Connection, The A controversial play by the US dramatist Jack Gelber, which helped to create the OFF-BROADWAY theatre of the 1960s. A partly improvised play about drug addiction, it was first produced in New York in 1959 by the LIVING THEATRE.

The story, such as it is, concerns the making of an avant-garde documentary film, also called *The Connection*. The producer and scriptwriter have gathered in a slum apartment to meet a group of drug-users and a jazz combo, all of whom will feature in the film. They wait for Cowboy, their supplier, who finally arrives with a stash of heroin; one character takes an overdose that puts him into a coma, from which the others help to revive him. Eventually the producer, anticipating the reaction of the theatre audience, complains about the lack of action, saying that he should have brought some girls. The original production used a number of devices to break the traditional barriers between the audience and the action, including having the supposed drug addicts beg from theatregoers during the interval.

Conquest family The English actor-manager Benjamin Conquest (Benjamin Oliver; 1805–72), his son George Augustus Conquest (1837–1902), who was a playwright, acrobat, pantomimist, and manager, and George's sons, the comedians George Conquest (1858–1926), Fred Conquest (1871–1941), and Arthur Conquest (1875–1945).

In 1851 Benjamin Conquest took over London's Grecian Theatre, previously a venue for light opera. After losing money producing Shakespeare, he staged more than 100 melodramas written by his son George, who was educated in France and adapted many works from the French theatre. George also collaborated with Henry Spry on nearly 50 pantomimes noted for their flying ballets, acrobatic effects, and stage mechanics (one play used 30 traps). He helped to manage the Grecian, which was rebuilt in 1858, and inherited it on his father's death.

George rebuilt the theatre again in 1876 and sold up three years later when he left for an ill-fated tour of America, during which he was crippled in a stage accident. In 1881 he took over the Surrey Theatre in Lambeth, where he continued to present his own sensational melodramas and Christmas pantomimes with great success. When he died his eldest son George, who excelled as a pantomime dame, ran the Surrey for three years before selling it. His younger brothers were both noted ANIMAL IMPERSONATORS, Fred being famous for his pantomime Goose, and

Arthur for his music-hall performances as Daphne, the chimpanzee.

Constant Wife, The A comedy by W. Somerset MAUGHAM, first performed in 1926 in New York and opening in London a year later for a run of 264 performances. An acclaimed 1974 revival in London starred Ingrid Bergman.

A year later John GIELGUD was weighing up an offer to direct the play in New York when he received a good omen at a second-hand bookshop in Manhattan. While he was browsing through the titles, a book toppled off the top shelf and landed at his feet. He picked it up and discovered *The Constant Wife*. He read it quickly and accepted.

The play, which has been called Maugham's wittiest, focuses on the marriage of Constance Middleton, who knows that her husband, John, is having an affair with her friend but takes it philosophically. When Constance meets a former sweetheart, Bernard, John encourages them to go out together. Constance finds a good job, becomes independent, and announces that she and Bernard are going on holiday to Italy. She adds, however, that she still loves her husband: "I may be unfaithful, but I am constant."

constructivism The use of abstract multilevel settings for a drama. The term was taken from the visual arts, having been first applied to abstract sculpture in about 1912. In the theatre constructivism was developed between 1922 and 1925 by the Soviet actor and director Vsevolod MEYERHOLD at the MOSCOW ART THEATRE. He removed the front curtain and replaced naturalistic sets with a practical "machine for acting" consisting of platforms, ramps, and rotating wheels. A typical example was his 1922 production of Molière's *Le Cocu imaginaire*, which features a constructivist machine-age setting by the designer L. Popova.

Contrast, The A work by the US playwright Royall Tyler (1757–1826), usually considered the first American comedy. It introduced the stock character of the rural Yankee who considers himself superior to other men. It was produced with great success by the AMERICAN COMPANY at the John Street Theatre, New York, in 1787. When it played in Tyler's hometown of Boston, it had to be disguised as a "moral lecture in five parts" because of prejudice against the theatre. George Washington was a subscriber when *The Contrast* was published in 1790.

The play is a light comedy that shows the influence of both Sheridan and Goldsmith. It contrasts the devious behaviour of Dimple, who deserts his fiancée for a wealthy woman, with the simple native honesty of Dimple's brother.

Cooke, George Frederick (1756–1812) British actor, whose brilliance on stage was obscured by his reputation for drunkenness and erratic behaviour. After 20 years languishing in the provinces, he suddenly found success in 1800 playing Richard III at Covent Garden. When John Philip Kemble (*see* KEMBLE FAMILY) saw the performance, he vowed never again to play the part. Cooke remained at the theatre for a decade but was constantly in trouble, in debt, or in jail. During one performance in Charles Macklin's *Love à la Mode*, he was too drunk to act and the show went on without anyone in the lead.

Cooke was one of the first British stars to be exported to America. He travelled to New York in 1810 to escape his reputation, appearing at the Park Theatre to great acclaim. His unreliability, however, wrecked his second New York season. On his own benefit evening, he tried to play *Cato* after a prolonged drinking bout and bewildered the audience by roaring out lines from Shakespeare interspersed with his own incoherencies. Afterwards he explained, "I always have a frolic on my benefit day. If a man cannot take a liberty with his friends, who the devil can he take a liberty with?"

Cooke later toured America and often spoke publicly on the evils of alcohol. He died in New York. Edmund KEAN, a great admirer, removed the body to a new burial place in the city and erected a monument. He also removed a toe-bone from the actor. When his Drury Lane company met him on his return, he commanded: "Behold! Fall down and kiss the relic! This is the toe-bone of the greatest creature that ever walked the earth." Each fell upon his knees and kissed it. Kean preserved the hallowed toe for years until one day his wife, in a pique, tossed it out of the window into a well. He rebuked her more in sorrow than in anger: "Mary, your son has lost his fortune. In possessing Cooke's toe-bone he was worth £10,000, now he is a beggar."

coon singer The music-hall term for a black-faced minstrel singer (*see* MINSTREL SHOW) who sang 'coon songs'. The most popular were Eugene STRATTON and G. H. Elliot, the CHOCOLATE COLOURED COON.

Cooper, Dame Gladys (1888–1971) British actress. She made her debut at the age of 17 in the lead role of Seymour Hicks's *Bluebell in Fairyland.* A year later she became a GAIETY GIRL, earning £3 a week for playing small singing and dancing parts. Her first serious acting role on the London stage came in 1906 with *The Belle of Mayfair.*

In 1917 Cooper became joint-manager of the London Playhouse with Frank Curzon (the only other woman running a London theatre at that time was Lilian Baylis at the Old Vic). She presented and acted in four Somerset Maugham premieres and enjoyed a great success in J. M. Barrie's PETER PAN. From the mid 1930s she worked mainly in America, making some 30 Hollywood films between 1940 and 1967. She became Dame Gladys in 1967.

Cooper always maintained that *Peter Pan* was for adults, not children. "Hook is a terrifying character," she pointed out, adding "When children are asked 'Do you believe in fairies?' they are egged on to call out 'Yes' by the elders." When one small boy visited her dressing room after the show he looked at her suspiciously for some moments and then commanded: "Well, now fly." Noted Cooper, "There absolutely does not seem to be any adequate answer to that sort of demand." Gladys Cooper was the mother-in-law of the actor Robert Morley (1908–92).

Co-Optimists One of the most famous PIERROT TROUPES, who successfully revived the old style of seaside show at the APOLLO THEATRE, London, from 1921 to 1927. They were led by Davy Burnaby (1881–1949).

copyright In the theatre, the legal protection afforded to the owner of a dramatic work, who is entitled to a royalty fee if his play is performed or published. Most countries recognize a copyright lasting at least 50 years after the author's death. Any infringement is a civil offence that can lead to an injunction or an action for damages.

In Shakespeare's time a playwright who published his work lost control of it to the printer. Throughout the 17th century the dramatist received no money from his work after its first run (which was rarely more than three performances), even if the work remained in a company's repertory.

The first English Copyright Act, passed in 1709, granted copyright for 14 years, renewable for 14 more. However, playwrights usually sold this to the theatre or a publisher for a small sum and throughout the 18th century depended upon BENEFIT PERFORMANCEs for adequate income.

Efforts by the Dramatic Authors' Society led in 1833 to England's first copyright law applying specifically to plays. This was followed by a detailed Literary Copyright Act in 1842. However, as acting rights to printed plays still belonged to the publisher, dramatists usually tried to keep their works out of print. Until the late 19th century the right of 'copyright performance' was traditionally considered lost if a play was published before being performed. This led George Bernard Shaw and others to hire actors for public readings in a hall or other public place, usually without costumes or scenery. Such 'copyright performances' have led to confusion in dating the premieres of many works.

The Berne Convention of 1886 established the International Copyright Union, amended in 1896 and 1908 and revised at Stockholm in 1967. Additional protection came from the Universal Copyright Convention signed at Geneva in 1952.

In Britain the Copyright Act of 1911 gave full protection to works intended for performance. The Copyright Act of 1956 was a revision to cover such modern media as films, records, radio, and television. Following the European Single Market Act (1992), copyright protection in EU countries was harmonized at 70 years after death.

US copyright law derives from the British Act of 1709. The first US Act was passed in 1790. The US dramatist George Henry Boker (1823–90) worked particularly hard to secure full legal protection for playwrights. An 1856 copyright act provided for registration of works in local courts (later the Library of Congress). The US Copyright Act of 1909 remains in effect today with amendments.

Cordelia The youngest of KING LEAR's three daughters. In the play's first scene she is disinherited for her inability to express her sincere love for her father in sufficiently flattering terms. She later rescues him from the ill-treatment of her sisters GONERIL and

REGAN. When she is hanged, Lear dies of a broken heart.

Coriolanus A tragedy by SHAKESPEARE, written *c.* 1607–08; no record of a Jacobean performance has survived.

The plot is taken from Plutarch's *Lives*. When the Roman general Caius Marcius captures Coriol from the Volscians, led by Tullus Aufidius, he is dubbed Coriolanus in honour of his victory and receives a hero's welcome in Rome. He is soon offered the consulship but his unwillingness to court the favour of the populace (together with the plotting of the tribunes) leads instead to his banishment. Enraged, he travels to Antium, where Aufidius is living, and offers to join the Volscians in an attack on Rome. Coriolanus soon has the city at his mercy and only relents when his wife and mother, Volumnia, plead for peace. On his return to the Volscians, Aufidius accuses him of treason and he is stabbed to death.

One of the most acclaimed modern performances was that of OLIVIER at the Old Vic in 1958. Laurence Kitchin wrote of the scene in which Coriolanus confronts the Roman mob, "There was the bizarre impression of one man lynching a crowd." During this unlucky production, Edith Evans (playing Volumnia) was involved in a car crash and Olivier missed six nights after hurting his leg. He was replaced by the young Albert Finney, who each day was fed a steak by the worried management. Olivier gave another brilliant performance in Peter HALL's 1959 Stratford production. Hall also mounted a celebrated production at the National Theatre with Ian McKellen in the title role (1984).

With his aristocratic pride and bitter contempt for the common herd, Coriolanus has divided opinion amongst critics and playgoers, provoking much debate about Shakespeare's own political views. Bertolt Brecht gave the play a Marxist slant when he adapted it as *Coriolan* (1962) while John Osborne rewrote it as *A Place Calling Itself Rome* (1973).

Corneille, Pierre (1606–84) French poet and playwright, considered the father of French classical tragedy. His reputation earned him the informal title **le grand Corneille** in his own lifetime.

Born into a family of lawyers, Corneille worked from 1628 to 1650 as crown counsel in a local government office in Rouen. The success of his first play, the farce MÉLITE (1629) encouraged him to concentrate on comedy for the next six years. In the 1630s he became one of a team of playwrights employed by Cardinal Richelieu, but the two men fell out in 1635, apparently because Corneille demanded an increased share of the takings. The same year saw the production of *Médée*, his first experiment in tragedy.

Corneille's great tragicomedy LE CID achieved instant success at the Théâtre du Marais in 1637. Ironically, the play that is now considered to have founded the French classical theatre was denounced by critics for disregarding the UNITIES. Following a critical report by the Académie Française (under Richelieu), the play was suppressed.

Le Cid was followed by a series of tragedies in the new classical style, the most notable being HORACE (1640), *Cinna* (1641), and *Polyeucte* (1643), often considered his finest work. The plays, written mainly in rhyming Alexandrines, are remarkable for their formal symmetry and stylized rhetoric. There is little external action, the main emphasis falling on the moral dilemmas of the heroic protagonists.

Despite his reputation as a tragedian, Corneille continued to write in other genres. His finest comedy, *Le Menteur*, was produced in 1643 with Floridor in the lead, while the spectacle play *Andromède* (1950) gave a starring role to Giacomo Torelli's stage machinery at the Salle du Petit-Bourbon (*see* GREAT MAGICIAN). *Psyché*, a COMÉDIE-BALLET produced in 1671, was written in collaboration with Molière.

After the failure of *Pertharite* in 1651 Corneille wrote nothing for the stage for seven years. In the 1660s he found himself rivalled by the young Jean RACINE, who gradually overtook him in public estimation. He died in comparative poverty.

Even in his declining days, however, Corneille knew the power of his reputation. When Molière and the actor Michel Baron admitted during rehearsals for *Titus and Bérénice* (1670) they did not understand a passage, Corneille confessed that neither did he. "Just say the lines as written," he shrugged. "There will be some in the audience who won't understand yet will deeply admire them."

> Corneille is to Shakespeare...as a clipped hedge is to a forest.
>
> SAMUEL JOHNSON.

Corneille de l'Isle The name adopted by the poet and playwright Thomas Corneille (1625–1709), Pierre Corneille's younger brother (by nearly 20 years). Thomas wrote more than 40 successful comedies and romantic tragedies before abandoning the stage for lexicography.

Cornell, Katharine (1893–1974) US actress who dominated the New York stage between the world wars and vied with Helen HAYES for the title of **First Lady of the American Theatre**.

Cornell grew up in Buffalo, New York, where her father managed a theatre. She made her Broadway debut with the Washington Square Players in *Bushido* at the Comedy Theatre. In 1921 she found acclaim with her performance as Sydney Fairfield in Clemence Dane's *A Bill of Divorcement* at the George M. Cohan Theatre. She subsequently married its director, Guthrie McClintic, and they worked together for the remainder of her career.

Her other successful roles included the title part in Shaw's *Candida* (1924) at the 49th Street Theatre and Iris Fenwick in *The Green Hat* (1925) at the Broadhurst Theatre. During the latter's run, she showed Leslie Howard how to make his face flush with false excitement before entering a tense scene by placing his hands on his knees and breathing heavily (*see* SHAKING THE LADDER).

Cornell's best known role was that of Elizabeth Barrett Browning in Rudolf Besier's *The Barretts of Wimpole Street* (1931). It ran at the Empire Theatre for a year and then toured. Cornell's appetite for touring was prodigious. In the 1933–34 season, for instance, she covered 75,000 miles to visit 77 US cities and perform to half a million people. She was joined by Edith Evans, Orson Welles, Brian Aherne, and Basil Rathbone for the three plays, *Romeo and Juliet, Candida,* and *The Barretts of Wimpole Street*. In 1934 she played Juliet on Broadway with Maurice Evans as Romeo and Ralph Richardson as Mercutio; Brooks Atkinson called the performance "a high plane of modern magnificence".

Later roles included that of Mrs Patrick CAMPBELL in Jerome Kilty's *Dear Liar* (1960); she retired the following year. She wrote two autobiographies, *I Wanted to be an Actress* (1939) and *Curtain Going Up* (1943). *See also* ANTONY AND CLEOPATRA.

Corn is Green, The A play by Emlyn WILLIAMS, first performed in London in 1938 at the Duchess Theatre. Williams himself directed and played the young Morgan Evans to Sybil Thorndike's Miss Moffat, his indomitable schoolteacher. It opened two years later in New York with Ethel Barrymore (*see* BARRYMORES) as the teacher.

The London producer Binkie Beaumont, Williams's friend and fellow Welshman, turned down the play, on the grounds that "Nobody wants to go to the theatre to see plays about people going to school." In fact, the drama proved a great success, transferring to the Piccadilly Theatre and completing a run of almost two years. The story was based on Williams's close relationship with Miss Cooke, the teacher who had discovered and nourished his writing ability. For the first production Williams, then 35, dyed his hair black to play the 18-year-old schoolboy. The play provoked Kenneth Tynan to write, "The most startling feature of the current theatre is plays *by* Emlyn Williams, *for* Emlyn Williams, and *about* Emlyn Williams."

The story shows Miss Moffat setting up a school in the Welsh village of Glansarno. She is impressed with Morgan Evans's ability to write about life in the mining community and insists that he attend university. Morgan, however, becomes involved with a young girl, who announces that she is pregnant by him as he awaits the results of his Oxford entrance examination. Although Morgan decides to do the honourable thing by the girl, Miss Moffat frees him to take up his Oxford place by adopting the child.

Cornish Rounds Ancient open-air theatres in Cornwall that were used to perform annual medieval MYSTERY PLAYS. They were carved into hill slopes to allow a large number of spectators to face the central acting area. An unusual feature was a trench used by actors for quick entrances. Documents suggest that the eastern end of the 'playing-place' was used to represent Heaven while Hell was to the north. Cornish Rounds were used for performances until the 17th century. In 1968 the cycle of Cornish mystery plays was given at the Piran Round, Perranporth, by drama students from Bristol University, who used original staging methods.

corrales de comedias (Sp. play-yards) The open courtyards used as public theatres during the Golden Age of Spanish drama. The first recorded use of such a venue for plays was in 1565 in Madrid. Nine years later Zan Ganassa's COMMEDIA DELL'ARTE company constructed an innovative covered stage in a *corral*. Madrid's two principal theatres were the Corral de la Cruz founded in 1579 and the Corral del Príncipe opened in 1582. The *corrales* declined from the middle of the 17th century as purpose-built theatres in the Italian fashion replaced them.

A theatre-goer had to pay to enter the *corral* and again to be seated. At one end of the yard was a projecting stage with trapdoors and devices for lowering divine characters; the back wall contained doors and windows and a curtained INNER STAGE. The theatre's *patio*, or pit, had benches around the sides, while the *aposentos*, or boxes, were window seats in houses overlooking the courtyard. Although men and women sat together in the best boxes, the remainder of the audience was divided by sex, with the uneducated women confined to their own gallery.

The companies, usually of from 12 to 14 actors, began their seasons at Easter. The continuous entertainment included music, dance, the *loa*, or prologue, and the *comedia* itself, with interludes (*see* ENTREMÉ; SAINETE) between the acts.

Corsican Brothers, The A spectacular melodrama by the British dramatist Dion BOUCICAULT. An adaptation of a French play, it was first performed at the Princess's Theatre, London, starring Charles KEAN, who played twin characters. The play introduced the so-called *Corsican Trap*, a variation of the GHOST GLIDE. It was during a revival of *The Corsican Brothers* at the LYCEUM THEATRE in 1880 that Henry IRVING introduced the practice of making scenery changes behind a curtain.

The story concerns the twins Louis and Fabien dei Franchi; Louis is killed in a duel and Fabien avenges his death. H. J. Byron (1834–84) later burlesqued the piece in his *The Corsican 'Bothers'; or, the Troublesome Twins*, while Willy Russell adapted the story for his musical BLOOD BROTHERS.

coryphaeus The leader of the CHORUS in Greek dramas; hence figuratively, the leader generally, the most active member of a board, company, expedition, etc. At Oxford University the helper of the CHOREGUS (assistant professor of music) was so called; both offices have long since disappeared.

The Coryphaeus of German Literature Johann Wolfgang von GOETHE, 'prince of German poets' (1749–1832).

Coryphée A ballet-dancer; strictly speaking, the leader of the ballet.

Costantini, Angelo (1655–1729) Italian actor of the COMMEDIA DELL'ARTE. In 1683 he joined the COMÉDIE-ITALIENNE in Paris meaning to share the role of ARLECCHINO with Giuseppe Biancolelli (1637–88). Instead, he enlarged the role of the character MEZZETINO, creating a distinctive red and white costume. He also wrote and published (1695) a somewhat inaccurate biography of his fellow actor, Tiberio Fiorillo, who had developed the role of SCARAMUCCIA. When the Court exiled the Italians from Paris in 1697, Costantini settled in the duchy of Brunswick; he was imprisoned for some 20 years after winning the heart of a woman also beloved by the Elector of Saxony.

Angelo's brother, Giovan Battista Costantini (d. 1720), was also a member of the Paris company, playing the role of Cintio, a young lover.

Costard A rustic clown in Shakespeare's LOVE'S LABOUR'S LOST, who apes the court wit of the period, but commits solecisms like Mrs MALAPROP or DOGBERRY.

The name is an archaic term for a large ribbed apple and, metaphorically, a man's head.

> Take him on the costard with the hilts of thy sword.
>
> SHAKESPEARE: *Richard III* (I, iv).

costumbrista In the early 19th-century Spanish theatre, a term for the technique of reproducing on stage the colour and customs of a specific region and its natives' accent and style. *Costumbrista* later became a characteristic of drama in the Spanish areas of Central and South America.

costume The clothing worn by an actor or other stage performer. Throughout the history of the theatre, fashions in costume have alternated between contemporary dress, attempts at historical representation, and symbolic costume.

The ancient Greeks introduced the wearing of MASKS, which allowed actors to play several parts, with long robes being worn for tragedy and short tunics for comedy.

Simple symbolic devices, such as the winged shoes of Hermes, were used to distinguish stock characters. The chorus often dressed symbolically to represent elders, townspeople, or birds or animals. Roman actors wore elaborate costumes for tragedy, using high boots, masks with high foreheads, and body padding to make themselves literally larger than life. Actors in comedies wore ordinary clothes. Stock characters had their own colours, with royalty being dressed in purple, slaves wearing red wigs, and prostitutes wearing yellow.

In medieval Europe elaborate costume was used to emphasize the supernatural aspects of the MYSTERY PLAYS. The faces of angels were painted red and those of the damned black. God appeared in gold cloth, Adam and Eve in leather suits, and the devil in grotesque masks. Less is known about the use of costume during the Renaissance. Elizabethan costume was a confused mixture of contemporary dress with occasional attempts to suggest historical period. The early 17th-century English court masques were notable for the ornate costumes of Inigo JONES.

In the Restoration period wildly exaggerated versions of the lavish fashions of the day were used in the comedies of Etherage and Congreve. Eighteenth-century costume was generally elaborate and fanciful until David GARRICK led a return to more naturalistic styles. Attempts at historical accuracy remained fairly notional, however. When portraying an ancient Greek in 1758, Garrick wore the costume of a Venetian gondolier, arguing that such men were usually of Greek origin. In France, where convention demanded that actors play MACBETH wearing a tail wig and 18th-century army officers' uniform, VOLTAIRE and the actor Henri-Louis LEKAIN campaigned for greater realism. In 1789 François-Joseph Talma made a great innovation by appearing in Voltaire's *Brutus* wearing a toga with bare legs and arms. The brief costume was not well received by the audience but by the end of the century realistic classical costume had become acceptable.

During the early 19th century, the dramatization of Sir Walter Scott's novels established a fashion for historical accuracy in costumes. For Charles Kemble's 1823 production of *King John*, James Robinson Planche dressed the king in clothes based on medieval manuscript illuminations.

However, by the beginning of the 20th century this trend had itself become restrictive. The modern theatre has embraced a variety of approaches to costume, ranging from the naturalistic to the wholly symbolic or abstract. The fashion for setting older works in fantasy worlds or historical periods other than that from which they originate has been used to particularly striking effect in Shakespearean productions. *See also* WARDROBE.

cothurnus *See* BUSKIN.

counterweight system A system for raising and lowering scenery by means of an arrangement of lines and weights. A theatre so equipped is (sometimes called a *counterweight house*) and does not require a fly floor (*see* FLIES).

The most spectacular counterweight system was that devised in 1641 by Giacomo Torelli (*see* GREAT MAGICIAN) for *La festa teatrale della finta pazzia* at Venice's Teatro Novissimo. Counterweights were connected to eight pairs of wings that could be changed simultaneously by one person. A similar system can still be seen at the Drottningholm Theatre and Museum, Sweden. *See also* HAND-WORKED HOUSE.

country. ***Country Girl, The*** A play by the US dramatist Clifford ODETS that provided his last great hit. First performed in 1950 in New York, it was seen in Britain two years later as *Winter Journey*. The 1954 film version starred Bing Crosby and Grace Kelly.

The country girl, Georgie, is married to the actor Frank Elgin, once a great star but now an alcoholic. Although he blames her for his failure, she adores him. When a director gives Frank the lead in a new play, the pressure induces the actor to go on a lengthy binge during the pre-Broadway tryouts. Although Georgie is attracted to the director, she remains faithful, and Frank is acclaimed on opening night in New York.

Country Wife, The William WYCHERLEY's robust Restoration comedy. First performed in 1675 at Drury Lane, it was his greatest triumph and probably the last play he wrote (although *The Plain Dealer* was staged a year later). *The Country Wife* became known as one of the lewdest plays in the language and, although popular in its day, was later supplanted by Garrick's bowdlerized version, *The Country Girl* (1766). No producer had the nerve to touch Wycherley's original until 1924, when it was staged at the Phoenix Society nightclub in London. It is now admired for its clever construction and mordant wit.

The play concerns the libertine Mr Horner, who feigns impotence in order to gain unrestricted access to women. Soon society women are flocking in droves to admire his 'china.' Mr Pinchwife, who has married the lusty country girl Margery, has not heard of Horner's supposed affliction and makes futile attempts to keep his young wife away from temptation.

coup de théâtre (Fr. stroke of the theatre) An unexpected turn in a drama producing a sensational effect; an astonishing piece of stagecraft; or an enormous theatrical success. More generally, the phrase is used of anything planned for effect, such as a dramatic political intervention, etc.

court. court fool In medieval and Tudor times, a member of the royal household given special licence both to amuse the monarch and to tell the truth, however unflattering. Certainly he was never simply a clown; his other roles included mascot, whipping boy, counsellor, poet, leader of revels, pet, and clairvoyant.

Famous court fools in England included Edward IV's John Scogan, Henry III's Ralph Simnel (who appears in Robert Greene's *Frier Bacon and Frier Bungay*), Henry VIII's Will Somers ("his plainness mixed with a kind of facetiousness, and tartness with pleasantness, made him very acceptable into the companies of all men"), and Elizabeth I's Richard TARLTON. According to tradition, Rahere, the founder of St Bartholomew's Hospital in London, was Henry I's fool. Some wealthy noblemen also kept a household fool. Sir Thomas More's fool, Henry Paterson, used to challenge his master's stance on papal supremacy after supper. Paterson appears in Holbein's famous portrait of the chancellor.

Shakespeare's interest in fools can be dated from 1599, when the comedian Robert Armin joined the Chamberlain's Men as a replacement for Will Kempe. Armin was an expert on court fools and had a fund of stories about them, later collected in *Foole Upon Foole* (1605) and *The Nest of Ninnies* (1609). It was Armin who created the roles of Touchstone in *As You Like It* (1599), Feste in *Twelfth Night* (1601–02), and the Fool in KING LEAR (1605). In the latter the Fool is a full participant in the tragic events, rather than a source of light relief.

The fool lost his central role at court in the 17th century; thereafter his place was sometimes taken by bands of rollicking grotesques, such as those who followed Marie Antoinette. The last court fool in England was Charles I's Muckle John. As late as 1728 Swift wrote an epitaph on Dickie Pierce, the Earl of Suffolk's fool, who is buried in Berkeley Churchyard, Gloucestershire. *See also* FOOL.

court theatre (in England) Although England never had an official court theatre to compare with that of Louis XIV at Versailles or Goethe's Court Theatre at Weimar, the English royal household had a long history of welcoming players. In the Elizabethan era many new works were first presented at court, including Shakespeare's *Twelfth Night*. Halls and other large rooms were adapted for the entertainments and if necessary the plays were altered to fit the available space.

In the early 17th century the elaborate court MASQUES favoured by the Stuart kings were held in more specialized venues, such as the Banqueting Hall and Masquing House in Whitehall and the Great Hall at Hampton Court. In 1604 Inigo JONES converted the Cockpit-in-Court into an intimate theatre. Although Charles II was a keen theatregoer the custom of presenting new works for purely royal pleasure declined after the Restoration; the era of English court theatre had effectively ended.

Covent Garden The familiar name of a theatre in Bow Street in the Covent Garden district of London; it is now known officially as the Royal Opera House, home of the Royal Opera and Royal Ballet.

Covent Garden is a corruption of *Convent* Garden, from the former garden and burial ground of the convent or Abbey of Westminster. A famous fruit, flower, and vegetable market was held in the district from the 17th century until 1974, when it moved to Battersea. In the 17th and 18th centuries the area was the stamping ground of the Mohocks and other semi-fashionable ruffians, and its coffee houses, bagnios, and taverns the favourite resorts of poets, actors, and artists.

The present theatre is the third on the Bow Street site. The first, the Theatre Royal, Covent Garden, was built in 1732 by John Rich the Harlequin (*see* RICH FAMILY). For the next 100 years Covent Garden and Drury Lane were the only fully licensed theatres in London (*see* PATENT THEATRES). Plays and operas (including several by Handel) alternated at the venue. Peg Woffington made her debut there in 1740 and gave her farewell performance in 1757. Goldsmith's *She Stoops To Conquer* received its premiere at Covent Garden in 1773 as did Sheridan's *The Rivals* two years later.

In the 18th century Covent Garden audiences were notoriously unrestrained. On one night alone, a riot started because "gentry in the upper gallery" demanded an unscheduled hornpipe, two playgoers fought a duel with swords, and an orange thrown at an actor "dented the iron of his false nose and drove it into his head."

John Kemble (*see* KEMBLE FAMILY) became manager in 1803 and appeared frequently with his sister, Sarah Siddons. Other leading attractions included the child prodigies Miss Mudie (*see* THEATRICAL PHENOMENON) and Master Betty, known as the Young ROSCIUS. In 1808 the theatre was destroyed by a blaze in which 23 firemen died; also lost were Handel's organ and some of his original scores. A new theatre, modelled on the Temple of Minerva, opened in 1809. With its capacity of 3013 it was said to be the largest in Europe.

The great clown Joseph GRIMALDI appeared regularly from 1806 to 1823. Sarah Siddons made her farewell appearance in 1812 and William MACREADY his debut four years later. In 1817, the year the theatre was lit by gas, the management passed to John Kemble's brother Charles. The theatre then declined somewhat, until it was saved by the popularity of Charles Kemble's actress daughter, Fanny.

In 1833 Edmund KEAN made a dramatic final appearance while playing Othello to his son Charles's Iago. Suddenly taken ill, he rested his head on his son's shoulder and whispered, "I'm dying, speak to them for me." He was carried from the stage and died weeks later.

In 1837 Macready became manager and introduced LIMELIGHT to the theatre. He was succeeded in 1839 by Madame VESTRIS and her husband Charles Mathews. In 1847 the theatre was reopened as the Royal Italian Opera House and in 1856 it again burned down.

The present opera house, designed by Sir Edward M. Barry, opened in 1858. Sir Thomas Beecham was musical director in 1919–20 and artistic director from 1933 until World War II. In 1946 the venue became the home of the Covent Garden Opera, renamed the Royal Opera Company in 1968, and of the Sadler's Wells Ballet Company, renamed the Royal Ballet in 1956.

Coward, Sir Noël (1899–1973) British playwright, composer, producer, and actor, who began his theatrical career at the age of 11, when his ambitious mother answered an advertisement for child actors in the *Daily Mirror*. The result was that Noël, so called because he was born just before Christmas, appeared in *The Goldfish* at Crystal Palace's Little Theatre. Thereafter, he became a successful child actor, although in his own view he was:

> ...when washed and smarmed down a bit passably attractive, but one of the worst boy actors ever inflicted on the paying public.

After World War I he began to write his own plays while continuing to appear in revues and comedies. His first major success as both actor and author came with THE VORTEX (1924), a domestic drama reflecting some of the desperation of postwar London society. It was, however, with HAY FEVER (1925) that Coward discovered his talent for writing and performing sharp social comedies. PRIVATE LIVES (1930; filmed 1931), DESIGN FOR LIVING (1933; filmed 1933), BLITHE SPIRIT (1941; filmed 1945), and PRESENT LAUGHTER (1943) followed in this vein. Meanwhile Coward was also writing musicals, including BITTER SWEET (1929; filmed 1933) and the patriotic CAVALCADE (1931; filmed 1932). During the 1930s Coward performed on both sides of the Atlantic, appearing with such stars as Alfred LUNT and Lynn Fontanne and Gertrude LAWRENCE, usually in his own plays. After World War II, while much in demand as a cabaret star, he never managed to achieve his former eminence as a writer: *Relative Values* (1951), *Nude with Violin* (1956), and *Suite in Three Keys* (1946), in which he made his farewell appearance, have not entered the repertory.

Coward, often referred to as the MASTER, was a prominent personality on the theatrical scene for over 50 years. His image – the dressing gown, silk scarf, and long cigarette holder – now seems to epitomize Europe's last attempt at frivolous sophistication before the onslaught of World War II.

Many anecdotes are told of him, most reflecting his skill at repartee. On one occasion Laurence Olivier's young son was accompanying the two theatrical giants on a walk along the front at Brighton, not far from St Dunstan's, the home for the blind. Noticing two dogs copulating, the young Olivier asked what they were doing. Coward replied:

> It's like this, dear boy, the poor little dog in front is blind and the kind one behind is pushing him all the way to St Dunstan's.

Cowell, Samuel *See* ROSCIUS, YOUNG AMERICAN *under* ROSCIUS.

coxcomb A term for a jester or FOOL, because they wore a cock's comb in their caps. In KING LEAR the Fool says of the disguised Duke of Kent, who has asked to follow Lear as a servant:

> Let me hire him too; here's my coxcomb.
> (I, iv)

The term was used by association of any empty-headed vain person.

Craig family The stage designer Gordon Craig (1872–1966) and his sister, the actress and director Edith Craig (1869–1947); they were the children of the actress Ellen Terry and the architect E. W. Godwin (*see* TERRY FAMILY).

Gordon Craig joined his mother on stage at the LYCEUM THEATRE when he was 16. His ego made him unpopular with fellow actors, who enjoyed landing blows on him during battle scenes. The first production he directed and designed was Alfred de Musset's *On ne badine pas avec l'amour* in 1893.

Craig spent much of his career on the Continent. In 1904 he travelled to Berlin, where he designed a memorable production of Otway's *Venice Preserv'd*, influenced Max REINHARDT, and had an affair with the dancer Isadora Duncan. Two years later he settled in Florence, where he founded *The Mask*, a theatre journal, and ran a school of acting. In 1912 he provided the designs for Stanislavsky's *Hamlet* at the Moscow Art Theatre. From 1929 he lived in France. He was made a Companion of Honour in 1955 but could not afford the trip to London to accept it.

Craig's theories were initially controversial – he was once labelled 'half-mad' – but many had become accepted internationally by the end of World War I. In particular, he advocated a new kind of 'total theatre' created by a master-artist combining the roles of director and designer. To Craig, a play was primarily a visual rather than a literary experience. He denounced playwrights for overemphasizing the role of words, and star actors for their self-importance. His most controversial idea was that actors should be reduced to the status of ÜBER-MARIONETTES, or super-puppets, in the hands of the master-artist.

Craig's designs were characterized by simple nonrepresentational sets and dramatic effects of light and shade. He also experimented with moving screens, rostrums, and stairways. These ideas were set out in his book *On the Art of the Theatre* (1911); other publications include a biography of his mother and an autobiography, *Index to the Story of My Days, 1872–1907*.

Edith Craig also began acting with Ellen Terry at the Lyceum. She managed her mother's 1907 US tour but soon afterwards left the theatre to study music in London and Berlin. From 1911 until 1921 she directed the Pioneer Players, also designing the costumes and scenery.

Crazy Gang A group of British comedians. Their comedy and variety act, which involved mixing with the audience and riotous impromptu routines, enjoyed success for some 30 years. The Gang comprised three double acts: Bud Flanagan (1896–1968) and Chesney Allen (1894–1982), famous for their many songs, including 'Underneath the Arches'; Jimmy Nervo (1890–1975) and Teddy Knox (1896–1974); and Charlie Naughton (1887–1976) and Jimmy Gold (1886–1967). They first appeared together on the stage of the London Palladium in 1932 and starred there almost continuously until 1940. After the war Chesney Allen retired, and the Gang reformed at the Victoria Palace in 1947, with the eccentric 'Monsewer' Eddie Gray (1897–1969). They disbanded in 1962.

Creditors, The A short tragicomedy by August STRINDBERG, given a single performance at his Scandinavian Experimental Theatre, Copenhagen in 1889. Four years later Lugné Poë, founder of the Théâtre Nouveau in Paris, revived the play with himself in the leading role.

Strindberg described the play – an original variation on the theme of the eternal triangle – as "humane, good-humoured, with all three characters sympathetic". Others have found it cynical and bitter. Like MISS JULIE, written in the same year, it deals with the psychological battle between the sexes and reflects the collapse of Strindberg's marriage to the actress Siri von Essen. In particular, it reflects his dread of ridicule for failing as a husband. He wanted Siri to play the role of the destructive wife, Tekla, but this was not to be.

The play's dialogue is frequently sardonic, as in this exchange between Tekla and her husband:

> TEKLA My sweet idiot, don't talk such nonsense!
> ADOLF You know it's risky to go round thinking everyone's an idiot but yourself.
> TEKLA Well, everyone does.

Cremorne Gardens Famous Victorian pleasure gardens opened in 1845 as a rival to VAUXHALL GARDENS on land formerly belonging to Thomas Dawson, Viscount Cremorne. A popular venue for fêtes and entertainments, they were closed in 1877 after complaints about their use by prostitutes. The now disused Battersea Power Station largely occupies their site. *See also* ROSHERVILLE GARDENS.

Crepuscolari, I (Ital. twilight) An artistic movement in early 20th-century Italy that found expression in a number of dramatic works. The movement was characterized by nostalgia, melancholy, and a pessimistic attitude to life.

The leading playwrights of the *Crepuscolari* were Fausto Maria Martini (1886–1931) and Cesare Vico Lodovico (1885–1968). The former is noted for his satires on middle-class attitudes, such as *The Black Lily* (1913), and *Laugh, Clown, Laugh!* (1919), while the latter dealt with the failure of human beings to communicate in such Chekhovian works as *Nobody's Woman* (1919) and *The Flaw, or Isa, Where Are You Going?* (1937).

cresset In the Elizabethan theatre, a crude form of stage lighting consisting of an iron cage or basket holding a knot of burning tarred rope. The cresset was usually mounted on the top of a pole or suspended from the ceiling. The word comes from the Old French *craisse*, grease.

> At my nativity
> The front of heaven was full of fiery shapes,
> Of burning cressets.
> SHAKESPEARE: *King Henry IV, Part I* (III, i).

Crispin In French comedy, a clever unscrupulous valet. The part derived ultimately from the character of SCARAMUCCIA in the COMMEDIA DELL'ARTE, who became Scaramouche in the French theatre. Paul Scarron introduced Crispin in his play *L'Écolier de Salamanque* (1654) while Jean-Francois Regnard made him the main figure in his works. In the 1650s the part was played by Raymond Poisson (1630–90) of the HÔTEL DE BOURGOGNE; his characterization retained some features of the traditional braggart soldier but added a new comic shrewdness. His son, Paul Poisson (1658–1735), completed the transformation of Crispin into a quick-witted rogue.

St Crispin's Day 25 October, the day of the battle of Agincourt. In Shakespeare's HENRY V the king says to his soldiers:

> And Crispin Crispian shall ne'er go by
> But we in it shall be remembered.
> *Henry V* (IV, iii).

Crispin and his brother Crispianus were Roman shoemakers, martyred in about 286.

Criterion Theatre A London theatre that was constructed below street level at Piccadilly Circus (then called Regent Circus) in the 1870s. Originally planned as a large restaurant containing a small concert hall, it was converted into a theatre during construction. Uniquely, the upper circle is reached by descending stairs. Contemporary press reports warned that it would be necessary to pump in air "to save the audience from being asphyxiated". The subterranean feature allowed the BBC to use the Criterion as a studio during the Blitz.

Today the theatre seats 602. It has beautifully preserved Victorian tiles and wall decorations, and renovations in the late 1980s uncovered remarkable murals.

The Criterion, managed by the actor Charles Wyndham until 1899, opened with H. J. Byron's comedy *An American Lady*. Terence Rattigan's *French Without Tears* opened in 1936 and ran for 1039 performances, while Ray Cooney's 1982 farce *Run for Your Wife* logged more than 2000 performances. In 1992 the Criterion presented Simon Moore's *Misery*, based on a novel by Stephen King.

critic. criticism

> See Hebrews 13:8.
> ROBERT BENCHLEY: criticism of the long-running play *Abie's Irish Rose*. The text is:

"Jesus Christ the same yesterday, and today, and for ever".

Listen, dear, you couldn't write 'fuck' on a dusty venetian blind.
CORAL BROWNE: to a Hollywood writer who had criticized Alan Bennett.

Two things should be cut: the second act and the child's throat.
NOËL COWARD: referring to a play featuring a child actor.

He played the King as though under momentary apprehension that someone else was about to play the ace.
EUGENE FIELD: referring to Creston Clarke's performance as King Lear.

Funny without being vulgar.
W. S. GILBERT: referring to Sir Henry Irving's *Hamlet*.

I have knocked everything except the knees of the chorus girls. Nature anticipated us there.
PERCY HAMMOND.

I could eat alphabet soup and *shit* better lyrics.
JOHNNY MERCER: describing a British musical.

She ran the whole gamut of the emotions from A to B.
DOROTHY PARKER: referring to a Broadway performance by Katharine Hepburn.

It had only one fault. It was kind of lousy.
JAMES THURBER: remark made about a play.

A strange, horrible business, but I suppose good enough for Shakespeare's day.
QUEEN VICTORIA: giving her opinion of *King Lear.*

I saw it at a disadvantage – the curtain was up.
WALTER WINCHELL.

critics

Critic, n. A person who boasts himself hard to please because nobody tries to please him.
AMBROSE BIERCE.

A critic is always serving the theatre when he is hounding out incompetence. If he spends most of his time grumbling, he is almost always right...he will see far more incompetence than competence in his theatre-going.
PETER BROOK.

A great deal of contemporary criticism reads to me like a man saying: "Of course I do not like green cheese: I am very fond of brown sherry."
G. K. CHESTERTON.

Tynan said I only had two gestures, the left hand up, the right hand down. What did he want me to do, bring out my prick?
SIR JOHN GIELGUD: on a hostile review by Kenneth Tynan.

Asking a working writer what he thinks about critics is like asking a lamp-post how it feels about dogs.
CHRISTOPHER HAMPTON.

You *may* abuse a tragedy, though you cannot write one. You may scold a carpenter who has made you a bad table, though you cannot make a table. It is not your trade to make tables.
SAMUEL JOHNSON: referring to the qualifications needed to be a literary critic.

Drama criticism should be concerned solely with dramatic art, at the expense of bankrupting every theatre in the country.
G. J. NATHAN.

Show me a critic without prejudices, and I'll show you an arrested cretin.
G. J. NATHAN.

The greatest part of critics are parasites, who, if nothing had been written, would find nothing to write.
J. B. PRIESTLEY.

A good drama critic is one who perceives what is happening in the theatre of his time. A great drama critic also perceives what is not happening.
KENNETH TYNAN.

Critic, The A burlesque by SHERIDAN, first performed at Drury Lane in 1779. Subtitled 'A Tragedy Rehearsed', it is much the best of the many satires of the theatrical world inspired by Buckingham's THE REHEARSAL. Sheridan was also writing from bitter experience as the manager of Drury Lane. His main targets were the vogue for heroic and sentimental drama, as represented in particular by the plays of Richard Cumberland (1732–1811), and the sorry state of contemporary theatrical criticism.

The main action takes place at a rehearsal of *The Spanish Armada*, a ludicrous work by the irrepressible Mr PUFF, who is also the producer. The play-within-a-play features historical characters such as Sir Walter Raleigh and Lord Burleigh (*see* BURLEIGH'S NOD) as well as a romantic subplot concerning the love between Tilburina of Tilbury and the Spaniard Don Ferolo Whiskerando. Also at the rehearsal are the amateur critics Dangle and Sneer and the writer Sir Fretful PLAGIARY, a character based on Cumberland. Their inept comments on the action provide one of the main focuses for Sheridan's satire.

Critique de l'Ecole des Femmes, La A comedy written by MOLIÈRE to answer the storm of protest provoked by his earlier play THE SCHOOL FOR WIVES (*L'Ecole des Femmes*). The controversial play was still running in Paris when Molière staged his reply in 1663. *La Critique de l'Ecole des Femmes* reassembled the characters of the first play to discuss both the merits of the work and the critical and moral attitudes of the day. A few months later Molière presented L'IMPROMPTU DE VERSAILLES another defence of *L'Ecole des Femmes*.

Crown Tavern A tavern in the Cornmarket in Oxford, where the playwright William DAVENANT was born in 1606. Davenant's father was the innkeeper there and one of the regular guests was Shakespeare, who is said to have stayed at the tavern on his journeys between Stratford-upon-Avon and London. Shakespeare became William Davenant's godfather but, according to the antiquaries John Aubrey and Anthony Wood, their relationship was even closer; it was popularly believed that Shakespeare was in fact the child's natural father. Although the truth of this has never been proved, Davenant himself made great capital out of his claim to being Shakespeare's son. One well known anecdote has the young Davenant hurrying home from school on being told that Shakespeare had arrived at the inn. When an acquaintance of the family asked where he was going in such haste, the boy said: "To my godfather, Shakespeare." "Fie, child," came the other's reply, "Have not you learned yet that you should not use the name of God in vain?"

Crucible, The Arthur MILLER's play about the notorious witchcraft trials in Salem, Massachusetts (1692). It was first performed in 1953 in New York and seen two years later in London at the Royal Court Theatre in a production by George Devine. The Salem trials resulted in some 20 executions and the indictment of scores of innocent people; Miller drew an easy parallel with McCarthyism and the investigations of the US House Un-American Activities Committee, then at their height.

When a number of Salem girls are seen dancing in the forest by the prim Reverend Parris, he suspects them of practising witchcraft. Among the group is Abigail Williams, the former servant of John and Elizabeth Proctor; to save herself she confesses to witchcraft and begins to accuse others. Because Abigail is in love with John, she names his wife as a witch. The investigators eventually indict John Proctor as well, along with many of his neighbours. Abigail disappears from town and Proctor is hanged.

Cruelty, Theatre of A theory of drama proposed by the French director, actor, and writer **Antonin Artaud** (1896–1948) in his book *The Theatre and its Double* (1938). Artaud was a follower of surrealism and sought to combine its theories with elements of Eastern dance drama to create a violent and ritualistic form of theatre. This was intended to be in direct opposition to the realistic theatre of the dominant rationalist culture. His aim was to shock his audiences into an awareness of basic human nature by releasing feelings usually repressed in conventional society. "Tragedy on the stage is not enough for me," Artaud once said. "I'm going to bring it into my life." He was certified insane and confined to psychiatric hospitals from 1937 until 1946, dying of cancer two years after his release. After Artaud's death playwrights such as Jean GENET and Fernando Arrabal, amongst others, experimented with the idea of a theatre of cruelty. Peter BROOK's 1964 production of Peter Weiss's MARAT/SADE, presented as part of a Theatre of Cruelty season at the Aldwych Theatre, London, is generally considered the definitive application of Artaud's theory.

crush bar A bar in a theatre that serves drinks during the intervals. A **crush room** is an old term for a room in a theatre or opera house, etc., where the audience could collect and talk during intervals, wait for their carriages, and so on.

Cuchulain or **Cú Chulainn** A legendary Irish hero. He acquired his name, which means the 'Hound of Culann' because, having accidentally slain the watchdog of the smith, Culann, he had to take the animal's place as a penance. He was brought up in the court of King CONCHOBAR of Ulster, whose kingdom he defended single-handed against the Queen of Connaught. His heroic life and death provide the subject matter for a cycle of plays by W. B. YEATS, including *On*

Baile's Strand (1904), *At the Hawk's Well* (1916), and *The Death of Cuchulain* (1939).

Cuckoo in the Nest, A The first of the 'Aldwych farces' written by Ben TRAVERS for the ALDWYCH THEATRE in London (although his *Tons of Money* had transferred there two years earlier from the Shaftesbury Theatre). First produced in 1925, *Cuckoo in the Nest* established Travers's reputation for madcap comedy and encouraged him to write eight more of the series. A filmed version was released in 1933.

cue A word, line, piece of business, etc., that notifies an actor that it is time to speak a particular line or perform a particular action.

> When my cue comes, call me, and I will answer
> SHAKESPEARE: *A Midsummer Night's Dream* (IV, i).

cup-and-saucer drama In the late 19th century, a realistic DRAWING-ROOM DRAMA that dealt with contemporary social issues. The term was first applied to the works of Tom ROBERTSON, whose play *Society* (1865) introduced a new realism to the London stage in the era of melodrama. The popularity of his *Caste* (1867) helped to ensure that a more naturalistic style of acting would permanently replace the bombastic delivery and sweeping gestures of the earlier Victorian stage.

The story of Robertson's conversion to cup-and-saucer drama provided the basis for Pinero's play *Trelawny of the 'Wells'* (1898), in which the character of Tom Wrench is closely based on Robertson.

curtain In a theatre with a PROSCENIUM ARCH, a cloth that screens the stage from the audience's view before and after a performance and between acts. It is either lifted vertically into the flies or divided centrally and drawn to the sides (sometimes the top outer corners).

Curtains were introduced to the stage by the Romans in the first century AD but were not used in early European theatres. In the Elizabethan theatre small curtains were used to hide DISCOVERY SPACES but the **house curtain** or **front curtain** was not introduced until the advent of the proscenium arch in the 17th century. By the mid 18th century the **act drop** was being used to mark the end of an act and as a background for entertainments between acts. Henry Irving first used a curtain to hide scenery changes at his LYCEUM THEATRE in about 1880.

The first **safety curtain** was installed at Drury Lane in 1794. Such a curtain is made of fireproof material (such as iron) in order to prevent a stage fire from spreading into the auditorium. It hangs in front of the house curtain and must by law be lowered once during a performance.

In the 1820s and 1830s the act drop was often lowered when the actors had frozen into a tableau (*see* LIVING PICTURE). This is the origin of **tableau curtains** or **tabs**. The term later came to be used of any theatre curtain and was often misapplied to a CURTAIN SET.

Towards the end of the 19th century the **traveller** or **running curtain** appeared; this was drawn across the back of a stage so that scenery could be changed behind it while the play continued in front. At about the same time the ADVERTISEMENT CURTAIN was introduced to carry information about the theatre's sponsors; this practice did not last beyond the early 20th century.

The advent of curtains introduced new scope for onstage disaster. Most actors have experienced curtains that failed to open, rose at the wrong time, or fell unexpectedly, sometimes upon the performers. When in 1936 Terence RATTIGAN's first play, *French Without Tears*, received rousing applause on its first night, the author was hurried onto the stage to thank the audience. A stagehand, not expecting a first-night speech, lowered the curtain unceremoniously on his head.

curtain call After the end of a play, the reappearance of the cast to take a bow in acknowledgement of the audience's applause. On opening night, the playwright and director may also appear on stage. In earlier days curtain speeches were also expected from stars. One actor who excelled at this was Fred Terry (*see* TERRY FAMILY), whose speech often included these words:

> If there is anything an actor values more than your applause, it is your silent attention to detail that enables us to give you of our best.

In the 18th century the great actors like Garrick and Kean began to take curtain calls after every scene (including death scenes), an absurd practice that lasted into the 1930s. Donald WOLFIT would shake the curtain from behind to encourage applause before stepping out, while Marlene Dietrich allowed 20 minutes for her curtain calls.

John Gielgud recalled how the ballerina Anna Pavlova, after taking endless bows and receiving a mass of flowers, would suddenly bound into the wings to reappear at once in a quite different part of the stage:

> The applause would grow more and more frantic as she floated on and off, running, tiptoeing, or leaping, surprising the enraptured audience with every reappearance.

curtain-raiser In the early 19th-century British theatre, a brief scene performed before the principal play. By mid-century the introduction of matinées had pushed the time of the main performance back until after dinner; as a result there was no longer time for such pieces.

curtain set A simple set consisting of an arrangement of curtains, usually without FLATS. This type of setting, popular with amateurs and LITTLE THEATRES, involves the use of a backcloth, BORDERS, and side curtains. In America it is sometimes called a **drapery setting**.

curtain-tune *See* ACT-TUNE.

to ring down the curtain To bring a matter to an end. From the practice of lowering the house curtain at the end of a theatrical performance.

> Let down the curtain, the farce is over.
> FRANÇOIS RABELAIS, reported last words.

Cushman, Charlotte (1816–76) The first great US-born actress. She was tall and rather plain, having masculine features and a rough voice, a combination that made her a natural for BREECHES PARTS. Acceptance in feminine roles was slower in coming, but after five years on the London stage, she returned to America in triumph, winning Walt Whitman's accolade as "the best living player."

Charlotte, who had originally intended to be an opera singer, made her acting debut in 1836 at the Bowery Theatre, New York, as Lady Macbeth, a role she repeated in London with William Macready. Other outstanding roles included Queen Katharine in *Henry VIII* and the intriguingly named Lady Gay Spanker in Boucicault's *London Assurance*. Her male roles included Hamlet and Romeo; both productions also featured her beautiful younger sister Susan (1822–59), as Ophelia and Juliet respectively.

In 1907 a Charlotte Cushman Club was established in Philadelphia; its clubroom contains paintings of the actress and many of her theatrical relics.

cut. cut-and-thrust dialogue *See* STICHOMYTHIA.

cut-cloth A CLOTH cut for decorative purposes or to reveal scenery behind it. In America this is usually called a **cut-drop**.

cyclorama A curved curtain, cloth, or other screen used to close off the back of the stage and part of the wings and create an impression of three-dimensional space. Sometimes called a *cyc* for short, it is hung to stage level and lit from top to bottom by floodlights. Since rigidity and an unbroken surface are essential, some theatres have permanent plaster or cement cycloramas. Partial and movable cycloramas have also been created with some success. The cyclorama was developed in Germany where it is called a *Rundhorizont* (round horizon).

Cymbeline A tragicomic romance by SHAKESPEARE, first performed in about 1611 at the Globe Theatre. One of his last plays, it draws its plot from legendary British history and an episode in Boccaccio's *Decameron*. The play's curious blend of fairytale, black comedy, and patriotic chronicle has provoked mixed responses. Tennyson loved it so much that he asked to be buried with his copy. Shaw, however, described the work as "stagey trash of the lowest melodramatic order" and rewrote the last act as *Cymbeline Refinished* (1936). Famous actresses drawn to the role of Imogen have included Ellen Terry (1896), Peggy Ashcroft (1957), Vanessa Redgrave (1962) and Judi Dench (1979).

In the plot Cymbeline, King of Britain, opposes the marriage of his daughter, Imogen, to Posthumus and banishes him. Posthumus travels to Rome, where he unwisely boasts of Imogen's purity to the treacherous Iachimo. In order to win a bet, Iachimo visits Britain and steals her ring as proof of Imogen's 'faithlessness'. Posthumus becomes insanely jealous and hatches a plot to kill her. Imogen puts on male dress and flees to Wales, where she lives in a cave with two young men who turn out to be her long-lost brothers, stolen from court as infants. Posthumus returns to Britain and saves Cymbeline's life in a battle between the British and the invading Romans. He and Imogen are reconciled and a peace treaty concluded between Britain and Rome. The play contains the celebrated lyric 'Fear no more the heat o' the sun'.

Cyrano de Bergerac A heroic comedy by Edmond Rostand, first performed in 1897 in Paris with the elder Constant-Benoît Coquelin in the title role. Although a lengthy verse play requiring a large cast, it has enjoyed numerous revivals. A film version starring Gérard Depardieu (1991) also enjoyed international success. Some, however, have found the play insubstantial. The critic James AGATE wrote: "Cyrano is the Crystal Palace of poetry. In this play, Rostand says nothing with unexampled virtuosity."

The play is based very loosely on the life of the historical Cyrano, a flamboyant soldier and writer famous for his enormous nose. Because of the latter, he hides his love for his cousin, Roxane, who loves the handsome but brainless Christian de Neuvillette. Cyrano helps Christian to court Roxane, even composing the tender love letters that thrill her with their heartfelt eloquence. When Cyrano is fatally wounded, Roxane belatedly finds out that he was their author.

The play was the cause of a rift between Laurence OLIVIER and Ralph RICHARDSON when they planned the 1947 Old Vic season together. Olivier wanted to play Cyrano on stage as a prelude to making a Hollywood film of the play with his wife, Vivien Leigh. Richardson, however, had first choice of roles, and took the part for himself. Olivier, believing that the other actor really coveted the part of Lear, made that his own choice – not because he wanted to play it, but in the hope of making a deal. Richardson declined, however, leaving Olivier to play the demanding role of Lear when he had little wish to do so. After this, the two men never acted together on the same stage.

When Robert Loraine played the part in 1927 in London, his rudeness to the stagehands during rehearsals caused resentment. In revenge, they deliberately left unfastened the cleats that secured the tree under which Cyrano sits in the final scene. Loraine suddenly found that in addition to acting the emotional death scene he had to hold up the leaning tree with his back.

D

Daly, Augustin (1839–99) US theatre owner, manager, director, playwright, and critic, who achieved fame on both sides of the Atlantic (*see* DALY'S THEATRE, NEW YORK and DALY'S THEATRE, LONDON). As a manager, Daly encouraged Bronson Howard, America's first playwright to live by his craft, by staging his first play, *Saratoga*, in 1870. As a dramatist, he wrote Westerns and melodramas such as *Under the Gaslight; or, Life and Love in These Times* (1867) as well as adapting some 90 plays, including many classics. In 1885 Daly broke up a Chicago pirating ring, an action that led to the formation of a society to protect the rights of playwrights, publishers, and managers. In the same year he defeated the infamous 'ticket scalpers' (operators who bought blocks of seats to resell on the street at up to 100% profit) by issuing unnumbered slips of paper that could subsequently be exchanged for real tickets prior to the performance.

Daly's Theatre, London A former theatre off Leicester Square, London, which opened in 1893. It was owned by and named after the US producer Augustin Daly. The theatre opened with a production of *The Taming of the Shrew* featuring the stars of Daly's US repertory company, Ada Rehan and John Drew (*see* DREW FAMILY). Subsequent performers there included Eleonora Duse and Violet Vanbrugh.

In 1895, discouraged that his British venture was not proving as successful as its New York counterpart, Daly sold the theatre to its manager, George EDWARDES, who made it a fashionable venue for musical comedy. This tradition continued after Edwardes's death in 1915.

In 1927 the theatre witnessed scenes of uproar on the first night of Noël Coward's *Sirocco* (*see* FLOP). After this failure, Daly's quickly returned to musical comedies but found little further success, eventually closing in 1937.

Daly's Theatre, New York A New York theatre that opened as Banvard's Museum in 1867 (changing its name to Wood's Museum the following year). At first the majority of productions were VARIETY and BURLESQUE, although more serious works were offered after 1872, when Laura Keene made her farewell performance in *The Sea of Ice*. After being remodelled by Augustin Daly it reopened in 1879 as Daly's Theatre, becoming one of New York's most fashionable venues.

In the 1880s Daly established one of America's last great repertory companies there, headed by John Drew (*see* DREW FAMILY) and Ada Rehan. One of their biggest hits was an 1887 revival of *The Taming of the Shrew*; other successes included the comedy *The Railroad of Love* (1888). Another of Daly's stars was Clara Morris, the Canadian-born US actress, who won particular acclaim as Lady Macbeth and in Wilkie Collins's *Man and Wife* (1872). Once a letter arrived for Morris from the rival Wallack's Theatre Company. Daly hid the letter, offered the actress a $20 rise if she immediately signed a new contract, then replaced the letter in her box. Although the rival offer was double Daly's salary, Clara remained with him for many years.

Daly managed the theatre until his death in 1899. Although it became a cinema in 1915, the venue retained his name until its demolition in 1920.

Daly's 63rd Street Theatre A New York theatre that opened in 1909 as the Davenport Theatre; it became a children's cinema in 1919, reopening in 1922 as Daly's. In 1928 it was renamed the Coburn Theatre, subsequently becoming the Recital Theatre (1932), the Park Lane Theatre (1932), and Gilmore's Theatre (1934). The Federal Theatre Project took on the lease in 1936 (renaming the venue the Experimental Theatre) and gave the New York premiere of Shaw's *On the Rocks* there. The building was demolished in 1957.

dame In English PANTOMIME, a comic female role that is traditionally played by a man.

The best-known such roles include Mother Goose, Cinderella's Ugly Sisters, Dame Trot, and Aladdin's mother Widow Twankey (described in 1844 as "a washerwoman with mangled feelings"). Dames became especially popular in the late 19th century when music-hall performers began working in pantomime. Famous Dames have included Dan Leno, George Robey, and Arthur Askey, who played numerous such parts in a panto career that lasted until he was 82.

Dandanata An Indian theatrical genre from the northeastern state of Orissa, thought to be one of the oldest forms of drama in the world. Various mythological characters are impersonated including Shiva, Krishna, Jogi, and the Gopis. Performances take place at night in an open arena and comprise music, dancing, and loosely connected dramatic episodes on religious and moral themes.

Dandy Dick A farce by Arthur Wing PINERO, first performed in 1887 at London's old Royal Court Theatre. The play has been revived with great success. The story involves a dean, the Rev. Augustin Jedd, and his extravagant daughters, Salome and Sheba, all of whom require money. The dean's sister, Georgiana, an ex-bookie, places the girls' savings on her horse Dandy Dick, a "certain winner". Even the dean makes a bet, via his butler, Blore. However, when he is found in the stables carrying a bottle of lotion, the dean is arrested for trying to nobble Dandy Dick (Blore, having bet on another horse, has tampered with the lotion). Through the intervention of his friend, Sir Tristram Mardon, the dean avoids custody. Dandy Dick wins the race, Sir Tristram weds Georgiana, and Salome and Sheba pay off their debts with their winnings.

Dane, Clemence (Winifred Ashton; 1888–1965) British playwright and novelist. She started acting under the stage name Diana Cortis in 1913, and published her first play, A BILL OF DIVORCEMENT, in 1921. This sensitive study of a woman's fear of hereditary madness received instant acclaim, and led Dane to turn to writing full time. Later works include *Will Shakespeare* (1921), *Naboth's Vineyard* (1926), and *Wild Decembers* (1932), a portrayal of the Brontës. However, none matched the success of her first play. She took her pseudonym from the name of her favourite church, St Clement Danes in London's Strand.

Dangerous Corner A play by J. B. PRIESTLEY, first performed in London in 1932. One of Priestley's 'time plays', it begins with a group of people listening to a radio play about a suicide. Conversation turns to a man called Martin Caplan, who had apparently stolen money from his employers and later committed suicide. One of the men now admits that he himself committed the robbery while one of the women reveals that Martin was in fact shot as he attempted to rape her. Following these revelations Martin's brother, Robert, who is present in the group, runs upstairs and shoots himself. The stage lights briefly fade and the drama restarts with the group again listening to the radio play; this time, however, someone switches to a music programme and the couples begin dancing.

When *Dangerous Corner* was seven months into its run, Priestley was approached by the producer Binkie Beaumont, who suggested that he write a play with a particular star in mind. Priestley responded vehemently to this suggestion: "I don't write vehicles, I write plays. And I've no time for bloody stars or the star system. If I had my way, we wouldn't have them. Just a lot of good actors."

D'Annunzio, Gabriele (Gabriele Rapagnetta; 1863–1938) The flamboyant Italian playwright, poet, and novelist. In 1894 he became the lover of the actress Eleonora DUSE, who helped to arrange the 1897 Paris production of his first play *The Dream of a Spring Morning*, as well as Italian performances of two of his tragedies, *La Gioconda* (1899) and *Francesca da Rimini* (1901).

D'Annunzio's dramas are noted for their intensity of language and feeling, which many now find excessive. His finest work, *The Daughter of Jorio* (1904), reveals a genuine and sensitive love of nature. D'Annunzio led an extravagant life and was forced to leave Italy in 1910 to escape his creditors. After settling in France, he wrote and staged the mystery play *Le Martyre de Saint-Sebastien* in 1911 (for which Debussy composed incidental music).

During World War I D'Annunzio served first in the army and then in the air force. After the war he became a vociferous nationalist and in 1919 led some 3000 volunteers to capture the Croatian port of Rijeka (Italian name: Fiume) for Italy. D'Annunzio proclaimed himself commandant of "the Italian regency of the Carnaro", but abdicated 15 months later when his headquarters were bombarded. He subsequently abandoned politics and retired to his villa on Lake Garda.

Danton's Death A play by the German dramatist Georg BÜCHNER, written in 1835 but not performed until 1903 in Berlin. The play uses the struggle between Danton and Robespierre during the French Revolution to present a pessimistic view of political life. Danton is portrayed as disillusioned and repulsed by the mass executions that have resulted from his efforts at reform. In writing the play, Büchner (who had been forced to flee Germany a year earlier for his revolutionary views) was expressing his own disenchantment with contemporary politics.

Despite its gloomy atmosphere, *Danton's Death* has been performed successfully in many countries, enjoying revivals in Berlin (1927), in New York (1939) by Orson Welles's Mercury Theatre, and in London (1971), where Christopher Plummer won acclaim as Danton.

Daskathia An Indian theatrical genre found only in the northeastern state of Orissa. The three-hour mythological drama uses two performers, the *Gayaka*, or main singer, and the *Palia*, who chants refrains about the epic hero Rama. The performers, who wear royal costumes and ankle bells, play several roles each and accompany themselves with cymbals and castanets. They also tell humorous stories and make satirical comments about society.

Davenant, Sir William (1606–68) English playwright, poet, and manager who claimed variously to be either the godchild or illegitimate son of William Shakespeare (*see* CROWN TAVERN). Davenant's first play, *The Cruel Brother*, was staged in 1627; during the 1630s he produced a number of MASQUES for the court, several plays, including *The Wits* (1633), and a volume of poetry, *Madagascar* (1638). In 1638 he also succeeded Jonson as the poet laureate.

Davenant supported King Charles during the Civil War, being knighted for his services to the royalist cause in 1643. While staying with the exiled Stuart court in France, he began to write his epic *Gondibert*. Having been sent by Queen Henrietta Maria on a mission to America, Davenant was captured by the Parliamentarians and suffered a spell of imprisonment in the Tower of London. He was released in 1654, according to tradition through the intervention of John Milton. Two years later he staged *The Siege of Rhodes*, a play that evaded the Puritan ban on drama by being set to music; it thus became the first English opera.

Following the Restoration, Davenant and Thomas KILLIGREW obtained royal patents from Charles II, which effectively gave them a theatrical monopoly in London. Killigrew moved his company to Drury Lane, while Davenant moved his Duke's Company, which included the young BETTERTON, into the LINCOLN'S INN FIELDS THEATRE. It was in this former tennis court that Davenant installed the first PROSCENIUM ARCH to be seen in a London theatre. His later works include several adaptations of Shakespeare, amongst them an operatic version of *The Tempest* (1667) written in conjunction with DRYDEN. He planned to move his company to the DORSET GARDEN THEATRE but died before the building was completed.

As a young man Davenant contracted syphilis from a prostitute, one physical consequence of this being the loss of his nose. His misfortune became the subject of many jokes. A fishmonger's apprentice, berated by Davenant for accidentally sprinkling him with water as he washed some fish, noticed the writer's disfigured face and complained: "Zounds, Sir, it's very hard I must be corrected for my Cleanliness, the Gentleman blew his Nose upon my Fish, and I was washing it off, that's all." Fortunately, Davenant saw the funny side and rewarded the boy with a coin. On another occasion he was accosted by a beggarwoman who repeatedly expressed hope that the writer's eyesight would never fail. When Davenant asked why she was so concerned about his eyesight, she replied: "Ah! good Sir! I wish you never may, for should your sight ever fail you, you must borrow a Nose of your Neighbour to hang your Spectacles on."

Davidge's Snake Shop A nickname for the Philadelphia Museum Theatre, where actor-manager William Davidge kept a display of stuffed reptiles in the foyer. The US actor Otis Skinner (*see* SKINNER FAMILY) made his debut at this rather shoddy venue, playing a Black character in *Woodleigh* (1887).

Day in the Death of Joe Egg, A A play by the British playwright Peter NICHOLS. First produced at the Glasgow Citizens' Theatre in 1967, it subsequently ran for several months in London with Joe Melia and Zena Walker heading the cast.

The play concerns the attempts of Bri and Sheila to care for their spastic daughter, Josephine (nicknamed Joe Egg). Because they have different ways of coping with the heart-rending strain of the child's handicap, their marriage begins to suffer, especially as Bri begins to suspect his wife of having an affair. Bri eventually has a breakdown and half-heartedly attempts to let Joe die of exposure. Sheila promises to find a nursing home for their child.

dead-heads Theatrical slang for those (such as critics and holders of complimentary tickets) admitted to theatres without payment – because they are considered 'dead' for the purposes of box office receipts.

death. ***Death of a Salesman*** Arthur MILLER's Pulitzer Prize-winning tragedy, first performed in New York in 1949, with Lee J. Cobb in the role of Willy LOMAN. Later that year the play opened at the Phoenix Theatre, London, with Paul Muni in the lead and Elia Kazan directing. In 1963 it was one of a quartet of plays that opened the first season at the Guthrie Theatre in Minneapolis. Other memorable revivals include the 1979 National Theatre production at the Lyttelton Theatre with Warren Mitchell in the lead.

Having been demoted by his company at the age of 60, Willy Loman, a once-successful salesman, is trying to come to terms with his life, which he regards as a failure. Willy, his wife Linda, and younger son Biff attempt to maintain an illusion of success, but their older son, Happy, despises his father's inadequacies. Eventually Willy's self-esteem collapses and he takes his own life. Miller's success in creating a tragedy from what appears to be an insignificant life has been much admired.

Deathtrap A thriller by the US playwright Ira Levin. First performed on Broadway in 1958, the play terrified its original audiences with its realistic gore-and-grime resurrection of a 'corpse' on stage. The first London production was staged in 1979 at the Garrick Theatre.

The plot involves Sidney Bruhl, a writer of thrillers who has run out of ideas. When an excellent script arrives from his protégé, Clifford Anderson, Sidney jokes with his wife, Myra, about killing Cliff to steal his plot. Sidney invites Cliff to his home and garrotes him in the living room. Myra's fragile heart begins to act up as Sidney buries Cliff, and when the dead man subsequently returns from the grave covered in blood, the shock is too much for her and she dies. The 'murder' is revealed as a set-up by Sidney and Cliff, who are both gay. Cliff soon becomes careless, however, suggesting that Sidney write a book based on the ghastly affair. Sidney decides that he has to murder Cliff who, in turn, resolves to strike first: both make several attempts to kill the other and both end up dead.

Deathwatch A one-act play by Jean GENET, first produced by Marcel Herrand in Paris (1949); it was subsequently seen in New York (1958) and London (1961).

Set in a prison, *Deathwatch* reflects Genet's experience of being incarcerated for burglary in 1942 at Fresnes. The plot involves three cellmates, the murderer Yeux-Verts, and two small-time crooks, Lefranc and Maurice, who aspire to emulate him. Lefranc eventually kills Maurice in order to increase his prestige with Yeux-Verts.

Deburau, Jean-Gaspard *See* BAPTISTE.

Décentralisation Dramatique *See* CENTRES DRAMATIQUES.

Deep Blue Sea, The A play by Terence RATTIGAN, first performed in 1952 in London, where it ran for 513 performances. The play won immediate critical approval, with Kenneth Tynan proclaiming it the most striking new English play of the decade. Peggy Ashcroft starred in the 1952 production, while the Austrian actress Elisabeth Bergner toured Germany and Austria in the role two years later.

The plot concerns Hester Collyer, a judge's wife, who lives with her younger lover, Freddie Page (played in the first production by Kenneth More). When Freddie accepts an overseas job, Hester refuses to accept that their relationship is over, and tries, unsuccessfully, to commit suicide. A second attempt at suicide is interrupted by a neighbour, a struck-off doctor; he tells her of his own experiences and his conclusion that life can be borne, even without hope.

Hester manages to come to terms with her life and accept Freddie's departure.

Deirdre of the Sorrows An unfinished tragedy by J. M. SYNGE, who wrote it while dying of Hodgkin's disease. It was first performed at the ABBEY THEATRE, Dublin (1910), a year after Synge's death.

The plot is drawn from Irish mythology. King Conchubor (*see* CONCHOBAR) becomes so obsessed with the beauty of his ward Deirdre that he keeps her sequestered until she is old enough to marry him. Deirdre, however, falls in love with the young warrior Naisi who, helped by his brothers, elopes with her to Scotland. Conchubor lures them back and Naisi is slain: Deirdre commits suicide. Synge's play is remarkable for its lyrical prose:

> Little moon, little moon of Alban, it's lonesome you'll be this night, and tomorrow night, and long nights after, and you pacing the woods beyond Glen Laoi, looking every place for Deirdre and Naisi, the two lovers who slept so sweetly with each other.

The same story inspired W. B. YEATS's play *Deirdre* (1907).

Delicate Balance, A A play by Edward ALBEE, first produced in 1966 in New York's Martin Beck Theatre with Jessica Tandy and her husband, Hume Cronyn, in the leading roles. The play opened in London in 1969 at the Aldwych Theatre with Peggy Ashcroft in the lead and Peter Hall directing. It combines social comedy with suggestions of allegory.

Set in 1960s America, the story focuses on Agnes (Mommy) and Tobias (Daddy), a retired couple. When Agnes accuses her husband of having an affair with her alcoholic sister Clair, Tobias responds by recalling how he once killed a cat who failed to love him. Harry and Edna, their best friends, arrive asking to spend the night because of a nameless dread of returning to their home. Agnes is fearful of letting the couple stay but Tobias extends the invitation. When Harry and Edna finally leave, Agnes, who believes herself close to madness, smiles sweetly:

> AGNES Don't become strangers.
> EDNA How could we? Our lives are the same.

Dench, Dame Judi (1934–) British actress, renowned internationally for her Shakespearean roles. Initially interested in set design, Dench was persuaded to attend London's Central School of Speech and Drama by her brother, the actor Jeffrey Dench. She made her debut with the Old Vic in London (1957), playing Ophelia to John Neville's Hamlet. After giving an acclaimed performance as Juliet in Franco Zeffirelli's 1960 production of *Romeo and Juliet*, Dench joined the Royal Shakespeare Company to play Anya in Chekhov's *The Cherry Orchard* at the Aldwych Theatre (1961). In 1968 Dench made her musical debut as Sally Bowles in *Cabaret* at the Palace Theatre. Subsequent successes have included Grace Harkaway in Boucicault's *London Assurance* (1970), Juno in O'Casey's *Juno and the Paycock* (1976), and Brecht's Mother Courage at the Barbican (1984).

In 1987 she was cast to play Shakespeare's Cleopatra at the National Theatre opposite Anthony Hopkins. In her characteristically self-effacing style she told the director, Sir Peter Hall, at rehearsals, "I do hope you know what you're up to, casting a menopausal dwarf as Cleopatra." The production went on to complete a record 100 performances.

In 33 years with the RSC Dench has played every major Shakespearean role for women. With Kenneth Branagh's Renaissance Theatre Company, she has recently turned to directing, staging *Much Ado About Nothing* in 1988 and a summer production of *Romeo and Juliet* at the Regent's Park Open Air Theatre in 1993. In the same year she played a vengeful wife in the RSC production of Peter Shaffer's three-hour *The Gift of the Gorgon*, a role she later described as the most demanding of her career.

Dench has also starred on television in situation comedies such as *A Fine Romance*, in which she appeared with her husband, Michael Williams (1935–). Her daughter Finty is also an actress.

design. designer A creative artist responsible for designing costumes, makeup, and scenery for stage productions; he or she often handles the lighting, sound, and other technical aspects as well. The designer needs to work closely with the director, and to have a thorough understanding of his or her idea of the text; for this reason some directors in the modern theatre assume the designer's role themselves.

The role of the designer developed principally in the courts of France and Italy. In the late 16th century Antoine Caron created festivals for Catherine de Medici in

France, while Tomaso Francini (1571–1648) was later brought to Paris to recreate the Italian scenic innovations at the French court. Georges Buffequin was the leading scenic designer of the first half of the 17th century in France.

Giacomo Torelli (*see* GREAT MAGICIAN) became Italy's most celebrated scene designer with his productions at the Teatro Novissimo in Venice from 1645 onwards. In Paris the designer Gaspare Vigarani (1586–1663) built the largest theatre in Europe, the Salle des Machines, to display his work. For the opening production, the opera *Hercules in Love* (1662), he designed machines to suspend the entire royal family and their attendants above the stage. Jean Berain *père* (1637–1711) produced ornate designs for the court and opera in the last 20 years of his life, a role in which he was succeeded by his son. The artist and stage designer Philippe James de LOUTHERBOURG (1740–1812) became the scenic director at Drury Lane in 1773 under David Garrick, for whom he created naturalistic details and invented new machines for SOUND EFFECTS.

Designers in the early 20th century sought unity of effect. The Swiss-born Adolph Appia (1862–1928) attempted this with a combination of simple three-dimensional units, such as steps, ramps, platforms, and skilfully deployed lighting. The most influential British designer of this period, E. Gordon Craig (*see* CRAIG FAMILY), worked on the Continent and made a great impression on German, Austrian, and Russian designers. Craig advocated the creation of a position of 'stage director', an all-powerful figure who would design the scenery and costumes before fitting in the actors and action.

The 20th century has seen a general movement towards more abstract stage designs. For his Moscow production of *The Life of Man*, a symbolistic drama by Leonid Andreyev (1871–1919), STANISLAVSKY used an arrangement of black curtains and white rope to represent walls, windows, and doors. Vsevolod MEYERHOLD experimented with non-naturalistic costumes and plain white furniture in a pioneering production of Ibsen's *Hedda Gabler*. Later Peter BROOK used a plain white set for his famous 1970 production of *A Midsummer Night's Dream*, employing coiled metal springs attached to fishing rods to suggest the forest and putting the actors on trapezes to represent flying. One of the most celebrated contemporary designers is the Czech Josef SVOBODA, who has experimented with FLEXIBLE STAGING, screens, mirrors, and cinematic projection.

Design for Living A comedy by Noël COWARD, first produced in 1933 at the Ethel Barrymore Theatre, New York, where it ran for a limited season of 135 performances. The play was written for the LUNTS, who appeared with the author in the Broadway production.

In Britain, the play's subject matter (a *ménage à trois*) caused some difficulties with the LORD CHAMBERLAIN. Coward, however, used his influence in Establishment circles to get the play performed at the Haymarket in 1939. In London, the leading men included Rex HARRISON and an Austrian refugee, Anton Walbrook, described by Harrison as "not, in my opinion, God's gift to the comedy stage." The relationship between the two men was not helped by the fact that Walbrook had been involved in an affair with the actress Coral Browne, who had previously rejected Harrison's advances. Knowing Walbrook's preference for German classical music, Harrison played jazz records each night in the adjacent dressing room. Of Diana Wynyard in the part of Gilda, Coward moaned, "Gilda needs to have a touch of the gipsy. She needs to be a bit common. Oh, if *only* Gertie [Gertrude Lawrence] was available."

Desiosi An Italian COMMEDIA DELL'ARTE company of the late 16th century. It was probably founded by the actress Diana da Ponti and included among its actors Tristano Martinelli, the famous ARLECCHINO. The company appeared in Paris in 1601 and when it disbanded some years later many of its members moved to the ACCESI company.

Desire Under the Elms A tragedy by Eugene O'NEILL, first performed in 1924 in New York, where the play's treatment of incest and infanticide provoked a police raid. Originally banned in Britain, the play opened in 1931 at the Gate Theatre Club, London, with Eric Portman and Flora Robson.

Set on a New England farm in the 1850s, the play focuses upon the triangle of the farmer Ephraim Cabot, his son Eben, and his new wife, Abbey. Eben hates his father for depriving him of his dead mother's farm. When Abbey arrives on the scene, Eben begins an affair with her, resulting in the birth of a child that must be passed off as Ephraim's. When told that the farm will now go directly to the baby, Eben decides to leave for California. Abbey, however, tries to prove her love for Eben by smothering the child to death. The lovers are arrested, and Ephraim abandons the farm.

desist, refrain, and cease A catchphrase meaning 'stop', popularized in the early 1910s by the British music-hall comedian George Robey, the self-styled PRIME MINISTER OF MIRTH. It is now rarely heard.

desultores Roman circus-riders who would leap from one horse to another (Lat. *desilio*, leap down, alight). This is the origin of the English word *desultory*, meaning jumping from one thing to another in a disconnected way.

detail scenery Small items of movable scenery such as BUILT STUFF, pictures, and chairs.

deus ex machina (Lat. god out of a machine) In a play, the unexpected appearance of a new character, who easily resolves the plot's main dilemma. The term derives from the ancient Greek theatre, in which the *deus ex machina* was traditionally a god who descended from Mount Olympus. The machine, or MECHANE, was a crane used to lower and raise the god. Modern playwrights generally shun any suspicion of a *deus ex machina*.

deuteragonist *See* PROTAGONIST.

Deutsches Theater A private theatre group founded in 1883 in Berlin to promote the performance of new works. It was founded by the playwright Adolf L'Arronge, who assembled a company under Josef KAINZ and Agnes Sorma (1865–1927). The group began by producing historical dramas in a realistic style using techniques pioneered by the MEININGER COMPANY. Otto Brahm took over the troupe in 1894 when his FREIE BÜHNE company was merged into it. The actors, who included Albert Basserman, were subsequently trained in the naturalistic principles of STANISLAVSKY.

With the MOSCOW ART THEATRE, the Deutsches Theater became one of the two leading European companies of the early 20th century. From 1906 onwards Max REINHARDT experimented with the idea of combining music, ballet, and mime with mainstream drama. Reinhardt's most famous star was Alexander Moissi, who was noted for his Shakespearean roles.

The theatre disbanded briefly at the onset of World War II but was revived by Heinz Hilpert (1890–1967), who maintained its popularity with German audiences during the war. In 1946 it became the National Theatre of East Berlin. From 1961 until 1969 it was run by the Swiss director Benno Besson (1922–), who produced works ranging from Aristophanes to Offenbach. The theatre is currently being reorganized following the reunification of Germany.

devil. Devil among the tailors A phrase used to describe a furious argument; it is also the name of a game in which a top (the 'devil') is spun among a number of wooden men (the 'tailors') with the intent of knocking down as many as possible.

The phrase is said to have originated from a BENEFIT NIGHT given in about 1805 for the actor William Dowton (1764–1851). The performance, a burlesque piece by Samuel Foote (*see* ENGLISH ARISTOPHANES) called *The Tailors: a Tragedy for Warm Weather*, resulted in a fracas outside the Haymarket Theatre among a large crowd of tailors, who considered the play a slur on their trade.

Devils, The A successful historical play by the British dramatist John Whiting (1917–63), first performed in 1961 by the Royal Shakespeare Company in London. Based on Aldous Huxley's novel of sexual hysteria *The Devils of Loudun* (1952), the play is set in a 17th-century French nunnery. Sister Jeanne, the prioress, invites the sensuous priest Urbain Grandier to become the convent's spiritual adviser: when he declines, the prioress and nuns develop hysterical symptoms and are assumed to have become possessed by demons. After their exorcism, Grandier is condemned, tortured, and executed. Ken Russell's notorious film version (1970), an extravaganza of bad taste, is based only loosely on the original play.

Devil's Disciple, The George Bernard SHAW's comedy satirizing MELODRAMA, first performed in Albany, New York (1897), then days later at the Fifth Avenue Theatre, New York. The play was produced by the US actor Richard Mansfield, who also played General Burgoyne, one of Shaw's wittiest characters (*see* GENTLEMAN JOHNNY). Set in

New Hampshire during the War of American Independence, the play tells the story of Dick Dudgeon, who has a reputation as a villainous free-thinker (the devil's disciple of the title); in fact, it transpires that he is both generous and self-sacrificing. When he is arrested by the English, who mistake him for the local minister, he declines to save his life by pointing out the error. This altruistic gesture wins the heart of Judith, the minister's wife. The minister, however, turns soldier and, rescuing Dick from the gallows at the last minute, wins back his wife.

Though Mansfield had great success with *The Devil's Disciple* (taking it on tour after a long New York run), he had an abiding dislike for Shaw as both man and author. When a senator suggested that Mansfield ought to thank God each night for finding such a play, he replied that he did, but always with the addition, "Why, O God, did it have to be by Shaw?"

Devine, George Alexander Cassady (1910–66) British actor and theatre director, who headed the original Young Vic and helped to found the ENGLISH STAGE COMPANY in 1955. A member of the OUDS while at Oxford, Devine made his professional debut in *The Merchant of Venice* at the Old Vic (1932). After a spell with John Gielgud's company at the Queen's Theatre, he worked with Michel Saint-Denis on the staff of the London Theatre Studio from 1936 until the outbreak of World War II. After war service he worked with Saint-Denis at the Old Vic School before taking responsibility for the Young Vic (1946–51).

As an actor, Devine won particularly good reviews for his Tesman in a 1954 production of Ibsen's *Hedda Gabler* (in which he played opposite Peggy Ashcroft); he also appeared in plays by Brecht and Ionesco. In 1955 Devine directed Gielgud in a celebrated production of *King Lear* with a Japanese setting. As artistic director of the English Stage Company (from 1956) he was responsible for staging new works by an entirely new breed of British dramatists. *Look Back in Anger* by OSBORNE, *Chicken Soup with Barley* by WESKER, and *Serjeant Musgrave's Dance* by ARDEN, just three of the plays Devine put on at the ROYAL COURT THEATRE in the 1950s, changed the face of the British theatre.

In 1966 the **George Devine Award** was instituted to recognize outstanding work by young people in the theatre.

Devrient family The great German actor Ludwig Devrient (1784–1832); his eldest nephew, the actor Karl August Devrient (1797–1872) and his son Max Devrient (1857–1929); another nephew, the opera singer, actor, and director Eduard Devrient (1801–77) and his son Otto Devrient (1838–94); and a third nephew, the actor Emil Devrient (1803–72).

Ludwig Devrient has been called the greatest tragedian of the Romantic stage in Germany. Ludwig, whose style has often been compared to Edmund KEAN's, performed at the Court Theatre in Dessau before moving to Berlin in 1814. Among his famous roles were Shakespeare's King Lear and Richard III and Franz Moor in Schiller's *Die Räuber*. A decision to assign him only comedy roles contributed to his later descent into alcoholism.

Karl Devrient began acting in 1819; he performed at the Court Theatre in Dresden (1821–35) and at Karlsruhe (1835–39) before moving to Hanover. He was acclaimed in works by Schiller, Goethe, and Shakespeare. Karl's son **Max Devrient** made his debut in 1878 in Dresden and later appeared in both tragedy and comedy at the Vienna Burgtheater and throughout Germany.

Eduard Devrient began as an opera singer in Berlin but from 1844 to 1852 worked at the Court Theatre in Dresden as an actor and director. In 1852 he became director of the Court Theatre at Karlsruhe where he concentrated on the German classics. In 1874 Eduard published the first history of the German stage, *Geschichte der deutschen Schauspielkunst*. Eduard trained his son **Otto Devrient**, who acted at Karlsruhe, Stuttgart, Berlin, and Leipzig before becoming stage director at Karlsruhe in 1863; ten years later he went to Weimar as a director and dramatist (writing three tragedies). In 1876 Otto produced a controversial version of Goethe's *Faust* in the style of a mystery play.

Emil Devrient began acting at Brunswick in 1821 and achieved some success before joining the Court Theatre in Dresden in 1831, where he remained until his retirement. He was highly praised for his performances as Goethe's Tasso and Egmont, and as Hamlet, a role that he played in London in 1852 and 1853.

Dhanu Jatra An Indian drama, performed at Baragarh in the eastern state of Orissa, that depicts events in the life of Krishna. Large replicas of palaces and other settings are erected on the outdoor stage. A special feature of the *Dhanu Jatra* is the participation of playgoers in the processions and dramatic scenes.

Dibdin family The British actor-manager, comedian, playwright, and composer Charles Dibdin (1745–1814) and his illegitimate children by the actress Harriet Pitt, Charles Isaac Mungo Pitt (1768–1833), a playwright and manager, and Thomas John Pitt Dibdin (1771–1841) an actor-manager, playwright, and songwriter.

Noted especially for naval ballads such as 'The Lass that Loved a Sailor' and 'Tom Bowling', **Charles Dibdin** wrote around 1000 songs, as well as BALLAD OPERAS like *The Waterman* (1774), which became part of the repertory of the Toy Theatre. Dibdin established his reputation as an actor in 1768, playing Mungo in Isaac Bickerstaffe's *The Padlock* (for which he also composed the music). In 1796 he built the Sans Souci Theatre in Leicester Square, where Edmund Kean performed as a boy acrobat. For many years Dibdin performed in the popular one-man show *The Whim of the Moment*, a miscellany of songs, anecdotes, and comic monologues.

Thomas Dibdin made his stage debut at the age of four, playing Cupid to the Venus of Sarah Siddons at Drury Lane. Following a period as an upholsterer's apprentice, Thomas ran away to act in the provinces. He later found success as an author of stirring naval dramas such as *The Mouth of the Nile* (1798) and *Nelson's Glory* (1805). After briefly managing the Haymarket, Thomas took over at Covent Garden; in 1806, following the defection of the theatre's resident clown to a rival company, he hired Joseph GRIMALDI to appear in his popular pantomime *Harlequin and Mother Goose*. Grimaldi remained at Covent Garden for 17 years, during which time he became recognized as the king of clowns. Thomas married the actress Nancy Hilliar and their four children, who used their grandmother's name of Pitt, all worked in the British and US theatre.

Charles Pitt, given the middle name of Mungo from his father's most famous role, managed Sadler's Wells and wrote several successful plays, pantomimes, and songs. In 1826 he published the valuable *History of the London Theatres*.

didascalia A term used in the ancient Greek theatre to mean a teacher of drama, a theatrical production, or a catalogue of dramatic works. Surviving examples of such catalogues (all fragmentary) contain the names of the dramatists, their plays, and the dates of production. The word *didascalic* entered the English language as an adjective meaning instructive.

dimmer An electrical or mechanical device used to dim the lighting on stage. Early expedients included the use of currents of air to extinguish candles and placing opaque screens in front of the lights. The first electric dimmers consisted of metal plates immersed in barrels of a brine solution (which apparently gave off a bad odour). In the modern theatre a central computerized dimmer board is used, enabling the operator to connect lights to dimmer switches in any required combination (a practice known as **patching**). Memory controls can also now be used to preset light levels in advance. *See also* GRAND MASTER CONTROL.

Dionysus The Greek god of fertility, wine, and ecstasy, also called BACCHUS or Iacchus, whose worship gave rise to the earliest form of Greek drama. According to Aristotle, the cult reached Greece from the Near East, though this has been disputed.

The rites of Dionysus were characterized by wild music, ecstatic dancing, and uninhibited sexuality. The antics of the god's attendants possibly mark the beginning of the SATYR-PLAY, while the wearing of symbolic phalluses survived as a tradition of Greek comedy. The DITHYRAMB, a hymn to the god sung by a chorus of 50 actors at the DIONYSIA, provides perhaps the strongest direct link between the rites of Dionysus and the drama proper.

Dionysia Annual spring festivals in ancient Greece honouring Dionysus; originally involving simple processions and rites, they evolved into drama festivals at which prizes were offered for the best plays. The **City Dionysia**, or **Great Dionysia**, held in Athens in late March and early April lasted five or six days with up to a dozen sets of plays being performed. Playwrights would submit a TETRALOGY consisting of three linked tragedies and a burlesque satyr play. Performances were supervised by the *archon*, or chief magistrate, with costs borne by rich citizens. Judges were chosen from a panel by drawing lots. The names of victorious poets, actors, and chorus leaders were inscribed on clay tablets. *See also* LENAEA.

The **Rural Dionysia** were local religious festivals, held annually in December, during which dramas were performed by troupes of travelling players. Many rural governments, or 'demes', constructed permanent theatres for the festival. One of the most important demes for drama was Piraeus, where Euripides is thought to have presented a play. According to Plato, the festivals were held on different days in different areas to allow people to see plays at more than one of them. Some scholars believe the Rural Dionysia provided an outlet for works turned down by the City Dionysia and Lenaea.

Artists of Dionysus Troupes of travelling players in ancient Greece who organized themselves into the first actors' guild or union in the 4th century BC. The Artists of Dionysus established rules and regulations for the profession and dealt with business and financial questions, such as actors' wages.

diorama A type of PANORAMA popular in the 19th century that created a three-dimensional effect through such devices as the TRANSPARENCY, cut-out scenery, and special lighting and gave the impression of movement. In 1823 a diorama was opened in Regent's Park, London, by Daguerre and Bouton, who put scenery on rollers to create moving backgrounds. Popular attractions included a representation of the changing view from a steamer sailing from Dover to Calais.

director The person who has overall responsibility for a stage production. His or her major tasks include interpreting the work in theatrical terms, rehearsing the actors, and coordinating the efforts of designers, technicians, and other workers. Until 1956, when the US terminology was officially adopted, a director was known as a producer in Britain.

Until the 20th century the responsibilities of the present-day director were usually undertaken by an author, manager, or leading actor. AESCHYLUS was a famous director in Athens in the 5th century BC. In medieval Europe the 'master of ceremonies' would often move about the stage during performances of miracle or mystery plays. In the COMMEDIA DELL'ARTE the most experienced actor often assumed the role of director.

The ACTOR-MANAGERS of the 18th and 19th centuries were gradually superseded by independent professional directors in the early years of this century.

Famous 20th-century directors include Harley GRANVILLE-BARKER, Joan LITTLEWOOD, Peter HALL, and Peter BROOK in Britain, Lee STRASBERG, Elia KAZAN, and Harold Clurman (1901–80) in America, Jacques Copeau (1879–1949), Georges Pitoëff (1887–1939), Jean VILAR and Ariane MNOUCHKINE in France, Leopold Jessner (1878–1945), Erwin PISCATOR, Bertolt BRECHT, Peter Zadek (1926–), and Peter STEIN in Germany, Giorgio STREHLER in Italy, V. E. MEYERHOLD, Konstantin STANISLAVSKY, Yuri LYUBIMOV in Russia, and Otomar Krejča (1921–) in the Czech Republic.

Methods of directing can be either autocratic or democratic. In the 18th century David GARRICK happily deleted and added scenes to the plays he staged, while GOETHE drew up a detailed list of rules for his actors. OLIVIER once said:

> I expect my actors to do exactly what I tell them to do and do it quickly, so I can see my own mistakes immediately if I have gone wrong. Arguing about motivation and so forth is a lot of rot.

Others, such as Peter Brook, believe that a director should consult with the actors and other workers at all stages of the production. Since the 1960s workshop sessions have developed to ensure this company input (*see* COLLECTIVE CREATION).

In recent years so-called **director's theatre** has come under attack from those who feel that an undue emphasis on the role of the director stifles the creativity of actors and can lead to unbalanced and eccentric interpretations.

> Theatre director: a person engaged by the management to conceal the fact that the players cannot act.
> JAMES AGATE (attrib.).

Dirty Linen* and *New-Found-Land A double bill of comedies by Tom STOPPARD that opened in 1976 at the Arts Theatre Club and ran for 1667 performances. *Dirty Linen*, in which a Parliamentary Committee discusses moral standards in public life, began as a salute to Ed Berman, a US dramatist and director who became a naturalized British citizen. Stoppard then added the one-scene *New-Found-Land*, in which two Home Office officials discuss an American's application to become a British subject; one of them eventually delivers a comically impassioned eulogy on America.

discovery space In the Elizabethan theatre, a space or spaces on the stage where concealed characters could be revealed or 'discovered'. The discovery space was at the back of the stage, though scholars disagree as to its nature. It may have been a pavilion structure, a medieval 'mansion', or a miniature proscenium stage screened by a curtain that would be opened for the discovery (*see* INNER STAGE). Large props and set pieces were probably stored there when not in use. Discovery scenes abound in Elizabethan and Jacobean drama; one of the best known occurs in the last act of Shakespeare's *The Tempest* (1611), when Ferdinand and Miranda are 'discovered' playing chess. The Cockpit in the Court Theatre, London, had five entrances apparently serving as discovery spaces. The Corral del Principe in Spain (*see* CORRALES DE COMEDIAS) had a central opening nine feet deep at the rear of the stage for this purpose.

diseuse An actress who performed dramatic recitals, including pieces sung or spoken to music. This popular Victorian entertainment continued into the 20th century, when the US actress Cornelia Otis Skinner became a celebrated diseuse on both sides of the Atlantic. The equivalent term for a male is a **diseur**.

disguising A form of dramatic entertainment at the English court in the 15th and 16th centuries. It involved the wearing of masks, music and dancing, and the exchange of gifts. Participants included both actors and nobility. In the 16th century, as Italian and French influence on the form grew, the word 'disguising' was gradually replaced by 'mask' or MASQUE.

dithyramb In the ancient Greek theatre, a hymn sung and danced to the god DIONYSUS. It was first recorded in the 7th century BC. According to Herodotus, the dithyramb was developed into a regular poetic form in about 600 BC by Arion of Lesbos, who has been called the father of dithyrambic poetry. The early form, which was improvised, dealt only with the life of Dionysus; it later expanded in scope to include stories of heroes. Competitions for the composition of dithyrambs were a feature of the DIONYSIA. The most celebrated composer of dithyrambs was Lasus of Hermione; only fragments remain of works by other writers.

In his *Poetics* Aristotle states that tragedy evolved from the dithyramb. It seems that the chorus leader became a soloist, the PROTAGONIST, and that his exchanges with the CHORUS led to the beginnings of dramatic dialogue.

'Dixie' One of the most famous US theatrical songs. Ironically, the tune that gave the South a nickname and became the unofficial anthem of the Confederacy during the American Civil War was written by a northerner, Daniel Emmett of Ohio, in 1859. Still more ironically, very recent research suggests that Emmett may have stolen the song from an obscure Black performer. The song became famous in the South following its inclusion in a burlesque drama, *Pocahontas*, at New Orleans' Varieties Theatre in 1861. It acquired its patriotic status after being played at the inauguration of Confederate President Jefferson Davis (18 February 1861).

The day after General Robert E. Lee surrendered his Confederate troops to General Ulysses Grant, Abraham Lincoln shocked White House celebrants by asking the Marine Band to play 'Dixie', which he called "one of the best tunes I have ever heard." Four days later he was assassinated.

dock *See* SCENE DOCK *under* SCENE.

Docteur amoureux, Le The partly improvised farce by MOLIÈRE that proved the turning point of his career. Molière's troupe presented the piece to the 20-year-old King Louis XIV in 1658, following a performance of Corneille's *Nicomède*. Molière introduced the surprise offering as one of the little pieces that had earned him some reputation in the provinces. The performance had the king crying with laughter and led to the company's adoption by his brother, Phillippe, later duc d'Orléans. The king allowed the troupe to establish itself in Paris and move into the Théâtre du PETIT-BOURBON.

Doctor's Dilemma, The George Bernard SHAW's tragicomedy satirizing the medical profession, first performed in 1906 at the Royal Court Theatre, London. When a

1941 Broadway revival starring Katharine Cornell was a great hit the 85-year-old Shaw gave his permission for a London revival at the Haymarket starring Vivien LEIGH. Shaw told the producer that the role of the doctor's wife was a difficult one. "Jennifer Dubedat is the sort of woman I really dislike," he said. "Perhaps you'll warn the young lady of this." In the event, the problem was the leading man, Cyril Cusack. Feeling ill after a few drinks one evening, Cusack forgot his lines and began quoting from the only play he could recall, Synge's *The Playboy of the Western World*. The audience did not realize that anything was amiss but Vivien Leigh was horrified. When the nervous understudy, Geoffrey Edwards, was called for, he was so unprepared that he had to read his part on stage. Cusack was dropped.

Despite these problems, the production was a success, largely owing to Leigh's recent fame from *Gone With the Wind* – a film that Shaw refused to see on the grounds that "Life is too short. I really can't afford to waste four hours of it watching a young woman winning the American Civil War single-handed."

After Tyrone Guthrie saw Michael Langham's 1947 revival of the play, he noted, "All you can do with Shaw is to fan the actors out in a semicircle, put the speaker at the top, and hope for the best."

The story, set in London in 1903, concerns Jennifer Dubedat, whose husband, Louis, is dying of consumption. The family doctor, Sir Colenso Ridgeon, decides to treat a fellow doctor instead of Dubedat and hands the case to a colleague, who administers the wrong injection, killing the patient. Ridgeon subsequently admits to Jennifer that he refused to treat her husband because he hoped to marry her after his death. She reacts furiously and informs him that, at her husband's last request, she has already remarried.

Documentary theatre or **theatre of fact** A genre of play based directly on historical and documentary records. Created in Germany in the 1950s, the form was much influenced by the US LIVING NEWSPAPER. The first work in the genre to attract international attention was *The Case of J. Robert Oppenheimer* by Heinar KIPPHARDT, which opened in 1964 in Berlin in a production directed by Erwin PISCATOR. The play dealt with the development of the atomic bomb and the allegations of disloyalty made against the nuclear scientist Oppenheimer during the McCarthy witch-hunts of the 1950s.

Other pioneers of the form were Peter Weiss (1916–82) and Rolf HOCHHUTH. Weiss's play *The Investigation*, about the Frankfurt trials of perpetrators of the Auschwitz atrocities, was produced simultaneously at 14 German theatres in 1965. His documentary about the Vietnam War, *Vietnam Discourse*, was produced in 1968 in Frankfurt. Hochhuth denounced Churchill for the bombing of Dresden in *Soldiers*, which had its first English-language production in 1968 in Toronto, then played Broadway and London. In Britain, Peter BROOK presented the experimental documentary work *US*, about US intervention in Vietnam, in 1966. When it opened at the Aldwych Theatre it was described as "the ultimate non-play so far".

Dogberry The ignorant, self-satisfied, but good-natured night-constable in Shakespeare's MUCH ADO ABOUT NOTHING. The name is sometimes applied to any foolish and meddling official. Shakespeare's character is famous for his preposterous verbal solecisms:

> Comparisons are odorous
> *Much Ado About Nothing* (III, v).

See also MALAPROP, MRS.

dog drama A 19th-century type of drama in which dogs appeared on stage as part of the cast. Originating in France, it became popular in London at Drury Lane and other theatres. The most successful play of this type was *Le Chien de Montargis; ou, le Fôret de Bondy* (1814) by Guilbert de Pixérécourt.

Parts written for dogs in 20th-century drama include Flush in THE BARRETTS OF WIMPOLE STREET and Sandy in the musical ANNIE.

Dogget's Coat and Badge The prize awarded in an annual rowing match for Thames watermen held on or about 1 August. The name comes from **Thomas Dogget** (*c.* 1670–1721), an actor of Drury Lane, who instituted the race in 1715 to mark the accession of George I. The race, from the Swan Steps at London Bridge to the Swan Inn at Chelsea, takes about 30 minutes. The coat is an orange-coloured livery jacket.

Doll's House, A Henrik IBSEN's classic drama about a woman who leaves her husband to seek fulfilment; it was first produced in 1879 at Copenhagen's Royal Theatre. Shaw, writing in 1897, saw the play's final scene as representing the end of the old sexual order: "the slam of the door behind her is more momentous than the cannon of Waterloo."

The plot concerns Nora Helmer, a young wife and mother, who has secretly forged the signature of her husband, Torvald, to help him in his financial troubles. Nils Krogstad, a man her husband had sacked, threatens to expose Nora unless he is reinstated. When she informs Torvald of her deed he is horrified and only forgives her when Krogstad backs down. Nora, however, cannot forgive his lack of support; realizing that she has been nothing to her husband but an amusing doll, she leaves him and sets off for a new independent life. At the first German production in 1880, the actress Hedwig Niemann-Raabe refused to perform the final scene, and Ibsen quickly wrote a happy ending in which the wife remains at home, sinking to the floor of her children's bedroom as the curtain falls.

The Austrian feminist writer Elfriede Jelinek (1946–) continued the story in her play *What Happened after Nora Left her Husband.*

Don Juan Don Juan Tenorio, the legendary Spanish hero of many plays, poems, stories and operas, is thought to have been based on the son of a notable family in 14th-century Seville. The story is that he killed the commandant of Ulloa after seducing his daughter. He then jokingly invited the statue of the murdered man (erected in the Franciscan convent) to a feast, at the end of which the sculptured figure indeed arrived to deliver him to hell.

His name is synonymous with rake, roué, and aristocratic libertine; in Mozart's opera *Don Giovanni* (1787; libretto by Da Ponte) the valet says that his master had "in Italy 700 mistresses, in Germany 800, in Turkey and France 91, and in Spain 1003." The story first appeared on the stage in Tirso de Molina's *El Burlador de Sevilla y Convidado de Piedra* in 1630; in this work the Don is presented as a troubled man who knows that his desires are sinful but remains unable to control them. Plays followed by MOLIÈRE, CORNEILLE, Shadwell, GOLDONI, and Rostand amongst others. George Bernard Shaw's MAN AND SUPERMAN is an ironic reworking of the legend in which Don Juan Tenorio becomes the English freethinker Jack Tanner. The character also appears in Tennessee Williams's fantasy play *Camino Real* (1953).

Donkey's Years A comedy by Michael FRAYN about a college reunion, first performed in 1976 at the Globe Theatre, London. The play won the Society of West End Theatres' Award for Comedy of the Year. Set at a lesser Oxford college, the play shows how a group of former students have changed over 20 years and then, as the evening wears on, how they revert to their undergraduate ways.

The story introduces such old boys as the government minister C. D. P. B. Headingly and the Reverend R. D. Sainsbury. Welcoming them back are a new lecturer, W. R. Taylor, and the Master's wife, Lady Driver, who is desperately searching for her former lover, the rough-and-tumble Roddy Moore. Moore has not turned up, however, and Lady Driver finds his old room occupied by K. Snell, who boarded out while in college and now wants to make up for lost opportunities. During the evening, the returnees become increasingly drunk; indeed Snell becomes so wild that he suffers a breakdown and has to be taken to the local mental hospital. The others pack and leave, but not before Lady Driver and the surgeon D. J. Buckley have planned an assignation.

Dorset Garden Theatre A former theatre situated on the north bank of the Thames, just off Fleet Street, London. It may have been designed by Sir Christopher Wren.

The theatre was planned by William DAVENANT, who died before its completion. Although it had an impressive proscenium arch, acting took place in front of it; productions had the advantage of the latest scenic effects, though the theatre's narrow auditorium made it somewhat cramped.

The Dorset Garden opened in 1671 with a revival of Dryden's *Sir Martin Mar-All.* From 1672 to 1674 it was the only theatre open in London, as Drury Lane was being rebuilt following a fire. The Dorset Garden's reputation for musical works began with two adaptations of Shakespeare: Davenant's musical *Macbeth* in 1673 and Thomas Shadwell's *The Enchanted Island*, a retelling of *The Tempest*, in 1674. Two works by Dryden received their premiere here; *The Kind Keeper; or, Mr Limberham* (1678) and *The Spanish Friar; or, The Double Discovery* (1680).

In 1682 financial pressures led the company to merge with that at Drury Lane, which became their headquarters. Dorset Garden was subsequently used mainly for opera, being renamed the Queen's Theatre in 1687 after Queen Mary II. Its popularity subsequently declined and it became a home for circus acts and wild animal shows before being demolished in 1709.

Dossenus A stock character of the Roman ATELLANA of the 1st century BC. He is assumed to have been a hunchbacked slave, the name Dossenus probably being derived from *dorsum* (Lat. back). He shared some of the traits of the greedy character MANDUCUS.

Dottore, Il A stock character of the COMMEDIA DELL'ARTE, usually played as a verbose physician or lawyer with the name of Graziano. Generally dressed in a black costume with a white ruff, the character often functioned as a counterpart to PANTALOON. Graziano's son, ARLECCHINO, and Pantaloon's daughter, Colombina, became the lovers Harlequin and Columbine in the English HARLEQUINADE. Graziano himself never reached the English stage, although the character was further developed in the French theatre by Molière.

double take The actor's device, often used for comic effect, of looking away from a person who has addressed a remark to you, and then looking back quickly as though the meaning of the remark has just sunk in. The phrase is used more generally to mean any delayed response to an event or comment.

downstage The area of a stage closest to the audience, usually the front third. The word is also used as a STAGE DIRECTION, meaning to move towards the audience. When an actor faces the audience, 'downstage right' is to his right and 'downstage left' is to his left. *See also* UPSTAGE; CENTRESTAGE.

D'Oyly Carte, Richard (Richard Doyle McCarthy; 1844–1901) British impresario, best known for his association with GILBERT AND SULLIVAN. The son of the musical-instrument maker who first imported the saxophone into Britain, D'Oyly Carte studied composition and was later appointed manager of the Royalty Theatre in London's Soho. As a concert agent he began promoting Gilbert and Sullivan with his production of *Trial By Jury* at the Royalty Theatre in 1875. He subsequently rented the OPÉRA COMIQUE to present other early works by Gilbert and Sullivan and continued to encourage the partnership, the success of which enabled him to build the SAVOY THEATRE in 1881. His own D'Oyly Carte Opera Company was formed in 1878 for the production of *HMS Pinafore*.

His flair for promotion and business made all three men wealthy, although D'Oyly Carte became the richest. Much of his time was spent smoothing over quarrels between his two stars; he generally favoured the even-tempered Sullivan, who was best man at his wedding. Following the first performance of *The Gondoliers* in 1889, D'Oyly Carte charged £140 for carpeting to a joint account. Gilbert contested this and went to court, only to find Sullivan testifying for D'Oyly Carte, who won the case.

In 1891 D'Oyly Carte built the Royal English Opera House (now the PALACE THEATRE) at London's Cambridge Circus. It opened with Sullivan's opera *Ivanhoe*, which ran for 155 performances, a record for grand opera. The theatre, however, was poorly designed for opera and D'Oyly Carte lacked a full repertoire. Consequently the project failed, losing its instigator a fortune.

drag artist *See* FEMALE IMPERSONATOR.

drama. drama school Courses provided by a theatre, academy, university, etc., to train actors, directors, and those involved in other areas of stagecraft. Until specialist schools began to be founded in the 18th century, virtually all training came from actual theatrical experience. One of the first great drama schools was the École de Déclamation, established in 1786 in Paris, and subsequently renamed the Conservatoire National d'Art Dramatique. The Conservatoire has had strong ties with the COMÉDIE-FRANÇAISE for more than 200 years. Famous graduates include Rachel and Sarah Bernhardt.

Britain's first drama school, the London Academy of Music and Dramatic Art (LAMDA), now in Cromwell Road with its own theatre, was founded in 1861 by T. H. Yorke-Trotter. The Royal Academy of Dramatic Art (*see* RADA) was established in 1904 by Beerbohm TREE in his theatre, His Majesty's; it is now in Gower Street. The Central School of Speech and Drama was opened two years later by the actress Elsie Fogerty (1866–1945) at the Royal Albert Hall (it subsequently moved to the Embassy Theatre in Hampstead).

The American Academy of Dramatic Arts was founded in 1884 in New York by Steele MACKAYE, Franklin Sargent, and others as the Lyceum Theatre School of Acting. Today it is associated with the State University of New York. Michael Chekhov, who had worked with STANISLAVSKY at the MOSCOW ART THEATRE, opened a noted acting school in New York in 1938. Stanislavsky's principles were also the inspiration for Lee Strasberg's ACTORS' STUDIO, which became the main training centre for the techniques of METHOD acting in the 1950s.

In Russia most major theatres have acting schools. The Lunacharsky State Institute of Theatrical Art (GITIS) was founded in 1878 and named in 1934 for the play-wright and Soviet official Anatoli Lunacharsky. It has supplied many actors to the Moscow Art Theatre.

The Carnegie Institute of Technology in Pittsburgh became the first US university to offer courses for actors and directors in 1914. In Britain the first university to provide such a course was Bristol in 1946 (with Manchester, Hull, and Birmingham following in the early 1960s).

dramatic unities *See* UNITIES.

dramatis personae The characters of a play, film, novel, etc. It is sometimes used by extension to mean the personalities involved in a particular situation or event.

drame In 18th-century France, a form of domestic drama that combined elements of comedy and tragedy while emphasizing middle-class moral concerns. The genre was named by Denis Diderot, who popularized it in such works as *Le Père de famille* (1761) and *Le Fils Naturel* (1771).

The *drame*, which developed from the COMÉDIE LARMOYANTE and from the *tragédie-bourgeoise* of Voltaire, usually ended agreeably with scenes of repentance and reconciliation.

drapery setting *See* CURTAIN SET *under* CURTAIN.

Drawcansir A character in Buckingham's THE REHEARSAL (1671), a parody of DRYDEN's heroic drama *Almanzor and Almahide* (1670). Drawcansir's opening speech:

He that dares drink, and for that drink dares die,
And knowing this, dare yet drink on, am I.
The Rehearsal (IV, i).

parodies Almanzor's:

He who dares love, and for that love must die,
And, knowing this, dare yet love on, am I.
Almanzor and Almahide (IV, iii).

In the past the name was sometimes used for any bustling braggart. *See also* BAYES.

drawing-room. drawing-room comedy An often derogatory description of a type of play that dominated the British stage in the early-to-mid-20th century. It alludes to the elegant upper middle-class settings favoured by authors such as Noël COWARD and Terence RATTIGAN. The term came to embody everything most disliked by the ANGRY YOUNG MEN of the later 1950s.

drawing-room drama A late Victorian genre characterized by respectable domestic settings and the examination of middle-class concerns and values. Similar works written by Tom ROBERTSON became known as CUP-AND-SAUCER DRAMAS. Other British playwrights associated with the genre included Arthur Wing Pinero and H. A. Jones.

Dream Play, A A fantasy play by August STRINDBERG, first performed in Stockholm in 1907. Strindberg wrote the play in 1902 during his 'spring in winter' marriage (his third) to the Norwegian actress Harriet Bosse (who left him in 1904).

The play, a passionate phantasmagoria that calls for a cast of 46 and such effects as an advocate's office that turns into a church and then into Fingal's Cave, is rarely performed. A highly poetic exploration of the unreality of existence, it has been called the first outstanding work of EXPRESSIONISM. The play ends with Strindberg's oft-quoted line:

Mankind's to be pitied.

dress. dress circle In a British theatre, the lower of two CIRCLES in the auditorium, the other being the 'upper circle' or, formerly, 'family circle'. The dress circle was so named because evening dress was once required there. In 1878, a correspondent for the *North American Review* marvelled at a London audience: "There they sit in splendid array in the dress circle, close to the royal box."

dressing room In a theatre, a backstage room where actors don costumes and put on make-up. Actors may also rest in the dressing room when not on stage and greet well-wishers there before and after a performance.

'Worst dressing room' stories are a favourite subject of conversation amongst actors and other performers. The Australian ballet dancer, actor, and director Sir Robert Helpmann (1909–86) endured his worst backstage experience when touring America with the ballet *A Midsummer Night's Dream*. For one performance, in a baseball stadium, he was given the 'star' accommodation of the umpire's changing room; Helpmann found he had to stand precariously on a chair balanced on a table in order to face the single light bulb so that he might put his eye make-up on. *See also* DUEL OF ANGELS.

dress parade *See* PHOTO CALL.

dress rehearsal A rehearsal during which the cast members wear their costumes and make-up as for a performance. Usually the last rehearsal before the opening night, it allows the cast to discover any problems with their costumes, furniture, or props. Publicity photographs are often taken at the dress rehearsal.

Drew family The US actress-manager Louisa Lane Drew (1820–97), her husband the Irish comedian John Drew (1827–62), their son the actor John Drew (1858–1927), and their daughter the actress Georgiana Drew (1856–92).

Louisa Lane Drew was born (as Louisa Lane) into a London family with theatrical connections going back to the Elizabethan theatre. A child star who once appeared with Macready, Louisa was taken by her widowed mother to America where, aged seven, she played in *Richard III* at the Walnut Street Theatre, Philadelphia. As an adult Louisa appeared with many famous actors, including Edwin Booth and Edwin Forrest. She had a strong personality and was singled out by the critic T. Allston Brown for her lofty intellect, passionate devotion to her art, and highly cultivated mind.

In 1850 Louisa married the Dublin-born actor **John Drew**, who specialized in comic Irish characters. John had made his New York debut in 1842 and the following year took out a lease on Philadelphia's ARCH STREET THEATRE. From 1859 he concentrated on touring, leaving Louisa to run the venue, which she continued to do until 1892. The first US woman to manage a major theatre, she presented several important plays as well as doing much of the all-round stage work, including carpentry, herself. From 1880 onwards she toured almost constantly in Sheridan's *The Rivals*, with the third Joseph Jefferson (*see* JEFFERSON FAMILY).

The younger **John Drew** made his debut at his mother's theatre in *Cool as a Cucumber* (1873). Two years later he made his New York debut in Augustin DALY's *The Big Bonanza*. In 1879 John joined Daly's new company, in which he played opposite Ada Rehan (1866–1916), also from his mother's theatre. In the 1880s Drew became a matinee idol popularly known as the **First Gentleman of the Stage**. In 1893 he and Rehan opened Daly's Theatre, London, with *The Taming of the Shrew*. John's last performance was in Pinero's *Trelawny of the 'Wells'*. *See also* BEERBOHM, SIR MAX.

Georgiana Drew, known as Georgie, made her debut in 1872 at the Arch Street Theatre, before also joining Daly's company. In 1876 she married the British actor Maurice Barrymore; their children, Ethel, John, and Lionel all later became stars (*see* THE BARRYMORES). Georgiana continued to act until her early death at the age of 36. Following her performance in *The Senator* in 1890, one critic had noted: "An actress to her fingertips, she captivated the audience at once and kept them in roars of laughter and applause."

droll A type of brief comic sketch that developed in England during the Puritan INTERREGNUM. Since plays were too long and elaborate to perform in secret, excerpts from well-known works, called *droll humours* or *drolleries*, were presented, usually followed by a dance.

Robert Cox (d. 1655) was the most famous exponent of drolls, adding juggling, conjuring, and rope-dancing to the performance. Cox appeared in London and at country fairs before being arrested and imprisoned in 1653 for presenting a droll at the Red Bull Theatre in Clerkenwell.

drop *See* CLOTH.

drum-and-shaft An early system for moving scenery, widely used in the Renaissance and Baroque theatre. Articles of scenery were attached by ropes to a shaft that could be rotated either by a lever or, for a steadier effect, another rope wound around a barrel attached to the end of the shaft (hence the mechanism's alternative name, the **barrel system**). In this way, several pieces of scenery could be moved simultaneously. Articles of scenery could also be made to move at different speeds by attaching drums of different diameters to the shaft and winding the ropes from the scenery around these instead of the shaft itself. The system was gradually superseded by more sophisticated equipment capable of moving several articles of scenery independently of each other.

Drury Lane The shortened name for the Theatre Royal, Drury Lane, the oldest and most famous of London's theatres. The thoroughfare itself takes its name from Drury House, built in the time of Henry VIII by Sir William Drury. Drury Lane and Covent Garden are Britain's only PATENT THEATRES, Drury Lane's charter having been granted in 1662 by Charles II.

The original theatre was opened by Thomas KILLIGREW in 1663, the first performance being Beaumont and Fletcher's *The Humorous Lieutenant*. Nell Gwynn made her debut there in 1665. It burned down in 1672 and was rebuilt to a design by Sir Christopher Wren, reopening in 1674 with John Dryden as resident playwright.

In 1682 Thomas BETTERTON's company occupied Drury Lane but poor management by Christopher RICH provoked a move to Lincoln's Inn Fields in 1695. Stability was achieved from 1711 onwards under the triumvirate of Colley CIBBER, Thomas Doggett, and Robert Wilkes. David GARRICK took over in 1746 to manage with distinction for 30 years. In 1775 Robert Adam renovated the interior and two years later R. B. SHERIDAN became manager and staged the premiere of his own *The School for Scandal*. Sarah Siddons and her brother John Kemble became stars there in the 1780s.

The third Drury Lane, seating 3611, opened in 1794 with a concert. One memorable first night was that of *Pizarro*, adapted by Sheridan from the German, in 1799. Sheridan was so behindhand with his translation that the actors, who included Siddons, Kemble, and John Barrymore, were obliged to perform the fourth act as Sheridan sat upstairs completing the fifth. They then had to attempt to memorize the new dialogue. The play did not finish until midnight; only 39 members of the exhausted audience remained for the farce that followed.

Sheridan was virtually ruined when the theatre burned down again in 1809. The fourth building was opened in 1812 with a prologue by Lord Byron; gas lighting was installed in 1817. Although successful seasons were given by Edmund KEAN and William MACREADY, Drury Lane declined after the patent monopoly was abolished in 1843. In 1878 F. B. Chatterton closed the theatre saying "Shakespeare spells ruin, and Byron bankruptcy." It reopened in 1879 under Augustus Harris, who enjoyed success with melodramas and an annual pantomime starring Dan LENO.

Henry IRVING appeared at Drury Lane from 1903 until his last London season in 1905. He was known for attaching flints to swords to create flying sparks. When electricity arrived, he wired up the weapons, and during one performance Romeo and Tybalt turned into livewires to the audience's enthusiastic cheers. Thereafter Irving insulated the weapons with rubber handles.

In the 1930s the theatre staged a series of musicals by Ivor Novello. It became the headquarters of ENSA during World War II and survived a bombing in 1940. After the war, it presented a string of successful Broadway musicals: *Oklahoma!* (1947), *South Pacific* (1951), *The King and I* (1953), *My Fair Lady* (1958), which ran for 2281 performances, *A Chorus Line* (1976), and *42nd Street* (1984). *Miss Saigon*, which opened in 1990, was still running in 1997. *See also* THEATRE GHOSTS *under* GHOST.

Druriolanus, Augustus The nickname of a 19th-century manager of Drury Lane, Augustus Henry Glossop Harris (1852–96). It is a humorously Latinized version of the theatre's name on the model of CORIOLANUS. The son of Augustus Glossop Harris (1825–73), who managed Covent Garden for 27 years, the younger Harris took over Drury Lane in 1879 and managed it for 17 years until his death.

Although Harris opened with *Henry V*, he soon turned to spectacular melodramas and extravagant annual pantomimes. He incurred some criticism by turning the Christmas productions over to the great music-hall stars, including knockabout comedians. In 1891 he was knighted – not for his work in the theatre but because he was a Sheriff of the City of London during a visit by the German kaiser.

Dryden, John (1631–1700) English poet, critic, and dramatist, responsible for nearly 30 plays. He was noted both for his elegant comedies and his heroic verse dramas, which introduced the principles of French neoclassicism to England (*see* NEOCLASSICAL DRAMA).

Dryden turned to drama following the reopening of the theatres at the Restoration; his first attempt, the comedy *The Wild Gallant*, was presented in 1663 at Drury Lane. The success of his heroic drama *The Indian Emperor* in 1665 established him as a leading playwright.

Another heroic drama, *Almanzor and Almahide* (1670), was burlesqued in Buckingham's THE REHEARSAL (1671), which ridiculed the play, the genre, and Dryden himself. When an actress paused with a distressed look after speaking Dryden's line, "My wound is great – because it is so small," Buckingham is said to have risen in his box and added sarcastically, "Then 'twould be greater, were it none at all." This roused the audience to hiss the woman from the stage. Following AURENG-ZEBE (1675), perhaps his best heroic work, Dryden abandoned the use of rhyming couplets, producing the oft-revived blank-verse tragedy ALL FOR LOVE (a retelling of Shakespeare's *Antony and Cleopatra*) in 1677.

Dryden was the first to write drama criticism in an informal modern style and the first to attempt a history of English drama in his essay *Of Dramatick Poesie* (1668). He eventually tired of playwriting, admitting in 1675 that "many of my Predecessors have excell'd me in all kinds; and some of my Contemporaries...have out-done me in Comedy." His final plays, such as the tragicomedy *Love Triumphant* (1694), were written to relieve financial problems after his fortunes fell with the abdication of James II. *See also* LISIDEIUS.

> If Dryden's plays had been as good as their prefaces he would have been a dramatist indeed.
>
> HARLEY GRANVILLE-BARKER: *On Dramatic Method.*

> His mind was of a slovenly character – fond of splendour, but indifferent to neatness. Hence most of his writings exhibit the sluttish magnificence of a Russian noble, all vermin diamonds, dirty linen, and inestimable sables.
>
> LORD MACAULAY: 'John Dryden' in the *Edinburgh Review* (Jan. 1828).

duchess. ***Duchess of Malfi, The*** A tragedy by John WEBSTER (1580–1634), first performed in London in about 1619. It is a violent and horrific work set in Renaissance Italy. The play describes the fate of the widowed duchess who, contrary to the wishes of her two brothers, the cardinal and Ferdinand, Duke of Calabria, secretly weds her steward, Antonio, by whom she becomes pregnant. Her brothers place in her service a spy, Bosola, who keeps them informed of events. Antonio and the duchess separate and flee. Captured by Ferdinand, the duchess and her children are murdered by Bosola with every refinement of cruelty. Bosola, now remorseful, realizes his master's wish to be rid of him; he kills Antonio and the cardinal, but is himself slain by the now insane Ferdinand. Ferdinand is, in turn, killed by friends of Antonio.

Perhaps the most memorable modern production of *The Duchess of Malfi* opened in 1946 in the Ethel Barrymore Theatre, with Elisabeth BERGNER in the title role. In 1980 the play was successfully revived by Adrian Noble at the Royal Exchange Theatre, Manchester, with Helen Mirren as the duchess.

> I suppose you could define a pessimist as a man who thinks John Webster's *Duchess of Malfi* a great play; an optimist as one who believes it actable.
>
> RONALD BRYDEN: 'Blood Soaked Circus', *The Observer*, 18 July 1971.

Duchess Theatre A theatre on Catherine Street, London, that opened in 1929 under the joint management of Jack de Leon and his sister, Delia. The exterior of the building, designed by Ewan Barr, has been described as 'Modern Tudor Gothic'.

The Duchess has an unfortunate place in theatrical history, having staged London's shortest ever running show, *The Intimate Revue* (1930), which closed before the end of the first performance. The individual sketches required so much scenery that it took about 20 minutes to change sets. A critic for *The Times* noted: "Each time the curtains parted, squads of scene-shifters might be seen in action or in horrid precipitate flight." The Duchess also drew the world's shortest review, the show *A Good Time* receiving the one-word critique: "No."

In the 1930s J. B. PRIESTLEY became associated with the theatre, which presented a number of his plays including *Eden End* (1934) and *Time and the Conways* (1937). Priestley's wife, Mary Wyndham Lewis, redesigned the interior of the theatre in 1934. Emlyn WILLIAMS's *Night Must Fall*, in which he also starred, opened in 1935 and ran for over a year. Later successes included works by Terence Rattigan and Agatha Christie. Kenneth Tynan's nude revue *Oh, Calcutta!* transferred from the Royalty Theatre in 1974 and ran until 1980. In 1991 the Duchess presented Marc Camoletti's comedy *Don't Dress for Dinner*, which was still running in 1997.

Duel of Angels (*Pour Lucrèce*) Jean GIRAUDOUX's last play, written in 1944 and performed in 1953 in Paris without great success. Christopher Fry's English translation opened in 1958 at the Apollo Theatre, London, with Vivien LEIGH as the evil Paola, who drives the virtuous Lucille to suicide by convincing her that she has committed adultery.

As was her custom during a London run, Leigh moved numerous personal items from her home – pictures, small furniture, even her dog and cat – into the dressing room to give it a cosy familiar look. For this reason, her room was the only one fitted with a lock. Her dresser, Roy Moseley, recalled how one night she let the entire cast change there, because they were worried about the risk of infection after discovering that someone was letting their dressing rooms out to prostitutes after the theatre closed at night. Leigh welcomed the other cast members into her pure quarters with great amusement.

Duenna, The A comedy by Richard Brinsley SHERIDAN, with music by his father-in-law, Thomas Linley. Opening in 1775 at Covent Garden, the work ran for 75 performances, exceeding the previous record of 68 set by Gay's *The Beggar's Opera* (1728). Indeed, the show was so successful that Sheridan was able to buy a controlling interest in DRURY LANE from David Garrick with the proceeds.

The story involves the ill-tempered Don Jerome, who wants his daughter Louisa to wed the rich Isaac Mendoza. Louisa, however, loves the poorer Antonio. The duenna (governess and chaperon) acts as a go-between for Louisa and Antonio; when Don Jerome discovers this he dismisses her and confines Louisa to the house. Louisa escapes disguised as the duenna, who stays behind in her place. Mendoza is then tricked into marrying the duenna.

Duke of York's Theatre A theatre on St Martin's Lane, London. It opened in 1892 as the Trafalgar Square Theatre, a name that was shortened to the Trafalgar Theatre two years later. It received its present name in 1895 in honour of the future King George V. From 1897 it was managed by Charles Frohman, Marie Tempest, Gerald Du Maurier, and Irene Vanbrugh, all of whom acted in productions. Frohman produced several of J. M. Barrie's plays, including *Peter Pan* (1904), which was revived each Christmas until 1914. Other Barrie plays first staged at the Duke of York's included *The Admirable Crichton* (1902) and *What Every Woman Knows* (1908).

From 1923 to 1928 the venue was managed by Violet Melnotte, who presented the revue *London Calling*, written mostly by Noël Coward. The Duke of York's was occupied by The People's National Theatre from 1933 to 1936. The theatre's longest run was *Is Your Honeymoon Really Necessary?*, which opened in 1944 for 980 performances. Later successes have included Frank Marcus's *The Killing of Sister George* (1965), Alan Ayckbourn's *Relatively Speaking* (1967), and Arthur Miller's *The Price* (1969).

In 1979 the Duke of York's became the first London theatre to be owned by a commercial radio station: Capital Radio purchased it during the run of Michael Frayn's comedy *Clouds* and closed it for refurbishment (which included installing a recording studio in the gallery). The theatre reopened in 1980.

Dumas family The French Romantic playwright and novelist Alexandre Dumas (Alexandre Davy de la Pailleterie; 1802–70), known as Dumas *père*, and his illegitimate son, Alexandre Dumas, known as Dumas *fils* (1824–95), also a playwright and novelist.

The son of a Napoleonic general, Dumas *père* adopted the surname of his grandmother, a Black San Domingan. In 1829 the Comédie-Française produced his *Henri III et sa cour*, the first triumph of the Romantic movement on the French stage. He followed this with a series of historical melodramas, including *Napoléon Bonaparte*

(1831) and *Antony* (1831). The latter was produced at the Porte Saint-Martin Theatre, as was his most successful play, the drama of terror *La Tour de Nesle* (1832). This led to a lawsuit and a harmless duel with Frédéric Gaillardet, whose manuscript Dumas had rewritten.

Dumas *père* also enjoyed success with *Kean, ou Desordre et genie* (1836), a play about the great English actor. The producer Dartois offered Dumas 2,000 francs if it took in 60,000 francs by its 30th performance. On the appointed night, Dartois came smiling to announce the total as 59,993 francs. Dumas, claiming he was broke, borrowed 20 francs from Dartois; five minutes later three more playgoers rushed into the orchestra seats and Dumas won the bet.

He is now mostly remembered for his novels, especially two that were subsequently adapted for the theatre, *The Three Musketeers* (1844) and *The Count of Monte Cristo* (1844–45). Both were produced at Dumas's own Théâtre Historique, whose eventual failure left him near bankruptcy. His later liaison with a US circus girl created a scandal; he died at Puys in the house of Dumas *fils*, his son by a Parisian dressmaker.

Although Dumas *fils* is sometimes credited with originating the realistic-social drama, he remains best known for dramatizing his own romantic novel THE LADY OF THE CAMELLIAS (1852). The character of the consumptive Marguerite Gautier, based in part on Dumas's mistress Marie Duplessis, provided a bravura role for such actresses as Sarah Bernhardt and Eleonora Duse.

His later moralizing dramas were sometimes known as the **useful theatre**: Dumas said that if he could persuade people to discuss a social problem and achieve a change in the law he had "done his duty as a man." *Le Demi-monde* (1855) gave the French and English languages a name for the social group it portrayed. *Le Fils Naturel* (1858) dealt with the stigma of illegitimacy, as did *Un Père Prodigue* (1859), which included an accurate portrait of his father.

dumb. dumb show *See* MIME.

Dumb Waiter, The A one-act play for two characters by Harold PINTER. It was first performed, as part of a double bill with *The Room*, in 1960 at the Hampstead Theatre Club in London. Both works later transferred to the Royal Court Theatre.

Set in a basement room in Birmingham, the play concerns two hit men, Gus and Ben, who are waiting for orders. They pass the time with small talk about how they will handle the assignment. An envelope is slid under the door but it is empty. The dumb waiter (service lift) descends bearing orders for a meal that the two men cannot supply. Gus uses a speaking tube to apologize to the unknown man upstairs.

Ben finally receives instructions on the tube, but Gus has gone outside for a glass of water, returning without his jacket, waistcoat, or revolver. The two men stare at each other for a long time in silence as the curtain falls.

dundrearies A Victorian nickname for long side-whiskers. The term came into usage in 1861, during performances at the Haymarket of Tom Taylor's play *Our American Cousin*, in which the US actor E. A. Sothern (*see* SOTHERN FAMILY) sported the style in his role as Lord Dundreary.

Dunlap, William (1766–1839) US dramatist and theatre manager. As a young man, Dunlap was sent to study art in England, where he developed his enthusiasm for the theatre and became a great admirer of Kemble and Sarah Siddons. He returned to America in 1787 and began to write plays. The first of his works to be performed, *The Father; or American Shandyism*, was produced at the John Street Theatre in 1789.

Several of his comedies were performed by the AMERICAN COMPANY and in 1796 he entered into partnership with the company's managers, Lewis Hallam and John Hodgkinson. Dunlap boosted the company's fortunes by introducing Joseph JEFFERSON as the leading actor. The company dominated the US stage for some twenty years under Dunlap's management. In 1798, after Hallam's retirement, Dunlap and Hodgkinson opened the PARK THEATRE, New York, with a production of *As You Like It*. Dunlap used the theatre to produce many of his own plays and adaptations including *André*, the first US tragedy, which dealt with the War of Independence. He also leased the Haymarket Theatre in Boston, to which many of his plays transferred.

In 1805 Dunlap was declared bankrupt, but continued his involvement with the theatre, first as an assistant stage manager at the Park Theatre and later touring with his own plays again. In 1832 he published a *History of the American Theatre*.

duologue or **duodrama** A short presentation or scene for two speaking characters (although other non-speaking actors may be present on stage). Duologues became popular as part of triple bills in Germany in the late 18th century.

Dürrenmatt, Friedrich (1921–90) Swiss dramatist and writer, considered one of the most important German-language playwrights in the second half of the 20th century. His first play, *It Is Written* (1947), demonstrated his indebtedness to the methods of Brecht and the expressionists. Subsequently he established his reputation with a series of black comedies on such themes as human greed, hypocrisy, and cruelty. *The Blind Man* (1948), *Romulus the Great* (1949), and *The Marriage of Mr Mississippi* (1952) shared the same sense of futility and desperation as other absurdist plays (*see* ABSURD, THEATRE OF THE), but were distinguished by their clever use of theatrical technique, which made them popular attractions in New York and London.

His best-known plays are THE VISIT (*Der Besuch der alten Dame*; 1956), about a rich old woman's revenge on her hometown for wrongs done to her many years before, and *The Physicists* (1962), a grotesque tragicomedy in which several fugitive scientists hide themselves in a lunatic asylum.

From the late 1960s Dürrenmatt turned increasingly to the novel, publishing a number of experimental works that incorporate speculative essays on politics, philosophy, and science. His other writings include several treatises upon the theatre, plays for radio, and a number of detective novels.

Duse, Eleonora (1859–1924) Italian tragic actress. Born into a family of poor strolling players, Duse had played Juliet by the age of 14. In 1878 she began touring with the great tragedian Ernesto Rossi (1827–96); three years later she acted in Russia, winning the admiration of Chekhov.

Duse's first London appearance was at the Lyric Theatre in 1893 in *The Lady of the Camellias*, a play she subsequently took to New York. In 1895 Duse and her great rival Sarah BERNHARDT both appeared in London as Magda in Sudermann's *Heimat*, Duse playing the role in Italian and Bernhardt in French. Critical opinion was divided, with George Bernard Shaw preferring Duse and Clement Scott Bernhardt. Duse's acting style was naturalistic, her costumes simple, and she wore no make-up, being noted for her ability to blush at will. The critic James Agate noted, "Her features have the placidity of long grief; so many storms have broken over them that nothing can disturb against this sea of calm distress."

Her finest roles were IBSEN's Rebecca West and Hedda Gabler, Zola's Thérèse Raquin, and SARDOU's Tosca, Fedora, and Theodora. In 1894 Duse appeared in *La Locandiera* at a command performance for the elderly Queen Victoria at Windsor Castle. That same year she fell in love with the Italian poet Gabriele D'ANNUNZIO, who wrote several florid melodramas for her, including *La città morta* (1898) and *Francesca da Rimini* (1902). Duse's performances in D'Annunzio's plays made him famous but dimmed her own reputation. She retired in 1913 but returned to the stage eight years later: she died whilst touring America. Mussolini, whom she hated, declared her a national hero and had her body returned for a state funeral in Rome.

Jewish Duse, The The nickname of the Polish actress Esther Rachel Kaminska (1862–1930), who was also called 'the Mother of the Yiddish theatre'. She began acting in 1892, being highly praised for her roles in such plays as *Mirele Efros* in which the daughter was played by her real daughter Ida Kaminska (1899–1970). The Kaminska family opened the Warsaw Yiddish Art Theatre (VYKT) in 1921. The E. R. Kaminska Theatre was built to house the Polish Jewish State Theatre, formed in 1950, and Ida became its artistic director.

Dust Hole The disparaging nickname for the Queen's Theatre, a former venue on Tottenham Street, London (subsequently replaced by the SCALA THEATRE). Owing largely to its unfashionable location, the Queen's was not a great success. The 'Dust Hole' appellation became widely used on account of the bleak uncrowded interior.

Dutch Courtesan, The A comedy by John MARSTON first performed in 1605 in London by the Children of the Queen's Revels, one of the BOY COMPANIES. The play has enjoyed several successful revivals.

The youthful Freevill, having become engaged to the virtuous Beatrice, wishes to end his relationship with Franceschina, the Dutch courtesan. Freevill introduces Franceschina to his puritanical friend Malheureux, who becomes infatuated with her. Franceschina agrees to become his mistress if he will murder Freevill and, as proof, bring her the ring that Beatrice gave him. Malheureux informs Freevill, who agrees to help by staging a bogus quarrel, giving him the ring, and disappearing. When Malheureux gives Franceschina the ring she immediately informs the fathers of Freevill and Beatrice. Malheureux is arrested for the murder and sentenced to death. He is freed, however, when Freevill suddenly reappears; Franceschina is flogged and imprisoned. The main plot is supported by rude farce involving the prankster Cocledemoy.

dwarfs In England, dwarfs or midgets were popular until the 18th century as court favourites. In later times they were often exhibited as curiosities at circuses and exhibitions. Famous dwarfs include Lucius (fl. 10 BC; 2ft), the dwarf of the Emperor Augustus, Xit (fl. 1550), the dwarf of Edward VI, John Jarvis (1508–56; 2ft), page of honour to Queen Mary, Copernin (fl. 1730), the last court dwarf in England, the Corsican Madame Teresia (2ft 10in), exhibited in London in 1773, Wybrand Lolkes (2ft 3in), exhibited at Astley's Amphitheatre in 1790, the Italian Caroline Crachami (1ft 8in), exhibited in London in 1824, the so-called Fairy Queen (1ft 4in), exhibited in London in 1850, the celebrated General TOM THUMB (1838–83), and the Zarate sisters (both under 2ft), exhibited in London as the Midgets in 1881.

dying words Some well-known final observations by some of the great figures of the theatre:

ADDISON, JOSEPH (*playwright and essayist*): See in what peace a Christian can die.

ALFIERI, V. A. (*playwright*): Clasp my hand, dear friend, I am dying.

BEHAN, BRENDAN (*playwright*; on having his pulse taken by a nursing nun): Bless you, Sister. May all your sons be bishops!

BYRON, LORD (*poet and playwright*): I must sleep now.

CHARLES II (*English monarch*; referring to his mistress the actress Nell Gwynn) Do not, do not let poor Nelly starve.

COOPER, DAME GLADYS (*actress*; on looking into her mirror): If this is what viral pneumonia does to one, I really don't think I shall bother to have it again.

COWARD, SIR NOËL (*playwright*): Good night, my darlings, I'll see you in the morning.

DIDEROT, DENIS (*playwright and critic*): The first step towards philosophy is incredulity.

DUNCAN, ISADORA (*dancer*; waving goodbye to friends from her car shortly before her scarf caught the wheel and strangled her): Adieu my friends, I go on to glory!

FAIRBANKS SNR, DOUGLAS (*actor*): I've never felt better!

GOETHE (*playwright and poet*): Light, more light.

HAZLITT, WILLIAM (*critic*): Well, I've had a good life.

IBSEN, HENRIK (*playwright*; on being told by the nurse that he was feeling better): On the contrary!

PALMER, JOHN (*actor*; a line in the last play in which he performed): There is another and a better world.

QUIN, JAMES 'BELLOWER' (*actor*): I could wish this tragic scene were over, but I hope to go through it with becoming dignity.

SANDERS, GEORGE (*actor*; his suicide note): Dear World, I am leaving you because I am bored. I am leaving you with your worries. Good luck.

SAROYAN, WILLIAM (*playwright*): Everybody has got to die, but I have always believed an exception would be made in my case. Now what?

SCARRON, PAUL (*playwright*): Ah, my children, you cannot cry for me so much as I have made you laugh.

SCHILLER, FRIEDRICH (*playwright*): Many things are growing plain and clear to my understanding.

TASSO, TORQUATO (*poet and playwright*): Lord, into Thy hands I commend my spirit.

THOMAS, DYLAN (*poet and writer*): I've had eighteen straight whiskies. I think that's the record.

VOLTAIRE (*writer*): Do let me die in peace.

WILDE, OSCAR (*dramatist*; contemplating the room in Paris in which he lay): Either that wallpaper goes, or I do.

E

Early Morning *See* BOND, EDWARD.

Earth Spirit A play by Frank WEDEKIND, first performed in 1902 with Wedekind's actress wife Tilly Newes (Mathilde Newes; 1886–1970) in the role of Lulu.

Earth Spirit was one of several dramas by Wedekind on the theme of repressed sexuality and its dangers. The plot centres on the beautiful and amoral Lulu, whose admirers always seek to change her and always fail. Wedekind continued her story in PANDORA'S BOX, first produced in 1905.

The British playwright Peter Barnes (1931–) adapted and merged the two plays in *Lulu* (1970).

Eastward Ho! A CITIZEN COMEDY by George CHAPMAN, John MARSTON, and Ben JONSON, first performed by the Children of the Revels at Blackfriars Theatre in 1605. Characters include the apprentices Golding and Quicksilver and the adventurer Sir Petronel FLASH.

The play is now mainly remembered for the distress it caused to its authors. Unluckily for them, a brief diatribe against the Scots in Act III was not well received at the court of the new king, the Scottish-born James I. Chapman and Marston were flung into the Old Marshalsea prison to await sentence; to show solidarity Jonson (who did not work on the passage in question) voluntarily joined them there. Rumours then circulated that the three authors would have their ears and noses split as punishment; only representations by influential friends secured their pardon and release.

Jonson was so relieved to escape this punishment that he threw a banquet for his friends and family to celebrate. In the middle of the party his old mother showed him some poison she had acquired; if the punishment was to have been carried out, she had planned to mix the potion in her son's drink and, being "no churl", to drink the remainder herself.

ecclesiastical drama *See* LITURGICAL DRAMA.

Edgar, David (1948–) British playwright, whose works are known for their strong political content. His reputation was established by *Destiny* (1976), which examines racist and fascist elements in British culture; it was first performed in a production by the Royal Shakespeare Company. His other works include *Wreckers* (1977), *Maydays* (1983), which explores the changes in British society since the mid 1950s, *That Summer* (1987), and *The Shape of the Table*, about the political upheavals in Eastern Europe during the late 1980s. In 1980 he enjoyed enormous critical and commercial success with an adaptation of Dickens's *Nicholas Nickleby* staged by the RSC.

Edgar has also been involved with COMMUNITY THEATRE projects and has enjoyed success with several screenplays.

Edinburgh Festival A major international festival, officially titled the Edinburgh Festival of Music and Drama, held annually in the Scottish capital for three weeks, usually from mid-August to mid-September. It was founded in 1947 by the Austrian-born Rudolph Bing, general manager of the Glyndebourne Opera Festival.

The Edinburgh Festival has shown the premieres of such works as T. S. Eliot's THE COCKTAIL PARTY (1949), *The Confidential Clerk* (1953), and *The Elder Statesman* (1958), and Thornton Wilder's THE MATCHMAKER (1954). It offers productions by major British companies, including the Royal Shakespeare Company, the English Stage Company, and the National Theatre Company, as well as foreign troupes, such as the Comédie-Française, the Théâtre National Populaire, and the Piccolo Teatro Della Città Di Milano.

In the 1950s the **Edinburgh Fringe** (*see* FRINGE THEATRE) grew up beside the official festival, attracting professional and amateur groups from around the world. Works made famous by the fringe include the revue BEYOND THE FRINGE (1960), and Tom Stoppard's ROSENCRANTZ AND GUILDENSTERN ARE

DEAD (1966). The 1996 fringe featured a record 14,060 performances of 1238 shows in 187 venues, making the 50th Edinburgh Festival the world's largest ever arts festival.

Edinburgh Festival Happening The sudden appearance of a naked woman on the stage during the Edinburgh Festival of 1963, which did much to intensify interest in the shortlived craze for theatrical HAPPENINGS.

Educating Rita A comedy by the Liverpool playwright Willy RUSSELL. *Educating Rita* opened in 1980 at the Donmar Warehouse Theatre, a fringe theatre in Covent Garden, London, and transferred later that year to the Piccadilly Theatre where it had a record run.

The play has only two characters: Rita, a bright but uneducated hairdresser with a desire to widen her horizons, and her Open-University English-literature tutor Frank, a cynical 50-year-old who has failed in his ambition to become a poet. Their tutorial sessions result in Rita leaving her husband and finding a better job; however, her new independence drives Frank to even heavier drinking and he is 'banished' by his university to a two-year teaching assignment in Australia. Before he departs, Rita's last act is to snip off his unruly locks of hair.

Russell later adapted the play for the cinema; the film version (1983) starred Julie Walters and Michael Caine.

Edward II A tragedy by Christopher MARLOWE, sometimes considered his masterpiece; it was a major influence on Shakespeare's RICHARD II. First performed in 1593 in London, it paints a bleak picture of power and human relationships.

Edward II was the first English play to feature homosexuality. The weak king is fond of the flatterer Gaveston, who has been forced into exile in Ireland. Queen Isabella hopes that her husband will now pay more attention to her, but he refuses unless she uses her influence to bring Gaveston back to court. When Gaveston is executed Edward shifts his affections to a new favourite, Spenser. The Queen and her lover, Mortimer, rebel against the king, who is eventually deposed and murdered.

In 1969 Ian McKellen played the roles of Marlowe's Edward II and Shakespeare's Richard II on alternate nights at the Mermaid Theatre, London.

Edwardes, George (1852–1915) British theatre manager, known as **the Guv'nor**, who pioneered the MUSICAL. Edwardes was business manager at the Savoy Theatre before taking over, with John Hollingshead (1827–1904), the old GAIETY THEATRE in 1885. In 1886 Edwardes became sole manager of the Gaiety and began to replace the burlesque shows with works in the new genre of musical comedy. He staged his first musical, *In Town*, at the Gaiety in 1892; the following year he produced *A Gaiety Girl* at the Prince of Wales's Theatre. Edwardes was the creator of the GAIETY GIRLS, a chorus line famous for their beauty.

In 1893 Edwardes opened DALY'S THEATRE, LONDON, for the American manager Augustin Daly (1839–99), and made it another home for musical comedy, achieving success with such productions as *A Country Girl* (1902) and *The Merry Widow* (1907).

Ten years later he opened his own new Gaiety Theatre, his greatest success there being *Our Miss Gibbs*, which had its premiere in 1909 and ran for 636 performances.

Eglinton Tournament A replica of a medieval tournament staged at Eglinton Castle, Scotland, in August 1839. Lady Seymour was made Queen of Love and Beauty and the Marquess of Londonderry was King of the Tournament. The ladies wore fashions of the 14th and 15th centuries and the gentlemen appeared in the role of Knights, among them Prince Louis Napoleon (later Napoleon III). The affair is magnificently depicted in Disraeli's novel *Endymion*.

Eidophusikon A moving dioramic exhibition, presented in 1871 in London by Philip James de LOUTHERBOURG who used it chiefly to demonstrate atmospheric lighting effects. Pieces of silk and glass were passed in front of lamps to create drifting clouds, falling rain, and changing seasons. The scenic entertainment, which included dramatic music, was given for two successful seasons on a stage only six feet wide.

The highlight of the show was a storm at sea. Clouds, painted on canvas, were hurried over the ocean by a winding machine while lightning flashed and the waves (carved in wood and varnished every night to reflect the lightning) rose menacingly and collapsed into foam, dimming as they receded. Another popular scene was a view of Greenwich, with the distant heights of Hampstead and other London high points in the background.

Ekhof, Konrad (1720–78) German actor and director, who greatly influenced the development of the German dramatic tradition. Born in Hamburg, Ekhof joined Johann Friedrich Schönemann's company in 1739 and remained with it for 17 years. During this period he introduced the new naturalistic style of acting in adaptations of French plays and in such works as George Lillo's *The London Merchant* and Lessing's *Miss Sara Sampson.*

In 1753 Ekhof opened an Academy of Acting at Schwerin; amongst the subjects discussed was the social responsibility of the actor. In 1767 he joined Konrad Ackermann in his attempt to establish a German National Theatre in Hamburg but left because of professional rivalry with Ackermann's stepson, the actor Friedrich SCHRÖDER.

Ekhof subsequently toured for several years with Abel Seyler (1730–1801) before joining the Court Theatre in Weimar where he acted under GOETHE; Ekhof was able to give the writer anecdotal material about the theatrical profession to use in *Wilhelm Meister.* In 1775 Ekhof became chief actor and director for the new Court Theatre at Gotha, inviting the 16-year-old August IFFLAND to join his company. Ekhof's farewell performance was as the Ghost in Schröder's version of *Hamlet.*

ekkyklema In the ancient Greek theatre, a movable platform that brought actors on stage. It may have been a wheeled platform, a couch on wheels, a pivoting turntable, or simply the opening of double doors in the centre of the stage wall to reveal a group of actors. The *ekkyklema* was often used by Euripides.

Electra The daughter of Agamemnon and Clytemnestra, who incited her brother Orestes to kill Clytemnestra in revenge for the latter's murder of Agamemnon. Electra is the eponymous heroine of tragedies by Sophocles and Euripides and also features in Aeschylus's ORESTEIA, on which Eugene O'Neill's trilogy MOURNING BECOMES ELECTRA is based.

In modern psychology an 'Electra complex' is a daughter's attraction towards her father accompanied by hostility towards her mother – a female equivalent of the Oedipus complex.

Eleusinian Mysteries The religious rites in honour of Demeter or Ceres performed at Eleusis in Attica and later partly celebrated at Athens. They were abolished by the Emperor Theodosius around the end of the 4th century AD.

Originally an agrarian cult, the rites included sea bathing, processions, and religious dramas; the initiated supposedly obtained a happy life beyond the grave. Little is known about the chief rites, hence the figurative use of the phrase to mean something deeply mysterious. *See also* DIONYSUS.

elevator *See* BRIDGE.

Eliot, T(homas) S(tearns) (1888–1965) US-born British poet, dramatist, and critic. Born in St Louis, Missouri, he studied philosophy at Harvard before leaving for Europe in 1914. In 1915 he decided to settle in the UK after marrying an English woman. Working first as a schoolteacher and then as a bank clerk, he managed to establish himself in his spare time as perhaps the most significant poet of the age; by the mid-1920s he had also become the poetry editor of Faber and Faber and the founder-editor of *The Criterion* (a literary journal).

Despite a long interest in the stage, it was not until the 1930s that Eliot's first important plays appeared. The poetic dramas MURDER IN THE CATHEDRAL (1935), about the martyrdom of Thomas à Becket, and THE FAMILY REUNION (1939) were not immediately accepted into the repertoire of the commercial theatre. In the 1950s, however, his prestige as a major poet entitled his three post-war plays THE COCKTAIL PARTY (1950), *The Confidential Clerk* (1954), and *The Elder Statesman* (1954) to prestigious West-End productions. All Eliot's plays reflect his preoccupation with religion (he became an Anglo-Catholic in 1927) and his own personal sense of guilt (largely connected with the mental illness of his first wife, their separation in 1933, and her death in 1947). In the later 20th century, however, those plays have been given very few revivals. Indeed, it is perhaps ironic that Eliot the playwright is now best known for the librettro of Andrew LLOYD WEBBER's musical CATS (1981), which is based on the light-hearted verse contained in his *Old Possum's Book of Practical Cats* (1939).

In 1984 Eliot's tortured marital life became the subject of the controversial play *Tom and Viv* by Michael Hastings.

Elizabethan drama English drama during the reign of Elizabeth I (1558–1603). England's first great era of the theatre was crowned by the emergence of the world's most renowned dramatist, William SHAKESPEARE. Other prominent writers of the Elizabethan age included the UNIVERSITY WITS – Christopher MARLOWE, Thomas KYD, John Lyly, and others – whose work for the stage shows the influence of ancient Greek and Roman playwrights, especially SENECA.

The first English tragedy, GORBODUC, was written and performed by law students of London's Inner Temple in 1562 with Elizabeth in the audience. The first extant English comedy, RALPH ROISTER DOISTER by Nicholas Udall, was performed around 1563. Distinct genres to emerge during the era include REVENGE TRAGEDY and the CITIZEN COMEDY.

Some 21,000 Londoners, or one-eighth of the population, attended the theatre at least once a week. Elizabeth herself saw only about five professional productions a year, for which she paid each company about ten pounds. She banned plays about religious or political subjects because these had been used as propaganda in earlier reigns; the MYSTERY PLAY was also prohibited.

As unlicensed actors were classified as vagabonds, they often sought the patronage of noblemen; among the companies supported in this way were the CHAMBERLAIN'S MEN and the ADMIRAL'S MEN, together with several BOY COMPANIES. During plague periods, the London theatres closed and actors went on gruelling tours of the region in order to survive. Many actors became famous, however, such as Richard Burbage (*see* BURBAGE FAMILY), Edward Alleyn, and William Kempe, while those who had financial interests in the theatres in which they performed also became wealthy.

The first permanent public playhouse in England, THE THEATRE, was opened in 1576 by James Burbage, Richard's father. Others quickly followed: the Curtain Theatre in 1577, the Rose Theatre in 1587, the Swan Theatre in 1594, and the famous GLOBE THEATRE, at which many of Shakespeare's works were given their first performances, in 1599. The average audience capacity was 2000 to 3000 people. The venues were classified as 'liberties' beyond the city's jurisdiction.

Elsinore A town in Denmark (Danish name Helsingør), which provides the setting for the story of HAMLET. Elsinore's Kronborg Castle has been the site since 1937 of an annual Shakespeare Festival in which international companies perform only that play.

The Old Vic company appeared in the festival's inaugural year, with Laurence OLIVIER as Hamlet. Although married, he was having an affair with the actress Vivien Leigh (his future wife), who persuaded him to give her the role of Ophelia, replacing the excellent Cherry Cottrell. The production, which also included Alec Guinness as Osric, was to be staged on the castle ramparts and terraces before the Danish royal family. On the day of performance, however, torrential rain forced the players into the ballroom of the Marienlyst Hotel for a THEATRE-IN-THE-ROUND production. Olivier improvised a new stage production that sometimes involved him moving into the audience. The critic J. C. Trewin called this "the performance of a lifetime – so new, astonishing and exciting".

Eltinge, Julian (William Dalton; 1883–1941) US actor who became the most famous FEMALE IMPERSONATOR of his day. Eltinge, who often appeared under the name **Mrs Lillian Russell**, specialized in playing glamorous women in extravagant gowns. His most popular sketch was one in which he appeared as a bathing beauty.

Eltinge first appeared in drag at the age of 10 with the Boston Cadets but his first professional success came in 1905 with the musical *Mr Wix of Wickham*. He subsequently toured with a Minstrel Show before winning great acclaim in the dual roles of Hal Blake and Mrs Monte in *The Fascinating Widow*, a musical comedy written especially for him. He starred in Vaudeville throughout the 1920s, made a few silent films, and retired in 1930, making a brief comeback in 1940 in Billy Rose's *Diamond Horseshoe Jubilee*.

Empire Promenade A once-famous feature of the former Empire Theatre, Leicester Square, London, consisting of an open space behind the dress circle where prostitutes would regularly parade. In 1894 Mrs Ormiston Chant of the London County Council campaigned for the closure of the Empire Promenade and its adjoining bars.

This led to the erection of canvas screens between them, but these were soon demolished by a riotous crowd, a prominent member of which was the young Winston CHURCHILL. Brick partitions were subsequently built.

> Thus the temples of Venus and Bacchus, though adjacent, would be separated, and their attack on human frailities could only be delivered in a successive or alternating and not in a concentrated form.
> WINSTON CHURCHILL: *My Early Life.*

encore A cry of enthusiastic admiration, calling for a repeat or supplementary performance. The term is also applied to the extra performance itself.

Although it is a French word (meaning 'again' or 'another'), encore is not used in the same way in France, where the audience cries *bis* (twice) for a repeat performance.

Endgame A one-act play by Samuel BECKETT. The original French version, *Fin de Partie*, received its first performance in London in 1957 at the Royal Court Theatre; the English version was published a year later.

The play has four characters: Hamm, blind and wheelchair-bound, is nursed by his servant son, Clov; his legless parents, Nagg and Nell, whom he continually berates, are stuffed in dustbins and speak nonsense as they slowly disintegrate. Clov announces from time to time that he is leaving but his father's influence prevents him from doing so. Beckett depicts with ironic humour this pitiful group, cut off from the dying world outside (which seems to have suffered some kind of holocaust), trying to come to terms with their own impending doom.

Enemy of the People, An A play by Henrik IBSEN, first performed in 1882 in Oslo. It was a combative answer to public and press criticism of his previous play, GHOSTS: in *An Enemy of the People* Ibsen defends the avant-garde minority and draws an unflattering portrait of a liberal newspaper. Ibsen's satire reveals his distrust of politicians and the blindly held beliefs of the majority.

The plot centres on the attempts of the physician Dr Stockmann to expose a pollution scandal in the spa town in which he lives. The local newspaper suppresses the story and when Stockmann appeals to a public meeting he is shouted down by the commercially-minded citizens. He calls them fools – and they call him an enemy of the people.

Ibsen admitted that the arrogant and muddle-headed doctor had "certain characteristics which will permit people to tolerate certain things from his lips which they might not accept so readily had they issued from mine".

Enfants Sans Souci (Fr: children without care) A medieval French society of actors, mainly young men of good family, who devoted themselves to the production of the SOTIE, a type of comedy that ridiculed public characters and the manners of the day. The head of the 'Care-for-Nothings' was called 'The Prince of Fools' (*Prince des Sots*), an office held for years by Pierre Gringore (*c.* 1475–1539).

English. English Aristophanes A nickname bestowed on the British actor-manager and playwright Samuel Foote (1720–77), who wrote sharp satirical sketches about contemporary manners. He has also been called 'the Father of the Burlesque'.

Foote began acting in 1744 and three years later took over the HAYMARKET. In 1749 he inherited a fortune and quickly spent it in Paris, returning to the Haymarket as actor-manager and playwright. His first successful farces were *The Englishman in Paris* (1753) and its sequel *The Englishman Returned from Paris* (1756). His best work *The Minor*, a satire on the Methodist movement, opened in 1760.

As manager, Foote used clever subterfuges to evade the Licensing Act of 1737. Although the Haymarket had no licence to present plays, he would invite 'guests' for tea or chocolate during which an entertainment would be given. In 1766 he obtained a limited patent for summer performances, as compensation for the loss of his leg as the result of a practical joke perpetrated by the Duke of York and others. He built a new Haymarket the following year.

Foote had a gift for bitter mimicry that made him feared. A frequent target of his wit was David GARRICK, known for his love of money. Foote once showed Samuel Johnson a bust of Garrick that he kept on his bureau. "You may be surprised that I allow him to be so near my gold," he said, "but you will observe he has no hands." Foote never ridiculed Johnson, for reasons the doctor explained to Boswell: "Sir, fear restrained him; he knew I would have broken his bones. I would have saved him the trouble of cutting off a leg; I would not have left him a leg to cut off."

Foote died on the way to France after selling his patent to George Colman the elder. His epitaph reads:

> Foote from his earthly stage, alas! is hurled;
> Death took him off, who took off all the world.

See also DEVIL AMONG THE TAILORS *under* DEVIL.

English Comedians Wandering troupes of English actors who travelled the Continent during the 16th and 17th centuries. Their repertoire of Elizabethan comedies and tragedies, usually abridged and always in English (sometimes interpreted), included a popular burlesque version of *Hamlet* (*Die bestrafte Brudermord*) that later became an essential part of the repertoire of German companies. The plays were supported by music, dancing, and comic sketches; the general comedy was broad enough to appeal to their foreign audiences. English clowns were popular, especially Robert Reynolds as PICKELHERING (upon whom the German clowns HANSWURST and THADDÄDL were modelled).

An early troupe performed in 1586 under William Kempe in Holland and Denmark, before moving on to Dresden and other German towns. The first company of English Comedians to achieve great acclaim and renown was led by Robert Browne, who produced plays in Leiden in 1591 and the next year took the group to the Frankfurt fair where they performed biblical plays, works by Marlowe, and GAMMER GURTON'S NEEDLE. Shortly afterwards, Thomas Sackville took a company to Wolfenbüttel and established it in the Court Theatre of Heinrich Julius, Duke of Brunswick, who was a playwright: the duke's extant plays show the influence of the English Comedians' repertoire.

The overall effect of these travelling actors was to bring action and passion to a German theatre preoccupied with lengthy speeches. By 1630 the printed repertoire of the English Comedians contained many works of German origin. They continued to play in Europe despite the Thirty Years' War, and returned in greater numbers during the Puritan INTERREGNUM, although there is no record of them after 1659.

English Stage Company A London theatre company founded in 1955 by George DEVINE to promote modern and experimental drama and encourage young playwrights. "A theatre must have a recognizable attitude," Devine stated. "It will have one, whether you like it or not."

The company made its permanent home at the ROYAL COURT THEATRE, opening in 1956 with Angus Wilson's *The Mulberry Bush*. An appeal by Devine for new scripts brought in 750 entries, including John Osborne's LOOK BACK IN ANGER, which was staged that same year and created a new trend in British drama. Other playwrights launched by the company include Arnold Wesker, John Arden, Edward Bond, and David Storey.

The ESC's controversial offerings created an uneasy relationship with the LORD CHAMBERLAIN, who banned *The Catalyst* by Ronald Duncan in 1957 and BOND's *Early Morning* in 1968.

ENSA Entertainments National Service Association. A British theatre organization established in 1938 to provide troops and war workers with entertainment ranging from plays to music and variety performances. It was managed by Basil Dean, who had organized similar shows during World War I, from offices in Drury Lane. The financial side was administered by the Navy, Army, and Air Force Institute (NAAFI).

All actors not called to active service were required to give six weeks to ENSA. These included John Gielgud, Edith Evans, Vivien Leigh, Emlyn Williams, and Beatrice Lillie. ENSA remained in business immediately after the war, when Laurence Olivier toured camps in Germany with the OLD VIC.

ENSA concerts greatly helped to boost morale during World War II, despite the joke among theatre people that ENSA stood for Every Night Something Awful.

enter *See* STAGE DIRECTION.

entertain. ***Entertainer, The*** A tragicomedy by John OSBORNE, first performed in 1957 at the Royal Court Theatre with Laurence OLIVIER in the title role of the seedy music-hall comic Archie RICE. When Olivier took the play to Broadway's Royale Theatre two years later, the New York critic Brooks Atkinson wrote, "If anyone doubts that Laurence Olivier is a versatile actor, consider the subject closed." Olivier went on to star in the film version (1960).

Osborne's story is set in 1956 in an English coastal resort. The Rice family struggles along as Archie continues his blatantly bad comic routines in the local halls. The play reflects the decline of Britain's political and economic roles and the rise of new forms of popular entertainment.

Entertaining Mr Sloane An anarchic comedy by Joe ORTON, first performed in 1964 in London. It was Orton's first play and established his reputation, receiving the *Evening Standard* Award for the best play of the year. Audiences, however, were shocked by the author's use of witty and elegant language to convey a story of murder and sexual perversion.

The plot centres on the amoral 19-year-old Mr Sloane, who takes lodgings in a house occupied by the three other characters. He inspires desire in Kath and her brother Ed, but disgusts their father Kemp. Sloane and Kath establish a sexual relationship, but the lodger avoids Ed's advances. When Kemp finally realizes that Sloane is the killer of his former employer, Sloane murders him too. This allows Kath, now pregnant, and Ed to blackmail Sloane, who is obliged to serve the two of them as a sexual plaything.

entremés In 16th-century Spain, a brief entertainment presented during a banquet; later, a comic piece (often ending in a dance) between the acts of a full-length play. Derived from Corpus Christi processions in Catalonia, the *entremés* became a respected genre adapted by such playwrights as Lope de Vega and Cervantes. It was similar to the English INTERLUDE and the Italian INTERMEZZO.

environmental theatre A form of theatre that emerged in the late 1960s, inheriting many ideas from the HAPPENING. The new term was popularized by the US director and critic Richard Schechner (1934–). In 1968 he published the axioms of environmental theatre, placing it between traditional theatre on the one hand and public events and demonstrations on the other; his examples of environmental theatre included the Polish Laboratory Theatre (*see* POOR THEATRE), the LIVING THEATRE, and the OPEN THEATRE.

The environmental theatre required no text, and its main feature was a mingling of actors and spectators. Schechner said "all the space is used for performance; all the space is used for the audience": members of the audience were both 'scene-makers' and 'scene-watchers', as bystanders are part of the street scene they view.

In 1967 Schechner formed his own company, the Performance Group, which was housed in a converted garage filled with towers and platforms used by actors and spectators. The following year he produced and directed their first offering, *Dionysus in 69*, an adaptation of Euripides's THE BACCHAE. In 1973 the group presented Sam Shepard's *The Tooth of Crime*, and in 1975 Bertolt Brecht's *Mother Courage and Her Children*. Schechner left the company in 1980.

Epic Theatre A form of political drama intended to appeal to reason rather than the emotions. Epic Theatre replaced the UNITIES with an episodic structure; an important feature was the ALIENATION EFFECT, in which actors and audiences were discouraged from identifying with the characters or scenes depicted. The name and theory were derived from Aristotle and pioneered in Germany in the late 1920s by Bertolt BRECHT and his associate Erwin PISCATOR (1893–1966). Both were avowed communists who sought an ideal theatre with social and political relevance that would stimulate playgoers into both thought and action; *Theatre of Commitment*, *Theatre of Social Action*, and *Theatre of Social Conviction* were alternative names for the genre. Brecht's MAN IS MAN (1926) is usually considered the first Epic Theatre play; Piscator's offerings included a dramatization of Tolstoy's *War and Peace*. The tradition was continued by many of the left-wing playwrights of the 1960s and 1970s.

Epidaurus The oldest surviving and best preserved ancient Greek theatre, located at the town of this name in Argolis on the Saronic Gulf. It was designed by the architect Polycleitus and built in about 340 BC. Partially restored in the late 19th century and now completely renovated, the theatre is used for an annual summer festival of drama.

The theatre once contained a raised stage and a SKENE. The circular orchestra is about 66 feet across, and the seating area, or *cavea*, accommodated some 14,000 spectators. Radiating from the orchestra are 24 flights of steps; there are 32 lower tiers of seats separated from 20 upper tiers by a wide passage, or *diazoma*.

epilogue A brief scene, speech, or short poem at the end of a play. It often explains the significance of the drama, a function made fun of in Shakespeare's *A Midsummer Night's Dream*, where Theseus appeals to Bottom at the end of the play-within-a-play PYRAMUS AND THISBE:

> No epilogue, I pray you; for your play needs no excuse. Never excuse; for when the players are all dead, there need none to be blamed.

John DRYDEN was an accomplished writer of epilogues. At the end of his *Tyrannic Love* (1669), he specified that the epilogue should be "spoken by Mrs Ellen [Nell GWYNN] when she was to be carried off dead by the bearers". In the role of Valeria, slain daughter of the Roman Emperor Maximin (who has executed St Catharine of Alexandria), Nell says to the bearer:

> Hold, are you mad? you damned
> confounded dog,
> I am to rise, and speak the epilogue.

The poem ends with Nell directly informing the audience that she will trust no poet to write her own epitaph, but will do it herself:

> Here Nelly lies, who, though she lived a
> slattern,
> Yet died a princess, acting in St
> Cathar'n.

See also PROLOGUE.

Epiphany play *See* LITURGICAL DRAMA.

episode Originally, the passages of dialogue that were interpolated between the choric songs in Greek tragedy. It was subsequently applied to an adventitious tale introduced into the main story, or an incident that stands by itself but is part of a wider series of events.

equestrian drama A type of drama, popular in 18th-century London, in which horses were a key element of the production. The most famous stage horse of the late Victorian era was the mare Lily, who appeared as Richard III's horse White Surrey. John Martin-Harvey, who rode her in this role, said "I suppose few leading ladies had played a wider range of parts than Lily." The only actor she allegedly refused to carry, for no known reason, was Beerbohm Tree.

The main London theatre for equestrian dramas was ASTLEY'S AMPHITHEATRE; its chief equestrian was Andrew Ducrow, who became joint owner in 1825. Other venues were Covent Garden and Drury Lane, with such actors as Henry Irving, who was no horseman, taking equestrian roles.

The most famous equestrian production was *Mazeppa*, based on a poem by Lord Byron and first performed in 1823 at the Coburg Theatre, London. Adah MENKEN played the title role "in a state of virtual nudity" in 1863 in California and the following year at Astley's.

Horses continued to occupy the early 20th-century stage: a chariot race in a 1902 production of *Ben Hur* employed four treadmills and a rapidly revolving background. In 1904, at the newly opened London Coliseum, six horses collided on a revolving platform and an actor was killed.

Equity. (American) Actors' Equity Association The US trade union for professional actors, founded in 1913. It was officially recognized in 1919 after calling a strike for better working conditions, and in 1924 it became a closed shop. The union gained a minimum-wage scale for its members in 1933; a strike in 1960 resulted in further improvements in members' contracts, and the following year brought a commitment to racial equality in the theatre.

Other US theatrical unions include the National Alliance of Theatrical Stage Employees (recognized in 1910) for stagehands, the United Scenic Artists (formed in 1918) for designers, and the Dramatists' Guild (formed in 1912) for playwrights.

(British) Actors' Equity Association The trade union for Britain's professional actors. The strict rules surrounding membership have made the **Equity card** much sought-after. The association is located at 8 Harley Street, London. It was formed in 1929 to deal with such important concerns as pay and conditions of employment. It also subsidizes professional companies in need of financial assistance, protects its members from an influx of foreign actors seeking work in Britain, and conducts research: a 1992 survey found that actresses earn an average of 50% less than actors and even those actresses with top billing earn 30% less. One of the hazards for aspiring British actors is that they need an Equity card to be given their first speaking part; however, in order to obtain their Equity card they need to be able to show that they have had professional engagements in the theatre!

The first actors' union was the Actors' Association founded in 1891 by the actor-managers H. B. Irving and Seymour Hicks, partly in response to the hiring of actors for parts rather than as members of a company. Another organization, the Variety Artists' Federation, began in 1906 but merged with Equity in 1968.

Equus A play by Peter SHAFFER, first produced in 1973 at the National Theatre, London, to great acclaim. The following year it opened in New York.

A psychological drama, the play explores the conflict between rational and instinctive behaviour. The plot involves the efforts of a psychiatrist, Martin Dysart, to cure a delinquent stable boy, Alan Strang, who has wilfully blinded six horses. Dysart goads Alan into confronting traumas from his childhood and his first love affair; Alan relives his relationships with horses, first worshipping them and then mutilating them.

The psychoanalytical sessions uncover the sources of his violence, and Alan becomes calmer. However, Dysart comes to wonder whether Alan's life of demented passion may not be preferable to his own drily rational existence. Richard Burton played the role of Dysart on Broadway in 1976, and again in the film version (1977) with Peter Firth and Jenny Agutter.

Erté The pseudonym adopted by the French artist and designer Romain de Tirtoff (1892–1990), noted in particular for his extravagant costumes and designs for the Folies Bergères in Paris. He derived it from the French pronunciation of the first letters of his Christian name and surname.

Essence of Eccentricity, the The nickname of Nellie Wallace (Eleanor Jane Wallace; 1870–1948), a British music-hall comedienne famous for her broad humour. She dressed as a tatty spinster in a tartan skirt, a hat with a skimpy feather, and a shabby fur, which she called "me little bit of vermin". She is remembered for such songs as 'I Lost Georgie in Trafalgar Square', 'My Mother Always Said Look Under the Bed', and 'Three Cheers for the Red, White, and Blue'.

Born in Glasgow, she made her debut in Birmingham in 1882 as a child clog dancer, became part of an act called the Three Sisters Wallace, and finally went solo. In 1910 she appeared on the opening bill at the Palladium. She eventually became one of the few successful female pantomime DAMES, making an appearance in 1935 as the Wicked Witch Carabosse in *The Sleeping Beauty* at the Vaudeville Theatre.

Etherege, Sir George (1634–91). The first major Restoration playwright and the creator of the English COMEDY OF MANNERS. His nickname, **Easy Etherege**, reflects his idle way of life and studiedly insouciant manner.

Etherege's first play, much influenced by MOLIÈRE, was the tragicomedy *The Comical Revenge; or, Love in a Tub*, which was produced in 1664 at Lincoln's Inn Fields Theatre and took £1,000 in one month. The tragic main plot (including a duel and suicide) was in verse, while the farcical subplot (including the imprisonment of a French valet for impertinence) was in prose.

In 1668 Etherege's SHE WOULD IF SHE COULD, considered the first pure comedy of manners in English, was produced at Lincoln's Inn Fields. His masterpiece THE MAN OF MODE, featuring the character Sir Fopling Flutter, the PRINCE OF FOPS, was performed with great success in 1676 at the Dorset Garden Theatre. The witty character of Dorimant was said to be based on the Earl of Rochester and that of Bellair on Etherege himself.

In 1668 Etherege was sent to Turkey as secretary to the ambassador, returning three years later to take up the life of a man-about-town in London. In 1676 he was involved in a riot in which one person was killed. He married a wealthy widow, Mary Arnold; it was suspected that his knighthood (1680) came with the marriage. From 1685 until 1689 he was an envoy of James II in Regensburg but apparently took a nonchalant attitude to his duties. He was equally casual about his marriage; he had affairs with a number of actresses and is said to have had a daughter (who died young) by Elizabeth BARRY. He eventually followed James II to Paris and died there a Jacobite exile.

Ethiopian opera In the 19th-century minstrel shows, a blackfaced burlesque of opera or of Shakespeare's plays. Often derived from routines by T. D. Rice, Ethiopian opera became a standard feature of the MINSTREL SHOWS third and final section.

Euripides (484–406 BC) Greek dramatist. The last major tragic playwright of the classical world, he has also been called "the first modern". Euripides was not highly successful in his lifetime, winning the first of only five victories at the DIONYSIA at the age of 43. While Aristotle called him "the most tragic of the tragic poets"; Aristophanes accused him of teaching Athenians "to think, see, understand, suspect, question everything". By the end of the 19th century, however, Euripides was the most acclaimed Greek playwright. Elizabeth Barrett Browning summed up the reasons for his popularity:

Our Euripides, the human,
With his droppings of warm tears,
And his touches of things common
Till they rose to touch the spheres.

When the Royal Shakespeare Company presented a ten-play cycle *The Greeks* in 1980, seven of the works were by Euripides.

He wrote 92 plays of which 17 tragedies survive, along with the only extant SATYR-PLAY, *Cyclops*. His tragedies include MEDEA, his masterpiece THE BACCHAE, the anti-war TROJAN WOMEN, and ELECTRA (413 BC) and its sequel *Orestes* (408 BC). Other works include tragicomedies, such as *Iphigenia in Tauris* (414 BC), the comedy *Helen* (412 BC), and the pageant play *Phoenician Women* (411 BC).

Euripides's innovations included the DEUS EX MACHINA and the formal PROLOGUE. He used simple everyday language, bringing a new realism to the stage. Although contemporaries accused him of killing tragedy, he humanized drama by adding elements of sentiment, romance, and even comedy. He was the first to argue against the social inferiority of women, and the first to show women in love. He was also the first to explore such subjects as madness and repression, thereby foreshadowing the psychological dramas of Seneca and the NEW COMEDY of Menander.

Euripides is believed to have been trained as an athlete by his father after an oracle predicted that he would win contests. (He later made fun of both athletes and oracles.) A recluse, he shunned Athenian civil and social affairs, and in later life would sit all day in a cave on Salamis overlooking the sea as he contemplated and wrote "something great and high". In 408 BC Euripides was exiled for his unorthodox views to Macedonia, where he died less than two years later. According to tradition, when the Spartans arrived to burn Athens, they desisted after a reminder that this was Euripides's city.

Evans. Dame Edith Evans (1888–1976) Outstanding British actress, who for over 60 years enchanted audiences in the theatre and the cinema both in comedy and high drama. She made her London debut in 1912, as Cressida in William Poel's production of *Troilus and Cressida*; her last appearance, at the Haymarket Theatre in 1974, was in an evening entitled *Edith Evans...and Friends*. Between these two milestones she acted in many productions of Shakespeare's plays (including two spells at the Old Vic), a number of Restoration comedies, and a great variety of modern works, including the first production of Shaw's HEARTBREAK HOUSE in 1921. Her performance as the haughty Lady Bracknell in Wilde's *The Importance of Being Earnest*, has been a favourite with two generations: she first appeared in the stage play in 1939 but gave a memorable reading in Anthony Asquith's 1952 film. Kenneth Tynan wrote of Dame Edith speaking the lines in "a voice which had lorgnettes implicit in every dragged and devastating syllable."

Maurice Herbert Evans (1901–89) British-born US actor who was praised for his performances in the plays of Shakespeare and Shaw. He was also well-known for his film and television roles.

Evans made his professional debut in 1926 as Orestes in the Oresteia of Aeschylus at the Festival Theatre, Cambridge. His first notable success came in 1928, as Lieutenant Raleigh in R. C. Sherriff's *Journey's End* at the Apollo Theatre, with Laurence Olivier as Captain Stanhope. When Olivier was subsequently offered the lead in *Beau Geste*, Evans turned down a part in the same production to avoid working with him again so soon in a supporting role. When Olivier played Romeo in 1940 on Broadway, US critics compared him unfavourably to Evans.

In 1934 Evans joined the Old Vic, playing the leads in *Richard II* and a full-length *Hamlet*, known to the company as '*Hamlet* in its eternity'. The US director Guthrie McClintic was in the audience, seeking a Romeo to play opposite his wife, Katherine Cornell; as a result Evans made his Broadway debut in 1935 in this role. He won his best reviews ever in 1937 for *Richard II*, which ran for 171 performances at the St James Theatre: the Drama League named him the best actor of the year, and the critic John Mason Brown wrote "It is one of the finest Shakespearian performances the modern theatre has seen." The British critic James Agate, however, thought Evans too boyish for tragedy.

In 1941, the year he became a US citizen, Evans played Macbeth at the National Theatre; some blamed the famous curse of the SCOTTISH PLAY when the Japanese attacked Pearl Harbor a month after the production opened. During World War II, he entertained the troops with his simplified *G.I. Hamlet*. His postwar work included four Shaw roles, including John Tanner in *Man and Superman* (1947) and Captain Shotover in *Heartbreak House* (1959). In 1961 he won an Emmy for his television performance as Macbeth. After a solo recital in 1973 (at the age of 72) of *Shakespeare and the Performing Arts* at the Kennedy Center for the Performing Arts in Washington, DC, Evans 'retired' to Britain but continued to appear on stage and screen until he was 80.

Evans's Supper Room One of the best-known centres of London night life in the 19th century, situated on the corner of King Street, Covent Garden. The premises, used by the National Sporting Club, were opened as a family hotel (1773) and in the 1830s were occupied by the Star Dinner and Coffee Room, much frequented by the nobility.

The name *Evans's Supper Room*, by which the premises were known until their closure in 1880, derives from their one-time owner W. C. Evans, a member of the chorus of the Covent Garden Theatre. He made it the most famous SONG-AND-SUPPER ROOM in London by specializing in 'blue' entertainment and allowing his acts to outdo each other in singing bawdy songs.

John Greenmore (Paddy Green) took over in 1844 and added a splendid new hall with a platform at one end. All the performers were male; women were only admitted after giving their names and addresses, and even then were only permitted to watch from behind a screen.

Evans's is generally regarded as the most important precursor of the MUSIC HALL. The Prince of Wales (later Edward VII) was a frequent visitor in the 1860s.

every. ***Everyman*** The best surviving example of the English MORALITY PLAY. Written by an unknown author, it was apparently derived from the Dutch drama *Elckerlyc* (1495), although some scholars have suggested that the English version came first. There is no original manuscript, but it was first performed in 1500 and first printed about thirty years later.

The play is an allegory in which each character's significance is defined by his name, such as Everyman, Confession, Kindred, etc. Its rough humour lies in the haste with which Everyman's false friends and relatives abandon him once he is summoned by Death. He then falls back on such virtues as Strength, Beauty, Intelligence, and Knowledge, who also fall away as he approaches the grave. The only virtue he retains is Good Deeds, the moral being that man can take nothing from the world but what he has given.

Everyman was unperformed for centuries before William Poel's Elizabethan Stage Society revived it in 1901. It is still performed for religious purposes: John Gielgud recalled watching one such production in the 1940s "on a very hard uncomfortable pew at a church off Regent Street".

Every Man in his Humour A comedy by Ben JONSON, first performed in 1598 at the Theatre, London, by the Chamberlain's Men with Shakespeare in the role of Knowell. The play centres on a group of riotous young men visiting the home of the merchant Thomas Kitely, who has a humour of jealousy (*see* COMEDY OF HUMOURS) and therefore suspects his visitors' intentions towards his young wife and his sister Bridget. One of the young men, Edward Knowell, has indeed fallen for Bridget. Others in the group, each of whom has his own particular humour, include the blustering but cowardly Captain BOBADIL, the gruff squire George Downright, and Edward's disguised servant Brainworm. A series of practical jokes, fights, and other disturbances bring them all before kindly old Justice Clement, who bestows peace and goodwill, allowing Edward and Bridget to marry. Jonson followed this success with *Every Man Out of His Humour* (1599).

Evita A musical by composer Andrew LLOYD WEBBER and lyricist Tim Rice, that won some 40 international awards. It was first performed in London in 1978 at the Prince Edward Theatre, directed by Hal Prince and starring Stephanie Lawrence and John Turner. When it moved to Broadway, it won the 1980 Tony Award with a cast headed by Elaine Page and Joss Ackland. Alan Parker's film version appeared in 1996, with Madonna in the title role.

The story follows the brief career of the glamorous and manipulative María Eva de Perón (1919–52), who was born in poverty and rose to become the wife of President Juan Perón of Argentina. Evita's charitable work, beauty, and early death all helped to create a popular myth around her name. The story, told in flashbacks by the cynical revolutionary Che Guevara, describes Eva's use of men to become a successful model, broadcaster, and film actress, before she meets Colonel Perón and inspires him to run for the nation's highest office. In her last hours, images of her life flow by and she wonders if she would have been happier as an ordinary person. The songs include 'Don't Cry for Me, Argentina' and 'Another Suitcase in Another Hall'.

existentialism A philosophical doctrine that developed in Germany after World War I and somewhat later in France and Italy; the term is a translation of the German *Existenzphilosophie*. Existentialists emphasize the freedom and moral responsibility of the individual and show a distrust of philosophical idealism. Much of their writing is characterized by disillusionment.

Atheistic existentialism was popularized in France during World War II by Jean-Paul SARTRE and underlies many of his plays, including *Les Mouches* (1942), *Huis-Clos* (1944), and *Les Mains sales* (1948).

exit *See* STAGE DIRECTION.

expanded cinema A type of film show in which live actors and musicians interact with the film being projected as part of a MIXED MEDIA performance.

expressionism A movement in the early 20th-century theatre that sought to replace REALISM with a type of psychological drama that expressed the inner motivation of characters. It was foreshadowed in the works of STRINDBERG at the turn of the century and in the grotesque plays of Frank WEDEKIND. It continued to dominate the stage until the 1930s, when playwrights took a renewed interest in realism.

Expressionism began with a reaction against realistic stage design, in which scenic detail sometimes seemed to reduce the significance of the actors. Realistic acting came under attack next: writers played down the individualism of their characters, and W. B. YEATS went so far as to hide his actors behind generalized masks.

Expressionism underwent its greatest development around 1910 in Germany, in the works of Georg KAISER, Ernst TOLLER, and others; it also influenced Brecht's development of EPIC THEATRE. In Britain such writers as W. H. Auden and T. S. Eliot were influenced by the movement, as were Thornton Wilder and Tennessee Williams in America.

Although pure expressionism went out of fashion before World War II, many playwrights have found commercial success by mingling it with realism; elements of expressionism can be found in the works of Harold Pinter, Arthur Miller, Samuel Beckett, Jean-Paul Sartre, and Eugene Ionesco.

extravaganza In the 19th-century British theatre, a lavish entertainment resembling the BURLESQUE but based on a myth or folk tale. Although satire was not the main aim of the extravaganza, a satirical element was often included along with the music and elaborate costumes. A leading writer of extravaganzas was James Robinson Planche (1796–1880), whose work influenced the librettist W. S. Gilbert. The actor H. J. Byron (1834–84) also wrote many extravaganzas and burlesques.

F

fabula In the ancient Roman theatre, the general term for a play. There were many subdivisions. One of the oldest native genres was the ATELLANA, a short impromptu farce, the name of which came from the town of Atella. Two similar forms were the *saltica*, in which the text was sung by a chorus, and the *riciniata*; both were mime plays.

The PALLIATA was a work of Greek NEW COMEDY translated into Latin. Evolving from this genre in the 2nd century BC, the TOGATA or *tabernaria* featured bawdy satire of the everyday life of the lower classes.

The *praetexta* was an original Latin play based on Roman legend or history, or dealing with contemporary themes. Naevius created the form, while other exponents included Accius, Ennius, and Pacuvius. The *rhinthonica* was a Roman burlesque of a Greek tragedy named after the Greek playwright Rhinthon of Tarentum (4th century BC).

fairground entertainment European fairs featured entertainers such as acrobats, jugglers, dancers, freaks, and trained animals from the 16th century onwards. In late-17th-century Paris a stronger link began to develop between fairs and dramatic entertainment with the presentation of COMMEDIA DELL'ARTE plays. After the expulsion of Italian actors from Paris in 1697 (*see* COMÉDIE-ITALIENNE) more permanent theatres were established at the fairs of Saint-Germain and Saint-Laurent in the early 18th century.

To avoid the licensing laws, which forbade them to use spoken dialogue, the fair companies created new dramatic forms involving music. By 1714, the Paris Opéra was in such dire financial straits that it agreed to allow fair companies to produce comic opera for a fee. Fairground troupes were suppressed in 1718 but resumed performances after the young Louis XV attended a play. In 1762 the Comédie-Italienne gained a monopoly on comic opera, so fairground performers returned to using songs set to popular tunes, a form they renamed *comédies-en-vaudevilles* or VAUDEVILLE. By the 18th century, the fairground playhouses remained open when the fairs were closed. The Théâtre de la Foire Saint-Laurent, built in 1721, was later demolished for the construction of the Opéra-Comique theatre in 1761.

In England, fairs never played such an important role in the early theatre, although there were notable exceptions. In the early 18th century Saint BARTHOLOMEW'S FAIR in London included Mrs Minn's BOOTH, where the well-known dramatist Elkanah Settle (1648–1724) performed as "a dragon in green leather". The fairs at Smithfield and Southwark offered everything from puppet shows to theatrical plays.

In Germany, the fair at Leipzig presented performances by the influential Caroline Neuber (1697–1760) while one at Frankfurt became the virtual home of the ENGLISH COMEDIANS.

fall. ***Fallen Angels*** A comedy by Noël COWARD, first performed in 1925 at the Globe Theatre, London, when it became one of four Coward plays running simultaneously in the West End (the others being *Hay Fever*, *On With the Dance*, and *The Vortex*). *Fallen Angels*, which starred Tallulah Bankhead, created a sensation with its story about two married women visited by their ex-lover. The last night's performance was attended by a crusader for public morality, Mrs Charles Hornibrook, who stood up in her box at the end of the second act and announced: "Ladies and Gentlemen, I wish to protest. This play should not go unchallenged." The audience hooted, the orchestra struck up with 'I Want To Be Happy', and Mrs Hornibrook was gently ejected from the theatre.

When it was revived in 1949 in Plymouth with Hermione Gingold and Hermione Baddeley, Coward was in the audience and recorded, "I have never yet in my long experience seen a more vulgar, silly, unfunny, disgraceful performance." When it proved to be a hit, he wrote, "*Fallen Angels* a terrific success. Livid."

falling flap A device formerly used for quick changes of scene, consisting of a hinged flat or canvas with scenes painted on both sides. The hinged section, kept up by catches, fell to reveal the other scene when these catches were released. Falling flaps were used in TRANSFORMATION SCENES in the English PANTOMIME.

false proscenium A construction of wings, flats, or cloths, used with a top border to reduce the size of the PROSCENIUM. The framework is painted to resemble draped curtains and can be employed with a CYCLORAMA to reduce the amount of scenery required. It is also called a **false pros** or **inner proscenium**; the term **portal opening** is usually used in America, and *le manteau d'Harlequin* in France.

Falstaff, Sir John The corpulent, self-indulgent knight, full of wit and exaggeration, who encourages Prince Hal to lead a dissolute life in Shakespeare's HENRY IV, *Parts I and II* (1596–98). His death is movingly described in *Henry V* while he also appears in diminished form in THE MERRY WIVES OF WINDSOR. The character was distantly based upon Sir John Oldcastle (d. 1417), a friend of Henry V, who was eventually executed for involvement in a Lollard plot against the king. Objections from the Oldcastle family apparently led Shakespeare to change the character's name; the new name was derived from that of Sir John Fastolf (1378–1459), a knight who was once unjustly suspected of cowardice and became a benefactor of Oxford and Cambridge. Shakespeare made clear the difference between his Falstaff and Sir John Oldcastle in the line "Oldcastle died a martyr and this is not the man."

Other traits of Falstaff may have been taken from Adrian Gilbert, the younger brother of the navigator Sir Humphrey Gilbert and half brother of Sir Walter Raleigh. He seems to have been similar in physique to Falstaff – "a gorbellied rascal" – and given to practical joking. John Aubrey called him "the greatest Buffoon of the Nation". Remains of Sir John Fastolf's house in London were unearthed in an archaeological dig in the 1980s.

DRYDEN called Falstaff "the best of comical characters...not properly one humour, but a miscellany of humours or images".

Family Reunion, The A poetic drama in two acts by T. S. ELIOT, first performed in 1939 in London without great success. Based upon THE ORESTEIA of Aeschylus, it describes the predicament of Harry, a contemporary man, who is obsessed with guilt about his wife's mysterious death. Despite the quality of Eliot's verse, critics have felt that the domestic drama does not blend well with the classical form of the play. The British actor Alec McCowen has described the play as splendid, sombre, and very innocent, "obviously written by a man who has no knowledge of psychiatry".

Peter BROOK directed a revival at the Phoenix Theatre starring Paul Scofield in 1956. The critic Philip Squire noted in *Plays and Players* that Scofield "brings a vibrant intelligence to Harry and speaks the character's mind as freely as the play allows though the blank verse occasionally halts for it."

Fanny's First Play The play that was the first great commercial success for George Bernard SHAW. First performed in 1911 in London and the following year on Broadway, the story follows the son and daughter of two respectable middle-class families who both marry unlikely partners after serving prison sentences. In addition to the play's satire on conventional social values, Shaw maliciously lampooned three contemporary London drama critics. Because of these contemporary allusions, the play is seldom revived.

farce A play characterized by broad humour and a complicated and improbable plot. The word comes from the Latin *farcire* meaning 'to stuff', which was originally used to refer to the explanatory sentences added to the liturgy, then in the theatre to the extra material interpolated into a play to delight and amuse.

Early types of farce included the ancient Greek SATYR-PLAY and the Roman ATELLANA with its stock clown characters. Later Roman dramatists such as PLAUTUS and TERENCE included farce in their works. It was also a characteristic feature of medieval and church drama, such as *The Second Shepherds Play* by the 15th-century Wakefield Master. Secular farces in the Middle Ages dealt with such subjects as marital infidelity and hypocrisy, the oldest surviving example being a 13th-century Flemish work, *The Boy and the Blind Man*. The roots of French farce can be found in the SOTIE, a political or religious satire in which all the characters were fools, and in the COMMEDIA DELL'ARTE, which influenced MOLIÈRE. Early German farces were called 'Shrovetime plays' with many of the best written by Hans Sachs (1492–1576).

Farce did not emerge as a distinct genre until the 16th century. In England an early example is John Heywood's *Johan Johan* (*c.* 1520), but English farce did not really come into its own until Edward Ravenscroft adapted Molière for *The Careless Lovers* (1673).

In the 18th and 19th centuries short farces were presented in the British and US theatres as light entertainment after a tragedy. France's master of the genre Georges FEYDEAU wrote some 40 in his lifetime. Famous examples of early full-length English farces were Arthur Wing PINERO's series in the 1880s for the Royal Court Theatre and Brandon Thomas's *Charley's Aunt* (1892).

The term is now most often applied to the BEDROOM FARCE, in which sexual innuendo is a major ingredient. Famous 20th-century British examples are the *Aldwych farces* of the 1920s and 1930s by Ben Travers, and the *Whitehall farces* of the 1950s and 1960s featuring Brian RIX.

> Farce is the essential theatre. Farce refined becomes high comedy: farce brutalized becomes tragedy.
>
> GORDON CRAIG: *The Story of My Days.*

Farquhar, George (1678–1707) Irish-born British playwright of the Restoration period (*see* RESTORATION DRAMA). During his ten-year career, he produced two brilliant comedies, THE RECRUITING OFFICER in 1706 and THE BEAUX' STRATAGEM the following year.

The son of a clergyman, he studied at Trinity College, Dublin, before briefly working as an actor at the Smock Alley Theatre in that city. Following an accident during a stage fight, when he mistakenly used a real sword and wounded a fellow actor so badly that he almost died, Farquhar renounced acting. Encouraged by his fellow actor Robert Wilks, he took up the pen and settled in London. His first play *Love and a Bottle* was well received at Drury Lane in 1698. The following year, *The Constant Couple; or, A Trip to the Jubilee* was an even greater hit with Wilks in the lead.

After *Sir Harry Wildair* (1701), a sequel to *The Constant Couple*, and *The Twin-Rivals* (1702), he wrote his first great play. The first production of *The Recruiting Officer* starred Anne OLDFIELD, with whom Farquhar supposedly had an affair. The following year Farquhar, with "not one shilling" in his pocket, was encouraged by Wilks to produce a hastily written play. The next day Farquhar delivered the plot for *The Beaux' Stratagem*, which was presented on stage within six weeks. He died from tuberculosis after the third performance, which included these lines in the Epilogue:

> Forbear, you fair, on his last scene to frown,
> But his true exit with a plaudit crown
> Then shall the dying poet cease to fear
> The dreadful knell, while your applause he hears.

Fart Fanatic, the (*Le Pétomane*) The billing for the French music-hall performer Joseph Pujol (1857–1945), who earned 20,000 francs at the Moulin Rouge for vibrating his sphincter. His specialities included imitations of his mother-in-law, a bride on her wedding night, and various animals. He also used this odd talent to produce music, smoke a cigarette, and extinguish a candle 20 centimetres away.

Fastnachtsspiel (Ger. carnival play) In medieval Germany, a type of one-act play that developed separately from the LITURGICAL DRAMA during the 15th century and was usually performed on Shrove Tuesday by craftsmen or students in the open air. The plays were crude comedies and ribald farces featuring as their main character a fool known as the NARR. Favourite subjects included the relationships between churchmen and their female parishioners, and doctors and their patients. The genre sometimes contained elements of the MORALITY PLAY. Many *Fastnachtsspiele* were written by Meistersinger, such as Hans Sachs and Hans Rosenplüt (*see* MEISTERSÄNGER).

fate drama (*Schicksaltragödie*) An early 19th-century German genre, initiated by Zacharias Werner's *The 29th of February* (1809). Typically, the lead character commits murder or some other heinous crime when destiny seems to leave no other choice. Other examples include Franz Grillparzer's first play *The Ancestress* (1817).

father. ***Father, The*** A tragedy by August STRINDBERG, first performed in 1887. It marked the transition from his early works, mainly rural farces and historical dramas, to the major plays in which he explores the depths of sexual conflict. In doing so it prepared the way for his masterpiece, MISS JULIE. Written during the first of Strindberg's three unhappy marriages, the misogynistic drama portrays Laura's callous manipulation of her husband and his subsequent descent into insanity.

father of comedy A name given to ARISTOPHANES.

father of Greek tragedy A name given to AESCHYLUS.

father of the halls Nickname for Charles MORTON, the theatre manager who pioneered music-hall entertainment in England.

father of variety Nickname for the British ventriloquist Fred Russell (Thomas Frederick Parnell; 1862–1957), because of the major role he played in the founding of the Variety Artists' Federation. In 1906 he also founded and edited *The Performer*, its official publication; he later became the Federation's president at the age of 90. Russell was also a founding member of the Grand Order of Water Rats and became its King Rat in 1903.

Having toured the world with his dummy Coster Joe, he was awarded the OBE in 1948 and three years later, at nearly 90, he performed in a televised music-hall programme. About 14 members of his family worked in VARIETY, including his son Val(entine) Charles Parnell (1894–1972).

father of vaudeville, The Nickname of Tony (Antonio) Pastor (1837–1908), the US variety performer and manager who created VAUDEVILLE entertainment suitable for the whole family. Pastor made his debut at the age of nine at Barnum's Museum, New York and subsequently travelled as a circus clown and minstrel, singing sentimental ballads, of which he had nearly 2000 in his repertoire. He also began arranging concerts in small towns and in 1861 booked his first variety acts into the disreputable American Theatre on Broadway.

In 1865, wishing to rescue variety from its vulgar reputation, he took over New York's Volksgarten and renamed it Tony Pastor's Opera House, billing the venue as 'The Great Family Resort'. He subsequently tried, with only moderate success, to lure women and children to matinées with door-prizes of turkeys and hams. In 1881 he moved his "straight, clean, variety show" to the small 14th Street Theatre and he achieved an unexpected success presenting wholesome family entertainment (such as comics, singers, jugglers, dancers, and dog acts). This encouraged other managers to offer what would later become known as vaudeville (a term Pastor never used), and led eventually to the Keith and Albee circuit of some 300 vaudeville houses.

Pastor, an overweight man with a waxed moustache, was a devout Catholic who kept a holy shrine backstage. Although an expert at booking and presenting acts, he eventually lost his best performers because he paid them so little. Despite being a pioneer showman, he died a poor man.

Faust. Johann Faust A German magician and astrologer (*c.* 1480–*c.* 1540), born in Württemberg, on whose life and legendary exploits many plays were based, including those by Goethe, Marlowe, and Lessing. In 1587 *The History of Dr. Faustus, the Notorious Magician and Master of the Black Art* was published by Johann Spies at Frankfurt. It immediately became popular and was soon translated into English, French, and other languages. Many other accounts followed and the Faust theme was developed by writers, artists, and musicians over the years. Notable amongst musical works inspired by the story are Berlioz's *Damnation de Faust* (1846), Gounod's *Faust* (1859), and Busoi's *Doktor Faust* (1925). The basis of the Faust story is that he sold his soul to the Devil in return for twenty-four years of further life during which he is to have every pleasure and all knowledge at his command. The climax comes when the Devil claims him for his own.

Faust A play in two parts by GOETHE. Although it is usually considered his masterpiece, it is too vast in concept to be conventionally staged. Disillusioned with his humdrum life of scholarship, Faust makes a pact with the demon Mephistopheles in order to taste hedonistic pleasures. However, unlike the hero of Marlowe's play, Goethe's character is not a mere pawn in the struggle between the forces of good and evil, neither does he forfeit his soul. Goethe's real theme is the restless striving of modern man, which, in conjunction with the power of love, ensures his salvation.

Goethe's less complex first draft, completed in about 1775, was discovered more than a century later to be published in 1887 as the *Urfaust*. Many modern producers prefer this manageable version to the completed work. Part I of the latter, which reflects the influence of the STURM UND DRANG, was published in 1808; Part II, containing the blinding of Faust along with much satire and scientific speculation, appeared posthumously in 1832. The complete drama was first staged in 1876 in Weimar.

STANISLAVSKY harboured a fearful superstition about performing the play. When encouraged by Vladimir Nemirovitch-Dantchenko (with whom he co-founded the Moscow Art Theatre) to play the role of Mephistopheles, Stanislavsky smiled and told him, "I've wanted to play Mephistopheles quite a number of times, but each time I tried it some kind of misfortune took place in my family."

The Tragical History of Dr Faustus A blank-verse tragedy written (c. 1592) by Christopher MARLOWE, which is probably the first dramatization of the medieval legend of a man selling his soul to the Devil. The climax of the play comes when the Devil claims Faust for his own.

> FAUSTUS *O lente, lente, currite noctis equi!*
> The stars more still, time runs, the clock will strike,
> The Devil will come, and Faustus must be damned.
> O' I'll leap up to my God! Who pulls me down?
> See, see where Christ's blood streams in the firmament!

The earliest known performance was given by the Admiral's Men in 1594.

Feast of Fools or **Feast of Asses** Festivities performed on the feasts of St Stephen (26 December), St John (27 December), and Holy Innocents (28 December) by the lower clergy in many European cathedrals and collegiate churches in medieval times. Apparently related to ancient Roman revels, it began in France in the 12th century and soon spread throughout Catholic Europe. In England it became a tradition at the cathedrals of Lincoln, Salisbury, and St Paul's, among others.

During the festivities, the minor clergy assumed the roles of their superiors and elected their own *dominus festi*, a King of Fools, or Boy Bishop, who evolved into an Abbot of Unreason or LORD OF MISRULE. The crude drama included a procession in which the King rode on an ass while wearing donkey's ears. An extant 13th-century manuscript of the *Festa Asinaria* at Beauvais Cathedral records the welcoming of the ass through its doors. The clergymen would feast and drink, sing ribald songs to the tunes of hymns, play dice at the altar, perform burlesques of sacred services in which braying often took the place of the customary responses, and act out licentious caricatures of bishops.

In 1207 Pope Innocent III banned these revels and later in the 13th century the Bishop of Lincoln called them "a vain and filthy recreation hateful to God and dear to devils." The English Church finally suppressed the Feast of Fools in 1500, but it lingered on for two more centuries in France. *See also* FOOL.

Fedeli One of the later COMMEDIA DELL'ARTE companies, formed at the beginning of the 17th century by a group that included the famous Giovann Andreini (1579–1654), known as Lelio, and Tristano Martinelli (1557–1603) who played the character of ARLECCHINO. It soon became a significant force, tempting players away from the GELOSI and ACCESI companies. The Fedeli, whose patron was the Duke of Mantua, continued to tour Italy until about 1650, when they disbanded.

Federal Theatre Project (FTP) The US government scheme that created work for more than 10,000 out-of-work actors, directors, playwrights, designers, stage hands, musicians, and others during the Great Depression. The Project produced more than 1000 amateur and professional plays, as well as operas, ballets, and puppet shows, plays for children, ethnic works, pageants, and vaudeville performances; all tickets were either free or low-priced.

The FTP began in 1935 as part of President Roosevelt's New Deal within the framework of the Works Progress Administration (WPA). Hallie Flanagan (1890–1969), director of the Experimental Theatre at Vassar College, was appointed the director and worked through regional assistants operating theatres in 40 states. She quickly made the FTP a pioneer of socially relevant drama and encouraged both new plays and experimental revivals. Orson WELLES and John Houseman produced an all-Black *Macbeth* in 1936, a Black company presented *Swing Mikado* in 1939, and Sinclair Lewis and John Moffitt's *It Can't Happen Here* (1939) received its premiere simultaneously in 21 cities.

The most controversial arm of the FTP was the **Living Newspaper**, a form of documentary theatre blending political satire and historical fact. Largely owing to the Living Newspaper, Flanagan was accused of being a communist, and increased political pressure forced the FTP to close abruptly in 1939.

feerie In 19th-century France, a spectacle drama that used elaborate machinery to produce illusions. The dream-like plots were based on fairy tales and romances and the *feerie* was a major influence in the development of BURLESQUE and the MUSICAL. An earlier type of extravaganza, the 17th-century *pièce à machines* was based on stories of classical mythology. The fantastic elements in the *feerie* derived largely from 18th-century fairground pantomimes.

The first *feerie* to achieve great success was *Le Pied du mouton*, presented at the Théâtre de la Gaîté, Paris, in 1806. A later hit was *Les Pilules du diable* at the Cirque Olympique in 1839. The stage illusions and transformation scenes required a large stage, limiting most *feerie* productions to such venues as the Théâtre de la Port Saint-Martin, which were able to accommodate them.

female impersonator A male actor who plays female roles. The intention may be either a realistic impersonation or a broad caricature of femininity, as in the traditional DAME of English Pantomime. A female impersonator is sometimes called a **drag artist** because the women's costumes dragged along the stage.

In the classical theatre the female roles were almost always played by boys or men. The Roman actor Bathyllus is one of the earliest impersonators whose name is recorded. Female impersonators have always been a part of drama in Japan (*see* ONNAGATA) and in China (*see* PEKING OPERA). In France, Alizon (1610–48) was famous for playing comic elderly maids. In the Elizabethan theatre, where it was illegal for women to appear on a public stage, Edward KYNASTON was the most famous boy actor to take female roles. The first professional actress in England, Margaret Hughes, did not appear on stage until 1660.

More recent examples of female impersonation in the legitimate theatre include Alec Guinness's portrayal of Mrs Artminster in Simon Gray's *Wise Child* in 1967 at Wyndham's Theatre. That same year Anthony Hopkins, Ronald Pickup, Charles Kay, and Richard Kaye played Phoebe, Rosalind, Celia, and Audrey in Shakespeare's *As You Like It* at the National Theatre. Famous drag artists in revue and on television include Danny La Rue and Barrie Humphries. *See also* BREECHES PART.

Fescennine verses Lampoons; so called after Fescennium in Tuscany, Italy, where performers at fairs and festivals used to extemporize scurrilous verses of a personal nature to amuse the audience.

Feydeau, George (1862–1921) French dramatist remembered for his FARCES, mostly on the traditional themes of adultery, mistaken identity, and misunderstanding. He is widely regarded as a master of plot and dialogue. Noël COWARD, who adapted his *Occupe-toi d'Amélie* (1908) as LOOK AFTER LULU (1959), thought otherwise, however:

> M. Feydeau is a *very* untidy playwright. He leaves characters about all over the place and disposes of them without explanation.
> *Diaries* (1982)

The best known of his nearly 40 plays are perhaps *L'Hôtel du libre échange* (1894; known in English as HOTEL PARADISO), *La Dame de chez Maxim* (*The Lady from Maxim's*; 1899), and *La Puce à l'oreille* (A FLEA IN HER EAR; 1907). His later plays were less successful. Feydeau himself designed the elaborate – sometimes split-stage – sets required by his works. He died of syphilis in a lunatic asylum.

fiabe A type of fairytale play created in 18th-century Italy by Carlo Gozzi (1720–1806), who was attempting to revive and reform the COMMEDIA DELL'ARTE. He retained the stock characters and comic improvisation, but used mythological subjects and added an element of fantasy. His work, more respected in Germany and France than his native country, influenced such German writers as GOETHE and SCHILLER.

L'Augellino belverde (1764) is usually considered to be Gozzi's best work. *Turandot* (1765) provided the libretto for an opera by Puccini, and *The Love of Three Oranges* (1761) inspired Prokofiev's opera of that name. His *The Stag King* (1761) was produced by the Young Vic in 1946.

Fiddler on the Roof A record-breaking musical by Joseph Stein (book), Jerry Bock (music), and Sheldon Harnick (lyrics). It was first performed in 1964 in New York with Zero Mostel in the lead. The London production opened in 1967 at Her Majesty's Theatre starring Topol, who also appeared in the film version and a 1983 stage revival.

When the play was being tried out in Detroit before moving to Broadway, *Variety* reported "No smash, no blockbuster". The show subsequently won the Tony Award as Best Musical and ran for eight years and 3242 performances, establishing a new record for musicals (broken by *Grease* in 1972).

Set in a Russian village in 1905, the play is based on Sholom Aleichem's short story *Tevye the Milkman*. It follows the fortunes of a Jewish community facing great social upheaval. The disintegration of the traditional way of life is reflected in the crisis faced by Tevye, whose daughters rebel against the old way of arranging marriages; one of the girls marries a young intellectual revolutionary and follows him into exile in Siberia whilst another elopes with a gentile. When Cossack soldiers arrive to enforce a pogrom against the Jews, the community fragments, with many leaving to seek a new future in Palestine and America.

The songs include 'Matchmaker, Matchmaker', and 'If I Were a Rich Man'.

Figaro The daring, cunning, and witty servant is in THE BARBER OF SEVILLE (1775), and THE MARRIAGE OF FIGARO (1784) by BEAUMARCHAIS.

Hence the name of the famous Parisian periodical which appeared from 1826 to 1833 and its daily successor which began life in 1854.

Fings Ain't Wot They Used T'be A musical by Lionel Bart with the book by Frank Norman. It was first performed in 1959 by Joan LITTLEWOOD's Theatre Workshop at Stratford East, subsequently transferring to the Garrick Theatre, where it ran for 897 performances and won the *London Evening Standard* Award as the year's best musical.

The plot concerns a middle-aged gangster, Fred Cochran, who runs an illegal gambling den in Soho with his lover, an ex-prostitute called Lil. When Fred is suddenly able to revamp and upgrade the club after a lucky win on the horses, he antagonizes an old criminal rival, who sends in his gang to teach Fred a lesson. Fred manages to outwit them and decides to go straight and marry Lil. Meanwhile the local sergeant takes over the club and looks forward to a new life of crime.

The songs include 'Fings Ain't Wot They Used T'be' and 'Big Time'.

Finney, Albert (1936–) British actor, who became known for his highly physical style of acting in the early 1960s. He began his career in 1956 at the Birmingham Repertory Theatre. In 1958 he went to Stratford-upon-Avon, where he played Edgar to Charles Laughton's King Lear and took over as Coriolanus after Laurence Olivier was injured (*see* UNDERSTUDY). He also appeared in London with Charles Laughton in Jane Arden's *The Party* (1958).

In 1960 Finney became widely known for creating the title role in Keith Waterhouse and Willis Hall's *Billy Liar*. The following year he took the lead in John Osborne's *Luther* at the Royal Court Theatre, later taking the play to the Théâtre des Nations in Paris and (in 1963) to New York. He joined the National Theatre in 1965, the year in which he created the role of John Armstrong in Arden's *Armstrong's Last Goodnight*.

In 1967 he co-starred in Peter Nichols's *A Day in the Life of Joe Egg* in London and New York. He was an associate artistic director at the Royal Court Theatre from 1972 to 1975 and performed as Hamlet, Macbeth, and Tamburlaine during the National Theatre's first season on the South Bank (1975–76).

Finney directed and starred in a revival of *Armstrong's Last Goodnight* at the Old Vic in 1983, and the following year directed and starred in Arden's *Serjeant Musgrave's Dance* at the same theatre. Later successes include major roles in Lyle Kessler's *Orphans* (1986), *J.J. Farr* (1987), *Another Time* (1989), *Chicago* (1991), and *Reflected Glory* (1992).

Finney has also found fame in films and television; he founded his own independent production company in 1965.

fire. ***Fire-Raisers, The*** A black comedy by Max FRISCH, considered one of the most significant works of the Theatre of the ABSURD. The play, originally meant for the radio, was first performed in Zürich in 1958 and opened at the Royal Court Theatre, London, in 1961. It was produced two years later in New York as *The Firebugs*.

The play attacks the moral complacency of modern society through the figure of Biedermann, a typical good citizen who nevertheless allows arsonists to start a fire in his attic. It is often interpreted as an allegory of the way in which respectable society permitted, and even condoned, the rise of the Nazis in prewar Germany.

fires In its earlier history the theatre was regularly plagued by fires, especially in the eras of candle, oil, and gas lighting. The first great loss was Shakespeare's GLOBE THEATRE, which was destroyed by fire in 1613 during a performance of *Henry VIII*, when a shot from a stage cannon set fire to the thatched roof. It was subsequently rebuilt with a tiled roof. London's patent theatres have both burned down twice; Drury Lane in 1672 and 1809 (although an iron safety curtain had been installed 14 years earlier) and Covent Garden in 1808, when 23 firemen lost their lives, and again in 1856.

A fire in a Liverpool theatre in 1878 prompted the passing of an act licensing English provincial theatres, but this did not prevent the worst fire disaster in the British theatre, which occurred nine years later at the Theatre Royal, Exeter, when 186 people died. The same venue had burned down two years earlier.

Fires were also a prominent feature in the early history of the US theatre. In 1798 Boston's Federal Street Theatre burned down. During the next 78 years 75 major theatre fires were recorded. One, in 1811 in Richmond, Virginia, cost 70 lives when the candles of the stage chandelier set fire to the scenery. In 1876, 300 people, including two actors, died at the Brooklyn Theatre, and this led to the introduction of stringent safety regulations. America's worst loss of life, however, came in 1903 at the supposedly fireproof Iroquois Theatre in Chicago. About 600 people died after a panic in the standing-room area, despite attempts by the performer, Eddie Foy, to calm the audience.

Elsewhere theatre fires have caused even greater loss of life. In 1837 some 800 theatregoers were killed in a fire in St Petersburg, Russia, and ten years later a similar number lost their lives in Karlsruhe, Germany. The worst-ever disaster occurred in 1845 in China, when 1670 people died. The introduction of electricity, fireproof scenery, and strict safety regulations have virtually eradicated the risk of serious fires, although London's Savoy Theatre was closed for refurbishment after a fire in 1991.

fireworks Fireworks have played a part in the theatre since the 14th century, when they were used in religious dramas to emphasize the terrors of Hell. In the 16th century they were shot from wooden figures during plays for the Feast of St John and the Assumption in Siena and Florence. But fireworks have always been dangerous, and by the 18th century the COMÉDIE-ITALIENNE in Paris was one of the few companies still using them indoors. In Britain they were mostly used in pleasure gardens or in pageants such as the Lord Mayor's show, in which actors representing the Green Man carried clubs spouting fire. By the 19th century they were considered somewhat old-fashioned.

The British actor Ralph RICHARDSON loved fireworks. As a young actor, he was placed beneath the stage with a stick of dynamite to help simulate a wartime Zeppelin raid. The cue for the explosion was to come from the actor F. R. Gowcott tapping on the stage with a stick. Richardson, however, mistook his tapping walk for the signal and before Gowcott could deliver his opening line, Richardson had blown him some 20 feet off the stage.

first. First Dancer *See* STOCK COMPANY.

First Folio The first complete collection of SHAKESPEARE's 36 plays. Under the title *Mr William Shakespeare's Comedies, Histories, and Tragedies*, they were published in 1623 for 20 shillings by his fellow actors Henry Condell (d. 1627) and John Heminge (1556–1630). Both were shareholders in the BLACKFRIARS THEATRE and GLOBE THEATRE. They added 20 plays to the 16 that had already been printed in quarto during Shakespeare's lifetime, ensuring that his works would survive (for none of his manuscripts have). No indication is given of the dates of composition.

The First Folio included Ben JONSON's poem declaring that Shakespeare "was not of an age, but for all time" and a title-page engraving by Martin Droeshout (1601–50), thought to be the only authentic likeness. It also included an invaluable list of contemporary performers who appeared in the plays. Condell and Heminge also edited the plays, dividing them (somewhat arbitrarily) into five acts in imitation of Ben Jonson (who was following Horace's advice).

The number of copies published is unknown, but a second printing was not ordered until 13 years later; two more printings were made in the 17th century.

First Gentleman of the Stage A nickname for the younger John Drew (*see* DREW FAMILY).

First Lady of the American Theatre An accolade bestowed on the actresses Helen HAYES and Katharine CORNELL.

first nighter One who makes a practice of attending the opening performances of plays.

First Singer *See* STOCK COMPANY.

Fiske, Minnie Maddern (Marie Augusta Davey; 1865–1932) US actress, who championed Henrik IBSEN's plays in New York. At a time when Ibsen was shocking America, Mrs Fiske called him "the genius of the age".

Born in New Orleans, she began acting at the age of three under her mother's name of Maddern. By the age of five she had made her New York debut; at 13 she began to play adult parts. She retired in 1890 on her marriage to her second husband, Harrison Grey Fiske (1861–1942), the wealthy owner of the *New York Dramatic Mirror*. However, she soon reappeared in a charity production of Ibsen's *A Doll's House* (1893), returning to the professional stage the following year in her husband's play *Hester Crewe*. She again played in *A Doll's House* in 1894 and took the title role in *Hedda Gabler* the following year. Her reputation was firmly established by her performance in Hardy's *Tess of the D'Urbevilles* in 1897. In 1899 she played the title role in *Becky Sharp*, a dramatization of Thackeray's *Vanity Fair*, at the Fifth Avenue Theatre. Because she fought with the all-powerful THEATRICAL SYNDICATE, who controlled the theatre, they evicted her in the middle of the successful run. In 1901 her husband bought the Manhattan Theatre, where Minnie played in *Hedda Gabler* (1903) and in Ibsen's *Rosmersholm* (1904). They left the Manhattan three years later.

In 1915 Harrison Fiske became bankrupt and she was forced to tour. His subsequent infidelity effectively ended the marriage and she devoted the rest of her life to the theatre and animal rights' campaigning.

Although Mrs Fiske was greatly admired for her intensity her delivery was often criticized, as noted by Franklin Pierce Adams:

Somewords she runstogether
Some others are distinctly stated,
Somecometoofast and s o m e t o o s l o w
And some are syncopated,
And yet no voice – I am sincere –
Exists that I prefer to hear.

Also see WOOLLCOTT, ALEXANDER.

Five Finger Exercise Peter SHAFFER's first play; a critical and commercial success, it established his reputation as a dramatist. It was first performed in 1958 at the Comedy Theatre, London, in a production by John Gielgud, and opened on Broadway the following year. The plot concerns tensions in the middle-class Harrington family. A German orphan, Walter Langer, is hired to tutor the daughter of the family, to which he becomes closely attached. The son is jealous of the intrusion of this outsider and untruthfully informs his father that his mother and Walter are having an affair. Giving up hope of being adopted, Walter attempts suicide.

Flare Path A play by Terence RATTIGAN, which opened in 1942 at the Apollo Theatre, London, and ran for 670 performances. Rattigan drew on his wartime experiences in the RAF to depict the tensions felt by pilots and their families during the Battle of Britain. The patriotism of the piece provided a considerable boost to the war effort in Britain; it was also well received in America.

Flash, Sir Petronel The penniless adventurer in the comedy EASTWARD HO! (1605) by George Chapman, Ben Jonson, and John Marston. A rogue who marries for money, Sir Petronel dupes everyone until his downfall by shipwreck (on his way to Virginia) on the Isle of Dogs.

flat A piece of stage scenery consisting of a wooden frame covered with stretched canvas, hardboard, or other material. It was introduced in the 17th century and has been in constant use ever since. Flats normally stand 18 feet high and up to eight feet wide, being supported by weights and braces (*see* STAGE BRACE). A **saddle-iron** (**sill-iron** in America) is a metal strip fastened across the bottom of a flat to provide support. When standing alone, a flat may have a small extension, a FLIPPER, for added strength.

Flats can be used in various combinations. A BOOK FLAT consists of two flats hinged together. A **French flat** is several flats battened together to create a back wall that can be 'flown' in one piece. A **backing flat** is placed outside a door, window, or other opening in a set to screen off the backstage area from the audience. A **tormentor** is a narrow flat or curtain that masks the wings, and a **return** is an additional piece to screen off areas not covered by the tormentor. Flats have also been put on rollers to create moving backgrounds. The stage directions for J. R. Planché's *Paris and London* (1828) instructed: "Deck of the steamer – Moving Panoramic View from Calais to Dover by various Painted Flats to the Scene."

Flea in Her Ear, A A farce by Georges FEYDEAU, first performed in 1907 in Paris. John MORTIMER provided the translation for the 1966 National Theatre production directed by Jacques Charon at the Old Vic; he also wrote the screenplay for the 1967 film version starring Rex HARRISON and Rachel Roberts. Mortimer changed Harrison's part slightly after the actor pleaded, "I don't think audiences would like a totally impotent man as the hero. They wouldn't accept me. Couldn't I be made just a little impotent now and then?"

The plot involves the love affairs, real and imagined, of the confused household of insurance agent Victor Emmanuel Chandebise. Tragedy looms but is averted when the misunderstandings and mistaken identities are cleared up.

Fletcher, John (1579–1625) English dramatist, who collaborated with Francis BEAUMONT on at least six plays. They began working together in about 1607 and had their first success in 1609 with *Philaster; or, Love Lies Bleeding*. Once, whilst sharing a bottle in a public house and dividing up their writing assignments for a new play, Fletcher was overheard to say: "You manage the rest and I'll undertake to kill the king." The two were overheard and immediately arrested; it was some time before they could convince the authorities of their innocence.

After Beaumont's retirement in 1613, Fletcher became chief playwright for the KING'S MEN, writing his own plays and apparently collaborating with Shakespeare on three works, THE TWO NOBLE KINSMEN, HENRY VIII, and a lost play, *The History of Cardenio*. He also collaborated with Nathan Field, William Rowley, and Philip Massinger, who succeeded him to the post in 1625.

His own plays included the pastoral *The Faithful Shepherdess* (1608), the tragedy *Bonduca* (1613), and the comedies *Wit Without Money* (1614), *The Wild Goose Chase* (1621), and *The Chances* (1625), which was revived at the Chichester Festival Theatre in 1962.

flexible staging A system of staging in which different acting areas can be created by moving platforms or other devices. The Czech designer Josef SVOBODA (1920–) created a totally flexible stage system based on platforms and steps that can be moved freely in several directions.

flibbertigibbet One of the five fiends that possessed 'poor Tom' in KING LEAR (IV, i). Shakespeare found the name in Harsnet's *Declaration of Egregious Popish Impostures* (1603) in which 40 fiends are cast out by the Jesuits, including 'Fliberdigibet', a name which had been previously used for a mischievous gossip. In A MIDSUMMER NIGHT'S DREAM the name is applied to PUCK.

flies The space above the stage where scenery, lighting, and other equipment can be suspended by ropes, out of sight from the audience. Scenery hung in this manner was called **flown scenery**. In the former HAND-WORKED HOUSE, a stagehand known as a **flyman** stood in the flies on a high **fly floor** or **fly gallery** along each side of the stage. He moved between the fly floors by means of a catwalk (*see* BRIDGE); the **flying lines**, or ropes, were usually tied on a rail on the PROMPT SIDE. British theatres normally had only a pair of fly floors, but the larger European ones had up to three pairs. Large theatres often had a higher **fly tower** to contain the flies.

flipper A brace for a FLAT, usually hinged and attached at right angles.

float *See* FOOTLIGHTS.

flop A play or musical that fails to run. Even the most famous playwrights have suffered humiliating disasters of this kind. At the height of his popularity, Noël COWARD suffered a major embarrassment with *Sirocco*, produced at Daly's Theatre, London, in 1927. Although the leading actress, Frances Doble, gave a quivering curtain speech calling it the happiest night of her life, the entire cast was booed for ten minutes.

Some playwrights and actors throw in the towel. When the audience began booing Charles Lamb's farce *Mr H* at Drury Lane in 1806, he joined in. Afterwards he explained that he booed and hissed so nobody would know he was the author. On one occasion Ralph Richardson stopped acting in mid-scene; walking towards the audience he asked, "Is there a doctor in the house?" When one stood up, Richardson said: "Doctor, isn't this play awful?"

Expensive musicals are by no means exempt. Stephen Sondheim's *Anyone Can Whistle* ran on Broadway for only eight nights in 1964; those who saw it are said to hold an annual reunion to analyse the disaster. The 1975 rock opera *Lieutenant*, about the My Lai massacre, came off after nine performances (with such songs as 'Kill' and 'Massacre'). Yul Brynner starred in a musical version of *The Odyssey* entitled *Home, Sweet Homer*, which ran for only one night in 1976. In 1981 a Broadway revival of CAN-CAN ran for five performances and lost over $2 million. The list of theatrical flops is long and distressing.

Flotsam and Jetsam The stage names adopted by two variety entertainers: B. C. Hilliam (1890–1968), English composer and pianist, took the name *Flotsam* and his partner, the Australian bass singer, Malcolm McEachern (1884–1945), that of *Jetsam*.

Flower Drum Song An unsuccessful musical by RODGERS AND HAMMERSTEIN. Set in San Francisco's Chinatown, it concerns the love affairs of two Chinese-American women (played in the original production by Japanese actresses). It was first performed in New York in 1958 and received unanimously bad reviews. The British critic Kenneth Tynan (remembering the film *The World of Susie Wong*) called the *Flower Drum Song* "the world of woozy song".

The songs included 'Grant Avenue', 'I Enjoy Being a Girl', and 'Sunday, Sweet Sunday'.

flown scenery *See* FLIES.

fly. fly floor or **fly gallery** *See* FLIES.

flying effect The illusion of flight on the stage. The ancient Greek theatre introduced the practice of lowering actors playing gods to the stage using ropes or wires, as well as the impressive DEUS EX MACHINA, which was operated by a form of crane. In Britain writers of the Restoration period often mention theatrical 'flyings', while the early 20th century even produced Kirby's Flying Ballet.

Perhaps the most famous flight on the British stage occurs in J. M. Barrie's PETER PAN (1904). Scores of leading ladies playing Peter have swooped across the stage suspended by wires attached to a special harness. When Gladys COOPER played Peter Pan, she squabbled with the stagehands; their revenge came during the performance when, instead of lowering her down gently into the Darlings' nursery, they bounced her off the walls "like a wrecking-ball on a building site".

flyman Formerly, a sceneshifter who worked in the FLIES, i.e. the gallery over the proscenium from which the curtains, scenery, etc., were controlled. He was also known as the **linesman** because he operated the 'lines' or ropes.

flyman's plot The list of all the articles required by the flyman in the play concerned.

flyting A stylized exchange of insults in prose or verse. In Italian carnival plays, a *contrasto a braccio* is a contest in satirical stanzas, in which pairs of competitors take opposite sides of an argument, such as city versus country or wine versus water. The winner may be decided by a panel of judges. Flyting also occurs in the INTERLUDES of the English dramatist John Heywood (*c.* 1497–1580) and the plays of the German Hans Sachs (1494–1576).

Fo, Dario (1926–) Italian actor, manager, and dramatist, whose political comment has enraged both conservatives and communists. Fo's theatrical career began in amateur theatre groups in Milan and continued with cabaret performances (from 1953) with his wife, the actress **Franca Rame**. The couple formed their own company in 1957, for which Fo wrote his first farces, including *Archangels Don't Play the Pin-Tables* (1959), *Stealing a Foot Makes you Lucky in Love* (1961), and *Seventh: Thou Shalt Steal a Little Less* (1964). Although these early farces contain a degree of political comment, they were written to appeal to conventional middle-class audiences. From the mid 1960s, however, Fo's work began to acquire a controversial reputation for its highly partisan comment on society and government.

Encouraged by the general political discontent of 1968, Fo abandoned the mainstream theatre and formed a new company, the Compagnia Nuova Scena. With this company he toured factories and halls with an increasingly political repertoire. In 1968 he presented *The Great Pantomime* and the following year *Mistero Buffo*, a unique one-man show designed to exploit his talents for comedy and mime. Fo has frequently revived *Mistero Buffo* and the show has toured widely in Europe. When it was televised in Italy in 1977 the Vatican called it "the most blasphemous spectacle in television history."

In 1970 Fo founded another company in Milan, La Comune, to specialize in left-wing drama. La Comune's first success was with his own ACCIDENTAL DEATH OF AN ANARCHIST (1970). This play, based upon the actual death of an anarchist railway worker while in police custody, has been widely translated and performed in many countries. Fo's more recent works include *Can't Pay? Won't Pay!* (1974), in which high prices provoke public unrest, *Trumpets and Raspberries* (1982), and *The Open Couple* (1987).

focus lamp A stage spotlight that uses a lens to focus and adjust the beam. It is also known as a **lens spot** and in Germany as a *Linsenscheinwerfer*. In most large theatres, the focus lamp has been superseded by the FRESNEL SPOT.

FOH Abbreviation for FRONT OF HOUSE.

folk theatre In Europe, a type of early drama that was performed by villagers at various agricultural festivals; in England these included PLOUGH MONDAY and MAY DAY, when ROBIN HOOD PLAYS were performed. Other folk festivals were held at the advent of spring (later linked to Easter), harvest home, and the winter solstice. Although few written records exist of the earliest folk plays, they influenced the well-documented MUMMERS' PLAYS and the tradition of LITURGICAL DRAMA. Folk theatre also included such ritual dances as England's MORRIS DANCE and Horn Dance.

follow spot A spotlight that is manoeuvred by hand to keep its beam upon a moving actor or object on stage.

fool In medieval Europe, a clown who appeared in the FEAST OF FOOLS and similar festivals and in various kinds of FOLK THEATRE. He wore a particoloured suit, known as motley, with a hood to which bells, horns, or asses ears were attached, and he carried a *marotte* or bauble made from a miniature fool's head on a stick. The fool played an important part in the MUMMERS' PLAY and the MORRIS DANCE. Similar in dress, but with a different role, was the COURT FOOL or jester.

Foote, Samuel *See* ENGLISH ARISTOPHANES *under* ENGLISH.

footlights. footlight One of the row of floodlights positioned on the floor across the front of the stage. Another British term is **float**. Once a major source of illumination, these lights are virtually unused today except for special effects, such as casting shadows around the eyes of an actor. The phrase 'the footlights' is also used to refer to acting and the theatre in general.

Footlights Club A small theatre group at Cambridge University, which has placed more performers on the professional stage than any other student organization. It was founded in 1883 in a clubhouse at 5 Falcon Yard and maintains a membership of 80. Women have been admitted since 1957, Eleanor Bron being the first female to be accepted.

The Footlights Club presents an annual REVUE at the Arts Theatre in May Week, has performed at the EDINBURGH FESTIVAL fringe (most notably with the revue BEYOND THE FRINGE in 1960), and tours internationally. Former Footlights members include Graham Chapman, John Cleese, Peter Cook, Russell Davies, Jimmy Edwards, Michael Frayn, David Frost, Eric Idle, Clive James, Jonathan Miller, Trevor Nunn, Bill Oddie, and Griff Rhys-Jones. It has also been the source of the television series *That Was the Week that Was* and *Monty Python's Flying Circus*, both of which became British institutions.

Cleese, noting that he spent much of his last two Cambridge years at the club because he enjoyed the company, said:

> We were rather in awe of the proper actors who wore jeans and black leather jackets and talked about motivation and Brecht. Someone a bit like this directed me in my first revuc. But he supported Ipswich Town and was really quite nice. His name was

Trevor NUNN. I always wondered what happened to him.

footlights trap In the 19th-century theatre, a long rectangular opening in the stage floor in front of the curtain into which the footlights could be lowered. This was done to dim or darken the scene, as well as to trim, clean, or repair the lamps in the cellar. The trap was controlled by a mechanism in the PROMPT CORNER.

footman's gallery *See* GALLERY.

fops' alley In the Restoration theatre, an area of the PIT or forestage, so called because the fops would gather there, in full view of the rest of the audience, to show off their finery and discuss the play.

Forbes-Robertson, Sir Johnston (1853–1937) British actor-manager noted for his bearing and beautiful voice. Trained by the Shakespearean actor Samuel Phelps, he made his debut in 1874 and became a member of Irving's company at the LYCEUM in 1882. After touring America, he took over the management of the Lyceum and played Romeo to Mrs Patrick CAMPBELL's Juliet. This led to an affair between them: after she eventually rebuffed him, he stunned her by marrying a younger actress. In the same season he gave an outstanding Hamlet, playing him as the archetypal "sweet prince" of tradition. His greatest commercial success came playing the Stranger in Jerome K. Jerome's *The Passing of the Third Floor Back* (1908). He retired in 1913, having been knighted during his last week at Drury Lane.

Forbes-Robertson wrote in his autobiography that he was only happy when he was a painter in his youth and that he left the theatre with "intense relief". He added, "Never at any time have I gone on the stage without longing for the moment when the curtain would come down on the last act. Rarely, very rarely have I enjoyed myself in acting." However, he was noted for his imperturbability. He was once nearly killed during rehearsals for *Caesar and Cleopatra* in Liverpool, when a carpenter dropped a hammer from the grid during one of his speeches. It missed the actor by inches, and he paused, looked up, and before continuing his speech, said quietly, "Please don't do that again."

His daughter, **Jean Forbes-Robertson** (1905–62), became a well-known actress, appearing in *Uncle Vanya* (1926), *The Constant Nymph* (1928), and *Time and the Conways* (1937). She also played Peter Pan for eight seasons.

Ford. John Ford (1586–1639) English playwright, whose works have often been cited as examples of the 'decadence' of CAROLINE DRAMA. In the 19th century he was admired by Charles Lamb but attacked by William Hazlitt and others, who accused him of lacking a sense of morality. However, many 20th-century critics have praised his insight into character and his skill in writing dialogue. Ford was captured in verse by a contemporary, William Hemminge:

> Deep in a dump Jack Ford alone was got
> With folded arms and melancholy hat.

Ford was born in Devonshire and trained as a lawyer. He wrote poetry and some pamphlets before turning to the stage at 35, when he seems to have collaborated with William Rowley and Thomas Dekker (*c.* 1570–1632) on *The Witch of Edmonton* (1621). He subsequently worked with Dekker on other plays, such as *The Sun's Darling* (1624). From 1625 to 1628 he wrote mostly for the private theatres, working at a time when drama was in decline.

His best-known play is the bloody tragedy 'TIS PITY SHE'S A WHORE (1627). Other works include *Love's Sacrifice* (1627), the tragicomedy *The Lover's Melancholy* (1628), and *Perkin Warbeck* (1634), described by T. S. Eliot as "one of the very best historical plays in the whole of Elizabethan and Jacobean drama".

Several of Ford's plays were lost for ever owing to the activities of WARBURTON'S COOK.

Ford's Theatre The theatre in Washington, DC, in which President Abraham Lincoln was assassinated on 14 April 1865 by the actor and Southern sympathizer John Wilkes BOOTH. While Lincoln watched Tom Taylor's play, *Our American Cousin*, Booth entered his box and fired a Derringer pistol into the back of the President's head. Waving a knife, the assassin leapt upon the stage and shouted, "*Sic semper tyrannis!* The South is avenged!" He escaped from the theatre but was found in hiding 12 days later and shot.

Ford's Theatre had opened three years earlier in a former church as Ford's Atheneum. It assumed its present name after rebuilding in 1863 but closed after Lincoln's death. It was designated a National Monument in 1932 and a meticulous restoration in 1968 has returned the interior to the way it looked on the fatal night. Visitors enjoying current productions can also see the basement museum, which is devoted to Lincoln's life. Items on show include the clothes he wore to the play, Booth's diary, and the pistol used in the assassination. Across the street is Petersen House, also open to the public, where the president died the next morning.

forestage *See* APRON.

formal stage A setting for a play in which the basic scene is left virtually unchanged throughout the performance, although items of DETAIL SCENERY are changed.

Forrest, Edwin (1806–72) The most renowned US tragedian of the 19th century. Despite being acclaimed on both sides of the Atlantic, he also made many enemies with his aggressive character, becoming a bitter and lonely man. The critic William Winter described him as "a vast animal, bewildered by a grain of genius".

Forrest, who first appeared on stage at the age of ten, made his adult debut at Philadelphia's WALNUT STREET THEATRE in 1820, playing Young Norval in John Home's *Douglas*. In his many Shakespearean roles he became known for his powerful and resonant voice, his expressive features, and grand style.

Forrest's offer of cash prizes for scripts by native Americans resulted in a number of parts that enhanced his reputation – particularly (in 1829) the title role in *Metamora* by John Augustus Stone, and (in 1831) the part of Spartacus in Robert Montgomery Bird's *The Gladiator*.

In 1836 Forrest made his London debut with great success; however, on a visit in 1845 he received bad reviews, which he attributed to the jealousy of the British actor William MACREADY. The critic John Forster (Macready's friend) wrote of Forrest's Macbeth, "our best comic actors do not often excite so great a quantity of mirth". The two actors' public quarrel culminated in the infamous ASTOR PLACE RIOT of 1849 in New York, when 22 people were killed.

In 1851 Forrest tried unsuccessfully to divorce his wife. A year later he virtually retired from the stage, retreating to his large Philadelphia home from which he continued to launch appeals against the court's decision for nearly 20 years. He gave his last performance in 1872, playing in Edward Bulwer-Lytton's *Richelieu* at the Globe Theatre, Boston.

Fortunatus A hero of medieval legend (derived from Eastern sources), who possessed an inexhaustible purse and a wishing cap. He appears in a German *Volksbuch* of 1509. Hans Sachs dramatized the story in 1553, while Thomas Dekker's *Pleasant Comedy of Old Fortunatus* was first performed in December 1599.

Fortune Theatre (1) A popular Elizabethan theatre in Cripplegate, London. It was modelled on the GLOBE THEATRE, and took its name from a statue of the goddess of fortune that stood over the entrance. It opened in 1600 with a performance by the ADMIRAL'S MEN, whose home it was for several years. Timber-built and brightly painted inside, it is the only Elizabethan playhouse whose dimensions are known (because its building contract has survived). The Fortune's site was 80 sq ft (24.4 sq m) and the inner space was 55 sq ft (16.8 sq m) with the stage being 43 ft (13 m) wide.

The first Fortune burned down in 1621 but reopened two years later, having been rebuilt in brick. After the theatres were closed by the Puritans in 1642 (*see* INTERREGNUM), the Fortune was one of the venues used for illegal performances, until 1649 when Commonwealth soldiers partially dismantled it. In 1661 it was totally demolished.

(2) The first London theatre constructed after World War I. It was opened by Laurence Cowen in 1924 in Russell Street, Covent Garden, on the site of the Albion Tavern, which had been frequented by actors in Georgian and Victorian times. Cowen took the name from the Elizabethan Fortune Theatre in Cripplegate.

During its first decade, the Fortune presented works by O'Casey, Galsworthy, and Lonsdale. After World War II, the theatre specialized in revue with *Joyce Grenfell Requests the Pleasure* (1954), *At the Drop of a Hat* (1957), and the highly successful BEYOND THE FRINGE (1961).

More recent successes have included Anthony Shaffer's *Sleuth* (1973), a revival of Agatha Christie's *Murder at the Vicarage* (1976), and *The Brothers Karamazov* (1981). In 1981 an attempt to present plays from provincial and fringe theatres proved financially disastrous. In 1990 *The Woman in Black*, a thriller adapted by Stephen Mallatratt from Susan Hill's novel, opened at the Fortune; it was still running seven years later.

'47 Workshop The influential playwriting laboratory at Harvard University founded by George Pierce Baker (1866–1935), Harvard's first professor of dramatic literature. It was a spin-off from his playwriting course 'English 47', which began in 1905. The workshop staged plays written by his pupils, who included Eugene O'NEILL, Edward SHELDON, and George ABBOTT.

In 1925 Baker moved to Yale University where he founded the department of drama. His courses always emphasized practical construction and creativity. He retired in 1933, having become one of the most influential figures in the modern theatre both in America and Europe.

foul papers In the Elizabethan theatre, the original manuscript of a play. To avoid plagiarism, the dramatist sold his 'foul copy' to his company, which would produce a 'scrivener's copy' from it. This would then be endorsed and licensed on its last page.

fourth wall, the A convention of acting in which the actors take no cognizance of the audience; the 'fourth wall' is an imaginary barrier sealing off the proscenium. The convention was advocated by the French playwright and critic Denis Diderot (1713–84), who argued that it would create a more natural interaction amongst performers and thus create greater realism. Diderot's *On Dramatic Poetry* noted in 1758:

> Imagine a wall across the front of the stage, dividing you from the audience, and act precisely as if the curtain had not risen.

The idea was enthusiastically adapted by André Antoine (1858–1943) for his naturalistic plays at the THÉÂTRE LIBRE. Actors were instructed to behave as if an audience did not exist, and Antoine would even construct his sets with four walls before deciding which one should be removed.

fox wedge On a raked stage (*see* RAKE), a wooden wedge that is positioned under a FLAT to adjust for the slant.

Foy, Eddie (Edwin Fitzgerald Foy; 1856–1928) Popular US VAUDEVILLE star and entertainer noted for his offbeat humour, strange mannerisms, lisp, and clown make-up. Born in New York, he danced as a child in the city streets to help support his family. Around 1878 he travelled West with a MINSTREL troupe, entertaining in boom towns and mining camps. From 1888 to 1894 he appeared in Chicago in such extravagant variety shows as *Bluebeard Jr* (1890) and *Little Robinson Crusoe* (1893). Foy was playing in Chicago's Iroquois Theatre in 1903 when it caught fire (*see* FIRES).

From 1904 to 1913 Foy starred on Broadway in several musicals, including *Up and Down Broadway* (1910). He took vaudeville by storm in 1913 when he appeared with his seven children billed as 'Eddie Foy and the Seven Little Foys'. He retired in 1923 but returned to the family act in 1927; he died a year later in Kansas City while on a farewell tour.

Foy's son, the comedian **Eddie Foy Jr**, impersonated his father in the 1943 film *Yankee Doodle Dandy*; this told the story of George M. COHAN, his father's main competitor. Bob Hope subsequently played Foy in a film about his life.

Fragson, Harry (Harry Potts; 1869–1913) Anglo-French MUSIC HALL entertainer, whose career was brought to a tragic end when his father, who was apparently jealous of his son's success, shot him dead during a fit of insanity.

Fragson began as a pianist and went to Paris to become a café concert singer before moving on to the halls. He was the first music-hall singer to accompany himself; his best-known song was 'Hullo Hullo, Who's Your Lady Friend?' He performed in Paris using his Cockney accent and switched to a French accent for his London appearances. He was a well-known figure in PANTOMIME at Drury Lane; when he played Dandini in *Cinderella* the character was renamed 'Dandigny' in allusion to his popularity on both sides of the Channel.

Frayn, Michael (1933–) British playwright, journalist, and novelist, who made his reputation with a series of dark comedies. He served in the Royal Artillery and Intelligence Corps before reading philosophy at Emmanuel College, Cambridge, where he joined the FOOTLIGHTS CLUB. In 1957 he became a columnist on the *Guardian*, joining the *Observer* in 1962.

Frayn made his theatrical debut in 1970, when the Garrick Theatre presented four short plays under the title of *The Two of Us*, starring Lynn Redgrave and Richard Briers. Later comedies include *Alphabetical Order* (1975), set in a newspaper library, DONKEY'S YEARS (1976), a tragicomedy about a college reunion, and *Clouds* (1976), starring Tom Courtenay as a journalist in Cuba. After a 1978 flop with *Balmoral*, Frayn was again successful in 1980 with *Make and Break*, about a businessman at a German trade fair, which won the *Evening Standard* Best Comedy Award. In 1982 his NOISES OFF, which skilfully parodies the conventions of farce, ran successfully at the Savoy Theatre.

In 1984 *Benefactors* won the *Evening Standard* Best Play Award and the Laurence Olivier Award for Play of the Year. It involves four characters, who exist in different times and hold different philosophies of life, addressing the audience and each other. More recent plays include the somewhat poorly received *Look Look* (1990) and *Here* (1993). Frayn has also won high praise for his translations of Chekhov, a writer with whom he evidently feels an affinity.

freie. **Freie Bühne** (Ger. Free Theatre) A Berlin theatre club founded in 1889 by Otto Brahm with Theodor Wolff and Maximilian Harden, all of whom were influenced by the French naturalistic dramatists and the director André Antoine (1858–1943). Freie Bühne, which was modelled on Antoine's THÉÂTRE LIBRE in Paris, presented the works of Ibsen, Strindberg, Hauptmann, Bjørnson, Anzengruber, and Zola, and published its own newspaper. The actress Agnes Sorma, who won great acclaim as Nora in Ibsen's *A Doll's House*, was a member of the club.

Brahm also influenced other experimental writers, for example Johannes Schlaf who wrote *Master Olze* (1890), and collaborated on *The Selicke Family* (1890) with Arno Holz. In 1894 the Freie Bühne merged with the Deutsches Theatre.

Freie Volksbühne *See* VOLKSBÜHNE.

French. **French brace** *See* STAGE BRACE *under* STAGE.

French flat *See* FLAT.

French Without Tears A farce by Terence RATTIGAN that opened in 1936 at the Criterion Theatre, London. The production made a star of Rex HARRISON, establishing his suave throwaway style of delivery; it also featured Kay Hammond and Trevor Howard.

French Without Tears was a great success despite disastrous rehearsals, a torrential downpour on the opening night, and Rattigan being hit on the head by the descending curtain when he took a curtain call. The play is set in a French resort, where candidates for the civil service are taking a French course. Rattigan makes fun of the art of translating idiom, having one character render "She has ideas above her station" as *"Elle a des idées au-dessus de sa gare"*. Harrison played the part of the Hon. Alan Howard, whose chauvinistic portrait of an ideal woman runs:

> First of all, she must not be a cow. Secondly, she will be able to converse freely and intelligently with me on all subjects...Thirdly, she will have all the masculine virtues and none of the feminine vices.

Fresnel spot A versatile spotlight able to produce a beam that is bright but softer than a PROFILE SPOT. Often used in combination with other lights, Fresnels can be adjusted using shutters (called BARNDOORS) or by changing the lamp's distance from the lens; the 1000-watt version can be used for lighting the FRONT OF HOUSE. The spot was named after Augustin Jean Fresnel (1788–1827), the French inventor of the Fresnel lens.

Friel, Brian (1929–) Irish playwright, born in Northern Ireland. The product of a strongly Nationalist background, Friel moved across the border to Co Donegal when the troubles erupted in the late 1960s. Much of his work is concerned with the political conflict in the province, particularly with its historical origins and the questions of cultural identity it raises. In *Philadelphia, Here I Come!* (1965), *The Gentle Island* (1971), and *The Faith Healer* (1979), he explores the plight of those who feel driven to exile from Ireland in order to escape from the cycle of violence; *Freedom of the City* (1973) and *The Volunteers* (1975) depict the suffering of the innocent. *Translations* (1981) illustrates the clash of Irish and English cultures through the Royal Engineers' attempts to conduct a Survey of Ireland in the 1830s; by the end of the play it is clear that in this failure of communication lies the seeds of Ireland's future problems. Friel's subsequent works have included a translation of Chekhov's *Three Sisters* (1981) and *Making History* (1988). In 1980 Friel was a cofounder of the Irish cultural organization Field Day; he was later nominated to the Irish Senate but did not take an active role.

Friel's masterpiece is *Dancing at Lughnasa* (1990), perhaps the most acclaimed English-language play of recent years. A poignant depiction of a family of sisters in pre-war Donegal, it is Friel's fullest treatment of his most distinctive theme – the supreme value but final untrustworthiness of memory. Subsequent plays include *Wonderful Tennessee* (1993).

fringe theatre Innovative and radical theatre that takes place outside the commercial mainstream; the phrase is the equivalent of the US OFF-OFF-BROADWAY. The term probably derives from the growth of unconventional theatrical productions on the 'fringe' of the EDINBURGH FESTIVAL during the 1950s. In 1960 the Cambridge Footlights team appeared at the Edinburgh Festival in the satirical BEYOND THE FRINGE. The first true fringe theatre was the Traverse Theatre, an Edinburgh studio venue that gave both Tom STOPPARD and C. P. Taylor their start in 1963. Fringe theatre, which included student and amateur productions, brought a new vitality to British drama in the 1960s. Plays were performed in pubs, parks, halls, universities, and other public places as well as in more conventional venues. Most productions were critical of the Establishment and appealed to younger audiences.

The abolition of stage CENSORSHIP in 1968 gave a further impetus to fringe theatres, which soon increased in number. By the 1970s the fringe companies began to receive grants from the ARTS COUNCIL and from local authorities. More than 50 London fringe theatres existed by the early 1980s, when a ticket agency was established for them at the CRITERION THEATRE. Well-known fringe groups have included the Pip Simmons Theatres, Shoestring, Bubble Theatre, Tricycle Theatre, Theatre of Black Women, the Portable Theatre (co-founded by the playwright David Hare), the King's Head, the Monstrous Regiment, the People Show, the Hull Truck Theatre Company, the 7:48 Touring Company, the GATE THEATRE and the Hampstead Theatre Club.

A variety of venues have housed the fringe groups: the Half-Moon Theatre is in a former synagogue, while the Bush Theatre in Shepherd's Bush, London, and the Orange Tree Theatre, Richmond are above pubs. Other venues for experimental productions include the ICA Theatre at the Institute of Contemporary Arts, the Riverside Studios Theatre, the Theatre Upstairs at the ROYAL COURT THEATRE, the Pit at the BARBICAN, and the Cottesloe Theatre at the ROYAL NATIONAL THEATRE.

Fringe successes that have transferred to the West End include *Accidental Death of an Anarchist* in 1979 and *Educating Rita* in 1980.

Frisch, Max (1911–91) Swiss playwright and novelist, who emerged as one of the leading writers in the German language in the late 1940s. He wrote his first play, *Now You Can Sing*, an exploration of individual guilt during wartime, in 1945 while working as an architect in Zürich. The plays that followed, which established his reputation for witty and socially challenging drama, included *The Great Wall of China* (1946), *When the War was Over* (1949), *Overland* (*Graf Öderland*; 1951), and THE FIRE-RAISERS (1958), a major contribution to absurdist theatre which remains his best-known work (*see* ABSURD, THEATRE OF THE). It attacks the moral complacency of Swiss society through the figure of Biedermann, a typical good citizen who nevertheless fails to prevent arsonists from starting a fire in his attic. Subsequent plays included *Andorra* (1961), which aroused controversy with its portrayal of the growth of anti-Semitism in a small and peaceful country, *Triptychon* (1979), and *Jonah and his Veteran* (1989), a drama about military service in Switzerland.

Frisch's novels include *Stiller* (1954), an exploration of the problems of personal identity, and *Homo Faber* (1957). He also published several volumes of diaries and literary sketchbooks.

Frogs, The A comedy by ARISTOPHANES produced in 407 BC at the LENAEA, when it won the first prize and was given the unusual honour of a repeat performance. The story centres on the god DIONYSUS, in whose honour all Athenian tragedy was written. Since Athens no longer has a worthy tragic poet, Dionysus travels to the underworld to bring back EURIPIDES, but he meets AESCHYLUS there who insists that it is he who should return since his achievements are greater. Euripides and Aeschylus engage in an absurd poetic debate. Dionysus sides with Euripides as the modern tragedian who best captured the city's mood during its decline, but eventually decides that Athens needs the old-fashioned Aeschylus, who had represented it in its heyday.

The Frogs, a gentle play for Aristophanes, anticipates MIDDLE COMEDY. It includes memorable comic scenes between Dionysus and his slave Xanthias as well as clever parodies of Aeschylean and Euripidean tragedy.

Frohman brothers Three US theatre managers: Daniel Frohman (1851–1940), Gustave Frohman (1855–1930), and the impresario who dominated Broadway for a quarter of a century, Charles Frohman (1860–1915).

Daniel Frohman began as business manager of New York's Fifth Avenue Theatre and the Madison Square Theatre, where he employed David BELASCO as his stage manager. Then, in 1885, Daniel and **Gustave Frohman** took over the LYCEUM THEATRE on Fourth Avenue and created an outstanding company that performed plays by such British dramatists as A. W. Pinero and H. A. Jones. The venue was demolished in 1902, and Daniel built a new Lyceum on 45th Street. He also managed DALY'S THEATRE from 1899 to 1903 and was president of the Actor's Fund of America.

Charles Frohman worked on newspapers before managing a tour for the Wallack Theatre Company in 1883. On one disastrous western journey, cowboys began to shoot at their train on the Northern Pacific Railroad; only when Frohman persuaded his actors to give a performance on the prairie did they calm down.

His first success was the production of Bronson Howard's civil-war drama *Shenandoah* in 1888. In 1893 he built and opened the Empire Theatre on Broadway,with John Drew (*see* DREW FAMILY) as the star of his stock company. In 1896, he led theatre owners, producers, and agents in forming the THEATRICAL SYNDICATE, which held a virtual monopoly on bookings in major US cities for about 16 years.

In 1893 Frohman took over the DUKE OF YORK'S THEATRE, London, where he established a repertory company whose successes included Barrie's PETER PAN (1904). When Frohman first read *Peter Pan* he was so excited that he would stop people in the streets and act out parts. Barrie, however, was so doubtful about "this dream-child of mine" that he wrote Frohman a second play, *Alice-Sit-By-the-Fire*, to make up for the expected failure of *Peter Pan*.

When Barrie informed Frohman that the child actor who was to play Peter was ill, Frohman boomed, "If the boy can't come to the play, we'll take the play to the boy." He assembled as many props as possible in the boy's sick room and had the cast perform it for him, apparently the only instance of a professional play presented in a child's bedroom.

Frohman died in the sinking of the *Lusitania*. During his lifetime he is credited with making many stars, including Ethel Barrymore (*see* BARRYMORES) and Maude Adams.

front. frontcloth *See* CLOTH.

front curtain *See* CURTAIN.

front of house (FOH) All the areas of a theatre in front of the stage, including the auditorium, bars, foyer, and the box office. These are the areas used by the audience. Just as the backstage area has a stage manager, so there is a front-of-house manager. The PROMPT BOOK direction 'On FOH clear' indicates that the play can begin when the audience has cleared the foyers etc. and is seated.

frontier theatre In 19th-century America, the theatre troupes that existed on the fringe of the western territory. Theatrical life began in America soon after settlements were established on the eastern coast; by the 1790s, drama was firmly established in such places as Philadelphia (the dominant theatrical centre from 1794 to 1815), Boston, and New York. Few performances were given west of the Allegheny Mountains before 1815, when Samuel Drake (1769–1854) took his company overland from Albany, New York, to Pittsburgh and down the Ohio to Kentucky. The plays in their repertory were all rewritten for the company's ten actors, who also doubled as stagehands. In the Mississippi Valley, from St Louis to Nashville, the early theatre was dominated by James H. Caldwell (1793–1863), an English light comedian, who emigrated to America in 1816. Most western theatres were located on rivers, and the SHOWBOAT became an important part of the frontier scene, especially along the Ohio and Mississippi rivers.

A year after the discovery of gold in California in 1848, the first professional English-language performances were given at the Eagle Theatre in Sacramento. The first theatre in San Francisco, which later became the western centre for drama, was opened in 1850, the year the Mormons began to produce plays in Utah; they built the Salt Lake Theatre in 1862. The transcontinental railway was completed in 1869, enabling many more troupes to travel west. Eastern actors playing the frontier included Edwin FORREST, Junius Brutus Booth, and his son Edwin Booth (*see* BOOTH FAMILY).

Fry, Christopher (Christopher Harris; 1907–) British playwright, a leading exponent of POETIC DRAMA in the late 1940s and early 1950s. "Poetry," Fry said, "is the language by which man explores his own amazement."

His first play, *The Boy with a Cart*, retold the story of St Cuthbert: it was given an amateur performance in 1937 and received its first professional production 12 years later at the Lyric Theatre, Hammersmith, starring Richard Burton.

In 1940 he became director of the OXFORD PLAYHOUSE and in 1946 enjoyed his first success as a dramatist with the one-act fantasy *A Phoenix Too Frequent*. Hope for a revival of poetic drama came with the popular success of Fry's THE LADY'S NOT FOR BURNING, which opened in 1948 at the Arts Theatre, and later transferred to the Globe Theatre; it starred John GIELGUD, Pamela Brown, Richard BURTON, and Claire Bloom. Burton's audition was so stumbling and confused that he had to be given a second chance to calm his nerves. The work opened in New York in 1950.

The same year saw the premiere of Fry's tragicomedy *Venus Observed*; this was a work written for Laurence Olivier, who starred as the Duke of Altair, an astronomer who learns that his son is his rival in love. *A Sleep of Prisoners* (1951) questioned the need for war through its story of four soldiers sheltering in a bombed church in enemy territory. It was first seen at London's St Thomas's church; it was later staged in a church in New York with a British cast.

In 1954 *The Dark Is Light Enough* ("Or *The Light is Dark Enough*," mused Noël Coward. "It comes to the same thing.") was less successful, despite the outstanding performance of Edith Evans. In the later 1950s the trend turned in favour of the KITCHEN-SINK dramas of John OSBORNE and others and Fry's reputation went into a decline from which it has never fully recovered. His 1961 drama *Curtmantle*, about Henry II and Becket, opened in Tilburg, The Netherlands, in Dutch, before being produced, rather unsuccessfully, by the RSC in London a year later. *A Yard of Sun* was produced at the Nottingham Playhouse in 1970 before transferring to London for a week's run. Later works have included translations and screenplays.

Fugard, Athol (1932–) White South African playwright and director, whose work is largely concerned with the social and racial problems of that country. The son of an Afrikaans mother and an English father, he served as a merchant seaman before entering the theatre as a stage manager. His early plays, which include *No Good Friday* (1959), and *The Blood Knot* (1961), explore the lives of Black and White workers in South Africa.

In the early 1960s Fugard and his actress wife, Sheila Meiring, formed an amateur theatre company of Black actors in New Brighton, Port Elizabeth. Amongst the plays he directed there were works by Sophocles, Machiavelli, and Brecht. In his own work for the company, he explored the ideas of improvisation and COLLECTIVE CREATION. This approach resulted in several acclaimed productions, notably *Sizwe Bansi is Dead* and *Statements after an Arrest under the Immorality Act* (both 1972).

Fugard's more recent work includes *A Lesson from Aloes* (1980), *My Children! My Africa!* (1990), and *Valley Song* (1996).

Funambules, Théâtre des A theatre on the Boulevard du Temple in Paris built in 1816 on the site of a former booth used by acrobats. *Funambulus* is the Latin word for a rope-walker and the first productions at the permanent theatre were mostly circus acts or harlequinades. In 1820 the pantomimist Jean-Gaspard Deburau (*see* BAPTISTE) appeared there as Harlequin with the young Frédérick (Antoine-Louis-Prosper Lemaître; 1800–76). Thereafter the theatre became known for its pantomimes, which were unrivalled for their elaborate technical effects. Deburau eventually replaced the character of Harlequin with his own version of PIERROT, which remained the star attraction until his death in 1846. The venue was demolished during the rebuilding of Paris in 1862.

Futurism A 20th-century movement in theatre and the other arts that glorified the dynamism of the machine age. It was launched in 1909 in Italy by Filippo Tommaso Marinetti (1876–1944), who coined the term. The movement, which reached its peak in the 1920s, called for the destruction of all libraries and museums and praised war as an example of supreme energy. It finally lost any intellectual respectability by endorsing the Fascist and Nazi philosophies of aggression.

Many of the Futurists' works were produced by Anton Guilio Bragaglia (1890–1960), who managed Rome's Teatro degli Independenti from 1922 to 1936. Advocates of Futurism rejected all former stage practices, denouncing traditional productions as too static and lengthy. Instead they proposed compressing a dramatic situation into a brief 'synthetic drama'. They also felt that the theatre of the future should incorporate the energy of music hall and circus. Enrico Prampolini (1894–1960), the main exponent of the genre in the 1920s, aimed to produce semi-religious dramas in which actors would be replaced by luminous forms, and moving 'stage architecture' substituted for painted scenery. Many of the innovations of the 1960s, such as the intermingling of actors and audience and the use of new technology to create MIXED MEDIA performances, had their roots in Futurism.

G

gaff Slang for a cheap public theatre or a low-class MUSIC HALL; such venues, which were often called *penny gaffs* from the price of admission, were once common on the south side of the Thames in London (*see* TRANSPONTINE MELODRAMA). They often provided violent and emotional melodramas, when they were known as **blood tubs**.

gag A theatrical term for an interpolation. When Shakespeare makes Hamlet direct the players to say no more "than is set down" (III, ii) he cautions them against gagging.

gaiety. Gaiety Girl One of the chorus for which the old Gaiety Theatre in the Strand, London, was famous in late Victorian and early Edwardian times. Such productions as *The Shop Girl* (1894) and *The Circus Girl* (1896) were designed to give full reign to the singing and dancing talents of the chorus, as well as to display their good looks. Several of the Gaiety Girls, many of whom came from humble origins, married into the peerage.

Gaiety Theatre, Dublin An intimate playhouse that opened in Dublin in 1871. It came under the auspices of the Irish Literary Theatre from 1900 to 1901. The theatre was renovated in 1955.

Gaiety Theatre, London A London theatre in the Strand, which opened in 1864 as the Strand Musick Hall. It was rebuilt and reopened in 1868, later becoming the first theatre to be lit by electricity on the outside. The chorus of GAIETY GIRLS first appeared in 1893 in a production of *In Town*, one of the first musical comedies. The theatre was demolished in 1903 for the widening of the Strand, but a new Gaiety was built in Aldwych and opened in the same year. It closed in 1939 and was finally demolished in 1957. *See also* EDWARDES, GEORGE.

Gaiety Theatre, Manchester The home of England's first REPERTORY company, founded by Annie HORNIMAN in a former music hall in 1908. Financial problems forced its closure in 1917 and the building became a cinema in 1921.

Gaiety Theatre, New York A theatre on Broadway, which opened in 1908. Those to make their names there included the young John Barrymore (*see* THE BARRYMORES). In 1932 the venue became a burlesque house and cinema, and in 1943 it was renamed the Victoria Theatre.

the gaiety of nations This phrase derives from Dr Johnson's words alluding to the death of David GARRICK – "I am disappointed by that stroke of death which has eclipsed the gaiety of nations and impoverished the public stock of harmless pleasure."

galanty show *See* SHADOW PUPPETS.

galère. Que diable allait-il faire dans cette galère? What the devil was he doing in that galley? A quotation from MOLIÈRE's comedy *Les Fourberies de Scapin* (1671). The rogue Scapin wants to bamboozle Géronte out of his money, and tells him that his son (Scapin's master) is being held prisoner on a Turkish galley, which he visited out of curiosity. The above phrase was Géronte's reply. It is applied to someone who finds himself in difficulties through being where he ought not to be, or to express astonishment that he should be found in such unexpected company, such a strange situation, etc.

Galileo A play by Bertolt BRECHT, based on the life of the astronomer Galileo (1564–1642). Premiered in 1943 in Zürich, the play concentrates upon the astronomer's struggle to maintain his integrity in the face of religious persecution.

Following the dropping of the atomic bomb on Hiroshima, Brecht revised the play to cast the scientist in a less heroic light. This revised version of the play (translated by Brecht and Charles LAUGHTON) opened at the Coronet Theatre in Los Angeles in 1947, the same year Brecht left America after having to testify before the House Un-American Activities Committee. A year later Laughton enjoyed a great success with the play on Broadway.

There have been many successful revivals, including productions by the National Theatre in 1980 and 1994.

gallery The highest rows of seats in a theatre, above the BALCONY and the CIRCLE. This is the cheapest area of the auditorium as the seating tends to be uncomfortable and the view of the stage poor. The reaction of the audience seated there was traditionally considered to be a measure of popular taste. In Elizabethan playhouses, however, gallery seats were more prestigious and expensive than places in the PIT.

In the 18th century the occupants of the gallery were nicknamed the **gods**, because of the elevated position of the seats and because blue sky, representing heaven, was painted on the ceilings of many theatres; the equivalent French term is *paradis*. British theatregoers would ask for seats up amongst the gods.

footman's gallery A gallery reserved for footmen, who were admitted free after the fourth act.

peanut gallery A US term for the gallery in a theatre, perhaps because the seats can be bought 'for peanuts' or because peanuts are sometimes thrown from these seats during unpopular performances.

to play to the gallery To appeal to the lower elements of one's audience, like an actor seeking popularity from those in the cheapest seats in the theatre (the gallery) by an exaggerated melodramatic display.

women's gallery A separate gallery (*cazuela*) for women in the Spanish CORRALES DE COMEDIA in the 16th century.

Game of Love and Chance, The A romantic comedy by Pierre MARIVAUX, first performed in Paris in 1730 by the Comédie-Italienne. It is often considered Marivaux's finest work, providing perhaps the best example of his skill in portraying the fine details of psychology and sentiment (a style now known as *marivaudage*).

The story centres on the marriage of Silvia and Dorante, prearranged by their parents on the condition that the young couple are willing to accept each other. The boy and girl, having never met, are sceptical about the match and each decides independently to observe the other in secret. Consequently Silvia disguises herself as her maid, Lisette, and Dorante changes places with his valet, Arlequin. After numerous confusions the couple fall in love without knowing each other's true identities.

Gammer Gurton's Needle The earliest extant English comedy apart from RALPH ROISTER DOISTER. It was written in verse, probably by one William Stevenson, in the early 1550s but not published until 1575. The lively comedy closes with the discovery of Gammer Gurton's missing needle in the seat of her servant Hodge's breeches.

García Lorca, Federico (1898–1936) Spanish poet and dramatist, considered one of the greatest influences on modern drama, especially in Spain. A composer in his youth, García Lorca believed that poetry was a form of music and established his reputation by performing rather than publishing his early verse. His first play *El maleficio de la mariposa* (*Butterfly's Evil Spell*) was produced in 1920 at the Teatro Eslava, Madrid, by Martinez Sierra, but was only performed once. It was followed by *Mariana Pineda* (1927) and *Amor de Don Perlimplin con Belisa en su jardin* (1931). In 1932 he founded *La Barraca*, a state-funded educational travelling theatre company, and thereafter served as its director, composer, and playwright.

With his hauntingly lyrical and experimental plays García Lorca opposed the contemporary fashion for REALISM. His poetic works depicted Andalusian peasant life, concentrating in particular on the conflict between love and honour. His best-known work is the trilogy comprising BLOOD WEDDING, THE HOUSE OF BERNARDA ALBA, and YERMA.

At the beginning of the Spanish Civil War, García Lorca was executed without trial by Nationalist partisans.

Garrick, David Garrick (1717–79) An extraordinary actor and director who ruled the British stage for some 30 years and who has been called "the first modern superstar". He introduced a more naturalistic style of acting to England and led the movement away from the vulgarity of RESTORATION DRAMA. He was also the author of more than 40 plays.

In 1737 he travelled to London with his friend Samuel Johnson, intending to study law. Instead, he became a wine merchant near Covent Garden, only later drifting into playwriting and acting. Drury Lane produced his first comedy *Lethe, or Esop in the Shades* in 1740; he made his acting debut there in 1742, playing 19 parts – including Lear and Hamlet – in his first season. Standing a mere 5′4″, he was an intensely active man, described by George III as "a great fidget who could never stand still".

In 1747 he became the artistic and administrative director of DRURY LANE. In this role Garrick is said to have been a harsh critic and a hard taskmaster. Playing opposite a new leading lady, whose delivery he considered too deadpan, he savaged her in rehearsal: "Can you chop cabbage?" he replied to her most passionate line, mimicking her lack of intonation. Under his management, Drury Lane competed fiercely with COVENT GARDEN; the theatres continually attempted to poach each other's actors and on one occasion staged *Romeo and Juliet* simultaneously, with Garrick claiming victory as his production lasted one day longer. His management was not without its disasters. In 1755 mobs wrecked the theatre after Garrick presented a French ballet when Britain and France were on the verge of war. More riots followed in 1762, after he abolished the traditional admission reductions for those who came late or left early.

Garrick is buried in the Poets' Corner in Westminster Abbey.

Garrick Club A London club in which "actors and men of education and refinement might meet on equal terms". The Duke of Sussex established it in 1831 in honour of David Garrick. It houses an extensive library, theatrical memorabilia, and a collection of theatrical portraits, including the painting by John Zoffany of Garrick and Susanna Cibber (*see* CIBBER FAMILY).

Membership of the Garrick Club is restricted to 700, and is only open to men. Among the first members were Charles Kemble, William Macready, and Charles Mathews; later members included Henry Irving, Beerbohm Tree, Johnston Forbes-Robertson, Laurence Olivier, John Gielgud, and Alec Guinness.

Garrick of Germany The posthumous nickname of Konrad EKHOF, the German actor and director.

Garrick Theatre A London theatre, off Charing Cross Road, designed by Walter Emden and decorated in the Italian Renaissance style. Built by W. S. Gilbert, the Garrick was partly underground, and initially had the problem of an underground river seeping into the foundations. After acquiring the site Gilbert is reported to have said that he could never decide whether to build a theatre or to lease the fishing rights. The theatre opened in 1889 with PINERO's *The Profligate*.

The first manager, John Hare, enjoyed a great success with the first production of Pinero's *The Notorious Mrs Ebbsmith* (1895), featuring Mrs Patrick CAMPBELL in the title role. In 1903 Arthur Bourchier, whose ghost is said to roam the theatre, became the first manager in Britain to ban a critic, A. B. Walkley of *The Times*.

In 1935 Wendy Hiller established her reputation in a production of Walter Greenwood's *Love on the Dole*, which ran for 391 performances.

From 1967 onwards Brian Rix presented a popular series of farces at the theatre, while Ira Levin's shocker *Deathtrap* drew large audiences in 1978. In 1992 Brian FRIEL's *Dancing at Lughnasa* won all London's major awards as Best Play.

A previous Garrick Theatre existed at Leman Street in Whitechapel from 1831 to 1881.

Gate Theatre. **Gate Theatre, Dublin** A theatre company formed by Hilton Edwards and Michéal MacLiammóir in Dublin in 1928. The company played at the Peacock Theatre (a smaller auditorium in the ABBEY THEATRE) before moving to its own venue in the Rotunda Buildings in 1930.

In 1931 the Sixth Earl of Longford (Edward Arthur Henry Pakenham; 1902–61), an Irish playwright and director, became associated with the Gate and in 1936 formed Longford Productions to stage classic dramas there. MacLiammóir performed in such Shakespearean roles as Hamlet, Romeo, and Othello. The Gate actively encouraged Irish playwrights while also producing modern plays from Britain, Europe, and America. After World War II, Lady Longford ran the theatre whose fortunes declined through the 1950s and 1960s; it was awarded a state renovation subsidy in 1969. After the death of MacLiammóir in 1978, it was taken over by a new management.

Gate Theatre, London A small club theatre founded by Peter Godfrey (1899–1971), a variety performer and Shakespearean actor. It opened in 1925 on the top floor of a converted warehouse in Floral Street,

Covent Garden. Finding himself unable to secure a licence for the venue, Godfrey made the Gate into a private club giving performances of noncommercial and foreign dramas.

In its first nine years Godfrey produced over 350 plays, gaining an international reputation as the principal exponent of expressionism in Britain. His productions employed stylized acting before black drapes, with unusual lighting effects.

The Gate opened with *Bernice* by Susan Glaspell and had its first success the following year with *From Morn to Midnight* by the German expressionist playwright Georg Kaiser. In 1927 it moved to Villiers Street near Charing Cross, where it occupied part of the old Hungerford Music Hall (later the home to the PLAYERS' THEATRE). Godfrey also used his club to stage such banned plays as Eugene O'Neill's DESIRE UNDER THE ELMS, presented in 1931 with Eric Portman playing Ebon Cabot and Flora Robson as Abbie Putnam.

The subsequent decline in its fortunes was halted when Norman Marshall (1901–80) took over the management in 1934; he presented Toller's *Miracle in America* that same year. Marshall subsequently produced several banned works, including Laurence Housman's VICTORIA REGINA (1935), Lillian Hellman's THE CHILDREN'S HOUR (1936), and Steinbeck's *Of Mice and Men* (1939). Marshall, who also revived the annual Gate Revue, managed the venue until 1940. In 1941 the theatre was badly damaged by bombing and was not reopened.

gatherer In the Elizabethan theatre, a man or woman who collected admission money at the entrances to the three main areas of the auditorium: the pit, public galleries, and private boxes.

gauze *See* TRANSPARENCY.

gel A colour filter for a stage light; they were originally made of gelatine but are now usually made from plastic. The gel was traditionally held in front of the light by a **gel frame**.

Gelosi One of the earliest and most famous of the COMMEDIA DELL'ARTE companies. Headed by Francesco Andreini (1548–1624), who created the character of IL CAPITANO, and his wife Isabella (1562–1604), who developed the role of *innamorata*, the company was attached to the household of the Duke of Mantua, who later supported the FEDELI troupe. The Gelosi played in France in 1571 and in 1577 were summoned to performances at Blois for Henry III. The company subsequently played in Paris, heralding the later invasion of Italian companies that were to have a profound influence upon the character of the French theatre (*see* COMÉDIE-ITALIENNE). The Gelosi toured Europe almost constantly, returning to perform in Paris in 1602. In 1604, on their return journey to Italy, Isabella died in childbirth in Lyons; her husband subsequently disbanded the company.

General Utility *See* STOCK COMPANY.

género chico Another name for the TEATRO POR HORAS.

Genet, Jean (1909–86) French playwright, novelist, and poet. His works for the stage shocked audiences with their blend of violence, lyricism, sexual perversion, and quasi-religious ritual.

Genet, born illegitimate and subsequently abandoned, spent much of his early life in reformatory and prison. His first play, THE MAIDS (1947), was produced in Paris by Louis Jouvet and performed five years later in French in London; an English version opened in New York in 1955. *The Maids* introduced Genet's idea of a play as a ritual, analogous to the Mass, in which the performers and the audience unite to share a transforming experience.

These notions were further developed in DEATHWATCH (1949), a play about the complex relationship between fellow-prisoners. THE BALCONY, a disturbing work about sex, fantasy, and power set in a brothel, received its première in London in 1957. The critic Kenneth Tynan commented: "For all its faults, it is a theatrical experience as startling as anything since Ibsen's revelation 76 years ago that there was such a thing as syphilis." THE BLACKS (1959) was a perverse study in prejudice and exploitation. Genet's last play *The Screen* (1966) dealt with the politically explosive situation in Algeria, thus ensuring a controversial opening at the Odéon in Paris.

Geneva A didactic play by George Bernard SHAW, first produced in 1938 at the Malvern Festival. Written during the years of Hitler's rise to power, *Geneva* has as its theme the idea that tyrants should face an international court of human justice; it also exposed the inadequacies of the League of Nations in dealing with Nazi Germany.

gentleman. ***Gentleman Dancing-Master, The*** A comedy by William WYCHERLEY, first performed in 1671 at the Dorset Garden Theatre, London. The play was revived in 1925 by the Phoenix Society, and in 1950 at Edinburgh's Gateway Theatre.

The story concerns Gerrard's attempts to win the hand of the beautiful Hippolita, who is being courted by her pretentious cousin. Gerrard poses as her dancing-master but, because of his clumsiness, is nearly discovered. However, Gerrard and Hippolita are eventually united and all ends happily.

Gentleman Johnny The nickname, acquired as a result of his elegance, of the British general and playwright John Burgoyne (1722–92). Following several undistinguished works, Burgoyne wrote *The Heiress*, a highly successful comedy, which was produced at Drury Lane by Sheridan in 1786. Burgoyne is probably better remembered, however, for his defeat at Saratoga (1777) during the American War of Independence. He appears as a character in George Bernard Shaw's THE DEVIL'S DISCIPLE.

gentlemanly melodrama A type of 19th-century MELODRAMA designed to appeal to a sophisticated audience; it was intended to encourage the upper classes to return to the English theatre. Until around 1840, melodrama was the favourite fare for the less well-educated playgoers. Gentlemanly melodrama was introduced by Sheridan Knowles (1784–1862) and was firmly established by Edward George Bulwer-Lytton (1803–73). William MACREADY, who had starred in some of Knowles's plays, encouraged the genre while managing Covent Garden and Drury Lane. He produced Bulwer-Lytton's works and even suggested material for such plays as *The Lady of Lyons* (1838).

Gentleman Smith Nickname for the English actor William Smith (1730–1819), because of his educated demeanour, elegant dress, and aristocratic wife.

Smith joined Covent Garden for the 1753 season and remained there for two decades. In 1774 he moved over to join David Garrick at Drury Lane and in 1777 created the role of the honest wastrel Charles Surface in Sheridan's *The School for Scandal*. Smith became best known for tragedy, however, playing Macbeth to Sarah Siddon's first portrayal of Lady Macbeth and alternating the roles of Hamlet and Richard III with Garrick. In 1788 he retired to live the life of a country gentleman in Bury St Edmunds. Of his acting career, Smith boasted that he had never played in farces or roles that required him to blacken his face or fall through a trap door.

Georges, Mlle *See* QUEEN OF BEAUTIFUL ACTRESSES *under* QUEEN.

Gershwin, George (1898–1937) US composer of Broadway musicals, often with his brother, **Ira Gershwin** (1896–1983), as lyricist.

Born in Brooklyn the son of Jewish-Russian immigrants, Gershwin first worked in a music publishing house. In 1919 his song 'Swanee' became highly successful as sung by Al JOLSON: that same year he also wrote his first Broadway show, *La La Lucille*. From 1920 to 1924 Gershwin contributed music to five editions of George White's *Scandals*, including such well-known songs as 'Somebody Loves Me'. After working with several lyricists, Gershwin collaborated with his brother Ira on the the successful jazz-orientated *Lady, Be good!* in 1924. Encouraged by this success, they rapidly produced a string of musicals, including: *Oh, Kay!* (1926), *Funny Face* (1927), *Strike Up the Band* (1927), and *Girl Crazy* (1930).

In 1931 the Gershwin brothers wrote *Of Thee I Sing*, which won the Pulitzer Prize for drama. Four years later they presented PORGY AND BESS, a 'folk opera' written in the jazz idiom for Black singers. Their last musical collaboration, *Porgy and Bess* was not a financial success during George Gershwin's lifetime. Since then it has acquired immense popularity and the status of a modern classic. Following George's death in 1937, Ira produced the lyrics for only another three shows.

George Gershwin was known for his egotistical nature, which prompted the pianist and pundit Oscar Levant to ask:

> Tell me, George, if you had to do it all over again, would you still fall in love with yourself?

ghost. **ghost glide** In the 19th-century, a TRAP used to create the illusion of a ghost rising from the stage floor and drifting across it. An actor would stand on a wheeled platform, which was pulled along an inclined cut in the stage floor; as the truck ascended, the actor would glide into view. A refinement known as the **Corsican trap** was introduced in Boucicault's *The Corsican Brothers* (1852). This involved covering the trap with SCRUTO, which would slide away as the truck moved through and then close again behind it.

Ghosts Henrik IBSEN's most controversial work, a tragedy that uses venereal disease as a symbol of inherited and collective guilt. The play, a landmark in the development of realist drama, was first performed in 1882 in Chicago before an audience of Scandinavian immigrants. Although presented earlier by the Independent Theatre Club, the play did not have a licensed production in Britain until 1914, when it was staged at the Theatre Royal, Haymarket; the *Daily Telegraph* critic Clement Scott described the play as "an open drain, a loathsome sore, an abominable piece, a repulsive and degrading work".

The plot concerns the widow Helen Alving, whose son Oswald has just returned from Paris. As a result of his father's debauchery, Oswald now suffers from a congenital disease. It also transpires that Regine, the woman with whom he has been having an affair, is his illegitimate half-sister. Upon learning of her parentage, Regine decides to leave Oswald, whose brain is now affected by the disease. As the curtain falls Oswald pleads with his mother to give him a fatal dose of pills.

Ghost Sonata, The A one-act drama by August STRINDBERG, first performed in Stockholm (1908) as one of five 'chamber plays' (*Kammarspel*) written for his Intima Teatern. The work has many 'grotesques' and dreamlike interruptions, thus anticipating some of the techniques of modern dramatists. The play especially influenced Eugene O'NEILL and the playwrights of the Theatre of the ABSURD.

The central theme of the work is the conflict between truth and pretence. The plot involves the plan of an embittered old minister, Hummel, to destroy a Colonel who, as a young rival, had taken the woman he loved. Only Hummel and Mummy, the Colonel's wife, know that the Colonel's much-loved daughter was actually fathered by Hummel. During a dinner at the Colonel's home, Hummel reveals to the other guests that their host is as phoney as his military rank. Mummy, however, exposes Hummel's deceitfulness and he commits suicide; their daughter is placed behind a "death screen" to wither and die.

Ghost Train, The A comic thriller by Arnold Ridley, first performed in London in 1925 at Saint Martin's Theatre. It was successfully revived in 1993 at the Lyric Theatre, Hammersmith.

The plot involves a group of travellers, including two young honeymooners, who miss their train and are forced to spend the night in a remote, and apparently haunted, Cornish railway station. It transpires, however, that the ghost train is an elaborate hoax to cover up a Bolshevik plan to smuggle weapons into Britain. The plan is thwarted by one of the travellers who, it emerges, is a secret agent.

The original production was noted for its elaborate SOUND EFFECTS; milk churns, garden rollers, and whistles were amongst the devices used to create the effect of the ghost train.

theatre ghosts Some of the best-known and most visible of all ghosts seem to haunt London theatres. Many sightings have been described in detail, such as that of the spirit that "flew up to the ceiling, made his way through the tiling, and tore away one-fourth of the house" after the final presentation at Lincoln's Inn Theatre in 1732. Tradition says that a sighting is a good omen for the play currently being performed.

The most famous of DRURY LANE's several ghosts is the so-called 'man in grey'. This is said to be the spirit of an actor who was stabbed to death during a stage fight in the 18th century. (When the theatre was demolished in 1791, a body was found bricked up in a wall with a knife in the ribs.) The man in grey is a brazen daytime ghost who frequents matinées; he has been seen in the upper circle and on stage. Drury Lane is also home to a screaming woman often heard backstage, and the spirit of the actor Clifford Heatherley, who died during the run of *Crest of the Wave* (1937).

Vying with the man in grey as London's most recognizable ghost is John Buckstone at the Haymarket Theatre. Buckstone (1802–79) had a long association with the theatre as actor, playwright, and manager; popular sentiment says he simply remained behind because of his love for the place. He has been seen by many actors, including Margaret Rutherford, while others have heard him rehearsing his lines in a dressing room. Buckstone is said to appear only when a production is going well.

A sadder ghost is that of the actor William TERRISS, who appears dressed in a frock coat and top hat in the Adelphi Theatre, the scene of his murder in 1897.

Three ghosts roamed the ROYALTY THEATRE in Dean Street before it was demolished in 1955. A lady in Queen Anne dress used to descend the stairs and disappear in the middle of the vestibule, a gypsy girl with a tambourine would appear when the orchestra played, and the 19th-century actress Fanny Kelly used to wander unconcernedly through the theatre in the daytime.

The resident ghost at the Bristol Old Vic is the great 18th-century actress Sarah SIDDONS, whose lover hanged himself there. The actor Frank Barrie once felt a tap on his shoulder after a rehearsal and turned around to see her sitting in a box at the edge of the stage.

the ghost walks An expression used by theatre people to mean that salaries are about to be paid. The phrase is an allusion to Shakespeare's *Hamlet* (I, i), where Horatio addresses the ghost:

> ...if thou hast uphoarded in thy life
> Extorted treasure in the womb of earth,
> For which, they say, you spirits oft walk
> in death...

Gielgud, Sir (Arthur) John (1904–) British actor and director, noted especially for his interpretations of Shakespeare. Gielgud's noble presence on the stage prompted OLIVIER to describe him as "always the poet, head upturned towards the stars". At RADA, however, he had been criticized for walking like "a cat with rickets". He was knighted in 1953 and appointed OM in 1997.

Gielgud's mother was the daughter of the actress Kate Terry-Lewis and a niece of Ellen Terry (*see* TERRY FAMILY). He was taken to the theatre from an early age and soon became stage-struck. He made his debut in 1921 as the herald in *Henry V*, having the one line "Here is the number of the slaughter'd French." In 1924 he joined the repertory company at the Oxford Playhouse and five years later moved to the Old Vic, taking a large salary cut in return for the chance to play Shakespeare. His great Shakespearean roles include Romeo, Macbeth, and especially Hamlet, which he would play more than 500 times in his career. In 1934 his performance of the part at Wyndham's Theatre inspired Sybil Thorndike to describe his interpretation as "hauntingly beautiful". When Olivier played the part in 1937, Gielgud went backstage and said, "Larry, it's one of the finest performances I have ever seen, but it's still my part."

During World War II Gielgud entertained the troops in Malta, Gibraltar, and Burma with plays by Noël Coward and others. After the war he developed as a director, presenting works ranging from Tennessee Williams's *The Glass Menagerie* (1948) to Berlioz's opera *The Trojans* (1957). In 1949 his production of Christopher Fry's THE LADY'S NOT FOR BURNING ran for 294 performances at the Globe, during which time Gielgud directed four other plays. Between 1956 and 1964, he successfully took his one-man Shakespearean anthology, *The Ages of Man*, around the world. His roles in contemporary British plays have included Harry in David Storey's *Home* (1970) and the depressed poet, Spooner, in Pinter's *No Man's Land* (1975). He has also appeared in numerous films, winning an Oscar for his performance as a supercilious valet in the comedy *Arthur* (1980).

gigaku A Chinese Buddhist dance drama imported to Japan in 612 by the Korean dancer, Mimaji. The performances consisted of processions followed by comic scenes performed on a temporary outdoor stage. Some 250 *gigaku* masks have been preserved in temple collections.

A typical performance of *gigaku* in the 13th century began with ritual Buddhist music (*netori*), followed by a procession (*gyodo*) of chanting monks masked as Buddhas. Ten or more actors representing stock characters such as a king, a Chinese woman, an Indian Brahman, and a lion tamer would then process before mounting the stage to enact a series of skits warning against various sins.

By the 12th century, *gigaku* had lost imperial support and was thereafter gradually replaced by BUGAKU.

Gilbert and Sullivan The playwright and lyricist Sir William Schwenk Gilbert (1836–1911) and the composer Sir Arthur Seymour Sullivan (1842–1900), who collaborated on a series of light operas between 1871 and 1896.

Gilbert, the son of a retired naval surgeon, claimed he had been kidnapped as a child in Naples and ransomed for £25. As a young man he briefly practised law while becoming increasingly involved in writing burlesques and extravaganzas for the theatre. Gilbert's more serious plays included *The Palace of Truth* (1870), *Pygmalion and Galatea* (1871), and *Dan'l Druce, Blacksmith* (1876). After his collaboration with Sullivan had made him rich, Gilbert invested some of his profits in the building of the Garrick Theatre. Although he wrote for other composers, only his libretti for Sullivan have survived.

Gilbert's notorious rudeness is said to have kept Queen Victoria from knighting him at the same time as Sullivan; the honour was finally granted after her death. Gilbert had a fascination with water and often spoke of dying in his garden on a summer's day; on 29 May 1911, when a visiting girl found herself in trouble swimming in the lake beside his house in Harrow Weald, on the outskirts of London, Gilbert gallantly plunged in to save her. Unfortunately the shock was too much for the 75-year-old man, who suffered a fatal heart attack.

The son of a theatre clarinettist, Sullivan was selected for the Chapel Royal Choir and won a scholarship to the Royal Academy of Music. He later studied in Leipzig where he was a classmate of Grieg's and also met Liszt and Schumann. Following a visit to Rossini in Paris, Gilbert decided to compose for the stage. His first success came with a version of *Cox and Box*, which was performed privately in London in 1866. He also composed 'Onward, Christian Soldiers!', 'The Lost Chord', and other familiar Victorian songs. Sullivan collaborated with several other dramatists before being introduced to Gilbert in 1871.

A warm host, gracious friend, and enthusiastic gambler at fashionable casinos, Sullivan was welcomed into London society. In this milieu he met Mary Ronalds, a beautiful, but married, American who became his mistress for the last 24 years of his life.

The relationship between the irritable Gilbert and the gentle Sullivan was prolific and highly successful – it was not, however, without its tensions. Their first collaboration was in 1871 with *Thespis; or, the Gods Grown Old*, an operatic extravaganza produced at the Gaiety Theatre. It was only after the first of their light operas, *Trial by Jury* (1875), that Richard D'OYLY CARTE commissioned further work. Their joint reputation was established by HMS PINAFORE (1878) and consolidated by THE PIRATES OF PENZANCE (1879). *Patience* (1881) was the first of the so-called SAVOY OPERAS presented at the purpose-built SAVOY THEATRE. It was followed by further successess including IOLANTHE (1882), *Princess Ida* (1884), THE MIKADO (1885), *Ruddigore* (1887), THE YEOMAN OF THE GUARD (1888), and THE GONDOLIERS (1889).

Gilbertian A term used to describe any humorously confused situation, such as those depicted in the Gilbert and Sullivan operas.

Gingold, Hermione (Ferdinanda) (1897–1987) British actress, who appeared successfully in revues on both sides of the Atlantic. She first appeared on stage at the age of 11 and six years later played Jessica in *The Merchant of Venice* at the Old Vic. In 1936 her skill as a comedienne was revealed when she appeared in Herbert Farjeon's revue *Spread it Abroad* at the Saville Theatre, London.

Gingold subsequently became one of the leading stars of intimate revue, appearing in the *Gate Revue* of 1938 and *Swinging the Gate* in 1940 before performing in the series of *Sweet and Low* revues at the Ambassadors Theatre (1943–47). In 1949 she appeared with her arch rival Hermione Baddeley in a revival of Noël Coward's *Fallen Angels*. Coward commented in his diary: "Gingold at moments showed signs that she could be funny. Baddeley was disgusting..." Gingold made her New York debut in revue in 1951 and toured in America with *Fallen Angels*. In the 1950s and 1960s she appeared in a number of Hollywood musicals, including *The Music Man* and *Gigi*. Her son, the actor and director **Stephen Joseph** (1927–67), created Britain's first permanent THEATRE-IN-THE-ROUND, the Victoria Theatre at Stoke-on-Trent in 1962.

Gingold was noted for her low husky voice which she often used to striking effect. She was once in an audience of children watching Joan Greenwood as Peter Pan. When Peter saves Tinkerbell's life by asking the audience if they believe in fairies, the chorus of 'yes' from the children was immediately followed by Gingold's roar: "*Believe* in them, darling? I *know* hundreds of them!"

Giraldi, Giovanni Battista *See* CINTHIO, IL.

Giraudoux, (Hippolyte) Jean (1882–1944) French novelist, playwright, and essayist, whose work combines fantasy with realism; his plots were often drawn from biblical and mythological stories. Giraudoux served as a diplomat and wrote several successful novels before trying his hand at drama. His first play, *Siegfried*, produced in Paris in 1928 when he was 45, initiated a long collaboration with the actor and director Louis JOUVET.

Giraudoux followed this with the highly successful *Amphitryon 38*, a work based on Plautus's *Amphitruo* (*see* AMPHITRYON). An adaptation of this work by S. N. Behrman for the LUNTS enjoyed successful runs on Broadway (1937) and in London (1938). *La Guerre de Troie n'aura pas lien*, which addressed the causes and dilemmas of the Trojan War, was first performed in Paris in 1935. Christopher FRY's translation TIGER AT THE GATES, with Michael Redgrave as Hector, had a successful London run in 1955 before transferring to New York's Plymouth Theatre, where it won a New York Drama Critics' Circle Award.

Ondine, based on the legend of a water-nymph who falls in love with a human, had its premiere in Paris in 1939; it was presented in London by the Théâtre National de Belgique in 1953 and revived by the Royal Shakespeare Company in 1961.

Giraudoux's THE MADWOMAN OF CHAILLOT was performed in Paris in 1945, opening three years later on Broadway with the British actress Martita Hunt in the lead. Elisabeth Bergner revived the part in Düsseldorf and returned to it at the Yvonne Arnaud Theatre, Guildford, in 1967. Two years later a Broadway musical version, *Dear World*, flopped.

Another play to be given a posthumous first performance was *Pour Lucrèce* (1953), translated by Christopher Fry as DUEL OF ANGELS.

giving out In the English theatre, the custom of announcing the next production at the end of a performance. This practice died out in the first half of the 19th century.

glamour girl, the A nickname for the actress Ethel Barrymore (1879–1959), a famous beauty. *See* BARRYMORES, THE.

glass. glass crash A theatrical SOUND EFFECT to simulate the breaking of a pane of glass. Before sound effects were taped, this was normally achieved by pouring pieces of broken glass and china from one bucket into another. The live method is still used in some productions.

Glass Menagerie, The Tennessee WILLIAMS's first successful play, produced in 1945 in New York. This semi-autobiographical work, described by Williams himself as a "memory play", won a New York Drama Critics' Circle Award; its language prompted the critic Stark Young to write: "Behind the Southern speech in the mother's part is the echo of great literature...It has the echo and the music of it." The role of Amanda, the emotionally fragile mother, provided the US actress Laurette Taylor (1884–1946) with her last major part.

The story, about the emotional tensions within an isolated Southern family, reflects Williams's own relationship with his mother and sister. The main characters are Amanda Wingfield, her grown son Tom, and her shy crippled daughter, Laura. The mother's chief mission in life is to see Laura marry well, but this pressure is driving the sensitive girl insane. Laura finally breaks down completely when her mother asks Tom to bring home a fellow employee, whom she pushes at Laura.

Globe Theatre Four theatres bearing this name have existed in London. The original Globe, a thatched three-galleried structure, was built by Richard and Cuthbert BURBAGE in 1599. It was constructed from timber originally used by their father, Thomas Burbage, to build THE THEATRE in 1576. The Theatre's landlord complained that the Burbage brothers had

> ...ryoutously assembled themselves together, and there armed themselves with dyvers and many unlawfull and offensive weapons...attempted to pull down the sayd Theater...and...carrye away from thence all the wood and timber thereof unto the Bancksyde...and there erected a newe playhouse with the sayd timber and wood.

Shakespeare, a shareholder in the Globe, acted there with the CHAMBERLAIN'S MEN, who performed many of his plays at the theatre. In 1613 the theatre was destroyed by fire, during a performance of Henry VIII, but it was rebuilt within a year with funds from a royal grant and from public subscriptions. The Puritans closed the theatre in 1642 (*see* INTERREGNUM) and two years later it was demolished.

The second Globe Theatre opened in Aldwych in 1868. Owing to their unstable appearance, the Globe and the Opera Comique next door were popularly known as the Rickety Twins. The 1800-capacity theatre, designed, built, and managed by Sefton Parry, had successes with two transfers, Charles HAWTREY's *The Private Secretary* (1884) and Brandon Thomas's *Charley's Aunt* (1893). In 1902, following a revival of *Sweet Nell of Old Drury Lane* with Fred Terry and Julia Neilson, the theatre was demolished for the Strand improvement scheme.

The Globe Theatre in Shaftesbury Avenue was originally named the Hicks Theatre after the actor-manager Seymour Hicks, who commissioned it with Charles Frohman. Designed by W. G. R. Sprague, it opened in 1906 and a year later enjoyed its first hit with *Brewster's Millions*. It was renamed the Globe in 1909. A riot took place at the theatre in 1917 when the French music-hall artiste Gaby Deslys appeared. The theatre's successes have included Terence Rattigan's *While the Sun Shines* (1943), Christopher Fry's *The Lady's Not for Burning* (1949), starring John GIELGUD, Robert Bolt's *A Man for All Seasons* (1960) with Paul Scofield, Terence Frisby's *There's A Girl in My Soup* (1966), and Peter Shaffer's *Lettice and Lovage* (1987) with Maggie Smith. In 1992 Sir Peter Hall staged a successful revival of Oscar Wilde's *An Ideal Husband*.

In the 1970s the US actor Sam Wanamaker embarked on a project to reconstruct Shakespeare's original Globe despite initial opposition from Southwark Council. The plans (by Theo Crosby) called for the first all-wooden building in London since the great fire of 1666. A German-language performance of *The Merry Wives of Windsor* was staged in the reconstructed theatre in 1993 to mark the 429th anniversary of Shakespeare's birth. Since its official opening in 1996 the Globe has rapidly become one of London's leading tourist attractions.

glory In RENAISSANCE DRAMA a tableau depicting a god descending to the stage in a shower of light. A DRUM-AND-SHAFT system would be used to lower the actor, who stood on one of several platforms painted to represent the heavens.

gobo A cut-out masking device used to create special lighting effects on stage. The gobo is placed in a PROFILE SPOT to shape the beam, creating such atmospheric effects as soft dappled woodland light, etc.

gods *See* GALLERY.

Goethe, Johann Wolfgang von (1749–1832) Germany's greatest literary figure, much of whose writing was for the theatre. The son of a lawyer, Goethe first became interested in drama after watching plays performed by French Army companies and enjoying the local marionette theatre (where he saw a piece that would later inspire his masterpiece FAUST).

In 1765 he attended the University of Leipzig to study law, but suffered a physical breakdown. While convalescing, he read, and was greatly influenced by, the plays of Shakespeare and the contemporary writings of the German dramatist G. E. LESSING. When he had recuperated, Goethe left Leipzig to complete his studies at the University of Strasbourg, where he met the writer Johann Gottfried Herder, in whose company Goethe saw his first Shakespeare play.

Soon after graduating, he published his first play, the historical drama GÖTZ VON BERLICHINGEN (1773). Despite its extreme length (54 scenes), the play created a sensation with its emotional intensity and racy plot; it is usually considered the first drama of the STURM UND DRANG movement. Two years later, Goethe settled in Weimar at the behest of the 18-year-old duke, where he directed entertainments, led the town's amateur theatrical group, and acted in his own works.

In 1786 Goethe visited Italy, and returned nearly two years later with a changed outlook on life and art; he had renounced youthful romanticism in favour of a more measured classicism. His drama of humanity and reconciliation *Iphigenie auf Tauris*, originally written in 1779 but recast in verse in 1787 (*see* IPHIGENIA) is evidence of this changed outlook. Friedrich SCHILLER called the work "astonishingly modern and un-Greek". Meanwhile Goethe fell in love with Christiane Vulpius and the couple created a scandal by living together for 18 years and having several children before eventually marrying in 1806. They remained together until Christiane's death 10 years later.

In 1790 Goethe published the first fragment of *Faust*, a play he had already been working on for some 20 years. The following year, the duke appointed Goethe as director of his new state theatre. With Schiller's encouragement, Goethe drew up a set of 91 rules to improve the resident company's acting technique and worked with individual actors for months before rehearsals. The result was the most integrated ensemble of the era and the creation of a new and influential style of acting (the so-called WEIMAR STYLE).

Schiller, who became co-director at the theatre, urged Goethe to finish the first part of *Faust*, which he did in 1808. Goethe produced most of his friend's plays and when Schiller died in 1805, lamented that he had lost "half of my existence." Subsequently Goethe's enthusiasm for the theatre diminished, and when the duke's mistress took control of the company in 1817 he resigned. Goethe continued to work on the second part of *Faust* until a few months before his death in 1832. The work, a drama of mankind's indomitable spirit, was his crowning achievement.

Gogol, Nikolai Vasilievich (1809–52) Russian playwright and novelist, a pioneer of realism in the Russian theatre. Born in the Ukraine, the son of a landowner, he acted in plays and wrote for magazines whilst at school. When he failed to secure an acting job at the St Petersburg state theatre, he decided to emigrate to America but only reached Sweden before changing his mind. In 1831 he met Alexander Pushkin, who suggested the plots for the novel *Dead Souls* (1842) and his most successful play THE GOVERNMENT INSPECTOR (1836).

Gogol's early works include the comedies *The Gamblers* (1832) and *An Utterly Incredible Affair* (1835) and a historical play, *Alfred the Great* (1835), which portrayed the English king as an ideal ruler. He abandoned his first attempt at a satire on Russian bureaucracy from fear of censorship, later destroying the manuscript. His satirical masterpiece *The Government Inspector* survived mainly owing to the support of Tsar Nicholas I, who enjoyed its performance in 1836. The play was attacked so severely by others, however, that Gogol left Russia for 12 years abroad, most of which he spent in Rome. He returned in 1848 in poor physical and mental health. Among the works written during this period abroad was *Marriage* (1842; produced in London on 1956 as *The Marriage Broker*). The novel *Dead Souls* was dramatized in 1928 by STANISLAVSKY at the Moscow Art Theatre and performed in 1964 in Russian at London's Aldwych Theatre as part of the WORLD THEATRE SEASON.

In 1959 the Moscow Transport Theatre was renamed the Gogol Theatre in honour of the 150th anniversary of his birth.

going up Theatrical jargon for the beginning of a performance, as in 'We're going up in five minutes.'

golden. ***Golden Boy*** A play by Clifford ODETS that opened in 1937 at the Group Theatre, New York, for a run of 250 performances; it was presented a year later in London. A successful musical version was staged on Broadway in 1964, starring Sammy Davis Jnr. The plot concerns Joe Bonaparte, a talented violinist who turns to boxing for money and prestige. He decides to return to music after killing an opponent in the ring, but he and his girlfriend are killed in a car crash before this can be accomplished.

Golden Foghorn Nickname of Ethel MERMAN, the US singer and actress known for her ability to be heard in the next block.

Golden Rump, The A play, by author or authors unknown, which helped to usher in tighter theatrical CENSORSHIP. In 1737 Robert Walpole, the prime minister, was the subject of a series of lampoons in the public theatres. Opportunely, Henry Gifford, then manager of Goodman's Fields Theatre, informed Walpole of a scurrilous manuscript he had received from an anonymous source. Walpole quoted extensively from the play in parliament, using it as a pretext to demand increased theatrical censorship. The play, *The Golden Rump*, called for a striking piece of scenery – a huge pair of golden buttocks from between which the various political figures being satirized would appear and disappear.

As a result of Walpole's use of the play in parliament, a new Licensing Act was brought in that caused the closure of some minor theatres and gave the LORD CHAMBERLAIN's office the power to demand the removal from plays of passages deemed offensive. Gifford received £1000 reward for his actions, although his theatre subsequently lost its licence. The manuscript of *The Golden Rump* disappeared, provoking speculation that Walpole himself may have commissioned the play to serve his political purpose.

Goldoni, Carlo (1707–93) Prolific Italian playwright, who made important reforms in the COMMEDIA DELL'ARTE and played a major role in the development of modern Italian drama. His works, written in Italian, Venetian dialect, and French, include more than 150 comedies, 10 tragedies, and 83 librettos. During the 1750–51 season alone he wrote 16 new plays to illustrate his dramatic theories.

The son of a Venetian doctor, Goldoni ran away from school with a troupe of actors when he was 14; in 1725 he was expelled from the Collegio Ghislieri, Pavia, for writing a satire about local ladies. He later studied law and practised in Venice and Pisa. In 1734 he joined the Imer company in Venice, who later that year produced his first play, the tragicomedy *Belisario*.

From about 1738 onwards Goldoni began to replace the traditional improvised comedy of the Commedia dell'arte with written parts. This was resisted by senior actors, as was his abandonment of the use of masks. Through these and other reforms Goldoni created a new comedy of character and social criticism comparable to Molière's. In works such as *La vedova scaltra* (1748) and *Il cavaliere e la dama* (1749) he similarly replaced traditional risqué farce with a more moral comedy of manners.

In 1746 Goldoni began a highly productive period writing for the company of Girolamo Medebac at the Teatro Sant' - Angelo. His realistic *Il teatro comico* (1750), presented on a bare stage, depicts a troupe of actors about to rehearse. A year later he wrote his comic masterpiece *La locandiera*, which includes the coquettish role of Mirandolina. The character became popular throughout Europe and became famous again in 1891 when Eleonora DUSE revived it for her world tours.

Goldoni subsequently moved to Francesco Vendramin's company at the Teatro San Luca (now the Teatro Goldoni). However, this venue proved too large for his intimate works and his reforms were strongly resisted by rivals including Carlo Gozzi. In 1762 Goldoni accepted an invitation to direct the COMÉDIE-ITALIENNE in Paris; during the next two years he produced French versions of his own works as well as new works in French. Despite wide acclaim Goldoni still found much opposition amongst the old school and in 1764 he retired. Thereafter he taught Italian to the French princesses and composed librettos for the *opera buffa*. Despite his many successes Goldoni died in poverty in Paris, having lost his pension following the French Revolution.

Goldsmith, Oliver (1730–74) The Irish-born poet, playwright, novelist, and journalist, whose two plays have outlived the efforts of all his contemporaries except SHERIDAN. Dr Johnson described him as "a very great man", while Goethe would later write, "To Shakespeare, Sterne, and Goldsmith my debt has been limitless."

Goldsmith's youth gave little promise of his future achievements. After attending Trinity College, Dublin, he abandoned plans to be ordained. He thought of emigrating to America but missed his ship. He then briefly studied medicine before travelling through Europe, partially supporting himself by busking. On his return, he earned his living by translating and reviewing; it was in this period that he emerged as an essayist of talent.

Goldsmith's first play, *The Good-Natured Man*, was turned down by Garrick; the elder Colman (*see* COLMAN FAMILY) subsequently produced it at Covent Garden (1768) though with only mild success. Goldsmith made his name as a playwright with the comedy SHE STOOPS TO CONQUER (1773), in which two men mistake a private house for an inn (a mistake the playwright had himself once made). In rehearsal, Goldsmith berated an actor for playing the part of Young Marlow (an Englishman) with an Irish accent. "Sir," replied the actor, "I spoke it as nearly as I could to the manner in which you instructed me, except that I did not give it quite so strong a brogue."

Goldsmith's only novel *The Vicar of Wakefield* (1766) was successfully adapted for the stage in 1878 with Ellen Terry (*see* TERRY FAMILY) in the role of Olivia, a part later played on tour by her sister, Florence Terry.

Goldsmith's Irish impudence and inconsequential style of chat often irritated his London contemporaries. Horace Walpole called him "an inspired idiot" while Samuel Johnson commented "No man was more foolish when he had not a pen in his hand, or more wise when he had."

goliard In medieval Europe, a wandering clerk or scholar attached to a band of travelling entertainers. Noted for their obscene ballads and short satirical plays, the goliards were infamous for their licentious lives and riotous behaviour. Many of their poems about wine and women appear in the *Carmina Burana*, a manuscript collection first published in the late 19th century. The goliards also specialized in religious satire, leading the Church to forbid clerics to act in 1281. The name comes from the mythical Bishop Golias, to whom the goliards pledged allegiance: it may derive ultimately from an Old French word for a glutton. The term eventually became more or less synonymous with MINSTREL and JONGLEUR.

Gombeyatta A genre of shadow puppet theatre performed in the Indian state of Karnataka. As many as 300 families are involved in producing these shadow plays which are mainly based on stories in the Ramayana and the MAHABHARATA. A *Gombeyatta* troupe usually consists of the main puppeteer, his wife who plays the harmonium and sings, other male family members who help in manipulating the puppets, and a *tabla* (drum) player. The companies, who perform on religious holidays, are generally associated with a particular Hindu temple.

The chief puppeteer often has over 100 figures under his control and may use as many as 50 in one performance. Several puppets can be used to represent the different moods of a single character. The social rank of the puppets is usually indicated by their size, with the largest being about 30 to 40 inches tall. Categories of puppet include gods, demons, humans, clowns, animals, and natural objects such as trees.

The BOMMALATTAM puppet theatre of southern India is also sometimes called *Gombeyatta*.

Gondoliers, The The happiest of GILBERT AND SULLIVAN's Savoy Operas. Subtitled *The King of Barataria*, the work was first performed in 1889 at the Savoy Theatre, London. The two men worked together amicably enough on the piece but fell out irretrievably shortly afterwards, a fact that probably explains the failure of their subsequent works.

Set in Venice, the story involves Marco and Giuseppe, two gondoliers whose weddings take place while the Duke of Plaza-Toro is visiting the city with his daughter. The Duke's daughter, Casilda, had 20 years earlier been married by proxy to the infant Prince of Barataria, who was abducted shortly afterwards. The circumstances suggest that one of the two gondoliers is in fact the prince, although it is not clear which. When informed, Marco and Giuseppe leave their new wives to share the throne of Barataria. Casilda intends to marry the true king as soon as he is identified by an old nurse. The nurse, however, reveals that she had switched her own child for the prince before the kidnapping. The true king is therefore Luiz, Casilda's attendant. The royal couple are united, and the gondoliers return delighted to their wives.

The Gondoliers was written four years after the publication of the second part of Marx's *Das Kapital* (1885), allowing Gilbert to lampoon the idea of communism in several verses:

> The Aristocrat who banks with Coutts,
> The Aristocrat who hunts and shoots,
> The Aristocrat who cleans our boots –
> They all shall equal be!

Goneril One of KING LEAR's three daughters. Having received her portion of Lear's Kingdom, the unnatural daughter first curtailed the old man's retinue, then gave him to understand that his company was troublesome. In Holinshed she appears as *Gonerilla*. *Compare* CORDELIA; REGAN.

Good Person of Setzuan, The A play by Bertolt BRECHT, written between 1938 and 1940 and first performed in Zürich in 1942. It is a complex parable about the role of individual goodness in a greedy and heartless world. Kenneth Tynan's review noted, "A fallacy has been exposed: that of seeking to be perfect in an imperfect society."

The play was first produced in 1956, as part of the English Stage Company's first season at the Royal Court Theatre. Peggy Ashcroft, who took the leading role of a prostitute who impersonates her male cousin, found the play "an adventure", having to sing and act half the time in a mask. Other members of the cast included Joan Plowright and John Osborne. Brecht's widow, the actress Helene Weigel, visited London during the rehearsals and returned in 1965 with the BERLINER ENSEMBLE to perform a German-language version of the play.

The play begins with three gods seeking shelter in the province of Setzuan, China. The only person willing to take them in is Shen Te, a warmhearted prostitute, to whom the gods gratefully give enough money to start a tobacco factory. Despite her benevolent intentions, Shen Te finds that she can only protect her interests by occasionally adopting the persona of a rough male cousin, Shui Ta. At one point the 'cousin' sings, "You can only help one of your luckless brothers by trampling down dozens of others." She later falls in love with a young aviator, until he admits to her 'cousin' that he only wants Shen Te's money. The aviator becomes foreman of the factory and, when Shen Te mysteriously disappears, he has Shui Ta arrested and accused of murdering her. Shen Te is forced to reveal her deception. The three gods listen sympathetically to her problem but are unable to offer any practical solution.

Gorboduc The earliest English tragedy, written by Thomas Norton (1532–84) and Thomas Sackville, later first Earl of Dorset (1536–1608). It was first performed on Twelfth Night in 1561. The play, which has the alternative title *The Tragedy of Ferrex and Porrex*, warns of the dangers to a nation of an unclear succession. It was seen by the childless Elizabeth I, although what she thought of it is not recorded. The play is also notable for the number of bloody deaths that occur during its performance – possibly a reflection of Sackville's duties as a commissioner at state trials (in which capacity he pronounced the death sentence on Mary, Queen of Scots).

The title character provided the basis for the figure of Gorbogud in Spenser's *The Fairie Queene*. Shakespeare also mentions King Gorboduc in *Twelfth Night*.

Gorki, Maxim (Alexei Maximovich Pyeshkov; 1868–1936) Russian playwright, novelist, short-story writer, and poet, who championed the cause of the socially outcast. Gorki, whose pen name means 'bitter', was one of the few Russian dramatists to find success in both the Tsarist and Soviet eras.

Gorki's first play *Scenes in the House of Bersemenov* was staged at the MOSCOW ART THEATRE in 1902 at the behest of Chekhov. Later that year STANISLAVSKY directed the same company in THE LOWER DEPTHS, Gorki's most influential work. It is a masterpiece of NATURALISM set amongst derelicts in a Moscow flop house. *The Lower Depths* opened in 1903 in London and in Berlin, where Max Reinhardt's production ran for over 500 performances. That same year, Chekhov wrote:

> Gorki is the first in Russia and in the world at large to have expressed contempt and loathing for the petty bourgeoisie and he has done it at the precise moment when society is ready for protest.

Between 1902 and 1915 Gorki wrote 14 plays, including *Summerfolk* (1904), *Children of the Sun* (1905), *Enemies* (1906), which was not produced in Russia until 1933, and *The Zykovs* (1913), which enjoyed a successful revival at the Aldwych Theatre in 1976, starring Mia Farrow and David Jones.

Gorki was known as 'the stormy petrel' of the Russian Revolution because of his political activism, which brought about his arrest in 1905. For several years he lived in exile in America, and some of his strongest works were not produced in his homeland until after 1917. During the 1920s Gorki lived abroad, returning to Russia in 1931 to begin work on a trilogy about the fall of the Russian bourgeoisie. Two parts of this trilogy were staged, *Yegor Bulychov and Others* (1932) and *Dostigayev and Others* (1933), but only part of *Somov and Others* was completed. He died in mysterious circumstances, leading some to believe he was eliminated by the state. The Grand Gorki Theatre in St Petersburg, which opened in 1919, is named in his honour. Gorki's birthplace, Nizhny-Novgorod, was also renamed after him in 1932 but reverted to its original name in 1991.

Gospel of Nicodemus, the An apocryphal book of uncertain origin, probably dating from between the 2nd and 5th centuries. The book, which provides elaborate descriptions of the trial, death, and resurrection of Jesus, was much used by writers of MYSTERY PLAYS and other medieval dramas. It names the two thieves and Pilate's wife and provides details of Christ's descent into hell. The book is also known as *The Acts of Pilate*.

Götz von Berlichingen The first play by Johann Wolfgang von GOETHE, historically important as the first German drama to be influenced by Shakespeare. Goethe wrote the play shortly after seeing several Shakespeare plays performed in Strasbourg in 1770. It was first produced in 1773 in Berlin by Friedrich SCHRÖDER's company.

The play gives a melodramatic picture of the life of the medieval robber baron Gottfriedens von Berlichingen (1480–1562), who is idealized by Goethe as a just man in rebellion against tyranny. It did much to inspire the developing STURM UND DRANG movement, and to end the era of French classical domination of the German stage. The play was widely imitated by other German playwrights, including Friedrich von SCHILLER, who followed nine years later with his equally intense and bloody DIE RÄUBER (*The Robbers*).

The historical Götz was known as *Iron hand* or *the iron-handed* after losing his right hand at the siege of Landshut (1505) and having one made of steel to replace it. Goethe's play was translated and adapted by John ARDEN as *Iron Hand* (1965).

Goulue, La The stage name of Louise Weber (1860–1919), a famous cancan dancer at the MOULIN ROUGE from 1889 to 1895; she appears in several paintings of the venue by Toulouse-Lautrec. A former washerwoman, the highly paid star became infamous in theatrical circles for her frightening temper and lesbian affairs. Following her years at the Moulin Rouge, she worked variously as a belly-dancer and lion-tamer, before finally succumbing to alcoholism.

Government Inspector, The (*Rivizor*) A satirical comedy by Nikolai GOGOL, written in 1835 and first performed the following year at the Alexandrinsky Theatre in St Petersburg. Although the play was banned by the censors Tsar Nicholas I overruled them, having enjoyed its ridicule of government bureaucracy. "Everyone has caught it," the tsar said of Gogol's satire, "but I have caught it more than anyone."

Attacks on the play prompted Gogol to write a defence of his work in which he stated: "Some of us who are ready to have a good laugh at a man's crooked nose, have not the courage to laugh at a man's crooked soul." In response to criticism that the play lacked a single honest character, Gogol claimed that there was one: "laughter". Nevertheless, continuing criticism led him to leave Russia in 1836.

The plot involves a petty clerk, Ivan Khlestakov, who is mistaken for a government inspector by the corrupt officials of a small provincial town. They smarten up the town and load him with bribes and gifts. By the time the mistake is discovered, Khlestakov has gone and the humiliated officials are left to face the real inspector.

The comedy was later interpreted by Soviet officials as criticism of the Tsarist regime, rather than as an attack on Russia's perennially inefficient and corrupt bureaucracy. *The Government Inspector* had its London premiere in 1920 and opened on Broadway three years later as *The Inspector-General*.

Gracioso A popular character in Spanish drama of the Golden Age. A comic servant who was used as a vehicle for satire and intrigue, Gracioso corresponded loosely to the fool of the Elizabethan stage. The character derived from Bobo, the clown of Lope de Rueda's PASOS, or short farcical interludes. In Lope de Vega's works the sharp-witted Gracioso was used to burlesque or parody the activities of his master. In Moreto's comedies, the character was employed to create complicated intrigues and to maintain the confusion.

grande *See* ZARZUELA.

grand master control A device added to a DIMMER board that allows simultaneous changes of lighting, either throughout a set or in one part of it. In recent years, this operation has been greatly enhanced by the introduction of more sophisticated computerized lighting systems, such as the Strand Lighting Console and the Strand System CD.

Granville-Barker, Harley (1877–1946) British actor, director, playwright, and critic, who exerted a major influence on British theatre in the early 20th century. He began his career as an actor, touring the provinces with various companies and appearing with William Poel and Mrs Patrick Campbell amongst others. In 1900 he appeared as Marchbanks in the London premier of CANDIDA, thus beginning a life-long association with the works of George Bernard SHAW. In the same year he directed the first major production of one of his own plays, *The Marrying of Ann Leete*. In 1904, together with J. E. Vedrenne, he took over the ROYAL COURT THEATRE, where they staged a successful season of Shaw's plays together with works by Ibsen and Yeats. The Royal Court seasons of 1904–07 were largely responsible for establishing Shaw as a major force in the British theatre. Granville-Barker's own plays, which include THE VOYSEY INHERITANCE (1905), WASTE (1907), and THE MADRAS HOUSE (1910), are written in a social-realist style much influenced by the early Shaw.

By 1907 he had largely abandoned acting to concentrate on directing. He was particularly admired for his productions of Shakespeare, which were more than usually faithful to the original texts. After marrying a wealthy divorcée in 1918, Granville-Barker retired from the stage and devoted himself to writing and lecturing. In 1919 he helped to found the British Drama League, of which he was chairman for 13 years. His many works of criticism include his famous *Prefaces to Shakespeare* (1927–46).

Graziano *See* DOTTORE, IL.

Grease Broadway's longest running musical, which opened in New York in 1972 and logged 3388 performances. The show became an international success, being known as *Glease* in Tokyo, *Vaselino* in Mexico, and *Brilliantine* in Paris. The songs, by Jim Jacobs and Warren Casey, include 'Summer Nights', 'Look at Me, I'm Sandra Dee', and 'Beauty School Dropout'.

The show takes a look at the rock 'n' roll youth scene of the 1950s. A reunion for Rydell High School's Class of '59 prompts much reminiscing. Most prominent are memories of romances between the Burger Palace Boys and the Pink Ladies, especially that between Danny Zuko and Sandy, the naive teenager who turns into a sex bomb. The finale takes place at the high school hop. The 1978 film version starred John Travolta and Olivia Newton-John. There was a successful West End revival in the mid 1990s.

great. **Great Dionysia** *See* DIONYSIA.

Great Magician, the (Il Gran Stregone) Nickname of the Italian architect and stage designer Giacomo Torelli (1608–78), bestowed because of the magical effects of his numerous inventions for the stage. Torelli apparently installed the first ever set of WINGS at the Teatro Farnese, while still a pupil of the theatre's architect, Giambattista Aleotti. From 1641 to 1645 he supervised the building of the Teatro Novissimo in Venice, where he invented the CARRIAGE-AND-FRAME SYSTEM.

In 1645 Torelli moved to the Salle du Petit-Bourbon in Paris to oversee the production of opera. While there he created various backstage mechanisms that helped to launch the genre of the MACHINE PLAY. When the Salle du Petit-Bourbon was demolished in 1660, most of Torelli's stage machinery was taken away and burned by a jealous rival, the court scene painter, Vigarani.

Great Piazza Coffee House A former coffee house, located at the northeast corner of the Covent Garden piazza, that opened in 1756. It was from here that the playwright Richard SHERIDAN (1751–1861) watched a fire destroy the DRURY LANE Theatre, of which he was manager. He remarked at the time: "A man may surely be allowed to take a glass of wine at his own fireside." The disaster ended his theatrical career. The building became a hotel in 1840 and was pulled down in 1865. *See also* FIRES.

Great Profile, the The nickname of the actor John Barrymore (1882–1942). *See* BARRYMORES, THE.

Great Schröder, the The nickname of Friedrich Ludwig SCHRÖDER (1744–1816), one of Germany's greatest actor-managers.

Great Vance The nickname of Alfred Vance (Alfred Peck Stevens; 1839–88), a British music-hall performer known for such comic Cockney songs as 'The Chickaleery Cove'. He adopted the role of a LION COMIQUE, developing a friendly rivalry with the first performer to earn that title, George Leybourne (*see* CHAMPAGNE CHARLIE). They both worked their way through comic songs listing the wines, with 'Cliquot' being the Great Vance's most popular offering.

After making his debut at the St James's Theatre, London, Vance appeared on the halls with his brother in a blackfaced act. He transformed himself into the first 'coster comedian' in 1864 becoming noted for moralistic 'motto' songs such as 'Act on the Square, Boys'. Vance died while performing at the Sun Music Hall, Knightsbridge.

Great White Way, the A once popular nickname for BROADWAY, the street running through the theatrical district of New York City. The name originated in the late 19th century because of the brilliant lighting used outside the theatres.

Greatest Show on Earth, the The name given to P. T. BARNUM's gigantic travelling show. A combination of CIRCUS, menagerie, and freak show, it was exhibited in America in 1871, making a fortune for Barnum and his partner (James Bailey). The show was presented at the London Olympia in 1889.

Greco-Roman drama The theatre of the Greco-Roman world between the close of the golden age of ATHENIAN DRAMA in about

300 BC and the later ROMAN DRAMA of the 1st century AD.

Many aspects of ancient Greek culture were adopted by the Romans, who had enormous respect for Greek intellectual and literary achievements. Greek colonists had lived in southern Italy and Sicily (where Greek theatres still stand today) since at least the 6th century BC and it was through these channels that the expanding Roman empire first came into contact with the Greek dramatic traditions. By the time of the Roman conquest of Greece in the 2nd century BC NEW COMEDY and romances had become popular, writers such as AESCHYLUS, EURIPIDES, SOPHOCLES, Plato, and Aristotle were revered historical figures, and Athens was established as an educational and cultural centre visited by Roman tourists.

The Romans adopted Greek mythology and were happy to retell Greek stories in both literature and drama. As the earliest Roman theatre consisted of little more than festival pageants and bawdy village rituals, the Romans copied Greek dramatic form, theatre design, costumes, and masks, and even used Greek actors. The first scripted Roman plays were translations from Greek by Livius Andronicus (*c.* 284–04 BC). Even SENECA, who lived in the 1st century AD reworked Greek tragedies. Roman comedy derived largely from the plays of MENANDER, with playwrights such as PLAUTUS and TERENCE managing to get laughs out of their admissions that they borrowed so much. Despite its great debt to the Greek theatre, however, Roman drama reflects the tastes, attitudes, and preoccupations of its own society.

Greek. Greek drama The theatre of ancient Greece, the fountainhead of the entire Western dramatic tradition. The earliest Greek drama is thought to have developed during the 6th century BC from imitative religious magic associated with the worship of DIONYSUS. The golden age of ATHENIAN DRAMA (the 5th and 4th centuries BC) saw the emergence of the genres of TRAGEDY and COMEDY and the production of the great works of AESCHYLUS (*c.* 525–456 BC), SOPHOCLES (*c.* 496–406 BC), and EURIPIDES (*c.* 484–406 BC). ARISTOPHANES (*c.* 448–385 BC) was the greatest comic playwright. The most important development of the later 4th century was the emergence of the NEW COMEDY of MENANDER. Although the Athenian tradition was in serious decline by about 300 BC, its influence had already spread to other parts of the Mediterranean world (*see* GRECO-ROMAN DRAMA).

The first Greek plays were performed in a circular dancing area known as an ORCHESTRA. Later a raised stage was added behind this area while a tent (SKENE) behind the stage functioned as both a stage set and a dressing room. Scenery became more elaborate and such devices as the EKKYKLEMA and the *mechane* for the DEUS EX MACHINA were added during the 5th century.

The influence of Greek theatre persists in the manifold translations, adaptations, and updatings that have appeared since the Renaissance. It also appears in numerous major and minor conventions of the Western stage; the issuing of a ticket (metal token) for each seat, and the habit of applauding to denote approval, and whistling to express disapproval were all originally Greek customs.

The Greeks Had a Word For it The title of a play by the US poet and playwright Zoë Akins, first produced in 1929. The phrase was originally included in the dialogue but was retained only as the title of the final version. The word alluded to is ετερο (*hetero*, other, different), describing certain characters in the play with rather outlandish personalities; it is not a reference to their sexual proclivities. The phrase became popular in the 1930s, when it was used of anything unusual or unconventional.

when Greek meets Greek, then is the tug of war When two men or armies of undoubted courage fight, the contest will be very severe. The line is slightly altered from Nathaniel Lee's play *The Rival Queens* (IV, ii), the reference being to the obstinate resistance of the Greek cities to Philip and Alexander, the Macedonian kings.

green. green baize *See* TRAGIC CARPET.

greencoat In the early Restoration theatre, a stagehand who changed furniture, scenery, and props between scenes. This was carried out in full view of the audience. The name comes from the stagehand's green livery.

green-eyed monster Shakespeare's description of jealousy in OTHELLO:

> O! beware my lord, of jealousy;
> It is the green-ey'd monster which doth mock
> The meat it feeds on.
> *Othello* (III, iii).

The phrase was probably based upon an analogy between jealousy and jaundice – a disease that causes a yellowy-greenish tinge in the whites of the eyes. Just as sufferers from jaundice were supposed (erroneously) to see everything tinged yellow or green, so those afflicted with irrational jealousy are presumed to find evidence of their suspicions in everything they look upon.

The Dublin actor Thomas Layfield (*fl.* 1750) once brought a performance of *Othello* to a sudden halt by declaiming:

O! beware my lord, of jealousy;
It is a green-eyed lobster.

This was the first sign of the madness that led to his spending his last years in a Dublin asylum.

green man In early English folk drama and rituals, a character dressed in green and adorned with leaves who represented spring and fertility. The character of Robin Hood in the English MAY DAY plays may have derived partly from the green man, also known as the woodman or JACK-IN-THE-GREEN. The green man was a feature of many MORRIS DANCES and even appeared in the Lord Mayor's show in London.

Green Pastures, The Mark Connelly's Black folk drama, first produced (with a Black cast) in New York in 1930. The work, which won a Pulitzer Prize, had the distinction of being the first US play to put God on stage, an innovation that earned it an automatic ban from the LORD CHAMBERLAIN in Britain. The role of God was played by a 62-year-old theatrical novice, Ricard B. Harrison, who found that his onstage persona followed him out of the theatre, often being called upon to use his healing powers and baptize the children of his admirers.

Connelly's fable, which he also directed, was set in a Black Louisiana church in which the preacher retells Bible stories in the simple language of his congregation. God becomes a tall cigar-smoking Black man who encourages his people to live it up, instructing Noah to take a barrel of liquor onto his ark and telling Moses to lead his people to "de choice piece of property".

green room A backstage room in a London theatre set aside for use by the cast and stage crew. The term was introduced in the late 17th century. Large theatres had several such rooms for relaxation, conversation, and the reception of visitors before and after a performance. Such areas were traditionally painted green, though it is also possible that the phrase was a corruption of the name 'scene' (scenery) room. The Drury Lane theatre and several other theatres still have a green room.

The **Green Room Club** was a social club founded in 1886 in Adam Street by members of the Junior GARRICK CLUB. Its members have mostly been actors and actresses.

green umbrella A US theatrical term for a prop, mannerism, or other detail that gives an actor a sudden insight into the characterization of a particular role. The phrase originated with the US actor Alfred LUNT, who was having difficulty interpreting the role of Professor Higgins in Shaw's *Pygmalion* (1927). According to his wife, Lynn Fontanne, her husband suddenly sat up in bed one night, exclaiming "I'll carry a green umbrella!" In Noël Coward's version of the story, the umbrella was Fontanne's suggestion.

Whatever the origin of the phrase, Lunt continued to use it. In 1937 during rehearsals for Giraudoux's *Amphitryon 38* at the Shubert Theatre on Broadway, Lunt called the cast together to announce that the play was off because "I can't find the green umbrella." Fontanne, who was sitting near the footlights, reassured the mystified cast, "Don't worry, we'll go on, and he will find it." Half an hour later, Lunt returned to announce delightedly that the umbrella had been found and the show would go on.

Gregory, Lady (Isabella) Augusta (1852–1932) Irish playwright, who with W. B. YEATS cofounded Dublin's ABBEY THEATRE. The first plays presented at the Abbey (on 27 December 1904) were her own one-act comedy *Spreading the News* and Yeats's *On Baile's Strand*. A daughter of the Anglo-Irish ascendancy who had been converted to nationalism and the Irish movement in the arts, she wrote her first play at the age of 51. Her best works were dialect comedies about Irish peasant life, including *Hyacinth Halvey* (1906) and *The Gaol Gate* (1906), although her tragedy *Dervorgilla* (1907) was also much acclaimed. As a manager of the Abbey, she championed the works of J. M. Synge, George Bernard Shaw, and Sean O'Casey. The success of the venture owed much to her formidable capacity for getting things done or persuading others to do them. In the cause of the Abbey she fought censors, braved rioting mobs, and, in the 1920s, obtained the first state subsidy for a theatre in the English-speaking world.

Lady Gregory also translated Molière's plays into Irish dialect as well as contributing to several works by Yeats, including *The Pot of Broth* (1902) and the fervently patriotic CATHLEEN NI HOULIHAN (1902).

> If the audience was poor, she would go out by the stage door when the curtain was up and come round to the front hall to enter the auditorium in the dark and pass as a new arrival, thus encouraging a thin attendance. She knew every aspect of her theatre...down to the bit of worn carpet leading to the stalls, the bit that must be cut out and have another sewn in because there wasn't enough money to buy a new carpet. The Abbey was the centre of her life, and because of her, and her partnership with Yeats, it survived.
>
> ULICK O'CONNOR: *Celtic Dawn.*

Grenfell, Joyce (Irene) (1910–79) British diseuse, whose one-woman show consisted of songs and sketches gently satirizing contemporary social mores. She made her debut in *The Little Revue* (1939) with a selection of monologues and mimicry. After World War II, during which she toured hospitals, she appeared in a series of West End revues by Noël Coward – *Sigh No More* (1945), *Tuppence Coloured* (1947), and *Penny Plain* (1951). In 1945 she made her first appearance in New York in *Joyce Grenfell Requests the Pleasure* and subsequently toured worldwide. Her books include *Nanny Says* (1972), *Joyce Grenfell Requests the Pleasure* (1976), and *George, Don't Do That* (1977).

grid Short for **gridiron**, the framework of pipes or BATTENS over the stage from which lighting equipment and scenery is hung. The acting area is also divided into a grid for the purpose of working out the positioning of the lights.

Griffiths, Trevor (1935–) British playwright, whose works express his commitment to socialism. Several of Griffiths's early one-act plays were presented by the 7:84 Company, while his first full-length work, *Occupations*, was produced by the Royal Shakespeare company in 1970. Among his better-known works are *The Party* (1973), a dramatized political debate first seen at the National Theatre with Laurence Olivier in the lead, and COMEDIANS (1975), which explores the nature of humour. He collaborated with Howard Brenton, David Hare, and Ken Campbell on *Deeds* (1978). His first wholly original work for the theatre for 17 years, *The Gulf Between Us* (1992) was a dream-like fantasy inspired by the Gulf War.

Griffiths's numerous works for television and the cinema include a dramatization of D. H. Lawrence's *Sons and Lovers* and episodes of *Dr Findlay's Casebook*.

Grillparzer, Franz (1791–1872) Austria's greatest 19th-century dramatist and a major figure in the European Romantic movement. Grillparzer began to study law at the University of Vienna but financial problems forced him to become a tutor and then a government clerk. The pessimistic outlook of his 12 tragedies reflected the unhappy events of his own life, in particular the early death of his father, his mother's suicide, and his own romantic failures.

His first play, *Die Ahnfrau*, was produced in 1817 at the Theater an der Wien by the director Josef Schreyvogle (1768–1832), who discovered and nurtured Grillparzer's talents. This was followed by *Sappho* (1818), a tragedy about the difficulty of reconciling art and life, and two years later by *The Golden Fleece*, a pessimistic reworking of the Greek legend in which Medea proclaims that life is not worth living.

Grillparzer's masterpiece, the historical play *König Ottokars Glück und Ende*, was written in 1823 but banned by the Metternich regime for two years because its leading character resembled Napoleon. The play received its premiere at the Burgtheater and became famous after transferring to the Theater an der Wien.

Grillparzer's other plays include *Des Meeres und der Liebe Wellen* (1831), which retells the story of Hero and Leander with a psychological insight that anticipates the work of Ibsen, and his adaptation (1834) of Calderóns *Life is a Dream*.

Grillparzer's only comedy, *Weh' dem, der lügt!* proved a failure when produced at the Burgtheater in 1838. Following this experience, he withdrew from the theatre and wrote only for his own amusement. After his death, three completed plays were found and produced, including the philosophical *Libussa* (1874), one of his finest works.

Grimaldi, Joseph (1778–1837), Britain's most famous clown. He played an important role in the development of English PANTOMIME from the HARLEQUINADE by emphasizing verbal comedy and introducing the now traditional story lines derived from nursery rhymes and fairy tales. His first success as a writer was *Harlequin and Mother Goose or The Golden Egg*, performed in 1806 at COVENT GARDEN, a venue he was to dominate for the next 17 years. Grimaldi also created the traditional clown-look of a white face with red cheeks, a bald wig with tufts of hair, and loose breeches. Clowns are often named Joey in his honour.

The illegitimate son of a Drury Lane ballet master, Grimaldi became a child actor at Sadler's Wells before moving into pantomime at Drury Lane. His famous routines included opening an oyster, riding a giant carthorse, grasping a red-hot poker, devouring a pudding, picking a pocket, and sneezing.

One contemporary wrote that "neither the wise, the proud, the fair, the young, nor the old were ashamed to laugh till tears coursed down their cheeks at Joe and his comicalities." He became a gifted mime artist, acrobat, dancer, and singer, and even tried serious acting, appearing in *Hamlet* in 1800 and 1805. Grimaldi damaged his health through overwork and retired at the peak of his career at Christmas 1823. Following a further decline in his health and the death of his son from alcoholism in 1832 he described his life as "grim all day".

Grock The stage name of Charles Adrien Wettach (1880–1959), a Swiss-born clown who became a star of the British music halls. Grock's mostly mute act was built around a series of calculated disasters and his ability to play over a dozen musical instruments.

The son of a watchmaker, Grock was performing acrobatics on the stage at the age of 12. After arriving in Britain he teamed up with another clown named Brick, but performed alone from 1911. Grock was one of the few clowns to be successful both on the music-hall stage and in the circus. He returned to the Continent in 1924.

When Kaiser Wilhelm I was introduced to Grock, he complimented him by saying, "I think you are even more famous than I am." The clown nodded appreciatively and replied, "Why not? I'm funnier."

grooves system A method of changing WINGS or FLATS that made use of wooden channels along which the pieces could slide. The system was introduced by Inigo Jones in his court masques and remained in use in the British theatre until the mid-19th century. The grooves system had the disadvantage of being noisy, however, and occasionally a flat would stick in the channel. The end of the system was hastened by the installation of the Continental CARRIAGE-AND-FRAME SYSTEM at Covent Garden. Irving removed the last remaining grooves in London from the Lyceum Theatre in 1880.

Grotowski, Jerzy (1933–) Polish director, whose avant-garde ideas have had a wide influence on European drama. As director of the 13 Rows Theatre in Opole (1959–64) he gained a reputation for his experimental work, which often involved audience participation. In 1965 he established the Institute for Research on Actor's Method Laboratory Theatre in Wrocław, which toured Europe and America with both established works such as Wyspiański's *Akropolis* and Calderón's *El Príncipe Constante*, as well as experimental works such as *Apocalypsis cum figuris*.

In the late 1960s Grotowski became celebrated for his concept of POOR THEATRE, which involved using the most basic setting and lighting in an attempt to break down barriers between performers and audience. He won the admiration of many contemporary directors, notably Peter Brook, who wrote the preface to Grotowski's book *Towards a Poor Theatre* (1968).

In 1976 Grotowski disbanded the Laboratory Theatre and embarked on a new programme of practical research, in which he explored the techniques of the theatre with actors and students but no audience.

ground. ground and lofty tumbling An 18th-century phrase for an acrobatic performance that took place both on the ground and on a tightrope.

groundrow A long irregularly shaped FLAT that stands on the stage floor, usually to mask the lights illuminating the lower part of a CYCLORAMA or CLOTH. It is normally painted to show such ground features as rocks or a horizon with hills or mountains. A groundrow depicting waves is called a **sea row** or **water row**. The term is also used for the row of lights masked by a scenic groundrow.

Group Theatre. Group Theatre, London A private society founded in 1933 to produce experimental and noncommercial plays at the Westminster Theatre. Rupert Doone (1904–66) directed the productions, which in 1935 included a double bill of T. S. Eliot's *Sweeney Agonistes* and W. H. Auden's *The Dance of Death*. Stephen Spender's *Trial of a Judge* was presented in 1938. Benjamin Britten wrote incidental music for some works. The Group Theatre closed during World War II but was revived for a while in the early 1950s, when performances included Sartre's *The Flies*.

Group Theatre, New York A theatre company founded in 1931, originally as an offshoot of the THEATRE GUILD. The cofounders were Lee STRASBERG (1901–82), Harold Clurman (1901–80), and Cheryl Crawford (1902–86). They sought to present serious plays that would not otherwise be seen on Broadway, while remaining commercially viable. The company was committed to ensemble acting and social realism and helped to popularize the theories of STANISLAVSKY.

The Group Theatre's first independent production was in 1932 with Maxwell Anderson's *Night Over Taos*; the following year it enjoyed its greatest hit with Sidney Kingsley's *Men in White*, which ran for 351 performances. The playwright Clifford ODETS began his career with the company, who mounted the first productions of his *Awake and Sing!* (1935), *Waiting for Lefty* (1935), and *Golden Boy* (1937). Other writers whose works were performed by the Group Theatre included William Saroyan, Irwin Shaw, Paul Green, and Robert Ardrey. Actors in the company included John Garfield, Elia Kazan, J. Edward Bromberg, Stella Adler, and Luther Adler.

The Group Theatre disbanded in 1941, much of its talent having defected to the commercial theatre.

Grundy, Mrs A character in Thomas Morton's play SPEED THE PLOUGH (1800), whose name has become a byword for narrow-minded bigotry. Although Mrs Grundy never actually appears in the play, she is frequently referred to by other characters, who anxiously ask: "What will Mrs Grundy say? What will Mrs Grundy think?" So notorious did her name become that Herbert Spencer was prompted to remark in *On Manners and Fashion*: "The tyranny of Mrs Grundy is worse than any other tyranny we suffer under." Thackeray wrote: "Who scorns? Who persecutes? Who doesn't forgive? – the virtuous Mrs Grundy. She remembers her neighbour's pecadilloes to the third and fourth generation, and, if she finds a certain man fallen in her path, gathers up her affrighted garments with a shriek, for fear the muddy, bleeding wretch should contaminate her, and passes on." When a performance of *Speed the Plough* was unexpectedly well received in Nashville it transpired that a real-life Mrs Grundy with not dissimilar views – including a deep loathing of the theatre – lived nearby; her husband, Judge Felix Grundy, later became US attorney-general.

Guerin, Auguste *See* BOBÈCHE AND GALIMAFRÉ.

Guignol A character in a popular 18th-century French puppet-show that involved macabre and gruesome incidents. The name subsequently came to be attached to short plays of a similar nature. Grand Guignol was the name of a theatre in Montmartre, Paris, that specialized in presenting sensational fare of this kind; hence the use of the term ***Grand Guignol*** to describe any bloody or horrifying entertainment.

Guinness, Sir Alec (1914–) One of the English theatre's most versatile talents, who has also enjoyed a distinguished career in films. He was knighted in 1959.

At 18 he joined an advertising agency but found the work so boring that he telephoned John Gielgud, then unknown to him, to ask his advice on becoming an actor. After taking voice lessons, Guinness won a scholarship to the Fay Compton Studio of Dramatic Art.

His first professional appearance was as a junior counsel in *Libel* (1934). Gielgud gave him several minor parts in his production of *Hamlet* (1935), despite having fired him during rehearsals. "You're terrible," Gielgud had told him one day. "I don't want to see you again." When Guinness asked him if he was sacked, the director spluttered "No! Yes! No, of course not. But go away. Come back in a week. Get someone to teach you how to act." Guinness was also unceremoniously dropped from the cast of the Old Vic's 1936 revival of Wycherley's *The Country Wife*, at the behest of the US actress Ruth Gordon. Despite these setbacks and a severe stage fright that afflicted him with crippling pain in his knees and back, Guinness showed considerable promise in several

Shakespearean roles and went on to take the lead in *Hamlet* (1938).

During the war Guinness was a lieutenant with the Royal Navy. While his ship was being repaired in New York, he would rush nightly to Broadway to play Flight-Lieutenant Graham in Rattigan's *Flare Path*. After the war, he returned to the Old Vic, becoming notable for his weary pale face and general air of frailty. Many of his greatest triumphs have been on the US stage. In 1950 he was voted Best Actor in the New York Drama Critics Poll for his appearance in T. S. Eliot's *The Cocktail Party* at the Henry Miller Theatre. He returned to New York in 1964 to play Dylan Thomas in *Dylan* at the Plymouth Theatre, earning three Best Actor awards, including a Tony.

In Britain, he created the role of T. E. Lawrence in Rattigan's *Ross* (1960), and made impressive work of playing the blind father in John Mortimer's *A Voyage Round My Father* (1971). He returned to the stage at the age of 70 to play Shylock in *The Merchant of Venice* (1984).

Guinness's many films include David Lean's *The Bridge on the River Kwai* (1957) and *Lawrence of Arabia* (1962); he also appeared in several Ealing comedies, including *Kind Hearts and Coronets* (1949), in which he played eight parts. His best-known television role was as the inscrutable spymaster George Smiley in *Tinker, Tailor, Soldier, Spy* (1979) and *Smiley's People* (1981–82).

> Olivier...ransacks the vaults of a part with a blowlamp, crowbar, and gunpowder; Guinness is the nocturnal burglar, the humble Houdini who knows the combination.
>
> KENNETH TYNAN: *Harper's Bazaar*, 1952.

Guthrie, Sir (William) Tyrone (1900–71) British actor, director, and producer, known for his innovative productions of Shakespeare and other classics at the OLD VIC. His hallmarks included the use of a THRUST STAGE and the creation of a swirling crowd movement within a scene. During his career Guthrie worked in several other countries, including Canada, America, Germany, and Israel. He received a knighthood in 1961.

Guthrie, known to all as Tony, once said that the director's duty was "to make each rehearsal so amusing that the actors will look forward to the next one". Laurence Olivier, however, described him as "shy of great human emotion". Directing Olivier and Jessica Tandy in *Henry V*, Guthrie told them "You two go and do the love scene by yourselves, will you. I can't be bothered with that".

The great-grandson of the American actor Tyrone Power (*see* POWER FAMILY), Guthrie made his debut in 1924 in a student production of *Henry IV* at Oxford. From 1929 to 1930 he worked as a director at the Festival Theatre, Cambridge, before directing his first London play, James Bridie's *The Anatomist*, which opened the Westminster Theatre in 1931. He became the Old Vic's youngest director in 1933 and was the administrator of both the Old Vic and Sadler's Wells Theatre during World War II. After the war he passed the management of the Old Vic to Olivier, Ralph Richardson, and John Burrell.

In 1944 Guthrie gave Olivier what the actor later called "the most priceless advice I've ever had from anybody". Olivier was complaining about his role of Sergius, a tediously conventional character in Shaw's *Arms and the Man*. Guthrie reproved him with the words "Well, of course, if you can't love Sergius, you'll never be any good in him, will you?"

Guthrie's celebrated Shakespearean productions at the Old Vic included *Measure for Measure* (1933) with Charles Laughton and *Hamlet* (1937) with Laurence Olivier. His production of Ibsen's *Peer Gynt* with Ralph Richardson and Sybil Thorndike opened the first season of the revived Old Vic at the New Theatre (now the Albery) in 1944.

In 1953 Guthrie helped to found the STRATFORD FESTIVAL in Stratford, Ontario, at which he directed works until 1957. In Stratford he indulged his love for the thrust stage by codesigning the Shakespeare Festival Theatre (with Tanya Moiseiwitsch). He also designed the Minneapolis Theatre, which opened in 1963, and worked as a director there until his death, when the venue was renamed the Guthrie Theatre in his honour.

Guv'nor, the A popular nickname for the British theatre manager George EDWARDES (1852–1915).

Guys and Dolls A musical by Jo Swerling and Abe Burrows with songs by Frank Loesser. The show opened on Broadway in 1950 and won the Tony award for Best Musical; three years later it enjoyed further success at the London Coliseum. Among its many revivals was a 1976 version with an all-Black cast and a famous London production by Richard Eyre (1982; revived 1996). In 1955 it was made into a film starring Frank Sinatra, Marlon Brando, and Jean Simmons.

The plot, based on stories by Damon Runyon, involves the attempts of Sister Sarah, a Salvation Army officer, to convert New York's gangsters to Christianity. Two apparent lost causes are Nathan Detroit and Sky Masterson. Nathan bets Sky he cannot lure Sarah away on a romantic trip to Havana. Sky accepts the challenge and offers Sarah "a dozen genuine sinners" if she agrees to come. Fearful that her mission may be forced to close, she accepts, not realizing that the 12 sinners are really seeking a place to hold a crap game. Goodness prevails, however, when the gang renounce their wicked ways at the mission, Sky joins the Salvation Army and marries Sarah, and Nathan weds his fiancée of 14 years.

Loesser's songs include 'Sit Down, You're Rocking the Boat', 'Luck be a Lady', and 'I've Never Been in Love Before'.

Gwynn, Nell (Eleanor Gwynn, Gwyn, or Gwynne; 1650–87) The beautiful English actress whose brief stage career ended when she became the mistress of Charles II and bore him two sons. The English public, starved by years of Puritanism, adored 'Pretty witty Nell' with her open indiscretions, high spirits, lovely heart-shaped face, and delicate but shapely figure.

Nell was also renowned for her profanity and bawdy humour. Samuel Pepys visited her dressing room after one ill-attended performance and recorded, "But to see how Nell cursed for having so few people in the pit, was pretty."

Her father died in a debtors' prison and her mother kept a brothel. Nell began her working life serving brandy to customers in Covent Garden and selling oranges in the King's Theatre. She subsequently became the mistress of the well-known actor Charles Hart, who trained her for the stage. After making her debut in 1664 as the courtesan Paulina in Thomas Killigrew's *Thomaso*, she became the leading comedienne of the King's Company, during which time she was mistress to Lord Buckhurst (later the 6th earl of Dorset). She also won praise as Cydaria in Dryden's *Secret Love* (1667) and Jacinta in his *An Evening's Love* (1668).

She became the king's mistress in 1669, and bore the first of his sons before giving her last performance as Almahide in Dryden's *Almanzor and Almahide*. The king gave her a house in Pall Mall, where Nell, still the illiterate street girl, mixed with court society, gave extravagant parties and lobbied successfully to have her son made duke of St Albans. She was in serious debt when Charles II died in 1685 but his deathbed wish to "Let not poor Nelly starve" was honoured by James II.

Hard by the Mall lives a wench call'd
  Nell,
King Charles the Second he kept her.
She hath got a trick to handle his pr---,
But never lays hands on his sceptre.
All matters of state from her soul does
  she haste,
And leave to the politic bitches.
The whore's in the right, for 'tis her
  delight
To be scratching just where it itches.

ANON.

gypsy Theatrical slang for a hard-working anonymous member of the CHORUS line in a big Broadway musical.

Gypsy Robe A white satin dressing gown that came to be considered a lucky charm on Broadway. The robe's original owner was Florence Baum, a 'gypsy' in *Gentlemen Prefer Blondes* (1949). During the show another dancer, Bill Bradley, sometimes wore it backstage for good luck; when the show was a great hit he lent it to a friend opening in *Call Me Madam* (1950). *Call Me Madam* was also a great success and a superstition was born.

The robe subsequently passed from company to company, always being presented to a member of the chorus who regarded it as a great honour. The recipient either wore it when the cast assembled or donned it for ritual visits to each dressing room before a performance. Eventually the robe became so covered with souvenirs (photos, a piece of costume, a programme, etc.), that it began to disintegrate. Although a wardrobe mistress for the revived CAN-CAN (1981) tried desperately to repair the robe, she failed and the show closed within a week. The robe was then presented to the drama collection at New York's Lincoln Center.

H

Habimah (Heb: stage) A Jewish theatre company, founded in 1917 in Moscow to produce plays in Hebrew (an earlier company with the same name was formed in 1909 in Bialystok, Poland). The second Habimah gained the support of Maxim Gorki and Konstantin Stanislavsky and became affiliated with the MOSCOW ART THEATRE. Its first director was Eugene Vakhtangov (1883–1922), a former pupil of Stanislavsky and director of the Moscow Art Theatre; Vakhtangov's most acclaimed Habimah production (in 1922, the year of his death) was *The Dybbuk* by Salomon Ansky.

In 1926 Habimah toured Europe and America with Jewish plays, such as Karl Gutzkow's *Uriel Acosta*, and mainstream classics, such as Shakespeare's *Twelfth Night*. The group went on to tour Palestine in 1928 and finally settled there in 1932. Habimah was named as Israel's official National Theatre in 1958 and reorganized in 1970, when it moved into a modern National Theatre building, which it opened with a Hebrew production of Thomas Dekker's comedy *The Shoemaker's Holiday*.

Hair The controversial rock musical by Gerome Ragni, James Rado, and Galt MacDermot that brought collective nudity to the stage during the hippie era. It was first performed in 1967, at the opening of Joseph PAPP's Anspacher Theatre, New York, where it ran for 1750 performances. A year later, just after the abolition of censorship in Britain, it began a record run of 1997 performances at the Shaftesbury Theatre, London. It was revived in 1993 at the Old Vic Theatre, but failed to attract large audiences.

The musical has little plot: a young man from Oklahoma becomes involved with the hippie culture of New York's East Village while on his way to enlist for the Vietnam War. One of the hippies is drafted and his friends lament the disaster. The anti-establishment stance of the show, blatantly pro-drug and anti-draft, was as controversial as the notorious nude scene.

The more memorable songs include 'The Age of Aquarius', 'Let the Sunshine In', and 'Good Morning Starshine'.

Hall, Sir Peter (1930–) British director and theatre manager.

Hall, who began directing as a student at Cambridge, made his name as an interpreter of Shakespeare with productions of *Love's Labour's Lost* (1956) and *Coriolanus* (1959) at Stratford-upon-Avon. In 1960 he established the ROYAL SHAKESPEARE COMPANY at the SHAKESPEARE MEMORIAL THEATRE, Stratford. He added modern plays to the repertoire and extended the season from six months to all year round by leasing the Aldwych Theatre in London. He also strengthened the company by introducing long-term contracts: his first contract players included Peggy Ashcroft, Peter O'Toole, and Dorothy Tutin.

Other changes made by Hall included the introduction of a simplified realism, influenced by Bertolt Brecht and emphasized by the sparse sets of John Bury (1925–). Among his most successful productions were THE WAR OF THE ROSES cycle (1963–64), Harold Pinter's *The Homecoming* (1965), and *Macbeth* (1967), a production subsequently taken to Moscow. In the same year, Hall resigned to become director of the Royal Covent Garden Opera Company.

In 1973 Hall replaced Laurence Olivier as head of the National Theatre (*see* ROYAL NATIONAL THEATRE). A noted early production was Samuel Beckett's HAPPY DAYS (1974). Beckett, who attended rehearsals, felt that the stage was not kept empty and open enough to show the characters' isolation. For his part, Hall thought the playwright "an absolute genius". The following year Hall directed the company's last play at the Old Vic, a production of *Hamlet* starring Albert Finney.

In 1976 the National Theatre finally moved into its new home on the South Bank. Hall was frequently criticized for the delay in relocation; his diary entry for a meeting with the royal family in 1975 noted:

> As we were presented, the Queen asked me when the National Theatre would open. I said I didn't know. The Queen Mother asked when the National Theatre would open. I said I didn't know. The Prince of Wales asked me when the National Theatre would open. I said I didn't know. At least they all knew I was running the National Theatre.

Hall's successes at the new venue included such varied works as Alan Ayckbourn's *Bedroom Farce* (1977), Peter Shaffer's *Amadeus* (1979), and Aeschylus's *The Oresteia* (1981). His diaries, published in 1983, give a fascinating picture of his often troubled tenure at the theatre. He resigned in 1988, following criticism of his outside activities, to create his own transatlantic company. This employed actors from Britain and America in productions that have transferred between London and New York, including *The Merchant of Venice* (with Dustin Hoffman) and Tennessee Williams's *A Streetcar Named Desire* (with Jessica Lange). In 1996–97 he directed a season of 12 plays at the Old Vic.

hall. **hall-keeper** A former name for a stage door-keeper (*see* STAGE DOOR).

halls A popular term for the British MUSIC-HALL theatres.

Hallam family A family of British and US actors and actresses. **Lewis Hallam** (1714–56), the son of the actor Adam Hallam, worked on the London stage before emigrating to America in 1752 with his family and a company of ten actors, who performed at Williamsburg, Virginia, in Shakespeare's *The Merchant Of Venice* and Jonson's *The Alchemist*. In 1753 Hallam created a company at the Nassau Street Theatre in New York. He died on a tour to Jamaica, and his widow married David Douglass, who founded the AMERICAN COMPANY.

Hallam's son and namesake, **Lewis Hallam** (1740–1808), became the leading actor with Douglass's American Company in 1758 in New York. He won acclaim in 1767 as Arsaces in the first professionally produced play, Thomas Godfrey's *The Prince of Parthia*. The American War of Independence drove the company to the West Indies; during this period its New York home, the John Street Theatre, was used for plays by British officers, including the notorious spy Major John André. After the war, Hallam co-managed the company at the John Street Theatre, which was visited several times by George Washington.

The elder Hallam's youngest daughter, **Isabella Hallam** (1746–1826), was left behind in London when the family emigrated to America. She was brought up by an actress aunt and first appeared on stage at the age of five, making her adult debut as Juliet in 1761. She married a provincial actor-manager, George Mattocks, and became known for light comedy, specializing in the role of chambermaid. Her last performance was in 1808 as Flora in Mrs Centlivre's *The Wonder, A Woman Keeps A Secret*.

ham actor An inferior actor, especially one who overacts (hence the phrase 'to ham it up'). There are a number of suggested origins: the use of ham fat to remove theatrical make-up in the 19th century; a certain Hamish McCullough (1835–1885), known as 'Ham', who toured with his company, known as 'Ham's actors', in Illinois; a popular US minstrel song, 'The Ham-fat Man', about an inept actor; an alteration of the word 'amateur'; and the claim of every down-at-heel actor to have performed the role of Hamlet in better days.

Shakespeare's *Hamlet* would be an appropriate source, since Hamlet in his speech to the players (III, ii) describes the essence of ham acting:

> Nor do not saw the air too much with your hand...it offends me to the soul to hear a robustious periwig-pated fellow tear a passion to tatters...

Hamburg style A realistic style of acting pioneered at the Hamburg National Theatre under Friedrich SCHRÖDER, who managed the company from 1786 to 1798. In the 19th century Hamburg style was considered the opposite of the formal WEIMAR STYLE of acting and the earlier LEIPZIG STYLE introduced by Johann Gottsched (1700–66).

Hamlet, Prince of Denmark SHAKESPEARE'S classic REVENGE TRAGEDY, probably the best-known play in the English language. It was written and first performed in 1600; according to tradition, Shakespeare himself played the ghost of Hamlet's father.

The plot was derived from a story told by the 13th-century Danish historian Saxo Grammaticus. Shakespeare's play centres on Hamlet's inability to avenge his father's death by killing Claudius, his father's brother and murderer, now married to Hamlet's mother Gertrude. He feigns madness and contemplates suicide, in the famous soliloquy beginning "To be, or not to be: that is the question"; his sweetheart Ophelia goes mad and drowns. The tragedy ends with the deaths of Gertrude, Ophelia's brother Laertes, Claudius (killed at last by Hamlet), and Hamlet himself.

The role of Hamlet is the longest (1530 lines) and most coveted in the Shakespearean canon. Max Beerbohm called it "a hoop through which every eminent actor must, sooner or later, jump". Those who have jumped include Henry Irving, Richard Burbage, Laurence Olivier, Richard Burton, and Albert Finney. Thomas Betterton took on the role in his seventies; Alec Guinness played it with a beard in 1951 to cries of outrage. Sarah BERNHARDT's performance as Hamlet in 1899 caused the *Punch* critic to remark that all the production needed for perfection was Irving as Ophelia. Edmund Tearle (1856–1913) was the fattest Hamlet, "a mastodon in tights", who always raised a laugh when he soliloquized, "O, that this too, too solid flesh would melt."

According to John GIELGUD, who has played the part more often than any other actor, "Hamlet is not a role that an actor should ever be asked to portray for a hundred performances on end." His 1934 London production, however, ran for 155 consecutive performances, beating all records since Irving.

A playbill issued in 1793 by the manager of the Theatre Royal, Kilkenny, announced "Hamlet by Mr Kearns who, between the acts, will perform several solos on the patent bag pipes ... Ophelia by Mrs Prior, who will introduce several favourite airs in character, particularly 'The Lass of Richmond Hill'."

G. I. Hamlet A simplified version of Shakespeare's famous play, as performed by the actor Maurice EVANS for US troops during World War II. "We are giving you," he informed the audience, "a *Hamlet* without the intellectual trimmings." The condensed drama, also known as the 'Jeep Version' made Hamlet a decisive man of action rather than the hesitant dreamer of tradition. The play proved so popular with the troops that Evans performed it in 1946 at the Columbus Circle Theater, New York, for 131 performances and then took it on tour.

It's (like) Hamlet without the Prince (of Denmark) A phrase used when the person who was to have played the principal role at some function is absent.

Hamlet was performed without the Prince of Denmark in 1787 at the Richmond Theatre, when an inexperienced actor named Cubit suffered an anxiety attack and refused to go on stage. Sir Walter Scott was present and said the audience thought the play much improved.

Hand. Handcuff King The nickname of Harry HOUDINI the US illusionist and escapologist.

hand-worked house A theatre that continued to raise and lower scenery by the old-fashioned method of manually adjusting the ropes after the advent of the COUNTERWEIGHT SYSTEM. Earlier terms for a theatre using the manual system were **rope house** and **hemp house**.

Handke, Peter (1942–) Austrian playwright and novelist, whose work dispenses with the usual dramatic conventions in order to highlight the problems of language and communication. Handke's first play, the provocative *Offending the Audience* (1966), did just that. In his subsequent works, Handke further examines the difficulties of communication; *Kaspar* (1968), for instance, revolves around a central character who is completely unable to speak, while *The Ride Across Lake Constance* (1971) seeks to show how people can become imprisoned by language; the work presents a group of characters whose only means of expression is through stale and sterotypical phrases. *They are Dying Out* (1974) which examines the effect upon a personality of pursuing a business career, is slightly more conventional in form and content. Handke has also written a dramatic monologue about his mother's suicide, *A Sorrow Beyond Dreams* (1977). His most recent work *The Hour In Which We Knew Nothing of Each Other* (1994) features some 300 characters (played by a cast of 35) and has no dialogue at all: the text consists of 60 pages of stage directions. It was described by one critic as "the most eloquent evening at the theatre available in Berlin today".

Hands, Terry (David) (1941–) British director, a cofounder of the Everyman

Theatre in Liverpool (1964), and sole artistic director of the ROYAL SHAKESPEARE COMPANY (RSC) from 1986 to 1991. Hands joined the RSC as a director for the touring Theatregoround Company in 1966. The following year he was appointed as an associate director of the RSC, being entrusted with the direction of several works at Stratford. Notable productions included Genet's *The Balcony* (1971), T. S. Eliot's *Murder in the Cathedral* (1972), and Arbuzov's *Old World* (1976). He is particularly noted for his productions of Shakespeare's history plays, having presented all of them by 1980.

From 1975 to 1977 Hands worked as a consultant director at the COMÉDIE-FRANÇAISE, where he produced several works. In 1978 he was appointed joint artistic director of the RSC with Trevor NUNN, becoming sole artistic director and chief executive in 1987, a position he relinquished in 1991.

Hanswurst A stock comic character in 18th-century Viennese theatre. Hanswurst's coarse mannerisms derived from the ZANNI of the COMMEDIA DELL'ARTE and from the clown Pickelhering, the fool Jan Bouschet, and other characters of the ENGLISH COMEDIANS.

A later version was originated by the actor-manager Joseph Stranitzky (1676–1726), who changed Hanswurst from a simple peasant to a sly knave. The character became even more sophisticated when played by Stranitzky's successor, the actor Gottfried Prehauser (1699–1769), and eventually appeared in all sorts of genres, disrupting the plot with improvisations.

Hanswurst was subsequently transformed by Joseph Kurz (1715–84) into the character of BERNADON.

happening A type of improvised artistic event that became popular in the 1960s. The events were spontaneous or made to appear so and usually involved a good deal of audience participation. They tended to be deliberately outrageous and confrontational in style.

The form was based on ideas introduced earlier in the century by the futurists, dadaists, and surrealists. A pioneer of happenings was the US painter and art historian Allan Kaprow (1927–), who presented a MIXED MEDIA '18 Happenings in 6 Parts' in an art gallery in 1959.

Happenings often took the form of unannounced street theatre, which spectators could mistake for a real event. The Brazilian playwright Augusto Boal specialized in this type of happening with his TEATRO INVISIBLE. Both the term and the concept are now dated.

See also ENVIRONMENTAL THEATRE.

Happy Days A tragicomedy by Samuel BECKETT, first performed in 1961 in New York. In the first act the main character, Winnie, is buried up to her waist in the sand of a desert but carries on an animated and happy monologue addressed to Willie, her taciturn husband.

Peter HALL directed Peggy Ashcroft in the role of Winnie in 1975 and again in 1976, in the opening production for the National Theatre's Lyttelton Theatre. While Hall was rehearsing the play, Beckett himself suddenly appeared on stage, concerned about a parasol that was supposed to burst into flames during the performance but which usually malfunctioned. Under pressure from the fire authorities and theatre managers, the playwright decided that the parasol should merely melt. He therefore cut out a page of text, which disturbed Ashcroft who, having learned the lines, was unhappy about losing them.

Hardwicke, Sir Cedric (Webster) (1893–1964) British actor and director, best known for his character roles. He was celebrated on both sides of the Atlantic as the quintessential Englishman and was knighted in 1934.

Hardwicke's theatrical ambitions began in childhood, when he learnt pages of Shakespeare by heart. His first appearance was in a minor role in *The Monk and the Woman* (1912) at the Lyceum Theatre. He scored two consecutive hits in the musical *Show Boat* (1928) at Drury Lane and the premiere of Shaw's *The Apple Cart* (1929) at the Malvern Festival. Shaw, who had written the part of King Magnus for him, called Hardwicke his fifth-favourite actor "after the Marx Brothers".

Hardwicke moved to New York in 1938, winning rave reviews as Canon Skerritt in *Shadow and Substance*. His success prompted a further move to Hollywood, where he made a string of films. In 1945 he directed Gertrude Lawrence in a New York revival of *Pygmalion*. After a brief spell with the Old Vic in London, he returned to America, spending most of the 1950s on Broadway.

where he gave a highly acclaimed performance in *Don Juan in Hell* (1951).

"I can't act," Hardwicke once claimed, "I have never acted. And I shall never act. What I do is to suspend my audience's power of judgment till I've finished." *See also* PICKWICK, ARISE SIR SAMUEL.

Hare, David (1947–) British playwright and director, noted for his critical examination of post-war British society. In 1968 he became a founder of the travelling FRINGE company, Portable Theatre, which performed some of his early plays. The following year he became resident playwright at the Royal Court Theatre, which gave the first performance of his play *Slag* (1970), about three teachers at a girls' school who decide to abstain from sex.

In 1973 Hare became resident playwright at the Nottingham Theatre, where he collaborated with the playwright Howard BRENTON on *Brassneck* (1973). The following year he became a cofounder of the Joint Stock Company, for which he adapted William Hinton's *Fanshen* (1975).

With the National Theatre's production of PLENTY (1978), the best known of his earlier plays, Hare began a long association with the company. In 1984 he was appointed an associate director of the National, which a year later produced Hare and Brenton's *Pravda*, a vigorous satire on the tabloid press. In 1986 Hare presented *King Lear* at the National, his debut as a Shakespearean director.

Hare's major work of the early 1990s was a much-praised trilogy of plays about British institutions; this began in 1990 with *Racing Demon*, about the Church of England, continued in 1991 with *Murmuring Judges*, about the judiciary, and concluded with *The Absence of War* (1993), about the decline of the Labour Party. In 1996 Hare's *Skylight* received the Olivier Award for best play of the year.

Harlequin A mischievous character in the English HARLEQUINADE and thereafter in PANTOMIME. He was usually supposed to be invisible to all eyes but those of his sweetheart COLUMBINE.

Harlequin wears a tight-fitting spangled or particoloured dress and is usually masked. He derives from ARLECCHINO, a stock character of the COMMEDIA DELL'ARTE, whose name probably originated as that of a sprite or hobgoblin (one of the demons in Dante's *Inferno* is called Alichino).

The prince of Harlequins was the actor John Rich (*see* RICH FAMILY).

harlequinade A forerunner of the English PANTOMIME. It evolved from John Weaver's ITALIAN NIGHT SCENES, which derived in turn from the COMMEDIA DELL'ARTE tradition.

The harlequinade began with a CURTAIN-RAISER, in which two lovers were transformed by a fairy into Harlequin and Columbine. In the main part of the entertainment they had to escape from Columbine's father, PANTALOON, and his servant PIERROT.

In 19th-century pantomime the curtain-raiser gradually became a full story featuring fairytale characters and the antics of Harlequin were reduced to a short AFTERPIECE. The harlequinade sequence was finally dropped during the early 1940s.

Harris, Sir Augustus *See* DRURIOLANUS, AUGUSTUS.

Harrison, Rex (1908–90) British actor. In the 1930s he pursued a successful career on the London stage, in such plays as Rattigan's *French Without Tears* and Eliot's *The Cocktail Party*; his prewar films included *The Citadel* (1938) and *Major Barbara* (1940). After wartime service in the RAF he returned to acting; the highlight of his careeer was the Broadway production of MY FAIR LADY (1956) and the subsequent (1964) film.

A debonair and charming man, who was six times married, Harrison was at his best in comedy; after seeing him in *Blithe Spirit* (1945), Noël COWARD is reputed to have said to him: "After me, you're the best light comedian in the world." According to some accounts he added: "If you weren't, all you'd be good for would be selling cars in Great Portland Street."

Hart, Moss (1904–61) US dramatist and director who collaborated on a number of successful plays with George S. KAUFMAN.

At the age of 15 Hart began working as an office boy for the Broadway producer Augustus Pitou, Jr, known as 'King of the One-Night Stands'. His first play, *The Beloved Bandit*, written in 1922 and produced by Pitou, had a disastrous opening night in Chicago. The curtain jammed, the set buckled, and a window came off in an actress's hands. At one point the Irish star Joseph Regan tripped and fell destroying the fireplace; on his next entrance he came through the hole where the fireplace had been, uttering the cryptic and unscripted line, "Every day's Christmas when the Irish come to town."

Hart survived this debut to become the entertainment director for the BORSCHT BELT in the Catskill Mountains. His first successful play, the satire *Once in a Lifetime*, was extensively rewritten by Kaufman before being produced in 1930. Together they wrote a series of light comedies, including *You Can't Take It With You* (1936), which won the Pulitzer Prize, and THE MAN WHO CAME TO DINNER (1939).

Among Hart's own works were *Winged Victory* (1943), *Christopher Blake* (1946), *Light Up the Sky* (1948), and *The Climate of Eden* (1952). He directed most of his plays and several hits by others, such as the famous Lerner and Lowe musicals MY FAIR LADY (1956) and CAMELOT (1960). In 1959 he published an excellent account of his early theatrical life, *Act One*.

Hassan A spectacular oriental melodrama by the poet James Elroy Flecker (1884–1915). It was first produced in 1923 by Basil Dean at His Majesty's Theatre, London (which had enjoyed a run of hit plays on oriental themes, including CHU CHIN CHOW in 1916). With its lavish costumes and scenery and incidental music by the composer Frederick Delius, the play proved a great success. It was revived unsuccessfully at the Cambridge Theatre, London, during the 1951 Festival of Britain.

Hathaway, Anne (*c.* 1555–1623) The wife of William SHAKESPEARE. Little is known of her life apart from the fact that she married Shakespeare – eight years her junior – in November 1582 and gave birth to Susanna (b. 1583) and the twins Hamnet and Judith (b. 1585); the marriage may have been occasioned by her pregnancy.

There has been much speculation about Anne's character. While many have suggested that Shakespeare's marriage was unhappy, the actor and songwriter Charles Dibdin credited her with divine charms:

> She hath a way so to control
> To rapture the imprisoned soul
> And sweetest Heaven on earth display,
> That to be Heaven Ann hath a way;
> CHARLES DIBDIN: 'Love's Ditty'.

In the late 19th century Samuel Butler, who had recently published *The Authoress of the 'Odyssey'* (in which he alleged that Homer was a woman) was teased by William Thackeray's daughter Anne: "Oh, Mr Butler, do you know my theory about the sonnets? They were written by Anne Hathaway."

Hauptmann, Gerhart (1862–1946) German playwright, novelist, and poet. A major figure in European NATURALISM, he was arguably the most notable German dramatist since Schiller. Hauptmann attended art school and worked as a sculptor in Rome before devoting himself to writing. His best work was done before World War I, earning him the Nobel Prize for literature in 1912. In the 1930s he initially condemned Nazism but eventually aligned himself with it, leading the British critic Eric Bentley to remark, "What Hauptmann lacks is the moral and intellectual stature of a great artist".

Hauptmann became an overnight success with his first play *Before Dawn*, produced in 1889 by Otto Brahm and his Freie Bühne in Berlin. The play shocked theatregoers with its frank depiction of alcoholism in a newly enriched peasant family. With its absence of a hero and lack of plot, *Before Dawn* was hailed as a new landmark in German drama and established Hauptmann's main theme of compassion for suffering.

Hauptmann's most famous work, *The Weavers* (1892), was a historical drama written in his native Silesian dialect. Using the case of a failed revolt by Silesian weavers in 1844 to highlight the cost of industrialization, *The Weavers* was the first tragedy in which the crowd assumed the role of hero; as such it was highly influential on later writers. The play received its premiere in New York in 1915 and was powerfully revived in the 1960s. Other works by Hauptmann notable for their social comment include *The Rats* (1911), a depressing play set in the slums of Berlin, and the satirical anti-Prussian comedy *The Beaver Coat* (1893).

Although mainly naturalistic, Hauptmann's work occasionally veered towards symbolism. His 'dream play' *The Assumption of Hannele* (1893) similarly prefigured EXPRESSIONISM. The romantic *The Sunken Bell* (1896) opened in New York in 1900 and London in 1907, while his mystical fairy drama *Und Pippa tanzt* (1906) was successfully performed throughout Europe.

Hauptmann's final work was *Die Atriden* (1945), a belated condemnation of Nazism. In 1962 Erwin PISCATOR produced this four-part dramatic cycle as one work, using a translucent stage lit from below and screens with back projections.

Haupt- und Staatsaktionen In the German and Austrian theatres of the 17th and 18th centuries, vernacular plays about violent and dramatic deeds in high places. These crude extempore performances were given by the first German-speaking professional actors. The plots, derived from plays presented by the ENGLISH COMEDIANS, combined melodrama with comic interludes supplied by the clown PICKELHERING, later replaced by HARLEQUIN and HANSWURST. Although the critic Johann Gottsched (1700–66) and the actress-manager Carolina Neuber (1697–1760) attempted to reform the *Haupt- und Staatsaktionen* by eliminating Harlequin, the older form remained popular throughout the 18th century.

Havel, Vaclav (1936–) Czech playwright, essayist, and politician; president of Czechoslovakia (1989–92) and subsequently of the Czech Republic (1993–).

Having been denied entry to a university drama course because of his 'bourgeois' background, Havel began his career in the theatre as a stagehand and lighting technician; eventually he worked his way up to become the resident playwright at the Balustrade Theatre in Prague, for which he wrote exclusively until 1968. Early absurdist dramas staged at the Balustrade included *The Garden Party* (1963), *The Memorandum* (1965), a satire on bureaucracy, and *The Increased Difficulty of Concentration* (1968). Following the Soviet invasion of Czechoslovakia in 1968 Havel's plays could no longer be staged in his own country, although they continued to be produced in the West.

Havel's support of the Committee for the Defence of the Unjustly Persecuted led to his being imprisoned from 1979 until 1983, by which time he had become recognized as a figurehead for the opposition movement in Czechoslovakia. Samuel BECKETT wrote the play *Catastrophe* (1982) in his honour and the international writing community showered him with awards.

Despite a further spell of imprisonment and almost constant surveillance, Havel continued to write; *Largo Desolato* and *Temptation* both appeared in 1985 and were produced successfully in the West. After the collapse of communism and his election to the presidency, Havel continued his literary output, writing a play, *Redevelopment* (1989), as well as several books of essays.

Hawthorne, Nigel (1929–) British actor. Hawthorne was born in the English Midlands but educated at Catholic schools in South Africa. Having become a professional actor in 1950, he returned to Britain and appeared in supporting roles for over 25 years without attracting special attention. This changed in 1978, when his performance in Peter Nichols's *Privates on Parade* earned several awards. Stardom followed with his depiction of the senior civil servant Sir Humphrey in BBC television's *Yes, Minister* (1980–83, 1985–86) and *Yes, Prime Minister* (1986–87). This gentle satire had the distinction of being Margaret Thatcher's favourite programme (Hawthorne was appointed CBE in 1987).

Owing to his new celebrity, Hawthorne was able to claim his first leading roles in the theatre. In 1983–84 he took the lead in both *Peer Gynt* and *Tartuffe* with the RSC. West End successes include *Hapgood* (1988) and *Shadowlands* (1989), in which he played the writer C. S. Lewis; the latter transferred to Broadway a year later, earning Hawthorne a coveted Tony Award. In 1992 Hawthorne enjoyed a personal triumph in the theatre when he starred in Alan Bennett's *The Madness of George III* at the National. His mastery of this demanding role was recognized with both Olivier and *Evening Standard* awards. The production toured in Europe and America and in 1994 was converted into a successful film that earned Hawthorne an Oscar nomination as Best Actor. Other film roles include Clarence in the Ian McKellen *Richard III* (1995) and Malvolio in *Twelfth Night* (1996).

Hawtrey, Sir Charles (1858–1923) British actor-manager, the leading British comedian of his day. He made his debut in 1881 at the Prince of Wales' Theatre in *The Colonel.* Two years later he raised £1,200 from friends to produce his own adaptation of Von Moser's comedy *The Private Secretary* with Beerbohm Tree in the lead. He became manager of Her Majesty's Theatre in 1885 and of the Comedy Theatre in 1887.

One of Hawtrey's most successful roles was Lord Goring in WILDE's *An Ideal Husband* (1895). With Charles Brookfield, who also played in *An Ideal Husband*, he helped to round up witnesses to testify against Wilde in the homosexuality trial of 1895.

In 1911 Hawtrey taught stage techniques to the child actor Noël Coward, who was among the cast of *Where the Rainbow Ends*. Coward always acknowledged his debt to Hawtrey's training: "I remember him standing over me at rehearsal, in front of the whole company, and saying, 'Now, boy, you've got to laugh.'"

Off stage, Hawtrey was a renowned gambler and *bon vivant* who always dressed immaculately. An extravagant spender, he was constantly pursued by creditors. He once received a writ-server in his office, offering the bewildered man his best cigars and insisting that he accept free tickets for a show. Hawtrey disappeared into an adjoining office and returned with an envelope: "There you are, my dear chap, two for tonight." Only after the man had stammered his gratitude and departed did he open the envelope and find the writ inside.

Hayduk In the Bulgarian theatre, a genre comprising stories about the *hayduks*, Bulgarian outlaws who were considered freedom fighters against Turkish rule. The plays, which were among the first works written in the modern Bulgarian language, inspired the nationalist movement of the 19th century and also led to a reaction against the authority of the Greek clergy.

Writers for the *Hayduk* theatre included Lyuben Karavelov (1834–79), whose realistic works centred on small-town everyday life, and Konstantin Velichkov (1855–1907). In the 20th century the genre continued to glorify Bulgaria's folk history, despite efforts by the communist authorities to suppress its intense nationalism.

Hayes, Helen (1900–93) US actress, known as the **First Lady of the American Theatre**. Hayes made her debut at the age of five and appeared on Broadway aged nine in the musical *Old Dutch*. ("I have never yearned to be an actress," she wrote in her autobiography, "because I always was one.")

As an adult she won acclaim in Kaufman and Connelly's 1922 hit *To the Ladies* and as Cleopatra in the THEATRE GUILD production of Shaw's *Caesar and Cleopatra*. To enhance her stage technique she studied boxing and fencing. Great success came the following year in J. M. Barrie's *What Every Woman Knows*. When she became pregnant during the run of *Coquette* (1929) and wished to leave the show, the producer Jed Harris sued and lost, leading to a clause in contracts that defines pregnancy as an 'act of God'. In 1931 Hayes went to Hollywood to make the first of her dozen films.

Although she was highly praised as Mary, Queen of Scots in Maxwell Anderson's *Mary of Scotland*, her greatest role came in 1935 when she played Queen Victoria, in Laurence Housman's VICTORIA REGINA which ran for 969 performances. Hayes never found the courage to play her two royal parts in Britain but in 1948 finally made her London debut in Tennessee Williams's *The Glass Menagerie*.

In 1955, when she celebrated her 50th year on the stage, the Fulton Theatre on 46th Street was renamed the **Helen Hayes Theatre** in her honour, making her only the second US actress so honoured (the first was Ethel Barrymore). She played there in 1958 in Eugene O'Neill's *A Touch of the Poet*.

In 1961 she toured 28 countries sponsored by the US State Department, and the next year joined the Shakespeare Festival Theatre in Stratford, Connecticut, for *Shakespeare Revisited* which then toured America. Two years later she founded the Helen Hayes Repertory Company to present Shakespeare readings at universities. She made her farewell performance in 1970 in O'Neill's *Long Day's Journey into Night*.

When the Helen Hayes Theatre was demolished in 1982, she was said to be proud that "I've outlasted all that brick and stone and steel".

Hay Fever A comedy by Noël COWARD. It opened in 1925 in London, running at the same time as three other Coward plays (*Fallen Angels*, *On with the Dance*, and *The Vortex*), which equalled Somerset MAUGHAM'S record. Coward commented: "Everyone but Somerset Maugham said I was a second Somerset Maugham."

The plot of *Hay Fever* centres on the four eccentric members of the Bliss family, each of whom has invited a weekend guest without telling the others. The group includes a writer, an actress, a diplomat, an artist, a flapper, and a vamp. The hosts' unconventional treatment of their guests during the course of the evening results in their hasty departure the following day.

Kenneth Tynan, who revived *Hay Fever* in 1964, was walking through Mayfair one day when a Rolls pulled up beside him; Coward wound down the window and drawled:

"Bless you, dear boy, for admitting that I'm a classic."

At rehearsals, Dame Edith Evans kept expanding the line "On a clear day you can see Marlow" to "On a very clear day you can see Marlow." Coward eventually interrupted: "Edith, the line is 'On a clear day you can see Marlow'. On a *very* clear day you can see Marlowe *and* Beaumont *and* Fletcher."

In 1968, as another revival was planned, Coward wrote in his diary, "Good old *Hay Fever* certainly has been a good friend. Written and conceived in exactly three days at that little cottage in Dickenfield in 1922! What a profitable weekend *that* was."

Haymarket The popular name for the Theatre Royal, Haymarket, London, a longstanding favourite of playgoers and the last theatre to be lit by candles. Built on the site of an old inn, it dates from 1721 when it was named the Little Theatre in the Hay and presented amateur performances. At that time, only Drury Lane and Covent Garden held patents to present public entertainment. Henry Fielding, who became manager in 1735, defied this by staging his own satires, causing the theatre to be closed in 1737. In 1747, Samuel Foote (*see* ENGLISH ARISTOPHANES) circumvented the law by charging only for 'refreshments'; he was later granted a patent to open when the two other theatres were closed for the summer. George Colman, who took over in 1776, obtained a full licence in 1777.

Foote's shadow continued to haunt the theatre 28 years after his death, when his play *The Tailors* was revived in 1805. Its portrayal of the profession caused a riot of hundreds of London tailors that had to be suppressed by troops (*see* DEVIL AMONG THE TAILORS).

The architect John Nash redesigned the theatre in 1821, adding its present Corinthian portico. John Poole's comedy *Paul Pry* was produced in 1825, and Julia Glover caused a sensation in 1833 as Falstaff in Shakespeare's *The Merry Wives of Windsor*. J. B. Buckstone was manager from 1853 to 1878, and his ghost is said to still haunt the theatre (*see* GHOSTS). In 1855 the venue became known as the Theatre Royal. Gas lighting and London's first 'picture frame' stage were later installed; the Haymarket was given its present regal look, inspired by the Grand Théâtre de Bordeaux, in 1879.

Beerbohm TREE, manager from 1887 to 1896, presented the first performances of Oscar Wilde's *A Woman of No Importance* (1893) and *An Ideal Husband* (1895). Tree used profits from the Haymarket production of *Trilby* in 1895 to build Her Majesty's Theatre across the road. The Haymarket was again remodelled in 1904 and between 1939 and 1941.

The longest run at the Haymarket was Terence Rattigan's ROSS, which opened in 1960 for 763 performances.

heart. ***Heartbreak House*** A sombre comedy by George Bernard SHAW, first performed in 1920 in New York and in 1921 at the Royal Court Theatre, London. Set during World War I, it depicts the boredom and frustration of the wealthy, who lack ideals and a purpose in life. The play shows the strong influence of CHEKHOV.

A number of friends gather at the house of 88-year-old Captain Shotover, a mad inventor of devices to annihilate the human race. (Cedric HARDWICKE greatly impressed Shaw when he played the role in 1922.) Shotover's daughter Hesione brings a young friend, Ellie, who becomes enamoured with her host; other guests include Hesione's husband, Hector HUSHABYE, and her sister, Lady Utterword. The play ends with an air raid.

The role of Hesione was inspired by Mrs Patrick CAMPBELL, but because of her on-and-off-again love affair with Shaw she was not allowed to play it.

When the play was produced in 1929 at the MALVERN FESTIVAL, Shaw complained during rehearsals that the explosion in the last act was not loud enough. The stage manager promised to provide an opening-night bang to remember, and warned the cast. When the cue came, Edith Evans (as Lady Utterword) spoke her line and covered her face but no sound effect was heard. The play had ended and the audience was leaving when the ceiling suddenly collapsed with a roar, sending two theatregoers to hospital. Noted Cedric Hardwicke later, "Shaw for once seemed happy."

'Hearts of Oak' A jingoistic sea song from *Harlequin's Invasion*, a pantomime by GARRICK with music by William Boyce. It was written in 1759, the year that saw victories over the French at Quiberon Bay, Quebec, and Minden; hence the allusion to 'this wonderful year' in the opening lines:

Come, cheer up my lads! 'tis to glory we steer,
To add something more to this wonderful year.

The title of the song refers to the timber from which the ships were built:

Hearts of oak are our ships,
Jolly tars are our men...

Heavens, the In the Elizabethan theatre, the canopy or roof over the stage (the below-stage area was known as **the Hell**). Also called **the Shadow**, it protected the open stage from rain and housed machinery and other devices for special effects. Such sound effects as thunder were created within the attic space, and flying props were lowered from there. Sometimes the underside of the Heavens was painted with the sky, sun, moon, stars, and signs of the zodiac. In many theatres, such as the Swan, the roof was supported by two pillars, but at the Hope it was cantilevered so that the stage could be removed for other entertainments.

heavy man In theatrical parlance, an actor who plays foil to the hero, such as Claudius in *Hamlet* or Iago in *Othello*.

Hedda Gabler A play by Henrik IBSEN, first produced in 1890 in Munich. The first London production, the following year, was at the Vaudeville Theatre with Elizabeth Robins in the title role.

Hedda, a bored and lonely woman, conceives a bitter jealousy of Eilert Loevborg, the rival of her academic husband, Jorgen Tesman. When Loevborg loses the manuscript of his important new book, Tesman finds it and Hedda destroys it. Loevborg is distraught and Hedda suggests he commit suicide. Instead he recovers the original notes and Tesman offers to help reconstruct the manuscript; it is Hedda who finally kills herself.

When the Italian actress Eleonora DUSE played the role of Hedda in London, critic Max Beerbohm was more impressed with the performance given by the prompter: "While Signora Duse walked through her part, the prompter threw himself into it with a will." The oddest interpretation was that given by Jenny Agutter in Charles Marowitz's free adaptation at the Round House in 1980. Agutter's Hedda was so sexually potent that one critic renamed her 'Hedda Gobbler'.

Heiress, The A play by Ruth and Augustus Goetz, based on Henry James's novel *Washington Square*. It was first produced in 1947 in New York and two years later at London's Haymarket, when John Gielgud directed a cast that included Peggy Ashcroft, Ralph Richardson, and Donald Sinden. Harold Hobson wrote of Ashcroft in the *Sunday Times*: "For her performance all superlatives are pale and feeble things." A film version in 1949 starred Olivia de Havilland and Montgomery Clift.

Set in New York in 1850, the story centres on Catherine Sloper, plain and unmarried, who lives in Washington Square with her widowed father, Dr Sloper, and her aunt. Morris Townsend charms Catherine and courts her for her inheritance; when Sloper threatens to disinherit his daughter, Townsend fails to turn up for their midnight elopement. Two years later Townsend returns penniless from California. Catherine agrees to elope with him as before, but when he knocks at the door it is her turn to reject him.

The play was originally given a happy ending, in which Catherine called Townsend back with the line "Morris, come home, you're home at last!" This was so mercilessly lampooned by the opening-night audience as they left the theatre that the authors went home and rewrote the final scene.

See also GENTLEMAN JOHNNY.

Helena The enigmatic heroine of Shakespeare's ALL'S WELL THAT ENDS WELL. The orphaned daughter of a physician, Helena loves the aristocratic BERTRAM and eventually, through much scheming, wins him. The role is a difficult one for an actress as it is easy for Helena to appear something of a golddigger. The first actress to have any real success with the role was Peg WOFFINGTON.

Hell, the *See* HEAVENS.

Hellman, Lillian (1905–84) America's most successful woman dramatist, who turned to writing plays after reviewing books and working as a press agent. Her tightly constructed works are examples of the WELL-MADE PLAY.

Hellman's first work, THE CHILDREN'S HOUR, was produced in 1934. Its subject of lesbianism resulted in a ban from the Lord Chamberlain, although it had run for 691 performances on Broadway. Her other plays include the powerful Southern drama THE

LITTLE FOXES, which opened in New York in 1939 and was seen in London in 1941, the anti-Nazi WATCH ON THE RHINE (1941), *Another Part of the Forest* (1946), and TOYS IN THE ATTIC, which opened in 1960 in both New York and London. She also worked on the libretto for Leonard Bernstein's musical *Candide* (1957). Her autobiographical volumes include *Scoundrel Time* (1976), which dealt with her summoning by the House Un-American Activities Committee in the 1950s.

Hellman was an abrasive character who met her match during preparations for *The Children's Hour*. The theatre owner Lee Shubert (*see* SHUBERT BROTHERS) saw an unknown woman watching a rehearsal from the stalls with her feet on the seat in front of her. "Take your dirty shoes off my chair!" he growled, pushing her leg down. Hellman retorted, "I don't like strange men fooling around with my right leg, so don't do it again." Having been informed who Hellman was, Shubert entered into a brief exchange:

> SHUBERT This play could land us in jail.
> HELLMAN I'm eating a frankfurter, and I don't want to think about jail. Would you like a piece of it?
> SHUBERT I forbid you to get mustard on my chairs.

Shubert departed with these words, and Hellman did not see him again until her play had run for six months, when she heard him loudly ask the doorman who she was.

Hello Dolly! A musical by Michael Stewart and Jerry Herman, based on Thornton Wilder's THE MATCHMAKER. Having been booed on its pre-Broadway tour, the show was extensively rewritten before opening in 1964 at the St James's Theatre; it subsequently ran for 2844 performances with Carol Channing in the lead, winning the Tony Award for Best Musical. The part of Dolly was later played by Betty Grable, Pearl Bailey (in an all-Black production), and Barbra Streisand in the film version. The London production opened in 1965 at Drury Lane.

The musical follows the story line of Wilder's play about a merchant from Yonkers who falls in love with the matchmaker Dolly Levi. The songs include 'Hello, Dolly!', 'Before the Parade Passes Me By', and 'It Only Takes a Moment'.

hemp house *See* HAND-WORKED HOUSE.

Henry. ***Henry IV, Part I*** The first of two plays by SHAKESPEARE about the reign of Henry IV, first performed in 1597 in London. The practice of presenting both parts together began only in the 20th century: the SHAKESPEARE MEMORIAL THEATRE at Stratford opened in 1932 with *Henry IV Part I* and *Part II* performed in one day.

Shakespeare apparently derived the story from an anonymous play called *The Famous Victories of Henry V* which was performed as early as 1588. The main plot deals with the rebellion of the Percy family, led by Harry Hotspur, against Henry IV. The king despairs of his elder son Henry (Prince Hal), who spends his time in taverns with Sir John FALSTAFF, a roguish liar and glutton; however, in the final battle against the rebels Prince Hal saves the life of his father and slays Hotspur. In performance the play is invariably stolen by the larger-than-life Falstaff, arguably the greatest (and most complex) comic creation in English drama.

Henry IV, Part II SHAKESPEARE's conclusion of the two-part story of Henry IV. It was first performed in 1598 in London with the comic actor William Kempe as Justice SHALLOW. In 1945 the Old Vic produced *Parts I* and *II* with Laurence Olivier as Hotspur in *Part I* and Justice Shallow in *Part II* and Ralph Richardson as FALSTAFF in both. Richardson was hailed by one critic as "the greatest of modern Falstaffs".

The plot begins three years after Hotspur's defeat and death, when a new insurrection looms. Falstaff, still leading a riotous life with his friends at the tavern, is asked to recruit soldiers. On the way to the battle he stays in Gloucestershire with his old friend Justice Shallow, taking advantage of his hospitality. Meanwhile Hal's brother, Prince John of Lancaster, uses treachery to capture the leaders of the insurrection without a fight, and the king dies in London. At the end of the play a reformed Prince Hal, now Henry V, banishes Falstaff "on pain of death...Not to come near our person by ten mile."

Once John GIELGUD was waiting with a fellow actor between takes on a film set, reading a book while the other man pored over his *Times* crossword. "Sorry," the man asked, "but is there a character in Shakespeare called the Earl of Westmorland?" Gielgud nodded, "Yes, in *Henry IV, Part II*." Scowling over his book, he added, "But it's a very poor part."

The US actor Henry Miller (1860–1926) once performed *Henry IV, Part II* with a touring company that outnumbered the paid audience two to one.

Henry V One of the best-known of SHAKESPEARE's history plays, which completes the trilogy (with *Henry IV Part I* and *Part II*) that charts the development of the young Prince Hal into a successful king. *Henry V* was written and first performed in 1599. It gives a strongly patriotic view of the early years of Henry's reign, culminating in the victory over the French at Agincourt (although some modern critics have detected a note of irony).

Producers of *Henry V* have gone to considerable lengths to recreate the battle scenes. Samuel Phelps, manager of Sadler's Wells Theatre from 1843 to 1862, had 40 actors marching behind a rock that only revealed their heads and shoulders. Strapped to each soldier's body were two dummies in armour, with heads modelled by Madame Tussaud's, so that there appeared to be 120 soldiers.

Laurence OLIVIER starred in the Old Vic's 1937 production. Charles Laughton once told him, "Do you know why you're so good in this part? You're England, that's all." After that, when people asked Olivier how he did it, he would say, "It's simple: I am England." Olivier also directed and starred in a stirring wartime film version in 1944.

One of the best known King Henrys of modern times is Kenneth BRANAGH, who played the part in 1984 at Stratford; at 22, he was the youngest actor the RSC had ever cast in the role. Branagh also made a film version in 1990, the first since Olivier's. He chose the play because "It has a crackling narrative, immense visual possibilities, and so many ideas – about politics, about war – that seem right for now."

Henry VI, Part I The beginning of SHAKESPEARE's story of Henry VI, first produced in 1593 in London. It was probably Shakespeare's first work for the stage. The uneven quality of the writing suggests that it was written in collaboration, probably with Robert Greene (1560–92) or Thomas Nashe (1567–1601). A modern version was produced in 1963 as part of the highly successful WARS OF THE ROSES cycle rewritten by John Barton for the Royal Shakespeare Company and directed by Peter Hall.

The play begins with news of a French rebellion against English rule. The dauphin, with the help of JOAN OF ARC, is gaining the upper hand, while in Britain, Richard Plantagenet (later Duke of York) and Beaufort, Earl of Somerset, are quarrelling as the weak young Henry VI desperately tries to make peace. Joan is finally defeated, taken prisoner, and burnt at the stake. Henry signs a truce with the enemy, and the Earl of Suffolk brings back Margaret of Anjou to be Henry's bride.

Henry VI, Part II The continuation of SHAKESPEARE's story of Henry VI, first produced in 1593 in London. This and *Part III* are superior in every way to the first part, and most scholars believe that Shakespeare was their sole author. *Part II* has 47 characters, more than any of Shakespeare's other plays.

The story continues as Henry's wife, Margaret, schemes with her lover Suffolk to discredit the Duchess of Gloucester. Suffolk has the Duke of Gloucester murdered and is later killed himself, leaving the way clear for the ambitious Duke of York to pursue his claim to the throne. Having gained Henry's permission to raise an army to quell a rising in Ulster, York plots with John Cade to start a peasant's revolt. Cade is at first successful, but his followers desert him and he is eventually killed. York refuses to disband his army until Somerset of the House of Lancaster is arrested; when Somerset is subsequently freed the two sides meet at St Albans in the first battle of the Wars of the Roses. York and his allies Warwick and Salisbury are triumphant, and the king and queen flee to London with the victors in pursuit.

Henry VI, Part III The conclusion of SHAKESPEARE's story of Henry VI, first produced in 1593 in London. Henry loses the Wars of the Roses and agrees that the House of York should succeed to the throne after his death, a promise that shocks Queen Margaret and her son, the Prince of Wales. York is killed in battle, Henry is imprisoned in the Tower, and York's son Edward, now on the throne, weds Lady Elizabeth Grey. When this news reaches the kingmaker Warwick and Queen Margaret in France, they join forces to invade England with a French army. The Yorkists triumph, and Edward's brother (the hunchbacked Richard, who has his eye on the crown) kills King Henry and the Prince of Wales.

Henry VIII A play about the English king, written by William SHAKESPEARE and John FLETCHER; the full title is *All is True* or *The*

Famous History of the Life of King Henry VIII. Apart from his contribution to THE TWO NOBLE KINSMEN, it was Shakespeare's last work for the stage. It was first produced in 1613 at London's GLOBE THEATRE, which was destroyed during the performance when a cannon shot announcing Henry's arrival set fire to the thatched roof. The theatre burned down in less than an hour. According to Sir Henry Wotton, "only one man had his breeches set on fire, that would perhaps have boiled him, if he had not by the benefit of a provident wit put it out with Bottle-Ale."

At a party thrown by Cardinal Wolsey, King Henry falls for Anne Boleyn, one of Queen Katherine's ladies-in-waiting. Wolsey persuades the Pope to declare Henry's marriage invalid, but secretly asks him to delay the annulment to prevent Henry from marrying the unworthy Anne. Having discovered Wolsey's machinations, Henry marries Anne at a private ceremony. Princess Elizabeth is born, and Archbishop Cranmer predicts she will have a glorious reign.

Despite its somewhat undramatic quality, the play's major roles have always attracted star actors. Sarah SIDDONS once gave a terrifyingly powerful performance as Queen Katherine in Edinburgh. In 1892 Henry Irving played Cardinal Wolsey at the Lyceum Theatre, in his own extremely expensive production which ran for six months but still lost money. Charles Laughton played Henry in 1933 just after filming *The Private Life of Henry VIII*.

Henslowe, Philip (d. 1616) English theatre-owner and impresario, whose diaries and notes are invaluable sources of information about the theatre of his time. They were inherited by his son-in-law, the actor Edward ALLEYN, and are now in Dulwich College (founded by Alleyn).

Henslowe built the ROSE THEATRE in 1587, the FORTUNE (with Alleyn) in 1600, and the HOPE in 1613. His papers show him to have been a shrewd businessman who made annual contracts with actors, paying them a fixed salary. He also leased his theatres to companies and provided costumes and properties in return for a large share of the profits from each production.

The accounts for Henslowe's theatres include loans made to actors. Some researchers suspect that Henslowe kept actors in debt to him in order to tie them to his theatre. In 1615 several actors drew up a document headed *Articles of Grievance, and Articles of Oppression, against Mr. Hinchlowe*, accusing him of embezzling their money and unlawfully retaining their property.

Hernani A Romantic verse drama by Victor HUGO, which caused a riot at its first performance on 25 February 1830 at the staid Comédie-Française, Paris. The plot involves the doomed love of Hernani, an outlaw, for Doña Sol. The older playgoers were offended by Hugo's breaches of classical decorum and began to shout "Racine! Racine!", provoking an equally passionate reaction from the younger advocates of Romanticism, mostly students. A turning point in the debacle occurred when the critic Théophile Gautier (1811–72) stood and shouted to the reactionaries, "Your Racine is a scamp, gentlemen!"

Nearly half a century later, in 1877, the role of Doña Sol was played with great sensitivity by Sarah BERNHARDT. Hugo was in the audience and said it was the first time he had seen the part properly acted.

Herne the Hunter A mythical wood spirit said to haunt Windsor Forest. Best known for his role in the downfall of Falstaff in Shakespeare's THE MERRY WIVES OF WINDSOR, Herne is supposed to appear wearing chains and a stag's antlers.

According to legend, a royal huntsman named Herne saved his king from injury by a wounded stag; he then enjoyed royal favour until jealous rivals had him dismissed. Herne subsequently hanged himself from a tree in the park, which he has continued to haunt – in 1962 some youths claimed to have been literally hounded out of the park by Herne after they blew hunting horns as a joke one night.

hero. Hero-Combat Play *See* MUMMERS' PLAY.

heroic drama A short-lived genre of English drama during the Restoration. In imitation of classical French tragedy, it obeyed the UNITIES of time, place, and action; the main theme, expounded in rhymed couplets, was the conflict of love and honour. The genre is represented by such plays as DRYDEN's *Conquest of Granada* (1671); it was dealt a fatal blow by Buckingham's burlesque THE REHEARSAL (1671). *See* NEOCLASSICAL DRAMA; RESTORATION DRAMA.

Herod. To out-herod Herod To outdo in wickedness, violence, or rant, the worst of tyrants. Herod, who destroyed the babes of Bethlehem, appeared in the medieval MYSTERY PLAYS as a ranting roaring tyrant. The phrase comes from *Hamlet* (III, ii). *See also* ADVICE TO ACTORS; PILATE, PONTIUS.

Heywood, Thomas (*c.* 1570–1641) English dramatist and actor, who claimed to have been involved in the writing of at least 220 plays, about 35 of which have survived. William Winstanley in his *Lives of the Most Famous English Poets* offers one possible explanation for the loss of so many of his plays:

> 'Tis said, that he not only acted himself almost every day, but also wrote each day a sheet: and that he might loose no time, many of his Plays were composed in the Tavern, on the back-side of Tavern Bills, which may be the occasion that so many of them be lost.

Although little is known of Heywood's early life, it is assumed that he must have been in London in the mid 1590s. In 1596 he appears to have begun writing plays for Philip HENSLOWE's company, the ADMIRAL'S MEN. Heywood is also known to have written for, and performed with, Queen Anne's Men.

Heywood's best-known surviving work is the domestic tragedy, A WOMAN KILLED WITH KINDNESS (1603). His diverse output includes a series of plays based on classical mythology called *The Golden Age, The Silver Age, The Brazen Age*, and *The Iron Age*, which were staged between 1611 and 1613. Other notable plays include *If You Know Not Me, You Know Nobody* (1605), *The Rape of Lucrece* (1607), and the two parts of *The Fair Maid of the West* (*c.* 1611, *c.* 1631), which chronicles the life of Elizabeth I. His romantic drama *The Four Prentices of London* (1600) was satirized by Francis Beaumont in THE KNIGHT OF THE BURNING PESTLE (1607). In 1631 Heywood appears to have taken over from Thomas Dekker (*c.* 1570–1632) as the writer of the Lord Mayor's Shows, a position he retained until 1639. Among Heywood's other writings is *An Apology for Actors* (1612).

Hill, Jenny *See* VITAL SPARK, THE.

Hindle Wakes A play by Stanley Houghton (1881–1913), a dramatist of the MANCHESTER SCHOOL. First performed in 1912 at the Aldwych Theatre, London, it was Houghton's only work not premiered at the Gaiety Theatre in Manchester. *Hindle Wakes* was the playwright's most successful and controversial work and has often been revived. Contemporary audiences were shocked by the heroine's attitude to her illicit affair with a rich man's son.

Fanny Hawthorne, a working girl, has been seduced by Alan Jeffcote, the son of a rich industrialist. Alan's father comes to an agreement with Fanny's father that a wedding must take place, but Fanny refuses to marry Alan, whom she does not love or even respect. Alan's family admires her, but Fanny's mother is humiliated and orders her out of the house. Thus liberated, Fanny sets out to take on the world.

hip bath The booming words used by the British actor Sir C. Aubrey Smith (1863–1948) to clear his throat before making his stage entrance. Audiences were often puzzled to hear the resonant voice offstage calling "Hip bath, hip bath, hip bath!"

Smith was also a fanatical golfer who would practise short approach shots in the wings with a club and paper ball. Once, during a performance, he chipped his paper ball through a window into the set. The US actor Raymond Massey, standing next to him, assured him that nobody would notice. "I know," growled Smith, "but I shanked [mishit] my shot!"

Hippodrome, the A theatre off Leicester Square, London, that progressed from circus to cabaret during its 80-year lifetime. It opened in 1900 with circus acts and aquatic spectacles (*see* AQUATIC DRAMA); after renovation, it reopened in 1909 as a music hall that also featured ballet. A series of popular revues was presented from 1912 to 1925 by Albert de Courville, and these were followed by musical comedies such as *Hit the Deck* (1927) and *Please, Teacher* (1935). Other great successes included the hit revue *The Fleet's Lit Up* (1938) and Ivor NOVELLO's musical comedy *Perchance to Dream* (1945), which prompted the critic James Agate to remark of the audience: "Mr Novello's nonsense had obviously suited their nonsense." The venue was reconstructed in 1958 as The Talk of the Town, a combined restaurant and cabaret that featured such stars as Eartha Kitt; it closed in 1982.

hired man In the Elizabethan theatre, an actor who was not a SHARER in the company's profits. Hired men, employees of the shareholders, lacked the privileges given to sharers by their patrons; their contractual weekly wage, which ranged from five to ten shillings, was often not fully paid. Hired men played minor roles on stage and also served as prompters, musicians, wardrobe keepers, and theatre cleaners.

Histrio-Mastix See NOTORIOUS WHORES.

HMS Pinafore A comic opera by GILBERT AND SULLIVAN, the first great success of their collaboration. Subtitled *The Lass that Loved the Sailor*, it opened in 1878 at the Opera Comique Theatre, London, for a run of 571 performances. Gilbert's knighthood was supposedly delayed for two decades because his characterization of Admiral Sir Joseph Porter was too close to Disraeli's First Lord of the Admiralty, W. H. Smith (the newsagent). Gilbert was also berated for his daring use of the word 'damn' on stage, having Captain Corcoran splutter "Damme!" when he hears that an officer's daughter is marrying one of the lower classes. The play also popularized the expression 'What, never?'

The story is set aboard *HMS Pinafore*, anchored off Portsmouth. The ship's commander, Captain Corcoran, has a lovely daughter, Josephine, who is engaged to Admiral Sir Joseph Porter but loves a humble sailor, Ralph Rackstraw. When it is revealed that Corcoran and Rackstraw were mixed up as babies Josephine, now a commoner, is able to marry Rackstraw, now a captain.

The songs include 'I'm Called Little Buttercup', 'I am the Captain of the *Pinafore*', and 'When I was a Lad I Served a Term'. *See also* PINAFORE RIOT.

hobby horse An animal character of European folk festivals. The hobby-horse actor rode on, or was disguised in, a wooden or wicker framework shaped like a horse. Probably derived ultimately from pagan animal worship, the character became a part of the MORRIS DANCE; it also appeared in some of the MUMMERS' PLAYS and in annual events such as the HOCK-TUESDAY PLAY. The term also refers to a child's toy in the form of a stick with a wooden horse's head on top.

Hobson's Choice A comedy by Harold Brighouse (1882–1958), first performed in 1916 and frequently revived. It is the story of the tyrannical shoe-seller Hobson and his strong-willed daughter Maggie, who marries the timid Willie Mossop against her father's wishes and ultimately takes over his business. David Lean's classic film version, made in 1954, starred Charles Laughton as Hobson and John Mills as Willie.

The phrase 'Hobson's choice', meaning no choice at all, derives from Thomas Hobson (1544?–1631), a Cambridge liveryman who offered his customers the choice of the horse nearest the stable door or none.

Hochhuth, Rolf (1931–) Swiss playwright writing in German. Hochhuth's first successful play, THE REPRESENTATIVE (1963), was a controversial but telling indictment of the Roman Catholic Church's indifference to the suffering of the Jews during the holocaust of World War II. *The Soldier* (1967) was no less contentious; it provided a critical examination of Winston Churchill's role in the bombing of Dresden and alleged that he was responsible for the death of General Sikorski, the wartime Polish leader in exile.

In general, Hochhuth's subsequent works have failed to generate the same level of controversy or interest; they include *Guerillas* (1970), *Lysistrata and NATO* (1973), and *Immaculate Conception* (1989), which deals with the subject of surrogate motherhood. The exception is Hochhuth's most recent work, *Wessis in Weimar* (1992), which accused Western economic interests of exploiting the former East Germany since reunification. The play includes a reference to the assassination of Detler Rohwedder, who had been in charge of privatizing the former East Germany's state-owned industry. The line "Anyone acting like Rohwedder should not be surprised to be shot dead" drew from Helmut Kohl, the German chancellor, the comment: "A German patriot is being slandered. It is a licence for murder..."

Hock-Tuesday play or **Hocktide play** or **Hock play** A form of traditional English FOLK THEATRE presented annually in Coventry, Worcester, Shrewsbury, Hungerford, and other English towns on the third Tuesday after Easter. It was banned in Worcester in 1450 and gradually ceased elsewhere, but was revived in 1575 during the Kenilworth Revels.

The play began with Captain Cox leading English knights (each on a HOBBY HORSE) to battle against the invading Danes; the captured Danes were finally led away and imprisoned by the English women. It was probably derived from an ancient custom in which women tried to catch ('hock') a man and demand a forfeit, the game being reversed the following day when the women were the prey.

Hofmannsthal, Hugo von (1874–1929) Austrian dramatist, poet, and essayist, who also wrote libretti for several operas by the German composer Richard Strauss. Hofmannsthal's first collection of poetry was published under the pseudonym Loris when he was 16. These poems, dream-like and highly lyrical, created something of a stir in German and Austrian literary circles. The following year his first verse play, *Yesterday*, appeared. Between 1891 and 1899 Hofmannsthal produced a number of these short poetic dramas, the most notable being *Death and the Fool* (1893) and *The Adventurer and the Singer* (1898).

In 1902, however, Hofmannsthal published an influential essay, *Ein Brief*, in which he renounced purely lyrical forms of writing. It later became evident that this essay represented not only a crisis of faith for Hofmannsthal personally, but was symptomatic of a larger disturbance involving both the expressionist and symbolist movements. Following the publication of *Ein Brief* Hofmannsthal experimented with several forms of drama, adapting and modernizing several classical works, such as EURIPIDES's *Electra* as *Elektra* (1903) and SOPHOCLES's *Oedipus* as *Odipus und die Sphinx* (1905). Hofmannsthal also produced an adaptation of OTWAY's *Venice Preserv'd* as *Das gerettete Venedig* (1905). *Jederman* (1911), later translated as *Everyman*, was an early 20th-century version of the medieval morality play; it was the first of a series of plays involving social and religious themes, which culminated in *Der Turm* (1925).

Hofmannsthal's works have failed to make much impact in the English-speaking world and his international stature rests mainly on his libretti for Strauss. He adapted his own play *Elektra* in 1909 and provided libretti for *Der Rosenkavalier* (1911) and *Ariadne auf Naxos* (1912). He was also one of the founders (with Max REINHARDT) of the Salzburg Festival in 1920.

hoist *See* SLOTE.

home. ***Home and Beauty*** A play by W. Somerset MAUGHAM, first performed in London in 1919. Its US title was *Too Many Husbands*. The plot concerns a woman who rejects the love of two World War I heroes after she falls for a civilian involved in black-market dealings.

In the 1950s, Noël COWARD invited the 80-year-old Maugham to a dinner party and expressed his desire to turn *Home and Beauty* into a musical. When Maugham reacted coolly, Coward slowly reviewed his guest's wrinkled face and horn-rimmed spectacles and nicknamed him 'The Lizard of Oz'.

Homecoming, The A comedy by Harold PINTER; first performed at the Aldwych Theatre, London, in 1965 by the Royal Shakespeare Company under Peter Hall, it went on to become Pinter's greatest Broadway success.

Ted, a lecturer at a US university, returns home with his new wife Ruth, introducing her into the all-male London household of his father Max, Max's brother Sam, and Ted's two brothers Lenny, who is a pimp, and Joey. When Ted finally goes back to America, Ruth accepts the degenerate family's invitation to stay. Lenny suggests that she may work for him in Soho, encouraging the other men to manoeuvre for her favours.

hook. Sling your hook! A phrase meaning 'Be off!' or 'Go away!' It derives from the long hooked pole used in some Victorian music halls to pull off performers who outran their time or outstayed their welcome.

Hope Theatre A theatre in Southwark, London, that was also a venue for bull- and bear-baiting. Philip HENSLOWE added theatre facilities in 1613, a year after the nearby Globe Theatre burned down, hoping to capture the latter's audience. The Hope had a roofed stage that could be removed for the baiting events and stables for six bulls and three horses.

The leading actor at the Hope was Edward ALLEYN, who was married to Joan Woodward, Henslowe's stepdaughter. A resident company, the Lady Elizabeth's Men led by Nathan Field (1587–1620), was engaged for the 1614–15 season and presented Ben Jonson's *Bartholomew Fair* amongst other works. Alleyn drew up a new contract with the actors, renamed the Prince Charles's Men, but disputes arose and continued to the point of litigation; eventually, the Globe was rebuilt before the new theatre could establish its popularity. It was demolished in 1687.

Hopkins, Sir Anthony (1937–) Welsh actor. Hopkins trained at RADA and made his stage debut in 1960 at the Library Theatre, Manchester, in Brendan Behan's *The Quare Fellow*. Following spells with a number of repertory companies, Hopkins first appeared in London in 1964 in a production of *Julius Caesar* at the Royal Court Theatre. In 1967 Hopkins joined the National Theatre Company at the Old Vic but was not given a leading part until 1971, when he played the title role in Shakespeare's *Coriolanus*; he appeared as Macbeth the following year.

After 1972 Hopkins worked mainly in America playing in films as well as on the stage. Notable stage roles from this period include the psychiatrist Dr Dysart in Peter Shaffer's *Equus*, a part Hopkins took over from Richard Burton.

Hopkins returned to the British stage in 1985, playing a monstrous newspaper tycoon in the National Theatre production of Brenton and HARE's *Pravda*. Memorable performances in *King Lear* (1986), *Antony and Cleopatra* (1987), and David Hwang's *M. Butterfly* (1989) followed.

Hopkins has also played in numerous television and film productions, achieving a new level of international fame with his portrayal of a cannibalistic serial killer in the 1990 film *The Silence of the Lambs*.

Horace. ***Horace*** A tragedy by Pierre CORNEILLE, first performed in Paris in 1640 at the Théâtre du Marais. Like its predecessor LE CID, *Horace* was a great success and was soon established as a landmark in the French classical tradition; VOLTAIRE said that moral convictions had never before been expressed with such sublimity on the stage.

The play drew parallels between ancient Roman history and the reigns of Louis XIII and Louis XIV. The plot is derived from an account by the Roman historian Livy (Titus Livius; 59 BC– 17 AD) of the battle betweeen the Horatii, three Roman heroes, and the Cuiratii. When the only surviving member of the Horatii returns to his pacifist sister, she curses him for causing the death of her lover. He kills her and must then argue his case before the king.

Horace of England A title given to the poet and playwright Abraham Cowley (1618–67) by George Villiers, Duke of Buckingham, the author of *The Rehearsal*. The reference is to the Roman lyric poet Horace (Quintus Horatius Flaccus; 65–8 BC).

In Ben Jonson's play *The Poetaster* (1601), a satire directed at his contemporaries Thomas Dekker and John Marston, the character of the poet Horace represents Jonson himself. Dekker responded with *Satiromastix* (1601), possibly written in collaboration with Marston, which features the same characters and ends with Horace as the butt of ridicule. *See* WAR OF THE THEATRES.

Hordern, Sir Michael (Murray) (1911–) British actor. Hordern made his first professional appearance in a 1937 production of *Othello*. After wartime service in the Royal Navy, he returned to the stage in a production of Ibsen's *A Doll's House* in 1946. Subsequent roles included Mr Toad in Christmas runs of *Toad of Toad Hall* (1948 and 1949). In 1950 he appeared in the title part in Chekhov's *Ivanov*. Hordern's reputation was firmly established by an excellent season with the RSC in 1952. The following year he joined the Old Vic, giving a highly acclaimed performance as Malvolio in *Twelfth Night*.

Following further success in Shaw's *The Doctor's Dilemma* (1955), Hordern played the senile old barrister in John Mortimer's *The Dock Brief* (1958). Subsequently he has specialized in playing mildly or wholly eccentric characters, such as the metaphysician George in Tom Stoppard's *Jumpers* (1972) and Captain Absolute in Sheridan's *The Rivals* (1983). He has also made many film and television appearances.

Horn Dance *See* ABBOTS BROMLEY HORN DANCE *under* ABBOT.

Horniman, Annie (1860–1937) British theatre patron and manager, who introduced modern REPERTORY THEATRE to Britain at the beginning of the 20th century. Impressed by the subsidized repertory scheme in Germany, she returned to fund the 1894 season at the Avenue Theatre, London, which included Shaw's *Arms and the Man*.

Horniman's most famous venture was financing the purchase of the ABBEY THEATRE in Dublin in 1904 and turning its management over to W. B. YEATS, whom she respected, and Augusta GREGORY, with whom she had a strained relationship. Horniman was often at odds with the company members and withdrew her patronage when they did not close on the day of King Edward VII's funeral in 1910.

In 1907 Horniman bought and renovated the Gaiety Theatre, Manchester, which became an inspiration for repertory theatres in Birmingham, Liverpool, and elsewhere. During her ten years as manager she produced 200 plays, many of them new works by local authors. Sybil Thorndike was a member of the company and married its director Lewis Casson. The Gaiety was not financially successful, however, and disbanded in 1917.

hotel. **Hôtel de Bourgogne, Théâtre de l'** The first permanent public theatre in Paris. Many of the most famous plays of the 17th century were produced there, including those of RACINE and CORNEILLE.

The theatre was constructed by the CONFRÉRIE DE LA PASSION in 1548 on the ruins of the former palace of the Dukes of Burgundy. It accommodated about 1000 people in its long and narrow space: a platform stage occupied one end, while a smaller upper stage was used to operate mechanical devices. There was a large pit for standing playgoers, with tiers of benches behind and boxes at the side. Performances, lit by candles, were presented in MULTIPLE SETTING.

Forbidden to perform religious plays and unable to survive on farces and romances, the Confrérie had to hire the theatre out to travelling troupes from France and Italy. In the early 17th century Valleran-Lecomte's company made the venue the best in Paris, a position that remained unchallenged until 1634 when the Théâtre du Marais opened. In 1647 the Hôtel de Bourgogne expanded its stage, added a front curtain, and copied the seating arrangements of the Marais.

More competition arrived in 1658 when MOLIÈRE became a favourite of Louis XIV and occupied the SALLE DU PETIT-BOURBON, moving two years later to the Palais-Royal. In 1665 he quarrelled with Racine for letting the Hôtel de Bourgogne company produce the latter's ALEXANDRE LE GRAND a fortnight after it had opened at the Palais-Royal.

In 1680 the companies of the Hôtel de Bourgogne and the Théâtre du Marais troupe merged to create the COMÉDIE-FRANÇAISE. The venue was later used by the COMÉDIE-ITALIENNE from 1680 to 1783.

Hotel Paradiso A farce by Georges FEYDEAU that opened in 1894 in Paris. It was not performed in London until 1956, when an adaptation by Peter Glenville, with Alec Guinness as Boniface, was the last important production at the Winter Garden Theatre before its demolition in 1965.

The builder Boniface makes an assignation at the infamous Hotel Paradiso with Marcelle, the frustrated wife of his architect friend Cot. Meanwhile Boniface's maid is after his nephew, and a friend arrives in Paris with his four daughters. Unfortunately, the friend's family stay at Hotel Paradiso the same night as Boniface and Marcelle, the maid and nephew, and even Cot himself who has been called to check the noisy plumbing. Rooms get mixed unintentionally and names intentionally, but the resulting embarrassments are smoothed over in the end.

hot spot, the An area of the stage that has just seen great acting. According to Laurence Olivier, other actors in the scene should avoid this space at all costs. "It's too hot," he once told actor Robert Lang. "The audience has used up this spot. Try somewhere else."

Houdini, Harry (Erik Weiz; 1874–1926) The world's most celebrated illusionist and escapologist. Born in Budapest of Jewish parents, who emigrated to New York, he began his career as a magician in 1890 but world fame began with his appearance in London in 1900. No lock could hold him, even that of the condemned cell at Washington gaol. He escaped from handcuffs, ropes, safes, etc., and was deservedly called the **Great Houdini** and the **Handcuff King**. He died from a punch in the stomach, delivered before he had tensed his muscles.

house. **house curtain** *See* CURTAIN.

housekeeper *See* SHARER.

houselights The lighting that illuminates the auditorium, rather than the stage. The houselights are turned on for the audience before and after the performance and during intervals.

House of Bernarda Alba, The A tragedy by GARCÍA LORCA, written in 1936 (the year of his death) and first performed in 1945 in Madrid, then in New York in 1951. The final part of a trilogy that also includes BLOOD WEDDING (1933) and YERMA (1934), *The House of Bernarda Alba* is widely considered to be the writer's best work.

The play is set in a Spanish village where Bernarda Alba, her insane mother, and her five daughters struggle to cope after the death of Bernarda's husband. The oldest daughter, Angustias, receives a marriage proposal, which causes jealousy among her sisters. The youngest, Adela, has an affair with Angustias's fiancé and commits suicide after her mother pretends to have him murdered.

House of Ostrovsky A former nickname for the Maly ('Little') Theatre, the oldest surviving theatre in Moscow. A statue of the playwright Alexander OSTROVSKY stands in the entrance. Between 1854 and 1885 he supervised the premieres of all his plays there, achieving great popular success. In 1885 Ostrovsky was named artistic director of the Moscow Imperial Theatres.

The Maly had opened in 1824 as the city's only state theatre for drama, becoming the home for a company founded in 1806. It was soon acclaimed for its productions of the classics, such as Shakespeare, and of the works of contemporary Russian dramatists, such as Gogol's *The Government Inspector*. The theatre survived the revolution and the transition to communism; in 1926 it premiered *Lyubov Yarovaya* by Konstantin Trenev (1884–1945).

House on Fire A play produced in Rome during the reign of NERO (54–68 AD), which combined drama with the era's love of spectacle. During one scene, a house filled with valuable furniture and other items was set on fire and the actors allowed to keep any piece they dared to rescue. Ironically, much of the city itself was destroyed in 64 AD by a fire allegedly started by the emperor, who is also said to have recited poetry and played his lyre while enjoying the spectacle.

To bring the house down To cause rapturous applause or uproarious laughter in a theatre.

How the Other Half Loves A comedy by Alan AYCKBOURN, first performed in 1969 at the STEPHEN JOSEPH THEATRE IN THE ROUND, Scarborough, where Ayckbourn is artistic director. In 1970 it transferred to the Lyric Theatre, London, and ran for two years with Robert Morley as Frank Foster. Morley subsequently toured with it in Canada and Australia.

The play has a complicated setting that works surprisingly well. Conversations taking place in two households are presented on the same split set: in one scene, two dinner parties occurring on separate nights are portrayed at the same time, with the main characters moving in swivel chairs back and forth between them. Frank Foster invites his employee Bob Phillips and his wife Teresa over for dinner, unaware that Bob is having an affair with his own wife Fiona; the following evening, Bob and Teresa have dinner with the company accountant and his wife. Ayckbourn said of this scene: "People will play any game you want in the theatre providing you set the rules out clearly."

huaju (Chin. talking drama) The Chinese term for Western-style dialogue plays. *Huaju* works were first performed in China in 1907. There was a resistance to translating Western works into the vernacular rather than classical language until the students' Literary Revolution of 1911; from 1915 to 1919 the Chinese were keenly translating and reading Western novelists and playwrights, especially Henrik Ibsen, who had set a powerful precedent by using the stage as a platform for social protest.

By the 1930s Chinese dramatists were imitating Western realism. A major breakthrough came in 1935 with Cao Yu's work *Leiyu*, which tackled modern social issues. It toured with a Western-style travelling repertory company that also performed Oscar Wilde's *Lady Windermere's Fan* as adapted by Hong Shen.

After World War II, *huaju* was reorganized by the communists. In 1950 the Central Drama Institute was opened in Peking to train actors, directors, and set designers for *huaju* with the aid of Russian advisers and teachers. During the Cultural Revolution of 1966 to 1976, however, all *huaju* works staged since 1949 were denounced and the companies and drama schools were closed. Since 1976 *huaju* has enjoyed a great renaissance: classical and modern plays have been presented from the Western repertoire, including a successful production of Arthur Miller's *Death of a Salesman* in 1983, directed by Miller himself and the actor Ying Ruocheng, who translated it.

hubris In classical Greek tragedy, the excess of pride and ambition that leads to the inevitable downfall and ruin of the protagonist. The drama presents this consequence as justified because the flawed hero has offended the gods.

Hugo, Victor (Marie) (1802–85) French dramatist, novelist, and poet who in 1830 was called "the most powerful mind of the romantic movement". His early success came in drama, and he used the stage as a platform for his social and political ideas.

Hugo published his forceful verse-drama *Cromwell* in 1824. Three years later, he added a provocative preface supporting the claims of romantic drama as against the French classical tradition and calling for works that combined tragedy and comedy in the free style of Shakespeare. The controversial HERNANI, presented at the Comédie-Française in 1830, marked the beginning of a prolific period of playwriting, which was partly inspired by his love for the actress Juliette Drouet. Their affair began in 1833; she eventually left the stage and became his intimate companion until her death in 1883.

Hugo's other works included the verse-drama *Le Roi s'amuse* (1832), which was banned from the French stage but subsequently used by Verdi as the libretto for *Rigoletto*, and the prose plays *Lucrèce Borgia* (1833) and *Marie Tudor* (1833). The failure of *Les Burgraves* (1843), together with the advent of realism in the mid 19th century, brought the romantic experiment to an end.

Owing to his opposition to the government, Hugo spent the years from 1851 to 1870 in exile, first in Brussels and then on the Channel Islands of Jersey and Guernsey. During his exile he wrote a few plays and the epic novel *Les Misérables* (1862), which returned to the stage as a highly successful musical more than a century later, in 1986. He returned to Paris after the proclamation of the Third Republic and died in 1885. He was buried in the Panthéon after being driven there, at his own request, in a poor man's hearse.

Human Billiard Table *See* JUGGLER.

hunger artist A sideshow performer who fasted publicly. Such acts were popular from the late 19th century until after World War II.

In 1880 Dr Henry Tanner, an American, fasted for 40 days to win a bet. Giacomo Succi was a popular hunger artist in Italy at the turn of the century, but the record of 47 days without food was established in 1926 by Ventego. The act was popular in Germany between the wars; it began to lose its appeal when political protesters began fasting in India and elsewhere. The problem of world hunger finally turned people against the use of starvation as a source of entertainment.

Related to the hunger artist was the sideshow performer billed as a **living skeleton**. In the 1820s the French living skeleton Claude Seurat kept thin by consuming a little wine and one roll each day; his skeleton stood clearly out and his heart could be seen beating.

Hurlo-Thrumbo A BURLESQUE by Samuel Johnson (1691–1773), a half-mad dancing master, which enjoyed an extraordinary run at the Haymarket Theatre from 1729 to 1730. So great was its popularity that a club called 'The Hurlo-Thrumbo Society' was formed. Johnson put this motto on the title-page when the burlesque was printed:

> Ye sons of fire, read my *Hurlo-Thrumbo*,
> Turn it betwixt your finger and your thumbo,
> And being quite undone, be quite struck dumbo.

Hushabye, Hector A character in the play HEARTBREAK HOUSE by George Bernard Shaw. A rogue and a liar notorious for his womanizing, Hushabye was largely based on Hubert Bland (1856–1914), a brush manufacturer and member of the Fabian Society. Bland was widely known for his profligacy, which continued long after his marriage to the writer Edith Nesbit. Although he professed highly moral views in public, he divided his time between his wife and another woman; he later took Edith's best friend as another mistress, persuading both to live in the same house with him. At one time both women were pregnant by him; all their children were looked after by Edith as though they were her own. Edith, meanwhile, had conceived a deep passion for Shaw, although the affair was never consummated.

I

Ibsen, Henrik (1828–1906) Norwegian dramatist and poet, who has been called the father of 20th-century drama. In his mature works Ibsen used naturalistic settings and dialogue to expose the corruption and hypocrisy of middle-class life. His work is valued for its technical mastery, penetrating psychological insight, and profound symbolism.

Ibsen was the son of a businessman, whose bankruptcy caused his family considerable social embarrassment. He left home at 15 to work as a chemist's assistant; an affair with an older woman at this time ended with the birth of a son. Ibsen secretly supported them both for the remainder of his life. By the age of 36, Ibsen was considerably in debt and subject to fits of depression. With the help of his friends, however, he paid off his debts and decided to move to Rome. He remained abroad, in Italy and Germany for 27 years.

His first play, the romantic *Catilina* (1850), written under the pseudonym of Brynjolf Bjarme, was followed by several historical dramas in verse; these included *The Burial Mound* (1854) and *The Feast of Solhoug* (1856), inspired by Norwegian folk songs. His most impressive works were written after he left Norway. The verse comedy PEER GYNT (1867), a portrait of the author as an undisciplined and unprincipled young man, established his international reputation. In 1871 Ibsen began the play that he considered his greatest work, *Emperor and Galilean* (1876), a 10-act 'double drama' based on the life of Julian the Apostate. It has seldom been revived.

The first of his four social plays, the works that represent the essence of IBSENISM, was PILLARS OF SOCIETY (1877). This was followed by A DOLL'S HOUSE (1897), which remains the most widely performed of his works, GHOSTS (1882), which uses venereal disease as a symbol of the guilt of a corrupt society, and AN ENEMY OF THE PEOPLE (1882). HEDDA GABLER (1890) explores the isolation of the individual, while THE MASTER BUILDER (1892) focuses on the psychology of the artist.

When Ibsen returned to Norway for good in 1891, it was as a world-famous author. A stroke in 1900 left him helpless for the remainder of his life.

Ibsenism A concern in drama with social problems, realistically rather than romantically treated, as in the works of Henrik IBSEN, whose plays, translated by William Archer and championed by George Bernard SHAW, infused new vigour into English drama.

Iceman Cometh, The A naturalistic tragedy by the US dramatist Eugene O'NEILL. Though written in 1939 the play remained unperformed until a New York production in 1946. The play, which has a cast of 19 and runs for around five hours, is one of O'Neill's most ponderous works.

Set in 1912 in Harry Hope's saloon bar, the play presents a group of down-at-heel alcoholics who indulge in nihilistic conversation about the failure of their dreams. The Iceman of the play's title, whose arrival is anticipated by the drinkers, is used as a symbol of death.

A 1956 off-Broadway production of the play made a star of the actor Jason Robards in the role of Hickey, a salesman. However, when nearly 30 years later Robards attempted to recreate the role on Broadway the production proved a failure. During a 1976 production of the play the actor Ian Holm developed such awful stage fright that he did not return to theatrical work until Harold Pinter's *Moonlight* in 1993.

Ideal Husband, An A comedy by Oscar WILDE, first performed in London in 1895 at the Haymarket Theatre. Charles HAWTREY created the part of Lord Goring and Charles Brookfield played his valet; both actors later testified against Wilde at his trial and held a celebration dinner when he was sentenced.

The play begins at a London party attended by the adventuress Mrs Cheveley. When the host, Sir Robert Chiltern, denounces the Argentine Canal Company as a swindle, she tries to blackmail him. However, when a brooch is later found to be missing, Lady Chiltern informs her husband that Mrs Cheveley was expelled from school for theft. Mrs Cheveley then tries to blackmail Lady Chiltern but is foiled. Sir Robert denounces the canal in Parliament and wins a Cabinet post.

idiot. idiot cards In America, the name given to large cards held up in the wings of a theatre to give a comedian on stage the cue for his next joke.

the Inspired Idiot The name the British writer Horace Walpole (1717–97) gave to the poet, dramatist, and novelist Oliver GOLDSMITH.

Iffland, August Wilhelm (1759–1814) German actor, dramatist, and director. Originally destined for the Church, Iffland began his acting career (in the face of strong parental opposition) under Konrad EKHOF at Gotha in 1777. Following Ekhof's death a year later the Gotha company transferred en masse to the newly opened National Theatre at Mannheim, where Iffland rose to a position of considerable influence.

Although his forte was sophisticated comedy, Iffland attracted much praise for his creation of Franz Moor in Schiller's DIE RÄUBER (1781). It was also at Mannheim that Iffland's own plays, sentimental melodramas that are now largely forgotten, were first produced to great acclaim.

Iffland remained at Mannheim until 1798, when he was appointed director of the Berlin National Theatre; in 1811 he became director-general of all royal theatres in Prussia.

I Have Been Here Before A play by J. B. PRIESTLEY, first produced in 1937 in London. Published with TIME AND THE CONWAYS as *Two Time Plays*, it deals with the metaphysical concepts of recurring and spiral time. The plot hinges upon the arrival of a strange German guest, Dr Görtler, at the Black Bull Inn in north Yorkshire. His theories of 'eternal recurrence' disturb the guests, who include the headmaster Oliver Farrant, the tycoon Walter Ormund, and his unhappy wife Janet. She and Oliver are in love, but Görtler persuades them to abandon their hopes of a future together by revealing that he has had a dream in which Walter commits suicide. Janet decides to remain with Walter, but he, invigorated by Görtler's theories, tells her to leave with Farrant so that he can begin a new life.

"ill Beest, an" A contemporary's description of the person who, in 1652, betrayed actors who were performing illegally at the Vere Street Theatre during the Puritan INTERREGNUM. According to the writer the "ill Beest" informed on the group "causing the poor actors to be routed by the soldiery". William Beeston (*see* THE BEESTONS) was suspected of being the Beest despite being imprisoned himself.

Imperial Theatre. Imperial Theatre, London A former theatre in Tothill Street, Westminster, which opened in 1876 as the Royal Aquarium Theatre (part of the Royal Aquarium Summer and Winter Garden complex). In 1878 Samuel Phelps made his farewell appearance there as Cardinal Wolsey in *Henry VIII*. That same year Marie Litton took over its management, changing the name to the Imperial in 1879.

In 1901 Lillie LANGTRY leased the theatre, redecorated it, and installed electricity; the venue reopened with *A Royal Necklace*, in which Langtry played the dual roles of Marie Antoinette and Mlle Olivia. In 1903 Ellen Terry (*see* TERRY FAMILY) took over the theatre but achieved little success with either Ibsen's *The Vikings at Helgeland*, in which she played the untypical role of a terrifying warrior mother, or *Much Ado About Nothing*, in which she played Beatrice. The final offering at the Imperial was Dix and Sutherland's *Boy O'Carrol* in 1906. The interior was then used for the Imperial Palace cinema in Canning Town, which was destroyed by fire in 1931.

Imperial Theatre, New York A large theatre on West 45th Street, between Broadway and Eighth Avenue, which opened in 1923. With its capacity of 1452 seats, it has been home to a string of highly successful musicals, including *Annie Get Your Gun* (1946), which ran for 1147 performances, *Call Me Madam* (1950), *Carnival* (1961), *Oliver!* (1963), *Fiddler on the Roof* (1964), *Zorba* (1968), *They're Playing Our Song* (1979), and *Chess* (1988).

Importance of Being Earnest, The Oscar WILDE's self-proclaimed "trivial comedy for serious people", first produced in London in 1895 at the St James's Theatre. Its many revivals include the 1943 production with

Edith Evans (as Lady Bracknell), John Gielgud, Peggy Ashcroft, and Cyril Richard.

In the play, Algernon Moncrieff poses as Jack Worthing's fictitious brother, Ernest, in order to court Jack's ward. Visiting them is Lady Bracknell, who opposes Jack's marriage to her daughter because of his uncertain lineage (he was found in a handbag in Victoria Station). His parentage is proven to be respectable, and both he and Algernon win their loves.

Wilde and his producer, Sir George Alexander, manager at St James's, once argued for almost an hour about trimming the original four-act version to three. Wilde finally relented with one last shot at Alexander:

> "The scene that you feel is superfluous cost me terrible exhausting labour and heart-rending strain. You may not believe me, but I assure you on my honour that it must have taken fully five minutes to write."

This brilliant comedy of manners did not delight everyone. George Bernard SHAW, as drama critic for *The Saturday Review*, noted:

> "I cannot say that I cared greatly for *The Importance of Being Earnest*...it leaves me with a sense of having wasted my evening."

impresario A person who organizes and presents theatrical entertainments, especially musical productions. An impresario is often a manager of a theatre or production company and may be a financial backer or ANGEL.

Famous impresarios have included the 19th-century American P. T. BARNUM and, in the British theatre, the brothers Prince Littler (1901–73) and Emile Littler (1903–), who staged numerous pantomimes and US musicals after World War II. They eventually owned nearly half the West End theatres. Another formidable impresario was their contemporary Binkie Beaumont who, as co-founder and managing director of H. M. Tennent Ltd, once had 14 productions running simultaneously in London.

Impromptu de Versailles, L' (*The Rehearsal at Versailles*) MOLIÈRE's second reply, presented in October 1663, to the criticism levelled at his *L'Ecole des Femmes*, which had opened in Paris the previous year (*see* THE SCHOOL FOR WIVES). His first response to the outcry against his play about raising girls to be perfect wives, LA CRITIQUE DE L'ÉCOLE DES FEMMES, was staged in June 1663.

L'Impromptu de Versailles was also part of Molière's running literary battle with Edmé Boursault, the resident playwright at the HÔTEL DE BOURGOGNE. Boursault had been offended by a supposed caricature of himself in *La Critique de l'Ecole des Femmes* and had responded with an attack on Molière in *Le Portrait du peintre* (1663). Molière's *L'Impromptu de Versailles* ridiculed both Boursault and the actors of the rival Hôtel de Bourgogne for their declamatory style of acting. It also reveals much about Molière's own ideas about acting and how he rehearsed his casts. The two dramatists later became friends.

Inadmissible Evidence A play by John OSBORNE, first performed in 1964 at the Royal Court Theatre in London. Nicol Williamson created the character of Bill Maitland, one of the theatre's most testing roles. The character has a number of long monologues about estrangement and isolation, both personal and professional.

The plot concerns the solicitor Bill Maitland who, despite leaving school at 15, has risen to the top of his legal practice. Now, almost 40, he is a bitter alcoholic whose relationships with his wife, his teenage daughter, and his mistress, are all failing. Professionally, he is ostracized by his colleagues for malpractice. His secretary and former mistress walks out, and Maitland pursues another secretary, who also rejects him. Nevertheless, he is sustained throughout his ordeal by the compassion he continues to feel for his clients.

Inchbald, Elizabeth (1753–1821) British playwright, actress, and novelist, who also edited several collections of English tragedies and comedies. Born Elizabeth Simpson, she left home at 18 to become an actress, despite suffering from a speech impediment. She married the actor Joseph Inchbald in 1772 and appeared with him in the provinces until his death in 1779.

She subsequently performed regularly at Covent Garden before retiring to write her own plays, mostly sentimental comedies and successful adaptations from French or German works. *A Mogul Tale, or Descent of the Balloon*, produced in 1784 at the Haymarket, was followed a year later by her most successful play, *I'll Tell You What*. Later offerings included *Wives as They Were, and Maids as They Are* (1797) and her last comedy, *To Marry or Not Marry* (1805).

She also wrote romantic novels. Charles Lamb once referred to Inchbald and Letitia Barbauld as his "two bald authoresses".

incidental music Music that is specifically written for a play but does not form an integral part of the work. Incidental music is often used to create mood or atmosphere. It is clear that Shakespeare sometimes used incidental music at the begining or end of a scene; for example, *Twelfth Night* begins with the line "If music be the food of love, play on" and at the close of *Much Ado About Nothing* Benedick calls "Strike up, pipers."

Some of the world's leading composers have contributed incidental music to drama, including Beethoven, Mendelssohn, Bizet, Tchaikovsky, Grieg, Debussy, Delius, Vaughan Williams, Elgar, and Britten.

Inge, William (1913–73) US playwright. He began his career as a theatre critic in 1943 and seven years later enjoyed his first Broadway hit with *Come Back, Little Sheba* (1950), which tells of the life of a lonely housewife. It opened two years later in London. Inge won a Pulitzer Prize in 1953 for his next offering, *Picnic*, about a small-town girl's seduction by a middle-aged drifter. He also won acclaim for *Bus Stop* in 1955 and *The Dark at the Top of the Stairs* (1957). All four works became popular films. His later less successful plays included *A Loss of Roses* (1959), *Natural Affection* (1962), and *Where's Daddy?* (1966).

In Good King Charles's Golden Days The last full-length play by George Bernard SHAW. First performed in 1939 at the MALVERN FESTIVAL, where Shaw was patron-in-chief, it relies on dialogue, having almost no action. Subtitled *A True History that Never Happened*, the play presents imaginary conversations between such historical figures as King Charles II, Sir Isaac Newton, George Fox (the founder of the Society of Friends), and the actress Nell Gwynn. The title comes from the opening lines of the 18th-century English song, *The Vicar of Bray*:

> In Good King Charles's golden days,
> When loyalty no harm meant...

inner stage A feature of the Elizabethan stage that was used to conceal actors who were then revealed at a certain point during the play. There is disagreement as to how such a DISCOVERY SPACE was designed, but it was probably an alcove covered by a curtain or a small structure projecting onto the stage.

inns Inn-yards were often used as theatres by strolling players in 16th-century Europe. The first recorded use of a galleried inn-yard for this purpose was in Malaga, Spain, in 1520 (*see* CORRALES DE COMEDIAS). The practice brought extra business to the inns, but often the performers were only paid by taking up a collection (known as BOTTLING). English inn-yards were well suited to hold a raised trestle stage: spectators could watch from the first-floor walkways, balconies, and the yard, some sitting on the acting area. All these features were adapted by James Burbage (*see* BURBAGE FAMILY) for England's first public playhouse, the THEATRE.

The first recorded performances at London inns were in 1557 at the Saracen's Head, Islington and the Boar's Head near Aldgate where a 'lewd' play, *A Sack Full of News*, was suppressed and the actors arrested. Within the City of London, the Queen's Men performed at the Bell in Gracechurch (then Gracious) Street and at the Bull in Bishopsgate, which began hosting drama before 1575 and continued for more than two decades. STRANGE'S MEN played at the Cross Keys Inn, also in Gracechurch Street, which served as a venue from before 1579 until about 1596. The Bel Savage on Ludgate Hill regularly presented plays from 1579 to 1588. Some inns were converted into permanent theatres, such as the Boar's Head near Aldgate, adapted in 1597–99, and the Red Bull in Clerkenwell, adapted in 1605.

Insect Play, The A comedy by the Czech brothers Karel and Josef ČAPEK. The allegorical fantasy, influenced by expressionism, satirized greed, social regimentation, and man's attempts to come to terms with life and death. It was first performed in 1921 in Prague and became the brothers' best-known work, opening two years later in London and in 1948 in New York (as *The Insect Comedy*). It has also been seen as *The Life of Insects*, *And So Ad Infinitum*, and *The World We Live In*.

In the story, a drunken tramp wakes to find a lepidopterist chasing butterflies because of his "great love of nature". The tramp, curious about the insects around him, is suddenly shrunk to their size and finds that they have recognizably human personalities. A beetle couple roll around their ball of dung for which they have "saved, scraped, toiled, and moiled", but another beetle steals it. The disgusted tramp pledges to sacrifice everything for the good of the State but then sees the well-regimented ants fighting amongst themselves until one proclaims himself leader. The tramp, convinced that he has become wise about the world, weakens and dies. A woman with a newborn baby stops and places a flower upon his body.

inset A small piece of scenery placed inside a larger one to allow a rapid change of set.

Inspector Calls, An A play by J. B. PRIESTLEY. It was first performed in 1946 at the New Theatre, London, starring Ralph Richardson, Alec Guinness, and Margaret Leighton with the Old Vic company. There was a much admired revival at the Aldwych Theatre in 1993–94.

A happy engagement party at the home of the prosperous Birling family is interrupted by the arrival of a mysterious Inspector Goole. The family clock stops as he announces that he is investigating a young girl's suicide. It transpires that each member of the family has contributed to the girl's tragedy, and all react in a hostile and guilty way. As he leaves, the Inspector reminds them:

> "We don't live alone. We are members of one body. We are responsible for each other."

The clock starts working again as the family checks with the local police to find that the inspector is unknown; consequently they return to their celebrations, assuming that they have been the victims of a hoax. The telephone then rings to inform them that an inspector is about to call to interview them about a suicide.

Not all critics liked the play. J. C. Trewin of the *Observer* wrote "we feel that the Birlings are hardly worth this elaboration, this prolonged rattling of skeletons (and, indeed, this high place in the Old Vic's repertory)." Lionel Hale of the *Daily Mail* called it "a pitiful play" and wondered who the inspector was and if the dead girl ever existed, adding, "The theatre hates indecision. Mr Priestley, not making up his own mind, does not persuade ours."

interlude A brief and usually comic dramatic piece in 15th- and 16th-century England. It represents a transitional form between medieval English theatre and the Elizabethan drama. Often performed at banquets, it was similar to the Italian INTERMEZZO and the Spanish ENTREMÉ. Such sketches were first performed in England by the Players of the King's Interludes (*Lusores Regis*) at the court of Henry VII. In the hands of its main exponent, John Heywood (1497–1580), the genre developed into a shorter piece performed between the acts of a full-length play. Heywood's most famous interlude was *The Four P's* (1520). The form disappeared entirely during the reign of Elizabeth I.

intermezzo In Italian drama, a brief and usually comic piece performed in the 15th and 16th centuries at banquets or between the acts of a full-length play or opera. The *intermezzo* was similar to the English INTERLUDE and Spanish ENTREMÉ. Its themes were often taken from mythology or classical history.

international. International Theatre Institute *See* ITI.

International Centre of Theatre Research An organization founded in Paris in 1970 by the directors Peter BROOK and Jean-Louis BARRAULT. The original aim of the project was to provide a point of contact between performers from different nations and diverse theatrical disciplines, and from this basis to work towards an "international theatre language". In 1972 the company performed *Orghast*, a play written in an invented language by Ted Hughes, at Persepolis, a ruined city in Iran. Two years later the organization moved from its original base in a disused tapestry factory to the Théâtre des Bouffes du Nord, a dilapidated former music hall in Paris. The venue is now established as one of the foremost centres of experimental drama in France.

The company also tours widely and has presented works in America, Australia, India, and Africa, where the actors performed improvisations in remote Saharan villages. The organization's most audacious production to date, however, is its 1985 staging of the nine-hour Indian epic THE MAHABHARATA, originally in a quarry near Avignon and subsequently at venues across Europe.

International Federation for Theatre Research An international theatre organization established in London in 1955 under the auspices of the British Society for Theatre Research. The Federation is dedicated to studying both traditional and contemporary theatre in its member countries, of which there are at present 34: to this end it assists in the coordination of national research organizations and publishes a periodical. It also manages an international institute for theatre research in the Casa Goldoni in Venice, in which summer schools and other courses are held.

Interregnum, the In the English theatre, the 18-year period from 1642 during which all public playhouses were closed by the Puritans. They reopened on the coronation of Charles II (1660).

As early as 1583 Philip Stubbes's *The Anatomie of Abuses* had given the Puritan view of the theatre as inducing "whoredom and uncleanness". The playhouses had already suffered closures due to outbreaks of the plague in 1625, 1630, and 1637, when, on 2 September 1642, Parliament published its *First Ordinance Against Stage Plays and Interludes* commanding that "public stage-plays shall cease and be foreborne" on religious and moral grounds. The closure order owed much to the fact that, with few exceptions, the theatrical world supported the Royalists, making London's theatres hotbeds of intrigue against the Puritan cause. Following the order most actors and playwrights joined the army, retired, went back to earlier trades, or left the country. After the Civil War orders were given to arrest any actors found giving a performance and to fine members of the audience.

Cromwell himself was not opposed to drama as such and allowed some private and school performances. William DAVENANT was one manager who protected his livelihood by cultivating Cromwell's love of music. In 1656 he was allowed to produce *The Siege of Rhodes*, a "representation of the art of perspective in scenes and the story sung in recitative musick" using singers instead of actors. This has been called the first English opera. Davenant staged other plays with music, such as *The Cruelty of the Spaniards in Peru* (1658) and *Sir Francis Drake* (1659). Both of these were given at the Cockpit Theatre, a venue that staged many illegal productions until it was raided by soldiers in 1649. Secret performances continued to take place both in private homes and in such venues as the Fortune Theatre (until soldiers dismantled it in 1649), the Vere Street Theatre (wrecked by soldiers in 1649), and the Red Bull Theatre, where several actors, including Robert Cox and Timothy Reade, were arrested. *See also* ILL BEEST.

Iolanthe One of GILBERT AND SULLIVAN'S Savoy Operas, subtitled *The Peer and the Peri.* It was first produced in 1882 at the Savoy Theatre and ran for nearly 400 performances.

The story involves the Arcadian fairy Iolanthe, who has been banished for 25 years by the Fairy Queen for marrying a mortal and having his son, Strephon. The young man now wishes to marry Phyllis, a ward in chancery who has also attracted the Lord Chancellor's interest. After Strephon becomes a member of parliament, Iolanthe names the Lord Chancellor as her mortal lover and Strephon's father. Wings sprout on the peers, and they fly off to Fairyland.

Iolanthe was intended as a satirical attack on women in politics and on the British legal and parliamentary systems. The message was softened when Gilbert and Sullivan removed the two most biting songs, but they still managed to score a few points, as in this Westminster sentry's song:

> When in that House MPs divide,
> If they've a brain and cerebellum, too,
> They've got to leave that brain outside,
> And vote just as their leaders tell 'em to.

The Fairy Queen has sometimes been played to resemble such figures as Queen Victoria or Margaret Thatcher.

Ionesco, Eugène (1912–94) Romanian-born French dramatist who pioneered the Theatre of the ABSURD. His plays, usually one-act dramas, deal with such themes as the absurdity of existence, the alienation and impotence of man, the fear of death, and the failure of language as a means of communication.

Under the influence of the dramatist Antonin Artaud (*see* CRUELTY, THEATRE OF), Ionesco rejected the realistic and psychological theatre but continued to use Freudian ideas to explore the subconscious and dreams. His famous 'anti-play' THE BALD PRIMA DONNA (1950) explores the paradoxical relationship of language to reality, as does THE LESSON (1951); THE CHAIRS (1952) is a study in nothingness. Criticized by Kenneth TYNAN and others for his works' lack of social relevance, Ionesco made fun of critics who demand a political message in *Improvisation* (1956). He also attacked Brecht as a 'postman' delivering messages.

Ionesco's full-length plays include *Amédée, ou comment s'en débarrasser* (1954) and *Tueur sans gages* (1959), translated as *The Killer* for its 1968 London run. The latter introduced his clownish but sympathetic hero Berenger, who in this play tries to attack the dwarf Death. Berenger reappeared in RHINOCEROS (1960), which had a successful run at the Royal Court Theatre in 1963 with Laurence Olivier and Joan Plowright. Characteristically, Ionesco uses logical language to destroy logic:

JEAN You're day-dreaming.
BERENGER But I'm wide awake.
JEAN Awake or asleep, it's the same thing.
BERENGER But there is some difference.
JEAN That's not the point.

Le Roi se meurt (1962), also featuring Berenger, was seen as *Exit the King* at the Royal Court in 1963 starring Alec Guinness. Later works include *Macbett* (1972) and *Journey Among the Dead* (1982).

Ionesco, describing the difficulties in writing a play, noted, "One has to get out of bed, which is unpleasant...."

Iphigenia In classical legend, the daughter of Agamemnon and Clytemnestra. One account says that her father, having offended Artemis by killing her favourite stag, vowed to sacrifice the most beautiful thing the year brought forth; this proved to be his infant daughter. He deferred the sacrifice until the Greek fleet that was proceeding to Troy reached Aulis and Iphigenia had grown to womanhood. Then the soothsayer Calchas told him that the fleet would be becalmed until he had fulfilled his vow; accordingly, the king prepared to sacrifice his daughter. At the last moment Artemis snatched Iphigenia from the altar and carried her to Heaven, substituting a hind in her place. The story has inspired tragedies by EURIPIDES, GOETHE, and RACINE, and an opera by Gluck.

Iphigenia in Aulis A tragedy by EURIPIDES that was left incomplete at his death. It was produced posthumously with additions that are now lost. In the surviving scenes an irresolute Agamemnon prepares to sacrifice Iphigenia.

Iphigenia in Tauris A tragedy by EURIPIDES, first performed in Athens (*c.* 414 BC). The play shows Euripides's mastery of a lighter more romantic style of drama.

In it Iphigenia, a priestess of Artemis, on discovering that her brother Orestes and his friend are the intended victims of a human sacrifice, outwits a barbarian king by organizing their escape.

Iphigenie auf Tauris A play by GOETHE, first written in prose (1779) and later in verse (1786–88). The earlier version was first performed at Weimar in 1779; the later version in 1802. Although based on the tragedy by Euripides, the second version of the play incorporates Goethe's highly personal views on the redeeming power of human love.

Ireland forgeries One of the most famous of all literary forgeries. William Henry Ireland (1777–1835) was the son of a bookseller and amateur antiquarian. At the age of only 19, young Ireland produced a number of seemingly ancient leases and other documents purporting to be in Shakespeare's handwriting, including a love poem to 'Anna Hatherrawaye'. Emboldened by their acceptance, he forged manuscripts of *King Lear* and *Hamlet* and even two 'lost' Shakespeare plays – *Vortigern and Rowena* and *Henry II*.

Ignoring the suspicions of KEMBLE, SHERIDAN produced *Vortigern and Rowena* at Drury Lane in 1796. Mrs SIDDONS and Mrs Palmer walked out during rehearsals and when it came to the performance Kemble helped to ensure that the play was laughed off the stage. When he spoke the line "When this solemn mockery is o'er", the house yelled and hissed until the curtain fell. Meanwhile the critic Edmond Malone had studied the *Miscellaneous Papers*, said to be Shakespeare's, and had declared them forgeries. Ireland confessed later that same year. His motive appears to have been a craving to secure the regard and admiration of his father, whose antiquarian interests amounted to an obsession.

The forgeries (of *Vortigern and Rowena* and *Henry II*) can now be seen in the British Museum. *See also* SHAKESPEAREANA.

iris An adjustable circular shutter of overlapping leaves used in spotlights to vary the diameter of the beam; it is also used in cameras and other optical instruments to vary the diameter of an aperture.

Iron, the Nickname of the first theatrical safety or fireproof CURTAIN, installed at Drury Lane in 1794.

Irons, Jeremy (1948–) British stage, television, and film actor. He began his career with the Bristol Old Vic company in 1966, appearing in such plays as Noël Coward's *Hay Fever* and Joe Orton's *What the Butler Saw*. After appearing in the musical *Godspell* from 1971–73 at the Round House in London, he played Don Pedro in a Young Vic production of *Much Ado About Nothing* and Mick in Pinter's *The Caretaker*, both in 1974. The following year he played Petruchio in *The Taming of the Shrew* at the Round House. In America he appeared in the Broadway production of Tom Stoppard's *The Real Thing* (1983) and later played Hamlet at the Globe Theatre in Utah. In 1986 he took leading Shakespearean roles at Stratford-upon-Avon and at the Mermaid Theatre, London.

Irons has starred on television in the award-winning *Brideshead Revisited* and in such films as *The French Lieutenant's Woman* (1981), *The Mission* (1985), and *Damage* (1992). He is married to the actress Sinead Cusack (1948–).

Irving, Sir Henry (John Henry Brodribb; 1838–1905) British actor who managed the Lyceum Theatre for 30 years and whose magnetic personality and mesmeric style of acting made him the greatest classical actor of the latter 19th century. Sarah Bernhardt, however, thought him "a mediocre actor but a great artist". He was knighted in 1895, the first actor to be so honoured.

The young Irving's desire to act was so strong that he cured his stammer with elocution lessons and swam in the Thames each morning to build up his lung-power. He made his professional debut in 1856 at the Lyceum Theatre, Sunderland, and spent the next seven years touring before making a successful London debut with the comedy *The Belle's Stratagem* in 1866. After captivating London as Mathias in THE BELLS (1871) he entered theatrical history in 1874 by creating a Hamlet of unprecedented tenderness; the play ran for a record 200 performances.

Four years later he acquired the lease of the Lyceum and engaged Ellen Terry (*see* TERRY FAMILY) as his leading lady for such productions as *The Merchant of Venice* (1879) and *Romeo and Juliet* (1882). In 1883 Irving took the Lyceum Company to America and during the next 18 years toured America six more times. Despite multiple successes at the Lyceum, Irving tended to overspend on special effects and in 1899 he had to give up sole ownership of the theatre. In 1902 Ellen Terry rejoined him for the Lyceum's final production, *The Merchant of Venice*, after which it became a music hall.

Irving collapsed and died in 1905 after performing *Becket* in Bradford. When his ashes were buried in Westminster Abbey, the ceremony was boycotted by George Bernard SHAW, who had never been able to convince Irving to stage his plays. "Irving would turn in his coffin if I came," said Shaw, "just as Shakespeare will turn in his coffin when Irving comes."

Isle of Dogs, The A comedy by Ben JONSON and Thomas Nashe, first performed in 1597 by Pembroke's Men at the Swan Theatre. The work, now lost, led to a temporary closure of the theatre and the imprisonment of the two authors and several others on charges of producing a "seditious comedy".

Italian night scenes An English dumb show (*see* MIME) that evolved into the HARLEQUINADE. Deriving from the COMMEDIA DELL'ARTE, it was brought to England from France in 1702 by John Weaver, who was the first to put the dances into a sequential story. Plays such as *Harlequin Jack Sheppard* featured HARLEQUIN in an English setting and made much use of TRICKWORK. John Rich (*see* RICH FAMILY) began his career performing in the Italian night scenes as Harlequin under the stage name of *Lun*.

ITI International Theatre Institute. An international theatrical organization, now based in Paris. It operates under the aegis of the United Nations Educational, Scientific, and Cultural Organization (UNESCO), which provides a yearly subsidy. ITI works through its 50 national centres to promote contracts between theatre workers in different countries and the exchange of information on specific problems, trends, and developments in the theatre.

The Institute was founded in 1948 in Prague as a branch of UNESCO. From 1950 until 1968 it published *World Theatre*, a quarterly illustrated journal, and from 1955 it sponsored an annual festival, the Théâtre des Nations. ITI also holds a world congress every two years and sponsors conferences and seminars on topics such as the training of actors and theatre architecture.

The individual centres provide information and research facilities. The British centre, one of the first national ITI groups established, is a clearing house for information on the British theatre. The US centre is housed in the Anta Theatre, New York.

It's All in the Family *See* BANKRUPT, THE.

Ivanov The first full-length play by Anton CHEKHOV, first performed in Moscow in 1887. The gloomy work opened to a decidedly mixed response, partly because the audience was expecting a light comedy in the vein of Chekhov's earlier humorous sketches and partly because only two of the cast knew their parts. It was revived with some success in 1889 at the Alexandrinsky Theatre in St Petersburg. The most celebrated British revival was in 1965 with John Gielgud (who also directed) and Claire Bloom.

Ivanov illustrates Chekhov's idea of himself as an "impartial witness", an aspiration that set him apart from his literary contemporaries. "I am not a Liberal, not a Conservative," he stated, "I should like to be a free artist." Ivanov is an extreme version of the neurotic anti-hero who appears in some form in all of Chekhov's serious plays. The character is a bored and melancholy intellectual, uncommitted and guilt-ridden, lost in endless reveries like Hamlet. Just before Ivanov is to marry Sasha, the young girl who has waited patiently for the death of his wife, he backs out. Before his suicide, he explains:

> I wander about among my friends like a shadow, and I don't know who I am or why I live or what I want.

Chekhov was upset at the audience's failure to understand that the ineffectual Ivanov was meant to show them the futility of their dreams. This was a theme that Chekhov was to develop further in his mature works.

J

Jack. Jack-in-the-Green A character in early English FOLK THEATRE; he probably originated as a fertility symbol in pre-Christian rituals. He took part in MAY DAY festivities and may have been a model for Robin Hood in the May Day play of that name. *See* GREEN MAN; JONKONNU; ROBIN HOOD PLAY.

jack-knife stage A method of staging that involves the use of platforms, or rostra, which pivot on castor wheels at one corner. In a **segment stage** these platforms are wedge-shaped and pivot on the upstage apex.

Jack Sprat A ten-inch-tall Amazona viridigena parrot who appeared in more than 1000 performances of *Treasure Island* in the 1950s and 1960s perched on the shoulders of six successive Long John Silvers. According to Sir Bernard Miles (1907–91), who played Long John each Christmas at the MERMAID THEATRE, the bird "travelled hundreds of miles with us on tour as a bona fide member of the cast". Jack Sprat eventually became the resident parrot in Miles's office.

Jack and the Beanstalk A nursery tale found among many peoples in varying forms: it is a favourite subject for English PANTOMIME. In the English version of the story Jack stupidly exchanges his poor mother's cow for a handful of beans. However, the beans, discarded in disgust by the mother, miraculously sprout overnight producing stalks reaching up to the sky. Clambering up the stalks, the intrepid Jack steals treasures from the giant's castle at the top of the beanstalk – a bag of gold, a wonderful lamp, and a hen that lays golden eggs. In the pantomime version, a young woman usually plays the part of Jack and a male comedian the role of his mother.

Jackson, Glenda (1936–) British actress, who has played many classic and contemporary roles on the stage and in films. The daughter of a bricklayer and a cleaning lady, she worked in a shop before taking elocution and fencing lessons at night and being accepted into the Royal Academy of Dramatic Art (*see* RADA). However, Jackson recalled, after graduating, "I spent the first ten years mainly out of work." She made her debut in London in 1957 at the Arts Theatre Club in *All Kinds of Men*, before appearing in the West End in Bill Naughton's *Alfie* (1963).

In 1964 Jackson joined the Royal Shakespeare Company and appeared in their celebrated Theatre of CRUELTY season, giving a highly praised performance as Charlotte Corday in Peter BROOK's production of Weiss's MARAT/SADE in London and on Broadway. In 1967 she played Masha in Chekhov's *Three Sisters* at the Royal Court Theatre and in 1975 toured Britain, America, and Australia in the title role of Ibsen's *Hedda Gabler*. Three years later Jackson appeared as Cleopatra in Peter Brook's production of *Antony and Cleopatra*.

In 1983 Jackson became director of the United British Artists production company, whose members include Diana Rigg, Albert Finney, and Ben Kingsley. She received outstanding reviews in 1984 as Nina in O'Neill's five-hour drama *Strange Interlude* at the Duke of York's Theatre, London, a production seen the following year on Broadway. In 1988 she starred in *Macbeth* on Broadway, and in 1990 in Brecht's *Mother Courage* in London.

Her international film career has included two Academy Awards as Best Actress, for *Women in Love* (1970) and *A Touch of Class* (1973). Her most successful television role came in 1971 when she played Queen Elizabeth I in *Elizabeth R*.

Jackson's career in the theatre came to a possibly temporary end when she was elected Labour MP for Hampstead and Highgate in 1992.

Jacobean drama The English theatre during the reign of James I (1603–25). Although SHAKESPEARE was still writing major works until around 1611, the leading dramatist of the era was Ben JONSON. Other noted Jacobean playwrights included John

MARSTON, Thomas MIDDLETON, Thomas HEYWOOD, John FORD, Thomas Dekker (*c.* 1570–1632), Cyril Tourneur (*c.* 1575–1626), and Samuel Rowley (*c.* 1575–1624).

In comedy the Elizabethan concerns with characterization and romantic love began to give way to a vogue for harsh satire and increased realism from about 1610. Jacobean tragedy, equally harsh, shows an obsession with the idea of moral corruption; examples include WEBSTER's *The White Devil* (1612) and *The Duchess of Malfi* (1619), as well as BEAUMONT and FLETCHER's *The Maid's Tragedy* (1610). The plays, which are often horrifically violent, show a generally cynical and pessimistic outlook on life. From 1605 Jonson collaborated with Inigo JONES to create the extravagant and scholarly court MASQUES beloved by James I and his queen.

Although James I was an enthusiast for the theatre, he imposed strict regulations on companies, specifying in which theatres they could play. One effect of this was to bring public performances into the cities of London and Westminster; before 1608 all theatres had to be outside the municipal boundaries. The leading troupe of the day, the CHAMBERLAIN'S MEN, became the King's Men on James's accession. Similarly the Blackfriars Boy Company became the Children of the Revels of the Queen, although the popularity of child actors came to an end during the Jacobean era. Other features of the period include the growing influence of neoclassical theories from the Continent (*see* NEOCLASSICAL DRAMA), increasingly violent opposition to the theatre from the Puritans, and a general decline in audience numbers.

Jacobi, Derek (George) (1938–) British classical actor, often considered the natural successor to Sir John GIELGUD. The son of London shopworkers, Jacobi appeared with the National Youth Theatre before making his professional debut in the Birmingham Repertory Theatre's 1961 production of N. F. Simpson's *One Way Pendulum*. Two years later he joined the National Theatre, with whom he made his London debut as Laertes in *Hamlet*. Since then Jacobi has played major roles in a broad range of plays, including Hamlet at Elsinore in 1979. As an associate actor of the RSC, he has starred in several notable productions, including *Peer Gynt* (1982) and an award-winning version of Rostand's *Cyrano de Bergerac* in 1983. In 1986 he was highly praised for his portrayal of the mathematician Alan Turing in Hugh Whitemore's *Breaking the Code*. More recently Jacobi has played the title roles in *Kean* (1990) and *Becket* (1991), as well as Byron in *Mad, Bad and Dangerous to Know* (1992). His keenly anticipated *Macbeth* opened in London in 1993. Jacobi remains best-known to the general public for his portrayal of the stuttering Emperor Claudius in the television series *I, Claudius* (1977).

Jam Factory, the Nickname for the Astoria Theatre, in London's Charing Cross Road. It was built on the site of a jam factory and opened in 1927 as 'London's Supreme Cinema', acquiring the nickname during its early years. In 1977 it was renovated as a theatre and opened with Jack Good's production of the multimedia musical *Elvis*. Since coming under new management in 1987, the venue has featured live music.

Jarry, Alfred (1873–1907) French novelist and playwright, chiefly remembered for his farce *Ubu roi* (1896), which began as a collaborative schoolboy satire on a physics teacher (*see* UBU). Jarry's other plays include *Ubu Enchaîné* (1900), *Ubu sur la butte* (1901), and *Ubu Cocu* (1944, written 1888), as well as the poetic drama *César Antechrist* (1894) and the farcical opera *Le Moutardier du Pape* (1907).

In life, Jarry contrived an eccentric persona that was as bizarre as his work. A keen athlete and marksman, he was rarely seen without his rusty Browning revolver and carbine. Anyone who bored or annoyed him was liable to be dismissed with a fusillade of blanks. On more formal occasions he wore paper shirts, on which he would draw a tie. His favourite drink was said to be absinthe diluted with red ink.

With its savage mockery of the French bourgeoisie and blatant disregard for theatrical form and convention, Jarry's work influenced both the Surrealists and the Theatre of the ABSURD. Jarry died at the age of 34, largely as a result of his alcoholism.

Jatra (Bengali: procession) A melodramatic hero-villain genre of Indian theatre; it is the most popular form of drama in rural Bengal and amongst Bengali speakers elsewhere. *Jatra* probably emerged in the 16th century from within the Vaishnava devotional movement; the first Bengali scripts still extant were written in the late 18th century.

Calcutta is the centre for about 20 travelling troupes controlled by owner-managers. The season runs from September to June, with companies performing for family events and major religious festivals. *Jatra* concentrated on religious themes until the early 19th century, but has since become largely secular. The Communist Party made use of the genre to win rural supporters in the 1930s and was later responsible for popularizing *Jatra* in the cities. In the mid-19th century, *Jatra* companies adapted Western styles of acting and writing.

The acting area, which is often outdoors, is made up of mats or carpets spread over the ground or a low wooden platform; the latter is usually connected to the dressing room by a ramp, which provides more acting space. There is no scenery and the only prop is a chair. The all-night performance opens with music, which can last for up to two hours. The musicians play the harmonium, violin, clarinet or flute, *pakhwaj* drum, and bell-metal cymbals. The melodrama follows, its scenes divided into acts by songs; the stories consist of battles between heroes and villains, interspersed with comic interludes. An allegorical character known as *bibek*, or Conscience, roams the stage commenting on the meaning behind the action and predicting its consequences.

Jefferson family US acting family. Its patriarch, the British-born Joseph J. Jefferson (1774–1832), had eight sons, seven of whom also became actors; his own father, Thomas J. Jefferson (1732–1897), had appeared at Drury Lane with Garrick.

Joseph Jefferson made his New York debut in 1796 in Vanbrugh's *The Provok'd Husband*. He was subsequently the leading actor at Philadelphia's CHESTNUT STREET THEATRE for nearly 30 years, where he appeared in such comic roles as Farmer Ashfield in Morton's *Speed the Plough*. His son, also Joseph J. Jefferson (1804–42), was a scenic artist and actor and the father of the third and most famous Joseph J. Jefferson (1829–1905), a leading comedy actor. He made his debut at the age of four in Washington, DC, singing 'Jump Jim Crow' with the black-faced comedy singer T. D. Rice. In 1857 he joined Laura Keene's company in New York and a year later became an overnight success as Asa Trenchard in Tom Taylor's *Our American Cousin*. He subsequently joined the Winter Garden Theatre in New York under the direction of Dion Boucicault, creating the role of Salem Scudder in Boucicault's *The Octoroon*.

After the death of his wife in 1861, Jefferson toured Australia. There, during a performance in the mining town of Castlemaine, he was horrified to see a barker standing on a barrel outside the theatre shouting "Step up, ladies and gentlemen. Now or never is your only chance to see the greatest living wonder of the age, Joseph Jefferson." The actor refused to go on unless the man desisted. When the barker refused, a tussle with the manager resulted in him falling through the barrel until, as Jefferson recalled, "only a fat head just appeared above the top. They tipped the barrel over and rolled him off inside, to the great amusement of the bystanders..."

In 1865 Jefferson went to London where he starred in Boucicault's adaptation of Washington Irving's *Rip Van Winkle*. It ran for 170 nights and Jefferson continued to play the part for the rest of his career.

Jersey Lily, the The nickname of Lillie LANGTRY, who was the daughter of the dean of Jersey.

Jesuit drama Plays performed and sometimes written by students at Jesuit colleges in Europe from the 16th to 18th centuries. The first such plays were written as school exercises to promote a greater understanding of theological and moral ideas; gradually they developed into more elaborate productions than the professional theatres were giving at that time.

The first Jesuit college, the Collegio Mamertino, opened in Messina, Sicily in 1548; the first recorded Jesuit tragedy was performed there three years later. The early plays had biblical or classical subjects, such as David, Saul, or Hercules, while later works dramatized the stories of saints and martyrs. As early as 1569 Latin began to give way to local languages, when Stefano Tuccio's *Christus Judex* was translated into Italian and German.

By the 17th century, Jesuit drama was being influenced by opera and ballet, especially in Vienna; this led to the use of large choruses and orchestras, lavish costumes and scenery, and elaborate stage machinery. In 1659 *Pietas Victrix* by the Austrian Nicolaus Avancini had 46 speaking parts and seven TRANSFORMATION SCENES. Productions of Jesuit drama in Paris were equal to those of the Paris Opéra; in Paris, too, such female characters as St Catherine and Esther were introduced.

By the mid-18th century Jesuit dramas were being performed at regular intervals in about 300 colleges. However, the excesses of these extravagant productions led to the imposition of restrictions and the dramas ceased altogether in 1773 when the order was suppressed. Some Jesuit dramas are occasionally revived; Jakob Bidermann's *Cenodoxus* (1602), for example, was performed in 1958 at the Residenztheater in Munich as part of the city's 800th anniversary celebration. Dramatists influenced by Jesuit drama include Calderón, Goldoni, Molière, Voltair, and Corneille.

Jesus Christ Superstar A rock opera based on the life of Christ, with music by Andrew LLOYD WEBBER and lyrics by Tim Rice. The stage musical was actually devised after the Webber-Rice songs had become a success on an LP record. The show opened in Pittsburgh in 1971 and moved to Broadway later that year; at London's Palace Theatre it ran for 3357 performances from 1972 and made £7 million at the box office (at that time a record for a British musical). It also established the unusual record of having the most actors (five) to play Christ in any production: Paul Nicholas, Steve Alder, Chris Neil, Richard Barnes, and Robert Farrant. After its Broadway opening, producer Robert Stigwood was heard to claim: "Jesus Christ could be the biggest thing in history." A highly praised revival opened at the Lyceum Theatre, London, in 1996.

The story is told by Judas Iscariot, who traces Jesus's life from his entry into Jerusalem until his Crucifixion. Songs include 'Superstar', 'I Don't Know How to Love Him', and 'Everything's All Right'.

Jew of Malta, The A play by Christopher MARLOWE, first performed in London in 1590; Edward ALLEYN created the role of the villainous Jew Barabas. Although a less three-dimensional character than SHYLOCK in *The Merchant of Venice*, the role of Barabas can be quite powerful on stage; Edmund KEAN excelled in both roles in the early 19th century. In 1965 the Royal Shakespeare Company presented both plays in repertory.

At the beginning of the play the Governor of Malta confiscates the wealth of Barabas, a Jew. Barabas, however, has more hidden in his house, which has been made into a nunnery. He persuades his daughter Abigail to convert to Christianity for long enough to retrieve the riches. Barabas also encourages her to arouse jealousy between her lover and the governor's son, who then kill each other. When Abigail chooses to enter the convent as a nun, Barabas and his Turkish slave, Ithamore, poison her along with all the other nuns. Barabas then poisons Ithamore for betraying him to the governor. He escapes punishment by swallowing a potion to feign death, surviving to betray the Christians and become governor himself. He then plots against the Turkish Prince Calymath but is double-crossed and dies in a pot of boiling oil.

jig In the Elizabethan theatre, a short musical farce presented by a clown and two or three other actors as an AFTERPIECE to full-length tragic works. Usually restricted to smaller theatres, the jig consisted of comic rhymes on topical subjects, sung to well-known tunes while the performers danced. The genre was popularized by Richard TARLTON and perfected by William Kempe.

Joan of Arc (Jeanne d'Arc; 1412–31) French patriot, who claimed to have been inspired by voices from heaven to liberate France from the English. She was captured and burnt at the stake as a heretic but canonized in 1920. Her career has inspired many literary and dramatic works, including plays by Schiller, ANOUILH (*The Lark*; 1943), and George Bernard SHAW. In Shakespeare's HENRY VI, PART I, she is portrayed as a coarse and treacherous instrument of the devil who trades her own soul for victory over the English; even her French allies regard her as little better than a witch.

By contrast, Shaw's SAINT JOAN (1924) presents her as a figure of total integrity who is at once saintly and completely down to earth. Consequently there was no shortage among Shaw's acquaintances of ladies claiming to be the author's model for the role. The credit goes, however, to Mary Hankinson (a suffragette and member of the Fabian Society), in whose copy of the play Shaw wrote: "To Mary Hankinson, the only woman I know who does not believe she was the model of *Saint Joan*, and also actually the only woman who was."

The true nature of the original Joan of Arc is notoriously hard to establish. One

17th-century investigation claimed that she had been married and that someone else had been burnt at Rouen in her place. The evidence for this theory consisted of documents relating to a marriage between "Robert des Armoyses and Joan of Arc, otherwise known as the Maid of Orleans" as well as several accounts of the reunion of Joan with her brothers after her supposed death.

Joe. **Joe Blatz** The ordinary US theatregoer as imagined by George M. COHAN when writing his musicals. He attributed his success to knowing Joe Blatz and said, "What the 15-year-old, clean-faced, fresh-minded, full-of-life American boy or girl likes, the Average American Audience will like." *Compare* AUNT EDNA.

Joey The familiar name for Joseph GRIMALDI England's most famous clown. Clowns are often called Joey in his honour.

John. ***John Bull's Other Island*** A play by George Bernard SHAW, first performed in 1904 at the Royal Court Theatre. Originally intended for Dublin's ABBEY THEATRE, it was meant to show an English character in the same ridiculous light as Irishmen were usually presented on the English stage. Shaw also argues for Irish independence, both in the play itself and in his provocative preface (written in 1906).

The plot concerns Larry Doyle, an Irish businessman who has been successful in England; on a visit to his home town with his partner, Thomas Broadbent, Doyle sees his ageing father, whose political views now clash with his, and Nora, his old sweetheart. The townspeople ask him to run for parliament but retract the offer when they realize how anglicized his views have become. Instead, they make the offer to the good-natured Broadbent, who also wins the heart of Nora. The local (unfrocked) priest, Father Keegan, becomes suspicious, however, as Broadbent makes plans to lure tourists into town with a new hotel and golf course. The role of Father Keegan was first played by Harley GRANVILLE-BARKER, who produced a series of Shaw's plays at the Royal Court.

John Paul II (1920–) The only reigning pope to have a play performed in the professional theatre. He wrote *The Jeweller's Shop* in 1960 (under his original name of Karol Wojtyła) while auxiliary bishop of Cracow, Poland. He became pope in 1978. The play, consisting of a series of monologues about marriage, opened in London in 1982, three days before his visit to Britain.

John Street Theatre New York's first permanent playhouse and one of George Washington's favourite venues. It opened in 1767 with Farquhar's *The Beaux' Stratagem*, and was home to THE AMERICAN COMPANY. The John Street Theatre presented the New York premieres of many plays by Shakespeare, including David Garrick's reduced version of *Hamlet*, which omitted the gravediggers and Osric. The theatre closed in 1798, when it was sold for £115.

Johnson Over Jordan A play by J. B. PRIESTLEY, first performed in London in 1939. It concerns Robert Johnson, a recently deceased businessman, who reviews his life and the highs and lows of his career. Ralph RICHARDSON gave a highly praised performance as Johnson in his last stage appearance before joining the Royal Navy in World War II.

Johnston, Henry Erskine *See* ROSCIUS, SCOTTISH *under* ROSCIUS.

Joking Apart A black comedy by Alan AYCKBOURN, first presented in 1979 at the STEPHEN JOSEPH THEATRE IN THE ROUND in Scarborough (where Ayckbourn is artistic director).

The play covers a 12-year span in the lives of its main characters; the four scenes are all set in the suburban garden of Richard and his wife Anthea. Quite inadvertently, this charming and successful couple wreak havoc on the lives of friends and neighbours by arousing envy and lust. The beautiful Anthea is still loved by her ex-boyfriend Brian and her husband's partner Sven. Next door, the tense young vicar Hugh also has a passion for Anthea, which has driven his wife Louise onto prescription drugs. Similarly, Richard's effortless superiority drives Sven into self-destructive bitterness. At a party given by Richard and Anthea for their daughter's 18th birthday, the daughter is perplexed by the antics of her parents and their friends.

Jolly Boys' Play *See* MUMMERS' PLAY *under* MUMMER.

Jolson, Al (Asa Yoelson; 1886–1950) US star of blackface revue and musical comedy who appeared in Hollywood's first talkie. Born in Russia, the son of a rabbi, he grew up in Washington, DC, and first appeared on stage at the age of 12. He first wore blackface in 1904 for an act with his brother Hirsh. Five years later he joined Lew Dockstader's minstrel troupe and quickly became a leading star. He began to sing his famous 'mammy songs' when the company played in San Francisco. Wearing blackface and white gloves Jolson delivered the sentimental tunes with sweeping gestures, often falling down on one knee. His hit songs included 'Mammy', 'Rockabye Your Baby with a Dixie Melody', 'Swanee', 'April Showers', and 'California, Here I Come'.

However camp and schmaltzy old films of him may now seem, Jolson had an undeniable power over the emotions of his audiences, often reducing them to tears. His famous catchphrase was "Wait a minute! You ain't heard nothin' yet!". His energy was boundless: he would often dismiss the entire cast of a show during a performance and continue alone on stage for hours.

In the 20 years between 1911 and 1931, Jolson appeared in many lavish productions, including several at the Winter Garden Theatre. His most successful shows included *La Belle Paree* (1911), *Honeymoon Express* (1913), *Robinson Crusoe Jr.* (1916), *Bombo* (1921), which opened the Jolson Theatre on 7th Avenue in New York, and *Wonder Bar* (1931), his first appearance without blackface in 27 years.

In 1927 Jolson starred in the cinema's first talkie, Warner Brothers' *The Jazz Singer*. Ironically, this and subsequent screen performances helped to speed the demise of his beloved vaudeville. The story of his own life was filmed in 1946 as *The Jolson Story*.

Jolson could not endure criticism of or apathy towards his act. Although he was offered enormous sums to perform in Britain, he was frightened by the idea of a strange foreign audience to which he might not be able to relate. "If there's just one guy who ain't enjoying the show, I'll know it," he explained, "and that'll kill me".

Jones. Inigo Jones (1573–1652) English architect and stage designer, whose work with court MASQUES brought several innovations to the English stage.

Jones, having visited Italy in 1603 and seen the great theatres at Vicenza and Parma, became an exponent of baroque theatre design. He also studied design and painting while employed at the court of Christian IV of Denmark, whose sister, Anne, was James I of England's queen.

In 1605 Jones was employed at the English court to design sets and costumes for masques by the dramatist Ben JONSON, the first being *The Mask of Blackness*. However, before long Jones's extravagant sets and costume designs, such as those for Oberon in *Oberon, the Fairy Prince* (1611), began to overshadow the dramatic content and a feud developed between the two men. Jonson savagely satirized Jones in several plays (*see* LANTHORN, LEATHERHEAD).

Jones also produced plays at Oxford's Christ Church Hall, where he introduced revolving Italian screens. He later pioneered the PROSCENIUM, the backcloth (*see* CLOTH), and painted FLATS that moved on a GROOVES SYSTEM.

During the Civil War, Jones's fortunes fell with the monarchy. He was captured and his estate was confiscated, but later restored; he died without adequate funds. More than 450 of his drawings and designs exist in the library of Chatsworth House, Derbyshire.

James Earl Jones (1931–) US Black actor, noted for his Shakespearean roles.

Jones, the son of the actor Robert Earl Jones, said of his father, "I saw how difficult it was for him. I knew I had to accept a low standard of living for some years". In 1957 he went to New York to study acting with Lee STRASBERG, making his debut in the city that year in *Wedding in Japan*. In 1960 he began his long association with Joseph PAPP at the New York Shakespeare Festival, where he appeared in *Henry V* and *Measure for Measure*; subsequent performances as Othello, Macbeth, and Lear at the Festival were much praised by the critics. Jones won the Village Voice OBIE AWARD for Best Actor (1961–62) for three off-Broadway plays, including *Moon of the Rainbow Shawl*, in which he appeared with his father.

Jones made his first European tour in the summer of 1967, playing the title role in O'Neill's *The Emperor Jones*. That same year he opened in Washington, DC, in *The Great White Hope*, in which he played the first Black heavyweight fighter, Jack Johnson (Jack Jefferson in the play), a performance that won him a Tony Award. The critic Martin Gottfried said, "Bravura actors are almost extinct in America and now there is Jones." He was also nominated for an Academy Award for playing the part in the 1970 film version.

Other successes include Athol Fugard's *Boesman and Lena* (1970), Chekhov's *The Cherry Orchard* (1973), Steinbeck's *Of Mice and Men* (1974), and Fugard's *A Lesson from Aloes* (1980). He was also the voice of the villain Darth Vader in the George Lucas film *Star Wars* (1977).

Robert Edmond Jones (1887–1954) US stage designer and director, who began a revolution in the US theatre and remained Broadway's leading designer for 30 years. Jones also helped to develop Technicolor for the cinema. His credo as a designer was "Keep in your soul some images of magnificence." In 1926 he published *Drawings for the Theatre*.

After graduating from Harvard in 1910, he studied in Berlin (1912–15) with Max REINHARDT and the designer Ernst Stern at the DEUTSCHES THEATER. On his return to New York in 1915, he launched the 'new stagecraft' with his designs for the New York Stage Society's production of *The Man Who Married a Dumb Wife*, directed by Harley Granville-Barker, in which Jones placed brilliantly coloured costumes in simple black and grey settings. Jones was also one of the first designers for the THEATRE-IN-THE-ROUND, producing sketches on Shelley's arena production of *The Cenci* in 1920. He was also influenced by Gordon Craig (*see* CRAIG FAMILY), as is clear from the Expressionist designs he created for John Barrymore's *Hamlet* in 1922. Two years later Jones directed and created a MULTIPLE SETTING for Eugene O'NEILL's *Desire under the Elms* (1924); this led to further designs for O'Neill's plays with the Provincetown Players, of which he became a joint manager. Despite using abstract designs, Jones worked from real life, travelling to England to see the Tower of London to prepare for *Richard III*, spending months in Venice for *Othello*, and studying original Chinese documents for Sidney Howard's *Lute Song*.

During one production the designer Jo Mielziner (1901–76) was summoned to the costume workshop to encounter a 17th-century lady in a splendid gown performing a genteel curtsy. Noting the richly trimmed wig and the baroque pearl necklace, he suddenly became aware that the face between them belonged to Jones. "You know, Jo," laughed Jones, "most actresses really don't know how to wear these things. I just had to see what it felt like."

jongleur A medieval minstrel and entertainer who recited verses to his or her own musical accompaniment as well as performing juggling and acrobatic acts. They were best known for wandering from castle to castle performing the *Chansons de Geste*, epic poems celebrating heroic deeds. The word comes from the Latin *joculator*, juggler. *See also* MINSTREL; TROUBADOURS; TROUVÈRES.

jonkonnu A masked and costumed street procession held in Jamaica at Christmas. First recorded in the 18th century, the *jonkonnu* apparently combines elements of the MUMMERS' PLAY and the West African masquerade. Members of the all-male troupes, who are accompanied by a fife and drum band, remain masked in public and disguise their voices. The various characters include the Devil, JACK-IN-THE-GREEN, Horse Head, Cow Head, and Belly Woman.

Jonson, Ben (1572–1637) English dramatist and poet, whose reputation amongst playwrights of the period is second only to Shakespeare's. Jonson was born in London and is thought to have received a good education. Despite this he worked as a bricklayer and served as a soldier in the Netherlands before turning to the theatre in around 1597. That same year Jonson was briefly imprisoned for his part in THE ISLE OF DOGS, a play written in collaboration with Thomas Nashe. In 1598 Jonson killed a fellow actor in a duel, escaping the death penalty, it seems, only because of his ability to read Latin, which allowed him to claim 'benefit of clergy'.

Although Jonson found little success as an actor, his reputation as a dramatist was firmly established in 1598 with EVERY MAN IN HIS HUMOUR. Shakespeare is thought to have acted in the play and, according to one account, was responsible for recommending the piece to the Lord Chamberlain's Men. This success was followed by another COMEDY OF HUMOURS, *Every Man out of His Humour* (1599), and the classically influenced satire *Cynthia's Revels* (1600). *The Poetaster* (1601) was an attack on his rival playwrights Thomas Dekker and John MARSTON (*see* WAR OF THE THEATRES). Jonson's Roman tragedy *Sejanus, His Fall* was staged in 1603.

In 1604 Jonson was again briefly imprisoned, this time for his part in EASTWARD HO!, a play whose sentiments offended the new king, James I. Considering the controversy of *Eastward Ho*, it is perhaps surprising that only a year later Jonson began collaborating with Inigo JONES on MASQUES for the Stuart court.

Jonson wrote all of the major comedies upon which his reputation is now based during the period 1605 to 1614. VOLPONE (1605), *Epicoene; or The Silent Woman* (1609), THE ALCHEMIST (1610), and BARTHOLOMEW FAIR (1614) were all hugely successful and have remained popular choices for revival. In particular the character of Abel Drugger in *The Alchemist* has provided generations of actors with a brilliant comic role.

The relative failure of *Catiline* (1611) and *The Devil is an Ass* (1616) seems to have prompted Jonson to take a break from writing for the stage, although he continued to work on the court masques. His late plays *The Staple of News* (1625), *The New Inn* (1629), and *A Tale of a Tub* (1633) did not prove popular and are now largely forgotten. In 1634 Jonson and Jones's long-running quarrel over whose contribution to the masque was the more important flared up again, leading to a final breach between the two men.

On his death Jonson was interred in Westminster Abbey (*see* RARE BEN).

Jordan, Dorothy (1762–1816) Irish-born English actress who excelled in boisterous tomboy roles and BREECHES PARTS. She was equally well-known for having 15 illegitimate children, 10 of them fathered by the future William IV when he was the Duke of Clarence. The duke was often in financial difficulties, and Dorothy would send him money when she was touring the provinces. When the government eventually insisted that he break off their liaison, she received a handsome payoff.

Herself the illegitimate daughter of an actress, Dorothy made her debut in 1779 at the Crow Street Theatre, Dublin, using the stage name Miss Francis. When, three years later, she became pregnant, she adopted the name Mrs Jordan.

In 1785 she was employed by Sheridan to understudy Sarah SIDDONS at Drury Lane. Thereafter she appeared in a succession of comic roles in works by SHAKESPEARE, Congreve, Farquhar, and Sheridan himself. The critic William Hazlitt said "her smile had the effect of sunshine". She was also a favourite with British artists. George Romney painted her in the role of Priscilla Tomboy in the musical farce *The Romp*.

When Mrs Jordan was beginning rehearsals at a provincial theatre for a play called *The Wonder*, someone pointed out her leading man. "Oh, I can't act with him," she moaned, "he's too little!" As she walked away the actor gave her a reproachful glance that she never forgot. Years later Mrs Jordan asked to be introduced to the most famous and fashionable actor of the day, Edmund KEAN. They met in the green room of the Drury Lane Theatre. "Great heavens!" she exclaimed, "the little man with the eyes!"

jornada The Spanish name for a division of a play, equivalent to an act; it was first used in the early 16th century by the playwright TORRES NAHARRO.

Journey's End A realistic anti-war play by R. C. Sherriff (1896–1975) that established his reputation. It was first performed (1928) in a Stage Society production at London's Savoy Theatre starring Laurence OLIVIER.

Set in a World-War-I-dugout in France, the play explores the relationship between two ex-school friends, the youthful Lieutenant Raleigh and Captain Stanhope. Raleigh hero-worships the older man, but becomes disillusioned with him when he turns to alcohol for comfort on hearing of the death of a friend. The next day the young officer is wounded, and Stanhope comforts him before he too enters battle.

Sherriff first thought of calling his play *Suspense* but rejected it "because I couldn't honestly claim that it had any". *Waiting* was the second choice, but one night in bed he was reading a book with a chapter that ended with the sentence, "It was late in the evening when we came at last to our Journey's End." He typed the last two words on the front page of his play and "the thing was done".

Sherriff later recalled his nervousness at the opening: "I was all over the theatre, running up to the gallery, walking round the pit, standing in a box. I couldn't sit down; I must have walked five miles in the theatre that night. I couldn't bear to look at the audience... When the curtain fell and there was no applause, I was pained, but thrilled, too."

Jouvet, Louis (1887–1951) French actor, director, designer, and stage technician, responsible for staging the first plays of both GIRAUDOUX and GENET. Jouvet made his Paris debut in an adaptation of *The Brothers Karamazov* (1910), before joining Jacques Copeau's at the Théâtre du Vieux-Colombier. In about 1920 he remodelled the stage there to resemble the acting area in an Elizabethan playhouse.

In 1922 Jouvet became director of the Comédie des Champs-Élysées, where he enjoyed a major success with *Dr Knock* (1923); he subsequently starred in both the 1933 film version and the 1950 remake. Five years later Jouvet co-founded the CARTEL, an association of four of the leading actor-managers in France. His direction of Giraudoux's *Siegfried* in 1928 led to a long collaboration between the two men, culminating in Jouvet's production of THE MADWOMAN OF CHAILLOT (1945) after Giraudoux's death. Two years later Jouvet staged Genet's first play, THE MAIDS (1947).

Juan, Don *See* DON JUAN.

juggler A performer who throws and catches objects (such as balls, plates, knives, etc.) in quick succession to create a variety of patterns in flight. The art was practised in ancient Egypt, China, and Greece; in Rome, knife jugglers were known as *ventilatores* and ball jugglers as *pilarii*.

During the Middle Ages jugglers featured at court entertainments, the best-known being Pierre Gringore (1475–1538), who was chief fool at the French court and also an actor and playwright. Juggling was a popular entertainment at fairs and, with the development of the CIRCUS during the 19th century, became a prominent feature of big-top performances. One Russian circus even claimed to have a bear who had been trained to juggle a flaming torch.

In the 19th century British music hall and variety stages offered both the 'strength juggler' and the 'salon juggler'. The former, which included Karl Rappo (1800–54), juggled heavy objects, including other human beings. The **antipodean juggler** lay on his back and tossed a heavy object from one foot to the other; if this were a young boy, the feat was called the **Icarus trick**.

The salon juggler tossed billiard balls, fans, and similar items, often balancing them on his head or chin. A famous example was Paul Cinquevalli (Paul Kestner; 1859–1918), known as **The Human Billiard Table**, who dressed in green baize with pockets at his waist, shoulders, and spine. He had the uncanny skill of juggling and rolling billiard balls over his body until they were all neatly pocketed. Another music-hall favourite was the restaurant scene popularized by the Charles Perzoff Troupe (1890–1910) during which waiters and customers end up wildly juggling a five-course meal. W. C. Fields (1879–1946) began his career as a stage juggler before becoming a Hollywood comedian. Jugglers have practised their art riding the unicycle, blindfolded on horseback, and on the high wire.

In Britain and America, juggling has recently undergone a revival in popularity as a sport, particularly the variety of club juggling introduced to Britain in the 19th century from India and formerly known as **Indian club swinging.** *See also* ACROBATICS.

Julius Caesar SHAKESPEARE's tragedy, believed to be the first play presented at the new GLOBE THEATRE in 1599 by the Lord Chamberlain's Men. Unusually for a tragedy, the title character is killed at the start of the third act. The play thereafter concentrates on the misgivings of his assassins. Shakespeare used Plutarch's *Lives* as his source, producing a straight-forward plot, which has no subplots or comic scenes.

There have been many notable performances on both sides of the Atlantic. In 1937 Orson Welles and John Houseman opened their Mercury Theatre with a modern-dress production, depicting Caesar as a Mussolini-type figure. John GIELGUD has played Cassius in two different films, with Marlon Brando and James Mason in 1953 and with Charlton Heston in 1969.

Laurence OLIVIER, famous for his laughing fits during performances in his early career, once played Flavius in *Julius Caesar*. The actor playing Murellus stood on a beer box to give the speech "Knew you not Pompey?" As Olivier watched, the man's long pants fell down underneath his toga and over the beer box, so preventing him from stepping down. Olivier laughed so much he had to leave the stage and was fired the next morning.

Jumpers A sophisticated comedy by Tom STOPPARD. It opened in 1972 with highly praised performances by Michael Hordern as George Moore, a Professor of Moral Philosophy, and Diana Rigg as his young ex-actress wife. Stoppard's satire on current fashions in academic philosophy has many revealing insights; it was called a "stark raving sane play" by the critic John Barber.

In the play Moore and his wife Dorothy are hosting a party during which Moore's colleague, Archie, apparently murders a rival for Dorothy's favours. Inspector Bones arrives to investigate and, taken by Dorothy's charms, dismisses the body's presence in her bedroom as an irrelevant detail. Archie continues to pursue Dorothy and directs a team of bouncing acrobats (jumpers) as George performs equally useless mental gymnastics, polishing his lecture on morals.

Juno and the Paycock A tragicomedy by Sean O'CASEY. It was first performed in 1924 at the ABBEY THEATRE, Dublin, opening in London the following year and in New York in 1926.

Set in Dublin's slums during the 'Troubles' of 1922, the plot concerns the disintegration of the Boyle family. The drunken 'Captain' Jack Boyle and his son Johnny, who has been wounded fighting for the IRA, leave all the work to the Captain's wife, Juno, and their daughter Mary. Life in the two-room tenement is bleak indeed, until the day Charles Bentham, the schoolmaster who loves Mary, announces that he has helped to draft a will that leaves the Captain a large amount of money. The family buy new furniture on credit before Bentham discovers that he has made an error and the family will receive nothing. Bentham departs for London leaving Mary pregnant and the furniture is repossessed. Worse, Johnny is executed for betraying the IRA cause. Finally, Juno and Mary leave the Captain in search of a less awful life.

Just Between Ourselves A bleak comedy by Alan AYCKBOURN, first presented in 1976 at the STEPHEN JOSEPH THEATRE IN THE ROUND, Scarborough.

The story takes place on the birthdays of the four main characters. On Pam's birthday, she and her husband Neil visit Dennis and Vera to look at Vera's car, which they are thinking of buying. Dennis, rearranging the mess in his garage, is reminded by his live-in mother, Marjorie, how much better his father was at DIY. Dennis ignores both her and his long-suffering wife, who yearns to be rescued from her dominating mother-in-law. On Dennis's birthday, Marjorie berates Vera for not making him his favourite cake. On Marjorie's birthday, Vera finally allows her fury free rein; by her own birthday, however, she is cowed and uncommunicative, huddled outside in the garden, while Marjorie happily rules the house and her son.

Justice The best-known play by John Galsworthy, first performed in 1910 at the Savoy Theatre, London. In the 1916 New York production John Barrymore (*see* BARRYMORES) established his name as a serious actor playing the leading role of the downtrodden clerk Falder. The *New York Times* stated that Barrymore "gained overnight a prestige which is priceless in the theatre, a prestige all his work in trivial entertainment would not give him". When she saw his performance the US actress and playwright Jane Cowl was so overcome that she fainted. Weeks later Barrymore was informed that she was again in the audience: "Is she?" he responded drily. "I do hope she'll give a good performance."

The plot concerns a junior clerk, William Falder, who, although usually honest, forges a cheque to assist Ruth Honeywill, a woman brutalized by her husband. His crime is discovered and he receives the maximum prison sentence; placed in solitary confinement, he has a mental breakdown. When he is released two years later, he applies to his old firm to be taken back. Told that he must first give up Ruth, who is now living with him, Falder refuses and later forges a reference for another job. When questioned by the police, Falder commits suicide rather than face prison again. The scene depicting Falder in solitary confinement is said to have helped reform the law relating to that form of punishment.

juvenile. juvenile drama *See* TOY THEATRE.
juvenile lead In the 18th- and 19th-century STOCK COMPANIES, an actor who played the part of a young man.

K

kabuki The most popular form of drama in Japan. Its name is derived from the Japanese verb *kabuku*, meaning to be modern and offbeat, and written using the Japanese symbols for singing (*ka*), dancing (*bu*), and art (*ki*).

Kabuki is said to have been invented by a priestess-dancer, which originated in the 15th century, who drew on the traditions of NŌ and Chinese theatre to depict subjects from everyday life. She was subsequently imitated by many women performers. In 1616, however, women were banned from the stage as most actresses were also prostitutes. Groups of boys replaced them, but in 1652 they too were banned for the same reason. Now *kabuki* players are all men, some of whom specialize in stylized female impersonations.

Kabuki plays range from farces to melodramas, drawing their plots from daily life, history, myth, *Nō* plays, and BUNRAKU puppet plays. The most popular *Kabuki* work is *Chushingura* (1748) by Takedo Izymo (1691–1756), which describes how faithful royal retainers avenge their master.

The stock *Kabuki* roles include courageous men (*tachiyaku*), evil men (*katakiyaku*), young men (*wakashukata*), comic roles (*dokekata*), and female characters (*onnagata*). The actors are not masked and wear extravagant costumes. Acting techniques were traditionally passed on from father to son; the Ichikawa family produced 12 generations of successful *kabuki* actors in this way. Scenery and staging are often elborate; *kabuki* companies made use of a revolving stage long before such a device was adopted in the West.

Kabuki has always tried to keep ahead of the times, incorporating innovative musical, choreographical, and artistic styles that have often been considered strange and shocking: the scholar Tsumbouchi Shoyo called it a "many-headed monster". Variations introduced during this century have included SHIMPA and SHINGEKI, both of which reflect the influence of European ideas. Despite its back-street origins, *kabuki* is now considered a high art form.

kagura A form of early Japanese dance drama imported from China in about 540 AD. The term embraces numerous ritual dances connected with the worship of nature and ancestors.

Kainz, Josef (1858–1910) Austrian actor, whose noble bearing and resonant voice made him the most popular German-language performer of his day. After training with the MEININGER COMPANY, Kainz acted with the Munich Court Theatre (1880–83), the Deutsches Theater in Berlin (1883–99), and the Vienna Burgtheater (1899–1910).

While performing in 1881 in Munich as Didier in Victor Hugo's *Marion de Lorme*, Kainz was seen by 'mad' King Ludwig II of Bavaria. The monarch subsequently wrote letters of admiration to the actor, showered jewels upon him, and brought him to his Schloss Linderhof to recite in his Blue Grotto. They became close friends, but Ludwig went too far during their visit to Switzerland when he forced Kainz to read a scene from *William Tell* on a mountainside in the middle of the night. The actor walked out and made a fortune by selling the king's personal letters to him.

Kaiser, Georg (1878–1945) German playwright, whose *From Morn to Midnight* (1917) is usually considered to have initiated EXPRESSIONISM in the theatre. The play was first seen at the Berlin Volksbühne in a production by Max REINHARDT, with imaginative sets by Hans Strohbach. The plot concerns a repressed bank clerk who searches for spiritual meaning in the modern world but is crushed and destroyed by society.

Kaiser's most ambitious work is a trilogy of plays in which he explores the hopelessness of the human condition: *Coral* (1917) shows the protagonist rejecting materialism, *Gas I* (1918) depicts his attempts to reform society, and *Gas II* (1920) ends in cataclysmic destruction.

Kaiser eventually abandoned expressionism and wrote such romances as *Alain und Elise* (1940). His condemnation of dictatorship led to a ban on his work by the Nazis in 1933; five years later he went into exile in Switzerland, where he died.

Kaminska, Esther Rachel *See* JEWISH DUSE *under* DUSE, ELEONORA.

Kamiriithu A Kenyan theatre project established in 1976 at Limuru by workers, peasants, and university staff to stage controversial plays about class and exploitation. Although it was closed down by the Kenyan authorities, this democratic experiment served as an inspiration to many African writers and artists.

The first *Kamiriithu* performance, put on in an open-air theatre built voluntarily by the local people, was *Ngaahika Ndeenda* (*I'll Marry When I Want*), which attacked the ruling classes for exploiting the workers and promoting foreign interests. The production was described by the *Sunday Nation* in Nairobi as "a play of the people...for the people, by the people". Within seven weeks, however, the play was banned and the project's leader, Ngugi wa Thiong'o, was arrested and imprisoned. After his release a year later he returned to help the community produce *Maitu Njugira* (*Mother Sing to Me*), a play about the early resistance to colonial domination. The government closed the community centre, razed the open-air theatre, and banned further performances of the play (although thousands of people turned out to see 'rehearsals' at the University of Nairobi).

Karagöz (Turk. dark eyes) An impudent and bawdy comic character in Oriental shadowplays. Karagöz was created in Turkey, apparently by a sheik called Kishteri; the name may have come from a 13th-century entertainer. Karagöz is a young reveller with a large penis and a quick and filthy wit. He is often accompanied by the boastful Hacivat and his wife, and sometimes by a selection of stereotyped national characters, all of whom serve as butts for his jokes. The character is known in North Africa as Karagush or Karogheuz. The Greek version, Karaghiosis, developed after the revolution of 1821; he was, in contrast to his Turkish counterpart, a decent fellow who travelled the country with a band of musicians promoting freedom and morality.

Kariyala An Indian theatre form popular among Hindu villagers in the state of Himachal Pradesh. The plays celebrate local traditions of dress, worship, and morality, by telling stories of ordinary life using a range of familiar characters. Music, dance, and satirical humour enliven the performances, which sometimes last all night. There is also a religious element with a chorus that sings praises to the gods. *See also* BHAND JASHNA.

Karno, Fred (Fred Westcott; 1866–1941) British showman, whose troupes of slapstick comedians (**Karno's Krazy Komics**) kept audiences entertained in the early 20th century. Both Charlie Chaplin and Stan Laurel began their careers with Karno. Hal Roach, the US film producer, once remarked:

> Fred Karno is not only a genius, he is the man who originated slapstick comedy. We in Hollywood owe much to him.

As a boy Karno ran away from home to become an acrobat with Ginetti's travelling circus. He later created the first famous comic duo of the musical halls – Jack Melville as MEREDITH and Fred Kitchen as Simpkins in *The Bailiffs*, a sketch first seen in 1907 at the Argyle theatre in Birkenhead. The bailiffs always found themselves in difficulties:

> MEREDITH Is this the house?
> SIMPKINS The number's on the warrant.
> MEREDITH Oh dear, I wish I'd brought the piano.
> SIMPKINS Why, what do you want a piano for?
> MEREDITH Well, that's where I left the warrant–on the piano!

By 1901 Karno had recruited **Karno's Army**, five touring companies that featured the combined talents of Chaplin, Laurel, Will Hay, and Bud Flanagan. In 1913 Chaplin took Karno's sketches to Keystone Studios in Hollywood; although he hardly changed them in his films, his former boss never complained.

That same year Karno built his 'Karsino' entertainment palace on Taggs Island in the Thames. By 1926 he was bankrupt, although he made a brief comeback in 1932 with *Laffs* at the London Palladium. In this show he assembled three double-acts, which became the core of the CRAZY GANG.

Five years later, Karno had lost all his money and retired to Dorset.

The nickname *Fred Karno's Army* was also given to the new British army raised during the war of 1914–18. The well-known army chorus, sung to the tune of 'The Church's one foundation', runs:

We are Fred Karno's army,
Fred Karno's infantry;
We cannot fight, we cannot shoot,
So what damn good are we?
But when we get to Berlin
The Kaiser he will say
Hoch, hoch, mein Gott
Vot a bloody fine lot,
Fred Karno's infantry.

In World War II 'Old Hitler' was substituted for 'The Kaiser'. The name Karno's Army is also applied derisively to other nondescript bodies.

Kasperl or **Kasperle** or **Kasper** The most popular puppet character in Austria and Germany, where he is the equivalent of Punch (*see* PUNCH AND JUDY). Kasperl was originally acted by Johann Laroche (1745–1806), a leading player at Vienna's Leopoldstadt Theater, who derived the character from HANSWURST. Laroche's Kasperl became a legendary figure in Viennese popular comedy; his leitmotiv was a cavernous moaning from the wings *"Auwedl"* ("Deary me!").

The character was first seen in puppet form in the Austrian Kasperltheater, where he was seen brandishing a bat against such characters as Gretel, Grandmother, the Devil, and Crocodile. The puppeteer Josef Leonhard Schmid (1821–1912) transformed him into an intellectual Bavarian gentleman named Kasper Larifari, while the writer Max Jacob (1888–1967) developed an acerbic self-important Kasperl in the 1920s. The name *Kasper* has subsequently become a German word for any puppet.

Kathakali (Malayalam: story play) A form of Indian dance-drama popular in the state of Kerala. It employs acting, dancing, and music to dramatize stories from the Ramayana, Mahabharata, and the Puranas. The genre, which is noted for its strong masculine dancing and use of facial and hand gestures to illustrate the action, developed from the earlier *Ramanattam* drama, which drew exclusively on the Ramayana. In the 16th century playwrights turned to popular epic material to find new plots, leading to the emergence of the new genre of *Kathakali*.

Although *Kathakali* was originally performed by *Nairs*, or martial arts experts, modern performances mix *Nairs* and other actors. Their training, which begins at the age of 10, takes up to 10 years, during which an actor must learn some 600 hand gestures, memorize the entire repertory of plays, and develop enormous physical stamina.

The performances, which last all night, may feature a main play chosen only hours beforehand. The presentation begins with a percussion overture and dances. This is followed by the main drama, which is chanted by the *ponnani* or leading singer, who strikes a gong, and another plays the cymbals. A *sanka* or conch shell represents the gods on stage. A *Kathakali* troupe successfully toured Britain in 1992.

Kathputli (Hindi: story puppet) A type of string puppet from the Indian state of Rajasthan. The traditional wooden marionettes are carefully crafted, decorated to represent specific characters, and dressed in long skirts as they have no legs or feet. They are now also mass-produced to sell to tourists.

Kathputli puppeteers work in travelling communities, taking their stories of the deeds of kings and heroes from village to village. The stage is constructed from upended wooden cots (*charphoys*), which are connected with a cloth to form a proscenium arch, known as the 'Taj Mahal'; a curtain hides the puppeteers.

A puppet is often inherited as a family heirloom. When it becomes too old and battered to be used, it is given a 'funeral' by being cast into a holy river to the sound of prayer. It is part of the tradition that the longer it floats the more it has pleased the gods.

Kaufman, George S. (1889–1961) US playwright, director, and critic, who dominated Broadway between the two world wars. Between 1903 and 1961 he wrote or collaborated on at least 70 plays and film scripts, included several for the Marx Brothers. He was also a member of the Algonquin Round Table of Wits. As a reviewer for the *New York Times* Kaufman proved to be a sharp critic. He wrote of one comedy:

There was scattered laughter in the rear of the theatre, leading to the belief that somebody was telling jokes back there.

After watching an unfortunate actor named Guido Nadzo, he wrote:

Guido Nadzo is nadzo guido.

Kaufman's cracks were legendary. He told the lyricist and playwright Howard Dietz:

I understand your new play is full of single entendre.

Once when bored during a play, he whispered to the woman in front of him:

Madam, would you mind putting on your hat?

When asked to write his own epitaph, he replied:

Over my dead body.

Kaufman's first successful play, written with Marc Connelly, was *Dulcy* (1921). Because he had only two successful solo efforts, he became known as the **Great Collaborator**.

Kazan, Elia (1909–) US theatre director. Kazan began his career as an actor with the GROUP THEATRE, making his debut as Agate Keller in Odets's *Waiting for Lefty* in 1935. In the 1940s he became increasingly interested in directing and attracted critical attention with his productions of Thornton Wilder's expressionist drama THE SKIN OF OUR TEETH (1942) and such plays as *One Touch of Venus* (1943), and *Jacobowsky and the Colonel* (1944).

After World War II Kazan became associated particularly with the works of Tennessee Williams and Arthur Miller, directing early productions of *A Streetcar Named Desire* (1947), *Death of a Salesman* (1949), *Cat on a Hot Tin Roof* (1955), and *Sweet Bird of Youth* (1959). In 1947 he was instrumental in founding the ACTORS' STUDIO, which helped to popularize the METHOD in America. After two years (1962–64) as co-director of the Lincoln Center for the Performing Arts in New York, he retired from the theatre to write novels.

The influence of Kazan's naturalistic style can be seen in many US films of the 1950s and 60s.

Kean, Edmund (1789–1833) English actor, who introduced romanticism to the London stage and fascinated the public both in his dramatic roles and in his private life. The poet Samuel Coleridge said of him:

To see him act is like reading Shakespeare by flashes of lightning.

Kean was the son of a failed actress who deserted him to join a group of strolling players. In 1814 he made a spectacular London debut as Shylock at the Drury Lane Theatre followed by a brilliant rendering of Richard III. Of this performance Lord Byron remarked:

Richard is a man and Kean is Richard.

By 1816 Kean was earning more than £10,000 a season. Unfortunately, his drinking was beginning to make him miss performances. After one spree, he sent word to the theatre that he had dislocated his shoulder in a carriage accident and was therefore unable to appear. The next morning, he was horrified to see friends and admirers streaming into the village where he was recovering. He had no option but to take to his bed with a bandaged arm, where he gave one of his best 'performances' for his sympathizers.

In 1925 Kean began an affair with Charlotte Cox, the wife of a City alderman, which was soon discovered. The scandal turned both the press and theatregoers against him; he was hissed on stage and met unfriendly demonstrations on provincial tours. He subsequently settled in Richmond, Surrey and managed his own theatre there. In 1833, he collapsed on stage, dying two months later after springing from his couch to shout:

A horse! A horse! My kingdom for a horse!

Keene, Laura (Mary Moss; 1826–73) The first US woman to open and manage her own theatre (in 1856). Although her production of Tom Taylor's *Our American Cousin* in 1858 proved a great success, her prosperity came to an end with the outbreak of the American Civil War in 1863. Keene subsequently toured with her company, which included Joseph Jefferson (*see* JEFFERSON FAMILY) and E. A. Sothern (*see* SOTHERN FAMILY), the latter starring with her in *Our American Cousin*. It was during a performance of this play in 1865 that President Lincoln was shot (*see* FORD'S THEATRE). Keene, who had toured Australia with Edwin Booth, was the first person to recognize the fleeing assassin as his brother, John Wilkes Booth (*see* BOOTH FAMILY). It was also Keene who held the dying president in her arms until he was carried out of the theatre.

She reopened New York's Fourteenth Street Theatre in 1871 and retired from the stage in 1872.

Kemble family A British theatrical family, the principal members of which were John Philip Kemble (1757–1823), his sister Sarah SIDDONS, his brothers Stephen Kemble (1758–1822) and Charles Kemble (1775–1854), and Charles's daughter Fanny (1809–93).

John Philip Kemble began his career as a child actor with his parents' touring company. His mother continued to act while raising 12 children, all of whom appeared on stage together in 1767 in Worcester. Although John was sent to study for the priesthood the lure of the theatre proved too great; he made his adult debut at Dublin's Smock Alley theatre before appearing as Hamlet at Drury Lane in 1783; of this performance one critic remarked: "How very like his sister!" Kemble subsequently appeared in most of the great tragic roles, winning particular acclaim for his *Lear* (1787). He became manager of Drury Lane in 1788 and of Covent Garden in 1802, where his decision to raise prices triggered the O.P. RIOTS. Kemble could hardly be persuaded to watch his great rival Edmund KEAN act; when someone asked if he had finally seen Kean, he replied:

> No, sir, I did not see Mr Kean. I saw Othello, and further, I shall never act the part again.

Stephen Kemble made his London debut in 1783, when he played Othello at Covent Garden. His choice of roles was somewhat restricted by his extreme corpulence. Hazlitt was among those unimpressed by his talents:

> We see no more reason why Mr Stephen Kemble should play Falstaff than why Louis XVIII is qualified to fill a throne because he is fat and belongs to a particular family.

Stephen was more successful as a manager, running theatres in Edinburgh, Glasgow, and Newcastle. He was briefly manager of Drury Lane (1818).

Charles Kemble made his first stage appearance in a Drury Lane production of *Macbeth* starring John and Sarah. He excelled in Romeo and other romantic roles; Thackeray later claimed that "the chivalrous Charles Kemble" was his favourite actor as a schoolboy. Kemble became manager of Covent Garden in 1817 but only survived bankruptcy through the help of his young daughter, **Fanny Kemble**. She had long wanted to be a novelist but took to the stage in 1829 in an attempt to save her father's fortunes. She was an instant success, playing Juliet to packed houses, despite being so nervous that she had to be pushed onto the stage. She later toured America with her father, and in 1834 married an American. In 1848, however, she returned to England to act with William MACREADY and her husband sued for divorce on the grounds of desertion. When Fanny died in 1893, the family's hold on the British theatre came to an end.

Kempe, William *See* THE NINE-DAYS' WONDER.

Kendals, the The actors **W. H. Kendal** (William Hunter Grimston; 1843–1917) and **Madge Sholto Robertson** (1848–1935), who married in 1869; thereafter they excelled in comedies and also managed St James's Theatre together. Madge Kendal, a lifelong rival of Ellen TERRY, was more brilliant and popular than her husband and had a wider range, sometimes playing such classical roles as Ophelia (1865).

In 1887 the Kendals gave a command performance for Queen Victoria at Osborne House on the Isle of Wight, when they played in W. S. Gilbert's comedy *Sweethearts*. The queen rewarded Madge with a brooch shaped like the royal crown made of diamonds, sapphires, and rubies.

The Kendals retired together in 1908, Madge being made a DBE in 1926. On her 80th birthday she recorded *As You Like It* for the BBC. The director politely pointed to the microphone and said, "and that, Dame Madge, is your Orlando". She returned a gracious smile and shook her head, "Ah, my husband was better-looking than that".

Khoktu kaksi A type of Korean puppet theatre dating back to at least 600 AD. The repertoire of a travelling *Khoktu kaksi* company would usually be made up of sketches dealing with such subjects as official corruption, domestic life, and even the sins of Buddhist monks. Korean puppets are unusual as they are manipulated using a combination of strings, rods, and the puppeteers' fingers.

Khyal or ***Khyala*** In India, a form of village theatre popular in the states of Uttar Pradesh and Rajasthan. The earliest evidence of the genre is found in Agra and dates from the 18th century. Although there are many variant forms, the dramas are usually mythological or historical with romantic and heroic themes; they are performed by elaborately costumed male actors, generally to a musical accompaniment.

The stage consists of a low-level acting area, the main stage, and a balcony; the main stage is often framed by four banana-tree trunks placed in the ground, from which colourful flags and lanterns are strung. Before the stage is constructed a pole is ritually planted in the ground; performances begin with prayers to Ganapati, the elephant-headed god, and other deities.

Killigrew, Sir Thomas (1612–83) English playwright and theatre manager. A member of the household of Charles I, Killigrew enjoyed moderate success with several comedies and tragicomedies before the INTERREGNUM, most notably with the bawdy comedy *The Parson's Wedding* (1641), based on a work by CALDERÓN de la Barca. Described as an "obscene, loose play" by Pepys, *The Parson's Wedding* was revived in 1664 after Killigrew had returned to London with his friend Charles II and was to influence the comedies of the Restoration period.

Killigrew is remembered less for his own plays than for his work in re-establishing the English theatre after the Restoration. Having been granted a patent (*see* PATENT THEATRES) by the king he founded (1662) the Theatre Royal, DRURY LANE, where he led a company that included Michael Mohun and Nell GWYNN. He also founded a training school for actors at the Barbican and in 1673 was appointed MASTER OF THE REVELS.

Kinet or ***Kinet Gwadd*** A revolutionary theatre company in Ethiopia. There are many such companies, all of which follow a policy of 'Art for Revolution', using political subject matter to influence their audiences. They are often made up of members of youth groups, women's associations, workers' cooperatives, or other organizations. The plays are usually devised and produced collectively with simple staging. Although *Kinet* companies sometimes employ *Azmareewoch*, or professional actors and musicians, audience participation is central to the productions – everyone joins in handling props and costumes, dancing, singing, and clapping to the beat of songs.

king. ***King and I, The*** The RODGERS AND HAMMERSTEIN musical about a Victorian English governess in Siam (modern Thailand), first performed in 1951 at New York's St James's Theatre. The King was played by Yul Brynner, Gertrude LAWRENCE played the governess, and 17 young Puerto Ricans appeared as the royal children. One of the best-known tunes, 'Getting to Know You', was added just before the New York opening after Gertrude Lawrence had asked for a number that she could sing with the children. Sadly, cancer forced Lawrence to leave the production during its run of 1246 performances (she died in 1952). Brynner also played the King in the 1956 film with Deborah Kerr and in the 1979 London Palladium production with Virginia McKenna.

The plot, based on Margaret Langdon's book *Anna and the King of Siam*, concerns the English governess Anna Leonowens, who goes to Siam to tutor the 67 children of the King. The King, with whom she falls in love, comes to rely on her advice in dealing with European powers but she resigns after he beats one of his concubines. As she is leaving, he falls mortally ill and they are reconciled before he dies. Songs from the show include 'Shall We Dance?', 'Hello, Young Lovers', and 'I Whistle A Happy Tune'.

King John, The Life and Death of A history play by SHAKESPEARE written in about 1596; the first recorded performance was a revival staged in 1737. Shakespeare appears to have based his work on an anonymous play called *The Troublesome Raigne of John King of England* (1591), although the true relationship between the two works is much debated. The witty and abrasive character of 'Bastard' Faulconbridge was added by Shakespeare, who also toned down the element of anti-Catholic propaganda in the other play.

John's throne appears to be threatened when the claims of his young nephew, Arthur of Bretagne, which are supported by King Philip of France. After an abortive invasion of France, John arranges to marry his niece to the Dauphin and cedes Philip some of his minor French possessions. However, this fragile peace is shattered when the Pope excommunicates John and calls on the French to attack England. When the French army is defeated, Arthur falls into the hands of John, who orders his murder (in the event Arthur dies while escaping from prison).

Assuming that John is responsible for his nephew's death, many of the English nobles desert to the French. John himself dies of poison administered by a monk.

King Lear SHAKESPEARE's great tragedy, often regarded as his finest work. It was first performed in 1606 in London. Lear's tragic journey from imperious rage, through madness and humiliation, to painful self-knowledge, makes the role perhaps the most demanding in the whole theatrical canon. Great Lears have included Irving, Wolfit, Olivier, and Paul Scofield. Nahum TATE's notorious rewritten version (1681) of *King Lear* had a happy ending: Cordelia and Edgar become lovers, while Lear survives and is restored to the throne.

The plot traces the fate of Lear, king of Britain, after he has decided to divide his realm between his three daughters according to the extent of their professed love for him; because she refuses to flatter his vanity he disinherits his favourite, CORDELIA. When his other daughters GONERIL and REGAN harass and mistreat him, Lear flees out on to the heath, accompanied only by his fool and the disguised Duke of Kent. In the ensuing storm he loses his mind. Although Cordelia returns from France with an army and the two are reunited, they are subsequently captured and imprisoned. In the last scene (which Dr Johnson confessed himself unwilling to reread) Cordelia is hanged, and Lear dies with her body in his arms. A parallel subplot deals with the fortunes of the Duke of Gloucester and his two sons.

In one 18th-century production at the Edinburgh Theatre the unfortunate actor playing Lear was obliged to leap over nine-pound cannon balls rolling across the stage. The balls were part of a contraption to create a thunder sound-effect, which had fallen over in the wings. A different problem faced William MACREADY when he played the role in Nottingham; when the moment came for Lear to divide his kingdom a slightly deaf props man handed the bemused actor not a map but a mop.

Shakespeare's immediate source for the story of Lear was the historian Holinshed, who in turn derived it from Geoffrey of Monmouth's *Historia Britonum*. Camden tells a similar story of Ina, King of the West Saxons. The earliest known version of the king is Lir, an ocean god of early Irish and British legend. In the romance *The Fate of the Children of Lir* his children are transformed into swans by the wicked Aoife. Lir appears in the *Mabinogion* as Llyr.

King of Misrule *See* LORD OF MISRULE *under* LORD.

King's Men *See* CHAMBERLAIN'S MEN.

Kipphardt, Heinar (1922–82) German playwright, noted for his pioneering work in DOCUMENTARY THEATRE. After training in medicine, Kipphardt became resident playwright for the Deutsches Theater in Berlin, for which he wrote such plays as *Wanted Urgently: Shakespeare* (1954). In 1959 he moved to West Germany. *In the Matter of J. Robert Oppenheimer* (1964), was his first important work to employ documentary techniques. Intended originally for television, the play broke new ground in its handling of recent historical facts, in this case the McCarthyist intrigues surrounding the US nuclear physicist Oppenheimer.

Joel Brand – the History of a Deal (1965) applied similar techniques to the subject of Nazi attempts to exchange Jewish prisoners for military equipment. Kipphardt's later documentary dramas included *The Life of the Schizophrenic Poet Alexander März* (1981) and *Brother Eichmann* (1983), which drew parallels between the beliefs of the notorious Nazi fugitive and military thinking in Cold War Europe. Among his other plays was the black comedy *The Night the Boss was Slaughtered* (1967).

Kiss Me Kate A musical comedy by Cole PORTER (libretto by Bella and Samuel Spewack) based on Shakespeare's THE TAMING OF THE SHREW. First produced on Broadway in 1948 starring Alfred Drake, it won a Tony Award. The critic Brooks ATKINSON wrote:

> In the part of the egotistical actor who plays Petruchio on stage, Mr Drake's pleasant style of acting and his unaffected singing are the heart of the show.

The show presents a play-within-a-play. A touring company is in Baltimore rehearsing *The Taming of the Shrew*, but rows break out between the star and his leading lady, who is also his ex-wife, and between the supporting actress and her boyfriend. Various romantic entanglements and financial problems ensue, so that the Shakespearean tussles on stage become almost indistinguishable from the 'real' lives of the 'cast'. Everything works out in the end, however, when even the mob become entranced by the Bard's poetry.

kitchen sink In the later 1950s, a term applied (often disparagingly) to the new wave of plays that dealt realistically with the domestic lives of working or lower-middle class characters. The use of humdrum or seedy settings in such plays as OSBORNE's *Look Back in Anger* (1956), Shelagh Delaney's *A Taste of Honey* (1958), and WESKER's *Roots* (1959), represented a decisive break with the elegant DRAWING-ROOM COMEDIES of (for instance) Noël Coward or Terence Rattigan. *Roots* actually begins with a character standing at a kitchen sink.

The term had previously been applied to the **kitchen-sink school**, a group of British artists, who held several joint exhibitions in the 1950s. They were known for painting scenes of working-class domesticity in a drably realistic style (e.g. Bratby's *Still Life with a Chip Frier*).

Kleist, Heinrich von (1777–1811) German playwright, who was virtually unrecognized during his lifetime.

His life was as strange and tragic as his plays. Kleist served in the Prussian army for what he called "the loss of seven valuable years" before leaving to devote himself to philosophy and literature. At one point during his travels the French imprisoned him for six months as a suspected spy, time he used to adapt Molière's *Amphitryon*. Over the next ten years he wrote some of the most remarkable plays in the German language while leading an eccentric wandering life in Germany, France, and Switzerland. In 1811 Kleist shot himself after first shooting a terminally ill woman who had pleaded with him to relieve her suffering by euthanasia.

Kleist's plays include THE BROKEN JUG (1808), which is now regarded as a comic masterpiece, the romantic medieval drama *Das Käthchen von Heilbronn* (1810), and *The Prince of Homburg* (1821), which has been highly praised for its psychological insight.

knight. ***Knight of the Burning Pestle, The*** A comedy written by Francis BEAUMONT for the boy company at the Blackfriars Theatre, London; it was first performed in 1607. The play lampoons both the pretensions of the rising middle class and the genre of romantic and fabulous histories.

The plot concerns the adventures of a grocer named Rafe and his wife, who are watching a play in which they are urged to participate by the cast. Rafe joins in as a 'Grocer-Errant, the Knight of the Burning Pestle' and defeats the monstrous barber-surgeon Barberoo; although he wins the heart of Princess Pomponia, he keeps his vow of fidelity to the maid Susan "as long as life and pestle last". The noble Grocer-Errant is killed by a forked arrow through his head but his soul ascends to the Grocers' Hall; Rafe and his wife leave the theatre having invited the players to their house for wine and tobacco.

Knights, The A comedy by ARISTOPHANES. Written during the Peloponnesian war, the play is a savage attack on Cleon, the Athenian demagogue, who had turned down a peace offer from the Spartans in 425 BC, on the entire political leadership in Athens, and on the nature of politics itself. Aristophanes had targeted the same Cleon in his play *The Babylonians* two years earlier; as a result he suffered a mild 'impeachment' from his victim.

When an oracle predicts that Cleon will be replaced by a demagogic sausage-seller, Demosthenes and Nicias conspire to put forward the first sausage-seller they meet. The conspirators are protected by a chorus of knights, and the sausage-seller, Agoracritus, wins over Demos (the populace), who decides to abolish Cleon's rule and restore honest government.

knockabout. **knockabout business** *See* BUSINESS.

knockabout turn A MUSIC HALL name for a noisy boisterous act, usually involving horseplay and slapstick.

Kolam (Sinhalese: appearance) A type of folk theatre from southern Sri Lanka. The form apparently developed from ancient fertility rites; the few surviving plays have pregnancy as a recurring theme. The plays are preceded by ceremonial dancing and chanting to honour the gods and to introduce the stock characters, who wear masks to indicate their status. The masks are ornate and are usually removed when the dialogue begins.

Kolam performances last all night; they were once an important focus for village life.

Krapp's Last Tape (*La Dernière Bande*) Samuel BECKETT's one-act play, first performed in 1958 at London's Royal Court Theatre. Alone on the stage, the old man Krapp, now nearly blind and deaf, listens to tapes he recorded some 30 years earlier; one tape, to which he keeps returning, was made after a failed love affair. He makes a new recording, commenting bitterly on his disappointments as a lover and a writer.

Two performances of the role stand out: one by the German actor Martin Held in Beckett's own production at the Berlin Schillertheater in 1969, and the other by Albert Finney at the Royal Court Theatre in 1973.

Kreeger Theatre *See* ARENA STAGE.

Krishnattam (Malayalam: stories of Krishna) A form of Indian dance-drama from the state of Kerala. Raja Manaveda, a Zamorin king, created the form in the 17th century to glorify Vishnu's incarnation as Krishna. Manaveda wrote the eight plays of the repertory, which dramatize events from the life of Krishna described in the *Bhagavata Purana*. Performances take place in the courtyard of the Guruvayur Temple for pilgrims with a special seating area being reserved for non-Hindus. Many of the all-male performers were given as young boys in service to the temple by their parents. *Krishnattam* has also toured India and played at both European and US venues.

For a fee, pilgrims can request a particular play, with favourites being Krishna's marriage, his miraculous birth, and his destruction of the wicked King Kamsa. Only rarely is the whole cycle of eight plays performed. When it is, the play about Krishna's birth must be acted at both the beginning and end of the cycle because it is considered a bad omen to end with his death. As in KATHAKALI, dance and gesture are used to tell the stories; both forms also share a flamboyant colourful style of costumes.

Kuchipudi A classical Indian dance-drama named after a village in the southern state of Andhra Pradesh. The name is now also applied to any dance of this style.

The first recorded performance was in 1505, when a Brahmin troupe performed for King Vira Narasimha Raya. In the late 17th century Siddhendra Yogi composed *Kuchipudi* plays, requiring members of Brahmin families to perform (once in their lives) the role of Satyabhama, Krishna's jealous wife, in his play BHAMAKALAPAM. This obligation is still in force.

The *Kuchipudi* companies have always toured. Performances, which last all night, are given in an open space in front of a temple and begin with a prayer to the goddess Amba. Dancers follow, before the stage manager (*sutradhara*) announces the play. A dancer enters wearing the mask of the elephant-headed god Ganapati, followed by the chief character, who enters with a spectacular flash produced by resin powder thrown onto an oil torch. Actors are required to be skilful and acrobatic dancers and to learn the repertoire of hand and body gestures; exceptional performers are honoured by members of the audience, who stop the show to adorn them with fresh flowers.

kunqu A Chinese theatrical form, which developed from an earlier musical style of the same name. In the 16th century Wei Liangfu and others created a more complex style from traditional *kunqu* music by combining a variety of local musical forms. This new style was adopted by the writer Liang Chenyu for his musical plays. It became immensely popular and soon became a genre in its own right, influencing the direction of the Chinese theatre. *Kunqu* dramas usually concern tales of young love and its attendant problems.

The genre began to decline during the late 18th century, when it was overshadowed by the more energetic form of the PEKING OPERA. However, in 1961 students from the Shanghai School of Dramatic Art staged a *kunqu* play after eight years of training under Yu Zhenfei. Although the Cultural Revolution temporarily halted its revival, *kunqu* is now undergoing a minor renaissance.

Kuppelhorizont (Ger: dome horizon) A device invented in 1902 by Mariano Fortuny (1871–1949) to reflect light onto the stage. Fortuny lined a huge plaster hemisphere with silk and suspended it above the stage to act as a reflector and diffuser of the rather harsh electric light. It was later superseded by the CYCLORAMA.

Kuravanji An Indian theatrical form that originated in the 17th century, possibly deriving from ritual dances at holy shrines.

The style of the performances and their associated customs differ slightly from one region to another. In Tamil Nadu the elephant-headed god of good fortune, Sri Vighneswara, is honoured before each performance and a clown (*kattiakaran*) announces the theme of the drama. The plays tend to tell love stories and focus almost exclusively on female characters.

The Maharaja Serfoji II (1798–1833) adapted *Kuravanji* dialogues so that one of the main characters, the gypsy, could describe her country of origin through song and dance. In this way the audience, who had few educational resources, could learn about the world outside their own village.

Kutiyattam A traditional form of Indian theatre from the state of Kerala. It is documented as an established form from around 950 AD and probably derives from the ancient Sanskrit theatre. *Kutiyattam* plays have been written in Sanskrit as well as in Prakrit and Malayalam.

The procedures to be observed during a performance are recorded in ancient manuals of instruction, which the actors follow closely. The performers, who traditionally come from the Cakyar caste, wear make-up and decorative costumes; a sophisticated code of exaggerated expressions and gestures is used.

Few *Kutiyattam* performances are held today. The Vatukumnathan Temple presents at least one a year, while others are sometimes presented in Kerala and elsewhere in India. A performance is always preceded by ritual worship, and continues throughout the night. In some cases a festival of performances can extend over several days.

Kyd, Thomas (1558–94) English playwright, about whose life and works little is now known. Kyd was a contemporary of Spenser and a friend of MARLOWE (although it has been suggested that he may have been implicated in the murder of the latter). He was criticized by the court poets for his lack of formal education but enjoyed great popularity as a dramatist. None of his early work having survived, he is chiefly remembered for THE SPANISH TRAGEDY (*c.* 1589), the first English REVENGE TRAGEDY. This violent and bloody play proved extremely popular and was revived after the Restoration in a production remarked upon by Samuel Pepys. Its influence can be seen in English tragedy throughout the 17th century, most notably in Shakespeare's HAMLET, which employs not only the revenge theme but also the use of a play-within-a-play to reveal the identity of the murderers. He is thought to have contributed to ARDEN OF FAVERSHAM.

Kynaston, Ned (Edward Kynaston; 1640–1706) The most celebrated FEMALE IMPERSONATOR of the Restoration theatre. Although women were permitted to act on the British stage after 1660 there was a shortage of willing performers. Samuel Pepys said that Kynaston made "the loveliest lady that ever I saw in my life" and added, after seeing him in Ben Jonson's *Epicoene*, that he was "clearly the prettiest woman in the whole house". Kynaston's most famous role was as Evadne in *The Maid's Tragedy*; he also played Juliet to Thomas Betterton's Romeo on several occasions.

The youthful beauty of Kynaston also attracted London's fashionable ladies, who would often call after a matinée to take him, still in costume, on carriage rides through Hyde Park.

On one occasion King Charles II was impatiently waiting for a tragedy starring Kynaston to begin; when the curtain failed to rise at the appointed time he sent word backstage asking for an explanation. The master of the company hurried to the royal box and informed His Majesty that "the Queen was not shaved yet".

As he approached middle age Kynaston began to play heroic male parts, such as Shakespeare's Henry V. In his later years, one young apprentice, Colley CIBBER, found that:

> his handsomeness was very little abated; even at past 60 his teeth were sound, white, and even as one could wish to see in a reigning toast of 20.

Kyōgen In Japan, a farcical interlude presented between NŌ plays. Its clowning is similar to that of the COMMEDIA DELL'ARTE, and forms a deliberate contrast with the nobility of *Nō*. The plots focus on such human weaknesses as greed and lechery. Unlike most Eastern drama *Kyōgen* is traditionally acted without music or masks; it is still popular today.

L

Labiche, Eugène (1815–88) French writer of FARCES solely or partly responsible for the creation of over 160 plays during a 40-year writing career. Labiche's first major success came in 1848 with the one-act *A Young Man in a Hurry*. His reputation was consolidated by the success of *An Italian Straw Hat* (1851) about a young man's attempts to replace a straw hat eaten by a horse on the day of his wedding. The play, which has been frequently revived, is best-known in Britain in the version by W. S. Gilbert. Other successes included *M Perrichon's Trip* (1860) and *The Piggy Bank* (1864). Towards the end of the 1870s interest in farce began to decline and Labiche ceased to write. In 1878 a massive, though by no means comprehensive, volume of Labiche's plays was published resulting in his election (1880) to the French Academy.

lady. Lady Bountiful The original character of this name appears in Farquhar's THE BEAUX' STRATAGEM (1707). The expression became part of the general language, meaning a benefactress, about a century later.

Lady of the Camellias, The The first play by Alexandre Dumas *fils* (*see* DUMAS FAMILY), adapted from his own romantic novel of the same name (1848). Also known as *Camille*, the play was banned from the French stage for three years because of its sympathetic treatment of its heroine, a courtesan; the character was based on Dumas's mistress, Marie Duplessis. It was first performed in 1852 in Paris and became one of the most successful plays of the late 19th century. The passionate and tragic role of Marguerite Gautier was much coveted by actresses. Eleonora DUSE made her first London appearance in the part in 1893 while Edwige Feuillère was acclaimed for her portrayal in 1940. The play was the source of Verdi's opera *La Traviata* (1853). Film versions include those starring Sarah BERNHARDT (1912) and Greta Garbo (1936).

Set in the Paris of the 1840s, *The Lady of the Camellias* is a romantic story about a prostitute who wins the love of the young Armand Duval and eventually dies pathetically from tuberculosis in his arms. One of Dumas's reasons for writing it was to appeal against the double standards that then existed between the sexual morals expected of men and those expected of women. Dumas subsequently turned to didactic dramas or 'thesis plays', confronting other contemporary social problems.

Lady Elizabeth's Men A Jacobean theatre company formed in 1611 under the patronage of James I's daughter, Elizabeth. The company appeared at court in 1612 and the following year absorbed the Revels Company. With Nathan Field as their leading player they appeared at Philip HENSLOWE'S Hope Theatre in 1614–15, giving the first performance of Ben Jonson's *Bartholomew Fair*. After Henslowe's death in 1616, the company disbanded, some members joining Prince Charles's Men and others dispersing into the provinces.

In 1622 Christopher BEESTON created a new company called Lady Elizabeth's Men to perform at his Phoenix Theatre (*see* COCKPIT THEATRE). They presented works by such dramatists as Thomas Middleton, Philip Massinger, William Rowley, and John Heywood. The company disbanded during the plague of 1625.

Lady's Not For Burning, The A verse play with a medieval setting by Christopher FRY, first produced in 1948 at London's Arts Theatre Club. It owed its success to an enchanting story, elegant language, and a cast that eventually included John Gielgud, Pamela Brown, Claire Bloom, and Richard BURTON.

Before one evening's performance, Richard Burton, who was continually in trouble with the management for his romantic escapades and practical jokes, decided to play a trick on the cast, which included the character actor Esme PERCY, who had a glass eye. Percy and the other actors were horrified to find glass eyes hidden in purses, drinking glasses, and even rolling across the floor.

The play begins with Thomas Mendip, a misanthropic soldier, confessing to murder and requesting to be hanged. The authorities ignore him, being preoccupied with the case of Jennet Jourdemayne, a young girl accused of witchcraft. Jennet's combination of beauty and sweetness finally convinces everyone of her innocence. Thomas then reveals that his 'confession' had been a diversion to save her, and the new lovers quietly leave together.

Lady Windermere's Fan A comedy of manners by Oscar WILDE, first produced in London in 1892. The young but priggish Lady Windermere has become disturbed by the friendship between her husband, Lord Windermere, and Mrs Erlynne, a woman with a scandalous past. Convinced that he is having an affair, she impulsively flees to her admirer, Lord Darlington. When her fan is found in Darlington's apartments, Lady Windermere is threatened with disgrace. Her reputation is saved by Mrs Erlynne, who claims that *she* dropped the fan, having taken it by mistake from the Windermeres'. This act of self-sacrifice is explained by the revelation that she is in fact Lady Windermere's mother.

Some critics complained that the play's action was constantly halted to enable the characters to deliver Wilde's epigrams. "English critics always confuse the action of a play with the incidents of a melodrama," snorted Wilde. "In the act in question [the one most complained about] there was absolutely no action at all. It was a perfect act."

Laird of the Halls, The The nickname of Sir Harry LAUDER, the Scottish singer and comedian who became one of the most successful music-hall stars of the early 20th century.

Lalee The name that Lillie LANGTRY gave to the railcar presented to her by Diamond Jim Brady for her tour of America in 1883. The Indian word sounds close to Lillie and means 'flirt'. The car had 10 rooms including a saloon with piano, a maid's room, a kitchen and pantry, and a bathroom with silver fittings. The roof had brass fitments in lily designs, while the blue exterior was also emblazoned with lilies. The suite was so heavy that the train had to avoid weak bridges.

Lambeth Walk A thoroughfare in Lambeth, London, leading from Black Prince Road to the Lambeth Road. It gave its name to an immensely popular Cockney dance performed by Lupino Lane (*see* LUPINO FAMILY) in the musical show *Me And My Girl* at the Victoria Palace, London (1937). Purporting to imitate the strutting walk of the typical Lambeth cockney, it came to symbolize the spirit of defiance of Londoners during the Blitz in World War II.

> Any time you're Lambeth Way
> Any evening, any day,
> You'll find us all,
> Doing the Lambeth Walk, Oi!

Lambs A London supper club founded by actors in the 1860s. The founding members included Henry IRVING, Squire Bancroft (*see* THE BANCROFTS), and the US actor Henry Montague. It always maintained 24 members, who met under their 'shepherd' first at the Gaiety Restaurant and then at the Albemarle Hotel. Lambs lasted for about 30 years, being disbanded in the 1890s. Montague began a counterpart club in New York in 1875, which still exists.

Land of Heart's Desire, The An early verse play by W. B. YEATS. It was first performed in 1894 at the Avenue Theatre, London, and later became part of the ABBEY THEATRE's repertory. Based on an ancient Irish legend about a fairy who takes on the disguise of a child in order to lure away the wife of an elderly farmer, the play also reflects Yeats's interest in the symbolist drama of Maurice MAETERLINCK and his unrequited love for the beautiful revolutionary Maude Gonne. Yeats wrote the play at the request of the actress Florence Farr, who managed the Avenue Theatre, to provide a part for her eight-year-old niece. It was staged in a double bill with Shaw's ARMS AND THE MAN, also receiving its first production.

Langtry, Lillie (Emilie Charlotte Le Breton; 1853–1929) British actress, famous for her beauty and her affair with the future King Edward VII. The daughter of the dean of Jersey, she married Edward Langtry as a passport to London society, becoming the toast of its fashion setters. When she became pregnant by the Prince of Wales she returned to Jersey for the secret birth of her daughter in 1881. That same year, she caused a sensation by becoming the first society woman to appear on the stage, when she starred in *She Stoops to Conquer* at the Theatre Royal, Haymarket.

Audiences loved her charm and freshness, but critics did not take her seriously either in Britain or America, where she made her debut in 1883. "The crudities of her performance were obvious," wrote one New York newspaper. She toured America in a private railcar (*see* LALEE) provided by Diamond Jim Brady, and earned an unprecedented $6000 a week while critics damned her performance in *As You Like It*. Indeed, she often created chaos on stage through her lack of professionalism, once accidentally handing an actor a piece of celery instead of the flower he expected. On another occasion, she told her leading man, "Let us retire and seek a nosy cook."

Lillie became a US citizen in 1887, the year in which she played Lady Macbeth on Broadway to unexpected critical acclaim. In 1895, her husband, whom she had supported for years, died in a lunatic asylum; she secretly married Sir Jugo de Bathe, the heir to a baronetcy, in 1899.

After a brief retirement, Lillie leased London's grand Imperial Theatre, remodelled and modernized it, and reopened it in 1902 with *Crossways*, which she cowrote. That year she gave a COMMAND PERFORMANCE at the Imperial and dined at the White House with President Theodore Roosevelt.

Lanthorn, Leatherhead A fairground crook and "profane professor of poetry" in Ben Jonson's BARTHOLOMEW FAIR (1614),who was intended by the playwright to represent the architect and stage-designer Inigo JONES. The long-running feud between the two men arose from a disagreement over the priority given to their names on the title-pages of the MASQUEs upon which they collaborated at the court of James I. At first Jonson, who was responsible for the texts of the masques and arranged their publication, gave Jones full credit for his contribution, writing in *Hymenaei* (1606): "The design and Act...belongs properly to the Merit and Reputation of Master Inigo Jones." Later, however, he belittled Jones's role and from 1614 onwards refrained from mentioning his collaborator at all, while caricaturing him in plays and verse. After *Bartholomew Fair* the feud smouldered for a few years before breaking into flame again in the 1630s. Their last collaboration was *Chloridia* in 1631. By this time Jones was preeminent and Jonson's star was on the wane; Jones wanted not only full acknowledgment but also a greater part in the intellectual content of the entertainments. To the irascible Jonson this was the height of pretension on the part of a "Master Surveyor" who had now "leapt forth an architect".

Jones continued in favour at court, planning the masques in personal consultation with Charles I; Jonson, by contrast, was almost penniless when he died in 1637.

Lark, The Jean ANOUILH's successful historical play (the first of his *pièces costumées*) about JOAN OF ARC's trial for heresy. It was first performed in Paris in 1953, translated by Christopher FRY for its opening in London in 1955, and adapted by Lillian HELLMAN for New York later that year.

In London the drama was compared unfavourably with Shaw's *Saint Joan*, which was then playing in the West End. Some critics also felt that the leading role had been miscast; Ronald Barker for one wrote "Dorothy Tutin is temperamentally wrong for Joan." In New York, however, Julie Harris won a Tony Award for her portrayal of Joan and toured with the play through 1956.

Larry Informal name for the LAURENCE OLIVIER AWARDS, probably in imitation of Oscar, the informal name for the Academy Award. 'Larry' was the nickname of Laurence OLIVIER, used both by those in the acting profession who knew him well and – with stagey familiarity – by others who aspired to be on first-name terms with him.

lashline *See* THROWLINE.

Last of the Red Hot Lovers, The A comedy by Neil SIMON, first performed in New York in 1969. The plot concerns the failed amours of Barney Cashman, a middle-aged restaurant owner. Despite being happily married, Barney aspires to be part of the 'swinging sixties', and yearns for an affair. His first assignation, in his mother's empty apartment, is with the unhappily married Elaine. Barney talks nervously throughout the meeting and the couple never reach the bedroom. He tries again with the glamorous but paranoid Bobbi, who talks endlessly about her aspirations to a Hollywood career; instead of sex, she gives Barney marijuana. Lastly, he tries Jeanette, the depressed wife of a philandering friend; realizing the depth of her misery, Barney decides to return to his wife.

lauda A type of early Italian religious drama that combined songs and dialogue. The genre, deriving ultimately from 12th-century hymns of praise was given impetus by a penitential and flagellant movement in the 13th century. The *laudi* began as narrative works but became steadily more dramatic, leading to the later SACRA RAPPRESENTAZIONE. Still later, the tradition of the *lauda* influenced the development of the oratorio.

Lauder, Sir Harry (Hugh MacLennan; 1870–1950), the Scottish ballad singer and comedian who became the first music-hall performer to be knighted. His sentimental songs included 'I Love A Lassie', 'Roamin' in the Gloamin', and 'Keep Right on to the End of the Road', while his comic offerings included 'That's the Reason Noo I Wear A Kilt' and 'Stop Yer Tickling, Jock'.

Curiously enough, Lauder began his career performing as a comic Irishman; only when the demand for encores exceeded his reserve of Irish songs, did he turn to familiar Scottish numbers. In 1900 he became an overnight success at Gatti's Music Hall, London and in 1907 made his US debut in New York. With his familiar stage costume of kilt, glengarry, and crooked walking stick, he became one of the few British music-hall stars to become famous in America, also playing successfully in Australia and South Africa. Lauder also appeared in revue and at least one serious play, Graham Moffat's *A Scrape o' the Pen* (1909). He was knighted in 1919 for entertaining troops during World War I.

Laughing Blacksmith, the The stage nickname of the British MUSIC HALL performer 'Jolly' John Nash (1830–1901), who perfected the laughing song (such as 'Little Brown Jug') and was known for his silly walks. Nash, originally a Gloucestershire metal-worker, made his debut at the Oxford Music Hall. He was the first music-hall artist to appear at a COMMAND PERFORMANCE and in 1874 became the first to tour America.

Laughton, Charles (1899–1962) British-born US actor, who made his professional stage debut in 1926 as Osip in Gogol's *The Government Inspector* and quickly built up a reputation as a character actor. From 1933 onwards he played under Tyrone Guthrie at the Old Vic, winning particular acclaim in Chekhov's *The Cherry Orchard* and as Prospero in *The Tempest*. A fluent French speaker, Laughton became the first British actor to star at the Comédie-Française, playing Sganarelle in Molière's *Le Médecin malgré lui* in 1936. That same year he played Captain Hook in *Peter Pan* at the London Palladium, while his wife, Elsa Lanchester (1902–87), took the title role.

In the 1930s and 1940s Laughton worked mainly in Hollywood, becoming famous for his outstanding character performances. He became a US citizen in 1950 but returned to London eight years later to appear in Jane Arden's *The Party*, which he also directed. In 1959 he was a "ginger-wigged, ginger-bearded" Bottom in Peter Hall's Stratford production of *A Midsummer Night's Dream* and two years later he directed his wife in her one-woman show, *Elsa Lanchester – Herself*.

One night at the Old Vic Laughton took a curtain call in response to cries from the gallery of "Good old Nero!" (referring to the part he had played in the recent film, *The Sign of the Cross*). The audience then called for Elsa Lanchester, who was in the audience. "Bring her up!" shouted a loud voice in the gallery. Laughton snapped back, "Many people have tried to do that, my friend, but they have not succeeded."

Laurence Olivier Awards Britain's most prestigious theatrical awards; first presented in 1976 as the **Society of West End Theatre Awards**, they were renamed in 1984 to honour Sir Laurence OLIVIER. The awards are given to outstanding actors, dancers, singers, playwrights, composers, directors, and designers. There are three adjudicating panels for theatre, opera, and dance, each of which includes representatives of both the theatre world and the general public. The awards are known colloquially as LARRYS.

Lawrence, Gertrude (Gertrud Alexandra Daymar Lawrence Klasen; 1898–1952) British actress, famous chiefly for her appearances in plays and revues by her friend Noël COWARD. The daughter of a British actress and a Danish music-hall singer, she made her debut in *Dick Whittington* at the age of 12. Her first successful appearance was in Coward's revue *London Calling* (1923). She subsequently worked closely with Coward, with whom she enjoyed a curious love-hate relationship. It was for her that he wrote the part of Amanda in PRIVATE LIVES (1930), in which she played opposite

Coward when it opened. Her Broadway appearances included roles in *Pygmalion* (1945) and *The King and I* (1951).

In 1965, thirteen years after her death, the biopic *Star* appeared with Julie Andrews playing Gertrude. Coward commented in his diary:

> ...about as suitable as casting the late Princess Royal as Dubarry [the mistress of Louis XV]...*Why* they are doing the film I shall never know. There isn't any real story beyond the fact that she started going in the theatre, became an understudy, then a star, lived with Philip Astley, Bert Taylor, etc., married Richard Aldrich, and died.

On the day after her marriage to Aldrich, a US theatre manager, Coward sent her a cable reading:

> Dear Mrs A. Hurray, hurray. At last you are deflowered.
> On this as every other day, I love you, Noël Coward.

lazzo An improvised comic interpolation used to enliven the main action of the COMMEDIA DELL'ARTE. Usually introduced when the action seemed in danger of flagging, the *lazzo* might consist of an unexpected pun, a topical allusion, or a piece of pantomime. *Lazzi* were often vulgar, sadistic, or slightly disgusting; a popular example involved HARLEQUIN catching and eating a fly. A longer version of the *lazzo*, known as the BURLA, frequently involved a practical joke. Both forms are thought to have influenced the SLAPSTICK antics of Charlie Chaplin, the Keystone Cops, and others.

Leather Lungs The nickname of the British singer and actress Elaine Paige (1948–), who appeared on the London stage in the musicals *Hair*, *Jesus Christ Superstar*, and *Grease*, before achieving stardom in the lead role in Andrew LLOYD WEBBER'S EVITA (1978). She subsequently enjoyed success as a pop singer and in the musicals *Cats* (1981) and *Chess* (1986). In the mid 1990s she found new stardom in the US in the Broadway production of Lloyd Webber's *Sunset Boulevard*.

Lecouvreur, Adrienne (1692–1730) French actress, who brought a delicate naturalistic style to the French stage during an era of bombastic overacting. VOLTAIRE called her "this incomparable actress, who almost invented the art of speaking to the heart". Unfortunately her success inspired jealousy in her fellow actresses. After making her Paris debut (1717) in Crébillon's *Électre* at the Comédie-Française, Lecouvreur went on to increase her reputation in works by Racine, Molière, and Corneille. She was equally famous for her beauty and her charm, and her salon became renowned as a meeting place for artistic Parisians.

In 1721 Lecouvreur became the mistress of Maurice Saxe, which made her the target of an attempt at poisoning by one of Saxe's better established mistresses. Lecouvreur took her revenge by stationing herself directly under the box of her rival to deliver a strong speech about those who commit crime and show an unblushing countenance. Saxe's desertion of Adrienne is said to have caused her sudden death six months later at the age of 38, although her public predictably blamed poisoning.

As an actress, the Church refused to allow her a Christian burial. Her body was interred at midnight in a corner of the Rue de Bourgogne with such secrecy that it has never been found. She had died in the arms of Voltaire, who wrote a furious poem against the Church in France, contrasting her funeral with that of the British actress Anne OLDFIELD, buried in Westminster Abbey earlier that year.

Lecouvreur was further immortalized in the successful but historically inaccurate play *Adrienne Lecouvreur* by Eugène SCRIBE and Ernest Legouve (1849).

Lee, Gypsy Rose Stage name of Rose Louise Hovick (1914–70), the US STRIPTEASE artist noted for the wit, sophistication, and style she introduced to her craft. Together with her sister (later the actress, June Havoc), she joined her mother on the vaudeville circuit at a very early age. At 14 she had her first engagement in BURLESQUE; within two years she was on Broadway, heading the bill at Billy Minsley's Republic Theatre. Dubbed the **Queen of Burlesque**, she was lionized by some of New York's most celebrated writers and intellectuals, and became a regular contributor to such publications as *Harper's* and *The New Yorker*. In 1937 she announced her retirement as a stripper; she then moved to Hollywood to make her film debut, in *You Can't Have Everything*. Over the next three decades she played in a further eight, generally rather mediocre, films. She quite regularly emerged from retirement to make stage appearances and wrote two popular thrillers, *The G-string Murders* and *Mother Finds a Body*. Her autobiographical book, *Gypsy* (1957), formed the basis for a successful Broadway musical of the same name (1959) and later for a rather less successful film version (1962).

> God is love, but get it in writing.
> GYPSY ROSE LEE.

leg *See* FLAT.

leg show A stage performance featuring a display of women's legs, this being a special feature of REVUE, US BURLESQUE, and some early musicals. The leg show can be traced back to the invention of tights for acrobats and dancers in the late 18th century (the Church permitted female performers to wear blue tights but considered pink ones indecent). The 'Spanish' dancer Lola MONTEZ scandalized her audiences in the mid 19th century by dancing without tights. Famous leg shows have included the can-can dance at the MOULIN ROUGE, Paris, in the late 19th century and the lavish display of showgirls in the ZIEGFELD *Follies*.

legitimate drama or **theatre** Serious theatrical work as distinguished from other stage presentations or from the output of such mass media as the cinema and television. The distinction originated in the 18th century, when unlicensed playhouses grew up all over London to compete with the two PATENT THEATRES, Drury Lane and Covent Garden (*see* LICENCE). These avoided the letter of the law by combining music, dancing, and other forms of entertainment with the drama they presented. The term 'legitimate drama' arose by contrast to describe the straight presentations of serious full-length plays offered by the patent theatres.

Leicester's Men England's first household company of actors, founded in 1559 under the patronage of the Earl of Leicester. The company included the carpenter and actor James BURBAGE, who in 1576 built the THEATRE, London's first purpose-built playhouse, and the comedian William Kempe. Leicester's Men performed in Burbage's Theatre and received royal support until 1583, when the rival Queen Elizabeth's Men was founded and poached some of their best actors. On the earl's death in 1588 the company merged with STRANGE'S MEN.

Leigh, Vivien (Vivian Mary Hartley; 1913–67) British stage and film actress, born in India, who made her stage debut in 1935 in Ashley Dukes's *The Mask of Virtue*. In 1937 Leigh played Ophelia to OLIVIER's Hamlet in an Old Vic production at Elsinore. Two years later she married Olivier and costarred with him in a New York production of *Romeo and Juliet*. By this time her popular fame had eclipsed her husband's, owing to her performance as Scarlett O'Hara in the film *Gone With the Wind*, for which she won an Academy Award.

In 1949 Leigh starred as the neurotic Blanche Dubois in the London production of Tennessee Williams's A STREETCAR NAMED DESIRE, which was directed by Olivier: Leigh won much acclaim for this performance and her reputation as a stage actress was greatly enhanced. She recreated her role for the 1951 film version, for which she won a second Academy Award. In that same year Leigh and Olivier played opposite each other in both Shaw's *Caesar and Cleopatra* and Shakespeare's *Antony and Cleopatra*. Leigh won further praise for her performance as Paola in Christopher Fry's translation of Giraudoux's DUEL OF ANGELS. Despite these sucesses, her later years were clouded by depressive illness. In 1960 her marriage to Olivier was dissolved. Following a tour of Australia in 1962, she made her musical debut in New York in *Tovarich* (1963); her final performance was in a New York production of Chekhov's *Ivanov* in 1966.

On Leigh's death from tuberculosis a year later the exterior lights of West End theatres were dimmed for an hour as a mark of respect.

Leipzig style A highly formal style of acting promoted in the early 18th century by the German playwright and literary critic Johann Gottsched (1709–66) through his collaboration with the actress Carolina Neuber (1697–1760). The new style, characterized by its formal florid gestures, transformed German acting, which had previously relied upon improvisation. The Leipzig style dominated until the latter half of the 18th century, when the new fashion for the BÜRGERLICHES TRAUERSPIEL led to a more realistic style of acting. *Compare* HAMBURG STYLE; WEIMAR STYLE.

Lekain, Henri-Louis (Henri-Louis Caïn; 1729–78) French actor generally considered the greatest tragedian of his day. Although he was a small man with unattractive features and a harsh voice, Lekain overcame these disadvantages through genius, hard work, and charm. He was often compared to his friend David GARRICK, each regarding the other as superior on stage. When Garrick visited Paris, the pair would go to the Champs Elysées and pretend to be drunk to amuse the crowd.

In 1748 Lekain, then an amateur, was discovered by VOLTAIRE, who took the 19-year-old into his own home, converting a room into a theatre for him. Lekain remained for six months, during which he trained with an amateur company composed of Voltaire's friends and family. In 1750 Lekain appeared for the first time at the COMÉDIE-FRANÇAISE in Voltaire's *Brutus*. By 1768 he was acknowledged as the best tragic actor in France.

Lekain was the first man in the French theatre to attempt historical accuracy in COSTUME and, with Voltaire's encouragement, adopted a more natural style of acting than that generally practiced at the time. However, his intensity as an actor often exhausted him, and he had to retire briefly in mid career because of ill health. He caught a chill after appearing as Vendôme in a revival of Voltaire's *Adélaïde du Guesclin* and died just as the author was making his triumphant return to Paris after a 28-year exile. This was the first news Voltaire heard on his arrival; he too died within months.

Leko *See* PROFILE SPOT *under* PROFILE.

Lenaea An ancient Greek festival honouring DIONYSUS. Held annually in January and February, it was important in the development of COMEDY from less theatrical revels. Competitive comedy performances were introduced in about 440 BC and works of tragedy about a decade later.

Leno, Dan (George Galvin; 1860–1904) British cockney star of the MUSIC HALLS, who specialized in comic songs and rambling monologues delivered at top speed. Leno was only five feet tall, had a squeaky voice, and, as Marie LLOYD said, "the saddest eyes in the whole world". He always feigned surprise when the audience laughed at his stories.

Leno made his debut at the age of four when he appeared at the Cosmotheka Music Hall, Paddington, as "Little George the Infant Wonder, Contortionist, and Posturer". He later began to sing and dance, winning the world clog-dancing championship at Leeds in 1880. He adopted his stage name in 1883. Five years later he made his Drury Lane debut as the Baroness in *Babes in the Wood*, going on to play pantomime DAMEs there for the next 15 Christmases, his best known roles being Widow Twankey and Mother Goose. On his death Max BEERBOHM wrote in the *Saturday Review*, "so little and frail a lantern could not long harbour so big a flame."

lens spot *See* FOCUS LAMP.

leotard The tight-fitting one-piece practice costume worn by ballet dancers and acrobats. It was popularized by **Jules Léotard** (1838–70), the French aerialist who invented the flying trapeze in 1859. The son of a gymnastics instructor, Léotard used his amazing agility and grace to perfect the trapeze act. He made a sensational debut at the Cirque Napoléon in Paris in 1859. His first London appearance, in 1861 at the ALHAMBRA Music Hall, inspired the song 'The Daring Young Man on the Flying Trapeze'. In 1959, on the centenary of his debut, a commemorative plaque was dedicated to Léotard at the Cirque d'Hiver.

Lessing, Gotthold Ephraim (1729–81) Germany's first great dramatist and drama critic, who greatly influenced the development of his country's theatrical tradition. Lessing studied with Carolina Neuber's company and she produced his early works, light comedies in the French tradition. However, as a critic he came to oppose the classical style adopted by Neuber and Johann Gottsched (*see* LEIPZIG STYLE) and in a series of critical essays, published as the *Hamburgische Dramaturgie* (1767–68), argued for a freer approach to both acting and writing, citing Shakespeare as an example.

His own plays included the realistic *Miss Sara Simpson* (1755), about a girl betrayed by her lover and poisoned by his mistress, which introduced Germans to domestic tragedy in prose. This was followed in 1767 by an important prose comedy, MINNA VON BARNHELM.

Lessing became Germany's first dramaturge, or dramatist associated with a particular company, when he took such a position with the Hamburg National Theatre in 1767. He was the first writer to make set changes only between acts rather than force delays between scenes. Lessing's final offering was the blank-verse drama NATHAN THE WISE, a plea for religious tolerance. Given its premiere two years after his death, it emerged as an important work when GOETHE revived it in 1801.

Lesson, The A one-act play for three characters by Eugène IONESCO, first seen in Paris in 1951. An early contribution to the Theatre of the ABSURD, it is a paradoxical exploration of the relationship between language and reality. A manic middle-aged professor gives an incoherent and rambling lecture on linguistics to a young student. As he overwhelms her with a torrent of words, she develops a terrible toothache, which he ignores. Then, as he rages on about the definition of the word 'knife', the student suddenly collapses, stabbed to death by the mere word. His maid rushes in to chastise him, reminding him that this is his fortieth victim of the day. As they place the girl's body in a coffin, another student arrives at the door.

lever de rideau Another term for CURTAIN RAISER.

Leybourne, George *See* CHAMPAGNE CHARLIE.

licence An official document permitting a venue or company to present drama or other entertainment. In 1559 Elizabeth I banned unlicensed works and by 1572 touring companies had to obtain a separate licence in each town they visited. Two years later, the MASTER OF THE REVELS was made the licenser of all plays and companies. During the reigns of James I and Charles I, all London companies were licensed to members of the royal family. In 1662 Charles II awarded monopoly patents for theatrical production in the city of Westminster to William DAVENANT at Lincoln's Inn Fields and Thomas KILLIGREW at Drury Lane (*see* PATENT THEATRES).

The **Licensing Act** of 1737 gave the LORD CHAMBERLAIN exclusive power to license theatres, halls, and other venues (except the patent theatres) and also to license (and thereby veto) new plays. A new bill in 1752 required licences for all places of public entertainment within 20 miles of London; this was extended to the whole country in 1788. The unrestricted Irish and US stages welcomed English actors and companies who could not obtain licences.

The exact conditions to be met for licensing were stipulated in the 1843 Theatres Act. This also reduced the Lord Chamberlain's powers, which were finally abolished in the Theatres Act of 1968. *See also* CENSORSHIP.

lie, the greatest *See* THE FOUR PS *under* P.

lighting Artificial light used to illuminate the stage. Lighting first became important during the Renaissance period in Italy, when performances moved indoors. Early forms included the candle, CRESSET, and BOZZE, actors and spectators alike preferring candles to oil lamps because they smoked and smelt less. Early lighting was often experimental: in 1539 San Gallo created a rising sun effect by filling a crystal sphere with water and illuminating it from behind, while in 1545 Sebastiano SERLIO put candles behind coloured glass to produce a romantic glow. Serlio also used barbers' basins as reflectors.

Candelabra were hung directly over the stage in the late 17th and 18th centuries. The main disadvantage was the glare; Samuel Pepys complained in his diary of headaches caused by looking into the candles. In the later 18th century David Garrick followed the lead set by French theatres and removed the overhead candelabra from Drury Lane. FOOTLIGHTS had been in use in England since 1672 but created heat and haze until Henry Irving sank them below stage level at his Lyceum Theatre. In 1876 the Lyceum also became the first theatre to darken the auditorium during a performance (disappointing those who attended the theatre to be seen).

In 1816 the Chestnut Theatre in Philadelphia became the first to be totally lit by gas, followed a year later by the Lyceum, London (which was two days ahead of Covent Garden). Some spectators, however, regretted losing the soft flickering candlelight. 1816 also saw the introduction of LIMELIGHT. Electric lighting was used for the first time at the Paris Opéra in 1864 but it buzzed and flickered and did not become popular until the invention of the incandescent bulb. In 1879 the California Theatre in San Francisco became the first to be lit completely by electricity, followed two years later by the Savoy Theatre, London; again, the change was regretted by some.

Lighting for the modern theatre is coordinated by computerized DIMMER boards. Recent developments include the use of lasers and holography.

lights, before the In theatrical parlance, on the stage, i.e. in front of the footlights.

Lillie, Beatrice (Constance Sylvia Munston, Lady Peel; 1898–1989) Canadian-born actress and singer, who became a star of sophisticated revues in Britain and America. She made her debut in 1914 in London as a ballad singer and later that year appeared in *Not Likely*, a revue by André Charlot. The following year she starred in another Charlot revue, *5064 Gerrard*, in which she dressed in farmer's overalls and sang 'Take Me Back to Michigan'. Her co-star, Jack Buchanan, was especially amused to see her walking about in men's clothing. "Tell me, Beattie," he asked one day "how do you dress, left or right?" Lillie, having no idea that he was referring to the old-fashioned bespoke tailors' question relating to the preferred position of his customer's genitals in relation to his fly, replied "In Number Five, stage left." Buchanan roared with laughter and, as Lillie recalled later, "thought I was brilliant."

In 1922 Lillie appeared in *The Nine O'Clock Revue* (with music written by her sister), which ran for a year in London. She then made her New York debut in *André Charlot's Revue of 1924* with Gertrude Lawrence and Jack Buchanan. She was also a favourite of Noël Coward's, playing in his *This Year of Grace* in New York in 1928.

Her first serious part came in 1932, when she played Sweetie the Nurse in the New York premiere of Shaw's *Too True to Be Good*. During World War II she appeared in sketches and short plays for ENSA. In 1952 she toured the world with her acclaimed one-woman show, *An Evening with Beatrice Lillie*. Her performance prompted Brooks Atkinson to write in the *New York Times* "Lillie is the funniest woman in the world". In 1964 the 68-year-old Lillie played in New York in *High Spirits*, a musical adaptation of Coward's *Blithe Spirit*.

Lillie acquired the title Lady Peel by marrying a descendant of the British prime minister Sir Robert Peel in 1925. She published an autobiography entitled *Every Other Inch a Lady* in 1973.

limelight A vivid light, giving off little heat, produced by the combustion of oxygen and hydrogen on a surface of lime. It was invented by Thomas Drummond (1797–1840) in 1816. Although it was tried at the South Foreland lighthouse in 1861, its main use developed in the theatre, where it was employed to throw a powerful beam upon one actor to the exclusion of others; the light could be adjusted manually to follow an actor around the stage. Hence the phrase **to be in the limelight**, meaning to be in the full glare of public attention. *See* LIGHTING.

Lincoln. Lincoln's Inn Fields Theatre A former London theatre, the first English venue to have a PROSCENIUM ARCH. Built in 1656 as Lisle's Tennis Court, it was converted into a home for the Duke's Company by William DAVENANT in 1661. A year later it became one of London's two PATENT THEATRES. The theatre opened with a revival of Davenant's *The Siege of Rhodes* starring Thomas BETTERTON. Known informally as the Duke's House, the theatre was equipped with movable scenery and staged the first scenic performance of *Hamlet* in 1661 with Betterton in the title role. Dryden's *Sir Martin Mar-All* (1667), written for the company's comedian James Nokes (d. 1696), was also an outstanding success. After Davenant's death in 1668, the company continued at the venue until 1671, when they moved to DORSET GARDEN THEATRE. Lincoln's Inn Fields subsequently reverted to being a tennis court, except for the period 1672–74 when Thomas Killigrew's company played there after fire destroyed the first Drury Lane theatre.

In 1695 Lincoln's Inn Fields was refitted for Betterton's company, which began a decade of performances there with Congreve's *Love for Love*. The company moved in 1705 to Vanbrugh's new Queen's Theatre in the Haymarket (*see* ACOUSTICS). After a period of disuse, Christopher Rich (*see* RICH FAMILY) began to restore Lincoln's Inn Fields shortly before his death; it was reopened by his son John Rich in 1714. Highlights of his management included the first English PANTOMIME (1716) and the first production of Gay's THE BEGGAR'S OPERA (1728).

In 1732 Rich transferred to his new theatre in COVENT GARDEN and Lincoln's Inn became a venue for operas, concerts, and balls, as well as some plays. After the theatre closed in 1744, the building served as a barracks, an auction room, and a china warehouse, before being demolished in 1848.

Lincoln's Men In the Elizabethan era, a small theatre troupe led by Laurence Dutton of the household of the first Earl of Lincoln; the company sometimes took the name of the earl's son, Lord Clinton. They were previously known as the Duttons. From 1572–75 they performed frequently at the court of

Queen Elizabeth I, and then toured the provinces for several years; they disbanded at the end of the decade. Another company of the same name toured the provinces from 1599 to 1610.

Linden Tree, The A two-act drama by J. B. PRIESTLEY; first produced in London in 1947, it ran for 422 performances. The original cast was headed by Lewis Casson and Sybil Thorndike.

The action takes place at the 65th birthday party of Professor Robert Linden in the dull provincial university town of Burmanley. The family, which includes the Professor's son Rex and his two grown-up granddaughters, gathers to celebrate but old wounds are soon reopened and the difference in values between the generations becomes glaringly obvious.

Linsenscheinwerfer *See* FOCUS LAMP.

lion comique In British MUSIC HALL, the character of an aristocratic young man-about-town who sings about the delights of drink. The first *lion comique* was George Leybourne (*see* CHAMPAGNE CHARLIE), while Alfred Vance (*see* GREAT VANCE) also became famous playing the type.

Lisideius One of the speakers in the *Essay of Dramatic Poesy* (1688) by John DRYDEN. Lisideius and his companions Eugenius (representing Charles Sackville), Crites (based on Sir Robert Howard), and Neander (Dryden himself) go boating on the Thames during the celebrated battle (1665) between the English and Dutch navies and discuss the art of playwriting. Lisideius was modelled upon the playwright **Sir Charles Sedley** (1639–1701), who was well known for his popular imitations of the drama of Molière and other French authors.

Sedley was once a favourite of James II but became deeply affronted when the king took his daughter, Catherine, as his mistress, granting her the title of Countess of Dorchester. James was unlucky in his mistresses, who were all notoriously unattractive, prompting wags to suggest that they were chosen for him by his priests. Sympathy was strong for the Sedleys when the news broke, as Sackville observed in *A Faithful Catalogue of Our Most Eminent Ninnies*:

> Poor Sedley's fall e'en her own sex
> deplore,
> Who with so small temptation turn'd
> thy whore.

Sedley longed for revenge; as a Member of Parliament, his opportunity finally came in 1688 when, following James's flight abroad, he voted in favour of the succession to the throne of William and James's daughter Mary. As he explained: "Since his majesty has made my daughter a countess, it is fit I should do all I can to make his daughter a queen."

In his youth the playwright himself was noted for his profligate ways. According to Pepys, he was brought before the courts in 1663 for having displayed himself naked (to a gathering crowd) upon a balcony "acting all the postures of lust and buggery that could be imagined, and abusing of scripture...And that being done, he took a glass of wine and washed his prick in it and then drank it off; and then took another and drank the King's health..."

little. ***Little Foxes, The*** Lillian HELLMAN's three-act drama about greed and corruption, usually considered her best play. It opened in New York in 1939, providing Tallulah BANKHEAD with one of her best-known roles. The 1941 film version starred Bette Davis. In 1981 the play was successfully revived on Broadway (moving to London the following year) with Elizabeth Taylor making a rare stage appearance.

The play depicts a ruthless Southern family, the Hubbards (Regina and her brothers Ben and Oscar), who place financial interests above all else. Regina's ailing husband, Horace, despises the family but lends them money to build a cotton mill. When he discovers that money is also missing from his safe-deposit box ('borrowed' by Oscar's son), Regina precipitates her husband's death by withholding his medicine.

Little Molière *See* under MOLIÈRE.

Little Theatres Small independent theatre companies relying upon unpaid volunteers and financial support from subscribers. In America the Little Theatre movement began at the turn of the century in emulation of the new European art theatres, such as the MOSCOW ART THEATRE. The impact of the first companies, which performed in any available venue (from stables to churches) with a minimum of scenery, was especially felt between 1912–20, when they introduced experimental plays and staging techniques.

The movement began with such companies as The Players in Providence, Rhode

Island (1909) and the Wisconsin Dramatic Society in Madison and Milwaukee (1911). Three important groups were founded in 1912: the Toy Theatre in Boston, '47 WORKSHOP at Harvard University, and the Little Theatre in Chicago. In 1915 three more well-known companies were set up: the Neighborhood Playhouse and the WASHINGTON SQUARE PLAYERS, both in New York, and the Provincetown Players in Provincetown, Massachusetts (which launched the career of Eugene O'NEILL). The famous Pasadena Playhouse opened in 1918 (closing in 1970).

The movement has continued to boom, with the number of Little Theatres increasing from about 50 in 1917 to more than 5000 today; some now have their own venues while others are based on university campuses. A number have acquired professional status. The Little Theatre movement has been supported by such organizations as the Drama League of America (1910–31), the American Community Theatre Association (ACTA; founded in 1958), and the American Association of Community Theatres (founded in 1985). The companies are mostly based outside New York, many being designated CIVIC THEATRES.

Britain's first theatre of this kind was the Stockport Garrick Society, founded in 1901, but the movement did not begin in earnest until the 1920s with the establishment of such companies as Maddermarket Theatre, Norwich (1921), the Village Players of Great Hucklow, Buxton, Derbyshire (1927), which has no members or subscribers and does not list actors' names in the programme, and the Questors Theatre, London (1929). Later companies include the Mountview Theatre, London (1947), which has had its own drama school since 1963, and the Tavistock Repertory Company, London (1932; revived in 1952). The British groups tend to produce from four to eight plays annually, while some also run courses for actors and directors. Most are affiliated to the **Little Theatre Guild of Great Britain**, established in 1946, which provides advice, information, and other assistance.

The Little Theatre movement was also significant in Canada, especially during the 1920s. Among the important Canadian companies are the Hart House Theatre in Toronto and the French-language Compagnons de Saint-Laurent.

Little Tich Stage name of the celebrated music-hall comedian Harry Ralph (1868–1928). As a podgy infant, he was nicknamed 'Tichborne' or 'Tich' in allusion to the corpulent claimant in the Tichborne case, a famous court case involving a false claim to a baronetcy. As he remained only four feet tall, he came to be called 'Little Tich'. He first appeared playing a tin-whistle and became renowned for his stage pranks and satirical humour. He subsequently appeared in pantomime at Drury Lane with Dan Leno and Marie Lloyd. His popularity in Paris gained him the Legion of Honour.

The English words 'titch' and 'titchy', applied to a small person or thing, derive from Little Tich. *See also* DWARFS.

Littlewood, (Maudie) Joan (1914–) British actress and director, who pioneered techniques of COLLECTIVE CREATION and was one of the first to apply the theories of BRECHT in the British theatre.

Littlewood trained at RADA but found both the atmosphere and the teaching stifling and left before completing her course. In the mid-1930s she moved to Manchester and became involved with the Theatre of Action, an innovative company organized by the dramatist and folk singer Ewan McColl, who became her first husband. Following World War II the Theatre of Action was reconstituted under the name of THEATRE WORKSHOP. The company toured extensively, performing a mixed repertoire of classic and modern drama until they found (1953) a permanent home at the **Theatre Royal, Stratford**, East London.

At the Theatre Royal the company embarked on a highly successful series of productions including, in 1955, the British premiere of Brecht's MOTHER COURAGE AND HER CHILDREN. In 1958 Brendan BEHAN's *The Quare Fellow* and Shelagh Delaney's A TASTE OF HONEY were both staged to great acclaim. However, the success of many of these productions often entailed a West End transfer and a subsequent loss of players from the company.

In 1961 Littlewood travelled to Nigeria and the Theatre Workshop staged no new productions for the next two years. Upon Littlewood's return in 1963 the Workshop enjoyed a major success with OH, WHAT A LOVELY WAR, an irreverent musical collage about World War I. Again, however, the subsequent West End transfer meant a loss of players for Littlewood. Other successes included the satirical *Mrs Wilson's Diary* (1967) and *The Marie Lloyd Story* (1967). Littlewood's last Theatre Royal production was *So You Want To Be in Pictures* (1973). Since 1975 she has worked mainly in France.

Those who have worked with Littlewood remember her, usually fondly, as a chain-smoking autocrat who bullied actors into giving performances they considered themselves incapable of. Kenneth Tynan, for instance, recalls her:

> Bellowing instructions through a megaphone in terms that would shame a Fascist traffic cop.

liturgical drama The earliest organized drama in medieval Europe, consisting of various types of play performed in church as part of the Christian liturgy. It developed in French and German Benedictine monasteries in the 10th century, mainly from the tradition of the TROPE, a brief interpolation in the plainsong liturgy. More theatrical elements were gradually introduced into services, especially during Holy Week, which often began with a procession to the church led by a performer in the role of Christ, riding a donkey. The earliest extant playlet survives in the *Regularis Concordia*, a document compiled in about 970 by Ethelwold, Bishop of Winchester.

Although other subjects were treated, the Easter story remained central, with more than 400 plays written on the visit of the three Marys to Christ's tomb. The PASSION PLAY depicted events from the Last Supper to the Crucifixion and the placing of Christ's body in the tomb. The **Nativity play**, telling the Christmas story, soon merged with the **Epiphany play** about the visit of the Wise Men. Other popular subjects included John the Baptist, the three children in the fiery furnace, the conversion of St Paul, and the raising of Lazarus.

The Latin plays were initially performed in church on small structures called 'mansions', which were arranged around a general acting area (*see* MULTIPLE SETTING). The performers usually wore church vestments. From about 1200, however, the plays began to be performed outside, a transition accelerated by the creation of the new feast of Corpus Christi, which falls in May or June. The directions for an early outdoor drama, *The Mystery of Adam*, performed in about 1150, state:

> Then let God go to the church, and let Adam and Eve walk about, innocently delighting in the Garden of Eden. Meanwhile, let demons run back and forth through the square, making suitable gestures.

By the end of the 13th century the dramas had lost their liturgical function and were mainly written in the vernacular, although they were still sometimes performed in churches until at least the 15th century. More secular elements were also gradually introduced. In one 14th-century German play, for example, the story of the three Marys was enlivened by the introduction of a comic spice seller. This comic element became more prominent as the liturgical drama developed into the more sophisticated MYSTERY PLAY. *See also* MEDIEVAL DRAMA.

liturgy (Gr. people work) In ancient Greece, a public service required of wealthy citizens in Athens. One such task was to assist in the staging of a drama – tragic, comic, or dithyrambic – by equipping and paying for a chorus. A patron of this kind, called a CHOREGUS, was chosen in rotation and excused that year from general taxes.

living. Living Newspaper A form of didactic DOCUMENTARY THEATRE that arose in America in the 1930s. Living Newspaper productions would usually define a social problem in a series of short scenes and then call for specific action; the tone was often satirical.

The FEDERAL THEATRE PROJECT, devised by the Roosevelt administration to create employment during the Depression, became particularly closely associated with the form. The Project's New York unit, composed of unemployed theatre personnel and newspaper workers, produced six Living Newspapers. The first, *Ethiopia*, about Italy's invasion of that country, was cancelled before the opening night following pressure from the US State Department. Subsequent presentations, staged by such eminent directors as Elmer Rice and Joseph Losey, dealt with poverty, housing, health care, and civil rights amongst other national issues. The most successful pieces were those written by Arthur Arent; his *Triple-A Plowed Under* (1936) encouraged farmers and consumers to unite against low salaries and food profiteering, *Power* (1937) advocated nationalization of the electrical power industry, while *One-Third of a Nation* (1938) called for low-cost public housing.

Several other Federal Theatre companies wrote Living Newspapers tackling local problems, though few were actually produced. The contentious opinions expressed in Living Newspaper productions led to numerous complaints, and this contributed to the government's closure of the Federal Theatre Project in 1939. However, the documentary techniques employed by the Living Newspapers continued to influence theatrical companies during and after World War II. Even the British army made use of the technique to keep troops up-to-date with political issues and conditions at home.

living picture A group of silent and motionless actors, usually arranged in imitation of a famous painting or to represent a biblical or historical scene. The term is a translation of the French **tableau vivant**. In the 18th century Denis Diderot advocated their use to illustrate emotional and moral states, while in Victorian melodramas they were often introduced at climactic moments and at the ends of acts. The 19th century period also saw the rise of the *pose plastique*, in which naked or near-naked women posed in imitation of classical statuary (such NUDITY being permissible as long as the actress remained motionless). In the music halls naked female performers were sometimes dusted white to resemble 'living statuary'.

In the early 20th century living pictures were an important element in such lavish US revues as the *Ziegfeld Follies* and George White's *Scandals*. A modern example of the *tableau vivant* occurs in Stephen Sondheim's musical *Sunday in the Park with George* (1983), in which Seurat's painting *Sunday on the Isle of La Grande Jatte* comes to life.

living skeleton *See* HUNGER ARTIST.

Living Stage *See* ARENA STAGE.

Living Theatre (LT) The experimental OFF-BROADWAY company founded in 1948 in New York by **Julian Beck** and his wife, **Judith Malina**. Their productions of plays by such writers as Brecht, Cocteau, and Pirandello profoundly influenced the experimental theatre of the 1960s. Beck called their presentations "an image for a changing society".

The Living Theatre acquired a permanent venue in 1959 but was evicted four years later for tax evasion. The company's last production was Kenneth Brown's *The Brig* (1963), an exposé of brutality in a US Marine Corps prison; to see it the audience had to enter the padlocked theatre through the windows. From 1964 until 1968 the LT toured Europe with several politically provocative productions, including a version of *Antigone* (1967) set during the Vietnam War. After a year in Brazil (1970) the Becks moved to Pittsburgh where they presented a series of plays using coal miners and steel workers as actors. The company returned to New York in 1984. Beck died the following year, but Malina and Hanon Reznikov kept the Living Theatre living. The ideas that inspired the company are set out in Beck's book *The Life of the Theatre* (1972) and Malina's *Diaries 1947–57* (1984).

Llareggub An imaginary Welsh seaside town, the setting of Dylan Thomas's UNDER MILK WOOD: *A Play for Voices* (1953). The original model for Llareggub was probably Laugharne, now in Dyfed, where the poet wrote most of his best-known work and is buried. Thomas, however, denied the link and claimed to have derived the name (which he first used in contributions to an Italian periodical in 1952) by spelling 'bugger all' backwards. A production of the work is staged once every three years in Laugharne itself.

Lloyd, Marie (Matilda Alice Victoria Wood; 1870–1922), the most famous of the British MUSIC HALL artists. She made her debut at the Royal Eagle Music Hall at the age of 15 and in 1891 starred with Dan LENO and LITTLE TICH in her first Drury Lane pantomime. By this time she was already well known for her naughty songs and mischievous wink. Her best-loved numbers included 'She'd Never Had Her Ticket Punched Before', 'A Little of What You Fancy Does You Good', and her famous charwoman number about 'The Old Cock Linnet'. These included lines like "If you show the boys just a little bit, it's the little bit the boys admire". A typical skit would have Marie enter holding her famous shabby handbag and battered birdcage and settle onto a park bench with wide slats and chirp, 'Oh dear, I'm nipped in the bud'.

Her admirer T. S. Eliot called Marie "the expressive figure of the lower classes", while James Agate wrote that "She had a heart as big as Waterloo Station", adding that her art "always envisaged the seamy side of life with gusto rather than deprecation."

Marie's private life was a well-known disaster, and her three marriages and two divorces were considered scandalous at the time; she was never invited to take part in a Royal Command Variety Performance. When she was excluded from the first one of these in 1912, she advertised her own shows with posters announcing "Every Performance by order of the British Public". She died three days after collapsing on stage at the Edmonton Empire.

Australian Marie Lloyd, the The Australian music hall singer **Florrie Forde** (Florence Flanagan; 1876–1940). She made her debut in 1894 at the Polytechnic, Sydney, singing 'He Kissed Me When He Left Me and Told Me To Be Brave'. She joined Harry Rickard's company there before settling in London in 1897.

Florrie's large figure became famous in the halls; she earned a reputation as a vivacious singer who could get even the most timid audience to explode into rousing renditions of such songs as 'Hold Your Hand Out, You Naughty Boy', 'Down at the Old Bull and Bush', and 'Has Anyone Here Seen Kelly?' On one occasion an audience had her repeat a popular tune 33 times. She also appeared as a principal boy in pantomime.

Lloyd Webber, Andrew, Baron (1948–) British composer of stage musicals, who in 1996–97 had six productions running simultaneously in London's WEST END. A revival of JESUS CHRIST SUPERSTAR joined five other shows already earning more than 20% of all West End box-office receipts between them. These were CATS (1981), THE PHANTOM OF THE OPERA (1987), *Sunset Boulevard* (1993), and revivals of both the roller-skating spectacular *Starlight Express* (1984), and *By Jeeves* (1975; lyrics by Alan AYCKBOURN). Lloyd Webber's personal fortune has been estimated at well over £300 million. He was raised to the peerage in 1997.

Lloyd Webber dropped out of Oxford after meeting lyricist Tim Rice during his first term. The two established their reputations by collaborating on the two biblical musicals *Joseph and the Amazing Technicolour Dreamcoat* and JESUS CHRIST SUPERSTAR (1971) while EVITA (1976) made them rich. Lloyd Webber's second wife (of three), the singer and dancer Sarah Brightman, starred in most of his musicals of the 1980s.

Aspects of Love (1989) was a more intimate piece, while the £3-million *Sunset Boulevard* was a spectacular reworking of the classic Billy Wilder film. Like most of Lloyd Webber's more recent shows, the latter was previewed in a chapel converted to a private theatre on his estate. The invited audience of 160 paid about £180 each for the privilege. His latest musical, *Whistle Down the Wind*, opened in America in 1997.

Despite his vast commercial success, the critics have often been less than kind to Lloyd Webber's work, accusing him of shallowness and unconscious plagiarism. Lloyd Webber believes he is successful because "the standard of musical being offered is, regrettably, not good. Broadway is worse than ever. Over the last ten years, I've been hoping a new team will emerge and things will change, but it hasn't happened." In 1992 the Master of the Queen's Music, Malcolm Williamson, commented bitterly:

> Lloyd Webber's music is everywhere, but so is Aids.

loa A type of short PROLOGUE used to preface Spanish dramatic works until the 17th century. It was often used to flatter an audience that included high officials; strolling players generally memorized several basic *loas* and reworded them to suit local dignitaries. Usually accompanied by music, the *loa* ranged from a short introductory monologue to a brief drama related in theme to the play that followed. By the 17th century, however, *loas* were normally reserved for new works or the religious plays called AUTOS SACRAMENTALES.

lobsterscope In theatre lighting, a device used to create the effect of slow motion on stage. It consists of a metal disc with slots that is rotated in front of a spotlight to create a flickering beam.

Locrine An anonymous tragedy published in 1595 bearing Shakespeare's initials (W.S.). Marlowe has also been suggested as its author. It is certainly not by either.

The story is taken from Holinshed and Geoffrey of Monmouth. In legendary British history Locrine was the eldest son of the mythical Brutus, King of Britain, and the father of Sabrina. On the death of his father he became King of Logres (Geoffrey of Monmouth: *Historia Britonum*, ch. I–V).

Loman, Willy The central character in the play DEATH OF A SALESMAN (1949) by Arthur Miller. Loman, a failure as a salesman and father, kills himself in a car crash to raise money for his family. The play, a sad commentary on the failure of the American dream, won a Pulitzer Prize.

> Attention, attention must be finally paid to such a person
> *Death of a Salesman.*

London. ***London Assurance*** A comedy by Dion BOUCICAULT, first produced by Madame VESTRIS at Covent Garden in 1841; it was the first play to use a complete BOX SET. The play's success restored the declining fortunes of the theatre and established the reputation of Boucicault (who wrote it under the pseudonym Lee Morton). The play tells the story of Dazzle, a poor young man, who is courting the beautiful and worldly Lady Gay Spanker. In the first New York production (1841), the role of Lady Gay was taken by Charlotte Cushman. The play was frequently revived during the late 19th century. The ROYAL SHAKESPEARE COMPANY's highly acclaimed 1972 production featured an outstanding performance by Donald Sinden as the Regency rake, Sir William Harcourt Courtly.

London Coliseum A large theatre in St Martin's Lane, London, now the home of the English National Opera. It was opened by Sir Oswald Stoll as a variety house in 1904. The theatre's many innovations included London's first REVOLVING STAGE, a mobile lounge to take royal parties to their boxes, lifts to carry audiences to the upper levels, and foyer facilities for typing and sending telegrams. In keeping with its name, the theatre was decorated in splendid Roman style with carved chariots and granite columns. Stoll intended the globe on top of the building to revolve but as this violated the building code he used flashing lights to create the illusion of movement.

The management initially found it difficult to fill the Coliseum's vast auditorium, which seats 2358, and the theatre closed briefly in 1906. Success eventually came with plays featuring stars such as Ellen Terry and Sarah Bernhardt. In 1930 the theatre gave the first stage demonstration of television. After World War II, it was used for presenting US musicals, notably *Annie Get Your Gun* (1947), which ran for 1304 performances, *Guys and Dolls* (1953), and *The Pajama Game* (1955). After some years as a cinema, the theatre became (1968) the home of the Sadler's Wells Opera Company, which became the English National Opera in 1974. In 1997 ENO announced its intention to leave the Coliseum, claiming that it needed some £100 million for refurbishment and expansion.

London Cuckolds, The A farce by Edward Ravenscroft (fl. 1680) that for 70 years was performed every Lord Mayor's Day (9 November) at both Drury Lane and Covent Garden. The tradition, which began in 1681, lapsed in 1751 at Drury Lane and the following year at Covent Garden. Since then the play has been revived only once, by the comedian John Quick in 1782.

London Idol, the The stage nickname of Vesta TILLEY, who became a great favourite of London music-hall audiences with her male impersonations. She was first billed as 'the London Idol' in 1880 and kept the title until her retirement 40 years later.

long. ***Long Day's Journey Into Night*** Eugene O'NEILL's tragedy of family life. Written in 1941 but not produced until 1956 (in Stockholm and New York), the play won O'Neill a posthumous Pulitzer Prize. Successful revivals have included the 1972 National Theatre production, starring Laurence Olivier.

O'Neill's drama of "old sorrow written in tears and blood" was based on his own family. The action takes place over one emotional day and night in 1912, when all the old frustrations, conflicts, and fears come to a climax. The Tyrone family is in the grips, as always, of the bullying miserly father, James, an actor. His wife Mary is going mad after failing to cure her drug problem, his younger son Edmund (O'Neill himself) is dying of consumption that James refuses to acknowledge or have treated, and his elder son Jamie is declining into alcoholism as he questions their worthless lives. As Mary sinks into madness, she closes the play with the pathetic line:

> I fell in love with James Tyrone and was so happy for a time.

Jamie's story was continued in A MOON FOR THE MISBEGOTTEN.

longest plays Honours for the longest play in English are shared. Edward Falconer's *Oonagh, or, The Lovers of Lismona* opened one evening in 1866 at half-past seven. By midnight most of the audience had left; by two o'clock in the morning only a few sleeping critics were still there. At three o'clock the stage crew brought the curtain down with the action still in progress and the play was taken off. More recently John ARDEN and his wife Margaretta D'Arcy attracted notoriety with *The Non-Stop Connolly Show* (1975), which lasted a record-breaking 26½ hours, including intervals. The fruit of Arden's ambition to express "noise, disorder, drunkenness, lasciviousness, nudity, generosity, corruption, fertility, and ease" on the stage, the show opened in Ireland and inspired one critic to call it "the cheapest doss in Dublin." *See also* SHORTEST PLAYS.

longest titles The longest play title of recent times was almost certainly *The Persecution and Assassination of Jean-Paul Marat as Performed by the Inmates of the Asylum of Charenton under the Direction of the Marquis de Sade* by Peter Weiss (1964). Publicists and playbill designers shortened this to the MARAT/SADE. Some other long titles in the theatre have included *The History of Two Valiant Knights, Sir Clyomon Knight of the Golden Shield, Son to the King of Denmark, and Clamydes the White Knight, Son to the King of Suavia*, a romantic comedy produced in London by the King's Men in 1577, *Oh Dad, Poor Dad, Mama's Hung You In the Closet and I'm Feeling So Sad*, a black comedy by the US playwright Arthur Kopit (1937–) produced in 1960, and *for coloured girls who have considered suicide when the rainbow is enuf* (1974) by Ntozake Shange. *See also* SHORTEST TITLES.

look. ***Look After Lulu*** Noël COWARD's adaptation of Georges FEYDEAU's 1908 farce *Occupe-toi d'Amélie!* The first production, directed by Coward and Tony Richardson, opened in London in 1959 at the Royal Court Theatre with a cast headed by Vivien LEIGH and Anthony Quayle. *The Times* reviewer wrote of Leigh: "Beautiful, delectably cool, and matter of fact, she is mistress of every situation."

Look Back in Anger A play by John OSBORNE that opened on 8 May 1956 at the ROYAL COURT THEATRE, London; it was Osborne's first play and the first production by the ENGLISH STAGE COMPANY under George DEVINE. The play's impact has been described as "a watershed in modern theatre", and "the beginning of a renaissance". However, most first-night reviews were merely lukewarm. The notable exception was Kenneth TYNAN, who wrote: "I doubt if I could love anyone who did not wish to see *Look Back In Anger*. It is the best young play of its decade."

Look Back in Anger expressed, for the first time on the London stage, youthful frustration at the post-war Establishment. Osborne's articulate anti-hero Jimmy PORTER, first played by Kenneth Haigh, was quickly dubbed the 'angry young man', giving the title of ANGRY YOUNG MEN to the new generation of anti-Establishment playwrights. The play's down-at-heel setting – a dingy bedsit – also began the vogue for KITCHEN SINK drama.

For his part, Osborne described *Look Back in Anger* as a "formal, rather old-fashioned play". It focuses on Jimmy Porter, a university-educated working-class market-stall owner, who spends most of his energy in merciless tirades against his middle-class wife, Alison, and her parents. When Alison becomes pregnant, her friend, Helena, comes to stay to offer support, much to Jimmy's disgust. After Alison finally walks out, Helena replaces her as Jimmy's lover – and as target for his invective. In the last act Alison returns, having suffered a miscarriage. Their coy, but touching, reconciliation shows Osborne in a gentler light.

Look Homeward, Angel A Pulitzer Prize-winning adaptation of Thomas Wolfe's novel by Ketti Frings, first produced in New York in 1957. The story concerns Eliza Gant, the proprietor of the Dixieland Boarding House, and her family, who are dependent on her business acumen and cowed by her authority. Eliza's husband, a stonemason, is saving a beautiful carving of an angel for his own headstone (hence the title, a line from Milton's *Lycidas*). Although Ben, her consumptive son, helps to support the family, his younger brother, Eugene, remains dependent and suffers from his lack of education. After Ben dies, Eliza offers to pay for Eugene's education, and he seizes this chance of independence.

Loot Joe ORTON's black farce about police corruption, first performed in 1965 at the Cambridge Arts Theatre before moving (in a heavily revised version) to London in 1966. Audiences were shocked by the use of a corpse as a comic prop.

Dennis, a hearse driver, and his friend Hal have robbed the bank next door to a funeral parlour. Bad taste abounds as Dennis woos Fay, a voluptuous nurse, while his recently deceased and embalmed mother lies upstairs. Hal and Dennis then hit upon the idea of hiding the money in the coffin, which means moving the corpse into a cupboard. The corrupt police inspector Truscott discovers that the dead woman had been poisoned by Fay, but the evidence (organs removed during embalming) is destroyed in a car crash. Inspector Truscott finds the money and is given a share.

Leonard Rossiter collapsed and died during a performance in 1984.

lord. **Lord Admiral's Men** *See* ADMIRAL'S MEN.

Lord Chamberlain The British public official who licensed and censored dramatic works and theatrical entertainment for more than 200 years before the office was abolished in 1968. Stage censorship was initially the responsibility of the MASTER OF THE REVELS, a minor official in the royal household of Henry VII, but the duties became so important that they were given to his superior, the Lord Chamberlain. His power was confirmed by an act of parliament (1713) that classified "common players of Interludes" as "rogues and vagabonds." The Licensing Act (1737) gave him the statutory right to issue licences for theatres (except Covent Garden and Drury Lane, the two PATENT THEATRES) and to license the performance of approved new plays.

The Lord Chamberlain could ban a play for profanity, sacrilege, sedition, indecency of dress, dance, or gesture, offensive portrayals of personalities, or anything likely to produce a breach of the peace. There was no appeal against his decision, which was made on the advice of the Examiner of Plays. Noted Examiners included George Colman the Younger (*see* COLMAN FAMILY) and Charles Kemble (*see* KEMBLE FAMILY).

The Theatres Act (1843) consolidated the Lord Chamberlain's authority. By the late 19th century, however, authors and managers were becoming restless under the sway of the censor, whose decisions often seemed absurd and arbitrary. In 1874 the Lord Chamberlain objected to the scanty costumes worn by a troupe of French dancers appearing in Offenbach's *Vert-Vert*; when the censor agreed to specify a length, the management announced that the new costumes were "designed by the Lord Chamberlain". In 1909 the censor complained about the line "My God, why has Thou forsaken me?" in Shaw's *Major Barbara*, asking if these were not the last words of Christ on the cross. When assured that they were also in the Psalms, he relented. Private theatre clubs were organized to circumvent the law but in 1966 the Lord Chamberlain ended their immunity. The Theatres Act (1968) finally abolished stage censorship.

During his active years, the Lord Chamberlain banned such plays as John Gay's *Polly* (1737), Ibsen's *Ghosts* (1881), Shaw's *Mrs Warren's Profession* (1893), Wilde's *Salome* (1893), Eugene O'Neill's *Desire Under the Elms* (1925), and John Osborne's *A Patriot for Me* (1965). The last play to be banned was Edward BOND's *Early Morning* (1968), which depicted a lesbian relationship between Queen Victoria and Florence Nightingale.

The correspondence of the Lord Chamberlain and his advisers, only released in 1991, provides a bizarre insight into the mentality of the censor:

> I have very grave doubts as to whether the public performance of *Oedipus* might not prove injurious.
>
> Of Sophocles's *Oedipus Rex* (1910).

> This picture of a frivolous and degenerate set of people gives a wholly false impression of society life...the time has come to put a stop to the harmful influence of such pictures on the stage.
>
> Of Coward's *The Vortex* (1924).

> In the first place there is the sordid and disgusting atmosphere which makes the immorality of the play glaring and crude. Then there is the very questionable theme in these days of the relations between masters and servants which this play tends to undermine.
>
> Of Strindberg's *Miss Julie* (1924).

> The Lord Chamberlain appreciates the atmosphere which the author is trying to produce, at the same time he objects, in principle, to the pulling of lavatory plugs and all that that stands for...From your point of view I realise that you have started with the idea of the symbolism which the lavatory creates and it is, therefore, difficult to think that anything else will produce the results you are after, but I suggest that...a sufficient atmosphere will be achieved by noises of water running out of a sink, washing etc. In fact I have heard many a sink make a noise like a well-behaved lavatory.
>
> Of Graham Greene's *The Living Room* (1952).

> Act I, page 11, alter "ass-upwards".
> Page 27 alter "pouf" (twice).
> Page 30 alter "shagged".
> Page 43 omit "rogered" (twice).
> Act III, page 3, alter "wet your pants".
> Page 4 omit "had Sylvia".
> Page 9 alter "camp".
> Page 21 omit "balls".
> Of Osborne's *The Entertainer* (1957).

> By presenting homosexuals in their most attractive guise – dressed as pretty women

– [it] will to some degree cause the congregation of homosexuals and provide the means whereby the vice may be acquired. Of Osborne's *A Patriot for Me* (1964).

See also CENSORSHIP; LICENCE.

Lord Chamberlain's Men *See* CHAMBERLAIN'S MEN.

Lord of Misrule In medieval and Tudor times the director of the Christmas-time festivities, also called the **Abbot** or **King of Misrule** and in Scotland the **Abbot of Unreason**. Lords of Misrule were appointed at the royal court, at Oxford and Cambridge, by the Lord Mayor of London, and in the households of noblemen. He ruled for a period varying from 13 days to three months (starting at Hallowe'en and lasting until the feast of the Purification), organizing all the entertainment and presiding over his own mock court. Philip Stubbes (*Anatomie of Abuses*, 1595) says that these mock dignitaries had from twenty to a hundred officers under them, equipped with hobby-horses, dragons, and musicians. At court, the function of the Lord of Misrule was eventually taken over by the MASTER OF THE REVELS.

Lorenzaccio A romantic tragedy written in 1834 by the French poet and playwright Alfred de MUSSET; he was helped with its construction by the writer George Sand, at that time his mistress.

Musset had taken a strong dislike to the theatre when his first play flopped in 1830; as a result he wrote *Lorenzaccio* to be read rather than staged. It was not produced until 1896, when Sarah BERNHARDT indulged her desire to play the hero, Lorenzo de' Medici. Having toured America to raise money, she gave an acclaimed performance at the Renaissance Theatre, Paris, as Lorenzo, a Renaissance nobleman whose search for goodness and beauty ends in debauchery and murder. The critic Jules de Tillet, not a Bernhardt lover, wrote "she gave full life to the part of Lorenzaccio, a part no one dared approach before her." However, owing to its extreme length and confusing plot the play closed within two months, leaving Bernhardt with heavy losses. In 1911 she decided to revive it, although aged 66 and a great-grandmother. Unfortunately she insisted on playing opposite her young lover, Lou Telegen, a former prize fighter, trapeze artist, gigolo, and self-confessed murderer. He was also a bad actor with a heavy Dutch accent, and the audience at the Théâtre Sarah Bernhardt in Paris was brutally frank, groaning and laughing throughout his performance.

Loutherbourg, Philip James de (Philippe Jacques de Loutherbourg; 1740–1812) One of the theatre's most innovative scenic designers. Loutherbourg, who was born in Alsace of Polish descent, lived in Paris from about 1755 as a landscape painter. After settling in England he worked at DRURY LANE for David Garrick (from 1771) and his successor Richard Sheridan (from 1776). He is mentioned by the playwright Mr Puff in Sheridan's *The Critic* (1779).

Before Loutherbourg introduced set scenes (often using the slope of the stage to create the illusion of perspective), scenery had consisted of little more than canvas flats. The backdrop featuring a romantic landscape that he created for Drury Lane in 1779 was probably the first scenic curtain used in Europe. He also introduced the CUT-CLOTH and experimented with transparencies to create such effects as fires, volcanoes, and moonlight. Loutherbourg was the first to use gauze to represent mist and to create atmosphere by placing silkscreens of different colours in front of the lights. He lit his scenery so well that actors at Drury Lane began to move back towards it to be better seen; as a result the audience often found it difficult to hear them.

In 1781 he devised the EIDOPHUSIKON, a type of panorama. After retiring from the theatre he became a faith healer.

love. ***Love for Love*** William CONGREVE's witty COMEDY OF MANNERS, first produced in London in 1695 with Thomas Betterton as Valentine and Anne Bracegirdle (Congreve's mistress) as Angelica. The critic Penelope Gilliatt has cited the play as a prime example of Congreve's depiction of sex as a form of currency "with every courtship in the plot wooing an estate: love for loot."

The young Valentine has wasted his fortune pursuing the beautiful but reluctant heiress Angelica. When his father, the bluff Sir Sampson Legend, agrees to settle his debts if he will sign over his inheritance to his brother Ben, a sailor, Valentine feigns madness to avoid signing. Angelica, who is not deceived, pretends to be in a love with Sir Sampson in order to charm the bond from him. When Valentine says he will sign the document if that will make her happy, she realizes the depth of his affection and reveals her own love for him. Other characters include the superstitious Foresight, the promiscuous Mrs Frail, and the feeble-minded beau Tattle.

Love in a Village A comic opera that provided the first theatrical success for the British dramatist Isaac BICKERSTAFFE. The rustic idyll, first performed in 1762, has music by Thomas Arne and others; the story was taken from Charles Johnson's *The Village Opera* (1728). Bickerstaffe's piece was frequently revived in the 18th and 19th centuries and greatly influenced the development of the light musical play in Britain.

Love of Four Colonels, The Peter USTINOV's fantasy on the *Sleeping Beauty* theme. It was first produced in 1951 in London with Ustinov in the leading role. The plot involves four colonels from the British, US, French, and Soviet occupying forces in Germany, all of whom are vying for possession of a castle in the village of Herzogenburg. Inside is a sleeping beauty, and they are invited by fairies to change into different forms to win her heart. The Englishman becomes an Elizabethan poet, the American an evangelist, the Frenchman a gallant, and the Russian a Chekhovian uncle. Mischief by the fairies ensures that all four prove unsuccessful suitors.

Love's Labour's Lost A comedy by SHAKESPEARE, first performed in 1594–95 in London. Until the 20th century this was perhaps the least popular of Shakespeare's plays; there is no record of a revival between 1605 and 1839. This neglect can be attributed mainly to the play's extravagant verbal wit, which involves numerous puns and allusions that are now incomprehensible without footnotes. Modern playgoers however, seem better able to appreciate the high spirits and human warmth beneath the verbal pyrotechnics. The many 20th-century revivals include Peter Brook's first production at Stratford-upon-Avon in 1946.

The play describes the doomed attempt of the King of Navarre and three of his nobles to dedicate themselves to a celibate life of study. This idealism is quickly undermined by the arrival of the Princess of France and her three beautiful ladies-in-waiting. The four young men embark upon a muddled but eventually successful pursuit of the ladies. The play's last scene brings a sudden change of mood when a messenger arrives with news of the death of the Princess's father. The four marriages are postponed for a year, during which time the fickle young men must show their steadfastness by engaging in good works. Other characters include the rustic clown Costard, the pedant Holofernes, and the affected Spaniard Don Armado. It is thought that some or all of these characters may have been suggested by living models (*see* CHAPMAN, GEORGE).

Lower Depths, The Maxim GORKI's internationally acclaimed drama, first produced by STANISLAVSKY at the MOSCOW ART THEATRE in 1902. It is considered Gorki's finest play and a key text in the development of 20th-century REALISM. The play provided Max REINHARDT with his first major success in 1903, running for more than 500 performances at his Kleines Theatre in Berlin.

The play explores the conflict between harsh reality and comforting lies. The pilgrim Luka enters a Moscow dosshouse and offers redemption to the inhabitants, who include a murderer, a thief, a prostitute, and a drunken actor. He brings them the illusion of hope (even urging Pepel, the thief, to start again in Siberia, "a land of gold"). In the event Pepel murders the dosshouse owner and goes to jail and the actor hangs himself. Luka disappears, leaving one character to explain: "He lied, but he lied out of sheer pity for you."

Ludi Romani (Roman games) In ancient Rome, a festival held each September in honour of Jupiter. The earliest performances of plays in Rome were given here as part of the free entertainment that accompanied the public games. Authors originally supervised the performances of their own plays; later, professional acting troupes hired out their services to the magistrate in charge of the festival. It was at the Ludi Romani in 240 BC that Livius Andronicus staged the first Latin translations of Greek tragedy and comedy. In later years the festivals included farces and MIME, although the latter was considered fit only for those at the bottom of the social scale.

Lun The stage name adapted by John Rich (*see* RICH FAMILY) to play the part of HARLEQUIN. His performances helped to establish and popularize the English PANTOMIME. Rich became especially acclaimed for his routine 'Harlequin Hatched from an Egg by the Sun' in *Harlequin Sorcerer*, first performed in 1741 at the Tottenham Court Fair.

Lun Junior was the name sometimes given to the actor Harry Woodward (1717–77), also known as 'the last of the great Harlequins'. In 1729 he joined John Rich's company at Lincoln's Inn Fields, where he performed in *The Beggar's Opera*. In 1738 he moved to Drury Lane and remained for 20 years, playing Harlequin and writing pantomimes for David Garrick. He joined the Covent Garden company in 1763 and created the part of Captain Absolute in Sheridan's *The Rivals* in 1775.

Lunts, the The US actor and director **Alfred Lunt** (1892–1977) and his British-born wife **Lynn Fontanne** (1887–1983), who became the most famous married couple in the US theatre. Ralph Richardson once said, "We often hear about the superiority of English stars. We have some very good performers, but America has something better – the Lunts." They appeared together in some 30 productions in four decades, specializing in sophisticated comedies. According to Noël COWARD, when they rehearsed for his *Quadrille* (1952), they performed "so exquisitely that the tears were in my eyes. They are *great* actors." The **Lunt-Fontanne Theatre** on West 46th Street in New York was named in their honour in 1958.

Fontanne was born in Woodford, Essex, and made her stage debut in 1904 in the chorus of the pantomime *Cinderella* at Drury Lane. Lunt was born in Milwaukee, Wisconsin, and made his Broadway debut in 1918 in *Romance and Arabella* at the Harris Theatre. They married in 1922 and joined the THEATRE GUILD in 1924, opening in Ferenc Molnar's *The Guardsman* and going on to enjoy such successes as Shaw's *Arms and the Man* (1925) and *Pygmalion* (1926). Later highlights included Robert Sherwood's *Reunion in Vienna* (1931), and Coward's *Design for Living* (1933), which was written especially for them.

For the play *At Mrs. Beam's* (1926), Fontanne was required to slap her husband but found in rehearsal that she could not. After she had tried several times and failed, Lunt shouted, "For God's sake, Lynn, you're the lousiest actress I've ever played opposite." She immediately gave him a good whack, and during each subsequent performance he had to whisper "Don't be lousy, dear" before the blow.

During the war the Lunts worked in Britain, where they performed in hospitals and military bases. In 1943 they were appearing in *There Shall Be No Night* at the Aldwych Theatre when a bomb fell nearby. The fire curtain was lowered, but Lunt yelled, "Take it up, we're going on" and the audience applauded. Terence Morgan, playing their son, had been blown out of the stage door by the explosion, but, smoothing his hair and somewhat shaken, he reappeared on cue. *See also* GREEN UMBRELLA.

Lupino family A theatrical family, claimed to be the oldest in Britain, members of which have included pantomimists, acrobats, dancers, comedians, and actors. The first known Lupino was a performer billed as 'Signor Luppino' in Italy in about 1612. Some years later **Giorgius Guillemus Luppino** (1632–93), a puppeteer and singer, settled in England as a political refugee; his son **Giorgius Carolus Luppino** (b. 1662), who later Anglicized his name to George Charles, became a puppeteer at the age of eight. In the late 17th century the family was granted a licence to perform for King Charles II. **Georgius Richard Eastcourt Luppino** (1710–87) was an apprentice to the harlequin John Rich (*see* RICH FAMILY); his son, **Thomas Frederick Lupino** (1749–1845) changed the spelling of the family name and became a dancer and scenic artist.

George Hook Lupino (1820–1902) claimed to have created the famous sketch in which a servant breaks a mirror and prevents his employer from discovering the accident by standing in place of the glass and mimicking his reflection. The routine has recurred throughout show-business history, appearing, for instance, in the Marx Brothers' *Duck Soup* (1933). George Hook had 16 children, 10 of whom became dancers. His eldest son, **George Lupino** (1853–1932), was born in a dressing-room at the Theatre Royal, Birmingham and brought on stage when less than an hour old. He became a clown and was still performing just hours before his death.

George Lupino's brothers, **Arthur** and **Harry**, became music-hall stars in the early 20th century; Arthur was also a noted ANIMAL IMPERSONATOR. George's son, **Barry** (1882–1962), became a dancer, actor, and for several years a stock comedian at the Britannia Theatre, Hoxton. He teamed up with Will Evans as 'Lupino and Evans', a popular comedy duo that performed in pantomimes, becoming especially famous for their role in *The Sleeping Beauty*. He also wrote some 50 pantomime librettos and starred in musical comedy, notably as Sir John in *Me and My Girl* (1941).

Barry's brother, **Stanley Lupino** (1894–1942), was an acrobat, comedian, and pantomimist at Drury Lane. He also wrote several plays and an autobiography, *From the Stocks to the Stars* (1934). His daughter, **Ida Lupino** (1918–) became a Hollywood film star.

Stanley's nephew, Henry George Lupino (1892–1959) was a renowned Cockney comedian who took the stage name of **Lupino Lane** from his grandmother. He first performed at the age of four as 'Nipper' Lane and subsequently became known in variety, pantomime, and musical comedy, especially as Bill Snibson in *Me and My Girl*, in which he created the LAMBETH WALK.

Lushington, City of A convivial society of actors that met at the Harp Tavern, Russell Street, until about 1895; it claimed to have existed since the mid 17th century. The name 'Lushington' (from *lush* in the sense of a drunk or alcoholic liquor) was formerly used in many jocular or euphemistic phrases alluding to excessive drinking. The City had a 'Lord Mayor' and four 'aldermen', who presided over 'wards' named Juniper (i.e. gin), Poverty, Lunacy, and Suicide. When a new member was admitted the Lord Mayor would deliver an ironic address on the evils of alcohol.

Lustige Brüder (Ger. Happy Brothers) The first signature tune used in British MUSIC HALL. The performer was the Australian comedian and singer Albert Whelan (Albert Waxman; 1875–1961), who first sang the song in 1901 at the Empire, Leicester Square, London, wearing evening dress with a tall hat and white gloves.

Luther John OSBORNE's powerful drama about the German Protestant reformer Martin Luther (1483–1546). It was first performed in 1961 by the English Stage Company at Nottingham's Theatre Royal, with Albert Finney in the title role. In his depiction of this 'angry young man' of the Church, Osborne concentrated on Luther's psychological and physical struggles (including his constipation), rather than on the theological issues. The dialogue makes use of many of Luther's own words.

The story begins with Luther joining the Augustinian Order after experiencing a religious vision that he will later come to doubt. His questioning of Church dogma leads to the decisive moment when he nails the 95 theses to the church door in Wittenberg. Refusing to recant, he is excommunicated but continues to question such practices as the sale of indulgences. Although he receives sympathy and recognition from some Church officials and support from his wife, Osborne's Luther remains consumed by self-doubt.

LX Short for 'electrics', the theatre term for stage lighting and electronic special effects.

Lyceum Theatre. Lyceum Theatre, London A venue in Wellington Street, off the Strand, which opened in 1771 to present concerts and exhibitions before being converted into a theatre in 1794. It acquired a licence to present plays in 1809, when the Drury Lane company was temporarily housed there after the Theatre Royal was damaged by fire. Rebuilt in 1812, it was renamed the Theatre Royal English Opera House in 1815; two years later it became the first British theatre to light its stage with gas (*see* LIGHTING). After a fire destroyed the venue in 1830 a new building was constructed and opened as the Royal Lyceum and English Opera House in 1834. Robert Keeley managed it successfully from 1844 until 1847, when Madame VESTRIS and her husband, the younger Charles Mathews took over. Their productions included spectacular works such as Planché's *The Vampire; or, the Bride of the Isles*. After they went bankrupt in 1856, the venue became home to the Covent Garden Theatre company for three years following a fire at their own theatre. Under the management of the French actor Charles Fechter new ideas for lighting and scene shifting were introduced. In 1871 the US impresario Hezekiah Bateman took over the theatre as a showcase for his daughters, Kate, Virginia, and Isabel. He also hired the 33-year-old Henry IRVING, whose performance that year in THE BELLS established both his and the theatre's reputation.

Irving himself became manager seven years later and began to perform with Ellen Terry (*see* TERRY FAMILY) in a series of plays that made the Lyceum the most prestigious venue in London. The two appeared together for the last time in *The Merchant of Venice* in 1902 and their departure sent the theatre's fortunes tumbling. In 1904 it was partly demolished. For the next 25 years, under the Melville brothers, Walter and Frederick, it turned to music hall, lurid melodramas such as Walter's *The Bad Girl of the Family* (1909), and a spectacular annual pantomime. When the Lyceum was scheduled for demolition in 1939, John Gielgud gave six farewell performances of *Hamlet* there. Ironically, the venue was saved by the start of World War II; it stood empty until 1945, when it became a dance hall. After extensive refurbishment it reopened as a theatre in 1996 with a revival of *Jesus Christ Superstar*.

Lyceum Theatre, New York The first Lyceum in New York was a small venue on 4th Avenue opened in 1885 by Steele MACKAYE, who established the city's first school of acting there. The opening play, Mackaye's *Dakolar*, proved so unpopular that he gave up the management shortly afterwards. Daniel Frohman and his brother Charles took it over and ran a successful stock company from the premises. The theatre itself was demolished in 1902.

A second Lyceum, on 45th Street and Broadway, was opened by Frohman in 1903. J. M. Barrie's comedy *The Admirable Crichton* had its US premiere there, and Charles Wyndham's London company visited for eight weeks. David BELASCO, who had been Frohman's stage manager at the first Lyceum, directed there for several seasons from 1916.

Successful productions have included *The Merchant of Venice* (1922), George S. Kaufman and Moss Hart's *George Washington Slept Here* (1940), Clifford Odets's *The Country Girl* (1950), John Osborne's *Look Back in Anger* (1957), Harold Pinter's *The Caretaker* (1961), and Arthur Kopit's *Wings* (1979).

Lyric Theatre. Lyric Theatre, Hammersmith A theatre that opened in 1888 in Hammersmith, west London, as the Lyric Hall. Two years later it was redesigned as the Lyric Opera House, after which it presented melodramas. After the King's Theatre, Hammersmith, opened in 1902, its fortunes declined until it became known locally as the 'Blood and Flea Pit.'

In 1918 Nigel Playfair took over the venue and renamed it the Lyric Theatre, making it fashionable with such productions as John Gay's *The Beggar's Opera*, which opened in 1920 to run for three and a half years and 1463 performances. Claude Lovat Fraser's romantic stage designs for the Lyric initiated a new trend in the 1920s. Playfair also revived two plays in which Edith Evans enjoyed major triumphs; Congreve's *The Way of the World* (1924), in which she played Millamant, and Farquhar's *The Beaux' Stratagem* (1927), in which she played Mrs Sullen. Ellen Terry made her final stage appearance here in 1925, as a ghost in Walter de la Mare's *Crossings*.

After Fairplay left in 1933 the theatre again declined. It remained closed for some time before Baxter Somerville took it over in 1944. He subsequently revitalized it with productions by John Mortimer, Harold Pinter, and others. In 1946 Alec Guinness appeared in his own adaptation of Dostoyevsky's *The Brothers Karamazov*, directed by Peter Brook, and in 1953 John Gielgud led the cast in Otway's *Venice Preserved*. Within three years of Somerville's death in 1963, however, the Lyric again closed.

In 1979 a new Lyric Theatre seating 537 was built on King Street using the original Victorian plasterwork. The opening production was Shaw's *You Never Can Tell*. The building also houses the smaller Lyric Studio Theatre.

Lyric Theatre, Shaftesbury Avenue The oldest surviving venue on London's famous theatrical thoroughfare (the original SHAFTESBURY THEATRE having been destroyed by bombing in 1941). Seating 948, the Lyric opened in 1888 with Marie Tempest in the comic opera *Dorothy*. This work had proved unsuccessful at two other theatres but after some judicious changes made a profit of some £100,000. The theatre continued to specialize in comic operas for several years.

The Italian actress Eleonora Duse made her first London appearance at the Lyric in 1892 in *The Lady of the Camellias*. US stars to appear included Tallulah Bankhead in *Let Us Be Gay* (1929) and Alfred Lunt and his wife Lynn Fontanne in *Reunion in Vienna* (1934) and Terence Rattigan's *Love-in-Idleness* (1944). Other successful productions included *The Little Hut* (1950), starring Robert Morley, which ran for 1261 performances, Alan Bennett's *Habeas Corpus* (1973), with Alec Guinness, and the National Theatre company's staging of Ayckbourn's *A Chorus of Disapproval* (1986). The Lyric is now managed by the Stoll Moss Theatres. In 1990 it staged the musical *Five Guys Named Moe*, which won a Laurence Olivier Award and ran for over five years.

Lysistrata A bawdy comedy by ARISTOPHANES, first performed in 411 BC in Athens. In the play the women of Athens, disgusted with the long-drawn-out war with Sparta, seize the Acropolis and the treasury at Lysistrata's instigation and refuse to sleep with their men until peace is made. The theme was apparently suggested by the contemporary Athenian military disasters in Sicily. Long considered too indecent for public performance, the play has been frequently revived in the late 20th century. The growth of women's peace movements in the 1980s also gave the work a renewed topical relevance.

Lyubimov, Yuri (1917–) Controversial Russian director who headed the Moscow Theatre of Drama and Comedy (*see* TAGANKA THEATRE) for 20 years from 1964. Despite mounting several experimental productions that incurred the displeasure of the authorities, in 1977 he was given permission to take the company on foreign tours and to direct in Western Europe. During one foreign visit in 1984, however, Lyubimov strongly condemned Soviet restrictions on the arts, an action that led the authorities to strip him firstly of his position at the Taganka and then of his citizenship.

Lyubimov subsequently directed in Europe and America, receiving particularly high acclaim for his adaptations of Dostoyevsky's *Crime and Punishment* and *The Possessed*, the latter being presented in 1985 at the THÉÂTRE DE L'EUROPE in Paris. Lyubimov's citizenship was restored during the era of *glasnost*, and he has since spent some time working in Russia. In 1989 he returned to the Taganka to present a revival of Boris Mozhaev's banned play *Alive* (1968), which exposes the bureaucratic mistakes of the 1930s. Recent work has included a production of Sophocles's *Electra* in Athens (1992).

M

Maach A musical folk theatre of central India performed in the villages of Madhya Pradesh; it originated in 17th-century Rajasthan, where it formed part of the spring celebration of Holi. The romantic and moral plays have complex plots and are usually based on social, religious, or historical themes. Men traditionally play all the roles, although women are now sometimes seen.

Performances take place in an open space on a three-foot-high stage, which has a border across the front to block off the view of the actors' feet. The all-night performances begin with the *bhisti raag*, a ceremony of blessing, which is danced as a summons to the villagers. This is followed by the *bhisti-farrasan samvad* overture in dance and song and the main *Maach* drama.

Macaire, Robert A typical villain of French comedy; from the character of this name who appeared in the plays *L'Auberge des Adrets* (1823) and *Robert Macaire* (1834) by Frédéric Lemaître and Benjamin Antier. Macaire has been described as:

> le type de la perversité, de l'impudence, de la friponnerie audacieuse, le héros fanfaron du vol et de l'assassinat.

Macbeth SHAKESPEARE's tragedy about the corrupting effect of ambition, written in 1605–06; the first recorded performance was in 1610. Shakespeare's company apparently desired the support of James I and this seems to have prompted them to choose a theme that flattered his descent from the Scottish kings and catered to his interest in witchcraft.

In the play Macbeth encounters three witches, who prophesy that he will become king. Inspired by this, Macbeth and his wife murder King Duncan and seize the throne. Despite suffering the tortures of a guilty conscience, Macbeth finds himself committing further crimes to consolidate his power, including the murder of the entire family of the nobleman Macduff. Lady Macbeth, engulfed by madness, commits suicide; finally Macduff returns from England to kill Macbeth in battle.

The play has always been one of Shakespeare's most popular works and the prized roles of Macbeth and Lady Macbeth have launched many careers. It has also seen some disastrous performances. Richardson's 1952 *Macbeth* was so ill-received that he was able to threaten an actor who hesitated to lend him money, "I'll have it put about that you were in my *Macbeth*." In 1980 Peter O'Toole's bombastic performance at the Old Vic had some members of the audience helpless with laughter.

The play has spawned numerous adaptations. In the late 17th century William DAVENANT (who claimed to be Shakespeare's illegitimate son) introduced dancing, singing, and flying witches. Other versions include Verdi's opera *Macbetto* (1847), Orson Welles's sombre film (1948), and the off-Broadway *MacBird* (1967), an attack on Lyndon Johnson that begins with the assassination of J. F. Kennedy.

Shakespeare's character bears only a loose resemblance to the historical Scottish king. According to Holinshed's *Chronicle of Scottish History*, which Shakespeare consulted, Duncan (1001–40) was a highly ineffective ruler and his murder was carried out by several nobles, not by Macbeth alone. The historical Macbeth – who had a good claim to the throne both in his own right and through his wife Gruoch – ruled well for 17 years (1040–57) and made a pilgrimage to Rome before eventually being killed in battle against Duncan's son. Shakespeare clearly drew on other incidents in Holinshed for his characters and plot; amongst these were the murder of King Duff by his trusted lieutenant and host Donwald, who was encouraged by his wife. The supposed line of descent from Banquo to James I may have prompted Shakespeare to portray that character as wholly innocent of Duncan's murder, whereas in Holinshed his role is far more ambiguous.

Macbeth's ghost is said to haunt Glamis Castle, lamenting Duncan's death; his body is reputed to lie on Iona – the traditional burial-place of Scottish kings. *See also* BIRNAM WOOD; SCOTTISH PLAY.

Maccus In the Roman theatre of the 1st century BC, a stock clown character of the ATELLANA. He often appeared as a stupid peasant in the farces of Novius and Pomponius.

machine play A type of dramatic spectacle in 17th-century France that depended on new scene-changing equipment and other mechanical devices. Corneille pioneered the genre with his *Andromède*, staged in 1650 at Molière's Théâtre du Petit-Bourbon. It was written in order to make full use of the elaborate Italian stage machinery introduced to France by Giacomo Torelli, the stage designer known as the GREAT MAGICIAN. His innovations included a revolving stage and the CARRIAGE-AND-FRAME SYSTEM for changing scenery. The machine play peaked with Molière's *Amphitryon* (1668) and *Psyché* (1671). Torelli's inventions were also embraced by Jean-Baptiste Lully, the founder of French opera.

MacKaye, (James Morrison) Steele (1842–94) US theatre designer, stage innovator, playwright, and actor-manager who has been called both a Renaissance man and "that strange genius".

MacKaye wrote some 30 plays and patented more than 100 theatrical inventions. He was the first US actor to play Hamlet in London, doing so in 1873. In 1885 he built the LYCEUM THEATRE, New York and founded the Lyceum Theatre School of Acting, which still exists today as the AMERICAN ACADEMY OF DRAMATIC ARTS.

His contributions to internal theatre design include being the first to use overhead lighting (1874), inventing folding theatre seats, and introducing the first moving 'double stage' (1879). He supposedly died from overwork and disappointment after planning a vast theatre, the SPECTATORIUM, which was never built.

McKellen, Sir Ian (Murray) (1939–) British actor, noted especially for his Shakespearean roles. McKellen made his first appearance in a 1961 Belgrade Theatre production of Robert BOLT's *A Man for All Seasons*. He played for several years in the provinces before making his London debut at the Duke of York's Theatre in James Saunders's *A Scent of Flowers* (1964). Following a season with the National Theatre in 1965, McKellen came to critical notice with his performance in *A Lily in Little India* (1966). His reputation as an actor of rare subtlety and intelligence was firmly established with his portrayals of Shakespeare's Richard II (1968) and Marlowe's Edward II (1969) with the Prospect Theatre Company.

In 1972 McKellen helped to found the Actors' Company, an actors' cooperative. Two years later he joined the Royal Shakespeare Company where his roles included Dr Faustus (1974), Romeo (1976), and a much-praised Macbeth to Judi Dench's Lady Macbeth at The Other Place (1976). In 1979 McKellen won a SWET award for his performance in Martin Sherman's *Bent*, about two homosexuals in a Nazi concentration camp. The following year he enjoyed a major success in New York as Salieri in Peter Shaffer's *Amadeus*. In 1984 McKellen was appointed an associate director of the National Theatre; that same year he appeared with the company in productions of Shakespeare's *Coriolanus* and the Chekhov adaptation *Wild Honey*. Recent performances have included Iago in Trevor Nunn's *Othello* (1989) and a modern-dress Richard III at the National Theatre (1990).

In the mid 1980s McKellen, a homosexual, emerged as a prominent spokesman for gay rights. His acceptance of a knighthood in 1991 prompted bitter attacks from more radical gay activists.

Macklin, Charles (Charles McLaughlin; *c.* 1700–97) British tragic actor and playwright, who was the first to play SHYLOCK in *The Merchant of Venice* as a tragic rather than a comic role. Unfortunately, he is mainly remembered for killing another actor while arguing over a wig. After stabbing the actor, one Hallam, through the eye with a stick in a fit of anger, Macklin attempted to help matters by urinating on the wounded area. At his trial for murder he conducted his own defence and had the charge reduced to manslaughter. Instead of going to jail, he was branded on the hand and paid compensation to the dead man's family.

Macklin made his last appearance playing Shylock at the age of 89. Becoming confused in the second act, he told the audience he was "seized with terror of mind" and begged their patience, adding:

> Should it be granted...you may depend upon it this will be the last night of my ever appearing before you in so ridiculous a situation.

Macklin also wrote several plays, including *Love à la Mode* (1759) and *The Man of the World* (1781).

Macready, William (1793–1873) British actor-manager. Known as the **eminent tragedian**, Macready was the chief rival of KEAN in the early 19th century.

Born in London of theatrical parents, he never wanted to be in the profession and never ceased to dislike it. When his father was imprisoned for debt, he was called in to manage the family's stock company, making his acting debut in 1810 as Romeo. Macready took over the management of Covent Garden in 1837 and of Drury Lane in 1841. He improved standards at both, restoring many of Shakespeare's original texts and insisting on thorough rehearsals.

An intensely emotional performer, he was often criticized for his exaggerated gestures and to cure this tendency sometimes rehearsed with his arms tied down with string. He could also use silence to great effect; the term **Macready pause** is still used of a long significant pause. When he performed in Paris in 1828, *La Réunion* expressed amazement at the histrionic powers of "a man to whom nature has refused everything – voice, carriage, and face."

Macready undoubtedly had an obsessive streak. One night when playing Macbeth in Manchester he was waiting in the wings for the imitation blood (cochineal) to smear on his hands. When it was not delivered and the moment for his entrance grew near, he walked over to a salesman whom the stage-manager had allowed backstage, struck the man violently on the nose, and rubbed his hands in the blood. After the play, he apologized for his 'rudeness' and gave the man a £5 note. *See also* ASTOR PLACE RIOT; KING LEAR.

Madame Sans-Gêne A historical play by Victorien SARDOU and Émile Moreau, first performed in 1893 in Paris. Madame Sans-Gêne ('without constraint' or 'free and easy') was the nickname of the wife of Lefebvre (1755–1820), one of Napoleon's marshals. She was originally a washerwoman and followed her husband – then in the ranks – as a victualler. She was kind and pleasant but her rough and ready ways and ignorance of etiquette made her the butt of Napoleon's court and earned her the nickname.

RÉJANE created the role and Sarah BERNHARDT later played it with great success. Ellen TERRY, however, had great difficulty learning the lines. On opening night, the director, Henry Irving, concealed prompters in every nook and cranny of the stage, including the fireplace. Whenever Terry hesitated, unintelligible voices would come at her from all directions. Finally, in utter despair, she clapped her hands and shouted, "Will *nobody* give me the word?"

Maddermarket Theatre *See* LITTLE THEATRES *under* LITTLE.

Madras House A satirical comedy by Harley GRANVILLE-BARKER. It was first performed with great success in London in 1910 at the Duke of York's Theatre. The play, which shows the influence of George Bernard SHAW in both its content and its style, has the repression of women as its main theme. The plot concerns the love affairs of six unmarried girls of the Huxtable family.

Madwoman of Chaillot, The A comedy by Jean GIRAUDOUX, first produced in Paris in 1945, the year after his death. It was an overnight success and (in an adaptation by Maurice Valency) went on to open in New York in 1948 starring Martita Hunt. The performance of the Austrian Elisabeth BERGNER in a 1967 revival led one critic to write:

> It takes a few minutes to adjust to the fact that her Madwoman isn't the huge painted crone Martita Hunt created, a few more to get used to her accent.

An unsuccessful musical version, *Dear World*, opened in 1969 on Broadway.

Giraudoux's play is an early appeal for ecological awareness. A group of eccentrics, led by the Ragpicker, approaches the madwoman, Countess Aurelia, to ask for her help, explaining that the world is being 'pimped' by greedy capitalists who now wish to destroy Paris by searching for oil. The Countess agrees to help and lures the capitalists to the cellar of her house. Led on by promises of untold wealth, they happily troop off down a tunnel that leads only to death. Countess Aurelia then closes the great stone door.

Maeterlinck, Maurice (1862–1949) Belgian playwright, poet, and essayist, who spent most of his life in France. A leading figure in the Symbolist movement, Maeterlinck was awarded the Nobel Prize for literature in 1911.

Maeterlinck's early dramas, *La Princesse Maleine* (1889) and *Les Aveugles* (1890), reflect the interest in mysticism that is characteristic of almost all his work. International recognition came with PELLÉAS ET MÉLISANDE (1892), first produced in Paris at the Théâtre de l'Oeuvre by the director Aurélian Lugné-Poë. With its dream-like action, enigmatic characters, and doom-laden atmosphere, the play is the epitome of Symbolist drama. It opened in London in 1893 with Mrs Patrick CAMPBELL in the role of Mélisande. The children's fantasy *L'Oiseau bleu*, first performed in 1908 by the MOSCOW ART THEATRE, also proved extremely popular during Maeterlinck's lifetime (a film version starring Shirley Temple being made in 1940). However, its allegorical treatment of the search for happiness in the world now appears somewhat glib. The patriotic play *Le Bourgmestre de Stilmonde* (1918) was once highly regarded, as were Maeterlinck's philosophical writings on themes from natural history, which are now largely forgotten. Although Maeterlinck's reputation has suffered with the passage of time, no other Belgian dramatist has made such an impact upon the development of world drama.

magazine batten *See* BATTEN.

maggio (It. May) In early Italian theatre, a type of spectacular entertainment that involved the staging of historical battles, natural disasters, and other sensational happenings. No works of this kind are now extant. Similar entertainments were staged by the late Roman emperors and it is thought these may have influenced the genre. The plays were so called because they were staged annually in May.

magic A form of entertainment found in many cultures throughout history. It features a performer who appears to accomplish impossible feats.

From the Middle Ages onward the fairground booth provided a venue for simple tricks, such as the classic cup-and-balls sleight-of-hand, in which a ball would appear to jump from beneath one cup to another. Isaac Fawkes (*c.* 1675–1731) and Christopher Pinchbeck (1670–1732) were early performers at London's Bartholomew and Southwark fairs. Magic shows began to be seen in the indoor theatre in the mid-18th century, enabling magicians to use more complicated equipment. The Scotsman 'Professor' J. H. Anderson (1814–74) was the first to employ concerted advertising, billing himself as "the Great Wizard of the North".

Until the 19th century magicians wore flowing robes as if practising witchcraft; the first to appear as drawing-room entertainers in evening dress were Wiljalaba Frikell (1816–1903) and Robert-Houdin (Jean Eugène Robert; 1805–71). Music hall magic acts tended to specialize in tricks involving spectacular effects. On occasions this proved dangerous, as when Chung Ling Soo (William Ellsworth Robinson; 1861–1918) was killed during a catch-the-bullet performance.

Harry Kellar (1849–1922) was the first magician to gain fame in America, while Harry HOUDINI, the illusionist and escapologist, attained almost legendary status. Other 20th-century stage magicians have included Harry Blackstone (1885–1959), the first to saw a woman in half. Magic has now found a wider audience through television, while more avant-garde acts thrive in cabaret.

Magic of the supernatural kind features in the plots of innumerable plays, some of which require illusionistic effects in their staging. The techniques used by magicians and creators of stage illusions have often coincided. The Elizabethan magus Dr John Dee (1527–1608) first acquired a reputation for magical powers through the stage effects he employed in a production of Aristophanes's *The Peace* at Trinity College, Cambridge. In the 17th century the designer Giacomo Torelli became known as the GREAT MAGICIAN for his use of elaborate stage machinery. Traditional devices for creating the 'magic of the theatre' include trapdoors, harnesses for 'flying', hidden entrances and exits, etc., – all aided, of course, by the audience's willingness to suspend its disbelief. More unusual effects include PEPPER'S GHOST, which uses a hidden mirror to reflect an apparition onto the stage. Albert A. Hopkins described many 19th-century stage tricks in *Magic: Stage Illusions and Scientific Diversions* (1897).

In the late 20th century technological developments such as computers, synthesizers, and holography have created a new arena of illusion for writers and directors.

Magistrate, The A play by A. W. PINERO that made his name when it opened in London in 1885. It was the first of three farces by Pinero staged at the old ROYAL COURT THEATRE before its closure in 1887.

The plot centres upon the friendly but incompetent magistrate, Mr Posket, whose disreputable stepson Cis lures him into a night of illegal drinking at the Hotel des Princes. A police raid results in the arrest of everyone except Posket and Cis, who escape. The next morning the magistrate has to sentence his drinking companions, including his own wife, to seven days in prison. Posket's coat, left behind during the raid, is subsequently traced to him. Before he too faces a magistrate, he gives Cis £1000 to emigrate to Canada.

Mahabharata One of the two great epic poems of ancient India, the other being the Ramayana. Its main story is the war between the Kauravas (descendants of Dhritarashtra) and the Pandavas (descendants of Pandu), but there are innumerable episodes. It contains the Bhagavad-Gita and provides the stories for many Indian theatrical genres, including KATHAKALI.

The *Mahabharata* is mainly known to Western audiences through Peter BROOK's nine-hour stage adaptation, first presented in a quarry near Avignon in 1985. The production, which subsequently toured internationally, drew eclectically on Western, Indian, and other theatrical traditions. The economy and craftsmanship of the staging prompted critical superlatives. The multiracial cast, assembled under the auspices of Brook's INTERNATIONAL CENTRE FOR THEATRICAL RESEARCH, had spent a month together in India before the first performance.

maid. Maid Marian A female character in the old MAY-DAY games and MORRIS DANCES, usually as Queen of the May. In the later Robin Hood ballads she became attached to the cycle as the outlaw's sweetheart, probably through the performance of ROBIN HOOD PLAYS at May-Day festivities. The part of Maid Marian, both in the games and the dance, was frequently played by a man in female costume.

> [The Courtier] must have his oil of tartar, his *lac virginis*, his camphor dissolved in verjuice, to make the foole as faire, for sooth, as if he were to play Maid Marian in a May-game or moris-dance.
>
> ROBERT GREENE: *Quip for an Upstart Courtier* (1592).

Maid Marian remains a familiar character from the numerous PANTOMIMES, films, etc. based on the Robin Hood story. In Britain, she became the feisty feminist heroine of a popular children's television series in the 1990s.

Maids, The The first play by Jean GENET, first seen in 1947 in Paris in a production by Louis Jouvet (1887–1951). The plot concerns two despised servants, the sisters Solange and Claire, who take it in turns to impersonate their mistress in a dangerous game that results in murder. The play exemplifies Genet's theory of drama as a masquerade, in which characters enact their secret desires and both actors and spectators put aside their usual assumptions about good and evil. *The Maids* was initially unsuccessful but did better when produced in New York in 1956 and in London the following year. The LIVING THEATRE staged a celebrated production in America in 1968.

Maisons de la Culture *See* CENTRES DRAMATIQUES *under* CENTRE.

Major Barbara A play by George Bernard SHAW, first performed at the Royal Court Theatre in 1905. In a 1956 revival at the Martin Beck Theatre, New York, Charles Laughton both directed and played the role of Andrew Undershaft.

The story involves a rich munitions manufacturer, Andrew Undershaft, his daughter Barbara, a major in the Salvation Army, and her fiancé, Professor Adolphus Cusins. Undershaft visits the Army's shelter and offers a large donation, but Barbara shudders at the thought of accepting money from arms sales. Later, however, she and her husband visit Undershaft's factory and find that he has built a model town to provide for all his workers' needs. After Undershaft delivers an eloquent defence of his trade Professor Cusins joins his staff while Barbara sets out on a new mission to convert the rich. For many, the character of Barbara Undershaft ranks only behind Saint Joan as Shaw's most inspirational heroine.

make-up The use of cosmetics, false hair and, more recently, prosthetics to suit the appearance of an actor to the character he or she plays.

Make-up has been widely used in the theatre since the decline of the MASK. In the medieval European theatre it was common for the actor's face to be painted in one symbolic colour: gold for God, red for seraphs, black for the damned, etc. By contrast, the elaborate facial make-up of the oriental theatre (or of the European CLOWN) involves the painstaking use of many colours to create a stylized face.

The practice of using cosmetics to enhance rather than to alter the appearance of actors seems to date from the 16th century. This kind of naturalistic make-up became more important with the introduction of larger auditoriums and new forms of theatrical lighting that rendered the performer's face pale and indistinct without make-up.

The make-up of the 16th and 17th centuries seems to have been rather crude, with reddened noses for drunkards and charcoal used to darken the skin for Black characters. In the 18th century David Garrick developed more naturalistic techniques and was much acclaimed for his use of cosmetics to convey age.

Early theatrical make-up usually consisted of a powder base mixed with water and some kind of grease. Often the white paint used for clowns, ghosts, or ladies of fashion was lead-based and dangerous as the poison could be absorbed through the skin. It was not until the mid 19th century that modern greasepaint was invented by Ludwig Leichner. The pre-mixed cosmetics bought in stick form were easier and more accurate to use and the colours long-lasting.

In recent years developments in plastics have allowed exotic prosthetic effects to be created. Although these have usually been developed for the cinema they are now used more widely in the theatre. However, such pieces are expensive to produce and uncomfortable to wear, as they are usually glued to the actor's skin.

Malade imaginaire, Le (*The Hypochondriac*) The last play by MOLIÈRE, who collapsed and died after his fourth performance in the title role at the Théâtre du Palais-Royal in 1673. His wife, Armande Béjart (1641–1700), played the role of his daughter, Angélique.

The play revolves around the hypochondriac Argan and his obsessive belief that there is something seriously wrong with his bowels. His doctor and pharmacist are happy to supply pills and purgatives. Argan wants his daughter, Angélique, to marry a doctor, and her fiancé agrees to take up the profession to win his approval. Finally, however, Argan's brother persuades the hypochondriac to become a doctor himself.

One of the least successful revivals of the play was that given in London by Elisabeth BERGNER and A. E. Matthews in 1951. The British press was particularly hostile to Bergner for deserting London during the war and she seems to have reacted by taking out her frustrations on her fellow actor. As John Gielgud recalled, "She had some fun in trying to upstage the redoubtable old war-horse A. E. Matthews, who was far too experienced a performer to let her get away with it."

Malaprop, Mrs A character in SHERIDAN's play *The Rivals* (1774). Named from the French *mal à propos*, meaning not to the purpose, she became one of the most memorable figures in British theatre through her comical misuse of language:

> If I reprehend anything in this world, it is the use of my oracular tongue and a nice derangement of epitaphs.

Celebrated 'malapropisms', as they came to be called, include:

> Illiterate him, I say, quite from your memory!
>
> He is the very pineapple of politeness
>
> and the famous solecism:
>
> as headstrong as an allegory on the banks of the Nile.

She may have been suggested by a similar character in Henry Fielding's novel *Joseph Andrews* (1742), a gentlewoman called Mrs Slipslop, who is described as a "mighty affecter of hard words", or possibly by Mrs Heidelberg in Colman and Garrick's *The Clandestine Marriage* (1766). Both characters hark back to an equally ponderous figure DOGBERRY, the Constable of the Watch in Shakespeare's *Much Ado About Nothing* (*c.* 1598).

Malcontent, The The tragicomedy by John MARSTON, often considered his best work. Written in about 1602, it was slightly expanded by John Webster for its first performance by the KING'S MEN in 1604.

In both its plot and its preoccupation with corruption in high places the play has strong affinities with Shakespeare's MEASURE FOR MEASURE, also first seen in 1604. The story centres on Altofronto, the banished Duke of Genoa, who disguises himself as the malcontent Malevole in order to warn his successor, Pietry, that his wife Aurelia is deceiving him. Altofronto also spies on the evil Mendoza as he plots to supplant Pietry, banish Aurelia, and even to marry Altofronto's own wife, Maria. The banished duke finally reveals himself to the sorrowful and repentant Pietry and together they triumph over Mendoza.

Malkin An old diminutive of Matilda; formerly used as a name for a puppet or MARIONETTE. The name was also sometimes given to the Queen of the May (*see* MAID MARIAN *under* MAID).

> Put on the shape of order and
> humanity.
> Or you must marry Malkin, the May
> lady.
>
> BEAUMONT and FLETCHER: *Monsieur Thomas* (II, ii).

Malvern Festival A theatre festival founded in 1929 at Malvern (now in Hereford and Worcester) by the British theatre manager and director Sir Barry Jackson (1879–1961). A number of Shaw's later plays, such as *The Apple Cart* (1929), received their first British performance at the Malvern Festival. New plays by J. B. Priestley, James Bridie, and other contemporary writers were also produced. In 1939 the festival was discontinued; it enjoyed a brief revival in 1949 and was re-established in 1977 as a festival of drama and music, giving special prominence to the works of Shaw and Sir Edward Elgar, who is buried at Malvern.

Malvolio The pompous and puritanical steward in charge of the countess Olivia's household in Shakespeare's TWELFTH NIGHT (1601–02). He is thought to have been based on Sir William Knollys, First Earl of Banbury (1547–1632), who was treasurer of the royal household of Elizabeth I. Stories were told of him appearing in a nightshirt to reprimand carousing courtiers, and of his inappropriate passion for Mary Fitton, the queen's maid of honour (who some scholars have identified as Shakespeare's 'Dark Lady of the Sonnets'). Knollys eventually married a much younger woman; he died believing that his two sons were fathered by somebody else and left them out of his will.

Memorable performances in the role include those of Laurence Olivier (who, according to John Gielgud, played the part "like a Jewish hairdresser"), Donald Sinden, and the comedian Ken Dodd.

Maly Theatre *See* HOUSE OF OSTROVSKY *under* HOUSE.

Mamet, David (1947–) US playwright and screenwriter. Mamet's principal theme is the debasement of ordinary people by American materialism, or what Mamet calls "the American dream gone bad." His characters, who are often trapped in stereotyped macho attitudes, seek power and money by bullying or manipulating others. Mamet is a master of naturalistic dialogue, capturing the speech patterns of his inarticulate characters with uncanny precision.

In 1973 Mamet co-founded the St Nicholas Theatre Company in Chicago. His early successes included the comedy *American Buffalo* (1975), about two second-rate crooks who attempt to steal a coin collection. The original Greenwich Village Theatre production starred Al Pacino and shocked audiences with its explicit dialogue. It was seen in London three years later at the National Theatre. *Glengarry Glen Ross* (1983; filmed 1992), another hit, won the Pulitzer Prize with its story of small-time real estate salesmen in cut-throat competition. Other plays by Mamet, all of which were first staged by the St Nicholas company, include *Sexual Perversity in Chicago* (1974), *A Life in the Theatre* (1977), and *Speed-the-Plow* (1988). OLEANNA (1992), about a young woman who ruins a man's career by making a false accusation of sexual harassment, bitterly divided audiences, critics, and commentators.

Since the mid 1980s Mamet has become increasingly involved in work for the cinema. As well as writing numerous screenplays, he has directed the films *House of Games* (1986) and *Homicide* (1992).

man. ***Man and Superman*** George Bernard SHAW's comedy about the battle of the sexes. Written between 1901 and 1903, it was first performed at London's Royal Court Theatre in 1905. The play, a paradoxical reworking of the DON JUAN theme, was a vehicle for Shaw's notion of a 'Life Force' and for his view that in sexual matters women are the hunters and men the hunted.

The play introduces the rich socialist Jack Tanner, whose ward, Ann Whitfield, has made up her mind to marry him. Frightened by her predatory guile, Jack flees to Spain, where he is captured by philosophical brigands. After awakening from a long dream he is rescued by Ann and her friends, who have pursued him from England. Although he continues to resist Ann's advances, he finally submits to her vitality, claiming that he has been vanquished by the 'Life Force'.

The dream fantasy 'Don Juan in Hell', which occupies the whole of Act Three, is often omitted or performed separately. In it, Jack's spiritual ancestor, Don Juan, joins the Devil and others in metaphysical speculations about life, death, and evolution. Don Juan maintains that man's self-consciousness is the glory of the 'Life Force' and finally resolves to leave the empty pleasures of hell for a duller but more satisfying existence in heaven.

Man for All Seasons, A Robert BOLT's play about the events that led to the execution of Sir Thomas More, Lord Chancellor to Henry VIII, in 1535. It was first produced in 1960 at London's Globe Theatre, with Paul Scofield in the lead. Bolt's script emphasized the conflict between More's duty to the king and the promptings of his conscience, which would not allow him to recognize the annulment of Henry's marriage or the Act of Supremacy. "He is more or less my ideal human being," Bolt said. The play used the Brechtian device of having a choric narrator, 'The Common Man'. In 1961 Scofield made his Broadway debut in the role, winning a Tony as Best Actor. In Fred Zinnermann's 1966 film version Scofield was joined by Wendy Hiller and Orson Welles.

More had been described as "a man for all seasons" by his contemporary Robert Whittington. The phrase is now often used to describe an adaptable and accomplished 'Renaissance man' who can be regarded as dependable in all situations.

Man is Man A one-act comedy by Bertolt BRECHT, the first of his works to employ the controversial *Verfremdungseffekt* (*see* ALIENATION EFFECT). The play, first produced in 1926 in Dusseldorf, is a satire on military valour. It has also been translated as *A Man's a Man* and *Man Equals Man*.

The story is set in British India. Galy Gay, a porter, goes out to buy a flounder for lunch. On the way he meets a British machine-gun crew, one of whose members has gone missing; they persuade Gay to impersonate the man at roll-call, promising to pay him for the inconvenience. When the missing soldier fails to report later, the crew decide to replace him permanently with Gay. Accordingly they trick Gay into making a fraudulent sale, arrest him, and only agree to forego his execution if he will assume the other man's identity. He agrees and the crew is sent to quell an uprising on the Tibetan border, where Gay, outshining the professional soldiers, becomes a hero.

Man of Mode, The The last comedy by Sir George ETHEREGE (1634–91), usually considered his best work. It was first performed at court in 1676 with the subtitle *Sir Fopling Flutter*. Much influenced by MOLIÈRE, the play set a new standard for the English COMEDY OF MANNERS. The lively characters include Sir Fopling Flutter, the 'prince of fops', the witty Dorimant, a character based in part on the Earl of Rochester, and the scheming lover Bellair, a self-portrait of Etherege.

Some 35 years later both play and author were attacked in *The Spectator* by Richard Steele, who wrote "I allow it to be Nature, but it is Nature in its utmost Corruption and Degeneracy." The critic John Dennis aggressively defended the work, saying Etherege's portrayal of Rochester "so burnished his vices that they appeared as virtues."

The play skilfully weaves together two plots. The rakish Dorimant gets rid of one mistress with the help of another only to propose to a third woman, the heiress Harriet Woodvil, following her into the countryside to receive her answer (never revealed). Harriet has another suitor in the reluctant Bellair, whose father is set on the match. For his part Bellair loves Emilia, a young woman who has also entranced his father. Bellair's aunt, Lady Towneley, helps him to outwit his father, who eventually comes to his senses and blesses his son's marriage to Emilia.

man who broke the bank at Monte Carlo, the Joseph Hobson Jagger, who in 1886 won over 2,000,000 francs in 8 days, inspiring the famous Victorian MUSIC-HALL ballad. Written and composed by Fred Gilbert, the song formed part of the repertoire of the inimitable Charles Coborn.

As I walk along the Bois Boolong, with
an independent air,
You can hear the girls declare – "He
must be a millionaire";
You can hear them sigh and wish to die,
You can see them wink the other eye
At the man who broke the bank at
Monte Carlo.

An engineer with an expert knowledge of spindles, Jagger suspected that one of the roulette wheels was faulty and had it watched for a week. Thereafter he backed the numbers that were turning up more frequently than their mathematical probability; it was, therefore, not to luck, but to his perspicacity, that he owed his fortune. He died in 1892, probably mainly from boredom.

Man Who Came to Dinner, The A comedy by George S. KAUFMAN and Moss HART, first performed in 1939 in New York. The play features a character based on the US playwright and theatre critic, Alexander WOOLLCOTT, who had previously collaborated with Kaufman and Hart on two plays. Although it gives a highly unflattering portrait, Woollcott later appeared in the role with a touring company. When the play ran in Washington, he stayed at the White House with his friends, President Franklin D. Roosevelt and his wife Eleanor. He later reported to Ethel Barrymore that "Mrs Roosevelt runs the best theatrical boarding house in Washington."

In the play, the famous critic Sheridan WHITESIDE falls and injures his hip outside the house of Richard and June Stanley in a small town in Ohio. The Stanleys have to nurse the pompous Whiteside over Christmas, during which they find him an eccentric and difficult guest. As he is finally leaving, Whiteside slips again and has to be returned to the family.

The play features the Cole Porter song 'What Am I To Do', written under the pseudonym 'Noël Porter' because it is sung by a character inspired by Noël Coward.

Manchester school A group of early 20th-century dramatists associated with the Gaiety Theatre in Manchester. Notable members of the Manchester school included Stanley Houghton (1881–1913), whose controversial play HINDLE WAKES was first performed at the Manchester Gaiety in 1912; Harold Brighouse (1882–1958), author of the comedy HOBSON'S CHOICE (1915); and Allan Monkhouse (1858–1936). The Gaiety Theatre company, the first modern English repertory company, was founded in 1908 by Annie Horniman (1860–1937); its first production was Allan Monkhouse's *Reaping the Whirlwind.*

Mandelot, Antoine *See* BOBÈCHE AND GALIMAFRÉ.

Manducus In the Roman theatre of the first century BC, a stock character of the ATELLANA. He was a clownish ogre with a large mouth and hooked nose, who shared some characteristics with the character DOSSENUS.

manet *See* STAGE DIRECTION *under* STAGE.

Mani-Rimdu A Buddhist dance-drama presented by monks for the Sherpa people of Nepal. The form apparently originated in Tibet, the Sherpas' ancient homeland. The plays extol the Buddhist faith and portray it as superior to Nepal's ancient Bon religion, which is frequently disparaged.

Performances are staged in temple courtyards during major religious festivals and usually last for three days. The audience wear their finest clothes; special guests join the religious authorities in reserved seats.

The festivities begin with a ceremony of 'Life-Consecration' featuring music played on such unusual instruments as 10-foot-long brass horns and trumpets made from human thigh bones. The second day's performance is divided into 13 segments of dance and comic antics lasting about 20 minutes each. The monks wear large colourful masks to represent deities, mythological beings, and ordinary mortals. When the day's drama ends, the playgoers dance and sing folk songs for most of the night. On the third day the chief abbot oversees rituals performed to symbolize the destruction of evil forces.

Marat/Sade, The The short title of the celebrated verse play by the German-born writer Peter Weiss (1916–82), first performed in Berlin in 1964. That same year Peter BROOK directed an acclaimed production for the RSC with Ian Richardson as Marat, Glenda Jackson as Charlotte Corday, and Patrick Magee as de Sade. Brook's savage production is usually considered the epitome of the Theatre of CRUELTY.

The play's full title is *The Persecution and Assassination of Jean-Paul Marat as Performed by the Inmates of the Asylum of Charenton under the Direction of the Marquis de Sade*. When the critic Alan Brien asked a friend if he had seen the play, he is reported by Brien to have replied, "No, but I've read the title".

Marceau, Marcel (1923–) French MIME artist, generally regarded as the greatest modern exponent of the form. Marceau trained under Charles Dullin, Etienne Decroux, and Jean-Louis BARRAULT before abandoning conventional acting for mime. In 1946 he introduced at the Théâtre de Poche in Paris his famous character of **Bip**, a whitefaced clown in a white costume, striped bow tie, and a stovepipe hat with a red flower in it. The character, essentially a development of the 19th-century PIERROT tradition, was named after Pip in Dickens's *Great Expectations*.

Marceau defined mime as "the art of expressing feelings by attitudes and not a means of expressing words through gestures." His best-known routines include one in which he tries to escape from an invisible box. In 1978 he founded his École de Mimodrame de Paris at the Théâtre de la Porte-Saint-Martin.

In 1975 Marceau appeared in Mel Brooks's film *Silent Movie*; he had the only speaking part.

Maria Stuart A historical play in verse by Friedrich von SCHILLER. Written while Schiller was suffering from tuberculosis, the play was first produced in 1800 by GOETHE at the Court Theatre in Weimar and has enjoyed regular revivals. The German actor Martin Held was particularly acclaimed for his performance in a 1952 production in Berlin. *Maria Stuart* is the only work of Schiller's to have held the stage in English; it was seen at Covent Garden in 1819, at the Royal Court Theatre in 1880, and (in a translation by Stephen Spender) at the National Theatre in 1958.

The play depicts the final days of Mary, Queen of Scots, emphasizing the spiritual and moral strength with which she accepts her fate. It includes a scene in which Mary meets Queen Elizabeth I, an event that never occurred.

Marie Tempest Theatrical jargon for a door hinge that has been reinforced by a screw lever to keep the door from opening by itself on the incline of a raked stage (*see* RAKE). It was named after the British actress Dame Marie TEMPEST, who insisted on their use.

Mari Lwyd *Singing with Mari Lwyd* (Holy Mary) is an old Welsh Christmas custom still surviving at Llangynwyd, South Wales. It may have derived from the old MYSTERY PLAYS. The chief character wears a white cowl and a horse's skull decorated with ribbons and is accompanied by two or three fantastically dressed followers. They sing outside houses, demanding to be let in. This is, at first, refused until the callers give evidence of their ability in song and repartee. They are then made welcome and suitably refreshed or recompensed.

marionette A puppet manipulated from above by strings (*see* PUPPET THEATRE). This form of puppetry is very old, marionettes having been found in ancient Egyptian tombs. The name may derive from the figurines of Mary in Nativity scenes. The marionette's strings are connected to a wooden cross called a **control** or **perch**, and the rack upon which the puppets are kept is known as a **perchery**.

The famous Salzburg Marionette Theatre was founded in 1913 by Anton Aicher, who specialized in Mozart operas, using trained singers to provide voices for the marionettes on stage. In the same year Vittorio Podrecca established the Teatro Dei Piccoli in Rome, which featured marionettes in lavish small-scale operas and fairy tales. It toured the world successfully for 40 years. Other famous marionette theatres include the Marionetteatern in Stockholm and the Toone Theatre in Brussels.

One of the best known 20th-century companies is Josef Skupa's Spejbl and Hujrvinek Company, founded in Plzeň before World War II and now based in Prague. During the German occupation Skupa was imprisoned for the anti-Nazi views expressed by his marionettes, and his puppets thrown on a rubbish dump. Children found the figures of Spejbl and Hujrvinek and returned them to Skupa after he was released.

The Union Internationale de la Marionette is a world organization for those involved in puppet theatre. The best known puppet museum is the Puppentheatersammlung in Munich.

Marivaux, Pierre (Carlet de Chamblain de) (1688–1763) French playwright, novelist, and journalist whose work is characterized by an extreme subtlety of language and feeling. This idiosyncratic style was referred to, originally disparagingly though now more respectfully, as **Marivaudage**.

> Ce qui constitue le marivaudage, c'est une recherche affectée dans le style, une grande subtilité dans les sentiments, et une grande complication d'intrigues.
> BOUILLET: *Dictionnaire Universel*

Marivaux began his career as a journalist and haunter of fashionable salons. In 1720, however, he lost his fortune and quickly produced three plays, two of which, *L'Amour et la Vérité* and *Arlequin Poli par l'Amour*, were performed by the COMÉDIE-ITALIENNE whilst the third, *Annibal*, was performed by the Comédie-Française. Although Marivaux continued to write for both companies, the majority of his plays were written for the Italian troupe, whose productions proved far more successful, perhaps because they better appreciated the refinements of his style.

In the 20th century Marivaux's sophisticated plotting, keen sense of psychological nuance, and strong female roles have gained increasing recognition. Recent decades have seen frequent revivals of his plays by the Comédie-Française. For many years it was thought that Marivaux's comedies were virtually untranslatable due to the subtlety of the language, but several of his works have been successfully performed in English since the mid 1970s.

Marlowe. Christopher Marlowe (1564–93) English playwright and poet, who through his establishment of blank verse as a medium for drama did much to free the Elizabethan theatre from the constraints of the medieval and Tudor dramatic tradition.

The son of a shoemaker, Marlowe was educated at Corpus Christi College, Cambridge, on a scholarship that may have been intended to provide for his taking holy orders. The university authorities seem to have been extremely reluctant to award Marlowe his MA, citing as grounds for their refusal his frequent term-time absences. They appear, however, to have relented upon receiving a letter form the Privy Council stating that Marlowe's absences were due to his employment "on matters touching the benefit of his country." The letter also made mention of Rheims, leading to speculation that Marlowe had been employed to conduct espionage work among the Jesuits resident there.

After leaving Cambridge in 1587 Marlowe settled in London and began to write for the theatre. His firse play TAMBURLAINE THE GREAT, was performed that same year, probably by the Admiral's Men with Edward Alleyn in the lead. With its swaggering power-hungry title character and gorgeous verse the play proved to be enormously popular; Marlowe quickly wrote a second part, which may have been produced later that year. Marlowe's most famous play, *The Tragical History of Doctor Faustus*, based on the medieval German legend of the scholar who sold his soul to the devil (*see under* FAUST) was probably written and produced in 1589, although it was not published until 1604. Historically the play is important for utilizing the soliloquy as an aid to character analysis and development.

THE JEW OF MALTA (*c.* 1590) has another unscrupulous aspiring character at its centre in the Machiavellian Barabas. By turns violent and grotesque, the play delivers a swingeing critique of contemporary religious values. EDWARD II (*c.* 1592), which may have influenced Shakespeare's *Richard II*, was highly innovatory in its treatment of a historical character and formed an important break with the more simplistic chronicle plays that had preceded it. Marlowe also wrote two lesser plays, *Dido, Queen of Carthage* (date unknown) and *The Massacre at Paris* (1593), based on contemporary events in France.

Marlowe was killed in a London tavern in 1593, apparently as the result of a quarrel with his drinking companions over the apportioning of the bill. Over the years, however, there has been a great deal of speculation concerning his death, with some writers suggesting that he might have been assassinated as a result of his activities as a spy. Other conspiracy theorists point to the fact that only twelve days before his death Marlowe had been summoned by the Privy Council to answer charges of atheism.

Although Marlowe's writing career lasted for only six years, his four major plays make him easily the most important predecessor of Shakespeare.

Julia Marlowe *See* SOTHERN FAMILY.

Marplot An officious person who ruins a plan by gratuitous meddling. The name is given to a silly cowardly inquisitive character in *The Busybody* (1709), by Susannah Centlivre. Similarly we have Shakespeare's **Sir Oliver Martext**, the clergyman in *As You Like It* (1599), and **Sir Martin Mar-All**, the hero of Dryden and the Duke of Newcastle's comedy of that name, which was based on Molière's *The Blunderer* (1655).

marriage. ***Marriage à la Mode*** A sophisticated comedy by John DRYDEN, first produced with great success in 1672 in London. The plot has two strands. One story traces the complex relationships of the lovers Rhodophil, Melantha, Palamede, and Doralice, whose dialogue is written in gentle courtly verse. Melantha's ridiculously affected use of French phrases gives the play its title. The other story is written in heroic verse and follows the struggle of Leonidas, prince of Sicily, to recover his throne from the usurper Polydamas.

Marriage of Figaro, The A comedy by Pierre de BEAUMARCHAIS, one of the most politically inflammatory works ever staged in Europe. It was first performed in 1784 at the Comédie-Française, Paris, after being banned for three years by Louis XVI because of its attacks on social injustice. When it finally opened, somewhat weakened by the censor, the city was tense with anticipation. Although the play's subversive ideas provoked Louis to call the text detestable and the production "a dangerous folly", it ran for 80 performances, a record in 18th-century France.

Beaumarchais's play was not performed in London until 1974, when Jonathan Miller staged it at the National Theatre. It was the source for Mozart's opera *Le nozze di Figaro* (1786; libretto by Da Ponte).

A sequel to THE BARBER OF SEVILLE, the play continues the story of Figaro, the shrewd valet to Count Almaviva. Figaro is about to marry Suzanne, maid to the Count's wife. The Count, however, desires Suzanne himself and tries to reinstitute his ancient right of *droit de seigneur*. At the same time Figaro's debts have put him in the power of Marceline, the Count's housekeeper, who is intent on marrying him. Figaro looks doomed until he learns the truth about his parentage (he previously believed himself an orphan). It turns out that Marceline is actually his cousin and that his father is rich enough to pay off his debts. Figaro and Suzanne are therefore free to marry.

Marston, John (*c.* 1575–1634) English playwright who wrote 12 plays between 1599 and 1609, his two finest being the tragicomedy THE MALCONTENT (1604) and the comedy THE DUTCH COURTESAN (1605). He is noted for his violent imagery and his preoccupation with mankind's failure to uphold Christian virtues. Other plays include the tragedies *Antonio's Revenge* and *Antonio and Mellida* (both 1599) and the comedy *What You Will* (1601).

At the turn of the century Marston became involved in the so-called WAR OF THE THEATRES, a prolonged feud with his rival Ben JONSON. Jonson repeatedly satirized him in such plays as *Every Man Out of His Humour* (1599) and *The Poetaster* (1601), while Marston replied in *Satiromastix* (with Thomas Dekker; 1601). Their squabble ended in time for the two to collaborate with George Chapman on the ill-fated EASTWARD HO! (1605), which resulted in all three authors being briefly imprisoned. Marston was later imprisoned for offending James I with his tragedy *The Insatiate Countess* (1610). After his release he took holy orders and wrote no more plays.

mask A covering for the whole or part of an actor's face. Masks have been worn since primitive times by those taking part in religious and magical rituals. They entered the theatre proper in Greece during the 6th century BC. The Greeks used a range of different masks, each of which represented a particular set of characteristics, such as sex, age, and emotion. Masks also allowed one actor to play several roles and may have assisted voice projection. Made of painted wood, linen, and leather, the masks used by the Greeks included false hair to cover the head and such details as beards and jewellery. When actors portrayed well-known Athenians, 'portrait masks' were worn.

Masks were also worn in the early Roman theatre. The Latin word *persona*, meaning mask, came to mean a dramatic role and still appears in this sense in the term DRAMATIS PERSONAE. The Roman masks for MIME had closed mouths and as this form of drama became increasingly popular, masks were often dispensed with.

In later European theatre masks have been the exception rather than the rule. In MYSTERY PLAYS golden masks were used to represent God and his archangels. 'Visors' were often worn in the Tudor and Stuart MASQUES. The characters of the COMMEDIA

DELL'ARTE wore small black 'cat-masks' that only covered the upper part of the face.

In modern Western theatre masks are usually only worn to create a specific dramatic effect. Modern playwrights to use masks have included Eugene O'NEILL, W. B. YEATS, Bertolt BRECHT, and John ARDEN. Masks are an important feature of the oriental stage, as in the Japanese NŌ drama.

masking piece A fabric or piece of scenery, such as a FLAT, used to conceal lights and other equipment or the backstage area from the audience's view.

masque A form of court entertainment, especially popular in England in the early 17th century, that greatly influenced the development of theatre, opera, and ballet. The amateur performances, often featuring courtiers, were held at banquets and receptions. Characters often included gods and goddesses and other supernatural beings as well as such PASTORAL figures as shepherds, fishermen, milkmaids, etc. The masque generally combined songs, dances, and short spoken scenes, all of which involved elaborate praise of the host, patron, or monarch. Since the performances were private, women were allowed to take part; even Charles I and his queen, Henrietta Maria, became performers and dancers.

The genre, which originated in the processions of masked figures in medieval MUMMERS' PLAYS, developed mainly in 16th-century Italy. In France it became known as the *Mascarade* and in England as the mask or masque, displacing the older term, DISGUISING.

The greatest master of the form was Inigo JONES, England's first scenic designer, who produced at least nine masques between 1605 and 1613. His most important collaborator was Ben JONSON. Their first joint production, presented in 1605 at Whitehall, was the *Masque of Blackness*, for which Jones designed an artificial sea, with the masquers performing in a large shell. Their formal innovations included the **antimasque**, a brief interlude of a contrasting character to the main piece (introduced in 1609), and the **double masque**, in which each performer played two roles. Some of Jones's technical innovations became a permanent part of the English stage. His decorative frame at Whitehall was the forerunner of the PROSCENIUM and, from his travels in Italy, he imported the idea of a painted backcloth with movable side wings set in grooves (*see* GROOVES SYSTEM). The overall effect was called a 'set scene', the origin of the modern term 'set'. Jonson became increasingly unhappy with the collaboration from about 1612 onwards, complaining that his poetry was being swamped by Jones's ornate scenery and costumes (*see* LANTHORN, LEATHERHEAD). When the Puritans closed the theatres in 1642, the masque was doomed by its royal associations. The form was not revived after the Restoration. *See also* CAROLINE DRAMA; JACOBEAN DRAMA.

Massinger, Philip (1583–1640) Versatile English playwright who wrote or collaborated on some 50 plays, of which nearly half are lost. At least eight of his works were mistakenly used as liners for pie-dishes by the servant of the antiquarian collector John Warbuton (*see* WARBURTON'S COOK).

In 1625 Massinger became chief dramatist of the King's Men and produced his best known comedy, A NEW WAY TO PAY OLD DEBTS. It was disregarded in the Restoration theatre but has been constantly revived since the 18th century. The role of the rapacious Sir Giles Overreach has provided a vehicle for such actors as the American Thomas Kean, who first played it in 1816, and for Donald Wolfit in the 1950s.

Massinger's other works include the romances *The Duke of Milan* (1620), *The Great Duke of Florence* (1627), and *The Roman Actor* (1626), the comedies *The City Madam* (1632) and *The Guardian* (1633), and the tragicomedies *The Bondman* (1623) and *The Renegado* (1624). He also collaborated on a number of plays with John Fletcher, and may have had a hand in Shakespeare and Fletcher's *Henry VIII* and *The Two Noble Kinsmen*.

master. Master, the Nickname of the British dramatist and entertainer Sir Noël COWARD. Coward himself disliked the name, possibly because it had already been given to the writer W. Somerset Maugham. It was also associated with the US film director D. W. Griffiths (1873–1948).

> I've over-educated myself in all the things I shouldn't have known at all.
> NOËL COWARD: *Wild Oats*.

Master Builder, The A tragedy by Henrik IBSEN. The play, written on Ibsen's return to Norway after many years of exile, was first performed in 1893 in Berlin. Contemporary critics found its symbolism "maddeningly obscure".

The play concerns the architect Halvard Solness, a man of great energy and iron will whose virility is now waning with age. A young woman, Hilda Wangel, appears one day to announce (with overt sexual symbolism) that she has worshipped him since the day, many years earlier, that she watched him climb to the top of a great tower he had built. Solness is both excited and troubled by her admiration. He has just built a house with a tower for himself and his wife, and Hilda insists that he climb to the top and crown it with a laurel wreath. Solness, overcome by her faith in him, struggles to the top before falling to his death.

Ibsen admitted that Solness was "a man somewhat like me". Both were inveterate wanderers, both had midlife crises involving brief infatuations with young women, and both failed to find happiness in success when it belatedly arrived.

Master of Santiago, The A play by the French dramatist Henri de Montherlant (1896–1972). First performed in 1948 in Paris, where it ran for more than a year, the work is very much in the classical tradition of Corneille and Racine. The 1957 London production, starring and directed by Donald WOLFIT did not find favour with British critics, who found the work too bleak, with one calling it "unrelievedly serious and sombre." Wolfit even tried, without success, to bar critic Kenneth Tynan from the theatre.

With its simple action and complex psychology, *The Master of Santiago* is considered Montherlant's most representative work. The emphasis falls on the sacrifices made by the main characters in order to live up to their own high ideals. The title character, Don Alvaro, is supported by his daughter Mariana when he refuses to compromise his pride and principles in order to regain his fortunes.

Master of the Revels An official who was in charge of court entertainments in England from 1494 until 1737. The first appointment was a temporary one for Henry VII's household. Sir Thomas Cawarden was the first permanent master of the revels, serving from 1545 to 1559; his duties included CENSORSHIP of the public theatre and supervising the festivities for Elizabeth I's coronation in 1558. In James I's reign Sir Edmund Tilney (1579–1610) did little more than license theatres for £3 a month and read plays for 7 shillings each. His nephew, Sir George Buck (1610–22), banned publication of several plays by George Chapman. Sir Henry Herbert was appointed in 1622 and served for 50 years, leaving extensive records that provide valuable information about the theatre of his day. The activities of Sir Thomas KILLIGREW, a theatre manager who misused the office to restrain rival theatres, helped to bring about the Licensing Act of 1737 (*see* LICENCE), which abolished the Office of Revels and made theatrical censorship the direct responsibility of the LORD CHAMBERLAIN.

mastersingers *See* MEISTERSÄNGER.

Matchmaker, The A play written in 1954 by Thornton WILDER that provided the basis for the 1964 hit musical HELLO DOLLY! It opened at the Edinburgh Festival before transferring to the Haymarket Theatre, London. Its plot was based on Wilder's earlier work *The Merchant of Yonkers* (1938), which was itself adapted from a 19th-century Viennese farce.

Peter O'Toole made his London debut with a seven-line part in the 1955 Old Vic production of *The Matchmaker*. In the audience was W. Duncan Ross who, three years earlier, had rejected O'Toole's application for an apprenticeship at the Nottingham Playhouse. When the two met backstage, O'Toole explained that the rejection had upset him so much that he had immediately hitch-hiked to London and demanded an interview at RADA, which resulted in the award of a scholarship.

The plot of *The Matchmaker* follows the amorous scheming of Horace Vandergelder, a rich widower who has decided to remarry, and various other characters including his new love, Irene Molly, his daughter, and her artist sweetheart. At the centre of the web is the matchmaker Dolly Levi, who wants and finally wins Horace for herself.

matinee An afternoon performance given at a reduced ticket price (although the word means 'morning'). The first recorded matinee performance was given at Mitchell's Olympic Theatre in New York on Christmas Day 1843; the Irish playwright Dion BOUCICAULT pioneered the matinee in Britain. By the end of the 19th century, 'matinees musicales' had become popular in London.

matinee idol A male actor who owes his success more to his romantic good looks than to his skill as a performer. The phrase came into use when matinee performances became popular, especially for coach parties of women from the suburbs and provinces.

Maugham, W(illiam) Somerset (1874–1965) British playwright, novelist, and short-story writer, who in 1908 had four plays running simultaneously in the West End, a record at that time. The plays were *Lady Frederick* at the Court Theatre, *Jack Straw* at the Vaudeville Theatre, *Mrs Dot* at the Comedy Theatre, and *The Explorer* at the Lyric Theatre. His work was noted for its clear style, solid construction, and shrewd perception of human nature.

Between 1898 and 1933 Maugham wrote 27 plays; the first to be produced was *Man of Honour* in 1904. His successes included *Our Betters* (1917), a satire on US social-climbers, HOME AND BEAUTY (1919), THE CIRCLE (1921), *East of Suez* (1922), THE CONSTANT WIFE (1926), and the anti-war play *For Services Rendered* (1932). After the comparative failure of *Sheppey*, directed by Gielgud in 1933, Maugham decided that he had lost touch with public taste and gave up writing for the theatre. Several of his short stories have been adapted by others for the stage, notably *Miss Thompson*, dramatized as *Rain* (1922) by John Colton and Clemence Randolph.

Maugham once complimented Noël COWARD on his dialogue but added:

> Good dialogue is like the most charming interior decoration of a house, but it is of little use if the foundations are insecure and the drains don't work.

Coward later wrote *A Song at Twilight* (1966), a play about an embittered homosexual writer, who was clearly based on Maugham. Fears of a possible libel suit evaporated when Maugham, who was 91, obligingly died just before the play opened. Coward, who had visited him three months before, remarked:

> Poor, miserable old man. Not very sadly mourned, I fear.

Mawworm A hypocritical pretender to sanctity, a pious humbug. From the character of this name in Isaac BICKERSTAFFE's *The Hypocrite* (1769), a play largely based on Molière's TARTUFFE.

May. May Day Spring time celebrations and fertility rituals have taken place throughout history and in many different cultures. The Romans used to leave their towns and cities for the open fields and spend the first of May dancing and singing in honour of Flora, goddess of fruits and flowers. The English have celebrated May Day for centuries with games and sports, particularly archery and MORRIS DANCES and the setting up of the maypole. In the 16th century May Day was known as Robin Hood's day and ROBIN HOOD PLAYS became an integral part of the festivities: performers dressed as Robin Hood and MAID MARIAN often presided as Lord and Lady of the May.

May Day was also formerly the day of the London chimney-sweeps' festival.

Mayfest An annual international festival of theatre and music held in Glasgow during the first three weeks of May. First held in 1990 to mark Glasgow's year as City of European Culture, it features comedy, cabaret, and children's shows as well as more mainstream theatrical events.

Mayakovsky, Vladimir Vladimirovich (1893–1930) Soviet poet, who became a major playwright of the FUTURISM movement. Mayakovsky's *Mystery-Bouffe*, produced in Moscow in 1918, is usually considered the first Soviet play. It depicted the triumph of the Unclean (proletarians) over the Clean (bourgeois) and parodied the Bible, the last scene showing the proletariat entering the Promised Land.

Although he was a fierce supporter of the Revolution and the Bolshevik regime, Mayakovsky later wrote two controversial plays satirizing Soviet bureaucracy. *The Bedbug (Klop*; 1929) showed the bedbug and the bourgeois, both survivors of the past, adjusting to the new regime. *The Bath House (Banya*; 1930) also satirized the survival of bourgeois traits in Soviet life.

The failure of these plays, the disapproval of the Soviet authorities, and a failed love affair, led Mayakovsky to shoot himself at the age of 37. After Stalin's death Soviet officials rehabilitated Mayakovsky and in 1954 Moscow's Theatre of the Revolution was renamed in his honour.

Measure for Measure One of SHAKESPEARE's so-called 'dark comedies', first performed in 1604 at court in London (although this version apparently differed considerably from the text we now have). Owing perhaps to its preoccupation with sex, death, and moral corruption, and to its complex and mostly unattractive characters, the play remained unpopular until the 20th century.

The 1933 Old Vic production at Sadler's Wells Theatre starred Charles Laughton as Angelo, a performance described as "magnificent" by John Gielgud. *Measure for Measure* was also the last play to be staged before the Old Vic disbanded in 1963. Jonathan Miller produced a memorable modern-dress version in 1975 at the Greenwich Theatre, while a production at the Lyttelton Theatre in 1981 set the action on a Caribbean island (with Angelo as a Black bishop).

The plot is derived mainly from George Whetstone's *Promos and Cassandra* (1578). Vincentio, the kindly but enigmatic Duke of Vienna, disguises himself as a friar in order to move unnoticed amongst his people and observe their morals at first hand. In his place he temporarily appoints the puritanical Angelo, who immediately sentences Claudio to death under a disused law against fornication. Isabella, Claudio's sister and a novice nun, pleads with Angelo for his life. Overcome with sudden lust, Angelo says he will only save Claudio if Isabella sleeps with him. Although Claudio begs her to do so, she indignantly refuses. Through a series of machinations the disguised Duke manages to save Claudio and shame Angelo. In the play's last moments he unexpectedly proposes to Isabella himself.

mechane (Gk. machine) A crane-like piece of machinery set up behind the stage in ancient Greek theatres. It was used to lower an actor playing a god from the roof of the SKENE onto the stage. The device was used when the only way to resolve a crisis or conclude a traditional plot was through divine intervention (hence the Latin phrase DEUS EX MACHINA, god from a machine). Sophocles used the device seriously but Euripides parodied the use of the contraption and Aristophanes made it seem ridiculous.

Medea A play by EURIPIDES; it was first performed in 431 BC in Athens, winning third prize at the City Dionysia. The play caused controversy because Euripides flouted tradition by allowing Medea, the child-murderer, to escape unpunished; in the play's final scene she even appears to have transcended human status and become a demigod or demon. ARISTOPHANES, who often made jokes about Euripides, wrote a scene in which the women of Athens rebuked the playwright for being a misogynistic child-hater. However, the play is now often seen as a proto-feminist statement. Medea speaks powerfully about the injustices she has suffered as a woman and a foreigner in Greece:

> I would rather stand three times in the front line of battle than give birth once.

The story depicts the ultimate revenge of a wronged woman on her treacherous lover. Medea's vendetta against Jason culminates in her killing their children in order to make him suffer. She finally escapes in a chariot belonging to her grandfather, the sun god.

Medea provides a complex, challenging, and prized role. In Gielgud's production, Dame Judith Anderson played Medea to Florence Reed's Nurse. The two actresses were bitter rivals. Dame Judith found it hard to achieve the concentration and intensity needed for her grand entrance at the speech beginning "Death! Death!" One night she sent a terse message to Reed through the stage manager:

> Tell that old bitch she is not to move a muscle, not a muscle, during my soliloquy. Now tell her that exactly.

Just before Dame Judith was due to go on, she asked the stage manager to tell her how Reed had reacted. The stage manager gave Reed's reply verbatim:

> Tell Judith to go fuck herself.

That night when Dame Judith stormed onto the stage shrieking "Death! Death!", there was a hidden agenda.

More recent revivals have included an acclaimed London production starring Diana Rigg (1992).

medicine shows A type of entertainment formerly presented from the wagons of itinerant pedlars of patent medicines in America. "Step right up," was the characteristic cry of travelling medicine men, who used a variety of short acts, from card tricks to banjo playing, to lure their rural customers. As VAUDEVILLE expanded, so did the medicine shows, which began to make more money from providing entertainment than from the sales of their dubious medicinal products. The presentations, interspersed with brief sales-pitches, usually lasted about two hours and offered up to a dozen acts, including burlesque comics, ventriloquists, banjo pickers, and blackfaced comedians usually named Sambo or Jake (*see* MINSTREL SHOW). The afterpiece was usually a farce, often involving a ghost. A few medicine shows, such as those run by Fred Foster Bloodgood and Tommy Scott, have continued into the late 20th century, but have had to abandon the preposterous medical claims, which would now breach consumer-protection legislation. A reconstructed performance, *The Vi-Ton-Ka Medicine Show*, was given in 1983 in New York's American Place Theatre.

medieval drama European drama from about 1000 to 1500. After about 400 years during which the theatre was virtually extinct in Europe, the seeds of a revival were sown in the 10th century when the Church began to introduce dramatic elements into the liturgy (*see* LITURGICAL DRAMA). By the 11th century short dramatizations of Biblical stories were being performed at Easter and Christmas in many parts of Europe. Gradually the vernacular replaced Latin and scenic devices, local subject matter, and humorous or dramatic touches were introduced to add to the interest.

The three main types of medieval drama – the MYSTERY PLAY, the MORALITY PLAY, and the MIRACLE PLAY – all achieved recognizable form during the 14th century. The mystery play developed directly from the tradition of liturgical drama but incorporated more humorous and secular material and shows a more sophisticated sense of theatre.

The development of religious drama in the middle ages appears to have been much influenced by a number of older secular traditions. These included the folk theatre of MAY DAY games, ROBIN HOOD stories, etc., and the tradition of jongleurs, minstrels, and other itinerant performers. Other secular influences on later drama include the elaborate pageantry of the courts and the outdoor festivities organized by town guilds and other local bodies.

Meek, Private Napoleon Alexander Trotsky A character in the play TOO TRUE TO BE GOOD, by George Bernard Shaw, first performed in 1932. Meek, an unassuming private soldier who proves himself effortlessly superior to his officers, was based on T. E. Lawrence in his Aircraftman Shaw phase. Although the two men became friends, the common assertion that Lawrence chose his pseudonym out of admiration for Shaw is untrue.

Meggs, Mary *See* ORANGE MOLL.

Meininger company A German court theatre group, which became one of the most influential companies in late 19th-century Europe. The company was founded in 1874 as the resident troupe at the court of Georg II, Duke of Saxe-Meiningen (1826–1914); it was strongly promoted by his wife, the actress **Ellen Franz** (1839–1923). The Duke himself directed the plays and designed the costumes and scenery. He was joined in 1876 by the actor and director Ludwig Chronegk (1837–1891). The company had performed in some 38 European cities by the time Chronegk's health failed in 1890. The directors Konstantin STANISLAVSKY and André Antoine (1858–1943) were amongst those influenced by the company's realistic style.

The Meininger troupe developed ensemble acting (occasionally requiring such stars as August Bassermann and Josef KAINZ to play minor roles), gave the director an enhanced interpretive role, demanded strict historical accuracy for sets and costumes, used experimental stage lighting, introduced the naturalistic BOX SET, and kept the stage action moving on different levels through the use of steps and ROSTRUMS.

Meistersänger (Ger. master singer) A member of one of the German guilds of poetry and music that flourished from the 14th to the 16th century. According to legend the *Meistersinger* were founded by 12 master poets of ancient times but in reality they probably developed from early fraternities of laymen who sang in church. Because in medieval Germany music and poetry were regarded as crafts to be learned, *Singschulen* (Ger. song schools) were formed on the same lines as the craft guilds; students had to pass several grades before becoming a 'mastersinger'. Music, subject matter, metres, and performance style were all restricted by codes called *Tabulatur*, thus originality was only possible during competitions, when poets fitted new words to old tunes.

In the 16th century, **Hans Folz** (*d.* 1515) campaigned successfully for a wider choice of subjects and the right to compose new music; this liberalization was extended by **Hans Sachs** (1494–1576), a leading *Meistersänger* and an important playwright. Sachs appears as a character in Wagner's opera *Die Meistersinger von Nürnberg* (1867). The *Meistersinger* were never generally popular and the *Singschulen* virtually disappeared after 1600 (although the last school, in Memminger, was not closed until 1875).

Mélite The first play by Pierre CORNEILLE, a comedy first performed in Paris by the Prince of Orange's Players in 1629. Although critics complained that the UNITIES were not observed and stock farce characters were omitted, the play surprised its author by becoming a great success. The plot involves the confused love affairs of two couples, Mélite and Tircis and Chloris and Philandre, complicated by the intrigues of Éraste, who also loves Mélite.

melo-. melodrama A form of sensational play that swept Europe in the 19th century. Mass audiences were attracted by its emphasis on fast implausible action and larger-than-life heroes and villains.

The term (from Greek *melos*, song and *drama*, action) was introduced by Rousseau to mean an entertainment in which dialogue was spoken to background music (*see* MÉLODRAME). In the late 18th century August Kotzebue (1761–1819) wrote numerous sentimental melodramas in Germany, while Guilbert de Pixérécourt (1773–1844) developed the form in France. British melodramas were often adaptions of Continental works; examples include Dion Boucicault's THE CORSICAN BROTHERS (1852), which was based on a French play of revenge.

In the mid 19th century the genre broadened to include domestic tragedies, realistic dramas set in the slums, moralizing works such as UNCLE TOM'S CABIN, and entertainments based on spectacular shipwrecks and disasters.

By the turn of the 20th century, theatregoers were turning to REALISM. Exaggerated plots and over-emotional acting soon survived only in grand opera and classical ballet, as well as in the new mass medium of cinema. One of the purest forms of melodrama was the cliff-hanging Hollywood serial, as exemplified by *The Perils of Pauline* (1914). Many of the elements of 19th-century melodrama were revived in television soap operas such as *Dallas* and *Dynasty* in the 1980s.

mélodrame A type of play combining spoken dialogue with passages of instrumental music. An influential example was *Pygmalion* (1770) with words by Jean-Jacques Rousseau and music by Horace Coignet (1735–1821). *Mélodrame* influenced the development of popular MELODRAMA but failed to develop as an independent form.

In opera the term means the use of spoken words for dramatic effect, either during a break in the music or to instrumental accompaniment. An example of *mélodrame* in this sense is the dungeon scene of Beethoven's *Fidelio* (1805).

melodramma An 18th-century Italian term for a serious play with music. Exponents of the genre included Apostolo Zeno and the librettist Pietro Metastasio (1698–1782).

Melpomene The MUSE of TRAGEDY in ancient Greek mythology.

Menander (343–292 BC) Greek exponent of the NEW COMEDY, whose witty and sophisticated plays had a major influence on the development of the modern comic tradition. Menander's plays gave a reduced role to the CHORUS and avoided serious treatment of heroic, religious, or political themes. His realism prompted one critic to ask:

> O Menander and life, which of you imitated the other?

Menander's plays are populated by conniving slaves, wily courtesans, domineering fathers, rebellious children, and other lively and bawdy urban characters. His complex plots often involve mistaken identities and problematic love affairs. These characteristics of his work influenced the Roman writers PLAUTUS and TERENCE, and, through them, Molière, Congreve, Wilde, and other writers of the COMEDY OF MANNERS.

Menander's popularity earned him invitations to royal courts in Egypt and Macedonia but he chose to remain in Athens, where he is thought to have drowned while swimming in the harbour.

Mendes, Sam(uel) (Alexander) (1965–) British director, who emerged as one of the country's most exciting theatrical talents while still in his mid twenties. After graduating from Cambridge in 1987, Mendes worked as a general assistant at the Chichester Festival, where he was given a chance to direct Chekhov for one night only. The response was so favourable that Mendes was made artistic director of the Festival's new studio theatre, the Minerva, at the age of 23. Over the next two years he established a national profile with a series of Stratford and West End productions including *Troilus and Cressida* for the RSC (1990),

Kean at the Old Vic (1990), and *The Rise and Fall of Little Voice* at the National (1992) – the last being a vehicle for the talents of his then-partner, the actress Jane Horrocks. Since 1992 Mendes has been director of the Donmar Warehouse Theatre, a venue that has been described as "the sexiest space in London." With productions that include revivals of Friel's *Translations* (1993), Mamet's *Glengarry Glen Ross* (1994), and the Sondheim musical *Company* (1995), it has undoubtedly become the capital's most fashionable and talked-about theatre. Mendes has continued to direct plays for other companies, including a successful revival of *Oliver!* at the Palladium (1994–) that has made him a wealthy man.

Menken, Adah Isaacs (Dolores Adios Fuertes; 1835–68) US actress, whose career was virtually confined to appearing bound to the back of a 'wild' horse in a skimpy costume in *Mazeppa*, a dramatization of Byron's poem. Menken, whose beauty was appreciated by Dickens and Swinburne, made her first appearance in this famous EQUESTRIAN DRAMA in London in 1861; after a year in America she returned to London in 1864 to appear in the same role at ASTLEY'S AMPHITHEATRE.

Merchant of Venice, The SHAKESPEARE'S tragicomedy about the attempted revenge of the Jewish usurer SHYLOCK. It was written in 1596 but the date of its first performance is unknown. Shakespeare's main sources were Giovanni Fiorentino's *Il Pecorone* (1558) and Marlowe's *The Jew of Malta* (1589). In the story Antonio, a Venetian merchant, borrows money from Shylock to help his friend Bassanio woo the heiress PORTIA. As security he is obliged to offer a pound of his own flesh, assuming that this is a friendly joke. When Antonio finds himself unable to return the money, Shylock, enraged by the constant insults of the Christians, demands his pound of flesh. In the play's climactic court scene Portia, disguised as a lawyer, saves Antonio's life by arguing that Shylock is entitled to a pound of the merchant's flesh but not to a drop of his blood. Shylock is stripped of his estate and compelled to become a Christian.

Between them Charles MACKLIN and Edmund KEAN revolutionized the interpretation of Shylock by turning him into a figure of tragic dignity. In 1889 Henry Irving and Ellen Terry presented the trial scene at Sandringham for the reclusive Queen Victoria. Other notable Shylock–Portia pairings have included Redgrave–Ashcroft in 1953 at Stratford and Olivier–Plowright in 1970 at the Old Vic.

Charles Macklin was so precise in his interpretation of the part that he once instructed Bobby Bates, playing Tubal, not to speak until Macklin had placed his right foot on a particular nail in the stage floor. Bates dutifully marked the spot with chalk, but Macklin forgot all about it once into his performance. When Bates missed his cue, Macklin growled under his breath, "Why the devil don't you speak?" "Sir," replied Bates, "put your right foot upon the nail."

In the 20th century the question of whether or not the play is anti-Semitic (and, if so, how this should affect our response to it) has received much anguished attention. In 1976 Arnold WESKER, himself a Jew, rewrote the story from Shylock's perspective as *The Merchant*.

Meredith. We're in, Meredith A catchphrase derived from the Fred KARNO sketch, *The Bailiff* (1907). It depicted the stratagems by which a bailiff and his assistant, Meredith, attempt to enter the house of a debtor. The phrase was used by the bailiff each time he thought he was on the verge of success.

mermaid. Mermaid Tavern A tavern in Bread Street, London, that was a meeting place of literary figures in the early 17th century. The **Friday Street Club**, which included amongst its members Sir Walter Raleigh, Beaumont and Fletcher, Jonson, and Shakespeare met here from 1603. According to Beaumont, in his verse epistle 'Master Beaumont to Ben Jonson', the conversation was inspirational:

> What things have we seen
> Done at the Mermaid! heard words that have been
> So nimble, and so full of subtle flame,
> As if that every one from whence they came
> Had meant to put his whole wit in a jest,
> And had resolv'd to live a fool the rest
> Of his dull life...

The tavern was destroyed in the Great Fire of London. John Keats wrote its epitaph in his 'Lines on the Mermaid Tavern':

> Souls of poets dead and gone
> What Elysium have ye known,
> Happy field or mossy cavern
> Choicer than the Mermaid Tavern?

Mermaid Theatre A riverside theatre in Blackfriars, London, built by the actor Bernard Miles (1907–91) and his wife, Josephine. The first Mermaid Theatre was a former schoolroom in the Miles's back garden in St John's Wood. This opened as a private venue in 1951. A year later the company moved to the City for a 13-week season on the piazza of the Royal Exchange; a replica Elizabethan stage was constructed on the same site in 1953.

In 1959 the theatre moved again, this time to a permanent home in a war-damaged warehouse at Puddledock. For the opening, the 4-year-old daughter of the actor Jack Hawkins was rowed up the Thames dressed as a mermaid. The first production was *Lock Up Your Daughters*, Miles's own musical adaptation of Fielding's *Rape upon Rape*. The Mermaid subsequently concentrated on Jacobean and Elizabethan revivals; revues and pantomime have also featured strongly.

The Mermaid closed for modernization in 1979 and reopened two years later as part of a controversial office-block complex. It now contains the Molecule Club studio theatre for schoolchildren, which brings science to life on the stage.

When a series of failures plunged the Mermaid into financial difficulties in the mid 1980s, it was bought by the entrepreneur Abdul Shamji, who was sentenced to 15 months imprisonment in 1989 for financial improprieties. In 1993 a one-man show about Muhammad Ali staged by Shamji's son ran up further large losses. The future of the Mermaid remains in considerable doubt.

Merman, Ethel (Ethel Zimmerman; 1909–84) US actress and trumpet-toned vocalist. Merman made her Broadway debut in a 1930 production of *Girl Crazy* at the Alvin Theatre; while singing 'I Got Rhythm' she held a note for 16 bars and stopped the show. It was said of her that she could "hold a note longer than the Chase Manhattan Bank", while *Time* magazine wrote:

> She aims at a point slightly above the entrails, but she knocks you out just the same.

In 1946 Merman opened in her most memorable part – Annie Oakley in Irving Berlin's ANNIE GET YOUR GUN, which ran for 1146 performances at the Imperial. It included her best-known song 'There's No Business Like Show Business'. Later triumphs included the roles of Sally Adams in Berlin's CALL ME MADAM (1950), Rose in *Gypsy* (1958), and the title character in *Hello Dolly!* (1970).

Merman's star quality owed a great deal to her contagious energy and enthusiasm. The *Saturday Review of Literature* once wrote "she works like a stable, not a horse", while Kenneth Tynan stated that in Merman's hands "musical comedy became a martial art." When Ralph Richardson was asked on television to define a star, he responded instantly, "Ethel Merman."

merry. Merry-Andrew A name for a clown on the Elizabethan stage; also a buffoon, jester, or attendant on a quack doctor at fairs. The term, which remained in use until the 19th century, may have derived from Andrew Borde (d. 1549), court doctor to Henry VIII and a celebrated eccentric. In 1668 Pepys noted in his diary that he saw a ridiculous play entitled *Marry Andrey* at Bartholomew Fair.

Merry Wives of Windsor, The A comedy by SHAKESPEARE, first performed in 1600 in London; according to tradition it was written in a hurry to please Queen Elizabeth, who had asked to see FALSTAFF in love. The play is generally considered one of Shakespeare's weakest works; in particular, the Falstaff of *The Merry Wives* seems a pale imitation of the great figure of the *Henry IV* plays. Nevertheless, Karl Marx later wrote:

> In the first act alone of *The Merry Wives of Windsor* there is more life and movement than in all German literature.

It is the only one of Shakespeare's plays to have a contemporary middle-class setting and to be written mainly in prose.

When Beerbohm TREE presented the play for the coronation of Edward VII in 1902, he deliberately cast Madge KENDAL and Ellen TERRY as the two wives, knowing how much they hated each other. Tree hid in a box to watch their encounter at the first rehearsal but was disappointed when they behaved with the utmost dignity.

In the 1833 production at the Haymarket Falstaff was played by the actress Julia Glover. Modern-dress versions include the 1986 Royal Shakespeare Company production, starring Peter Jeffrey as Falstaff.

The story concerns Falstaff's attempts to seduce Mistress Ford and Mistress Page, the two wives of the title, as a means of getting his hands on their husbands' wealth. The wives discover that he has sent them identical love letters and devise a series of plots to humiliate him. Accordingly Falstaff is forced to hide in a basket of stinking linen, thrown into a ditch, beaten by Ford, and tormented by a troupe of bogus fairies. *See also* HERNE THE HUNTER.

mescidato A form of Italian secular drama that developed from the SACRA RAPPRESENTAZIONE. The *mescidato* retained the basic structure of the liturgical drama but dealt with nonreligious themes. By the end of the 16th century, it had evolved into the PASTORAL.

Method, the An acting technique developed from the theories of Konstantin STANISLAVSKY and taught from 1950 onwards at the ACTORS' STUDIO, New York, under the directorship of Lee STRASBERG. Strasberg was a former pupil of Richard Boleslavsky, who had brought Stanislavsky's ideas to America in the 1920s. The most important principle of the Method is the actor's total understanding of and identification with his character's motivation; to grasp this, the actor is encouraged to draw on comparable experiences in his or her own life, including painful ones that have been buried in the subconscious. This is intended to produce a greater realism in the actor's subsequent portrayal of the character. The technique was widely criticized, but remained an important influence on stage and screen acting in the latter half of the 20th century. Notable exponents of the Method include Marlon Brando and Dustin Hoffman.

Enthusiasm for the Method led Eli Wallach into trouble when he was appearing in a Broadway production of *Antony and Cleopatra* in 1948. One night Wallach rushed to the theatre inspired by Strasberg's classroom exhortation, "If you go on stage to do something, do it!" In his role as a messenger he became so eager to deliver his news about Antony's marriage that he kept on interrupting Cleopatra's lengthy soliloquy. The exasperated actress, Katharine CORNELL, finally slapped him hard and walked offstage. At his next class, Wallach complained to Strasberg, "What the hell kind of Method is that?" The director merely shrugged: "Wait for your cues".

Meyerhold, Vsevolod Emilievich (1874–1940) Russian actor and director. Meyerhold trained as an actor under Vladimir Nemirovich-Danchenko, a co-founder of the MOSCOW ART THEATRE, which Meyerhold himself joined in 1898. He made his first appearance in STANISLAVSKY's famous naturalistic production of Chekhov's THE SEAGULL.

In 1902 Meyerhold formed his own company and spent a time touring the provinces; he also worked briefly at the theatre of Vera Komisarjevskaya, a noted Russian actress, in 1906–07. By this time, he had already formulated his controversial theory of BIO-MECHANICS and his opposition to the naturalism of Stanislavsky led to conflict between the two men and Meyerhold's final departure from the Moscow Art Theatre. Meyerhold subsequently directed at theatres in St Petersburg, notably at the Aleksandrinsky, where his productions reflected his growing interest in Oriental theatrical conventions.

Following the 1917 Revolution Meyerhold was amongst the first directors to offer his services to the new regime. In 1918 he became the first director to stage new Soviet drama with his production of MAYAKOVSKY's *Mystery-Bouffe* (1918). Meyerhold later produced the same author's *The Bed-Bug* (1929) and *The Bath House* (1930).

In the mid 1930s, however, Meyerhold became increasingly unpopular with the Soviet authorities: his formalist leanings were regarded as suspect, as was his unwillingness to embrace the new socialist realism. In about 1937 his theatre company was closed. Details of the end of Meyerhold's life are sketchy. Shortly after his arrest in late 1938 or early 1939, his wife, an actress, was found murdered at their home; nothing more was heard of Meyerhold until the late 1950s, when a Soviet encyclopedia stated that he had died in 1942. A later edition of the book, however, gave his death date as 1940.

mezzanine floor A floor or gallery below the stage used to operate traps, etc. In America the term is also applied to the first GALLERY of the auditorium (or its first few rows). **Entresol** is another rarer term, used in both Britain and America, for the mezzanine floor in this second sense.

Mezzetino One of the ZANNI of the COMMEDIA DELL'ARTE. Angelo COSTANTINI transformed the role in the 1680s, making Mezzetino a more sophisticated character than the comic rogue of tradition and replacing the green stripes of the costume with red ones. The French name for the character was

Mezzetin; Preville of the COMÉDIE-FRANÇAISE was famous for playing this role.

Mickery-theatre An Amsterdam theatre that imports productions of new works by leading foreign companies, thereby introducing new theatrical trends to the Netherlands. It was founded in 1965 by Ritsaert Ten Cate, who held the first performances on his farm in the village of Loenersloot. In 1970 the theatre began to receive public funding and moved into a disused cinema in Amsterdam. The building was not divided into a conventional stage and auditorium and the Mickery-theatre chose to retain this arrangement, so as not to introduce barriers between audience and actors. A number of experimental seating arrangements have been used, including the use of movable cubicles supported by air-cushions to lead the audience from scene to scene in such works as *Fairground* (1975), *Cloud Cuckooland* (1979), *Outside* (1979), and *Fairground '84* (produced for the Holland Festival).

Companies closely associated with the Mickery-theatre include the Pip Simmons Theatre Group and the People Show in London, the Traverse Theatre in Edinburgh, La Mama in New York, and the Tenjo Tsukiji company in Tokyo. During the 1984–85 and 1985–86 seasons, the Pip Simmons company explored the relationship between theatre and television in *La Ballista*.

middle. Middle Comedy One of the three periods of ancient Greek comedy. The term is applied in particular to ARISTOPHANES's last two plays, *Ecclesiazusae* (*Women in Parliament*; 392 BC) and *Plutus* (*Wealth*; 388 BC), as well as to works by his immediate successors in the early-to-mid 4th century BC. Middle Comedy dispensed with much of the festive exuberance and bawdy revelry found in OLD COMEDY; there was less singing and dancing, plots became more complex, and the dramatic illusion more sophisticated. Although plays of the Middle Comedy retained a political dimension, they showed a greater concern with personal and social issues, preparing the way for the shift to NEW COMEDY in the middle of the 4th century.

middle theatre The US term for a middle-sized New York theatre that is considered to be neither on BROADWAY nor OFF-BROADWAY.

Middlesex Music Hall *See* OLD MO.

Middleton, Thomas (1570–1627) English dramatist, whose comedies provide penetrating insight into 17th-century London society. He is also noted for his richly poetic verse, his intricate plots, and his understanding of feminine psychology. His admirer, T. S. Eliot, wrote:

> Middleton was a great observer of human nature, without fear, without sentiment, without prejudice.

Middleton's first plays were acted by BOY COMPANIES at Blackfriars Theatre and other venues. He often worked in collaboration with other dramatists for the theatre owner Philip HENSLOWE. With Thomas Dekker (*c.* 1570–1632) he wrote *The Honest Whore* (1604) and *The Roaring Girl* (1610), and with William Rowley such plays as THE CHANGELING (1622).

Middleton's social comedies include *A Trick to Catch the Old One* (1604–05), which provided the basis for Philip Massinger's A NEW WAY TO PAY OLD DEBTS (1623), *A Mad World, My Masters* (1605), which introduced Sir Bounteous Progress, a lively country gentleman who is generous to all except his heir Dick Follywit, and *A Chaste Maid in Cheapside* (1619), which satirized ordinary Londoners. Other works include the tragedy WOMEN BEWARE WOMEN (1621) and the political satire *A Game of Chess* (1624), about the futile efforts to unite the royal houses of England (represented by the White Knight) and Spain (the Black Knight):

> The White Knight, with wit-wonderous
>   strength
> And circumspective prudency,
> Gives check-mate by discovery
> To the Black Knight...

The play drew huge crowds to the Globe Theatre but the Spanish ambassador protested and James I had *A Game of Chess* banned after only nine performances. It proved equally popular in print.

Midsummer Night's Dream, A SHAKESPEARE's comedy of romantic entanglements; it was probably written in 1595 and performed a year later in London.

Having been forbidden to marry, the lovers Hermia and Lysander flee from the Athenian court to the forest of the Fairy King, OBERON; they are followed by Demetrius, who also loves Hermia, and Helena, who loves Demetrius. Oberon, who has fallen out with his Queen, TITANIA, orders the spirit PUCK to sprinkle a magic potion on her eyes so that she will fall in love with the first creature she sees on waking. This turns out to be one of a troupe of amateur players, BOTTOM THE WEAVER, whom Puck has also bewitched, replacing his head with that of an ass. Puck also uses the potion to cause multiple confusions amongst the young lovers, until Oberon eventually orders him to undo the damage. The last act includes the amateur theatricals of the Athenian artisans, as presented at the wedding of Duke Theseus (*see* PYRAMUS AND THISBE).

One of the most continuously popular of Shakespeare's plays, the *Dream* has been staged in an extraordinary variety of styles over the years. In 1856 Charles Kean, manager of London's Princess Theatre, took realism to extremes by building a full-scale workshop for Quince the Carpenter and claiming "the furniture and tools introduced in this scene are copied from discoveries at Herculaneum." In 1900 Beerbohm TREE set live rabbits to run across the stage during the woodland scenes at his theatre, Her Majesty's. By contrast, Peter BROOK's celebrated 1970 production for the RSC used a plain white setting, placing the actors on trapezes, swings, and other such devices. It enjoyed the longest tour of any RSC production, with performances in 13 countries in 1972–73.

Mikado, The GILBERT AND SULLIVAN's popular comic opera with a Japanese theme; subtitled *The Town of Titipu*, it opened in 1885 at the Savoy Theatre. The subject matter is said to have suggested itself to Gilbert when an ornamental Japanese sword fell from the wall of his library. Sullivan, who had announced his intention of writing no more comic operas, was persuaded to relent when he saw the libretto.

The opera traces the fate of Nanki-Poo, the son of the Mikado (emperor), who has disguised himself as a minstrel in order to woo Yum-Yum, the ward of Ko-Ko, the Lord High Executioner. Unfortunately Ko-Ko intends to marry her himself. The Mikado has complained to Ko-Ko about the lack of executions, so, unaware of Nanki-Poo's true identity, he agrees to let him marry Yum-Yum as long as he consents to be executed for the Mikado's visit a month later. When Ko-Ko realizes that according to the law Yum-Yum must also die (by being buried alive) he draws up a certificate saying the execution has already taken place. When the Mikado visits and asks about Nanki-Poo, his lost son, the shocked Ko-Ko brings the boy back from the dead.

In 1907 performances of *The Mikado* were banned by the Lord Chamberlain during a visit by the Japanese Prince Fushimi. It was felt that Gilbert's depiction of Japanese judicial procedures might give offence:

> To sit in silence in a dull, dark dock,
> In a pestilential prison, with a life-long lock,
> Awaiting the sensation of a short, sharp shock,
> From a cheap and chippy chopper on a big black block!

The phrase **short sharp shock**, was used in 1983 by William Whitelaw (then Home Secretary) to promote a system of harsher punishment for young offenders and in the early 1990s to describe the purpose of allied bombing raids on military installations in Iraq.

Miles Gloriosus A stock character of the Greek NEW COMEDY, a braggart soldier who proves to be a coward. He appears in later Roman plays, including those by Plautus, and in the *Commedia dell'arte* as Il CAPITANO. The Miles Gloriosus also provided the basis for various characters of Elizabethan and Jacobean comedy, including Shakespeare's FALSTAFF and PAROLLES.

Miller. Arthur Miller (1915–) US dramatist, considered one of the most significant of the 20th century. Born into a Jewish New York family that suffered badly during the Depression of the 1930s, he held various odd jobs after leaving school, enabling him to pay for a course on journalism at the University of Michigan. Here he started writing. Miller's first successful play, the Ibsenesque ALL MY SONS, was produced in 1947; like his later plays, this examination of the private and public guilt of a man responsible for producing faulty war materials stressed the need for self-knowledge and a true sense of values. The same year saw the production of DEATH OF A SALESMAN (1947), the Pulitzer-Prize-winning tragedy of US middle-class life that established Miller's reputation as a great modern playwright. This reputation was consolidated by THE CRUCIBLE (1953), a play about the 17th-century Salem witch trials that was clearly relevant to the anticommunist witchhunts of the 1950s. Miller was himself questioned by the Un-American Activities Committee, before which he refused to divulge the names of people said to have attended a communist writers' group; his conviction for contempt was quashed on appeal.

A VIEW FROM THE BRIDGE and *A Memory of Two Mondays* were staged together as a double-bill in 1955. AFTER THE FALL (1964), a painful examination of a failed human relationship, reflected some of the unhappiness of Miller's highly publicized marriage (1955–60) to Marilyn Monroe. During their marriage the world's press had catered extensively for the insatiable curiosity of its readers in the unlikely relationship between a Jewish intellectual Pulitzer Prize-winner and a world-famous sex symbol (whose brain had been described by Billy Wilder as being "...like a Swiss cheese, full of holes"). Miller wrote the screenplay for Monroe's last film, appropriately called *The Misfits* (1961).

Miller's later plays include *The Price* (1968), *The Archbishop's Ceiling* (1977), *Playing for Time* (1981), *The Ride Down Mt Morgan* (1991), and *The Last Yankee* (1992).

> I am simply asking for a theatre in which an adult who wants to live can find plays that will heighten his awareness of what living in our time involves.
>
> ARTHUR MILLER

a Joe Miller An old joke that is no longer funny. In 1739 an enterprising person called John Mottley compiled a book of jokes which (without permission) he entitled *Joe Miller's Jest-Book*, from Joseph Miller (1684–1738), a popular comedian of the day who could neither read nor write. A 'Joe Miller' is applied to an old joke implying that it is stolen from Mottley's compilation.

Mills, Sir John (Lewis Ernest Watts; 1908–) British actor who began in musicals before diversifying into both comedy and serious drama, as well as making more than 100 films. He changed his name while still a schoolboy, because it was "too sissy".

Mills was inspired to go on the stage by his older sister Annette, who had revived the Charleston in New York in the 1920s (and later partnered Muffin the Mule on British television). He made his debut in 1929 as a chorus boy at the London Hippodrome. Two years later he starred in the first production of Coward's CAVALCADE, becoming the first actor to sing 'Mad Dogs and Englishmen'. Laurence Olivier subsequently made arrangements for him to play *Hamlet* and *Richard III* at the Old Vic, but World War II intervened. Olivier later directed him in such serious works as Tyrone Guthrie's *Top of the Ladder* (1949).

Mills first appeared on Broadway in 1961, playing T. E. Lawrence in Terence Rattigan's ROSS. He was paralysed by stage-fright but Olivier built up his confidence, telling him to peek through the curtain 15 minutes before the performance and whisper to the audience, "You lucky people – you'll find it impossible to take your eyes off me!"

Mills's wife, Mary Hayley Bell, is a playwright while his daughters Juliet Mills (1941–) and Hayley Mills (1946–) are both actresses.

mime A wordless form of entertainment, in which movement and gesture are used to communicate. The term comes from the Greek word *mimos*, meaning imitator. Early Greek mime is thought to have originated in about 581 BC in Megara; it had some basic dialogue but emphasized physical action. Surviving examples of Greek mime are mainly burlesques of myths or satirical playlets about domestic situations.

Small troupes of Greek mime artists probably performed at banquets in the 5th century BC, making them the earliest known professional entertainers. The troupes included women, many of whom were also prostitutes. The performers wore distinctive costumes but no masks; mime performers were never admitted to membership of the Artists of DIONYSUS. In Greek southern Italy a type of mime play known as the PHLYAX became popular.

The earliest mime artist known to us by name was the Roman Livius Andronicus (284–204 BC). According to tradition, he turned to mime when his voice failed after a series of performances. In Imperial times the *mimus*, a type of bawdy knockabout farce, and the performances of the lascivious PANTOMIMUS became popular. The former often involved displays of NUDITY and sometimes included real on-stage executions. The licentiousness and anti-Christian satire of these performances led to the Church excommunicating all mime performers in the 5th century AD.

Many elements of the Roman pantomime survived in the 16th-century COMMEDIA DELL'ARTE, which was in turn the main source of modern mime. In England the **dumb show**, a section of a play performed without words, was popular in the Elizabethan and Jacobean periods but almost disappeared after 1620. HAMLET (1600) includes a dumb show enacted as part of the play-within-a-play, while Webster's THE WHITE DEVIL (1612) features two dumb shows.

Modern mime is usually performed to music and without props (although they may be used). Many of its conventions were devised in the early 19th century by the great French Pierrot Jean-Gaspard Deburau (*see* BAPTISTE). Another Pierrot, Étienne Decroux (1898–1991) was sometimes known as 'the father of modern mime' because he developed a systematic language of gesture for the genre. Other famous French mimes include Jean-Louis BARRAULT, who played the part of Deburau in *Baptiste* (1946) and the film *Les enfants du paradis* (1945), and Marcel MARCEAU.

mimodrame A type of drama without words that became fashionable in France after the Revolution. It was popularized at the Cirque Olympique, Paris.

Minna von Barnhelm A play by Gotthold Ephraim LESSING, first staged in 1767 in Hamburg, that ushered in a new era of German comedy with its lively dialogue and in-depth characterization. Set in the aftermath of the Seven Years' Wear, the play deals with the unfair dismissal of an army officer, who decides that he can no longer marry his fiancée because of his Prussian sense of honour.

minstrel Originally, someone who had some official duty to perform (from Lat. *ministerialis*). In the middle ages the term became restricted to someone whose duty it was to entertain his employer with music, storytelling, juggling, etc.; hence a travelling entertainer.

minstrel show An indigenous US entertainment consisting of lively songs, sentimental ballads, comic routines, and soft-shoe dancing, performed by White artistes in blackface. It dominated the popular stage in America from 1840 to 1880. The songs and antics were based on stereotyped notions of Blacks from the US South. Wearing costumes of striped trousers and waistcoats with tall white hats, the performers would sit in a semicircle with banjos, tambourines, bones, and other instruments. Besides music, there was witty wrangling between the white-faced master-of-ceremonies, Mr Interlocutor, and the two 'end-men', Mr Tambo and Mr Bones. Speciality acts included the stump speech, the wench impersonation, and the plantation sketch.

Minstrel shows descended directly from the popular performances of T. D. Rice (known as Jim Crow), who in 1828 began to sing Negro patter songs, play the banjo, and perform burlesques of Shakespeare and opera, while imitating the idiosyncracies of an elderly Black man he knew in Baltimore. Among the most popular troupes were Bryant's Minstrels, who gave the South its unofficial anthem, DIXIE, and the CHRISTY MINSTRELS, who once gave 2500 performances in one season in New York.

After the Civil War, competition from VARIETY encouraged the minstrel masters to make their shows more professional and spectacular: in 1878 J. H. Havelry combined four troupes into his United Mastodon Minstrels. The first real Blacks to appear in minstrel shows were Haverly's Coloured Minstrels. Although the genre began to decline before the turn of the century, US entertainment remained influenced by the minstrel show and those performers trained in it, such as Al Jolson and Eddie Cantor. Complaints about the insulting caricatures of Blacks presented by the shows gathered pace with the rise of the Civil Rights Movement in the 1950s and 60s, leading to the genre's demise.

Britain had its own minstrel troupes, who played at St James Hall, Piccadilly, from 1859 to 1904, the most popular being the Moore and Burgess Minstrels, The Mohawks, and Sam Hague's Minstrels. In the 1960s the Black-and-White Minstrel Show became a fixture on television and at the Victoria Palace, London. The company's reformation in 1992 caused much controversy, despite their abandonment of blackface.

miracle play In medieval England, a term used interchangeably with MYSTERY PLAY. Elsewhere in Europe it meant a play depicting the life and martyrdom of a saint and the miracles he or she had performed. The most popular subjects were legends associated with the Virgin Mary and St Nicholas. Cathedrals and abbeys would often perform such a play on the feast day of their patron saint. In England plays of this kind were known as **saints' plays**. Most of the English saints' plays were destroyed during the Reformation but many survived in France.

Misalliance George Bernard SHAW's one-act comedy, first produced in 1910 at the Duke of York's Theatre, London. The fast-paced and rather strange story focuses on Hypatia Tarleton, a young woman who seeks excitement to enliven the monotony of her life. Hypatia seems set to wed Bentley Summerhays for his social position until the day an aircraft crashes into the garden. From the wreckage emerge Joseph Percival and the beautiful acrobat Lina Szczepanowska. Hypatia falls in love with Joseph, despite her father's disapproval, and Bentley is smitten by Lina. As always, Shaw mixes social comment with the humour, here most notably in the speeches of a demented gunman who arrives to kill Hypatia's father for seducing his mother. Some recent critics see the play as an anticipation of the work of IONESCO and the Theatre of the ABSURD.

Misanthrope, The MOLIÈRE's comedy about the hypocrisy of polite society, first produced in 1666 in Paris. The bitterness of the play is thought to reflect the unhappiness of Molière's marriage to the actress, Armande Béjart (1641–1700), who was 20 years his junior; the role of the insincere Célimène was created for her.

The misanthrope of the title is Alceste, a man blind to his own faults but so disgusted with the hypocrisy of his contemporaries that he tries to lure them into agreement or flattery to expose their insincerity. Unfortunately, he falls in love with Célimène, one of the most hypocritical women in Paris, who enjoys playing off Alceste and a rival. When Alceste decides to renounce polite society and go into solitary exile in the countryside, Célimène says that she will marry him as long as they can live in Paris. Alceste rejects this and, at the play's end, leaves for the country followed by friends who hope to change his mind.

mise en scène (Fr. setting on stage) The stage setting of a play, including the scenery, properties, etc., and the general physical arrangement of the production. It is also used metaphorically to mean the setting in which an event occurs.

Miser, The MOLIÈRE's comedy about the evils of greed and selfishness. The play, inspired by Plautus's *Aulularia*, was first produced in Paris in 1668, with Molière's young wife, Armande Béjart playing the part of Elise. It has remained popular.

The plot concerns a rich miser, Harpagon, who opposes the marriage of his daughter, Elise, to his steward, Valere. He, himself, intends to marry his pretty neighbour Mariane, unaware that his son, Cleante, is in love with her. To prevent this disaster, Cleante's servant steals Harpagon's gold, holding it as a ransom until he breaks off the match. Harpagon meanwhile discovers that Mariane and Valere are the long-lost children of his friend, Seigneur Anselm. He allows his children to marry their sweethearts and recovers his gold.

Miss Julie A one-act play by August STRINDBERG, first performed in 1889 in Copenhagen and described by the author as "the Swedish drama's first naturalistic tragedy." Strindberg's lengthy preface is one of the most important statements of 19th-century NATURALISM.

The plot, about a fatal sexual liaison within a decaying aristocratic household, gives Strindberg (a noted misogynist) ample scope to deplore female sexuality in particular and human nature in general. The play was written during the collapse of his first marriage. Miss Julie is the daughter of a Swedish count and his working-class feminist wife. The tension between her parents has made the sensual girl wary of love, but this changes when she celebrates Midsummer Night with the family servants and is seduced by an ambitious footman, Jean. When Julie makes it clear that she regrets the incident, Jean reacts with deliberate cruelty, driving her to suicide.

Mistinguett The stage name of the French actress and singer Jeanne-Marie Bourgeois (1873–1956). Mistinguett was a star of the music halls of Paris between the wars, notably the MOULIN ROUGE and the Folies-Bergère, where she danced and sang with Maurice CHEVALIER. She also performed in comedy. Mistinguett was famous for her spectacular hats, her elaborate costumes, and her long shapely legs, which were said to be insured for a huge sum of money.

Mitre Tavern The name of three London inns with literary and theatrical connections.

The Mitre Tavern in Wood Street was used by Ben JONSON as the setting for scenes in *Bartholomew Fair* and *Every Man in His Humour*; subsequent visitors included Samuel Pepys. The building was destroyed in the Great Fire of 1666.

In the late 17th century the Mitre Tavern in St James's Market was run by a Mrs Voss, the aunt of Anne OLDFIELD. The playwright George Farquhar was impressed when he heard Anne rehearsing passages from *The Scornful Lady* by Beaumont and Fletcher while she was working behind the bar; they subsequently became lovers. Anne's mother mentioned Farquhar's admiration for her daughter to another guest, John Vanbrugh, who – anxious not to lose such a promising talent to a rival – found her work at Covent Garden. By the time of her death in 1730 Anne Oldfield was the most famous actress in the country.

The Mitre Tavern in Mitre Court, Fleet Street, was a meeting-place for Dr Johnson, Oliver GOLDSMITH, and other figures from the literary world of the time. It was here that Johnson made his famous remark that a seat in a tavern is "the throne of human felicity." Later landlords capitalized upon the tavern's history, even preserving Johnson's chair; the building was demolished in 1829.

mixed media The combined use of live action, video, photography, music, and animation in an artistic or educational presentation. The earliest mixed-media presentations included the documentary dramas presented in the 1930s by the LIVING NEWSPAPERS; later examples included the popular musical OH, WHAT A LOVELY WAR! (1963). **Multimedia** is an associated term used of specialized computer software that combines on-screen graphics, animation, music, and voice synthesis for educational and other presentations.

Mnouchkine, Ariane (1934–) French theatre director, noted for her commitment to COLLECTIVE CREATION. Mnouchkine studied in Paris and Oxford and travelled extensively around the Orient before returning to France to form the **Théâtre du Soleil** in 1964. The company came to public attention in 1967 with a highly successful production of Arnold Wesker's *The Kitchen*. A first attempt at collective creation, *The Clowns* (1969), was followed in 1970 by *1789*, an epic retelling of the French revolution as seen through the eyes of ordinary people. The play, which was created through group improvisation backed by historical research, involved actors playing multiple roles and the use of no less than five stages. *1789* was followed by *1793* (1972), a similar work dealing with the Terror. In 1972 the company was offered cheap premises in the form of a disused munitions warehouse at a defunct army training ground. At this new base the company presented another collaborative work, *The Golden Age* (1975) before disbanding a year later. Mnouchkine and some other members of the troupe subsequently made a film about Molière, exploring the way in which his theatre company managed to live and work together for so long.

In 1979 the Théâtre du Soleil regrouped and staged *Mephisto*, Mnouchkine's adaptation of the Klaus Mann novel. Subsequent productions have included a number of Shakespearean plays presented using oriental staging conventions, *The King of Cambodia* (1983), a play about Prince Sihanouk by Hélène Cixous, and *Les Atrides*, a cycle of Greek tragedies consisting of Euripides's *Iphigenia in Aulis* and Aeschylus's *Oresteia* trilogy. The Théâtre du Soleil is still run on a firmly egalitarian basis; Mnouchkine herself can sometimes be found collecting tickets on the door.

Molière (Jean-Baptiste Poquelin; 1622–73) French playwright and actor-manager. The son of a wealthy upholsterer in the service of the king, Molière was expected to take his father's place at the court. Instead, at the age of 21, he became involved with an acting family, the Béjarts, turning his back on his father's business and changing his name to Molière. With the Béjarts, Molière attempted to found a new theatre company in Paris; the result was a short lived enterprise called the Illustre-Théâtre, which ran into debt as early as 1645, leading to a brief spell in a debtor's prison for Molière.

Upon his release, Molière and a few other members of the now defunct company (including the Béjarts' eldest daughter Madelaine, with whom Molière was in love) headed for the provinces and joined forces with a touring troupe. He spent the next 13 years in almost constant touring, mainly playing farces inspired by the COMEDIA DELL'ARTE. It was during these years in the provinces that Molière wrote his first plays such as *L'Étourdi ou les Contretemps* (1655) and *De Dépit Amoureaux* (1656).

In 1658 the company returned to Paris and obtained, through the patronage of the king's brother, a command performance before Louis XIV. The company performed two works, a tragedy by Corneille and one of Molière's own farces, LE DOCTEUR AMOUREAUX, which was an instant success and led to the king providing them with the use of the Salle du PETIT-BOURBON on a time-share arrangement with an Italian *commedia* company. The following year Molière enjoyed his first Paris success with LES PRÉCIEUSES RIDICULES. Following the demolition of the Petit-Bourbon in 1661, Molière and his company were installed the following year at the Palais-Royal.

In 1662 Molière married Armande Béjart, the younger sister of Madelaine, who was almost 20 years his junior. At the time of the marriage there was much gossip, most of it spread by theatrical rivals, to the effect that Armande was actually Molière's own daughter by Madelaine. That same year saw the production of Molière's first full-length comedy, THE SCHOOL FOR WIVES, which encountered a storm of criticism from those who considered the work to be immoral. The following year much of the gossip was silenced when the king commissioned Molière to write L'IMPROMPTU DE VERSAILLES (1663), in which the playwright ridiculed his rivals and detractors.

No less controversial were Molière's next two plays, TARTUFFE (1664) and DON JUAN (1665). Following its first production *Tartuffe* was withheld from performance until 1667, whereupon it was denounced for immorality by the Church and banned until 1669. Similarly *Don Juan* was withdrawn from the stage following its first production and not performed again until after Molière's death. However, successful productions followed of THE MISANTHROPE (1666), possibly Molière's greatest play, THE MISER (1668), *Les Fourberies de Scapin* (1671), *Les Femmes savantes* (1672), and LE MALADE IMAGINAIRE (1672). It was during an early performance of *Le malade imaginaire* that Molière, playing the role of the hypochondriac, was seized by a real coughing fit and collapsed; he died hours later.

Molière's main achievement was in raising the standard of French comedy to a level commensurate with French tragedy. In doing so he created a body of work that would continue to be performed for the next three centuries, providing generation after generation of performers with some of their finest roles.

Little Molière (*le petit Molière*) The nickname of the French actor Jean-Baptiste Raisin (1655–93), alluding to his acclaimed comedy performances at the HÔTEL DE BOURGOGNE. With his wife Fanchon (Françoise Pitel de Longchamp; 1661–1721) he was a founding member of the COMÉDIE-FRANÇAISE in 1680. After he died, Fanchon became the mistress of the Dauphin, by whom she had two daughters.

Momus The Greek god of mockery and ridicule, and subsequently of clowns, who was banished from heaven for criticizing the other gods. When Zeus created man, Momus complained that he should have put a window in his chest, so that men could look into each other's hearts. Momus frequently appeared as a character in the MASQUE and HARLEQUINADE. In the 19th century the name was often used as a synonym for clown; Joseph GRIMALDI, for instance, called himself "the once Merry Momus." The name was also used to describe any excessively critical person.

monodrama A type of play featuring a single speaking character that developed in late 18th-century Germany; other silent characters sometimes appeared. Often accompanied by music (when they were sometimes called MELODRAMAS), these short pieces were usually presented as part of the triple bills then fashionable. The form was popularized by the playwright and actor Johann Christian Brandes (1735–99). Also popular was the DUOLOGUE for two actors; both forms were often extracts from longer plays in the manner of the English DROLL.

Montdory Stage name of the French actor Guillaume des Gilberts (1594–1651), who in 1636 was suddenly afflicted with paralysis of the tongue while performing before Cardinal Richelieu in Tristan's *La Mariane.* He was forced to retire from the stage and did not speak again for 14 years.

At the time of this tragedy, Montdory was the most famous actor in France, the first to be known by name throughout the country. Although his declamatory style was most suitable for tragedy, his first success was in CORNEILLE's comedy *Mélite* (1630). Seven years later he enjoyed one of his greatest triumphs when he created the role of Rodrigue in Corneille's tragicomedy LE CID. Montdory founded the Théâtre du Marais where he built up an excellent company whom he trained and directed. After his enforced retirement, the Marais never regained its former reputation.

Montez, Lola (Maria Dolores Eliza Rosanna Gilbert; 1818–61) Irish dancer and beauty, who began her notorious career in 1843. Despite her slender talent, she became internationally famous when Ludwig I of Bavaria was forced to abdicate as a result of an affair with her. Her New York debut in *Betley the Tyrolean* (1851) was followed a year later by an appearance in C. P. T. Ware's *Lola Montes* [sic] *in Bavaria*, a brazen attempt to cash in on her infamous past. She then toured the Gold Rush country and California with her 'spider dance', which was so risqué that it even shocked liberal San Francisco. While out West she took an interest in a young miner's daughter, Charlotte Crabtree (1847–1924), and began training her for a career on the stage. After beginning as a child actress Charlotte became a leading BURLESQUE comedienne as **Lotta Crabtree**, making her New York debut in 1865. In her later years Montez lectured on fashion and spiritualism, to which she had been converted.

Montfleury (Zacharie Jacob; *c.* 1600–67) French actor, who performed in tragedies at the HÔTEL DE BOURGOGNE from the late 1630s onwards. Montfleury, who was frequently ridiculed for his extreme corpulence and his declamatory style of acting, is now mainly remembered for his feud with MOLIÈRE in the 1660s. When the playwright married a much younger woman Montfleury accused Molière, before the king, of marrying his own illegitimate daughter by a former lover. The king showed his faith in Molière's innocence by acting as godfather to the couple's first child. Molière himself struck back by writing L'IMPROMPTU DE VERSAILLES (1663), which cruelly parodies Montfleury and his company.

Montfleury was also unpopular with Cyrano de Bergerac, who, according to legend, once interrupted the actor in mid performance and ordered him off the stage for his abominable overacting. The incident appears in Rostand's CYRANO DE BERGERAC. Montfleury collapsed and died during a performance of Racine's *Andromaque*, after apparently bursting a blood vessel during a particularly emotionally charged scene.

Month in the Country, A Ivan TURGENEV's psychological comedy of love pursued and evaded. It was written between 1848 and 1850 in Paris as *The Student*, but censorship delayed its first performance in Moscow until 1872. With its emphasis on the motivation of its characters, the play anticipates the drama of Chekhov. It is considered Turgenev's finest work for the stage and was one of the plays made popular outside Russia by STANISLAVSKY's influential school of acting.

The plot centres on a tutor, the young and naive Beliaev, who arrives at the estate of Yslaev to educate his son. As soon as Beliaev walks through the door, however, he unwittingly captures the hearts of Yslaev's wife Natalia, his ward Vera, and the attractive maid Katia. Life becomes so complicated within the household that Vera decides to marry an old wealthy neighbour, Katia postpones her engagement to another servant, and Beliaev eventually resigns.

Moon for the Misbegotten, A A play by Eugene O'NEILL – the last of his works to be staged in his lifetime. It was first performed in out-of-town trials in 1947 and did not open on Broadway until ten years later. Jason Robards Jr., who has played more O'Neill leads than any other actor, starred as James Tyrone Jr. He returned to the role at New York's Morosco Theatre in 1973, a year after a car accident had disfigured his face, requiring three operations and $50,000 to rebuild it.

The play, a sequel to LONG DAY'S JOURNEY INTO NIGHT, depicts the continuing self-destruction of Jim Tyrone, the alcoholic son in the earlier play, who is now the owner of a Connecticut farm. The other major characters are Phil Hogan, a farmer whose bullying has driven his three sons off the land, and Josie, his rough-hewn daughter, who loves Jim.

moral. moral interlude In the 16th-century theatre, a short drama intended both to entertain and to edify. It developed from the medieval MORALITY PLAY but featured more humour; the personified vices of the earlier genre often appear in the moral interlude as realistic comic characters. Successful English pieces included the anonymous *Hickscorner* (*c.* 1513) and Wever's *Lusty Juventus* (1550).

morality play In medieval Europe, a type of allegorical drama in which personified vices and virtues are usually shown struggling for the soul of Mankind. Morality dramas began to appear in about 1400, the first important example being the English *The Castle of Perseverance* (*c.* 1405). During the later 15th century the genre overtook the MYSTERY PLAY in popularity. Other well-known examples are the anonymous EVERYMAN (*c.* 1500), John Skelton's *Magnyfyence* (*c.* 1520), and Sir David Lyndsay's *Ane Pleasant Satyre of the Thre Estaitis* (1552). The morality play developed into the MORAL INTERLUDE during the later Tudor period. *See also* MEDIEVAL DRAMA.

moresca A dance-drama found in the Mediterranean region and in Central America. The blend of Christian and Muslim influences found in the dance is reflected in the name, which comes from a Spanish word for a Moor. The English term MORRIS DANCE probably derived from *moresca*, although the two forms have nothing in common. The *moresca*, which is often performed at carnivals or local feasts, contains a prologue, a drama, and a concluding sword-dance. The plot often portrays legends or events from local history.

Morosco Theatre A former New York theatre that presented the premieres of four Pulitzer Prize-winning plays: Eugene O'Neill's BEYOND THE HORIZON (1920), George Kelly's *Craig's Wife* (1925), Arthur Miller's DEATH OF A SALESMAN (1949), and Tennessee Williams's CAT ON A HOT TIN ROOF (1955).

The theatre was built by the SHUBERT BROTHERS and opened in 1917 with *Canary Cottage* by Elmer Harris and Oliver Morosco, after whom it was named. It started a vogue for mystery thrillers in 1920 by producing *The Bat*, by Mary Roberts Rinehart and Avery Hopwood. Other hits have included Edwin Meyer's *The Firebrand* (1924), Gore Vidal's *The Best Man* (1960), and Arthur Kopit's *Oh Dad, Poor Dad, Mamma's Hung You in the Closet and I'm Feeling So Sad.*

Many British plays have made a successful transition from the West End to Broadway via the Morosco, including works by Noel Coward, Peter Shaffer, David Storey, Simon Gray, Terence Rattigan, and Alan Ayckbourn. The Morosco Theatre was demolished in 1982.

morris dance A traditional English folk dance. It is related to similar dances performed by the Basques of southern France, the Calusari of Romania, and other ethnic groups in Europe and India. The name suggests Moorish influence (*see* MORESCA) and this may explain why some dancers perform with blackened faces. The dance may have its origin in pre-Christian rituals, celebrating the resurrection of a pagan god; the English version seems to be more directly associated with the traditions surrounding harvest and MAY DAY, with its ROBIN HOOD folk theatre.

English morris dancing was in danger of dying out until the folklorist Cecil Sharp led a revival at the beginning of the 20th century. The morris men wear white clothes decorated with small bells, flowers, and ribbons; they hold white handkerchiefs or staves, which are struck together in some dances. The best-known groups are those from the Cotswolds, but other regions have their distinctive traditions. Derbyshire morris dancers wear distinctive hats and are accompanied by a King and Queen and a black-faced clown; Lancashire groups once pulled a rush-cart while being driven on by a 'whiffler' carrying a whip. Some groups are accompanied by a joker who bangs the heads of the audience with an inflated pig's bladder on a stick. The dance was previously an all-male preserve but a number of women's groups now exist. *See also* HOBBY HORSE.

Mortimer, John (Clifford) (1923–) British playwright, novelist, and barrister, whose works have often drawn on his legal career. He is best known to the general public for his television series *Rumpole of the Bailey*.

Mortimer's first one-act plays, *The Dock Brief* and *What Shall We Tell Caroline?*, were produced in 1957 as a double bill. His first full-length drama, *The Wrong Side of the Park*, opened four years later at the Cambridge Theatre. The moving autobiographical play *A Voyage Round My Father* was first produced in 1971 at the Haymarket Theatre with Sir Alec Guinness in the lead; a later television production starred Sir Laurence Olivier in the role of Mortimer's blind father.

Mortimer has also adapted several farces by the French playwright Georges FEYDEAU; these include *A Flea in Her Ear* (1965) produced by the National Theatre Company at the Old Vic, *Cat Among the Pigeons* (1969), and *A Little Hotel on the Side* (1984).

Morton, Charles (1819–1904) British pioneer of MUSIC HALL entertainment, who was known as the **Father of the Halls**. Born in Hackney, he became the landlord of the Canterbury Tavern there in 1848 and constructed a venue for entertainment on the tavern's skittle alley. This later became the famous CANTERBURY MUSIC HALL.

In 1861 Morton opened the OXFORD MUSIC HALL in London, the first purpose-built music hall of its kind; he gave up the Canterbury six years later. His skilful management of his halls and the stars who performed in them led to his being asked to run and revitalize the faltering London Pavilion in Westminster and the Tivoli Music Hall in the Strand (*see* TIV).

Moscow. Moscow Art Theatre The world-famous theatre in Moscow, founded as a cooperative in 1898 by Konstantin STANISLAVSKY, who oversaw staging and production, and the playwright and director V. I. Nemirovich-Danchenko (1859–1943), who was in charge of the administration. Its aim was to produce works using the naturalistic style of acting that became Stanislavsky's hallmark.

The opening production was Alexei Tolstoy's *Tsar Fyodor Ivanovich*, a historical drama about the son of Ivan the Terrible, which was staged using authentic sets and costumes. Stanislavsky's productions of CHEKHOV were responsible for making the playwright's name and, less happily, for establishing the rather ponderous style of presenting his plays that held sway until quite recently. A successful revival of the THE SEAGULL in the theatre's first year was followed by productions of UNCLE VANYA (1899), THREE SISTERS (1901), and THE CHERRY ORCHARD (1904); the last two were written specially for the theatre. Gorki's masterpiece of naturalism THE LOWER DEPTHS had its first production there in 1902.

The Moscow Art Theatre company survived the revolution and civil war to tour Europe and America in 1922–23. Works presented in the post-revolutionary era included plays by Vsevolod Ivanov and Mikhail Bulgakov, whose *The Days of Turbins* (1926) proved an irritant to the Bolshevik authorities. Bulgakov later satirized the theatre in his banned novel *Black Snow* (1936). During the Cold War period the theatre was largely used as a showcase for Soviet cultural achievement. In 1973 the company moved into larger premises, retaining its existing base and drama school. Since 1985 the two halves of the company have functioned virtually independently of each other.

Moscow Theatre of Drama and Comedy *See* TAGANKA THEATRE.

most unkindest cut of all Treachery from a friend; the proverbial 'last straw'. The phrase comes from Shakespeare's JULIUS CAESAR (III, ii). When Mark Antony shows the crowd the dagger cuts in Caesar's mantle, he thus refers to the thrust made by Brutus, Caesar's great friend:

> This was the most unkindest cut of all;
> For when the noble Caesar saw him stab,
> Ingratitude, more strong than traitor's
> arms,
> Quite vanquished him.

Mother Courage and Her Children Bertolt BRECHT's sombre play about individual and collective responsibility during wartime. First produced in 1941 in Zürich, it was revived after the war by Brecht's own BERLINER ENSEMBLE, with his wife, Helene Weigel, playing Mother Courage. In Britain, the role provided a triumph for Judi Dench at the Barbican Theatre in 1984.

The play, set in Germany during the Thirty Years' War, was written just before World War II as a warning against the evils of war profiteering. In performance, however, the leading character tends to win the audience's admiration as an indomitable survivor, rather than arousing their disgust as a profiteer. Brecht is more successful in establishing the connection between small civilian contributions to the war effort and great military atrocities.

The plot follows the career of Anna Fierling, a Swedish army canteen worker. Although Anna intends to profit from the war, she is determined to keep her three children (who haul her wagon) out of it. To her grief, they are all arrested on various charges and one is executed; nevertheless she tenaciously carries on, hauling the wagon herself in search of business amongst the warring troops.

motion A type of puppet play that was presented in Britain by travelling showmen in the 16th and 17th centuries. The earlier motions were based on Bible stories; Shakespeare's *The Winter's Tale* mentions "a motion of the Prodigal Son." Later subject matter included tales from mythology, history, and medieval romance.

Moulin Rouge A famous cabaret and dance hall that was opened in 1889 in Montmartre, Paris, by Joseph Oller and the former butcher Charles Zidler. A giant windmill adorned the entrance, while the garden used for outdoor dancing and summer concerts had a hollow stucco elephant for decoration. In 1903 a music-hall stage was built and the size of the dance-floor reduced. Although the cancan dance did not originate there, the Moulin Rouge was the first venue of any size and respectability to present it. Celebrity dancers such as la Goulue and la Mome Fromage led a high-kicking chorus famous for their ability to perform the *grand ecart* (splits) and *porte d'armes* (holding the uplifted ankle head-high). Yvette Guilbert sang her sultry songs and Toulouse-Lautrec captured the gaiety of the scene in his famous paintings and posters. Mistinguett, France's leading star of music hall, was a regular performer before World War I (later becoming part-proprietor for several years).

After a fire in 1915 the Moulin Rouge was rebuilt to offer both cancan and ballet as dinner shows. Jacques-Charels revitalized its fortunes in the late 1920s with a series of risqué revues. The building subsequently became a cinema, but the Moulin Rouge reopened as a cabaret venue in 1953. It now continues to provide a popular tourist attraction, with the original cancan as one of several cabaret items, including a topless chorus line.

Mourning Becomes Electra A trilogy of plays by Eugene O'NEILL, dealing with the tragic cycle of love and revenge within a single family. Often considered his masterpiece, the work was first performed by the Theatre Guild in 1931 in New York starring Alice Brady and the Russian actress Alla Nazimova; the first London production was in 1937. The film version (1947) starred Rosalind Russell and Dame Judith Anderson, while an operatic adaptation of the play was produced in 1967 at the Metropolitan Opera in New York.

The sequence of three plays (*Homecoming, The Hunted*, and *The Haunted*) is based on AESCHYLUS's great trilogy THE ORESTEIA, with the action updated to New England at the end of the Civil War. Although O'Neill himself felt that the work lacked great language, it proved his most successful play. "It is uneven," wrote one reviewer, "but so are the Himalayas." The critic Alexander Woollcott, however, described the work as "a grumbling and belated review of the remorseless and venerated trilogy (i.e. *The Oresteia*) by the same sacred cow who wrote *Strange Interlude*". He later called it "that glum three-decker."

Homecoming begins with Lavinia, O'Neill's Electra figure, discovering that her mother, Christine Mannon, is having an affair. Christine sends her lover away but decides to murder her husband when he comes back from the war. He returns with a weak heart and she confesses her affair, hoping that the shock will induce a heart attack. When it does and he dies, Lavinia decides to murder her mother.

In *The Hunted* Lavinia's brother, Orin Mannon, returns from the war to find his father dead. When Christine reestablishes contact with her lover, Orin lies in wait and murders him. As a result, Christine commits suicide and Orin suffers a breakdown. Lavinia promises to take care of him.

In *The Haunted* Lavinia attempts to arrange a marriage between Orin and his boyhood sweetheart, Hazel Niles, while she herself plans to wed Hazel's brother, Peter. Orin, however, is still consumed with guilt over his mother's death and kills himself. Lavinia admits to Peter that she too has had an affair, and he abandons her.

Mousetrap, The A murder mystery by Agatha CHRISTIE that has become the longest continuously running play in theatrical history. It opened at London's Ambassadors Theatre in 1952 and ran there for 8862 performances before transferring in 1974 to St Martin's Theatre, where it is still showing. It has been seen by more than 9.5 million people.

Christie wrote the piece in one week in 1947 as a 20-minute radio play called *Three Blind Mice*, which was broadcast to mark the 80th birthday of Queen Mary. The BBC had offered to broadcast anything the queen wanted to hear, and she had requested a new Christie play. As there was already a play called *Three Blind Mice*, Christie's son-in-law, Anthony Hicks, suggested *The Mousetrap* as a title, this being an allusion to Hamlet's play-within-a-play (III, ii). Initially *The Mousetrap* received poor reviews, but the producer, Peter Cotes, and the gloomy cast, headed by Richard

Attenborough and his wife Sheila Sim, received encouragement from Christie who said: "Don't worry children, I'm sure we will get a nice little run out of it." She gave the play's copyright to her grandson Matthew as a tenth birthday present.

The show's longevity has owed much to its popularity with US and other tourists to London. Cunningly, the producers banned Broadway productions or any US road shows until the end of the London run. The ban also applies to Australia, but the play has been staged in 44 other countries in 24 languages. The British film producers Eddie Small and Victor Saville paid £5,000 each for the film rights to *The Mousetrap* with a proviso that no film could be made until the play finished its London run. Both Small and Saville are now dead.

In 1981 *The Mousetrap* became the first West End play to be performed for an audience made up entirely of deaf people, being translated into sign language by interpreters at the side of the stage. On 25 November 1992 *The Mousetrap* held its 40th anniversary performance; the audience included prime minister John Major, who reminisced nostalgically about the 1950s when the play opened

> I was in short trousers...no-one had ever heard of Maastricht. They were, I remember, happy days.

moutons. ***Revenons à nos moutons*** (Fr. Let us come back to our sheep) A phrase used to mean "Let us return to the subject". It is taken from the 14th century French comedy *La Farce de Maître Pathelin*, or *l'Avocat Pathelin*, in which a woollen-draper accuses a shepherd of ill-treating his sheep. In telling his story he continually wanders off the subject and, to throw discredit on the defendant's attorney (Pathelin), accuses him of stealing a piece of cloth. The judge has to pull him up every moment, with "*Mais, mon ami, revenons à nos moutons.*" The phrase is frequently quoted by Rabelais.

Mr. **Mr and Mrs Wood in front** A theatrical catchphrase, first heard in the early 20th century, meaning that the auditorium is virtually empty, the performers being greeted with the sight of rows of empty wooden seats.

Mr Lillian Russell Stage nickname of Julian ELTINGE, the famous female impersonator.

Mr Show Biz An accolade applied to various leading actors, singers, composers, impresarios, etc., often as an introduction: "Here's Mister Show Biz, himself..."

Mrs. **Mrs Pat** Affectionate name for the British actress Mrs Patrick CAMPBELL. Born Beatrice Stella Tanner, she eloped with Patrick Campbell, an army officer, at the age of 19. Campbell was killed in the Boer War (as was their son) but she continued to use his name professionally for the rest of her career.

Mrs Warren's Profession A play by George Bernard SHAW, written in 1893 and first performed in 1902 in a private theatre club production in New Haven. Its candid approach to the subject of prostitution had resulted in a ban by the LORD CHAMBERLAIN and the play did not receive a public performance in Britain until 1925.

The story centres on Vivie Warren, a young woman whose expensive education was paid for by a mother she hardly knows. When Mrs Warren finally visits her daughter she reveals that she made her wealth by running a brothel. Vivie is strangely impressed, but when she tells her boyfriend, Frank, he abandons her in disgust. Vivie finally rejects the opportunity of a reconciliation with her mother, being determined to make her own life.

Much Ado About Nothing A comedy by SHAKESPEARE, first performed in 1598 in London. It was revived in 1613 before James I with the title *Benedick and Beatrice*. The action of the play arises from the visit of Don Pedro, Prince of Aragon, to Leonato, Governor of Messina. He is travelling with his malevolent half-brother, Don John, and the noblemen BENEDICK and Claudio. The latter falls in love with Leonato's daughter, Hero. Don John and his follower Borachio convince Claudio that she has been unfaithful, and he publicly rejects her at their wedding ceremony. Friar Francis persuades Hero to hide until he proves her innocence, and then reports that she is dead. Finally Don John's plot is uncovered, he is arrested, and the lovers are reunited.

For most audiences, however, the main action is totally overshadowed by the subplot, which concerns the "merry war" of wits between Benedick and BEATRICE, Leonato's niece. The two, who have a history of pretended antipathy, are finally tricked into declaring their love for each other. The play also includes the comic constable DOGBERRY, whose pompous character is said to have been based on a constable at Grendon,

Buckinghamshire, which was on Shakespeare's route from Stratford to London. The part was created by the clown William Kempe.

In 1879 the first SHAKESPEARE MEMORIAL THEATRE in Stratford-upon-Avon opened in 1879 with a production of the play in which the cast was led by Barry Sullivan and Helen Faucit (in her last role). The theatre's GREEN ROOM had been beautifully decorated as a dressing room for Faucit and when Sullivan saw this he refused to appear unless he received equal treatment. Charles Flower, who had built the theatre, told his wife, "You, my dear, must send across silver candlesticks, vases of flowers, and a lace pincushion for Mr Sullivan." Sullivan was mollified and the production was a success.

Henry Irving and Ellen Terry gave famous performances as Beatrice and Benedick in the 1882 production at the Lyceum Theatre. In 1906 all 22 members of the TERRY FAMILY appeared in the play's masked dance for Ellen's Jubilee Matinee at Drury Lane. Sir John GIELGUD directed and starred in a high Renaissance version at Stratford in 1949, while Franco Zeffirelli's stunning production for the National Theatre in 1965 starred Maggie SMITH and her then husband Robert Stephens. John Barton staged a British Raj version at Stratford in 1976, with Judi Dench and Donald Sinden. Kenneth Branagh's successful film version, in which he starred with his wife Emma Thompson, was released in 1993.

mug A slang word for face. In the theatre, **to mug** is to pull exaggerated grimaces while acting. The phrase **to mug up**, meaning to study hard for an exam, etc., may also derive from the theatre, where an actor, while making up his face or 'mug' would hurriedly read over his lines.

multiple setting In medieval drama, a convention whereby several different locations were represented on the stage at the same time. This practice originated with the LITURGICAL DRAMA, in which several 'mansions' or performing areas were arranged about the church. The convention survived until the early 17th century on the Continent and in English court masques, although the Elizabethan stage had dispensed with it. In France, the single set became standard with the advent of classical tragedy. The convention has sometimes been revived in the 20th century, for instance in the staging of John ARDEN's play *Armstrong's Last Goodnight* (1964).

mummer A contemptuous name for an actor; from the parties that formerly went from house to house at Christmas *mumming*, i.e. performing shows such as St George and the Dragon etc.

> We call strolling acting 'mumming', and the actors 'mummers'. All spouting is mumming.
>
> HENRY MAYHEW: *London Labour* (1861).

Mummers' Play or **Mumming Play** A type of European folk play that was widespread in the 16th and 17th centuries but probably has its roots in pre-Christian traditions. The name may come from German *Mumme*, meaning mask or from Greek *mommo*, meaning a frightening monster.

Mummers were part of the European tradition of street performers. Often masked, they dressed in exotic and colourful clothes or disguised themselves as animals to parade singing and dancing through towns and villages. They would perform their plays in the open air or in private houses.

Different types of mummers' plays occur throughout Europe, but most have as an underlying theme the death of the old year and the rebirth of the new. They were usually performed at Christmas and other winter festivals. In England many plays featured St (or Sir, Prince, or King) George, the green knight, a figure who is probably a Christianized version of an ancient spirit of vegetation and fertility. In the plays St George, a Crusader, is killed by a Turkish knight and subsequently resurrected. The story occurs in Richard Johnson's *Famous History of the Seven Champions of Christendom* (1596).

Other English plays include the Hero-Combat play, in which the performers black their faces and dress in rags or torn paper (as in the Paper Boys' Play of Marshfield in Avon), and the Wooing Ceremony from the Midlands, in which men dress as women. The Sword Play of northeast England may have evolved from a traditional sword dance, in which the theme of death and rebirth was symbolized by a sword held above a dancer's head. Scottish mummers were called **guisards** or **guisers** and usually featured the hero **Galatian** or **Golashans**. In Germany the **Perchten runners** paraded on Twelfth Night.

Mummers' plays are still performed at Christmas in some villages in Britain and Northern Ireland.

municipal theatre *See* CIVIC THEATRE.

Murder in the Cathedral T. S. ELIOT's verse play about the events leading to the martyrdom (29 December 1170) of St Thomas à Becket. It was first staged in Canterbury Cathedral, the scene of the murder, in 1935 with Robert Donat as Becket. Usually considered Eliot's most effective work for the stage, the play combines elements of Greek tragedy and the medieval MORALITY PLAY. It has often been revived; Richard Pasco assumed the title role in a successful 1972 production.

The play begins with the CHORUS of the poor women of Canterbury giving voice to their sense of expectation and dread. Becket returns from seven years of exile to resume his confrontation with King Henry II, who is seeking to control the Church. After refusing to compromise and giving himself up to God's will, Becket is accused by the king's knights of treason. The Chorus despairs as Becket refuses to go back into exile and is consequently murdered by the knights. After the killing the assassins take it in turns to justify their actions in a series of direct addresses to the audience. The play ends with the Chorus and priests praising God for Becket's martyrdom and for the benefits it will bring to the Church.

Muses In Greek mythology, the nine goddesses of the arts. The three associated with drama were **Melpomene**, the muse of tragedy, usually depicted as holding a tragic mask and wearing a COTHURNUS; **Thalia**, the muse of comedy, holding a comic mask; and **Terpsichore**, the muse of dancing and the choral songs that accompanied it, holding a lyre. Ancient authors would invoke the Muses, asking for inspiration and artistic success; later this invocation became a literary and dramatic convention.

musical or **musical comedy** A stage entertainment or film that tells a story using a mixture of dialogue, songs, and dance routines. Probably the single most impressive contribution made by BROADWAY to the modern theatre, the musical developed from many sources, including vaudeville, revue, melodrama, and operetta.

The first work to combine these influences to create a recognizably new genre was William Wheatley's spectacular ballet-melodrama THE BLACK CROOK, first produced in New York in 1866. George EDWARDES's *In Town*, produced at his old Gaiety Theatre, London, in 1892, is usually considered the first British musical. Edwardes developed a highly successful formula that involved the use of a sketchy plot as a framework for memorable songs and expensive production numbers featuring attractive chorus girls (*see* GAIETY GIRL).

In the early 20th century US musicals remained heavily indebted to the tradition of European operetta. After World War I, however, a more energetic and sophisticated, but still essentially lightweight, type of show was pioneered by such writers as Irving BERLIN, Cole PORTER, the GERSHWIN brothers, and Rodgers and Hart. In 1928 Jerome Kern's SHOW BOAT gave a new prominence to plot and demonstrated that the musical could encompass more serious themes.

These developments were taken further in RODGERS AND HAMMERSTEIN's landmark production OKLAHOMA! (1943). The same combination of an exciting plot, memorable songs, vigorous professional dancing, and extravagant costumes and sets characterized their subsequent hits CAROUSEL (1945), and SOUTH PACIFIC (1949). The tradition they had established was continued by Lerner and Loewe in international successes such as MY FAIR LADY (1956) and CAMELOT (1960). Other hits of the 1950s and 1960s included WEST SIDE STORY (1957), HELLO DOLLY! (1963), FIDDLER ON THE ROOF (1964) and CABARET (1966).

In the late 1960s and 1970s the tradition of the classic Broadway musical appeared to decline. The only important US writer to continue in the genre was Stephen SONDHEIM, whose sophisticated and idiosyncratic works won critical praise but lacked popular appeal. The main development of this period was the advent of the rock musical, as represented by HAIR (1967) and Andrew LLOYD WEBBER and Tim Rice's *Joseph and the Amazing Technicolour Dreamcoat* (1968), and JESUS CHRIST SUPERSTAR. In the 1970s and late 1980s Lloyd Webber led a revival of the large-scale spectacular musical with a series of shows that proved immensely successful on both sides of the Atlantic: these included EVITA (1978), CATS (1981), PHANTOM OF THE OPERA (1986), and *Sunset Boulevard* (1992).

music hall A highly popular form of variety entertainment that flourished in Britain in the late 19th and early 20th centuries. It had its origins in the 'Free and Easy' of public houses in the SONG-AND-SUPPER ROOMS of early Victorian London. Food, drink, and song were the music hall's first ingredients. Singers, comedians, dancers, and other performers took 'turns' entertaining the patrons, who came from the working classes. The first music hall proper, the CANTERBURY MUSIC HALL, was opened in 1852 by the so-called 'Father of the Halls' Charles MORTON, a native of Hackney. He went on to open the OXFORD MUSIC HALL in 1861 and ran several others.

The music halls flourished at the turn of the century, when leading performers included Harry LAUDER, Marie LLOYD, Dan LENO, LITTLE TICH, and George Robey. After World War I new media such as films, radio, and, later, television, helped to bring about their demise.

Music halls once outnumbered regular theatres in London and the provinces but have now disappeared or become civic theatres, cinemas, or bingo halls, keeping on the the traditional names such as Palladium, Palace, Alhambra, Coliseum, Empire, and Hippodrome. They have, however, left a legacy of popular song and memories of great entertainers whose fame depended upon the individuality of their acts.

Musset, Alfred de (1810–57) French playwright, poet, and novelist, who was a leading figure of the Romantic movement in France. His bittersweet comedies and dramas are noted for their poetic language.

As a young man Musset painted for a while before turning to writing. He became a fashionable man-about-town, leading a dissipated social life that eventually led to his early death. Several of his works were rediscovered in Russia 20 years later by a French actress, who returned them to Paris.

His first play, the one-act *La Nuit vénitienne*, was a failure when presented at the Théâtre National de l'Odéon in 1830, and he resolved thereafter to write only CLOSET DRAMAS. In 1833 Musset and the writer George Sand began an intense but short-lived affair. During their trip to Italy in 1834 Musset became ill and Sand fell in love with the doctor she summoned. By this time he had already created (with Sand's help) his best work, the historical drama LORENZACCIO. It later provided Sarah Bernhardt with one of her most celebrated *travesti* roles.

In the 1840s Musset enjoyed great success with a series of *Comédies et proverbes*, light comedies and short plays illustrating proverbs. Although they were not intended for the stage, in 1847 one of them, *Un Caprice*, was given at the Comédie-Française to such acclaim that the following year saw the staging of three more works, *Le Chandelier*, *Il faut qu'une porte soit ouverte ou fermée*, and *Il ne faut jurer de rien*.

In 1851 he successfully blended classical and romantic styles in his play *Caprices de Marianne*. There was also a posthumous production of the tragicomedy *On ne badine pas avec l'amour*. In 1893 this became the first play to be produced by Britain's E. Gordon Craig (*see* CRAIG FAMILY), who directed, designed and painted scenery, and created 14th-century costumes.

My Fair Lady A musical by Alan Jay Lerner and Frederick Loewe, one of the most successful ever staged on Broadway. Based on Shaw's PYGMALION, it opened at the Mark Hellinger Theatre in 1956 with Rex HARRISON as Henry Higgins, the linguistics professor, and Julie Andrews as Eliza Doolittle, the cockney flower-seller. Like the 1938 film, the musical substituted a conventional romantic ending – Higgins and Eliza fall in love – for Shaw's more prosaic conclusion. In 1964 *My Fair Lady* became a film itself, starring Harrison and Audrey Hepburn.

Mary Martin thought the show would fail when she first heard the songs, commenting "Those dear boys have lost their talent." However, *My Fair Lady* won the 1957 Tony Award as Best Musical and eventually ran for 2717 performances. Opening in London in 1958, it established Drury Lane's longest run with 2281 performances. When Rex Harrison revived the show in 1981 at the Pentagess Theatre, Los Angeles, the first week's box-office receipts of $409,884 set a record.

mystery play The most important form of medieval European drama. Unlike the early LITURGICAL DRAMA, from which it developed, the mystery play was written in the vernacular, spoken rather than sung, and performed out of doors. Although the subject matter remained exclusively biblical, the plays also featured an element of coarse humour that probably derived from the folk theatre. The individual plays were organized into lengthy cycles covering the whole of history from the Creation to the Day of Judgment. These would be presented over a period of one or more days. The most important mystery cycles in England included those performed at Chester, Lincoln, Wakefield, and York.

The name 'mystery play' has no reference to the religious subject matter but comes from the Middle English word *misteri* (Lat. *ministerium*), meaning a trade or skill. In the later 14th century the plays were performed by members of trade or craft guilds, each of which undertook an episode relevant to their calling, so that the carpenters, for instance, presented the story of Noah's Ark while the fishmongers played Jonah and the Whale. The plays were usually performed on converted wagons known as PAGEANTS. In England the mystery play was sometimes called a MIRACLE PLAY, although strictly this was a distinct genre dealing with the lives of the saints. Another name is **Corpus Christi play**, because the dramas were generally performed during the feast of Corpus Christi, which falls in May or June. The Continental equivalents to the English mystery play included the German *Mysterienspiel*, the French *mystère*, the Spanish AUTO SACRAMENTAL, and the Italian SACRA RAPPRESENTAZIONE. *See also* MEDIEVAL DRAMA.

N

Nadagama A type of rural folk theatre in Sri Lanka. Originally a form of religious drama, it was introduced in the early 19th century by Catholic missionaries from southern India; secular stories about local heroes were soon, however, added. The so-called **Father of Nadagama** was the blacksmith Phillipu Sinno, who wrote more than a dozen plays. Nadagama is acted in the open air with the audience seated on the ground or (for a higher fee) in chairs. The stage, a raised and roofed platform without a curtain, is separated from the dressing room by painted scenery.

The drama begins when the presenter (*Pote Gura*), invokes the deities and prays for a successful performance. He then outlines the plot and introduces each of the stock characters, including a jester, a wise man, and two soothsayers. The introductory chants, which last for about three hours, are followed by the appearance of the king, who summons various members of his court who enter with ceremonial song and dance. The scene is now set for the main dramatic action, which is narrated by the *Pote Gura*. Nadagama plays are generally long and episodic, and may run for up to seven evenings.

Naluyuks (Eskimo: heathens) Eskimo MUMMERS of northern Labrador, who disguise themselves with masks and bearskins to visit children at their homes on Twelfth Night. The Naluyuks question the children about their conduct before presenting them with gifts. The children respond by singing Christmas carols. Outside, the Naluyuks make a loud display of taunting spectators and chasing them from the scene.

Nancy, Miss A popular name for the beautiful but narcissistic actress Mrs Anne OLDFIELD (1683–1730). After her death the name came to be used of any person, especially a man, who was unusually fastidious about his or her dress.

In his *Moral Essays* (1731–35) Alexander Pope referred to Mrs Oldfield under the name of **Narcissa**. There was at the time of the actress's death a law, enacted for the benefit of the wool trade, that required all shrouds to be made of wool. On her deathbed, however, Mrs Oldfield insisted that she be buried in "a very fine Brussels lace headdress, a Holland shift with a tucker and double ruffles of the same lace, a pair of new kid gloves, etc." Her instructions were lampooned by Pope:

> Odious! In woollen! T'would a saint provoke
> (Were the last words that poor Narcissa spoke).

nap Theatrical slang for a blow to the face in SLAPSTICK comedy. After taking part in a Christmas pantomime that involved a slapstick altercation with the clown, the humorist Jerome K. Jerome (1859–1927) wrote:

> He rushes at me and hits me, and I take the nap from him, and then he takes a nap from me (it wakes you up, this sort of nap, I tell you)...

The term nap was usually reserved for a pulled punch while a **straight nap** was one that connected.

Naqal A form of rural entertainment once popular in the Kashmir, Punjab, and Uttar Pradesh regions of northern India, though now seldom seen. It consisted mostly of hectic farce, with clowns providing wit and tumbles as well as harassing and satirizing the audience. The all-male troupes travelled through towns and villages to perform at weddings and other celebrations. The 'theatre' was usually a street, yard, private home, or other setting that allowed them to mingle with their audience. The group's leader was called the *khalifa*, a term that probably reflects the Naqal's origin during the Muslim Mogul dynasty.

Narcissa *See* NANCY, MISS.

Narr The medieval German equivalent of the English FOOL. The Narr, who wore the cap and bells of the court jester, became a traditional part of early German farce; he later took on some characteristics of the *zanni* of the COMMEDIA DELL'ARTE. In the 16th century he developed into the central comic character of the carnival play, the FASTNACHTSSPIEL. A number of his clownish traits were adopted by English fools and by this route may have influenced some of Shakespeare's comic figures. Aspects of the Narr's character were adopted by the English actor Thomas Sackville (1590–1613) to create the clown Jan Bouschet.

Nash, John *See* LAUGHING BLACKSMITH, THE.

Nathan the Wise A verse play by G. E. LESSING, first performed in Berlin in 1783. It won high praise in Goethe's production in 1801 at the Court Theatre in Weimar. The work, a plea for religious freedom and the brotherhood of man, was written as a tribute to Lessing's friend the Jewish philosopher Moses Mendelssohn.

In the play Nathan, a Jewish merchant, visits Muslim-held Jerusalem to seek his adopted daughter, Recha, who has been saved from a fire by a German crusader, Conrade. Nathan is accused by a Christian of kidnapping Recha in her infancy, but he is able to disprove the allegation. Finally he establishes harmony between the contending faiths by revealing that Recha and Conrade are brother and sister, and that their father is the Sultan's brother.

national. ***National Health, The*** A black comedy by Peter NICHOLS. It was first performed at the National Theatre, London, in 1969, although Nichols had originally written it for television. The play, which contrasts hospital soap operas with the reality of a ward for terminally ill men, was voted best play of the year by the London theatre critics.

The plot involves the love affair between two members of the staff of a London hospital, Dr Neil Boyd and Nurse Norton, a West Indian. Their story is told with cynicism by Barnet, an orderly who prepares the bodies of dead patients for the undertaker, and then in absurdly romanticized form in the television soap 'Nurse Norton's Affair'.

National Theatre *See* ROYAL NATIONAL THEATRE.

National Youth Theatre of Great Britain (NYT) A theatre organization founded in 1956 by the actor, director, and schoolmaster Michael Croft (1924–86). The NYT was originally created to give school-age actors a chance to appear in professionally directed summer productions of Shakespeare; these early efforts were praised both at the Edinburgh Festival and in the West End. In 1965 the NYT began to stage contemporary plays, beginning with David Halliwell's *Little Malcolm* at the Royal Court Theatre and Peter Terson's *Zigger-Zagger* (1967), which addressed the problem of soccer hooliganism.

In 1971 the NYT moved from its original base in Dulwich to the Shaw Theatre, London; in the same year it launched a professional organization, the Dolphin Company, which presented several works by Terson as well as plays by Arnold Wesker and Barrie Keeffe. The company was temporarily disbanded after the NYT lost its Arts Council grant in 1981. Commercial sponsorship has since been found and the company, which remains amateur, makes regular provincial and foreign tours; in 1989 it performed T. S. Eliot's *Murder in the Cathedral* at the Moscow Art Theatre. Actors who began their careers with the NYT included Derek Jacobi and Helen Mirren.

Nativity play *See* LITURGICAL DRAMA.

naturalism In the later 19th century, a movement in the theatre (as in the other arts) that aimed to present ordinary life as accurately as possible, without romantic illusions or literary artifice. Theatrical naturalism was essentially a development of the REALISM of IBSEN. The other dominant influence was the novelist and playwright Emile Zola, who published *Le Naturalisme au théâtre* in 1878. In France the movement was centred upon the Théâtre Libre in Paris, where the director André Antoine (1858–1943) produced the bitter comedies of Henri Becque and others (*see* COMÉDIE ROSSE). In Germany the Freie Bühne theatre club produced Arno Holz's gloomy *Die Familie Saliche* (1890) and HAUPTMANN's *Die Weber* (1892).

The harsh and dreary subject matter of most naturalistic plays, which tended to emphasize the boredom, depression, and frustration of contemporary life, frequently alienated 19th-century audiences. The treatment of topics such as divorce and prostitution also caused outrage. Naturalistic playwrights aimed as far as possible to eradicate any sense of the theatrical from their work, employing such techniques as making real time and fictional time the same. There was also an emphasis on accurate documentation, especially of social detail. The behaviour of the characters was often explained in terms of heredity or environmental factors, as in Strindberg's early masterpiece of naturalism MISS JULIE.

By the end of the century many young writers had begun to experiment with SYMBOLISM and naturalism soon came to be regarded as old-fashioned.

naumachia (Lat. naval battle) In ancient Rome, a mock sea battle staged in a flooded amphitheatre as an extravagant entertainment; also the venue in which such battles were enacted. The earliest recorded *naumachia* was that held in 46 BC, when Julius Caesar presented a battle between 'actors' representing Tyrian and Egyptian fleets on a specially constructed lake in the Campus Martius. The bloody event involved around 4000 rowers and 2000 combatants. In one battle held under Claudius in 52 AD, 19,000 gladiators and condemned criminals fought to the death in the roles of Rhodians and Sicilians. In the later *naumachia*, crocodiles were often added as a special terror to participants.

Even when the battles were presented as friendly entertainment, with the combatants being told to do as little damage as possible to each other or the expensive decorative ships, the scene usually ended in slaughter. After one battle, a report noted that the bodies of dead 'actors' were dragged away to the animals' dens.

Caesar's *naumachia* was reputedly some 2000 feet long and 200 feet wide, being capable of containing 50 triremes. The Colosseum at Rome and the amphitheatre at Pozzuoli could both be flooded for sea fights. The Emperor Augustus gave the name *Naumachia* to an amphitheatre on the bank of the Tiber.

Nautanki A form of theatre practised in the Indian states of Uttar Pradesh, Punjab, Rajasthan, Hariyana, and Bihar. The genre is a modern development of the 16th-century SVANGA. The moralistic plays, which are performed to mark special occasions such as a wedding or a birth, are generally melodramas or romances with stories taken from history, folklore, and mythology. Most troupes have from 10 to 12 actors, usually lower-caste Hindus; female performers were introduced in the 1930s. Players collect donations from the spectators during the performance. The musicians, who are normally Muslims, play the harmonium, drums, bell-metal cymbals, and, more recently, the clarinet. Plays are usually presented on a raised stage in an open field, courtyard, or tent. Additional acting space may be found on the balcony of a house or an area of raised ground (marked off by a special post).

Modern *Nautanki* style was pioneered in the cities of Hathras and Kanpur. The Hathras version was popularized in the 19th century by Indarman and his disciple Natharam, who established a centre where actors trained under strict master-teachers and published and distributed scripts. The Hathras actor-singers, who use a distinctive high-pitched style, perform on a nearly bare platform stage, the audience being seated in a three-sided arena space.

Kanpur style was created in the 20th century by Sri Krishna Pahalvan, who defied the rule that only disciples of recognized master-teachers could enter the profession. Kanpur productions emphasize plot rather than singing, feature detailed sets, and use a proscenium-style stage with wings.

nautical drama A typically British form of melodrama that was introduced in the 1750s and remained popular for over a century. Its hero was the 'Jolly Jack Tar,' a stock figure based largely on the naval characters created by the novelist Tobias Smollett (1721–71). In 1757 David Garrick produced Smollett's successful and much imitated nautical farce *The Reprisal* at Drury Lane. The actor Charles Dibdin the Elder (*see* DIBDIN FAMILY) became particularly popular in the Jack Tar roles. In the 19th century Douglas Jerrold's BLACK-EY'D SUSAN (1829) presented a sentimental picture of the relationship between a sailor and his faithful wife. Nautical drama continued to attract London audiences into the 1880s, especially at the Surrey Theatre. By this time, however, it had become fair game for parody, the most notable burlesque of the genre being Gilbert and Sullivan's HMS PINAFORE (1878).

Nazimova, Alla (1879–1945) Russian actress, who became known as a leading interpreter of the works of Ibsen and Chekhov after settling in America. Nazimova began her career with the MOSCOW ART THEATRE before becoming leading lady of the St

Petersburg theatre, which toured Europe and America in 1904. Following six months of intensive study she appeared in the title role of an English-language production of Ibsen's *Hedda Gabler* at New York's Princess Theatre in 1906.

Nazimova remained in America thereafter. In 1910 the Shubert Theatre Corporation (*see* SHUBERT BROTHERS) built and named the Nazimova Theatre after her; she opened the theatre with a six-week run as Rita in the US premiere of Ibsen's *Little Eyolf*. After a year the venue was renamed the 39th Street Theatre. In 1918 Nazimova won special acclaim in Ibsen's *The Wild Duck*, though her popularity was by this time beginning to decline.

Nazimova made a number of silent films in Hollywood, including *Camille* (1921) with Rudolph Valentino and *A Doll's House* (1922). Her later work for the New York stage included the 1931 Theatre Guild production in which she created the role of the lethal Christine Mannon in Eugene O'Neill's *Mourning Becomes Electra*. A year before her death she appeared in the highly successful film *The Bridge of San Luis Rey*.

neoclassical drama A concept of drama that originated in the writings of 15th-century Italian scholars and came to dominate the stage in 17th- and 18th-century France. Neoclassical theorists advocated a return to the values and conventions of classical Greek drama as these were then understood. In particular, they ascribed a great importance to the *Poetics* of Aristotle, and to the UNITIES of time, place, and action that they deduced from this work.

In France, where the unities became rigidly formalized, the neoclassical style achieved its fullest expression in the works of CORNEILLE and RACINE (although Corneille's tragicomedy, LE CID (1637) provoked a storm by deviating from the unities).

By contrast, neoclassicism never took root in the English theatre, despite the support of distinguished advocates such as Jonson and DRYDEN, whose rhymed heroic tragedies enjoyed some success. Joseph Addison's blank-verse tragedy *Cato* (1713) was probably the most popular neoclassical work on the English stage.

In France neoclassical tragedy eventually gave way to the bourgeois DRAME, although it enjoyed a brief revival in some of the works of VOLTAIRE. The movement as a whole was swept away by the advent of Romanticism. *See also* AUGUSTAN DRAMA.

Nero (37–68 AD) Roman emperor (54–68 AD), whose downfall was hastened by his love of the theatre. Although drama and entertainers had a low status during his reign, Nero was fascinated with both. Proud of his own abilities as a performer, he often became involved in productions, playing the lyre, singing, acting as a PANTOMIMUS, and appearing in dramatic roles such as Oedipus, Hercules, and Orestes. Like other actors of the time, Nero wore a mask; in his case, however, this was generally modelled either upon his own features or those of a current mistress.

In 66 AD Nero undertook a tour of Greece, during which he gave increased rein to his artistic pretensions. The tour, and especially his portrayal of low characters and morally ambiguous Greek heroes, cost Nero a great deal of credibility at home, prompting one of his legates to complain that he had witnessed Nero "on stage playing pregnant women and slaves about to be executed." These factors combined with growing political unrest and revolts throughout the empire to precipitate Nero's downfall and his eventual suicide.

neume In early church plainsong, a group of notes sung as a rhythmic expansion of the melody. The neume developed into the illustrative TROPE, which is usually regarded as the starting-point for the LITURGICAL DRAMA. *See also* MEDIEVAL DRAMA.

new. New Comedy The third and final division of ancient Greek comedy, dating from the end of the 4th century BC to the middle of the third century BC. New Comedies, which were less bawdy and satirical than the OLD COMEDY of Aristophanes, featured complex plots revolving around such problems as mistaken identity, unrequited love, and household disputes.

The leading exponents of the form were the Sicilian, Philemon (*c.* 368–*c.* 264 BC), who worked in both Athens and Alexandria, and MENANDER (*c.* 341–*c.* 290 BC). Only fragments of Philemon's work survive, but one complete play by Menander, the *Dyscolus*, was discovered on a papyrus in Egypt in 1958. In the 2nd century BC playwrights TERENCE and PLAUTUS translated and adapted New Comedy for the Roman stage, introducing audiences to a more subtle kind of humour than that found in the early Roman farces.

Through the Roman playwrights, the Greek New Comedy has exerted a profound influence on the development of the later COMEDY OF MANNERS in Europe. Comic playwrights from Shakespeare and Molière to Alan Ayckbourn have used similar themes, situations, and stories.

New Drama A movement in British drama from approximately 1890 to 1914 that introduced a new NATURALISM and advocated the use of the theatre as a forum for social and political debate. Much influenced by Continental dramatists such as IBSEN, STRINDBERG, MAETERLINCK, and HAUPTMANN, the movement received early impetus from Henry Arthur Jones who, in 1884, adapted Ibsen's *A Doll's House* as *Breaking a Butterfly*.

The New Drama found its most powerful voice when George Bernard SHAW's first play *Widowers' Houses* was produced in 1892. Shaw went on to use the stage as a platform from which to expound his views on a variety of social questions. The development of the so-called 'problem play' received early support from J. T. Grein, who encouraged the new realistic drama at his Independent Theatre. By 1893 even the farceur Arthur Wing PINERO had turned to the genre with *The Second Mrs Tanqueray*.

Interest in realism was also generated by Harley GRANVILLE-BARKER's seasons at the Royal Court Theatre (1904–07), which inspired the creation of new repertory theatres for the performance of naturalistic works at Birmingham, Manchester, Liverpool, and Glasgow. Granville-Barker's own plays included *The Voysey Inheritance* (1905), which concerned the ethical dilemmas of business, and *The Madras House* (1910), which dealt with the repression of women. Another writer associated with the New Drama was John Galsworthy, whose works included *Justice* (1910), which is thought to have prompted reforms to the laws concerning solitary confinement, and *The Eldest Son* (1912).

New Theatre *See* ALBERY THEATRE.

New Way to Pay Old Debts, A A comedy by Philip MASSINGER, written in 1625 and first performed in 1632 in London. The play is still a popular choice for revival, largely because its larger-than-life villain, the extortioner Sir Giles Overreach, offers superb opportunities to actors. Edmund KEAN was the first to excel in the part, playing the role so powerfully in his 1816 production at Drury Lane that Lord Byron reportedly went into a convulsion and several ladies in the audience fainted. When Kean took the play to Birmingham and failed to make a similar impact he went into a rage, replying to another actor's line about the marriage of a lady:

> Take her, Sir, and the Birmingham audience into the bargain.

Other actors to make an impression as Overreach include Edwin Booth and Donald Wolfit, who first played the role in a production at the Richmond Theatre, Surrey in 1950.

In the play, the grasping Overreach reduces his nephew Frank Wellborn to utter poverty and then treats him with contempt. Lady Allworth, a rich widow, helps matters by pretending that she has plans to marry Wellborn, thereby prompting Overreach to suddenly shower kindnesses upon him. Meanwhile Tom Allworth, Lady Allworth's stepson, has fallen in love with Overreach's daughter, Margaret, who returns his affection. As Overreach wants his daughter to wed Lord Lovell and become 'right honourable', it is an easy matter for Lovell to pretend to woo Margaret while in fact advancing Tom's suit. When Overreach realizes the deception he becomes insane and is committed to Bedlam.

New York Shakespeare Festival *See* PAPP, Joseph.

New York Theatre, Bowery *See* BOWERY THEATRE.

nice. It's turned out nice again The catchphrase of the Lancashire comedian George Formby (1904–61), with which he used to open his shows. It also featured frequently in his films, especially as he rose to his feet and shook himself down after yet another mishap had befallen him.

Nichols, Peter (1927–) British author of dramas for both television and the stage. Of his often strongly autobiographical works Nichols has said: "I can only write dialogue when I hear people's voices in my mind," and "my writing...comes from memory and imitation". Although several of Nichols's plays deal with the anguish of physical suffering, he denies that his vision of the world is a tragic one on the grounds that "my characters meet adversity cheerfully and humorously". Roger Woodis has noted of

Nichols that "he disturbs us because he is honest. He is a worried man, and that is his strength."

Nichols's best-known work, A DAY IN THE DEATH OF JOE EGG (1967), reflects his own experience of caring for a severely handicapped daughter. His black comedy THE NATIONAL HEALTH (1969) contrasts glamorous hospital soaps with the reality of a ward for the terminally ill. Later works include *Forget-me-not-Lane* (1971), in which Nichols recalls his adolescence, the musical PRIVATES ON PARADE (1977), which starred Denis Quilley as a captain in a song-and-dance military unit, the comedy *Born in the Gardens* (1979), with Beryl Reid as an eccentric widow, PASSION PLAY (1980) a tragicomedy about marriage, *Poppy* (1982), an idiosyncratic musical about Britain's involvement in the Opium Wars with China, and *A Piece of My Mind* (1986).

night. ***Night and Day*** A play by Tom STOPPARD, first performed in 1978 at the Phoenix Theatre, London, with Diana Rigg and Peter Machin in the leads. Rigg was named best actress of the year by *Plays and Players* for her performance, with Jack Kroll noting in *Newsweek*: "Beauty, wit, bitchery and vulnerability seem to whirl about her like a pride of playfully savage ocelots." Before the play moved to Broadway, however, Rigg developed back trouble and was replaced by Maggie Smith.

The play explores the concept of press freedom. A group of journalists are covering an African rebellion from the house of the White mining engineer Carson and his wife, Ruth. The *Sunday Globe*'s reporter Wagner and his photographer Guthrie are at odds with a freelancer, Milne, whose exclusive interview with the rebel leader Shimbu has outclassed their best efforts. Professional jealousies are exacerbated by the fact that Ruth, who once spent a night with Wagner in London, now fancies Milne. Guthrie and the freelancer travel to the rebel camp on a mission to bring Shimbu to meet President Mageeba, but Guthrie soon returns to announce that Milne has been killed.

Night Must Fall A thriller by Emlyn WILLIAMS. His first major success, the play had its premiere in 1935 at the Duchess Theatre, London, and ran for a year. Williams was also praised for playing the leading role – a maniacal baby-faced murderer. The critic Audrey Williamson wrote that "his dramatic power held the stage and, with a perverted charm, wrung pity from the pitiless." A year later the play opened on Broadway at the Ethel Barrymore Theatre, where it enjoyed similar success.

The play, set in a bungalow in an Essex forest, involves Mrs Bramson who lives with her niece Olivia, her maid Dora, and her cook Mrs Terence. When Dora becames pregnant, Mrs Bramson decides to put pressure on her boyfriend, Dan, to marry her. Meanwhile, the police have begun to investigate the disappearance of a woman from a nearby hotel; Olivia suspects Dan, who is a bell boy there. Dan works himself deeper into Dora's affections, however, and leaves his hotel job to move into the bungalow. The police discover the missing woman's headless body, and Olivia becomes convinced that the head is in Dan's hatbox. One night, while alone with Mrs Bramson, Dan smothers her. When Olivia returns unexpectedly, he decides that she, too, has to be murdered; she is only saved by the arrival of the police. Olivia, who has become fascinated with Dan, now tries to cover up for him. He rejects her help, however, and leaves with the police.

Night of the Iguana, The A play by Tennessee WILLIAMS that was first performed in 1961 on Broadway at the Royale Theatre, winning the New York Drama Critics' Circle Award. The critic Brooks ATKINSON wrote that the cast, headed by Margaret Leighton, Bette Davis, and Alan Webb, "acted with an eerie sense of foreboding". Leighton received a Tony Award, Variety Award, and Newspaper Guild Page One Award for her performance. The play opened in London in 1965 at the Ashcroft Theatre, Croydon, with Sian Phillips, before transferring to the West End.

The story, set in Mexico in 1940, involves the widow Maxine Faulk, who runs the Costa Verde, a small hilltop hotel surrounded by jungle. Nearby are a family of Germans who cheer at Nazi broadcasts claiming victory in the Battle of Britain. One day, a busload of Baptist women teachers arrives, guided by the Rev. Shannon, a former priest who has seduced several of his younger charges. Shannon is suffering from a fever and is close to a breakdown, so Maxine asks him to stay on and manage the hotel. However, Shannon's attention is diverted by the arrival of Hannah Jelkes, a painter, and her 97-year-old grandfather, Jonathan Coffin, known as Nono the Poet.

Maxine, seeing that Hannah and Shannon are attracted to each other, becomes jealous. Shannon cannot decide whether to move in with Maxine, move on with Hannah, or go back to the Church; eventually he decides to stay, mainly because he lacks the energy to do anything else. Nono finishes his last poem and dies, leaving Hannah alone.

nine-days wonder, the A feat performed in the spring of 1599 by the English clown William Kempe (*fl.* 1600), who appeared with the CHAMBERLAIN'S MEN in many of the earlier plays of Shakespeare. For a wager, Kempe danced from London to Norwich in nine days (not including several days spent resting on the way). When he arrived, the mayor of Norwich gave Kempe £5 and entertained him. His accomplishment was recorded in 1600 in the book, *Kempe's Nine Daies Wonder*. The expression is now used to describe an event that arouses great interest for a very short time.

Nō or ***Noh*** A formal Japanese dance drama that utilizes courtly language, music, and dance to create an emotional mood rather than tell a story. The material for *Nō* drama comes from Buddhist scriptures, Japanese and Chinese mythology, poems, novels, and other sources, while the dancing is derived from ancient temple and folk dances. *Nō* seeks the quality of *yugen*, or gentle gracefulness, by using indirectness, restraint, and suggestion. In performance the plays, which all end in a stately dance, are interspersed with comic interludes called KYŌGEN ('mad words').

The genre was created by Kiyostsugu Kanami (1333–84), who combined a style of dancing and tumbling known as *sarugaku-nō* ('monkey music') with Zen Buddhist themes. The name of the new drama was eventually shortened to *Nō*. The form was developed by Kanami's son Zeami (1363–1443), who wrote some 200 plays in the style. Kanami's aristocratic entertainments were supported by the shoguns, and performers were accorded the status of samurai warriors.

The dramas are acted on a raised stage with a square roof supported on four pillars; there is no scenery and very few props. *Nō* drama involves two main actors, the secondary *waki* and the principal *shite*, who performs the ritual dances. Both wear painted wooden masks and dress in magnificent silk costumes based on ancient models. In addition to the principals, there are about 10 members of the chorus, four musicians, and two assistants, who appear on stage during the action but are regarded as invisible by both audience and actors.

Originally, programmes of *Nō* always contained five types of play: the *kamimono* praising the deities, the *shuramono* concerning warriors, the *kazuramono* about women, the *kuruimono* involving insane persons or spirits, and the *kirinomono* about demons and other supernatural beings. Since World War II, however, programmes usually consist of only two or three main plays. With the *Kyōgen* interludes a performance can still last for up to seven hours.

In the 20th century several prominent Western playwrights have been influenced by the *Nō* drama, most notably W. B. YEATS who, after 1916, made great use of masks, music, dancing, and chanting in his works.

noises off All theatrical SOUND EFFECTS that are produced offstage. The form is also employed as a stage direction, sounds from offstage suggesting a disturbance or commotion.

Noises Off A farce by Michael FRAYN, first performed in London in 1982. The play is chiefly remarkable for having what has been called "the most difficult single act to perform ever written." The act in question presents a third-rate travelling company's production of the feeble sex comedy *Nothing On*. During this farce-within-a-farce everything that could go wrong does go wrong, as lost contact lenses, missed cues, drunkenness, and backstage squabbles combine to produce a terrifying descent into chaos.

No Man's Land A play for four characters by Harold PINTER. First performed in 1975 at the Old Vic, it subsequently transferred to Wyndham's Theatre and then to the National Theatre. The play was directed by Peter HALL and starred John GIELGUD as Spooner, Ralph RICHARDSON as Hirst, Michael Feast as Foster, and Terence Rigby as Briggs. The critic Michael Coveney called Gielgud and Richardson's performances "the funniest double-act in town."

The plot centres on two men in their sixties, the poor poet Spooner and the wealthy literary figure Hirst, who meet in a pub and return to Hirst's home. There they drink and chat and ramble on until Hirst collapses. Foster and Briggs, members of the same homosexual household, then enter and attend to Hirst, showing hostility to Spooner's presence. Briggs locks Spooner in the room overnight. When he recovers the next day, Hirst becomes convinced that Spooner is someone he had known many years previously at Oxford. The two men recall mutual friends and lovers, until Hirst suddenly declares that he once had an affair with Spooner's wife. The play ends with the two men continuing to wander through their no-man's-land of memory and fantasy.

Norman Conquests, The A sequence of three two-act comedies by Alan AYCKBOURN, first performed in 1973 at the Stephen Joseph Theatre-in-the-Round, Scarborough, where Ayckbourn has been artistic director since 1970. In 1993, 20 years after its premiere, Ayckbourn directed a revival of the work at the same theatre.

The plays depict the same dreadful but hilarious event, a weekend family reunion, from different vantage points: *Table Manners* takes place in the dining room during a disastrous meal (with one guest sitting on a low stool with his head barely above the table), *Living Together* in the sitting room, and *Round and Round the Garden* outside. Although this is the official sequence, the comedies can be seen separately or in any order.

The story begins with a married couple, Reg and Sarah, arriving at the house of his invalid mother to give Reg's sister, Annie, a weekend's break from caring for her. They are joined by Norman, Reg's brother-in-law, and Tom, Annie's wishy-washy boyfriend. Unknown to the others, Norman, a lustful assistant librarian, is taking Annie away for a dirty weekend. Sarah, who also fancies Norman, tries to keep him free for herself by goading Tom into proposing to Annie. When Annie backs out of the dirty weekend, Norman gets drunk and reveals their affair. Sarah rings Norman's wife Ruth, who arrives the next day quite unperturbed. On Sunday, the family lunch degenerates into bitter squabbling. As the visitors begin to leave on Monday morning, Norman deliberately crashes the family cars to cause a delay in which he can continue his flirting.

"notorious whores" The unfortunate phrase used by the Puritan **William Prynne** (1600–69) to describe actresses at the very moment (1633) that Queen Henrietta Maria was rehearsing for an amateur pastoral. As a consequence, Prynne was sentenced to life imprisonment, fined, and placed in the pillory, where both his ears were cut off. He later had the letters SL (seditious libeller) branded on both cheeks. The offending phrase appeared in Prynne's 1100-page tract *Histrio-Mastix: The Players Scourge, or Actors Tragedie*, which recited the immoralities of the stage throughout history. It had been inspired by the first appearance of French actresses upon the London stage. Despite this treatment, Prynne was one of the few Puritans to publicly oppose the execution of Charles I – a stand that led to a further spell of imprisonment. After the Restoration Charles II appointed him keeper of records in the Tower of London.

History remembers him as one of the most vitriolic and unswervable critics of the stage. Samuel Butler wrote an epitaph for him:

> His brain's career was never stopping,
> But pen with rheum of gall still
> dropping,
> Til hand o'er head brought ears to
> cropping.

nous avons changé tout cela (Fr. we have changed all that). A phrase, originating in MOLIÈRE's *Le Médecin malgré lui* (1666), that is used as a facetious reproof to a person who harks back to old or authoritarian ways.

Novello, Ivor (David Ivor Davies; 1893–1951) British actor-manager, playwright, and composer, whose light musical plays dominated the West End stage in the 1930s.

Novello was born in Cardiff, the son of musical parents; by the age of 10 he had won a prize at the National Eisteddfod. In 1914 he was provoked into writing 'Keep the Home Fires Burning' by his mother, who had composed a dreadful patriotic song that she threatened to sing in public unless he wrote a better one. It was to be the most popular song of World War I and earned Novello £15,000 in its first five years. During the war, Novello served in the Air Ministry and wrote *Theodore and Co.*, which opened in 1916 for an 18-month run at the Gaiety Theatre, London.

Novello made his acting debut in 1921 in Sacha Guitry's *Deburau* at the Ambassadors Theatre. The following year he left for America to become a silent film actor. Hollywood made much of his famous profile and he became an international star; however, he was to return to the London stage declaring, "I want to show them that there is an art beyond the reach of mechanical devices of black and white shadows chasing each other round a white screen."

In 1924 Novello co-wrote and starred in *The Rat*, which opened in Brighton (where he took 39 curtain calls on the first night) before transferring to the Prince of Wales's Theatre, London. In 1929, a year in which Novello was Britain's top cinema attraction, his *Symphony in Two Flats* opened at the New Theatre. The following year Novello made his New York debut in the play at the Shubert Theatre. In America, however, *Symphony in Two Flats* ran for only seven weeks, prompting Novello to say "we opened in a heat wave and closed in a heat wave...unfortunately it was the same heat wave."

He then wrote the script for MGM's *Tarzan, the Ape Man* before returning to London to stage his *Party* (1932) at the Strand Theatre. This play about two theatrical rivals featured characters based on Tallulah BANKHEAD and Mrs Patrick CAMPBELL; the latter played the character based on herself in a New York production in 1933. *Fresh Fields* also opened that year at the Criterion Theatre, its run overlapping with those of *Sunshine Sisters* at the Queen's Theatre and *Proscenium*, a sentimental comedy about the theatre, at the Globe.

Novello's romantic musicals, all staged at Drury Lane, included *Glamorous Night* (1935), *Careless Rapture* (1936), which Novello liked to call "Careless Rupture", *Crest of the Wave* (1937), and *The Dancing Years* (1939), in which he played a Viennese composer. In 1949 Novello enjoyed further success with *King's Rhapsody*, in which he was starring at the time of his death two years later.

nudity Stage nudity has a long history. In the first century AD Roman MIME featured scenes in which female performers would undress. Following the adoption of Christianity as the state religion, however, and especially after the reign (527–65) of the emperor Justinian, nudity was restricted. Throughout the Middle Ages public nudity continued to be banned by the Church, although some royal pageants were exempt. Theatrical nudity was eventually reinstated in France where, despite the disapproval of the Church, many 17th-century plays would feature an occasional uncovered bosom. When governmental restrictions came into effect in the 1780s, creative designers introduced tights (*see* LEG SHOW) and the tutu for ballet.

The English-language stage was not far behind. In 1861 the US actress Adah MENKEN was billed as 'The Naked Lady' for wearing a scanty costume in a dramatization of Byron's *Mazeppa*. Nudes were sometimes seen on the 19th-century English stage in *poses plastiques*, LIVING PICTURES that imitated famous paintings or sculptures. The convention that discreet stationary nudity was permissible was endorsed by the Lord Chamberlain's 1931 ruling on *Revuedeville* at the Windmill Theatre: "If it moves, it's rude."

Modern STRIPTEASE is supposed to have originated in 1893 at the MOULIN ROUGE and by 1920 had become a popular US BURLESQUE attraction. The genre was made semi-respectable by the sophisticated routines of Gypsy Rose LEE. Performers generally retained 'pasties' to cover their nipples and the famous 'G-string' until the early 1950s when total nudity was introduced at the Crazy-Horse Saloon.

In Britain the abolition of stage censorship in 1968 (*see* LORD CHAMBERLAIN) was followed within days by the London premiere of HAIR, which featured full-frontal nudity. Earlier that year Maggie Wright, playing Helen of Troy, had become the first legitimate actress to appear totally nude on the British stage in the Royal Shakespeare Company's production of *Dr Faustus*. In 1969, Kenneth TYNAN's revue *Oh, Calcutta!* featured ensemble nudity and was advertised as "the hottest show in town." A year later Diana Rigg appeared nude in Ronald Millar's *Abelard and Heloise*, prompting the critic John Simon to write, "Diana Rigg is built like a brick mausoleum with insufficient flying buttresses." As late as 1980, however, audiences were still shocked by male nudity in Howard Brenton's *The Romans in Britain*. In Nell Dunn's play STEAMING (1981), set in a women's Turkish bath, the all-female cast spend most of the production without clothes. Indeed, nakedness has now become so ubiquitous on both stage and screen that some drama schools now make learning to perform in the nude an obligatory part of the course.

Occasionally, nudity has continued after the fall of the curtain. The distinguished alcoholic British actor, Robert Newton, once entered Anna Neagle's dressing room naked except for his socks and suspenders. He was introduced to three ladies who had just attended the matinée, engaged them in lively conversation, escorted them out of the stage door, and, still naked, hailed them a taxi.

Nunn, Trevor Robert (1940–) British director noted for his long association with the ROYAL SHAKESPEARE COMPANY. After gaining experience with the Marlowe Society at Cambridge, Nunn joined the Belgrade Theatre, Coventry, as a trainee director in 1962.

Three years later Nunn left the Belgrade to become a director at the RSC. His first production, codirected with John Barton, was *Henry V* at the Aldwych Theatre, London. In 1966 Nunn directed the first revival for 300 years of Tourneur's *The Revenger's Tragedy*; he successfully revived Vanbrugh's *The Relapse* the following year. In 1968 he was named artistic director of the RSC on the departure of Peter HALL; later that year he directed *Much Ado About Nothing*, *King Lear*, and *The Taming of the Shrew*.

In 1972 Nunn was involved in an acrimonious and well-publicized dispute with John ARDEN and his wife Margaretta D'Arcy, who disowned Nunn's production of the play *The Island of the Mighty*. During his time as director Nunn opened two small venues for the company, the Other Place in 1974 in Stratford and the Warehouse in 1977 in London. In 1976 Nunn directed a sinister *Macbeth* at the Other Place and (with Guy Woolfenden) turned *The Comedy of Errors* into an exuberant musical. Two years later, he was named chief executive of the RSC and became joint artistic director with Terry Hands. In 1980 the RSC had a landmark hit at the Aldwych when Nunn, with John Caird, staged David Edgar's adaptation of Dicken's *Nicholas Nickleby*; the show later enjoyed a massive success on Broadway.

Since the 1980s Nunn has been much in demand as a director of large-scale musicals. With the RSC he created the enormously successful *Les Misérables* (1985) and the notorious horror musical *Carrie* (1986), a critical and commercial disaster. Working as a freelance he directed the Andrew LLOYD WEBBER musicals *Cats* (1981), *Starlight Express* (1984), and *Aspects of Love* (1989). In the mid 1980s his prolonged absences from the RSC and his lucrative outside interests provoked much criticism. An apocryphal story from this time has a group of actors writing to Jimmy Savile requesting him to "fix it" for them to meet their director. Nunn resigned his posts at the RSC in 1986, since when he has held the title of director emeritus. He took up a new appointment as artistic director of the Royal National Theatre in 1997.

nurseries The acting schools of the Restoration theatre in London. The first one, the Nursery, was established in about 1662 at Hatton Garden by Thomas KILLIGREW and later moved to the Vere Street Theatre. By the time the Nursery closed in 1671 two other schools had opened: the Barbican Nursery, run by Sir William DAVENANT's widow, and the Bun Hill Nursery. *See* DRAMA SCHOOL.

O

Oakley, Annie *See under* ANNIE.

Oberammergau Passion Play The best-known surviving PASSION PLAY. In 1633 the Black Death swept through Bavaria; when it abated, the inhabitants of the village of Oberammergau vowed to enact the Passion of Christ every ten years in gratitude for having been spared. This they have done ever since, with one or two exceptions. The play is now a highly commercial undertaking, although the cast is still taken from the villagers. In recent decades there has been some controversy over the allegedly anti-Semitic overtones of the traditional text.

Oberon In Shakespeare's A MIDSUMMER NIGHT'S DREAM the King of the Fairies, whose quarrel with his wife TITANIA leads indirectly to the various confusions on which the plot depends.

The name Oberon is possibly connected to Alberich, who is the King of the Dwarves in Scandinavian mythology. The character first appeared in *Huon de Bordeaux*, a medieval French romance, in which he is described as being the son of Julius Caesar and Morgan le Fay (in Celtic legend, the fairy sister of King Arthur). According to *Huon de Bordeaux*, Oberon was only three feet high and at birth had received magical gifts from the fairies.

Obie The annual theatre award, established in 1955 by *The Village Voice*, for OFF-BROADWAY productions. The name is a phonetic rendering of OB (off-Broadway).

O'Casey, Sean (John Casey; 1880–1964) Irish dramatist, whose greatest plays depict life in the slums of Dublin during the 'Troubles' of 1915 to 1922. Recurring preoccupations of his work include the waste of war, man's willingness to sacrifice life for a cause, and the contrast between blustering parasitic Irishmen and their long-suffering womenfolk.

Born to a poor Protestant family in Dublin, O'Casey lacked formal education and taught himself to read at the age of 14. For many years he worked as a labourer, also becoming involved with labour movements, including the paramilitary Irish Citizens Army. By late 1914, however, he was sufficiently disillusioned to have withdrawn from active politics.

O'Casey's first work to be produced was THE SHADOW OF A GUNMAN (originally titled *On the Run*), which was staged in 1923 at the ABBEY THEATRE. The play, which centres on the brutal conflict between Irish nationalists and the British army in Dublin in 1920, was followed by two more tragicomedies at the Abbey. The success of JUNO AND THE PAYCOCK (1924), allowed O'Casey to give up his manual work; he later recalled: "I decided then that one job is enough for any man." THE PLOUGH AND THE STARS (1926), which gave an unromantic view of the 1916 Easter rising, provoked a riot among the fiercely patriotic audience. These two plays, both of which move dexterously from tragedy to farce, have been frequently revived in London, New York, and elsewhere.

O'Casey's next play, the anti-war THE SILVER TASSIE (1928), was rejected by W. B. YEATS, the manager of the Abbey, who disliked both the move towards EXPRESSIONISM and the didactic tone. O'Casey quarrelled violently with Yeats and decided to settle in England; thereafter he rarely returned to his native land.

His later, more symbolic, works are generally considered weaker than the plays he wrote for the Abbey. These include the expressionist *Within the Gates* (1933), the anti-fascist *The Star Turns Red* (1940), RED ROSES FOR ME (1942), about the 1913 Dublin General Strike, and *Cock-a-Doodle Dandy* (1949), which berated the puritanism he believed to be destroying Ireland. He also wrote six volumes of autobiography (1939–51) and two volumes of dramatic criticism (1937 and 1957).

Odd Couple, The A comedy by Neil SIMON, first performed in 1966 in New York and subsequently at the Queen's Theatre, London. The play, which was later made into a well-known film (1968) starring Jack Lemmon and Walter Matthau, also spawned a highly successful US television series. In 1985 it was revised by Simon for a female cast.

The story concerns two men sharing a Manhattan apartment. Oscar Madison, an unkempt sportswriter who is behind on his alimony, invites his friend Felix Ungar, who has just divorced, to move in. The meticulous Felix devastates Oscar by cleaning up the apartment, arranging Oscar's junk into neat piles, drawing up schedules for the week's meals, and insisting that they stick to a budget. When two Englishwomen visit and take to the refined Felix, this is the last straw; Oscar throws his friend out and returns to his poker games and slovenly habits. However, he discovers that he can now pay his alimony thanks to Felix's economic reforms.

odeon *See* ODEUM.

Odéon, Théâtre National de l' A theatre in the Latin Quarter of Paris, which opened in 1781 as the home of the COMÉDIE-FRANÇAISE. In 1784 Beaumarchais's *The Marriage of Figaro* had its premiere there. The venue was renamed the Odéon in 1795, becoming one of France's four state-supported theatres in 1807. It was reconstructed by the playwright and manager Louis-Benoît Picard (1769–1828) in 1816 but burned down two years later. Picard rebuilt it as a theatre for light comedy and operetta and continued as manager until 1821.

The Odéon established a reputation for serious drama in the 1830s. Sarah BERNHARDT, who first played there in 1866, was responsible for converting the theatre into a field hospital during the siege of Paris (1870). In 1906 André Antoine (1858–1943) was appointed director and completely modernized the building. Under the leadership (1922–30) of the director Firmin Gémier (1869–1933) the Odéon became virtually an avant-garde National People's Theatre. After World War II the Ministry of Arts merged the Odéon company with the Comédie-Française, renaming the theatre the Salle Luxembourg. The Odéon became independent of the Comédie-Française once more in 1959 when Jean-Louis BARRAULT was appointed director; the venue was now renamed the Théâtre de France. In 1966 riots occurred inside and outside the theatre when Barrault produced Genet's play about the Algerian war, *The Screens*. Further trouble erupted in 1968 following a performance given as part of the Théâtre des Nations festival, when the theatre became a base for student rioters. Barrault was dismissed and took his troupe away, leaving the theatre without a company. The Odéon reverted to this name and was reassigned in 1971 to the Comédie-Française, which uses it mostly as a venue for new and avant-garde works or for visiting provincial and foreign companies. In 1983 it became home to Giorgio STREHLER's THÉÂTRE DE L'EUROPE.

Odets, Clifford (1906–63) Left-wing US playwright best known for the influential dramas of social protest he wrote in the 1930s. He has described his work as an attempt to explore how a person can retain "the conviction of innocence" in a materialistic world. Odets, who was a founding member (1931) of the GROUP THEATRE, New York, made his name with his first play, the six-scene WAITING FOR LEFTY (1935). The play, about a cab strike in New York, also finds time to attack such varied targets as the US medical system and chemical warfare.

His other plays include *Till the Day I Die* (1935), about the anti-Nazi underground in Germany, AWAKE AND SING! (1935), concerning a Jewish working-class boy, GOLDEN BOY (1937), about professional boxing, and *The Big Knife* (1949), an exposé of Hollywood decadence reflecting his own experience as a scriptwriter. THE COUNTRY GIRL (1950) tells the story of an alcoholic actor and his wife; it was seen in London two years later as *Winter Journey* and was filmed in 1954 with Bing Crosby and Grace Kelly in the leading roles. Odets's last play, *The Flowering Peach* (1954), is a retelling of the story of Noah set in modern Brooklyn.

> He hits hard, and below the belt if need be. But at least he hits.
>
> JOHN MASON BROWN: *Dramatis Personae*.

odeum In ancient Greece and Rome, a roofed building for performances of vocal and instrumental music. The term (also given as **odeon** and **odeion**) derived from the original Odeion music hall built by Pericles in about 440 BC next to the Theatre of Dionysus in Athens. This hall was also used for musical competitions and for a preliminary ceremony held before poetry contests that included a parade of dramatists, actors, and chorus members dressed in their costumes. A public announcement was also made of the names of the playwrights and their works and of the names of the *choregi* (*see* CHOREGUS). In the 18th and 19th centuries the name odeum or odeon was often given to theatres and halls used for musical performances. Odeon was the tradename of a British cinema chain founded in 1933.

Oedipus. ***Oedipus Rex*** or ***Oedipus Tyrannus*** A one-act play by SOPHOCLES that is perhaps the best known of all Greek tragedies. Considered by many to be Sophocles's finest work, it was first performed in 429 BC and followed by a sequel OEDIPUS AT COLONUS. In his *Poetics,* Aristotle held up *Oedipus Rex* as the paradigm of the genre. The theme, of a son murdering his father and marrying his mother, was adopted by Freud as a symbol of the hidden desires that (supposedly) exist in all male children.

Oedipus Rex has been frequently revived. In 1585 the play was the opening production of the Teatro Olimpico, Vicenza. Max Reinhardt presented a famous staging in London in 1912 at Covent Garden starring John Martin-Harvey (1863–1944). A legendary Old Vic revival took place in London in 1945 at the New Theatre, with Laurence OLIVIER in the title role and Michel Saint-Denis directing. Olivier shocked the audience with two blood-curdling screams, one offstage and one when he entered with blood flowing from his eyes and hands. The critic John Mason Brown wrote: "They are the dreadful, hoarse groans of a wounded animal. They well out of a baby that has been clubbed by fate." Olivier claimed he was imitating the cry he had once heard from a Canadian skunk, trapped by its tongue sticking to a block of salt.

The play is set in Thebes after Oedipus has become king and wed Jocasta, wife of his murdered predecessor, Laius. Oedipus pronounces a curse on the murderer and swears to avenge Laius. When Teiresias, the blind prophet, accuses the king himself, Oedipus banishes him along with Creon, Jocasta's brother, whom he suspects of plotting against him. Jocasta tells Oedipus that he must be innocent, since an oracle said that Laius would be killed by his own son. But she also reveals that Laius was killed at the junction of three roads, reminding Oedipus that he once killed a man at such a place. Oedipus gradually realizes that he is the dead king's son and has married his own mother. Jocasta commits suicide and Oedipus blinds himself, leaving Thebes to be ruled by Creon.

Oedipus at Colonus A tragedy by SOPHOCLES that forms a sequel to OEDIPUS REX, being considered by some critics as an even finer work. The play, written when Sophocles was nearly 90, was first produced posthumously in 406 BC in Athens by the author's grandson, also named Sophocles.

A classic story of redemption through suffering, the play has often been revived and adapted. In 1984 the US dramatist Lee Breuer (1937–) wrote *Gospel at Colonus,* which combined Sophocles's work with contemporary Black gospel music.

The plot shows Oedipus some 20 years after the events of *Oedipus Rex*. Now old, blind, and exiled, he has been led to Athens by his loyal daughter ANTIGONE. Oedipus seeks a haven in Athens but finds himself an object of horror as well as pity. King Theseus, however, sees a divine purpose in the life of the old man and believes that Oedipus will bring victory and blessings to the place where he dies. The Thebans also wish Oedipus to return, and their king, Creon, abducts his daughters, Antigone and Ismene, in an attempt to force him to follow. The daughters are rescued by Theseus, however, and Oedipus commends them to his protection, as he himself is now summoned by the gods who have caused him so much pain.

off-Broadway In New York, a type of theatrical production that arose as an alternative to the commercial tradition of BROADWAY in the 1950s. Off-Broadway theatres became popular venues for low-budget productions of plays by such contemporary dramatists as Tennessee WILLIAMS and Edward ALBEE, and helped to launch the careers of such stars as Geraldine Page. The start of the movement is usually dated from the production of Williams's *Summer and Smoke* given at the CIRCLE-IN-THE-SQUARE in 1952. Inevitably, when the success of these productions was recognized, business interests moved in and theatres began to stage more commercial plays.

off-off-Broadway In New York, the alternative theatre that developed in the early 1960s in the coffee houses and other small venues of Greenwich Village and the Lower East Side. The off-off-Broadway scene arose as OFF-BROADWAY productions became more professional and profit-conscious (although today it is itself often used to test the commercial value of experimental works).

The first off-off-Broadway venue was the Caffe Cino on Cornelia Street, a small coffee house where Joe Cino presented plays from 1958 until 1967. By the mid-1960s several small off-off-Broadway companies existed, who introduced such new US playwrights as Sam Shepard, Terrence McNally, Israel Horowitz, Adrienne Kennedy, and Charles Ludlam. Noted off-off-Broadway groups have included the avant-garde Open Theatre, founded in 1963 by Joseph Chaikin, the Performance Group, founded in 1967 by Richard Schechner and re-formed in 1970 as the Wooster Group, and the socialist Bread and Puppet Theatre, founded in 1961 by Peter Schumann. The Play-House of the Ridiculous opened in 1967 (*see* RIDICULOUS, THEATRE OF THE).

Oh, What A Lovely War! A musical lampoon of World War I that was created by Joan LITTLEWOOD's Theatre Workshop in 1963 at the Theatre Royal, Stratford East. The play was a 'documentary collage' that juxtaposed sentimental songs of the period with poignant scenes and harrowing wartime photos projected on a screen to create a powerful anti-war message. The work soon transferred to Paris and New York. Richard Attenborough's 1969 film version featured an all-star cast that included Laurence Olivier, John Geilgud, Ralph Richardson, Maggie Smith, and Vanessa Redgrave.

oil the knocker, to To tip a doorman or gatekeeper. The expression derives from RACINE's comedy *The Litigants* (1668): *"On n'entre point chez lui sans graisser le marteau"* (no one enters this house without oiling the knocker).

Oklahoma! RODGERS AND HAMMERSTEIN's musical about cowboys and farmers in the American West, first staged by the THEATRE GUILD in 1943. It received rave reviews and ran for 2212 performances; the 1947 London production at Drury Lane lasted for 1543 performances. Together with *Annie Get Your Gun*, which opened a few weeks later, *Oklahoma!* changed the face of the stage musical by blending music, dance, and story as never before. It was also the first musical for which an original cast album was recorded.

Oklahoma!, originally to be called *Oklahoma and Away We Go!*, was based on Lynn Rigg's play *Green Grow the Rushes*. When the musical played in New Haven, Connecticut, before its Broadway opening, one local critic dismissed it with the comment "no legs, no jokes, no chance". Following its New York success, Hammerstein took out a self-congratulatory ad in *Variety* announcing "I've done it before and I can do it again!" which, rather than mentioning *Oklahoma!*, listed his many earlier flops.

The plot concerns Curly, a cowboy, who loves Laurie, a farmer's daughter. Curly has a dangerous rival, however, in Jud Fry, the hired hand. Jud dies on his own knife in the final fight and the couple ride off together. The songs include 'Oklahoma!', 'Oh, What a Beautiful Mornin'', and 'People Will Say We're in Love.'

old. ***Old Bachelor, The*** A comedy by William CONGREVE, first performed in 1693 at Drury Lane where it ran for a record two weeks with a cast headed by Thomas Betterton, Anne Bracegirdle, and Mrs Mountfort. According to Congreve, the play had been written to pass the time during a convalescence three years earlier. When he saw the script Dryden remarked that he had never seen such a brilliant first play and used his influence to have it produced.

The plot involves a surly old bachelor, Heartwell, who marries the young Silvia before learning that she is a discarded mistress of Vainlove. Heartwell is delighted when he discovers that the 'marriage' ceremony was performed by a sham vicar, Vainlove's friend Bellmour, who has disguised himself to get close to Laetitia, the wife of old Fondlewife. Eventually Sir Joseph Wittol, a foolish fellow, genuinely marries Silvia, thinking her to be the rich Araminta, and the cowardly Captain Bluffe weds Silvia's maid under the same false assumption. Vainlove, however, finds that the real Araminta is not ready to marry him.

Old Comedy The early Greek comic tradition of the 5th and 4th centuries BC. It is thought to have derived from the *komoidia*, the song accompanying the *komos* or revel at the festival of DIONYSUS; the use of a large chorus, masks, and costumes imitating the phallus and female genitals probably reflects these origins (*see* COMEDY). Fragments exist from several Old Comedy writers – Magnes, Cratinus, Crates, Eupolis, Pherecrates, Ameipsas – but the only major works extant are the 11 plays of ARISTOPHANES. They are full of obscene language, extravagant mockery, personal abuse of politicians (as in *The Knights*; 424 BC), and attacks on contemporary life and philosophy (as in *The Clouds*; 423 BC).

The tradition of Old Comedy was sufficiently confident for Aristophanes's violent attacks to continue to flourish even in the desperate days of the Peloponnesian War. Other writers addressed similar themes, with Ameipsas ridiculing Socrates in one of his plays as Aristophanes had in *The Clouds*.

Aristophanes's later works sometimes omitted the choral lyric and his last two plays were noticeably less confident and powerful (*see* MIDDLE COMEDY). Old Comedy faded away after the tragic conclusion of the war in 404 BC, probably because Athenian society had become too fragile for such harsh attacks. The NEW COMEDY of Menander would be gentle by comparison.

Old Corrector The name given to the supposed author of certain amendations to a Second Folio edition of Shakespeare's plays that the eminent Shakespearean scholar John Payne Collier (1789–1883) claimed to have discovered in 1849. Collier ascribed the comments to Richard Perkins, a Jacobean actor, and maintained that this version overturned all previously known texts. When the so-called **Perkins Folio** arrived at the British Museum for examination, however, pencil marks in a modern hand were discovered beneath the 'ancient' amendations in ink. The true identity of the Old Corrector was soon revealed and Collier's reputation was ruined. Towards the end of his life the once-respected scholar admitted: "I am such a despicable offender. I am ashamed of almost every act of my life." Nevertheless, at the age of 86 he attempted to arouse interest in a newly discovered Milton folio...

Old Drury The nickname of two US theatres, the CHESTNUT STREET THEATRE in Philadelphia and the PARK THEATRE in New York. The name, taken from London's DRURY LANE Theatre, was bestowed in honour of their seniority and importance in establishing the US theatre.

Old Dutch Nickname of the music-hall singer and comedian Albert CHEVALIER. The phrase is an informal Cockney expression for one's wife (an abbreviation of 'duchess'); it was associated with Chevalier after his success with the sentimental song 'My Old Dutch'.

Old Man *See* STOCK COMPANY.

Old Mo Nickname for the Middlesex Music Hall in Drury Lane, London. The name referred to the original building on the site, the 17th-century Mogul Tavern, which had an association with Nell GWYNN who had lived nearby. The Mogul Saloon began to present entertainment in 1847 and was renamed the Middlesex Music Hall in 1851. The venue was rebuilt in 1872, 1891, and 1911, when it was renamed the New Middlesex Theatre of Varieties. Music hall and revue dominated the programme until 1919, when the theatre, now known as the Winter Garden, was used for musicals.

old stager Originally an experienced stage player; now used more generally to refer to anyone of long experience.

> All the girls declare
> That I'm a gay old stager,
> Hey! Hey! clear the way
> Here comes the galloping major!
> F. W. LEIGH and G. BASTOW: 'The Galloping Major'.

Old Vic, the A famous London theatre, situated south of Waterloo Bridge. It opened in 1818 as the Royal Coburg Theatre and became something of a conversation piece because of its looking-glass curtain. In 1833 the theatre was refurbished and renamed the Royal Victoria Theatre. It soon began to acquire a reputation for rowdiness, and in 1858 a bogus fire alarm in the gallery resulted in several playgoers being trampled to death. The name changed in 1871 to the New Victoria Palace and in 1880 to the Royal Victoria Hall and Coffee Tavern, when the social reformer Emma Cons offered it as "a cheap and decent place of amusement on strict temperance lines", reversing its earlier reputation as a disreputable BLOOD-TUB. On Cons's death in 1912 her niece Lilian Baylis assumed control and introduced performances of Shakespeare's plays at reasonable prices. She would devote nearly 40 years of her life to the Old Vic (whose circles are named in her honour). In 1923 it became the first theatre anywhere to have produced all the plays in the First Folio.

Ballet arrived in 1931 with the first performance of the Vic-Wells Ballet (which later became the Royal Ballet) under Ninette de Valois. Two years later the opera and ballet programmes transferred to the SADLER'S WELLS THEATRE (which Baylis had rebuilt) while drama remained at the Old Vic. In the 1930s the remarkably talented company included Gielgud, Olivier, and Richardson. The Old Vic was severely damaged during the Blitz and despite the survival of the auditorium remained closed from 1941 until 1950.

In 1963 the Old Vic company disbanded and the theatre became a temporary home for Olivier's National Theatre company (*see* ROYAL NATIONAL THEATRE), which arrived with an initial offering of *Hamlet*, starring Peter O'Toole. In 1976 the National Theatre company moved to the South Bank and a new Old Vic Company was formed from the Prospect Company. This collapsed, however, following disasters such as Peter O'Toole's notorious *Macbeth* (1980). In 1981 public subsidy was withdrawn, resulting in the Old Vic's closure until 1983. Then, after a £2.5 million renovation by the new owner, the Canadian entrepreneur 'Honest' Ed Mirvish, the theatre reopened with the Tim Rice musical *Blondel*. A 1991 production of Hammerstein's *Carmen Jones* won five major awards, including the 1992 Laurence Olivier Award for Best Musical. From late 1996 Sir Peter Hall directed a season of plays at the theatre with his own informal ensemble. *See also* YOUNG VIC, THE.

Old Woman *See* STOCK COMPANY.

Oldfield, Anne (1683–1730) English actress, the first to be buried in Westminster Abbey; no monument was erected as she had borne two illegitimate children.

The dramatist George FARQUHAR discovered her while she was working at the MITRE TAVERN; she subsequently became his mistress and is probably the 'Penelope' of his love letters. Her children were fathered by Arthur Manwaring and John Churchill, the Duke of Marlborough. When the Princess of Wales congratulated Mrs Oldfield on her 'marriage' to the Duke the actress replied, "So it is said, may it please your royal highness, but we have not owned it yet."

Her acting career began when the playwright Sir John VANBRUGH found her a place on the Drury Lane stage in 1699. She excelled in comedy and made her name in 1704 in the role of Lady Betty Modish in Colley Cibber's *The Careless Husband*. Two years later she appeared as Millamant in Congreve's *The Way of the World*, and in 1707 she created the roles of Silvia in Farquhar's *The Recruiting Officer* and Mrs Sullen in his *The Beaux' Stratagem* (1707).

Mrs Oldfield was noted for her beautiful diction; indeed, Voltaire claimed that she was the only English actress he could understand without effort. In 1728, the year of her retirement, she gave one of her most acclaimed performances as Lady Townly in Cibber's *The Provoked Husband*. Her last appearance was in Henry Fielding's *Love in Several Masques*. *See also* NANCY, MISS.

Oleanna A play by the US dramatist David MAMET that confronts the controversial subjects of sexual harassment and political correctness. The play opened on Broadway in 1992 and created an uproar among both feminists and anti-feminists, with the cast being subjected to frequent heckling from the audience. A year later it was seen in London at the Royal Court Theatre in a production by Harold Pinter starring Lia Williams and David Suchet.

The plot explores the conflict between Carol, an insecure college student, and John, a middle-aged professor. During a tutorial, Carol appears to be on the verge of a nervous breakdown because she cannot understand John's academic jargon; when she begins to cry, John paternally puts an arm round her shoulders. This is followed by a mildly risqué joke. Encouraged by campus feminists, Carol accuses him of sexual harassment and attempted rape, a charge that results in John losing his job and facing criminal charges. Exasperated by the injustice John eventually loses his self-control, knocks her to the floor and kicks her violently as she cowers under the table – an action that provoked cheers from male members of the audience in both New York and London. Recovering himself, John apologizes but realizes it is too late.

Oliver! Lionel Bart's musical adaptation of the Dickens classic *Oliver Twist*. First produced in 1960 at London's Albery Theatre, it ran for 2618 performances with Ron Moody as Fagin and striking sets by Sean Kenney (1932–73). Moody also appeared in the 1968 film version and returned for a 1983 revival at the Aldwych Theatre. A further revival, starring Robert Lindsay, opened at the London Palladium in 1994.

Bart's free adaptation follows the orphan Oliver from the cruelty of the workhouse, through his experiences in the underworld with Fagin and his gang of pickpockets, to eventual happiness with a wealthy grandfather. The songs include 'Food, Glorious Food', 'Oliver', 'Consider Yourself', 'I'd do

Anything', 'You've Got to Pick a Pocket or Two', and 'As Long as He Needs Me'.

Olivier, Laurence (Kerr), Baron (1907–89) British actor, director, and manager, generally considered the leading classical actor of his time. The son of an Anglican clergyman, he made his first stage appearance as Katherine in a school production of *The Taming of the Shrew* (1922). Two years later he made his professional debut in *Byron* at the Century Theatre, London. During the 1930s Olivier came to critical notice in Shakespearean roles, including Hamlet (1937), and became known to a wider public through Hollywood films such as *Wuthering Heights* (1939). After war service he became a codirector of the OLD VIC with Ralph RICHARDSON (1944) and gave a series of outstanding performances in plays by Shakespeare, Chekhov, and Sophocles (*see* OEDIPUS REX). The 1950s saw Olivier managing his own company and extending his range by taking roles in contemporary British works, notably that of Archie Rice in Osborne's THE ENTERTAINER. After a year as director of the CHICHESTER FESTIVAL, he became founding director of the National Theatre (*see* ROYAL NATIONAL THEATRE) in 1962, a post he held for 11 years. His film work included the Shakespearean trilogy *Henry V* (1944), *Hamlet* (1948), and *Richard III* (1956), each of which he directed as well as playing the leading role. Olivier was knighted in 1947 and became the first actor to be created a life peer in 1970. He was married three times, his most celebrated and stormy marriage being to the actress Vivien LEIGH and his last to the actress Joan Plowright (1929–), who survives him.

Olivier's early career was not auspicious, with Sir Cedric Hardwicke for one remembering him as noisy and unsubtle. He was also prone to giggle nervously on stage, a maddening habit that cost him one job and threatened his career. Olivier credited Noël Coward with curing him. During the first run of *Private Lives* (1930), Coward and Gertrude Lawrence engaged in a deliberate policy of making Olivier corpse at every opportunity. By the end of its seven-month run, Olivier was laughed out.

Olivier was also notoriously accident-prone; during his career, he suffered one broken ankle, two torn cartilages, two torn calf muscles, and three ruptured Achilles tendons. Other mishaps included a 30-foot fall onto the stage from a rope ladder and the occasion on which he landed "from considerable height, scrotum first, upon an acrobat's knee." He also inflicted injuries on others. Wielding a sword during the fight scene in *Romeo and Juliet* (1935), he cut Geoffrey Tonne's thumb so badly that the young actor had to leave the cast for four weeks.

Olivier himself had moments of self-doubt. After one triumphant performance of *Othello*, he stormed back to his dressing room and slammed the door. The cast waited outside until one summoned up the courage to knock and ask, "What's the matter, Larry? It was *great*!" Olivier shouted back: "I know it was great, damn it, but I don't know how I did it, so how can I be sure I can do it again?"

His name is commemorated in the LAURENCE OLIVIER AWARDS, given annually for the best West End productions, and in the Olivier Theatre, opened in 1976 as one of the three auditoriums of the National Theatre.

Ollantay A play in the Quechuan language, performed near Cuzco, Peru, in around 1780 under the direction of Padre Antonio Valdés. Whether Valdés created the work himself or transcribed it from oral tradition is somewhat contentious, though scrutiny of the play's structure suggests the former. The work has been variously adapted and translated by late 20th-century writers.

Olsen and Johnson The US VAUDEVILLE stars Ole Olsen (John Olsen; 1892–1963) and Chic Johnson (Harold Johnson; 1892–1962), who billed themselves as the "Comic Nuts, Kings of Cacophony, Unconventionality and Conviviality." Their "screamlined" masterpiece *Hellzapoppin* (1938) still holds the record run for a revue, lasting for 1404 performances before becoming a film in 1942. Despite its original success, a 1977 revival starring the comedian Jerry Lewis flopped.

Olsen, who began as a vaudeville pianist, teamed up with Johnson, a violinist, at the 14th Street Music Hall in 1915. By 1922 the pair had become stars of the ZIEGFELD FOLLIES. They appeared on Broadway in *Monkey Business of 1926* and had another success with *Atrocities of 1932*. After filming three comedies for Warner Brothers, Olsen and Johnson took Broadway by storm with *Hellzapoppin* at the 46th Street Theatre. In 1941 they returned with a similar format in *Sons of Fun* at the Winter Garden Theatre.

ombres chinoises *See* SHADOW PLAY.

omnibus box A theatre box paid for by the subscription of several different parties, all of whom have the right to use it.

One and Only, the Nickname of the US STRIPTEASE artiste of the 1940s Phyllis Dixey, since applied almost universally to show-business stars, regardless of their merits. The British comedian Max Miller was also known by this nickname.

O'Neill, Eugene (Gladstone) (1888–1953) US playwright, often regarded as the first serious and distinctive voice in American drama. His father, James O'Neill, was a touring actor, and Eugene was born in a Broadway hotel. He attended Princeton University for one year but dropped out to become a seaman, after which he led an itinerant existence in Europe and South America. During this period he became an alcoholic, attempting suicide on at least one occasion. While recovering from tuberculosis at a sanatorium in 1912 he began to write melodramas as part of his 'rebirth'.

O'Neill's first work to be produced was the one-act nautical drama *Bound East for Cardiff*, staged by the experimental Provincetown Players in Massachusetts in 1916. The group formed the Playwrights' Theatre in New York later that year and continued to produce his plays. His first full-length work, BEYOND THE HORIZON, opened in 1920 at Broadway's Morosco Theatre and won a Pulitzer Prize. Three more Pulitzers were awarded for ANNA CHRISTIE (1922), STRANGE INTERLUDE (1928), and the autobiographical LONG DAY'S JOURNEY INTO NIGHT (posthumously awarded in 1957). He received the Nobel Prize in 1936. Other full-length plays include DESIRE UNDER THE ELMS (1924), about the love-hate relationship between a New England farmer and his son, MOURNING BECOMES ELECTRA (1931), a reworking of Aeschylus's *Oresteia*, AH! WILDERNESS (1933), his only comedy, and THE ICEMAN COMETH (1946), a highly charged drama about the death of a disillusioned man.

O'Neill's tragic outlook on life may well have stemmed from the grim family background depicted in *Long Day's Journey into Night*; it was undoubtedly exacerbated by his three disastrous marriages and the problems he had with his children. He was devastated by the suicide of his eldest son, Eugene, and furious when his daughter, Oonagh, married Charlie Chaplin, who was O'Neill's contemporary. During his last years, O'Neill was crippled by Parkinson's disease. He died, as he had been born, in a hotel.

one-night stand A single evening performance by a touring company, etc., or a town that is likely to provide an audience for one night only. The phrase is also used of a casual sexual relationship lasting for a single night.

onnagata In the KABUKI theatre of Japan, a male actor who plays female roles. When boys and women were banned from performing in the 17th century, female roles began to be played by men with shaved foreheads. Until quite recently, the actors were expected to conduct themselves in a feminine manner even when they were not on stage.

The *onnagata* actor applies white make-up to the face before drawing false eyebrows and adding rouge to the mouth and the corners of the eyes. The role of a married woman is played with blackened teeth and no eyebrows. *See also* FEMALE IMPERSONATOR.

open. open-air theatre The first Greek and Roman theatres were in the open, and medieval travelling players also erected their temporary stages outside. Plays were first produced indoors in Renaissance Italy. In England the PUBLIC THEATRES of the Elizabethan era were open to the sky except for roofs over the stage and galleries. Although theatre came firmly inside with the introduction of the PROSCENIUM arch, open-air drama, whether on the streets or in municipal parks, has never died out.

Britain's best known outdoor venue is the Open Air Theatre in Regent's Park, London. Ben Greet began to stage plays in the park with his Woodland Players in 1900. Sydney Carroll revived the tradition in 1932, and in 1962 the New Shakespeare Company was formed to carry it on; three productions are now given each summer, two of which are Shakespearean works. The theatre was reconstructed in 1975 with an auditorium complex being added to replace the old rows of deck chairs. The Open Air Theatre's bar is famous for its 'Puck's Fizz' cocktail.

Europe's largest open-air theatre, with a seating capacity of 7000 and standing room for 9000, is at Scarborough in North Yorkshire. The theatre closed in 1968 but reopened in 1982 with a production of *Magical Musical Time Machine*.

open stage *See* THRUST STAGE.

Open Theatre, the An OFF-OFF-BROADWAY theatre company founded in New York in 1963 by Joseph Chaikin, formerly of the LIVING THEATRE, and Peter Feldman. The group pioneered a form of COLLECTIVE CREATION, in which the cast would improvize around a script that the dramatist would then rewrite incorporating their ideas. Their first full-length play, *Viet Rock* (1966) by Megan Terry (1932–), addressed the horrors of the Vietnam war. Other productions included *The Serpent* (1968), *Terminal* (1969), *Mutation Show* (1971), and *Nightwalk* (1973).

The group borrowed many of its ideas from Jerzy Grotowski's POOR THEATRE, employing minimal scenery, props, and lighting. Actors moved freely from one role into another and appeared in their rehearsal clothes without make-up. The company was reorganized as a collective in 1970 and subsequently performed mainly for university and prison audiences until its dissolution in 1973.

opera. opera house In America, any building in a small town that can be used as a theatre for travelling entertainers, lecturers, etc.

Opera Comique A former London theatre in Aldwych that was opened in 1870. The following year, a group of actors from the Comédie-Française, all refugees from the Franco-Prussian War, performed there under Edmond-François-Jules Gôt. The theatre continued to appeal to international performers such as the Italian actress Adelaide Ristori, who visited in 1873, but its French name made London theatregoers suspicious and the venue often remained unused. From 1877 Richard D'OYLY CARTE and his Comedy Opera Company produced a series of works by GILBERT AND SULLIVAN at the venue; *The Sorcerer* (1877) was followed by *HMS Pinafore* (1878) and *The Pirates of Penzance* (1880). *Patience* (1881) had its premiere at the Opera Comique but transferred to the SAVOY THEATRE, which D'Oyly Carte opened later the same year.

After a period during which it was closed for redecoration the theatre presented the young Marie Tempest as Lady Blanche in *The Fay o' Fire*. It enjoyed little subsequent success, however, and became a venue for special performances and try-outs. It was partially rebuilt in 1895, closed in 1899, and demolished in 1902. *See also* RICKETY TWINS.

Ophelia In Shakespeare's HAMLET, the daughter of Polonius, lord chamberlain at the Danish court. Ophelia loves Hamlet but is sufficiently dutiful to repel Hamlet's romantic overtures on the instruction of her father. Hamlet's subsequent cruelty towards Ophelia, and his accidental slaying of her father, finally drive her mad and she drowns herself. The actress Ellen TERRY was especially well received in the role.

opposite prompt side (OP) *See* PROMPT SIDE *under* PROMPT.

O.P. riots A series of riots that took place at COVENT GARDEN in 1809. Following the destruction by fire of the first Covent Garden theatre in 1808, a new theatre was quickly constructed and opened the next year. Due to the smaller capacity of the new theatre, however, admission prices were raised. Riots broke out and continued for three months, with crowds disrupting performances with shouts of "O.P." (old prices) and doing considerable damage to the theatre itself. The ferocity of the riots eventually forced the theatre's management into submission and the old prices were brought back.

Orange Moll Nickname for Mary Meggs (d. 1691), a seller of oranges and other refreshments at the Drury Lane Theatre for nearly 20 years from its opening in 1663. One of her orange girls, most of whom doubled as prostitutes, was Nell GWYNN, the future actress and mistress of Charles II. Meggs, a widow, became a popular fixture at the theatre and delighted Samuel PEPYS by passing on scandalous gossip about Gwynn and other theatrical personalities, many items of which ended up in his *Diary*.

When Drury Lane was destroyed by fire in 1672, a report pinpointed the source as being under the stairs "where Orange Moll keeps her fruit"; thereafter suspicion lingered that she or one of her girls (including Gwynn) might have been searching the area with a candle.

In 1682 the companies of Drury Lane and Dorset Garden were combined and became more businesslike. When it was discovered that Meggs was in arrears, she was replaced. Since her original licence was for 39 years, she initiated a protracted legal claim that was still unresolved on her death.

orchestra In the ancient Greek theatre, the circular or semicircular area where the CHORUS chanted and danced. It was positioned between the audience and the raised stage used by the principals. The word is derived from the Greek *orcheesthai* meaning 'to dance'.

The orchestra was one of the most ancient features of the Greek theatre. In the 6th century BC a dancing place was laid out around the *thymele* or altar in the Theatre of Dionysus, Athens. A raised wooden stage was added about a century later, this being connected to the orchestra by steps or ramps. Some scholars believe that orchestras were rectangular until the 4th century, although the theatre at Epidaurus, built in about 350 BC, has a well-preserved circular orchestra with a diameter of about 66 feet.

orchestra pit The sunken area in front of a stage in which musicians perform. The orchestra pit was an innovation of the Georgian theatre, musicians having sat aloft in a gallery in Elizabethan times and in a box in the Restoration theatre. The term (and, indeed, the use of the word orchestra to mean a musical ensemble) derives from the space reserved for the chorus in the ancient Greek theatre.

orchestra seat *See* STALLS.

Oresteia, The A sequence of three tragedies by AESCHYLUS, the only complete Greek trilogy to have survived (the accompanying SATYR-PLAY is lost). Consisting of the plays *Agamemnon*, the *Choephoroi (Libation Bearers)*, and the *Eumenides* (*Furies*), it was first performed in 458 BC in Athens and won first prize at the City DIONYSIA. Often considered the profoundest of all tragic works, *The Oresteia* has many complex themes, but concentrates particularly on guilt and its expiation, the conflict between vengeance and justice, and the nature of the relationship between human beings, the gods, and destiny.

In the first play Agamemnon, king of Argos, returns home from the Trojan War to be murdered by his wife, Clytemnestra, who has taken a lover. She has sent their infant son, Orestes, into exile but in the *Choephoroi* he returns as a young man to avenge his father. The pivotal moment in the trilogy occurs when Orestes has to choose between avenging his father by committing the heinous crime of matricide, or letting his father remain unavenged, an equally grave offence. A stunning theatrical innovation was deployed by Aeschylus at this point. In all previous Greek tragedies the hero was attended by a mute companion figure, and Aeschylus uses this character (who speaks only four lines in the play) to advise Orestes. Orestes kills his mother but is pursued by the Furies, who demand that she, in turn, be avenged. In the *Eumenides* Orestes pleads before the Athenian court, the Areopagus, to be released from his guilt. Eventually the goddess Athena acquits him, breaking the cycle of vengeance.

Orpheus. ***Orpheus Descending*** A tragedy by Tennessee WILLIAMS. Originally written as *Battle of Angels* in 1940, it was reworked for production on Broadway in 1957. The play was later made into a heavily bowdlerized film.

The plot is a loose reworking of the legend of Orpheus, the poet-musician who descended into the infernal regions to rescue his wife, Eurydice, but lost her for a second time when he turned to look back. After his return to earth, he was torn to pieces by a mob of Bacchantes. The play's Orpheus figure is Val Xavier, a drifting guitarist who runs out of money in a small town in the South. He is taken on at the general store by Lady Torrance, whose husband, Jabe, is dying of cancer. Val finds several eager admirers amongst the town's women but maintains his distance from all except Lady, with whom he begins a love affair. The sheriff, who wrongly suspects Val of trying to seduce his wife, orders him out of town. Before he can leave, however, Lady discovers that she is pregnant by him – and also that her husband had helped to murder her father. Lady begs Val to stay until she has had revenge on her husband by watching his slow death. Jabe, however, finds them together and kills Lady, before running into the street to accuse Val of the murder. The sheriff hunts down Val who is carried away to his death by an angry mob.

Orpheus of Highwaymen A name bestowed on the English playwright John Gay (1685–1732) on account of his BEGGAR'S OPERA (1728).

> I have been told of an ingenious observation of Mr Gibbon, that *The Beggar's Opera*

may, perhaps, have sometimes increased the number of highwaymen: but that it has had a beneficial effect in refining that class of men, making them less ferocious, more polite, – in short, more like gentlemen." Upon this, Mr Courtenay said that "Gay was the Orpheus of Highwaymen."
JAMES BOSWELL: *Life of Samuel Johnson* (1791).

Orton, Joe (John Kingsley Orton; 1933–67) British playwright noted for his black comedies, which combine genteel dialogue with violent and shocking action. Orton left home at 16 to train as an actor. His subversive style of humour first revealed itself in a bizarre incident in 1962, when he and his lover, Kenneth Halliwell, were gaoled for defacing library books. The two had carefully removed jacket blurbs from middlebrow novels and substituted their own, mostly scatological, counterfeits. Orton's best-known works are ENTERTAINING MR SLOANE (1964), LOOT (1966), a satire on the genre of detective fiction in which much of the comedy revolves around a corpse, and WHAT THE BUTLER SAW, a farce about a deranged psychiatrist that was first produced in 1969, with Ralph Richardson in the lead.

Orton was a flamboyant homosexual in a period before the liberalization of the British law, and this side of his life is described graphically in his posthumously published diaries. He was battered to death by Halliwell (who subsequently committed suicide) during a domestic argument in 1967.

Osborne, John (James) (1929–94) British playwright and actor, who became the leading representative of the so-called ANGRY YOUNG MEN of the 1950s. Osborne's LOOK BACK IN ANGER (1956), the first of his plays to be accepted for production, ushered in a new era in British theatre with its attacks on conventional middle-class values and its vituperative antihero, Jimmy PORTER. The forerunner of many so-called KITCHEN SINK dramas, it provided the English Stage Company at the ROYAL COURT THEATRE with one of its greatest triumphs. Although the initial notices were indifferent, *The Observer*'s Kenneth TYNAN wrote a powerful review in which he said he would be unable to love anyone who did not wish to see it. Both Osborne and *Look Back in Anger* leapt to fame overnight. Osborne consolidated his success with THE ENTERTAINER (1957), about a seedy music-hall comedian, Archie RICE, which was first produced with Olivier in the role. This, too, was highly praised and like his first play now forms part of the Eng. Lit. school syllabus. Among the plays that followed, the best received have been LUTHER (1961), INADMISSIBLE EVIDENCE (1964), *The Hotel in Amsterdam* (1968), and A PATRIOT FOR ME (1969). In the 1970s, however, such plays as *West of Suez* (1971) and *A Sense of Detachment* (1973) failed to please either audiences or critics. Osborne had no new play produced on the British stage between the failure of *Watch It Come Down* (1975) and the premiere of *Déjà Vu* (1992), a sequel to *Look Back in Anger* that looks at Jimmy Porter 35 years after his first appearance. The first production of *Déjà Vu* was postponed for several months following a bitter dispute between Osborne and Peter O'Toole, who was to have played Porter.

Osborne also wrote for television and the cinema, winning an Oscar for his screenplay for *Tom Jones* (1964). He produced two volumes of autobiography: *A Better Class of Person* (1981) deals with his early life and draws a deeply hostile picture of his mother, while *Almost a Gentleman* (1991) has been described by a critic as "dancing on the graves" of his two deceased wives, the actresses Mary Ure and Jill Bennett.

Ostrovsky, Aleksandr Nikolaevich (1823–86) Russian dramatist, considered by many the virtual founder of the Russian theatre. Ostrovsky wrote some 47 plays which, at the time, constituted a large proportion of the Russian theatrical repertoire. Most of these were first produced under his personal supervision at the Maly Theatre in Moscow, which became known as the HOUSE OF OSTROVSKY.

The son of a government clerk, Ostrovsky studied law at the University of Moscow; after failing an examination he obtained employment as a clerk at the Moscow juvenile court. Ostrovsky was dismissed from this post, however, following the publication of his second play, THE BANKRUPT (1848), which exposed dubious business practices. *The Bankrupt*, revised two years later as *It's a Family Affair, We'll Settle It Among Ourselves*, was considered to be an insult to the Russian merchant classes and was banned by the censor, production not being allowed for over a decade. As a result of this debacle and a rather indiscreet affair with an actress, Ostrovsky's family deprived him of all financial support.

However, after the popular success of his comedy *Poverty is No Disgrace* in 1853, Ostrovsky enjoyed an unrivalled position in Russian drama, which continued until his death. Other notable works include the domestic tragedy THE STORM (1860), *The Scoundrel* (1868), *The Forest* (1870), and *The Snow Maiden* (1873), which provided the basis for an opera by Rimski-Korsakov. His plays, which are realistic in style, are set almost exclusively amongst the merchant class.

The year before his death Ostrovsky was appointed the artistic director of all the imperial theatres in Moscow.

Othello SHAKESPEARE's tragedy of the Moorish general who "loved not wisely but too well." It was written in about 1602 and first performed in 1604. Shakespeare based the play on a story in IL CINTHIO's *Hecatommithi* (1595), but made important changes to both plot and characterization.

As the play begins we learn that the Black Othello, a general in the Venetian army, has secretly married Desdemona, the daughter of a senator. The main action of the play, which occurs in Cyprus, depicts the destruction of this relationship through the plotting of Othello's trusted ensign Iago, a consummate hypocrite whose malevolence is never adequately accounted for. Iago's insinuations that Desdemona is having an affair with Cassio, another officer, appear to receive support when one of her handkerchiefs is found in Cassio's possession. Further prompting from Iago leads Othello, now reduced to a state of psychotic jealousy, to smother Desdemona in bed. When the lie is revealed, Othello commits suicide.

The demanding roles of Othello and Iago have boosted or bedevilled many careers. The most famous Othello of the 19th century was Edmund KEAN, who enjoyed his first triumph in the role at Drury Lane in 1814. During a later performance in the part at Covent Garden in 1833, he collapsed into the arms of his son Charles (who was playing Iago), dying two months later. In 1937 a production boasting Ralph RICHARDSON as Othello and Laurence OLIVIER as Iago proved a surprise flop. Following the performance, Richardson is reported to have paced back and forth in the corridor asking, "Has anyone seen my talent? It was always small, but it used to be shining."

On another occasion, Olivier was playing Othello at an open-air theatre in America when a woman called at his portable dressing room during the interval to ask for directions to the exit. When Olivier asked why she was leaving so early, the lady shrugged: "Frankly, I saw it years ago back in Brooklyn. It was in Yiddish and it hurts me to hear how much it loses in translation."

In 1951 Orson WELLES made his London debut playing Othello in a production that he also directed. The critic T. C. Worsley wrote that Welles "gave off an aura of terror such as I have seen no actor before produce." Kenneth Tynan, however, commented "Welles's Othello is the lordly and mannered performance we saw in *Citizen Kane* slightly adapted to read *Citizen Coon.*" Welles also released a film version in 1955.

Three Black US actors have proved particularly outstanding in the role of Othello. Ira Aldridge, the so-called African ROSCIUS, played the part in his London debut in 1826. Paul ROBESON starred with Peggy Ashcroft in a 1930 production of the play at the Savoy Theatre, leading to an off-stage love affair between the two. In 1945 Robeson enjoyed a run of 295 performances in the part on Broadway, a record for a US production of a Shakespeare play. More recently James Earl JONES was praised for his Othello in two productions (in 1964 and 1981).

Despite its acknowledged greatness, the play has often induced a queasy reaction in critics and audiences – partly because of the squalor of the tragedy but partly, no doubt, because of its affront to racial and sexual sensitivities. In the late 17th century the critic Thomas Rymer denounced the play as a barbarous farrago, valuable only as "a warning to all good wives that they look well to their linen." A later critic, S. T. Coleridge, proved to his own satisfaction that Othello was not really Black. To avoid the strictures of Puritans, when the play was staged in Newport, Rhode Island in 1761, it was advertised as "Moral Dialogues in Five Parts, Depicting the evil effect of jealousy...and proving that happiness can only spring from the pursuit of virtue." *See also* GREEN-EYED MONSTER.

Otway, Thomas (1652–85) English playwright best known for *Venice Preserv'd; or, A*

Plot Discovered (1682), one of the very few Restoration tragedies still staged. Dryden wrote a prologue for the play and was lavish in his praise:

> Nature is there, which is the greatest beauty.

Although many of the finest British actors of the 18th and 19th centuries appeared in *Venice Preserv'd*, the first 20th-century presentation was not until 1953, when John GIELGUD and Paul Scofield appeared in Peter Brook's production at the Lyric, Hammersmith. The production lost money, however, and critic Kenneth TYNAN complained:

> The play's major flaw is that Otway allows Jaffier far too much self-pity, a mood of which John Gielgud as an actor is far too fond. The temptation sometimes proves too much for him: inhaling passionately through his nose, he administers to every line a tremendous parsonical quiver.

The son of a vicar, Otway left Oxford without a degree. He made only one appearance as an actor, in Aphra Behn's *The Forced Marriage* in 1670. His first play to be produced was the rhyming tragedy *Alcibiades*, staged in 1675 at Dorset Garden. It starred Thomas Betterton and Elizabeth Barry, with whom Otway was in love. Otway's greatest success in his own lifetime was *The Cheats of Scapin*, an adaptation of Molière's farce *Les Fourberies de Scapin*, first presented in 1676 as an AFTERPIECE to his *Titus and Berenice*. In 1678 he was serving in an English regiment in the Netherlands when his comedy *Friendship in Fashion* was produced in London. After his return to London in 1679, Otway fought a duel with John Churchill, later Duke of Marlborough, without harm to either party. Later plays included *The Orphan; or, The Unhappy Marriage*, a domestic tragedy starring Betterton and Mrs Barry, and the comedy *The Soldier's Fortune*, both of which were produced in 1680.

Despite his fame, Otway spent the last years of his life in great poverty. According to Theophilus Cibber in his *Lives of the Poets* (1753), he died after ravenously eating a bread roll bought with money donated by a compassionate stranger.

OUDS Oxford University Dramatic Society. An amateur theatre club founded in 1885 by a group of Oxford undergraduates that included Arthur Bourchier, who would later become manager of the Garrick Theatre. Until 1939 female roles were always played by professional actresses. The society is respected for its presentations of Shakespeare and other classics, which are often directed by professionals. OUDS is now based in the renovated Oxford Playhouse, which reopened in 1992.

Early OUDS productions had their share of mishaps. During a performance of Shakespeare's *King John* in 1891, the combined British and French armies (60 performers) were trapped on stage when a drawbridge would not lower. Later in the play the actors playing King John and King Philip became hooked together by their chain armour during their quarrel scene and had to leave the stage like Siamese twins.

Our Town Thornton WILDER's Pulitzer-Prize-winning play about smalltown America, first performed on Broadway in 1938. *Our Town* takes a somewhat nostalgic look at everyday life in the small community of Grovers Corner, New Hampshire, at the turn of the century. The style contains elements of expressionism. A 'stage manager' guides the audience through the action, explaining and commenting upon events and relationships, whilst also participating in the action.

The plot revolves around the romance of Emily Webb and George Gibbs. Wilder uses flashbacks to show the daily existence of the Webb and Gibbs families together with their friends and neighbours. The youthful love of Emily and George matures into a happy marriage that ends with her death in childbirth. At the funeral Emily's spirit appears and desperately tries to convey her past happinesses to her mother. When this fails, Emily returns to the grave despairing at the way in which most people allow the joys of life to pass them by.

Oxford. Oxford Music Hall The first purpose-built London music hall. It was opened in 1861 by Charles MORTON in an old galleried tavern at the corner of Oxford Street and Tottenham Court Road. Early bills offered a mixture of music and slapstick comedy. The Oxford remained one of the leading music halls despite increasing competition and destructive fires in 1868 and 1872. George Robey made his West End debut there in 1891. Two years later a new hall was built on the site, opening with such top names as Marie Lloyd, Bessie Bellwood, and Harry

Champion. The Scottish comedian Harry Tate made his first London appearance there in 1895.

Serious drama first appeared on the Oxford stage in 1906, when the Italian actress Eleonore Duse starred in Ibsen's *Ghosts*. In 1917 Charles Cochran presented Bruce Bairnsfather's play *The Better 'Ole*, based on his famous World War I cartoon. The venue was renamed the New Oxford Theatre in 1920, reopening with the Dolly Sisters in *The League of Notions*. In 1924 the Old Vic Company presented a season of Shakespeare under the direction of Robert Atkins. Two years later the Oxford closed and the site became a Lyons' Corner House.

Oxford's Men The name of two early English theatre companies, both of which became embroiled in controversy. The first was formed in about 1492 from the household of the Earl of Oxford. In 1547 the company caused outrage when it performed in Southwark while a dirge was being sung in a nearby church for Henry VIII. The first company disbanded in 1562 and it was not until 1580 that a new troupe was formed under the patronage of the 17th Earl of Oxford, Edward de Vere (a minor poet believed by some to have been the true author of Shakespeare's plays: *see* BACONIAN THEORY). Later that year the players were banished to the provinces after becoming involved in a brawl at the THEATRE. In 1584 boys from Oxford's Men played at BLACKFRIARS with members of other BOY COMPANIES. The company disbanded in 1602.

Oxford University Dramatic Society *See* OUDS.

P

P. ***The Four Ps*** A "merry interlude" by John Heywood, written *c.* 1520. The four principal characters, a Palmer, a Pardoner, a Potticary (apothecary), and a Pedlar, have a dispute as to which of them can tell the greatest lie. When the Palmer says he has never seen a woman out of patience the other three concede defeat, declaring that such falsehood cannot possibly be outdone. The piece is considered an important link between the medieval and Elizabethan dramas. *See* INTERLUDE.

The Five Ps William Oxberry (1784–1824) was so called, because he was Player, Printer, Poet, Publisher, and Publican. He published the *Dramatic Mirror* and wrote the farce *The Actress of All Work* (1819). His son, William Henry Oxberry (1808–52), was also an actor, playwright, and publisher.

Pace-Egg Play *See* MUMMERS' PLAY *under* MUMMER.

pageant Originally, a cart that served as a movable stage for the presentation of medieval religious dramas. The lower half of the wagon usually served as a dressing room. In the Tudor and Elizabethan period the term was applied to both the wood or canvas stages used for MASQUES and the permanent stages developed for royal visits or ceremonies.

The modern sense of the word developed by association. During the later medieval period it came to be applied to a secular festivity organized by a town guild and consisting of a procession of decorated carts. London's prime surviving example is the Lord Mayor's Show, in which the Lord Mayor's horse-drawn carriage is accompanied by a procession of vehicles decorated to illustrate various themes.

In the early 1900s open-air patriotic and civic festivals known as pageants became popular in both Britain and America. These historical celebrations were usually performed by local townspeople directed by professionals. Some theatres also presented pageants depicting their own histories, such as the 1918 Pageant of DRURY LANE.

pageant lantern In stage lighting, a spotlight or footlight unit that produces a narrow beam. The usual US term is a **projector unit**.

Pakhomushka A type of Russian farce acted by amateurs at parties, celebrations, and other social gatherings. Performances are usually impromptu, with the props and costumes being selected from whatever is available. The main characters are the idiot Pakhomushka, who has a humped back and fanged teeth, and his wife Pakhomikha, whom he has sexually deprived. The plot involves the cuckolding of Pakhomushka and his subsequent revenge. At one point in the performance a male actor usually selects a 'bride' from the women in the audience, who must then go through a sham marriage and wedding night. This always produces witty sexual banter between the actors and members of the audience.

Pala An Indian theatrical genre that honours the deity Satyapir, who is worshipped by Hindus in the eastern state of Orissa. There are two traditional styles of performance, one in which the actors are seated and one in which they stand dressed in royal attire. Groups of *Pala* players sometimes compete for prizes.

The *Pala* is performed in any suitable open space. The *gayaka*, or chief player (who hold a yak's-tail fly whisk and plays small bell-metal cymbals), explains the songs in the audience's local language. Other players make up the chorus.

Palace Theatre. Palace Theatre, London A theatre in Cambridge Circus, London. It was opened in 1891 by Richard D'OYLY CARTE as the Royal English Opera House; the first work to be staged was Arthur Sullivan's romantic opera *Ivanhoe*. Following a string of commercial failures, D'Oyly Carte's dream of a London opera house came to an abrupt end in 1892, when the theatre was sold and renamed the Palace Theatre of Varieties.

Stars to appear at the Palace included Marie TEMPEST, who performed in variety in 1906, and Maud Allan, who shed a series of white veils in what was then considered an erotic ballet, *The Vision of Salome*. Anna Pavlova, the Russian ballerina, made her London debut there in 1910. The following year the theatre acquired its present name and hosted the first of the Royal Command Variety Performances.

Since the success in 1925 of *No, No, Nanette* starring Binnie Hale, which ran for 655 performances, the Palace has specialized in musicals. During World War II Cicely Courtneidge appeared with Jack Hulbert in several musical comedies, while subsequent offerings have included *The Song of Norway* (1946), Ivor Novello's *King's Rhapsody* (1949), and *The Sound of Music*, which ran from 1961 until 1967. Andrew Lloyd Webber and Tim Rice's *Jesus Christ Superstar* logged 3357 performances between 1971 and 1980. The Royal Shakespeare Company's *Les Misérables* transferred from the Barbican Theatre in 1985 and was still running in 1993.

Palace Theatre, New York A Broadway theatre, the legendary Mecca for VAUDEVILLE performers for two decades. The ultimate ambition of every US variety act was to 'play the palace!' The 1800-seat theatre was built and opened in 1913 by Martin Beck, manager of the Orpheum circuit.

In 1931 the comedians Eddie Cantor and George Jessel teamed up for a record run of nine weeks, returning to top the bill in 1937. One evening during a routine together Cantor told an ad-lib joke that drew a great laugh. Jessel quickly topped him and Cantor, at a loss for words, took off his shoe and thumped Jessel on the head: it got the evening's biggest laugh. Jessel walked to the footlights and announced:

> Ladies and Gentlemen, this so-called grown-up man, whom I have the misfortune to be working with, is so lacking in decorum, breeding, and intelligence that, when he was unable to think of a clever retort, he had to descend to the lowest form of humour by taking off his shoe and striking me on the head. Only an insensitive oaf would sink so low.

Cantor strolled over and hit Jessel on the head again.

By 1942 the Palace had begun to combine filmed newsreels and cartoons with live performances and later that year became a cinema. Vaudeville's domination of US entertainment ended that night. The Palace briefly became a burlesque house, returned just as briefly to vaudeville in 1950, then converted in 1965 into a 1358-seat theatre for musical comedy. Subsequent productions include Neil Simon's *Sweet Charity* (1966), Betty Comden and Adolph Green's *Applause* (1970), a revival of Rodgers and Hammerstein's *Oklahoma!*, and Peter Stone's *Woman of the Year* (1981).

Pal Joey A musical by Richard Rodgers and Lorenz Hart, notable for being the first work in the genre to take a bad character as its 'hero'. Rodgers claimed that *Pal Joey* had finally forced the musical comedy theatre to "wear long pants". It was first performed in New York in 1940 at the Ethel Barrymore Theatre, when it launched Gene Kelly to stardom. The show was even more successful in a 1952 Broadway revival. Frank Sinatra starred in the film version (1957). In 1980 the London FRINGE THEATRE company, New Half Moon, staged a revival that transferred to the Albery Theatre.

The story concerns Joey (Evans), a disreputable nightclub dancer, who tries to seduce the young and naive Linda English by promising to write a book about her. However, the fickle Joey is soon distracted by Vera Simpson, a rich married woman, who sets him up in an expensive apartment and opens a nightclub named after him. Eventually both Vera and Linda realize they are being duped and together plot revenge. Joey, having overheard the plan, suddenly disappears from their lives.

The songs, with music by Rodgers and lyrics by Hart, include 'I Could Write a Book', 'That Terrific Rainbow', and 'Do It the Hard Way'.

Palladium The name by which the London Palladium Theatre is usually known. In this Soho theatre, top stars from both sides of the Atlantic have performed in VARIETY; they include Max Miller, Frankie Howerd, Ken Dodd, Judy Garland, Liza Minnelli, Bing Crosby, Danny Kaye, Bob Hope, and Jack Benny. The theatre became a household word in the 1960s with the popular TV variety show, 'Sunday Night at the London Palladium'. It has often been the venue for the Royal Variety Show. The critic Alan

Brien once described it as the only London theatre that Bertolt BRECHT would have enjoyed.

The Palladium was built in Argyll Street in 1910 by the circus manager Charles Hengler, who had staged his Grand Cirque on the site since 1871. He named the theatre on the false assumption that the Palladium of classical legend (a statue of Pallas Athena removed from Troy by the victorious Greeks) was a circus like the Roman Colosseum.

The theatre had the largest seating capacity in London (2306) and drew big audiences for its revues, variety bills, and musicals. Its first great success was *The Whirl of the World* (1924), with the comedienne Nellie Wallace. The CRAZY GANG first appeared together in a show at the Palladium in 1932. Barrie's PETER PAN was presented every Christmas from 1930 to 1938. The musical *Barnum* (1981) had the longest run in the theatre's history and was also the show carrying the highest insurance (£5 million) in British history. Its star, Michael Crawford, who had to walk the high wire and slide down a rope from the theatre's highest box, was himself insured for £3 million. A revival of Lionel Bart's *Oliver!* opened in 1994 and was still running more than two years later.

palliata A form of Roman comedy that used plots taken from Greek NEW COMEDY of the 4th and 3rd centuries BC. The actors wore the *pallium*, a type of Greek cloak, and the characters were given Greek names. The action was always set in the street. The leading exponents of the *palliata* were TERENCE, Caecilius Statius, and PLAUTUS, who adapted the form to give it a more Roman flavour. The *palliata* seems to have died out around the beginning of the first century BC.

Palmer, John *See* PLAUSIBLE JACK.

Pandora's Box A play by Frank WEDEKIND; written in 1894, it was first performed in 1905 in Vienna with his wife Tilly Newes (1886–1970) in the leading role. It was a sequel to EARTH SPIRIT, which introduced the beautiful and promiscuous *femme fatale* Lulu. *Pandora's Box* depicts her total ruin and eventual murder. Denounced at the time as pornographic, it is now more frequently criticized for misogyny. The two stories were combined in Alban Berg's opera *Lulu* in 1937 and again in 1970 by the British dramatist Peter Barnes, whose *Lulu* opened at the Nottingham Playhouse with Julia Foster in the title role and transferred to the Royal Court Theatre, London.

Pandora's Box begins with Lulu, who has been imprisoned for killing a lover, escaping with the help of the lesbian Countess Geschwitz. Once outside, Lulu seduces her dead lover's son and moves to Paris, where she survives relationships with several unsavoury men, including her father, an incestuous pimp. She agrees to sleep with him again if he will kill one of her lovers of whom she has grown tired. Having moved on to London, Lulu goes on the streets, where she and the countess are murdered by one of her clients, Jack the Ripper.

Panjandrum A nonsense character created by Samuel Foote, the so-called ENGLISH ARISTOPHANES, as part of a challenge to test the memory of the actor Charles MACKLIN. In 1755 Foote responded to a boast by Macklin that he could remember any speech perfectly after hearing it once by composing a piece beginning: "So she went into the garden to cut a cabbage leaf to make an apple pie; and at the same time a great she-bear, coming up the street, pops its head into the shop – What! no soap? So he died and she very impudently married the barber; and there were present the Picninnies, and the Joblillies, and the Garyalies, and the grand Panjandrum himself, with the little round button at top..." Unsurprisingly Macklin had to concede defeat; indeed, it is said that he was so indignant at the nonsense that he refused to repeat a word of it. The phrases "no soap" and "the grand Panjandrum" have since entered the language.

Panopticon of Science and Art *See* ALHAMBRA.

panorama A background scene painted on a long piece of canvas that is unrolled from one side of the stage to the other, thus giving the impression of motion to a stationary vehicle, etc., by presenting a changing landscape. *See also* CYCLORAMA; DIORAMA.

Pantaloon A lean and foolish old Venetian merchant with a large nose in the 16th-century COMMEDIA DELL'ARTE. His name, originally Pantalone, is said to come from San Pantaleone, the patron saint of physicians, who was very popular in Venice. In the later HARLEQUINADES and PANTOMIMES the character is the father of Columbine and fiercely opposed to her association with Harlequin.

He is the main butt of the clown's jokes. Pantaloons, a type of trousers, and pants both get their name from the character, who always dressed in loose trousers and slippers.

pantomime An English theatrical form that developed from the HARLEQUINADE in the 18th century. It was also influenced by the 18th-century French *ballets-pantomimes*, which were distantly related to a Roman tradition called pantomime consisting of a dumb show performed by a single masked dancer (*see* PANTOMIMUS). The development of pantomime as a distinct form owed much to the famous harlequin, John Rich (*see* RICH FAMILY), who emphasized the comic aspects of the Harlequinade in his productions. In the early 19th century the genre was transformed by Joseph GRIMALDI, who introduced many of its now-established conventions.

Traditionally, pantomime is a Christmas entertainment, intended particularly for children. The sketchy plots, which are usually based loosely on fairy tales, are embellished with music, dancing, TRANSFORMATION SCENES, slapstick, audience participation, and topical references. A woman in tights usually plays the part of the PRINCIPAL BOY, while a man plays the part of the DAME. Today professional productions are usually spectacular affairs, with leading TV personalities and comedians playing the main roles.

Popular traditional pantomimes include ALADDIN, ALI BABA, CINDERELLA, JACK AND THE BEANSTALK, and Dick WHITTINGTON.

pantomimus In ancient Rome, a masked performer in dumb shows. The name means 'imitating everything'. Making stylized movements and gestures to a musical accompaniment, he played all the roles of the short scene himself, wearing a different mask for each character. A chorus explained the story, usually drawn from mythology or history, in Greek. The librettos were sometimes written by such distinguished poets as Lucan and Statius.

These dances, known as *fabulae salticae*, were introduced in about 22 BC by Pylades of Cilicia and Bathyllus of Alexandria. One exceptional *pantomimus*, Paris, was executed by NERO, who had became jealous of his popularity. The Church was later outspoken in its condemnation of the audacious and often seductive dance of the *pantomimus*; St Augustine considered it more corrupting than the circus, although the dances were never as obscene as the Roman MIME.

paper. Paper Boys' Play *See* MUMMERS' PLAY *under* MUMMER.

paper the house, to In theatrical jargon, to fill empty seats with DEAD-HEADS, or non-paying spectators, admitted by paper orders.

Papp, Joseph (Joseph Papirofsky; 1921–91) US director and producer, who founded the New York Shakespeare Festival in 1954 and the PUBLIC THEATRE in 1987. A leading figure in US drama for nearly 40 years, he enjoyed successes ranging from *Hamlet* to HAIR.

Papp's first shows were produced on board an aircraft carrier that toured the Pacific during World War II. The New York Shakespeare Festival, with which his name will always be associated, began life at the Emanuel Presbyterian Church on East 6th Street, with most of the actors performing for no fee. In 1957 it moved to the open-air Belvedere Lake Theatre in Central Park and five years later to the open-air Delacorte Theatre, on the west side of the park, given by the city as a permanent home for Papp's summer 'Shakespeare in the Park'. In 1971 Papp produced an acclaimed musical version of *Two Gentlemen of Verona*, which won the Tony Award as Best Musical. At the same time, he developed an offshoot group, the Mobile Theatre, which took plays to people throughout New York's boroughs.

Papp's Public Theatre company gave its first performance at the Anspacher Theatre in the outrageous hippy musical *Hair*, which ran for 1750 performances. Another great success was Jason Miller's *That Championship Season*, which won the New York Critics Circle Award as the Best Play of 1972 and transferred to Broadway. The following year Papp became director of the Vivian Beaumont Theatre and the Mitzi E. Newhouse Theatre at New York's LINCOLN CENTER, but left after a financial crisis. By 1980 money problems also dogged the Shakespeare Festival and that year it staged only one production, an updated version of Gilbert and Sullivan's *The Pirates of Penzance*. It was a hit, moving to the Uris Theatre for a long run and then finding equal success in London (despite the horror of traditionalists). The city of New York responded by giving the Festival a permanent subsidy, making it both a private and public enterprise. In the later 1980s Papp began to feature television and film stars in his Shakespearean productions, which had already drawn such names as Julie Harris and Colleen Dewhurst.

Pappus A stock character of an old man in the Roman ATELLANA farces of the 1st century BC. He was probably presented as incompetent and gullible.

parade In 18th-century France, a brief sketch presented by fairground actors to lure spectators into their booths. *Parades* were also acted on the first-floor balcony of the Théâtre de la Foire Saint-Germain. The sketches combined elements of the COMMEDIA DELL'ARTE and of medieval French farce. They disappeared along with the fair booths in the middle of the 18th century. The genre was revived later in the century by BEAUMARCHAIS and continued into the 19th century in the repertoire of such performers as BOBÈCHE AND GALIMAFRÉ at the Boulevard du Temple.

paradiso A piece of stage machinery consisting of a copper dome in which saints, angels, and other heavenly beings were raised and lowered over the stage. The device was invented by Filippo Brunelleschi (1377–1446) for the annual Annunciation play in Florence's church of San Felice. A group of choir boys, representing angels, and an actor playing the archangel Gabriel were suspended in the *paradiso* and lowered by crane to a platform from which the actor recited his part before being lifted back to heaven. The device remained in use until the late 18th century. *See also* GLORY.

parallel *See* ROSTRUM.

Paris-Garden A famous Tudor bull-BAITING and bear-baiting garden in Bankside, in the London borough of Southwark. It was established on the site of a house owned by Robert de Paris, who held the manor in the reign of Richard II. In about 1595 the SWAN Theatre was erected on the site and, in 1613, this was replaced by the HOPE. The name Paris-Garden was sometimes used to mean any noisy or disorderly place.

> Do you take the court for Paris-garden?
> SHAKESPEARE: *Henry VIII* (V, iv).

Park Theatre A New York theatre opened by William DUNLAP and John Hodgkinson in 1798; the first production was Shakespeare's *As You Like It*. The theatre's early success was largely owing to appearances by Thomas Cooper, an English-born actor who had come over in the troupe hired by Thomas Wignell for the CHESTNUT STREET THEATRE. In 1805, however, the managers fell out and Hodgkinson resigned. Dunlap continued for a year but went bankrupt and was replaced by Cooper.

The Park Theatre began to flourish again when Stephen Price took over its management in 1808. A year later he produced the first US play with a Native American theme, *The Indian Princess; or, La Belle Sauvage* by J. N. Barker. The theatre burned down in 1820 just as Edmund Kean was due to appear. After it was rebuilt the following year, it became the most distinguished venue in the country, earning the nickname 'Old Drury of America'. Despite such later successes as Boucicault's *London Assurance* in 1841 and a production of *Macbeth* featuring Charles Macready in 1843, the theatre went into decline after Price's death in 1840. Thomas Hamblin rented and redecorated it in 1848 but three months later it burned down and was never rebuilt.

parlyaree In the 18th and 19th centuries, an Italian-based language used as the lingua franca of non-legitimate theatrical performers. Early users of the language were circus artists and other performers whose work involved foreign tours. In the mid- to late-19th century the language became current in the underworld and the homosexual community. Since the early 1970s *polari* has been a term for gay slang and it is possible that the two words are connected. Although parlyaree became fairly widespread it never achieved respectability.

parody In drama, as in literature and the other arts, a work or part of a work that mimics in a humorous and distorted way the style of an author or genre. The word comes from the Greek *paroidiā*, meaning a song that mocks another song.

Examples survive from the earliest days of the theatre. Aristophanes parodied both Aeschylus and Euripides, making the two great tragedians compete against each other in his comedy THE FROGS (405 BC). *The Second Shepherd's Play* of the medieval Towneley mystery cycle contains a parody of the Nativity scene, in which a stolen sheep is disguised as a baby. The heroic dramas of the 17th and 18th century were parodied in

Buckingham's THE REHEARSAL (1671) and Sheridan's THE CRITIC (1779), as well as in numerous BURLESQUE plays. Gay's THE BEGGAR'S OPERA (1723) parodied the fashionable operas of his day. Modern examples include Tom Stoppard's *The Real Inspector Hound* (1968), which sends up the conventions of the murder mystery, and Michael Frayn's *Noises Off* (1982), which parodies bedroom farce.

Several passages in Shakespeare reveal him as a master of linguistic parody. In the play-within-a-play in *A Midsummer Night's Dream* (*see* PYRAMUS AND THISBE) he burlesques the exaggerated rant of much Elizabethan tragedy:

O grim-look'd night! O night with hue
so black!
O night, which ever art when day is not!
O night! O night! alack, alack, alack,
I fear my Thisbe's promise is forgot!

Parolles A comic character in Shakespeare's ALL'S WELL THAT ENDS WELL. He is a faithless, bragging, slandering rogue who calls himself 'captain', pretends to knowledge that he doesn't have, and to sentiments he never feels. After his exposure and disgrace he comforts himself with the famous line:

Simply the thing I am
Shall make me live.
(IV, iv).

Pasadena Playhouse *See* LITTLE THEATRES *under* LITTLE.

Pasku A PASSION PLAY presented in Sri Lanka. The performances began in the late 19th century in the northern port of Jaffna and then spread throughout the Catholic population. From 1923 onwards K. Lawrence Perera wrote and produced several plays in imitation of the famous OBERAMMERGAU PASSION PLAY. His first piece, the spectacular Shridhara Boralessa Passion Play, used more than 100 villagers and other amateur actors. The venue was constructed like a RUKADA puppet theatre, with a central stage and side wings. Controversy arose in 1939 when it was announced that actresses were to play the female roles, a decision that was reversed after the Archbiship of Colombo banned the performance as a violation of decorum.

The *Pasku*, which is performed in Holy Week, depicts the key episodes in the story of Christ's Crucifixion and Resurrection. Apart from the numerous actors, the performances involve a narrator and the use of life-size effigies, which are dressed in historical costume and arranged to create tableaux. The plays are accompanied by church music.

paso In 16th-century Spanish drama, a short comic interlude performed between the acts of a serious play. The term was first used by Lope de Rueda (1562–1635), the best-known writer of *pasos*, who turned out 19 such pieces. The simple farces relied on familiar low-life characters from the COMMEDIA DELL'ARTE, such as the rustic clown, **Bobo**, and were popular for their quick repartee. The *paso* subsequently developed into the more sophisticated ENTREMÉ. *See also* INTERLUDE; INTERMEZZO.

Pasquin A witty roguish character in 16th and 17th century comedy; also a name adopted by many writers of anonymous lampoons and satires.

The association of the name with satire goes back to the early 16th century. In 1501 an ancient mutilated statue was dug up in Rome and placed near the Piazza Navona. Each St Mark's Day students and others dressed it up to represent some historical figure and placed satirical Latin verses around its base. The statue was given the name Pasquino after a witty schoolmaster (in other accounts a barber or tailor) who had formerly lived nearby.

The first dramatic character to bear the name was Pasquino, one of the ZANNI of the COMMEDIA DELL'ARTE. In 17th century France this character developed into the valet Pasquin, who appears in plays by Destouches (1680–1754) and others. The member of a troupe who specialized in playing the satirical roles in the comedies of Jean-François Regnard and Charles-Rivière Dufresny was often referred to as the 'Pasquin of the Company'.

In the 18th-century English theatre a *pasquinade*, *pasquin*, or *pasquil* was any lampoon or satirical piece. Henry Fielding satirized the government in his play *Pasquin* (1736) and often signed articles and letters 'Mr Pasquin'.

pass door A door linking the auditorium in a theatre with the backstage areas; its use is usually restricted to theatre staff.

Passion play A type of medieval LITURGICAL DRAMA depicting the Passion (sufferings) of Christ from the Last Supper to the placing of his body in the tomb. It was traditionally presented on Good Friday. The earliest Passion plays were performed in church buildings and combined mime with readings from the Bible. Later the plays were staged in the open air.

The play presented at Valenciennes, France, in 1547 provides the earliest record of stage settings for a Passion play; these included city gates, a temple, a dungeon, and the popular Mouth of Hell, with its flames and moving jaws.

The genre remained popular throughout Europe until the Reformation. In Germany the Passion play was given a second lease of life by the Catholic revival in the 16th century. The best-known German example is the OBERAMMERGAU PASSION PLAY, which is still performed once every 10 years.

Passion Play A tragicomedy of marital life by Peter NICHOLS, first performed in London in 1981 by the Royal Shakespeare Company. When Nichols and the director Mike Ockrent squabbled about the staging, the playwright took over the production himself.

In *Passion Play* Nichols uses the unusual device of having the two main characters shadowed by alter egos who voice the true feelings that the characters are repressing.

The play depicts the breakdown of James and Eleanor's marriage after he is seduced by Kate, who is young enough to be his daughter. The couple remain outwardly civil towards each other, but their alter egos reveal their real sentiments. James convinces his wife that he has called the affair off, but she subsequently learns that this is a lie. Thinking that it might help the situation, Kate decides to visit the couple, with the result that she finds herself in love with Eleanor as well as her husband. When Eleanor takes an overdose of pills James nurses her back to health (although his alter ego again reveals his true feelings). Later, he meets Kate at a Christmas party and the two make love – or is this perhaps *her* alter ego?

Pastor, Tony *See* FATHER OF VAUDEVILLE *under* FATHER.

pastoral A genre of drama, popular from the 15th to the 17th centuries, that depicted an innocent rustic world of shepherds and maids. Pastoral drama drew most of its elements from the pastoral poetry of Greek and Roman writers, notably Theocritus and Virgil. The genre developed in Italy and had a lasting influence on the French drama; its impact on theatre in England was more limited.

Although Angelo Poliziano's *Favola d'Orfeo* (1472) and Agostino Beccari's *Il Sacrifizio* (1544) both anticipated the genre, Torquato Tasso's story of rustic love *L'Aminta* (1573) is considered the first important pastoral play. Another significant writer of pastorals was IL CINTHIO, whose most notable work in the genre was the tragicomedy *The Faithful Shepherd* (1598).

Italian pastoral had a major influence on such 17th-century French playwrights as Seigneur de Racan, who enjoyed a great success with *Les Bergeries* (1620), and Jean Mairet, whose *Silvie* (1626) is considered one of the finest of all pastorals. The genre survived into the era of NEOCLASSICAL DRAMA, with Corneille amongst others continuing to present an idealized picture of rural pleasures in his comedies. Mairet's *La Silvanire ou la morte vive* (1630) was the first pastoral to respect the UNITIES.

English pastorals included John Lyly's comedies on mythological subjects, John Fletcher's *The Faithful Shepherdess* (1608), and Shakespeare's AS YOU LIKE IT (1599). Pastoral elements played an important part in the Stuart MASQUES.

Pataphysics The so-called "science of impossible solutions" devised by the French playwright Alfred JARRY. Essentially an anticipation of surrealism and the Theatre of the ABSURD, it is exemplified in Jarry's grotesque farce *Ubu Roi* (*see* UBU, PÈRE).

patch A FOOL. The first to be so-called was Cardinal Wolsey's jester, Sexton, who got his nickname either from the Italian *pazzo*, a fool, or from the motley of patched dress worn by licensed fools.

> What a pied ninny's this! thou scurvy
> patch!
>
> SHAKESPEARE: *The Tempest* (III, ii).

patent theatres The two London theatres, DRURY LANE and COVENT GARDEN, that hold Letters Patent and the title of Theatre Royal, as granted in 1662 by Charles II. The charters, which were intended to revive the English theatre after the Puritan INTERREGNUM, gave a monopoly within the City of Westminster to two managers, Thomas Killigrew of Drury Lane and William Davenant of LINCOLN'S INN FIELDS THEATRE. The Lincoln's Inn charter passed in 1671 to the Dorset Garden Theatre and then in 1732 to the new theatre at Covent Garden.

Restrictions on serious acting in London's other theatres were reaffirmed by the Theatres Act of 1737, but these gradually weakened and were abolished in 1843. Although the Letters Patent made Drury Lane and Covent Garden free of licensing (*see* LICENCE) by the Lord Chamberlain, they were still answerable to censorship until its abolition in 1968. Both theatres are still leased under the terms of the original charters.

Patriot for Me, A John OSBORNE's play about the career of Alfred Redl, a homosexual officer in the Austro-Hungarian Army at the turn of the century. Some critics consider it Osborne's best work. Based on fact, the play describes how Redl was blackmailed into becoming a spy because of his homosexuality. It includes a transvestite ball scene that caused particular offence to the LORD CHAMBERLAIN, who withheld a licence. The play was first performed in 1965 at the ROYAL COURT THEATRE as a club production for the English STAGE SOCIETY. Maximilian Schell created the part of Redl. A successful revival was staged in 1983 at the Haymarket with Alan Bates in the leading role.

patter The running talk of conjurers, entertainers, and comedians, etc. The term derived from Paternoster, i.e. the Lord's Prayer. When saying Mass the priest often recited in a low rapid mechanical way until he came to the words "and lead us not into temptation", which he spoke clearly and deliberately.

pavai. Pavai Kathakali A type of Indian glove-puppet theatre, in which the puppets are designed and decorated to resemble characters of the KATHAKALI dance-drama. Performances are rare and usually held on religious occasions. The puppets stand 12 to 18 inches tall and have wooden heads and hands. They are operated by teams of four or more puppeteers from the village of Kavadi Parambu in the Palghat district. The stories come from the MAHABHARATA and follow its narrative sequence. Musical accompaniment is provided by a drum and bell-metal cymbals.

Pavai Koothu (Tamil. Woman Play) A type of glove-puppet theatre performed in the city of Thiruchendoor, Tamil Nadu, India. It is thought to have originated in the 16th century. The foot-tall puppets have papier-mâché heads and arms and wear simple cloth costumes festooned with paper or coconut fibre. The manipulator sits behind a wooden box that hides him from the audience's view. An *idakka* drummer and a singer provide music selected from regional folk melodies.

The plot concerns Vali, a female attendant of the Hindu god Siva, and her love for his son Subramanya. Vali was born to a deer in the forest and raised by a hunter and his wife. Narada sees her one day in the forest and describes her beauty to Subramanya, who disguises himself as a seller of bangles to enter the hunter's cottage. He lures Vali away and reveals his divine form to her. They embrace with the blessings of Ganesh, the god of good fortune.

Pavaikuthu (Tamil. Figure-of-a-Shadow Play) A type of shadow-puppet theatre from the southern Indian state of Kerala. Also called *tholpavaikuthu*, the genre is based on stories from the *Kambar Ramayana*, a 9th-century Tamil version of the Ramayana. The puppets, which are made of antelope skin, range from 4 to 36 inches high and are held against the screen by a bamboo strip. The main characters have movable heads, arms, and hands.

Performances are given in Tamil although the audiences of the region speak Malayalam. The plays are usually presented in a temple compound as an entertainment for Kali, the Hindu goddess of destruction. The manipulators, who are hidden by a black curtain, operate the puppets in the light from a row of coconut-oil lamps set in coconut halves or earthen vessels.

Peace, The A comedy by ARISTOPHANES, first performed in 421 BC in Athens as an appeal for an end to the Peloponnesian War between Athens and Sparta. The plot concerns a farmer who flies to heaven on a dung-beetle and discovers that Zeus has allowed War to imprison Peace in a cavern. The play was staged a few weeks before the ratification of the peace of Nicias and several months after the deaths of the two main advocates of the war, the Athenian Cleon, whom Aristophanes had abused in *The Knights* (424 BC), and the Spartan Brasidas.

peanut gallery *See* GALLERY.

Pedrolino One of the ZANNI of the COMMEDIA DELL'ARTE. The actor Giovanni Pellesini (1526–1612) created the role of this simple and honest servant who always dressed in white. Later, the actor Giuseppe Giaratone (or Giratoni), who joined the Comédie-Italienne in Paris in 1665, emphasized Pedrolino's naive and awkward qualities, and dressed him in a loose white garment and large floppy hat. In doing so he created the character of PIERROT.

Peer Gynt Henrik IBSEN's fantasy comedy, published in Oslo in 1867. Grieg's incidental music was written for the first performance in 1874. Although a long verse play of considerable complexity, it is still regularly revived. A particularly memorable revival was that given by Ralph Richardson and the Old Vic Company at the New Theatre in 1944.

The title character – a reckless liar and egotist who remains essentially lovable – was based partly on Ibsen's younger self and partly on his perception of the Norwegian national character. The play, which is set mainly in rural Norway, begins with the young Peer boasting about his (imaginary) hunting exploits to his mother, Åsa. When he is slighted by Solveig, the girl who really loves him, Peer abducts another village girl, Ingrid, on her wedding day. Pursued by villagers, they flee to the mountains. After abandoning Ingrid, Peer falls for a mysterious beauty who leads him to the underground kingdom of the trolls; she subsequently bears him a hideous troll baby. In the fourth act Peer, now middle-aged, has drifted to North Africa after making his fortune in the slave trade. He attracts a following by posing as a prophet but then loses everything through his infatuation with a dancing girl. He returns home a saddened old man to find Solveig, now blind, still waiting for him.

Peking Opera The most popular form of drama in China. Although the tradition began in about 740 with the founding of China's first drama school, the Pear Garden, the style did not achieve cultural preeminence until the 19th century.

The plays of the Peking Opera combine dialogue, orchestral music, song, dance, and acrobatics. Works are classified as civil (*weu*) or military (*wu*), with the subject matter drawn from mythology, history, and fiction. The melodramatic stories usually deal with the triumph of good over evil.

The productions are presented on a bare stage, using minimal props and furniture. Some props have traditional symbolic meanings: a table represents a bridge, three chairs indicate a bed, a whip implies a horse, a hat wrapped in red cloth means a decapitated head, and a folded red cloak on the floor is a corpse. Costumes follow similar conventions: emperors wear yellow, important officials wear red, and warriors have magnificent embroidered costumes and impressive headdresses.

There are four traditional types of role: male (*sheng*), female (*dan*), large males with painted faces (*jing*), and comedians (*chou*); until 1911 female roles were taken by men. The most famous female impersonator of modern times was Mei Lan-Fang (1894–1961), whose skill and renown greatly enhanced the importance of the heroine's role. During the Chinese Civil War he refused to act, letting his beard grow in protest.

The actors, who are trained to use very little movement, improvise from an outline script, somewhat in the manner of the European COMMEDIA DELL'ARTE. Their speech is mostly delivered in a falsetto voice accompanied by music. Character is indicated by expressions drawn on the face, by props (such as a fan for frivolity), by colours of dress (blue for good citizens and black for bad ones) or make-up (red for courage, yellow for strength, white for treachery, and blue for ferocity).

In the early 1960s the Peking Opera made a successful tour of Europe and Canada. The Opera, which has resisted radical changes in presentation, recovered quickly after the Cultural Revolution, during which only state-sanctioned dramas on revolutionary themes were permitted.

Pelléas et Mélisande The best-known play by Maurice MAETERLINCK, a pseudo-medieval fantasy first performed in 1893 in Paris. The acknowledged masterpiece of theatrical SYMBOLISM, it was the first play staged by Aurélien-François Lugné-Poë at his Théâtre de l'Oeuvre. Mrs Patrick CAMPBELL played Mélisande in the first London production at the Prince of Wales's Theatre in 1898; she also took the play to New York four years later. J. M. Barrie wrote that "Mrs Campbell is beyond comparison, better than she has ever been in anything else." In the play her jealous husband was played by Mrs Pat's real-life lover Johnston FORBES-ROBERTSON. Fauré later provided INCIDENTAL MUSIC, while Debussy's opera *Pelléas et Mélisande* was first staged in 1902.

Wandering in the forest, Golaud meets and falls in love with the beautiful but enigmatic Mélisande. He marries her and takes her to live in his castle by the sea. However, an intense relationship soon develops between Mélisande and Golaud's younger brother, Pelléas. Conscience stricken, Pelléas bids her farewell for ever, but Golaud, misunderstanding the situation, stabs him to death in a frenzy. Mélisande bears Golaud's child and, forgiving him, dies.

The play is best known for the 1904 French-language production at London's Vaudeville Theatre in which Sarah BERNHARDT, then aged 59, played the youthful Pelléas to Mrs Pat's Mélisande. It was during this production that one of the theatre's longest-running on-stage jokes began. When Mrs Pat complained that a fishpond used in one scene was a shoddy cut-price job compared to that used in the first London production, Bernhardt, piqued at this one-upmanship, arranged for a hideous-looking fish to be placed in the pond; when Mrs Pat bent to gaze dreamily into its depths during the performance, she became helpless with laughter. A year later the two stars took the play on a provincial tour. Mrs Pat, informed that nothing could make Bernhardt laugh on stage, bought a tobacco pouch in the shape of a fish, painted on gills and scales, and tied it to the bottom of the pond. When Bernhardt saw the fish she was unperturbed and bent gracefully down to scoop it out; however, since it was secured firmly to the bottom of the pond, the actress lost her balance and nearly fell in. Neither mentioned the incident after the curtain fell. At the next day's matinée, in a scene in which Bernhardt was required to take Mrs Pat's hand tenderly, the Frenchwoman slipped a raw egg into her palm and squeezed. Mrs Pat continued without a smile, although Bernhardt was shaking with mirth, tears running down her cheeks. During a later performance, when Bernhardt caressed Mrs Pat's hair, the latter used the cover of her long tresses to slip a live goldfish into her partner's hand. Bernhardt continued unperturbed, holding the squirming goldfish for the rest of the tender scene. Again nothing was said.

Pembroke's Men An Elizabethan theatre company formed in about 1592 from the household of the Earl of Pembroke. Shakespeare worked with the company for two years, during which they presented his *Titus Andronicus* (1592), *The Taming of the Shrew* (1593), and *Richard III* (1592–93); he left to join the CHAMBERLAIN'S MEN in 1594. Pembroke's Men also performed Christopher Marlowe's *Edward II* (1593).

In 1597 the company was involved in the production of *The Isle of Dogs*, the 'seditious' play by Ben JONSON and Thomas Nashe that landed the authors in prison and closed the Swan Theatre. It also precipitated the eventual demise of the company, as their actors began to leave for other troupes. Pembroke's Men were last heard of in 1600, when they performed at the Rose Theatre in London.

penny. penny gaff *See* GAFF.

Penny for a Song, A A comedy by the British playwright John Whiting (1917–63), first produced in London by Binkie Beaumont in 1951. The production starred Ronald Squire (as a squire) and Virginia McKenna; costumes and sets were designed by the *Punch* cartoonist Rowland Emett. Despite critical praise, the play was a box-office failure. Whiting revised the text for a successful 1962 production by the Royal Shakespeare Company at the Aldwych Theatre.

A Penny for a Song is a whimsical farce set in Britain during an invasion scare in 1814. When an eccentric squire dresses up as Napoleon to confuse the French army, he is captured by the English Home Guard who believe he is the real thing.

People's National Theatre *See* PRICE, NANCY.

Pepper's Ghost A striking Victorian stage effect used to create the appearance of a ghostly figure on stage. The illusion was the origin of the expression "It's all done with mirrors". Henry Dircks, a retired engineer, was the first to suggest that a piece of glass held at an angle of 45° to the front of the stage could be used to throw the image of an actor concealed in the orchestra pit onto the stage. John Henry Pepper (1821–1900), director of the Royal Polytechnic Institution in London, bought the idea from Dircks in 1862 and renamed it 'The Ghost Illusion'. Dickens used it that Christmas Eve for a dramatic reading of his *The Haunted Man and the Ghost's Bargain* (1848).

Pepper's Ghost, as it became known, first appeared on the professional stage in 1863, when it was used at the Britannia Theatre, London, and at Wallack's Theatre, New York. The effect's novelty value soon wore off, however, mainly because the reflected ghost could not speak and was difficult to position. It survived into the 20th century at provincial fairs, but was superseded on stage by back-lit gauze.

Pepys, Samuel (1633–1703) English diarist and playgoer, whose journal provides a record of London's early Restoration theatre that is both personal and precise. The diary, which he kept from 1660 to 1669, includes notes about the plays he saw as well as backstage gossip and scandals. His sources included Drury Lane's orange seller ORANGE MOLL and the actress Mary Knepp.

Pepys's diary entries also record his observations on the audience and its behaviour. After taking his wife and her maid to a play, he was "a little shamed" that their clothes were not appropriate, "all the ladies being finer and better dressed in the pitt than they used, I think, to be." He often complained about the unruly conduct of other theatregoers: when he saw *Heraclius* at the Duke of York's House (*see* DORSET GARDEN THEATRE) he thought the audience "did so spoil it with their laughing...and with the noise they made within the theatre." On another occasion "a lady spit backward upon me; but after seeing her to be a very pretty lady I was not troubled at it at all."

In 1668 he went to see *The Tempest* at the Duke of York's House.

> But there happened one thing which vexed me, which is that the orange-woman did come in the pit and challenge me for twelve oranges which she delivered by my order at a late play, at night, in order to give to some ladies in a box, which was wholly untrue, but yet she swore it to be true. But, however, I did deny it, and did not pay her; but, for quiet, did buy 4s. worth of oranges of her at 6d. apiece.

Pepys also provided brief personal critiques of the many works he saw. He thought *The Tempest* "no great wit, yet good, above ordinary plays". *The History of Henry the Fifth* by the Earl of Orrery was "full of height and raptures of wit and sense". He found *The Parson's Wedding*, performed by an all female cast, indecent.

Pepys himself appears as a character in at least two plays; Frederick Ranalow played him in *Mr Pepys* (1926) while Leslie Henson took the role in *And So To Bed* (1951).

perch A position for additional lighting units behind the PROSCENIUM ARCH on one side of the stage. Older theatres may have small raised platforms for such units. *See also* MARIONETTE.

Percy, Esmé (Saville) (1887–1957) Eccentric British actor and director, whose glass eye often posed problems for his fellow cast members. Percy trained in Sarah BERNHARDT's company, but she advised him to leave because he was too much like her. The versatility of his voice was extraordinary; he once did a radio version of *Hamlet* in which he played the Ghost, the Player King, and Osric.

In 1913 Percy formed a touring company that specialized in works by Oscar Wilde and George Bernard Shaw. After World War I, he ran a theatre in Cologne for British troops, persuading Mrs Patrick CAMPBELL to appear there as Eliza to his Henry Higgins in *Pygmalion*. As was Mrs Pat's habit, she bullied him mercilessly on stage, telling him in a whisper to hurry up, and then to slow down. She finally gazed in horror at his suede shoes and, turning her back to the audience, growled, "Oh you're quite wrong. He's not that kind of man at all."

Percy subsequently became general producer of the Shaw Repertory Company; one of his most acclaimed roles with the troupe was Dobelle in Denis Johnston's *The Moon in the Yellow River* (1934). He spent the last years of his career with the ENGLISH STAGE COMPANY at the Royal Court Theatre.

Percy was short and plump and had a broken nose as well as the glass eye (replacing the one he lost when attacked by a Great Dane). One night in 1949 the eye fell out during his big scene as Matthew Skipps, a drunken tinker, in Christopher Fry's THE LADY'S NOT FOR BURNING. "We were all too dismayed to move," recalled John Gielgud who was in the cast with Richard BURTON. Percy frantically whispered, "Oh, do be careful, don't tread on it, they cost £8 each." Percy wore a black patch for the subsequent performances.

Perdita In Shakespeare's THE WINTER'S TALE, the daughter of Leontes, King of Sicily. By order of her father, she was abandoned as an infant on "the sea-coast of Bohemia", where she was discovered by a shepherd, who brought her up as his own daughter. In time, Florizel, the son and heir of the Bohemian King Polixenes, fell in love with the supposed shepherdess. The match was forbidden by Polixenes and the young lovers fled to Sicily, where Perdita's true identity was revealed. Finally she is restored to her parents and marries Florizel.

Mary Robinson (1758–1800), the actress and mistress of George IV when Prince of Wales, was specially successful in the part of Perdita, by which name she came to be known (the Prince being known as Florizel).

periaktoi Early scenic devices of the Greek and Roman theatre, probably consisting of painted prisms that were rotated to indicate a change of scene. Each of the surfaces bore a traditional image to suggest a location, such as waves, trees, or the column of a building. They also helped to project sound from the stage.

When details of the *periaktoi* were discovered in the writings of the Roman Marcus Vitruvius Pollio (70–15 BC), architects of the Renaissance theatre adopted and improved the devices under the name of **telari**. Removable canvas panels were introduced for the prism faces.

Pericles, Prince of Tyre A romance by SHAKESPEARE, first performed in 1608 by the King's Men at the GLOBE THEATRE. Although published in 1609 as "the late and much admired Play", it is usually considered one of the least successful of Shakespeare's works. Some scenes may have come from another pen, possibly that of George Wilkins, who in 1608 published *The Painful Adventures of Pericles Prince of Tyre* as "a poor infant of my brain". The uneven quality of the first two acts suggests that the printed version may have been written down by actors from memory.

The story derives from an episode in John Gower's *Confessio Amantis* (1390), and Shakespeare includes "Gower, as Chorus" in the cast. When Pericles, Prince of Tyre, discovers the incestuous secret of Antiochus, the Greek emperor, he takes to the sea to save his own life. Pericles survives a shipwreck to wed Thaisa, daughter of the King of Pentapolis. When Antiochus is killed by a bolt of lightning, Pericles sets sail for home but is again caught in a storm, during which Thaisa gives birth to a baby girl, Marina, and appears to die. She is buried at sea but gets washed ashore and is revived. Believing her husband dead, she enters the service of the Goddess Diana. Marina, now grown up, is captured by pirates and forced into a brothel in Mitylene, where her uncompromising virtue preserves her from would-be seducers. In the last act she is reunited with her father in an intensely moving scene; a vision of Diana finally leads Pericles to Thaisa and the entire family is reunited.

The play, a peculiar mixture of styles and genres, is seldom revived. One memorable production was that presented in 1973 at Her Majesty's Theatre, London, starring Derek Jacobi; this version was also an off-Broadway hit in 1980.

Perish the thought! Do not entertain such an idea for a moment! A quotation from Colley Cibber's version (1700) of Shakespeare's RICHARD III. This version also contains the famous line "Off with his head! So much for Buckingham.", which is often taken as being Shakespeare's own.

Perkins folio *See* OLD CORRECTOR.

Persians, The A tragedy by AESCHYLUS, first performed in Athens in 472 BC. It is the only surviving Greek tragedy to be based on a contemporary historical event, the defeat of the Persians at Salamis in 480 BC. Aeschylus had himself fought against the Persians at Salamis (and at Marathon and Platea). *The Persians* is also unusual amongst Greek tragedies in probably not being part of a TETRALOGY.

The play, set at the palace of Xerxes, the Persian king, begins with the chorus of councillors expressing concern at the lack of news from their expedition against the Greeks. The mother of Xerxes enters to tell them of an ominous dream, and soon a messenger brings news of the defeat. The humiliated Xerxes returns from Salamis, and the spirit of King Darius is called from his tomb to explain the defeat as part of the moral order of Zeus. The play ends with the king and chorus lamenting the Greek victory.

person The word comes from the Latin *persona*, which meant originally a MASK worn by actors (perhaps from *per sonare*, to sound through), and later the character or personage represented by the actor. The word subsequently came to mean any role, function, office, etc., assumed by someone; it had acquired its modern sense of an individual human being by the time it entered English in the 13th century.

Peter Pan A play for children by J. M. BARRIE, first produced in London in 1904 with Nina Boucicault (*see* BOUCICAULT FAMILY) as Peter. The title character is a little boy who never grows up, the leader of the **Lost Boys** of **Never Never Land.**

One night Peter flies in through the nursery window of the Darling family's house to recover his shadow and then flies home to Never Never Land with the Darling children. They are all captured by pirates, except Peter, who manages to secure their release and defeat the villainous Captain Hook. The children return home with their new friend but Peter refuses to stay because he does not want to grow up.

The character of Peter was inspired by the five sons of Barrie's friends Arthur and Sylvia Llewelyn Davies (who appear as Mr and Mrs Darling). Barrie took the Llewelyn Davies boys into his house after the deaths of their parents and explained in the play's dedication "I made Peter Pan by rubbing the five of you violently together, as savages with two sticks produce a flame."

In their later lives, the boys seemed doomed to be haunted by tragedy. In 1915 George died fighting in World War I, while in 1921 Michael drowned in mysterious circumstances in Oxford, possibly in a homosexual suicide pact. Of all the boys, Peter was the one most closely linked with his fictional namesake. He himself was named after the title character of *Peter Ibbetson*, a novel by his grandfather, George Du Maurier. At Eton, his identification with Peter Pan caused him considerable suffering. His life ended tragically in 1960, when – by then a well-known publisher – he threw himself under a train in the London Underground. Michael Llewelyn Davies was the model for Sir George Frampton's statue of Peter Pan in Kensington Gardens, which was placed there by Barrie in 1912. Peter Pan may also have reflected some of Barrie's own problems – notably his impotence and his inability to come to terms with the death of his own brother at the age of 12.

The play is still regularly revived, particularly at Christmas. Barrie arranged for all copyright fees from the play to go to the Great Ormond Street Hospital for Sick Children, London.

Petit-Bourbon, Salle du The first court theatre in Paris, located in the palace of the dukes of Bourbon. It was designed for ballets and balls and first used for professional drama in 1577 by the GELOSI, an Italian *commedia dell'arte* troupe.

From 1645 the famous Italian scene painter and machinist Torelli (*see* GREAT MAGICIAN) supervised the production of opera at the venue. MOLIÈRE's provincial company took up residence there in 1658, opening with five plays by Corneille before presenting some of the playwright's own early works, including *Les Précieuses ridicules* (1659). In 1660 the Petit-Bourbon was suddenly scheduled for demolition, and Molière found himself briefly without a venue until Louis XIV provided a vacant theatre in the Palais-Royal.

Before the Petit-Bourbon was demolished, however, Molière was allowed to take away furniture, fittings, and equipment. Torelli's scenery and machinery were collected and carried away by the court scene painter Vigarani, supposedly for the Salle des Machines he was designing and building for the king in the Tuileries. However, Vigarani was jealous of Torelli's talent and fame and burned every item he collected.

Pétomane, Le *See* FART FANATIC, THE.

Petrified Forest, The A play by Robert SHERWOOD, first performed in 1935 in New York. It starred Humphrey Bogart, who later appeared in the film version. The play, written two years after Hitler came to power, is a semiallegorical piece about the corrupting effects of fascism. Set in the Arizona desert, it shows how the gangster Duke Mantee and his gang take over a café by terrorizing the family who own it. The central character, a failed writer who has fallen for the café-owner's daughter, Gabby, begins to see some benefits in Mantee's power, calling him "the last great apostle of rugged individualism". He asks Mantee to kill him after making Gabby the beneficiary of his life-insurance policy. After the gangster has complied, the writer, as he had requested, is buried in the nearby petrified forest.

Phantom of the Opera, The A musical by Andrew LLOYD WEBBER, with lyrics by Charles Hart; Lloyd Webber wrote the book with Richard Stilgoe, who also contributed additional lyrics. First performed in London in 1986 at Her Majesty's Theatre, it was still running in 1997. It received the Laurence Olivier and *Evening Standard* Awards for Best Musical of 1986 and a year later repeated its success on Broadway.

The plot, based on Gaston Leroux's gothic novel, tells of a disfigured and deranged composer who haunts the labyrinth beneath the Paris Opéra. Lloyd Webber's version downplays the original horror story in favour of the romance between the masked Phantom and the opera singer Christine (played in the original version by Lloyd Webber's then wife, Sarah Brightman). The musical's success owed much to a bravura performance by Michael Crawford as the Phantom.

The songs include 'The Point of No Return', 'The Music of the Night', and 'Wishing You Were Somehow Here Again'.

Phèdre A tragedy by Jean RACINE, usually acknowledged as his masterpiece, that was first performed in Paris in 1677. Critics have praised its lyrical dialogue, subtle psychology, and intricate plot. The title role was first played by Mlle CHAMPMESLÉ, the leading tragic actress with the Comédie-Française, and Racine's mistress. Glenda Jackson played the role to great acclaim in Philip Prowse's 1984 London production.

Phèdre has been called "the keystone in French tragic drama". Racine is said to have written it to prove that "a good poet could get the greatest crimes excused and even inspire compassion for the criminals." The plot, based on the *Hippolytus* of EURIPIDES, concerns Phèdre's passion for her stepson, Hippolyte. Hearing that her husband, Thésée, has died in Athens, Phèdre confesses her passion to Hippolyte, who is deeply shocked. When Thésée unexpectedly returns, Phèdre pretends to him that Hippolyte has tried to seduce her. The deceit results in Hippolyte's death and Phèdre's suicide.

Phelps, Samuel (1804–78) British actor-manager, best known for his Shakespearean productions at SADLER'S WELLS Theatre.

Phelps began acting in 1826 and for 11 years toured the provinces, earning a reputation as an excellent tragedian. In 1837 he was engaged by Ben Webster (*see* WEBSTER FAMILY) at the Haymarket, where he gave well received performances as Hamlet, Shylock, and Richard III. Later he joined William MACREADY's company at Covent Garden, appearing as Othello to Macready's Iago.

When the monopoly of Covent Garden and Drury Lane was abolished by the Theatres Act of 1844 (*see* PATENT THEATRES), Phelps immediately took over Sadler's Wells Theatre and began to produce serious drama. During his management (1844–62) he staged 34 of Shakespeare's 37 plays, including *Macbeth* (1844), *Antony and Cleopatra* (1849), and *Pericles* (1854). Despite his usual striving for historical accuracy in costume, Victorian propriety demanded "a very demure and much petticoated Cleopatra". His *Pericles* made use of the original text for the first time since 1661. Phelps appeared in most of the productions himself with Mrs Warner as his leading lady. After leaving Sadler's Wells, Phelps returned to acting in Shakespeare and dramatizations of Scott's novels. His last performance was as Cardinal Wolsey in *Henry VIII* in 1878.

Phelps was also renowned as a teacher. Having learned traditional techniques passed down from David GARRICK through Macready and Sarah Siddons, he helped to launch the successful careers of many young actors, including Johnston FORBES-ROBERTSON (who painted a well known portrait of Phelps in the role of Cardinal Wolsey). *See also* HENRY V.

Philanderer, The A play by George Bernard SHAW. It was written in 1893 but owing to its somewhat risqué subject did not find a producer until 1905, when it was presented in London as a private club production. The play satirizes two causes that Shaw himself supported, Ibsenite free-thinking and feminism. Shaw's main character, Charteris, is largely a self-portrait, while he wrote the part of the tempestuous Julia for Mrs Patrick CAMPBELL, with whom he was infatuated. In the event Mrs Pat never played the part.

The story centres on Leonard Charteris, a philandering Ibsenite, who is unable to decide between two women – an old sweetheart, the volatile Julia Craven, and a new love, the widow Mrs Grace Tranfield. Charteris attempts to resolve his dilemma by persuading the physician Dr Percy Paramore to propose to Julia, whose acceptance frees him to concentrate on Grace. For her part, however, Grace decides that she would rather have Charteris's respect than his love.

Philipe, Gérard (1922–59) French actor, whose spectacular career was cut short by his sudden death at the age of 37. He was buried in the costume he wore in Corneille's *Le Cid*.

Philipe made his debut in 1943 in the first production of Jean Giraudoux's *Sodome et Gomorrhe*. Two years later he made his name in the title role of Albert Camus's *Caligula*. In the late 1940s he became a film star, but returned to the stage in 1951, joining the Théâtre National Populaire under Jean VILAR. After drawing in youthful playgoers in Paris with such successes as *Le Cid*, he toured America, Canada, and Russia. He remained with the TNP until his death.

Philipe was particularly praised for performances in Heinrich von Kleist's *Prinz Friedrich von Homburg* (1951), the first French production of Brecht's *Mother Courage* (1951), Shakespeare's *Richard II* (1954), and Musset's *Les Caprices de Marianne* (1958) and *On ne badine pas avec l'amour* (1959).

Philoctetes A play by SOPHOCLES, one of the best known of Greek tragedies, first performed in 409 BC in Athens. Sophocles wrote it at the age of 87.

In Greek legend Philoctetes was a famous archer, Hercules having given him his arrows on the point of death. In the tenth year of the Trojan War Odysseus commanded that Philoctetes be sent for, as an oracle had declared that Troy could not be taken without the arrows of Hercules. Philoctetes went to Troy, slew Paris, and Troy fell. Sophocles's play, however, tells a later story of Philoctetes being cast away on a desert island, from which he fears he may never escape.

phlyax In the GRECO-ROMAN DRAMA, a type of MIME popular in the 4th and 3rd centuries BC. The comic playlets, which were probably mostly improvised, combined burlesque with scenes from everyday life. Writers of the *phlyax* in the 4th century BC included Rhinthon of Tarentum. Information about the form comes mainly from vase paintings, which reveal that it was performed on a primitive stage consisting of a wooden platform supported on posts. The *phlyax* was eventually absorbed into the Roman ATELLANA.

phoenix. Phoenix Society A British theatre group founded in London in 1919 to perform early English drama. It was set up under the aegis of the STAGE SOCIETY, which had already revived a number of works by Farquhar, Congreve, Vanbrugh, and others. The Phoenix Society presented 26 important productions between 1919 and 1925. These drew support from such leading theatrical figures as Edith Craig, who managed the productions, Allan Wade, who directed all but two, and Norman Wilkinson, who designed sets. Sir Thomas Beecham arranged the music for the 1923 production of John Fletcher's *The Faithful Shepherdess*. Other dramatists whose work was produced included John Dryden, Ben Jonson, Thomas Otway, and Francis Beaumont. In many cases the Society's revival of forgotten or neglected works led to subsequent productions by other companies.

Phoenix Theatre A theatre on Charing Cross Road, London, opened by Sidney Bernstein in 1930 on a site once occupied by the Alcazar Music Hall. It opened with the first production of Noël COWARD's *Private Lives*, starring the author and Gertrude LAWRENCE. The Phoenix maintained its association with Coward for many years and in 1969 he opened the theatre bar that had been named after him.

Coward and Lawrence appeared together again in *Tonight at 8.30*, a series of one-act plays presented in 1936. During World War II John Gielgud starred in Congreve's *Love for Love* (1943) and Cicely Courtneidge in *Under the Counter* (1945). Subsequent productions have included works by Thornton Wilder, Terence Rattigan, John Osborne and Bertolt Brecht. The Phoenix's longest run was a musical adaptation of Chaucer's *The Canterbury Tales* (1968) which logged 2082 performances. Recent successes have included Coward's *Design for Living* (1973), Stoppard's *Night and Day* (1978), Simon Gray's *The Common Pursuit* (1988), and Willy Russell's musical *Blood Brothers* (1993).

photo call or **picture call** A prearranged session during which cast members are photographed in costume, wigs, and make-up for publicity purposes. This is normally carried out within a stage set to give the impression of a live production. In Britain, photo calls are sometimes held during the dress rehearsal but in America they tend to be held at **dress parades** several days earlier.

Piaf, Edith (Giovanna Edith Gassion; 1915–63) The internationally famous French singer and entertainer. Her assumed name *Piaf* is French slang for sparrow – a reference to her tiny stature. Despite a poverty-stricken childhood and a disastrous private life, Piaf's indomitable spirit, distinctive voice, and emotional style brought her enormous success in cabaret and music hall. She was loved by Parisians, who thronged the streets on the day of her funeral, causing total traffic chaos, and admired throughout the world for such songs as 'La Vie en rose', which she wrote herself, 'Pigalle', 'Mon legionnaire', 'Je ne regrette rien', and 'Pour deux sous d'amour'. Jean COCTEAU, an ardent admirer, wrote *Le Bel Indifferent* (1941) to provide her with one of her infrequent theatrical roles. She also appeared in Marcel Achard's *La P'tite Lili* (1951). Her own disastrous childhood and emotional instability, which resulted in failed marriages, alcoholism, and drug addiction, were depicted in Pam Gems's play *Piaf* (1980); Jane Lapotaire gave a moving interpretation of the singer in the first English production. The play was revived in 1993 with Elaine Paige in the lead.

Piccolo Teatro della Città di Milano *See* STREHLER, GIORGIO; TEATRO STABILE.

Pickelhering The German term for a CLOWN or buffoon, from a humorous character of that name in an early 17th-century play. It was adopted in England (in the Anglicized form *Pickleherring*) through Addison's use of the term in *The Spectator* (1711).

"Pickwick, Arise, Sir Samuel" The words uttered by George V when knighting the actor Sir Cedric HARDWICKE in 1934. The king, who was somewhat deaf, was responding inaccurately to a prompt from his equerry.

Pierrot A tall thin melancholy clown who appears in whiteface wearing a loose white costume with very long sleeves and a row of big buttons down the front. A traditional figure in French pantomime, he developed from the character of PEDROLINO in the Italian *Commedia dell'arte*. The character's melancholy demeanour was largely the creation of the famous 19th-century Pierrot BAPTISTE. In England the character featured in the HARLEQUINADE and the later PIERROT TROUPES.

Pierrot troupes British seaside song-and-dance companies of the late 19th and early 20th centuries, all members of which dressed in the traditional white costume of Pierrot. In 1891 the London success of *L'Enfant prodigue*, a mime Pierrot play, inspired Clifford Essex to introduce a troupe in Ireland and the Isle of Wight; other groups were formed by such showmen as Carlton Frederick in Weymouth (1894) and Edwin Adeler in Southport (1898). After the turn of the century, Pierrot troupes performed at London's Apollo Theatre in such productions as H. G. Pelisser's *The Follies* (1908, 1910) and THE CO-OPTIMISTS (1921–27). The troupes were vividly portrayed in Joan Littlewood's revue OH, WHAT A LOVELY WAR! (1963).

Pilate, Pontius. ***Acts of Pilate, The*** *See* GOSPEL OF NICODEMUS.

Pilate voice A loud ranting voice, especially as used by an actor. In the medieval MYSTERY PLAYS tyrannical characters such as Pontius Pilate were made to speak in a rough ranting manner. Similarly, Shakespeare uses the expression "out-herods Herod" of a bombastic declamatory actor in *Hamlet* (III, ii).

> The Miller, that for-drunken was al
> pale...
> In Pilates vois he gan to crye...
> CHAUCER: *The Miller's Prologue.*

Although a link has been suggested, there is no connection between the name of the squawking ruffian Mr PUNCH and *Pontius* Pilate.

Pillars of Society, The first of the 'social' dramas in prose with which Henrik IBSEN revolutionized the theatre of the late 19th century. First performed in 1877 in Copenhagen, it quickly established the author's reputation in Germany, with five theatres in Berlin presenting the play within five months of its publication. It was also the first Ibsen play to be translated (by William Archer) for production in London, opening as *Quicksands; or, The Pillars of Society* in 1880 at the Gaiety Theatre.

The story focuses on Karsten Bernick, the moral and financial pillar of the small Norwegian community in which he lives. Bernick, however, has a secret. Some fifteen years earlier he had been involved in underhand dealings and had let his brother-in-law, Johan, take the blame and flee to America. When Johan returns, Bernick is terrified that the truth will be revealed, ruining another illegal venture that he has recently become involved in. Although Johan sails for America without saying anything, Bernick cannot shake off his guilt; when the local newspaper pays tribute to him, he is prompted to reveal the truth about his illegal dealings past and present, a confession that brings his family closer together.

Pinafore Riot A dispute that occurred in 1879 over rival productions of Gilbert and Sullivan's HMS PINAFORE. Richard D'OYLY CARTE had financed his Comedy Opera Company by luring wealthy backers, making them directors, and then failing to renew their contracts. Since the ex-directors had been making £500 a week each from the production of *HMS Pinafore* that opened at the Opera Comique in 1878, they hired a team of hooligans to steal the play's scenery from the theatre in order to stage their own version. The cast and stage staff chased them off, however, and the rival production proved a failure. D'Oyly Carte sued the ex-directors and won his case.

Pinero, Sir Arthur Wing (1855–1934) A popular and prolific British playwright, who began his career as an actor with Irving's Lyceum Company (1876–81). At Irving's encouragement, he wrote his first play, *£200 a Year*, in 1877. He enjoyed early success at the Royal Court Theatre with a series of farces that included THE MAGISTRATE (1885) and DANDY DICK (1886). The light comedy *Trelawny of the 'Wells'* (1898) follows the actress Rose Trelawny through the West End of the 1860s. Pinero is now best known for the serious social dramas he wrote in the 1890s under the influence of Henrik IBSEN. These include THE SECOND MRS TANQUERAY (1893), which ends with a suicide, and *The Notorious Mrs Ebbsmith* (1895). The latter made the reputation of Mrs Patrick CAMPBELL, who excelled in a scene calling for her to rescue a Bible from the flames and press it to her bosom.

pin spot A SPOTLIGHT that throws a tiny brilliant beam of light onto the stage. It is used to dramatically highlight a special object or to isolate a person's face.

Pinter, Harold (Harold Da Pinta; 1930–) British dramatist, director, and screenwriter, regarded as one of the most original writers of the post-war period. Like BECKETT, with whom he is often compared, Pinter resolutely refuses to analyse his works, although he did once rather cryptically suggest that his plays were about the "weasel under the cocktail cabinet."

Born in the East End of London, Pinter briefly attended RADA and the Central School of Speech and Drama before joining Sir Donald Wolfit's touring company as an actor (using the name David Baron). Curiously, Pinter appeared alongside two other as yet undiscovered playwrights, Ronald Harwood and Alan AYCKBOURN.

Pinter's first play, the one-act THE ROOM, was staged at Bristol University in 1957; his first full-length play, THE BIRTHDAY PARTY appeared the following year, much to the bewilderment of both audiences and critics. THE DUMB WAITER (1960) received its premiere in Hamburg, being followed later in the year by THE CARETAKER, which enjoyed successful productions in both London and New York, establishing Pinter as a major writer for the theatre. Although *The Caretaker* has only three characters and very little in the way of plot, it effectively established a new theatrical style in which tension, suspicion, and ambiguity combine to create a 'comedy of menace'. Subsequent plays, such as THE HOMECOMING (1965), *Old Times* (1971), NO MAN'S LAND (1975), and *Betrayal* (1978) are much concerned with the subjective nature of time and memory. During the 1980s he spent much of his time writing for the cinema and campaigning for political causes. The enigmatic *Moonlight* (1993), his first major play for 15 years, was followed by *Ashes to Ashes* in 1996.

Pinter's first wife, Vivien Merchant (1929–82) played many of his early female roles. After their divorce he married the historian Lady Antonia Fraser in 1980.

Pinteresque Resembling the work or style of Harold Pinter. It is used especially of dialogue that resembles Pinter's in being oblique, repetitive, interspersed with lengthy pauses (*see* PINTER PAUSE), menacing, and loaded with hidden meanings. One critic has called the imitators of this style the **Pinteretti**.

Pinter Pause A long significant pause in stage dialogue. The name derives from Harold PINTER's characteristic use of the device; notoriously, he indicates his pauses explicitly in his texts rather than leaving them to the discretion of the actors. John Gielgud has noted, "The 'Pinter Pause' is now a kind of copyright in the theatre world as it was once the traditional property of the actor MACREADY in the nineteenth century."

pipe *See* BATTEN.

Pirandello, Luigi (1867–1936) Italian dramatist, actor, critic, novelist, and short-story writer. With Strindberg, Ibsen, Chekhov, and Shaw he is considered one of the founders of the 20th-century theatrical tradition. His philosophy of the absurdity of human existence struck a chord with the disillusioned generation of the 1920s: "I think that life is a very sad piece of buffoonery" he wrote, adding "My art is full of bitter compassion for all those who deceive themselves..." In their reaction against realism Pirandello's works have had a major influence on French drama, particularly on the Theatre of the ABSURD that developed after World War II.

Born in Sicily, he attended universities in Palermo and Rome and received a doctorate in philosophy from the University of Bonn. In 1894 marriage to the daughter of a wealthy sulphur merchant gave him the security to write; this, however, proved shortlived as the family lost all their money in a mine disaster in 1903 and Pirandello was obliged to take a lecturing post. Over the following years his wife became mentally ill, developing a persecution mania and a frantic jealousy of her husband. He cared for her at home for 15 years before she was confined in a sanatorium.

Although Pirandello's first play, *L'epilogo*, was produced in 1910, he did not find success on the stage until 1917, when *Right You Are (If You Think So)*, a dramatization of one of his short stories, was performed. Like many of his later works, this proclaimed the relativity of truth, undermining the whole notion of objective reality.

Pirandello's most famous work, SIX CHARACTERS IN SEARCH OF AN AUTHOR, had its premiere in Rome in 1921 and was produced the following year in both London and New York. Its paradoxical exploration of the relationship between theatre and reality was continued in two more plays, *Each in His Own Way* (1924) and *Tonight We Improvise* (1929). In 1922 he wrote the powerful tragedy, *Henry IV*, which examines the concepts of sanity and madness; it was first seen in London in 1925 and in New York in 1947.

In 1925 Pirandello established his own company at the Teatro Odescalchi, Rome, with Ruggero Ruggeri (1871–1953) and Marta Abba (1900–88) as its leading players. He produced and directed his own plays at the theatre and toured Europe and America with the company. In 1934 he was awarded the Nobel Prize for Literature.

Pirates of Penzance, The GILBERT AND SULLIVAN's light opera about a band of soft-hearted plunderers. It was first produced in 1879 at the Royal Bijou Theatre, Paignton, Devon, and then a day later at the Fifth Avenue Theatre, New York; the first London production was in 1880 at the Opera Comique. The work is full of larger-than-life comic characters who owe a great deal to the English MUSIC HALL tradition. The songs include 'I am the Very Model of a Modern Major-General', 'Oh, Dry the Glistening Tear', and 'With Cat-like Tread'.

The story's hero is the well-meaning Frederick. When he was a boy, his father had instructed a servant to ensure that the boy was apprenticed as a sea pilot: unfortunately, the slightly deaf servant thought the word was 'pirate'. As a result Frederick, now 21, is a rather reluctant novice pirate. When the gang attacks a Major-General's house, Frederick defends it until the Pirate King reminds him that he is bound by the terms of his apprenticeship. However, when the prostrate Sergeant of Police calls, "We charge you yield, in Queen Victoria's name!" the pirates suddenly recall their love for Queen and country and surrender; they subsequently settle down and marry the Major-General's daughters.

The opera's subtitle, *The Slave of Duty*, highlights Gilbert's malicious pleasure in poking fun at this most Victorian of virtues. When the Pirate King reminds Frederick of his obligation to continue in his calling, he sees no way out:

> Well, you have appealed to my sense of duty, and my duty is only too clear. I abhor your infamous calling; I shudder at the thought that I have ever been mixed up with it; but duty is above all – at any price, I will do my duty!

Piscator, Erwin (Friedrich Max) (1893–1966) German director, noted for his ingenious staging techniques and his influence on the development of EPIC THEATRE and DOCUMENTARY THEATRE. A member of the German Communist Party from 1918, Piscator saw the theatre as a means of both explaining issues and influencing voters.

Piscator's innovative productions made use of machinery, newsreels, film clips, photographs, and audio recordings to create an experience of total theatre. Notable among his early productions were *Despite All!* (1925), which gained him a job at the Berlin VOLKSBÜHNE, *Storm Over Gottland* (1927), which lost him the job, *Rasputin* (1927), and *The Good Soldier Schweik* (1928). The last two productions were staged in collaboration with BRECHT.

The Political Theatre, Piscator's book of photographs and writings on the theatre, was published in 1929 and had a profound effect upon the Federal Theatre Project's LIVING NEWSPAPER productions, as well as Joan LITTLEWOOD's Theatre Workshop productions.

Following his arrest in 1931 for failing to pay entertainment tax, Piscator moved to the Soviet Union; in 1938 he moved to New York, where he remained until 1951. During this time in America Piscator taught at the Dramatic Workshop, where he influenced such writers as Arthur Miller and Tennessee Williams.

After returning to West Germany in 1951, Piscator remained largely inactive until his appointment (1962) as artistic director of the West Berlin Volksbühne. Here he staged a number of highly controversial works of documentary theatre by such writers as HOCHHUTH and Peter Weiss.

Pistol FALSTAFF's 'ancient' (i.e. ensign) in Shakespeare's HENRY IV, PART II, HENRY V, and THE MERRY WIVES OF WINDSOR. A cowardly braggart, Pistol finally gets his comeuppance in *Henry V* from Captain Fluellen, who forces him to eat a raw leek for mocking the Welsh. Following this humiliation, Pistol announces his intention to return home to a life of crime: "To England will I steal and there I'll steal." His bombastic language parodies the ranting style of many Elizabethan tragedies.

pit In the Elizabethan theatre, the central unroofed area of the auditorium that offered the cheapest places. The name comes from the cockpits used for cockfighting. The pit (sometimes called the **yard**) provided standing room only and was used mostly by the lower classes. This tended to place the most rowdy theatregoers nearest to the stage, increasing the accuracy with which oranges and other missiles were hurled at the actors. Similarly in the French theatre, the area corresponding to the pit often contained 1000 spectators standing, jostling, and fighting one another (a serious matter, since they could wear swords).

In the early English playhouses the stage and lower boxes were at ground level and the pit was sunk between them. In the 16th century admission to the pit cost a penny, rising in the 17th century to two pennies. After the Restoration, the three grand theatres – Drury Lane, Lincoln's Inn Fields Theatre, and Dorset Garden Theatre – introduced slanted pits to improve visibility and began to provide backless benches for everyone. One reason for the demise of the APRON stage was the need to create more seats in the pit. In the early 19th century, a raised circle replaced the lower boxes and the pit was extended backwards underneath it. Soon afterwards, the cheap pit benches were replaced by the STALLS, which became the highest priced seats in the house; only the back rows were still referred to as the pit. Modern theatres have no pit.

Plagiary, Sir Fretful A character in SHERIDAN's comedy THE CRITIC (1779), who was intended as a caricature of the playwright Richard Cumberland (1732–1811). Cumberland, the author of several popular comedies, found his sentimental style suddenly outmoded when GOLDSMITH and Sheridan enjoyed their first successes. Anxious to see these new comedies for himself, he took his children to the first night of *The School for Scandal* (1777); when the children laughed at the play he furiously tried to restrain them, coldly informing them that there was nothing at all to laugh at. Sheridan was incensed when he heard of the incident: "It was very ungrateful in Cumberland to have been displeased with his poor children for laughing at my comedy; for I went the other night to see his tragedy, and laughed at it from beginning to end." Sheridan took his revenge by satirizing Cumberland at Sir Fretful, one of his great comic creations.

Plain Dealer, The A harsh comedy by Sir William WYCHERLEY, sometimes considered his best play. Loosely based on Molière's THE MISANTHROPE (1666), it was first performed in 1676 at Drury Lane. The identification of the misanthropic title character, Manly, with the author himself led to the latter being nicknamed 'Manly' Wycherley. The play's satire is strident and frequently obscene. At one point Manly anticipates the objections of the audience by asking, "Is railing satire... and roaring and making a noise humour?" In the later 18th century the play generally appeared in a bowdlerized version by Isaac BICKERSTAFFE. The Renaissance Theatre Company presented a noted revival of Wycherley's original at London's Scala Theatre in 1925.

Manly, a plain-dealing naval captain, returns from the Dutch wars with a distrust of all mankind except his fiancée Olivia, to whom he has entrusted his money, and his best friend Vernish. He is shocked, therefore, to find them married to each other. Fidelia, a young woman who had followed Manly to sea disguised as a male, tries to intervene on his behalf but the treacherous Vernish attempts to rape her. When she is wounded defending Manly from an attack by Vernish, the captain realizes that it is Fidelia who loves him and vows to marry her.

Planchon, Roger (1931–) French actor, director, and dramatist, who had formed his own company before he reached the age of twenty. The company, which lived and worked as a commune, built its own theatre, where Planchon produced plays ranging from the classical to the avant-garde. In particular, he championed the work of ADAMOV and BRECHT. In 1954 he met Brecht and subsequently became the leading French director of his plays.

The company was invited, in 1957, to take over the Théâtre de la Cité, a huge municipal theatre at Villeurbanne, an industrial suburb of Lyons. At Villeurbanne, Planchon managed to build up a substantial working-class audience, for which he directed mainly Marxist interpretations of classical plays, including works by Shakespeare, Marivaux, Molière, and Jonson. Following a successful production in Paris in 1961 the company was given a government grant, making it the first provincial theatre to receive a government subsidy.

Planchon himself has written a number of dramas, many of which he has also directed and performed in; his most notable plays are *La remise* (1962), *Dans le vent* (1968), and *Gilles de Rais* (1976). In 1972, following the closure of Jean VILAR's theatre at Chaillot, Planchon inherited the name THÉÂTRE NATIONAL POPULAIRE for his theatre at Villeurbanne.

platt In the Elizabethan theatre, the outline of a play posted backstage to cue the stage crew for such duties as calling actors and moving properties.

Plausible Jack The nickname given to the actor John Palmer (1742–98) by Richard Brinsley SHERIDAN, because of Palmer's fame as a liar. The son of a doorkeeper at Drury Lane, Palmer began his career as a strolling player. He opened the Royalty Theatre in London in 1787 but, as this was unlicensed (*see* LICENCE), he was soon arrested and made no further attempts at theatre management. He died on stage in Liverpool (*see* DYING WORDS).

Plautus, Titus Maccius (254–184 BC) Roman playwright, whose comedies were the most popular dramatic works of their day. He was originally an actor or clown. Twenty-one of his 130 plays survive, revealing his theatrical craftsmanship and total mastery of farce. Although his works were PALLIATA, adaptations of Greek NEW COMEDY originals now lost, he shifted the scene to Rome and based much of the humour on Roman manners and customs. His comedy, which was broader than that of TERENCE, still works today. Stock characters of Plautus's plays include the bragging soldier, the miser, the old man in love, the parasite, identical twins, the wily slave, and the courtesan.

Later European dramatists influenced by Plautus include Shakespeare, Jonson, Dryden, and Molière. His comedy was often based on disguises and mistaken identities; Shakespeare's THE COMEDY OF ERRORS (1592) was based on Plautus's *Menaechmi*, about the confusions caused by a pair of long-separated identical twins. Several of his plays were combined for Stephen SONDHEIM's 1962 Broadway musical *A Funny Thing Happened on the Way to the Forum* (although only one line from Plautus was retained: "I am a parade").

Plautus was eventually forced to work in a grain mill after losing most of his theatrical earnings in unsuccessful business ventures.

play. playbill Either a poster advertising a play or a programme handed out to the audience. The poster or circular usually lists the title, date, time, theatre, cast, and other information; it may quote favourable reviews. The audience playbill is a small programme with basic information and perhaps advertising. These are free in Britain and sold at a nominal price in America. Most theatres also sell quality colour programmes.

The first poster playbills were printed in London in 1737 by the managements of Drury Lane and Covent Garden. They were quarto sheets circulated to coffee houses and stuck up outside the theatres. The first programme playbills were handed out in 1850 at the Olympic Theatre to occupants of the more expensive seats.

Players' Club A gentleman's club in New York, established in 1888 by the actor Edwin Booth (*see* BOOTH FAMILY) as the US equivalent of London's GARRICK CLUB. Booth, the first president, donated a house for its foundation. He died in office in 1893, as did the next two presidents, Joseph Jefferson (*see* JEFFERSON FAMILY) and John Drew (*see* DREW FAMILY). The fourth president was Walter Hampden, who served for 27 years (1918–55) and after whom the club library is named. Subsequent presidents have included Howard Lindsay (1955–65) and Alfred Drake (1970–78). In 1994 Lynn Redgrave became the first female president. The Players Club maintains an extensive collection of theatrical mementos.

Players' Theatre A London theatre club that opened in 1927 as Playroom Six at No. 6, New Compton Street, later changing its name to the Players' Theatre. In 1936 it moved into Evans (late Joys) Song and Dance Rooms in Covent Garden. The following year Peter Ridgeway acquired the theatre; as Ridgeway's Late Joys it offered evenings of songs and sketches, which survived Ridgeway's death in 1938 and a move to Albermarle Street in 1940; finally, the Players' Theatre moved in 1946 to a theatre under the arches of Charing Cross Station in Villiers Street. Here it continued to give Victorian music-hall entertainments with Leonard Sachs and Don Gemmell as masters of ceremonies and a great deal of audience participation. Curiously, the name Late Joys still featured in its programmes. In 1953 Sandy Wilson's musical *The Boyfriend* had its premiere at the Players' Theatre. In 1987 the Players' moved temporarily to the Duchess Theatre, before returning to a renovated theatre under the arches in 1990.

Playhouse A theatre on the Embankment near Charing Cross, London. It was opened under this name by Cyril Maude (1862–1951) in 1907; the original building on the site, the Royal Avenue Theatre, was very severely damaged in 1905 when part of Charing Cross Station collapsed onto it, causing six deaths. Maude and his wife, Winifred Emery (1862–1924), performed regularly at the Playhouse from 1907 until 1915.

Frank Curzon and Gladys COOPER became the new managers in 1917; Cooper starred there in the 1922 revival of Pinero's *The Second Mrs Tanqueray* before running the theatre alone from 1927 to 1933. She produced several of Somerset Maugham's plays, including *The Letter* (1927).

During World War II, the Playhouse offered a varied menu, including a 1943 Old Vic production of Reuben Simonov's *The Russians.* It became a BBC studio in 1951 and did not reopen as a theatre until 1987, when it presented the musical *Girl Friends.* In 1992 Ray Cooney's farce *It Runs in the Family*, starring John Quayle, was produced.

The original theatre on the site, the Royal Avenue Theatre, opened in 1882. High points in its history included the 1894 premiere of George Bernard Shaw's *Arms and the Man.*

to play to the gallery *See* GALLERY.

Playboy of the Western World, The J. M. SYNGE's comic masterpiece, which provoked some of the worst riots in theatrical history when first performed in 1907 at Dublin's ABBEY THEATRE. The main action begins with Christy Mahon's arrival at a pub in a wild part of Mayo, where his story of slaying his bullying father makes him a hero amongst the local women. Later, Christy's father appears with a fractured skull and berates his son so furiously that Christy attacks him again. Believing the man dead, the villagers try to hang Christy, but his father recovers once more and the two indignantly leave the pub together.

Trouble began on the first night of the Abbey production and continued throughout the run. The audience hissed and stamped their feet, sang patriotic songs, and shouted "Kill the author!" There were fights and demonstrations at every performance until 500 police "thick as blackberries in September" were brought in to maintain order. Those outraged by the play included Irish nationalists, who were upset by the unsentimental portrayal of peasant life, and pious Catholics, who complained about what *Sinn Fein* called "the foulest language we have ever listened to on a public platform". (The word 'shift', meaning petticoat, caused particular offence.) Others denounced the supposed insult to Irish womanhood, or condemned the comic treatment of patricide.

Yet more protests came from Irish Americans when the play toured America in 1911–12. In New York stink bombs, potatoes, a cigar tin, and an old watch were amongst the objects thrown on stage: the owner of the watch later called at the stage door and asked for its return. In Philadelphia the whole company was arrested for performing a play "likely to corrupt morals". (Hearing this, George Bernard Shaw commented: "All decent people are arrested in the United States.")

Plenty A play by David HARE, first performed in 1978 by the National Theatre company at their Lyttleton Theatre with Hare directing. A film version appeared in 1985. The drama, set in the two decades after World War II, uses the traumatic decline of the Resistance heroine Susan Traherne as a symbol for the decay of political idealism in Britain.

Susan, now married to Raymond Brock, a career diplomat, finds her peacetime life dull and meaningless and becomes increasingly disillusioned by Britain's complacent class-ridden society. Her eccentric behaviour becomes a burden to her husband and friends and she eventually leaves Raymond and drifts into drugtaking. A wartime comrade, Codename Lazar, traces her and they spend a night together, two pathetic figures living in the past.

Plinge, Walter An imaginary name that sometimes appears on British playbills, especially for productions of Shakespeare, to disguise the fact that the same actor is playing two roles. Its use dates from about 1900, when the name was used by the versatile actor Oscar Asche (1871–1936), and it is still occasionally seen. The original Walter Plinge is thought to have been the landlord of a public house near the Lyceum Theatre, London. The US equivalent is the name **George Spelvin**, which first appeared on the bill for the 1886 New York production of Charles A. Gardiner's *Karl the Peddler*. Estimates suggest that the name Spelvin has been used on Broadway more than 10,000 times for actors, gag writers, animals, dummies, and dolls posing as babies.

plot sheet A schedule drawn up and kept by the STAGE MANAGER that details the requirements of each actor in a play, such as his make-up and wardrobe, as well as his entrances and exits. It also includes a **furniture plot**, specifying which pieces are to be arranged where during each scene, a **property plot**, listing all props and where they are to be kept offstage, and a **sound** or **special-effects plot**. *See also* PROMPT BOOK.

plough. ***Plough and the Stars, The*** A tragicomedy by Sean O'CASEY, first performed at the ABBEY THEATRE, Dublin, in 1926. It is set in the slums of Dublin (which O'Casey knew at first-hand) during the 1916 Easter Rising. O'Casey angered Irish patriots by emphasizing the antiheroic aspects of the rebellion and its destructive effects on the lives of ordinary people.

The Plough and the Stars is the Abbey Theatre's most performed play but also one of the most troubled. On the fourth night of the first production, police had to quell rioting members of the audience as they stormed on stage to attack the cast. W. B. YEATS, one of the theatre's founders, cried at the audience (in allusion to the riots that greeted Synge's THE PLAYBOY OF THE WESTERN WORLD nearly 20 years earlier), "You have disgraced yourselves again. You are rocking the cradle of a new masterpiece." After a revival in 1951, the Abbey burned down (ironically, the play ends with soldiers singing 'Keep the home fires burning'). When the theatre reopened in 1966, *The Plough and the Stars* was the second play to be presented. Many Irish actors have excelled in the leading role of the antiheroic Fluther Good; one of the most acclaimed recent performances was that of Cyril Cusack (1910–93) in a production at the National Theatre in 1977.

Plough Monday The Monday after Twelfth Night (6 January), a day on which plays were traditionally performed in some English villages; where the custom still occurs it is usually on the first Saturday after Plough Monday. The plays, which derive from primitive folk theatre and the ancient rite of blessing the plough, centre upon the accidental death of one of the farm workers who are the drama's principal characters. In this respect they seem to be related to the Christmas MUMMERS' PLAYS, in which the hero is killed in a fight only to be resurrected.

poet. **poetic drama** A play written wholly or mainly in verse. As this was the norm in early drama (a tradition crowned by the works of Shakespeare), the term is usually reserved for works written since the Restoration (1660); by this time only tragedies were still composed in verse, comedies being more commonly written in prose.

In the late 17th century the great works of CORNEILLE and RACINE established the rhyming couplet as the standard form for tragedy and serious historical dramas. Despite the efforts of DRYDEN, however, the form never took root in the English theatre. In the early romantic era a revival of verse drama was led by the Germans GOETHE and SCHILLER, whose early works consciously invoke the example of Shakespeare. Goethe's greatest poetic drama was the two-part FAUST (1829 and 1854), while Schiller's historical plays *Maria Stuart* (1801) and *Wilhelm Tell* (1804) have held the stage in German-speaking countries.

In Britain, the romantic poets Wordsworth, Coleridge, Byron, Shelley, and Keats all wrote plays, although most of these come into the category of CLOSET DRAMAS; only Coleridge's *Remorse* (1813) and Byron's *Marino Faliero* (1821) were staged during the lifetimes of the authors. Shelley's THE CENCI, a gothic tale of incest and murder written in 1819, was produced in 1886 and is still sometimes revived. The pitfalls of verse drama were demonstrated even more thoroughly by the Victorian poets Tennyson and Browning, whose work for the stage rarely rises above the feeblest Shakespearean pastiche.

Although Ibsen's early works BRAND and PEER GYNT are amongst the most successful poetic dramas to have been written since the Jacobeans, his later plays were chiefly responsible for establishing prose as the natural vehicle for serious modern drama. The triumph of REALISM in the late 19th century has made verse drama seem an increasingly marginal form. Amongst those to lead a reaction against prose realism was W. B. YEATS, who turned to the Japanese NŌ theatre for inspiration.

The attempt to find a contemporary idiom for verse drama did not really bear fruit until the 1930s, when poets such as T. S. ELIOT and W. H. Auden began to use free verse. In Britain there was a shortlived vogue for poetic drama in the years after World War II, when such plays as Christopher FRY's *The Lady's Not for Burning* (1948) and Eliot's *The Cocktail Party* (1949) were presented successfully in the West End. In 1945–46 the actor and director E. Martin Browne (1900–80), who directed all of Eliot's plays, produced a season of new verse drama at London's Mercury Theatre.

Poet Laureate A court official who composes odes in celebration of royal birthdays and state occasions. The appointment dates essentially from the time of James I, although there had been an occasional *Versificator Regis* in earlier times. The laurel crown was an ancient mark of distinction and honour.

Oddly enough, the great majority of 17th- and 18th-century laureates were principally men of the theatre rather than poets *per se*. Although Ben Jonson (1619–37), Sir William Davenant (1638–68), and John Dryden (1670–88) were poets of distinction as well as successful playwrights, this can hardly be said of Thomas Shadwell (1688–92), Nahum Tate (1692–1715), Nicholas Rowe (1715–18), Colley Cibber (1730–57) or William Whitehead (1757–85).

This trend reached the point of absurdity in the appointment of Cibber, a comic actor and playwright who demonstrated little ability to write verse, let alone poetry. The laureate was mercilessly ridiculed by such literary figures as Alexander Pope, who wrote:

> Cibber! write all thy verses upon Glasses,
> The only way to save 'em from our A---s.
> 'Epigram Occasioned by Cibber's Verses in Praise of Nash'.

poetomachia *See* WAR OF THE THEATRES.

Poet's Corner The southern end of the south transept of London's Westminster Abbey, where many leading British writers are buried. Chaucer was buried there in 1400 and many later poets desired to be laid to rest near his bones, including Edmund Spenser, whose funeral took place in 1599. The playwright Francis BEAUMONT was interred here in 1616; he had once written of the Abbey:

> Think how many royal bones
> Sleep within this heap of stones:
> Here they lie had realms and lands,
> Who now want strength to stir their
> hands.

SHAKESPEARE (buried in Stratford-upon-Avon) is commemorated by a monument bearing lines from *The Tempest*. Legend has it that Ben JONSON, whose grave is nearby, was buried upright, having bargained for a space only two feet wide and two feet long. A certain nobleman, who happened to visit the Abbey while Jonson's grave was being completed, paid for the carving of the famous inscription "O rare Ben Jonson" (*see* RARE BEN).

Other playwrights buried in Poet's Corner include Aphra Behn, William Congreve, Nicholas Rowe, Joseph Addison, John Gay, Samuel Foote, and Richard Brinsley Sheridan. There are also memorials to more recent writers for the stage, including Noël Coward.

Curiously, Poet's Corner also includes the graves of 'old Parr', whose claim to fame was his survival to the age of 152 (having done penance for fornication at the age of 105), and 'Spot' Ward, who won a vote of thanks from the House of Commons for curing George II of an injury to his thumb. The name Poet's Corner was first applied by Oliver GOLDSMITH. Addison had previously referred to it as the 'poetical quarter' in 1711, observing: "I found there were Poets who had no Monuments, and Monuments which had no Poets."

Perhaps the most poignant epitaph of all is that of the poet Samuel Butler, who died in poverty:

> The Poets Fate is here in emblem shown:
> He asked for Bread and he received a
> Stone.

Polonius The garrulous old courtier in Shakespeare's HAMLET, a pompous, sententious, interfering old man. He is the father of Ophelia and Laertes and lord chamberlain to the king of Denmark. Taking him for the king, Hamlet stabs Polonius to death while he is hiding behind an ARRAS to spy.

Pooh Bah Pooh Bah, The Lord High Everything Else, is a character in Gilbert and Sullivan's THE MIKADO, who was First Lord of the Treasury, Lord Chief Justice, Commander-in-Chief, Lord High Admiral, Master of the Buckhounds, Groom of the Back Stairs, Archbishop of Titipu, and Lord Mayor. The name is used of one who holds numerous offices simultaneously, usually from motives of self-interest.

poor theatre A term devised by the Polish director Jerzy GROTOWSKI to describe a type of essential drama that can be arrived at by eliminating traditional 'theatrical' extras. As he explained in his book *Towards a Poor Theatre* (1968):

> By gradually eliminating whatever proved superfluous, we found that theatre can exist without make-up, without autonomic costume and scenography, without a separate performance area (stage), without lighting and sound effects, etc.

By contrast, Grotowski describes the contemporary commercial theatre as the "Rich theatre – rich in flaws". He rejects the dictatorial powers of the modern director and believes that the only element essential to effective drama is the direct actor–spectator relationship. By encouraging audience members to participate in the drama, he has attempted to create a revolutionary **Theatre of Involvement.**

Many of these concepts were put into practice by Grotowski through his involvement with the Polish Theatre Laboratory in Warsaw, which he directed from 1964 to 1976. He was a major influence on Britain's Peter BROOK (who wrote a preface to *Towards a Poor Theatre*) and on such US experimental groups as the LIVING THEATRE.

Porgy and Bess A musical by George GERSHWIN, often described as the first US folk opera. The show was not an immediate success, losing the entire production cost of $70,000 when first presented in 1935. Gershwin's musical was based on the 1927 play *Porgy* by Du Bose Heywood, who collaborated with Ira Gershwin on the lyrics. The songs include 'Summertime', 'I Got Plenty O' Nuttin'', 'It Ain't Necessarily So', and 'Bess, You Is My Woman Now'.

The story is set in Catfish Row, a Black ghetto in Charleston, South Carolina. After Bess's boyfriend, Crown, murders a man during a dice game and flees, she settles down with the crippled beggar Porgy. When Crown returns to claim Bess, Porgy kills him, becoming a fugitive himself.

pornographic theatre Plays or exhibitions that are designed to arouse sexual excitement. Erotica has been an element of the theatrical tradition since earliest times. In ancient Greece an association between comedy and sexual licence carried over from the rites of DIONYSUS. The Roman MIME often combined scenes of nudity and simulated sex with real on-stage violence.

In Europe graphic depictions of sexual acts were mainly confined to brothels until the later 20th century. The first pornographic theatre was opened in Paris in 1741 by a madame named Lacroix. In the same city the Theatron Erotikon presented pornographic puppet shows from 1862 onwards. In Britain, erotic plays were written to be read rather than acted (though one 1879 work was humorously advertised as having been produced at the Theatre Royal Olimprick).

The sexual liberation of the 1960s and the easing of stage censorship in most Western countries brought a new sexual explicitness to the legitimate stage. Kenneth TYNAN's 1969 hit *Oh, Calcutta!* included a simulation of the sex act, while Lennox Raphael's *Che!* (1969) featured a naked Uncle Sam practising oral sex and sodomy (before the show was closed and the cast arrested). A scene of simulated buggery in Howard Brenton's THE ROMANS IN BRITAIN (1980) provoked a private prosecution (subsequently withdrawn). When the revue *Porno-Erotico* was presented in 1974 in Cantanzaro, Italy, the cast was tipped off that the public prosecutor had their production targeted. Accordingly the actors confined themselves to singing Neapolitan love songs and juggling oranges. The disappointed audience of some 500 businessmen rioted and ripped up the theatre's seats. The police arrived with smoke bombs and machine-guns but took four hours to subdue the barricaded theatregoers. *See also* NUDITY; STRIPTEASE.

Porter. Cole Porter (1892–1964) US composer and lyricist, whose stylish and witty songs appeared in some 27 musicals and revues. Born into a wealthy family, he began to write songs while studying law. His first musical, *See America First* (1916), a satire on the jingoism of George M. COHAN, was a total flop. During World War I he served briefly in the French Foreign Legion and thereafter lived the life of a wealthy socialite in Europe while continuing to write songs.

Porter's early musicals included *Wake Up and Dream* (1929) and *The Gay Divorce* (1932). Mary Martin made her Broadway debut in Porter's *Leave It To Me* (1938), which includes the song 'My Heart Belongs to Daddy'. Ethel MERMAN starred in four hits, namely, ANYTHING GOES (1934), in which she performed the title song and 'I Get a Kick Out of You', *Dubarry Was a Lady* (1939), *Panama Hattie* (1940), and *Something for the Boys* (1943), in which she sang 'Hey, Good Lookin''. Porter's KISS ME KATE (1948) was a backstage musical based loosely on Shakespeare's *The Taming of the Shrew*. His last works for the stage were CAN-CAN (1953), another hit, and *Silk Stockings* (1955).

A serious riding accident in 1937 left Porter in poor health for the rest of his life: one of his legs had eventually to be amputated. Despite being a homosexual he had married in 1919 and after his wife's death in 1954 lived as a virtual recluse.

Other popular songs by Porter include 'Night and Day', 'Begin the Beguine', and 'Let's Do It'.

Jimmy Porter The central character in John Osborne's play LOOK BACK IN ANGER (1956), whose rantings were taken as typical of the ANGRY YOUNG MEN of the period. The frustrated product of a working-class background and a provincial university, Porter lived in a drab bedsit with his middle-class wife, Alison, who served as the butt for most of his invective.

> She's so clumsy. I watch for her to do the same things every night. The way she jumps on the bed, as if she were stamping on someone's face, and draws the curtains back with a great clatter, in that casually destructive way of hers. It's like someone launching a battleship. Have you ever noticed how noisy women are? Have you? The way they kick the floor about, simply walking over it? Or have you watched them sitting at their dressing tables, dropping their weapons and banging down their bits of boxes and brushes and lipsticks?

At the time, his self-pitying harangues were thought to articulate a general disillusionment with postwar Britain. Porter, now in irritable middle age rather than angry youth, made a second appearance in Osborne's recent play *Déjà vu* (1992).

When the original production of *Look Back in Anger* became a *succès de scandale*, George DEVINE had the idea of asking the audience to remain in their seats after the performance to discuss the play with himself, Osborne, Tony Richardson (the director) and the cast (led by Kenneth Haigh as Porter and Mary Ure as Alison). One evening the discussion centred on whether Jimmy Porter was psychotic or merely neurotic. This led to an appeal for a clear distinction between these states. Two definitions were offered, both by psychiatrists in the audience. One: "a neurotic builds castles in the air; a psychotic moves into them"; the other: "a neurotic *thinks* that two and two make four, but is worried that this may not be the case; a psychotic is quite sure that two and two make five and sees no reason to worry about it."

Portia A rich heiress in Shakespeare's THE MERCHANT OF VENICE (*c.* 1596). By the terms of her father's will she is bound to marry the suitor who chooses from three caskets (one each of gold, silver, and lead) the one containing her portrait. Her preferred suitor, Bassanio, chooses correctly. Later, disguised as a doctor of law, she successfully defends Bassanio's friend Antonio from SHYLOCK's claim for a pound of his flesh.

pose plastique *See* LIVING PICTURE.

pound of flesh The whole of the bargain, to the last letter of the agreement. The allusion is to Shakespeare's THE MERCHANT OF VENICE, in which the Jewish moneylender SHYLOCK demands a pound of Antonio's flesh in fulfilment of his bond. He is foiled in his suit by PORTIA, who argues that the bond was expressly a pound of flesh, and therefore (1) Shylock must cut the exact quantity, neither more nor less than a pound; and (2) in so doing he must not shed a drop of blood.

Power family A family of actors, most notably the Irish actor Tyrone Power (David Powell; 1795–1841), his grandson Tyrone Edmond (1869–1931), and his great-grandson, the US actor Tyrone Power (1914–58).

The first **Tyrone Power** made his debut in 1815 and became known for his comic Irish parts, such as Sir Lucius O'Trigger in Sheridan's *The Rivals*. He also appeared in his own comedies and farces, including *St Patrick's Eve* (1832) and *O'Flannigan and the Fairies* (1836). He drowned in the sinking of the SS *President* while making the return voyage from his third tour of America. Of his eight surviving children, one son Maurice Power (d. 1849) entered the profession.

Another son, Harold Power, was the father of **Tyrone Edmond**, who became a member of Augustin DALY's American company from 1890–98 and later specialized in Shakespearean parts. Harold's niece, Norah, was the mother of the British theatre director, Sir Tyrone GUTHRIE.

Tyrone Edmond's son, the second **Tyrone Power**, found fame primarily in films, although he also gave impressive stage performances in such plays as *Romeo and Juliet* (1935), Shaw's *Saint Joan* (1936), Christopher Fry's *The Dark is Light Enough* (1955), and Shaw's *The Devil's Disciple* (1956).

praetexta See FABULA.

Prahlada Nataka In India's eastern state of Orissa, a unique style of drama performed in villages of the Ganjam district. Some 40 troupes perform the *Play of Prahlada* during festivals. Derived from a classical text popularized by a local 19th-century ruler, Raja Ramakrishna Deva Chotterai, the plays tells of a little prince's persistent worship of Vishnu despite the opposition of his wicked father, the king. Performances take place in an open field on a platform stage. The actors dance to musical accompaniment provided by the harmonium, wind instruments, drums, cymbals, and conch shells. At the climax of the play, the actor playing Narsimha, the incarnation of Vishnu, dons a man–lion mask that is believed to have special power. When he does so, he is believed to become possessed by the god and must be restrained by attendants to protect the actor playing the evil king. When Vishnu destroys the king order is restored.

précieuses, les The ladies of the intellectual circle that gathered at the Hôtel de Rambouillet in 17th-century Paris. The term can be translated as 'persons of distinguished merit'. Their affected airs were the subject of MOLIÈRE's comedy *Les Précieuses Ridicules* (1659), the work that proved his first major success.

prelude In the British theatre of the late 18th century, a brief introductory sketch performed when the theatrical season began or a new venue was opened. The prelude was usually a satirical piece dealing with topical issues within the theatrical profession.

première (Fr. first) A first performance. It is an abbreviation of the French *la première d'une pièce*.

Present Laughter Noël COWARD's last major comedy, first performed in London in 1943. It was to have been produced in 1939 but the war interrupted rehearsals and Coward was sent to Paris to open a British bureau of propaganda. In 1943 he played the lead, calling it "a wonderful part for me and I shall not be too dependent on fractious leading ladies." The plot concerns the relationship between Gary Essendine, a self-obsessed actor, and his estranged but still adoring wife. Approaching 40 and a mid-life crisis, Gary indulges in brief affairs and ends up being pursued simultaneously by a married woman and a young girl. As his emotional life becomes intolerably complicated, he flees back to his wife.

The play was revived in 1947 at the Theatre Royal, Haymarket, but Coward thought the cast "tatty and fifth rate". He was deeply mortified when his star, the US actress Mary Martin, said to Princess Margaret, "Give my best to your sister. Bye-bye for now." When CBS television made plans to broadcast the play in 1956, they told Coward that the script would provoke anguished protests from "outraged Methodists in Omaha complaining about illicit love being brought into their very homes by me." He therefore wrote an expurgated version.

Price, (Lilian) Nancy (Bache) (1880–1970) British actress and theatre manager, who in 1930 founded the **People's National Theatre** in London. Price joined Frank Benson's company at the age of 19 and made her name three years later as Calypso in Stephen Phillips's *Ulysses*. The People's National Theatre opened with a revival of Anstey's *The Man from Blankley's* at the Fortune Theatre; she subsequently produced more than 50 plays for the company at the Little Theatre. These included Susan Glaspell's *Alison's House* (1932), S. I. Hsiung's *Lady Precious Stream* (1934), and Mazo de la Roche's *Whiteoaks* (1936), in which Price played the part of Adeline Whiteoaks. The Little Theatre was destroyed in 1941 by wartime bombing.

Price gave her last performance in Eden Phillpott's *The Orange Orchard* at the New Lindsey Theatre in 1950 (the same year that she was awarded a CBE). She was married to the actor Charles Raymond Maude (1882–1943), grandson of the singer Jenny Lind.

Priestley, J(ohn) B(oynton) (1894–1984) British dramatist, novelist, and man of letters. His first work for the stage, *The Good Companions* (1931), was a dramatization of his own successful novel about a touring theatre company. It was followed in 1932 by DANGEROUS CORNER, the first of several expressionist works exploring the nature of time and presenting alternative versions of the same series of events. TIME AND THE CONWAYS and I HAVE BEEN HERE BEFORE (both 1937) employ similar ideas and are amongst Priestley's most frequently revived works. They were followed by the farce WHEN WE ARE MARRIED (1939), set in Priestley's native Yorkshire; in the first production the author himself played a role. *They Came to a City* (1943), Priestley's most overtly political play, was followed by the popular mystery drama AN INSPECTOR CALLS (1946), which starred Ralph Richardson, and THE LINDEN TREE (1947), in which Lewis Casson and Sybil Thorndike played husband and wife. Priestley's later plays were generally less successful. He was the first president of the INTERNATIONAL THEATRE INSTITUTE.

Prime Minister of Mirth Nickname of the British actor and music-hall performer Sir George Robey (1869–1954). He became known as the **Darling of the Halls** for an act featuring such characters as Daisy Dilwater, the Mayor of Mudcumdyke, and a red-nosed vicar with staring eyes and a lewd smile. Robey later appeared in plays and films and was in great demand as a pantomime dame.

prince. Prince of Fops The nickname of the dandy Sir Fopling Flutter, the title character in THE MAN OF MODE; *or Sir Fopling Flutter* (1675) by Sir George ETHEREGE.

Prince of Humbugs The nickname of the US showman P. T. BARNUM (1810–91), who used the title himself during his 50 years of deceiving the public (who never tired of coming back for more). His motto was "There's a sucker born every minute" and one of his three autobiographies bore the title *Humbugs of the World* (1865). Amongst his spurious exhibits were Joice Heth, a Black woman advertised as being more than 160 years old, and George Washington's former nurse, and a fake mermaid.

> He will ultimately take his stand in the social rank...among the swindlers, blacklegs, pickpockets, and thimble-riggers of his day.
>
> *Tait's Edinburgh magazine*, 1855.

Prince of Wales' Theatre A theatre in Coventry Street, London, associated with successful musicals and revues. The first venue on the site was built as The Prince's Theatre by the actor-manager Edgar Bruce; it was noted for its foyer decorated in the Moorish style and a circular Moorish 'grotto' under the street (used as a smoking room). The first production was W. S. Gilbert's *The Palace of Truth* (1884). Later that year Beerbohm Tree scored a great success in *The Private Secretary*, while Lillie LANGTRY's 1885–86 repertory season included Sheridan's *The School for Scandal*. The theatre's present name was adopted in 1886. Between 1918 and 1926 several revues were presented by André

Charlot. Edith Evans briefly managed the venue in 1930.

The Prince of Wales' Theatre was rebuilt in 1936, the interior being redesigned in a stark simple style by Robert Cromie. It reopened in 1937 with *Les Folies de Paris et Londres*. Sid Field had a successful run in *Harvey* (1949) before musical comedies and revues returned in the 1950s, attracting such international stars as Mae West and Barbra Streisand. *The World of Susie Wong* opened in 1959 and ran for 824 performances, while *The Danny La Rue Show* was a highlight of 1973. Recent revivals have included Rodgers and Hammerstein's *South Pacific* (1988) and Irving Berlin's *Annie Get Your Gun* (1992).

princes in the tower The young Edward V and his brother Richard, Duke of York; the sons of Edward IV, they disappeared in mysterious circumstances in the Tower of London in about 1483. Richard III, the original 'wicked uncle', has traditionally been held responsible for their deaths, largely due to Shakespeare's portrayal of him as the archetypal villain – grotesquely deformed, innately malevolent, and driven to murder by his lust for power (*see* RICHARD III). Shakespeare relied heavily for his interpretation on the historians Raphael Holinshed and Edward Hall – themselves influenced by Sir Thomas More's *History of King Richard III* (written 30 years after the event). The continuing popularity of Shakespeare's play has done much to foster this interpretation.

In truth, very few facts can be stated regarding the boys' disappearance: they were last seen alive, in the Tower, in the summer of 1483 and it was soon common rumour that they were dead and that Richard was responsible. According to More, Sir James Tyrell – condemned to death for treason in 1502 – admitted to suffocating the princes on Richard's orders. In this century writers and historians have seized on the gaps in the evidence to argue Richard's innocence. However, if the boys were killed in the Tower in 1483 (as seems likely), it is improbable that anybody would have dared carry out the deed without explicit authorization from the king; moreover, from Richard's point of view, it would have been a prudent political decision to order their deaths. Bones of two boys of the appropriate ages were discovered in the Tower in 1674 and 1987.

principal boy The leading male role in English PANTOMIME, traditionally played by a woman. The characters derive ultimately from the role of Harlequin. One of the most popular, Cinderella's Prince Charming, did not appear on the London stage until 1915. Principal boys were especially popular in the late Victorian era, when they were usually played by buxom music-hall stars, whose plumpness in tights led to the familiar thigh-slapping routine. The roles have attracted such famous performers as Vesta Tilley, Nellie Stewart, and Fay Compton; more recently principal boys have been played by soap-opera stars with good legs.

private. ***Private Lives*** A comedy of manners by Noël COWARD, first produced in London in 1930. The plot revolves around the acerbic divorcees Amanda and Elyot, who both happen to be honeymooning in the same hotel with their new spouses. On the verandas of their adjacent rooms, the old love-hate relationship is rekindled:

> AMANDA Have you known her long? [referring to his new wife]
> ELYOT About four months, we met in a house party in Norfolk.
> AMANDA Very flat, Norfolk.

The play was written by Coward as a vehicle for himself and Gertrude LAWRENCE. It has been suggested that the intense love-hate relationship between Elyot and Amanda – who find being together almost as painful as being apart – reflects some of the tensions in the relationship between Coward and Lawrence themselves.

In the first production, Laurence OLIVIER made an early West End appearance as Amanda's new husband, Victor Prynne. It was during the long opening run of *Private Lives* that Olivier's notorious tendency to giggle on stage was addressed. Coward told Olivier that he would make him laugh in every performance during the breakfast scene until he could control himself. After seven months, Olivier confessed himself cured.

Privates on Parade A play (with music) by Peter NICHOLS, first performed in 1977 by the Royal Shakespeare Company at the Aldwych Theatre, London. Denis Quilley (1927–) won the Society of West End Theatres Award for Best Comedy Performance as the outrageously camp captain with a song-and-dance unit of soldiers. In a drag skit, he impersonated Marlene

Dietrich, Carmen Miranda, and Vera Lynn. The US director Charles Marowitz noted how Quilley restrained himself from going over the top, "producing instead a delicately controlled performance which perfectly balances comment and caricature".

Set in Malaya a few years after World War II, the story centres upon the activities of SADUSEA (Song and Dance Unit South East Asia). Apart from the captain, Terri Dennis, the wandering troupe includes the unscrupulous Sergeant-Major Reg Drummon, the good-natured Corporal Len Bonny, and the beautiful Anglo-Indian Sylvia Morgan. In the plot the racketeer Reg fakes his own murder in order to evade a crackdown on his criminal activities. One performance by the troupe ends in a shootout during which Len dies and a flight-sergeant is crippled. The action is interspersed with lively songs and skits.

private theatres The indoor London playhouses of Elizabethan, Jacobean, and Caroline times. The most notable were the Boys of St Paul's (1575), the BLACKFRIARS (1576), the second Blackfriars (1600), the Whitefriars (1605), the COCKPIT (1616), and Salisbury Court Theatre (1629). In practice, the 'private' theatres were open to the public, although they charged a higher admission price than the open-air PUBLIC THEATRES. By declaring their theatres private, managers could avoid censorship and other interference from the authorities. The productions were sometimes described as 'rehearsals' of works to be presented at the genuinely private court theatres.

producer Until 1956, the usual British term for the person having overall control of a production; the US term DIRECTOR was officially adopted in that year.

In both Britain and America, the term producer is now used to mean a person who organizes the administrative and financial aspects of a production. His or her duties usually include engaging actors and staff, dealing with copyright, renting the theatre, buying special equipment, drawing up and keeping the budget, arranging for advertisements and press releases, organizing ticket sales and complimentary tickets, overseeing the design and selling of programmes, handling receipts, and taking responsibility for the house regulations concerning fire prevention and other such matters.

professor. ***Professor Taranne*** An early work by the Russian-born French playwright Arthur ADAMOV. It was first performed in 1953, when Roger PLANCHON directed it at the Théâtre de la Comédie, Lyons; it was produced in English translation in 1962. The play, a striking example of the Theatre of the ABSURD that shows the influence of both Kafka and Strindberg, was based on a dream. It centres on the plight of a university professor who comes under attack for 'obscene' behaviour. This short play remains Adamov's best known and most frequently revived work.

Professor Wallofski A grotesque character created by the British variety comedian Max WALL. The antics of the professor, an outrageous pianist in a black shoulder-length wig, black tails, black tights, and large black boots, derived ultimately from the musical nonsense of the great Swiss clown GROCK. Wall invented the character while serving with the Royal Air Force during World War II but did not present him on stage until 1946, when he appeared in the revue *Make It A Date* at the Duchess Theatre, London.

Professor Wallofski was usually introduced by a statuesque lady, who would attempt to engage him in polite conversation:

> LADY What are you going to play for us, Professor?
> PROF Liszt's Hungarian Rhapsody, number two.
> LADY Oh, Liszt! I love him!
> PROF Do you really? Well, perhaps you'd like me to dig him up?

Infuriated by such exchanges the woman would lift the professor up to her height by his lapels. When he finally reached the piano the professor would go through such absurd routines as finding a little potty inside the piano stool, attempting to play with the keyboard lid down, crushing his fingers, etc. As he played the piano, one arm would appear to become longer than the other.

profile. profile board A piece of canvas or board projecting from a FLAT to create a three-dimensional scenic effect, such as an awning projecting from the painted front of a shop, etc.

profile spot A spotlight that throws a bright sharp beam on stage. When used in conjunction with shutters or masking devices (such as a GOBO or IRIS) the beam can be used to create an outline or 'profile' of a chosen shape. Profile spots, generally known in America by the tradename **Leko**, provide good long-range coverage on stage and excellent side or special lighting.

projector A projection unit that uses glass slides to create atmospheric lighting on stage. Less frequently, projectors are used to project still or moving images behind actors, as in the Polykran and Laterna Magica of Josef SVOBODA and in such plays as Joan Littlewood's musical documentary OH, WHAT A LOVELY WAR! (1963). When certain weather and natural effects are required (such as stormy skies, snow, rain, and fire, etc.) special-effects projectors are employed. In America, this latter device is known as a **sciopticon**, which is the old Victorian name for a magic lantern used to project photographs (one was exhibited in London's South Kensington Museum in 1876).

projector unit *See* PAGEANT LANTERN.

prologue An introductory speech or scene given before the main play. EURIPIDES introduced the use of a prologue to recount the events leading up to those presented in the play, thereby avoiding the need for too much exposition in the first act. Some Roman dramatists, such as Plautus, turned out elaborately written poems to introduce their plays – a practice continued by Molière in, for example, his *Amphitryon* (1668).

In medieval England, mystery and miracle plays were often introduced by homilies, while in the Elizabethan theatre the prologue, when it occurred, was usually called the 'chorus'. It was during the Restoration period that the prologue, along with the closing EPILOGUE, truly came into its own. Spoken by the leading actor or actress, these pieces were always in rhymed verse and often full of sharp witty comments on topical issues. John DRYDEN wrote numerous prologues for his own and others' plays, which are not only fine poems in their own right but also a valuable source of information about the theatrical world of the time. David Garrick was a noted writer of prologues in the 18th century. George Bernard Shaw replaced the prologue with a 'preface' for readers, creating long polemical pieces that were usually provocative and entertaining. The critic James Agate went so far as to remark "Shaw's plays are the price we pay for Shaw's prefaces".

promenade A THEATRE-IN-THE-ROUND production in which the audience moves between several locations to follow the action. One of the most celebrated promenade plays was *1789*, an epic work about the French Revolution created by Ariane MNOUCHKINE's Théâtre du Soleil; the production used five stages and involved the audience in the action as members of the mob. The Scottish director and playwright Bill Bryden (1942–) staged several influential productions 'in promenade' after taking over the Cottesloe Theatre (*see* ROYAL NATIONAL THEATRE) in 1978; these included *The Mysteries* in 1985 and plays by Eugene O'Neill and Arthur Miller.

Prometheus Bound A tragedy by AESCHYLUS, the first part of a tetralogy that was first performed in about 460 BC. The work was controversial during its day for presenting Zeus as a tyrant. The plot centres on Prometheus, bound to a rock for stealing fire from heaven for mankind. Although he faces the implacable power of Zeus and is tormented by an eagle that continually feasts on his liver, Prometheus remains defiant.

Prometheus Bound is an unusually static play, featuring a motionless hero and little action; long expository speeches are exchanged between Prometheus and such visitors as a chorus of sea nymphs, their father Oceanus, the "cow-headed" goddess Io, and Hermes. It also poses a number of questions about Greek staging conventions. The play calls for a rugged mountain locale, which is destroyed by an earthquake in the final scene. Some scholars believe a special mountain-cliff set was built and tipped over during the earthquake scene, some think the SKENE was already in use at this early date and decorated to suggest mountains, while others argue that the earthquake was conveyed by the spoken lines alone.

Aeschylus continued the story in *The Loosing of Prometheus* and (it is thought) *Prometheus the Firebearer*, neither of which survives. In these plays, Heracles shoots the tormenting eagle and frees Prometheus, who is then reconciled with Zeus.

Prometheus Unbound (1820) was the title of a CLOSET DRAMA by the poet Percy Bysshe Shelley.

prompt. prompt book The master copy of a play kept by the stage manager or PROMPTER. It is a log that records all actors' moves, technical cues, and props involved in the production. One page contains the final script and the facing page charts the moves, lighting, etc.: essential directions are recorded next to the relevant line. Cues for lighting and sound are written in different colours for quick identification. Advance warnings for upcoming cues are recorded in the book as 'WARN' and the exact moment of operation is labelled 'GO'. *See also* PLOT SHEET.

prompt corner An area concealed behind the PROSCENIUM ARCH in which the PROMPTER sits at a desk or table with his prompt book, ready to feed lines to forgetful actors. The prompt corner is traditionally located downstage left in Britain (*see* PROMPT SIDE) and downstage right in America. In Continental theatres and opera houses the prompter sits downstage centre hidden by a semicircular hood.

The US actor George Nash once appeared in a Broadway play when he barely knew his lines. The prompter, who disliked Nash, made a point of prompting him slightly before it was really necessary just to demonstrate how poorly he was prepared. After six prompts, Nash stalked over to the prompt corner and hauled the man out on stage, growling, "Since you know the part so well, you have a go." In the second act, the prompter remained silent and only pulled funny faces at Nash when he appealed for words. Finally, when the actor pleaded, "Give me a word," the prompter offered an obscene one. Nash stormed over to the prompt corner and kicked the man, who pursued him back on stage uttering threats.

prompter A person employed to whisper key words to an actor who has forgotten his next line. He attends all rehearsals and records stage moves and script changes in his book. Prompt copies from the early days of the theatre often provide the only reliable information on the actors and playwright involved in a production.

In 14th-century England, the prompter was also employed to revise and copy texts of the mystery plays, supply costumes, and provide refreshments. In the Elizabethan theatre he was called the **book-holder**. A well-known prompter of the Restoration era was John Downes (d. 1710), who took up his duties at Lincoln's Inn Fields Theatre in 1661. Prompting is one of the theatrical practices satirized by R. B. Sheridan in his farce THE CRITIC (1779). By the 18th century, the prompter's duties included securing licenses for plays, copying scripts, holding rehearsals, and cueing the music and scene changes.

Prompting sometimes comes from unexpected quarters. When Alan Ayckbourn's *How the Other Half Loves* toured America in the 1970s, the role of Frank Foster was taken by Phil Silvers, who had a dreadful time remembering his lines. At the theatre in Palm Springs, California, the director Gene Saks had a hole cut in the wide aluminium forestage and placed his assistant director, Tom Erhardt, there as prompter. During the performance Silvers dried and Erhardt, who was not a professional prompter, seemed unable to help the struggling actor (who also suffered from buzzing in his ears). At one point Silvers hesitated with his line:

> SILVERS Well, Bob, I think...I think...I think...where are you, Tom?
> ERHARDT Possibly.
> SILVERS Well, Bob, I think...I think...I think...

Finally, a frustrated man in the rear stalls shouted: "Possibly!" Silvers never forgot the humiliation of having been prompted by a member of the audience.

prompt side (PS) In the British theatre, a term sometimes used for the side of the stage where the PROMPTER sits (stage left in Britain). The other side of the stage is referred to as the **opposite prompt side** (OP).

prop or **property** Any inanimate object used on stage during a play, not including costumes, scenery, or furniture. The term is short for *stage property*. Articles carried on to the stage by actors are called **hand props**, those for personal use (e.g. glasses, cigarettes) being **actor's props** and the remainder **manager's props**. All props are ultimately the responsibility of the stage manager.

property plot *See* PLOT SHEET.

proscenium Originally, the *proskenion* or stage area of the ancient Greek theatre. The term was retained for the rectangle stage of the English Restoration playhouse. The proscenium in Wren's second Theatre Royal, Drury Lane (1674), was about 20 feet deep, occupying more than a third of the auditorium; actors entered by PROSCENIUM DOORS in each side wall. Today the word is used to mean either the stage or (more commonly) the PROSCENIUM ARCH.

proscenium arch The opening that separates the stage from the audience. It normally has a curtain (and the safety curtain demanded by fire regulations). One of the first proscenium arches was built for the Teatro Farnese, which opened in 1628 in Parma, Italy. Early English examples had APRONS, or forestages, for acting in front of the proscenium arch; these began to disappear in the early 19th century, reinforcing the sense of the action taking place within a picture frame. The opening can be reduced in size by using FLATS or cloths to create a **false proscenium** (known in America as a **portal opening**). Many modern directors regard the proscenium arch as a barrier to interaction between actors and audience, and for this reason modern theatre designs often use an open stage plan or arena setting (*see* THEATRE-IN-THE-ROUND).

proscenium border *See* BORDER.

proscenium doors One or more pairs of doors on each side of the stage in the English Restoration playhouse. Also called **doors of entrance**, they provided a means of entrance to and exit from the acting area. By theatrical convention, if an actor left by one door and returned through the one next to it, he was presumed to be in another room. In the early 18th century the doors were reduced to one on each side and by the 19th century they were used only by actors taking bows (being known then as **call doors**).

Prospero The deposed Duke of Milan in Shakespeare's THE TEMPEST, a powerful magician living in exile on an island to which he brings his enemies. He controls the events in the plot like a dramatist but has to learn to control his own vengeful temper. In this century the most notable Prospero has been Sir John GIELGUD, who has returned to the part many times.

protagonist The principal character in a play. In ancient Greece, this was the term for the principal actor. According to legend, THESPIS became the first protagonist by expanding the role of the actor who led the chorus in the DITHYRAMB. The protagonist was subsequently joined by the **deuteragonist** and the **tritagonist** (second and third actors) in the works of EURIPIDES and SOPHOCLES.

Provok'd Wife, The Sir John VANBRUGH's comedy about the marriage between a wavering wife and her drunken husband; it was first performed in 1697 at London's Drury Lane. Unfortunately, *The Provok'd Wife* provoked England's increasingly respectable middle classes with a scene in which the debauched Sir John Brute disguised himself as a clergyman. In 1706 Vanbrugh rewrote the part so that Sir John dresses as a bonneted lady instead. David Garrick appeared in the role in 1744 and made it one of his most famous parts. An admired revival was staged by John Wood at the National Theatre in 1980.

In the play Sir John's long-suffering wife, Lady Brute, is pursued by Mr Constant, while her neice, Belinda, is courted by Constant's friend, Heartfree. The two couples retire to Lady Brute's home while her husband is out revelling. Disaster looms when Sir John returns unexpectedly to find the two men hidden in the closet; fortunately he accepts their explanation that the gathering was to arrange the marriage of Heartfree and Belinda.

Pry, Paul An idle meddlesome fellow, who has no occupation of his own, and is always interfering with other people's business. The name comes from the hero of John Poole's comedy, *Paul Pry* (1825).

public. Public Theatre A theatre in Lafayette Street, New York, that is permanently subsidized by the city. Its complex of seven separate auditoriums, the most under any one roof, was created by converting the former Astor Library, work carried out in 1967 under the director and producer Joseph PAPP. Amongst its distinguished premieres have been Jason Miller's *That Championship Season* (1973), which won a Pulitzer Prize, and Marvin Hamlisch's musical *A Chorus Line* (1975), which received both a Tony Award and a Pulitzer Prize.

The four main auditoriums are the 275-seat Anspacher Theatre, which opened in 1967 with the hippy musical HAIR, the 108-seat Other Stage, which opened the following year as a venue for playwriting workshops, the 300-seat Newman Theatre, which opened in 1970 with Dennis Reardon's *The Happiness Cage*, and the 191-seat Martinson Hall, which opened in 1971 with the musical *Blood*.

public theatres Open-air theatres in Elizabethan London. They were called 'public' playhouses to distinguish them from the roofed PRIVATE THEATRES, which were no less public but served a more educated and aristocratic audience.

The use of open-air venues developed from the outdoor tradition of medieval drama and the later custom of performing plays in the yards of INNS. The public theatres continued in use throughout the Jacobean and Caroline eras but from about 1610 were used mainly as summer venues, covered theatres being used in the winter.

At least nine public theatres were constructed before 1642; all were built outside the City boundary, mainly on the south bank of the Thames. The venues were: the THEATRE (1576–97), the Curtain (1577–*c.* 1627), an unnamed theatre at Newington Butts (*c.* 1579–*c.* 1599), the ROSE (1587–*c.* 1606), the SWAN (*c.* 1595–*c.* 1632), the first and second GLOBE (1599–1613 and 1614–44), the first and second FORTUNE (1600–21 and 1621–61), the RED BULL (1605–63), and the HOPE (1613–17).

Puck A mischievous fairy character in Shakespeare's A MIDSUMMER NIGHT'S DREAM, in which he is servant to OBERON. Also known as Robin Goodfellow, he appears in English folklore as a wayward household sprite who delights in playing cruel tricks. However, for a reward of a little bread and milk, he will also undertake various household chores. He featured in the anonymous 16th-century collection *Mad Pranks and Merry Gests of Robin Goodfellow* and is mentioned in Spenser's *Epithalamion* (1594).

puff An onomatopeic word, suggestive of the sound made by puffing air from the mouth; since at least the early 17th century it has been applied to extravagantly worded advertisements and reviews, with the implication that they have as much lasting value as a 'puff of wind'.

In Sheridan's THE CRITIC (1779), the character **Mr Puff** describes himself as "a practitioner in panegyric, or, to speak more plainly, a professor of the art of puffing" and gives a catalogue of puffs:

> Yes, sir – puffing is of various sorts, the principal are, the puff direct, the puff preliminary, the puff collateral, the puff collusive and the puff oblique, or puff by implication. These all assume, as circumstances require, the various forms of letter to the editor, occasional anecdote, impartial critique, observation from correspondent, or advertisement from the party.
>
> *The Critic* (I, ii).

Pujol, Joseph *See* FART FANATIC, THE.

Pulcinella The forerunner of Mr Punch in the English PUNCH AND JUDY show. Pulcinella, one of the comic servants or ZANNI of the COMMEDIA DELL'ARTE, was probably created by the actor Silvio Fiorillo at the start of the 17th century. The Italians considered him to have typical Neopolitan attributes. A dullard with a hooked nose and a hunched back, he probably derived from MACCUS, a stock character of the Roman ATELLANA. In the French Comédie-Italienne he became the more cunning and witty Polichinelle before evolving, in England, into the irascible Punch.

un secret de Polichinelle No secret at all; an open secret. In the old French puppet-shows Polichinelle's secrets are stage whispers addressed to all the audience.

Pulitzer Prizes Awards for literary work (both fiction and nonfiction), drama, poetry, journalism, and music, that are awarded annually by New York's Columbia University from funds left for the purpose by Joseph Pulitzer (1847–1911), a prominent and wealthy US newspaper proprietor. The Pulitzer Prize for Drama now stands at $3,000 and is given annually to the US writer of an outstanding play, preferably dealing with life in America. It was first presented in 1918 to Jesse Lynch Williams for *Why Marry?* Eugene O'NEILL won four prizes, the last being awarded posthumously for *Long Day's Journey Into Night* in 1957. Robert E. Sherwood won three Pulitzers. Other playwrights honoured have included Tennessee Williams, Thornton Wilder, William Inge, Arthur Miller, Edward Albee, and Sam Shepard.

Punch. Punch and Judy The central tradition of the English puppet theatre. The play is traditionally presented by a single puppeteer in a small booth of striped cloth. Originally, the puppets were marionettes but by the early 19th century almost all Punch-and-Judy men used glove puppets. The name of Mr Punch, the antihero, probably derives ultimately from the Italian *pulcinello*, a diminutive of *pulcino*, a young chicken (*see also* PULCINELLA). The identification of Punch with Pontius PILATE and of Judy with Judas is imaginary.

The story roughly in its present form is attributed to a 17th-century Italian comedian, Silvio Fiorillo and appeared in England at about the time of the Restoration. Punch, a crafty hunchbacked character with a hooked nose and a vile temper, strangles his infant child in a fit of jealousy, whereupon his wife Judy belabours him with a bludgeon until he retaliates and beats her to death. He flings both bodies into the street but is arrested and shut in prison, whence he escapes by means of a golden key. The rest is an allegory showing how Punch triumphs over (1) Ennui, in the shape of a dog; (2) Disease, in the disguise of a doctor; (3) Death, who is beaten to death; and (4) the Devil himself, who is outwitted. Other characters in the show include TOBY the dog, the Hangman (who instead of hanging Punch gets hanged himself), and the Crocodile.

pleased as Punch Greatly delighted. Punch is always singing with self-satisfaction at the success of his evil actions.

puppet theatre A form of dramatic entertainment in which the characters are represented by dolls. The best known form in Britain and America is the PUNCH AND JUDY show while popular figures elsewhere include GUIGNOL in France, KASPERL in Austria, and Petrushka in Russia. Varieties of doll include glove puppets manipulated by hand, MARIONETTES operated by string or wire, rod puppets, and shadow puppets.

Most ancient civilizations had highly developed puppet theatres. Far from being aimed at children, as is now the case in the West, the puppet plays depicted the religious, historical, and ethical traditions of a culture. Puppets have a long history in Java and India, and are still used in both countries at religious festivals. In Japan, puppetry has been traced back to the Heian era (781–1185); the famous life-size BUNRAKU puppets (*ningyo shibai*) achieved great popularity in the 18th century.

Puppet theatre was probably brought to Europe from the East through Turkey and Greece. Early religious puppet plays in England were called **motions**. However, puppetry never became a part of the mainstream European theatre, being relegated to fairs and streets and practised largely by itinerant showmen. The early 20th century saw a renewed interest in puppetry as a serious art form. George Bernard Shaw wrote a playlet for marionettes, while the designer E. Gordon Craig (*see* CRAIG FAMILY), wrote in his *The Art of the Theatre*:

> In the puppet we have all those elements necessary to interpretation and in the puppet stage every element necessary to a creative and fine art.

Purim play In the Jewish theatre, a traditional play performed during the festival of Purim (14 Adar). The genre developed from a 14th-century drama influenced by the Italian carnival. Mostly performed in rural areas, the improvised plays were usually one-act comic interludes with songs and dances. They were based on the story of the deliverance of the Jews from the massacre planned by Haman, which is celebrated at Purim. Playwrights later began to treat other subjects from Jewish scripture, such as the lives of Joseph, Moses, and David.

The Purim plays contributed to the development of a distinctly Jewish dramatic tradition and became popular throughout Europe in the 17th century. Later influences included the COMMEDIA DELL'ARTE and, in Germany, the ENGLISH COMEDIANS. The genre declined during the 18th century, when the Jewish religious authorities found its depiction of comic rabbis, midwives, and devils too irreverent. The Haskala groups in Germany later restored the genre's original didactic intention. The Purim play was eventually absorbed by the Yiddish theatre established by Abraham Goldfaden (1840–1908).

Putul Nautch A rod puppet theatre in India's eastern state of Bengal. The name, which means 'dancing dolls', refers to the fact that the puppets are attached to long rods held in a cup on the waistband of the puppeteer, whose dancing action activates the dolls. Individual parts of the figures can be manipulated by strings. The stories come from the MAHABHARATA and from such folk tales as that of Manasa, the snake goddess. Performances occur during rural festivals and fairs but are otherwise seldom seen today.

The wooden puppets are two to three feet tall and hollow. Earlier dolls were made of bamboo and plaster overlaid with banana leaves.

Pygmalion George Bernard SHAW's comedy of linguistic manners. In order to demonstrate his point about the role of accent in the English class system, Henry Higgins, a professor of phonetics, undertakes to transform a cockney flower girl, Eliza Doolittle, into a 'duchess' in six months. Although he succeeds, the play ends with Eliza at odds with the overbearing Higgins, who persists in seeing her as an experimental subject rather than a human being. The play, one of Shaw's most popular works, was first produced in Vienna in 1913; the part of Eliza was written for Mrs Patrick CAMPBELL. For the 1938 film version, Shaw approved the scripted 'happy ending', with a reconciliation between the Professor and Eliza (played by Leslie Howard and Wendy Hiller). This modified plot was adapted for the Lerner and Loewe musical MY FAIR LADY (1956). Shaw is said to have based the Higgins character on the distinguished Oxford phonetician, Henry Sweet (1845–1912).

In Greek legend Pygmalion was a sculptor and king of Cyprus, who, according to Ovid's *Metamorphoses*, fell in love with his own ivory statue of the ideal woman. At his earnest prayer the goddess Aphrodite gave life to the statue, and he married it. The story was adapted by W. S. Gilbert in his comedy of *Pygmalion and Galatea* (1871), in which the sculptor is a married man. His wife, Cynisca, becomes jealous of the animated statue (Galatea), which, after considerable trouble, returns voluntarily to its original state.

Not Pygmalion likely! A popular British euphemism of World War I and thereafter; it alludes to Shaw's *Pygmalion*, in Act III of which the expletive 'bloody' was first heard on the British stage. The word occurs during a tea party in which the cockney Eliza Doolittle, played in the first London production by Mrs Patrick Campbell, has been introduced to polite society. Although she has learned to speak in the accents of the upper classes, her conversational habits remain those of the East End streets. When a dashing young man inquires if she is walking home, she replies: "Walk? Not bloody likely! I am going in a taxi."

The morning before the play opened in London in 1916, the *Daily Sketch* thundered, "It is a word which the *Daily Sketch* cannot possibly print and tonight it is to be uttered on the stage...this evening the most respectable audience in London is to hear this appalling word fall with bombshell suddenness from Mrs Pat's lips." Shaw's biographer, Hesketh Pearson, noted that when the offending word was spoken the opening-night audience gasped as one, "their intake of breath making a sound that could have been mistaken for a protracted hiss." The laughter that followed was timed at 75 seconds by the stage manager's stopwatch.

Pyramus and Thisbe The 'play within a play' performed by BOTTOM THE WEAVER and the other Athenian artisans in Shakespeare's A MIDSUMMER NIGHT'S DREAM. The "tedious brief scene" is a travesty of the legend of Pyramus, as found in Ovid's *Metamorphoses*. Pyramus and Thisbe, two lovers who have been forbidden by their parents to marry, exchange vows through a chink in a wall. On arriving at a rendezvous by a mulberry tree, Pyramus finds Thisbe's veil, covered in blood; believing her to be dead, he stabs himself in despair. Thisbe, who had in fact fled when attacked by a lion, returns to find her lover's body. She also kills herself. According to the legend, the mulberry tree has borne blood-red fruit ever since. The story may also have influenced Shakespeare's *Romeo and Juliet*, which he wrote in the same year.

Q

Q Theatre A small London repertory theatre, on the north side of Kew Bridge. Jack de Leon renovated the former Prince's Hall and opened it as the Q in 1924 with a revival of Gertrude Jennings's *The Young Person in Pink*. He remained manager for nearly 30 years, producing such plays as Frederick Knott's *Dial M for Murder* and Philip King's *See How They Run*, as well as numerous revivals. The theatre closed in 1956.

In 1928 Mrs Patrick CAMPBELL and Nancy PRICE appeared together at the Q Theatre in Ibsen's *John Gabriel Borkman*. The notoriously temperamental Mrs Pat began by informing de Leon that he was too young to manage a theatre, and then turned on the noted Ibsen actor Rupert Harvey, who was directing:

> MRS PAT Mr Harvey, I have *forgotten* more about Ibsen and about acting than you will ever *learn*!
>
> HARVEY You have indeed forgotten it *all*!

Harvey stormed out and never returned. Mrs Pat then locked horns with her co-star, demanding a pink spotlight while Nancy Price insisted upon a straw-coloured one; the nervous technician had to keep both lights working without allowing the beams to cross. The feud intensified to the point that the two actresses refused to look at each other on stage, even during the most intimate scenes.

Quality Street A romantic comedy by J. M. BARRIE, set in the Regency period and usually played as a lavish costume drama. It was first performed in 1901 in London. The plot concerns Phoebe Throssel and her sister Susan, who live in Quality Street. Phoebe is in love with Valentine Brown, who is sent with his regiment to fight in the Napoleonic wars. When he returns 10 years later, Phoebe is worried that he will no longer love her now that she has aged; consequently she dresses brightly and arranges her hair in a youthful style. When Valentine fails to recognize her she pretends to be an imaginary niece, Miss Livvy. As soon as she realizes that Valentine is attracted to her, she woos him brazenly, as a test of his loyalty. Valentine, however, realizes her true identity and confesses his steadfast love for Phoebe. Phoebe gives up her false identity, Valentine proposes to her, and she modestly accepts.

queen. **Queen Anne's Men** A 17th-century English theatre company, commonly known as the Queen's Men, who appeared successfully in both London and the provinces. The company was created by former members of Worcester's Men and Oxford's Men on the accession of James I in 1603. Among the actors were Thomas Heywood and Christopher Beeston (*see* BEESTONS), who became their business manager in 1612. They performed regularly at London's Curtain Theatre and at the Red Bull Inn until 1616, when they moved to Beeston's new COCKPIT THEATRE. The company disbanded on the death of Queen Anne in 1619.

Queen Henrietta's Men An English theatre company, usually known as the Queen's Men, that was founded by Christopher Beeston (*see* BEESTONS) after his LADY ELIZABETH'S MEN dispersed during the plague of 1625. It received the patronage of the new Queen, Henrietta Maria. The company performed at Beeston's Phoenix Theatre from 1625 until 1636; their resident dramatist was James SHIRLEY. They also performed in such court MASQUES as *Love's Mistress* (1634), for which Inigo Jones designed scenery. Another outbreak of the plague in 1636 forced the company to disband, the actors eventually being absorbed into other companies. Beeston then formed Beeston's Boys, one of the BOY COMPANIES.

A second company with the same name performed at the London Theatre, Salisbury Court, from 1637 until 1642, when the Puritans closed the theatres.

Queen of Beautiful Actresses The extravagant billing for the French tragic actress Mademoiselle Georges (Marguerite-Josephine Weymer; 1787–1867). In 1824 she was billed as "Queen of Beautiful Actresses – the most beautiful woman at present on the stage". The manager of the theatre in Angers went further, advertising her as "the most beautiful woman in Europe". Mademoiselle Georges made her debut at the Comédie-Française in 1802 and won acclaim as Lady Macbeth. In 1808 she eloped with a dancer to Russia, where she joined a French company and became a bitter rival to the actress Yekaterina Semyonova (1786–1839). She returned to the Comédie-Française five years later, but her furious temper caused so much trouble in the company that she was forced to leave in 1817.

Her lovers were said to include Napoleon, Talleyrand, and Metternich. In her old age, Mlle Georges asked Arsene Houssaye to help her to write her memoirs; he could not control his curiosity about her supposed affair with the emperor:

> HOUSSAYE Is it true that he sent for you long after midnight and that he forgot that you were there until morning, absorbed as he was in the map of Europe?
>
> MADEMOISELLE GEORGES Pure slander. His map of Europe! *I* was his map of Europe.

Queen of Burlesque Nickname of the striptease artist Gypsy Rose LEE.

Queen of the Halls Nickname of Marie LLOYD, the most famous of the British music-hall singers. Her alternative nickname **Our Marie** indicates the warmth of feeling with which she was regarded by the British public.

Queen's Theatre A London theatre in Shaftesbury Avenue, which was a twin to the Edwardian GLOBE THEATRE. When John Vedrenne opened it in 1907, George Bernard SHAW remarked, "He is after a knighthood. It is not for nothing that he called his theatre *The Queen's*..." The elegant interior, largely preserved despite wartime bomb damage, combined Italian, Georgian, and Edwardian styles.

By 1913 business had become so bad that 'tango teas' with dancing and a fashion show were introduced. A year later, however, the theatre had its first great success with the US comedy *Potash and Perlmutter* (1914). It was managed from 1929 to 1933 by Barry Jackson, who presented Shaw's *The Apple Cart* (1929; with Cedric Hardwicke and Edith Evans); other notable productions included Rudolf Besier's *The Barretts of Wimpole Street* (1930). The manager from 1937 to 1939 was John Gielgud, who during the 1938 season alone performed in *Richard II*, *The School for Scandal*, *Three Sisters*, and *The Merchant of Venice*. More recent successes have included the musicals *Stop the World, I Want to Get Off* (1961), *Wonderful Town!* (1986), and *Radio Times* (1992).

Quem Quaeritis? (Lat. Whom are you looking for?) In the early medieval Church, the most famous example of a TROPE, a short piece of sung dialogue added to the liturgy. It comes from a 9th-century manuscript from St Gall, France. On Easter Sunday a priest dressed in a white robe to represent the angel at Christ's empty tomb addressed three choirboys representing the three Marys:

> *Quen quaeritis in sepulchro, O Christocolae?*
> (Whom seek you in the sepulchre, O Christian women?)

After explaining that Christ had already risen, the priest and choirboys led the congregation in an Easter hymn. By the 10th century this simple sequence had become more elaborate, with monks in Winchester and elsewhere miming the action; additional scenes and even comic characters were sometimes added. Other dialogues were devised with the famous introduction, including a Christmas trope:

> *Quem quaeritis in praesepe, pastores, dicite?*
> (Whom are you looking for in the crib, shepherds, tell us?)

quick-change. quick-change room A small area just offstage in which actors can quickly change their costumes and make-up when there is not enough time for them to return to their dressing rooms.

quick-change variety A format for variety shows initiated at the LONDON COLISEUM when it opened in 1904. The bill consisted of two distinct programmes every day, each of which featured a succession of different acts. On the first day the 24 acts included 'Coon Songs and Dance', 'Signor Peppo's Wonderful Performing Monkeys', and 'Military Evolutions by the Lady Troupe of Japanese Guards'.

quidnunc (Lat. What now?) Someone who is curious to know everything that's going on, or pretends to know it; a self-important newsmonger and gossip. It is the name of the leading character in the farce *The Upholsterer, or What News?* by Arthur Murphy (1727–1805).

Quinapalus A high-sounding pedantic name invoked by Feste the clown in Shakespeare's TWELFTH NIGHT, when he wished to make a saying or proverb sound impressive. The name is used to mean someone 'dragged in' when one wishes to clinch an argument by some supposed quotation.

> What says Quinapalus: "Better a witty fool, than a foolish wit."
> *Twelfth Night* (I, v).

Quotidien, Théâtre du (Fr. theatre of everyday) A style of theatre popularized in the 1970s by the Comédie de Caen and the Théâtre National de Strasbourg. Their productions were realistic in style and presented ordinary, even rather boring characters faced with the problems of contemporary day-to-day existence. The characters were mainly working class, alienated from mainstream society, and inarticulate. The first writer in the genre was Georges Michel, who presented a brutal picture of modern society in such plays as *The Sunday Walk* (1966) and *A Little Love Nest* (1970). Other important playwrights of the Théâtre du Quotidien have included Franz Xaver Kroetz, who dramatized the harsh realities of peasant life in such plays as *Homework* (1971) and *Ghost Train* (1972), Martin Sperr, whose powerful and violent dramas include the much-revived *Magic Afternoon* (1968), Jean-Paul Wenzel, who enjoyed success with *Far from Hagondange* (1977), and Michel Deutsch, whose *Convoy* (1980) deals with the failure of communication between a French peasant woman and the young Jewish girl she shelters during the Occupation.

Quyi A generic term for China's vocal arts, which encompasses about 350 provincial styles of story-telling and balladry, often accompanied by gestures and mime. The performers sing or recite to traditional rhythmic accompaniment from drums, wooden clappers, or stringed instruments. The subject matter is taken from epics and romantic novels about China's past, as well as from contemporary events and issues, which are often presented in comical and satirical skits.

Early sources for the *Quyi* (as for Chinese acting in general) were the Buddhist sutras, the entertainments presented by jesters at the Han courts, and comedy routines from the *zaju* variety plays. Public story-telling flowered during the Sung dynasty (960–1279). Although the *Quyi* story-tellers were later banished to the streets and were banned altogether during the Cultural Revolution, their skills are highly valued in China today.

R

Rabinal Achí A Guatemalan folk drama that is believed to be the only form of theatre to have survived from the pre-Columbian Americas without European influence. The Quiché Mayan Indians had a rich oral tradition but the dialogue for the *Rabinal Achí* was not written down until 1850, when it was also translated into Spanish, French, and English. A performance is still put on by the surviving Quiché Mayans, each year in January.

The *Rabinal Achí* was originally known as the Dance of Tun; music and dancing form an important part of the spectacle. The drama tells the story of the Quiché Warrior and the Rabinal Warrior, who fight a ceremonial battle against death.

Rachel (Elisabeth Félix; 1821–58) French tragic actress, born in Switzerland. The daughter of poor Jewish pedlars, she began her career by singing in the streets of Paris and Lyons as a child. She subsequently attended the Conservatoire, where she was trained in the French classical tradition by Joseph-Isidore Samson, before joining the COMÉDIE-FRANÇAISE in 1838. Her first great triumph came in 1843, when she played the lead in Racine's *Phèdre.* As Adrienne LECOUVREUR in Scribe's play of that name (1848) she confirmed her position as one of the greatest tragic actresses of the age. Rachel did much to revive the reputation of the Comédie-Française and toured widely in Europe: she also became known for her many love affairs. Despite her small frame she gave performances of great physical force. Her early death was caused by consumption aggravated by overexertion.

Racine, Jean(-Baptiste) (1639–99) French playwright who is considered the greatest master of French classical tragedy. An orphan, he was educated by Jansenists at Port Royal, where he read Sophocles and Euripides. His tutor twice surprised him secretly reading the Greek romance *The Loves of Theagenes and Chariclea*, and both times threw the book into the fire. Racine found another copy, memorized it, and took it to the tutor, saying "You may now burn this as you burned the others." This tutor subsequently described writers as "public poisoners." Racine's interest in drama and his debauched personal life subsequently led to his estrangement from the movement.

Racine wrote his first serious poems while studying at the University of Paris. In 1664 he met MOLIÈRE, who produced his first play, *La Thébaïde*, at the Palais-Royal. Racine subsequently alienated him by taking his next offering, ALEXANDRE LE GRAND (1665), to a rival theatre, the HÔTEL DE BOURGOGNE, shortly after its opening. To add insult to injury, Racine then seduced Molière's actress mistress, Mlle Du Parc, and employed her as his leading lady. She appeared in his tragedy ANDROMAQUE (1667), which won the acclaim of Paris playgoers and the support of Louis XIV.

Racine's other works of this period include his only comedy, *The Litigants* (1668), and the tragedies *Britannicus* (1669), *Bérénice* (1672), BAJAZET (1672), *Mithridate* (1673), and *Iphigénie* (1674). His literary style is highly formal and employs an unusually restricted vocabulary (some 2000 words). In 1677 he produced his masterpiece PHÈDRE, which emphasized the destructive power of irrational passions. Within a year of this triumph, at the height of his powers, he retired from the theatre and became court historiographer to Louis XIV. His son later attributed this to Racine's return to Jansenism and his wish to atone for a dissolute life. His last two plays, *Esther* (1689) and ATHALIE (1691), were based on biblical material and written for the girls' school run by the King's morganatic wife, Madame de Maintenon. Neither was performed publicly in Racine's lifetime.

Racine fell out of favour at court by criticizing Louis's warmongering. The king complained, "Because he is a great poet, does he fancy himself a minister?"

After his death from cancer, Racine was buried in the monastery at Port Royal.

When Louis issued an anti-Jansenist decree and destroyed the monastery and school, Racine's remains were moved to the church of St Étienne du Mont in Paris.

RADA (The Royal Academy of Dramatic Art) The best-known British drama school, founded in 1904 by Herbert Beerbohm TREE, manager of His Majesty's Theatre. Later that year he handed the Academy over to an independent governing body and it moved to the present Gower Street site. Its theatre, the Vanbrugh, opened in 1954 and is named after Irene and Violet Vanbrugh, the actress sisters of Sir Kenneth Barnes (1878–1957), who ran RADA for many years. George Bernard Shaw was a noted supporter of the Academy, which has trained such renowned actors as John Gielgud, Margaret Lockwood, Richard Attenborough, Alan Bates, and Glenda Jackson. In recent years, the Academy has added the George Bernard Shaw (GBS) Theatre and a small studio theatre. It trains students in acting and stage management as well as offering specialist courses in stage carpentry, scene painting and design, and property making.

Radio City Music Hall The world's largest theatre, which also claims to possess the world's largest Wurlitzer organ and chandeliers. Part of the Rockefeller Center in New York, it opened in 1932 with variety acts before switching to a mixture of top Hollywood films and spectacular variety shows featuring the Rockettes precision chorus line. Radio City announced its closure in 1979 but in response to a public outcry and nationwide campaign it has remained open.

Radius In Britain, a nondenominational Christian organization that promotes and coordinates religious drama. It was founded in 1929 as the **Religious Drama Society of Great Britain** with George Bell, then the Dean of Canterbury, as its first president. The society commissioned Christopher FRY's *A Sleep of Prisoners* for the 1951 Festival of Britain.

Radius sponsors productions of religious plays, offers advice, and holds an annual summer school to train directors and actors. It also maintains a large reference and lending library and is associated with the **Sesame** organization, which promotes drama as therapy for the physically and mentally handicapped.

rag opery US slang for a travelling TENT SHOW.

rain. rain barrel A metal container with perforations in the underside, used to sprinkle water on stage for the visual simulation of rainfall.

rain machine In the theatre, a device used to create the sound of rain, hail, or waves (*see* SOUND EFFECTS). It was normally a large cylinder that could be filled with such items as pebbles, marbles, dried peas or beans, etc., to create a variety of different sounds when rotated. The sound could also be varied by changing the rotation speed. The device was popularized by the French stage designer Philippe Jacques De LOUTHERBOURG. A wind machine with a ribbed drum could usually be converted into a rain machine when required.

Raisin in the Sun A play by Lorraine Hansberry (1930–65), first performed in 1958 in New York. The first play by a Black woman to be produced on Broadway, it had a Black director and cast and found financial backing from the Black business community. It was very successful and won the New York Critics' Circle Award for 1959. In 1961 the story was made into a film starring Sidney Poitier and Ruby Dee.

The plot concerns the struggles of a Black family, in the inner city of Chicago. When her husband dies, Mama Younger receives a large sum of insurance money and buys a house in an all-White neighbourhood. This causes bitter disappointment to her son, Walter Lee, who had hoped to use the money to open a liquor store, but his pregnant wife, Ruth is delighted. Walter's sister, Beneatha, is only concerned with her plans to study medicine. Mama finally gives Walter the remaining money, including Beneatha's share, for his store, but his business partner runs off with the cash. Walter feels humiliated but wins back the respect of his family by insisting they still move into the new house.

rake The slope of a stage floor from the back down towards the front. It was introduced in the Renaissance period to enhance the illusionistic effect of scenes painted in perspective; a rake appears in the basic design for a theatre published by Sebastiano Serlio in 1545. However, the rake, which could be up to a 4% slope, caused problems with jointed scenery and movable platforms (*see*

BOAT TRUCK). In modern theatres the stage is level while the auditorium floor is raked to enable those sitting at the back to see over the heads of those in front of them.

Ralph Roister Doister The first English comedy on classical lines. It was written in 1534 by the Oxford scholar Nicholas Udall (1505–56) and received its first performance at Eton, where he was headmaster. Udall composed the play, which shows the influence of PLAUTUS and TERENCE, for performance by his pupils instead of the usual Latin comedies. It was not printed until about 1566. Despite its crude action and doggerel verse, the play influenced generations of comic dramatists in England. The story follows the wooing of a wealthy London widow, Dame Christian Custance, by the pompous fool, Ralph Roister Doister.

Ramlila (Hindi: play of Rama) A form of Indian theatre, especially popular in northern villages, which depicts episodes from the life of the Hindu god Rama. *Ramlila* is a generic term for a range of dramatic events performed in honour of Rama, mainly during festivals in September, October, and November, and at Diwali. It takes place throughout India and has many local variants. In Ramnagar (which means 'Rama's city') 30 days are devoted to the *Ramlila* and more than a million pilgrims as well as non-Hindus attend the processions and performances. *Ramlila* probably dates back to ancient India, with stories taken from the *Ramayana* and music that blends religious, classical, and folk traditions.

The main characters are Rama, his wife Sita, and his three brothers Lakshmana, Bharata, and Saturgna, all of whom are played by Brahmin boys who have not reached puberty. They are believed to become embodiments of the gods during the performance. The actor playing Ravana, the king of the demons, wears a mask showing his 10 heads. There are opportunities for hundreds of other youths to take part as the warring monkey soldiers of Rama and the demon soldiers of Ravana. The battle ends with the burning of huge effigies of Ravana and his brothers, which are set alight by burning arrows; fireworks are also set off as the crowd chants "Victory to Rama".

Ranelagh A former place of amusement in London, on the site that now forms part of the grounds of Chelsea Hospital. It was named after Richard Jones, 1st Earl of Ranelagh, who built a house and laid out gardens there in 1690. From 1742 to 1803, Ranelagh was famous for its masquerades, etc. A notable feature was the Rotunda, built in 1742. It was similar to the Albert Hall in design, with numerous boxes in which refreshments were served, while the brightly lit floor served as a promenade. There was also a Venetian pavilion in the centre of a lake. *See also* CREMORNE GARDENS; VAUXHALL GARDENS.

rare. rare Ben The inscription on the tomb of Ben JONSON, in the north nave aisle of Westminster Abbey (*see* POET'S CORNER). According to the author John Aubrey, it was "done at the charge of Jack Young (afterwards knighted), who, walking there when the grave was covering, gave the fellow eighteenpence to cut it." *Rare* in this case means unusual, remarkable, from the Latin *rarus*. It has been suggested that the inscription was originally meant to read "Orare Ben Jonson", Latin for "Pray for Ben Jonson".

raree show A peep-show; a show carried about in a box. In the 17th century, most of the travelling showmen were Savoyards, and perhaps this represents their pronunciation of *rare* or *rarity*.

Rasdhari The version of RASLILA that has developed in the northwest Indian state of Rajasthan. The travelling performers who brought *Raslila* to Rajasthan in the mid 19th century were called *Rasdharis*, a term that was later applied to the genre itself. Local people formed their own troupes and diverse styles developed; while some were overtly devotional others adapted stories from mythological and historical sources and drew on regional musical traditions. Today's fast-paced energetic performances are put on by peripatetic actors and musicians in village meeting areas. Costumes are based on local styles and the actors often improvise to suit the mood or habits of the villagers or to satirize individuals.

Rasdhari productions take place on a simple stage without scenery: basic props are often borrowed from the villagers. In contrast, the prose and songs are elaborate and detailed to create vivid pictures of other places and times for the audiences.

Raslila (Hindi: dance play in a circle) In India, a general term for various dance-dramas and dances; the word refers to Lord Krishna's dance with the wives of Vrindavan. Performances often occur in a temple or sacred resting place for travellers. The most famous version is the *Raslila* of Vrindavan, a holy city in northern India close to where Krishna is believed to have been born.

Raslila is a sacred ceremony in itself: performances must end before midnight and the audience must remove their shoes, refrain from talking and smoking, and never sit or stand higher than the actors playing Krishna and Radha. The *Raslila* troupe consists of 10 to 18 male performers. The actors who play Krishna and Radha are traditionally drawn from Brahmin families while Krishna's other chief consorts are played by pre-pubescent boys. When the actors don their crowns, they are believed to become incarnations of the gods they portray and are carried to the acting area so that their feet do not touch the ground. The drama combines dancing, songs, dialogue, monologue, and tableaux. When it ends the audience shouts "Victory to Krishna of Vrindavan!"

Rattigan, Sir Terence (1911–77) British playwright, whose well-structured plays enjoyed enormous success in the years before and after World War II. At one time three of his works were running simultaneously in the West End. Rattigan was knighted in 1971, the only dramatist so honoured since the war.

When Rattigan was a young man his father, a wealthy diplomat, agreed to finance his writing for a maximum of two years. After 23 months, Rattigan produced his first comedy, FRENCH WITHOUT TEARS (1936), about young British students learning French for the diplomatic corps. It ran for 1049 performances at the Criterion Theatre, providing Rattigan with the greatest success ever enjoyed by a West End newcomer. Rattigan was emotionally devastated by the play's opening night. When the audience rose to its feet with cries of "Author, author" he vanished and was found looking ill and supporting himself against a back wall. When Rattigan finally stepped forward to acknowledge the applause, the curtain landed heavily upon his head.

His second success, *After the Dance*, dealt with the danger of stifled passion; it was revived by the BBC in 1993. His great wartime successes included a drama inspired by his days in the RAF, FLARE PATH (1942), and *While The Sun Shines* (1943), which ran for 1154 performances. THE WINSLOW BOY (1946) which won many awards, told the true story of a father's campaign to prove his son innocent of theft. Later outstanding works included THE BROWNING VERSION (1948), THE DEEP BLUE SEA (1952), a moving story about adultery and suicide (written after the suicide of his lover Kenneth Morgan), SEPARATE TABLES (1955), and ROSS (1960) in which Sir Alec Guinness starred as T. E. Lawrence.

Rattigan lived an extravagant life, driving a Rolls-Royce with a personalized number plate and gambling away the £25,000 he made from *French Without Tears* in three weeks. His lifestyle and attitudes were diametrically opposed to those of the ANGRY YOUNG MEN of the mid 1950s, who tended to regard his work as the epitome of everything they disliked most in contemporary drama. Rattigan stated publicly that he hated Osborne's LOOK BACK IN ANGER (1956) and as the new KITCHEN SINK realism became popular his reputation waned, along with that of Noël Coward and others of his generation. "We were told we were old-fashioned, effete, and corrupt," he said. Recently, however, there has been more interest in his work: a production of *The Deep Blue Sea* opened in 1993 at the Almeida Theatre, the first major revival since its premiere in 1952. *See also* AUNT EDNA.

Räuber, Die (Ger. *The Robbers*) The first play by Friedrich von SCHILLER; its first production in 1782 caused a sensation and is now accepted as a watershed in the German theatre. "Complete strangers fell sobbing into one another's arms," wrote one observer, "and fainting women tottered towards the exits." Schiller wrote *Die Räuber* at the age of 21 and used borrowed money to publish the text himself; a few months later Baron von Dalberg accepted the drama for production at his National Theatre at Mannheim. The famous actor August IFFLAND created the role of Franz Moor. Younger theatregoers flocked to see the play, stirred by Schiller's attacks on tyranny, corruption in high places, and stifling social conventions.

Schiller, an officer in a Stuttgart regiment, travelled to Mannheim to see the premiere without obtaining the permission of the autocratic Duke Karl Eugen of Württemberg. When the duke sentenced him to a fortnight's detention and ordered him to stop writing plays, Schiller fled to Baron von Dalberg, who eventually appointed him as resident dramatist to his theatre.

Die Räuber made a major contribution to the STURM UND DRANG movement in Germany and also influenced the development of romantic melodrama in England and elsewhere. An adaptation, *The Red-Cross Knights* was produced at the Haymarket in 1799.

Raupach, Ernst *See* SHAKESPEARE OF TRIVIALITY *under* SHAKESPEARE.

Ravana Chhaya (Oriyan: Ravana shadow) An almost extinct form of shadow-puppet theatre from the Indian state of Orissa. Performances last for seven nights and can involve up to 700 different puppets. In Hindu mythology *Ravana* is the ten-headed Hindu demon-king who rules the kingdom of Lanka. He is the villain of the epic *Ramayana*, which tells of his battles with, and defeat by, the hero-god Rama. The stories told in *Ravana Chhaya* are all to do with this conflict, and come from the *Vichitra Ramayana*, the Oriyan version of the *Ramayana*, which was written around 1700.

It seems strange that the genre should be named after its chief villain; some suggest that this is owing to the influence of the Jains, who are more sympathetic to Ravana than most Hindus, or possibly to that of the Tamils, who take Ravana to be a symbol of resistance to invaders from the north, assuming Lanka represents Sri Lanka. A more likely explanation is that the name *Rama Chhaya* was rejected because it was considered unlucky to speak of the god Rama as a shadow.

Performances are always preceded by sacrifices to Rama and other gods, although they can be held at any time and place and are not related to any particular festivals. The puppets themselves are considered to be ceremonial objects. When a new puppet is made it is blessed before it is used, and worn out puppets are cremated and their ashes scattered into a river or stream.

realism A movement in late 19th-century drama that aimed to replace the artificial romantic style with accurate depictions of ordinary people in plausible situations. In attempting to create a perfect illusion of reality, playwrights and directors rejected dramatic conventions that had existed since the beginnings of drama. EURIPIDES had taken a tentative step towards realism in the 5th century BC but in later European theatre ordinary people speaking colloquially had only appeared in comedy or farce; even in such plays no attempt was made to create realistic sets or scenery. The 19th-century realist movement revolutionized contemporary theatre in every aspect, from scenery, to styles of acting, from dialogue to make-up.

The first moves towards modern realism were made in 16th-century Italy with the introduction of perspective scenery. By the mid 19th century realistic gas lamps had exposed the unnatural appearance of canvas backdrops; the realistic BOX SET with three walls and furnishings was subsequently popularized by the US director and playwright David BELASCO. The Victorians also pioneered mechanical devices that were capable of producing convincing scenic illusions and sensational effects, such as fires and train crashes. In the 18th century David GARRICK initiated the use of historically accurate costumes and sets, a trend that was followed by directors including Sir Henry Irving and Sir Herbert Beerbohm TREE.

Despite these developments, it was not until the end of the 19th century that the drama began to emulate the serious treatment of contemporary themes achieved in the novel. The move away from melodrama and stilted dialogue to "the plain truthful language of reality" was led by Henrik IBSEN, who is often called the father of modern realism. Ibsen also broke with convention by taking the everyday lives of his middle-class audience as subject matter for serious drama. In this he was followed by the Russians CHEKHOV and GORKI: while the former explored the ennui of outwardly uneventful middle-class lives, the latter depicted the drudgery and suffering of the poorest classes. The first serious steps to codify realism in acting were made by Konstantin STANISLAVSKY for productions at the Moscow Art Theatre. Before his production of Gorki's THE LOWER DEPTHS (1902), Stanislavsky sent his actors into the Moscow slums to prepare for their roles as beggars. This technique was later developed and systematized by Lee Strasberg as the METHOD.

Other playwrights to contribute to the realist movement included T. W. ROBERTSON, Henry Arthur JONES, Harley GRANVILLE-BARKER, and George Bernard SHAW in Britain, Eugene O'NEILL in America, Victorien SARDOU and Augustin Eugène SCRIBE in France, and Gerhart HAUPTMANN in Germany. *See also* CUP-AND-SAUCER DRAMA; KITCHEN SINK; NATURALISM.

Real Thing, The A comedy by Tom STOPPARD, which became an instant success when first performed at the Strand Theatre, London, in 1982 in a production starring Felicity Kendal, Tom Conti, and Roger Rees.

Max thinks his mistress, Charlotte, has another lover when he overhears her acting out a scene from a drama written by her playwright husband, Henry. The play reflects the real affair taking place between Henry and Max's wife, Annie. Both marriages crack under the strain enabling Henry and Annie to wed. Two years later, Annie meets the peace-protester Brodie; they become lovers until he is arrested and jailed for burning the Cenotaph wreath. Annie then embarks on an affair with a young actor, but manages to save her marriage with Henry because their love is 'the real thing'.

Recruiting Officer, The A comedy by George FARQUHAR, who based it upon his own experiences as a recruiting officer. It was first performed in 1706 in London with Anne Oldfield in the role of Sylvia; later 20th-century actresses to excel in the part have included Edith EVANS in 1927 and Maggie SMITH in 1970. The play has been constantly revived and was an early colonial favourite; it was performed during the 1730s at Charleston's Dock Street Theatre in Sydney in 1789 (the first recorded stage performance in Australia). The plot was used by BRECHT in his *Trumpets and Drums.*

In 1963 the new National Theatre staged a production directed by William Gaskill and Laurence OLIVIER, who also took a minor role. Although keen to enter into the spirit of experiment that prevailed during the theatre's first year, Olivier was not happy with Gaskill's idea of improvisation at rehearsals. "I don't like improvisation in rehearsal," he complained. "As soon as a director says, 'Try this, try that,' I think, 'Listen, chum, I can do that at home'." At one rehearsal Gaskill, Kenneth Tynan, and John Dexter all criticized Olivier for overacting; he was shocked at such an accusation but nevertheless moderated his performance.

The play concerns Captain Plume and Captain Brazen, who are recruiting for the Army in Shrewsbury. They are assisted by the disreputable Sergeant Kite, who is not above lying, cheating, and disguising himself as a fortune-teller to dupe naive youths into enlisting. Plume has fallen in love with Sylvia, but her father, Justice Balance, has forbidden the marriage. Sylvia disguises herself as a man and Plume tricks her father into handing her over as a recruit. When the truth is discovered Balance relents and allows the match. Plume vows to give up recruiting in order to "breed recruits".

red. **Red Bull Theatre** A London courtyard theatre established on the premises of the Red Bull Inn, Clerkenwell. The galleried inn had occasionally presented plays in its large square yard before 1605, when Aaron Holland converted the space into a permanent theatre and QUEEN ANNE'S MEN moved in for an 11-year residency. Although in its heyday it promoted the works of Thomas HEYWOOD and saw the acting of Christopher BEESTON, the Red Bull later acquired a somewhat disreputable reputation because of its rowdy audiences and its propensity for staging sensational plays. After Queen Anne's Men left, the Red Bull brought in several other companies and underwent major renovation in 1625, apparently adding a roof. During the Puritan INTERREGNUM (1642–60), it drew crowds to illegal productions; Robert Cox was imprisoned after performing a comic DROLL there in 1653. After the Restoration Thomas KILLIGREW brought a company there that featured the actor Michael Mohun. Killigrew's later decision to leave with some of the best actors proved a serious blow. Samuel Pepys recorded watching a dismal play at the Red Bull on 23 March 1661. Audiences declined and the theatre was demolished in 1665.

red-hot poker In the English HARLEQUINADE, a comic prop of Clown, who would place it maliciously under the seat of some unsuspecting character's trousers. As PANTOMIME became more popular than the harlequinade, which was often relegated to the position of an AFTERPIECE, so the red-hot poker was used less frequently. In 1864 *Chambers Journal* published an imaginary letter to Clown, which included the complaint: "What has become of the red-hot poker? On behalf of the entire community, I repeat, with becoming warmth of expression, WHAT HAS BECOME OF THE RED-HOT POKER?"

Red Megaphone, the (*Das Rote Sprachrohr*) Germany's first and most famous AGITPROP company, which performed communist propaganda plays, revues, and choral works at factories, workers' clubs, and similar venues. It was established in 1927 by M. Valletin and the following year presented *Hallo, Kollege Jungarbeiter* (*Hello, Young Colleagues*), an episodic piece about the exploitation of workers. In 1929 the Red Megaphone toured the Soviet Union with its choral presentation *Dritte Internationale* (*Third International*). In 1931 the company adapted EPIC THEATRE techniques for *Song of the Red United Front*. It was disbanded and some members arrested when the Nazis came to power in 1933.

Red Roses for Me A play by Sean O'CASEY, first performed in Dublin in 1943. It is the most frequently revived of the later expressionist works that he wrote in 'exile' in England after his rift with W. B. Yeats and the ABBEY THEATRE. The play was based on O'Casey's own experiences during the General Strike in Dublin (1913). It expresses anti-fascist ideals using powerful colloquial language and also features dance and mime. Although the play has been criticized for its structural clumsiness, it is nevertheless regarded as one of O'Casey's most moving works.

Redgrave family A British theatrical family that has now produced three generations of famous actors: Sir Michael Redgrave (1908–85), his daughters Vanessa Redgrave (1937–) and Lynn Redgrave (1943–), his son, Corin Redgrave (1939–), and Vanessa's daughters, Natasha Jane Richardson (1963–) and Joely Richardson (1966–).

Sir Michael Redgrave was the son of the actor Roy Redgrave and the actress Margaret Scudamore. His mother insisted that at 6′ 2″ he was too tall to be an actor so he became a schoolmaster and did not embark on his acting career until his mid twenties. In 1934 he joined the Liverpool Repertory Theatre, where he met and married the actress **Rachel Kempson** (1910–). Two years later they both joined the Old Vic, where Michael made his London debut as the King of Navarre in *Love's Labour Lost*. He then worked with Sir John Gielgud at the Queen's Theatre.

During World War II Redgrave served in the Royal Navy and starred in several wartime films. In 1943 he played Rakitin in Turgenev's *A Month in the Country*, a role he repeated in 1949 for the Old Vic Company. During one matinée performance, he was playing a love scene with Valerie Taylor in a somewhat desultory fashion when he heard a lady in the stalls whisper pointedly to her friend, "I like *her*." Noted Redgrave "I was noticeably quicker on my cues after that."

In 1959, the year he was knighted, Redgrave found further acclaim in his own dramatization of Henry James's *The Aspern Papers*. Three years later he joined Olivier's company for the first CHICHESTER FESTIVAL, when he starred in the title role of Chekhov's *Uncle Vanya*. After a spell of ill health he returned to the stage in 1971 in William Trevor's *The Old Boys* at the Mermaid Theatre; a year later he played Father in a production of John Mortimer's *A Voyage Round My Father* which toured Canada and Australia.

Vanessa Redgrave studied at the Central School of Speech and Drama and made her professional debut in 1957 at the Frinton Summer Theatre in *The Reluctant Debutante*. She made her first London appearance in 1958, acting beside her father in N. C. Hunter's *A Touch of the Sun*. In 1961 she won rapturous praise for her performance as Rosalind in an RSC production of AS YOU LIKE IT. Her other early successes included playing Nina in a production of Chekhov's *The Seagull* directed by her then husband, Tony Richardson (1964). More recently she has appeared in Shaw's HEARTBREAK HOUSE at the Haymarket (1992) and Ibsen's *John Gabriel Borkman* at the Royal National Theatre (1996). Her films include *Howard's End* (1992). Referring to her many political activities, including membership of the Workers' Revolutionary Party, her father commented: "There are some days when her politics drive me mad and other days when I see her touch greatness as an actress and am immensely proud."

Corin Redgrave starred in Ronald Millar's *Abelard and Heloise* in 1971 but soon afterwards gave up acting to work for the Workers' Revolutionary Party. He has made a return to TV and film work in the 1990s.

Lynn Redgrave performed with the National Theatre company before moving to America in 1983. She returned to Britain in 1990 to star with her sister Vanessa and Vanessa's daughter Natasha Richardson in a highly publicized production of Chekhov's THREE SISTERS at the Queen's Theatre. Subsequent Broadway productions have included Ibsen's *The Master Builder* (1992). In 1996 she opened in *Shakespeare for My Father*, a one-woman show reflecting her difficult relationship with Sir Michael Redgrave. She has also had a successful film career.

Natasha Richardson made her adult debut in a production of *The Seagull* in 1985 at the Lyric Theatre, Hammersmith. In 1992 she gave an award-winning Broadway performance in *Anna Christie*. Her films include *Patty Hearst* (1988) and *Widow's Peak* (1994).

Joely Richardson began acting in 1985, when she appeared with her mother in the film *Wetherby*. She has also appeared on television, notably in *Lady Chatterley's Lover* (1993), and in the films *Drowning by Numbers* (1988) and *Shining Through* (1991). Her London stage debut was in 1989.

reflector A spotlight or floodlight unit that contains both the lamp and a shiny back surface to intensify and focus the beam of light.

Regan The second of the king's unfilial daughters in Shakespeare's KING LEAR. In one scene (IV, ii) she is called "most barbarous, most degenerate". In Geoffrey of Monmouth's *Historia Britonum* from which the story originally comes, she is called *Regau*. *See also* CORDELIA; GONERIL.

regional theatre *See* RESIDENT THEATRE.

rehearsal A session in which the director, cast, and staff of a play prepare for a performance. Usually, the first rehearsals are read-throughs in which the cast simply read aloud from the script. Entrances, exits, movements, and gestures are added next, usually by BLOCKING. Technical rehearsals are also held for the stage crew, lighting technicians, etc. The final run-through before the opening night is the DRESS REHEARSAL.

Except in rare cases of improvisation, rehearsal is now regarded as essential in the Western theatre. This has not always been the case; rehearsals were virtually unknown to medieval performers. That Elizabethan actors met to practice is shown by Shakespeare's *A Midsummer Night's Dream* (1595), which includes a scene in which a group of amateur players rehearse. Organized rehearsals had become standard practice by the 19th century, when they were directed by the stage manager. The standard of rehearsals is often no indication of how well a performance will go. Terence RATTIGAN's first play, *French Without Tears* (1936), had disastrous rehearsals but ran for 1000 performances in the West End.

Rehearsals are often intense and stressful, providing a battleground for egos and temperaments. Sir Alec GUINNESS was fired twice during rehearsals in the early part of his career. Dame Madge KENDAL, who managed St James's Theatre in the 1880s, once gathered her cast round and insisted that they kneel to pray, "Oh Lord, we pray Thee out of Thy infinite mercy that Thou will cause some notion of the rudiments of acting to be vouchsafed to this company for Jesus Christ's sake, Amen." She then stood up and growled, "Well, now we'll see what *that* will do!"

Horror stories about never-ending rehearsals abound. The longest rehearsal period at the Royal National Theatre was for Marlowe's *Tamburlaine the Great* in 1976; owing to construction work the original 10-week schedule was extended to nearly six months. The ancient Greek CHORUS would rehearse full time for at least 3 months before giving their single performance. The record-holder, however, is STANISLAVSKY who once spent two years rehearsing the Moscow Art Theatre's production of *Hamlet*, which finally opened in 1912.

Rehearsal, The A comedy first performed at Drury Lane in 1671; although it is attributed to George Villiers, 2nd duke of Buckingham (1628–87), it is likely that several other parties had a hand in its authorship.

The Rehearsal is a BURLESQUE of the popular Restoration genre of HEROIC DRAMA. Its main character, BAYES, was intended to pillory the playwrights William DAVENANT and John DRYDEN. The plot revolves around a rehearsal for a heroic tragedy that magnifies all of the failings and absurdities of the genre. Notable among the characters in the play-within-a-play are the bombastic DRAWCANSIR and Prince Pretty-man. *The Rehearsal* was one of the earliest examples of the English dramatic burlesque. It had many imitators during the 18th century, most notably Sheridan's THE CRITIC.

Reigen (Ger. round dance) A one-act play by the Austrian playwright Arthur Schnitzler (1862–1931). It was written in 1896–97 and first performed in 1912 in Budapest, where the audience was shocked by its frank portrayal of casual and heartless sexual encounters. Schnitzler was a friend of Sigmund Freud and had been influenced by his idea of sex being paramount in human behaviour. The play caused riots when performed in Vienna in 1921 and was not staged again until 1982. It has been translated into English as *The Round Dance, Merry-Go-Round,* and *Hands Around,* and has twice been filmed in France as *La Ronde* (1950 and 1964).

The play, set in turn-of-the-century Vienna, presents a daisy chain of sexual liaisons: a prostitute is picked up by a soldier, who meets a housemaid, who is seduced by her master, who sleeps with a young married woman, and so on. The 'round dance' is completed when an army officer picks up the original prostitute. The characters all deceive or are deceived, excusing their infidelities to themselves with a variety of pretexts.

Reinhardt, Max (Max Goldmann; 1873–1943) Austrian director, actor, and manager. The first modern director to gain an international reputation, Reinhardt was regarded as either a genius or a vulgar showman. He dominated the European stage for more than 25 years, directing more than 600 productions, and was a major influence on drama in Britain and America. His innovations in staging and the use of colour and movement (especially in crowd scenes) are considered particularly important. It was largely owing to Reinhardt's fame and influence that productions began to be attributed to the director rather than to author or the leading actor.

After studying drama in Vienna, Reinhardt spent a year with the resident theatre company in Salzburg. He subsequently became a leading performer under Otto Brahm at the Deutsches Theater, Berlin. In 1903 he founded the Neues Theater in Berlin, where in one year he produced and directed 42 works by such varied dramatists as Wilde, Schiller, and Gorki. In these productions he reacted against NATURALISM and he adopted many of the ideas of the British designer Gordon CRAIG, using steps, runways, and rostrums, to divide the stage horizontally and vertically. With the Swiss designer Adolf Appia, he pioneered new lighting effects and the use of THEATRE-IN-THE-ROUND.

Reinhardt initiated a revival of classical Greek drama and also made an impact with his striking productions of Ibsen, Strindberg, Wedekind, and Shakespeare. His inventive and much revived staging of *A Midsummer Night's Dream* was first seen in 1905.

Reinhardt was famous for his lavish spectacles. In 1920 he founded the Salzburg Festival and thereafter directed the morality play *Jedermann* (Hugo von Hofmannstal's adaptation of EVERYMAN) in front of the cathedral every year until 1934. He was equally comfortable with intimate work, founding Berlin's Kammerspiele (chamber theatre) in 1906 and the avant-garde Das Junge Deutschland theatre in 1917.

When the Nazis took power in 1933 Reinhardt was abroad. He left his theatres to the German people, having sent a bitterly ironic letter to the Nazi government. He settled in America, where he directed and produced a successful film version of his famous *A Midsummer Night's Dream* starring James Cagney as Bottom and Mickey Rooney as Puck. His final production was Franz Werfel's *The Eternal Road* (1937), an interminable biblical pageant with music by Kurt Weill. The performances, at the Manhattan Opera House in New York, lasted from 8 p.m. until 3 a.m. The play drew full houses for 153 performances but lost $5000 a week owing to high production costs.

Réjane (Gabrielle-Charlotte Reju; 1857–1920) French actress and comedienne, whose performances enchanted Paris at the turn of the century, although most of the plays she appeared in are now forgotten. She made her Paris debut at the Théâtre du Vaudeville in 1875 and later appeared in both London and New York. She was known for her eccentricities, such as driving about Paris in a carriage drawn by two mules.

Réjane's appearances in serious roles tended to divide the critics. Some, including Shaw, admired her mastery of pathos, comparing her with Sarah BERNHARDT and Eleonora DUSE. Many of her best roles were in works by SARDOU; in 1893 she created the part of MADAME SANS-GÊNE, taking the play to New York two years later. She also appeared in Sardou's *Divorçons*, Alexandre Dumas's

La Dame aux camélias, and Ibsen's *A Doll's House*.

She opened her own Théâtre Réjane in Paris in 1906 and remained on the stage until the year she died; her last performance was in a production of Henri Bataille's *La Vierge folle*.

Relapse, The Sir John VANBRUGH's successful first play, a comedy subtitled *Virtue in Danger*. It was first performed in 1696 at Drury Lane. Vanbrugh wrote the play as a parodic sequel to Colley CIBBER's sentimental comedy *Love's Last Shift*, staged earlier that year at the same theatre. Ironically, Cibber gave a brilliant performance as the main character, Lord Foppington (based on his own play's Sir Novelty Fashion).

The pamphleteer Jeremy COLLIER was outraged by the Foppington character and specifically attacked Vanbrugh (along with Congreve) in his influential *A Short View of the Immorality of the English Stage* (1698). When Sheridan rewrote *The Relapse* as a musical play, *A Trip to Scarborough* (1777), he eliminated much of Vanbrugh's bawdiness for the more prudish audience of his day. Vanbrugh's original has enjoyed many revivals in the 20th century, including an RSC production in 1967 at the Aldwych Theatre.

The play has two plots. The first involves Loveless, a reformed philanderer, who is now living peacefully in the country with his wife, Amanda. He accompanies her to London and suffers a relapse when he meets a young widow, Berinthia. Worthy, Berinthia's former lover, discovers that the rake has returned to his old ways and prevails on her to disclose Loveless's infidelity. In this way he hopes to alienate Amanda from her husband and seduce her himself. Amanda, however, remains loyal and virtuous.

The second (and more amusing) plot concerns the empty-headed Lord Foppington, who has bought his title and wants a wealthy wife to go with it. He arranges to marry an heiress but before he can meet her his younger brother, Young Fashion, who also wants the woman's money, arrives on the scene pretending to be Lord Foppington and marries her in secret. When the real Foppington arrives to claim his bride he is thought to be the impostor and is accused of impersonating himself.

Relatively Speaking The comedy by Alan AYCKBOURN that brought him recognition. It was first performed in 1965 as *Meet My Father* at the Stephen Joseph Theatre in the Round, Scarborough, and then under its current title in 1967 at the Duke of York's Theatre, London.

The play, based on a series of farcical misunderstandings, has a lighter tone than most of Ayckbourn's later comedies. The story involves the lovers Ginny and Greg. When Greg finds evidence that Ginny is being unfaithful, he seethes with jealousy but nevertheless proposes marriage to her. She says she is leaving to visit her parents in their country home, and Greg later follows, intending to surprise her there. Somehow he arrives first and receives a bewildered reception, because this is actually the home of Ginny's married lover, Philip, with whom she is determined to break. When Ginny arrives she continues the pretence that Philip is her father. Philip and his wife go along with the deception, fooling Greg, who leaves happily with Ginny.

renaissance. Renaissance drama European drama from about the 15th to the early 17th centuries. During this period the rediscovery and imitation of classical works established the foundations of the modern theatre. England's major contribution was the lively Elizabethan stage that produced SHAKESPEARE.

Renaissance drama began in Italy, with scholars initially attempting to recreate the original stagings of Greek and Roman plays, then adapting them to contemporary dress and speech. The new interest in classical drama was fired by the rediscovery of texts by Euripides, Seneca, Plautus, and Terence. Aristotle's *Poetics*, which defined the classical genres of tragedy and comedy, came to light in the 15th century. The disreputable profession of acting began to assume a new dignity and the first professional companies were formed.

In the field of tragedy, the main influence on Renaissance writers was the work of SENECA. As early as 1315, Albertino Mussato (1261–1329) wrote a Latin tragedy, *Ecerinis*. The first important Renaissance tragedy was Giangiorgio Trissino's *Sophonisba*, which was written in 1515. Other authors of tragedy included Italy's Pietro Aretino (1492–1556), Giovanni Giraldi (1504–73) (*see* CINTHIO, IL), and Torquato Tasso (1544–95); France's Étienne

Jodelle (1532–73); Spain's Juan de la Cueva (*c.* 1543–1610), and Miguel de Cervantes (1547–1616); as well as England's Shakespeare, KYD, and MARLOWE.

In the Renaissance theatre the solemn scenes of tragedy were often interspersed with *intermezzi* (*see* INTERMEZZO), song and dance interludes that borrowed from the Greco-Roman SATYR-PLAY. These interludes ultimately developed into the court MASQUE in England, the opera in Italy, and ballet in France.

The discovery of Roman comedy, with its stock characters and intricate plots, inspired Renaissance dramatists to write similar works, such as Udall's RALPH ROISTER DOISTER (*c.* 1534). The first significant comedy written in Italian was *Calandria* (1506) by Bernardo Dovizi da Bibbiena (1470–1520). In 16th-century Italy authors of the COMMEDIA ERUDITA began to combine aspects of Roman comedy and tragedy with elements of the liturgical drama. A leading writer of the *commedia erudita* was Lodovico Ariosto (1474–1533). This new genre, however, provoked an important reaction in the form of the improvised COMMEDIA DELL'ARTE. Major comic playwrights of the era included England's Shakespeare and Ben JONSON; France's Jacques Grévin (1538–70) and Pierre de Larivey (*c.* 1540–1619); and Spain's Bartolomé de Torres Naharro (*c.* 1485–*c.* 1524).

Renaissance stage design also harked back to classical models, especially to Vitruvius (1st century BC), whose ideas influenced the construction of the first permanent playhouses in Italy and France (although theatres in Britain and Spain adapted features from the inn courtyards in which drama had previously been performed). Greco-Roman ideas influenced such Italian theatre architects as Sebastiano SERLIO (1475–1554), Andrea Palladio (1508–80), Giovanni Aleotti (1546–1636), and Vincenzo Scamozzi (1552–1616). Their designs incorporated classical devices like the PERIAKTOI, although new features such as the PROSCENIUM ARCH were also introduced.

Renaissance Theatre Company *See* BRANAGH, KENNETH.

Théâtre de la Renaissance The first theatre of this name opened in Paris in 1826 as the Salle Ventadour. Amongst the works staged there were plays by Victor Hugo and the elder DUMAS. In 1838 the theatre enjoyed an enormous success with Hugo's RUY BLAS, but its fortunes began to decline soon afterwards and it closed in 1841.

The second theatre to bear the name opened in 1873 on the site of the Théâtre de la Porte-Saint-Martin, which had burnt down two years earlier. The Renaissance began by staging serious dramas by such writers as Emile Zola but within a few years had moved to the lighter material of FEYDEAU and LABICHE. In the 1890s the theatre came under the management of Sarah BERNHARDT, who appeared there in a series of her great classical and modern roles. When Bernhardt left the Renaissance it was taken over by the actor-manager Firmin Gémier (1869–1933). In the early 20th century the theatre was badly hit by the rise of the cinema, although it enjoyed a run of successful revivals in the 1930s. In the mid 1950s the Renaissance was taken over by the actress Vera Korene, who did much to restore the building as well as to establish a more contemporary repertoire.

repertory or **repertoire** or **rep** A list of plays that a theatre company performs on a rotating basis, usually on a weekly schedule, or has ready to be presented at short notice. The repertory system was the norm in former years, although early travelling companies could repeat the same play at different locations. Once permanent playhouses were built, different plays had to be presented in rotation to attract a larger nightly audience. During the 18th and 19th centuries, repertory companies were called STOCK COMPANIES, the name by which they are still known in America. At the beginning of the 19th century, most US cities had a resident repertory company. London's Royal Court Theatre operated as a repertory theatre from 1904–07 under Granville-Barker. By the early 20th century the rising expense of producing commercial plays in London and New York had led to the practice of staging a continuous run of a single play in the hope of achieving a long-running hit. There are now two repertory companies in London, the Royal Shakespeare Company and the ROYAL NATIONAL THEATRE, and several in Britain's regional theatres. 'Repertoire' theatres also still exist on the Continent.

The terms 'repertory' and 'repertoire' also refer to the collection of roles played by an individual actor or actress, especially those parts for which he or she is especially known.

repertory movement A campaign in early 20th-century Britain to restore a true REPERTORY system by creating repertory theatres throughout the country. It began as a reaction to the commercial thinking that favoured long-run productions. The movement's success came mostly in the provinces. Leaders of the repertory movement included Frank Benson with his summer festival (1886–1916) at Stratford-upon-Avon, Annie Elizabeth Horniman who established Manchester's Gaiety Theatre as the first permanent repertory theatre in 1907, and Frank Waring who founded the Glasgow Repertory Theatre in 1909. The oldest surviving repertory theatre in Britain is the Liverpool Playhouse, which opened in 1911. These venues proved excellent training grounds for young actors, who could learn a range of parts by appearing in a series of productions that usually lasted no longer than a week at a time.

More than 100 repertory theatres existed in the early 1950s, but by 1960 the number had fallen to 44. A summer venue was established in 1951 at the Pitlochry Festival Theatre in Scotland, while the Belgrave Theatre with its resident repertory company opened in 1958 in Coventry. Since the 1960s there has been a revival in regional theatres, where short-run productions usually last for three or four weeks.

Representative, The A controversial documentary drama (*see* DOCUMENTARY THEATRE) by the Swiss playwright Rolf HOCHHUTH. It was first performed in an abridged version in 1963 in Berlin; English-language versions were seen in London that same year and in New York (as *The Deputy*) a year later. The lengthy detailed play caused an outcry by placing much of the blame for the massacre of the Jewish population in Nazi-occupied Europe on Pope Pius XII's refusal to intervene. The play includes harrowing film sequences of Auschwitz. Although Hochhuth's virulent attack on the Catholic Church resulted in *The Representative* being banned in many countries, it effectively launched the documentary drama movement and thereby helped to revitalize the German theatre.

resident theatre or **regional theatre** or **repertory theatre** Regional nonprofitmaking US theatres run on a professional basis. The various companies and theatres are used as educational resources and as training grounds for actors and directors: they are funded by public and private subsidies. Although the 1980s saw a decline in venues, by 1990 there were still more than 200 resident theatres mounting more than 3000 productions a year.

Although the first resident theatre, the Cleveland Play House, was founded in 1915 the movement only really gathered momentum after the establishment of amateur LITTLE THEATRES in the 1920s. Congress provided a great impetus in 1935 when it chartered the American National Theatre and Academy (*see* ANTA) to revive drama outside New York. In 1947 Margo Jones (1913–55) founded Theatre '47 in Dallas, which became the prototype for later regional theatres. That same year Nina Vance founded Houston's Alley Theatre: in 1949 Zelda Fichandler cofounded the Arena Stage in Washington, DC and in 1952 Jules Irving and Herbert Blau began the Actors' Workshop in San Francisco.

The 1960s saw a great expansion of resident theatre, encouraged by new financial support. In 1959 the Ford Foundation made generous grants to several small companies, allowing them to become totally professional. More help came from the federal government in 1965 with the establishment of the National Endowment for the Arts. By 1966, for the first time in the 20th century, New York had fewer professional stage actors than the rest of the country. Resident companies established in the 1960s include the Minneapolis Theatre (1963) founded by Tyrone GUTHRIE (and later renamed after him), the American Place Theatre company (1964), the Actors' Theatre of Louisville (1964), now the State Theatre of Kentucky, the American Conservatory Theatre (1967) in San Francisco, Long Wharf Theatre in New Haven, Connecticut (1965), and the Mark Taper Forum (1967) in Los Angeles.

During this period, Chicago became a leader in resident theatres and by the end of the 1980s had 110 companies, including the Steppenwolf Theatre (1976). The Goodman Theatre, which became a resident venue in 1977, gained national recognition under Gregory Mosher.

Resident companies have premiered many shows that subsequently became Broadway hits and Pulitzer Prize winners. David Mamet's *Glengarry Glen Ross*, which won the 1984 Pulitzer, was first seen at the Goodman Theatre and Sam Shepard's

Fool for Love (1983) originated at San Francisco's Magic Theatre.

The Theatre Communications Group, founded in 1961 in New York, provides a communications link between regional theatres; the League of Resident Theatres (LORT) in Baltimore, Maryland, was formed in 1965.

resting An actor's euphemism meaning that he or she is temporarily unemployed.

Restoration drama The revival of drama in England after the restoration of the monarchy (1660).

Its main features were the reopening of the theatres after the Puritan INTERREGNUM, the formation of new acting companies, and the first appearance of women on the English stage. The dominant genres of the era were the COMEDY OF MANNERS and the HEROIC DRAMA of Dryden and others, both of which show a strong French influence. This was encouraged by the king himself, who had become familiar with the works of Corneille and others while in exile in France.

In the two decades without drama many actors, playwrights, and regular theatregoers had died. The early Restoration audience was made up largely of courtiers and of aristocrats, although the influence of the middle classes became greater as the era wore on. Charles himself kept a tight control on the new theatres, issuing patents to only Thomas Killigrew of the King's Men, who played at DRURY LANE, and William Davenant of the Duke's Men at LINCOLN'S INN FIELDS THEATRE. The new audience was so small, however, that it barely supported two theatres; the two companies merged in 1682 and separated again in 1695.

Because of their novelty value, the most famous performers tended to be women. By 1670 actresses were well established, the favourites being Nell GWYNN, Anne OLDFIELD, Elizabeth BARRY, Anne BRACEGIRDLE, and Mary Saunderson, the wife of the era's most renowned actor Thomas BETTERTON.

The greatest achievement of the Restoration theatre was in comedy. The English comedy of manners was pioneered by Sir George ETHEREGE, who took his cue from the works of Molière and other French and Spanish masters. The form was subsequently perfected by CONGREVE in such sophisticated works as *Love for Love* (1695) and *The Way of the World* (1700). Other writers to produce witty comedies of intrigue and sentiment included Aphra BEHN and John VANBRUGH: the works of William WYCHERLEY are darker and more satirical. George FARQUHAR, who enjoyed success with *The Beaux' Stratagem* in 1707, is usually considered the last true exponent of Restoration comedy.

In tragedy, the attempt to imitate French NEOCLASSICAL models spawned a number of high-flown works in rhyming verse, notably Dryden's *Tyrannick Love* (1669) and *Almanzor and Almahide* (1671). The only Restoration tragedies to enjoy regular revivals today are Dryden's *All For Love* (1678) and Thomas Otway's *Venice Preserv'd* (1682), both of which are in blank verse.

The Restoration style of comedy fell out of favour in the early 18th century, when middle-class audiences began to reject its cynicism and licentiousness (*see* COLLIER, JEREMY). Samuel Johnson summed up the attitude of his age to the Restoration wits when he wrote:

> Themselves they studied, as they felt they writ;
> Intrigue was plot, obscenity was wit.
> Vice always found a sympathetic friend;
> They pleas'd their age, and did not aim to mend.

The comedies were generally staged in bowdlerized form until the mid 20th century.

return *See* FLAT.

Revels Office *See* MASTER OF THE REVELS *under* MASTER.

revenge. ***Revenger's Tragedy, The*** A violent tragedy published anonymously in 1607 and performed in London at about the same time. Scholars are divided over the authorship, some favouring Cyril Tourneur (*c.* 1575–1626) but others supporting Thomas MIDDLETON. It was revived in 1966 at Stratford-upon-Avon with Tourneur given as the author; the production moved to the Aldwych Theatre three years later.

The plot revolves around Vindice's desire to avenge the death of his mistress, who was poisoned by the duke after she rejected his advances. Vindice enters the court in disguise and eventually murders the duke by having him kiss the poisoned skull of his victim. Other characters are killed in a final orgy of bloodletting. Vindice confesses to murdering the duke and is led to his execution.

revenge tragedy A popular genre of the Elizabethan and Jacobean stage, in which the main character seeks revenge on the murderer of a relative or friend. The action was often precipitated by a ghost returning to a descendant or friend, who promises to exact retribution. The genre usually combined violent and sensational action with intense meditations on the morality of revenge. The first Elizabethan revenge tragedy was Thomas KYD's *The Spanish Tragedy* (1585–89), in which Hieronimo seeks revenge for his son's murder. Shakespeare wrote two, the grotesquely violent *Titus Andronicus* (1592) and *Hamlet* (1600), the masterpiece of the genre. Other examples include George Chapman's *Bussy d'Ambois* (1604), the anonymous *The Revenger's Tragedy* (1607), Cyril Tourneur's *The Atheist's Tragedy* (1611), John Webster's *The Duchess of Malfi* (1619), Thomas Middleton and William Rowley's *The Changeling* (1622), John Marston's *Antonio's Revenge* (1599), and James Shirley's *The Traitor* (1631).

reverberator A reflective metal device, used to increase the strength of stage lighting in the Restoration theatre. The forerunner of the floodlight, it was used mainly to illuminate the APRON.

revista (Port. revue) In Portugal, a type of satirical variety entertainment, ranging from intimate sketches to small-scale musicals, performed in the large theatres of Lisbon. *Fossilismo e progresso* (*Fossil-Worship and Progress*; 1859) was the first of the annual *revista do ano* (reviews of the year). Originally little more than brief sketches lampooning politicians and royalty, by the early 20th century they usually had a plot (often drawn from mythology) and employed an orchestra and chorus line. The satire was often virulent. The *revista* gained in popularity and respect under the dictatorship of Salazar (1932–68), despite repressive censorship that reduced the number of new offerings from 122 in the 1930s to 68 in the 1960s.

revolving stage A stage with a large circular area that can be rotated about a central axis, either as part of the dramatic action or to reveal new sets. The idea originated in Japan's KABUKI theatre, the first efficient revolving stage being built in 1758 at the Kado-za doll theatre in Osaka. The turntable stage did not appear in Europe until the end of the 19th century. Britain's first revolving stage was introduced by Sir Oswald Stoll at a cost of £70,000 when he opened the LONDON COLISEUM in 1904. Its first year saw one of the theatre's worst accidents: during a Derby scene featuring six live horses ridden by professional jockeys at 15 mph, two horses collided and one rolled over the footlights, killing its jockey. Stoll merely roped off the footlights and ran the Derby again for the next performance. The Royal National Theatre has revolving stages in both its Lyttelton and Olivier theatres.

revue A form of VARIETY popular in Britain and America between the world wars, in which a group of performers presented a programme of songs, dances, and sketches. In this it differed from English music hall and US vaudeville, which featured a series of different acts.

Revue was first introduced at the Théâtre de la Porte-Saint-Martin in Paris in the late 19th century and subsequently became the rage at the Folies-Bergères. The first English revue was *Under the Clock* (1893) by Seymour Hicks (1871–1949), although *Pot-Pourri* (1899) was the first to be so designated on the playbill.

Broadway's first revue was *The Passing Show* (1894), which ran for 12 seasons; it opened in London in 1914, inaugurating a series at the Palace Theatre by Alfred Butt (1878–1962). The fashion for costly spectacles was set by ZIEGFELD'S FOLLIES, which became the longest-running annual revue (1907–57) with its chorus girls and stars like Fanny Bryce and Bert Williams. Al JOLSON made his name in 1911 with his black-faced revue *La Belle Paree* at the new Winter Garden Theatre.

In Britain, the smaller-scale *intimate revue* arrived in 1914 with *Odds and Ends*, presented at the Ambassadors Theatre by Charles COCHRAN. In the 1920s such shows were presented regularly at the Hippodrome Theatre by Albert de Courville (1887–1960) and at the Alhambra by André Charlot (1882–1956). Gertrude Lawrence, Beatrice Lillie, and Jack Buchanan made *Charlot's Revue of 1924* a Broadway hit, although electrical problems with the neon sign often billed it as *Harlot's Revue of 1924*. Noël Coward starred in his own *This Year of Grace*.

In America, *George White's Scandals* an intimate version of Ziegfeld's *Follies*, ran from 1919 to 1931; it emphasized comedy, featuring stars like Eddie Cantor and W. C. Fields. *Earl Carroll's Vanities* ran from 1923 to 1932 and *The Greenwich Village Follies* from 1919 to 1928. New York's longest-running revue was OLSEN AND JOHNSON's *Hellzapoppin* (1938), which logged 1404 performances at the 46th Street Theatre.

In Britain the success of the satirical revue BEYOND THE FRINGE helped to bring about the demise of the more expensive type of stage revue (which briefly found a new home on television). So-called *continuous revue* or *non-stop variety*, such as *Revuedeville* at the WINDMILL THEATRE (with its famous nudes) died out at much the same time.

Rhinoceros An absurdist satire by Eugène IONESCO that was first performed in 1959 in Paris. The story is set in a small French town and centres upon the reluctant clerk Bérenger (a character from Ionesco's 1959 play *The Killer*), who is having a drink in a café with his friend Jean when a rhinoceros thunders past. Bérenger ignores this, but the next day rhinoceroses appear everywhere and even Jean turns into a vicious specimen. When his girlfriend makes a similar transformation, Bérenger begins to find the breed attractive. Soon he finds himself the last non-rhino in the town, but bravely resists the temptation to conform.

The first London production opened in 1960 at the Royal Court Theatre, later transferring to the Strand Theatre for a total of over 100 performances. The part of Bérenger was played by OLIVIER in one of his rare ventures into contemporary drama. The leading lady was originally Joan Plowright, who was to become Olivier's third wife. When Vivien Leigh, to whom he was still married, issued a statement in New York saying she was seeking a divorce, Plowright withdrew from the cast and Maggie Smith took over her role.

The Royal Court production was designed and directed by Orson WELLES, who complained bitterly that Olivier was constantly undermining his authority:

> He took every actor aside and said that I was misdirecting them. He got them off in little groups and had little quiet rehearsals having nothing to do with me.

Olivier, who felt that Welles was too bombastic and temperamental, asked him to leave several days before the premiere and took over the direction himself.

rhinthonica *See* FABULA.

Rice. Archie Rice The central character in John Osborne's play THE ENTERTAINER (1957), a struggling survivor from the great days of music hall, partly based on the veteran comic Max Miller (1895–1963). The role was originally played by Laurence OLIVIER, in a notable departure from the classical repertory in which he had made his name.

Elmer Rice (Elmer Reizenstein; 1892–1967) The most important US expressionist playwright. Also a director and producer, Rice was responsible for introducing a number of innovatory techniques, including the flashback, which he used in his first play *On Trial* (1914). In 1936 he became one of the founders of the Playwright's Producing Company. A socialist and rationalist, Rice had a love–hate relationship with the theatre; when he accepted the Pulitzer Prize for STREET SCENE (1929), he stunned the audience by announcing, "I do not like playgoing".

Rice's other outstanding and influential play was his harsh satire on automation, THE ADDING MACHINE (1923); he also wrote *We, The People* (1933), the anti-Nazi *Judgement Day* (1934), *Dream Girl* (1945), and *Cue for Passion* (1958).

Richard. *Richard II* SHAKESPEARE's history play, written in 1595 and first performed that year in London. The plot follows the conflict between the weak and capricious king and the ambitious Bolingbroke (later Henry IV). When Richard returns from the Irish wars, he is taken prisoner and yields the crown to Bolingbroke, who eventually has him poisoned. In the first production the deposition scene was omitted so as not to offend Queen Elizabeth.

The GLOBE THEATRE staged a revival in 1601, when supporters of the Earl of Essex bribed the Lord Chamberlain's Company to stage a special performance on the night before Essex's planned uprising against Queen Elizabeth's counsellors. The conspirators seem to have believed that this play about the deposition of an incompetent monarch would win public support for their actions. The plot was foiled and Essex executed. The actors were apparently wholly unaware of the plan; far from blaming them, the queen asked them to play at court six days later.

The Edwardian actor-manager Beerbohm TREE was known for his penchant for using live animals on stage. In his production of the play at Her Majesty's Theatre, Tree had the king accompanied by a dog, who waited until the deposition scene to turn from Richard to lick Bolingbroke's hand. On another occasion, IRVING was hiring a horse for a play. Just as the owner informed him that Tree had recently ridden the beast in *Richard II*, the horse yawned. "Ah!" smiled Irving, "he's a bit of a critic too, I see."

Richard III SHAKESPEARE's history play about Richard's ruthless campaign to seize the throne, his bloody rule, and his death in battle at the hand of Richmond (Henry VII). It was written between 1592–93 and first performed in 1593. Although the historical accuracy of Shakespeare's portrait has been attacked, there is no doubt that the deformed and malevolent Richard offers one of the great bravura roles in the English-speaking theatre. The part is the longest in the Shakespearean canon (1164 lines) after Hamlet. GARRICK made his London debut in 1741 as Richard; Edwin Booth (*see* BOOTH FAMILY) played him at 18; and the part established John BARRYMORE as the greatest US actor of his day. The finest performance of recent times is usually thought to be that of Anthony Sher, who was first seen in the role in 1984 at Stratford.

The most celebrated Richard of the 20th century, however, was OLIVIER, whose 1944 performance with the Old Vic, depicting the king as an evil joker, has been called "one of the legendary nights of theatre history". Critic Kenneth TYNAN called it "energetic evil in all its wicked richness". Olivier made a film version in 1955.

Richard's most famous line is his last: "A horse! A horse! My kingdom for a horse!". One night when the Irish tragedian Barry Sullivan spoke the line, a voice in the pit yelled out, "And wouldn't a jackass do as well for you?" Shot back Sullivan: "Sure, come around to the stage door at once!"

There is a story that when Richard BURBAGE played the role, a female admirer invited him to come to her house under cover of darkness, where he should identify himself as 'Richard the Third'. Shakespeare, overhearing this, went ahead to the woman's dwelling and gained admittance. He was being entertained when a message came from Burbage saying that Richard the Third had arrived. The Bard sent a message back that William the Conqueror came before Richard the Third. *See also* PERISH THE THOUGHT!; PRINCES IN THE TOWER.

Richardson. Sir Ralph Richardson (1902–83) British actor. Richardson's first job in the theatre was to simulate the sound of a Zeppelin raid using two empty petrol cans; in his enthusiasm, he drowned the leading man's speech with the noise. He made his acting debut as Lorenzo in *The Merchant of Venice* in 1921, subsequently joining Barry Jackson's Birmingham Repertory Theatre. After successful seasons at the Old Vic and the Malvern Festival, he made his name in the West End in plays by Shakespeare and J. B. Priestley.

In 1944, after wartime service with the Fleet Air Arm, he became joint director of the Old Vic company with Laurence OLIVIER. During this period he consolidated his reputation as one of Britain's greatest actors in a series of classic roles that included Ibsen's Peer Gynt, Rostand's Cyrano de Bergerac, and Chekhov's Uncle Vanya. He later appeared opposite John Gielgud in both David Storey's *Home* (1970) and Harold Pinter's *No Man's Land* (1975).

In his long career Richardson appeared in over 200 parts on stage and some 50 film roles, the latter including the 'Supreme Being' in Terry Gilliam's *Time Bandits*. His greatest success, however, was as Falstaff, a role to which he returned many times.

Richardson was well known for his eccentricities, which included riding around Hampstead on a motorbike with his pipe in his mouth and a pet parrot called José seated on his shoulder. On one occasion he is said to have walked up to Alec Guinness in a hotel in Madrid and knocked him to the floor, saying "Who can one hit if not one's friends?"

Richardson's Show A touring English variety show of the early 19th century, whose fairground performances were a forerunner of MUSIC HALL. John Richardson (1766–1836), a mild-mannered publican and itinerant actor who had once been a workhouse boy, erected his first theatre booth at London's BARTHOLOMEW FAIR in 1798 using scenery borrowed from Drury Lane. During its heyday, Richardson's Show could seat some 1000 spectators in its 100 ft × 30 ft booth, which also accommodated 1500 lamps and an elevated stage with crimson curtains. Within a span of 25 minutes, the audience was treated to a fast-paced overture, comic songs, a melodrama, and a pantomime (with three murders and a ghost, noted Dickens). Many distinguished actors, including Edmund Kean began with Richardson, who is credited with spreading popular drama to the provinces. In 1826 he tried to auction off the show but inadequate bids made him persevere for another decade until his death. Nelson Lee then acquired the property, disposing of it in 1853.

Rich family The British theatre managers Christopher Rich (d. 1714) and his son, the Harlequin John Rich (1681–1761).

Christopher Rich was a lawyer who bought a share in DRURY LANE, subsequently taking control of the theatre in 1693. He spent much of his time in lawsuits and became notorious for manipulating and bullying actors and cutting their salaries. All this caused the great actor Thomas BETTERTON and most of his company to walk out, leaving Rich with a group of second-rate performers. After the Lord Chamberlain closed Drury Lane, Rich bought the deserted LINCOLN'S INN FIELDS THEATRE to refurbish but died before he could reopen it.

His son, **John Rich**, who inherited Lincoln's Inn Fields, became a successful Harlequin using the stage name of LUN. Virtually illiterate, he did more than anyone else to create the English PANTOMIME, producing one such show annually from 1717 to 1760. In 1725 he devised *Harlequin Sorcerer, with the Loves of Pluto and Proserpine*, in which the title character knocked down traders, leapt through glass, climbed walls, and dashed down chimneys while being chased by a village constable. Many contemporaries paid tribute to the brilliance of his miming and his agility on stage:

> He hides where it is impossible to hide, he passes through openings that are smaller than his body, he stands on supports that are too weak to support his weight, he balances on an umbrella, he curls up inside a guitar-case – and throughout, he flees, he escapes, he leaps.
>
> THÉODORE DE BANVILLE

One night in 1721 a drunken earl was backstage and, seeing friends in the opposite wing, walked across the stage disrupting the scene then being acted. When tongue-lashed by Rich, he struck the Harlequin, who hit back. A riot ensued between actors and aristocrats, the latter storming the boxes with swords before the actor James Quin (*see* BELLOWER QUIN) overpowered them with the help of a constable and theatre watchmen. The king, informed of the riot, posted soldiers in the theatre for the next few performances.

Rich's outstanding success as a manager was Gay's THE BEGGAR'S OPERA, which was produced in 1728 at Lincoln's Inn Fields. Its record run of 62 performances led to the quip that it had "made Gay rich and Rich gay". It provided him with the funds to build the first COVENT GARDEN Theatre in 1732.

riciniata *See* FABULA.

Rickety Twins, the Nickname for two London theatres off the Strand that were built back-to-back, the GLOBE THEATRE, which opened in 1868, and the OPERA COMIQUE, which opened two years later. They had been jerry-built with the expectation of additional funds that did not materialize.

Riders to the Sea A one-act tragedy by J. M. SYNGE that has been described as the finest short play in any language. It was inspired by his visits to the Aran Islands off Galway each summer from 1898 to 1902 and uses the speech patterns of the Aran peasants. *Riders to the Sea* was first performed in 1904 at the Abbey Theatre in Dublin. In 1937 Vaughan Williams adapted it as an opera. The main character is Maurya, an old woman who loses the last of her six sons to the sea and discovers a strange peace in her life because fate can no longer harm her. She concludes:

> No man at all can be living for ever, and we must be satisfied.

Ridiculous, Theatre of the A theatrical movement that began in 1967 with the opening of the Play-House of the Ridiculous on OFF-OFF-BROADWAY. It was characterized by outrageous dialogue, bad taste, double entendre, and witty word-play. The first offering was Ronald Tavel's *The Life of Lady Godiva* (1967), directed by John Vaccaro, with Charles Ludlam as the leading actor. That same year, Ludlam wrote and Vaccaro directed *Big Hotel* and *Conquest of the Universe*. Ludlam shortly afterwards left to form his own company, writing, directing, and acting in such plays as *Turds in Hell* (1968), *Camille* (1973), and *Der Ring Gott Farblonjet* (1977). Vaccaro remained with the Play-House company, which toured Europe and subsequently found a home in New York's La Mama Experimental Theatre Club. It disbanded in 1972.

ring. ***Ring Round the Moon*** (*L'Invitation au château*) A play by Jean ANOUILH that opened in 1947 at the Théâtre de l'Atelier, Paris. The plot concerns the tangled love affairs of identical twins, the shy romantic Frederic and his cynical brother Hugo.

In 1950 the play was staged in London in a translation by Christopher Fry; the production was directed by Peter Brook and starred Paul SCOFIELD as both the twin brothers. Claire Bloom, Cecil Trouncer, and Margaret Rutherford also appeared. Having left the stage as one brother, Scofield was frequently obliged to make an athletic backstage dash to the opposite wing in order to reappear moments later as the other. In one scene, one of the brothers left the stage to be called back by the butler, briefly revealing his back to the audience; a split second later, Scofield appeared at the opposite side of the stage to gasps from the audience, who had not detected that a double was used.

According to Binkie Beaumont, the Paris production was terrible, with dull costumes and settings. In London Beaumont had expensive Edwardian costumes designed and created a great winter garden in an onstage conservatory. When Anouilh saw the London production, he told Beaumont, "I had no idea that my little play could look so marvellous."

to ring up the curtain To order the curtain to be raised or opened, the signal originally being the ringing of a bell. The phrase is often used metaphorically, meaning to initiate an enterprise, etc. Similarly to **ring down the curtain** is to terminate or bring to an end.

rise-and-sink A former method of rapidly changing a set for a TRANSFORMATION SCENE, as in English pantomime; a low grid beneath the stage roof was used to raise the upper half of the scenery while SLOTEs were used to lower the bottom half into the cellar. This revealed the new set behind.

Ritchard, Cyril (Cyril Trimnel-Ritchard; 1898–1977) Australian-born British actor and director, described by the critic Michael Billington as the "etiolated dandy-mincing revue star".

Ritchard made his debut in 1918 at His Majesty's Theatre, Sydney, in the chorus of *A Waltz Dream*. In 1925 he made his first New York appearance in the revue *Puzzle of 1925* and his London debut in the revue *Bubbly* at the Duke of York's Theatre. He subsequently remained in Britain for several years, appearing in revue, cabaret, and such roles as Algernon in Wilde's *The Importance of Being Earnest* (1942).

After the war Ritchard alternated between Britain and America. Highlights of his later career included playing Sir Novelty Fashion in a London production of Vanbrugh's *The Relapse* (1947) that later transferred to Broadway (1950). The critic Harold Hobson called his performance "a gorgeous creation of wit, wigs, taste, and paste".

Ritchard is best remembered, however, for playing the dual role of Mr Darling and Captain Hook in the 1954 musical version of *Peter Pan* at New York's Winter Garden. He remained in America for the last two decades of his career, ending as he began: his farewell performance in 1975 was a revue, *A Musical Jubilee*.

Ritterdrama (Ger. knight drama) In late 18th-century German theatre, a genre of historical drama that depicted the heroic days of medieval knights. It derived from the STURM UND DRANG movement, taking its romantic and patriotic themes from the historical plays of Goethe and Klinger. With its staging of battles, jousting, and other pageantry, the genre established new standards for historical realism in settings and costumes.

Successful *Ritterdrama* plays included *Agnes Bernauerin* (1780) by Josef August von Törring (1753–1826) and *Otto von Wittelsbach* (1782) by Joseph Marius Babo (1756–1822). At the end of the century the genre was banned from the Munich stage for emphasizing Bavarian patriotism, but its popularity continued in Austria and elsewhere.

Rivals, The A comedy by Richard Brinsley SHERIDAN, first performed in London in 1775. The play, Sheridan's first, did not meet with immediate success, being an hour longer than most works of the time; the character of Sir Lucius O'Trigger also caused offence. After Sheridan had drastically revised it, the play enjoyed a great success on its second performance 11 days later. He used its profits to buy Garrick's share of DRURY LANE and become manager there in 1776. The play's many revivals have included Peter Wood's 1983 production for the National Theatre with Geraldine McEwan and Michael Hordern.

In the story, Lydia Languish longs for a romantic elopement rather than a more conventional marriage. Accordingly, Captain Jack ABSOLUTE woos her in the guise of a penniless ensign. Confusions mount as her aunt, Mrs MALAPROP, decides to disinherit her and Bob ACRES, a cowardly rival for Lydia's hand, challenges the ensign to a duel. When the elderly Sir Lucius O'Trigger comes courting, Lydia decides to accept Jack. The play is best known for the outrageous verbal solecisms of Mrs MALAPROP, which gave the word 'malapropism' to the language.

In accordance with an old theatrical superstition (*see* TABOOS AND SUPERSTITIONS), Ellen Terry once played Lydia's cousin, Julia, without having rehearsed the play's final line. When she came to speak the unfamiliar words on stage, she delivered the line on an upward inflection. The curtain stayed up and John Buckstone, a deaf actor playing Bob Acres, stunned the audience by shouting across the stage at the prompter, "Eh! Eh! What does this mean? Why the devil don't you bring down the curtain?"

Rix, Sir Brian (1924–) British actor-manager, who played in bedroom farces for over 30 years, a career that he has described as one of "diving under beds and into cupboards and pinching girls' bottoms".

The son of a shipowner, Rix made his stage debut with Donald Wolfit's company in 1942; his early roles included a courtier in *King Lear* and Sebastian in *Twelfth Night*. In 1943 he joined the White Rose Players, a Harrogate repertory company, and played farce for the first time in *Nothing but the Truth*.

After wartime service in the RAF, Rix toured with his own Viking Theatre Company in the army farce *Reluctant Heroes*. In 1950 he brought the play to the WHITEHALL THEATRE, London, where it ran for nearly four years. His next farcical offering, *Dry Rot*, enjoyed a similarly long run; Rix eventually set a record by staging more than a decade of continuous farces at the same theatre. In 1967 he moved to the Garrick Theatre, where he appeared in *Stand by Your Bedouin*, *Let Sleeping Wives Lie*, and *She'd Done It Again* during the first year of his management. He has published two volumes of memoirs, *My Farce from my Elbow* (1975) and *Farce about Face* (1989).

In 1982 Rix became secretary-general of the charity for the mentally handicapped, MENCAP; six years later he retired from the theatre to become the organization's chairman. "It's a great relief to make the break," he said when leaving the stage, "I just got so tired of the eternal cry of 'Drop 'em!'" He was knighted for his services to charity in 1986, and became the first Baron Rix of Whitehall in 1992.

Robert and Elizabeth *See* BARRETTS OF WIMPOLE STREET.

Robertson, T(homas) W(illiam) (1829–71) British playwright, who introduced a new NATURALISM to the London stage in the 1860s. Robertson came from a large theatrical family; his 21 brothers and sisters included the future Madge KENDAL. As a child he appeared on stage with his father, and subsequently wrote songs and plays and worked as a stage manager. His first success as a playwright came with his adaptation of *David Garrick*, produced at the Haymarket in 1864. SOCIETY (1865) proved a great popular success when produced at the Prince of Wales Theatre by the BANCROFTS; the first of his realist plays, it established the genre of CUP-AND-SAUCER DRAMA. Robertson wrote 22 plays in all, the most famous being CASTE (1867). *See also* SHORTEST TITLES *under* SHORT.

Robeson, Paul (1898–1976) The Black US actor; despite outstanding performances in Shakespeare, he is best remembered for singing 'Ol' Man River' in SHOW BOAT. The son of a former slave, Robeson studied law before making his professional acting debut in 1921 at New York's Lafayette Theatre in *Simon the Cyrenian*. In 1924 he played Jim Harris in Eugene O'Neill's play about a mixed marriage, ALL GOD'S CHILLUN GOT WINGS. When word got out that the play featured a scene in which a White woman knelt down before the Black actor, cast members were threatened by the Ku Klux Klan. O'Neill was so impressed with Robeson that he revived his earlier play *The Emperor Jones* (1920) for him to appear in. It opened in 1925 at London's Comedy Theatre, transferring to Broadway the following year.

Robeson won international fame for his role as Joe in the Jerome Kern musical *Show Boat*, which he played in the first London production of 1928 and the 1932 Broadway revival. Further success came with OTHELLO (1930), in which he played opposite Peggy Ashcroft at the Savoy Theatre, sparking an off-stage romance. He was the first Black Othello since Ira Aldridge (the so-called African ROSCIUS) in the 1860s. In 1943 he returned to America to play the part in a Theatre Guild production that ran for 295 performances on Broadway, a record for a US Shakespeare production.

During the McCarthy era Robeson's outspoken sympathy for left-wing causes attracted much criticism and he was prevented from travelling abroad. It was not until 1959 that he returned to Britain, to sing at the Albert Hall and play *Othello* at the Shakespeare Memorial Theatre in Stratford. Robeson subsequently went into semi-retirement in America, while continuing to sing and campaign for civil-rights causes. He had already done much to open the mainstream theatre to other Black actors.

Robey, Sir George *See* PRIME MINISTER OF MIRTH.

Robin Hood Play In the English FOLK THEATRE, a type of play recounting the legendary exploits of Robin Hood and his band of outlaws. Such plays were performed at various festivals throughout the agricultural calendar, particularly at MAY DAY celebrations. The character of Robin Hood seems to have become identified with JACK-IN-THE-GREEN, a figure from pre-Christian religion in England.

robot (Czech *robota*, forced labour) An automaton with semi-human powers and intelligence. The name comes from the mechanical creatures in Karel ČAPEK's play *R.U.R.* (Rossum's Universal Robots), which opened in 1921 in Prague and was successfully produced in London in 1923. The play was a futuristic fantasy warning of the dangers of uncontrolled technological development.

Robson, Dame Flora (1902–84) British actress, who was created a dame in 1960. Raised in London, Robson studied at RADA and made her professional debut in 1921 as a ghost in *Will Shakespeare* by Clemence Dane. When further offers dried up, she worked in a Shredded Wheat factory for four years.

With the encouragement of Tyrone Guthrie she returned to the theatre and in 1931 won encouraging reviews as Abbie Putnam in O'Neill's *Desire Under the Elms*. She enjoyed another triumph that same year in Bridie's *The Anatomist*. The critic St John Ervine wrote, "If you are not moved by this girl's performance, then you are immovable and have no right to be on this earth. Hell is your place." In 1949 she was a great success as a disturbed mother in *Black Chiffon* at the Westminster Theatre, playing the part on Broadway a year later. She won the 1960 *Evening Standard* Award for Best Actress for her depiction of Miss Tina in *The Aspern Papers*.

In 1934 Robson played the title role in *Mary Read*, the violent story of a woman pirate, at His Majesty's Theatre. At one point in the performance, she was required to fire a prop gun at Robert Donat, playing her stage lover. One night, when she fired at Donat's chest his shirt burst into flames. She watched in horror as he fell to the ground and rolled over to put out the fire. When the curtain fell, Donat sat up with a black face and yelled, "Flora has singed my navel!"

Rodgers and Hammerstein The US composer Richard Rodgers (1902–79) and his lyricist Oscar Hammerstein II (1895–1960), who were the stage's most successful musical team since Gilbert and Sullivan. Their main contribution to the 20th-century musical was to blend bright strong tunes with sophisticated plots. Beginning in 1949, they became producers of their own musicals and those of others.

Hammerstein, who came from a family of theatre managers and producers, began his career as a stage manager on Broadway before turning to writing lyrics. His first work on a musical was creating the book and lyrics for *Always You* (1920). Success came with *Rose Marie* (1924; music by Rudolf Friml), *The Desert Song* (1926; music by Sigmund Romberg), and the epoch-making SHOW BOAT (1927; music by Jerome Kern).

Rodgers, who began to write songs at an early age, met the witty lyricist **Lorenz Hart** (1895–1943) at Columbia University and the two collaborated on a 1920 varsity show. Later they enjoyed success with such offerings as *The Garrick Gaieties* (1925), *A Connecticut Yankee* (1927), *On Your Toes* (1936), which was the first Broadway musical to feature a ballet ('Slaughter on Tenth Avenue' choreographed by George Balanchine), *Babes in Arms* (1937), THE BOYS

FROM SYRACUSE (1938), and PAL JOEY (1940), which made Gene Kelly a star.

Rodgers and Hammerstein's first collaboration was the epoch-making OKLAHOMA! (1943), which won a Pulitzer Prize and ran for 2248 performances on Broadway and 1543 at London's Drury Lane. It was followed by Hammerstein's personal favourite CAROUSEL (1945), which has been called their best show musically and dramatically, and the unsuccessful *Allegro* (1947). SOUTH PACIFIC (1949) took another Pulitzer Prize, and was followed by the exotic THE KING AND I (1951), starring Yul Brynner and Gertrude Lawrence, who died during its run, FLOWER DRUM SONG (1958) set in San Francisco's Chinatown, *Pipe Dream* (1955), a relative failure that ran for only 246 performances, and, a year before Hammerstein died, THE SOUND OF MUSIC (1959).

After Hammerstein's death, Rodgers worked on several musicals with Stephen SONDHEIM.

roll-out *See* TRICKWORK.

Roman. Roman drama The theatre flourished in ancient Rome for about 800 years, during both the Republic and the Empire. It developed from village entertainments such as the ATELLANA, and from GREEK DRAMA (*see* GRECO-ROMAN DRAMA).

The earliest Roman drama probably evolved from jolly carnivals and bawdy fertility rites performed on religious occasions. Its development was influenced greatly by the traditions of Greek colonists living in southern Italy and Sicily. The first documented Roman playwright was Lucius Livius Andronicus (*c.* 280–204 BC), a freed Greek slave who translated Greek works into Latin. The first recorded production took place in 240 BC at the Roman Games (LUDI ROMANI). Unlike their Greek predecessors Roman playwrights, such as Ennius, Naevius, and Andronicus wrote and published non-dramatic poetry.

Few Roman tragedies survive; most of the plays seem to have been adaptations of Greek originals, although Lucius Accius is thought to have written some original works. The role of the CHORUS diminished, until it functioned as little more than a source of interlude music during scene changes. At the same time rhetoric grew increasingly important, with plays containing long set speeches. It is not even certain that the nine gory tragedies of SENECA were written to be performed on stage.

Roman comedy derived from the Greek NEW COMEDY, with such authors as PLAUTUS and TERENCE basing many of their works directly on plays by Menander and others. Although the plays were often set in Greece they tended to satirize Roman society and featured stereotypical Roman characters. Bawdy and brutal MIME and the performances of the PANTOMIMUS eventually superseded literary comedy.

Roman drama was generally performed on festival days, together with gladiatorial contests, circuses, and races; popular actors could be very highly paid, one of the most successful being ROSCIUS. Theatre buildings were originally wooden, and took their design from Greek theatres. The first stone theatre was built in Rome in 55 BC. Roman theatres became considerably more elaborate than the original Greek models; they were built to be freestanding, and had complex arrangements of curtains and scenery. There were even some indoor theatres. The AMPHITHEATRES designed as arenas for races were also used for theatrical shows. Performances were sometimes given in private; players could be hired to entertain dinner guests, while members of the literary elite would hold prestigious private readings of their works.

Roman drama disappeared in the 6th century AD when Christian opposition to acting resulted in the emperor Justinian closing down all the theatres.

Romans in Britain, The A play by Howard BRENTON, which in 1980 caused one of the greatest controversies in the history of the National Theatre, who put it on. The play included a scene between nude actors, in which a group of druids were buggered by Roman centurions. This resulted in the Greater London Council threatening to reduce its grant to the National Theatre, inquiries by Scotland Yard, and a private prosecution of the director, Michael Bogdanov (1938–), for procuring an act of gross indecency. The case, which had been brought by Mary Whitehouse, was eventually dropped. The play also caused political outrage by drawing a parallel between the Roman conquest of Britain and the contemporary stationing of British forces in Northern Ireland.

Romeo and Juliet SHAKESPEARE's tragedy of two young lovers from rival families. It was probably written in 1595, when the London theatres were closed owing to the plague, and first performed a year later.

Shakespeare based his play upon Arthur Brooke's long narrative poem, *The Tragicall History of Romeo and Juliet* (1562), which was derived ultimately from an earlier Italian story (1535) by Luigi da Porto. Romeo, of the house of Montague, falls in love with Juliet, one of the Capulet family, who are long-standing enemies of the Montagues. On the day that Romeo and Juliet are secretly married, Romeo is banished from Verona as punishment for his unintentional killing of a Capulet in an affray. Old Capulet then orders Juliet to prepare herself to marry Count Paris. To avoid disclosing that she is already married to Romeo, she drugs herself into a death-like trance. Romeo, hearing that she has died, returns, enters the tomb where Juliet lies, and kills himself. Juliet, awakening to find her husband dead, dispatches herself with Romeo's dagger.

The play is remembered for its famous balcony scene, which includes the often misinterpreted line, "O Romeo, Romeo, wherefore art thou Romeo?" (Juliet is asking why Romeo is a Montague, not where he is). The work also contributed the still popular curse, "A plague o' both your houses", uttered by Romeo's friend Mercutio, when he is fatally wounded in a brawl between Montagues and Capulets. SHAW, who was never shy of straightening out Shakespeare's literary problems, complained that some of Romeo's fanciful lines "make you curse Shakespeare's stage-struckness and his youthful inability to keep his brains quiet".

Before actresses were accepted on the British stage, the part of Juliet was played by boy actors, one famous pairing being that of Thomas Betterton as Romeo and Edward Kynaston as Juliet. By contrast, in an 1845 production at the Haymarket Theatre, the sisters Charlotte and Susan Cushman played the parts. Asked if he might one day play Shakespeare, the ageing Noël Coward replied: "I might play the nurse in *Romeo and Juliet*."

The most famous modern production (and, with 186 performances, the most successful) was that staged in 1935 at the New Theatre (now the Albery) with Olivier, Gielgud, Ashcroft, and Edith Evans in the cast. Gielgud and Olivier alternated between the roles of Romeo and Mercutio. Another much admired production was Franco Zeffirelli's boisterous interpretation with John Stride and Judi Dench (1960). Shakespeare's story has often been updated and reworked, notably in the musical WEST SIDE STORY (1957).

The worst actor to play Romeo seems to have been Robert 'Romeo' Coates (1772–1842), who was eventually forced to abandon the role because no actress would play opposite him. Coates insisted on playing the part in an outlandish sky-blue costume decorated with diamonds. When, as often happened, the audience crowed at him and jeered he would halt the action to crow back. During one performance in 1807 in Bath, the audience rioted when Coates carried a crowbar on stage to prise open the Capulets' tomb.

Romeo and Juliet has been made into several films, an opera, and a ballet by Prokofiev. In 1994 the ballet caused some perplexed hilarity when a London headmistress refused to allow her pupils to attend a performance at the Royal Opera House at reduced prices, on the grounds that Shakespeare's play was "blatantly heterosexual".

Romanoff and Juliet A comedy by Peter USTINOV that updates the story of ROMEO AND JULIET to a Cold War setting. Often considered his best play, it was first performed in London in 1956 at the Piccadilly Theatre, with Ustinov himself playing the General. The British critic Caryl Brahms wrote, "Never can so many twitches, squeaks, skips, hops, winks, blinks, nods and finger flutterings have afflicted one and the same elder statesman, poor gentleman." The play ran for a year, winning the *Evening Standard* Award for Best New Play, before opening on Broadway in 1957. It subsequently toured America and was made into a film.

The story, set in a tiny European country, involves the love between Igor Romanoff, the son of the Soviet ambassador, and Juliet Moulsworth, the daughter of the US ambassador. Trouble brews when the fiancés of both Igor and Juliet arrive on the scene. The country's leader, the General, worries that this inconvenient love affair will ruin his country's standing in both the communist and capitalist worlds. However, he eventually helps to unite both Romanoff and Juliet and the two discarded fiancés as well.

Rookery Nook The best-known of the Aldwych farces written by Ben TRAVERS for

London's ALDWYCH THEATRE. It opened in 1926 in a production starring Tom Walls, Ralph Lynn, and Robertson Hare and ran for 409 performances. The farce has been a popular choice for revival by repertory companies and amateur groups.

The plot involves the priggish Mrs Gertrude Twine, who is staying in a holiday cottage, Rookery Nook, with her brother-in-law Clive and his cousin, Gerald. The arrival of a young woman in pyjamas, who has been thrown out of her house by her stepfather, sets off a chaotic sequence of events, as Clive and Gerald scheme to keep Mrs Twine from discovering their compromising situation.

Room, The The first play by Harold PINTER, a one-act drama that was written in a few days and first performed in 1957 by the drama department of Bristol University. First seen in London in a 1960 double bill with *The Dumb Waiter*, it shows all the hallmarks of the later PINTERESQUE style.

The plot centres on Bert and Rose, an elderly couple who live in a drab bed-sitting room. Their landlord, Mr Kidd, arrives in an agitated state but leaves without explaining his behaviour. Bert also leaves on some unknown errand. Subsequently a blind Black man, called Riley, appears; he calls Rose 'Sal' and says he has a message for her. Bert suddenly returns and beats Riley to death, whereupon Rose screams that she has now also gone blind. The room appears to be a symbol of refuge in a menacing world.

Roots The second play in Arnold WESKER's famous trilogy about the lives of a Jewish family in the years 1936 to 1959. The other plays in the sequence are CHICKEN SOUP WITH BARLEY (1958) and *I'm Talking About Jerusalem* (1960). *Roots* is probably Wesker's best-known and most optimistic work. It was first performed in 1959 at the Belgrade Theatre, Coventry, in a production directed by John Dexter and starring Joan Plowright as Beatie Bryant. The production moved to London's Royal Court Theatre for a month before transferring to the Duke of York's Theatre.

Set in the 1950s, the play revolves around Beatie Bryant, who comes up from London to visit her family in Norfolk. She is critical of her family's ignorance and prejudice, constantly quoting the ideas of her Jewish boyfriend Ronnie Kahn, a socialist (and a character in *Chicken Soup with Barley*). Beatie has asked Ronnie to meet her family but on the day he is expected, she receives a letter from him ending their relationship. She blames her family, and when her mother angrily reproaches her, Beatie responds assertively. She realizes that she is no longer parrotting Ronnie, having found an articulate voice of her own.

Kenneth TYNAN praised the original production but added, "Joan Plowright's Beatie seemed to me a touch too pawky, suggestive less of rural Norfolk than of urban Lancs."

rope house *See* HAND-WORKED HOUSE.

Rosalind The daughter of the banished Duke in AS YOU LIKE IT. Rosalind is the longest female role in any Shakespearean play. Famous performances in the part include Vanessa REDGRAVE's in 1961. She spends most of the play disguised as a young man (Ganymede) in the Forest of ARDEN. The witty and engaging Rosalind lampoons romantic love, while clearly being deeply in love with Orlando.

Roscius A name for a first-rate actor; after the Roman comic actor Quintus Roscius Gallus (120–62 BC), who was unrivalled for his physical grace, melodic voice, conception of character, and delivery.

> What scene of death has Roscius now to act?
>
> SHAKESPEARE: *Henry VI, Part III* (V. vi).

The name was used in the title of Charles Churchill's satirical poem *The Rosciad* (1761), which shocked the London theatre with its savage mockery of nearly all the famous actors of the day.

Roscius, the African Nickname for Ira Frederick Aldridge (1804–67), who is recognized as the first great Black actor. Aldridge began performing in New York in 1821 with James Brown's African-American company at the African Grove tea garden. As racial barriers prevented him from developing a theatrical career in America, he moved to Britain, making his London debut in 1826 at the Royalty Theatre.

In the course of his highly successful career, Aldridge played not only Othello but also Shylock, Macbeth, Lear, and other major Shakespearean roles. He made his first tour of the Continent in 1853, becoming especially popular in Germany, where he acted in English while his supporting cast spoke German. His only performances of

Lear were in Russia, where he played with a whitened face but black hands. Aldridge's success brought him considerable wealth and decorations from monarchs in Prussia, Russia, and Saxe-Meiningen. He became a naturalized British subject in 1863.

Roscius, another Richard Burbage (*see* BURBAGE FAMILY), the first great English actor, was so described by William Camden.

Roscius, the British The great Restoration actor Thomas BETTERTON, of whom Colley Cibber said, "He alone was born to speak what only Shakespeare knew to write." The title was also given to David GARRICK, who revolutionized the English stage with his new style of acting.

Roscius, the Dublin or **Hibernian** The Dublin-born actor Gustavus Vaughan Brooke (1818–66). After touring the British provinces, he made his London debut at the Olympic Theatre in 1848 and went on to play Othello, Hamlet, Richard III, and Shylock. His career was damaged by his intemperance, which on one occasion landed him in Warwick jail. He made successful tours of America and Australia; on the way to a second tour of Australia his ship sank in the Bay of Biscay. His second wife was the US actress Avonia Jones (1839–67).

Roscius of France Nickname for Michel Baron (1653–1729), a leading actor with the Comédie-Française.

rose. rose, the Early 19th-century theatre jargon for the cluster of footlights at the centre of the stage. When an actor had important lines to deliver, he or she would move to this bright spot, stepping away after the speech to allow the next major speaker to approach the rose. Such formal movements were typical of acting at this time.

Rose Tattoo, The A play by Tennessee WILLIAMS, first performed in 1950 in New York and seen in London in 1959. When the play was presented at the first Dublin Festival in 1957 its treatment of illicit love led to a ban; the festival founder Alan Simpson was arrested, resulting in the suspension of the event the following year. The film version (1955) starred Burt Lancaster and Anna Magnani.

The story, set within the Sicilian community of New Orleans, centres on the pious Serafina Delle Rose, a 30-year-old dressmaker, who still mourns the death of her truck-driver husband, Rosario, three years earlier. She talks to his ashes (kept in an urn) and locks up Rosa, her 15-year-old daughter, to keep her from her sweetheart, Jack. When Serafina hears gossip of her dead husband's infidelity, she is distraught. However, at this point Alvaro, a young truck driver, comes into her life. Because he reminds her of Rosario, even having the same rose tattoo on his chest, Serafina accepts him as a lover. Rosa accuses her mother of hypocrisy, and Serafina allows her to go to Jack. Serafina then feels the tattoo appearing on her own breast and knows she has conceived.

Rose Theatre An octagonal Elizabethan theatre built in 1587 in London by Philip HENSLOWE. The Rose, thatched and built of wood and plaster on a brick foundation, stood on Bankside at the corner of Rose Alley and Maiden Lane on a site that was once a rose garden.

Between 1592 and 1594 the theatre was occupied by STRANGE'S MEN, who probably performed Shakespeare's *Henry VI* plays during their stay. The actor Edward ALLEYN made his name at the Rose as the leading player with the ADMIRAL'S MEN, who were based at the theatre from 1594 to 1640, when they left for the Fortune Theatre. The Rose was dismantled when its lease ran out in 1605. In December 1989 part of the site was uncovered during development work, leading to a campaign for its preservation, which was supported by leading theatrical personalities.

Rosencrantz and Guildenstern Are Dead The first major success of Tom STOPPARD. It was produced by the Oxford Theatre Group for the 1966 Edinburgh Festival and subsequently enjoyed a lengthy West-End run at the Old Vic. In the play, which is written loosely in the tradition of the Theatre of the ABSURD, Stoppard brings two minor characters from *Hamlet* centre-stage to contemplate their own existence. While waiting for instructions, they discuss the meaning of their roles in the tragic events of *Hamlet* (which take place entirely offstage) and pass the time in word-play and philosophical logic games. Critics saw parallels between Stoppard's protagonists and Vladimir and Estragon in Beckett's WAITING FOR GODOT.

Rosherville Gardens In Victorian times, "the place to spend a happy day". These gardens were established by Mr Rosher in disused chalk quarries at Gravesend. A theatre, zoological collections, and music formed part of their attraction, and the gardens were particularly favoured by river excursionists. The site was subsequently given over to industry. *See also* CREMORNE GARDENS; VAUXHALL GARDENS.

Ross Terence RATTIGAN's drama about the later years of T. E. Lawrence, as he sought anonymity. It opened in 1960 at the Haymarket and ran for two years with 762 performances. Alec GUINNESS was highly praised in the title role, winning the *Evening Standard* Best Actor Award. The critic Caryl Brahms thought the play "fragmentary", but said the actor had "the timing of a histrionic angel, the sweetness from which Guinness is never wholly divorced".

The play begins and ends in a British RAF depot in 1922. Hoping to escape his fame as 'Lawrence of Arabia', Lawrence has enlisted in the ranks under the assumed name of Ross. Eventually another airman recognizes him and attempts to blackmail him with the threat of press exposure. Lawrence rejects his demand for money, and the subsequent publicity forces him to leave the RAF. Flashbacks are used to present key events in Lawrence's earlier career, including the incredible desert march to capture Akaba, his capture and sexual abuse at the hands of a Turkish official, the deaths of his two beloved bodyguards, and the historic capture of Damascus.

rostrum Any platform used to create different levels of staging. Known in America as a **parallel**, it can be either permanent or collapsible for transport and storage. A rostrum usually has steps or a ramp and sometimes a canvas 'rostrum-front' to disguise the platform.

In the late 19th century rostrums were used extensively by the famous MEININGER COMPANY to keep the action moving on several different levels. They can be especially effective on the modern open stage: the Stratford Festival Theatre in Ontario, Canada, employs eight acting levels.

Rover, The A witty comedy of intrigue by Aphra BEHN. Subtitled *The Banished Cavalier*, it was first performed in two parts in 1677 and 1681. It was often revived in the 18th century and was performed in 1979 in Colchester with a cast led by Lynn Dearth. The story involves the romantic adventures of a band of hot-blooded English cavaliers in Naples and Madrid, during the exile of Charles II. The play's hero, the dissolute Willmore, is thought to have been based on either the Earl of Rochester or Behn's lover John Hoyle.

royal. Royal Arctic Theatre A 19th-century custom of the Royal Navy, whereby plays were presented on board ice-bound ships off the coasts of Canada. The earliest known performances occurred in about 1819; they appear to have involved both officers and ordinary seamen, who would play male and female roles. Performances of Garrick's *Miss in her Teens* and even Shakespeare's *Hamlet* are known to have been put on. The productions, which were often quite intricately staged, are thought to have ceased in about the mid- to late 1870s.

Royal Avenue Theatre *See* PLAYHOUSE.

Royal Court Theatre The name of two theatres in London's Sloane Square. The earlier Royal Court, on the south side of the square, was originally called the New Chelsea. Until 1870 the building had been a Nonconformist chapel, and locals joked that it had always had bad acting, a pit, and payment at the doors. After remodelling in 1871, the theatre changed its name to the Royal Court. Successful productions included several early pieces by W. S. Gilbert and a series of farces by A. W. Pinero in the 1880s.

Following the theatre's demolition for road widening in 1887, its manager John Clayton built the present building on the east side of the square. Opening in 1888, it slowly earned a reputation for innovative drama, staging 10 of George Bernard Shaw's plays between 1904 and 1907. The Royal Court became a cinema in 1932 and suffered from wartime bombing in 1940. It remained derelict until 1952, when Robert Cromie renovated it for the London Theatre Guild. The theatre then entered another exciting phase of its history in 1956, when the ENGLISH STAGE COMPANY took up residence. Under its artistic director George DEVINE, the company produced such controversial new plays as John Osborne's LOOK BACK IN ANGER (1956) and Arnold Wesker's *Chips with Everything* (1962). In 1969 the old rehearsal rooms, which had also been used as a nightclub, were converted into the **Theatre Upstairs** for experimental productions. The Royal Court, which seats only 401, has maintained its challenging approach. In 1987 protests by Jewish groups forced it to withdraw the play *Perdition* by

Jim Allen, which suggested the complicity of some Zionists in the Holocaust.

Royal Hunt of the Sun, The Peter SHAFFER's epic tragedy about the culture clash between the Old and the New World, as exemplified by the relationship between the Inca king Atahualpa and the Spanish conquistador Pizarro. It was first shown at the 1964 CHICHESTER FESTIVAL, and subsequently enjoyed a successful run in a National Theatre Company production at the Old Vic. Colin Blakely played Pizarro and Robert Stephens Atahualpa, while John Dexter was responsible for the majestic staging, which featured mime, dance, and ritual processions. Dexter claims that he decided to direct the play the moment he saw the stage direction "They cross the Andes".

When they first meet, the sun-worshipping Atahualpa believes that Pizarro is the awaited White god. Pizarro promises that no harm will come to the king if the Incas fill a great room with gold for the conquistadors. After this has been done, Pizarro decides that Atahualpa must die. When Atahualpa offers to prove his divinity by dying and being reborn overnight, Pizarro almost believes his claim. However, when the king has been crucified and failed to rise by the morning sun, Pizarro is overcome with remorse.

I and Albert (1972), a much-criticized play about the sex-life of Queen Victoria and the German Prince Albert, was later dubbed 'Royal Cunt of the Hun' by its detractors.

Royal National Theatre Britain's state-supported national theatre company was finally established in 1962 after over a century of discussion. The National Theatre Board was set up in 1962, partly through the efforts of Sir Laurence OLIVIER, who became the first artistic director. The company was formed from the OLD VIC company, which had been performing Shakespeare's plays since 1912. Olivier's successor, Peter HALL, took over in 1975 and oversaw the company's move into its own theatre complex (designed by Denys Lasdun) on the South Bank a year later, ending a lengthy stay at the Old Vic Theatre.

The complex, with terraces overlooking the Thames, has been variously called "a great building", "a concrete fortress", and by Prince Charles:

> A way of building a nuclear power station in the middle of London without anyone objecting.

It houses the UK's most versatile and technically advanced drama facilities and stages a great variety of classic and modern drama. The three theatres are the Olivier, holding 1160 people in its fan-shaped auditorium; the Lyttleton, a proscenium theatre that accommodates 890 people; and the Cottesloe, whose flexible seating for up to 400 can be removed for experimental plays.

Hall was succeeded by Richard Eyre in 1988; at the same time the theatre was granted the right to add the prefix 'Royal', in recognition of its 25th anniversary. Trevor NUNN took over as artistic director in 1997.

Royal Shakespeare Company (RSC) One of the world's leading theatre companies, originally formed in 1879 as the company of Stratford-upon-Avon's newly opened SHAKESPEARE MEMORIAL THEATRE; it was incorporated by royal charter in 1925. The name of the theatre was changed in 1961 to the 'Royal Shakespeare Theatre' and the company then adopted its present title. Peter HALL was the new company's first director. Although the RSC now stages a wide variety of plays in its five auditoria, the company remains faithful to its prime role – performing the works of Shakespeare.

The original Shakespeare Memorial Theatre was destroyed by fire in 1926 and replaced by the present building, which opened in 1932. The company established its first London base in 1960, at the Aldwych Theatre, followed by The Warehouse, a studio theatre opened in 1977. In 1982 both operations were transferred to the new BARBICAN CENTRE in the City of London. Meanwhile, Stratford had seen the opening of its own studio theatre, the Other Place, in 1974. In 1986 the Elizabethan-style Swan Theatre, built inside the shell of the original Shakespeare Memorial Theatre's auditorium, came into use. The current artistic director is Adrian Noble (1950–).

royalty. **royalty** The legal obligation to pay dramatists a small percentage of the box-office receipts or a set fee each time their work is performed. In Elizabethan times, plays were purchased by a company from its resident playwright, who also received a payment if the work was later printed. The first British dramatist to receive a percentage of the profits was Dion Boucicault (*see* BOUCICAULT FAMILY), who in 1860 was paid £10,000 by Benjamin Webster (*see* WEBSTER FAMILY), manager of the Adelphi Theatre, for either *The Colleen Bawn* or *The Octoroon*.

The first US royalty went in 1886 to David BELASCO for his play *Valerie*; this was paid as a fee of $250 a week. The rate of royalties has risen through the years from a standard 5% to, in some cases, 20% or more. *See also* COPYRIGHT.

Royalty Theatre The name of three London theatres, the first standing from 1787 to 1828 in Well Street, the second from 1840 to 1955 in Dean Street, and the third opening in 1960 in Portugal Street.

John Palmer (*see* PLAUSIBLE JACK) opened the first unlicensed Royalty in 1787 with Shakespeare's *As You Like It* and Garrick's farce *Miss in her Teens*. Palmer was arrested and the theatre closed, however, after complaints by the PATENT THEATRES. Under subsequent managers, the Royalty turned to burlesque and pantomime, changing its name in 1813 to the East London Theatre. It burned down in 1826 and reopened two years later as the Royal Brunswick Theatre; only three days after the opening the structure collapsed, killing 15 people.

The second Royalty was a small venue in Soho built for Fanny Kelly's acting school: it opened in 1840 with a mixed bill. A horse drove the original stage machinery, which was so noisy that it had to be removed. Kelly closed the Royalty in 1849 but it opened a year later. After a series of name changes, it became the New Royalty Theatre, with a company that included the young Ellen Terry. Although it specialized in melodrama, in 1875 it staged the premiere of *Trial by Jury*, the first collaboration between Gilbert and Sullivan.

The theatre then took up the cause of modern drama, presenting the first English productions of two of Ibsen's plays, *Ghosts* (1891) and *The Wild Duck* (1894), as well as Shaw's *Widowers' Houses* (1892) and *You Never Can Tell* (1899). Mrs Patrick Campbell starred in a series of revivals, and in 1904 the ABBEY THEATRE Players made their first London appearance at the Royalty. Other hits included John Galsworthy's *The Pigeon* (1912), Noël Coward's *The Vortex* (1924), Sean O'Casey's *Juno and the Paycock* (1925), and J. B. Priestley's *I Have Been Here Before* (1938), its last major success. The Royalty was bombed during the Blitz and did not reopen.

The third Royalty was opened in 1960 on the site of the earlier Stoll Theatre. The first production was Dürrenmatt's *The Visit*, starring Alfred Lunt and Lynn Fontanne. A year later, it became a cinema, reopening as a theatre with the revue *Birds of a Feather* in 1970. The nude revue *Oh, Calcutta!* opened that same year, later transferring to the Duchess Theatre for a total of 2434 performances. Another hit was the musical *Bubbling Brown Sugar* in 1977. The Royalty briefly became a television studio in 1981 before Stoll Moss Theatres took it over as a venue for plays, concerts, and conferences. The Royalty Theatre Company was formed in 1987 and that year successfully staged *Winnie-the-Pooh* along with a series of revivals.

RSC *See* ROYAL SHAKESPEARE COMPANY *under* ROYAL.

Rukada A genre of Sri Lankan puppet theatre that is believed to have developed from the NADAGAMA folk theatre in the early 19th century. The stories and songs come from the Nadagama and are set to traditional Hindustani tunes. The dolls are three- to four-feet tall and are manipulated by strings held by puppeteers sitting on a ledge above the stage. The acting area is divided into three sections, each with a black curtain.

run A series of consecutive nightly performances of a play. A *long run* means the play was performed repeatedly over a long period, owing to its popularity. A *short run* means that the show failed to find favour with the public and was soon withdrawn.

The longest continuously running play in theatrical history is Agatha Christie's THE MOUSETRAP, which opened in the West End in 1952 and is still showing at St Martin's Theatre. The shortest run on record is that of Bulwer Lytton's *The Lady of Lyons*. On the play's opening night (26 December 1838) technical problems prevented the raising of the curtain: the audience waited in the seats for an hour before going home.

run-through A reading or REHEARSAL of a play, especially one that is allowed to continue without interruptions from the director or others.

runway A bridge-like walkway from the stage over the orchestra pit; it often extends the auditorium, allowing performers to approach the audience more closely. The device is mainly employed in musical entertainments; in Andrew LLOYD WEBBER's *Starlight Express* the roller-skating cast make "white-knuckle runs" (as the advertising puts it) towards the audience. Runways are also a feature of beauty pageants.

In the Japanese NŌ drama a runway called a *hashigakari* (bridge) allows performers access to the stage through the auditorium.

RUR A satirical play by the Czech dramatist Karel ČAPEK, first performed in 1921 in Prague and subsequently in London and New York. The initials stand for Rossum's Universal Robots. The play, which introduced the word ROBOT to the language, depicted a futuristic society in which technology is used to create a regimented working class. The robotic machine men eventually go out of control and begin to take on human characteristics. Čapek's play was highly influenced by German expressionism and also employed some features of revue.

The dramatist R. C. Sherriff (1896–1975) wrote of the opening night of his own *Journey's End* (1928): "I couldn't bear to look at the audience. I remember thinking they looked like the robots in *RUR* standing outside the wire."

Russell. Fred Russell *See* FATHER OF VARIETY *under* FATHER.

Willy Russell (1947–) British dramatist and song writer, born and brought up in Liverpool. After leaving school, Russell became a ladies' hairdresser, an experience to which he ascribes his ability to write convincingly for women. He later went to college as a mature student and became a schoolteacher. His first work to be performed was a musical about the Beatles, *John Paul George Ringo...and Bert* (1974), which opened at the Everyman Theatre in Liverpool before transferring to London and New York. A subsequent two-character play, EDUCATING RITA (1980), reflected his own struggle to acquire an education long after leaving school. His one-woman show *Shirley Valentine* (1988), about the self-discovery of a frustrated working-class Liverpool woman, was also shown at the Everyman before transferring to London. BLOOD BROTHERS (1983) was another successful musical.

Rutherford, Dame Margaret (1892–1972) British actress known especially for her portrayals of astute though eccentric middle-aged ladies. Having spent several years working as a piano and elocution teacher, Rutherford began her acting career when she enrolled at the Old Vic school in 1925. She attracted critical attention in a 1934 production of Ibsen's *The Master Builder*, though her first major success was as Miss Bijou Furse in Farrell and Perry's *Spring Meeting* (1938). Other notable roles incouded Miss Prism in Gielgud's production of Wilde's *The Importance of Being Earnest* (1939), Madame Arcati in Noël Coward's *Blithe Spirit* (1941), and Lady Wishfort in Congreve's *The Way of the World* (1953).

Rutherford was also noted for her frequent film appearances, especially her portrayal of Agatha Christie's amateur sleuth, Miss Marple.

Ruy Blas A poetic drama by Victor HUGO, first performed in 1838 in Paris and frequently revived. In the 20th century, it provided a famous role for the romantic actor Gérard PHILIPE. Hugo used this story of the valet and poet Ruy Blas, who disguises himself as his master's cousin in order to enter the Spanish court, to put forward his democratic views. At court Ruy Blas finds that his passionate love for the queen is returned, and he is appointed prime minister. When his lowly origins are revealed, however, he commits suicide. The play's darker moments are relieved by the farcical antics of the character Don César.

S

sacra rappresentazione An early form of religious drama in Italy, equivalent to the English MYSTERY PLAY, French *mystères*, Spanish *auto sacramentales*, and German *Geistspiele*, all of which derived from the earlier LITURGICAL DRAMA. *Sacra rappresentazione*, which retained aspects of the earlier LAUDA devotional drama, developed to its highest form in 15th-century Florence. It was produced by educational and religious groups and usually consisted of re-enactments of biblical stories. Writers included Feo Belcari (1410–84) and Lorenzo de' Medici (1449–92).

The decline of *sacra rappresentazione* began in the late 15th century; although comic interpolations and other secular elements had been introduced it was overtaken by the new demand for drama based on classical models. The genre had a minor influence on Renaissance drama.

saddle-iron *See* FLAT.

Sadler's Wells A theatre in Finsbury, London, formerly renowned for its productions of opera and ballet. The name derives from a holy well that was once located on this site; it was blocked up at the Reformation but rediscovered by Thomas Sadler in 1683, when workmen were digging for gravel. (It still remains under a trap door beneath the theatre's stalls.) At first Sadler opened a medicinal spring here; when attendances declined, he erected a wooden 'Musick House' to provide entertainment, and from the 1690s this became the chief attraction under the management of James Miles.

In 1765 a builder named Thomas Rosoman built a proper stone theatre, which became famous for burlettas, musical interludes, and pantomimes. Edmund Kean, Dibdin, and Grimaldi all appeared here. In 1844 Samuel Phelps took over and specialized in productions of Shakespeare's plays but, after his retirement, the boom in WEST END theatres left Sadler's Wells somewhat isolated. It became, in turn, a pickle factory and boxing arena, was revived as a music hall, and eventually became a cinema, which closed in 1916.

A new theatre, built with the help of the Carnegie United Kingdom Trust, opened in 1931 under Lilian Baylis of the Old Vic. This became one of the leading houses in London for the production of ballet and opera. In 1946 the ballet company transferred to the Royal Opera House, Covent Garden, later (1956) combining with another troupe to form the Royal Ballet. In 1968 the opera company moved to the London Coliseum, becoming known as the English National Opera (1974). The theatre is currently being rebuilt.

sainete In the 18th-century Spanish theatre, a one-act farce or satirical sketch on an urban theme performed between the acts of a full-length play. Derived from the PASO and ENTREMÉ of the 16th and 17th centuries, the *sainete* introduced an element of social criticism and foreshadowed the TEATRO POR HORAS. A leading writer of the genre was Ramón de la Cruz (1731–94).

saint. patron saints of the theatre:

of actors St Genesius
of comedians St Vitus
of musicians and singers St Gregory the Great, St Cecilia, St Dunstan

St George Play *See* MUMMERS' PLAY.

Saint Joan SHAW's historical drama about JOAN OF ARC, often regarded as his masterpiece. It was first performed in 1923 in New York and opened the following year at London's New Theatre, becoming Shaw's greatest commercial success. Sybil THORNDIKE played the title role for 244 performances at the New Theatre with another 321 at the Regent Theatre. The critic James Agate described her characterization of Joan as "boyish, brusque, inspired, exalted, mannerless, tactless and...a nuisance to everybody."

Shaw wrote the play for Thorndike and read it to her in his room. "Shaw himself was a perfect Saint Joan," she said later. "He could have played it far better than any of us." He wrote on her rehearsal book, "To Saint Sybil Thorndike from Saint Bernard Shaw."

Shaw was fascinated by Joan of Arc's genius. "She had an unbounded and quite unconcealed contempt for official opinion," he said. The play climaxes in the scene of Joan's trial, which Shaw based on actual court records.

St Martin's Theatre A London theatre that stands next door to the AMBASSADORS THEATRE. The two theatres were built as a pair, but the opening of St Martin's was delayed until 1916 because of the outbreak of World War I. Both were designed by the architect William Sprague, who followed the new classical (neo-Georgian) style rather than the older fashion for ornate French decor. The façade of St Martin's was damaged during World War II.

In 1923 St Martin's was one of the first London theatres to introduce matinée performances, under the title of 'The Playbox Theatre'. Arnold Ridley's *The Ghost Train* was produced in 1925 with extraordinary SOUND EFFECTS, and Edward Percy's *The Shop at Sly Corner* was presented in 1945. Anthony Shaffer's *Sleuth* opened in 1970 with Anthony Quayle and ran for three years before transferring to the Garrick and then the Fortune for a total of 2359 performances. THE MOUSETRAP transferred from the Ambassadors in 1974; and on 25 November 1991 the cast celebrated the play's 40th anniversary with the prime minister, John Major, in attendance.

saint play *See* MIRACLE PLAY.

Saint's Day A play by John Whiting (1917–63), first performed in London in 1951 at the Arts Theatre Club. The play's violence and black humour were several years ahead of contemporary taste. The plot centres on Paul Southman, a reclusive poet who is lapsing into senility, together with his granddaughter Stella, and her husband Charles. Southman hates the local villagers and is not upset to hear that three soldiers on the run have ransacked the village. Convinced that the villagers have poisoned his dog, Southman insists that Robert Procathren, visiting the old man on his birthday, help him with his revenge. The poet hands him a gun, but it discharges and kills Stella. Procathren flees and tells the soldiers to kill Southman and Charles, which they do without remorse.

Saint-Denis, Michel Jacques (1897–1971) French actor and director, who founded the Compagnie des Quinze in Paris, the London Theatre Studio, the Centre Dramatique de l'Est in Strasbourg, and the Bilingual National Theatre School of Canada in Montreal.

Saint-Denis began his acting career under his uncle Jacques Copeau (1879–1949) at the Théâtre du Vieux-Colombier. In 1930 he founded the Compagnie des Quinze from his uncle's troupe, which made its debut the following year with André Obey's *Le Viol de Lucrèce, Noé* and *La Bataille de la Marne*, all of which Saint-Denis directed. Although the company achieved a high reputation in Paris and London, it disbanded in 1934.

In 1936 Saint-Denis founded the London Theatre Studio to train young actors, but it closed three years later at the outbreak of World War II. In 1937 he directed Laurence OLIVIER and Judith Anderson in *Macbeth* at the Old Vic. Fulfilling the curse of the SCOTTISH PLAY, Saint-Denis narrowly escaped death in a taxi accident, Olivier was nearly crushed by a falling sandbag on stage, and Lilian Baylis, the theatre's manager, died on the eve of the opening night. Nevertheless, Olivier said he had had immediate faith in Saint-Denis: "I'll believe in you, boy. Whatever you say, I'll believe in you."

During the war Saint-Denis headed the French section of the BBC under the name of Jacques Duchesne, for which he was made an honorary CBE. After the war he again directed at the Old Vic, becoming head of the theatre's drama school (with George Devine and Glen Byam Shaw) in 1946. The drama school was closed in 1952 after a purge by the administrator Llewellyn Rees (who also closed the Young Vic and fired Olivier and Ralph Richardson for being too interested in outside activities).

Saint-Denis subsequently returned to France to establish the Centre Dramatique de l'Est in Strasbourg. In 1957 he became artistic adviser to the Vivian Beaumont Repertory Theatre Project at the Lincoln Center in New York and in 1962 joined Peter Hall at the Royal Shakespeare Company as general artistic adviser. In 1960 he published *Theatre: The Rediscovery of Style*, on the subject of training for the stage.

Sakhi Kundhei A type of Indian puppet show found in the eastern state of Orissa. The plays are usually performed at village festivals or fairs and the travelling puppeteers are often families, who depend upon donations collected from the villagers. The form is also known as *Sakhi Nata, Kundhei Nata*, and *Gopa Lila*, terms which refer to the dancing of the marionettes. The puppets have heads and hands made of paper or light wood and stand about 18 inches tall. Animal puppets also exist, especially elephants, tigers, horses, and goats.

The stage, resembling that of the KATHPUTLI of Rajasthan, has a curtain about three feet high to mask the puppeteers and is often decorated with pieces of colourful cloth. The stories, which are based on events in the life of Lord Krishna, are narrated by musicians, who sing folk tunes or adapt popular songs from films. The musical accompaniment is provided by a harmonium, cymbals, and *pakhavaj* drum.

Sakuntala The heroine of Kalidasa's great Sanskrit drama *Abhijnanasakuntala*. The daughter of a sage, Viswamita, and a water nymph, Menaka, she is brought up by a hermit. King Dushyanta visits the hermitage and persuades her to marry him but later, he returns to his throne, leaving her a ring as a gift. Sakuntala bears a son, Bharata, and sets out with him to find his father. On the way she loses the ring, and the king fails to recognize her. The ring is subsequently found by a fisherman, the king recognizes his wife and she is publicly proclaimed his queen. Bharata becomes the founder of the glorious race of the Bharatus. Sir William Jones (1746–94) translated the drama into English.

Salacrou, Armand (1899–1989) French playwright and journalist. His first success, *Patchouli*, was produced in 1930 by Charles Dullin, who also staged Salacrou's hit comedy *Atlas-Hôtel* (1931) and the historical drama *La Terre est Ronde* (1938). Some of Salacrou's themes were later developed by SARTRE, who apparently used *L'Inconnue d'Arras* (1935) as a source for his *Huis-Clos*.

Salacrou became internationally known in 1946 with *Les Nuits de la Colère*, about the collaboration and Resistance in German-occupied Chartres. First produced by Jean-Louis Barrault at the Théâtre Marigny, Paris, it was presented in New York in 1947 as *Nights of Wrath*. Barrault brought the French-language version to London in 1951 and the BBC broadcast it in English as *Men of Wrath*.

Salacrou also contributed the new social drama that emerged after World War II as part of the decentralization movement associated with the CENTRES DRAMATIQUES. His documentary drama *Boulevard Durand* was performed in Le Havre by the Centre Dramatique du Nord in 1961.

Salmacida Spolia The last English court MASQUE. Written by William DAVENANT and designed by Inigo JONES, it was first staged in 1640 at Whitehall, with King Charles I and Queen Henrietta Maria among the performers. Jones had introduced four sets of flat wings and several back shutters sliding on grooves for rapid changes, creating possibly the first completely changeable setting on an English stage.

Salmacida Spolia was an allegorical glorification of Charles's reign. In the anti-masque Discord and other evil spirits arrive to disturb England, "envying the blessing and tranquillity we have long enjoyed". This is soon halted by the arrival of Wisdom (Charles), titled Philogenes or 'lover of his people'. The Queen is then sent down from heaven as a reward to Wisdom for turning the storm into calm. The final scene included a GLORY, in which eight actors richly attired in clouds appeared high above the stage: as music filled the theatre, the heaven opened to reveal its deities.

Salomé A one-act play by Oscar WILDE, based on the biblical story of Salome, who danced for her father Herod and demanded the head of John the Baptist in return. The play, which was written in French for Sarah BERNHARDT in 1891, was banned from performance in England by the Lord Chamberlain. Bernhardt finally produced it in Paris in 1896, by which time Wilde had been imprisoned for sexual offences. *Salomé* was not allowed on the British stage until 1931, although the operatic version by Richard Strauss, with a German libretto, was presented in 1905. The Strauss version was Peter BROOK's first Covent Garden production in 1949, with designs by Salvador Dali.

saltica *See* FABULA.

sandae-togam-guk A form of Korean masked dance-drama, also called *Kamyon-guk*, which has many local variations. The *sandae-togam* was originally the authority in the Choson court that supervised and controlled all forms of entertainment. The modern dance-drama is derived from rituals formerly used to exorcize evil spirits, ensure a plentiful harvest, and bring health and happiness to the population. It involves vigorous dancing, traditional gestures, singing, jesting, and commentaries on everyday life. A musical accompaniment is provided by string, woodwind, and percussion instruments.

Sandow, Eugene (1867–1925) German weightlifter and strongman, who won international fame by presenting the first 'Hercules' act on stage. Sandow had developed his physique through a system of body building that concentrated on muscle groups. His stage programme mostly consisted of lifting enormous weights: at his London debut in 1889 he lifted a 600-pound carthorse. In a blaze of publicity orchestrated by Florenz ZIEGFELD, he appeared at the 1893 Columbian Exposition in Chicago, wearing brief costumes and lifting his pianist together with the grand piano. Sandow increased his income by endorsing such products as health oils and corsets. He retired at 40 and died at the age of 58, while attempting to lift a car out of a ditch.

Sanger, George (1827–1911) British circus proprietor, known as *Lord George Sanger*, who originated the three-ring CIRCUS. He adopted his unofficial title after the US showman BUFFALO BILL had been referred to as 'the Honourable' William Cody during a lawsuit. "If Cody is an Honourable," Sanger remarked, "then I am a Lord!" Queen Victoria made a point of using the title on greeting Sanger.

Sanger launched his first circus at Charter Fair in Kings Lynn, Norfolk. In 1860, at Plymouth Hoe, he created the first three-ring circus, but expenses later forced him to reduce this to one large ring. He also popularized the circus street parade, which passed through the town to the tent; on one occasion he joined his ornate circus wagons to a procession escorting Queen Victoria through London.

In 1871 Sanger and his brother John bought ASTLEY'S AMPHITHEATRE, enlarged it, and returned it to its former use as a circus under the title of Sanger's Grand National Amphitheatre. He staged extravagant spectaculars at the venue until 1893, when the amphitheatre had to be closed as unsafe; it was subsequently demolished.

Sanger, who was married to the lion-tamer Ella Chapman, continued with his famous show until 1905. Six years later he was axed to death by an insane farmhand. Sanger's Variety Circus continued to perform for another half century; after World War II it provided the scene for the debut of a young comedy duo, Morecambe and Wise.

Sardou, Victorien (1831–1908) Prolific French dramatist, who dominated the Parisian stage in the late 19th century with his well-crafted melodramas. The successor to Eugène SCRIBE, he influenced A. W. Pinero, Henry Arthur Jones, and numerous other playwrights.

Sardou scored his first success in 1860 with *Les Pattes de mouche*, seen a year later in London as *A Scrap of Paper*, and went on to produce 20 plays in the next six years. Of his 50 subsequent works, one of the most popular was the melodrama *Fédora* (1882) which starred Sarah Bernhardt when first staged in Paris. In the 1895 London production, Mrs Patrick Campbell played Fédora, a role that Beerbohm Tree, playing opposite her, called "a part to tear a cat in".

Bernhardt also starred in Sardou's *La Tosca* (1887), which Puccini turned into the opera *Tosca* in 1900, and several other dramas written especially for her by Sardou. His other successes included the historical drama *Patrie!* (1869), MADAME SANS-GÊNE (1893) and the social drama *Dora* (1877), which was produced in London as *Diplomacy* in 1878.

Sardoodledom George Bernard SHAW's disparaging term for the type of WELL-MADE PLAY written by the French dramatist Victorien Sardou.

> Sardou's plan of playwriting is first to invent the action of his piece, and then to carefully keep it off the stage and have it announced merely by letters and telegrams.
>
> GEORGE BERNARD SHAW.

Saroyan, William (1908–81) US novelist and playwright, born in California of Armenian parents. In 1939 the GROUP THEATRE's production of Saroyan's first play, the one-act *My Heart's in the Highlands*, established him as one of the leading experimental dramatists of the period. His next play, THE TIME OF YOUR LIFE (1939), was an innovative but accessible piece in which a group of barroom eccentrics discuss their lives and philosophies. The play was an enormous commercial success and became the first drama to win both a Drama Critics' Circle Award and a Pulitzer Prize. However, Saroyan turned down the Pulitzer Prize on the grounds that material awards were dangerous to the recipient and that *The Time of Your Life* was "not any more good or great" than anything else he had written.

Although Saroyan continued to write plays throughout the 1940s and 1950s, none of them captured the success of the first two. These later works include *Hello, Out There* (1942), about the lynching of a harmless tramp, and *The Cave Dwellers* (1957), a strange play set in an abandoned theatre. In 1960 Saroyan wrote *Sam, the Highest Jumper of them All* for the THEATRE WORKSHOP. After the failure of this play Saroyan wrote little else for the theatre, concentrating on novels and autobiographical writings.

Sartre, Jean-Paul (1905–80) French existentialist philosopher, novelist, and playwright who, with Jean ANOUILH, dominated the postwar French theatre. In 1964 he refused the Nobel Prize for literature.

In 1929 Sartre graduated from the École Normale Supérieure, where he formed a lifelong partnership with his fellow student Simone de Beauvoir, the writer and feminist. His melodramatic plays explore moral conflicts with a deep Gallic pessimism, while also functioning as sounding boards for the EXISTENTIALISM he popularized in the 1940s. The first, *Les Mouches*, an interpretation of the Orestes story, opened in 1943 in Paris. As *The Flies* it was produced in New York in 1947 and in London in 1951. The one-act *Huis-Clos* opened in Paris in 1944 and was subsequently produced in London as *Vicious Circle* and in New York as *No Exit*. The plot involves a man and two women who are imprisoned in an ornate sitting-room; it transpires that they have recently died and are condemned to spend eternity together. As each begins to taunt the other two they gradually realize that they have been thrown together to create a special hell for one another: in Sartre's celebrated phrase "Hell is other people."

Morts sans sépultures (1946), about a group of captured Resistance fighters, was seen in London as *Men Without Shadows* (1947) and in New York as *The Victors* (1948). *Le Diable et le bon dieu* (1951), based on the *Faust* of Goethe, is often regarded as Sartre's best dramatic work. His other plays include *Nekrassov* (1955), about a confidence trickster who assumes the identity of the Soviet ambassador, and the wartime drama *Les Séquestrés d'Altona* (1959), produced in 1961 in London as *Loser Wins* and in 1965 in New York as *The Condemned of Altona*. Sartre's adaptation of the elder Dumas's *Kean* was seen in 1953 in Paris, reworked as a US musical in 1961, and produced at the Oxford Playhouse in 1970 (later transferring to London).

Satin Slipper, The The last play by the French poet and playwright Paul Claudel (1868–1955), written between 1919 and 1924 and regarded as his masterpiece. Because of its length and complex symbolism (at one point the hemispheres converse and at another the earth becomes a bead on a rosary), it was considered impossible to stage until 1943, when it was produced at the Comédie-Française by Jean-Louis BARRAULT. Barrault drew on all his technical resources to present Claudel's work, evolving the approach that became known as THÉÂTRE TOTAL. The play has recently proved popular in a new shortened version.

Set in the late 16th century, the action of *The Satin Slipper* ranges from Spain, Italy, and Africa, to America; the play also includes scenes on board ships in the Mediterranean and Atlantic. Its main characters, Don Rodrigue and Doña Prouhèze (who rarely appear together), resist their earthly passions in order to attain Christian salvation.

satire The use of ridicule to expose the pretensions, folly, and evils of human beings and their institutions. The word comes from the Latin *satira*, meaning a dish of mixed fruit, because the first satires were long verses containing a mixture of numerous literary devices. Satire has been employed by dramatists since it was first used on the stage by ARISTOPHANES, who drew upon it to attack his country's political and military leaders, as well as fellow playwrights. Some scholars have suggested that masks were worn in the ancient Greek theatre so that actors could remain anonymous while delivering their satirical lines.

Satire was also prominent in the MYSTERY PLAY of the Middle Ages. John Skelton's MORALITY PLAY *Magnyfycence* was an early 16th-century satire condemning Church abuses. Romantic love was a favourite target of Shakespeare and the Elizabethans. By the late 16th century, satire had become an essential part of European comedy: it has been estimated that three-quarters of the plays produced in London between 1599 and 1613 were satires. Ben JONSON was the chief satirist of the Jacobean period.

In Restoration England the men and women of society were satirized in the COMEDY OF MANNERS of Congreve and others, while in France, MOLIÈRE's clever use of satire drew attention to such vices as greed, snobbery, and religious hypocrisy. In 18th-century England satire became increasingly political; John Gay's THE BEGGAR'S OPERA (1728) was so pointed and successful in its attacks on the government of Robert Walpole that strict controls were imposed on drama. Although the 19th century saw a reaction against satire, 20th century writers have used the theatre to expose and attack social, political, and economic ills. Two of the greatest satirists of the modern era have been George Bernard SHAW, who attacked conventional attitudes to a wide variety of subjects, ranging from prostitution to war, and Bertolt BRECHT, who ridiculed military valour in *Man is Man* (1926).

satyr-play In the ancient Greek theatre of the 5th century BC, an obscene farcical play that burlesqued tragedy. Aristotle claimed, perhaps incorrectly, that Greek tragedy was directly derived from the satyr-play. A dramatist presenting his three tragedies at the DIONYSIA contest was required to add a satyr-play as an afterpiece: it was usually related to the tragedies in theme, making ribald comments on the gods and legendary heroes. These pieces were characterized by swift action, vigorous dancing, and indecent speech and gestures. The form was named after its CHORUS of satyrs, companions of Dionysus later depicted by the Romans as half-goat, half-man. Each member of the chorus wore a mask and goatskin loincloth that included a phallus and a horse-like tail. The chorus leader, Silenus, wore an animal-skin cloak over fleecy tights.

The satyr-play was supposedly created by Pratinus of Philius at some time between 534 and 500 BC. Other famous exponents included Euripides, whose *Cyclops* is the only complete surviving example, Aeschylus, and Sophocles, whose *The Trackers* has survived in fragments.

Satyr-plays gradually diminished in popularity: by about 431 BC the City Dionysia was recording only one such production each year.

Saved A play by Edward BOND; the LORD CHAMBERLAIN's refusal to grant it a licence helped to speed the abolition of stage censorship in 1968. The play was first performed in 1965 as a club production of the English Stage Company at the Royal Court Theatre; controversy immediately arose over a scene in which a baby was stoned to death in its pram. The Director of Public Prosecutions issued 18 summonses against the company and ordered them to pay £50 costs.

The play is set in south London: Len has moved in with Pam and her parents, but Pam breaks with Len and becomes pregnant by his friend, Fred. One day, pushing the baby in the park, she meets Fred and his gang. The youths shove the pram, spit into it, and then stone the baby to death. Fred goes to prison; on his release he rejects Pam, who wants him back. Len, still a lodger, refuses to leave Pam's parents' house, and they welcome him into the gloomy atmosphere of the family.

Savoy. Savoy Operas A name given to the series of eight light operas written by GILBERT AND SULLIVAN for production at the SAVOY THEATRE: the operas were *Iolanthe* (1882), *Princess Ida* (1884), *The Mikado* (1885), *Ruddigore* (1887), *The Yeoman of the Guard* (1888), *The Gondoliers* (1889), *Utopia (Limited)* (1893), and the unsuccessful *The Grand Duke* (1896). Prior to their Savoy works, Gilbert and Sullivan had established their reputations on both sides of the Atlantic with *HMS Pinafore* (1878) and *The Pirates of Penzance* (1880), written for London's Opera Comique.

Savoy Theatre A theatre in the Strand, London, designed and built by Richard D'OYLY CARTE as a home for Gilbert and Sullivan's light operas and the D'Oyly Carte Opera Company. The original Savoy had some 1000 seats in three tiers, and was the first public building in the world to have electric lights. It opened in 1881 with Gilbert and Sullivan's *Patience*, which had transferred from London's Opera Comique; *Iolanthe* (1882) was the first of the so-called SAVOY OPERAS. In 1907 Harley Granville-Barker and J. E. Vedrenne became managers and began to present works by Shaw and Shakespeare. R. C. Sherriff's realistic play about World War I, *Journey's End*, was staged in 1929, the year the building closed for reconstruction.

The remodelled Savoy, with 1121 pink and gold seats in two tiers, opened in 1929 with a revival of Gilbert and Sullivan's *The Gondoliers*. The influence of Broadway was felt in the 1940s, when Kaufman and Hart's long-running *The Man Who Came to Dinner* (1941) was followed by further US comedies, including Ruth McKenney's *My Sister Eileen* (1943) and Clarence Day's *Life with Father* (1947). Later successes have included William Douglas Home's *The Secretary Bird* (1968), which had the Savoy's longest run (1463 performances), and the Royal Shakespeare Company's productions of Shaw's *Man and Superman* (1977) and the musical *Kiss Me, Kate* (1988). The theatre was severely damaged by fire in 1990 but has since been restored.

Scala Theatre A theatre in Tottenham Street, London, opened (as the King's Concert Rooms) in 1772. Despite several changes of name and management in the first half of the 19th century, it failed to dispel a somewhat second-rate and down-at-heel reputation. In 1865, however, the actress Marie Wilton leased the Queen's, gave it a luxurious remodelling, and reopened it (in the presence of the future Edward VII) as the **Prince of Wales's Theatre**. That same year she produced T. W. Robertson's *Society* (the first of his CUP-AND-SAUCER DRAMAS), and *A Winning Hazard* with Squire Bancroft, whom she married two years later. The BANCROFTS made the Prince of Wales's the leading comedy theatre in London, playing together in such hits as *The School for Scandal*, *London Assurance*, and *Diplomacy*. It became one of London's favourite venues, drawing such famous names as Ellen Terry (*see* TERRY FAMILY) and the KENDALS.

In 1880 the Bancrofts left for the Haymarket and the theatre went downhill again. The Prince of Wales's was condemned and closed, being used for a time as a Salvation Army hostel, before being demolished in 1903. The old portico survived as the stagedoor entrance for a new theatre, the Scala, which opened in 1905. The new venue had little success, however, and turned to amateur shows, dance exhibitions, and films. In World War II it was used as the headquarters of the US Army Theatre Unit. The Scala was eventually demolished in 1972.

Scapino In the 17th-century COMMEDIA DELL'ARTE, one of the crafty ZANNI servant characters. Traditionally dressed in green and white, Scapino was a quick-witted rogue who, true to his name (which means 'run off'), would flee at the first sign of real danger. The role was created by the Italian actor Francesco Gabrielli (1588–1654) and ultimately evolved into **Scapin**, the cunning and unprincipled character of the COMÉDIE-ITALIENNE. Scapin is the principal character in Molière's *Les Fourberies de Scapin* (1671).

Scaramuccia *See* CAPITANO, IL.

scenario A name formerly used for the synopsis of a dramatic work; it originated in the early 18th century for the largely improvised plots of the COMMEDIA DELL'ARTE. These were informal outlines of the action, including some stage directions. In modern usage the word more commonly describes the storyline of musicals or films.

scene A subdivision of a play, consisting of a single episode with one setting and a continuous time frame; its end is usually marked by the fall of the curtain or an empty stage. In ancient Roman and classical French dramas, the beginning of a new scene was marked by the entrance or exit of any actor. *Compare* ACT.

scene dock or **dock** A backstage area of a theatre used for the storage of scenery and flats. Also called the **scene bay**, it is usually situated near the stage for the convenient movement of scenery.

scene of releave or **scene of relief** In Restoration drama, a three-dimensional scenic effect created by the use of cut-out scenery. It was usually viewed through open shutters.

scenery Anything placed on stage to indicate the location of the action. Scenery consists chiefly of painted FLATS, CLOTHS, furniture, and PROPS. The use of scenery is a comparatively recent development in the history of the theatre. Greek plays were acted against a stage wall, which the Romans turned into a grand façade, the *scaenae frons*; in the Middle Ages plays were staged in church or in the open air using the convention of MULTIPLE SETTING. Scenery first became important during the Renaissance, with the introduction of wings and perspective painting in the mid-15th century. In the 16th century Sebastiano SERLIO created three basic stage settings that were used for nearly 300 years.

In the Elizabethan theatre, location was evoked by a few props, such as a tent or throne, and by the poetry of the dramatist. Heavy scenic devices were left on stage and ignored when they were inappropriate. Inigo JONES was the first to copy the painted scenes used on the Continent and to adopt sliding side wings. His example was generally followed in the English theatre after the Restoration.

In the 17th century the BIBIENA FAMILY introduced diagonal perspective scenery to the Continental baroque theatres. The 18th century was marked by a growing taste for naturalistic and historically accurate scenery, as in William Capon's designs for John Philip KEMBLE's revivals of Shakespeare (1794–1802) at Drury Lane. In 1832 the London stage saw its first BOX SET, with three walls and a ceiling, real furniture, and working doors and windows.

In the early 20th century the movement against realism was led by Gordon Craig (*see* CRAIG FAMILY), V.E. MEYERHOLD, and the advocates of expressionism. The vogue for nonrepresentational staging was introduced to America as the 'new stagecraft' by Robert Edmond JONES. In the contemporary theatre scenic designs range from the naturalistic to the abstract. *See also* DESIGNER.

Scheifflin, Eugene (1827–1906) US theatrical enthusiast, whose fascination with Shakespeare was such that in the 1890s he conceived the idea of introducing all the bird species mentioned in Shakespeare's plays into America. He accordingly released flocks of imported birds in Central Park; it was thus that the ubiquitous sparrow and starling entered US skies for the first time.

Schembartläufer Masked participants at the Fastnachtszeit carnival in Austria and Bavaria, particularly in Nuremberg. Carrying staves, they variously parade, run, and leap wildly at spectators, tossing ashes over them. The name is derived from the German *Schönbartläufer*, meaning 'pretty beard runner', the masks, even those for women, being generally bearded.

Schicksaltragödie *See* FATE DRAMA.

Schiller, (Johann Christoph) Friedrich von (1759–1805) One of Germany's greatest playwrights and poets, whose lengthy works for the stage are noted for their lyrical beauty. After Shakespeare, he was the most popular dramatist in 19th-century Germany.

Schiller's first play, DIE RÄUBER, was produced in 1782 at Mannheim by Baron von Dalberg. It was an astounding success, especially with younger playgoers, who fainted and embraced one another in the theatre. Somewhat belatedly, it provided the STURM UND DRANG movement with one of its most characteristic works, fraught with emotional intensity and great dramatic drive.

Having left his military post (as medical officer with a Stuttgart regiment) without authorization to see the première of *Die Rauber*, Schiller was ordered to stop writing plays. Instead he fled to Baron von Dalberg, but failed to interest him in his second play, *Fiesko*. This was primarily because Schiller insisted on reading it aloud to the director and company: he was such a bad actor (although he had once considered the profession) that the reading came to a grinding halt after the first act. Years after Schiller's death, *Fiesko* was rediscovered and staged.

Schiller briefly became the official dramatist to the Mannheim theatre, living in debt and under an assumed name to avoid the military. An admirer, Christian Gottfried Körner, became his patron and close friend, supporting Schiller as he finished his first historical verse tragedy, *Don Carlos* (1789), which at 6000 lines was nearly twice as long as Shakespeare's *Hamlet*.

In 1790 Schiller married Charlotte von Lengefeld. By this time, however, he was suffering from tuberculosis and his health soon began to fail. He earned a meagre living as a professor of history at the University of Jena, where he carried out research on the Thirty Years' War that led to his great historical trilogy, WALLENSTEIN. This work was completed in 1799, the year he became co-manager of the Weimar Court Theatre with GOETHE. Despite their very different personalities, their collaboration continued successfully until Schiller's death six years later.

Owing to his disillusionment with the outcome of the French Revolution, Schiller's later historical dramas are concerned less with politics than with the psychological mainsprings of human action.

MARIA STUART (1800), *Die Jungfrau von Orleans* (1801), *Die Braut von Messina* (1803), and WILHELM TELL (1804), all of which were staged by Goethe at Weimar, treat history in an increasingly mythical light. Schiller died while writing *Demetrius*, a drama with a Russian theme: its brief fragments suggest that the work could have become a masterpiece.

Schnozzle Nickname of the US comedian Jimmy Durante (James Francis Durante; 1893–1980), who was famous for his bulbous nose (his *schnozz* or *schnozzle*), his gravelly New York accent, and his unsophisticated humour. He later confessed that he greatly disliked his nose until it became a factor in his commercial success. Durante started his show-business career as a pianist, working first at Diamond Tony's Saloon on Coney Island. He subsequently teamed up with Eddie Jackson and Lou Clayton, and throughout the 1920s the trio worked New York's vaudeville and nightclub circuit. Durante's contribution to the act included such songs as 'Ink-a-Dink-a-Doo' and 'It's my Nose's Boithday Today', which later became stock items in his solo cabaret act, films, and radio and television appearances.

school. **school drama** Plays written in Latin during the Renaissance by European scholars for performance by pupils at schools and colleges. The genre began under the influence of the humanists. One important branch was JESUIT DRAMA, although these plays soon began to be written in the vernacular.

School plays flowered in England in the 16th century, outstanding examples being RALPH ROISTER DOISTER, presented originally at Eton, and the comedy GAMMER GURTON'S NEEDLE, first produced at Christ's College, Cambridge. The only English school play still regularly performed is the WESTMINSTER PLAY, which has been presented annually in Latin at Westminster School, London, since 1560.

School for Scandal, The A comedy of manners by Richard Brinsley SHERIDAN, which opened on 8 May 1777 at Drury Lane. George Washington called it one of his very favourite plays, and Charles Lamb later recalled, "Amidst the mortifying circumstances attendant upon growing old, it is something to have seen *The School for Scandal* in its prime." The play has survived two centuries of changing tastes and fashions in the theatre, one of the most acclaimed modern versions being Jonathan Miller's 1968 production.

The comedy lampoons the activities of scandalmongers. Two of the worst, Lady Sneerwell and Joseph Surface, circulate rumours about Joseph's brother Charles, an honest wastrel, to prevent him from marrying Maria, a ward of Sir Peter Teazle. The duplicitous Joseph wants Maria for himself and shamelessly flatters Lady Teazle to further his suit. The brothers' rich uncle, Sir Oliver Surface, dons a disguise to find out their true feelings towards him; as a result, he chooses to reward Charles's basic honesty with his financial support.

School for Wives, The (*L'École des femmes*) A comedy by MOLIÈRE, first produced in 1662 at the Théâtre du Palais-Royal. The controversy aroused by the piece provoked three more plays, all produced the following year. LA CRITIQUE DE L'ÉCOLE DES FEMMES, written by Molière in response to criticism of the original play, included a caricature of the playwright Edmé Boursault. Boursault responded with an attack on Molière in *Le Portrait du peintre*, causing Molière to counterattack with L'IMPROMPTU DE VERSAILLES, which again ridiculed Boursault and the Hôtel de Bourgogne company. The two dramatists were later reconciled.

The plot of *The School for Wives* involves a middle-aged Parisian, Arnolphe, who intends to marry his ward, Agnès. To ensure her innocence he has had her raised by nuns; however, the sheltered Agnès falls for Horace, the son of Arnolphe's friend Oronte. Arnolphe discovers the affair and nearly kills Horace, but Oronte convinces him that the lovers should marry.

Schröder, Friedrich Ludwig (1744–1816) Germany theatre manager, and playwright. Schröder was a dominant force during the most formative period of the German stage and introduced theatregoers to Shakespeare and Goethe.

Friedrich was born in Schwerin, the son of an alcoholic father and the actress Sophia Schröder (1714–92), who subsequently left her husband to join the travelling company of Konrad Ackermann (whom she eventually married). The young Schröder began as a child actor in his stepfather's company. At the age of 12 he accidentally became separated from it and survived by working as an acrobat and rope-dancer until he found the company again in Switzerland. Schröder was trained by the company's most renowned actor, Konrad EKHOF. From 1767 onwards they both assisted Ackermann in his efforts to establish the first German National Theatre in Hamburg. Mismanagement doomed the project, however, and when Schröder began to take over most of Ekhof's parts, the older actor decided to move on.

Following Ackermann's death in 1771, Sophia retained financial control of the company and Schröder, by now the leading actor, became artistic director. Schröder improved the company's standards and reputation, producing such important works as G. E. Lessing's *Emilia galotti* in 1772 and Goethe's first play *Gotz von Berlinchingen* the following year. In 1771 he became manager of the Hamburg theatre, where he introduced his own adaptations of Shakespearean works including *Hamlet* and *Romeo and Juliet*. In 1782, after years of tension with his mother, Schröder moved to the BURGTHEATER in Vienna where, as guest-artist for four years, he established the refined ensemble acting that was to remain a feature of the company. In 1786 he returned to his mother's company and finally assumed complete control, prospering sufficiently to retire to a country estate in 1798. *See also* HAMBURG STYLE.

sciopticon *See* PROJECTOR.

scissor. scissor cross *See* STAGE DIRECTION *under* STAGE.

scissor stage *See* BOAT TRUCK.

Scofield, (David) Paul (1922–) British actor, who made his first professional appearance in 1940 at the Westminster Theatre. Scofield subsequently joined the Birmingham Repertory Theatre under the direction of Sir Barry Jackson, whom he followed to the SHAKESPEARE MEMORIAL THEATRE at Stratford-upon-Avon in 1946. At Stratford, Scofield embarked on a series of prominent Shakespearean roles that greatly enhanced his reputation; these included Hamlet in a 1955 production that toured to America and Russia and Lear in Peter BROOK's celebrated 1962 production for the RSC. Scofield has since played almost all of the major Shakespearean roles.

He was also highly praised for his portrayal of Sir Thomas More in Robert Bolt's A MAN FOR ALL SEASONS (1960) as well as powerful performances in works by contemporary dramatists as diverse as John OSBORNE, Christopher Hampton, and Peter SHAFFER. Highlights of his later career include West End productions of Herb Gardner's *I'm Not Rappaport* (1986), Shaw's *Heartbreak House* (1992), and Ibsen's *John Gabriel Borkman* (1996).

scop From the 5th to the 8th centuries, a singer and storyteller in Germanic or Teutonic areas of northern Europe. His performances were a major part of feasts and other celebrations. In the pre-Christian era, he was an honoured member of society as the chief preserver of a tribe's history. However, with the advent of Christianity in the 7th and 8th centuries, the scop became classified with mimes and other disreputable entertainers.

Scottish Play An alternative title used by actors for Shakespeare's MACBETH, in deference to the curse allegedly attaching to the play. 'That play' and 'the unmentionable' are amongst the other euphemisms used. Popularly regarded as the unluckiest play in the dramatic repertory, *Macbeth* has become the focus of many theatrical traditions and superstitions. If an actor refers to the play in a dressing room by its original title he or she must immediately leave the room, turn around three times, break wind or spit, knock on the door, and ask permission to re-enter. Alternatively the line "Angels and ministers of grace defend us", from *Hamlet* (I, iv), may be quoted.

Nobody knows the origin of the superstition, but the witches' incantations on stage may be responsible. The history of bad luck began with the first performance, on 7 August 1606 at the Globe Theatre, when the boy-actor playing Lady Macbeth died of a sudden fever in the middle of the play. More recent years have seen the postponement of Olivier's first production at the Old Vic due to the death of Lilian Baylis on the opening night (1937), three deaths in the company during the first production with Gielgud (1942), and – on an eventful tour in 1954 – an attempted suicide, an accident in which the company manager broke both legs, the electrocution of an electrician, and the death of a visitor from a blow by a stage spear after a member of the crew uttered the fateful word to him in conversation.

Many attempts have been made to ward off the curse, including an exorcism of evil spirits in 1926 by Sybil Thorndike and Lewis

Casson at the Princes Theatre. A more powerful defence was used during Orson Welles's famous 1928 all-Black *Macbeth* in Harlem's Lafayette Theatre. John Houseman recalled, "Our supernatural department was very strong at the Lafayette." It included an authentic witch doctor who sacrificed live goats in the theatre at night. When the critic Percy Hammond attacked the production, the witch doctor led a voodoo session and Hammond died a few days later of a sudden illness. A similar tradition is associated with the play in China, where it is often referred to by the title *The Bloodstained Hands*. *See* TABOOS AND SUPERSTITIONS.

Scribe, (Augustin-)Eugène (1791–1861) French playwright, who developed the WELL-MADE PLAY with its close-knit plot. He dominated the Paris theatre for more than 30 years of the early 19th century, earning a fortune from his output of over 400 works (many of which were written in collaboration). Most of his works were light vaudevilles; he also wrote 35 plays – comedies, tragedies, and historical dramas – as well as opera libretti and a ballet. His work was an important influence on Eugène LABICHE, Victorien SARDOU, and even Henrik Ibsen's first play *Catilina* (1850). Scribe was elected to the Académie Française in 1836.

He began writing for the theatre in 1810 and became known in 1815 with the vaudeville success *Encore une nuit de la Garde Nationale*, in which he substituted figures from contemporary society for the conventional characters of the genre. His most successful play was *Adrienne Lecouvreur* (1849), written in collaboration with Ernest Legouvé (1807–1903); the first production featured Rachel in the title role of the 18th-century actress, who was supposedly poisoned by her rival (*see* LECOUVREUR, ADRIENNE). Sarah Bernhardt played Adrienne for the first time in 1880 and it subsequently became one of her most famous roles.

By the latter half of the 19th century Scribe's dull characterization, contrived plots, and feeble language were increasingly recognized. Even Bernhardt decided in 1905 that the original version of *Adrienne Lecouvreur* was too bad to perform ("I don't know how Rachel managed...I can't do a thing with it") and wrote her own version for a US tour. Later generations blamed Scribe for corrupting the art of playwriting, and none of his works are performed today. It is said that when the German poet Heinrich Heine was dying he was asked if he could hiss: "No, not even a play of Scribe's," he replied weakly.

scruto A flexible sheet of scenery made from thin strips of wood fastened to a piece of canvas. It may be used for a TRANSFORMATION SCENE or to conceal an opening, such as the Corsican trap (*see* GHOST GLIDE *under* GHOST), through which an actor can make a surprise entrance or exit.

Seagull, The A play by CHEKHOV, first performed in 1896 at the Alexandrinsky Theatre in St Petersburg, where it was a total disaster. One critic wrote, "We have not been present for a long time at so complete a failure." Chekhov had tried to introduce naturalistic acting, but admitted that the audience showed "a strained state of boredom and confusion". However, when *The Seagull* was revived in 1898 at the Moscow Art Theatre under STANISLAVSKY's watchful direction, it was an enormous success, establishing Chekhov's reputation as a serious playwright. In London, the play ran for 109 performances in 1936 at the New Theatre.

The plot centres on the unsuccessful playwright Konstantin Trevlev and his actress girlfriend Nina. When Nina falls in love with the successful writer Boris Trigorin, Trevlev kills a seagull and places it at her feet. Trigorin takes Nina as his mistress and later marries her, but their baby dies, her career fails, and he finally leaves her. When Nina tells Trevlev that she still loves Trigorin, Trevlev shoots himself.

Second Mrs Tanqueray, The A serious 'problem play' by A. W. PINERO, first performed in 1893 at St James's Theatre with Mrs Patrick CAMPBELL as Paula Tanqueray. Although Pinero thought the subject (a mother and stepdaughter having an affair with the same man) likely to cause offence, the play was an overwhelming success. Mrs Pat became famous overnight, entering what George Bernard Shaw called "the heyday of her Tanqueradiance". She later toured in the role and, according to the critic James Agate, "burst upon the provincial darkness".

Gladys Cooper starred in a 1922 revival at the Old Vic with Mrs Pat in the wings as drama critic of the *Daily Mail*. Another revival at the Haymarket in 1950 had Eileen Herlie as Paula and Leslie Banks as her husband, with sets by Cecil Beaton. Mrs Pat's daughter refused an invitation to the premiere, having been badly treated by her mother and not wishing to be reminded of her.

The plot concerns Aubrey Tanqueray's second marriage, to Paula. Eileen, his 18-year-old daughter from his first marriage, comes home and falls in love with Captain Hugh Ardale. Paula, to protect her, must reveal that she also had an affair with the man. Paula then kills herself, convinced that she cannot escape her fate: "I believe the future is only the past again, entered through another gate."

segment stage *See* JACK-KNIFE STAGE *under* JACK.

Seneca, Lucius Annaeus (4 BC–65 AD) Roman tragedian, philosopher, and statesman. Seneca's nine surviving tragedies on legendary Greek subjects are the only plays from the Imperial era to have survived. The plays (dates unknown) are *Phaedra, Thyestes, Troades, Medea, Agamemnon, Hercules Furens, Hercules Oetaeus, Oedipus*, and *Phoenissae*. They were all written for recitation, rather than stage production.

Seneca's plays are flawed by their artificial language, stereotyped characters, and melodramatic plots. Nevertheless, they had a great influence on the drama of Renaissance Europe, especially the REVENGE TRAGEDIES of the Elizabethans. Shakespeare's TITUS ANDRONICUS (1592) borrowed the device of a pie made of human flesh from Seneca's *Thyestes*.

Seneca himself led a dangerous and eventful life: the emperor Caligula, jealous of his success, refrained from executing him only because he thought Seneca was already dying; the wife of Claudius I subsequently exiled him to Corsica on charges of adultery with the emperor's niece. He later became Nero's tutor, and committed suicide at Nero's command after being accused of conspiracy.

sentimental comedy A popular form of comedy in the 17th and 18th centuries. Moralistic and redolent with pathos, sentimental comedies were a reaction against the licentiousness of the Restoration stage; they appealed especially to the new middle-class audience, which included many women.

Colley Cibber's *Love's Last Shift* (1696) is usually considered the first sentimental comedy. The leading exponent of the genre in England was Richard Steele, whose final comedy and greatest success, *The Conscious Lovers*, opened in 1722 at Drury Lane under Cibber's management. The work was translated into German and French, giving impetus to the wave of sentimentality engulfing Europe. The French version of the genre, COMÉDIE LARMOYANTE, was led by the dramatist Le Chaussée, whose offerings included *L'École des mères* (1744) and *La Gouvernante* (1747).

Separate Tables Two one-act plays on a single bill by Terence RATTIGAN, first performed in 1954 at St James's Theatre, London. The two plays, *Table by the Window* and *Table Number Seven*, evoke the sadness and isolation of life in a small residential hotel. The opening production, directed by Peter Glenville, starred Eric Portman (giving "as good a performance as England can show" according to critic Ronald Barker) and Margaret Leighton. In 1956 it opened at the Music Box in New York, where Leighton won the Tony Award for her performance. During the run her husband Max REINHARDT divorced her on the grounds of misconduct with the actor Laurence Harvey, whom she married the following year. The play was filmed in 1958 with David Niven (who won an Oscar for his performance as Major Pollock), Burt Lancaster, Wendy Hiller, Deborah Kerr, and Gladys Cooper.

Set in the dining room of the Beauregard Hotel, Bournemouth, the play explores the lives of its lonely and ageing residents. In *Table by the Window*, the ex-wife of the disgraced politician John Malcolm discovers that he is having an affair with the manageress. Malcolm still loves his former spouse, despite their stormy past, and they depart together. In *Table Number Seven* Mrs Railton-Bell uncovers the fact that Major Pollock's military credentials are bogus and incites the other residents against him. Her plain and timid daughter Sibyl, finding that she has much in common with Pollock, defies her mother and persuades him to stay.

Serjeant Musgrave's Dance A play protesting against war and violence by John ARDEN. This "historical parable" was first performed in 1959 at the Royal Court Theatre, London; its action was quickly compared with events during the last days of British rule in

Cyprus. Although the original production was a failure, the work has since been hailed as a classic and is frequently revived.

Set in Victorian England, the story follows four soldiers who desert their overseas unit after the death of their comrade, Billy Hicks. Musgrave leads them to Billy's home town, a northern mining community weakened by a coal strike. Here they show Billy's skeleton to the local people in order to turn them against the colonial war. They receive no support from the townspeople and after the accidental death of one of the soldiers they decide to kill "five times five" civilians as a lesson to the community. Another soldier is killed, but a massacre is prevented by the arrest of the two remaining deserters. The innkeeper comments that "you can't cure the pox with further whoring" – a pithy reflection on Serjeant Musgrave's problem.

Serlio, Sebastiano (1475–1554) Italian painter and architect, who was the first scenic artist to publish his drawings. They appeared in 1545 in the second part of his *L'Architettura*, translated into English as *The Second Book of Architecture* in 1611. Serlio's designs dominated the European stage for some 400 years. His ideas were followed by Inigo Jones, Molière, and others, and copies of his sets appeared as late as the 19th century in scenery for melodramas.

Serlio designed for temporary theatres set up in aristocratic banqueting halls. He was a clever fund-raiser among his patrons, explaining:

> The more costly these things are, the more they are worthy of praise, because in truth they then express the generosity of rich lords and their enmity to ugly stinginess.

His sets featured wooden or painted canvas houses with a painted backcloth behind. In his book he illustrated three types of perspective set, each of which featured central avenues with houses or trees on either side: the *scena tragica* depicted palaces, the *scena comica* had city houses, and the *scena satyrica* portrayed a landscape of trees, hills, and cottages.

Another section of Serlio's book concerned lighting, including coloured light, sunshine, and moonlight. Among his suggestions for the production of red lighting on stage was a bottle of red wine placed in front of a torch. He also dealt with the creation of thunder and lightning effects. *See also* SCENERY; SET.

Sesame See RADIUS.

set The scenery, props, and lighting used to evoke the location or mood of the drama. The word 'set' comes from *set scene* – a term formerly used to distinguish an arrangement of scenery, furniture, and props set in place for the duration of a scene from a *flat scene*, consisting of flats that could be slid on and off stage. The BOX SET, representing the three walls and ceiling of a room, was introduced in the early 19th century.

In the later 19th century the movement towards REALISM demanded a new style of set design incorporating many details from everyday life. The director André Antoine (1858–1943) insisted on using real furniture and even had real beef hanging in his set of a butcher's shop. Beerbohm TREE ordered real broom for his production of *Richard II* at the Haymarket but prickly gorse was installed by mistake, causing the leading actor to leap up in agony after pronouncing the lines "For God's sake, let us sit upon the ground and tell sad stories of the death of kings." Perhaps the grandest attempt to create a totally realistic set came from David BELASCO, who had a real New York boarding-house bedroom ripped out and installed on stage for a play called *The Easiest Way*. Many theorists have pointed out that since the audience knows the set is not real, it is pointless to try to create the illusion of reality. Ellen Terry once described stage realism as "real goats, real dogs, and real litter".

Expressionist or experimental plays usually have abstract sets to represent themes or moods. *See also* SCENERY.

set a stage To arrange scenery and props on a stage. The New York *Daily Tribune* explained in 1889: "An elaborate scene is 'set' when it is arranged upon the stage, and 'struck' when it is removed." *See also* STRIKE.

set the scene To indicate to an audience where the action of the play is taking place, and what has prompted it.

Seven Against Thebes A tragedy by AESCHYLUS, first performed in 469 BC in Athens. One of the first plays to be dominated by the PROTAGONIST rather than by the chorus, it is the third and only surviving part of a tetralogy based on the legend of Oedipus, his father Laius, and his sons. The first two dramas, *Laius* and *Oedipus*, showed how Laius had disobeyed the oracle and fathered a son, bringing doom on his family and peril for their city.

The play opens with a prologue explaining that Oedipus is dead. Thebes is besieged by an army from Argos, that wishes to place Polyneices, Oedipus's son, on the throne. His brother Eteocles promises the chorus of fearful women that he will defend the city as one of the seven champions placed at the gates. Polyneices is the enemy champion at Eteocles's gate and the brothers meet in combat, fulfilling Oedipus's curse that his sons shall divide their inheritance with the sword. At the end of the play a messenger announces that the brothers have killed each other, but that Thebes has been saved.

shadow. ***Shadow of a Gunman, The*** Sean O'CASEY's first play, which opened in 1923 at the ABBEY THEATRE, Dublin, and later in London (1927) and New York (1932).

The melodramatic story is set in 1920 in Dublin, where the young poet Donal Davoren and the pedlar Seamus Shields share a basement. The landlord and Minnie Powell, believing that Davoren is an IRA gunman, treat him royally. Shields's pedlar friend Maguire leaves his case of 'samples' with them and is later shot as a member of the IRA. Davoren and Shields discover that the case contains bombs, and when the British army raids the house Minnie hides it in her room. She is arrested and taken away in an army lorry that is then ambushed by the IRA. Minnie yells "Up the Republic!" but is killed as she tries to escape.

shadow puppets Two-dimensional puppets whose shadows are cast on a translucent screen illuminated from behind; they are usually manipulated by rods or wires. Shadow-puppet theatre originated in the Orient: in India, shadow puppets have been used since ancient times to enact the Hindu national epics Mahabharata and Ramayana, and in China they were used to present miniature operas in the Song Era (960–1279), while their use is also traditional in Bali, Java, Burma, and Cambodia.

In France the puppets were known as *ombres chinoises*. Dominique Séraphin opened a shadow theatre in 1774 in Versailles; this later moved to the Palais Royal in Paris and was continued by Séraphin's descendants until 1859. From 1887 Henri Rivière devised sophisticated plays for the Chat Noir cabaret in Montmartre.

Shadow puppets were taken to America in the 18th century, and in 1893 Léon-Charles Marot presented the *Théâtre des Ombres Parisiennes* at the Chicago World's Fair. In Britain shadow plays known as **galanty shows** were presented in conjunction with PUNCH AND JUDY in the late 19th century. In the Germany of the 1920s and 1930s Lotte Reiniger made black-silhouette films such as *Prince Achmet* (1926); her puppets, like those used in France and Britain, were cut out of tin.

Shaffer, Peter (1926–) British dramatist, who has said that a great play must come "bolting out like rabbits out of the hedge". His brilliant first play FIVE FINGER EXERCISE, directed by Gielgud at the Comedy Theatre in 1958, ran for 607 performances; this was followed by further success with two one-act plays billed together, *The Private Ear* and *The Public Eye* (1962).

Shaffer's next play, the epic tragedy THE ROYAL HUNT OF THE SUN (1964), gave the National Theatre Company its first triumph with a contemporary work. In this play, set in Peru following the arrival of the conquistadors, Shaffer began to explore his characteristic themes of reason versus faith and greatness versus mediocrity. The National Theatre also staged the two plays that are probably Shaffer's best-known works: EQUUS (1973) and AMADEUS (1979). His subsequent plays include the comedy *Lettice and Lovage*, which opened in 1987 with Maggie Smith, and *The Gift of The Gorgon* (1992).

Shaffer collaborated with his twin brother, **Anthony Shaffer** (1926–), on three detective books in the early 1950s. Anthony found success with his first play, SLEUTH (1970), and has written other stage thrillers, such as *Murderer* (1975).

Shaftesbury Theatre A theatre in Shaftesbury Avenue, London, that opened in 1911 as the New Prince's Theatre. The management intended to specialize in popular melodrama, with seat prices ranging from sixpence to five shillings. Since 1916, however, musicals and light opera have predominated. In 1919, when the theatre was managed by C. B. COCHRAN, an association began with the D'Oyly Carte Opera Company which was to last more than 40 years. When the Astaires performed in Gershwin's *Funny Face* in 1928, the run was interrupted by a gas explosion. Regular drama was also produced: Sarah Bernhardt appeared in 1921 in Louis Verneuil's *Daniel*, Sybil Thorndike in 1926 in *Macbeth*, and

Michael Redgrave and Peggy Ashcroft in 1953 in their highly praised *Antony and Cleopatra*.

After refurbishment in 1963 the theatre reopened under its present name with the musical *How to Succeed in Business Without Really Trying*. History was made in 1968 when the controversial 'hippie' musical HAIR opened the day after censorship by the Lord Chamberlain was abolished. It logged 1997 performances before literally bringing the house down: as celebrations were being organized for its 2000th performance, part of the roof collapsed and the theatre was closed for repairs. Under threat of demolition, it was rescued by the efforts of the Save London's Theatres campaign; having been listed as "a building of special architectural or historic interest", it reopened in 1974. Recent musicals to have played in the 1358-seat auditorium include *Kiss of the Spider Woman*, which won the 1992 Evening Standard Drama Award for Best Musical.

The first theatre to be constructed in Shaftesbury Avenue, also called the Shaftesbury, opened in 1888 with *As You Like It*. It also found success with musicals, such as *The Belle of New York* (1898) and *The Arcadians* (1909), which starred Cicely Courtneidge and ran for more than two years. The theatre was destroyed by bombs in 1941.

Shakespeare, William (1564–1616) English dramatist, poet, and actor, widely regarded as the greatest playwright of all time. His works have been performed more frequently and in more languages than those of any other dramatist in history. The Shakespearean canon comprises the 36 plays of the FIRST FOLIO (1623), which include several collaborative contributions that cannot be determined with certainty, the *Sonnets*, the long poems *The Rape of Lucrece* and *Venus and Adonis*, and a few lyrics.

Of Shakespeare's life little is certainly known apart from the approximate dates of his birth, marriage to Anne HATHAWAY, and death. After 1590 it is possible to find references to Shakespeare's early plays in the works of other writers; contemporary records show that as well as being a well-regarded actor he was much admired for his poetry. Despite this, reliable information about Shakespeare's personal life, character, and opinions remains virtually nonexistent, leading to much speculation on the basis of the plays.

Shakespeare's first work for the stage is usually considered to be the three parts of *Henry VI*, although the imprecise dating of his plays makes even this is uncertain. By the mid 1590s Shakespeare was a shareholder in the CHAMBERLAIN'S MEN, who were later to become the King's Men. By about 1610 he had made enough money to retire to the second largest house in Stratford. He had been dead for seven years before two of his friends arranged and paid for the publication of the First Folio.

The theory that Shakespeare was not the writer of the works attributed to him was first put forward by Herbert Lawrence in 1769 (*see* BACONIAN THEORY).

> The striking peculiarity of Shakespear's mind was its generic quality, its power of communication with all other minds – so that it contained a universe of thought and feeling within itself, and had no one peculiar bias, or exclusive excellence more than another. He was just like any other man, but that he was like all other men. He was the least of an egotist that it was possible to be. He was nothing in himself; but he was all that others were, or that they could become.
>
> WILLIAM HAZLITT: *Lectures on the English Poets* (1818).

anti-Shakespeareana William Shakespeare is undoubtedly the preeminent English man of letters. Or is he? Many have disagreed...

> An upstart crow beautified with our feathers.
>
> ROBERT GREENE.

> The most insipid, ridiculous play that ever I saw in my life.
>
> SAMUEL PEPYS: referring to *A Midsummer Night's Dream*.

> Shakespeare never had six lines together without a fault. Perhaps you may find seven, but this does not refute my general assertion.
>
> SAMUEL JOHNSON.

> I cannot read him, he is such a bombast fellow.
>
> GEORGE II.

> Shakespeare, – what *trash* are his works in the gross.
>
> EDWARD YOUNG.

> One of the greatest geniuses that ever existed, Shakespeare, undoubtedly wanted taste.
>
> HORACE WALPOLE.

His rude unpolished style and antiquated phrase and wit.
LORD SHAFTESBURY.

A disproportioned and misshapen giant.
DAVID HUME.

I have tried lately to read Shakespeare, and found it so intolerably dull that it nauseated me.
CHARLES DARWIN: *Autobiography*.

With the single exception of Homer, there is no eminent writer, not even Sir Walter Scott, whom I can despise so entirely as I despise Shakespeare when I measure my mind against his. The intensity of my impatience with him occasionally reaches such a pitch, that it would positively be a relief to me to dig him up and throw stones at him, knowing as I do how incapable he and his worshippers are of understanding any less obvious form of indignity.
GEORGE BERNARD SHAW: after seeing Irving's production of *Cymbeline*.

Shakespeareana Relics said to be linked to William Shakespeare. In 1787, 171 years after the playwright's death, the only genuine relic – apart from certain legal documents – appeared to be his chair. However, by the late 19th century inhabitants of Stratford-upon-Avon had mysteriously unearthed Shakespeare's walking-stick, gloves, tobacco box, cutlery, and many other curiosities associated with him – even the sword he is supposed to have used while playing Hamlet (despite the well-established tradition that the author took only minor roles in his own works). The owners of two local hotels claimed to have Shakespeare's clock and shovel-board, while his old school proudly displayed the actual desk at which he sat.

The most spectacular items of Shakespeareana were the forgeries of William Henry Ireland (1777–1835), which included the play *Vortigern and Rowena* and letters between 'Willy' Shakespeare and 'Anna' Hathaway (*see* IRELAND FORGERIES). He was so insistent that these were genuine that several distinguished visitors, including James Boswell, were persuaded to sign a 'Certificate of Belief', attesting to their origin. Others remained sceptical: at the height of Ireland's success the *Telegraph* printed its own satirical item of Shakespeareana, a letter from Shakespeare to his cheesemonger:

Thee chesesse you set mee werree tooee sweattie, and tooe rankee inn flauvorre, butte thee redde herringges were addmirablee.

Shakespeare Memorial Theatre A theatre in Stratford-upon-Avon, built by public subscription in 1879 on land donated by the owners of a local brewery. It was the venue for an annual festival of Shakespeare's plays from 1886 until 1926, when the theatre was destroyed by fire. A new theatre, designed by Elizabeth Scott, was built on the same site and opened in 1932. After World War II the theatre became increasingly influential under the successive managements of Sir Barry Jackson (1945–47), who brought in such talented newcomers as Peter BROOK, Anthony Quayle (1948–56), whose production featured such well-known actors as John Gielgud and Peggy Ashcroft, and Glen Byam Shaw (1956–61). In 1961 a new director, Peter HALL, took over the theatre, renaming it the Royal Shakespeare Theatre, and founding the resident ROYAL SHAKESPEARE COMPANY.

The Shakespeare of Triviality A malicious nickname given to the German playwright Ernst Raupach (1784–1852) by the theatre manager and playwright Heinrich Laube (1806–84). Jealousy may have played a part, since Raupach was the most popular and prolific dramatist of his time, turning out well-constructed histories, such as the 16-play cycle *The Hohenstaufens* (1837). The epithet may have been prompted by Raupach's output of melodramas.

The German Shakespeare A name sometimes given to the German dramatist August von Kotzebue (1761–1819), noted for his prolific output of sentimental melodramas.

The Spanish Shakespeare A name sometimes given to the Spanish playwright Pedro CALDERÓN de la Barca.

Shakespeare villages A group of villages near Stratford-upon-Avon in Warwickshire, made famous by a rhyme traditionally attributed to Shakespeare:

Piping Pebworth, dancing Marston,
Haunted Hillbro', hungry Grafton,
Dudging Exhall, papist Wicksford,
Beggarly Broom and drunken Bidford.

The verse is supposed to have been written after Shakespeare and some friends accepted a drinking challenge from the men of Bidford-on-Avon. Shakespeare and his companions lost the contest and had to sleep off the effects before returning to Stratford the next day. According to another legend, it was alcohol that precipitated

Shakespeare's death: having fallen down some steps after a drinking bout with Drayton and Jonson, he subsequently contracted the fever from which he died.

Shaxpur, William A character in *1601, or a Fireside Conversation in ye Time of Queen Elizabeth* (1876) by Mark Twain. A thinly disguised portrait of William Shakespeare, Shaxpur is seen in discussion with Queen Elizabeth, Ben Jonson, Francis Beaumont, and the Duchess of Bilgewater. Their conversation ranges from the source of a fart produced by one of the company to a frank discussion of sexual practices at the court. This obscene piece of writing was dedicated by Twain to his friend the Rev. Joseph Twitchell and published only as a private edition. Twain said of it: "If there is a decent word findable in it, it is because I overlooked it."

shaking the ladder A technique formerly used by actors for to build up their nervous tension offstage, merely enabling them to enter a scene in a state of excitement. Actors waiting for their cue used to shake the rope ladders hanging from the flies to raise their pulse rates and quicken their breathing. This technique has given way to other devices, such as breathing exercises.

Shallow, Justice A foolish country judge in Shakespeare's plays THE MERRY WIVES OF WINDSOR and HENRY IV, PART II. The character is allegedly based on Sir Thomas Lucy (1532–1600), a justice of the peace who owned Charlecote Park near Stratford-upon-Avon. Legend has it that the young Shakespeare was arrested and brought before the magistrates for poaching deer in the park. In revenge, the future playwright wrote a doggerel attack on Sir Thomas:

> A Parliament member, a Justice of the Peace,
> At home a poor scarecrow, at London an asse;
> If lowsie is Lucy, as some folks miscalle it,
> Then Lucy is lowsie whatever may befall it.

Significantly, in *The Merry Wives of Windsor*, Falstaff is caught poaching Shallow's deer; Shallow's coat of arms is also markedly similar to that of the Lucy family, containing "a dozen white luces" or pikes.

shaman A tribal priest or witch doctor believed to have supernatural powers, including gifts of healing, cursing, and foreseeing the future. Their methods involved ritual dances and other dramatic techniques. Shamanism was especially prevalent amongst Siberian nomads and Native American tribes; the word comes from a Siberian language. In the 20th century, directors such as Antonin Artaud (*see* CRUELTY, THEATRE OF) and Peter BROOK have attempted to rediscover the shamanistic roots of theatrical performance.

sharer In the Elizabethan theatre, a member of a company who held shares in the PROMPT BOOKS, costumes, and properties. The financial risks were divided among the sharers, as were the profits. The evening's take was split up after each performance on a **sharing table** marked out like a draughtboard with the sharers' initials chalked inside the squares.

Sharers normally made up less than half the employees. Important actors were encouraged to put up the money necessary to become shareholders, as this would ensure their loyalty. The sharers formed a self-governing body that chose and produced plays. Members usually had other duties, such as acting, writing plays, or supervising props or costumes.

In 1635 a witness in a court case stated that sharers in the King's Men earned about £180 annually, although others claimed the figure was nearer £50. A nonsharing member, or HIRED MAN, worked under contract for very little money. By 1690 the sharing system had been dropped in London as theatres declined and actors demanded fixed salaries.

Those who had shares in the theatre building but not in the scripts and costumes were known as **housekeepers**. They paid the building's rent and maintained it, receiving an agreed percentage of the admission receipts. Shakespeare was a housekeeper at the Globe Theatre.

Other countries also had sharing troupes. In 16th and 17th century Spain they were called *compañias de parte*, while in early 17th-century France all companies were organized in this way.

Shaw, George Bernard (1856–1950) Irish playwright and critic, whose many plays have been frequently revived throughout the 20th century.

Born and educated in Dublin, he moved to London in 1876 to join his mother and two sisters. By the mid-1880s he had established himself as a critic on the *Pall Mall Gazette* (books), *World* (art), and *Star* (music). Over the next decade he emerged as a powerful advocate of both Wagner and IBSEN. Inspired mainly by the social dramas of Ibsen, he began to write plays of his own, although they were not performed until later. *Plays Pleasant and Unpleasant*, published in 1898, included MRS WARREN'S PROFESSION, which was banned by the LORD CHAMBERLAIN until 1925, WIDOWERS' HOUSES, an exposé of slum landlordism, and THE PHILANDERER. The other plays in the collection, ARMS AND THE MAN, YOU NEVER CAN TELL, CANDIDA, and THE MAN OF DESTINY reveal the author's gift for sparkling comedy. Unable to find commercial audiences for these plays, Shaw wrote extensive Prefaces for them, elaborating on the social and moral themes that they explore. These pieces reflected the socialist beliefs that had led him to become a founding member of the Fabian Society in 1884.

His next collection, *Three Plays for Puritans* (1901), included THE DEVIL'S DISCIPLE, CAESAR AND CLEOPATRA, and CAPTAIN BRASSBOUND'S CONVERSION. Although these plays were performed (indeed Mrs Patrick CAMPBELL appeared in the first performance of *Caesar and Cleopatra* in 1899) Shaw's reputation as a dramatist was not established until JOHN BULL'S OTHER ISLAND and MAN AND SUPERMAN had been seen in the London theatre in 1904. Subsequent plays included MAJOR BARBARA (1905), THE DOCTOR'S DILEMMA (1906), MISALLIANCE (1910), FANNY'S FIRST PLAY (1911), ANDROCLES AND THE LION (1913), and PYGMALION (1914; filmed in 1938 and produced as the musical MY FAIR LADY in 1955). During World War I Shaw's reputation suffered seriously from his pacifist essay *Common Sense About the War* (1914). However, the London theatregoing public had forgiven him by 1921, when HEARTBREAK HOUSE appeared (one year after its first performance in New York). The series of plays BACK TO METHUSELAH was staged later that year. SAINT JOAN (1924), in which Sybil Thorndike played Joan of Arc, was another great success and is often regarded as his most important play. His later plays include THE APPLE CART (1929).

Shaw was a determinedly controversial figure, who could be relied on to be provocative and witty in almost any situation. If some of his plays have dated, this is partly because the avant-garde opinions of nearly a century ago are now accepted as commonplace. Others still retain their poignancy – largely because of the eloquence of his characters. He was awarded the Nobel Prize for literature in 1925.

> His brain is a half-inch layer of champagne poured over a bucket of Methodist near-beer.
>
> BENJAMIN DE CASSERES: *Mencken and Shaw.*

Shaw Festival An international theatre festival held annually from May to October at Niagara-on-the-Lake, Canada. When the festival was founded in 1962 by the playwright Brian Doherty (1906–74) it concentrated exclusively on the works of George Bernard Shaw. It now features works by a variety of dramatists.

Shaw's Corner The name by which George Bernard Shaw's house at Ayot St Lawrence, Hertfordshire, became known. Shaw acquired the house in 1906, the decisive factor being a gravestone he spotted in the village cemetery with the legend: "Jane Eversley. Born 1825. Died 1895. Her time was short." Shaw, with his philosophy of human longevity (*see* BACK TO METHUSELAH), instantly declared "this is the place for me." His confidence was well placed; at the age of 94 he was still able to prune the trees in his garden there – although it was a fall while doing so that hastened his death in 1950. His ashes were mixed with those of his wife and scattered in the garden. The National Trust received the house and grounds, complete with 'The Wilderness' – the hut in which Shaw wrote and which he could rotate to catch the sun's rays – under the terms of the author's will. The house itself has few aesthetic merits: one National Trust inspector described it as "very ugly" and another as "an example of the nadir of taste to which a distinguished writer could sink."

she. ***She Stoops to Conquer*** Oliver GOLDSMITH's classic comedy, first performed in 1773 at Covent Garden. On opening night, Goldsmith's friends stationed one of their number with "the most contagious laugh" in an upper box, hoping that every time he laughed the rest of the audience would join in. The ploy was unnecessary, as the play proved an immediate success and has remained popular ever since.

In the plot Young Marlow and a friend are tricked into mistaking Mr Hardcastle's house for an inn; consequently they treat him as the landlord and his daughter, Kate, as a servant. Marlow, who is painfully shy with women of his own class but forward with serving wenches, pays avid court to Kate while his friend pursues her cousin. By the time the misunderstanding is cleared up, two matches have been made.

Goldsmith had himself made a similar mistake. When travelling in Ardagh he had asked for "the best house" in the area, meaning an inn, and was directed to the home of Sir Ralph Featherstone. Sir Ralph saw the mistake but played along, allowing Goldsmith to treat the family to their own wine and not ending the joke until, on departing, his visitor asked for the bill.

She Would if She Could A comedy by George ETHEREGE, first performed at Lincoln's Inn Fields Theatre, London, in 1668. Much influenced by Molière, it was the first English comedy of manners to be written entirely in prose.

In the play Sir Oliver and Lady Cockwood, together with Sir Joslin Jolley and his nieces Ariana and Gatty, travel from their country homes to London, seeking dubious pleasures. Lady Cockwood pursues Mr Courtal who, with his friend Freeman, escorts the three women to the Bear Tavern in Drury Lane. Sir Joslin and Sir Oliver also arrive at the tavern, where Sir Oliver, too drunk to recognize his own wife, dances with her. The ladies flee home with their men friends. When Sir Oliver arrives, Courtal and Freeman attempt to hide but are discovered and matched with the nieces. For her part, Lady Cockwood resolves to "give over the great business of the town" and attend to her own family.

Sheldon, Edward Brewster (1886–1946) US dramatist who pioneered REALISM on the US stage with his first play *Salvation Nell.* First produced at Hackett's Theatre on Broadway in 1903, it starred Minnie FISKE as a parish scrubwoman, Nell Sanders, and was directed by her husband, Harrison Grey Fiske. Sheldon, who had been a member of '47 WORKSHOP at Harvard University was instantly acclaimed as the leader of a new US school of naturalistic playwrights. This standing was confirmed by subsequent works such as *The Nigger* (1904), which explored the race problem, and *The Boss* (1911), about contemporary employment abuses.

Sheldon's biggest hit, however, was *Romance* (1913), a far less realistic piece in which Doris Keane starred in the role of an Italian opera singer. The play, one of the first to use flashbacks, enjoyed long runs in New York and London. Owing to his ill health most of Sheldon's later work was in collaboration with other writers.

Sher, Antony (1949–) British actor, best known for his daring interpretations of Shakespeare. A native South African, Sher travelled to Britain in the late 1960s to train as an actor. He made his West End debut (1975) in the musical *John, Paul, George, Ringo...and Bert* and that same year he gave a much-praised performance as Khlestakov in Gogol's *The Government Inspector.* In 1982 he became an associate member of the RSC and played his first major Shakespearean role, that of the Fool in *King Lear.* He also became known to a wider public as the devious Eng. Lit. lecturer Howard Kirk in television's *The History Man.*

Charismatic but dangerously manipulative characters have since become a speciality for Sher, the best known being his startling RICHARD III (1884–85). Against the modern trend, Sher chose to emphasize the character's physical deformity, playing him as a grotesque spider-like creature on crutches. The result was hailed as the strongest interpretation since Olivier's 40 years earlier. Sher went on to give similarly bold readings of Shylock and Malvolio (both 1987). His non-Shakespearean roles have included the drag queen Arnold in *Torch Song Trilogy* (1985), an Auschwitz survivor turned ruthless slum landlord in Peter Flannery's *Singer* (1987), the title character in Brecht's *The Resistible Rise of Arturo Ui* (1991), and the artist Stanley Spencer in *Stanley* (1996). In 1995 he returned to South Africa in a production of *Titus Andronicus* directed by his partner, Gregory Doran.

Sher is also a talented writer and illustrator; his books include *The Year of the King* (1986), about his preparations for the role of Richard III, and several novels.

Sheridan, Richard Brinsley (1751–1861) Dublin-born British playwright and theatre manager, who produced three classic comedies within a five-year writing career. "Whatever Sheridan has done or chosen to do," Lord Byron wrote, "has been, *par excellence*, the best of its kind."

The success of Sheridan's first great comedy, THE RIVALS (1775), allowed him to buy Garrick's share in DRURY LANE; he became manager in 1776 and sole owner two years later. Another brilliant COMEDY OF MANNERS, THE SCHOOL FOR SCANDAL, opened in 1777 at Drury Lane to universal acclaim. He also wrote a burlesque of heroic drama, THE CRITIC (1779). All are high comedies, featuring such memorable characters as MRS MALAPROP, Lady Teazle, and Mr PUFF.

Unfortunately he was not so brilliant in his management of Drury Lane. His love of extravagant spectacles almost led to bankruptcy, and he constantly became embroiled in legal action against managers of unlicensed theatres (*see* LICENCE). In 1794 he rebuilt his theatre to such vast proportions that Mrs Siddons called it "a wilderness of a place".

In 1780 Sheridan abandoned the theatre to enter parliament, where he gained a reputation as a fine orator. When Drury Lane caught fire in 1809 he drank a leisurely glass of wine at the GREAT PIAZZA COFFEE HOUSE, watching the flames consume his theatre and remarking "A man may surely be allowed to take a glass of wine at his own fireside."

Sherlock Holmes A play by the US actor and playwright William Gillette (1855–1937) that opened in 1899 in Buffalo. At its London opening (1905) at the Duke of York's Theatre, the role of the page Billie was played by the young Charles Chaplin for 50 shillings a week. Gillette, who played the title role for nearly 40 years, had obtained Conan Doyle's permission to present his detective on the stage (and later the radio). From the play's profits, he built Gillette Castle in Hadlyme, Connecticut, an eccentric mansion with its own miniature railway in the grounds.

Sherwood, Robert (1896–1955) US playwright, whose works emphasize the role of personal sacrifice in both peace and war. Sherwood himself had dropped out of Harvard in 1917 to enlist in the Canadian Black Watch Battalion, with which he served in France. After his discharge he worked as the drama editor of *Vanity Fair* (1919–20), becoming a member of the famous Algonquin Round Table of Wits. In 1938 he was cofounder with Maxwell ANDERSON and others of the Playwrights' Company.

Sherwood's first successful play was *The Road to Rome* (1927), an anti-war satire about Hannibal's crossing of the Alps. Subsequent works included *Reunion in Vienna* (1931), starring the LUNTS, and the tragedy THE PETRIFIED FOREST (1935), starring Humphrey Bogart. In 1936 he won a Pulitzer Prize for *Idiot's Delight*, in which the Lunts appeared as US actors working in Europe who decide to become social activists. He also won Pulitzer Prizes for *Abe Lincoln in Illinois* (1938) and *There Shall Be No Night* (1940), in which a group of Finnish pacifists resolve to take up arms against the Soviet invaders. When the play moved to London in 1943 it had to be reset in Greece, as the Soviet Union had become an ally.

During World War II Sherwood served as President Franklin D. Roosevelt's speech writer and subsequently as head of the overseas branch of the Office of War Information. In 1946 he scripted the film *The Best Years of Our Lives*, which won eight Academy Awards, including Best Screenplay. A fourth Pulitzer Prize came in 1949 for his book *Roosevelt and Hopkins: an Intimate History*.

shimpa (Jap. new school) A modern version of the Japanese KABUKI drama that reflects Western influence, even allowing women to appear on stage. Beginning in the 1880s, the movement reached a peak in the early years of the 20th century and then declined. Attempts have been made to revive *shimpa* in the post-war era, usually with works that are rather sentimental.

shingeki (Jap. new drama) A 20th-century movement that aimed to create a more Western style of drama in Japan. It began early in the century with a commitment to realism and the principles of STANISLAVSKY. Many Japanese dramatists, actors, and playgoers still have difficulties accepting the genre, partly because the Japanese tradition of stylized acting does not fit easily with realistic Western staging, and partly because women appear on stage.

The *shingeki* repertory includes works by Western playwrights as well as modern Japanese dramatists like Kobo Abe (1924–) and Yukio Mishima (1925–70). Abe, who was much influenced by Bertolt Brecht, wrote several protest plays, including *Slave Hunt* (1952), which attacked the traffic in the remains of those killed in war. Mishima wrote such works as *The Nest of the White Ant* (1955), about the dismal lives of Japanese living in Brazil. In recent decades *Shingeki* has become more experimental and aware of international trends.

Shirley, James (1596–1666) English playwright, who was the last important pre-Restoration dramatist. His 40 plays, which include five masques, reflect the influence of Ben Jonson and John Fletcher. More interestingly, his satirical comedies of fashionable London society can be seen as foreshadowing the Restoration COMEDY OF MANNERS. At least eight of his works were revived after the Restoration.

Shirley's first offering, *Love Tricks, or the School of Compliments,* was produced in 1625 at the Phoenix Theatre. Subsequent comedies included *Hyde Park* (1632), *The Gamester* (1633), which David Garrick later adapted, and *The Lady of Pleasure* (1635). He also wrote a number of successful revenge tragedies including *The Traitor* (1631) and *The Cardinal* (1641), which Samuel Pepys saw twice. Shirley's most elaborate masque was *The Triumph of Peace* (1634), performed at the Inns of Court with scenery by Inigo JONES.

When the plague closed the theatres in 1636, Shirley moved to Dublin to become the resident dramatist at St Werburgh's Theatre. On the death of Philip Massinger in 1640 he returned to London to become playwright with the King's Men (*see* CHAMBERLAIN'S MEN) at Blackfriars Theatre. He was thus England's leading writer for the stage when the Puritans closed the theatres in 1642 (*see* INTERREGNUM). After returning to his old profession of teaching he produced few works, the best-known being the 'semidramatic entertainment' *The Contention of Ajax and Ulysses,* in which the two characters contend for the armour of Achilles. The famous dirge that closes the piece alludes to the fate of Charles I:

> Sceptre and crown
> Must tumble down,
> And in the dust be equal made
> With the poor crooked scythe and spade.

Shirley and his wife died of exposure after being forced from their Fleet Street home by the Great Fire of London.

Shoemaker's Holiday, The A boisterous comedy by Thomas Dekker, subtitled "A pleasant comedie of the gentle craft". It was first performed in London in 1599 and proved the most popular of the author's works. Dekker derived the story from *The Gentle Craft* by Thomas Deloney (1560–1600), which included the story of Simon Eyre, the 15th-century shoemaker's apprentice who became Lord Mayor.

The Shoemaker's Holiday was among the plays presented on Broadway in 1938 by the Mercury Theatre company of Orson Welles and John Houseman. Another notable revival was John Dexter's 1981 production at the National Theatre, starring Alfred Lynch.

In the play Rowland Lacy, a relation of the Earl of Lincoln, loves Rose, the daughter of the Lord Mayor of London. The Earl, intent on breaking up the match, sends Lacy off to France to command a company; Lacy, however, resigns and returns in the disguise of a Dutch cobbler. Finding employment with the eccentric Simon Eyre, a master shoemaker, who supplies the Lord Mayor's family, Lacy continues his pursuit of Rose. They are married, Lacy is pardoned by the king, and Eyre becomes Lord Mayor.

shortest. shortest plays The shortest play ever written is almost certainly Samuel BECKETT's *Breath* (1969), which lasts about 35 seconds. It has no dialogue or actors, using recorded human sounds and changing lighting to depict life from the cradle to the grave. The piece begins with a newborn baby's cry and ends with the dying gasp of an old man. *Breath* was 'written' on the back of a postcard for Kenneth TYNAN's 1969 revue *Oh, Calcutta!* but subsequently withdrawn when Tynan attempted to incorporate mass onstage nudity. *See also* LONGEST PLAYS.

shortest runs. *See under* RUN.

shortest titles There are many one-word play titles, but the shortest are probably *Eh?* (1964) by Henry Livings (1929–) and *X* (1972) by Barry Reckford. T. W. ROBERTSON specialized in one-word titles such as *Society* (1865), *Ours* (1866), *Caste* (1867), *Play* (1868), and *School* (1869). *See also* LONGEST TITLES.

showboat The US riverboat theatres that were an institution for more than a century, during which flatboats were replaced by steamers and paddlewheelers. They plied the larger western rivers, such as the Mississippi and Ohio, to bring entertainment to the backwoods regions of the developing country.

Although records exist of river-borne actors performing on shore as early as 1817, the first purpose-built showboat was that launched in 1831 in Pittsburgh by the British-born actor William Chapman (1760–1841). His crude 'floating theatre' was lit by candles and poled down the river to New Orleans. During the voyage Chapman's family, including his five children, would perform such dramas as Shakespeare's *The Taming of the Shrew* and Kotzebue's *The Stranger*. His imitators replaced drama with song-and-dance to attract larger audiences. Before the Civil War interrupted operations in 1861, the trade produced such spectacular enterprises as the 'Floating Circus Palace', launched in 1851 in Cincinnati, which carried a large menagerie and had seating for 3400.

After the war, the new showboats relied on VAUDEVILLE. Augustus Byron French managed five boats from 1878 to 1901 and pioneered the use of marching bands on shore to drum up business. However the settling of the frontier, the development of films and radio, and the Great Depression of 1929, all spelled doom for the big boats. Their numbers fell from 26 in 1910 to five in 1938, the last authentic showboat being Philip Graham's *Goldenrod*, which was still running in 1943.

Show Boat A nostalgic musical about Mississippi riverboat days by Jerome Kern and Oscar Hammerstein (*see* RODGERS AND HAMMERSTEIN), first produced on Broadway in 1927. It created a new direction for the musical by integrating the songs with the action; another innovation was to open the show with a group of Black dockworkers instead of a conventional chorus line. Florenz ZIEGFELD of the *Ziegfeld Follies* was brought in to stage the lavish first production. The London premiere, given at Drury Lane in 1928, saw Paul ROBESON's first performance of the show-stopper 'Ol' Man River'. The role had been written for Robeson, but production delays in New York meant that Jules Bledsoe became the first to sing the song. Hammerstein had to remove the word 'nigger' from the lyrics after Black groups protested.

The story, based on Edna Ferber's novel, follows the Cotton Blossom showboat down the Mississippi. Along the way, the players encounter problems with their love lives or with racial prejudice, but all ends well during a reunion years later. The songs include 'Only Make Believe', 'Why Do I Love You?', and 'Can't Help Lovin' That Man'. Besides its many stage revivals, *Show Boat* was filmed in 1929, 1936 (with Robeson), and 1951.

Shubert brothers Three US brothers who held a virtual monopoly of theatres in New York and other cities in the early 20th century through their Shubert Theatre Corporation. Lee Shubert (1875–1953), Sam S. Shubert (1876–1905), and Jacob J. Shubert (1880–1964) were instrumental in breaking up the THEATRICAL SYNDICATE but replaced that vast theatrical empire with one of their own, estimated to be worth $4 million.

The brothers were born in Syracuse, New York, and managed their first theatres in that town. In 1900 they leased Broadway's Herald Square Theatre, the first of many they would acquire during the VAUDEVILLE era. Sam died in 1905, however, at the age of 29.

David BELASCO and other independent producers backed the Shubert's organization during the battle against the syndicate. The brothers made a point of renting venues to producers who had been hurt by the monopoly. After their victory, which had become clear by about 1912, the two surviving Shuberts opened the Sam S. Shubert Theatre in their brother's memory (*see* SHUBERT THEATRE). The Shuberts now began to produce so many plays that they booked out most of their theatre chain, stifling competition. Their contracts were so unfair that Equity called a successful strike in 1919, in which both stars and stagehands joined.

A lesser defeat came in 1919 when Tallulah BANKHEAD, appearing in *39 East* at the Broadhurst Theatre, refused to wear stockings on stage in the hot summer weather and was hissed by outraged ladies in the audience. It was Lee Shubert, always the dominant brother, who had to plead with her to cover her legs. She refused.

The Shuberts moved into London's West End in the 1920s but were unable to meet the strong British competition. In 1950 the US government accused the Corporation of violating the law prohibiting monopolies. After Lee's death the surviving brother, Jacob, sold 12 theatres in 1956 to meet the government's demands.

Shubert Theatre A New York theatre on West 44th Street, opened in 1913 by Lee Shubert and Jacob J. Shubert, who named it after their late brother Sam S. Shubert. Although originally intended as a venue for musicals, it began by presenting serious drama, the opening production being *Hamlet*, starring Johnston Forbes-Robertson.

Other successes included *The Copperhead* (1918), starring Lionel Barrymore (*see* BARRYMORES), James Fagan's *And So To Bed* (1927), with Yvonne Arnaud as Mrs Pepys, and Sinclair Lewis's *Dodsworth* (1934). The THEATRE GUILD sponsored productions of Margaret Kennedy's *Escape Me Never* (1935), which gave Elizabeth Bergner her Broadway debut, Robert Sherwood's *Idiot's Delight* (1936), with the LUNTS, and Jean Giraudoux's *Amphitryon 38*.

The first musical (1937) to play at the Shubert was *Bloomer Girl*, which ran from 1944 to 1946; it has been followed by Lerner and Loewe's *Paint Your Wagon* (1951), Anthony Newley and Leslie Bricusse's *Stop the World – I Want to Get Off* (1962), Neil Simon and Burt Bacharach's *Promises, Promises* (1968), and Marvin Hamlisch's *A Little Night Music* (1973) and *A Chorus Line* (1975).

shund theatre In the late 19th century, a term used in the US Yiddish theatre for the melodramas and sentimental works that found great popularity among the unsophisticated immigrant audiences. 'Shund' means 'nonsense' or 'rubbish'.

Shylock The vengeful Jewish usurer in Shakespeare's THE MERCHANT OF VENICE (1596). Shakespeare is thought to have created the part in response to the anti-Semitic feelings aroused by the execution in 1594 of Dr Roderigo Lopez, a Jewish physician convicted of trying to poison Queen Elizabeth. Shakespeare's consumate skill as a dramatist, however, prevented him from creating a one-dimensional villain. His portrait of Shylock evokes both revulsion for the businessman insisting on his POUND OF FLESH and compassion for the man's dilemma. Shakespeare gives him a good and memorable case:

> Hath not a Jew eyes? Hath not a Jew hands, organs, dimensions, senses, affections, passions?...If you prick us, do we not bleed? If you tickle us, do we not laugh? If you poison us, do we not die? And if you wrong us, shall we not revenge?

This aspect of the role was first emphasized by Charles MACKLIN's performance in 1741, when he played Shylock as a tragic and dignified figure. A similar interpretation persisted in many 19th-century productions; William Hazlitt noted in 1818 that Shylock "becomes a half-favourite with the philosophical part of the audience...Shylock is a *good hater*; a man no less sinned against than sinning." This is even more true today, when an anti-Semitic caricature would be totally unacceptable to most audiences.

Siddons, Sarah (Sarah Kemble; 1755–1831) One of the great British actresses of all time. William Hazlitt wrote of her, "She was tragedy personified. To have seen Mrs Siddons was an event in everyone's life." Siddons's furious performance as Queen Katherine in *Henry VIII* so frightened an actor playing one of the minor roles that he vowed he would "not for the world meet her on the stage again".

Her acting once made George III weep. The king, who could not stand even a hint of tragedy in a play, went to see her in the comedy *The Mysterious Husband*, not realizing that the last act contained a death scene. When the actors reached this part of the play he sobbed loudly and said to his wife, "Charlotte, don't look, it's too much to bear!" The play, by royal request, was never performed again.

Sarah was the eldest of 12 children of Roger Kemble and Sarah Ward, who managed a touring company; her brothers John, Charles, and Stephen Kemble were all actors (*see* KEMBLE FAMILY). She made a poor debut in *The Merchant of Venice* in 1775 at Garrick's Drury Lane but seven years later won renown there as a tragic actress in Garrick's *Isabella*. Later in her career she became known for her Shakespearean roles, most notably Lady Macbeth; her performance in the sleepwalking scene was particularly celebrated. In 1802 Siddons and her brother, John Philip Kemble, took over Covent Garden. She continued to appear there until her last season (1811–12), during which she gave an amazing 57 performances.

Off stage Siddons was unpopular: actors found her unapproachable and she gained a reputation for being discourteous to her admirers. She never forgot the hardships of her childhood; even when she was well off she was known for her stinginess, gaining the nickname 'Lady Sarah Save-all'.

A play about her, *Mrs Siddons*, starred Sybil Thorndike in 1933. She is also said to be the resident ghost at the Bristol Old Vic (*see* GHOSTS).

sightline The line of vision from a member of the audience to the action occurring on stage. Visibility varies greatly from one theatre to another, and set designers must keep these individual factors in mind. Walls can be dispensed with and doors and windows reduced to simple frames to solve sight-line problems. When a director blocks out the movements of actors (*see* BLOCKING), he usually views these from seats in every section of the house to ensure that all of the audience can see the main action.

silence. Silence, Theatre of A theatrical movement of the 1920s, characterized by the use of long pauses in the dialogue to allow the audience to imagine the unstated meanings or emotions. The symbolist playwright Maurice MAETERLINCK was a founder of the genre, which the French call *le Théâtre de l'Inexprimé*. Jean-Jacques Bernard (1882–1972) contributed such works as *The Sulky Fire* (1926) and *The Springtime of Others* (1934).

The rest is silence The last words of the dying HAMLET (Shakespeare: *Hamlet*, V, ii).

silver. ***Silver Box, The*** The first play by the British author John Galsworthy (1867–1933). It was highly praised after its first performance at London's Royal Court Theatre in 1906. The play presents the parallel experiences of two families in order to point a moral about the legal system's unequal treatment of two men, one rich and one poor, who have both been accused of theft.

Silver Tassie, The A play by Sean O'CASEY. It employs a markedly different style from his previous work, moving from realism to expressionism in the second act. Owing mainly to this change of style, the ABBEY THEATRE, which had produced all his earlier work, declined to produce *The Silver Tassie* when O'Casey offered it to them. This rejection prompted O'Casey's decision to leave Ireland for good and the work was premiered in 1929 in London with Charles Laughton in the lead. For several years following his rift with the Abbey, O'Casey would not allow his work to be performed in Ireland; when *The Silver Tassie* was finally produced there in 1935, it was attacked by both the critics and the Church.

In the play O'Casey expresses his opposition to war through the experiences of two World War I soldiers, Harry Heegan and Barney Bagnal, who return home on leave from the Western Front. While there Harry leads the local football team to win a trophy, the Silver Tassie of the title. After they return to the Front, Harry is wounded and his life saved by Barney, who carries him to safety while still under fire. When Harry's girlfriend Jessie sees his crippled state, she switches her attentions to Barney, and Harry sinks into depression, smashing the Silver Tassie. Notable revivals have included the 1969 RSC production with Richard Moore in the lead.

Simon, Neil (1927–) US playwright, whose numerous comedies have made him the most financially successful playwright in the history of the theatre. In the 1960s he produced six successive hits and at one time had four plays running simultaneously on Broadway. Simon owns the 1075-seat Eugene O'Neill Theatre in New York, finances his own productions, and adapts his works for films (which in Britain have been more successful than his plays). Reviewing his career, Simon commented, "When I was good, I was very, very good. When I was bad, we folded."

Simon began by collaborating with his brother, Daniel, on sketches for revues; in 1961 they wrote their first full-length work *Come Blow Your Horn*. Simon's first solo work was the book for the musical *Little Me* (1962). His string of hits began with BAREFOOT IN THE PARK (1963), followed by THE ODD COUPLE (1966), and *Plaza Suite* (1968). Four serious comedies followed, THE LAST OF THE RED HOT LOVERS (1969), *The Gingerbread Lady* (1970), about an ageing alcoholic singer, *The Prisoner of Second Avenue* (1971), about an unemployed man heading for a breakdown, and *The Sunshine Boys* (1972). In 1976 he returned to writing playlets, combining four short pieces in the hit *California Suite*.

In the 1980s Simon produced several autobiographical works, including BRIGHTON BEACH MEMOIRS (1983), *Biloxi Blues* (1985), which won a Tony Award, and *Broadway Bound* (1986). His most recent offerings have included *Rumours* (1988), *Lost in Yonkers* (1991) which won both a PULITZER PRIZE and a Tony Award, and *Jake's Women* (1992).

Singspiele *See* BALLAD OPERA.

siparium *See* CURTAIN.

Sisterly Feelings An experimental comedy by Alan AYCKBOURN, in which the course of the plot is determined by the toss of a coin in the first scene and subsequently by the choice of an actress. It was first performed at the Stephen Joseph Theatre-in-the-Round, Scarborough in 1980, subsequently transferring to the National Theatre.

The story begins on the day after the funeral of Dr Ralph Matthews's wife, Amy, when Matthews takes his family to the remote site where he had proposed to her. Ralph's son, Melvyn, is infatuated with Brenda Grimshaw, while his daughters, the unmarried Dorcas and Abigail, whose husband is away on business, are attracted to Brenda's brother Simon. Because the car is full, one sister must walk home with Simon, and a coin is tossed to determine whether Dorcas or Abigail will accompany him in the next scene. When Dorcas's boyfriend, the poet Stafford, arrives, she must choose between the two, a choice (left to the actress) that determines the next two scenes. The play ends with the marriage of Melvyn and Brenda.

Six Characters in Search of an Author A play by Luigi PIRANDELLO. First seen in 1921 in Rome, it made Pirandello internationally famous when it was produced a year later in London and New York. The play, a paradoxical exploration of the nature of fiction and theatrical illusion, forms part of a trilogy with *Each in His Own Way* (1924) and *Tonight We Improvise* (1929). Memorable revivals include the 1963 production at the Mayfair Theatre, London, in which Ralph Richardson starred as the Father.

The play begins with a producer and cast rehearsing Pirandello's play *Rules of the Game*. Six fictional characters suddenly appear, looking for the author who created them but has now rejected them. In an attempt to take control of their own fate, they perform a drama in which a father is reunited with his family, including his stepdaughter, in a brothel; then a silent little girl drowns as a silent little boy looks on before shooting his stepbrother. This impresses the producer so much that he begins to assign his own actors to play the parts. The 'real' characters, however, complain that they are closer to the roles and that the actors would distort the truth. The producer and actors eventually go home leaving the characters to themselves.

skene In the ancient Greek theatre, a wooden building behind the PROSCENIUM used as a dressing room and backstage area. The front of the *skene* was decorated with painted panels, from which the English word 'scene' derives. The building had three doors (later five) through which the actors made their entrances and exits; each of these had a symbolic meaning, for example, one entrance was reserved for an arrival from a distant place. During the 5th century BC the *skene* became stone rather than wood. A century later it acquired a long platform that elevated the principal actors above the chorus in the orchestra.

skin. ***Skin Game, The*** A play by John Galsworthy (1867–1933), first performed in 1920 in London. The story involves the conflict between the families of a country gentleman and a prosperous manufacturer. Squire Hillcrist is furious with his loud nouveau-riche neighbour, Hornblower, for going back on his promise and evicting tenants from cottages that he had bought from Hillcrist. When the squire's wife snubs Chloe, the pregnant daughter-in-law of Hornblower, the gloves come off and 'the skin game' (or bare-knuckle fight) begins. Hornblower buys land overlooking the Hillcrist house and announces his intention to build kilns on it. Hillcrist's agent, Dawker, investigates the other family and finds that Chloe was once a 'professional co-respondent' in divorce cases. The squire blackmails Hornblower, who agrees to sell the land to Hillcrist at a loss and reinstate the tenants if Chloe's secret is kept. However, Chloe's husband is suspicious and makes Dawker reveal the truth. She tries to end the marriage and commit suicide. Hillcrist, the victor, is left with a sense of shame at having abandoned his own principles.

Skin of Our Teeth, The An idiosyncratic comedy by Thornton WILDER, first produced on Broadway in 1942 with Tallulah Bankhead in the leading role. The play, which won a Pulitzer Prize, tells the story of mankind through the fortunes of one family, the Antrobus's. Mr and Mrs Antrobus survive the Ice Age by burning furniture and relive the Adam and Eve story: Mr Antrobus is made President of the Order of Mammals and invents the wheel. The conclusion is that mankind has always managed to pull through by the skin of its teeth.

The London opening on 18 May 1945, starring Vivien Leigh, was also memorable as the night Laurence Olivier punched the *The Sunday Times*'s critic James AGATE.

Skinner family The US actor Otis Skinner (1858–1942) and his daughter Cornelia Otis Skinner (1902–79), who were among the theatre's most versatile performers. Otis was a classical tragedian, romantic hero, comedian and character actor, while his daughter became an actress, singer, diseuse, humorist, poet, and dramatist.

Otis Skinner worked as a clerk before making his debut in 1877 at the Philadelphia Museum Theatre (*see* DAVIDGE'S SNAKE SHOP). He played 92 different roles during his first year in the professional theatre before making his Broadway debut in *Enchantment* in 1879. In 1884 he acted with Edwin Booth (*see* BOOTH FAMILY) and Augustin Daly at Toole's Theatre, London. After several years touring with Helena Modjeska, he started his own touring company in 1894, hiring Maud Durbin as leading lady and marrying her a year later.

Skinner's most famous role was Hajj the beggar in Edward Knoblock's fantasy *Kismet*, which he created in 1911 at the Knickerbocker Theatre. He played Hajj for a year on Broadway and then toured in the part for a further three years, making a silent film version in 1916 and a 'talkie' in 1930.

Skinner mostly concentrated on Shakespeare in his later years; one of his last roles was that of the title character in *Uncle Tom's Cabin* at the Alvin Theatre in 1933. He wrote several volumes of reminiscences, including *Footlights and Spotlights* (1924) and *The Last Tragedian* (1939).

Cornelia Otis Skinner made her debut beside her father in 1921 in *Blood and Sand*. She later wrote and performed in MONODRAMAS, which she toured in America and Britain. These one-woman shows included *The Wives of Henry VIII* (1931), *The Empress Eugénie* (1932), and *The Loves of Charles II* (1933). They were generally well-received, but the critic George Jean Nathan noted "A woman talking steadily for two hours is hardly my idea of entertainment whether in the theatre or in private."

Cornelia also starred in *Candida* (1939), *Lady Windermere's Fan* (1946), and *The Pleasure of His Company* (1958), written in collaboration with Samuel Taylor. She wrote several acclaimed theatrical biographies including *Madame Sarah* (1967) about Sarah Bernhardt.

skomorokhi Traditional itinerant players of Imperial Russia. The *skomorokhi*, who included musicians, dancers, boxers, and other entertainers as well as actors, were condemned by the Church as heathens and pagans in the 11th century. Traditionally, they would dress as women and animals on New Year's Eve and paint their faces for Easter.

By the late 16th century these troupes, often consisting of more than 100 players, were extremely popular. The leading entertainers wore peasant costumes decorated with ribbons, adopted names such as Foma and Erema, and drew large crowds with their stories, puppet shows, and trained bears, dogs, and rats. However, after an uprising in Moscow, the *skomorokhi* were once more banned in 1648 by Tsar Aleksey Mikhailovich; they retreated to the rural north to preserve their traditions, working mainly as entertainers at private functions. They exerted an important influence on the development of the Russian circus and variety acts.

sky. sky border *See* BORDER.

sky cloth *See* CLOTH.

slapstick Originally, the name of the divided paddle used by HARLEQUIN to strike other performers with a resounding slap or crack but without injury. The term later came to encompass all boisterous comedy involving knockabout action and horseplay. Modern stage practitioners have included THE CRAZY GANG in Britain and Olsen and Johnson in America. The slapstick tradition was continued in the cinema by Charlie Chaplin, Laurel and Hardy, the Marx Brothers, the Three Stooges, and Abbott and Costello and on television by Benny Hill. Slapstick can also be entirely verbal, as demonstrated by The Goons, whose zany radio shows became cult listening (1952–60):

> SEAGOON Listen, that tricycle against the wall – whose is it?
> ECCLES Mine – a present from an admirer.
> SEAGOON Could you drive me to town on it?
> ECCLES No, the tricycle ain't mine, the wall was the present.

Sleuth An ingenious two-act thriller by Antony Shaffer (1926–), twin brother of the playwright Peter SHAFFER. After opening in 1970 at London's St Martin's Theatre it transferred to the Garrick and Fortune for a total run of 2359 performances. It also ran for 1222 performances on Broadway. The 1973 film version brought together Laurence Olivier (then 65) and Michael Caine. Olivier was paid $200,000, his highest-ever single fee, for the performance.

The plot introduces Andrew Wyke, a successful writer of detective fiction who lives in a remote manor house in Wiltshire. When his wife's lover, Milo Tindle, visits, the two begin a series of dangerous psychological games, which escalate out of control towards a violent denouement.

slips A British 19th-century name for the seats at the extreme right and left of the gallery in a theatre. Covent Garden still retains the term.

slote or **sloat** In the 19th-century British theatre, a mechanical arrangement of weights and rails used to raise or lower actors or pieces of scenery, often through a TRAP. The slote was invented in the early 1800s and had become standard equipment in London theatres by the middle of the century. In 1853 a theatre article in *Punch* mentioned the "workings of various mysterious engines of machinery, called 'sloats' and 'scruto-pieces'". Henry Irving described in 1887 how a slote once struck him on the head instead of carrying him up into the FLIES. The usual US term is **hoist**.

Sly, Christopher A drunken tinker, also a keeper of bears, who appears in the Induction of Shakespeare's THE TAMING OF THE SHREW. Shakespeare mentions him as a well-known character of Wincot, a hamlet near Stratford-on-Avon, and it seems possible that in him we have an actual portrait of a contemporary.

Sly is found dead drunk by a nobleman, who commands his servants to put him to bed, and on his waking to attend upon him like a lord and bamboozle him into the belief he is a great man; the play that follows is performed for his delectation.

In *The Taming of a Shrew*, another Elizabethan play with the same plot, Sly interrupts the performance more than once before going home resolved to tame his own wife. Modern producers of Shakespeare's play sometimes incorporate the additional Sly scenes from *A Shrew*.

SM A common abbreviation for STAGE MANAGER.

Smith, Dame Maggie Smith (1934–) British actress and comedienne, known for playing "the impossible nanny goat" roles. The critic Alan Brien wrote in 1974 that "it is Maggie Smith, all those knees and elbows and pointed toes like an umbrella in a thunderstorm, or a sleepwalking bat, or a spider escaping from treacle, who keeps us continually watching her in incredulous delight."

She made her debut in 1952 in the OUDS production of *Twelfth Night*. After training at the OXFORD PLAYHOUSE School, she appeared on Broadway in the revue *New Faces of '56* at the Ethel Barrymore Theatre. The following year she was back in London in Bamber Gascoigne's revue *Share My Lettuce*, in which she appeared with Kenneth Williams. She claimed to have picked up her nasal delivery from Williams. One night he unexpectedly added new material and ruined her next line; Smith rushed angrily to his dressing room, where Williams explained it seemed such a good joke that he couldn't wait for the next rehearsal to add it. Smith defused the situation by leaning over his dressing-room sink and asking "Have you been peeing in here? I suppose you couldn't wait for that either?"

In 1959 she joined the Old Vic company and a year later replaced Joan Plowright in Ionesco's *Rhinoceros*. She joined Olivier's National Theatre company at the Old Vic in 1963, playing the role of Desdemona to this Othello in 1964. In the same year she appeared in a revival of Noël Coward's *Hay Fever* directed by the Master himself; when Smith starred in another Coward hit *Private Lives* in 1972 he praised her as being "much better than Gertie" (his beloved Gertrude LAWRENCE).

Her later plays have included the one-woman show *Virginia* (1980), based on the life of Virginia Woolf, Ronald Harwood's *Interpreters* (1985), and Peter Shaffer's *Lettice and Lovage* (1987). In 1993 she starred as Lady Bracknell in Nicholas Hytner's revival of Wilde's *The Importance of Being Earnest* at the Aldwych Theatre.

Maggie Smith is probably best known for creating the title role in the film *The Prime of Miss Jean Brodie* (1969), for which she won an Oscar for Best Actress.

William Smith *See* GENTLEMAN SMITH *under* GENTLEMAN.

socialist realism The approved theory and practice of visual and literary composition in the Soviet Union from the 1930s onwards. Its aim was to educate the Soviet workers in Marxist doctrine through simple naturalistic works. Although the application of the theory produced some interesting results in the early years, the style later degenerated into idealistic representations of the heroic successes of the Soviet economy and society, which are almost totally devoid of merit.

The playwright and commissar for education, Anatoli Lunacharsky (1875–1933), was an early advocate of using the theatre as an instrument of propaganda. Such experimental directors as Vsevolod MEYERHOLD and Alexander Tairov fell out of favour, their work being declared too abstract to forward the socialist dream. Two leading playwrights who worked within the tenets of socialist realism were Maxim GORKI (1868–1936) and Vladimir MAYAKOVSKY (1893–1930).

sociétés joyeuses In medieval France, amateur theatrical societies of 'companies of fools'. When the Church suppressed the FEAST OF FOOLS in the 15th century the *sociétés joyeuses* took over many of its features, thereby creating the first secular drama in France. The local groups, mostly composed of young men, produced two kinds of farce, the SOTIE, in which all the characters were fools, and the *sermons joyeux*, which were burlesque sermons.

society. ***Society*** The first of the so-called CUP-AND-SAUCER DRAMAS of Tom ROBERTSON, which began a new fashion for realistic plays about domestic problems. It was first produced in London in 1865 at the Prince of Wales' Theatre by the actor–managers Squire Bancroft and Marie Wilton (*see* BANCROFTS), who also starred in the roles of Sydney Daryl and Maud Hetherington. *Society* established their reputations as well as Robertson's. In the play the gentleman Sydney Daryl is approached by a father and son, who want to use him to gain access to high society. When Daryl refuses to cooperate, the son tries to ruin him without success.

Society for Theatre Research A scholarly body dedicated to research into the British theatre and to the preservation of its buildings, records, and other historical remains. It was founded in 1948 at the Old Vic Theatre with the theatre historian Gabriele Enthoven as its first president. The Society makes annual grants towards theatre research and sponsors lectures. In 1987 it helped to found the national THEATRE MUSEUM, to which it donated its library. It also publishes a thrice-yearly journal, *Theatre Notebook*, along with other publications and pamphlets.

The Society hosted the first international conference on theatre history in 1955 in London, an event that led to the foundation of the International Federation for Theatre Research. An associated body, the American Society for Theatre Research, was founded in 1956 in New York.

Society of West End Theatre (SWET) The trade association founded in 1908 to represent the West End theatre owners, managers, and producers. The Society, based in Covent Garden, presents the annual LAURENCE OLIVIER AWARDS to the profession and promotes the 45-or-so central London theatres through the Leicester Square ticket booth and its various publications. These include the free *The London Theatre Guide*, published every two weeks with details of plays, times, and venues, and the organization's bimonthly journal, the *West End Theatre Magazine*, containing articles on all aspects of the theatre as well as details of current and upcoming productions.

sock Comedy. The term comes from the *soccus*, a type of light low-heeled shoe worn by actors in the classical Greek and Roman comedies. The term **sock and buskin** is sometimes used to refer to comedy and tragedy, or drama in general. Hence Dryden's line, which appears so ludicrous to modern readers:

> Great Fletcher never treads in buskins here
> Nor greater Jonson dares in socks appear.

See also COTHURNUS.

Sokari One of Sri Lanka's oldest forms of theatre, performed after the Sinhalese New Year as an offering to the goddess Pattini. The sexual symbolism of the drama links it with earlier fertility celebrations. The all-night presentations are given in the open air; the performers, male peasants wearing masks, use dance and mime to depict the actions described in song.

Though the story differs slightly in the various villages, the basic plot involves the Indian Guru Hami and his wife, Sokari, who sail to Sri Lanka with their servant, Paraya, and are caught up in a series of humorous adventures. Sokari, young and beautiful, becomes involved with a local doctor and at the end of the play has a child.

Sondheim, Stephen (Joshua) (1930–) US composer and lyricist, noted for his innovative and sophisticated musicals. Sondheim's first music for the theatre was written for the play *Girls of Summer* (1956). He subsequently supplied the lyrics for Leonard Bernstein's WEST SIDE STORY (1958) and for *Gypsy* (1959). In 1962 he wrote both the lyrics and music for *A Funny Thing Happened on the Way to the Forum*, a hit show based on the farces of the Roman author PLAUTUS. After the failure of *Anyone Can Whistle* (1964), a series of highly successful and often quite experimental musicals followed; *Company* (1970), *Follies* (1971), *A Little Night Music* (1973), which was written entirely in three-four time, and *Sweeney Todd* (1979), all won New York Drama Critic's Circle awards. In 1983 Sondheim won a Pulitzer Prize for *Sunday in the Park with George*, inspired by the works of the French pointillist painter Georges Seurat. More recent works include *Into the Woods* (1987), a witty reworking of several familiar fairy-tales, and the macabre *Assassins* (1991). The revue *Side by Side by Sondheim*, produced in London in 1976, featured a selection of his songs, as did *Marry Me a Little* (1981) and *You're Gonna Love Tomorrow* (1983). In 1990 Sondheim was appointed visiting professor of drama at Oxford University.

son et lumière (Fr. sound and light) A type of outdoor dramatic spectacle presented after dark in appropriate natural settings or around historic buildings. Such entertainments are dependent on lighting effects (such as coloured floodlights or laser beams), music, and a recorded narrative, often punctuated by dramatic sound effects; there may or may not be a cast of performers involved. The first *son et lumière* was staged in 1952 at the Château de Chambord on the Cosson River in France. The first British production of this kind was staged in 1957 at Greenwich Palace; the first US one was in 1962 at Independence Hall in Philadelphia.

song-and-supper rooms Small British venues that featured popular entertainment in the early 19th century. They developed from earlier traditions of tavern entertainment, such as the 'sing-song' taproom concerts given at Sadler's Wells, the Coal Hole, and the Cyder Cellars. When the Licensing Act of 1751 was passed (*see* LICENCE), 'musick' or 'harmonic' clubs were formed to avoid the new restrictions. Those attending the song-and-supper rooms were served food and drink at their tables while being entertained by 'free' programmes of variety that included ballads and comic songs, jugglers, acrobats, and monologues.

The most popular of these venues was EVANS's in Covent Garden, London, which opened in about 1820 in the cellar of a tavern. Entertainers such as Sam Cowell and Charles Sloman performed there and early MINSTREL SHOWS were introduced. Like many other song-and-supper rooms, Evans's eventually became a MUSIC HALL.

Sophocles (496–406 BC) One of the three tragic playwrights of ancient Greece; he wrote 123 plays during a career of 60 years and was still writing at the age of 90. His plays dwell on the conquest of suffering. Only seven tragedies survive: *Ajax* (450 BC), ANTIGONE (442 BC), OEDIPUS REX, also known as *Oedipus Tyrannus* (429 BC), TRACHINIAE (425 BC), ELECTRA (409 BC), PHILOCTETES (409 BC), and OEDIPUS AT COLONUS (401 BC).

Sophocles studied tragedy under Aeschylus, whom he defeated in the DIONYSIA in 468 BC. He went on to win a further 18 contests in less than 30 years. However, his most famous work, *Oedipus Rex*, won only second prize (as one of a group of three plays judged together).

Sophocles's formal innovations included adding a third principal actor, limiting the role of the chorus to one of commentary, and making plots more complex. He remains popular with modern audiences largely because of his sympathetic approach to his characters.

Oedipus Rex, which gave Freud the term 'Oedipus complex', is the story of the King of Thebes who unwittingly murders his father and marries his mother. The most renowned modern performance of Oedipus was given by Olivier in 1945 with the Old Vic at the New Theatre. The production is remembered by those who saw it for Olivier's searing cry when Oedipus learns he has murdered his father. Olivier claimed he was imitating a cry he heard in a Canadian forest, where skunks were caught by making their tongues stick to a block of salt.

Sothern family The British–US actor Edward Askew Sothern (Douglas Stewart; 1826–81), his son Edward Hugh Sothern (1859–1933), and Edward Hugh's wife

Julia Marlowe (Sarah Frances Frost; 1866–1950).

E. A. Sothern was born in Liverpool and acted in the provinces before travelling to America, where he joined Lester Wallack's company at Wallack's Theatre in New York (*see* WALLACK FAMILY). His first success came in 1858, when he played Lord Dundreary in Tom Taylor's *Our American Cousin*, a triumph he repeated at London's Haymarket three years later (*see* DUNDREARIES). It was during a performance of *Our American Cousin* by the same company that President Lincoln was assassinated (*see* FORD'S THEATRE). Other noted successes included leading roles in Tom Robertson's *David Garrick* (1864), which was written especially for Sothern, *Brother Sam* (1865), which he co-wrote, and H. J. Byron's comedy *A Crushed Tragedian* (1878).

E. H. Sothern made his debut in his father's play *Brother Sam* at the Park Theatre, New York. He was a light comedian like his father but also played romantic leads. He made his London debut in 1881 and from 1885 to 1897 was leading man at the Lyceum Theatre, New York. In 1900 Sothern played a spectacular Hamlet at the Garden Theatre, New York, but the production was cancelled after less than a week when he was stabbed in the foot during swordplay and contracted blood poisoning. In 1904 Sothern began to act with Julia Marlowe, whom he married in 1911. He frequently revived his father's famous role of Lord Dundreary and in 1916 played his role in *David Garrick*. When his wife retired in 1924 they donated the scenery, costumes, and properties from 10 Shakespearean plays to the Shakespeare Memorial Theatre at Stratford-on-Avon. Sothern continued to act occasionally until 1927.

Julia Marlowe appeared as a child in *HMS Pinafore* and other productions, making her adult debut in 1887 in New York in Mrs G. W. Lovell's *Ingomar* (1887). She excelled in Shakespeare (especially as Juliet and Lady Macbeth) and in classic comedy, starring as Lydia Languish in Sheridan's *The Rivals*. In 1897 the theatre manager Daniel Frohman wrote: "This is the greatest emotional actress in America but it will be a heart-breaking task to find plays equal to her strength".

sotie A type of satirical play, usually with a political or religious theme, performed in medieval France. The playwright Pierre Gringore (1475–1538) was one of the most successful writers in the genre. A *sotie* was often performed as a prelude to a MORALITY PLAY; the performers, drawn from either amateur or permanent companies, were called *sots* (Fr. fools) and dressed in the traditional fool's costume of dunce's cap, short jacket, and tights with bells on the legs. Few extant texts exist, one of the best known being the *Recueil Trepperel*. The form was prohibited in the 16th century. *See also* SOCIÉTÉS JOYEUSES.

soubrette A minor female role in comedy, especially a lady's maid who is pert or flirtatious. The soubrette (from a French word for maidservant) became a key role in 17th-century French comedy. One British critic wrote of a 19th-century actress: "Tragedy queens and comic soubrettes were alike to her, and she did not present them very differently to her audience."

Soul-Cakers Play *See* MUMMERS' PLAY *under* MUMMER.

sound. sound effects The production of special sounds required during a play. They are used to establish locale, weather, and time of day or year, as well as to reproduce the sound of physical events crucial to the plot (e.g. gunshots). Before the era of recording, sound making was a technical art assigned to the property department. Many of the traditional effects were carried over to radio drama.

In the late 1940s recorded sound began to be used but many theatres continued to employ live effects to save money. The first major London production to use taped sound effects was *My Fair Lady* in 1957 at Drury Lane. Despite the sophisticated technology now available, theatrical wisdom has it that live effects are to be preferred because of their spontaneity and clarity.

One of the greatest ever challenges to the sound-effects men was Arnold Ridley's *The Ghost Train* (1925), first staged at the St Martin's Theatre, London. Six sound technicians were required to create train noises by using whistles, garden rollers, bells, drums, wire brushes, milk churns, galvanized iron tanks, air cylinders, mallets, and thunder sheets.

Traditional methods of creating live sound effects include:

Thunder Created by means of a galvanized iron 'thunder-sheet' vibrated by jerking a handle at the bottom. This replaced the 18th-century 'thunder-run' in which cannon balls rumbled down wooden troughs to fall with a crash. Such a device can still be seen as the Theatre Royal, Bristol. *See* STEAL ONE'S THUNDER *under* THUNDER.

Wind Created by using a mechanical 'wind machine', in which wooden slats attached to a revolving drum rub against a piece of canvas.

Rain, surf, and *hail* Created by shaking dried peas, marbles, or lead shot in a box or cylinder.

Explosions Created by fireworks placed and activated in tanks.

Gunfire Created by using a starting pistol or by hitting wood with leather.

Horses' hooves Created by striking coconut shells together or on a hard surface like slate.

Slamming door sounds are best created by slamming a real door offstage, *breaking glass* is best done by breaking glass, and *bells* should be bells. To avoid comical bad-timing, actors should press working doorbells themselves and be able to cut off a ringing telephone by lifting the receiver.

Sound of Music, The RODGERS AND HAMMERSTEIN's musical based on the true story of the Von Trapp Family Singers. The original 1959 Broadway production featured Mary Martin in the leading role and won a Tony Award. In the 1961 London production at the Palace Theatre Jean Bayless appeared as Maria, while the extraordinarily popular 1965 film version starred Julie Andrews and Christopher Plummer. A 1981 revival at the Apollo Victoria Theatre set a record for a single week's attendance figure (2600 seats overbooked at 101%). The musical is one of the few to feature Nazi characters.

Set in Austria in the 1930s, the story concerns Maria Rainer, a postulant nun, who becomes governess to the seven children of Captain Georg Von Trapp, who has recently lost his wife. Maria's high spirits soon cheer the family, and a hesitant romance with the captain leads to their marriage. The Nazis gain power, however, and the singing family use their appearance at the Salzburg Festival of Music to flee over the mountains to Switzerland. The songs include 'The Sound of Music', 'Climb Every Mountain', 'Maria', 'My Favourite Things', and 'Do Re Mi'.

> This last, most remunerative and least inspired...of the Rodgers and Hammerstein collaborations is square and solid sugar.
>
> JUDITH CRIST

South Pacific A musical with a World War II setting by RODGERS AND HAMMERSTEIN, first produced on Broadway in 1949 starring Mary Martin and the operatic bass Ezio Pinza. It ran for 1955 performances and won the 1950 Tony Award as Best Musical. The London production, also with Martin, opened in 1951. The plot follows a US Navy nurse, Nellie Forbush, who is stationed on a Pacific island during the war and falls in love with a French planter, Émile de Becque. A widower with two children, de Becque has fled France after killing a local bully. A subplot concerns US Lieutenant Joseph Cable who becomes the lover of Liat, the daughter of islander Bloody Mary. Both this relationship and that of Nellie with Émile are overshadowed by racial prejudice. Cable and de Becque are sent on a dangerous mission in which the lieutenant is killed. The Frenchman survives, however, and returns to Nellie.

The quality of the songs led some critics to label *South Pacific* as a masterpiece. They include 'Some Enchanted Evening', 'There is Nothing Like a Dame', and 'I'm Gonna Wash that Man Right Outa My Hair' (memorable for being sung by Mary Martin, in both New York and London, while shampooing her hair).

Southwark An ancient suburb on the south bank of the Thames, annexed to the City of London in 1327. It has a wealth of literary and historical associations including the site of the Tabard Inn of Chaucer's *The Canterbury Tales.* In Elizabethan times the **Bankside** area had numerous theatres, including the GLOBE, the ROSE, the HOPE, and the SWAN, as well as one of London's best known bull-and-bear-BAITING venues.

Southwark Theatre The first permanent theatre built in Philadelphia and possibly the first in America. David Douglas, manager of the AMERICAN COMPANY, opened it in 1766 on South Street outside the city's jurisdiction. The red building had a brick lower storey and a timber upper half topped by a cupola. The first production on its stage, lit by oil lamps, was Vanbrugh's *The Provoked Wife*, presented on 12 November. A year later the Southwark presented Thomas Godfrey's *The Prince of Parthia*, the first work by a US-born playwright to receive a professional staging.

The Southwark, known informally as the South Street Theatre, was closed by the Continental Congress in 1774 and briefly became a hospital during the War of American Independence. British troops reopened it in 1778 to raise money for widows and orphans; a drop curtain added by a British major at this time continued in use for the life of the theatre. The American Company returned in 1784 to give 'moral lectures' – a device to avoid a local prohibition against play-acting. From 1789 the Southwark returned to regular presentations. However, new competitors reduced its profits and a fire in 1821 was the *coup de grâce*.

Soyinka, Wole (Akinwande Oluwole); (1934–) Nigerian dramatist, poet, and novelist, considered to be one of the foremost playwrights of his generation. In 1986 Soyinka became the first Black African recipient of the Nobel Prize for literature.

Soyinka was educated at the University of Ibadan and subsequently at the University of Leeds. After Leeds, Soyinka moved to London where he became associated with the Royal Court Theatre and George Devine's Writer's group, which at the time also included the dramatists Edward Bond, Arnold Wesker and Ann Jellicoe. In 1959 Soyinka's play, *The Invitation*, was staged at the Royal Court under his own direction.

Following his return to Nigeria, Soyinka formed the theatre group the 1960 Masks, which subsequently became the Orisun Theatre Company. In 1960 his play *The Dance of the Forests* was staged as part of the celebrations for Nigerian independence. Other notable plays include *The Trials of Brother Jero* (1960), *Kongi's Harvest* (1964), which opened the first Festival of Negro Arts in Dakar in 1966, *Madmen and Specialists* (1970), which was first produced at a Playwright's Conference in America, *Death and the King's Horseman* (1976), *A Play of Giants* (1985), and *A Scourge of Hyancinths* (1992).

In his other writings, which include collections of poetry and several highly acclaimed novels, Soyinka similarly attempts to fuse Western literary influences with African tradition. A politically active writer, Soyinka was imprisoned briefly in 1965 and again from 1967 until 1969. In the mid 1990s he emerged as a leading critic of the military regime of General Abacha and was obliged to flee to America for safety. He was formally charged with treason – a capital offence – in 1997.

Spanish Tragedy, The A play in blank verse by Thomas KYD. First performed in 1592 in London, it was one of the most popular dramas of its day, initiating the fashion for REVENGE TRAGEDIES. Since its plot is similar to that of HAMLET, some scholars have suggested that Kyd wrote an earlier, now lost, play about Hamlet that Shakespeare drew upon to create his masterpiece. *The Spanish Tragedy* was certainly one of Shakespeare's sources. The play was frequently revived, sometimes with additions by other hands. The continuing popularity of the work is demonstrated by Samuel Pepys's note that he saw it in 1668.

Set in Spain in 1592, the play focuses on the plight of Hieronimo, marshal of Spain, whose son Horatio has been murdered for political reasons. Having failed to secure justice, he carries out his personal revenge by having a play acted out in which the two murderers, employed as actors, are killed. Hieronimo himself bites off his tongue before running from the stage to commit suicide.

spectacle theatres Europe's earliest purpose-built playhouses, dating from the 16th century. They were ornately decorated and had stages equipped with an array of mechanical devices. The only surviving examples, all in Italy, are Andrea Palladio's Teatro Olimpico in Vicenza (1585), Vincenzo Scamozzi's Court Theatre at Sabbioneta (1589), and Giovanni Battista Aleotti's Teatro Farnese at Parma (1619).

spectator. Spectatorium A gigantic theatre designed by Steele MACKAYE for the 1893 Chicago World's Fair but never built. MacKaye intended it to seat 12,000; the 25 moving stages would have incorporated the most advanced European stage equipment. The first production was to have been *The World Finder*, for which Dvořák composed his *New World Symphony*.

Financial problems prevented the grand design from being realized and MacKaye died the following year. A scale model had been constructed and demonstrated, however, and theatre architects later employed some of its new ideas for the stage.

spectatory An early Victorian word for an auditorium. It was also sometimes used as a collective noun for the mass of spectators themselves, this being considered a more accurate term than 'audience' (meaning 'hearers').

Speed the Plough A sentimental comedy by the British playwright Thomas Morton (*c.* 1764–1838), first performed in 1800. The play is mostly remembered for the unseen character Mrs GRUNDY, who became a popular symbol of rigid middle-class respectability. The main plot centres on Sir Philip Blandford, who mistakenly thinks he has killed his own brother.

The US dramatist David MAMET also wrote a play with the title *Speed-the-Plow* (1988).

Spelvin, George *See* PLINGE, WALTER.

Spieltreppe A form of multilevel staging introduced by Leopold Jessner (1878–1945) during his period as director of the Berlin State Theatre (1919–30). He replaced conventional sets with a number of different acting levels connected by stairways. This innovation was also called *Jessnertreppe*. The many plays he staged in this way included Shakespeare's *Richard III* and Wedekind's *Der Marquis von Keith*.

spill Stage lighting that spills or scatters from a spotlight into areas that should not be lit. The problem can be corrected by adjusting the BARNDOOR shutters to tighten the beam.

spill and pelt A routine of the English HARLEQUINADE in which a costermonger's barrow is overturned and the fruit and vegetables are thrown by Clown and Pantaloon at a mob of greengrocers, fishwives, bakers, police, and others.

spot. spot bar *See* BATTEN.

spotlight In the theatre, a light that produces a bright narrow beam that can be focused on a particular actor or area of the stage. It is usually mounted so that the beam can be directed as required. The spotlight is one of the most powerful symbols of the theatre and acting, and the term has come into general use in such expressions as *in the spotlight*, meaning to be the centre of attention.

In the early 19th century LIMELIGHT was used to create a spotlight effect. An arrangement of electric arc-lighting behind glass lenses was first used to spotlight the actors at the Paris Opéra in 1846. In 1907 improved filaments in incandescent lamps, enabling a much higher wattage to be used, led to the creation of the first modern spotlights. By World War I 1000–watt lamps were in common use in Europe and spotlights began to replace footlights as the primary source of illumination. More complex arrangements of spotlights and DIMMERS were developed on the US stage. Modern spotlights are often equipped with such devices as BARNDOOR shutters and a COLOUR WHEEL. *See also* LIGHTING.

spring. ***Spring Awakening*** The first major play by Frank WEDEKIND, written in 1891 and given its first public performance 15 years later in Berlin. In its attack on sexual repression it anticipates the themes of Wedekind's subsequent dramas. Subtitled *A Children's Tragedy*, the play depicts the tragic love affair between two 14-year-olds; the disapproval of their tyrannical parents leads to an abortion and both their deaths.

In 1901 the work was privately performed in London by the STAGE SOCIETY. Owing to its controversial subject matter, it was not produced for public performance in Britain until 1965, when it was seen at the Royal Court Theatre. In 1974 it was revived by the National Theatre in a translation by Edward Bond.

Spring '71 A play by the Russian-born French dramatist Arthur ADAMOV. It was first performed in 1961 in Paris and then a year later in London at the communist Unity Theatre. The play, which shows the influence of Bertolt Brecht's EPIC THEATRE, provides a sweeping history of the Paris Commune of 1871 interspersed with contemporary political and social comment.

Staberl, Chrysostomos A comic character of the 19th-century Viennese theatre, who is usually portrayed as a happy but crafty umbrella-maker. His character is similar to that of the earlier clowns HANSWURST and KASPERL. Introduced by the Austrian playwright Adolf Bäuerle in his *Bürger von Wien* (1813), he featured in numerous later comedies by Bäuerle and others. The role was created by Ignaz Schuster and refined by Karl Carl, who introduced Staberl to the

Munich stage, from whence the character spread throughout Germany.

Stadt Theatre *See* BOWERY THEATRE.

stage. **stage brace** or **brace** A piece of wood attached to the back of scenery to support it. One end is attached to the FLAT by a hook-and-eye, while the other end is weighted down or secured to the floor by a stage screw. It is usually adjustable. A **French brace** is a nonadjustable triangular piece of wood attached to the flat as a permanent support. It is hinged to fold flat for storage or transportation.

stage business *See* BUSINESS.

stage cloth A CLOTH consisting of canvas or other material that is laid on the stage floor. It can be either plain or painted to complement the other scenery. Some stage cloths have specific purposes, such as the **sand cloth** used for desert settings.

stage crew A general term for the backstage theatre staff under the direction of the STAGE MANAGER. The crew includes stage hands who move scenery and props and operate the curtain, traps, and flying devices, as well as those who build and set the scenery, handle lighting, and operate sound effects.

stage direction A theatrical instruction, usually written into the script, telling an actor to move to a certain area of the stage, or asking the stage manager for a specific stage effect.

Movements by actors are always described from the point of view of someone looking from the stage towards the auditorium; therefore when an actress moves 'stage left' a member of the audience sees her moving from left to right. The primary movements on stage are labelled UPSTAGE (away from the audience) and DOWNSTAGE (towards the audience), terms that derive from the early 'raked' stages that sloped upwards towards the back. The stage is divided into nine main zones: the three at the back are labelled 'up left', 'up centre', and 'up right'; the three middle ones are 'left', 'centre', and 'right'; and three at the front are 'down left', 'down centre', and 'down right'. Directions of this kind are normally abbreviated, as 'UR' for 'up right', etc.

If an actor is directed to stand **above** a piece of furniture or other object he should stand upstage of it, while **below** indicates the opposite. **Cross** means that the actor should move across the stage from one side to the other, while **scissor cross** means that two actors should exchange sides of the stage. **Enter** and **exit** require no explanation. **Manet** (Lat. he remains) was formerly used to indicate that the actor should remain on stage.

Stage directions are also given in regard to scenery and stage effects. These are normally self-explanatory but can be complicated, as this direction from Thomas Shadwell's production of *The Enchanted Island* (1674) shows:

> This tempest...has many dreadful Objects in it, as several Spirits in horrid shapes flying down amongst the sailors then rising and crossing in the Air. And when the Ship is sinking, the whole house is darken'd, and a shower of Fire falls upon 'em. This is accompanied with Lightning, and several Claps of Thunder.

stage door The door at the back or side of a theatre for actors and staff. It is the normal gathering place for autograph seekers and was formerly the haunt of **stage-door Johnnies** enamoured of chorus girls. *Stage Door* was the title of a play by the US dramatist Maxwell Anderson.

The private entrance is usually guarded by the stage door-keeper, who ensures that no unauthorized person gains access. London's favourite example was the former music-hall artist Harry Loman, who in 1955 became stage door-keeper of the Criterion Theatre at the age of 74 and remained in his post until he was 96.

stage-keeper In the Elizabethan theatre, the person who maintained the stage in a clean and orderly condition for performances.

stage manager (SM) The person who coordinates the physical aspects of staging a production. In the first place he determines whether the visions of the director and stage designer can be physically staged; thereafter he coordinates the efforts of the STAGE CREW to realize them. He also draws up a PLOT SHEET listing the properties, makeup, and costumes, etc. needed by each character in the play.

In addition, the stage manager is responsible for keeping order backstage during the performance and for ensuring the safety and security of the area. He is supposed to be the last to leave the theatre each evening. He also keeps copies of the PROMPT BOOK and maintains the CALL BOARD. In large theatres, he is helped by an ASSISTANT STAGE MANAGER

(ASM) who sometimes serves as the PROMPTER.

The role of stage manager was established during the second half of the 19th century. Before the position of director developed in the early 20th century, the stage manager often ran the rehearsals. The designer Gordon Craig (*see* CRAIG FAMILY) believed that all actors should serve a spell as stage manager during their careers, as this was the best way of learning what was effective and beautiful on stage. Many modern directors (examples include Sir Peter Hall and Peter Brook) have also assumed the duties of stage manager.

Stage Society A British theatre organization that was founded in London in 1899 to present plays with artistic merit that were unlikely to be produced as commercial ventures. The private Society was also able to perform works that had been refused a licence by the LORD CHAMBERLAIN. The plays were usually presented in West End theatres on Sunday nights. Many plays introduced by the Society later transferred successfully to the commercial theatre.

The first Stage Society production was George Bernard Shaw's *You Never Can Tell*, presented at the Royalty Theatre in 1899. Later Shaw productions included *Captain Brassbound's Conversion* (1900), *Mrs Warren's Profession* (1902), and *Man and Superman* (1905). Other dramatists whose works were performed included Clifford Odets, Frank Wedekind, Maxim Gorki, Luigi Pirandello, and Jean Cocteau.

In 1919 the Stage Society sponsored the foundation of the **Phoenix Society** to perform early English drama. During the six years of its existence, the Phoenix produced 26 works, all but six of which were directed by Allan Wade. Its successes included Fletcher's *The Faithful Shepherdess* in 1923, for which Sir Thomas Beecham arranged the music.

In 1926 the Stage Society merged with the Three Hundred Club, an organization with similar aims and methods. During the 1930s, however, it was largely superseded as a patron of new experimental drama by the GATE THEATRE and other London venues; it was disbanded during World War II, the last production being García Lorca's *Blood Wedding*, given at the Savoy Theatre in 1939.

During its 40-year lifespan, the Stage Society attracted some of the theatre's finest talent, including Laurence Olivier, Edith Evans, and Peggy Ashcroft. Theodore Komisarjevsky, married for a time to Ashcroft, created innovative scenery for the Society's productions.

stage whisper A 'whisper' intended to be heard by people other than those to whom it is addressed, as one on the stage is heard by the audience.

Stainless Stephen Nickname for the English comedian Arthur Baynes (1892–1971), who displayed his Sheffield origins on stage by wearing a stainless steel shirt front and hat band. His act included being overly proper with his speech; he always recited both the punctuation in the script and his stage directions.

stalls The theatre seats nearest to the stage. The US term for any stall seat is an **orchestra seat**, whereas in Britain the term **orchestra stalls** applies only to the first row or rows (*see* ORCHESTRA). Among the most expensive seats in a theatre, stalls were introduced in the 1830s when many venues extended the pit of the auditorium further back. The close proximity to the stage sometimes prompts those seated in the stalls to hurl remarks at the actors. During the first London run of Beckett's WAITING FOR GODOT, for instance, Vladimir's remark to Estragon "I am happy" and the latter's reply "I am happy too", drew the loud comment from the stalls, "Well, I'm bloody well not."

Stanislavsky, Konstantin (Konstantin Alekstzev; 1863–1938) Russian director who sought "inner realism" by insisting that his actors find the truth within themselves and "become" the characters they portrayed. His painstaking approach meant that he would sometimes rehearse a cast for a year before feeling satisfied that they understood their roles. His work brought international fame to the Moscow Art Theatre, which he had cofounded with Vladimir Nemirovich-Danchenko in 1897.

The son of a wealthy industrialist, Stanislavsky began as an amateur actor before founding a popular theatrical company, the Society of Art and Literature, in 1888. During his early years at the Moscow Art Theatre he directed the first productions of CHEKHOV's *Uncle Vanya* (1899), *Three Sisters* (1901) and *The Cherry Orchard* (1904) as well as a series of celebrated versions of

Shakespeare. Stanislavsky toured America with the company in 1923.

After World War II the US edition of Stanislavsky's treatise AN ACTOR PREPARES (1926) became the bible of the METHOD school of acting.

star A top entertainer or performer in films, theatre, television, etc. The term is recorded as early as the 1770s, when it was applied to the actor David GARRICK (who has been called "the first modern superstar"). The Hollywood star system was created by the studios in the 1910s as a means of enhancing box-office receipts; before this, the film companies tended not to identify actors and actresses in order to hold down their salaries. In the 20th century the term has been devalued by indiscriminate use, leading to such aggrandized versions as **superstar** and **megastar**.

star trap A circular stage TRAP consisting of several triangular flaps of wood that are hinged to the rim and open outwards in the shape of a star. As it allows an actor to make a sudden appearance on stage it is often used for ghosts or other supernatural characters. The **bristle trap** is a similar contrivance in which bristles are attached to the rim of the opening.

Stationers' Company An organization, incorporated by royal charter in 1537, that played a key role in the earliest literary CENSORSHIP in England. Under the terms of the charter only members of the company or holders of special patents could print any work for sale in the country.

By the end of the 16th century state censorship was much in evidence. The activities of professional informers, employed by the state to search out seditious meanings, were a particular source of annoyance. In his *Sonnets*, written in the 1590s, Shakespeare complains bitterly of "art made tongue-tied by authority".

In 1599 the Archbishop of Canterbury and the Bishop of London, who were mainly responsible for licensing books, issued an order for the suppression and burning of seven satirical works, three books of allegedly immoral tendency including Marlowe's poems, and all the controversial works of the feuding pamphleteers Gabriel Harvey and Thomas Nashe. Verse satire consequently died out until after the deaths of these licensers, but the satirical spirit reasserted itself with extra vigour on the stage. At the beginning of James I's reign there was a spate of prosecutions against Jonson and others (*see* EASTWARD HO!).

The control exercised by the early censors did, however, have one beneficial effect in that the register of published works compiled by the Stationers' Company provided the basis for the first rules of COPYRIGHT.

steal one's thunder *See* THUNDER.

Steaming A play by the British writer Nell Dunn (1936–) that caused considerable interest because of the NUDITY of its all-female cast. It was first performed in 1981 at the Theatre Royal, Stratford, and subsequently transferred to London's Comedy Theatre. The title refers to the play's setting in a Ladies' Turkish bath. This required the creation of a stage pool containing 2000 gallons of water, heated and filtered by a mechanical unit that ran for 21.5 hours a day; it was only turned off during the performance to eliminate its noise.

The plot concerns six women who regularly meet in a council-run bath in London's East End. The place answers different needs for each woman, providing a refuge from men for the party-girl Josie, a place to renew an old friendship for Nancy and Jane, and a haven from poverty for Mrs Meadow and her daughter Dawn. Trouble starts when the council decides to convert the baths into a library. The women unite to petition the council, with Josie finding a new self-confidence as she presents their case at the hearing. When the demolition order is confirmed the women barricade themselves into the building in a last desperate attempt to save the baths.

Stein, Peter (1937–) German theatre director, whose work with the Berlin Schaubühne in the 1970s had an international influence. In 1969 Stein's production of Goethe's *Torquato Tasso* at Bremen was hailed as a milestone for the German theatre. His radical interpretation of this work criticized Goethe for avoiding political reality and compared artists who accept state subsidies with Tasso's subordination to his aristocratic patrons. The director and several of his actors were dismissed when they insisted on reading left-wing political statements to the audience.

Stein and his colleagues then established a theatre collective, based in West Berlin's Schaubühne (a venue opened in 1962). The company, which included such leading actors as Bruno Ganz, Edith Clever, and Michael König, soon established a reputation as the most exciting troupe in Germany with innovative productions of Shakespeare's *As You Like It*, Ibsen's *Peer Gynt*, Edward Bond's *Saved*, and Heinrich von Kleist's *Prince of Homburg*. Stein and the company made exhaustive research into the ideology of the plays and dramatists, often rewriting the texts to draw out the contemporary parallels.

In 1982 Stein's company moved into a new $30-million theatre in West Berlin, the Schaubühne am Lehniner Platz; it featured an open acting space with 76 movable floor sections.

During the 1980s Stein dropped his didactic leftwing approach and began to concentrate on fidelity to the written text. His naturalistic presentation of Chekhov's *Three Sisters* in 1984 became the company's most popular production. For his subsequent Chekhov productions Stein consulted STANISLAVSKY's notebooks in an attempt to reconstruct the original Moscow staging. In 1987 he left the Schaubühne to concentrate on opera production, earning particular acclaim for his work with the Welsh National Opera. In 1992 he became director of theatre at the Salzburg Festival.

Stephen Joseph Theatre in the Round A theatre in Scarborough, North Yorkshire. The original theatre was established in 1955 by the director Stephen Joseph (1927–67) to produce THEATRE-IN-THE-ROUND. Since 1959 most new works by Alan AYCKBOURN have been premiered at the theatre; Ayckbourn became artistic director in 1970. The company moved in 1976 to a new 300-seat arena theatre.

In 1993 a campaign was launched to finance the creation of a new theatre in a former cinema. Ayckbourn contributed £400,000 to the project. The theatre, which opened in 1996, has both a 400-seat theatre-in-the-round and a 150-seat conventional auditorium. Despite its national reputation, the theatre ran into grave financial problems within months of opening; after fierce local controversy, the town council agreed to a hefty grant.

stichomythia A type of dialogue in which actors exchange short remarks; it is usually characterized by repetition and antithesis and delivered at speed. It has also been called **cat-and-mouse dialogue** and **cut-and-thrust dialogue**. The device was first used in the ancient Greek theatre to intensify the drama of an exchange. It is now mainly used for comic effect or to create tension. Noël Coward was a master of comic *stichomythia*, especially in his early plays, and the technique was also used to great effect in Beckett's *Waiting for Godot* (1955). Perhaps the most famous example of *stichomythia* in English literature is the tense exchange between Macbeth and his wife immediately after the murder of Duncan:

> LADY MACBETH My husband!
> MACBETH I have done the deed. Didst thou not hear a noise?
> LADY MACBETH I heard the owl scream and the crickets cry.
> Did not you speak?
> MACBETH When?
> LADY MACBETH Now.
> MACBETH As I descended?
> LADY MACBETH Ay.
> MACBETH Hark!
> Who lies i' the second chamber?
> LADY MACBETH Donalbain.
> MACBETH This is a sorry sight.
> [*Looking on his hands.*]
> LADY MACBETH A foolish thought, to say a sorry sight.

stock company In the 18th and 19th centuries, a permanent troupe of actors who performed a limited repertory at one or more theatres. The term **summer stock** is still used in America for productions at provincial summer theatres. The first stock companies were those of London's Drury Lane and Covent Garden theatres in the early 18th century; the tradition continued with the CIRCUIT companies in both Britain and America. They reached the height of their strength in the 1850s; within 30 years, however, railways allowed professional touring companies to move easily about both countries, putting stock companies out of business. The last true example was Henry Irving's company, which gave its final performance at London's Lyceum Theatre in 1902.

The stock company was an excellent training-ground for young actors, who were called upon to play a variety of parts. Players eventually developed specialities in the set roles. The company was led by the **Tragedian**, who would star in parts such as Hamlet, Lear, and Macbeth; second in importance was the **Low Comedian**, who played the leading parts in farcical comedies and minor roles and tragedies. Other set parts were the **Juvenile Lead**, a youthful hero or heroine, the **Juvenile Tragedian**, the **Old Man** and the **Old Woman**, the **Heavy Father** (or **Heavy Lead**) who came into his own in the 1830s as a villain in melodrama, and the **Heavy Woman**, who played roles such as Lady Macbeth. Minor parts were played by the **Walking Lady** and **Walking Gentleman**, **General Utility** or **Utility** with minor roles, and the **Supernumerary**, or **Super**, who had a walk-on part. Specialized parts also existed, such as the **First Singer** and the **First Dancer**.

stooge A comedian's accomplice who acts as the foil for his jokes, usually by assuming a stupid or naive character. The term is sometimes used as a verb: *Time* magazine noted in 1946 that "Entertainer Danny Kaye stooged for other entertainers". The chaotic Hollywood film trio The Three Stooges began as comedians' stooges who were often planted in the balconies of vaudeville houses as if regular audience members. A **straight man**, the serious and sometimes bullying member of a two-man comedy act, differs from a stooge in being less of a victim.

Stoppard, Tom (Tom Straussler; 1937–) British playwright, born in Czechoslovakia. His ingenious comedies of ideas are noted for their verbal brilliance, structural deftness, and concern for such serious moral issues as the freedom of the individual.

Stoppard worked as a journalist before beginning to write radio and television plays in the 1960s. In 1966 ROSENCRANTZ AND GUILDENSTERN ARE DEAD (1966) was produced by the National Theatre at the Old Vic six months after being staged by the Oxford Theatre Group at the Edinburgh Festival fringe. Stoppard won immediate acclaim for this absurdist drama about two minor characters from *Hamlet* who find no meaning outside their roles in the play. This was followed two years later by a West End production of *Enter a Free Man*, first performed in 1963 in Hamburg and on British television (as *A Walk on the Water*).

The successful one-act comedy *The Real Inspector Hound* (1968) was a spoof on detective thrillers; during the play two drama critics in the audience become drawn into the murder mystery they are reviewing. The comedy JUMPERS, presented at the National Theatre in 1972 was widely regarded as an intellectual *tour de force*; the production featured Michael Hordern as George, the confused professor of moral philosophy, and Diana Rigg as his wife Dottie, as well as a team of acrobats. TRAVESTIES, first performed by the Royal Shakespeare Company in 1974, was a dazzling piece set in World War I Zürich; the characters include James Joyce, Lenin, and the unsophisticated British consular official Henry Carr. The double-bill of the short farces DIRTY LINEN AND NEW FOUND LAND (1976) ran for four years.

Stoppard's play *Every Good Boy Deserves Favour* (1977), with music by André Previn, was the first play ever to feature a full symphony orchestra as an element of its cast. The plot concerned a political dissident in a Soviet psychiatric hospital. The following year saw the production of NIGHT AND DAY (1978), a defence of press freedom. THE REAL THING (1982) was a tragicomedy starring Felicity Kendal and Tom Conti, the latter playing a dramatist whose writings contrast with the sorry state of his own marriage. Stoppard's own marriage to the well-known TV personality and doctor, Miriam Stoppard, collapsed some years later following a well-publicized affair with Kendal. *Hapgood* (1988) was a cerebral spy thriller. After a few years of silence, Stoppard produced another major play, ARCADIA, in 1993.

Other works have included translations of plays by García Lorca and Václav Havel as well as screenplays and works for television.

Storey, David (1933–) British playwright, whose dramas reflect his working-class Yorkshire background. His plays have been compared to those of Pinter and Chekhov for their realism and ambiguity.

The son of a miner, Storey became a professional rugby player at the age of 17 while also studying to be a painter. He enjoyed his first literary success with the novel *The Sporting Life* (1960), which drew upon his rugby-playing experiences. The cost of social mobility was also a theme of Storey's first play, *The Restoration of Arnold Middleton*, which was a hit in 1967 at the Royal Court Theatre. It told the story of an uprooted schoolmaster driven mad by his bourgeois marriage and his homesickness for the North.

Storey's second play *In Celebration* (1969), used a fortieth wedding-anniversary party to contrast two generations of the Shaw family, who find that success does not guarantee happiness. Lindsay Anderson directed this and several other Storey plays including *The Contractor* (1970), in which the assembling and dismantling of a marquee for a wedding reception reveals the different attitudes of the workmen and their employers. The same year saw the first production of *Home*, an examination of life in a mental institution, with John Gielgud and Ralph Richardson in the leads. It subsequently transferred to Broadway and was named the best play of the season; *The Changing Room* (1971), about the relationships between members of a rugby team, was similarly acclaimed in both London and New York.

His other dramas have included *The Farm* (1973), *Cromwell* (1973), *Life Class* (1974), the black sex farce *Mother's Day* (1976), *Sisters* (1978), *Early Days* (1980), in which an elder statesman (originally played by Ralph Richardson) reviews his past, *Phoenix* (1984), and *The March on Russia* (1989).

Storey is noted for his temper, having once thumped Michael Billington about the head in the bar at London's Royal Court Theatre after the critic had written a caustic review of *Mother's Day*.

Storm, The A tragedy by the Russian dramatist Alexander OSTROVSKY, which is regarded as his masterpiece. It was first performed in Moscow in 1859 at the Maly Theatre (*see* HOUSE OF OSTROVSKY). The play was presented in New York in 1900 but was not seen in London until 1929; it was revived by the National Theatre company in 1966 at the Old Vic. It is the only work by Ostrovsky to be well known in English.

The Storm, one of a cycle of plays dealing with Moscow's merchants, was interpreted as an attack on the greed, ignorance, intolerance, and brutality of the trading class. Set in a small town on the Volga, the play explores the plight of a young woman married to a trader who is shown to be a weakling but nevertheless cruel. In love with a man powerless to help her, she takes her own life.

Straker, Henry The chauffeur of John Tanner in the play MAN AND SUPERMAN (1903) by George Bernard Shaw. Straker is intended to represent the 'New Man' of the polytechnic revolution. Skilled, confident, and a scientific socialist, he is superior in all practical respects to his master, whose gentlemanly class, Shaw believed, was doomed to extinction by the new economic and political forces embodied by Straker.

Strand Theatre A London theatre in Aldwych. It was built in the fashionable Louis XIV style by William Sprague as one of a pair with the Aldwych Theatre. A special feature was the circular ceiling with its grand picture of Apollo in his chariot. The 925-seat theatre was opened in 1905 as the Waldorf Theatre under the SHUBERT BROTHERS, who began with a season in which Italian opera alternated with plays starring Eleonora Duse. The present name was adopted in 1909 (although it was known as the Whitney Theatre between 1911 and 1913).

In 1930 the Strand was refurbished and opened with the play *It's a Boy*. Other successes were *1066 and All That* (1935) and *Arsenic and Old Lace*, which opened in 1942 for a run of 1337 performances. Donald Wolfit presented lunch-time performances of Shakespeare during the Blitz. Post war successes have included *A Funny Thing Happened on the Way to the Forum* (1963) starring Frankie Howerd and the farce *No Sex Please – We're British*, which began its record run of 4419 performances in 1971 (transferring to the Garrick in 1982).

An earlier Strand Theatre stood in the Strand itself, opening in 1832 to stage burlesque and melodrama, reopening the next year as a theatre school, then becoming a theatre again in 1836. In 1850 it was renamed Punch's Playhouse, becoming associated in 1858 with H. J. Byron's burlesques. In 1905 it closed and was demolished to build Aldwych tube station (now closed).

strange. *Strange Interlude* A nine-act drama that earned Eugene O'NEILL his third Pulitzer Prize. It was first produced in 1928 by the THEATRE GUILD in its Guild Theatre, New York. The production starred Lynn Fontanne, who played with "power, concentrated aggression, and magnetism", according to the critic Brooks Atkinson. In the play O'Neill presents a psychological portrait of Nina Leeds, who enacts the 'seven ages of woman': daughter, fiancée, wife, adulteress, mother, widow, and child once more. He often freezes the action on stage to allow Nina and the other characters to deliver asides or soliloquies that explain their motivation. In Nina's case, this is primarily a search for love and acceptance. In the end, Nina regards her experiences with wonder:

> Strange interlude! Yes, our lives are merely strange dark interludes in the electrical display of God the Father!

Strange's Men An Elizabethan theatre company that probably included SHAKESPEARE amongst its members. With Lord Strange as its patron, the company toured the provinces before making an appearance at court in 1582. Lord Strange's father also had a company at this time, a fact that has caused confusion for theatrical historians. Strange's Men, who included such leading actors as Richard Burbage and William Sly, performed works by Shakespeare, Marlowe, and Robert Greene, amongst others. As was the usual practice of the time, Strange's Men would perform with actors from other companies in public theatres. They joined the Admiral's Men for performances in 1590–91 at the Theatre and in 1592–93 at the Rose, where they may have performed Shakespeare's *The Comedy of Errors* and the first part of *Henry VI*. They also produced several plays now lost, including *Titus and Vespasian* (1592), which may have been the prototype for Shakespeare's *Titus Andronicus*, and Richard Tarlton's *The Seven Deadly Sins*. When Strange's Men returned to the provinces after 1594, several of its members, including Shakespeare, formed one of England's most famous troupes, the CHAMBERLAIN'S MEN.

Strasberg, Lee (1901–82) US director, producer, and drama teacher who formulated the system of METHOD acting from the ideas of STANISLAVSKY. Born in Austria, Strasberg entered the theatre in 1924 as an assistant stage manager at London's Garrick Theatre. He subsequently studied at the American Laboratory Theatre and acted with the Theatre Guild. In 1931 he helped to found the GROUP THEATRE, and during its ten-year existence directed plays such as Maxwell Anderson's *Night over Taos* (1932) and Sidney Kingsley's *Men in White* (1933).

In 1950 Strasberg became director of the Actors' Studio, New York, and turned it into a school for Method acting; his teaching placed stress on improvisation and the actor's use of 'affective memory' to supply appropriate emotions for stage roles. Professional actors rushed to retrain under the Method; Strasberg's students included Ann Bancroft, Montgomery Clift, James Dean, Robert De Niro, Julie Harris, Marilyn Monroe, Paul Newman, Al Pacino, Maureen Stapleton, Shelley Winters, and Joanne Woodward. The name most closely associated with the Method was Marlon Brando.

However, not all professionals were enthusiasts for the Method. When Charles Laughton began directing *Major Barbara* in 1956 on Broadway, he approached Eli Wallach, a student of the Method, and said firmly, "I don't want any of that Stanislavsky shit from you." Nor was Strasberg always successful with his own productions. His version of Chekhov's *Three Sisters*, presented at London's Aldwych Theatre during the World Theatre Season of 1965, was a memorable disaster. When Sandy Dennis delivered the line, "Oh it's been a terrible evening", someone in the audience called out, "It sure has been!" and the house roared with laughter.

Stratford. Stratford Festival The summer drama and music festival held annually in Stratford, Ontario. The first summer Shakespeare Festival was held in 1952 under the direction of Tyrone GUTHRIE and the designer Tanya Moiseiwitsch who created a temporary theatre featuring an Elizabethan open stage under a canvas roof. The event subsequently expanded into a major showcase for classical drama, with concerts, opera, and a film festival being added later.

In 1956 Guthrie handed over control to another Englishman, Michael Langham, whose first presentation was *Henry V* starring Christopher Plummer. The following year an innovative permanent theatre was built featuring a semicircular auditorium and the world's largest open stage. Despite the size of the theatre an intimate atmosphere is retained since no seat is more than 65 feet from the stage. A tent-like effect was created by having girders reach up to the conical roof like the spokes of a wheel. The design has been the inspiration for new theatres in New York, London, Minneapolis, Chichester, and other cities. In 1963 the Festival opened a second theatre, the Avon, a proscenium design that seats 1100.

The Canadians Jean Gascon and John Hirsch succeeded Langham in 1968 and began an ambitious expansion. Plays by Ben Jonson and John Webster were added to the repertoire, together with less familiar Shakespeare works, such as *Cymbeline* and

Pericles. Gascon served alone from 1969 until 1974 and in 1971 opened an experimental venue, the Third Stage. The Festival company toured worldwide and in 1978 completed its ambition of presenting all of Shakespeare's plays with a production of *Titus Andronicus*.

When Gascon resigned in 1974, the young English director Robin Phillips was appointed to succeed him, provoking a storm of nationalistic protest. He resigned in 1980 and after bitter infighting within the selection committee, John Hirsch became artistic director. Many leading actors protested and boycotted the Festival, which suffered a financial crisis. This was eased when John Neville took over in 1986 and presented popular revivals, such as Rodgers and Hart's *The Boys from Syracuse* and Brecht's *Mother Courage and Her Children*.

Stratford Jubilee The celebrations organized by David GARRICK and others in 1769 to mark the bicentenary of SHAKESPEARE's birth. Undaunted by the fact that the true date had passed in 1764, Garrick set the celebrations for September (although Shakespeare had been born in April) and arranged for lavish displays of fireworks, cannonades, music, fancy dress, and parades.

The first of the four days of the festival went well, with 30 cannons firing a salute and musicians serenading the crowds. The spectators included James Boswell and the composer Thomas Arne, with whom Garrick had collaborated upon an *Ode upon Dedicating a Building to Shakespeare*, specially written for the occasion. On the second day, however, the rain began. The triumphal procession never took place, the river burst its banks as the soprano Mrs Baddeley sang "Soft thou gently flowing Avon", and guests at the fancy dress ball found themselves dancing minuets ankle-deep in water. On leaving the ball, 150 guests fell into a flooded ditch; the rest waited in the marquee until daybreak before attempting to escape. On top of all this, the only lines from Shakespeare that were spoken during the festival were misquoted – nonetheless, they remained singularly appropriate:

> If there be any, speak, for him have I
> offended.

One hundred years later it was almost inevitable that the idea of another jubilee should be mooted. In 1863 it was announced that a National Shakespeare committee had been formed to oversee celebrations of Shakespeare's tercentenery – among its members were Sir Edward Bulwer-Lytton, Tennyson, and Charles Dickens.

The committee was dominated by Hepworth Dixon, editor of the *Athenaeum*, who – unknown to his colleagues – harboured a deep grudge (based on an old quarrel) against William Thackeray, who was strongly favoured to join the committee's ranks. Through a series of manoeuvres Dixon succeeded in having a resolution passed to the effect that Thackeray would not be invited to join the committee. This led to a furore in the press, which only ended when on Christmas Eve the novelist was found dead in his bed. Somewhat taken by surprise, Dixon hastily delivered a laudatory speech in Thackeray's memory at the committee's next meeting and suggested that his resolution be deleted from the minutes. However, this time he had miscalculated; his outraged fellow-committee members not only insisted that the resolution remain on the minutes for all time but passed a further resolution regretting the whole affair. Within weeks the organization had disbanded in disgust.

The 400th anniversary of Shakespeare's birth was marked by the opening of the Shakespeare Centre next to the playwright's birthplace.

Stratton, Eugene (Eugene Augustus Ruhlmann; 1861–1918) US entertainer who graduated from MINSTREL SHOWs to become a popular MUSIC HALL star. Wearing black-face make-up, he sang 'Lily of Laguna', 'Little Dolly Day Dream', and other sentimental 'coon songs'. He also danced in white hat and gloves with a cane, whistling as he glided silently across the stage under a single following spotlight.

At the age of 17 Stratton joined J. H. Haverly's United Mastodon Minstrels and accompanied them to London in 1880. The next year he remained in Britain to become a member of the Moore and Burgess troupe, staying with them until their popularity waned. In 1892 he took to the halls, performing without black-face at the Royal Holborn. When this was not successful, he returned to his minstrel act and immediately became London's top black-face performer until he retired in 1914.

street. Streetcar Named Desire, A The Pulitzer Prize-winning play by Tennessee WILLIAMS; it opened on Broadway in 1947 under the direction of Elia KAZAN. Jessica Tandy starred as the neurotic Southern Belle Blanche DuBois, who is brutalized and eventually driven insane by her brother-in-law, Stanley (played by Marlon Brando). Williams later recalled how Brando arrived to audition for the part at his beach cottage; when the electricity failed the young actor immediately repaired both the lights and the bad plumbing. Williams, who was openly gay, recalled, "He was just about the best-looking young man I've seen, but I have never played around with actors and anyhow Brando was not the type to get a part that way."

Kazan directed a somewhat censored screen version of *Streetcar* in 1951. Brando was joined by Vivien Leigh, who used her best Scarlett O'Hara Southern accent to deliver Blanche's famous line, "I have always depended on the kindness of strangers."

During a revival of *Streetcar* at Los Angeles's Ahmanson Theatre in 1973, a woman in the audience turned around to berate the man behind her for sniggering through the performance. "Don't you realize this is a serious play?" she reprimanded him. The offender was Tennessee Williams, who could never restrain himself from laughing at his own dialogue. "My tragedies are funnier than my comedies," he later told a journalist.

The play's curious title comes from Desire, a street in New Orleans. The tram bearing the street's name rumbled past Williams's tiny French Quarter apartment several times a day; he is said to have drawn inspiration from its clanging bell. The streetcar has been preserved as a historic and literary monument.

Street Scene An expressionist play by Elmer RICE about the futility of life in a New York slum neighbourhood. It was first performed in New York in 1929 with a striking set based on a real house at 25 West 65th Street. A film of the play was made in 1931, while Kurt Weill produced a musical version in 1947.

In the play characters from a variety of ethnic backgrounds chat and gossip on a hot summer night. The most titillating subject is the love affair of the Irishwoman Anna Maurrant and the romance of her daughter, Rose, with the Jewish boy Sam Kaplan. Tension is introduced with the arrival of Anna's husband, Frank, who discovers his wife with her lover and shoots them both. He is arrested, and Rose leaves her boyfriend to live with her brother. Neighbours decide she is being taken care of by a rich admirer. As events settle down, a new couple arrives to enquire about the now empty apartment.

Strehler, Giorgio (1921–) Italian theatre director, who has been one of the most influential figures in post-war Italian drama. In 1947 Strehler cofounded (with the actor-director Paolo Grassi) the **Piccolo Teatro della Città di Milano**, the company with which he continued to work for the next 45 years. The establishment of the Piccolo Teatro marked the beginning of the TEATRO STABILE movement in Italy. Under Strehler's guidance the company developed an extensive repertoire, establishing a particularly distinguished record for productions of Brecht, Shakespeare, Goldoni, and Pirandello.

Between 1968 and 1972 Strehler also worked with the Gruppo Teatro e Azione, which he established in order to explore more overtly political forms of theatre. From 1983 until 1990 he was also artistic director of the Théâtre de l'Europe in Paris. In late 1992 Strehler resigned from the Piccolo Teatro, following allegations that he had seriously mismanaged a grant of £300,000 from EC funds. The 71-year-old director announced his resignation in these words:

> I resign from Italy...I resign from civilized life, society, the theatre and culture. I shall retain only my poetry, my talent and the purity of my heart.
>
> *The Independent*, 1 December 1992

Strife A play by the British writer John Galsworthy (1867–1933). It was first performed in 1909 in London and revived regularly for the next 25 years. In the play Galsworthy presents the obstinacy and suffering on both sides of a prolonged industrial dispute.

Set at the turn of the century, the play shows how a Welsh village is torn apart by the strike at the Trenartha Tin Plate Works. John Anthony, the company founder and chairman of the board, refuses to compromise with the strikers despite great financial losses. On the other side David Roberts, the firebrand head of the Workman's Committee, refuses to yield even though the employees' families are suffering. The strike becomes a personal struggle between the two men. Roberts's wife dies of malnutrition, and Anthony's son tries in vain to convince his father to relent. The workers finally accept a compromise worked out by their negotiator, Simon Harness, while Roberts is absent and the board of directors agrees, outvoting and ousting Anthony. The two broken enemies finally acknowledge their respect for each other, and the play ends with a conversation between Harness and the board's Henry Tench.

> TENCH D'you know, Sir, those terms, they're the very same we drew up together, you and I, and put to both sides before the fight began? All this – all this – and – and what for?
>
> HARNESS That's where the fun comes in!

strike To take down or dismantle a stage set, or to remove an item from it. The *Pall Mall Gazette* was amazed in 1891 to note that, "It took 12 hours of work by a very large staff to 'strike' *Ivanhoe* and mount *La Basoche*." The word also means to turn off a stage light or terminate a sound effect. *See also* SET A STAGE.

strike an attitude To assume an exaggerated or theatrical pose for the sake of effect. The phrase originally referred to the stereotyped poses denoting grief, horror, anger, etc. adopted by actors.

Strindberg, August (1849–1912) Swedish playwright, novelist, and poet. Although hailed in his own lifetime as a pioneer of NATURALISM, his most lastingly influential works were the symbolic dramas he wrote towards the end of his life. Strindberg, who had an interest in hypnosis, was the first dramatist to explore the role of the subconscious – an approach more easily accepted by later audiences familiar with the theories of psychoanalysis. Although his works have never enjoyed wide popular appeal, Strindberg was one of the most famous writers in the world when he died.

Strindberg was the son of a shipping agent who married his housekeeper after a long illicit relationship; his unstable childhood is described in the autobiographical work *The Son of a Servant* (1886). After leaving Uppsala University without a degree he worked as a freelance journalist in Stockholm while writing the historical drama *Master Olof* (1872) in a style influenced by Shakespeare and Ibsen. The play was rejected by the Royal Theatre. In 1877 he married the actress Siri von Essen, a relationship that was soon soured by Strindberg's pathological jealousy.

In 1883, prompted by his involvement in a bitter literary controversy, he left Sweden with his family to travel somewhat aimlessly in Europe. Meanwhile he established his reputation as a naturalistic dramatist with THE FATHER (1887) and MISS JULIE (1888), grimly pessimistic plays about the inevitable (as Strindberg saw it) conflict between the sexes. After returning to Sweden in 1889 he wrote THE CREDITORS (1891), a manically bitter play that reflects the breakdown of his marriage. He was divorced in 1891 and lost custody of his children.

The following year he travelled to Berlin, where he married the Austrian journalist Frida Uhl. When this marriage collapsed after two years Strindberg suffered a mental breakdown during which he became obsessed with the occult and experimented with alchemy. He emerged from this period as a disciple of the mystic Swedenborg. In 1901 he married the Norwegian actress Harriet Bosse but, again, the relationship failed. His most innovative works were written during this time. Inspired by MAETERLINCK, Strindberg wrote a number of symbolic 'dream' plays, including the trilogy *The Road to Damascus* (1898–1901) and THE DREAM PLAY (1902). He said of the form, "Anything may happen; everything is possible and probable. Time and space do not exist. The characters split, double, multiply, vanish, solidify, blur, clarify."

Strindberg returned to Sweden again for the last four years of his life. Although his plans for a Scandinavian Experimental Theatre were never realized, from 1907 to 1910 he helped August Falck (1882–1938) to run the 161-seat Intima Teatern (Intimate Theatre) in Stockholm. It was for this venue that he wrote his five 'chamber plays', the best known being THE GHOST SONATA (1907). His last play, *The Great Highway* (1909) was an allegory of his life.

strip. strip light *See* BATTEN.

striptease A theatrical or cabaret performance in which a woman undresses herself slowly and provocatively to music. This erotic entertainment was introduced to US BURLESQUE shows in about 1920 to counteract the lure of films; its effect, however, was to provoke tougher censorship laws that led to the closure of many burlesque houses. Traditional burlesque-style stripping continues today in striptease clubs and some nightclubs, notably those of New Orleans's French Quarter. The performer is variously called a 'striptease dancer', 'striptease artiste', 'stripper', 'exotic dancer', or 'ecdysiast' (a term coined in 1940 by H. L. Mencken). The most famous and elegant stripper was Gypsy Rose LEE, who became the subject of the Broadway musical *Gypsy* (1959; filmed in 1962).

stroboscope A unit of stage lighting that produces a series of rapid flashes of light to create an effect of slow or jerky motion similar to that in early cinema film. It is also called a **strobe** or **strobe lighting**. Strobe lighting can have a dangerous effect on those prone to fits and should be used with care.

Student Prince, The A romantic operetta by the prolific Hungarian-born US composer Sigmund Romberg (1887–1951). It was first performed in 1924 in New York under the full title of *The Student Prince of Heidelberg*. The plot, which is based on the play *Old Heidelberg* by Wilhelm Meyer-Foerster, concerns the careless life and loves of a prince studying in Heidelberg, especially his romance with a local barmaid. Two years later Romberg followed this hit with another successful operetta, *The Desert Song*. Although the film version of *The Student Prince* (1954) featured the voice of Mario Lanza, he was considered too fat to play the hero on screen (the part was taken by Edmund Purdom).

Sturm und Drang (Ger. Storm and Stress) A German literary and dramatic movement of the later 18th-century. The term came from the title of a preposterous play by Friedrich von Klinger (1776). The movement, essentially a reaction against 18th-century neoclassicism, was greatly influenced by the idealism of Rousseau and the example of Shakespeare.

The plays of the *Sturm und Drang* are characterized by an emphasis on passionate emotion, a disdain for the UNITIES and other literary conventions, and a concern with the individual's struggle against tyranny and oppression. Leading works of the movement include Goethe's play GÖTZ VON BERLICHINGEN (1773), his novel *The Sorrows of Young Werther* (1773), and Schiller's play DIE RÄUBER (1781). Other writers associated with the *Sturm und Drang* include Johann Gottfried Herder (1744–1803), the movement's main theorist, and Jakob Lenz (1751–92), who formulated the rules of Romantic drama in his treatise *Anmerkungen übers Theater* (1774). *Sturm und Drang* was imitated throughout Europe and influenced early 19th-century English melodrama. It also spawned a sub-genre called the RITTERDRAMA (Knight drama).

Sub-Plot A nickname for the AMERICAN PLACE THEATRE.

Suddenly Last Summer A play by Tennessee WILLIAMS, first produced in 1958 in New York and London as part of the double bill *Garden District* (which also included *Something Unspoken*). A 1959 film version starred Katherine Hepburn, Elizabeth Taylor, and Montgomery Clift.

Following the death of her son, Sebastian, Mrs Veneble offers to finance the building of a new wing for a mental asylum in his name. She stipulates, however, that this will only happen if the surgeon Dr Cukrowicz agrees to perform a lobotomy on her niece Cathy, who has suffered a breakdown. Cathy was with Sebastian when he died mysteriously during a European holiday. She now has a memory block, which Cukrowicz tries to break. Mrs Veneble, fearful of what might emerge, pushes for the operation but the doctor resists. When Cathy recovers her memory she reveals that Sebastian, a homosexual, had used her to lure boys to his rooms. Suddenly, last summer, he became ill and the hungry local boys pursued, murdered, and cannibalized him. The doctor makes Cathy reveal everything to Mrs Veneble, who is understandably led away in shock.

summer. ***Summer and Smoke*** A play by Tennessee WILLIAMS with loneliness as its main theme. The drama had a long and tortuous route to success. First produced by Margo Jones in 1947 at her experimental theatre in Dallas, it failed when she directed it a year later in New York. London first saw *Summer and Smoke* in 1951, when it received moderate reviews. A year later the play contributed to the rise of the OFF-BROADWAY theatre when the Circle-in-the-Square presented a highly acclaimed production. Williams later rewrote the piece as *The*

Eccentricities of a Nightingale and it was revived under this title at the Yvonne Arnaud Theatre in Guildford in 1967.

The plot involves Alma, an ageing spinster, and her avid suitor John. She rejects him but after John becomes a respected physician the roles are reversed, with Alma hopelessly trying to win his love.

summer stock *See* STOCK COMPANY.

super Short for *supernumerary*, one of the traditional roles in a stock company. The super took silent walk-on parts and was not usually paid. Dickens wrote of "wretched supernumeraries or sixth-rate actors". The term is still used in the theatre, often for amateurs in crowd scenes.

Suppliant Women, The (*Hiketides*) A tragedy by AESCHYLUS. Once thought to be the oldest surviving Greek play, it has now been redated to about 463 BC, making it less old than either THE PERSIANS or SEVEN AGAINST THEBES.

The CHORUS of suppliant women which speaks more than half the lines, is the true protagonist of the work, which has little dramatic action and is noted for its lyrical poetry. The 50 women, all daughters of Danaus, king of Egypt, have fled to Argos, the home of their ancestors, to escape marriage to their 50 cousins, the sons of Aegyptus. They beg the king of Argos for protection, placing him in a grave dilemma: he knows he faces war with Egypt if he protects them and the wrath of Zeus if he does not. He asks the people of Argos to decide, and they welcome the fugitives. A herald comes ashore from the Egyptian fleet and begins to drag the suppliants violently from the altars where they have taken refuge but the king rescues them. The play ends with the Danaids imploring the gods for a favourable outcome.

The Suppliant Women was the first play in the Danaid trilogy, the other parts of which are now lost. *The Aegyptii* apparently portrayed a battle in which the king of Argos was killed and his city besieged by the Egyptians; in *The Danaides* the women are forced to wed their cousins but, on Danaus's advice, kill them on their wedding night. Only Hypermestra spares her husband, Lynceus; in time their descendants become the Argive kings.

Another tragedy with the same title but a totally different plot was written by EURIPIDES.

Surgeon of His Own Honour, The (*El médico de su honra*) A tragedy by CALDERÓN. First produced in 1635, the year of Lope de VEGA's death, the play confirmed Calderón's standing as Spain's supreme dramatist. This grim and macabre work remains controversial. Some critics accuse Calderón of justifying the murder of an innocent woman to meet the requirements of an inhuman code of honour, while others say his purpose was to attack the code by creating a feeling of horror and sympathy.

In the play Don Gutierre de Solis's wife is admired by the King's brother but remains entirely faithful. Don Gutierre, however, becomes convinced of her infidelity. He grants her two hours to live, during which she prepares herself for a holy death. Don Gutierre blindfolds a surgeon and brings him home to bleed his wife to death. Afterwards, the physician marks the door of the house with his bloody hand and informs the King. Don Gutierre, purely for honour's sake, says his wife died accidentally. When the King orders him to marry a certain Leonore, Don Gutierre agrees but warns her that if necessary he will once more defend his honour:

> And mark me, too, that, if already once
> Unto mine honour I have proved a leech,
> I do not mean to lose my skill.

Susie *See* TOBY.

Svanga A type of theatre found in the villages of the northern Indian states of Harayana, Uttar Pradesh, and the Punjab. It is performed at Hindu festivals and family celebrations such as weddings and births of sons. Also called *Swang*, *Sang*, or *Sangeet*, the form dates from the late 18th century and has spread to some urban areas.

Svanga dramas usually have moralistic themes of love, honour, and duty. The plots are loosely derived from history and popular ballads. The all-male dramas are performed in an open space or occasionally on the veranda of a patron's house. The actors dress in ordinary village garments set off with elaborate headdresses and colourful cloth pieces; they also use false wigs and beards. The spectacle begins with songs praising the Hindu gods, especially the elephant-headed Ganapati, the god of good fortune. The plays are acted in regional dialect and usually include a number of romantic love songs.

Svoboda, Josef (1920–) Influential Czech stage designer, noted for introducing MIXED MEDIA technology into the theatre. An example of his innovative work was his 1965 production of Luigi Nono's opera *Intoleranza*. He linked several studios to the main stage by two-way television, allowing performers some miles away to see the conductor and follow the main drama.

In 1948 Svoboda became head designer of the National Theatre in Prague, where he presented a stunning production of Gogol's *The Government Inspector*. However, he was given little chance to develop his ideas until the communist regime eased restrictions in the late 1950s, allowing him to create an unconventional *Hamlet* in 1959.

His multimedia ideas developed from experimental work carried out in the 1930s by E. F. Burian (1904–59) and Miroslav Kouril (1911–), the latter offering Svoboda the support of his Prague Institute of Scenography. In 1958 Svoboda collaborated with the director Alfred Radok in devising a means of combining still and moving pictures on screens. This *Polyekran* project was followed by the development of the **Laterna Magika**, which combined live actors with projections. The two techniques were a great hit at the 1958 Brussels World's Fair, and the following year Svoboda began to incorporate them into his stage work, projecting images onto such surfaces as plastic, mirrors, and netting. The Laterna Magika established a base in Prague's famous Theatre Behind the Gate and Svoboda created designs for many of the productions there.

During the 1960s Svoboda also experimented with flexible staging using movable platforms. For the 1963 production of Sophocles's *Oedipus Rex* at the Prague National Theatre, Svoboda constructed a 30-foot wide semitransparent staircase rising from the bottom of the orchestra pit up to the grid above the stage. Svoboda's work was seen in London during the 1965 WORLD THEATRE SEASON and a year later at the Edinburgh Festival. He was subsequently commissioned by the National Theatre to create abstract sets for Ostrovsky's *The Storm* (1966) and Chekhov's *Three Sisters* (1967). In 1970 he designed the sets for Simon Gray's adaptation of Dostoevsky's *The Idiot* (1970) at the Old Vic. Despite the communist authority's clampdown on the Czech theatre in the late 1970s, Svoboda was allowed to continue his work because of his international reputation.

swan. The Swan of Avon SHAKESPEARE; a nickname coined by Ben Jonson in allusion to his birthplace at Stratford-upon-Avon and the legend that Apollo, the god of poetry and music, was changed into a swan. According to Pythagoras, the souls of all good poets passed into swans.

Swan Theatre An Elizabethan playhouse, the fourth built in London; it opened in 1595 despite opposition from the Lord Mayor. The theatre was situated on Bankside and named after the swans on the Thames. Resting on a brick foundation, it was constructed of wooden pillars with flint-and-mortar work between. The interior was sketched by a visiting Dutch student in 1596 and a copy of this drawing is the only contemporary depiction of an Elizabethan theatre known to survive. It reveals a large raised platform stage and three galleries running round the building.

The Swan had no permanent company. PEMBROKE'S MEN were the first to lease the theatre, but in 1597 a performance of the "seditious comedy" *The Isle of Dogs* by Ben Jonson and Thomas Nashe led to the suspension of stage performances for several months. The venue also hosted sports, exhibitions, and other entertainments, such as a contest of wit and versification in 1598. Plays were again halted in 1602 when the interior was wrecked by the audience after Richard Vennar was arrested just before presenting his spectacular play *England's Joy*.

Thomas Middleton's *A Chaste Maid in Cheapside* was presented at the Swan in 1611. LADY ELIZABETH'S MEN performed there from 1612 until 1614, when they moved to Philip Henslowe's HOPE THEATRE, which was modelled on the Swan. The success of this new venue was the Swan's death blow. Prize fights took over after 1621 and according to a contemporary pamphlet it thereafter dwindled "like a dying Swanne".

swazzle A device held in the mouth of a puppeteer that enables him to speak in the high-pitched voice of Mr Punch in the PUNCH AND JUDY shows. It was first used in the early 18th century.

Sweet Bird of Youth A play by Tennessee WILLIAMS, first performed in 1959 at the Martin Beck Theatre, New York. Paul Newman created the role of Chance Wayne, while Geraldine Page won the New York Drama Critics Award for Best Actress with her performance as Princess Kosmonopolous. Brooks Atkinson described her characterization as "loose-jointed, gangling, raucous of voice, crumpled, shrewd, abandoned yet sensitive about some things that live in the heart". The two stars also appeared in the filmed version (1962).

The story focuses on the Hollywood drifter Chance Wayne, who has become a gigolo to the ageing film star Princess Kosmonopolous. He now brings her to his home-town of St Cloud, unaware that during his last visit he impregnated Heavenly, the daughter of the local politician, Boss Finlay. When Chance hears the news, he refuses to leave despite threats. Boss Finlay had once castrated a Black man, and Chance now quietly awaits his fate.

Sword Play *See* MUMMERS' PLAY *under* MUMMER.

symbolism A French-led movement in the theatre and other arts that reacted against REALISM in the last decade of the 19th century. Symbolist writers strove to penetrate beyond what they saw as the superficial trappings of physical existence to express the inner meaning of life. In the theatre this usually involved a deliberately artificial style of staging, the use of poetic language, and themes chosen from myth or fairytale rather than contemporary life. The first symbolist plays were presented at the Theatre d'Art from about 1890 by Paul Fort, who produced *The Intruder* (1890) and *The Sightless* (1891), atmospheric works by Maurice MAETERLINCK, the leading writer of symbolist drama. Other symbolist playwrights included the Austrian, Hugo von HOFMANNSTHAL, in his *Everyman* (1911); the Irishman, William Butler YEATS, in early works such as *The Land of Heart's Desire* (1894), and the French Catholic dramatist, Paul Claudel (1868–1955). The later plays of STRINDBERG are often described as symbolist works, as are the dramas of Eugene O'NEILL.

Fort was succeeded at the Theatre d'Art in 1893 by Aurelien-Francois Lugne-Poe (1869–1940), who renamed the venue the Theatre de l'Oeuvre. It closed in 1929.

symphonic dramas A series of 15 plays based on events in US history by the US dramatist Paul Green (1894–1981). They were all staged out-of-doors in his native state of North Carolina with a mixture of professional and amateur actors. The first of the series was *The Last Colony* (1937). Green had previously won the Pulitzer Prize for his play *In Abraham's Bosom* (1926), about the decadence of the South.

Synge, J(ohn) M(illington) (1871–1909) Irish playwright, whose six produced plays established him as a leading figure in the Irish dramatic renaissance.

Synge studied languages at Trinity College, Dublin and music at the Royal Irish Academy. Hoping to become a musician, he spent much of his youth wandering in Germany, Italy, and France. In 1897 he experienced the first symptoms of Hodgkin's disease, from which he would die 12 years later at the age of 38.

In Paris Synge had a crucial meeting with W. B. YEATS, who encouraged him to visit the primitive Aran Islands in search of material; if he lived amongst the peasantry as one of themselves he would be able to "express a life that has never found expression". Synge took the advice and spent his summers on the islands from 1898 to 1902. The stories he heard in his first week there inspired his early one-act plays *In the Shadow of the Glen* (1903), which aroused hostility when produced by the Irish Literary Theatre, and the tragic RIDERS TO THE SEA (1904). The distinctive speech rhythms of the Aran Islanders echo through all his works.

The Well of the Saints (1905) was followed by Synge's comic masterpiece, THE PLAYBOY OF THE WESTERN WORLD (1907). Its unsentimental depiction of the Irish peasantry provoked riots and demonstrations amongst nationalists when it was staged at Yeats's ABBEY THEATRE. Synge's other major plays are *The Tinker's Wedding* (1908) and DEIRDRE OF THE SORROWS, based on a famous love story from Irish mythology. A seventh play, *When the Moon has Set*, was rejected three times by Yeats and not published until 1968.

T

tableau vivant *See* LIVING PICTURE.

table legs The nickname devised by Gordon Craig (*see* CRAIG FAMILY) for loyal supporting actors.

taboos and superstitions Few professions have more taboos and superstitions than the theatre. Lucky items include three-leaved clovers, horseshoes, and anything made of ivory, while unlucky ones include peacock feathers, green clothes, and real flowers on stage. STANISLAVSKY would not play Mephistopheles because he believed that something bad always happened to him afterwards. Eleonora DUSE once talked a chimney-sweep into giving her his broom as a good-luck token for opening night, while Katharine Hepburn still crosses herself when entering a theatre in which she once flopped. Florenz ZIEGFELD carried a tiny red elephant for luck and left his name off the billing for *Follies of 1907* to avoid having more than 13 letters in the title. Noël Coward once claimed his only superstition was never to sleep 13 in a bed.

Many actors believe it is a sign of good luck to fall flat on one's face when making a first entrance, since nothing worse can then happen. Most superstitions, however, are about bad luck. They include:

Never calling *Macbeth* by its title (*see* SCOTTISH PLAY).

Not rehearsing the last line of a play.

Not wishing an actor good luck on opening night (the jovial injunction 'Break a leg!' is preferred).

Not unpacking your make-up box until the reviews appear.

The belief that whistling in the dressing room will lead to a short run.

The belief that a good dress rehearsal portends a disastrous opening night.

The belief that leaving a bar of soap behind in the dressing room means that you will never play that theatre again.

The belief that it is unlucky for a visitor to enter the dressing room with the left foot first.

tabs *See* CURTAIN.

Taganka Theatre The popular name for the **Moscow Theatre of Drama and Comedy**, Taganka being the suburb in which it is located. Founded in 1946, it has enjoyed a reputation as the most experimental and controversial theatre in Russia since the mid 1960s. Under Yuri LYUBIMOV, who took over in 1964, the Taganka won the loyalty of students and young playgoers but aroused official disapproval by staging works that were critical of Soviet values. Lyubimov was also criticized for employing 'formalistic' production techniques, such as the use of dance, mime, projections, puppets, and masks. The authorities banned or censored several of the Taganka's offerings. In 1977 the company was given permission to tour internationally. Finally, while working abroad in 1984, Lyubimov was removed as head of the theatre and stripped of his citizenship.

His replacement was an equally controversial director, Anatoly Efros (1925–87), whose productions at other theatres had often been censored. When he died, Nikolai Gubenko (1941–) was appointed to run the theatre, which benefited greatly from the new era of *glasnost*. In 1989 Gubenko was named Soviet Minister of Culture, the first professional artist to hold this post since the 1920s; and Lyubimov was reappointed to his old position at the Taganka.

tail *See* BORDER; FLAT.

Tale of Mystery, A A sensational play sometimes described as the first English MELODRAMA. First produced at Covent Garden in 1802, it was an adaptation by Thomas Holcroft (1744–1809) of the French drama *Coelina, ou l'enfant de mystère* (1800) by Guilbert de Pixérécourt (1773–1844), who was not acknowledged. The plot involves a murder planned by Count Romaldo in order to marry a rich heiress. *A Tale of Mystery* was a great success, and the melodrama soon became a mainstay of the secondary theatres.

Talma, François-Joseph (1763–1826) The greatest French tragedian of the Napoleonic era, sometimes considered the finest of all French actors. He made numerous reforms to the theatre of the day, adopting historically accurate costumes and a naturalistic acting style.

The son of a French dentist who had moved to London to practise, the young Talma organized amateur theatre performances for the French community, acquiring a love for the comparatively restrained English acting style. He returned to Paris in 1786 to become one of the first students at the newly opened Ecole de Declamation, where he trained under François-René Molé (1734–1802).

Talma made his professional debut at the Comédie-Française in 1787 in Voltaire's *Mahomet*. He soon became known as a troublemaker because of his revolutionary ideas in both politics and the theatre. He disliked bombastic acting, elaborate staging, and the use of contemporary costume. In 1787 he stunned audiences by appearing on stage in a toga with bare arms and legs. Despite his unconventional ideas the strikingly handsome and spirited Talma became an immense star. The intensity of his performances led the critic Abbé Geoffroy to write: "His triumph lies in the portrayal of passion worked up to delirium, to insanity."

In 1789 Talma played the king in Marie-Joseph de Chénier's anti-monarchical *Charles IX*, provoking demonstrations in the theatre with his passionate performance. He also fought a duel with the royalist actor Naudet, who had avoided playing the role by feigning illness. The bitter divisions between monarchists and republicans led to the disintegration of the company in 1791.

The following year, Talma and a number of likeminded actors from the Comédie-Française joined those from the Variétés Amusantes to form a company in the Théâtre de la rue de Richelieu, which they renamed the Théâtre de la Révolution. It soon became France's premiere theatre (partly because many conservative actors were in prison at the time). Talma continued to appear in works by Corneille and Shakespeare, his usual companion in tragedy being Mlle Duchenois (*c.* 1777–1835).

In 1803 Talma reunited the old Comédie-Française at his theatre and Napoleon, a great admirer of the actor, subsequently restored the company's pensions and subsidies. Talma travelled with the emperor throughout Europe, playing in 1803 in Erfurt, Germany, to an audience that included five crowned heads. He also had an affair with Napoleon's beautiful sister Pauline, the duchess of Guastalla. After the return of peace, he was a frequent visitor to London, appearing at Covent Garden in 1817.

Talma gave his last performance in 1826 in Delaville's *Charles VI*, dying four months later. His last words were "*Voltaire!...comme Voltaire...toujours comme Voltaire...*"

Tamasha A popular type of folk theatre in India's west-central state of Maharashta. Its origin is uncertain, although it is thought to have been introduced to the region in the early 18th century by Mogul armies. The name *Tamasha* is Persian for 'fun' or 'entertainment'. The plays adapt themes from history or mythology to satirize politicians, businessmen, priests, and others.

There are various kinds of companies. The *dholki-barris* folk-drama troupes have a leading actor, clown, six actor-singers, one or more female dancer-singers, and several musicians. The *loknatya*, or people's theatre, perform for urban playgoers in the modern theatres of Bombay, Nagpur, and elsewhere. In the 1960s government programmes were introduced to help companies with financial problems.

Tamasha is either performed outside in any open space or, especially during the monsoon season, in roofed theatres. The entertainment opens with a *gan*, or song praising the deities. This is followed by the *gaulan*, a humorous skit featuring Krishna and his clown attendant. Next is the *vag*, a brief humorous dialogue play. This was only added in the 19th century, but is now the main feature of the drama.

Also popular are the *lavani*, or love songs, which are now sung by professional dancing girls (they were performed by male singers disguised as women until the late 19th century). *Tamasha* dance combines classical and folk forms.

Tamburlaine the Great A tragedy in blank verse by Christopher MARLOWE, written in two parts and first produced in London in 1587. It is based on the career of the Mongol conqueror Timur Leng (1336–

1405). The first part describes how Tamburlaine, a Scythian shepherd, becomes king of Persia, goes on to defeat the Turkish emperor BAJAZET, and woos Zenocrate, daughter of the Sultan of Egypt. The second part of the play shows how the hero's pride and lust for power lead eventually to his ruin.

Taming of the Shrew, The SHAKESPEARE's comedy of marital strife, written in 1593 with the first date of performance unknown. Its precise relationship to another anonymous play called *The Taming of a Shrew* has sparked much scholarly debate.

The play opens with an Induction in which Christopher SLY, a drunken tinker, is tricked into believing that he is a lord. The story of Katharina and Petruchio is then performed for his pleasure by a troupe of strolling players. Katharina, the shrew of the title, and Bianca, her beautiful sister, are the daughters of a rich Paduan merchant. While Bianca has numerous wooers, the older Katharina, whom her father is determined to see married first, drives men away with her furious temper. Eventually Petruchio, a blatant fortune-hunter, marries the unwilling Katharina and carries her off to his home in Verona. Here he successfully tames her into a submissive wife. In the final scene Katharina astonishes her family by delivering a long speech on marital obedience.

The Taming of the Shrew was rewritten by Garrick in 1754 as the popular *Catherine and Petruchio*. Cole Porter later adapted Shakespeare's original for his Broadway musical KISS ME KATE (1948). In 1967 the Richard Burton and Elizabeth Taylor film of *The Taming of the Shrew* credited three writers, none being Shakespeare.

In 1978 at Stratford Jonathan Pryce played the drunken Sly so convincingly, fighting in the stalls and ripping down scenery, that several members of the audience left their seats to call the police. The 14-year-old Olivier gave one of his first stage performances as Katharina in an all-male schools production at Stratford in 1922. "I can't remember any actress in the part who looked better," wrote the critic W. A. Darlington.

'Ta-Ra-Ra-Boom-De-Ay' The song, written by Harry Sayers (1857–1934), that transformed the career of Lottie Collins (1866–1910), the British music-hall performer. She began as a skipping-rope dancer, but became an overnight star in 1891 when she introduced 'Ta-Ra-Ra-Boom-De-Ay' with a high-kicking dance in the pantomime *Dick Whittington* at the Grand Theatre, Islington. She also sang it in the burlesque *Cinder-Ellen-Up-Too-Late*, which she was appearing in at the Gaiety, dashing from one theatre to the other to perform it. Collins eventually went to America, where she was paid £200 a week for her one-song act.

Tarlton, Richard (d. 1588) England's first professional comic actor. Scholars believe he inspired the characters of Bottom in *A Midsummer Night's Dream* and Yorick in *Hamlet*. Tarlton was short and slightly hunchbacked with a squint and a flat nose (this had been damaged while he was separating dogs and bears during bear-baiting). He joked that he still had "sagacity enough to smell a knave from an honest man". In 1583 he joined the Queen Elizabeth's Men and remained the queen's favourite jester until she banned him from court for telling jokes about Sir Walter Raleigh and the Earl of Leicester.

Tarlton wrote the successful play *The Seven Deadly Sins* (1585) and several other lost works, while many of his witticisms are recorded in *Tarlton's Jests*, published posthumously in 1611. He also popularized the comic JIG and was famous for improvising on stage. Hamlet's comment to the players, "Let those that play your fools speak no more than is set down for them" was apparently written with Tarlton in mind.

Tartuffe MOLIÈRE's comedy about religious hypocrisy, first performed in 1664 before Louis XIV at Versailles. Molière's young wife, Armande Béjart (1641–1700), played Elmire while he himself played Orgon (wearing a black satin cloak lined with shot silk trimmed in English lace and with lace on his shoes and garters). When Molière revised the play for the Palais Royal, it was immediately banned. The chief judge of Paris told the author, "You are an honour and a glory to France, but it is not the theatre's business to dabble in religion." The king was baffled by the strength of feeling aroused by the play, which does not directly attack Christianity or the Church, until a member of his court explained: "Molière mocks the men themselves. That's what they cannot bear." Molière, who was determined that the comedy should be staged, revised it twice and added a final speech praising the king. When finally produced in 1669, it was an instant success.

In the plot, Tartuffe uses his false religiosity to win the admiration of the gullible merchant Orgon. While feigning abstinence, he is eating, drinking, and even stealing from his supporter. When Tartuffe is finally caught trying to seduce his wife, Orgon throws him out.

The word *tartuffe* is still used in France to mean a sanctimonious hypocrite.

Taste of Honey, A A two-act play by Shelagh Delaney (1939–). It was first performed in 1958 at the Theatre Workshop, London, where it enjoyed great success before transferring to Wyndham's Theatre. The story centres upon the love–hate relationship between the working-class Helen and her rebellious daughter Jo, who live together in a drab Manchester flat. When Helen leaves with her boyfriend, Peter, the neglected Jo has an affair with a Black serviceman. She becomes pregnant and takes in Geoff, a homosexual art student. Together they prepare for the coming of her baby, but Helen reappears and forces Geoff out. When Helen learns that the baby will be Black, she rushes off to the pub, leaving Jo deserted again.

The play won awards in both Britain and America and was made into a successful film, starring Rita Tushingham, in 1961.

Tate. Harry Tate (Ronald Macdonald Hutchison; 1872–1940) British music-hall comedian, who perfected a series of riotous sketches about motoring, golfing, fishing, and other sports. They usually featured an elderly man and his moronic fat son. Tate's motoring sketch became one of the most renowned on the halls, while the fishing sketch ended with dozens of prop fish of all shapes flying through the air on rods.

Born in Scotland, Tate took his stage name from his former employer, the sugar refiners Henry Tate and Sons. He made his debut in 1895 as a mimic at the Camberwell Empire and went on to perform at the London Hippodrome in such successful revues as *Business as Usual*.

The name *Harry Tate* soon came to be used to designate anything disorganized or chaotic. *Harry Tate's Navy* was a good-humoured sobriquet applied to the Royal Naval Volunteer Reserve from about the time of World War I.

Nahum Tate (1652–1715) Irish-born writer who has been described as "a poor poet and worse playwright". Despite this handicap, he was appointed poet laureate in 1692 (and historiographer royal in 1702).

Tate's own works include the farce *A Duke and No Duke* (1684); he also collaborated with Dryden on the second part of *Absolom and Achitophel* (1682). He is mostly remembered, however, for his eccentric adaptations of Shakespeare's plays. When he adapted *Richard II* as *The History of King Richard II* (1680), his work was banned for emphasizing usurpation and abdication at a time of political tension. His response was to move the action to Sicily, retitling the word *The Sicilian Usurper* (1681). Tate's *The Ingratitude of Common-Wealth* (1681) was adapted from *Coriolanus*, but incorporated part of *Titus Andronicus* in the last act.

Tate's most infamous adaptation was his rewriting of *King Lear* (1681), in which he omitted the character of the Fool, allowed Cordelia to survive to marry Edgar, and introduced a happy ending with Lear restored to the throne. This farrago replaced Shakespeare's play on the British stage for over 150 years, until William Macready resurrected the original, at Covent Garden in 1838.

Although Tate's adaptations were subsequently ridiculed, they were extremely popular in their day, winning the admiration of Dr Johnson amongst others.

Tavistock Repertory Company *See* LITTLE THEATRES *under* LITTLE.

Taylor, Tom (1817–80) British playwright, who was the author of around 100 dramatic works and often took part in the private amateur productions organized by Charles Dickens. He also edited *Punch* (1874–80).

Taylor's first play, *A Trip to Kissingen*, was produced in 1844 at the Lyceum. Subsequent works included *To Parents and Guardians* (1846), *Masks and Faces* (1852; with Charles Reade), which was based on the life of Peg WOFFINGTON, *Still Waters Run Deep* (1855), which was considered sexually frank in its day, and the influential melodrama THE TICKET-OF-LEAVE MAN (1863).

Taylor's successful comedy *Our American Cousin* is now mainly remembered as the play Abraham Lincoln was watching when he was assassinated in 1865. It was first produced in 1858 by the actress-manager Laura KEENE at her theatre in New York; E. A. Sothern (*see* SOTHERN FAMILY) starred as the simpleton Lord Dundreary (*see* DUNDREARIES). Keene's company was performing the play in FORD'S THEATRE when the president was shot by John Wilkes Booth (*see* BOOTH FAMILY).

teatro. ***Teatro Abierto*** (Sp. Open Theatre) An Argentine theatre movement founded in 1981 to fight political repression and revitalize the country's drama. Osvaldo Dragún was amongst those who launched an appeal for new works that resulted in the choice of 20 one-act plays for production. These were staged by 20 different directors at the Teatro Picadero in the space of a week. Suspiciously, the theatre burned down at the week's end, but public demand ensured that further performances took place at the Teatro Tabarís. The impact of the second season was weakened by mediocre scripts and the outbreak of the Falklands War; the movement has since been less influential owing to Argentina's return to democracy.

Teatro Campesino *See* CHICANO THEATRE.

Teatro del grottesco (It. Theatre of the Grotesque) A movement in modern Italian drama that originated in World War I as a reaction against the heroic plays of Gabriele D'ANNUNZIO. The movement, which lasted through the 1920s, sought to renew the Italian theatre by introducing elements of parody, irony, violent realism, and grotesque humour. The works explored hypocrisy and the gap between illusion and reality.

Teatro del grottesco derived its name from the subtitle to one of its best-known works, the 1916 farce *Le Maschera e il volto* (*The Mask and the Face*) by Luigi Chiarelli (1884–1947). This satirical look at modern society has been widely translated and performed. Other important writers were Pier Maria Rosso di San Secondo (1887–1956), who wrote *Marionette, che passione!* (*Puppets, What Passion!*; 1918) and *La Scala* (*The Ladder*, 1926), and Massimo Bontempelli (1878–1960). Italy's greatest 20th-century dramatist, Luigi PIRANDELLO, was also associated with the movement.

Teatro Farnese A majestic RENAISSANCE THEATRE in Parma, Italy, famous as the oldest surviving venue with a PROSCENIUM ARCH. It is now seldom used for performances. Designed by Giovanni Aleotti (1546–1636), it was begun in 1619 and opened in 1628. In addition to the proscenium arch, it had two similar frames further back on the deep stage, allowing actors to use the entire area. The theatre originally had a set of wings, which are also thought to have been designed by Aleotti. In front of the proscenium arch, which had a Roman-type curtain, there was a large open space used for dancing; on one occasion this was flooded for a water spectacle. The auditorium was that of a traditional court theatre, providing raised seating in a horseshoe arrangement for 3500 spectators.

teatro invisible (Sp. invisible theatre) In Argentina in the 1970s, a type of HAPPENING presented in public places to unsuspecting audiences by the Brazilian playwright and director Augusto Boal (1931–). An exile from his own country because of his Marxist views, Boal also devised the **teatro jornal**, a type of LIVING NEWSPAPER. His first work of protest theatre was the drama *Revolução na América do Sul* (*Revolution in South America*), presented in 1961. Boal's ideas about the revolutionary potential of the theatre are set out in the 1975 volume *Teatro do Oprimido* (*Theatre of the Oppressed*).

Teatro Olimpico The oldest surviving RENAISSANCE THEATRE. The magnificent venue in Vicenza, Italy, was built by the Olympic Academy of Vicenza, a body founded in 1555 for the study of Greek drama. It was designed by Andrea Palladio (1518–80), who aimed to create the effect of an indoor Roman theatre. Palladio died soon after beginning the construction work in 1580 and the theatre was completed four years later by Vincenzo Scamozzi (1552–1616). The theatre's semicircular raised seating curves around a small ORCHESTRA and the raised acting area. Behind the stage is an elaborate stone wall with five openings, three being doors painted with perspective views of streets leading away. The Teatro Olimpico opened in 1585 with Sophocles's *Oedipus Rex*.

teatro por horas In late 19th-century Spain, a type of light comedy drama. Derived from the SAINETE, it began in about 1868 and reached the height of its popularity just before the turn of the century. The one-act plays satirized everyday Spanish life, especially in Madrid. The vogue for the *teatro por horas* was associated with the revival of the musical ZARZUELA. They were superseded by the *astracanadas*, comic sketches noted for their bad puns and unrealistic plots.

Teatro stabile One of the permanent acting troupes formed in Italy after World War II in an effort to establish regional theatres. Ten existed by the 1960s, and others have now been formed throughout the country. The best known include the Teatro stabile in Genoa, founded in 1952 and headed by Luigi Squarzina (1922–), and the Teatro stabile in Turin, founded in 1955 and headed by Gianfranco de Bosio (1924–).

The first and most famous, however, was the **Piccolo teatro della città di Milano**, founded in 1947 by the director Giorgio STREHLER, who has directed about three-quarters of the plays, and the actor-director Paolo Grassi (1919–81). The company was given rent-free use of a theatre by the city of Milan, and later received the first state subsidy awarded to an Italian drama company. It opened with a production of Gorki's *The Lower Depths* starring Marcello Moretti (1910–61), the famous Harlequin. The company later developed its own training school. Today it has an international reputation, being considered one of the best regional theatre companies in Europe. It introduced Brecht to Italian audiences, and is equally respected for its revivals of works by Shakespeare and Goldoni, as for its productions of works by contemporary Italian dramatists.

technical rehearsal or **tech** A REHEARSAL, usually held shortly before opening night, at which sound, lighting, and other technical operations are practised. The director usually runs through the show 'cue-to-cue', i.e. jumping from an actor's entrance to the next sound cue, lighting change, etc., without reading the dialogue. If actors have quick changes, however, these will be rehearsed while the text is read. A production generally hopes to have one technical rehearsal and two dress rehearsals.

tempest. Dame Marie Tempest (Mary Susan Etherington; 1864–1942) The leading British comedienne of the early 20th century. She made her debut in 1885 in Suppé's comic opera *Boccaccio*, later winning acclaim as Kitty Carol in *The Red Hussar* (1889), which she took to New York the same year. Her greatest success came in 1902, when she played Kitty Silverton in *The Marriage of Kitty*, a play adapted from the French by her husband Cosmo Gordon-Lennox. She kept the piece in her repertoire for 30 years. Another triumph was provided by Noël Coward, who wrote the part of Judith Bliss in HAY FEVER (1925) especially for her; the play ran for 3367 performances. In 1934 she played opposite Olivier in Kaufman and Ferber's *Theatre Royal*, a play about the Barrymores. Her last big success came when she appeared in Dodie Smith's *Dear Octopus* (1938) at the age of 74.

Short and plump, Tempest was fastidious about clothes and would never sit down in her dressing room when in costume. Once when an emotional young actress flung herself at Tempest's feet to beg forgiveness for being late, the grand lady commanded, "Get up! Get up! Have you no respect for your management's clothes?"

Rex Harrison recalled that she was so nervous on opening nights that during the tea party scenes (that always seemed to feature in her plays) her cup had to be glued to the saucer. He also noted that whenever they left a scene, Dame Marie would wait until she was out of sight of the audience and then begin clapping; the audience, thinking the sound came from their midst, would take up the applause. She also milked extra applause by having her maid shoo her Sealyham dog on stage during the last CURTAIN CALL; she would appear surprised that the dog had followed her and take it lovingly in her arms while the audience roared approval, resulting in two or three extra calls. *See also* MARIE TEMPEST.

The Tempest The last play that SHAKESPEARE wrote without a collaborator. A romantic fantasy, it was first performed before James I at Whitehall in 1611; two years later it was staged to celebrate the wedding of Princess Elizabeth and the Elector Palatine.

The story is set on an enchanted island ruled by PROSPERO, the deposed Duke of Milan, who lives there with his beautiful daughter Miranda. A potent yet benevolent magician, he is served by various spirits, including the delicate ARIEL, and by CALIBAN, the misshapen son of a witch. In the opening scene a ship carrying Antonio, the brother who usurped Prospero's dukedom, and Alonso, king of Naples, is wrecked through Prospero's magic. The courtiers are cast onto the island, where Prospero uses a variety of supernatural devices to bring his enemies to a sense of their guilt. Finally he forgives them and renounces his art in a speech that has often been interpreted as Shakespeare's own farewell to the stage.

When Beerbohm Tree produced *The Tempest* in 1904, the opening shipwreck scene was staged using an entire ship that rocked in a sea with waves that splashed over the deck, making some in the audience seasick. The play has inspired many adaptations, from an unfinished opera by Mozart to the 1954 science-fiction film *Forbidden Planet*. The most renowned Prospero of modern times has been Sir John Gielgud, who has played the part more often than any other living actor.

Ten Times Tables A comedy by Alan AYCKBOURN that opened in 1977 at the Stephen Joseph Theatre in the Round, Scarborough (where Ayckbourn is artistic director) and transferred the next year to the Globe Theatre in London. The story centres on the Pendon Civic Society which, inspired by an idea from its chairman, Ray, initiates a fund-raising PAGEANT based on the martyrdom of the 'Pendon Twelve'. When Eric, a leftist schoolteacher, decides to turn the festivities into a propaganda show, the organizing committee splits into two groups responsible for rehearsing the workers and the military. Eric handles the workers' group adroitly but Ray's gang have to bring in the neo-fascist Tim, who carries a real revolver and directs his group like General Franco. On the big day there is much disarray, but Ray has already hatched a plan for the next pageant: Romans battling Britons.

tent show In America, a travelling company that staged plays under canvas. One of the first tent shows was that organized in 1851 by Fayette Lodowick 'Yankee' Robinson in the Midwest states of Iowa and Illinois. Before the turn of the century, such outdoor offerings as the Harley Sadler Show had become popular summer entertainment. Known humorously as **rag opries**, the plays were performed in a tent about 60 feet wide on portable platform stages with basic props and scenery; the audience sat on wooden benches.

The earlier tent shows generally produced pirated or poorly rewritten melodramas, but the advent of tougher copyright laws forced them to commission original plays, mostly dealing with rural themes. A popular moralistic work was Charles Harrison's *Saintly Hypocrites and Honest Sinners* (1915). Many comedies were written featuring the rustic hero TOBY. By the late 1920s, some 400 tent shows were drawing an audience of around 78 million. The shows were doomed, however, by the Depression of the 1930s and the growth of cinema.

Terence (Publius Terentius Afer; *c.* 190–159 BC) Roman playwright, who was a Carthaginian slave educated and freed by his Roman master. Six of his plays, all based on works of the Greek NEW COMEDY, have survived: *Andria* (166 BC), *Hecyra* (165 BC), *Heauton Timoroumenos* (163 BC), *Eunuchus* (161 BC), *Phormio* (161 BC), and *Adelphi* (160 BC). They show Terence's comedy to be more original and subtle with thoughtful characterization and a graceful style. His plotting and characterization influenced many Renaissance playwrights, amongst them Molière and Shakespeare.

In his own day Terence was always overshadowed by PLAUTUS, who produced more topical and less refined comedies. Julius Caesar criticized Terence's plays for lacking the true comic spirit. The playwright's later prologues sharply answer these attacks and also complain of the fickleness of the public, which was developing a preference for circuses and gladiatorial combats.

Termagant The name given by the Crusaders and by the writers of medieval romances to an idol or deity that the Saracens were popularly supposed to worship. Termagant was subsequently introduced into the MORALITY PLAYS as a violent ranting character in long flowing Eastern robes. This dress led to the character being identified as a woman, whence the name later came to be applied to a shrewish virago.

o'erdoing Termagant Acting with ranting raging pomposity. In medieval drama, the degree of rant was the measure of villainy and Termagant (like HEROD and PILATE) being considered the nadir of evil was always played in an exaggerated bawling style. The phrase comes from Hamlet's instructions to the players (*Hamlet*, III, ii), in which the Prince tells them not to overdo the shouting.

Terpsichore The MUSE of dancing and the dramatic chorus in ancient Greek mythology. Hence the adjective *Terpsichorean*, pertaining to dancing.

Terriss, William (William Charles James Lewin; 1847–97) British actor. Terriss spent part of his youth as a sheep farmer in the Falkland Islands before returning to Britain, where he became a successful actor at the age of 26. His legions of fans brought him constant presents, but Terriss always passed them on to the call boy or other behind-the-scenes workers. His daughter Ellaline became an actress and music-hall performer.

Terriss became well known for playing alongside IRVING in melodramas at the Adelphi. Irving was particularly fond of the younger actor, and would tease him during rehearsals. "Bill, my boy," he said on one occasion, "what do those last two lines mean?" Terriss put off the answer for a minute, then admitted, "So help me goodness, guv'nor, I'm blowed if I know what they *do* mean." Irving joined the cast in laughter: "No, I thought not."

Ironically, the much loved Terriss became the only actor to be murdered outside a London theatre. On 16 December 1897 he was stabbed to death as he made to enter the Adelphi by a jealous small-time actor, Richard Prince. Irving bitterly predicted, "Terriss was an actor. His murderer will not be executed." Prince indeed escaped the hangman to spend the remainder of his life in Broadmoor Asylum.

Terry family A British family of actors, consisting of Benjamin Terry (1818–96), his wife Sarah Ballard (1817–92), their four daughters Kate Terry (1844–1924), Ellen Terry (1847–1928), Marion Terry (1856–1930), and Florence Terry (1855–1896), and their son Fred Terry (1863–1933).

The elder Terrys were provincial actors. Ben, the son of an Irish publican, never rose above mediocrity as an actor. Sarah, the daughter of a Scottish Wesleyan lay preacher, was more successful; using the stage name of Miss Yerret she once played Gertrude to William Macready's Hamlet. Of their 11 children, nine survived and five went on the stage. When young, the children slept in drawers in Sarah's dressing rooms.

Kate Terry danced hornpipes on the stage when three, played Prince Arthur in Charles Kean's production of *King John* at eight, and at 14 was the youngest ever Cordelia in a professional production of *King Lear*. In 1862 she went on as an understudy in Victorien Sardou's *Nos Intimes* and overnight became "the stage divinity of her day". In 1865 she won acclaim in Tom Taylor's *The Ticket-of-Leave Man* and the following year took the female lead in Dion Boucicault's *Hunted Down*, the play in which Henry Irving made his spectacular London debut. Some critics considered her superior to her famous sister Ellen, but in 1867 Kate married and left the stage, giving an emotional farewell performance as Juliet. Her eldest daughter, also called Kate, was the mother of Sir John GIELGUD.

Dame Ellen Terry was the most famous member of the family and one of the most adored of her profession. Oscar Wilde once described her as "like some wan lily overdrenched with rain".

Ellen made her debut at the age of nine as Mamillius in Charles Kean's production of *The Winter's Tale*. In 1861 she joined the Haymarket Company and three years later, at 17, married the painter G. F. Watts, who was 47. The marriage lasted less than a year. She later lived with the stage designer E. W. Godwin, bearing him two children, Edith and Gordon Craig (*see* CRAIG FAMILY).

In 1878 she married the actor Charles Kelly (Charles Wardell; 1839–85). That same year she joined Henry IRVING's company at the LYCEUM THEATRE to begin a famous partnership that lasted for a quarter of a century. The highlights included numerous performances of Shakespeare – she excelled as Beatrice, Cordelia, Desdemona, Olivia, and Viola – and the famous melodrama *The Bells*, which Terry and Irving gave as a command performance for Queen Victoria.

Terry was infamous for forgetting her lines. Mrs Patrick CAMPBELL recalled a performance of *Cymbeline* in which Terry, playing Imogen, "forgot her words and, giving a delicious look at the audience and then towards heaven, spoke three times in a voice that melted your bosom, this word: 'Beyond...Beyond...beyond'. There was no 'beyond' in the text, but it was the loveliest word I ever heard, and described her Imogen."

After Irving's retirement from the Lyceum she became manager of the Imperial theatre in 1903 and produced several plays with scenery by her son Gordon Craig. In 1906 she celebrated her golden jubilee with a spectacular matinée at Drury Lane, in which 22 members of the Terry family appeared. She was then playing Lady Cicely Waynflete in CAPTAIN BRASSBOUND'S CONVERSION, a part created especially for her by George Bernard Shaw. He based the character on the personality she had revealed in the flirtatious love letters they had exchanged since 1897 (the two had never met). Playing opposite her was the 30-year-old US actor James Carew (James Usselman; 1876–1938), who became her third husband.

In 1917 Terry attended a schools performance of *Julius Caesar* at All Saints' School near Oxford Circus. Her companions expressed admiration for the young actors playing Caesar and Antony, but Terry put aside her bag of boiled sweets and said, "No." A long silence sat upon the group. "The boy who played Brutus," she said finally, "the dark little boy – he is a born actor." The 10-year-old boy's name was Laurence Olivier.

In 1925 she gave her last performance, in Walter de la Mare's *Crossings* at the Lyric Theatre, Hammersmith. That same year she was created DBE, the second actress so honoured.

Marion Terry, known to the family as Polly, was noted for her refined manner, which brought her many parts as titled ladies; even in old age Ellen delighted in spreading wild stories about her well-bred sister. In 1892 Marion created the part of Mrs Erlynne in Wilde's *Lady Windermere's Fan* (1892) and in 1902 the role of Susan Throssel in J. M. Barrie's *Quality Street*. At 64 she played the aristocratic Mrs Higgins in a revival of Shaw's *Pygmalion*. Marion retired in 1923, owing to arthritis.

Florence Terry, known as Floss or Flossie to the family, was considered the happiest and kindest of the sisters. She began acting as a child and later played a supporting role to Ellen's Portia in *The Merchant of Venice*. She would also stand in for Ellen and Marion when required. Critics expected her to become a star, but Florence had little ambition and appeared mainly in amateur productions after marrying in 1882.

Fred Terry, known as the **golden Terry**, was a romantic actor who retained his florid acting style into the 20th century. He disliked his famous sister Ellen, who used to lock him in cupboards when they were children. When he was 17 and his voice broke on stage, Ellen, instead of covering for him, imitated him to draw a laugh. From 1905 to 1913 Fred occupied the New Theatre for a six-month season with his actress wife Julia Neilson, during which he gave an acclaimed performance as Sir Percy Blakeney in *The Scarlet Pimpernel*. Their actor son Dennis Neilson-Terry (1895–1932) died in South Africa while touring. Fred also had two actress daughters with his second wife Mary Glynne (Mary Aitken; 1898–1954).

tetralogy In the ancient Greek theatre, a series of four works by the same dramatist, consisting of three tragedies followed by a SATYR-PLAY. These were presented in drama contests at the City DIONYSIA. In the early competitions, the four plays had a common theme and were given a common name. No complete tetralogies are extant; THE ORESTEIA of AESCHYLUS is the only surviving trilogy.

Thaddädl A stock figure in Viennese comedy. A ridiculous young man with a high voice, Thaddädl was created by the Austrian actor Anton Hasenhut (1766–1841) and proved a great success in Kringsterner's *Der Zwirnhändler* (1801). He did not retain his popularity beyond the 1820s.

Thalia The MUSE who presided over comedy and pastoral poetry.

Thalia Theatre *See* BOWERY THEATRE.

thanigratha In the Crow Indian tribes of North America, a class of designated fools. Their traditional comic instrument was a tortoiseshell rattle. Much of their humour involved satirizing the White man through such antics as riding backwards, shooting arrows over their shoulders, etc. They also mimicked the drunken White man and his inept encounters with nature: when one of the *thanigratha* forded a stream, he would carefully roll up one trouser leg and then hop across on the other leg.

THE Theatre in Health Education. A number of British companies that travel to schools, colleges, and universities to present dramas with health-education messages. The subjects have included AIDS, drugs, and smoking. Funding comes from fees as well as from private and government sources. West Midland companies, including Birmingham's Theatre in Health Education Trust, charge no fees because they are financed by the regional health authority. The Contagious Theatre Company is funded totally by Femidom, the manufacturer of female condoms.

theatre. Theatre, the Britain's first public theatre, built in Shoreditch, London, in 1576 (sometimes called "the most significant date in the history of English drama"). It was situated just outside the City limits, a little to the north of the present London Wall. This was to avoid the jurisdiction of the Puritan authorities, who were strongly opposed to the project. The Theatre was constructed by the actor James BURBAGE and played host to such early theatrical companies as LEICESTER'S MEN, the QUEEN'S MEN, and the CHAMBERLAIN'S MEN (which included Richard Burbage and Shakespeare amongst its members). The audience, who paid one penny for standing room, had a wide choice of entertainments on different nights. Straight theatrical performances had to compete with swordplay, athletics, and bear-baiting. In 1596 the Chamberlain's Men gave the first performance of HAMLET. Being used to so much ephemera, it is doubtful if the first-night audience guessed that the play they had just seen would still be at the head of the international repertory 400 years later.

In 1597 the lease on the land on which the Theatre stood ran out and the landlord, Giles Alleyn, refused to grant a new one. Accordingly, on the night of 28 December 1598, a number of conspirators led by Richard Burbage dismantled part of the building and carried the timbers across London to a new site on Bankside, south of the Thames. Relying on an obscure clause in the lease to protect themselves from the remonstrances of the irate Alleyn, they used these timbers to build the largest playhouse in Elizabethan England, the GLOBE THEATRE.

The Theatre, or what remained of it, was never used again for drama; it was eventually pulled down.

Théâtre de l'Europe A theatre established in 1983 by the European Parliament at the urging of the Italian director Giorgio STREHLER, director of the Piccolo Teatro della Città di Milano. Strehler was appointed head of the new organization, which was given the Odéon Theatre in Paris as a permanent home (*see* ODÉON, THÉÂTRE NATIONAL DE L').

The Théâtre de l'Europe was established by the European Parliament as a symbol of Europe's common cultural heritage. Major theatre companies from the member states of the EC contribute productions, which tour the larger cities of Europe and overseas. The Théâtre's first offering was a production of THE TEMPEST, directed by Strehler himself, which eventually toured as far as the Olympic Art Festival in Los Angeles. The director won great praise for turning Shakespeare's play into a story about the theatre, transforming the character of Prospero into a director-magician who creates all the characters and the dramatic illusions of the storm, etc.

Strehler's subsequent productions for the Théâtre de l'Europe have included works by Strindberg, Corneille, and Lessing.

Théâtre des Nations A major subsidized theatre festival. It was first organized in 1954 in Paris by the INTERNATIONAL THEATRE INSTITUTE, as a summer season of works by foreign companies. A. M. Julien directed the festival at the Théâtre Sarah-Bernhardt (now the Théâtre de la Ville). In 1957 alone, 16 companies performed in nine languages; between 1955 and 1965 companies from 50 countries appeared. The French actor and director Jean-Louis BARRAULT took over its management in 1965; three years later the festival was disrupted by the *événements* of May and June 1968, leading to its suspension (and to Barrault's dismissal from the management of the ODÉON theatre). The festival has since been revived irregularly in other countries. The organization produces its own journal *Théâtre: drame, musique, danse*, and also helped to found the International Association of Theatre Technicians.

Theatre Guild The New York production company founded in 1918 by Lawrence Langner (1890–1962) to provide theatregoers with the best of European and US drama. It was based at the Garrick Theatre until 1925, when a string of successes prompted a move to its own Guild Theatre. In the 1920s the Guild helped to establish the international reputation of George Bernard SHAW. After staging the world premiere of Shaw's *Heartbreak House* (1920), the Guild acted as his US agent and went on to produce 15 more of his plays, including world premieres of *Back to Methuselah* (1922), *Saint Joan* (1923), *The Apple Cart* (1929), and *Too True To Be Good* (1932).

Other European plays produced during the early years included Ferenc Molnár's *Liliom* (1921), Leonid Andreyev's *He Who Gets Slapped* (1922), and Henrik Ibsen's *Peer Gynt* (1923). The Guild also presented work by Tolstoy, Strindberg, Chekhov, and Marlowe.

The company was equally important in developing the careers of contemporary US playwrights. In 1928 it produced *Marco Millions* (1928) by Eugene O'NEILL, who maintained a long association with the company after his rise to fame. It also gave crucial early encouragement to the Pulitzer Prize-winners Maxwell Anderson, Robert Sherwood, and William Saroyan.

Amongst the famous actors the Guild nurtured were Helen HAYES, the Russian actress Alla NAZIMOVA, and Lynn Fontanne and her husband Alfred Lunt (*see* LUNTS, THE), who appeared together (for only the second time) in the Guild's 1924 production of Molnár's *The Guardsman*.

In musical theatre, the Guild made an outstanding contribution by producing Gershwin's PORGY AND BESS and by bringing together Richard Rodgers and Oscar Hammerstein to create the innovative musical OKLAHOMA! (1943).

In 1950 the Guild came under the aegis of the American National Theatre and Academy (ANTA), and the Guild Theatre was renamed the Anta Theatre. The company's 'Theatre Guild on the Air' presented the nation with distinguished radio and television play productions from 1945 to 1963.

Theatre in Education *See* TIE.

Theatre in Health Education *See* THE.

theatre-in-the-round A form of staging that places the acting area in the centre of the theatre with the audience on all sides. It provides an intimate atmosphere but creates technical problems with lighting, sound, and the movements of actors. Although theatre-in-the-round is often considered a modern development, this was the earliest way of staging drama, being used in open-air and street presentations. After centuries during which the actors and the auditorium were separated by the PROSCENIUM ARCH, some companies felt the need to be released from this confinement. In the 1930s the Soviet director Nikolai Okhlopov introduced theatre-in-the-round for his experimental Realistic Theatre. In 1937 Britain's Robert Atkins, who ran the Open Air Theatre in Regent's Park for over 30 years, presented Shakespeare in the round in the Ring, Blackfriars.

America's first permanent theatre-in-the-round was the Penthouse Theatre on the University of Washington campus in Seattle, which opened in 1940. The off-Broadway CIRCLE-IN-THE-SQUARE opened in 1951 in Sheridan Square, and the ARENA STAGE in Washington, DC, opened in 1961. This form of staging became a familiar part of US university drama during the 1960s and 1970s, largely because of the scope it gave for free interaction between actors and audience.

British examples of permanent theatres-in-the-round include the New Victoria Theatre in Newcastle-under-Lyme, the Stephen Joseph Theatre in Scarborough, and Manchester's Royal Exchange Theatre. Many other venues have flexible staging. An innovative offshoot of theatre-in-the-round has been the PROMENADE PRODUCTION, in which the audience remains standing and accompanies the actors from one acting area to another.

Théâtre Libre A private theatre founded in Paris in 1887 by André Antoine (1858–1943) to present contemporary works of NATURALISM. Antoine, who was much influenced by the work of IBSEN, produced the first French version of *Ghosts* at the theatre, playing the role of Oswald Alving himself. Other Ibsen plays were produced, as well as works by Hauptmann and Strindberg, and adaptations of Zola's naturalistic novels. The Théâtre Libre became a rallying point for the 'plays of ideas' of young French playwrights such as Georges de Porto-Riche (1849–1930), Henri Lavedan (1859–1940), and Eugène Brieux (1858–1932). It was not a great financial success and closed in 1896. *See also* COMÉDIE ROSSE.

Theatre Museum A London museum that opened in Covent Garden in 1987 to house materials relating to drama, music hall, opera, ballet, circus, the puppet theatre, and even pop music. It is a branch of the Victoria and Albert Museum, which created the collection in 1974 when materials of the British Theatre Museum Association were transferred to the V & A to join those already held.

The museum maintains a permanent exhibition on the history of the theatre from the 18th century onwards, galleries for temporary exhibitions, research and reading facilities, and a 70-seat theatre. The items on view include playbills, programmes, scripts, costumes (including those of the Diaghilev Ballet), theatrical paintings and engravings, props, and stage designs. Special exhibits include the Hinkins Collection of Toy Theatre sheets, the Houston Rogers Collection of theatrical photographs, and the Anthony Hippisley Coxe Collection of circus materials.

Théâtre National Populaire (TNP) The government-supported French National People's theatre. The original organization of this name, founded in 1920 by Firmin Gémier, occupied premises in the Paris suburb of Chaillot. When he died in 1933, the theatre lay dormant until Jean VILAR, who had founded the Avignon Festival, reestablished it as 'a public service' in 1951. Vilar introduced a number of radical innovations, such as dispensing with the curtain, footlights, and painted scenery. The TNP's administrator, Jean Rouvet, also abolished evening dress and tipping.

Under Vilar the TNP performed a mixed repertoire of French classics, Shakespeare, and such modern works as Brecht's *Mother Courage* and Eliot's *Murder in the Cathedral*. He was succeeded in 1963 by the actor Georges Wilson, who faced dwindling audiences. In 1972 the company's title was transferred to Roger PLANCHON's subsidized provincial company in Lyon. This has since toured nationally with a series of politically radical productions intended to expose the social divisions in modern France. "Our job," Planchon has said, "is to keep the wound open."

Theatre of Cruelty *See* CRUELTY, THEATRE OF.

Theatre of Fact *See* DOCUMENTARY THEATRE.

Theatre of Satire A theatre in Moscow that became noted for its avant-garde staging in the 1950s. It opened in 1924 with a series of revues and subsequently produced works of satire and comedy under Nicolai Gorchakov. In 1954 Valentin Pluchek created a sensation by staging MAYAKOVSKY's *The Bedbug* and *The Bathhouse* in a formalist manner similar to that of V. E. MEYERHOLD, who had been officially denounced under Stalin. Pluchek became artistic director of the theatre in 1957. The Theatre of Satire's resident company transferred to a larger theatre in the 1960s, a move that reflected their success.

Theatre of Silence *See* SILENCE, THEATRE OF.

Theatre of the Ridiculous *See* RIDICULOUS, THEATRE OF THE.

Theatre Royal A title bestowed on the new theatres in DRURY LANE and LINCOLN'S INN FIELDS when they were granted Letters Patent by Charles II in 1662 (*see* PATENT THEATRES). The Lincoln's Inn title eventually passed to COVENT GARDEN. Many provincial British theatres later adopted the name Theatre Royal. The Theatre Royal, Stratford East, was for 20 years (1953–73) the home of Joan Littlewood's THEATRE WORKSHOP.

Theatres Act *See* LICENCE.

theatre time A phrase alluding to the tendency of stage managers to keep backstage clocks running at least five minutes fast, as a safeguard against lateness.

théâtre total A theory of theatrical technique that gained widespread currency in Europe after World War II. According to this theory, responsibility for all matters of interpretation and artistic control lies solely with the director (contrast COLLECTIVE CREATION). Sometimes the director's influence has even been extended to the text itself; Jean-Louis BARRAULT, one of the best-known advocates of *théâtre total*, often had a hand in creating the scripts of his productions.

Theatre Workshop An experimental left-wing drama group founded in Kendal in 1945 by a group of actors dissatisfied with the mainstream theatre. From 1953 the Workshop was based at the Theatre Royal, Stratford East, London, with Joan LITTLEWOOD as artistic director, Gerald Raffles as general manager, and Ewan McColl (Littlewood's husband) as writer or adapter of many of the group's productions. Theatre Workshop sought to revitalize the British theatre with challenging adaptations of the classics and new works dealing with working-class issues. Many of these, including Brendan Behan's *The Quare Fellow* (1956) and Shelagh Delaney's *A Taste of Honey* (1958), later transferred to London's West End. In 1961 Littlewood left the group, disillusioned by the dilution of the radical content of its output as a result of the pressure for commercial success. She did, however, return to direct the occasional production, notably the musical OH, WHAT A LOVELY WAR! (1963). She eventually left the UK in 1975 to work in France; the Workshop disbanded soon afterwards.

Theatrical Phenomenon, the Billing for the 8-year-old child actress Miss Mudie, whose performance in 1805 at Covent Garden in the adult role of Miss Peggy in *The Country Girl* has been called "the most imperfect performance ever witnessed on a London stage". The precocious Miss Mudie, who had received rave reviews in the provinces, enraged a tough London audience when she attempted to play the ludicrously inappropriate role of wife and mistress with the otherwise adult cast. She was tiny for her age and theatregoers found the love scenes she played with the actor John Brunton either absurd or distasteful.

Hissing and cries of "Off! Off!" resulted in Miss Mudie stopping the play, coming forward to confront the audience, and complaining: "Ladies and gentlemen, I have done nothing to offend you, and as for those who are sent here to hiss me, I will be much obliged to you to turn them out." When a further plea from the manager Charles Kemble (*see* KEMBLE FAMILY) fell on deaf ears, an adult actress, Miss Searle, was substituted; nevertheless the uproar continued and the evening ended in chaos.

Kemble was not above enjoying the furore generated by the small girl. When asked if she was really a child, and not, as some alleged, a midget he replied:

> Child! Why, Sir, when I was a very young actor in the York company, that little creature kept an inn at Tadcaster and had a large family of children.

Theatrical Syndicate An organization of US theatrical managers that held a monopoly on productions in the early 20th century. Formed by a group of businessmen in 1896, it took advantage of the country's new railway system to book travelling troupes into venues that had once been dominated by local STOCK COMPANIES. The association began to exert a stranglehold when Charles Frohman arranged a cooperative agreement between the booking agency of Marc Klaw and Abraham Erlanger and two groups that controlled theatres throughout the east and west. Performers were required to sign exclusive contracts that dictated the time and place of bookings. Within seven years, most of the important productions in New York and the regions were controlled by the Syndicate.

This dominance continued for about 16 years and was only broken by the emergence of a new national monopoly. Performers, such as the US actress Minnie Fiske and France's Sarah Bernhardt, began to object to the Syndicate's rough treatment, as did David BELASCO, Frohman's former stage manager, who owned his own Broadway theatre. This encouraged the SHUBERT BROTHERS, Sam, Lee, and Jacob, to build up their own chain of theatres, which, by 1913, had twice the number of the Syndicate. Three years later, the Syndicate disbanded.

theatrum mundi A type of miniature theatre that was used to recreate current events, especially military battles and natural disasters, in the early 19th century. The figures, which were operated by strings, could be moved backwards and forwards along a track through a wing-and-border set. In Britain, a well-known example was Brown's Theatre of Arts, which toured fairs from 1830 to 1840 presenting scenes of Napoleon's campaigns. The *theatrum mundi* was especially popular in Germany. Goethe is known to have possessed one, while a popular venue in the Luisenstrasse, Berlin, presented such attractions as 'The Battle of Schleswig-Holstein'.

Theoric Fund In ancient Athens, a state grant made to poor citizens to allow them to attend the theatre during the DIONYSIA. This small financial assistance was introduced during the rule of Pericles. After being suspended by the Peloponnesian War, it was reinstituted in 394 BC and continued until 338 BC.

Thérèse Raquin A play by Émile Zola, based on his naturalistic novel (1867) of the same name. It was first performed in 1873, setting a fashion for theatrical NATURALISM that spread throughout Europe. It was seen in London in 1891 and subquently revived as *Thou Shalt Not* in 1938 in London and *Thérèse* in 1945 in New York.

The story is set in Paris. Mme Raquin is grieving for her son, whom she believes to have been killed in a boating accident; in fact, he was drowned by his wife Thérèse and her lover, the painter Laurent. With Mme Raquin's approval they marry, but she overhears them discussing the murder and suffers a paralysing stroke. Overcome by guilt, Thérèse and Laurent accuse one another of instigating the crime; the animosity so aroused destroys their love. Mme Raquin recovers sufficiently to explain that she did not denounce them earlier because she wished to see them suffer. Their response is to commit suicide in front of her.

Therukoothu (Tamil. street play) A traditional theatrical genre of south India, popular mainly among the rural and urban lower classes in the state of Tamil Nadu. Its origins are obscure. The most acclaimed troupe is the Raghava Thambiran Company, named after its founding member.

The plays, which are presented in Tamil, are improvised around stories from the *Puranas*. They are performed in any open space, the acting area being designated by tall bamboo posts with colourful banners stretched between. Actors wear skirts of cloth and grass, crowns, colourful ornaments, and blue and red make-up; heroes have waxed moustaches.

The nine-hour entertainment begins with a religious procession. The drama is explained by the *kattiakaran*, a stage manager who also performs comic antics. The actors dance to express emotion or to represent such action as a battle. After the performance members of the audience join the company in walking across hot coals to demonstrate their faith.

About half of the performance is sung. The musicians sit upstage centre and are joined by actors who sing when they are not performing. Accompaniment is by harmonium, *kurukuzhal* (a wind instrument), hand drums, and cymbals.

Thespis (6th century BC) Greek poet, playwright, and chorus leader who is traditionally considered the founder of acting. According to tradition he was the first performer to separate himself from the CHORUS, thereby introducing an element of dialogue to the choric lyric. A native of Icaria in Attica, Thespis won the prize at the first contest for tragedies at the DIONYSIA in 534 BC. None of his works is extant.

It is generally supposed that Thespis, who managed a travelling company, transported his actors in wagons, which also served as their stage. John Dryden wrote:

> Thespis, the first professor of our art,
> At country wakes sang ballads from a
> cart.

The term **thespian**, used as both an adjective and a noun, came into use in the early 19th century to refer to actors and the acting profession. Amateur companies often used the word in their titles, and a Victorian journal of the theatre was called *Theatrical Times, a Weekly Magazine of Thespian Biography*. The term is now mainly used facetiously.

Thieves' Carnival (*Le Bal des voleurs*) An early play by Jean ANOUILH, later classified by the author as one of his *pièces roses*, or romantic light comedies. It was first performed in 1938 in Paris and first seen in English translation in 1952. The director, André Barsacq (1909–73), was so impressed by the potential shown by the young playwright that he chose to direct most of Anouilh's works for the next 10 years.

In the play Lady Hurf willingly allows three confidence tricksters into her home disguised as Spanish grandees. After an appropriate amount of suspicion and confusion, two of them develop romances with her nieces.

This Happy Breed A patriotic play by Noël COWARD, sentimentally extolling the values of the British middle class, from which he himself had sprung. "You must never, never forget your roots," he once told a producer. The work was originally scheduled to open with PRESENT LAUGHTER in 1939 but the plays were postponed when Coward, who intended to star in both, took an intelligence job on the outbreak of World War II. The two plays were finally given a brief run at the Haymarket in 1943, after which they toured the provinces with the original cast of Coward, Joyce Carey, Judy Campbell, and Dennis Price.

The plot provides an episodic history of a lower middle-class family in the London suburb of Clapham from 1919 to 1939. Frank and Ethel Gibbons share a house with Frank's unmarried sister Sylvia, Ethel's mother, and their children Reg, Queenie, and Vi. The play deals mainly with the love affairs and marriages of the three children, and ends with Frank and Ethel moving into a flat with Queenie's illegitimate son.

Thorndike, Dame Sybil (1882–1976) Versatile British actress, who played parts ranging from Shaw's Saint Joan to the fool in *King Lear*. John Gielgud described her as "lively, passionate, argumentative." She was created a DBE in 1931.

The daughter of a clergyman, Sybil began to perform as a child in family plays that she and her brother, Russell, had written. She subsequently studied at Ben Greet's Academy, making her professional debut with his company, the Pastoral Players, in 1904. During her three years with Greet, she performed 112 parts.

She married the actor-director Lewis Casson in 1908 while performing with Annie Horniman's company in Manchester; they appeared together in many plays over a span of 55 years. In 1914 she joined the OLD VIC under Lilian Baylis; during the four years she spent with the company she built up a reputation as one of the foremost tragic actresses of her day. Celebrated roles included Hecuba in *The Trojan Women* (1919) and the title role of *Medea* (1920).

In 1924 she created the title character of Shaw's SAINT JOAN, a part the author had written especially for her. Of the role she later said, "I felt I'd reached something I could never reach again, and I was just so grateful that the audience was there night after night to see me do it."

During World War II, she and her husband took Shakespeare and Greek classical drama to the mining villages of Wales; after one performance of *Medea* an elderly miner told her, "It kindles a fire." In her later years, she created outstanding portraits of elderly women and undertook many demanding overseas tours. In 1963 she was called out of retirement by Laurence Olivier to appear in *Uncle Vanya*, the first production of the National Theatre company. Her last performance, as one of the murderous old women in *Arsenic and Old Lace*, was given at the age of 84.

three. Three Hundred Club *See* STAGE SOCIETY *under* STAGE.

Threepenny Opera, The A musical drama by Bertolt BRECHT and Kurt Weill. The play was first performed in 1928 at the Theater am Schiffbauerdamm in Berlin, where it ran for 4000 performances. Brecht derived the plot from John Gay's THE BEGGAR'S OPERA, but used it to emphasize the corrupting effect of bad social conditions and to satirize contemporary German society. Hitler banned it in 1933, the year that it flopped in New York. Duke Ellington later wrote a version for Broadway entitled *Beggar's Holiday* (1946). Brecht's original was finally performed successfully off-Broadway in 1954 and ran for 2611 performances; the first London production followed in 1956 at the Royal Court Theatre. The musical's opening song 'Mack the Knife' became an international hit.

Three Sisters Anton CHEKHOV's poignant drama of lost illusions and thwarted hopes. It was first presented in 1901 at the MOSCOW ART THEATRE; the cast included Chekhov's actress wife, Olga Knipper-Chekhova, and STANISLAVSKY, who also directed. The play was not seen in London until 1926. A highly acclaimed modern production was Peter Ashmore's 1951 version, starring Ralph Richardson and Margaret Leighton. In 1991 the sisters were played for the first time by three members of the same family – Vanessa REDGRAVE, her sister Lynn, and Vanessa's daughter Natasha Richardson.

The story concerns the three Prozorov sisters, Olga, Masha, and Irina, who live a dreary provincial life with their brother in a large country house in the north of Russia. All three reminisce wistfully about their happy childhood in Moscow and talk of the great day when they will return. The arrival of a military unit seems to offer a way out of their constricted existence, but the lieutenant Irina hopes to marry is killed in a duel and Masha's love affair with a married officer ends when the troops move on. Meanwhile Olga is promoted to headmistress of the local school and abandons her dream of moving to Moscow. Despite the failure of all their hopes, the sisters face the future with determination.

> IRINA A time will come when people will understand what it was all for, what the purpose was of all this suffering, and what was hidden from us will be hidden no more. In the meantime, though, we have to live...

throwline A thin rope used to join together FLATS and other parts of a set. The usual US term is **lashline**.

thrust stage A stage that extends forwards into the auditorium, with seating on three sides. This arrangement, also called an **open stage**, can improve the interaction between the actors and the audience. It resembles the **platform stage** of the Elizabethan and Restoration theatre, thereby permitting more authentic revivals of work from the early modern period.

thunder. *Thunder Rock* An allegorical antiwar play by the US dramatist Robert Ardrey. It was first performed in 1939 in New York by the GROUP THEATRE. The first London production, which starred Michael Redgrave, opened in 1940 at The Neighbourhood, a fringe theatre in Kensington, before transferring to the Globe Theatre. The plot concerns Charleston, a young lighthouse keeper, who faces the approach of World War while being haunted by the ghosts of those drowned in a shipwreck a century earlier.

The London production was performed at the height of the Blitz. When the air-raid warnings sounded, Redgrave would stop the drama, walk to the front of the stage and offer to entertain the audience "in a rather more basic manner" until the all-clear. He would then give rousing renditions of music-hall and wartime songs, such as 'Run, Rabbit, Run' and 'We're Going to

Hang Out the Washing on the Siegfried Line'. These performances were soon the talk of London, and members of the audience from other theatres began to swell the ranks of the Globe whenever a siren sounded. For many it was a disappointment when the performance of *Thunder Rock* resumed.

steal one's thunder To reduce the effect of a person's words or actions by forestalling them. It originated from an incident involving the English playwright and critic John Dennis (*see* APPIUS). Dennis was the inventor of the **thunder-run**, a device in which cannon balls were rolled down wooden troughs to create a sound effect for thunder (*see* SOUND EFFECTS).

He introduced the thunder-run in his drama *Appius and Virginia*, which was produced at Drury Lane in 1709 but was taken off after a few performances. Soon afterwards, while watching *Macbeth* at the same theatre, Dennis heard his thunder-maker in action. He leaped up, faced the audience, and yelled, "The villians! That's my thunder they're using. They won't play my play, but they will steal my thunder!"

Ticket-of-Leave Man, The A contemporary melodrama by the British playwright Tom TAYLOR, which featured the first stage detective and the first set of a London restaurant. Adapted from *Léonard* by Edouard Brisbarre and Eugène Nus, it was first performed in 1863 and had a considerable influence on later writers of melodrama.

The story involves Robert Brierly, a naive young Lancastrian, who arrives in London and falls in with the low-life character James Dalton. Brierly is arrested and imprisoned for innocently passing counterfeit money given to him by Dalton. After serving a year, he receives a 'ticket of leave' for good conduct. Despite losing his job and sinking into poverty, he resists Dalton's attempts to lure him back into crime. Instead, he works with Detective Hawkshaw to bring Dalton to justice.

Tidings Brought to Mary, The (*L'Annonce faite à Marie*) A poetic drama in the style of a medieval mystery play by the French poet and playwright Paul Claudel (1868–1955). Often considered his best work for the stage, it was first performed in 1912 in Paris, then seen in London two years later in a production by the Pioneer Players under Edith Craig (*see* CRAIG FAMILY). It was not produced in America until 1923, when its complex structure provided an opportunity for experimental staging.

The play is based on Claudel's earlier work *La Jeune Fille Violaine*, (1898). It involves Violaine, an innocent young woman who contracts leprosy after miraculously curing a victim of the disease.

TIE Theatre in Education. A British movement, founded in 1965 at the BELGRADE THEATRE, Coventry, to establish companies to perform in schools. Since then, the use of drama as an educational tool has spread throughout the country. Equivalent movements have been established in America, Canada, and Australia.

The companies, which receive funding from local education authorities, use drama to illuminate subjects ranging from social history to racism, and the dangers of drug abuse. They also provide information about the theatre itself. Audience participation is usually encouraged and students are often involved in making decisions about the content and staging of the play.

TIE has also provided an outlet for new writing: Willy Russell's successful musical BLOOD BROTHERS was originally a Theatre-in-Education production.

Some well-known London TIE companies are the Half Moon, Greenwich Young People's Theatre, Curtain Theatre, and the Cockpit. Provincial companies include Pit Prop in Wigan, Theatre Venture in Newham, and Theatre Foundry in Wolverhampton. Some of Britain's best-known theatres, including the National Theatre and the Theatre Royal, Stratford East, also do educational work.

Tiger at the Gates (*La Guerre de Troie n'aura pas lieu*). A play by Jean GIRAUDOUX, first performed in 1935 in Paris. It did not open in London until 1955, when it was seen at the Apollo Theatre in a translation by Christopher Fry. Michael Redgrave, who starred as Hector, gave a performance described by Kenneth Tynan as "a monumental piece of acting". He went on to play the role at New York's Plymouth Theatre, receiving the New York Drama Critics' Award for 1955.

The play, which is set during the Trojan War, explored the conflict between pacifism and patriotism. Hector, Troy's greatest hero, returns from war intent on keeping the peace. However, he soon learns that the Greeks, under Odysseus, are coming to try to force his brother, Paris, to release the abducted Helen. Although the populace, urged on by the war-mongering poet Demokos, cries out for battle Hector negotiates with Odysseus for the return of Helen. However, when Demokos falsely claims to have been attacked by the Greek Ajax this further inflames Trojan passions and war becomes inevitable.

Tilley, Vesta (Matilda Alice Victoria Powles, 1864–1952) The most famous male impersonator in British music hall. She made her provincial debut at the age of four and her first London appearance ten years later as 'The Great Little Tilley', singing such songs as 'Following in Father's Footsteps' and 'Near the Workhouse Door'.

Although famous for her tailored masculine attire, she sang such hits as 'After the Ball' and 'Jolly Good Luck to the Girl Who Loves a Soldier' in a very feminine soprano voice. Well known for her impersonations of soldiers, she helped to recruit during World War I by donning uniform to sing 'The Army of Today's All Right'. She also performed as a principal boy in pantomimes, usually at Drury Lane. After her retirement in 1920 she spent the remaining 30 years of her life as a charity worker.

time. ***Time and the Conways*** A play by J. B. PRIESTLEY, published in 1937 with I HAVE BEEN HERE BEFORE as *Two Time Plays*. They were both performed that year in London at the Duchess Theatre. The story centres upon the middle-class Conway family. In the first act, set in 1919, the widowed Mrs Conway and her six children gather to celebrate the 21st birthday of Kay, one of the daughters, who hopes to be a novelist. The second act moves to 1937 to contrast their earlier hopes with reality: they variously face money problems, disappointed ambitions, and failed marriages, while one of the daughters has died. The third act returns to 1919. Kay's brother, Alan, explains his theory of time as a continuum, and this helps them to accept their changing world.

Time and Time Again A comedy by Alan AYCKBOURN, first performed in 1971 at Scarborough's Stephen Joseph Theatre-in-the-Round (where Ayckbourn is artistic director) and subsequently transferring to the Comedy Theatre, London. The play, set in a suburban family garden, involves Anna and her husband Graham, who have inherited her mother's house. Unfortunately the property is occupied by her eccentric brother Leonard, who gardens endlessly and talks to the resident gnome. When the sports-loving Peter and his fiancée Joan come to visit, Graham makes several passes at her, only to see Joan fall for the unworldly Leonard.

Time of Your Life, The The second play by the US dramatist William SAROYAN. It was first performed in 1939 in New York, winning the New York Drama Critics' Award and the 1940 Pulitzer Prize, which Saroyan refused. A 1948 filmed version starred James Cagney and William Bendix.

The play is set in a waterfront bar in San Francisco. The regulars are a crowd of lovable eccentrics whose conversation reflects Saroyan's belief in the value of the weak, poor, and obscure members of society.

Timon of Athens A little-known tragedy by SHAKESPEARE, written between 1604 and 1608. No performances are recorded until 1678, when Thomas Shadwell presented an adaptation entitled *The Man-Hater*. Shakespeare's version does not seem to have been revived in London until 1851, when Samuel Phelps produced it at Sadler's Wells Theatre. Some scholars believe that the loose plot, uneven writing, and thin characterization indicate that the surviving play is a draft or incomplete version.

More recently, Paul Scofield won acclaim for his performance as the misanthropic Timon in a 1965 Stratford production, while Peter BROOK chose the play as the first full-scale production for the International Centre for Theatre Research in Paris (1970).

The plot centres upon Timon, a rich Athenian noble noted for his generous benefactions. When his funds become depleted, he asks his friends for help but they all turn him down. Stung by their ingratitude, he invites them to a feast where the beautiful covered dishes turn out to contain warm water. Timon turns his back on the city to become a misanthropic hermit. While digging for roots one day, he finds gold, which he gives to the rebel general Alcibiades, who is about to lead an army against Athens. The corrupt senators visit Timon's cave and beg him for help but he refuses. Soon afterwards he dies and is buried on the seashore. Alcibiades takes the city and offers peace.

Tingeltangel A type of cheap music hall in Berlin in the late 19th and early 20th centuries. The most successful included the Singspielhalle, the Kuhstall, the Silberhalle and Elysium, and the Klosterstiebel. The name came from the title of a comic song made famous by the performer Tange at the Triangel Theater. The entertainment, designed for an audience of male students and workers, consisted mainly of ribald songs performed by female singers to piano accompaniment. The audience would sing along and goosestep backwards and forwards around the small stage.

Tinker Bell In J. M. Barrie's children's play PETER PAN (1904), a female fairy who accompanies Peter and the Darling children on their adventures. When she 'dies', the audience is required to declare its belief in fairies in order to bring her back to life.

tiring house or **tire house** The wardrobe room in an Elizabethan theatre. The name derives from *attire*. The theatre employee in charge of the wardrobe was called the *tireman*; besides looking after costumes, he often provided stools for members of the audience and attended to the lights.

'Tis Pity She's a Whore John FORD's violent tragedy of incestuous love, first performed in 1627 in London. The play presents a largely sympathetic picture of the doomed relationship between Giovanni and his sister Annabella. When Annabella weds her suitor Soranzo, he is enraged to find that she is already pregnant. On discovering that her brother was responsible, he invites Giovanni to a feast intending to kill him. Giovanni acts first, however, killing his sister and returning to the table with her heart impaled on his dagger. He then slays Soranzo, upon which he is in turn killed by Soranzo's followers.

Titania In Shakespeare's A MIDSUMMER NIGHT'S DREAM the wife of OBERON and Queen of the Fairies. The name was used by Ovid in his *Metamorphoses* for Diana, Circe, and other female descendants of the Titans.

Titus Andronicus SHAKESPEARE's first tragedy, a brutal and sometimes absurd work in which nearly all of the characters die a violent death. It was first performed in 1593 in London. Because of its crudeness, scholars have sometimes tried to attribute the play to another author. It was not performed at Stratford until 1955, making it the last of Shakespeare's works to be staged there; OLIVIER played the demented Titus with Peter BROOK directing.

In the story, which is set in ancient Rome, the emperor Saturninus and his wife Tamora determine to destroy the general Titus Andronicus. Tamora's sons rape and maim his daughter, Lavinia, cutting off her hands and tongue, and two of Titus's sons are falsely condemned to death. In revenge, Titus kills Tamora's sons and bakes them in a pie, which he serves to her and Saturninus. Titus then kills his shamed daughter and Tamora before being slain by Saturninus who, in turn, is killed by Titus's remaining son. The play is notorious for its grisly stage directions, which include:

> Enter a messenger, with two heads and a hand.
>
> She takes the staff in her mouth and guides it with her stumps.

Olivier, who was accident prone, once took a frightening backward fall down a flight of stairs during the play. He told Anthony Quayle that the worst thing about the role was having to complain all the time:

> What you hate about Titus, he's always going 'oh, oh, oh, fancy them doing that to me, oh, oh, oh.' And how many ways are there of saying 'oh, oh'? It's very tough on your imagination, it's very tough on your resourcefulness of variations of all kinds, and, therefore, it's also a very great strain physically.

Quayle nodded and replied, "Othello is all of that *and* you have to black up as well."

Tiv, the Nickname for the Tivoli Music Hall in the Strand, London. It was named after the beer-hall that had previously stood on the site. The Tiv opened in 1890 but was unsuccessful until Charles MORTON, the so-called Father of the Halls, was hired to manage it three years later. Under his direction it became one of the country's top music halls. When this type of entertainment waned, however, the Tiv closed in 1914 and was demolished to make way for a cinema.

Toby In Britain, the name given to the live dog that features in the PUNCH AND JUDY show; in America, a stock character in the early 20th-century TENT SHOWS.

The dog Toby began to appear in Punch and Judy shows in the first half of the 19th century. His name was probably derived from the biblical story of Tobias, a favourite subject for puppeteers, in which a dog appears. Punch and Judy are usually accompanied by a sprightly terrier wearing a ruff, sometimes with bells on. He sits on the ledge of the booth during the performance and afterwards circulates amongst the audience to collect money in a small bag carried in his mouth.

In US tent-shows, Toby was a naive country bumpkin with a freckled face and blacked-out front tooth, who wore a red wig, a calico shirt, and farmer's working jeans. Despite his simplicity, he usually managed to triumph over the sophisticated 'city slicker'. Eventually a female companion, **Susie**, was added. The performer who played the role needed considerable gymnastic abilities, because of the many comic falls involved. The part is still played sporadically in rural areas.

togata In the ancient Roman theatre, a type of FABULA that superseded the PALLIATA in the 2nd century BC. The name came from *toga*, the traditional garment of the Roman citizen. Also known as the *tabernaria*, the genre had fewer actors and simpler plots than the *palliata*; it was also more satirical, lampooning the urban lower classes in their everyday life.

The leading writer of the *togata*, with 44 works to his credit, was Lucius Afranius (2nd century BC), who is thought to be the first dramatist to introduce the subject of homosexuality on stage. Other exponents of the genre included Titus Quintius Atta (d. 77 BC), noted for his characterization of women, and Titinius (2nd century BC), who was influenced by Menander. Only fragments of their comedies survive.

Toller, Ernst (1893–1939) German playwright and poet, who pioneered expressionism in the theatre. His earliest and most important plays were written during the five years (1919–24) he spent in prison for leading strikes and demonstrations in post-war Munich. The first of these works to be produced was *Die Wandlung* (*Transfiguration*), which was staged in Berlin in 1919. Based loosely on the events of Toller's own life, it depicts the evolution of an enthusiastic volunteer soldier into a revolutionary pacifist. *Masse-Mensch* (*Man and the Masses*), first seen at the Volksbühne in 1920, showed working men rebelling against their condition of near-slavery. It was also one of the first modern dramas to introduce the *Sprechchor*, or speaking chorus.

A number of Toller's plays dealt with historical subjects. The verse play *Die Maschinenstürmer* (*The Machine Wreckers*; 1922) explored the causes of the Luddite riots of 1815, while *Feuer aus den Kesseln* (*Draw the Fires!*; 1930) depicted the 1917 Kiel mutiny that helped to spark the Bolshevik revolution. Another major work was *Hoppla, wir leben!* (*Hurrah, we Live!*; 1927), staged in 1929 as *Hoppla!* at the Gate Theatre, London. The protagonist commits suicide when he discovers that the former revolutionaries are now living comfortable and satisfied lives.

When the Nazis took control in 1933, Toller was driven into exile. He committed suicide in New York shortly after Germany's invasion of Czechoslovakia.

Tollu Bommalu A popular form of shadow-puppet theatre in the southern Indian state of Andhra Pradesh. According to tradition it began in 200 BC, but evidence only dates back to the 16th century. Stories are taken from the *Ramayana*, the *Mahabharata*, and the *Puranas*. The leather puppets have movable parts; they are translucent and dyed with black, red, and green pigments. More than one figure may be used for the same character.

The puppeteers use thorns to pin the figures onto a white screen stretched between two poles. The chief manipulator wears a set of bells on one ankle to jingle during dance sequences. The improvised dialogue is interspersed with songs from classical and folk traditions as well as from Indian films.

Performances last from four to eight hours; the chief divisions are the introduction of characters, songs sung in homage to Hindu deities, a comic interlude between the drunken Katikayata and his fat wife Bangavaka, and the main drama.

Tom Thumb Originally, the tiny hero of an old nursery tale, popular in the 16th century. *The History of Tom Thumb* was published by Richard Johnson in 1621.

General Tom Thumb was the name given to the US DWARF Charles Sherwood Stratton (1838–83) when first exhibited by Phineas T. BARNUM. The 'General' was then under five years of age and less than 24 inches in height but eventually grew to 40 inches. When in London he was summoned to Buckingham Palace by Queen Victoria and subsequently visited King Louis Philippe in France. He married another US dwarf, Lavinia Warren in 1863.

Tom Thumb the Great A BURLESQUE by the novelist and dramatist Henry Fielding, first performed in London in 1730. The full title was *The Life and Death of Tom Thumb the Great; or, the Tragedy of Tragedies.* The tiny figure of Tom Thumb was used to mock the bombastic heroes of contemporary tragedy. Other characters included Mr Noodle, Mr Doodle, Queen Dollaholla, and Mustacha. Tom becomes engaged to Princess Huncamunca but after defeating his rival Lord Grizzle, he is eaten by a cow. In the final 12 lines of the play all remaining nine characters are killed, including Tom's ghost.

Too True to be Good A play by George Bernard SHAW. One of his last works, it was first performed in 1932 in Boston when Shaw was 76 years old. There is little plot. Instead, the characters, who include a thinly disguised caricature of Lawrence of Arabia (*see* MEEK, PRIVATE NAPOLEON ALEXANDER TROTSKY), take part in lengthy debates about the virtues and vices of capitalism and the sorry moral state of mankind.

top drop *See* BORDER.

Torelli, Giacomo *See* GREAT MAGICIAN *under* GREAT.

Torres Naharro, Bartolomé de (*c.* 1485–*c.* 1524) One of Spain's first important dramatists. He founded the comic tradition in the Spanish theatre (although his comedies were so bawdy they were banned by the Church) and wrote the first published Renaissance theory of drama.

Torres Naharro was ordained as a young man and spent much of his adult life in service to noblemen in Italy. His plays were published in 1517 in one volume, *Propalladia*. In the preface he divided his plays into *comedias a noticia*, involving things "noted and seen in true reality", and *comedias a fantasía*, about things "fantastic or feigned, which though not true have the colour of truth". His realistic works included *Comedia soldadesca*, concerning a bragging Spanish captain, and *Comedia tinellaria*, about the lives of servants in an Italian palace. An example of his fantastic plays is *Comedia Himenea*, his most famous work; based on LA CELESTINA by Fernando de Rojas, the piece foreshadows the later CLOAK-AND-SWORD PLAY.

Touch of the Poet, A A play by the US dramatist Eugene O'NEILL. It was written in about 1940 and first performed in 1957 in Stockholm. Helen Hayes starred in the original Broadway production, while Jason Robards Jr won great acclaim in a 1977 revival. The story involves the growing cultural gap between Con Melody, an immigrant, and his US-born son.

The drama was intended to be one of an 11-play cycle about the same family, tracing its fortunes from the early 19th to the mid 20th century. Although outlines of several others were drawn up, *A Touch of the Poet* was the only play completed before a crippling disease brought O'Neill's writing career to an end.

touring company A theatre company that travels to different venues, either with a single hit play or with a more varied repertory. This may be on a set CIRCUIT within range of its home city or theatre, but often involves venturing into unknown territory. If the company is financially secure, it may be accompanied by elaborate scenery and its own technicians. Touring is as old as the early Western theatre, being a feature of the 16th-century COMMEDIA DELL'ARTE. Before West End plays came to rely upon tourists, productions were often tried out on provincial tours before they were seen in the capital. Likewise, many West End hits would subsequently tour the provinces rather than move to Broadway. In modern Britain touring companies have proliferated with the decline of REPERTORY companies.

Noël COWARD was a veteran tourer who often squabbled with fellow actors on the road. One of the worst incidents occurred early in his career, when he toured with Esme Wynn Stoj and Arnold Raynor in *Charlie's Aunt*. The producer, knowing that Coward was a homosexual, insisted that he share a room with the actress as if he shared with Raynor this might give the company a bad name. Coward and Stoj had their first row when he used her make-up; after several further disagreements, she threw a punch at him backstage, knocking him to the floor just before his entrance in Act III. Coward staggered on stage and afterwards cornered Stoj in her dressing room, where the fist fight continued, with Coward getting much the worst of it. Only when Raynor dashed in and hit Stoj on the head with a hairbrush did they all make up.

toy. ***Toys in the Attic*** A play by Lillian HELLMAN, first performed in 1950 in New York. A 1963 film version starred Geraldine Page and Dean Martin. The drama is set in New Orleans and concerns two middle-aged spinsters, Carrie and Anna Berniers, who live together in their old family home. For years they have gladly sent money to their younger brother Julian, who has not contacted them since his marriage to the emotional Lily. They are disconcerted when he suddenly arrives with $150,000 and tickets for a European holiday for the sisters. He has profited from an investment tip from an old girlfriend, and Lily is frightened she will lose him. However, when Julian is robbed and beaten, the sisters happily resume their old routine of supporting him.

toy theatre A type of children's play theatre that became very popular in the mid 19th century. With their accurate replicas of contemporary sets and costumes, the toy theatres are now a valuable source of information for researchers. The child constructed the theatre by cutting out drawings from a sheet and mounting them on cardboard. Figures representing popular actors and actresses could then be drawn across the stage on metal slides. Simplified texts of well-known plays were also available, so the child could present a complete performance.

The first toy theatre sheets were issued in 1811 by William West; between 1815 and 1835 some 50 publishers are known to have existed. The sheets, available in penny-plain and twopence-coloured versions, covered about 300 plays, including Boucicault's *The Corsican Brothers* and Pocock's *The Miller and His Men*. The original blocks were being used to print sheets as recently as 1932.

Miniature theatres for children were also popular in Europe, especially in Germany, Denmark, and Spain, but these only reproduced juvenile drama.

trabeata See FABULA.

Trachiniae (*The Women of Trachis*) A tragedy by SOPHOCLES, first performed in about 420 BC in Athens. It shows the influence of EURIPIDES in its use of a Prologue and in the reduced role given to the chorus; there are also specific similarities to the plot of MEDEA. Sophocles was criticized for using a plot in which one of the two main characters (Deianira) commits suicide two thirds of the way through the play, and the other (Heracles, her husband) does not appear on stage until after that event.

The story begins with Deianira waiting patiently for Heracles to return from battle. First, however, he ravages a city, killing its men and sending a captured girl back to live with Deianira as his mistress. Hoping to regain his affection, Deianira sends him a shirt soaked in what she believes to be a love potion; in fact, it is a deadly poison supplied by an enemy of Heracles. When she learns the truth Deianira kills herself. Finally Heracles arrives in mortal torment and dies.

Sophocles made the wronged wife Deianira a moving and fascinating character, who has been called "one of the most delicately beautiful creations in literature". By contrast the great hero Heracles emerges as a somewhat inglorious character. The Women of Trachis act as the chorus of the play.

tragedy A serious play with an unhappy ending. The word means, literally, a goat-song (Gr. *tragos*, goat; *ode*, song), though why the form should be so called is not clear.

It was Aristotle (in his *Poetics*) who said that tragedy should move one "by pity and terror" (*see* CATHARSIS):

> The plot ought to be so constructed that, even without the aid of the eye, he who hears the tale told will thrill with horror and melt to pity at what takes place.

The genre developed in ancient Greece, where tragedies were expected to follow a fairly strict form. Tragic protagonists were drawn only from deities, royalty, and the upper classes, and their inevitable suffering and downfall was brought about by a combination of fate and their own HUBRIS. The three great authors of classical tragedy were AESCHYLUS, SOPHOCLES, and EURIPIDES, all of whom wrote in the 5th century BC.

The rules of classical tragedy were rediscovered at the Renaissance, as were many of the Greek and Roman texts. The gory tragedies of the Roman SENECA proved particularly influential on the playwrights of the time. Typically, the tragedies of the Elizabethan and Jacobean eras combined violent and sensational action with acute psychological insight and intense poetry. The great tragedies of SHAKESPEARE are usually considered the pinnacle of world drama. In the 17th century the Frenchmen CORNEILLE and RACINE led a return to the stricter Greek forms of tragedy.

Thereafter the tradition of serious tragic writing declined, being largely displaced by sentiment and MELODRAMA. It did not revive until the late 19th century, when such writers as IBSEN, STRINDBERG, and CHEKHOV managed to combine the sombre themes and moral seriousness of tragedy with a realistic depiction of contemporary life. Perhaps the only modern writer to attempt the classic tragic form was the US dramatist Eugene O'NEILL.

tragedian An actor who specializes in tragic roles; the equivalent term for an actress is **tragedienne**. The term now has a somewhat old-fashioned or facetious ring. The leading character in a STOCK COMPANY was called the Tragedian.

tragédie-Bourgeosie *See* DRAME *under* DRAMA.

tragic carpet In the 17th-century English theatre, a green baize cloth that was traditionally spread on the dusty stage boards during a tragedy to protect actors' clothes when their characters collapsed and died. The practice, often mentioned in theatrical memoirs, continued into the 19th century.

tragicomedy A genre that blends elements of tragedy and comedy. Tragicomedies tend to fall into two main categories; those in which a potentially tragic series of events is resolved happily and those in which the comedy has dark or bitter overtones.

Although the form can be traced back to EURIPIDES and PLAUTUS, tragicomedy first emerged as a recognizable genre in the Renaissance. In Spain, Fernando de Rojas's frequently staged dialogue novel LA CELESTINA (1499) was subtitled the *Tragicomedia de Calisto y Melibea*, while in 16th-century Italy the term was applied to several plays by Giovanni Giraldi (*see* CINTHIO, IL). A number of Shakespeare's works – most notably, perhaps, THE MERCHANT OF VENICE, MEASURE FOR MEASURE, TROILUS AND CRESSIDA, and CYMBELINE – are regularly described as tragicomedies.

Many PASTORAL works of the 16th and 17th centuries are essentially romantic tragicomedies. The first French tragicomedy, Robert Garnier's *Bradamante*, was published in 1582. Alexandre Hardy (*c.* 1575–*c.* 1632) developed the genre in the early 17th century, influencing his countrymen Molière and Corneille, whose LE CID (1637) has been called the perfect tragicomedy. He was also imitated by the Jacobean and Caroline dramatists in England. The last example of a romantic tragicomedy in English is probably Dryden's *Secret Love, or the Maiden Queen* (1667).

Although it has disappeared as a distinct genre, tragicomedy has arguably become the dominant mode of serious dramatic writing in the 20th century. The works of CHEKHOV, O'CASEY, BRECHT, BECKETT, and PINTER could all be described as tragicomic.

transformation scene A sudden and spectacular change of scene in the English PANTOMIME. It is usually effected using such devices as FALLING FLAPS, RISE-AND-SINK mechanisms, and transparent backcloths (*see* TRANSPARENCY). The purpose is generally to suggest a magical transformation, such as the transportation of Aladdin's castle by the sorceror Abanazer.

transparency A piece of gauze, linen, or other thin fabric that can be made to appear either transparent or opaque. If a backcloth made of such material is painted with a transparent dye and lit from the front it appears to be a normal painted scene, but if lit from behind the fabric becomes transparent, revealing whatever lies behind. If a transparency is gradually illuminated from behind, the original scene fades or is supplemented by additional painting on the back. This can create such illusions as bare winter trees blossoming in spring or a house suddenly catching on fire.

The US stage designer Lee Simonson (1888–1967) used transparencies to great effect in the original 1949 Broadway production of Arthur Miller's *Death of a Salesman*.

transpontine melodrama A derogatory term for a crudely sensational play. In 19th-century London the word transpontine, meaning 'across a bridge', was applied to the MELODRAMAS produced on the south side of the Thames at such theatres as the Old Vic and the Surrey. By the turn of the century, the label was applied to any sensational work; in 1901 a reviewer in *The Scotsman* wrote of "a new drama strongly seasoned with transpontine flavour".

trap An opening cut into the stage floor or scenery to allow actors to appear suddenly and dramatically on stage. They were often used for the entrances and exits of ghosts in 19th-century melodrama. The device made English actors internationally renowned for their TRICKWORK. Traps are also used to raise and lower stage equipment and for rapid scenery changes in pantomime.

Traps became established in the English theatre in the late 17th century, the Drury Lane stage having several. It was not until the 19th century, however, that the SLOTE and the corner trap became favourite devices for moving actors quickly on or off stage.

Particular kinds of trap were often named after a play or scene. The long narrow **Corsican trap** (a type of GHOST GLIDE) was devised to make a ghost appear to float across the stage in Boucicault's THE CORSICAN BROTHERS (1852). The VAMP TRAP, an opening with spring-leaves used to create the impression of an actor passing through a solid wall, was first used in the melodrama *The Vampire* (1820). The **cauldron trap** was named after its use in the witches' scene in *Macbeth*, and the **grave trap** after the gravediggers' scene in *Hamlet*.

Other traps included the STAR TRAP, which opened in the shape of a star, and the **bristle trap**, an opening covered with flexible bristles. The **footlights trap**, a long opening in front of the curtain, was used to lower lamps into the cellar, either to darken the stage or so that they could be trimmed.

Traps could be a source of considerable danger to performers. During one scene in *The Fire Worshippers*, a melodrama presented at the Surrey Theatre, an actor was required to ride across the stage on a live camel. Unfortunately the animal's weight released a trapdoor and, although the actor leaped safely away, the camel fell through and broke its neck. The play proceeded as workmen cut the dead animal out piecemeal from below.

The casualty rate among pantomime stars was especially great. When the great clown GRIMALDI was shot up through a trap one night in Manchester the ropes on the counterweight broke and he tumbled back into the cellar. Stunned and in dreadful pain, he completed the scene. When the company reached Liverpool, Grimaldi got a pledge from the master carpenter that the accident would not be repeated. However, just as his head appeared above stage to great applause, the ropes again snapped, dropping the clown into the machinery below.

traveller. traveller, the In the late 19th-century British theatre, the nickname for a sliding CURTAIN pulled across the back of a stage to allow scenery to be changed while the action continued in front.

Traveller Without Luggage, The The play that gave Jean ANOUILH his first great success. One of his melancholy *pièces noires*, it was first produced in 1937 by Georges Pitöeff (1885–1939) at the Théâtre des Mathurins, Paris. The title refers to an ex-soldier who is suffering from amnesia. When he finally learns the facts about his disreputable youth, he decides to concoct a new identity to escape his past. Anouilh's own early life is reflected in the numerous bitter references to the effects of poverty.

Travers, Ben (1886–1980) British playwright, who was the king of farce in the 1920s. He wrote his first, *The Dippers*, in 1922. His subsequent comedies were known as the *Aldwych farces*, being first performed at the ALDWYCH THEATRE, London. This series began with three works acknowledged as his best: A CUCKOO IN THE NEST (1925), ROOKERY NOOK (1926), which ran for 409 performances, and *Thark* (1927), which was included in the National Theatre's opening repertory in 1976. While *Plunder* (1928) was his last great success, Travers continued to write such farces as *A Bit of a Test* (1933) and *Banana Ridge* (1939). His last, *The Bed Before Yesterday* (1975), was produced in his 90th year. Travers enjoyed the longest career of any playwright in the British theatre, exceeding even that of George Bernard Shaw.

Travesties A comedy about politics, art, and memory by Tom STOPPARD, first performed in London by the Royal Shakespeare Company in 1974. The production, directed by Peter Ward, opened at The Place before transferring to the Aldwych Theatre. *Travesties* consolidated Stoppard's reputation as a writer with an amazing flair for witty dialogue and intricate plot construction.

The story is based on the memories of Henry Carr, a retired diplomat who served as a British consulate official in Zürich during World War I, when the city was also home to Lenin, James Joyce, and the Dadaist Tristan Tzara. Carr recalls playing Algy in an amateur production, organized by Joyce, of Oscar Wilde's *The Importance of Being Earnest*. This allows Stoppard to set up a dazzling series of parallels between the action of Wilde's play and events in Zürich. Literary and other confusions abound, with Lenin's writings getting mixed up with sections of Joyce's *Ulysses*. Carr becomes embroiled in a trivial legal battle with Joyce over production expenses and fails to prevent Lenin from leaving for Russia and a date with destiny. Like the title characters in Stoppard's earlier ROSENCRANTZ AND GUILDENSTERN ARE DEAD, he remains unaware to the end of the significance of the events taking place around him.

Tree, Sir Herbert (Draper) Beerbohm (1853–1917) British actor-manager, a flamboyant showman who excelled in large-than-life costume roles. The half-brother of the caricaturist and critic Sir Max BEERBOHM, Tree made his acting debut in 1878. His first real success did not come until 1884, when he played the Rev. Robert Spalding in Charles Hawtrey's popular farce *The Private Secretary*.

Tree became manager of the Comedy Theatre in 1887 before moving later that year to the more prestigious HAYMARKET THEATRE, where he remained for nine years. At the Haymarket, Tree staged works by Ibsen, Wilde, and Shakespeare, enjoying an enormous personal success as Falstaff and an equally resounding failure as Hamlet: a performance damningly described by W. S. Gilbert as "funny without being vulgar".

Tree's success at the Haymarket enabled him to build Her Majesty's Theatre, where between 1897 and 1915 he staged a series of lavish Shakespearean productions. As an actor, Tree enjoyed two major successes at Her Majesty's: the first, playing Fagin in an adaptation of *Oliver Twist* (1905) and the second, as Henry Higgins in Shaw's *Pygmalion* (1914).

Tree was married to the actress Helen Maud Holt (1863–1937), by whom he had three children; he also had a further six children by a woman called May Pinney, with whom he appears to have conducted a simultaneous family life. A minor actress, Muriel Ridley, gave birth to Tree's last child in 1917.

Tree, who was knighted in 1909, is also remembered for founding the Royal College of Dramatic Art (*see* RADA) in 1904. *See also* RICHARD III.

tree border *See* BORDER.

trickwork A general term for stage devices that create illusions. One of the earliest records of trickwork describes how a garden scene was suddenly changed into a house during a production at Covent Garden in 1743. The art depended heavily upon the use of TRAPS, which allowed actors to appear as if from nowhere, or to pass through apparently solid walls, etc.

Trickwork was especially popular during the Victorian era, when British actors became famous throughout Europe and America for the tumbling and other acrobatic skills that were required by many of the commonest illusions. Two popular feats were the **roll-out**, in which an actor rolled through loose canvas at the bottom of the scenery to appear as if from thin air, and what was probably the most difficult physical stunt, the **leap**, an acrobatic jump up through a hidden opening in the scenery. Trickwork is still sometimes seen in pantomime.

trilogy *See* TETRALOGY.

tritagonist *See* PROTAGONIST.

Triumph of Horus, The or ***Abydos Passion Play*** An Egyptian drama written around 3200 BC and usually considered the world's oldest known play. Although a few scholars discount this claim, saying it was a religious ceremony rather than a true drama, it seems clear that some type of dramatic performance did take place in Abydos as part of the worship of Osiris. Our knowledge of the play comes from a papyrus account written by Ikhernofret, a performer of the 19th century BC, that was found at Luxor, the ancient Thebes. Professional actors apparently played the leading roles and pilgrims the minor parts.

The play concerns the death, burial, and resurrection of Osiris. At the start of the play he has married his sister, Isis, and is ruler of Egypt. His evil brother, Set, is jealous of Osiris's power and murders him, scattering his limbs far and wide. Isis and their son, Horus, gather the pieces together and resurrect Osiris, who goes to dwell in the afterworld to become the judge of souls. Horus fights and defeats Set, and the drama ends with his coronation as king of Egypt.

Triumvirate, the The celebrated partnership of the three managers Colley Cibber, Robert Wilks, and Thomas Doggett, who took over the running of DRURY LANE in 1710. Barton Booth later replaced Doggett. Under the triumvirate arrangement, which lasted until 1733, the theatre prospered as never before.

Troilus and Cressida SHAKESPEARE's bitter tragicomedy of war and sex, which was probably written in 1602. The date of the first production is unknown; it has been conjectured that the play may have been written for private performance, possibly at the Inns of Court. It was seldom seen before the 20th century. Dryden rewrote Shakespeare's play as *Truth Found Too Late* (1679), in which Cressida remains faithful.

In 1923 Lilian Baylis produced *Troilus and Cressida* at the Old Vic to complete the first-ever staging of all the works in the First Folio by the same company. (The marathon project had started in 1914). When Luchino Visconti directed an outdoor production in Florence's Boboli Gardens in 1949, he put half the cast on horseback. Peter Hall and John Barton directed a 1960 Stratford production staged in a sandpit.

The main sources for the story are Chaucer's *Troilus and Criseyde* (1385) and Chapman's translation of *The Iliad* (1598). The play is set during the Greek siege of Troy. Troilus, a Trojan prince, loves Cressida, the daughter of a Trojan priest who has gone over to the Greeks. When the armies agree to send Cressida to the Greeks in exchange for a Trojan prisoner, she and Troilus vow constant fidelity. Once in the Greek camp, however, Cressida forgets Troilus and falls for the handsome Greek hero, Diomedes. Troilus challenges Diomedes in battle but is defeated and killed. Shakespeare's play presents a cynical picture of both military heroism and romantic love. The anti-heroic tone is set by the foul-mouthed Thersites, who provides a scurrilous commentary on the action.

Trojan Women, The An anti-war play by EURIPIDES, first performed in 415 BC during the Peloponnesian War. The message is summed up in a speech by Poseidon, the god of the sea:

> Foolish is the man who sacks cities and gives over to destruction temples and tombs which are sacred to the dead, only to perish himself.

The play reveals the brutal cost of the Greeks' victory over the Trojans in a series of episodes: Cassandra is carried off as the concubine of Agamemnon, and becomes half mad; Hecuba, the queen, becomes a slave of Odysseus and learns of her daughter's murder. The play ends with the cries of the Trojan women as the Greeks burn their city.

In one recent revival at the Long Wharf Theatre in New Haven, Connecticut, the young actress playing the distraught Cassandra would work herself up into a frenzy on stage and strike the nearest actor. This was normally David Spielberg; although his fellow actor Martin Macguire advised "Hit the bitch back". Spielberg took the blows patiently until one night, when the actress drew blood with a direct blow to his mouth, he turned to two sentinels on the parapet of Troy and ordered, "Guards, take her away." The two extras carried the stunned actress off in the middle of her scene.

trope In the early Middle Ages, a brief sung passage interpolated in the Christian liturgy to illustrate the meaning of a particular festival. It was a natural development from the chanted NEUME and the beginning of the tradition of LITURGICAL DRAMA. The earliest recorded trope featured in an Easter service at the Monastery of St Martial at Limoges in the 10th century. The most famous trope was the Easter Day QUEM QUAERITIS? a brief dialogue between a priest representing the angel at Christ's empty tomb and three choirboys representing the three Marys.

troubadours Poets of the south of France in the 11th to 14th centuries, whose works were often performed and sung by wandering MINSTRELS or JONGLEURS; so called from the Provençal verb *trobar*, to find or invent. They wrote in Provençal, principally on themes of love and chivalry. *See also* GOLIARD; TROUVÈRES.

trouvères Poets of central and northern France in the 12th to 14th centuries. Many were also JONGLEURS, performing their own works in public. The *trouvères* were so-called from the French verb *trouver*, to find or invent (*compare* TROUBADOURS). They wrote mainly of love, but also composed narrative and dramatic verse.

truck *See* BOAT TRUCK.

tumbler A BATTEN around which canvas scenery can be rolled to prevent creasing. Also an acrobat who performs such stunts as handsprings and somersaults.

Turgenev, Ivan Sergeivich (1818–83) Russian playwright and novelist, who laid the foundations of the modern Russian theatre with his realistic dramas of everyday life. His skilful use of domestic details to evoke the inner feelings of his characters is seen most clearly in A MONTH IN THE COUNTRY, the first Russian psychological drama. The play was a major influence on Anton CHEKHOV.

Turgenev was still a student at the university of St Petersburg when he published his first play, *Steno* (1834), a poetic melodrama influenced by Byron. After returning from further studies in Berlin, he fathered an illegitimate daughter by his mother's seamstress. The following year he began an affair with the married opera singer Mme Viardot, a relationship that lasted for the rest of his life.

Between 1846 and 1852 Turgenev wrote a series of satirical comedies that he intended to be read rather than acted. His second play, written in the style of Nikolai GOGOL, was *Moneyless; or, Scenes from the Life of a Young Nobleman* (1846). This was followed by *Where It's Thin It Tears* (1848), *The Bachelor* (1849), which was written for the great comic actor Mikhail Shchepkin, *The Boarder* (1850), and *A Provincial Lady* (1851). Turgenev's masterpiece, A MONTH IN THE COUNTRY, was written in 1850 but not staged until 1872.

Censorship, imprisonment, and exile eventually drove Turgenev from the stage. In 1852, he was imprisoned for a month and then exiled to his estate, Spasskoe, for 18 months under police supervision. This was ostensibly because of an obituary he had written praising the officially disgraced Gogol, but was actually a result of hostility to his criticism of serfdom. From 1856 Turgenev lived mostly in Germany and France, becoming the best-known Russian writer in the West with a series of masterful novels and stories.

turkey Broadway slang for a dull or bad production that is doomed to fail. Reviewing a play called *My Dear Children* in 1951, the critic Gene Fowler wrote, "The management prudently kept the turkey out of town." *See also* FLOP.

Turlupinades Popular farces presented at the Hôtel de Bourgogne, Paris, from 1618 to about 1630 by a trio of comedians, the red-bearded Turlupin (Henri Legrand, 1587–1637), the corpulent Gros-Guillaume (Robert Guérin, 1554–1635), and the thin Gaultier-Garguille (Huges Guéru, d. 1633). Turlupin, after whom the farces were named, apparently began his act at Parisian fairs before joining a professional company in about 1615. The antics of the three derived ultimately from the *commedia dell'arte*; their interaction is considered to have been at its most inspired in Gougenot's *La Comédie des comédiens* (1631).

Twelfth Night 5 January, the eve of the Feast of the Epiphany, which is the twelfth day after Christmas. Formerly this was a time of revels and merrymaking, when plays, and masquerades were performed. The tradition may derive from the ancient Roman Saturnalia, which were held at the same season.

Twelfth Night; or, What You Will Shakespeare's last romantic comedy, often regarded as his finest work in the genre. It was written in 1599, probably for Twelfth Night festivities, and received its first public performance in 1602 in London. The play has been consistently popular. Granville-Barker produced the comedy in 1895 on a reconstructed Elizabethan stage and then in 1912 in black-and-white at the Savoy Theatre. Productions of the play opened the Sadler's Wells Theatre in 1931 and the Regent Park's Open Air Theatre in 1933. Modern players in *Twelfth Night* have ranged from Peggy Ashcroft (1950) to the comedian Ken Dodd (1971). In 1969 it became a Broadway musical entitled *Your Own Thing*.

The main story, which derives ultimately from an Italian play called *Gl'ingannati* (1531), involves the twins, VIOLA and Sebastian, who are separated by a storm at sea. Viola disguises herself as a boy, and becomes page to Orsino, Duke of Illyria, with whom she falls in love. The duke loves Olivia, but she becomes enamoured of the disguised Viola. Eventually the twins are reunited, Olivia marries Sebastian and Orsino Viola. The romantic plot is offset by a comic subplot involving the revenge of Sir Toby BELCH and Sir Andrew AGUECHEEK on Olivia's pompous steward MALVOLIO. Tricked into believing that Olivia is secretly in love with him, he behaves so absurdly that he is taken for a madman and imprisoned. The melancholy tone of the play, which in places seems to anticipate the tragedies that Shakespeare would write in the next few years, is perfectly encapsulated in the three songs of Feste the clown: 'O Mistress Mine', 'Come Away Death', and 'When that I was and a Little Tiny Boy'.

two. **two-fold** *See* BOOK FLAT *under* BOOK.

Two Gentlemen of Verona, The SHAKESPEARE's first and least successful attempt at romantic comedy, written in about 1594; the first recorded performance was in 1672. The plot, which is derived mainly from Jorge de Montemayor's romance *Diana*, involves two friends, Valentine and Proteus (the gentlemen of the title). Their friendship is severely tested when they both fall for Silvia, daughter of the Duke of Milan. In order to further his own suit, the deceitful Proteus betrays Valentine to the Duke, who banishes him. Meanwhile, Proteus's former love, Julia, disguises herself as a boy and becomes his page, even carrying his love messages to Silvia. After a series of highly implausible adventures – including Silvia's capture by a group of bandits led by Valentine, and Proteus's bungling attempt to rape her (for which he is immediately forgiven) – the friends are reconciled. Valentine weds Silvia, and Proteus weds Julia. It is the Bard's only play to feature a dog (called Crab).

In most modern productions of the play the serious romantic plot is played mainly for laughs. The Royal Shakespeare Company chose Peter Hall's production as their first offering in 1960. A modern-dress version presented in 1975 at Stratford featured actresses in bikinis beside a swimming pool. There was a musical adaptation in 1927 called *Two Gentlemen of Soho*, while Joseph PAPP later produced a Broadway musical version that won the Tony Award for 1971.

Two Noble Kinsmen, The A little-known tragicomedy by SHAKESPEARE and John FLETCHER; it is probably the last play that Shakespeare worked on. It was first performed at court in about 1619 and published in a 1634 quarto, whose title page credits "the memorable Worthies of their time; Mr John Fletcher, and Mr William Shakespeare, Gent". It is believed that Shakespeare wrote the first and fifth acts, and Fletcher the rest. The main plot was adapted from Boccaccio's *Teseida* and Chaucer's *The Knight's Tale*.

The story centres upon the cousins Palamon and Arcite, who have been captured in war by Theseus, Duke of Thebes. While in prison both fall in love with Emilia, Theseus's sister-in-law. After Arcite is released and Palamon escapes, the two cousins meet to fight a duel over Emilia. Theseus interrupts the proceedings and, when Emilia fails to decide between them, orders them to fight again in a month's time; the winner will have Emilia and the loser will die. Arcite wins the encounter only to suffer a fatal fall from his horse. Dying, he requests that Emilia should wed his cousin, thereby saving him from execution. There is also a lively subplot involving a jailor's daughter who goes mad from unrequited love for Palamon.

Tynan, Kenneth (Peacock) (1927–80) British theatre critic, who wrote witty, acerbic, and controversial columns for *The Observer* (1954–58, 1960–63) and the *New Yorker* (1958–60). As literary adviser to the new National Theatre (1963–69), he promoted the works of Anouilh, Brecht, and Beckett before clashing with the governors over his desire to stage Rolf HOCHHUTH's *Soldiers*, which presented Churchill as a war criminal. When censorship was abolished in 1968, Tynan co-produced it at the New Theatre (now the Albery). The following year he devised and produced the sex revue *Oh, Calcutta!*, a self-styled "evening of elegant erotica" that ran for 1314 performances in New York (1969) and for 2434 in London (1970).

After leaving Oxford Tynan directed a provincial repertory company and even acted as First Player to Alec Guinness's Hamlet (1951) before moving into journalism. His sarcasm could devastate a play. Reviewing *The Glorious Days* (1953), he wrote, "There was a heated division of opinion in the lobbies during the interval but a small conservative majority took the view that it might be as well to remain in the theatre." Sir Donald Wolfit and several other managers tried unsuccessfully to bar Tynan from seeing their plays, while Richard Burton once physically attacked him.

tyrant's vein, a A ranting bullying manner. In the medieval MYSTERY PLAYS the tyrants were made to rant, and the loudness of their rant was proportionate to the villainy of their dispositions. *See* HEROD; PILATE, PONTIUS; TERMAGANT.

U

über. ***Überbrettl*** A type of CABARET venue in early 20th-century Germany. The first *Überbrettl* (literally, 'super-gaff') was the Bunte Bühne (Motley Stage), which was opened in 1901 by Baron Ernst von Wolzogen and Otto Julius Bierbaum. The Bunte Bühne is usually considered the first modern cabaret.

Über-marionette The ideal actor envisioned by the designer Gordon Craig (*see* CRAIG FAMILY); he or she would be an egoless 'super-puppet', wholly at the bidding of the play's director. He insisted that "acting is not an art" and believed that actors should represent a character's emotions by "feeling as little of them as is necessary".

Ubu, Père The outrageous character created by the French playwright Alfred JARRY. Ubu was a fat, cowardly, greedy, stupid, and cruel bourgeois modelled upon one of Jarry's schoolmasters. He was introduced in the farce *Ubu Roi*, a brutal and scatalogical work generally considered to have launched the modern avant-garde theatre. The satirical drama, written when Jarry was 15, was first performed in 1888 as a marionette play. It was first produced on stage in Paris in 1896, when the director, Firmin Gémier, used many props and conventions of the marionette theatre. The play was revived successfully by Jean VILAR at the Théâtre National Populaire in 1958, while an English version was presented in 1966 at the Royal Court Theatre with costumes and decor by David Hockney.

Ubu Roi ridiculed both bourgeois morality and the conventions of the naturalistic theatre. In the plot, which is based loosely on that of *Macbeth*, Ubu and his wife, Mère Ubu, conspire to kill the Polish king, assisted by Captain Bordure. Once the deed is done, Ubu double-crosses Bordure, forcing him to flee to Russia. Ubu and his wife rule Poland with great cruelty, until Prince Bourgrelas, the dead king's son, recaptures Warsaw. They escape to Lithuania, where Ubu throws Mère Ubu to a bear, but then rescues her when he finds that he needs her help against Bourgrelas, who has pursued them. They escape once more, and the play ends with Ubu eagerly preparing for his new post as minister of finance in Paris.

Jarry continued Ubu's story with less freshness in *Ubu enchaîné* (1899) and *Ubu sur la butte* (1901).

uncle. ***Uncle Tom's Cabin*** The most popular play of the late 19th-century US theatre. The first stage version of Harriet Beecher Stowe's famous anti-slavery novel was presented in 1852 in Baltimore, the year that the book was published. From then on, certain US actors made an entire career of 'Tomming'. London saw seven productions in 1852 and an 1878 spectacular featuring "a hundred real American freed slaves". In 1879 almost 50 travelling troupes were performing the work under tents in America and by the 1890s this had reached about 400. Soon, the plot became so well known that individual companies began to introduce special attractions, such as real bloodhounds to chase the escaped slave Eliza across the river (a scene that does not appear in the book). Productions ranged in size from one using only three actors to William Brady's spectacular staging of 1901, which involved 200 dancers and singers and 21 TRANSFORMATION SCENES. A dozen companies were still touring with the play in 1927, but the melodramatic style of dialogue led to the play falling out of favour soon afterwards.

Uncle Vanya Anton CHEKHOV's painful drama of purposeless lives, rewritten from an earlier unsuccessful play called *The Wood Demon* (1889). *Uncle Vanya* was first seen in STANISLAVSKY's production at the MOSCOW ART THEATRE in 1899. The first British production was that mounted by the Stage Society at the Aldwych Theatre in 1914. Olivier played the complex role of Astrov at the Old Vic in 1944 and again for the famous 1963 production at the CHICHESTER

FESTIVAL, which had Michael Redgrave in the title role and Joan Plowright as Sonya.

Professor Serebryakov and his lovely but lethargic wife Yelena retire to his country estate. This has been managed for many years by Vanya, a futile character eaten up with a sense of his own failure. Also in the household is the professor's daughter Sonya, who nurses a hopeless love for the local doctor, Astrov. When Serebryakov suggests selling the estate, Vanya goes berserk and tries to shoot him. Characteristically, despite firing at point-blank range, he misses. The professor and his wife leave, and Vanya sinks back into his life of hopeless routine.

In the words of the critic Desmond McCarthy, the play ends with "that dreariest of all sensations: beginning life again on the flat when, a few hours before, it has run shrieking up the scale of pain till it seemed the very skies might split".

under. ***Under Milk Wood*** A "play for voices" by the Welsh poet Dylan Thomas (1914–53), featuring a cast of characters numbering more than 60. Originally commissioned by the BBC for radio, *Under Milk Wood* was first broadcast in 1954; it later transferred successfully to the stage, being performed in Edinburgh and London in 1956. Thomas had died in 1955, before he was able to complete the final revision of the stage version.

The play depicts the life of LLAREGGUB, a Welsh seaside village, through a series of stories told by the villagers about themselves and their neighbours. They include the blind seaman Captain Cat, Mrs Ogmore-Pritchard and her two dead husbands, and the local flirt, Polly Garter. Other characters include Nogood Boyo, Willy Nilly, Nasty Humphrey, Bessie Bighead, and Dai Bread. The play is notable for its rich poetic prose.

understudy An actor who learns the part of another, especially that of a principal actor, in order to substitute for him at short notice in case of an emergency such as illness. In the 18th-century French theatre, this substitute was called a *double*, and young actors usually began their careers in this way.

Albert FINNEY first achieved recognition in 1959, when, as a 23-year-old understudy he replaced Laurence OLIVIER who injured his knee whilst performing in *Coriolanus* at Stratford-upon-Avon. Finney had previously experienced great nervousness on the Stratford stage, but when he replaced the star "all the difficulties I seemed to be going through left me". He summed up the advantages of the understudy, noting: "It didn't matter what happened. It didn't matter if I dried; they'd expect it. If I fainted, well it's a lot of pressure on the lad, you know. So I didn't worry."

One case of an understudy imitating the star too closely occurred at the Mermaid Theatre during a revival of Shaw's THE PHILANDERER. A new polished parquet floor had been installed and when the actress Jane Arden made her entrance, she slid straight off the stage into the lap of a woman in the stalls. Arden was too shaken to continue, and the understudy was called for. When this actress appeared on stage she too skated right into the same woman, who left the theatre indignantly, thinking she had been the victim of a deliberate practical joke.

unities The NEOCLASSICAL doctrine that a play should have a unity in three aspects: time, place, and action. In practice this meant that a play should present one basic action occurring in one place during the course of a single day. Although Aristotle's *Poetics* was cited as the authority for these rules, only the unity of action was stressed in this work, the other two unities being derived from Renaissance misreadings of the text. The unities were introduced to French classical tragedy by Jean Mairet (1604–86), whose *Sophonisbe* (1634) was the first modern work to embody them. In the writings of such French critics as Boileau (1636–1711) the need to maintain the unities became a rigid dogma. The unities also influenced the neoclassical drama of Spain and Italy but never replaced the tradition of Shakespearean free structure in England.

University Wits The name given to a group of Elizabethan playwrights educated at Oxford or Cambridge and noted for their wild and dissolute behaviour. It was coined by the Victorian critic George Saintsbury (1845–1933). Among the wits were Christopher MARLOWE (1564–93), Robert Greene (1560–92), Thomas Nashe (1567–1601), George Peele (1556–96), and the less well-known Thomas Lodge (1557–1625), whose pastoral romance *Rosalind* (1590) inspired Shakespeare's *As You Like It*.

upstage The area of a stage furthest from the audience, usually the back third. The word is also used as a STAGE DIRECTION, meaning to move away from the audience. When an actor faces the audience, 'upstage right' is to his right and 'upstage left' is to his left.

The phrase to *upstage someone* has entered the general language, meaning to draw attention to oneself at the expense of another; it derives from the fact that an actor moving upstage of another obliges the latter to act with his back to the audience. *See also* CENTRESTAGE; DOWNSTAGE.

useful theatre *See* DUMAS FAMILY.

Ustinov, Sir Peter (Alexander) (1921–) British actor, playwright, director, and raconteur, noted for performing in his own successful comedies. He comes from a famous Russian theatrical family, one ancestor having been the architect of the Bolshoi Theatre. Ustinov trained at the London Theatre Studio where his final report was unpromising:

> He has a long way to go. He is still lamentably stiff. He seems to have great difficulty in walking, or running, or jumping. His mind wanders during gymnastics. His voice is unresonant and monotonous.

Ustinov made his professional debut at the Players' Theatre, London, in 1939, appearing in his own sketches. His first produced play was *Fishing for Shadows*, a translation of Jean Sarment's *Le Pêcheur d'ombres*, which was staged at the Threshold Theatre in 1940. After serving in World War II, during which five of his plays were produced, he returned to the stage as Petrovich in an adaptation of Dostoevsky's *Crime and Punishment* (1946). He then went to Hollywood to begin a successful career in films.

As a playwright, Ustinov has written strong leading roles to suit his own comic abilities, which include a gift for mimicry. His successes have included THE LOVE OF FOUR COLONELS (1951) and ROMANOFF AND JULIET (1956), a comedy of diplomatic life. While the latter was running, he was challenged to a tennis match by a Mr Romanov, minister-counsellor at the London Soviet Embassy, who was amused by the use of his name. During the match, Ustinov strained his back and had to leave the play, remaining strapped to a board for eight weeks.

At the 1968 Chichester Festival, he performed in his play *The Unknown Soldier and His Wife* and at the 1979 Stratford (Ontario) Festival as Lear. His recent works have included *Beethoven's Tenth* in 1987 at the Vaudeville Theatre and his acclaimed one-man show, *An Evening with Peter Ustinov*, in 1990 at the Haymarket.

Utility *See* STOCK COMPANY.

V

vagante (Lat: wanderer) Another word for a GOLIARD.

Valdéz, Luis *See* CHICANO THEATRE.

vamp trap or **vampire trap** A type of TRAP introduced in James Robinson Planché's melodrama *The Vampire; or, the Bride of the Isles* in 1820 at the Lyceum Theatre. Consisting of two spring leaves or flaps in a canvas FLAT, it was used to create the illusion of a ghost or other supernatural character passing through a solid wall.

Vanbrugh, Sir John (1664–1726) English playwright of the later Restoration era; also the architect who created the English Baroque style in architecture, designing Blenheim Palace in Oxfordshire and Castle Howard in Yorkshire.

The son of a sugar baker, Vanbrugh became an officer with the Earl of Huntingdon's regiment in 1686. Four years later he was arrested and imprisoned in Calais as a suspected spy, being moved in 1692 to the Bastille. The regime was not brutal: he enjoyed four-course dinners and three bottles of wine a day and amused himself by writing a draft of THE PROVOK'D WIFE.

Vanbrugh's first successful play was THE RELAPSE; *or, Virtue in Danger*, a comedy about a libertine and his long-suffering wife. It was written and produced in 1696 as an ironic sequel to Colley CIBBER's *Love's Last Shift*, which was staged earlier that year. Vanbrugh used his share of the profits from *The Relapse* to pay off the debts of one of the owners at Drury Lane; similarly, he took no payment for his *Aesop*, produced the following year.

At Lord Halifax's urging Vanbrugh revised *The Provok'd Wife* for production at Lincoln's Inn Fields Theatre in 1697; it was a comedy about a miserable marriage in which David Garrick donned female clothes. The robust action and bawdy realism of his plays, however, were beginning to attract attention from moralists. Both works were singled out by Jeremy COLLIER in his celebrated pamphlet *A Short View of the Immorality of the English Stage*.

Two later and lesser works, *The Country House* (1703) and *The Confederacy* (1705), were produced by Thomas Betterton at the Queen's Theatre, Haymarket, which Vanbrugh had designed. The Queen's was built as an opera house, but its acoustics proved so unsuitable for drama that alterations had to be made while the company moved temporarily to Lincoln's Inn Fields.

After the playwright's death, an unfinished work called *A Journey to London* was found amongst his papers and completed by Cibber as *The Provok'd Husband* (1728). Cibber once described Vanbrugh's witty and natural dialogue as "his common conversation committed to paper".

Vance, Alfred *See* GREAT VANCE *under* GREAT.

variety In Britain, a type of popular entertainment that developed from MUSIC HALL in the late 19th century. It was characterized by the presence of diverse acts on the same bill. In America the term was used more or less synonymously with VAUDEVILLE.

The variety era saw the replacement of the earlier halls and clubs, in which the audience had been able to eat, drink, and smoke while being entertained, with specially built variety theatres. These were more comfortable, more expensive, and more respectable, lacking much of the old boisterous atmosphere. The entertainment was often spectacular, with the HIPPODROME offering aquatic dramas and the LONDON COLISEUM presenting chariot races. The famous ALHAMBRA Music Hall in London became the Alhambra Palace of Varieties.

The continuous programmes of the old music halls, which often ran to midnight, were replaced by twice-nightly bills that combined songs, comedians, ballet, spectacle, and short dramatic 'snippets' that ran for less than 30 minutes. The popularity of these dramatic pieces even attracted such stars of the legitimate theatre as Beerbohm TREE and Sarah BERNHARDT. In 1918

Diaghilev's Ballets Russes company appeared at the Coliseum on the same bill as jugglers and comedians. With the advent of talking pictures, many variety theatres were converted into cinemas; attempts to combine the new medium with old-style variety acts proved futile (*see* CINE-VARIETY).

vaudeville A US form of VARIETY entertainment that was popular in the late 19th and early 20th century.

The name, which is French in origin, may be a corruption of *vaux-de-vire* (songs of the Vire), referring to a region of Normandy famous for satirical songs in the 15th century. An alternative derivation is from *vaux des villes* (songs of the city streets). In the late 17th century the French critic Boileau applied the term to satirical ballads and to the dumb shows (*comédies en vaudeville*) presented in Paris's booth theatres. It later came to be applied to the popular musical dramas presented at the Opéra-Comique and other venues.

In the later 19th century, the term vaudeville came to be used of variety performances, especially in America, where a tradition of beer-hall entertainment had developed in parallel to the MUSIC HALL in Britain. Other influences on early US vaudeville included MINSTREL SHOWS, MEDICINE SHOWS, and 'dime museums' of freaks and trained animals, such as P. T. BARNUM's American Museum in New York. The first regular vaudeville programmes were presented at the Franklin Theatre, New York, in 1842. Like US BURLESQUE, vaudeville remained rather suspect until Tony Pastor created the "straight, clean variety show" in the 1860s at New York's American Theatre. A typical bill would include juggling, a musical act, trained animals, a dramatic skit, a comedy sketch, an acrobatic act, and a magic performance. At the turn of the century, short films would often be shown to clear the house. By this time vaudeville was big business: the agency of B. F. Keith and Edward Franklin Albee booked acts for 400 theatres east of Chicago, while Martin Beck ran the Orpheum Circuit of theatres with houses from Chicago to California. After the advent of talking pictures in 1927, however, vaudeville performers began to dwindle into support acts for films. New York's PALACE THEATRE, the nation's top vaudeville house, closed in 1932.

Vaudeville produced many of America's early film stars and radio performers, some of whom survived into the television era. The impressive list includes Danny Kaye, Harry Houdini, Al Jolson, Sophie Tucker, W. C. Fields, Will Rogers, Jimmy Durante, Burns and Allen, the Marx Brothers, and the Three Stooges. Europeans introduced to the US audience through vaudeville included Harry Lauder and Vesta Victoria.

Vaudeville Theatre A London theatre in the Strand, opened in 1870 by C. J. Phipps. It was noted for its elegant interior and an innovative lighting system with brilliant 'sun-burners' in the centre of the ceiling and hidden footlights. The Vaudeville was reconstructed in 1891, with a facade of Portland Stone that remains today. In 1926 the inside was drastically altered and in 1969 it was completely refurbished with a gold and cream decor, 694 seats, and a great chandelier in the foyer.

The Vaudeville is best known for its comedy and musical productions. Early in its history it drew such renowned performers as Henry IRVING, Seymour Hicks and his wife Ellaline Terriss, and Charles Hawtrey. One of the theatre's early successes was H. J. Byron's comedy *Our Boys*, which ran for 1362 performances from 1875 to 1879. Ibsen's *Hedda Gabler* had its first English production at the Vaudeville in 1891. André Charlot presented a popular series of revues at the theatre beginning in 1915.

Later successes included William Douglas Home's comedy *The Chiltern Hundreds* (1947) and Julian Slade's musical *Salad Days*, which ran for 2283 performances between 1954 and 1960. In 1969 the Gatti family, who had owned the theatre for 78 years, sold it to Peter Saunders. Recent hits have included John Chapman and Ray Cooney's farce *Move Over Mrs Markham* (1970), Agatha Christie's *A Murder is Announced* (1977), and a revival of Chekhov's *Uncle Vanya* (1988).

Vauxhall Gardens A very popular pleasure resort for Londoners, first laid out in 1661 as Spring Gardens and finally closed in 1859. Pepys referred to it as Fox Hall. In the 19th century it was mentioned by both Dickens and Thackeray. It was a place of musical entertainment, fireworks, displays of pictures and statuary, etc., and at night was lit by over 1000 lamps. *See also* CREMORNE GARDENS; ROSHERVILLE GARDENS.

Veedhi Natakam A form of rural theatre in the southern Indian state of Andhra

Pradesh, where the tradition can be traced back at least as far as the 16th century. The name means 'street drama'. The travelling players perform in any open space, such as the square in front of a temple, with the acting area surrounded by rugs and mats for the spectators. The audience is segregated by sex. Songs are performed to the accompaniment of a harmonium and tabla (drums), although film music has virtually replaced traditional folk melodies.

Vega (Carpio), Lope (Félix) de (1562–1635) Spain's first great playwright. The most prolific dramatist in the history of the theatre, he is believed to have written some 1500 plays of which about 470 survive. He established the conventions for the Spanish COMEDIA in the last decade of the 16th century, influenced the development of the ZARZUELA, and wrote numerous AUTO SACRAMENTALes. He is regarded as the founder of the Spanish commercial theatre and the most influential writer of Spain's Golden Age.

In his *New Art of Writing Plays* (*c.* 1609), Lope analysed the essentials of drama and admitted that he played to the popular taste. "I allow myself to be borne along in the vulgar current," he wrote, "wherefore Italy and France call me ignorant."

His personal life was as flamboyant as his dramas. The son of an embroiderer, he took part in the conquest of Terceira in the Azores (1583) and sailed with the Armada in 1588, an event that inspired his epic poem *La Dragentea* (1597), which attacks Drake and England. He was also known for his passionate love affairs, which continued after he became a priest in 1614 and created a great scandal.

Lope wrote initially for Madrid's open-air theatres and subsequently for the royal court, drawing his subject matter from history and chivalric legend, peasant life, and biblical and mythological stories. His lyrical verse plays, most of which have happy endings, are noted for their dramatic action, use of suspense, and lively and natural dialogue. Many were based on the conflict of love and honour.

Among his many notable works are *Fuenteovejuna* (*c.* 1614) in which villagers murder their tyrannous feudal lord and are saved by the king's intervention, and *El castigo sin venganza*, in which a licentious duke maintains his public reputation by killing his adulterous wife and her illegitimate son.

Venice Preserv'd *See* OTWAY, THOMAS.

ventriloquism The trick of producing vocal sounds so that they appear to come not from the person producing them, but from some other quarter. The name is derived from Latin *venter*, belly, *loqui*, to speak (speaking from the belly), reflecting the erroneous notion that the voice of the ventriloquist proceeded from his stomach. In the Middle Ages it was often regarded as a sign of witchcraft or demonic possession. The modern type of ventriloquist act, in which a performer speaks without moving his lips while making his voice appear to issue from a dummy, became a popular feature of MUSIC HALL and VAUDEVILLE in the later 19th century.

Vere Street Theatre A former London theatre in Clare Market, close to Lincoln's Inn Fields. During the Puritan INTERREGNUM William DAVENANT used this former tennis court to present what he termed "music and instruction", thereby evading the law forbidding stage performances. In 1652 a group of actors who performed there were betrayed to the authorities by an unknown person whom a contemporary named an ILL BEEST.

On the Restoration of the monarchy (1660) Thomas KILLIGREW reopened the Vere Street with Shakespeare's *Henry IV, Part I*. That same year Margaret Hughes became the first professional actress to appear on the English stage when she played Desdemona there in *The Moor of Venice*, Killigrew's adaptation of *Othello*. Killigrew remained at the Vere Street for three years before moving to his new theatre at DRURY LANE. Owing to new regulations that gave the PATENT THEATRES a virtual monopoly in the City of London, his successor, George Jolly was obliged to run the theatre as an acting school, or NURSERY. In 1675 the building became a Nonconformist meeting-house, and in 1809 it burned down.

Verfremdungseffekt *See* ALIENATION EFFECT.

verismo A movement towards greater NATURALISM in the Italian theatre in the late 19th and early 20th centuries. Playwrights turned to social and political themes, setting their plots in working-class and regional settings. The leading exponents of the style were Giovanni Verga (1840–1922), whose tragedies of Sicilian life include *Cavalleria Rusticana* (1884), and Luigi Capuana (1839–1915), who wrote *Malia* (1859) and other works in Sicilian dialect. Other playwrights associated with the movement included Giuseppe Giacosa (1847–1906), Luigi PIRANDELLO, and Gabriele D'ANNUNZIO. The style also influenced the earlier operas of Puccini. Although *verismo* was Italy's first distinctively national form of drama, it was suppressed by the Fascists during the 1920s.

Vestris, Madame (Lucy Elizabeth Bartolozzi; 1797–1856) British actress and singer. She was the first British actress to manage a theatre, and became the first PRINCIPAL BOY in English pantomime (playing Ralph in *Puss and Boots*).

After studying music she married the French dancer Armand Vestris (1788–1825), at the age of 16. Vestris was ballet master at the King's Theatre, where she made her debut in 1815 in Peter von Winter's opera *Il Ratto di Proserpina*. Her first great success came at Drury Lane in 1817, when she played the title-role of Moncrieff's *Giovanni in London*, a burlesque of Mozart's *Don Giovanni*. After performing in Paris, where her husband deserted her in 1820, she returned to London to star at both Drury Lane and Covent Garden. She excelled in high comedy, playing fashionable ladies such as Lydia Languish in Sheridan's *The Rivals* (1826).

In 1830 she took over as manager of the Olympic Theatre, opening with *Olympic Revels* by James Planché, who continued to write farces and burlesques for her. An excellent if somewhat stern manager, Vestris introduced a number of important innovations, including the BOX SET in 1832. Other reforms included the use of accurate costumes, realistic scenery, and real props, and shortening presentations from the usual six hours to five. Although the plays that she presented were popular, the theatre still lost money owing to the small auditorium: she declared bankruptcy in 1837.

In 1838 Vestris married the actor Charles James Mathews the younger (1803–78), a member of the Olympic company, who was one of the best light comedians of his day. They immediately toured America, where she received ecstatic reviews acting and singing in *The Loan of a Lover*. The couple took over the management of Covent Garden in 1839, drawing large audiences for such productions as the 1841 comedy *London Assurance* by Dion Boucicault (*see* BOUCICAULT FAMILY), in which Mathews starred as Dazzle. The cost of their opulent productions, however, led to bankruptcy and imprisonment for Mathews in 1842.

In 1847 the couple took over the Lyceum Theatre, where they introduced further innovations, such as the first TRANSPARENCY for Planché's extravaganza *The Island of Jewels*, and the abolition of half-price tickets for those arriving late. By 1854, however, they were once more experiencing financial problems. Vestris gave her final performance that year in *Sunshine Through the Clouds*. When they left the Lyceum in 1855 Mathews was once again imprisoned for debt. He was released a week before his wife died.

Vice The buffoon in the old English MORALITY PLAYS. He wore a cap with ass's ears, and was generally named after some particular vice, such as Gluttony or Pride. The character appeared in some of the later MORAL INTERLUDES and influenced the creation of such comic figures of the Elizabethan stage as FALSTAFF.

Victoria, Queen Victoria (1819–1901) Queen of the United Kingdom (1837–1901), who supported the theatre throughout her life and helped to change its disreputable image by knighting the actor Henry IRVING in 1895. Both Irving and the queen regarded the honour as one bestowed on the whole profession. Although Victoria rarely made personal comments at investitures, when she knighted Irving she leaned towards him and announced, "We are very, very pleased."

As a child Victoria had loved the theatre's depiction of an exciting world beyond her restricted life at Kensington Palace. The Royal Coburg Theatre was renamed the Royal Victoria in her honour in 1833; it subsequently became the OLD VIC.

As queen, Victoria attended the theatre up to three times a week; it was one of the few places where she could behave informally. Once, when attending the Haymarket Theatre she was met at the entrance by the manager, comedian John Buckstone, who (following tradition) walked backwards with lighted candles to direct her to the royal box. A sudden draught blew out the candles leaving them in total darkness. "Now just look at that!" chirped Buckstone, using one of his famous catchphrases. The queen laughed, and even let him take her by the hand to guide her through the dark.

Victoria encouraged her children to put on their own plays for guests. In one drama presented at Balmoral, a gallant knight (the Prince of Wales) returned from battle to rejoin his loyal wife (the Princess Alice). The knight recounted his valiant adventures in a lengthy speech to which his wife replied "And we, too, my lord, have not been idle during your absence!", as she gestured towards their 'children', a vast array of dolls.

After the death of Prince Albert in 1861, Victoria never visited a theatre again. However, in 1881, after years as a recluse, she began to ask such actors as Henry Irving, John Hare, Ellen Terry, Eleanora DUSE, Sarah BERNHARDT, the KENDALS, and the Bancrofts to put on private shows for her in the Waterloo Chamber at Windsor and at other royal residences. London's actor-managers kept special scenery for these royal engagements and would close their theatres for the night. In her last 20 years, Victoria viewed 28 of these command performances.

For years after her death the British censors would not allow Queen Victoria to be portrayed on the London stage. She was, however, represented in New York in 1923 by Beryl Mercer in *Queen Victoria* and in 1935 by Helen Hayes in VICTORIA REGINA. She has since been played by Anna Neagle in *The Glorious Days* (1951), by Dorothy Tutin in *Portrait of a Queen* (1965), and by Polly James in the musical *I and Albert* (1972). In 1968 Edward BOND's *Early Morning* was refused a licence for its scurrilous portrait of the queen as a lesbian.

Victorian theatre slang The following is a selection of the slang terms used in the London theatre during the late 19th century:

bus (pronounced 'biz') short for stage BUSINESS

corpse originally, to cause confusion on stage through any kind of unprofessional behaviour; now applied almost exclusively to cases in which an actor falls out of character and laughs at an inappropriate moment.

daddy a stage manager

ducats money

fox to criticize a fellow actor's performance

goose to hiss a play

make-up a personal appearance

menagerie the orchestra

mug-up to paint one's face (*see* MUG)

mutton-walk the saloon at Drury Lane

sal a salary

stab to help yourself; the expression 'stab yourself and pass the dagger' meant 'help yourself and pass the bottle'

stall to act a part

supe supernumerary

trunks short trousers worn over hose or tights

Victoria Palace Theatre A London theatre opposite Victoria Station, noted mainly for its musicals. It was built on the site of the Royal Standard Music Hall, when that venue was demolished in 1910. The new theatre, designed by architect Frank Matcham, featured an entrance hall of grey marble and pillars of white Sicilian marble. The classical facade later bore a statue of Pavlova, the famous Russian ballerina, who made her first London appearance there in 1912. The dancer was too superstitious to look at it; during the Blitz the statue was removed and subsequently lost.

The Victoria Palace opened in 1911 as a music hall and quickly drew all of the great stars. The venue added Theatre to its name in 1934, the year it staged the much-ridiculed patriotic melodrama YOUNG ENGLAND, which ran for 278 performances, attracting theatre-goers with its reputation for unintentional comedy. Successes followed with revues and musical comedies. *Me and My Girl* (1937) ran for 1646 performances, CRAZY GANG revues were produced between 1947 and 1962, and *The Black and White Minstrels* opened in 1962 to run for 4344 performances. Later offerings included *Annie* (1978) and *Winnie* (1988), a musical based on the life of Winston Churchill. In 1994 the rock musical *Buddy*, about the pop star Buddy Holly, entered its fifth year.

Victoria Regina A series of one-act plays by Laurence Housman (1865–1959), dealing with the reign of Queen Victoria. Housman, the brother of the poet A. E. Housman, wrote and published some 30 plays about the queen but the Lord Chamberlain consistently banned them from public performance. In 1935 a selection was privately performed at the Gate Theatre, London, under the title of *Victoria Regina* with Pamela Stanley playing the queen.

A Broadway production opened the same year at the Broadhurst Theatre, starring Helen HAYES in the title role. She won the Drama League of New York Medal for her performance and continued to play the part, which she based on her Victorian grandmother, for three years. The role required her to age from 18 to over 80, leading the critic Brooks Atkinson to write:

> The girlish innocence, the eager propriety of her wooing of Albert, the unaffected joy of her devotion to him, her pettish anger when her authority was challenged, the moving humility of her surrender from queen to wife, her courage and her simplicity were parts of a memorable stage composition.

In 1936 Edward VIII intervened personally to ensure that the play was granted a licence for public performance in Britain. It was produced in 1937 at the Lyric Theatre with Pamela Stanley once more in the lead.

Victor, ou l'Enfant de la forêt A melodrama by the French dramatist Guilbert de Pixérécourt (1773–1844). It was first performed in 1789 in Paris and helped to establish the standard form of French melodrama for the BOULEVARD THEATRES. Based on a novel by François-Guillaume Ducray-Duminil, the play explores the moral dilemma of Victor, who must kill his natural father (a bandit) in order to protect his adoptive father.

View from the Bridge, A A tragedy by Arthur MILLER. Originally a one-act play, it was first performed in a double-bill with another one-act work by Miller, *A Memory of Two Mondays*, in 1955 in New York. Although banned from public performance in Britain by the Lord Chamberlain, it was produced privately by the New Watergate Theatre Club at the Comedy Theatre in 1956. Miller expanded the text into three acts for later productions.

The play concerns the New York longshoreman Eddie Carbone. He and his wife, Beatrice, have raised her niece, Catherine, but Eddie finds himself increasingly attracted to the young woman. Further problems arise when Beatrice's two Sicilian brothers, both illegal immigrants, arrive on the scene and one of them, Marco, wins Catherine's love. Jealous and fearful of losing her, Eddie informs immigration officers about the brothers. The play ends with a fight in which Marco kills Eddie. The lawyer Alfieri is used throughout as a CHORUS.

Vilar, Jean (1912–71) French theatre director and actor, noted for his attempts to make the theatre accessible to provincial and working-class audiences. After training as a stage manager under Charles Dullin, Vilar began to direct in Paris with a small travelling company called La Roulette. In 1945 he staged a memorable production of T. S. Eliot's *Murder in the Cathedral* at the Vieux-Colombiers, in which he also starred; this aroused considerable interest, especially when it was subsequently staged in the open in front of the Abbey de Bec-Hellouin. The production undoubtedly contributed to Vilar being asked to organize an open-air drama festival at Avignon in 1947; he remained closely associated with the AVIGNON FESTIVAL for over 20 years.

His efforts to open up the theatre to all classes were rewarded in 1951, when Vilar was appointed head of the revived THÉÂTRE NATIONAL POPULAIRE, based at the Palais de Chaillot in Paris. He managed the TNP for over a decade, during which time he also returned annually to Avignon; his productions of classical and contemporary plays were equally admired. In 1962 he resigned from the TNP because funding was not sufficient to allow for expansion. Vilar continued to stage productions at Avignon until 1968, when he undeservedly became the target for left-wing demonstrators.

Viola The heroine of Shakespeare's TWELFTH NIGHT. Having been shipwrecked on the coast of Illyria, she disguises herself as a page under the name Cesario. In this guise she woos the lady Olivia on behalf of Orsino, Duke of Illyria, with whom she herself is in love. Eventually the various misunderstandings are unravelled and Viola weds Orsino. She speaks mainly in prose as Cesario and in verse as herself.

Visit, The (*Der Besuch der alten Dame*) A black comedy by Friedrich DÜRRENMATT, first performed in 1956. It was immediately hailed as one of the most accomplished works by a German-language playwright since World War II. The plot revolves around the figure of Claire Zachanassian, a rich old woman, who returns to her home town to seek revenge on those who wronged her many years before. A scathing satire on the corrupting influence of wealth, the play ends with the death of her oldest enemy at the hands of the townspeople, who will do anything for a share in her fortune.

Vital Spark, the The usual billing for Jenny Hill (Elizabeth Pasta; 1851–96), an early MUSIC HALL performer at the Pavilion in London. She began her career by entertaining in East End public houses. After being deserted by her acrobat husband, she lived for years in poverty. Her act at the Pavilion included such songs as 'The Little Stowaway', dancing, and male impersonations. Ironically the 'Vital Spark' retired to Streatham in poor health and died at the age of 45.

Vivat! Vivat Regina! A chronicle play by Robert BOLT, which explores the relationship between Elizabeth I and Mary Queen of Scots. It opened at the Chichester Festival Theatre in 1970, later transferring to London's Piccadilly Theatre, where it ran for over a year with 442 performances. Bolt's wife, Sarah Miles, played Elizabeth and Eileen Atkins appeared as Mary.

The play begins with the young Mary's assumption of the Scottish throne. Her imprudent political dealings and disastrous marriages soon alienate the Scottish nobles, who eventually ask Elizabeth to depose her. The English queen replies that she will not act unless she has proof that Mary has conspired with English Catholics. Confined to Sheffield Castle, Mary is almost inadvertently drawn into a Catholic plot, an act that leads to her execution. The play originally concluded with a long and thrilling speech by Elizabeth but was revised to end with the execution of Mary.

volks. **Volksbühne** (Ger. People's Theatre) A subscription organization founded in 1890 in Berlin (as the Freie Volksbühne) to bring quality drama to a working-class audience. In 1914 it opened its own 2000-seat theatre on the Bülowplatz. The Volksbühne produced socially committed work in the new naturalistic style, introducing SHAW to German theatregoers and fostering the early careers of the directors Max REINHARDT, Jürgen Fehling, and Erwin PISCATOR. By 1930 the Volksbühne boasted more than 300 branches and some 500,000 members throughout Germany.

Although the Nazis closed the Volksbühne in 1937, it experienced a postwar renaissance in 1948 in both West and East Germany. In East Berlin, the rebuilt Volksbühne Theatre opened in 1954 and went on to stage impressive work under the management of the Swiss director Benno Besson (1969–79). The playwright Heiner Müller directed his popular version of *Macbeth* there in 1982. In West Berlin, the Volksbühne company returned to its original ideals, moving into a new theatre in 1963 under Piscator. In the former West Germany, there were about 65 towns with resident companies. Reunification of the country in 1990 has resulted in a merger of the divided Volksbühne.

Volksstück (Ger. popular drama) An often scurrilous form of Viennese dialect comedy popular in the 18th and 19th centuries. The most famous example is Mozart and Schikaneder's opera *The Magic Flute* (1791). The genre developed from the improvisational works of two Austrian actors – Joseph Anton Stranitzky (1676–1726), who created the comic figure of HANSWURST, and Gottfried Prehauser (1699–1769), who inherited and refined the stock character. Philipp Hafner (1731–64) was a leading exponent of the *Volksstück*, his most notable work being *Megära, the Terrible Witch* (1755). Although the Austrian censors banned improvisation in 1768, some playwrights, such as Joseph Felix von Kurz (1715–84), continued the tradition. Kurz, who created the popular character of BERNADON, and wrote more than 300 plays.

During the 19th century, the *Volksstück* produced two offshoots. The *Zauberstück* (Ger. magic play) used music and spectacle to create a fairytale atmosphere; Ferdinand Raimund (1790–1836) wrote and acted in many of these farces. The more realistic *Lokalstück* satirized Viennese manners; Johann Nestroy (1801–62) produced the best of these caustic works. The *Volksstück* declined at the end of the 19th century and was absorbed into either operetta or broader-based comedy.

Volpone Ben JONSON's satirical comedy about human greed, subtitled 'The Fox'. It was first performed in 1606 by the King's Men and has often been revived. The drama was first seen in New York in 1928 in a production by the THEATRE GUILD and in Paris in 1931, when it was directed by Charles Dullin. Volpone was one of Donald WOLFIT's most celebrated roles; he first played it in 1938 at London's Westminster Theatre, and it was included in his repertoire for his New York debut in 1947. During the play's subsequent run at the Savoy Theatre, the critic Harold Hobson wrote, "*Volpone* has the teeming life of worms in a rotting corpse, and Mr Wolfit plays it with all the 57 kinds of relish." A musical version entitled *Foxy* opened in 1964 at New York's Ziegfeld Theatre. Despite critical reviews, its leading man, Bert Lahr, received the Tony Award for Best Musical Star Actor. Jonson's play was later seen in National Theatre productions by Tyrone Guthrie and Peter Hall.

The story concerns Volpone (the fox), a cunning Venetian who feigns a terminal illness; aided by his 'parasite' servant Mosca (the fly), he dupes three Venetians into showering him with expensive gifts, in the hope of inheriting his wealth. The would-be heirs are Voltore (the vulture), Corbaccio (the crow), who disinherits his own son to show his loyalty to Volpone, and Corvino (the raven), who even offers his wife. Volpone goes too far, however, when he pretends to have died and left everything to Mosca. When the treacherous servant tries to blackmail him, Volpone reveals all to the authorities. The magistrates give his fortune to the infirm, order his imprisonment until he becomes as weak as he pretended to be, and have Mosca flogged and sent to the galleys.

Voltaire (François-Marie Arouet; 1694–1778) French writer and thinker, whose attacks on political and religious tyranny made him a leading figure of the Enlightenment. Amongst his numerous writings are 53 plays, more than half of which are tragedies: others belong to the genres of the COMÉDIE LARMOYANTE and the *drame bourgeois* (*see* DRAME).

The son of a notary, Voltaire was educated at a Jesuit school in Paris. While serving a prison sentence in the Bastille for writing a satire on the regent, he finished his first play, the tragedy *Oedipe* (1718), which was performed to great acclaim. While living in England (1726–29), he visited the elderly William CONGREVE and discovered the works of Shakespeare. On his return to Paris, he wrote several plays on Shakespearean themes, such as *Brutus* (1730), and his great success, ZAÏRE (1732). He also adopted his pen name, an anagram of Arouet l(e) i(eune).

Voltaire, a good amateur actor, promoted restrained acting styles and spectacular stage effects. He also campaigned successfully against the practice of seating a section of the audience on the stage. Among his theatrical acquaintances were the actor Henri-Louis LEKAIN, whom he discovered and trained, and his close friend, the actress Adrienne LECOUVREUR. However, he also had his detractors; when Voltaire asked the French playwright Alexis Piron (1689–1773) his opinion of a new play, Piron predicted that it would be hissed. Voltaire invited him to the first night, and, when the piece finished to moderate applause, pointed out that nobody had hissed. "My dear Sir," replied Piron, "how can people hiss when they yawn?"

After publishing *Lettres philosophiques* (1734), which compared France unfavourably with England, Voltaire had to take refuge for 15 years with Madame du Châtelet at Cirey. Whilst there, he wrote a number of successful tragedies, including *Alzire* (1736), *Mahomet* (1742), and *Mérope* (1743). *Mahomet* was banned until Voltaire passed off a commendatory letter from the pope about one of his poems as an approval of his play. He also embarked on a battle of plays with his adversary, the former dramatic censor Prosper Jolyot de Crébillon; *Sémiramis* (1748) and five other works by Voltaire trumped plays by Crébillon on the same subjects.

When Madame du Châtelet died in 1749, Voltaire moved to the court of Frederick the Great. In 1758 he settled at Ferney, Switzerland, where he wrote *Tancrède* (1760), which began a vogue for plays based on French history. His fame was now so widespread, and visits by the famous so numerous, that he became known as the 'Innkeeper of Europe'.

In 1778, after an exile of 28 years, he returned triumphantly to Paris to direct the rehearsals for *Irène*. At its sixth performance, his bust was ceremoniously crowned on stage while he watched from his box. He died two months later, and was hastily interred by the priests of the Abbey of Scellières before the authorities could refuse a Christian burial.

vomitory In a THEATRE-IN-THE-ROUND, a gangway running underneath the auditorium to provide access to the stage. The term comes from the ancient Roman theatre, when it referred to a large door in an AMPHITHEATRE.

Vormingstoneel (politiek) (Dutch: (political) educational drama) A left-wing movement in Dutch and Belgian theatre in the 1970s. As in SOCIALIST REALISM, the theatre was seen as an instrument to further the class struggle through political education. The Dutch companies included Proloog (1964–83), De Nieuwe Komedie (1969–85), and Sater (1971–85); while the main Belgian troupes were Kollektief Internationale Nieuwe Scene, Mannen van de Dam (Men of the Dam), and Het Trojaanse Paard (The Trojan Horse).

The scripts were often the product of COLLECTIVE CREATION. Performances took place in such venues as factories and schools, or during political demonstrations, and were usually followed by discussions relating the drama to social needs and conditions. This activist approach, especially strong amongst the Dutch companies, led in the 1980s to the withdrawal of their subsidies and the collapse of the movement.

Vortigern and Rowena *See* IRELAND FORGERIES.

Vortex, The The controversial play that established the reputation of the 24-year-old Noël COWARD, who wrote, directed, and starred in it. *The Vortex* was first performed in 1924 at the Everyman Theatre in Hampstead, London. Coward later claimed that its *succès de scandale* had caused him a nervous breakdown. He was succeeded in the lead role by John Gielgud. Audiences were shocked by the play's treatment of adultery, drug addiction, and (indirectly) homosexuality; one critic referred to it as "this dustbin of a play". *See also* LORD CHAMBERLAIN *under* LORD.

The plot involves Florence Lancaster (originally played by Lilian Braithwaite), a society hostess, whose despair at her fading beauty leads her into an affair with the young Tom Veryan. When her adult son Nicky returns from France with his fiancée, Bunty Mainwaring, they throw a party in their country house. After Nicky and Bunty break off their engagement, Florence finds Tom and Bunty kissing; Florence's tantrum provides Nicky with the opportunity to confront his mother about her adultery and confess his drug addiction. She breaks down, promising to be a better mother.

Voysey Inheritance, The A comedy by Harley GRANVILLE-BARKER, first performed in 1905 at London's Royal Court Theatre, which he co-managed with J. E. Vedrenne. The story involves an ethical dilemma faced by Edward Voysey, a partner in a solicitors' firm in Lincoln's Inn. He is mortified to find that his father (his senior partner) has illegally speculated with clients' funds and run the family business deep into debt. When his father dies unexpectedly, Edward informs his family of the problem and his intention to call in the police. They dissuade him from doing so, leaving Edward to tackle the problems on his own. His honesty and assertiveness win the love of Alice Maitland.

W

wagon *See* BOAT TRUCK.

wait Originally a medieval nightwatchman whose duty was to sound the hours on various musical instruments. In Elizabethan times groups of four to nine waits would serve a town as resident musicians much in the manner of a modern town band; alternatively, they were sometimes employed by a nobleman, in which case they wore his livery. Their connection with the theatre began when, to earn extra money, they hired themselves out to provide music for plays. By the time nightwatchmen were replaced by organized police forces in the early 19th century the waits' main function was to serenade householders and perform street music at Christmas time.

waiting. ***Waiting for Godot*** A tragicomedy by Samuel BECKETT, considered by many critics to be the most important work written for the European stage since World War II. This two-act play, originally written in French as *En Attendant Godot* in 1949, was given its first performance at the Théâtre de Babylone, Paris, in 1953. The first English production was staged in 1955 by Peter HALL at the Arts Theatre, London. The drama critic Penelope Gilliatt said the play arrived in London "like a sword burying itself in an over-upholstered sofa." The 1956 Broadway cast included the comedian Bert Lahr, best known for his Cowardly Lion in the film *The Wizard of Oz* (1939). The play later toured America billed as "the laugh sensation of two continents."

Beckett's play variously bewildered, fascinated, exasperated, or intrigued audiences and critics. The symbolism of the two despairing tramps (Vladimir and Estragon), waiting in vain for the mysterious Godot to arrive and bring meaning to their lives has been a subject of debate ever since. The play has been regularly revived. *See also* ABSURD, THEATRE OF THE.

Waiting for Lefty An influential play by the left-wing US playwright Clifford ODETS, on the theme of trade unionism. It was first performed in 1935 at the GROUP THEATRE, New York; three years later it was presented with equal success at the Unity Theatre, London. *Waiting for Lefty* helped to raise the profile of drama as a medium for social comment.

The play tells the story of a New York taxi drivers' strike in six scenes. Other subjects raised include the failings of the US medical system, the problems of an actor seeking work, and the ethics of manufacturing poison gas.

Wakefield Master, the The unidentified author of the five extant MYSTERY PLAYS of the 32 in the early 15th-century Wakefield Cycle, performed at Wakefield, Yorkshire; they are also known as the Towneley Cycle. The works attributed to the Wakefield Master are *Processus Noe cum Filiis* (*The Pageant of Noah and his Sons*), *Pagina Pastorum* (*The Shepherds' Play*), *Secunda Pastorum* (*The Second Shepherds' Play*), *Magnus Herodes* (*Herod the Great*), and *Coliphizacio* (*About the High Priest Caiaphas*).

The plays are all written in the nine-line stanza used only in the Wakefield Cycle (other cycles use a 13-line stanza). The language is colloquial. Despite the biblical subject matter, humour and farce both feature strongly; the Wakefield Master is considered to be one of the wittiest and most accomplished of the authors of mystery plays.

walk. **walk through a part** To repeat one's part at rehearsal verbally, but without dressing for it or acting it.

walking gentleman *See* STOCK COMPANY.

walking lady *See* STOCK COMPANY.

walk-on part A part in a play in which the actor has only to walk about on stage, sometimes with a word or two to say.

Wall, Max (1908–90) British variety comedian. The son of Jack Lorimer, an eccentric dancer known as the 'Hielan Laddie', Wall made his variety debut as a child, when he was billed as 'The Boy with the Obedient Feet'. As an adult he appeared in cabaret as 'Max Wall and His Independent Legs', making his West End debut in 1925 in *The London Review*. His eccentric dance would begin with a few quiet taps, before building into a mad frenzied whirl, during which he would rip off clothes and tear out his hair. In the 1920s and 1930s Wall toured Europe and America, making his first New York appearance in *Earl Carroll's Vanities* in 1932. It was during this period that he first began to intersperse his physical routines with sardonic one-liners (example: "If they sawed a woman in half, I'd get the half that eats").

Wall's stage genius, mournful eyes, and lantern jaw proved just as effective in serious drama; he undertook his first 'legitimate' role in 1956, when he appeared as UBU in Jarry's *Ubu Roi*. He later gave acclaimed performances in both Osborne's THE ENTERTAINER (1974) and Beckett's WAITING FOR GODOT (1981). In 1973 he played the British impresario Sir Charles COCHRAN in Peter Saunders's musical comedy *Cockie* at the Vaudeville Theatre. Two years later he successfully revived his old variety act as *Aspects of Max Wall*, and received a special award from the Variety Club. *See also* PROFESSOR WALLOFSKI.

Wallace, Nellie *See* ESSENCE OF ECCENTRICITY, THE.

Wallack family A British-US theatrical family that produced four noted actors: Henry John Wallack (1790–1870), his son James William Wallack (1818–73), Henry's younger brother, also named James William Wallack (1791–1864), and his son Lester Wallack (John Johnstone Wallack; 1820–88), who was also a playwright.

Henry John Wallack was born in London, the son of William Wallack, a star of Astley's Amphitheatre, where young Henry appeared with his father. In 1818 he emigrated to America and joined Thomas Wignell's company at Philadelphia's CHESTNUT STREET THEATRE. He acted at the Chatham Theatre, New York, in 1924, taking over its management two years later. In 1837 he became stage-manager at his brother James's National Theatre in New York, where he achieved considerable success in 1847 as Sir Peter Teazle in Sheridan's *The School for Scandal*.

James William Wallack II, was born in London and served an apprenticeship with his father before joining his uncle James's company at the National in 1837. He specialized in tragedy and melodrama, playing many leading Shakespearean roles. In 1865 he joined his cousin Lester at Wallack's Theatre, New York. His later successes included Fagin in *Oliver Twist* and Mathias in *The Bells*.

The elder **James William Wallack** began acting at the age of 12, and subsequently spent nearly 10 years at Covent Garden. From 1818 onwards he played romantic and tragic roles in both America and Britain. He was general manager of the National Theatre, New York, from 1837 until 1839, when it burned down. In 1852 he reopened the New York Lyceum as Wallack's Theatre, which became one of the city's leading venues. He made his farewell performance there in 1859; two years later he opened a second Wallack's on Broadway, shortly before retiring and leaving the theatre to his son Lester and nephew James.

James's son **Lester Wallack** was born in New York but began his career in the provincial theatre in Britain. His New York debut came in 1847 in Boucicault's *Used Up*; he subsequently played romantic and comic roles before joining his father at Wallack's Theatre. He took over the management of Wallack's in 1861; amongst his many successes was his own play, *Rosedale*, which opened in 1863. He opened a third Wallack's in 1882 and managed both venues until his retirement five years later.

Lester collected theatrical spoonerisms. His favourite occurred in a production of *The School for Scandal* at Wallack's Theatre, when the actor H. B. Crabtree tried to say "a bullet in the thorax" but came out with "a thullet in the borax". None of the audience noticed until his fellow actor John Brougham (who never failed to inflate others' mistakes) boomed out, "What the devil is his borax?"

Wallenstein Friederich von SCHILLER's dramatic masterpiece, a historical trilogy completed in 1799. No record exists of its first performance at the Weimar Court Theatre, which Schiller managed with Goethe from 1799 to 1805. The last two parts of *Wallenstein* were translated into English in 1800 by Samuel Taylor Coleridge, who called it "not unlike Shakespeare's historical plays – a species by itself".

Wallenstein follows the career of the Austrian general Albrecht von Wallenstein

(1583–1634), who was victorious in the Thirty Years' War until his defeat in 1632 by Gustavus Adolphus at Lützen. He was later murdered by his officers, who thought he was going to defect to the Swedish enemy. Schiller first became attracted to the story while carrying out research as a professor of history at the University of Jena. The drama explores the corrupting effect of power.

Walnut Street Theatre A theatre in Philadelphia, the oldest US theatre still in use today. Built in 1809 as a circus venue, it was converted to use as a theatre in 1811 to compete with the established and successful CHESTNUT STREET THEATRE. The rivalry between the two theatres was such that both lavished vast amounts of money on importing fashionable British and European acts in attempts to outdo each other. The appearance of another rival, the ARCH STREET THEATRE, in 1828 proved too much for the two better-established venues, both of which became bankrupt in 1829 as a result of their wild extravagance.

The Walnut Street Theatre recovered, however, and went on to support a talented stock company, even though New York was already replacing Philadelphia as the centre of the US theatre. The Walnut Street Theatre was redesigned in 1970 to accommodate an audience of 1052. The Philadelphia Drama Guild was based there from 1971 until 1980.

Waltz of the Toreadors, The One of Jean ANOUILH's *pièces grinçantes*, or harsh comedies. It was first performed in 1952 in Paris. The first London production (1956) was staged by Peter Hall at the Arts Theatre Club and featured strong performances by Hugh Griffith and Beatrix Lehmann. A film version was later made with Peter Sellers.

The story concerns General St Pé, who has kept his lover Ghislaine waiting for 17 years because he cannot bring himself to desert his wife, who pretends to be crippled. Ghislaine, who once danced the Waltz of the Toreadors with the general, becomes so frustrated that she leaps from a window. Fortunately she lands in the arms of St Pé's young secretary Gaston, who is actually the general's illegitimate son. The ensuing romance between Gaston and Ghislaine drives St Pé to enter into an affair with his maid.

war. ***Wars of the Roses, The*** The four Shakespeare plays set during the Wars of the Roses – the three parts of HENRY VI and RICHARD III – adapted for performance as a cycle. The Royal Shakespeare Company has given two highly praised productions of the sequence. The first, in 1963–64, was directed by Peter Hall with Peggy Ashcroft as Queen Margaret, David Warner as Henry VI, Donald Sinden as York, and Ian Holm as Richard III. The second, in 1978, was directed by Terry Hands and starred Alan Howard as Henry VI.

war of the theatres or **poetomachia** A battle of insults between three of England's leading Elizabethan dramatists. The opening shot was Ben JONSON's *Every Man out of His Humour* (1599), which presents bitter portraits of his contemporaries John MARSTON and Thomas Dekker. Jonson struck again in 1600 with *Cynthia's Revels* and in 1601 with the devastating *Poetaster*. Marston counterattacked weakly with *What You Will* (1601) before collaborating with Dekker to give an offensive portrait of Jonson as an inflated pedant in *Satiromastix* (1602). The cause of the quarrel is now obscure and some theatre historians believe that the entire exercise may have been a publicity stunt for all three writers.

Warburton's cook The servant of the English antiquarian and book collector John Warburton (1682–1759), who was responsible for the destruction of some 60 unique manuscripts of Elizabethan and Jacobean plays, collected by her master. Betsy Baker by name, she was clearly unaware or unheedful of the value of the manuscripts assembled by Warburton, the Herald of Somerset:

> After I had been many years collecting these MSS playes, through my own carelessness and the ignorance of my servant in whose hands I had lodged them, they was unluckely burnd or put under pye bottoms...

Of the total collection only three plays and a fragment of a fourth were saved from an ignominious fate at Betsy's hands and John Warburton has gone down in history as "the pie-eating herald". Although many of the lost manuscripts were probably of little interest, it has been conjectured that they may have included works by Thomas Dekker, John Ford, Philip Massinger, Cyril Tourneur, and William Shakespeare.

Ward, Dame (Lucy) Geneviève Teresa (1838–1922) US actress, who in 1921 became the first actress to be created a Dame of the British Empire. Born in New York, she began her career as an opera singer using the stage name Madame Ginevra Guerrabella, but turned to acting when she lost her singing voice through illness. Her career as an actress began in 1873 when she appeared in Manchester as Lady Macbeth, a part that she also performed in French at the Théâtre de la Porte-Saint-Martin in Paris. A year later she won acclaim in the role of Portia in *The Merchant of Venice*.

Ward made her New York debut in 1878 in the tragic title role of *Jane Shore* by W. G. Wills. In 1879 she produced and starred in *Forget-Me-Not* by Herman Merivale and F. C. Grove at the Lyceum Theatre, London, a venue which she briefly managed. In 1891 she joined Henry Irving at the Lyceum, appearing first as Queen Eleanor in Tennyson's *Becket*. She made her farewell appearance in 1920, playing Queen Margaret to Frank Benson's Richard III.

wardrobe All the costumes assembled for a stage production. These are either specially created for a play or taken from a large permanent collection kept in the theatre's wardrobe room. Larger theatres have their own wardrobe mistress or master, whose duties include buying cloth, sewing the costumes, fitting actors, and making modifications, as well as cleaning, repairing, and storing costumes.

Theatre properties can also be stored in the wardrobe room. Joseph Addison wrote in 1711 of a visit to a playhouse wardrobe in which he saw "daggers, poniards, wheels, bowls of poison".

Washington Square Players A US theatre group formed in 1914 by amateur players to perform a summer repertory season at Provincetown, Massachusetts. The founders included the Welsh-born producer Lawrence Langner, who later helped to found the Theatre Guild in 1919. In 1915 the Washington Square Players moved into a former stable in New York's Greenwich Village, before taking over the 40-seat Bandbox Theatre, where they presented one-act plays. In 1916 the company transferred to the 600-seat Comedy Theatre, where they performed their first full-length productions, including Chekhov's *The Seagull*, Ibsen's *Ghosts*, and Shaw's *Mrs Warren's Profession*.

Members of the company included the actress Katharine CORNELL, who made her professional debut there in *Bushido* in 1916, the set designer and director Robert Edmond JONES, and the theatrical designer Lee Simonson (1888–1967), who was later a founder and director of the Theatre Guild. The Washington Square Players broke up in 1918, as a result of financial difficulties.

Waste A tragedy by the British dramatist Harley GRANVILLE-BARKER. It was first performed privately in London in 1907 by the Stage Society, after the Lord Chamberlain refused to license it for performance at the Royal Court Theatre. The ban, which was imposed because one of the characters has an illegal abortion, was not lifted until 1936.

Watch on the Rhine, The Lillian HELLMAN's anti-Nazi drama, first produced in 1941 in New York, where it ran for 378 performances.

The play opens with Sara Muller returning to America from Europe in 1940 to find the Romanian aristocrat Teck de Brancovis staying with her mother and brother in their country home. Teck discovers that Sara's German husband Kurt is a member of the anti-Nazi resistance with a price on his head. After the Romanian attempts to blackmail Kurt, Kurt kills him and leaves immediately for Germany. As a Jewish writer, Hellman was attempting to warn America of the tyranny and evil that the Nazis were imposing upon Europe.

During the performances, the actor Charles Goldner ran a sweepstake in which members of the cast guessed the evening's box office takings. Goldner always won because he made the first entrance, walked to centre stage to kiss the leading lady's hand, then straightened up and let his eyes roam slowly from stalls to gallery, to assess the number of empty seats.

water. water puppet show A form of puppet theatre in Vietnam, said to have been performed for 1000 years. Several troupes still exist. The plays are performed on pavilions built on landing stages in lakes. The puppeteers stand up to their waists in water behind reed screens, and move the brightly coloured puppets over the surface of the lake with underwater rods.

The chief character is the smiling Teu, who often wears a red loincloth. The plays also feature an array of animals including the unicorn, phoenix, dragon, and tortoise, together with fish, ducks, and other creatures swimming, flying, dancing, and fighting on and below the water. The performance is accompanied by music provided by an orchestra of flutes, drums, and gongs.

water row *See* GROUNDROW *under* GROUND.

way. ***Way of the World, The*** William CONGREVE's finest comedy of manners, which was initially such a failure that he retired from the theatre. It was first performed in 1700 at Lincoln's Inn Fields Theatre, which was managed by Congreve and Thomas Betterton. The play's cool reception was mainly owing to its convoluted plot and sophisticated dialogue, both of which were difficult to follow. Critical opinion has since recognized the skill of its construction and its serious appraisal of sexual morality.

Following the first production, which starred Betterton, *The Way of the World* enjoyed only two revivals in the following 50 years. Thereafter it was considered too old fashioned and too bawdy for the public stage: it even shocked theatregoers as late as the 1920s, when it was revived at the Oxford Playhouse to packed student audiences. A highly successful production was staged in 1953, with John Gielgud as Mirabell, Pamela Brown as Millamant, and Margaret Rutherford as Lady Wishfort.

Mirabell is in love with the witty and spirited Millamant, but conceals his pursuit by courting her aunt Lady Wishfort, who is opposed to the match. The lovers eventually agree to marry after the famous 'bargaining scene', in which they negotiate an agreement as to their rights within marriage.

Way Upstream A comedy by Alan AYCKBOURN, first performed in 1981 at the STEPHEN JOSEPH THEATRE IN THE ROUND, Scarborough, where Ayckbourn is artistic director; it was produced at the National Theatre a year later.

The plot centres on Keith and June, who are taking a canal-boat holiday with another couple, Alistair and Emma. The domineering Keith orders his companions about as they wend their way upriver, squabbling all the way. Keith's secretary continually interrupts their holiday with news of a growing labour dispute at his factory, until Keith finally has to leave, and soon the boat runs aground. The remaining holiday-makers are rescued by Vince, who claims to be an old hand with narrow boats. Vince soon takes over the expedition, subjecting the others to a dictatorial regime and revealing himself as a sadistic maniac. He seduces the grateful June, and becomes involved in a brawl with the mild-mannered Alistair. Eventually Vince is overthrown and Alistair and Emma head upstream alone. The element of political allegory was not missed by the original critics.

Weaver, John (1673–1760) English dancing-master, who helped to create the English HARLEQUINADE. Weaver introduced French balletic mimes or 'scenical dancing' to the English theatre in his ITALIAN NIGHT SCENES, which were based on the scenarios of the *commedia dell'arte*. In 1728 he published a *History of Mimes and Pantomimes*.

Weber and Fields A US BURLESQUE comedy team consisting of Joseph Weber (1867–1942) and Lew Fields (Lewis Maurice Shanfields; 1867–1941). Fields, who was tall and thin, played the devious character Mayer, while the short plump Weber played the innocent Mike. Both wore ridiculous padded suits and small bowler hats.

The sons of Polish Jewish immigrants, Weber and Fields appeared together in minstrel routines from the age of nine. They later created a slapstick 'knockabout Dutch act' featuring comic broken English. In 1885 they formed their own company for writing and acting burlesques at the Broadway Music Hall; 10 years later they opened their own theatre. Weber eventually went on to direct shows, while Fields moved into musical comedy and took over the Wallack Theatre in 1904. They performed together for the last time in 1912. Weber retired in 1918 and Fields in 1929.

Webster. John Webster (*c.* 1580–1634) English playwright. Little is now known about Webster's life. He was the son of a London coachmaker and appears to have studied law at the Middle Temple. Although he is recorded as the author of several other works, incuding a history play, *Lady Jane*, his only surviving works are *Westward Ho!* and *Northward Ho!* (1604–05), written in collaboration with Thomas Dekker, the comedy *The Devil's Law Case* (1620), and the two tragic masterpieces, THE WHITE DEVIL (1612) and THE DUCHESS OF MALFI (1614).

With their eloquent poetry and superbly crafted plots, the two plays are amongst the most compelling of Jacobean REVENGE TRAGEDIES. Nevertheless, Webster has often been criticized for the violence and morbidity of his work: George Bernard Shaw called him the "Tussard Laureate" of English literature, while Rupert Brooke described his plays as "full of the feverish and ghastly turmoil of a nest of maggots". Both *The White Devil* and *The Duchess of Malfi* have enjoyed frequent modern revivals.

> Webster was much possessed by death
> And saw the skull beneath the skin;
> And breastless creatures under ground
> Leaned backwards with lipless grin.
>
> T. S. ELIOT: *Whispers of Immortality*.

Webster family The English actor-manager and dramatist Ben Nottingham Webster (1797–1882); his grandson the actor Ben Webster (1864–1947) and his actress wife Mary Whitty (1865–1948); and their daughter Margaret Webster (1905–71), who became an actress, director, and author.

The elder **Ben Webster** began his theatrical career playing the violin at the Croydon Theatre; for six weeks he walked from Shoreditch to Croydon on twopence a day ("one pennyworth of oatmeal and one pennyworth of milk"). Webster's special treat came when the gallery pelted the orchestra with mutton pies, which he collected and ate under the stage.

His first parts were as Harlequin and Pantaloon in the provinces and subsequently at Drury Lane. He performed in broad comedy at the Olympic Theatre before turning to managing and acting at the Haymarket from 1837 to 1853. He wrote comedies, farces, and adaptations, including one of Dickens's *The Cricket on the Hearth*. Webster's finest role was as Triplet in Taylor and Reade's *Masks and Faces*, which he produced in 1852 at both the Haymarket and the Adelphi. He went on to manage the Princess's Theatre in 1869 and retired in 1874.

The younger **Ben Webster** first appeared in London in 1887, going on to establish a reputation with his performances in the works of Shakespeare and Shaw. Webster, who emigrated to America in 1939, was surprised at the US custom of rewriting a play during rehearsals. When he asked the actress Grace George which version of a particular play she intended to act, she replied, "Whichever I can remember when I get to it." He earned a distinguished name on Broadway, making his farewell appearance there in 1940 as Montague in *Romeo and Juliet*.

Mary Whitty married Ben Webster in 1892. She made her debut in Liverpool in 1881 and a year later played at the St James's Theatre, London. Eventually she joined Henry Irving's company at the Lyceum, touring America with the troupe in 1895. She appeared in Harley Granville-Barker's *The Madras House* (1910) and Emlyn Williams's *Night Must Fall* (1935). Whitty went to New York with Webster in 1939.

Margaret Webster, daughter of Webster and Whitty, first appeared on stage at the age of 12. She made her adult debut in 1924 in the chorus of Euripides's *The Trojan Women*. The production starred Sybil Thorndike, with whom she later toured in Shaw's *Saint Joan*. Webster joined Gielgud's Old Vic company in 1929 and played in his *Hamlet* the following year. In 1937 she directed Maurice Evans in a successful Broadway production of *Richard II*. Webster's 1943 production of *Othello*, in which she played Emilia to Paul Robeson's Moor, broke all records for Shakespeare on Broadway. In 1946 she helped to found the American Repertory Theatre, directing and acting in the opening production of *Henry VIII*.

Wedekind, Frank (Benjamin Franklin Wedekind; 1864–1918) German playwright and actor, whose sexual, violent, and grotesque themes shocked his audiences. His dramas mark a transition between REALISM and EXPRESSIONISM in the theatre. Wedekind was a major influence on Bertolt Brecht who said, "Like Tolstoy and Strindberg, Wedekind was one of the great educators of modern Europe. His greatest work was his own personality."

Wedekind worked as a journalist, advertising manager, and secretary to a circus before becoming a cabaret singer and actor in Leipzig. Excited by the new drama of Strindberg and Hauptmann, he turned to playwriting in 1889, provoking a sensation with his portrayal of adolescent sexuality in *The Young World* (1890) and SPRING AWAKENING (1891). The latter, featuring adolescent deaths resulting from abortion and suicide, was banned in Britain until 1965.

Themes of sex and death were also explored in Wedekind's plays about the amoral Lulu, EARTH SPIRIT (1898) and PANDORA'S BOX (1903). The part of Lulu was created by Wedekind's wife, Tilly Newes (Mathilde Newes; 1886–1970), who appeared in many of his plays.

After Wedekind's death the director Leopold Jessner enjoyed a great success at the National Theatre in Berlin with his 1920 production of Wedekind's play about sophisticated crooks, *Der Marquis von Keith* (1900).

Weimar style A style of acting outlined by GOETHE in his 'Rules for Actors', written when he was a director at the Weimar Court Theatre (1791–1817). The detailed code of rules, which dealt with articulation, ways of controlling tempo and tone when speaking, principles of posture and movement, and social conduct offstage, was prompted by the regional accents and undisciplined stage behaviour of members of Goethe's poorly educated company. Goethe expected his actors to be models of decorum, both on and off stage. His aim was grace, formality, and dignity – although some thought the end result rather stiff.

The Weimar style did, however, create the most integrated ensemble of Goethe's era, and influenced many actors in the early 19th century. Goethe also expected high standards of conduct from his audiences and was known to reprimand them during a performance for indecorous behaviour. *See also* HAMBURG STYLE; LEIPZIG STYLE.

Welles, (George) Orson (1915–85) US director, actor, writer, and producer. Welles made his acting debut at the age of 16 in *Jew Süss* (1931) at Dublin's Gate Theatre, after falsely telling the management that he was a member of the THEATRE GUILD. He subsequently toured in plays by Shakespeare and Shaw before collaborating with John Houseman (1902–88) on the FEDERAL THEATRE PROJECT. As part of the Project he directed a successful *Macbeth* (1936) with a Black cast at Harlem's Lafayette Theatre (*see* SCOTTISH PLAY). In 1937, when they devised a controversial 'labour opera' *The Cradle Will Rock*, Project officials closed the theatre two hours before the curtain was due to go up. Welles and Houseman simply moved the audience to another theatre and performed without scenery.

That same year the two men opened their renowned Mercury Theatre with an anti-fascist interpretation of *Julius Caesar* in modern dress, featuring Welles as Brutus. In 1938 the Mercury's radio version of H. G. Wells's *The War of the Worlds* caused panic among listeners, who thought that Martians were genuinely invading New Jersey. In 1940 Welles took several of the Mercury players to Hollywood, where he wrote, produced, directed, and starred in the film classic *Citizen Kane* (1941).

After a decade in Hollywood, Welles returned to the theatre in 1951, making his London debut in the title role of *Othello*; in 1955 he played Ahab in *Moby Dick* with "a voice of bottled thunder" (in the words of Kenneth Tynan). He designed and directed a production of Ionesco's *Rhinoceros* at the Royal Court Theatre, London, in 1960.

Welles, as a true showman, was never at a loss on stage. When his false nose fell off during *Moby Dick*, he kicked the putty appendage straight into the stalls. In 1956, when he broke one ankle and sprained the other playing King Lear in New York, he disguised a wheelchair as a throne and rolled through the part.

well-made play English translation of the French phrase *une pièce bien faite*, used in the early 19th century to describe plays that depended on a well-crafted plot. In the hands of Eugène SCRIBE, the well-made play developed a formulaic structure still sometimes used today: the protagonists meet with complications that build towards a climax followed by a denouement. By the late 19th century, however, 'well-made play' became a pejorative term because characterization was subordinated to an articifial action that depended upon such manipulations as coincidental meetings and mistaken identity. The genre was particularly ridiculed by Zola, who helped to usher in the fashion for NATURALISM.

Besides Scribe, French exponents of the well-made play included SARDOU, LABICHE, and FEYDEAU. In Britain its techniques were adopted by Henry Arthur Jones, A. W. Pinero, Terance Rattigan, Noël Coward, and even George Bernard Shaw (who once attacked Sardou's high-class melodrama as 'Sardoodledom'). Well-made plays were also turned out by such US playwrights as Lillian Hellman.

Wendy The young girl in J. M. Barrie's children's play PETER PAN (1904), who exercised motherly control over Peter and her younger brothers during their visit to Never Never Land. The character has given her name to the 'Wendy house', a child's toy house that is large enough to enter. It is named after the little house that Peter and the Lost Boys build around Wendy.

Werkteater (Dutch: work theatre) A cooperative theatre society founded in 1970 in Amsterdam to investigate and develop new directions for drama. The company urges its actors to identify totally with their roles and encourages a highly physical style of acting. It also aims to explore the interrelationship between actors and their audiences. Like the US LIVING THEATRE, the Werkteater emphasizes collective creation – many of its plays come from improvisations built on an actor's personal experiences – and is committed to airing social issues. These are highlighted in such works as *Situations* (1972), about conditions in mental hospitals, *Sunset Sky* (1973), dealing with old age, *Forest and Air* (1979), about mentally handicapped people, and *In For Treatment* (1979), showing a cancer patient's treatment in hospital. The last-named play has been filmed as *Opname* by Enkuan Zuylen. In the early 1980s Shireen Strooker formed Werkteater II for younger theatre workers.

Wesker, Arnold (1932–) British playwright, who made his name with a trilogy about the history of a Jewish family from 1936 to 1959. His own Jewish East-End background was the basis for the three plays CHICKEN SOUP WITH BARLEY, which opened in 1958 at the Belgrave Theatre, Coventry, and transferred to the Royal Court Theatre, London; ROOTS, which followed in 1959; and *I'm Talking About Jerusalem*, which appeared in 1960. The trilogy shows how the socialism and idealism of the younger members of the family are often in conflict with the disillusionment of the older members. *The Kitchen* (1959) made use of Wesker's memories of his four years working as a pastry cook, while CHIPS WITH EVERYTHING (1962) was based on his National Service with the RAF.

Many of Wesker's plays deal with the struggles of the idealist in unsympathetic surroundings, a situation in which he has often found himself in real life: a natural supporter of liberal causes, he was imprisoned briefly for his commitment to the antinuclear movement. In 1961 he established the CENTRE 42 project with the aim of bringing the arts to working-class audiences; the centre was wound up in 1971 for financial reasons. Although Wesker's best-known plays belong to his early period, he has continued to please audiences, if not always the critics, with such pieces as *The Merchant* (1976), a reworking of Shakespeare's *The Merchant of Venice*, *Caritas* (1981), about a medieval anchoress, the monologues *Mothers* (1982) and *Annie Wobbler* (1983), *Whatever Happened to Betty Lemon* (1986), and *Blood Libel* (1991). He has also written for television and radio.

west. West End The western district of inner London, which contains most of the capital's principal theatres. The term is used as a synonym for the commercial theatre in London (as BROADWAY is used in America). The main concentration of theatres is in the area bounded by Shaftesbury Avenue and the Strand.

West Side Story The highly successful Broadway musical set in New York's gangland, with music by Leonard Bernstein and lyrics by Stephen SONDHEIM. The idea of setting a modern version of *Romeo and Juliet* in downtown New York was first suggested by Jerome Robbins, who subsequently directed and choreographed the musical. Arthur Laurents wrote the book. The first performance was in 1957 in New York; the show opened a year later at Her Majesty's Theatre, London, and won the *Evening Standard* Award. Songs include 'Maria', 'Tonight', 'America', 'I Feel Pretty', and 'There's A Place for Us'.

The first scene introduces two rival West Side gangs, the Jets and the Sharks. Tony, a member of the Jets, falls in love with Maria, the sister of the Shark's leader, Bernardo. Tony accidentally stabs Bernardo to death whilst trying to prevent a fight; although Maria is devastated, she forgives him and they plan to elope. Whilst waiting for her to join him, Tony is deceived into believing that Maria has been murdered. Devastated, he seeks out Maria's former fiancé Chino, who shoots him and leaves him to die in Maria's arms.

Westminster play A play presented in Latin by the 'Scholars in College' at Westminster School in London, Britain's only surviving

SCHOOL DRAMA, the Westminster play has been staged since 1560 with two short breaks during the Civil War and World War II. In the 18th and 19th centuries the play was noted for its topical prologues and epilogues; the former became an annual review of school news while the latter satirized contemporary events.

The tradition was begun by the headmaster Dr Alexander Nowell (1507–1602) and reaffirmed by Queen Elizabeth I, who attended performances, of Plautus's *Miles Gloriosus* in 1564 and the anonymous *Sapientia Salomonis* two years later. The works normally come from the plays of Plautus, Terence, or other classic authors. The most famous performer was Barton Booth (1681–1733), who attended the school from 1689 to 1698 and appeared in a cycle of plays by Terence, later becoming a leading tragedian.

The Westminster play was performed in the New Dormitory in Little Dean's Yard until this was damaged by bombs in World War II; the performances moved into the open air in 1954, and are now given biennially in contemporary dress.

what. ***What the Butler Saw*** The last full-length play by Joe ORTON, first performed in 1969 two years after his murder. A Freudian farce, it was a box-office success, although some audiences were shocked by its explicit discussions of sexual perversions; some critics believed Orton would probably have revised the work had he lived. The story takes place in the private clinic of Dr Prentice and involves rape, blackmail, transvestism, incest, and the private parts of Sir Winston CHURCHILL.

What Every Woman Knows A social comedy by J. M. BARRIE, first produced at the Duke of York's Theatre, London, in 1908.

The play is set in a small town in Scotland, where the parents of plain Maggie Wylie promise to pay for the education of drab John Shand if he will marry her. When Shand becomes an MP, the couple marry; he soon becomes known for his witty speeches, largely written by his new wife. When he is attracted to another woman, Maggie cleverly lets him discover this woman's failings for himself. At last, John comes to appreciate his wife's wit and charm.

Helen Hayes scored a great success in the role of Maggie Wylie in a 1926 performance on Broadway. She played the part for so many years, and revised her interpretation so thoroughly that the critic Brooks Atkinson became totally confused. In 1926 he wrote that Hayes "is not quite up to the interpretation of so full-bodied a part...this Maggie is a woman of tougher substance than Miss Hayes communicates..." Years later, he noted, "She was perfectly cast when she played in Barrie's *What Every Woman Knows* – a mousy, unassertive woman..."

Whelan, Albert *See* LUSTIGE BRÜDER.

when. ***When We Are Married*** A farce by J. B. PRIESTLEY, first produced in 1938 in London. The plot involves three respectable Yorkshire couples, who were married in the same church on the same day and are now gathering 25 years later to have a photograph taken for the local press. The Helliwells, Parkers, and Soppitts celebrate happily until the chapel organist, Gerald Forbes, reveals that a clerical error 25 years ago made their marriages invalid. All three couples now re-examine their commitment to each other; when the press photographer discovers that they are all legally married after all, Parker bribes him to keep the whole affair secret. During the original production Priestley himself played the part of the photographer for several performances when the actor concerned was injured.

When We Dead Awaken The last play by Henrik IBSEN, subtitled "a dramatic epilogue". It was first performed with great success in 1899 in Oslo, being seen three years later in London, and in 1905 in New York. The drama received high praise in the *Fortnightly Review*, in an article by the 18-year-old James Joyce. The story centres on the character Rubek, a sculptor, and examines the relationship between artistic creativity and truth.

white. ***White Devil, The*** A tragedy by John WEBSTER, written some time after 1609 and first performed in 1612. The passionate drama is loosely based on real events in 16th-century Italy. Modern revivals include Frank Dunlop's 1969 production for the National Theatre, with Geraldine McEwan, Edward Woodward, and Derek Godfrey.

The play centres on the adultery of the Venetian lady, Vittoria Corombona, with the Duke of Brachiano. Aided by her brother Flamineo, she incites the duke to kill her husband and his wife, Isabella. In a famous scene, Vittoria is tried for both adultery and murder but defends herself with considerable intelligence. She is sentenced to confinement but escapes to become Brachiano's duchess. However, Isabella's avengers, prompted by her ghost, poison Brachiano before murdering Vittoria and Flamineo.

White-eyed Kaffir, the The stage name of George H. Chirgwin (1854–1922), a popular British music-hall performer. His high-pitched singing and banjo-playing predated a similar act by George Formby. Chirgwin first appeared on stage at the age of seven and toured with a minstrel show before playing the halls. He was first billed as the White-eyed Kaffir in 1877, owing the nickname to the white patch make-up around his right eye. His most famous songs were 'The Blind Boy' and 'My Fiddle is My Sweetheart'. Chirgwin celebrated his golden jubilee in 1911 at London's Oxford Music Hall.

Whitehall Theatre A London theatre in Whitehall, near Trafalgar Square. It opened in 1930 and has long been identified with farces and sex revues. The striptease artiste Phyllis Dixey appeared there in 1943. After the war, a run of R. F. Delderfield's *Worm's Eye View* marked a return to comedy. An almost continuous string of Brian RIX farces opened in 1950 with Colin Morris's army play *Reluctant Heroes*, which ran for four years. Rix managed the theatre from 1950 to 1967, bringing the era of the **Whitehall farces** to a close with his own *Uproar in the House*. Paul Raymond found equal success in 1969, when his nude show *Pyjama Tops*, opened to run for 2498 performances. Two years later he bought the lease. In recent years the Whitehall has offered more varied fare, including John Wells's political spoof *Anyone for Denis* (1981), the thriller *Murder by Misadventure* (1992) and a dramatization of Irvine Welsh's *Trainspotting* (1995).

Whiteside, Sheridan The central character, a venomous theatre critic, in THE MAN WHO CAME TO DINNER (1939) by George S. KAUFMAN and Moss HART. The play was inspired by a visit from the notoriously outspoken US critic Alexander WOOLLCOTT to the house of Hart's family. Woollcott proved an impossible guest; among his many acid comments during his stay was the observation on Hart's home: "Just what God would have done if he had the money". Surprisingly, Woollcott was amused by the piece – he even toured in the role himself with great success.

Whittington, Dick Hero of the popular legend and PANTOMIME, a poor boy who made his way to London when he heard that the streets there were paved with gold. He found shelter as a scullion in the house of a rich merchant, who permitted each of his servants to take part in sending a cargo of merchandise to Barbary. Dick sent his cat, but subsequently ran away from the cook's ill-treatment. He was recalled by the sound of Bow bells seeming to say: "Turn again Whittington, Lord Mayor of London." He returned to find that his cat had been purchased for a vast sum by the King of Barbary, who was much plagued by rats and mice. He married his master's daughter Alice, prospered as a merchant, and became Lord Mayor.

The real Richard Whittington, a wealthy aristocrat who was three times Lord Mayor of London, died in 1423. The familiar legend first appeared in 1605 and was adapted as a theme for pantomime in the 19th century.

Who's Afraid of Virginia Woolf? Edward ALBEE's harrowing drama about an unhappily married couple. It was first performed in New York in 1962 and received its London premiere two years later, with Uta Hagen in both productions. The play established Albee's reputation and has enjoyed several revivals, including a 1996 London production with Diana Rigg and David Suchet. The 1966 film version starred Richard Burton and Elizabeth Taylor as the battling couple.

The play is set in a small New England college, where George, a history professor, and his wife Martha are entertaining a young couple, Nick and Honey. The evening degenerates as George and Martha pursue their drunken game of embarrassing their guests and humiliating each other.

Widowers' Houses The first play by George Bernard SHAW; written in 1885–87, it was first performed privately in 1892 at London's Independent Theatre Club. *Widowers' Houses* was published as one of the three 'unpleasant' plays in Shaw's *Plays Pleasant and Unpleasant* (1898). It was originally planned as a collaboration between Shaw and his friend William Archer, the critic who popularized the works of Ibsen through his English translations. The play addressed the contemporary problem of slum landlords and their exploitation of the poor.

The plot centres upon an honest young doctor, Harry Trench, who falls in love with and proposes to Blanche Sartorius. Later he learns that her father's fortune comes from the ownership of slum houses. The horrified Trench refuses Sartorius's financial help, but Blanche rejects her lover. Eventually Trench joins Sartorius in a philanthropic but profitable deal and is reunited with Blanche.

wild. ***Wild Duck, The*** Henrik IBSEN's tragicomedy about the damaging effects of idealism. Sometimes regarded as his masterpiece, it was first performed in 1884 in Bergen. The idealistic Gregers Werle attempts to save Hjalmar Ekdal's family from a life based on lies by telling Hjalmar that his beloved 14-year-old daughter, Hedvig, is not his child. Although Hedvig worships him, Hjalmar turns against her. Gregers advises the girl to shoot the wounded duck, which the family keeps in the attic, to prove to her father that she will sacrifice her greatest treasure for him. Instead, she shoots herself.

There has been much speculation as to what the captive duck symbolizes; suggestions have ranged from the family's self-delusions, to human weakness, to misplaced idealism. Ibsen himself gave no clue. Neither would he suggest how the parts should be played. He once attended a performance of *The Wild Duck* in Copenhagen to the great excitement of the cast, who asked if their interpretations had been satisfactory. Again, the playwright refused to offer any opinion.

Wild West exhibition A show featuring a demonstration of US frontier survival skills and scenes of Native American life. This type of entertainment was popular in America in the late 19th century and continued in some rural areas until shortly after World War II.

The first such entertainment was P. T. BARNUM's *Indian Life, or A Chance for a Wife* (1874). A vogue was then established by William Cody, known as BUFFALO BILL, who collaborated with Ned Buntline on the play *Scouts of the Prairie* and starred in it at New York's Bowery Theatre in 1874. By 1884 Cody was touring with his own Wild West show, with the sharp-shooter Annie Oakley as one of its stars (*see* ANNIE). The following year the show became part of Steele Mackaye's *Drama of Civilization* in New York. Cody's troupe merged with Pawnee Bill's in 1909 and eventually went bankrupt.

The Miller Brothers and Edward Arlington's Wild West Show flourished between 1908 and 1916 and was revived in the late 1920s. After this Wild West acts were mainly limited to brief exhibitions in rodeos and closing acts at circuses.

Wilde, Oscar (Fingal O'Flahertie Wills) (1854–1900) Irish playwright, who wrote one of the best loved comedies in the English language – THE IMPORTANCE OF BEING EARNEST (1895). A leading wit and conversationalist in London society, his career was destroyed at its height when he was imprisoned for homosexual offences.

Wilde was born in Dublin and educated at Trinity College, Dublin, and Magdalen College, Oxford. Settling in London, he became famous for his extravagant dress, long hair, and paradoxical views on art, literature, and morality. His first play, *Vera* (1880), a tragedy about Russian nihilists, was produced in New York to poor reviews. Success in the theatre came with the elegant drawing-room comedy LADY WINDERMERE'S FAN. After its opening night at the St James's Theatre, a friend asked how the performance went. "Oh, the play was a great success," Wilde replied, "but the audience was a total failure." A WOMAN OF NO IMPORTANCE (1893) was another success; when the audience called for the author at the end of the first performance, Wilde rose from a box and announced "Ladies and Gentlemen, I regret to inform you that Mr Oscar Wilde is not in the house." His other works for the theatre were AN IDEAL HUSBAND (1895) and the biblical SALOME (1896), written in French for Sarah Bernhardt.

Wilde flaunted his homosexual affairs, including his ill-fated liaison with Lord Alfred Douglas. Following a celebrated trial in 1895 he was sentenced to two years' imprisonment with hard labour. This led to public humiliation, poor health, and bankruptcy. On his release in 1897 he left for France and remained in exile there until his death.

> He belongs to our world more than to Victoria's. Now beyond the reach of scandal, his best writings validated by time, he

comes before us, still a towering figure, laughing and weeping, with parables and paradoxes, so generous, so amusing, and so right.

RICHARD ELLMANN: *Oscar Wilde* (1987).

Wilder, Thornton (1897–1975) The US 'anti-naturalist' playwright and novelist, who won Pulitzer Prizes for his expressionist dramas, OUR TOWN (1938), about small-town America, and THE SKIN OF OUR TEETH (1942), about humanity's ability to survive the disasters of history.

Wilder's early plays include the Civil-War drama *The Trumpet Shall Sound* (1927). He established his reputation with three one-act plays performed in 1931: *Pullman Car Hiawatha*, *The Happy Journey to Trenton and Camden*, a look at rural US life performed on an empty stage, and *The Long Christmas Dinner*, later adapted by the author as the libretto for Hindemith's 1961 opera.

Influenced by Strindberg, whom he called the "fountainhead of virtually all modernism in the drama", Wilder adopted a range of anti-naturalistic devices in his plays. His characters sometimes address the audience directly, as in *Our Town* and THE MATCHMAKER (1954). In 1955 Tyrone Guthrie commissioned him to adapt Euripides's *Alcestis* as *A Life in the Sun* for the Edinburgh Festival. Wilder's *Three Plays for Bleeker Street*, a triple-bill of one-act dramas, was produced at New York's Circle-in-the-Square in 1962.

Wilhelm Tell The last finished play by Friedrich von SCHILLER. It was first staged by Goethe at the Weimar Court Theatre in 1804, a year before Schiller's death. As Germany was then experiencing a new spirit of idealism, Schiller chose the legendary Swiss hero as a symbol of the struggle for individual and political freedom. His source was a 16th-century chronicle, *Chronicon Helveticum* (1834–36), by Gilg Tschudi. It was Schiller's play, however, that first brought the legend to worldwide attention. Albert Basserman (1867–1952), one of Germany's best-known naturalistic actors, took the title role in 1919. The play was also the basis for Rossini's 1829 opera.

The story, set in the 13th century, centres on the Swiss peasant Tell and his defiance of the tyrannical Austrian governor Gessler. It contains the famous incident of Tell shooting an apple from his small son's head with a crossbow, a punishment imposed by Gessler because Tell refused to bow to a symbol of Austrian power. Tell's assassination of Gessler raises moral questions as to whether violence may be justified in the struggle against oppressive rule.

A play also titled *William Tell* (1825) was written by the British actor-dramatist Sheridan Knowles (1784–1862).

Williams. Bert Williams (Egbert Austin Williams; *c.* 1876–1922) US comedian, who was the first Black entertainer to perform in a White show, and the first to be recorded on gramophone records. Williams also organized the first society for Black actors in 1906.

Born in the Bahamas, he began his career in MINSTREL SHOWS, in which he had to blacken his light complexion and adopt the comic dialect and shuffling gait of the stage Negro. Whenever he could Williams underplayed his characters, foregoing the traditional eye-rolling exaggerations.

A modest, sensitive, and scholarly man, Williams was humiliated by the indignities he endured before White audiences. "I'd like to stop doing piffle," he once said, "and portray the *real* Negro on stage." W. C. Fields called him "the funniest man I ever saw and the saddest man I ever knew."

From 1893 to 1908 he teamed up with George Walker (1873–1911), who played a flashy city slicker to Williams's shiftless melancholy dupe. After a spell with Sieg's Mastodon Minstrels, the duo appeared in New York in 1896 with *The Gold Bug*, becoming famous with their song 'Good Morning Carrie'. They then starred in several all-Black musicals, the most successful being *In Dahomey* (1902), which Williams produced in New York and subsequently in London (with a command performance at Buckingham Palace).

When Walker retired in 1909, Williams continued alone; a year later, despite protests from some cast members, he joined the previously all-White *Ziegfeld Follies*.

(George) Emlyn Williams (1905–87) Welsh playwright and director, who also made a reputation as a leading character actor. He made his acting debut in London in 1927 and produced his first work for the stage, *A Murder Has Been Arranged*, in 1930. Three years later he adapted Fauchois's *Prenez-garde à la peinture* as *The Late Christopher Bean*, which ran for more than a year with Edith Evans in the lead role.

Williams's first great hit as both actor and playwright came in 1935 in London with the thriller NIGHT MUST FALL. Other successful roles included Angelo in *Measure for Measure* (1937) and Sir Robert Morton in Rattigan's *The Winslow Boy* (1946). He also gave outstanding performances in his own works, particularly THE CORN IS GREEN (1938), in which he played a young Welsh miner.

In 1962 Williams replaced Paul Scofield as Sir Thomas More in the US production of Bolt's *A Man for All Seasons*. In the 1950s he toured widely in a one-man show in which he played the role of Charles Dickens. He followed this with *A Boy Growing Up* (1955), a sequence of readings from the works of Dylan Thomas.

Tennessee Williams (Thomas Lanier Williams; 1911–83) US playwright, whose controversial plays dealt with themes of repressed sexuality and family conflict. Williams was the most popular playwright in America between 1945 and 1960, winning the Pulitzer Prize twice and the New York Drama Critics' Circle Award four times. Amongst serious playwrights, only Eugene O'Neill equalled his achievements on the Broadway stage; several of Williams's plays were also made into successful films.

Williams, the son of a shoe salesman, grew up in some poverty in Mississippi and Missouri. Many of his early frustrations, which are reflected in his plays, arose from the prudery of his mother and the coarseness of his womanizing father, who, as his son's homosexuality became apparent, invariably referred to him as "Miss Nancy". The playwright revealed his homosexuality in his *Memoirs* (1975), having previously explored the subject in CAT ON A HOT TIN ROOF and SUDDENLY LAST SUMMER.

Williams tried his hand at fiction and poetry before turning to drama in the late 1930s, winning a Theatre Guild prize for the four one-act plays entitled *American Blues* in 1939. Recognition as a major playwright came with THE GLASS MENAGERIE, a tender work based largely on his own family. His next play, the brutal A STREETCAR NAMED DESIRE, opened in 1947, winning the Pulitzer Prize and making a star of Marlon Brando. It was followed a year later by SUMMER AND SMOKE. In 1949, these three plays were running simultaneously in London.

His later works included THE ROSE TATTOO (1951), *Camino Real* (1953), *Cat on a Hot Tin Roof* (1955), which won another Pulitzer Prize, ORPHEUS DESCENDING (1957), *Suddenly Last Summer* (1958), and SWEET BIRD OF YOUTH (1959), which opened with Paul Newman and Geraldine Page in the leads. By the late 1950s, Williams was being accused of repeating himself, and after *Period of Adjustment* (1960) and THE NIGHT OF THE IGUANA (1961), his plays were received unenthusiastically.

During his later years, Williams became dependent on drugs and alcohol, suffering a nervous breakdown in 1969. The critic Eric Bentley commented that Williams's problem was "an ambiguity of aim: he seems to want to kick the world in the pants and yet be the world's sweetheart..."

Will's Coffee House Will Unwin's famous tavern in London's COVENT GARDEN, which became a meeting place for writers, wits, and theatrical people during the Restoration and later. Also known as the Rose Tavern, the Russell Street Coffee House, and the Wit's Coffee House, the building stood on the corner of Bow Street and Russell Street. John Dryden and Dr Johnson were among the notables who frequented the after-theatre gatherings in a room on the first floor.

wind machine *See* SOUND EFFECTS *under* SOUND.

Windmill Theatre "We never closed" was the slogan of the Windmill, the only London theatre to keep its doors open throughout World War II. The theatre was built in 1910 as a small cinema in Great Windmill Street, near Piccadilly, on the site of an 18th-century windmill. The building, which has 326 seats on two levels, reopened as a theatre in 1931 with Michael Barrington's *Inquest*. A year later the owner, Laura Henderson, and her manager, Vivian Van Damm, began a programme of nonstop variety acts entitled *Revuedeville*. The theatre subsequently became famous for its tableaux of nearly nude girls (the Windmill Girls) interspersed with young comedians. Jimmy Edwards, Harry Secombe, and Tony Hancock, all learnt their trade there, finding laughs hard to achieve from an audience who had paid for titillation. Nevertheless, *Revuedeville* continued until 1964, when the building reverted to being a cinema. The impresario Paul Raymond purchased it in 1974 and opened with the sex comedy *Let's*

Get Laid, followed by another nude revue, *Rip-Off*. The Windmill was converted into a theatre-restaurant in 1981.

wings In popular usage, the space offstage on either side of the acting area. In a more technical sense, wings are FLATS at each side of the stage, used both as scenery and to screen off the backstage area from the audience.

Pairs of flats were first used in this way in late 16th-century Italy, whence they were introduced to England by Inigo JONES. Wings were eventually replaced by the BOX SET (first seen in London in 1832) but remain in use as scenery pieces for pantomime, opera, and ballet.

The expression *waiting in the wings* is used metaphorically to mean being ready to step in when needed. To *wing it* is to improvise or partly improvise a performance at short notice – the implication being that the actor has only had time to look at his or her part whilst standing in the wings.

Winslow Boy, The A play by Terence RATTIGAN, first performed in London in 1946, when it won the Ellen Terry Award as best play of the year; it moved to Broadway the following year to take the New York Drama Critics' Circle Award as best foreign play.

The story concerns the young naval cadet Ronnie Winslow, who is expelled from college for stealing a postal order. Rattigan's play, which concentrates on the struggles and sacrifices of the boy's father in his campaign to clear Ronnie's name, was based on the true case of George Archer-Shee, who was expelled from Osborne Naval College on the Isle of Wight in 1908 after being accused of petty theft. The cadet's father engaged the famous barrister Sir Edward Carson to represent his son in suing the Admiralty. The case ended with George Archer-Shee receiving £7000 compensation from the Admiralty. He was killed at Ypres in World War I.

winter. Winter Garden Theatre *See* OLD MO.

Winter's Tale, The SHAKESPEARE's tragicomic romance about the destructive power of jealousy and the healing power of love. One of his last plays, it was first performed in 1611 at the Globe Theatre, London and revived in 1612–13 to celebrate the marriage of Princess Elizabeth and the Elector Palatine. It contains Shakespeare's famous stage direction: "Exit, pursued by a bear."

In 1755 Garrick wrote and performed in his own adaptation, *Florizel and Perdita*. The US actress Mary Anderson made history by playing roles of both Hermione and her daughter PERDITA at London's Lyceum Theatre in 1887, a feat not repeated until 1969, when Judi Dench successfully performed the roles with the Royal Shakespeare Company. A film version of *The Winter's Tale* was released in 1966, with Laurence Harvey as Leontes.

In the story, King Leontes of Sicily believes his wife, Hermione, to be pregnant by his friend King Polixenes of Bohemia, and orders the child to be abandoned. Hermione apparently dies of grief and Leontes is repentant. Years later his abandoned daughter, Perdita, who has been brought up by shepherds, is courted by Polixenes's son, Florizel. Finally, Perdita's identity is revealed, Leontes is reconciled with Polixenes, and Hermione is revealed to be alive.

Wizard of Oz, The A fantasy by Frank L. Baum (1856–1919), which first appeared on the stage in 1902. Baum wrote the original book, *The Wonderful Wizard of Oz*, in 1900 and turned it into a musical play two years later. The story tells of young Dorothy, who is blown by a cyclone from her Kansas farm to the strange land of Oz, where she meets the Tin Woodman, the Scarecrow, and the Cowardly Lion. Other stage versions followed, including the 1975 Broadway musical, *The Wiz*, which featured an all-Black cast and music and lyrics by Charlie Smalls. The famous film starring Judy Garland was released in 1939.

Woffington, Peg (Margaret Woffington; *c.* 1714–60) Dublin-born actress, noted for her beauty. After her father died a pauper she joined a children's acting troupe, playing roles that included Polly Peachum in *The Beggar's Opera*. In 1740 she joined the Covent Garden company and made her reputation in the BREECHES PART of Sir Harry Wildair in Farquhar's *The Constant Couple*. She immediately became the toast of the town and her portrait was painted by Hogarth. Off-stage, however, she constantly quarreled with other actresses, particularly Mrs George Ann Bellamy, whom she is said to have wounded with a dagger on one occasion.

After one season, she argued with manager John Rich over her salary and moved to the Drury Lane Theatre, where she became the mistress first of Charles Macklin and then of David GARRICK (who wrote the song 'My Lovely Peggy' for her). When Garrick brought in the actress Kitty Clive, however, Peg returned to Covent Garden, playing such roles as Lady Macbeth to less popular acclaim.

In 1751 she joined SHERIDAN's company at Dublin's Smock Alley Theatre, opening the season with *The Provok'd Wife*; she soon became a famous figure in the city, even though she annoyed the Irish by presiding over the Beefsteak Club, which entertained English aristocrats with luxurious meals. In 1754 Sheridan took a chance by staging Voltaire's politically dangerous play *Mahomet* with Peg as Palmyra. The audience rioted and nearly destroyed the theatre; it was, however, refurbished later that year, with Peg appearing in a benefit performance of *All for Love*.

In 1757 Peg was starring as Rosalind in *As You Like It*, when she collapsed as she came to the end of the epilogue. She immediately retired, having played more than 125 leading roles in 30 years. She apparently repented of her former lifestyle, amazing friends and foes alike by her piety in her last years. Her life became the subject of Reade and Taylor's play *Masks and Faces* (1852), in which Sybil Thorndike starred in 1915.

Wolfit, Sir Donald (Donald Woolfitt; 1902–68) The last of Britain's great actor-managers. His famous roles included Shylock, Volpone, Richard III, King Lear, and Solness in Ibsen's *The Master Builder*. He was knighted in 1957. Believing that everybody should have the opportunity to see Shakespeare's plays, Wolfit spent much of his career making gruelling provincial tours.

Wolfit made his debut in 1920 in *The Merchant of Venice* at York's Theatre Royal. He founded his own Shakespeare company in 1937 and began to tour, visiting London only occasionally. Complaints were sometimes made that Wolfit surrounded himself with inferior actors in order to appear more impressive himself; he was also said to hurry his company players through their parts to make more time for his own lines. Once he omitted a scene in *Twelfth Night*, saying it was the work of another writer. "I cannot learn it," he declared, "and if I cannot learn it, Shakespeare did not write it!" One young actor appeared in Wolfit's *Macbeth* for several seasons. In his role as a messenger, he would come on crying "My Lord, the Queen is dead." After asking Wolfit several times for a more demanding role and receiving no response, he took revenge one evening by rushing on stage to announce, "My Lord, the Queen is much better and is even now at dinner."

When Wolfit played Falstaff he discovered that his padding had to be completely removed if he was to relieve himself during the performance. Luckily, Falstaff is offstage for some time during the play. "Brilliant craftsman, Shakespeare," Wolfit acknowledged. "Knew the actor would want to pee and constructed the play accordingly. A master, a master!"

woman. ***Woman Killed with Kindness, A*** A domestic tragedy by Thomas HEYWOOD, often regarded as one of the finest of the genre. It was first performed in 1603 in London and often revived. In 1913 Jacques Copeau's famous Théâtre du Vieux-Colombiér in Paris, opened with the drama.

The story involves the happily married Frankfords. Their domestic peace is ruined, however, when Frankford welcomes Wendoll into his home and soon finds his wife in the arms of their guest. Instead of taking immediate retribution, Frankford determines to "kill her even with kindness". He banishes her to a comfortable manor house but forbids her ever to see him or her children. Before she dies of remorse, his wife sends for him to beg forgiveness, which he grants.

Woman of No Importance, A Oscar WILDE's society comedy, first performed in 1893 at the Theatre Royal, Haymarket. Wilde wrote the lively first act in answer to criticisms that LADY WINDERMERE'S FAN lacked action. In the story, Lord Illingworth decides to employ Gerald Arbuthnot, the son of a former mistress, whom he dismisses as "a woman of no importance". When Mrs Arbuthnot reveals to Lord Illingworth and Gerald that they are in fact father and son, Gerald demands that his parents wed. Lord Illingworth is willing but Mrs Arbuthnot turns him down. The play contains many of Wilde's best epigrams; Lady Hunstanton, says of Lord Illingworth, for example:

> I was in hopes he would have married Lady Kelso. But I believe he said her family was too large. Or was it her feet? I forget which.

woman scorned, hell hath no fury like a A popular saying derived from CONGREVE's *The Mourning Bride* (III, viii):

Hev'n has no rage, like love to hatred turn'd
Nor Hell a fury, like a woman scorn'd.

women. ***Women, The*** A comedy by the US dramatist Clare Boothe Luce. The play, which features an all-female cast, was first performed in New York in 1936 at the Ethel Barrymore Theatre; a revival in 1973 with Rhonda Fleming and Alexis Smith leading the cast was well received. The story involves the lives, loves, and intrigues of a coven of Park Avenue matrons.

Women Beware Women A tragedy by Thomas MIDDLETON, often considered his masterpiece; it was first performed in 1621 in London but not published until 1657. The play was revived by the Royal Shakespeare Company at the Arts Theatre Club, London in 1962.

Set in Renaissance Florence, the play is based on historical events. Bianca Cappello, the wife of the poor clerk Leantio, is seduced by Francesco de' Medici, grand duke of Tuscany, who contrives her husband's murder. The play ends with a scene in which the main characters die by drinking poison during a masque. The remorseful Bianca drinks deliberately from the poisoned cup.

Woodward, Harry *See* LUN.

Wooing Ceremony *See* MUMMERS' PLAY *under* MUMMER.

Woollcott, Alexander Humphreys (1887–1943) US drama critic, who was portrayed as Sheridan WHITESIDE in the 1939 comedy THE MAN WHO CAME TO DINNER. Woollcott went on to star in the part himself and also appeared in S. N. Behrman's comedies *Brief Moment* (1932) and *Wine of Choice* (1938). He helped write two plays himself, collaborating with George S. Kaufman and Moss Hart on *The Channel Road* (1929) and *The Dark Tower* (1932).

Woollcott wrote for *The New York Times, The New York Herald, The Sun,* and *The New York World,* before retiring to broadcast, write for magazines, and lecture. His books include a biography of Minnie FISKE (1917) and *The Story of Irving Berlin* (1925).

Although he was an accomplished writer with engaging wit, his theatre criticism was sometimes surprisingly naive. Tallulah Bankhead said "To him the acting nobility was confined to Minnie Maddern Fiske and Harpo Marx." Since he valued players more than plays, he had difficulty analysing complex works, leading him to call Eugene O'Neill's contributions "worthless".

Woollcott's scathing notice of their French farce *Taking Chances,* provoked the Shubert management to attempt to ban him from their Broadway theatres. Although *The New York Times* won an injunction restraining the Shuberts from barring him, they subsequently had this reversed. When the paper refused to accept the Shuberts' advertising, they backed down and sent the critic a box of cigars. "The whole thing went up in smoke," noted Woollcott.

working lights In a theatre, ordinary lights that can be used when a play is not being performed for an audience, as when actors rehearse or the stage crew constructs a set.

World Theatre Season An annual theatre festival in London for foreign plays; it ran from 1964 to 1973 with a revival in 1975. Sir Peter Daubeny (1921–75) founded the event as part of the celebrations for the 400th anniversary of Shakespeare's birth. Works were presented at the Aldwych Theatre in their original languages by such renowned companies as the COMÉDIE-FRANÇAISE, the MOSCOW ART THEATRE, and the ABBEY THEATRE, as well as companies from America, Sweden, South Africa, Uganda, Turkey, Greece, India, Israel, and Japan.

Worthington, Mrs The lady to whom Noël COWARD addressed his advice in his song 'Don't Put Your Daughter on the Stage, Mrs Worthington'.

She has nice hands, to give the wretched girl her due
But don't you think her bust is overdeveloped for her age?
I repeat Mrs Worthington, sweet Mrs Worthington,
Don't put your daughter on the stage.

Mrs Worthington was, in fact, 'Glitters' Worthington, the wife of a Birchington GP who had an affair with the playwright Frederick Lonsdale (1881–1954). Their illegitimate daughter, Angela, had early aspirations to become an actress. Coward's song was well-intentioned advice to Angela's mother to resist the temptation. Although Angela did not herself tread the boards she did marry Robin Fox, the theatrical agent and impresario. Her main contribution to the theatre was through her illustrious sons – the actors Edward and James Fox and the theatrical producer Robert Fox.

Woyzeck An uncompleted play by Georg BÜCHNER, who died of typhoid fever at the age of 23. It was written in 1836, but not published until 1879; the first performance was given in Vienna in 1913. Since World War II it has enjoyed numerous successful revivals; the Austrian composer Alban Berg (1885–1935) used it as the libretto for his first opera, the expressionist *Wozzeck* (1925).

The play deals with an illiterate soldier's mental disintegration and suicide after murdering his wife. It is one of the first dramas to sympathize with a working-class protagonist, anticipating the social dramas of the 1890s with their concern for society's oppressed. *Woyzeck* foreshadowed both expressionism in its style and NATURALISM in its subject matter.

Wycherley, William (1640–1716) English playwright of the Restoration era, whose bawdy and satirical plays contain elements of biting social criticism. Despite their harshness, his works enjoyed a great vogue, and Wycherley became a favourite of King Charles II. Congreve was amongst those who saw Wycherley as an essentially moral writer appointed "to lash this crying age".

As a young man Wycherley studied law but became bored and abandoned it: his first play, *Love in a Wood, or, St James's Park*, was produced at Drury Lane in 1671. He followed this success with THE GENTLEMAN DANCING-MASTER (1672) and his two great plays THE COUNTRY WIFE (1675), and THE PLAIN DEALER (1676). However, as a result of his somewhat dissolute lifestyle, he spent seven years in debtors' prison until rescued by James II.

Once, when Wycherley was driving down Pall Mall in his coach, he passed the carriage of one of King Charles's beautiful mistresses, the Duchess of Cleveland. She called out to him, "You, Wycherley, you are a son of a whore." He invited her to the next performance at Drury Lane, where she sat in the first row of the king's box. Wycherley and the king eventually came to share the duchess's favours.

Wyndham's Theatre An intimate London theatre in the Charing Cross Road. The Marquess of Salisbury allowed it to be built on his land because he admired the actor-manager Sir Charles Wyndham, who opened the venue in 1899. The architect Sprague designed the 759-seat theatre in Louis XVI style; the bust over the proscenium is said to be of the actress Mary Moore, Wyndham's wife. The opening production, a revival of Tom Robertson's *David Garrick*, was followed in 1900 by Henry Arthur Jones's *Mrs Dane's Defence*, which ran for over 200 performances.

Frank Curzon, who became manager in 1903, was joined the following year by Gerald Du Maurier. In 1916 they produced J. M. Barrie's *A Kiss for Cinderella* and the next year his *Dear Brutus*. Tallulah BANKHEAD made her sensational London debut there in 1923 in *The Dancers*. From 1926 to 1932 Wyndham's produced six thrillers by Edgar Wallace, after which the management was taken over by Wyndham's son, Howard, and his stepson, Sir Bronson Albery.

Post-war successes have included James Bridie's *Daphne Laureola* (1949) with Edith Evans and Peter Ustinov's *The Love of Four Colonels* (1951) with the playwright in the lead. Transfers have also provided hits: *The Boyfriend* from the Players' Theatre in London had a record-breaking run of 2084 performances at Wyndham's in 1954. Shelagh Delaney's *A Taste of Honey* (1958), Brendan Behan's *The Hostage* (1959), and *Oh, What a Lovely War!* (1963) all transferred from Joan Littlewood's THEATRE WORKSHOP. Transfers from Broadway have included *Godspell* in 1972 and *Side by Side by Sondheim* in 1976.

In 1978 Ian Albery, the great-grandson of Mary Moore, became Wyndham's new manager. His greatest success of the 1980s was Dario Fo's *Accidental Death of an Anarchist*, which opened in 1980 for 622 performances.

Y

Yates, Richard (1706–96) English comedian, who won fame playing clown roles in Shakespeare's plays. He began his career in a booth at London's BARTHOLOMEW FAIR in which he played PANTALOON to Ned Shuter's HARLEQUIN. After becoming a member of Giffard's company at Goodman's Fields Theatre he moved on to play at Covent Garden and Drury Lane for many years. He created the role of Sir Oliver Surface in the first production of Sheridan's THE SCHOOL FOR SCANDAL (1777). Yates's second wife was the actress Mary Ann Graham (1728–87), who played at Drury Lane from 1754 to 1785, becoming one of her era's most respected tragic actresses.

Yeats, William Butler (1865–1939) Irish poet and playwright, who led the Irish dramatic renaissance in the early 20th century and, with the help of Lady GREGORY, created the ABBEY THEATRE. The first play performed at the Abbey (on 27 December 1904) was Yeats's *On Baile's Strand*. It remained part of the theatre's repertoire with his other works, which include THE LAND OF HEART'S DESIRE (1894) and *Deirdre* (1907). Yeats, who was awarded a Nobel Prize for Literature in 1923, gave strong encouragement to other Irish playwrights including J. M. Synge and Sean O'Casey.

The first of his 30 plays was the symbolist drama *The Countess Cathleen* (1892), the heroine of which was modelled on Maud Gonne, a beautiful nationalist friend who remained a source of inspiration throughout Yeats's life. In 1902 Maud took the title role in his fiercely patriotic play CATHLEEN NI HOULIHAN. Yeats reacted strongly against the fashion for NATURALISM in the theatre; in his later works he aimed to create a form of ritual drama analogous to the Japanese NŌ, making use of dance, poetry, and masks. Many of his plays deal with themes from Irish mythology (*see* CUCHULAIN).

Yeats was a great stickler for detail. The actor Sir Cedric Hardwicke recalled him trying for hours to find the right lighting effect for a sunset. After the electricians had tried all the possible colour combinations, Yeats saw a glow and shouted, "That's it! Hold it, hold it!" A stage hand gave a quick embarrassed reply, "We can't hold it, Sir. The bloody theatre's on fire."

Yeoman of the Guard, The A light opera by GILBERT AND SULLIVAN, set in the Tower of London in the 16th-century and subtitled *The Merryman and His Maid*. It was first produced in 1888 at the SAVOY THEATRE. Gilbert is said to have taken the idea from a poster of a Beefeater advertising the Tower Furnishing Company. For his part, Sullivan wrote the piece during a bout of depression in which he accused himself of wasting his talents on musical comedies instead of writing grand opera; consequently *Yeoman* is one of his more serious works.

The plot concerns the plight of Colonel Fairfax, due to be beheaded in the Tower on false charges based on the evidence of a cousin, who will inherit his estate if he dies unmarried. Accordingly, he persuades Elsie Maynard, a singer, to marry him in return for 100 crowns. Meanwhile, Phoebe, the daughter of a Yeoman warder, has fallen in love with Fairfax. She steals the keys to his cell, and Fairfax assumes the identity of her brother, Leonard. When she discovers that Fairfax has fallen in love with Elsie, Phoebe discloses his true identity to Wilfred Shadbolt, the Head Jailer and Assistant Tormentor. To protect Fairfax and escape a treason charge, Elsie now promises to wed Shadbolt "in a year – or two – or three, at the most".

Yerma A poetic tragedy by Federico GARCÍA LORCA, first performed in 1934 in Madrid and first seen in London in 1937. *Yerma* is the second play in a trilogy of folk tragedies that begins with BLOOD WEDDING (1933) and is completed by THE HOUSE OF BERNARDA ALBA (1936). The plot involves the suffering of a childless gypsy woman who murders her sterile husband.

you. ***You Can't Take It With You*** A comedy by the US playwrights George S. KAUFMAN and Moss HART. It won the Pulitzer Prize after opening in New York in 1936. The play is set in the eccentric New York household of Grandpa Martin Vanderhof. His granddaughter Alice has invited her fiancé, Tony Kirby, and his strait-laced parents to dinner, and she is concerned about the impression that her unconventional family will make. Grandpa avoids taxes by pretending to be dead, his son-in-law Paul makes fireworks, and granddaughter Essie takes ballet lessons from the flamboyant Russian Boris Kolenkhov. Tony's family arrive on the wrong night to find the usual chaos; they leave in disgust, as the fireworks factory is raided by the authorities. When Tony returns on the next evening, followed by his father, Grandpa succeeds in persuading Mr Kirby to take a more relaxed view of life, and the engagement is saved.

You Never Can Tell A light comedy by George Bernard SHAW, written between 1895 and 1897, published in 1898 in *Plays Pleasant and Unpleasant*, and first performed in 1900 at the Strand Theatre, London. *You Never Can Tell* was one of 10 Shaw works presented in repertory (1904–07) by John Vedrenne and Harley GRANVILLE-BARKER at the Royal Court Theatre.

A farcical tale set in an English seaside hotel, the play deals with the intrigues of the Clandon family and their guests, the womanizing Valentine and the 'new woman', Gloria. A case of mistaken identity is resolved and the Clandons are reunited with their missing father. The play ends with the conversion of Gloria and Valentine to a more conventional way of life and their decision to marry.

young. ***Young England*** A play intended as a stirring morality tale, which opened at the Victoria Palace in September 1934 and convulsed audiences with its unintentional comedy. Essentially a wholesome entertainment about young lovers beset by a variety of villains, the play featured a troop of Boy Scouts and Girl Guides, who foil the plans of a devious scoutmaster. The performances quickly degenerated into a riot of audience participation as theatregoers joined in with or supplemented the dialogue. The author, Walter Reynolds, an 83-year-old dramatist and proprietor of the Theatre Royal, Leeds, used to sit in a box glaring at the audience as they joined in the Boy Scouts' Song or shouted lewd remarks at younger female characters. It is estimated that 250 000 people saw the play, before it finally closed in May 1935 after 278 performances.

> Away we go to camp and all its
> pleasures,
> A merry mob, a merry mob!
> 'Boy Scouts' Song'.

Young Vic, the A theatre in Lambeth, London, near the OLD VIC THEATRE, that offers professional productions for young people at reasonable prices. The theatre has a 456-seat main auditorium and a studio auditorium seating 100. The Young Vic was founded by Frank Dunlop under the auspices of the National Theatre and opened in 1970 in a converted butcher's shop. The first production was *Scapino*, an adaptation from Molière, which Dunlop directed in a modernized *commedia dell'arte* style.

In 1974 the Young Vic became independent of the National Theatre and Dunlop gave up his management role, although he continued to direct from time to time. Michael Bogdanov served as director from 1978 to 1980. The company, which likes to maintain an informal atmosphere, has presented a wide variety of plays to its young audience, including Beckett's *Waiting for Godot*, Shakespeare's *The Comedy of Errors*, Andrew Lloyd Webber's musical *Joseph and the Amazing Technicolor Dreamcoat*, and Ibsen's *Ghosts*, which transferred in 1986 to Wyndham's Theatre. In 1992 the Young Vic staged an adaptation of *The Snow Queen*.

A previous Young Vic Theatre was opened in 1945 under George DEVINE as part of the Old Vic Drama School. The company began on a high note with Carlo Gozzi's fantasy *The King Stag* and followed with other successes, but financial problems forced it to disband in 1951.

Z

Zaïre A tragedy by VOLTAIRE, often regarded as his best work for the stage. First performed in 1732 in Paris, it is strongly influenced by Shakespeare, whose works Voltaire had become familiar with during his stay in England (1726–29). The dedication mentions Shakespeare's historical plays, while the plot suggests *Othello* as another source.

Set in the Middle East during the Crusades, the story concerns Zaïre, a slave, who is loved by her master, the sultan Osman. She discovers that she is really the daughter of another slave, Lusignan, the former king and a Christian. She also finds that she has a long-lost brother, Nerestan. Zaïre keeps this information from the sultan, and when he discovers her meetings with Nerestan he becomes furiously jealous and murders them both.

Zanni The comic servant characters of the COMMEDIA DELL'ARTE. They included ARLECCHINO, PANTALOON, PULCINELLA, and SCAPINO. Several of the *Zanni* later became major figures in the English HARLEQUINADE. In English *Zani* became a term for a clown or buffoon, giving rise to the modern adjective *zany*.

> He's like the zani to a tumbler
> That tries tricks after him to make men
> laugh.
>
> BEN JONSON: *Every Man out of his Humour* (IV, i).

zarzuela A type of Spanish musical play or operetta that developed as a popular court entertainment in the mid 17th century; the name comes from the Palacio de la Zarzuela, a royal hunting lodge near Madrid. The first *zarzuela*, combining narrative passages with music and dance, was *El laurel de Apolo* (1658), by Pedro CALDERÓN de la Barca. Another notable exponent of the genre was Lope de VEGA. The *zarzuela*'s popularity at court owed much to its heroic and mythological subjects. By the 18th century, however, Italian opera had become the fashion and the *zarzuela* had to be revived by Ramón de la Cruz (1731–94), who created works with plots taken from everyday life. Although he experienced great success, the genre faded again after his death and remained in obscurity until 1856, when the Teatro de la Zarzuela opened in Madrid. Over the years, the *zarzuela* evolved into two forms, the one-act comedy known as the TEATRO POR HORAS and the opera-like version called the *grande*. The modern *zarzuela* has been greatly influenced by international musicals.

Ziegfeld, Florenz (1867–1932) US impresario and theatre manager, who became a US institution with his **Ziegfeld Follies**, which ran continuously from 1907 until his death in 1932, and then periodically until 1957. The *Follies* were an expensive REVUE (modelled on Paris's Folies Bergères), which featured seminude girls, glamorous costumes, and spectacular sets. As an impresario, Ziegfeld developed the careers of several stars, including W. C. Fields, Will Rogers, Eddie Cantor, Paulette Goddard, and Fanny Brice and imported such international talent as Maurice CHEVALIER. He also worked with a number of America's top composers, including Irving BERLIN, and GEORGE GERSHWIN.

Ziegfeld began his career in entertainment at the World's Columbian Exposition in 1893, when he acted as publicist for SANDOW the strongman. From 1896 he promoted the musical comedy performer Anna Held (1873–1918), whom he married the following year. They were divorced in 1913 and Ziegfeld subsequently married the light comedian Billie Burke (who later appeared as Glinda, the Good Witch of the North, in the film of *The Wizard of Oz*).

In 1927 he opened his own Ziegfeld Theatre on Sixth Avenue and 54th Street with the musical *Rio Rita*. That same year he produced the musical SHOW BOAT, which was an enormous success in London the following year. When Ziegfeld died (leaving debts of around $500,000), his theatre became a cinema. It was reopened by Billy

Rose under its old name in 1944 with the revue *Seven Deadly Arts*, starring Beatrice LILLIE. From 1953 onwards it was used for television broadcasts but in 1963 returned to live entertainment, with Maurice Chevalier presenting an evening of songs and sketches. The Ziegfeld Theatre was demolished in 1967.